CENTAUR CLASSICS

GENERAL EDITOR: J. M. COHEN

THE PENTATEUCH

PREFACE.

Like a traveller who at the end of a long and difficult voyage has safely reached the haven where he would be, I offer to Almighty God the tribute of praise and thanksgiving for the blessings of unbroken health, of journeying mercies throughout the progress of this work, and of much kindness from friends, old and new, on both sides of the Atlantic, without which it could not have been done at all.

Having stated elsewhere the origin, character and aims of this book, it is my pleasing duty to enumerate here the sundries of a heavy debt incurred, in payment of which I can only tender this note of gratitude, which I hope will be strongly endorsed by the public, and graciously received by the good friends to whom it is offered.

The Trustees of the Lenox Library will please accept my thanks for the hospitality of the Institution and the unrestricted use of the rich Collection of which they are the custodians. To one of their number, George H. Moore, Esq., LL.D., Superintendent of the Library, I am under special obligation for the courtesy and readiness with which he has met my wants and facilitated my work. The valuable help afforded me by S. Austin Allibone, Esq., LL.D., the Librarian, is duly recorded in another place, but I have yet to add that he has enriched this volume by an Index to the Prolegomena.

The contributions enumerated below excepted, this is the first book which has been entirely prepared in the Library from material drawn from its shelves, and for this reason is inscribed to the memory of the good man who founded it.

For the collation of Genesis of 1530, with Genesis *Newly correctyd and amendyd by W. T. 1534*, and of several of the Prologues with those in Daye's Folio of 1573, as well as for the reading of the proof-sheets of the entire Pentateuch, I am indebted to the kindness of The Reverend James Culross, D.D., President of the Baptist College, Bristol. I have also to thank Edward Augustus Bond, Esq., LL.D., Principal Librarian of the British Museum, George Bullen, Esq., Keeper of the Printed Books of the British Museum, and The Reverend J. E. Sewell, D.D., Warden of New College, Oxford, for valuable contributions duly acknowledged in the proper places. To the kindness of Francis Fry, Esq., of Bristol, I owe the photograph of Tyndale's Autograph Letter, which faces the Title Page, and much useful information, some of which I have been able to print.

The technical finish of this Volume is due to the skill and interest of Mr. John F. McCabe, the Superintendent of the Stereotype Foundry at St. Johnland; his interest has been shared by the compositors, whose carefulness has not a little lessened the work of correcting the proof-sheets.

Although great pains have been taken to secure accuracy, the imperfection which marks all human effort, especially where it aims to avoid it, may have caused some things to escape the observation of my kind friends, and myself, which others perhaps will notice. I shall feel grateful to have pointed out to me any real blemishes, that they may be removed from the plates.

Several months ago the Earl of Shaftesbury unveiled the monument on the Thames Embankment in honor of the Apostle of Liberty, who, at the cost of his life, gave to the people of English tongue much of the English Bible, and it is now my privilege to unveil the monument which William Tyndale himself erected in restoring to use by all lovers of the English Bible, and of the same glorious liberty, the long buried volume of the first English Version of the Pentateuch made from the Sacred Original.

J. I. MOMBERT.

LENOX LIBRARY, *August, 1884.*

CONTENTS.

ILLUSTRATIONS.

INDEX TO PROLEGOMENA.

By Dr. Allibone.

PROLEGOMENA.

PROLEGOMENA.

CHAPTER I.

BIOGRAPHICAL NOTICE OF WILLIAM TYNDALE.

Obscurity shrouds the first forty years of the life of William Tyndale, uncertainty and mystery involve the remainder. We may trace him from Gloucestershire to Worms to lose sight of him during eight eventful years and to find him permanently settled at Antwerp. The details of his manner of life there, of his arrest, imprisonment, trial, and martyrdom, which have come down to us in the shape of history and tradition, are few and unsatisfactory, and mainly contained in the sketch of John Foxe described as *The hiſtorie and diſcourſe of the lyfe of William Tyndall out of the Booke of Notes and Monumentes Briefly extracted* by him in *The Whole workes of W. Tyndall, John Frith, and Doct. Barnes, three worthy Martyrs*, &c , London, John Daye, An. 1573. in-folio. The most important of these are the following:

A.iiij. "Firſt touching the birth and parentage of this bleſſed Martyre in Chriſt, hee was borne in the edge of Wales, and brought vp from a childe in the vniuerſitie of Oxforde, where hee by long continuance grew, and encreaſed aſwell in the knowlege of tongues, and other liberall artes, as eſpecially in the knowlege of Scriptures, whereunto his mind was ſingularly addicted: Inſomuch that hee liyng in Magdalene hall, read priuelye to certaine ſtudentes, and felowes of Magdalene College, ſome percell of Diuinitie, inſtructing them in the knowlege, and trueth of the Scriptures. Whoſe maners alſo and conuerſation being correſpondent to the ſame, were ſuch that all they which knewe him, reputed, and eſteemed him to bee a man of moſt verteous diſpoſition, and of a life vnſpotted. Thus hee in the vniuerſitie of Oxford encreaſyng more and more in learning, and proceeding in degrees of the ſchooles, ſpiyng his tyme, remoued from thence to the Vniuerſitie of Cambridge, where, after he had likewyſe made his abode a certayne ſpace, and beeing now farther rypened in the knowlege of Gods worde, leauing that vniuerſitie alſo, he reſorted to one *M. Welſhe* a knyght of Gloceſter ſheare, and was there ſchoole maſter to his children, and in very good fauour with his maſter. This gentleman, as hee kept a very good ordinary commonly at his table, there reſorted vnto him many tymes ſondry Abbottes, Deanes, Archdeacons, with other diuers Doctours, and great beneficed men: Who there togither with *M. Tyndall* ſittyng at the ſame table, did vſe many tymes to enter communication and talke of learned men, as of *Luther* and *Eraſmus*, and of diuerſe controuerſies, and queſtions vpon the ſcripture. At which time *M. Tyndall*, as he was learned, & wel practiſed in Gods matters, ſo he ſpared not to ſhew to them ſimply, and playnely his iudgement in matters as he thought. And when as they at that tyme did varie from *Tyndall* in opinions, and iudgment, he would ſhewe them the booke, and lay playnely before them the open, and manifeſt places of the ſcriptures to confute their errours, and to confirme his ſayinges. And thus continued they for a ſeaſon, reaſoning, and contending togither diuers and ſondry tymes, till at the length they waxed wery of him, and bare a ſecret grudge in their hartes againſt hym.

B.j. *sqq.* "To bee ſhort *M. Tyndall* beeing ſo moleſted and vexed in the countrey by y[e] Prieſts, was conſtrayned to leaue that Countrye, and to ſeeke another place: and ſo comming to *M. Welſhe* hee deſired him of his good will, that hee might depart from hym, ſaying thus vnto him: Syr I perceaue I ſhall not bee ſuffered to tarye long here in this countrie, neither ſhall you bee able (though you woulde) to keepe mee out of the handes of the ſpiritualtie, and alſo what diſpleaſure might growe to you by keeping mee God knoweth: for the which I ſhulde bee right ſory. So that in fine *M. Tyndall* with y[e] good will of his Maſter departed, and eftſones came vp to London, and there preached a while according as hee had done in the countrye beefore. At length hee beethought hym ſelfe of *Cuthbert Tunſtall* then Byſhop of London, and eſpecially for the great commendatiō of *Eraſmus*," etc. (See the Prologue "When I had tranſlated, &c.," from which this part of Foxe's account is taken.)

"And ſo he remayned in London the ſpace almoſt of a yeare, beholding and marking with him ſelfe the courſe of the world and eſpecially y[e] Demeanour of the preachers, how they boaſted them ſelues, & ſet vp their auctoritie & kingdome; Beholding alſo the pompe of the Prelates, with other thinges that greatly miſliked him. Inſomuch, as he vnderſtoode not onely to be no roome in y[e] Biſhops houſe for him to tranſlate the new Teſtament: but alſo that there was no place to doe it in all England. And therefore fynding no place for his purpoſe within the Realme, and hauing ſome ayde and prouiſion, by Gods prouidence miniſtred vnto him by *Humfrey Mommouth* Merchaunt, who after was both Shirife and Alderman of London, and by certaine other good men, he tooke his leaue of the Realme, and departed into Germany. Where the good man being inflamed with a tender care and zeale of his countrey refused no trauell, or diligence, how by all meanes possible to reduce his bretheren & Countrymen of England to the same tast and vnderstanding of Gods holy worde, and veritie which the Lorde had endued him withall. * * *

"For these and such other considerations, this good man was moued (and no doubte styrred vp of God) to translate the Scripture into his mother tongue, for the publique vtilitie and profit of the simple vulgar people of his coũtrey: First setting in hand with the new testament, which he first translated about the yeare of our Lord .1527. After y^t he tooke in hande to translate the olde testament, finishing the .V. bookes of Moses, with sondry most learned and godly prologues prefixed before euery one of them most worthy to be read, and read againe of all Christians, as the like also he did vpon the new testament.

"He wrote also dyuerse other woorkes vnder sondry titles, among the which is that most worthy monument of his intuled the obedyence of a Christian man, wherein with singular dexteritie he instructeth all men in the office, and duetie of Christian obediẽce, with dyuerse other treatises as may apere in the contentes of this booke.

"So soone as these bookes were compiled, and made by *William Tyndall*, and the same were published and sent ouer into England, it can not bee spoken what a dore of light they opened to the eyes of the whole Englishe nation, which before were many yeares shut vp in darknes. * * *

"After that *William Tyndall* had translated the fysth booke of Moses called *Deuteronomium*, and he mynding to print the same at Hamborough, sayled thitherward: and by the way vpon the coast of Holland, he suffered shipwracke, and lost all his bookes, writinges, and copyes: and so was compelled to beginne all agayne anewe, to his hynderaunce and doublyng of his labours. Thus hauyng lost by that ship both money, his copyes and tyme, he came in an other shippe to Hamborough, where at his appointment *M. Couerdale* taryed for hym, and helped hym in the translatyng of the whole fiue bookes of Moses. And after hee returned to Andwarp, and was there lodged more than one whole yeare in the house of *Thomas Pointz*, an English man, who kept a table for Englishe marchauntes, etc.

"About which tyme, an Englishe man whose name was *Henry Phillips*, whose father was customer of *Poole*, a comely man, and seemed to be a gentleman. This man sodainely entred into the great loue and fauour of *Willam Tyndall*, who greatly commended his curtesie and learning, and in the ende fell into famylier loue and acquaintance with him. And *Thomas Pointz* their host espying such great loue and familiaritie to be betweene *M. Tyndall* and this

Philippes, which vnto hym was but a mere ſtrainger, did much meruell thereat, and fell into a geloufy, and ſuſpition that this *Phillipes* was but a ſpye, and came but to betraye *M. Tindall*, wherefore on a time, the a fore ſayd *Thomas Poyntz* aſked *M. Tyndall* how he came acquainted with this *Phillipes: M. Tyndall* aũſwered that he was an honeſt man, handſomely learned, and very conformable. Then *Poyntz* perceauing that he bare ſuch fauour vnto him, ſayd no more, thinking that hee had beene brought acquainted with him by ſome frende of his. The ſayd *Phillipes* being in the towne .iij. or iiij. dayes did then depart to the Court at Bruxelles, which is from Andwarp .xxiiij. myles and did ſo much there that he procured to bring from thence with him to Andwarp the procuror generall, which is the Emperours attorney with certaine other officers. And firſt the ſayd *Phillipes* ſeruaunt came vnto *Poyntz* and demaunded of him whether *M. Tyndall* were there or not, for his maſter would come and dyne with him. And forthwith came *Phillipes* and aſked *Poyntz* wife for *M. Tyndall* and ſhe ſhewed him that he was in his chamber, then ſayd he, what good meate ſhall we haue to dinner for I entend to dyne with you, and ſhe aunſwered they ſhould haue ſuch as the market would geue. Then went *phyllipes* ſtraight vp into *M. Tyndales* chamber, and tolde him that by the way as he came he had loſt his purſſe, and therefore prayed him to lend him .xl. ſhillings, which he forthwith lent, for it was eaſie inough to be had of him if he had it. For in the wilie ſubtilnes of this world, he was ſymple and vnexpert.

"Then ſayd *Phillipes* you ſhall be my gueſt here this day. No, ſayd, *Tyndall*, I goe forth this day to dynner, and you ſhall goe with me and be my geſt where you ſhall be welcome. And when dynner tyme came *M. Tyndall* and *Phillipes* went both forth togither. And at the going forth of *Poyntz* houſe was a long narrow entrey, ſo that .ii coulde not goe on a front. *Tyndall* would haue put *phillipes* before him, but *Phillipes* would in no wiſe, but put *Tyndall* beefore him, for that hee pretended to ſhew great humanitie. So *Tyndale* being a man of no great ſtature went before, and *Phillipes* a tall perſon folowed behinde him, who had ſet officers on either ſyde of the dore vpon .ii ſeates, which beeing there might ſee who came in the entrye. And comming through yͤ ſaid entrye, *Phillipes* pointed with his finger ouer *M. Tyndales* head downe to hym, that the officers which ſat at the dore, might ſee that it was hee whom they ſhould take, as the officers that tooke *Tyndall* afterward tolde to the a fore ſayde *Poyntz*, and ſayd that they pitied to ſee his ſimplicitie when they tooke him. But *Tyndall* when hee came nere the dore eſpied the officers and woulde haue ſhronke backe: nay ſayd *Phillipes* by your leaue you ſhall goe forth, and by force bare hym forward vpon the officers. And aſſone as the officers had taken him, they forthwith brought him vnto the Emperours attorney, or procurour generall, where hee dyned. Then came the procurour generall to the houſe of *Poyntz*, and ſent awaye all that was of *Tyndales*, aſwell his bookes as other thinges: And from thence *Tyndall* was had to the Caſtell of filforde, xviij. Engliſhe myles from Andwarpe, where hee remayned priſoner more than a yeare and a halfe, and in that meane tyme, came vnto him diuerſe lawyers, and Doctours in Diuinitie, aſwell fryers as other with whom hee had many conflyctes: But at the laſt *Tyndall* prayed that hee might haue ſome Engliſhe Deuines come vnto him, for the maners and Ceremonies in Douch land (ſayd hee) did much differ from the maners and Ceremonies vſed in England. And then was ſent vnto him dyuerſe Deuines from Louayne whereof ſome were Engliſhmen, and after many examinations, at the laſt they condemned him by vertue of the Emperours decree made in the aſſembly at Auſbrough, and ſhortly after brought him forth to the place of execution, and there tyed him to a ſtake, where with a feruent zeale, and a loud voyce hee cried, Lord open the eyes of the King of Englande, and then firſt he was with a halter ſtrangled by the hangman, and afterward conſumed with fier. In the yeare of our Lord .1536.

"Such was the power of his doctryne, and the ſinceritie of his lyfe, that during the tyme of his impriſonment, which (as aforeſayd) endured a yeare and a halfe, hee conuerted his keepers Daughter, and other of his houſholde. Alſo ſuch as were with him conuerſaunt in the Caſtell reported of him, that if hee were not a good Chriſtian man, they could not tell whom to truſt. The Procurour generall the Emperours attorney beeing there, left this teſtemony of him, that he was *Homo doctus pius et bonus*, that is, a learned, a good, and a godly man. * * *

"And here to ende and conclude this hiſtory with a fewe notes touching his priuate behauiour in dyet, ſtudy, and eſpecially his charitable zeale, and tender releuing of the poore: Fyrſt he was a man very frugall, and ſpare of body, a great ſtudent and earneſt laborer, namely in the ſetting forth of ye Scriptures of God. He reſerued or halowed to hym ſelfe .ij. dayes in the weeke, which he named his dayes of paſtime, and thoſe dayes were Monday the firſt day in the weeke, and Satterday the laſt daye in the weeke. On the Monday he viſited all ſuche poore men and women as were fled out of England by reaſon of perſecution into Antwarp, and thoſe well vnderſtanding their good exerciſes and qualities he did very liberally comfort and relieue: and in like maner prouided for the ſicke and deceaſed perſons. On the Satterday he walked round about the towne in Antwarpe, ſeeking out euery Corner, and hole where he ſuſpected any poore perſon to dwell (as God knoweth there are many) and where he found any to be well occupied and yet ouerburdened with children, or els were aged, or weake, thoſe alſo hee plentefully releued. And thus he ſpent his .ij. dayes of paſtime as he cauled them. And truely his Almoſe was very large and great: and ſo it might well bee: for his exhibition that he had yearely of the

Englishe merchauntes was very much, and that for the most parte he bestowed vpon the poore as afore sayd. The rest of the dayes in the weke he gaue hym wholy to his booke where in most diligently he traueled. When the Sonday came, then went he to some one merchaunts chamber, or other, whether came many other merchauntes: and vnto them would he reade some one percell of Scripture, eyther out of the olde testament, or out of the new, the which proceded so frutefully, sweetely and gentely from him (much like to the writing of S. John the Euangelest) that it was a heauenly comfort and ioy to the audiēce to heare him reade the scriptures: and in likewise after dinner, he spent an houre in the aforesayd maner. He was a man without any spot, or blemishe of rancor, or malice, full of mercy and compassion, so that no man liuing was abie to reproue him of any kinde of sinne or cryme, albeit his righteousnes and iustification depended not there vpon before God, but onely vpon the bloud of Christ, and his fayth vpon the same: in the which fayth constantly he dyed, as is sayd at Filforde, and now resteth with the glorious campany of Christes Martyrs blessedly in the Lord, who be blessed in all his saintes Amen. And thus much of *W. Tyndall*, Christes blessed seruaunt, and Martyr."

Within this framework lie the earliest *indicia* of the history of Tyndale, confirmed, disproved, or augmented by contemporary evidence, and collected by the unremitting zeal and patient research of earnest students. The *results* of their labors will now be considered.

In the latest, exhaustive, and best, biography of Tyndale extant,[1] Mr. Demaus demonstrates that the Martyr was neither born at Hunt's Court in Gloucestershire, nor a member of the Tyndales who obtained possession of it not till long after his birth. *Their* son William was alive six years after the Martyr's death, and could not, of course, have been identical with him. The same writer has shown that Tyndales were settled as farmers at Melksham Court in the parish of Stinchcombe, and others at Slymbridge; also, that Edward, a brother of the subject of this notice, was under-receiver of the lordship of Berkeley,[2] and rendered it not improbable that

[1] The authorities are given by Demaus: *William Tyndale, a Biography*, &c., London, no date, pp. 1–8.

[2] Burke: *History of the Commoners*, IV., p. 546; Rudder: *Gloucestershire*, p. 756, cited hy Demaus, *l. c.*, p. 7. Also Atkyns: *The Ancient and Present State of Glocestershire*, 2d ed., London, 1712.

Slymbridge was the birthplace of the Reformer. This inference conflicts, however, with the genealogy compiled by the heraldic historians, according to which Edward Tyndale was the fourth son of Sir William Tyndale, of Hockwold, Norfolk, whose elder brother William lived till 1558. In the pedigree printed by Mr. Offor,[1] Edward is not mentioned at all; it deserves to be preserved, however, on account of the reference to the name of Hutchins (spelled also Huchyns,

[1] Pedigree of William Tyndale the Martyr, as preserved by one branch of the family, communicated to G. Offor, Esq., by J. Roberts, Esq. From *Advertisement* to NEW TESTAMENT, &c., Lond. 1836.

Hugh, Baron de Tyndale, of Langley Castle, Northumberland, escaped from the field of battle when the Yorkists were overcome by the Lancastrians: lost his title and estate: he took refuge in Gloucestershire, under the assumed name of Hutchins. = Alicia, daughter and sole heiress of Hunt, of Hunt's Court at Nibley, in Gloucestershire.

John Tyndale, otherwise called Hutchins, of Hunt's Court at Nibley, Gloucestershire.

John Tyndale, otherwise Hutchins, an eminent merchant of London, persecuted by bishop Stokesley.

William Tyndale, otherwise Hutchins, strangled and burnt at Vilvoorde, near Brussels, September, 1536.

Thomas Tyndale, whose descendant, Lydia Tyndale, married the celebrated Quaker, honest John Roberts, of Lower Siddington, near Cirencester.

Mr. James Herbert Cooke, F. S. A., in a paper *The Tyndales in Gloucestershire*, states:

"'In a deed of entail executed by Alice Tyndale in her widowhood, date 20th January, 1541–2, by which she entails the Hunt's Court Estate on her five sons'; 'she had five sons, Richard, Henry, William, Thomas, and John, and two daughters, Joan and Agnes.' William is named one of the valuers of his mother's household effects in her will dated 3rd Feb. 1542–3, he resided at Nibley, probably at Hunt's Court, as he is assessed to the subsidy of 1543 of goods in that parish of the value of £4.'

"'It seems therefore fair to conclude with Mr. Greenfield that Edward Tyndale, and William the Martyr, were in all probability brothers of the first Richard Tyndale, of Melksham Court, to whom we may add a fourth brother, viz. John Tyndale, a Merchant, of London, who was punished by the Star Chamber in 1530 for assisting William in the circulation of his New Testament.'"

For these extracts I am indebted to the Note on the Pedigree of W. Tyndale, drawn up for insertion before the Introduction to the *New Testament, Translated by W. Tyndale, Reproduced in Facsimile*, by Francis Fry, F. S. A., 1862.

Atkyns, *l. c.*, p. 303, says that William Tyndale was born at Nibley, apparently on the authority of the *History of the Hundred of Berkeley*, written by John Smith of Nibley; it is in MS. and at present the property of Mr. Cook of Berkeley Castle.

Hitchens, Hychins, &c.) assumed by the Martyr on the Continent, to which, according to the pedigree, he appears to have had a right.

The origin of Tyndale is still uncertain. William was a favorite name among the Tyndales; it was borne by one to whom thus far I have seen no reference except in Wood's *Athenæ Oxon.*,[1] by another ordained by the bishop of Pavada in 1503; and by a third, who took monastic vows at Greenwich in 1509; the identity of either and both with the Reformer has been challenged.

Equal uncertainty attaches to the date of his birth. The incidental statement in Tyndale's *Anſwer to Sir Thomas More*,[2] that "theſe things to be even ſo, M. More knoweth well enough, for he underſtandeth the Greek, and he knew them long ere I", has been adduced as proof that Tyndale was younger than More and that he was born after 1480.

The want of documentary evidence that More was born in 1480, precludes all inference as to the date of Tyndale's birth, nor does it follow from Tyndale's words that More was his senior, for the latter may have known the things referred to much longer than Tyndale and yet have been his junior. A young person may have been possessed of information for many years which has not come to the knowledge of a much older person. If Tyndale at the time of his martyrdom in 1536 was a middle aged man, the earliest date of his birth would be 1476 and the latest 1486. This is as near as we can get.

The statement of Foxe (see p. xvii.) that Tyndale was "brought vp from a child in the vniuerſitie of Oxford, where hee by long continuance grew, and encreaſed aſwell in the *knowlege of tongues, and other liberall artes, as eſpecially in the knowlege of Scriptures*" warrants our connecting his stay at Oxford with Grocyn,

[1] Wood, *Ath. Oxon.*, II., col. 781.: [1493. Ioh'es Malett de Irby generosus presentat Jacobum Malett cl'icum ad ecclesiam de Irby predict. in dioc. Linc. vac. per mort. d'ni Willelmi Tyndall, dat. 21 Apr., 1493. *Autogr. in Reg. Buckden.* KENNET]

[2] Works, III., p. 23.

who after 1491 "taught and read the Greek tongue to the Oxonians after that way, which had not before, I suppose, been taught in their University, became a familiar friend of, or rather tutor to, Erasmus, and a person in eminent renown for his learning."[1] While Grocyn may have taught him Greek, there is but little doubt that John Colet, who continued to lecture at Oxford until 1505, influenced and shaped the theological education of Tyndale.

Wood[2] confirms the statements of Foxe, and a portrait of Tyndale formerly in the library, now in the refectory of Magdalen Hall, bears the inscription:

Gulielmus Tyndalus, Martyr.
Olim ex Aul: Magd:

Refert hæc Tabella (quod solum potuit Ars) Gulielmi
Tindale effigiem, huius olim Aulæ Alumni simul & Ornamenti;
Qui post felices purioris Theologiæ primitias hic depositas
Antwerpiæ in Nouo Testamento, necnon Pentateucho
In vernaculam transferendo operam nauauit, Anglis suis eo
Vsque salutiferam, ut inde non immerito Angliæ Apostolus
Audierat. Wilfordæ prope Bruxellas martyrio coronatus
An: 1536. Vir, si vel aduersario (procuratori nempe Imperatoris
Generali) credamus, perdoctus, pius & bonus.

Lewis[3] says, "Of this picture I would have here given the Reader a copy, but on view of it by an engraver for that purpose, it was judged to be so ill done, as that it was not worth while to copy it." An engraving of it is found in Offor's reprint of Tyndale's New Testament[4] and one made from another picture in the Manuscript of Tyndale described on a subsequent page.

The meagre and vague account of Foxe embraces all that is known of Tyndale from the undefined time of his removal to Cambridge, and his continuance there, to his appearance about 1521 as tutor in the family of Sir John Walsh at Little Sodbury in Gloucestershire.

Three documents have been discovered which will

[1] Foxe, *The Whole works of Tyndale*, &c., London, John Daye, An. 1573, in-folio.

[2] Wood, *Athenæ. Oxon.*, I., col. 94.

[3] *A Complete History of the Several Translations of the Holy Bible*, &c., p. 57, note, London, 1818, in-8.

[4] *The New Testament*, &c., London, 1836, in-8.

now be considered. The first is a Manuscript containing translations from the Gospels marked W. T. and bearing the dates 1500 and 1502, described at length p. lvi. *sqq.* The second is the following entry in the Register of Warham, then bishop of London, communicated by G. Offor, Esq., to Professor Walter and transcribed from his *Biographical Notice of William Tyndale*, p. xv., prefixed to *Doctrinal Treatises*, &c., Cambridge, 1848. in–8.:

"Ordines generaliter celebrat. in ecclesia conventuali dom. sive prioratus Sancti Barthi in Smythfelde Londin. per Rev. prem. Dmn. Thomā Dei gratia Pavaden. epm. aucte Rev. Pris Domini Willem permissione divina Londin. die sabbati iiii[or]. temporum, viz. undecimo die mensis Martii Ann. Dom. Millmo Quingentesimo secundo. Presbri. Willms Tindale Carlii Dioc. p. li. di. ad ti[m] domus monialium de Lambley."

Concerning this record of a general ordination it is claimed that the William Tyndale, ordained priest, could not have been the Reformer, because he was neither a native of the diocese Carlisle nor connected with its jurisdiction. This is the statement of Professor Walter (*l. c.*), to which Mr. Demaus adds, that, "according to ecclesiastical precedent, the person who was ordained priest in March, 1503, could not have been born later than 1478; but this was two years *before* the birth of Sir Thomas More, and is, therefore, incompatible with what we know of Tyndale's age."[1] These inferences appear to me to be untenable for the reasons stated p. xxiv., and without pretending to affirm that the William Tyndale named in the Register is the subject of this notice, I feel bound to insert the entry.

The third document is an inscription on the title-page of *Sermons de Herolt*, a small folio, printed in 1495, in the Cathedral Library of St. Paul's, worded as follows:

"Charitably pray for the soul of John Tyndale, who gave this book to the monastery at Greenwich of the obseruance of the minor brothers, on the day that brother William, his son, made his profession, in the year 1508."[2]

The readiness and frequency with which Sir Thomas

[1] Demaus, *l. c.*, pp. 35, 36.

[2] Offor, *Memoir of William Tyndale*, prefixed to his edition of Tyndale's New Testament, p. 8.

More flung the epithets *friar* and *apostate* at Luther, Œcolampadius, Jerome, and Roye, render it highly probable that Tyndale would have been regaled with them had he deserted the said monastery close to a favorite residence of Henry VIII. The circumstance must have been known to Sir Thomas, and his silence on the subject may be regarded as strong proof that the inscription relates to another person who bore the name of William Tyndale.[1]

The account of Foxe, given above, with which should be compared the much fuller narrative in the first edition of his *Actes and Monumentes* of 1563, appears to have been derived from contemporary and authentic sources; it covers the period of Tyndale's life at Little Sodbury and in London; viz., from A. D. 1521 to May, 1524. Mr. Demaus has collected every available authority and produced two exceedingly interesting chapters.[2]

For Tyndale's movements on the Continent the account of Foxe is singularly unsatisfactory. The points established by documentary evidence are the following: Tyndale arrived in Hamburg sometime about May, 1524, and revisited that city in April, 1525.[3] The interval he spent, according to contemporary authority, with Luther at Wittenberg.[4] In September of that year he was at Cologne with Roye and superintended the printing of his English version of the New Testament which had advanced as far as the letter "K" in the signature of the sheets, when, chiefly through the instrumentality of Cochlæus, further progress was arrested. Most probably in October of the same year, Tyndale and Roye fled to Worms where six thousand copies of the first complete New Testament in English were printed during the ensuing winter.[5] For some time, perhaps a year, he remained unmolested

[1] Walter, *l. c.*, p. xv. [2] Chapters II., III. [3] Demaus, *l. c.*, p. 91.

[4] The authorities are given by Demaus, *l. c.*, p. 93 *sqq*.

[5] *Ibid.*, p. 140 *sqq*. See also, *Doctrinal Treatises*, Parker Soc. ed., p. xxv., and Arber, *The First Printed English New Testament*, pp. 1–24.

at Worms. Probably early in 1526 he met Hermann von dem Busche (a pupil of Reuchlin, the earliest German Hebraist), who mentioned the matter to Spalatin in a conversation which took place on, or the day after St. Lawrence, that is, Aug. 11, 1526. The entry in Spalatin's Diary, bearing that date, is given in Schelhornii, *Amœnitates Literariæ*, IV., p. 431, under the head, *Excerpta quædam e diario Georg. Spalatini*, and reads:

"Dixit nobis in coena Matthias Leimbergius, Erasmum Rot. miro consternatum editione Servi Arbitrii, ei libello non responsorum, jam scribere de conjugio Buschius vero a Rege Gallorum revocatum Jacobum Stapulens. & nonnullos alios, & reversos liberatos XII captivos, quos Evangelii nomine Parlamentum conjecisset in carcerem. Item Wormatiæ VI mille exemplaria Novi Testamenti Anglice excusa. Id operis versum esse ab Anglo, illic cum duobus aliis Britannis divertente, ita VII linguarum perito, Hebraicæ, Græcæ, Latinæ, Italicæ, Hispanicæ, Britannicæ, Gallicæ, ut, quamcunque loquatur, in ea natum putes. Anglos enim, quamvis reluctante & invito Rege, tamen sic suspirare ad Evangelion, ut affirment, sese empturos Novum Testamentum, etiamsi centenis millibus æris sit redemendum. Adhæc Wormatiæ etiam Novum Testamentum Gallice excusum esse."

The publication by Tyndale of the *Prologe vpon the Epiſtle to the Romans* (1526) and of *The Parable of the Wicked Mammon*, 8th of May, 1527, as well as the continuous influx of his Translation into England, rendered it unsafe for him to continue at Worms, where the said works had been printed, and led him to seek and find a hiding place so secure and well chosen that the most diligent search of the emissaries of Henry VIII. and Wolsey, set to possess themselves of his person, proved wholly unavailing, and that to this hour no authentic intelligence of its mysterious location has come to light.

The meeting of Tyndale with Busche has given rise to the wide spread story that the town of Marburg in Hesse was his home in Germany. The account is purely inferential, and rests on two circumstances utterly disconnected. The first is the undoubted fact that Hermann von dem Busche was appointed professor of

Hebrew in the University of Marburg; the second is the publication of a number of Tyndale's works containing, some on the title-page, others in the colophon, the notice that they had been printed by Hans Luft at Malborow in the land of Hesse. Connecting these data with the entry in Spalatin's Diary it has been rashly inferred that Tyndale followed Busche to Marburg, translated the Pentateuch there, wrote and printed a number of pamphlets, held delightful and sympathetic intercourse with leading personages connected with the Reformation, and much more to the same effect. These statements were current and accepted as history until the following facts, developed by inquiries addressed to the authorities of the University of Marburg, were printed in the *Hand Book of the English Versions*, p. 110 *sqq.*, London and New York, 1883, and are here reproduced:

It occurred to me that the best and surest way might be to open direct communication on the subject with the authorities of the University of Marburg, and for that purpose I took occasion on November 7th, 1881, to address a letter to the Rector Magnificus of that university, inquiring among other matters:

1. If Hans Luft had a printing-press at Marburg? and

2. If William Tyndale, as well as John Frith and Patrick Hamilton, ever studied there?

Professor Ennetterus very courteously handed my letter to Professor Dr. Julius Cæsar, the librarian of the University, and author of *Catalogus studiorum scholæ Marpurgensis*, Marburg, 1875, who having thoroughly explored the archives of the University, and the documents in the library of the same, is unquestionably the most competent scholar to testify on the subject under consideration. This scholar, in a letter to me, bearing date November 26th, 1881, after briefly traversing the field of inquiry, informs me:

1. *That Hans Luft never lived, and never had a printing-press, at Marburg.*

2. That while the Album of the University enumerates among the matriculates for the year 1527 the following persons—thus:

PATRITIUS HAMILTON, A LITGAU, SCOTUS, MGR. PARISIENSIS,
IOANNES HAMILTON, A LITGAU, SCOTUS,
GILBERTUS WINRAM, EDINBURGENSIS,

there is no entry in the Album, or a trace in any document whatever in the archives of the University, that Tyndale and Frith ever were at Marburg.

Professor Cæsar, moreover, agrees with me in the opinion that the name of the printer, Hans Luft, and of the place of printing, Marburg, *i. e.*, Marlborow, in the land of Hesse, are fictitious, and were probably selected to conceal the real place of printing from Tyndale's enemies in England. He further coincides with me in the belief that the statement of Tyndale having followed Hermann von dem Busche to Marburg is simply an inferential conjecture . . .

The importance of the subject appears to me to render it desirable that the correspondence on it should be preserved; it is therefore produced here in the original, and the translation accompanying it may prove useful to persons not familiar with German.

Novr. 7, 1881.

DEM RECTOR MAGNIFICUS DER UNIVERSITÆT MARBURG.

Hochgeehrter Herr:—Im Verfolg einer geschichtlichen Untersuchung wage ich es mich an Sie um Aufschluss über eine Sache zu wenden, die auch für Sie nicht ohne Interesse sein dürfte.

Bei Gelegenheit der Bearbeitung eines Aufsatzes über den englischen Bibelübersetzer William Tyndale fand ich, dass eine Notiz folgenden Inhalts in verschiedenen älteren Werken vorkömmt, die von den Neueren immer wiederholt wird, und die, wie es mir scheint, bis jetzt noch nicht durch historische Belege erwiesen ist.

Die betreffende Notiz behauptet dass William Tyndale einer der ersten Studirenden in Marburg gewesen, und dass verschiedene seiner Werke von *Hans Luft in Marburg gedruckt seien.*

John Frith und Patrick Hamilton sollen auch in Marburg studirt haben, und der Name des Letzteren auf der ersten Seite des Universitäts-Registers eingetragen sein.

Da es Ihnen vermöge Ihrer amtlichen Stellung wohl nicht schwer sein dürfte, diese Uberlieferungen zu verificiren, erlaube ich mir bei Ihnen anzufragen,

1. Ob Hans Luft eine Buchdruckerei in Marburg gehabt hat, und

2. Ob das Universitäts-Register irgend welche authentische Nachrichten über die in Frage stehenden Persönlichkeiten enthält?

Novr. 7, 1881.

TO THE RECTOR MAGNIFICUS OF THE UNIVERSITY OF MARBURG.

Very honored Sir:—In the prosecution of an historical inquiry, I venture to address you for information in a matter which may not be void of interest to you.

Engaged on the preparation of an essay on the English Bible translator, William Tyndale, I find the following notice in older writers, which, though persistently repeated by modern authors, does not appear to me proven by historical evidence.

The notice in question asserts that William Tyndale was one of the first students at Marburg and that several of his works *have been printed by Hans Luft at Marburg.*

John Frith and Patrick Hamilton are also said to have studied at Marburg, and that the name of the latter is recorded on the first page of the University Register.

As you, in virtue of your official position, may not find it difficult to verify these traditions, I beg leave to inquire

1. If Hans Luft ever had a printing-press at Marburg? and

2. If the University Register contains authentic notices of the persons in question?

In der Hoffnung dass Sie die Gewogenheit haben mögen mir im Interesse geschichtlicher Wahrheit das mitzutheilen, was Sie darüber ermitteln können, und mir die Freiheit, mit der ich mich an Sie wende, nicht verübeln wollen, empfiehlt sich mit ausgezeichneter Hochachtung,

Ergebenst

J. I. MOMBERT.

Marburg, 26 Nov., 1881.

DEM EHRW. HERRN, DR. MOMBERT.

Hochgeehrter Herr: — Der zeitige Rector unserer Universität, Herr Professor Ennetterus, hat mir Ihren an ihn under dem 7. d. M. gerichteten Brief zur Beantwortung überlassen, da ich mich schon früher mit der von Ihnen gestellten Frage genauer beschäftigt habe. Obgleich mir aug blicklich nicht Alles gegenwärtig ist, was ich einmal darüber gewusst habe, vnd auch die Zeit fehlt, die Nachforschung von Neuem zu beginnen, so glaube ich Ihnen doch über einen Hauptpunkt eine bestimmte Antwort geben zu können.

Es hat nie einen Buchdrucker Hans Luft in Marburg gegeben Allerdings existiren verschiedene Drucke mit seinem Namen und dem Druckort Marburg (Ma[r]lborough, Malborow, u. a.) in the land of Hessia, die Sie unter den Werken von Tyndale und von Fryth bei Lowndes, in dem Oxforder Katalog u. sonst angeführt finden, aber es ist nicht zu bezweifeln, dass so wohl der Druckort als der Name des Druckers fingirt ist, vielleicht um den wahren Druckort in England zu verbergen. Man hat sich dabei der in der Geschichte der Reformation berühmten Namen der Universität Marburg und des Wittenberger Druckers bedient, und diese in eine durch Nichts gerechtfertigte Verbindung gebracht.

Es ist richtig dass Patrick Hamilton in Marburg immatriculirt war; und sein Name unter dem J. 1527 sich fol. 5 b.

Hoping that in the interest of historical truth you may be obliging enough to communicate to me what you may be able to learn on this subject, and that you will kindly pardon the trouble to which I put you, I beg you to believe me, with high regards,

Yours very truly,

J. I. MOMBERT.

Marburg, 26 Nov., 1881.

TO THE REV. DR. MOMBERT.

Very honored Sir:—The temporary Rector of our University, Professor Mr. Ennetterus, has requested me to answer the letter you addressed to him on the 7th inst, as I have already more fully considered the question you have submitted to him. Although I do not at this moment recollect all that at one time I knew on the subject, and lack the necessary leisure to begin the research anew, I nevertheless believe to be able to give you a definite reply concerning a principal point.

There has never existed at Marburg a printer of the name of Hans Luft. There exist, to be sure, sundry printed works with his name and Marburg (Ma[r]lborough, Malborow, etc.) in the land of Hesse, as the place of printing, which you will find under the works of Tyndale and Fryth in Lowndes, in the Oxford Catalogue, and elsewhere, but it cannot be doubted that both the place of printing and the name of the printer are fictitious, probably for the purpose of concealing the true place of printing (from the authorities) in England. For that purpose the names of Marburg and of the Wittenberg printer, celebrated in the history of the Reformation, have been employed and connected together without anything to justify it.

It is correct that Patrick Hamilton matriculated at Marburg, and that his name is entered under the year 1527

unseres Albums eingetragen findet, und zwar in Verbindung mit zweien seiner Genossen, in folgender Weise:

PATRITIUS HAMILTON, A LITGAU, SCOTUS, MGR. PARISIENSIS.

JOANNES HAMILTON, A LITGAU, SCOTUS.

GILBERTUS WINRAM, EDINBURGENSIS (CF. CATALOGUS STUDIORUM SCHOLÆ MARPURGENSIS. ED. JUL. CÆSAR, P. I. MARB., 1875, 4, P. 2).

Aber dass Tyndale und Fryth wirklich hier in Marburg gewesen seien, davon habe ich nirgends eine *urkundliche* Spur finden können; in unserm Album kommen sie nicht vor. Was Lorimer in seinem Buch über Hamilton (Edinb., 1857), p. 93 f. erzählt, indem er sich auf Anderson's *Annals of the Bible*, I., p. 139, 167 beruft, habe ich leider bis jetzt nicht controliren können, da wir nur die zweite abgekürzte Ausgabe des Andersonschen Werkes besitzen (das auch in Göttingen nicht vorhanden ist.) Ich weiss nicht wo der von ihm erwähnte Brief von Hermann von dem Busche an Spalatin gedruckt ist. Geht daraus hervor, dass Tyndale bei diesem im J. 1526 in Worms war, so scheint das Weitere, dass er dem im J. 1527 nach Marburg übergesiedelten B. dahin gefolgt sei, nur eine auf jenen fingirten Druckort gestützte Vermuthung zusein.

Es würde mir sehr interessant sein, wenn Ihre Forschungen über Tyndale zu sichereren positiven Resultaten führten.

Mir selbst haben die Mittel nicht zu Gebote gestanden, um dasu zu gelangen, und die Zeit um die Sache durch Nachfragen an grössere Bibliotheken, oder in England weiter zu verfolgen, doch habe ich sie nicht aus dem Auge verloren.

Hochachtungsvoll und ergebenst,

DR. JULIUS CÆSAR,

Professor und Bibliothekar an der Universität Marburg.

on folio 5 b. of our Album, and that in connection with two of his comrades as follows:

PATRITIUS HAMILTON, A LITGAU, SCOTUS, MGR. PARISIENSIS.

JOANNES HAMILTON, A LITGAU, SCOTUS.

GILBERTUS WINRAM, EDINBURGENSIS (CF. CATALOGUS STUDIORUM SCHOLÆ MARPURGENSIS. ED. JUL. CÆSAR, P. I. MARB. 1875, 4, P. 2).

But that Tyndale and Fryth were really here at Marburg, I have not been able to find a documentary trace thereof anywhere; their name does not occur in our Album. What Lorimer in his book on Hamilton (Edinb., 1857), p. 93, sq. narrates with reference to Anderson's *Annals of the Bible*, I., p. 139, 167, I regret to have been thus far unable to verify, as we have only the second abridged edition of Anderson (nor is there a copy of it at Göttingen). I do not know where the letter of Hermann von dem Busche to Spalatin, to which he refers, is printed. If it states that Tyndale was with him at Worms in 1526, the rest, that he followed B. on his removal to Marburg in 1527, appears to be a conjecture based on the fictitious place of printing.

It would be interesting to me if your researches respecting Tyndale should lead to more certain and positive results.

I myself did not possess the means to accomplish it, nor the time to prosecute the matter by inquiries directed to larger libraries, or in England, but I have not lost it out of sight.

With high regards, etc.,

DR. JULIUS CÆSAR,

Professor and Librarian of the University of Marburg.

In the absence of all authentic data as to the place covered by the pseudonyme *Malborow in the lande of Hesse*, we only know from the foregoing correspondence that it does not designate Marburg on the Lahn, and in the endeavor to identify that mysterious abode it is proper to remember that it must have been a place of safety and ready access, affording to Tyndale facilities in the pursuit of his literary labors and conveniences for the printing of his works.

As the emissaries of Henry VIII. and Wolsey had scoured the valley of the Rhine in pursuit of the exile, Cologne, Mayence, Worms, Speyer, and Strassburg must be ruled out, and as inquiries for him had been made at Nürnberg and Frankfurt, those cities also must be excluded. This narrows the inquiry and, if his place of concealment was in Germany, limits it to two places, Hamburg and Wittenberg.

Foxe, after his account of the shipwreck and visit to Hamburg, given p. xix., adds in *Actes and Monumentes* after "the whole fiue books of Mofes" the words, "from Easter till December, in the houfe of a worfhipful widow, Mrs. Margaret Van Emmerson, anno 1529, a great sweating ficknesse being at the time in the town. So having dispatched his bufiness at Hamborough, he returned afterward to Antwerp again."

The circumstantial character of the narrative invests it with a certain degree of authority, for the "sweating ficknesse" did rage in 1529 in Hamburg, and the name of the lady has been verified as that of a person then living there, who was the relict of a senator, and entitled to be called *worshipful*. The only inaccuracy appears to be the notice of the strange appointment with Coverdale, for though the meeting may have occurred, the assistance, as stated, could hardly have been rendered by him at that early date, when his knowledge of Hebrew must have been in a stage of tenderest infancy.

It has been rather rashly asserted that Tyndale could not have *mynded to print* Deuteronomy at Hamburg, there being no evidence that a printer existed there in 1529. This is clearly wrong, for Panzer, *Annales Typogr.*, vol. i., p. 453, has, under HAMBURGI, the following entry:

MCCCCXCI.

Laudes beate MARIE virginis. *Hæc in fronte fol. I. a. Fol. 2. a. col. I.* Incipiunt laudes beate Marie virginis. Cogitaui dies antiquos et annos eternos, &c. *In fine fol. 152. b.* Finem accipiunt beate virginis marie laudes magna cum diligentia emendate. atque de verbo ad verbum per totum attente reuiſe *In mercuriali oppido Hamborgenſi loco famatiſſimo impreſſe. Per me Ioannem et Thomam borchard'. Anno dni. M.CCCC.XCI. ſecunda feria poſt martini. De quo dns deus glorioſus cum ſua benedicta matre ſit eternaliter benedictus.* AMEN. *Sequitur* tabula fol. 1½. *In fine:* Explicit Tabula. *Char. Goth. mai. Sine cuſt. & pagg. num. cum ſign. col. 2. fol.*

Maitt. Ind. II. App. p. 535. ex March. Hiſt. p. 86. *Primi et unici huius, Sec. XV. Hamburgi typis expreſſi libri exemplum extat in Bibl. Gœtting. et in collectione noſtra.*

It is therefore not by any means improbable that Tyndale should have been *mynding* to print at Hamburg. Foxe seems to imply that the first four books of the Pentateuch were already printed, and to contradict himself in saying that Coverdale "helped hym in the translatyng of the whole fiue bookes of Moſes." Or are we to infer that Coverdale was engaged on the work during Tyndale's absence at Antwerp? The case is rather knotty, but perhaps not impossible to solve. Tyndale might have translated at Hamburg and have the printing done at Wittenberg, for the traffic on the Elbe is of very ancient date.

But, on the whole, probability seems to point to Wittenberg as the place where Tyndale translated the Pentateuch and had it printed.

The repeated use of the name of *Hans Luft*, the famous printer at Wittenberg (in *The obedience of a Chriſtian Man*, in 1528, *The Expoſition in to the ſeuenth Chaptre of the firſt piſtle to the Corinthians*, in 1529, in the *Boke of Geneſis* and the *Practiſe of popiſhe Prelates*, in 1530), appears to indicate some distinct connection. Luft's well-known interest in the movement of the Reformation renders it not improbable that he would sanction the employment of a pseudonyme which, though it could not hurt him, might aid Tyndale and mislead his pursuers. Wittenberg again was a much safer place than Hamburg—it was especially a spot which men of the Rinck and Cochlæus stamp shunned like the pestilence, and where the powerful influence of the Reformers would shield the desolate English exile. The printing press of Luft was one of the best and most busy in Germany and the literary resources of the place were certainly equal, probably superior, to every other seat of learning in Germany. After Tyndale's death John Rogers, his literary executor, is said to have lived at Wittenberg, to have filled an ecclesiastical position there, and to have produced there the book known as Matthew's Bible.

The appearance of Rogers at Wittenberg, so remote from Antwerp, appears to favor the supposition that he went there at the instance of Tyndale, or in consequence of information received from him.

Attention is called to a circumstance of peculiar interest, which possibly may shed light on the question in hand: it is the undoubted fact, proved by the notes in this volume, that Tyndale and Rogers made use of the Chaldee Paraphrase, which, as far as I have been able to learn, existed, down to the date of the preparation of Tyndale's Pentateuch, only in costly folio editions of the Hebrew Bible. Wherever Tyndale kept concealed, he must have had access to one or other of the works mentioned in *Helps used by Tyndale*, and in this respect again, Wittenberg seems to meet the requirements of the case.[1]

The facilities of travel to and from Wittenberg, deserve also to be considered. The bad and insecure state of the highways of Germany in the sixteenth century rendered travel not only difficult but very expensive. The frequent journeys of Tyndale suggest the probability that he chose the safest and cheapest mode of travel. He was practically regarded as an outlaw, and

[1] Additional details relating to the Pentateuch are given in the bibliographical notice of the volume, Chapter III. I understand that an octavo edition of the Chaldee Paraphrase was also in circulation.

it is difficult to surmise the expedients by which on overland journeys he could have eluded the vigilance of those who tried their utmost to seize him. He ran no such risk on the water route from Wittenberg down the Elbe to Hamburg and thence by sea to Antwerp; this appears a not improbable solution of the suddenness of his movements in that city.

But wherever he had made his home, we know that he left it on at least two occasions, to visit Antwerp. His first visit took place in 1529, and is thus referred to by Hall:

"Here it is to be remembered that at this present time William Tyndale had newly translated and imprinted the New Testament in English; and the Bishop of London, not pleased with the translation thereof, debated with himself how he might compass and devise to destroy that false and erroneous translation (as he said); and so it happened that one Augustine Packington, a merchant and mercer of London, and of a great honesty, the same time was in Antwerp where the Bishop then was, and this Packington was a man that highly favoured Tyndale, but to the Bishop utterly showed himself to the contrary.

"The Bishop, desirous to have his purpose brought to pass, communed of the New Testaments, and how gladly he would buy them, Packington, then, hearing that he wished for, said unto the Bishop, 'My lord, if it be your pleasure, I can in this matter do more, I dare say, than most of the merchants of England that are here; for I know the Dutchmen and strangers that have bought them of Tyndale and have them here to sell; so that if it be your lordship's pleasure to pay for them (for otherwise I cannot come by them but I must disburse money for them), I will then assure you to have every book of them that is imprinted and is here unsold.' The Bishop, thinking he had God by the toe, when indeed he had, as after he thought, the Devil by the fist, said, 'Gentle Mr. Packington, do your diligence and get them; and with all my heart I will pay for them whatsoever they cost you, for the books are erroneous and nought, and I intend surely to destroy them all, and to burn them at St. Paul's Cross.' Augustine Packington came to William Tyndale, and said, 'William, I know thou art a poor man, and hast a heap of New Testaments and books by thee, for the which thou hast both endangered thy friends and beggared thyself; and I have now gotten thee a merchant, which with ready money shall despatch thee of all that thou hast, if you think it so profitable for yourself.' 'Who is the merchant?' said Tyndale. 'The Bishop of London,' said Packington. 'Oh, that is because he will burn them,' said Tyndale. 'Yea, marry,' quoth Packington. 'I am the gladder,' said Tyndale, 'for these two benefits shall come thereof: I shall get money to bring myself out of debt, and the whole world will cry out against the burning of God's Word, and the overplus of the money that shall remain to me shall make me more studious to correct the said New Testament, and so newly to imprint the same once again, and I trust the second will much better like you than ever did the first.' And so, forward went the bargain; the Bishop had the books; Packington had the thanks; and Tyndale had the money.

"After this Tyndale corrected the same New Testaments again, and caused them to be newly imprinted, so that they came thick and threefold into England. When the Bishop perceived that, he sent for Packington, and said to him, 'How cometh this, that there are so many New Testaments abroad? You promised me that you would buy them all.' Then answered Packington, 'Surely, I bought all that were to be had: but I perceive they have printed more since. I see it will never be better so long as they have letters and stamps [for printing with]: wherefore you were best to buy the stamps too, and so you shall be sure:' at which answer the Bishop smiled, and so the matter ended.

"In short space after, it fortuned that George Constantine was apprehended by Sir Thomas More, who was then Chancellor of England [made Chancellor October 24, 1529], suspected of certain heresies. During the time that he was in the custody of Master More, after divers communications, amongst other things Master More asked of him, saying, 'Constantine, I would have thee be plain with me in one thing that I will ask; and I promise thee I will show thee favour in all other things, whereof thou art accused. There is beyond the sea, Tyndale, Joye, and a great many of you: I know they cannot live without help. There are some that help and succour them with money; and thou, being one of them, hadst thy part thereof, and therefore knowest from whence it came. I pray thee, tell me, who be they that help them thus?' 'My lord,' quoth Constantine, 'I will tell you truly: it is the Bishop of London that hath holpen us, for he hath bestowed among us a great deal of money upon New Testaments to burn them; and that hath been, and yet is, our only succour and comfort.' 'Now, by my troth,' quoth More, 'I think even the same, for so much I told the Bishop before he went about it.'"[1]

In connection with this visit to Antwerp, preceding the printing of the Pentateuch at the mysterious "Mal-

[1] Hall's *Chronicle;* Foxe, Vol. IV., p. 670, etc., cited by Demaus, *l. c.*, p. 221 *sqq*.

borow in the lande of Hesse," Mr. Demaus[1] has suggested, with great show of probability, that part of the money proceeding from the sale of New Testaments to the bishop of London, was applied to the purchase of the blocks of the eleven woodcuts of the tabernacle and its furniture scattered over the book of Exodus.

The cuts appear in Vostermann's Dutch folio Bible of 1528, a copy of which has been kindly loaned me for comparison with the illustrations in Tyndale's Pentateuch. They are doubtless identical, although actual measurement shows that some have been slightly trimmed and others slightly enlarged, but the reduction and extension applies only to the edges and does not touch the objects represented.

Mr. Demaus has called attention to the circumstance that a subsequent edition of the same Bible published in 1532 contains a new set of illustrations, from which he infers that the change was due to the sale of the first set to Tyndale, and states: "whatever else, therefore, Tyndale may have done with any money received from Tunstal, it seems highly probable that he purchased with it the blocks which were employed in the book of Exodus; and the rude woodcuts of this rare work are thus invested with a curious interest, when we look at them as virtually the contribution of that prelate, who prided himself on his zeal in condemning and burning the English Bible."

Tyndale paid a second visit to Antwerp in the spring of 1531, doubtless in response to a letter from Stephen Vaughan, envoy to the princess-regent of the Netherlands, holding out to the exile hopes of pardon. Vaughan, as appears from a despatch to Henry VIII., dated Barrugh, Jan. 26, 1530 [*i. e.*, 1531] had tried to open communication with Tyndale. He says. ". . . I have written three sundry letters unto William Tyndale, and the same sent for the more safety to three sundry places, to Frankforde, Hanborughe, and Marleborugh. I then not [being] assured in which of the same he was,

[1] *William Tyndale*, p. 226, 227.

and had very good hope, after I heard say in England, that he would, upon the promise of your Majesty, and of your most gracious safe conduct, be content to repair and come into England."[1]

That letter reached Tyndale, and hardly three months later he sought an interview with Vaughan, who narrates it in his letter to the king as follows:

"The day before the date hereof [*i. e.*, April 17] I spake with Tyndale without the town of Antwerp, and by this means: he sent a certain person to seek me, whom he had advised to say that a certain friend of mine, unknown to the messenger, was very desirous to speak with me; praying me to take pains to go unto him, to such place as he should bring me. Then I to the messenger, 'What is your friend, and where is he?' 'His name I know not,' said he; 'but if it be your pleasure to go where he is, I will be glad thither to bring you.' Thus, doubtful what this matter meant, I concluded to go with him, and followed him till he brought me without the gates of Antwerp, into a field lying nigh unto the same; where was abiding me this said Tyndale. At our meeting, 'Do you not know me?' said this Tyndale. 'I do not well remember you,' said I to him. 'My name,' said he, 'is Tyndale.' 'But Tyndale!' said I, 'Fortunate be our meeting.' Then Tyndale, 'Sir, I have been exceedingly desirous to speak with you.' 'And I with you; what is your mind?' 'Sir,' said he, 'I am informed that the king's grace taketh great displeasure with me for putting forth of certain books, which I lately made in these parts; but specially for the book named the Practice of Prelates; whereof I have no little marvel, considering that in it I did but warn his grace of the subtle demeanour of the clergy of his realm towards his person, and of the shameful abusions by them practised, not a little threatening the displeasure of his grace and weal of his realm: in which doing I shewed and declared the heart of a true subject, which sought the safeguard of his royal person and weal of his commons, to the intent that his grace, thereof warned, might in due time prepare his remedy against their subtle dreams. If [it be] for my pains therein taken, if for my poverty, if for mine exile out of my natural country, and bitter absence from my friends, if for my hunger, my thirst, my cold, the great danger wherewith I am everywhere compassed, and finally if for innumerable other hard and sharp fightings which I endure, not yet feeling of their asperity, by reason I hoped with my labours to do honour to God, true service to my prince, and pleasure to his commons; how

[1] The letter is preserved in the Cotton MSS. *Galba*, B. X. 46; it has been printed in Anderson, *Annals*, B. I., § 8, and by Demaus, *l. c.*, p. 288 *sqq*.

is it that his grace, this considering, may either by himself think, or by the persuasions of other be brought to think, that in this doing I should not shew a pure mind, or true and incorrupt zeal and affection to his grace? Was there in me any such mind, when I warned his grace to beware of his cardinal, whose iniquity he shortly after proved according to my writing? Doth this deserve hatred? Again, may his grace, being a Christian prince, be so unkind to God, which hath commanded his word to be spread throughout the world, to give more faith to wicked persuasions of men, which presuming above God's wisdom, and contrary to that which Christ expressly commandeth in his testament, dare say that it is not lawful for the people to have the same in a tongue that they understand; because the purity thereof should open men's eyes to see their wickedness? Is there more danger in the king's subjects than in the subjects of all other princes, which in every of their tongues have the same, under privilege of their sufferance? As I now am, very death were more pleasant to me than life, considering man's nature to be such as can bear no truth.'

'Thus, after a long conversation had between us, for my part making answer as my wit would serve me, which were too long to write, I assayed him with gentle persuasions, to know whether he would come into England; ascertaining him that means should be made, if he thereto were minded, without his peril or danger, that he might so do: and that what surety he would advise for the same purpose, should, by labour of friends, be obtained of your majesty. But to this he answered, that he neither would nor durst come into England, albeit your grace would promise him never so much surety; fearing lest, as he hath before written, your promise made should shortly be broken, by the persuasion of the clergy, which would affirm that promises made with heretics ought not to be kept."

"After this, he told me how he had finished a work against my lord chancellor's book, and would not put it in print till such time as your grace had seen it; because he apperceiveth your displeasure towards him for hasty putting forth of his other work, and because it should appear that he is not of so obstinate mind as he thinks he is reported to your grace. This is the substance of his communication had with me, which as he spake, I have written to your grace, word for word, as near as I could by any possible means bring to remembrance. My trust therefore is, that your grace will not but take my labours in the best part I thought necessary to be written unto your grace. After these words, he then, being something fearful of me, lest I would have pursued him, and drawing also towards night, he took his leave of me, and departed from the town, and I toward the town, saying, 'I should shortly, peradventure, see him again, or if not, hear from him.' Howbeit I suppose he afterward returned to the town by another way; for there is no likelihood that he should lodge without the town. Hasty to pursue him I was not, because I was in some likelihood to speak shortly again with him; and in pursuing him I might perchance have failed of my purpose, and put myself in danger.

"To declare to your majesty what, in my poor judgment, I think of the man, I ascertain your grace, I have not communed with a man"—[1]

The effect of this letter on Henry is clearly stated in the reply written by Cromwell, who appears to have substituted, not improbably at the King's dictation, the harsh expressions given in the text for the more temperate forms of the original draft, as printed in the footnotes.

"Stephen Vaughan, I commend me unto you; and have received your letters, dated at Andwerpe, the xviii. day of April, with also that part of Tyndale's book inclosed in leather, which ye with your letters directed to the king's highness; after the receipt whereof I did repair unto the court, and there presented the same unto his royal majesty, who made me answer for that time, that his highness at opportune leisure should read the contents as well of your letters as also the said book. And at my next repair thither it pleased his highness to call for me, declaring unto me as well the contents of your letters, as also much matter contained in the said book of Tyndale. * * *

"Albeit that I might well perceyue that his Maiestee was right well pleased, and right acceptablie considered your diligence and payns taken in the wryting and sending of the saide boke, as also in the perswading and exhorting of Tyndall to repayre into this realme; *yet his Highness nothing lyked the sayd boke, being fyllyd wt scedycyous, slanderous lyes, and fantasticall oppynyons, shewing therin nother lernyng nor trewthe; and ferther, cõmunyng wt his grace, I myght well mind and conject that he thought that ye bare*[2] moche affection towards the saide Tyndall, whom in his maners and *knowlage in woordlye thinge*[3] ye vndoubtedlie *in yor l̃res* do moch allowe and cõmende; whos works *being replet wt so* abhominable sclaunders *and lyes*, imagened and *onlye* fayned to infecte the peopull, *doth declare hym bothe to lake grace, vertue, Lernyng, discrecyõ and all other good qualytes, nothing ells pretending in all his worke but to seduce* . . . dyssayve (that ye in such wise *by yr Lr̃es*,

[1] Cotton MSS., *Titus*, B. I.

[2] Originally: "in the accomplishement of his high pleasure and commaundment. Yet I might conjecture by the ferther declaracyon of his high pleasure, which sayed unto me that by yr wryting it manifestlie appered how *moche affection* and zele ye do berc"

[3] Originally: "modestie and symplycitee"

prayse, set forth and avaunse hym which nothing ells pretendeth) *and sowe sedycion among the peopull of this realme. The Kinge hignes therfor*[1] hathe cōmaunded me *to advurtyse you that is plesure ys*, that ye should desiste and leve any ferther to persuade or attempte *the sayd Tyndalle to cum into this realme:* alledging, that he p̄ceyuing the malycyous, perverse, vncharytable, *and Indurate* mynde *of the sayd Tyndall, ys in man*[er] *wt owt hope of reconsylyacyon in hym, and is veray joyous to have his realme destytute of such a p̄son*, then that he should retourne into the same, there to manyfest his errours and sedycyous opynyons, which (being out of the realme by his most vncharytable, venemous, and pestilent boke, craftie and false persuasions) he hath partelie don all redie; *for his highnes right prudentlye consyderyth* if he were present by all lykelohod he wold shortelie (which God defende) do as moche as in him were, to infecte and corrupt the hole realme to the grete inquietacyon and hurte of the cōmen welth of the same. Wherefore, Stephen, I hertelie pray you, in all your doing, proceding, and wryting to the King's highnes, ye do iustely, trewlie and vnfaynedlie, *wt owt dyssymulatyon, shew your self his trew, louyng, and obedyent subjecte, beryng no maner favor, loue, or affeccyon*[2] to the sayd Tyndale, ne to his worke, in any man[er] of wise; but utterlie to contempne and abhorre the same, assuring you that in so doing ye shall not onely cause the King's royall maieste, whose goodnes at this tyme is so benignelie and gracyouslie mynded towards you, as by your good dyligence and industrie to be used to serve his Highnes, and extewing and avoyding . . . favor, and allow the saide Tyndale his erronyous worke and opynions so to sett you forwardes, as all yor louers and frendes shall have gret consolacyon of the same; and by the contrarie *doing, ye shall* acquire the indignacyon of God, displeasure of yor sov'eigne lorde, and by the same *cause* yor good frends which have ben euer glad, prone, and redie to *bryng* you into *his gracyous* fauours, to lamente and sorow that their sute in that behalf should *be frustrate and* not to take effecte, according to their good intent and purpose."

Cromwell then adverts to Frith (or Fryth) saying that the King, "hearing tell of his towardness in good letters and learning, doth much lament that he should apply his learning to the maintaining, bolstering, and

[1] Originally: "Tyndale assuredly sheweth himself in myn oppynion rather to be replete with venymous envye, rancour and malice, then wt any good lerning, vertue, knowledge or discression:" this was changed into: "declareth hymself to be envyous, malycyous, slanderous and wylfull, and not to be lerned;" then erased, and given as above.

[2] Originally: "to shew yourself to be no fautor."

advancing the venemous and pestiferous works, erroneous and seditious opinions of Tyndale;" and begging Vaughan to use his influence with Frith "to leave his wilful opinions, and like a good Christian to return unto his native country, where he assuredly shall find the king's highness most merciful, and benignly, upon his conversion, disposed to accept him to his grace and mercy." The letter concludes with an exhortation to Vaughan, "for his love of God, utterly to forsake, leave and withdraw his affection from the said Tyndale, and all his sect."[1]

Cromwell added a postscript, after the letter had been read and approved by the king, which virtually nullified its contents, for he said: "Notwithstanding the premises in my letter, if it were possible by good and wholesome exhortations to reconcile and convert the said Tyndale . . . I doubt not but the king's highness would be much joyous of his conversion . . . and if then he would return into this realm . . . undoubtedly the king's majesty refuseth none."[2]

Upon the receipt of Cromwell's letter, Vaughan had a second interview with Tyndale, the account of which is given in his reply, dated Bergen-op-Zoom, May 18, as follows:

"I have again been in hand to persuade Tyndale. And to draw him the rather to favour my persuasions, and not to think the same feigned, I shewed him a clause contained in master Cromwell's letter containing these words following: *And notwithstanding other the premises, in this my letter contained, if it were possible, by good and wholesome exhortations, to reconcile and convert the said Tyndale from the train and affection which he now is in, and to excerpte and take away the opinions sorely rooted in him, I doubt not but the kings highness would be much joyous of his conversion and amendment; and so being converted, if then he would return into his realm, undoubtedly the king's royal majesty is so inclined to*

[1] The quotations, transcribed from the original, in the Brit. Museum, MSS. Cotton, *Galba*. B. X. fol. 338, for the Parker Society's edition of the *Doctrinal Treatises*, &c., of William Tyndale, have been taken from that volume. The brief paragraph relating to Frith I have extracted from Demaus, *l. c.* p. 305.

[2] From the text given by Demaus, *l. c.*, p. 306. See the full text in Vaughan's reply, p

mercy, pity, and compassion, that he refuseth none which he seeth to submit themselves to the obedience and good order of the world. In these words I thought to be such sweetness and virtue as were able to pierce the hardest heart of the world; and, as I thought, so it came pass. For after sight thereof I perceived the man to be exceedingly altered, and to take the same very near unto his heart, in such wise that water stood in his eyes; and he answered, 'What gracious words are these! I assure you,' said he, 'if it would stand with the king's most gracious pleasure to grant only a bare text of the scripture to be put forth among his people, like as is put forth among the subjects of the emperor in these parts, and of other Christian princes, be it of the translation of what person soever shall please his majesty, I shall immediately make faithful promise never to write more, nor abide two days in these parts after the same; but immediately repair into his realm, and there most humbly submit myself at the feet of his royal majesty, offering my body to suffer what pain or torture, yea, what death his grace will, so that this be obtained. And till that time I will abide the asperity of all chances, whatsoever shall come, and endure my life in as much pains as it is able to bear and suffer. And as concerning my reconcilation, his grace may be assured, that whatsoever I may have said or written in all my life against the honour of God's word, and so proved, the same shall I before his majesty and all the world utterly renounce and forsake; and with most humble and meek mind embrace the truth, abhorring all error soever, at the most gracious and benign request of his royal majesty, of whose wisdom, prudence and learning I hear mo great praise and commendation, than of any creature living. But if those things which I have written be true and stand with God's word, why should his majesty, having so excellent a gi of knowledge in the scriptures, move me to do any thing against my conscience?'—with many other words which be too long to write. I have some good hope in the man; and would not doubt to bring him to some good point, were it that something, now and then, might proceed from your majesty towards me, whereby the man might take the better comfort of my persuasions. I advertised the same Tyndale that he should not put forth the same book, till your most gracious pleasure were known: whereunto he answered, 'mine advertisement came too late; for he feared lest one that had his copy would put it very shortly in print, which he would let if he could; if not, there is no remedy.' I shall stay it as much as I can, as yet it is not come forth; nor will not in a while, by that I perceive."[1]

[1] Offor's *Mem. of Tyndale*, pp. 67–9. Anderson, pp. 277–9. *Doctr. Treat.* p. xlviii. *sqq.* The original is in the British Museum, Cotton MSS. *Galba.* B. X. 7, new notation. Also in Demaus, *l. c.*, p. 306 *sqq.*

Vaughan had yet another conversation with Tyndale, for he writes on June 19: "I have spoken with Tyndale, and shewed him as you wrote me the king's royal pleasure was, but I find him always singing one note."[1]

This concludes the negotiations set on foot by Cromwell to induce Tyndale to return to England, and our knowledge of him, except through his writings, until his final settlement at Antwerp in the summer of 1534.

The following passage in a letter of Poyntz, bearing date August 25 (Cotton MSS. *Galba*. B. X.) fixes the date of Tyndale's final settlement at Antwerp. "This man [William Tyndale] was lodged with me three quarters of a year, and was taken out of my house by a sergeant-at-arms, otherwise called a dore-wardore, and the Procureur-General of Brabant." Reckoning backward from the day of his arrest, established by the official statement given in the note[2] to have occurred on the 23rd or 24th of May, 1535, Tyndale seems to have reached Antwerp sometime in August, 1534.

The extract from Foxe (p. xxi.), gives a clear account of his life there. It is perhaps not unnecessary to add that he held no official position, but engaged in the voluntary work of an Evangelist. Rogers arrived at Antwerp sometime in the autumn of that year as English Chaplain and his acquaintance with Tyndale speedily ripened into friendship. He worked with him and there

1 State Paper Office: *Miscellaneous Letters*, Second Series; printed by Sir Henry Ellis in his collection of *Original Letters*.

2 "Account of Master Ludwig von Heylwygen of the confiscated goods of the Lutherans and heretical sects beginning from the year 1533, and ending in 15—

"Fol. viii. Expenses in vacation and other expenses in affairs of justice of the Lutherans.

"Paid to Adolph Van Wesele on account of the business done by him as well in keeping of a certain prisoner named *William Tyndale*, a Lutheran, as for his money expended, done and expended therein at the request of the Procureur-General, for a year and one hundred and thirty-five days, at forty stivers the day, as appears by the taxation, assignment and quittance pertaining thereto, the sum of . . . £102." This is the translation appended to the original document, given by Demaus, *l. c.* p. 498. The date of Tyndale's martyrdom, according to Foxe, is October 6, 1536, and his arrest consequently occurred on the 23rd or 24th of May, 1535.

is no reason to doubt the statement that the papers of Tyndale passed into his hands, and that he embodied in his edition of the Bible, known as Matthew's Bible, the remaining books of the Scripture which Tyndale had translated, viz., the books of Joshua, Judges; 1 and 2 Samuel, 1 and 2 Kings, 1 and 2 Chronicles.[1] His literary labors at Antwerp resulted in the revised edition of the book of Genesis and the revision of the New Testament; both were published in 1534. How much of the other books just named was done between 1534 and 1536 is not known.

The letter of Tebold or Theobald, a godson of Cromwell, who seems to have been instructed to collect information on the circumstances connected with the arrest of Tyndale, is a valuable addition to the narrative of Foxe (see page xx.).

"News here, at this time, be none, but that here is most earnest communication that the French Queen [Leonora, sister of the Emperor; Charles V.] and her sister the Queen of Hungary [the Regent of the Low Countries], shall meet together at Cambray now afore Michaelmas. All these Low Countries here be most earnest with the Bishop of Rome and his traditions; and therefore he hath now sweetly rewarded them, sending them his deceitful blessing, with remission of all their sins, so [on the condition that] they fast three days together, and this is given *gratis* without any money. Here is an evil market [a bad bargain for the pope], that whereas he was wont to sell his pardons by great suit and money, now he is glad to offer them for nothing. And yet a great many make no haste to receive them where they be offered. I do hear of certain that the Bishop of Rome is contented, and doth desire to have a General Council, and that this matter is earnestly entreated of divers. I am sure, if this be truth, your Lordship have heard of it or this time, more at large.

"*He that did take Tyndale is abiding at Louvain, with whom I did there speak; which doth not only there rejoice of that act, but goeth about to do many more Englishmen like displeasure; and did advance this, I being present, with most railing words against our King, his Highness, calling him* 'Tyrannum ac expilatorem reipublicæ' [*tyrant and robber of the Commonwealth*]. He is appointed to go shortly from Louvain to Paris in France, and there to tarry, because he feareth that English merchants that be in Antwerp will hire some men privily to do him some displeasure unawares.

[1] "The boke of Ionas" is Coverdale's Version.

"Pleaseth it your Grace that I have delivered your letters unto Mr. Thomas Leigh [a merchant held in much esteem by Cranmer and Vaughan], which, according to your writing, hath delivered unto me twenty crowns of the [same], which money, God willing, I will deliver where your Grace hath assigned. Within these sixteen days I take my journey from Antwerp about the last day of July [letter begun, therefore, July 15th]. And because at my first arrivance to Antwerp I found company ready to go up withal to Cologne [on his way to Nuremberg], I went to see my old acquaintance at Louvain; whereas [where] I found Doctor Bockenham, sometime prior in the Black Friars in Cambridge; and another of his brethren with him. I had no leisure to commune long with them; but he showed me that at his departing from England he went straight to Edinburgh in Scotland, there continuing unto [Easter] last past [March 28]; and then came over to Louvain, where he and his companions doth continue in the house of the Black Friars there; having little acquaintance [or] comfort but for their money; for they pay for their [meat] and drink a certain sum of money in the year. All succour that I can perceive them to have is only by him which hath taken Tyndale, called Harry Philips, with whom I had long and familiar communication, [for] I made him believe that I was minded to tarry and study at Louvain. I could not perceive the contrary by his communication, *but that Tyndale shall die;* which he doth follow, [*i. e.*, urge on], and procureth with all diligent endeavour, rejoicing much therein; saying that he had a commission out also for to have taken Doctor Barnes and *George Joye* with other. Then I showed him that it was conceived both in England and in Antwerp that George Joye should be [*i. e.*, had been] of counsel with him in taking of Tyndale; and he answered that he never saw George Joye to his knowledge, much less he should know him. This I do write, because George Joye is greatly blamed and abused among merchants, and many other that were his friends, falsely and wrongfully.

"But this foresaid Harry Philips showed me that there was no man of his counsel but a monk of Stratford Abbey, beside London [Stratford-le-Bow], called Gabriel Donne, which at that time was student at Louvain, and in house with this foresaid Harry Philips. But now within these five or six weeks he is come to England, and, by the help of Mr. Secretary, hath obtained an abbey of a thousand marks by the year in the west country.

"This said Philips is greatly afraid, (in so much as I can perceive,) that the English merchants that be in Antwerp, will lay watch to do him some displeasure privily. Wherefore of truth he hath sold his books, in Louvain, to the value of twenty marks worth sterling, intending to go hence to Paris; and doth tarry here upon nothing but of the return of his *servant which he has long since sent to England with letters. And by cause of his long tarrying, he is marvellously afraid lest he be taken and come into Master Secretary's handling, with his letters.* Either this Philips hath great friends in England to maintain him here; or else, as he showed me, he is well beneficed in the bishopric of Exeter. He raileth at Louvain and in the Queen of Hungary's Court, most shamefully against our King his Grace and others [Cranmer and Cromwell probably]. For, I being present, he called our King his Highness, *tyrannum, expilatorem reipublicæ,* with many other railing words, rejoicing that he trusteth to see the Emperor to scourge his Highness with his Council and friends. Also he saith, that Mr. Secretary hath privily gone about matters, here in Flanders and Brabant, which are secretly come to the knowledge of the Queen of Hungary, the Governess here, which she reckoneth, one day, at her pleasure and time, to declare to his rebuke. What this meaneth I cannot tell, neither I could hear no farther; but if I had tarried there any time, I should have heard more," etc.

"Written at Antwerp the last day of July, by your bedeman and servant, ever to my small power,—Thomas Tebold."[1]

The plot to seize Tyndale and to bring him to trial for heresy was doubtless due to astute contrivance in England, but thus far no positive evidence has been discovered to fasten the charge either on Gardiner or any one else. Donne and Phillips are admitted to have acted under instructions of persons strong in pecuniary ability, adepts in craft, and invincible in hatred. Henry VIII. and Cromwell cannot be charged with complicity, but may not be exonerated from indifference and neglect. Once in the meshes of the law, as administered in Flanders, the fate of Tyndale was sealed, but though his extradition could not be demanded *de jure*, the influence of an accredited "man of reputation" might have secured his liberation.[2]

The chief promoter and agent in stirring up interest on behalf of Tyndale was Poyntz, whose narrative given by Foxe at great length cannot be reproduced here. In re-

[1] Cotton MSS. *Galba*, B. X. cited by Demaus, *l. c.* pp. 430–433. The italics and matter in brackets are given as presented by him.

[2] Such seems to have been the impression of Stephen Vaughan who wrote "it were good the King had one living in Flanders that were a man of reputation." *Chapter House Papers*, State Paper Office, cited by Demaus, *l. c.* p. 439.

sponse to his indefatigable energy and self-denial he obtained letters from Cromwell, but his efforts were cut short by his own arrest and imprisonment, brought about by Phillips, who had preferred against him also the charge of heresy.[1]

The record of the trial of Tyndale appears to have been destroyed or lost. From a document in the Archives of the *Chambre des Comptes* at Brussels the names of the leading members of the commission nominated for his trial by the Regent, Mary of Hungary, have been obtained.[2] The Procureur-General has been represented as a monster of wickedness and cruelty; the Dean of St. Peter's is charged with holding the maxim that "It is no great matter, whether they that die on account of religion be guilty or innocent, provided we terrify the people by such examples; which generally succeeds best when persons eminent for learning, riches, nobility, or high station,

[1] The narrative of Poyntz is found in Foxe and has been reprinted in full by Demaus, *l. c.* p. 443 *sqq.* In the same work may be read the letter of Poyntz to his brother, Cotton MSS. *Galba*, B. X., as well as a letter from Flegge, an English merchant at Antwerp, to Cromwell advising him what had been done on behalf of Tyndale. Cotton MSS. *Galba*, B. X.

[2] The document printed by Demaus, *l. c.* p. 498 *sqq.* is here reproduced. The very able and interesting account he has constructed of the probable order observed in the trial of Tyndale is perhaps the most successful portion of a volume which should be read by all desirous to understand the case. He has furnished also sketches of Pierre Dufief, the Procureur-Général, and of two of the most prominent clerics on the commission, Ruwart Tapper and Jacques Lathomus. The document reads as follows:

"Archives of Belgium: Chambre des Comptes, No. 19,1662.

"Paid to the Procureur-General of Brabant for himself £128. 8s. 6d.; also for Mr. Ruwart Tapper, Dean of St. Peter's at Louvain, Jacques Lathomus, Jan Doye, canons there, all Doctors in theology, William Van Caverschoen, amounting for them all to £149: to Godfrey de Mayere £54; Charles T'Serraets £5. 8s.; Theobald Cotereau £6. 6s.; Mr. Jacob Boonen £10. 10s.; Councillors in Brabant: to Mr. Henry Vander Zypen £3. 12s.; to Marcellis van Immerseel £4. 10s.; Peter de Brier £6. 10s.; Cornelius Vander Bruggen £2.; Henry Van Pellen £10. 10s.; Bartholomew Vander Broecke, Nicolas Borreman, Jan Vander Biest and Dierick Cappellemans £6. 15s.: executioners and messengers of the Council, who have been engaged, by the ordinance of the Queen [Mary of Hungary] as they say, in prosecution of the process directed by the said Procureur-General against William Tyndale, a priest, a Lutheran prisoner, and executed by fire at Vilvorde for entertaining certain wicked opinions touching the Holy Catholic faith; so that they have been occupied at Vilvorde and elsewhere on different days, as appears from the contents of their declaration of their engagements, amounting for the said engagements to the sum of £312. 9s. 6d., and over and above to the sum of £16 for behoof of the Doctors only: this appearing from the declaration, taxation and assignment and receipt thereto belonging in all to . . . . £407. 9s. 6d."

are thus sacrificed;" and of Lathomus, the third of the leading members of the commission, it is narrated that the part he had taken in the conviction of Tyndale filled him with remorse, if not despair.[1] Tried by such a commission, condemnation was inevitable, for the writings of Tyndale abound in sentiments which the Louvain theologians could have had no difficulty in proving to have been rank heresy. The passage in Foxe that "there was much writing and great diſputation to and fro between him [Tyndale] and them of the Vniversitie of Louvain, in such sort that they had all enough to do, and more than they could well wield, to answer the authorities and testimonies of the Scripture, whereupon he most pithily grounded his doctrine," sheds light upon the manner in which the trial was conducted. It was all in writing; Tyndale's own defence has not yet come to light, but the reply of Lathomus, printed in his Works, has been preserved. The publication of that treatise would be a valuable contribution to the history of Tyndale.

This notice is concluded with a precious memento of William Tyndale in the text of a touching letter written by Tyndale in his prison at Vilvorde in the winter of 1535. It is without date and superscription, and was doubtless addressed to Antoine de Berghes, Marquis of Bergen-op-Zoom, who held the office of Governor of the Castle of Vilvorde in 1530. M. Galesloot found it in the Archives of the Council of Brabant, and M. Gachard permitted Mr. Francis Fry of Bristol to have it photographed; from a

[1] "Jacobus Lathomus, omnium theologorum Lovaniensium, sine controversiâ, princeps, posteaquam stultâ et puerili concione quam Bruxellæ habuit coram Imperatore, se toti aulæ ridendum exhibuisset, mox ubi Lovanium rediit, pernicioso quodam furore correptus, cœpit insanire, ac in ipsâ etiam publicâ prælectione voces edere plenas desperationis atque impietatis. Quod cum cæteri theologi animadvertissent, præcipue Ruardus Enchusanus [*i. e.* Tapper], homo miserabili balbutie, et crudelitate atque impietate inauditâ, apprehenderunt furentum Lathomum, eumque domi clausum tenuerunt. Ab eo tempore usque ad postremum spiritum nihil aliud clamavit Lathomus quam 'se condemnatum esse, se a Deo rejectum esse, nec ullam spem salutis aut veniæ sibi amplius esse reliquam, ut qui veritatem agnitam impugnâsset.'" The last clause appears to refer to Tyndale. The whole passage is taken from Demaus, *l. c.* p. 456, who says, that it is given by H. Janssen, *Jacobus Præpositus*, on the authority of Diaz.

copy of this photograph of the only known autograph letter written by William Tyndale, kindly sent me by Mr. Fry, has been made the photo-engraving which faces the title page of this volume. But as the handwriting may not be easily read by those unfamiliar with the written characters of the sixteenth century, I subjoin a transcript in ordinary Roman letter, literary accurate in all respects except the contractions, which, for want of proper types, had to be avoided. I have also added an English translation.

Credo non latere te, vir preſtantiſſime, quid de me ſtatutum ſit. Quam ob rem, tuam dominationem rogatum habeo, idque per dominum Ieſum, vt ſi mihi per hyemem hic manendum ſit, ſollicites apud dominum commiſſarium, ſi forte dignari velit, de rebus meis quas habet, mittere, calidiorem birretum, frigus enim patior in capite nimium oppreſſus perpetuo catarro, qui ſub teſtudine nonnihil augetur. Calidiorem quoque tunicam, nam hec quam habeo admodum tenuis eſt. Item pannum ad caligas reficiendas, Duplois detrita eſt: camiſee detrite ſunt etiam. Camiſeam laneam habet, ſi mittere velit. Habeo quoque apud eum caligas ex craſſiori panno ad ſuperius induendum. Nocturna birreta calidiora habet etiam: vtque veſperi lucernam habere liceat, Tedioſum quidem eſt per tenebras ſolitarie ſedere. Maxime ante omnium, tuam clementiam rogo, atque obſecro, vt ex animo agere velit, apud dominum commiſſarium, quatenus dignari velit, mihi concedere bibliam hebreicam, grammaticam hebreicam et vocabularium hebreicum, vt eo ſtudio tem-

I believe, most excellent Sir, that you are not unacquainted with the decision reached concerning me. On which account, I beseech your lordship, even by the Lord Jesus, that if I am to pass the winter here, to urge upon the lord commissary. if he will deign, to send me from my goods in his keeping a warmer cap, for I suffer greatly from cold in the head, being troubled with a continual catarrh, which is aggravated in this prison vault. A warmer coat also, for that which I have is very thin. Also cloth for repairing my leggings. My overcoat is worn out; the shirts also are worn out. He has a woolen shirt of mine, if he will please send it. I have also with him leggings of heavier cloth for overwear. He likewise has warmer nightcaps: I also ask for leave to use a lamp in the evening, for it is tiresome to sit alone in the dark. But above all, I beg and entreat your clemency earnestly to intercede with the lord commissary, that he would deign to allow me the use of my Hebrew Bible, Hebrew Grammar, and Hebrew Lexicon, and that I may

pus conteram. Sic tibi obtingat quod maxime optas, modo cum anime tue ſalute fiat, Verum ſi aliud conſilium de me ceptum eſt, ante hyemem perficiendum, patiens ero, dei expectans voluntatem, ad gloriam gratie domini mei Ieſu chriſti, cuius ſpiritus tuum ſemper regat pectus. Amen.
W. TINDALUS.

employ my time with that study. Thus likewise may you obtain what you most desire, saving that it further the salvation of your soul. But if, before the end of winter, a different decision be reached concerning me, I shall be patient, and submit to the will of God to the glory of the grace of Jesus Christ my Lord, whose spirit may ever direct your heart.
W. TINDALUS.

The evidence, furnished on every page of the present volume, that Tyndale translated the Pentateuch direct from the Hebrew, is strikingly confirmed by the passage in which he entreats and beseeches the Governor to send him his Hebrew Bible, Hebrew Grammar and Hebrew Dictionary.

CHAPTER II.

THE WRITINGS OF WILLIAM TYNDALE,

EITHER PUBLISHED WITH HIS NAME OR ASCRIBED TO HIM.

1. Translations, probably anterior to 1524: a. *Enchiridion Militis Christiani.* b. *Iſocrates, Orationes.*

2. *The Newe Teſtamente.* 1525–26. Revised edition 1534. Upwards of eighty editions have been printed. See Lists of Archbishop Newcome, Dr. Cotton, and Mr. Anderson; for historical details the writer's *Hand Book of the English Versions*, &c., Ch. IV., and for bibliographical purposes, Francis Fry: *A Bibliographical Description of the Editions of the New Testament, Tyndale's Version in English, with Numerous Readings, Comparisons of Texts, and Historical Notices; the Notes in full, from the Edition of Nov. 1534. An Account of two Octavo Editions of the New Testament of the Bishops' Version without Numbers to the Verses. Illustrated with Seventy-three Plates, Titles, Colophons, Pages, Capitals.* London, 1878.

3. *A Pathway into the holy Scripture,* 1525 to 1532.

4. *The parable of the wicked Mammon, May* 8, 1527 [28] in-4 and 8.

5. *The obedience of a Chriſten man, and how Chriſten rulers ought to gouerne, wherein alſo (if thou marke diligently) thou ſhalt finde eyes to perceaue the craftie conueyaunce of all iugglers.* May and Octob. 2, 1528. 1535. 1561.

6. *An exhortation to the diligent ſtudye of the ſcripture, made by Eraſmus Roterodamus. And trāſlated into engliſh.* ¶ *An expoſition in to the ſeuenth chaptre of the firſt piſtle to the Corinthians.* Colophon: At Malborow in the londe of Heſſe. M.D.xxixx. xx. daye Iunii. By me Hans Luft.—Herbert's Ames, III., p. 1538.

7. *Treatise on Matrimony*, 1529.

8. *Translation of the Fiue bokes of Moses called the Pentateuch*, with Prologues into the several books, 1530 (*Geneſis, correctyd*, etc. 1534), alleged to have been reprinted in 1534, 1544, 1551. Each book of the Pentateuch has a separate title; there is no *general* title in the edition of 1530; for information concerning editions see Ch. III.

9. *The Prologue of the Prophete Jonas and Translation of the Book*, 1530 [31].

10. *A Compendious Olde treatiſe, ſhewynge howe that we ought to haue the Scripture in Englyſſhe.* Hans Luft. 1530.

11. *The Practyſe of Prelates.* ❨ *Whether the Kings grace maye be ſeparated from hys quene, becauſe ſhe was his brothers wyfe.* Marborch. In the yere of our Lorde, Mccccc. & xxx. (Copy in the Cambridge University Library, marked F. 13, 40)— ¶ *The Practiſe of papiſticall Prelates, made by William Tyndall.* ❨ In the yeare of our Lorde. 1530. (Title of the reprint in Daye's folio of 1573.)

12. *An aunſwere vnto Syr Thomas Mores Dialogue, made by William Tyndall.* 1530. ☞. Firſt he declareth what the Church is, and geueth a reaſon of certaine wordes which Maſter More rebuketh in the tranſlation of the new Teſtament. ❨ After that he aunſwereth particularly vnto euery Chapter which ſemeth to haue any appearaunce of truth thorough all his foure bookes, ❨ *Awake thou that ſlepeſt and ſtand vp from death, and Chriſt ſhall geue the light.* Epheſians. 5. (Title of reprint in Daye's folio of 1573.) 1531.

13. *The expoſition of the firſt Epiſtle of S. Iohn*, set forth by M. William Tyndall in the yeare of our Lord. 1531. Septemb. (Title in Daye's folio of 1573.)

14. ¶ *An expoſition vppon the V. VI. VII. chapters of Mathew, which three Chapters are the keye and the dore of the ſcripture, and the reſtoring agayne of Moſes law corrupte by the Scribes and Phariſes. And the expoſition is the reſtoring agayne of Chriſtes lawe corrupte by the Papiſtes.* ¶ *Item before the booke, thou haſt a Prologe very neceſſarie, contayning the whole ſumme of the couenaunt made betwene God and vs, vppon which we be baptiſed to keepe it.* Set forth by William Tyndall. (Title in Daye's folio of 1573.) 1532.

15. *The Souper of the Lorde. wher vnto, that thou mayſt be*

the better prepared and ſuerlyer enſtructed: haue here firſt the declaracion of the later parte of the .6. ca. of S. Iohā., beginninge at the letter C. the fowerth lyne before the Croſſe, at theſe wordis: Verely, vere. etc. *wheryn incidently M. Moris letter agenſt Iohan Frythe is confuted.* Colophon: Imprinted at Nornburg, by Niclas Twonſon, 5 April. An. 1533. (Herbert's Ames, III., p. 1541.) *The Supper of the Lorde. After the true meanyng of the ſixte of John, and the .xi. of the fyrſt epyſtle to the Corynthians; whereunto is added an Epyſtle to the reader. And incidently in the expoſicion of the ſupper is confuted the letter of Maſter More agaynſt Ihon Fryth.* 1 Cor. xi. Whoſoever ſhall eate of this bread and drinke of this cuppe of the Lorde unworthely, ſhall be gyltye of the body and bloud of the Lorde. Anno Mcccccxxiii. v day of Apryll. ("Title of edition in the Archbiſhop's Library, Lambeth." Prof. Walter in Vol. *An Anſwer*, &c., by Tyndale, Parker Soc. ed. 1850.)

16. *A frutefull and godly treatiſe expreſſing the right inſtitution and vſage of the Sacramentes of Baptiſme, and the Sacrament of the body and bloud of our Sauiour Ieſu Chriſt.* Compiled by William Tyndall. (Title of Reprint in Daye's folio of 1573.) 1533 or 1534? See below in Wood's list No. 10.

17. *A Proteſtation made by William Tyndall, touching the Reſurrection of the bodyes, and the ſtate of the ſoules after this life.* Adſtracted out of a Preface that he made to the new Teſtament, which he ſet forth in the yeare 1534. (John Foxe in Daye's folio 1573.)

18. *The Teſtament of maſter William Tracie Eſquier, expounded* by William Tyndall. *Wherein thou ſhalt perceiue with what charitie the Chaunceler of Worceter burned, when he tooke vp the dead carkaſſe and made aſhes of it after it was buried.* 1535. (This Title and an address ¶ *To the Reader*, as they appear in Daye's folio of 1573, are due to John Foxe.)

19. *A Letter ſent from William Tyndall, vnto Iohn Frith, being priſoner in the Tower of London.* (Title of reprint in Daye's folio of 1573.) 1532.

20. *An other notable and worthy Letter of maiſter William Tyndall ſent to the ſayd John Frith, vnder the name of Iacob.* (Title of reprint in Daye's folio of 1573.) 1533. See also below in Wood's List, No. 1.

21. *Preface* to Wiclif's *Wicket.*

22. The Books of Joshua, Judges, Ruth, 1, 2 Samuel, 1, 2 Kings, 1, 2 Chronciles as they appear in Matthew's Bible, 1537, are believed to have been translated by William Tyndale.

23. [Wood, *Athenæ Oxonienses*, &c., vol. i., col. 94 *sqq*, ed. London. 1813, in-4., states: "The following additional treatises remain to be mentioned. 1. *Summæ S. Scripturæ.* This is noted by Henry Stalbridge, in his Epistle to Henry VIII.—2. *Translation of the*

Psalms, MS. in New college library, Oxford, No. 320.*—Besides these he wrote, 3. A preface to *The prayer and complaint of a plowman.*—4. One to *The examinations of William Thorpe and Sir John Oldcastle.*—5. *Exposition on 1 Cor. vii. with a prologue*, 120, 1529. (See No 6 above.)—6. *A boke concerning the church.*—7. *A godly disputation between a christian shomaker and a popish persone.*—8. *The disclosyng of the man of sin.*—9. *The matrimonye of Tindall*, 1529. TANNER, *Bibl. Brit.* 450.—10. *A brief declaration of the ſacramentes expressing the first originall and how they came up and were instituted, with the true and most sincere meaninge and understandynge of the ſame, very necessarye for all men that will not erre in the true use and receauinge thereof. Compyled by the learned and godly man William Tyndall. Imprinted at London by Robert Stoughton dwellinge within Ludgate at the sygne of the bishoppe's miter.* 8vo. KENNET.—11. *Epistolas ad Joh. Frith tres;* quarum ultima continet Expositionem vi capitis Iohannis et 1 Corinth. xi. contra Tho. Morum; sed nomen Tindalli non subscribitur.' TANNER, *Bibl. Brit.*—Foxe, *Actes and Monumentes*, B. v., under date of 1360 mentions the title of No. 3 thus: *The Prayer and complaint of the Ploughman, concerning the abuses of the world, as the book was faithfully set forth by William Tyndale;* and that

* In response to an inquiry on this MS. addressed by me to the Rev. T. E. Sewell, D.D., Warden of New College, Oxford, that gentleman has kindly informed me that MS. 320 is the work of Wiclif, not of Tyndale, and sent me the following extract from *Catalogus Codicum* MSS. *qui in Collegiis Aulisque Oxoniensibus hodie observantur*, by H. O. Coxe, late Librarian of the Bodleian.

¶ "CCCXX.

¶ "Codex chartaceus, in folio minori, ff. 45, sec. xv; olim Thomæ Smythe.

¶ "*The Psalms of David, according to the earlier version of Wycliffe's translation, with two prologues.* The Version agrees with that of MS. No. 66 above described.—At the end are,

1. "The songs of Moses, Anna, Simeon, &c. taken from the Old & New Testament,
2. "The Creed of St Athanasius,
3. "An hymn to the Virgin by William Huchen: Beg.

"Swete and benygne moder and may
Turtill true flower of women alle,
Aurora bryght clere as the day,
Noblest of hewe thus we the calle."

Dr. Sewell adds: "The words *By William Huchen* are found at the bottom of the page on which the hymn to the Virgin occurs, being the last page of the *MS.* There is no doubt that there is nothing of Tyndale's in the *MS.* the date of which is of the fifteenth century. The *MS.* No. 66, which Mr. Coxe refers to contains *The Books of the Old Testament, according to the later version of John Wycliffe*, &c., &c. I have compared the versions of the song of Simeon by Tyndale and by Wyckliffe, and am sure that the version in the *MS.* in the Library of New College is Wyckliffe's and not Tyndale's."

The name William Huchen resembling Tyndale's pseudonyme has probably occasioned the erroneous notice in Wood's list, taken from Tanner.

of No 4: *William Thorp's account of his Examination, when brought before Thomas Arundel, archbishop of Canterbury, as corrected by master William Tyndale.* Advertisement in *Doctrinal Treatises,* p. ix. Parker Society's edition, Cambridge, 1848. See also note on p. x.]

24. *Portions of the New Teſtament translated from the Greek into English by that noble and venerable Martyr William Tyndale who first published the New Testament in English in 1525 In his own handwriting and accompanied by his own drawings in 1502.*

This is the Title, drawn up by Mr. George Offor, of a Manuscript now (1884) in the Lenox Library, New York, concerning whose acquisition Mr. Offor says in the Preface: "In 1808 it came into the possession of my kind old antiquarian friend, the Revd. Henry White of Lichfield Cathedral, and from about the year 1815 it became the pearl of my great collection of English Bibles."

No account in print having come to the notice of the present writer, he here presents the following description of this interesting Manuscript.

An antique ecclesiastical oaken case, richly carved, showing on the upper cover a Madonna seated, on the lower cover, a figure of Justice with sword and scales, enclosing a volume bound (1850) in morocco, in–4, the cut page 10⅞ *in.* × 8¾ *in.*, 46 ff. in the following order: Fly leaves, 2 ff.; two engravings of Tyndale, 2 ff.; Title Page,* 1 f.; engraving of Tyndale, 1 f.; The Tyndale Manuscript, being an account of it by George Offor, 9 ff.; pen and ink sketch of Christ, shewing underneath a pasted slip with the name of the former owner: "HENRY WHITE, Close, Lichfield, November 13th, 1808" in his handwriting, 1 f.;—then follow 26 ff., each displaying on the recto a full page drawing in India ink, water colours, and gold, of Scripture topics connected with the Gospels given on the verso of each preceding leaf, except the first two, illustrating the Presentation of John Baptist and the Purification of the Virgin. The Gospels appear in illuminated borders in compartments of unequal size, the largest measuring 6 *in.* × 3⅞ *in.*, the smallest 5½ *in.* × 3¼ *in.* Recto of Fo. 3, illustrating Luke vii, 36, &c., contains the date 1500. The verso of Fo. 23, giving Luke xviii, 9–17, contains in the right hand border a column with the legend: TIME TRIETH., and the date 1502. The initials W. T. occur eight times. The Gospels supplied are the following: Fos. 3. Luke vii, (erroneously viii. in the Ms). *And one of the Pharises* &c.; 4. Marke xi, *And on the morowe* &c.; 5. Iohn ii, *And the thyrde daye* &c.; 6. Matthew viii, *And when he entred* &c.; 7. Matthew viii, *When muche people followed him* &c.; S. Luke vii, *And it fortuned after this* &c.; 9. Matthew xi, *When Iohn beinge in preſon*

* Title Page: In border with ecclesiastical emblems: Title as given above.

&c.; 10. Luke viii, *The ſower wente oute* &c.; 11. Luke xvii, *Ieſus toke vnto him the twelue* &c.; 12. Matthew xx, *For: the kyngdome of heauen is lyke vnto a man that is an houſholder* &c.; 13. Matthew iv, *Then was Ieſus led a waye of ẏ ſprete* &c.; 14. Matthew xv, *And Ieſus wente thence, and departed into the coſtes of Tyre* &c.; 15. Luke xi, *And he was caſtyng oute a deuell* &c.; 16. Iohn v, *When Ieſus lifte vp his eyes* &c.; 17. Iohn viii, *Whiche of you rebukethe me of ſinne?* 18. Iohn xvi, *After a while ye ſhall not ſe me* &c.; 19. Iohn iii, *There was a man of the Phariſes* &c.; 20. Mathew xxii, *The kyngdome of heauen is lyke vnto a man that was a kynge* &c.; 21. Luke xvi, *There was a certeyne richeman, whiche was clothed in purple and fine white* &c.; 22. Luke v, *It came to paſſe (when the people preaſed vpon him to heare the worde of god)* &c.; 23. Luke xix, *And when he was come* &c.; 24. Luke xviii, *And he tolde this parable vnto certayne wich* &c. The date 1502 occurs on this page. 25. Luke xvii, *And it chaunced as he wente to Ieruſalem* &c.; 26. Iohn i, *When the Iewes ſent prieaſtes and Leuites* &c.—Verso of fo. 26 has the usual border but the panel is left blank;—Morton, the bookbinder's receipt for £4. 4.—Verso blank, 1 f.; 1 f. blank; fly leaf, 1 f.—The volume on both morocco covers has in gilt: NEWE TESTAMENT. 1502. W. TYNDALE.

The MS. is written on paper with the water mark of an open hand surmounted by a stellar flower; this mark, and the bull's head and star, are said not to have been used since 1510. The character is Black Letter, but the handwriting appears to be due to several writers; several hands may also be traced in the ornamental borders and the full page illustrations; the anachronisms are striking; on f. 18 Nicodemus, in the costume of the sixteenth century, holds a rosary; the Pharisee and the Publican, f. 24, also carry rosaries, and on the same page two saints appear as mural ornaments of the Temple; on the verso of f. 4 St. George is represented in the act of killing the Dragon in order to relieve the Virgin Mary; the border of f. 7 depicts an angel with a Maltese cross over his head; churches with spires and a liberal supply of crosses in strictly oriental scenes are of constant occurrence.

The portrait of Henry VII., identified by the emblematic union of the two roses supporting his throne, occurs twice in the ornamented borders.

Among the orthographical characteristics may be named: *stode a farr*, *thorowe*, *fownde*, *aduouterers*, *deuell*, *a broode* (abroad); also such divisions of words as: *di-sciples*, *th-en*, *m-en*, *pray-yse*, *we-ddyng*.

Some of the translations *must* have been made from the Greek, but it is incredible that Tyndale who in 1525 rendered ἄνωθεν *a newe* and *agayne*, should have translated that word in 1500 or 1502 *from above*. This last rendering, as far as I am advised, appeared for the first time in the version of Pagninus, who discards the old Vulgate rendering, *renatus fuerit denuo*, and gives, *natus fuerit superne*. Similar renderings from the Greek have been noted by others. Other translations, however, seem to have been made from the Latin.

Subjoined is a specimen, selected solely on account of its brevity, accompanied by the Latin from the edition of Stephanus, 1528, collated with the text of Jenson's *Biblia*, Venetiis, 1479, in–folio., which contains only two variations, viz., v. 37 *diſcendentium* and v. 40 *quia ſi tacuerint*.

Luke The .XIX. Chapter.

37 And when he was come: nye to the goynge | downe of the
mounte Olyuete: the hole multitude | of the dyſcſiples began to
reioyce and to praiſe- | God wyth a loude voyſe, for all the mirac-
38 les that | they had ſene, ſayinge: :·: Bleſſed be the kynge y^{t} |
commeth in the name of the Lorde: peace in hea- | uen, and glory
39 in the hyeſt. And ſome of the pha | riſes of the company ſaide
40 vnto him: Maſter, | rebuke thy dyſciples. He ſaide vnto them:
I- | tell youe, that yf theſe holde there peace: :·: then | ſhall the
41 ſtones crye: And when he was come | nyare, he behelde the citie
42 and wepte on it ſayin- | ge: If thou haddeſt knowne thoſe thinges
w^{lch} | be longe vnto thy peace, euen in this thy day, | thou
43 woldeſt take hede: But nowe are they, | hydde frome thine
eyes: For the dayes ſhalle | come vpon the. :·: that thy enemyes
alſo ſhall | caſte a banke aboute the, and compaſſe the ro- | unde,
44 and kepe the in of, euery ſyde, and make | the euen with the
grounde: and the childeren wh^{ch} | are in the: And they ſhall not
leaue one ſtone a pon a nother: because thou knoweſt not the
tyme | of thy viſitacion.: :·: ‖ :·: ‖ :·: ‖ :·: ‖ : : ‖ :·: ‖ :·:

Luc .XIX., 37–44. From Stephanus, *Biblia*, 1528, in-folio.

37 Et cum appropinquaret iam ad descensum montis Olivueti, cœpe-
runt omnes turbæ discentium gaudentes laudare deum voce mag-
38 na super omnibus quas viderant, virtutibus, dicẽtes, Benedictus
qui venit rex in nomine domini, pax in cælo, & gloria in excelsis.
39 Et quidam Pharisæorum de turbis dixerunt ad illum, Magister,
40 increpa discipulos tuos. Quibus ipse ait, Dico vobis quia si hi ta-
41 cuerint lapides clamabunt: ¶ Et vt appropinquauit, videns ci-
42 uitatem, fleuit super illam, dicens, Quia si cognouisses & tu, &
quidem in hac die tua, quæ ad pacem tibi. nunc autem abscon-
43 dita sunt ab oculis tuis. Quia venient dies in te: & circundabunt
44 te inimici tui vallo, & circundabunt te, & coangustabunt te vndique,
& ad terram prosternent te, & filios tuos qui in te sunt. & non
relinquent in te lapidem super lapidem: eo quod non cognoueris
tempus visitationis tui.

Mr. Offor's Title must be deemed infelicitous, for 1. it is not certain that the letters W. T. denote the author; 2. it cannot be proved that they designate William Tyndale; 3. it may be demonstrated that portions, perhaps the greater part of the MS., are translations from the Latin.

The Author of the *Historical Account*, &c., prefixed to the first edition of Bagster's *Hexapla* (p. 41, n.,) believed it to have been written and translated by the Martyr; Anderson, *Annals*, &c., Vol. II., App., iii., n., ridicules the notion; Professor Westcott, *History of the English Bible*, p. 25, n., 2d edition, declares the MS. to be spurious.

CHAPTER III.

THE PENTATEUCH OF 1530.

To the best of my knowledge only *one perfect* copy has been discovered. It is in the Grenville Library of the British Museum. The copy in the Lenox Library is all but perfect, the only parts wanting being, Folios XLIV.

and XLV., containing Ex. xxv. 37 to xxvi. 14 and two of the eleven woodcuts contained in the volume, which have been supplied in *facsimile* by H.; see *Bibliographical Notice.* The copy in the Baptist College, Bristol, contains Genesis of 1534, but the remaining books of the Pentateuch are of the edition of 1530. A copy, recently discovered and given to the Astor Library, lacks the book of Genesis.

The Lenox copy, from which the present edition is made, is a 12mo volume, without a general title. A full account of it is now presented.

1. *Bibliographical Notice of the Copy of Tyndale's Pentateuch of 1530, in the Lenox Library, New York.*

Title page displaying in fancy border: | The fyrſt | boke of | Moſes called | Geneſis. | ∴—Verso: | W. T. To the Reader. | "When I had," &c., to "more correcte"; in Dutch or German Black Letter, 4 ff.— | ¶ Aprologe ſhewinge the vſe," &c., to "thorow him. AMEN.," in German Black Letter, 4 ff.; in all, 8 ff. of signature A. not marked.—The pages number 30 and 31 lines.—.1. Chapter. Fo. 1. | The fyrſt boke | of Moſes called Geneſis | The fyrſt Chapiter. | on signature B 1. to "The end of the firſt boke of Moſes." on recto of f. LXXVI. being the fourth folio of signature L. in eights, 76 ff. Verso of f. LXXVI.: "¶ A table expoundinge certeyne wordes," &c., to Colophon: ¶ Emprented at Malborow in the lan | de of Heſſe, by me Hans Luft, | the yere of oure Lorde .M. | CCCCC.xxx. the .xvij. | dayes of Ianu | arij. | three additional folios, making in all 79 ff., in Dutch or German Black Letter, 32 and 33 lines to a page. The page from head line to signature inclusive measures 5¼*in.* and crosswise 2⅝*in.* approximately.—One blank leaf. —Title Page: | A PROLO | GE INTO THE SECON- | de boke of Moſes called | Exodus. | Verso: | 𝔚 T | "Of the preface vppō Geneſis, &c.," to "ād handes with oure face to the grounde," 8 ff., or one signature not marked. Title Page displaying in fancy border: | The ſecon | de boke of Mofes, cal- | led Exodus. | Verso, blank. Fo. II. | ℭ The feconde boke of Mofes | called Exodus. | ℭ The firft Chapter. | , on signature A.ij, to "The ende of the feconde boke of Mofes": recto of f. LXXVI., verso blank, in all 76 ff., in Dutch or German Latin Letter. The Prologe and the boke of Exodus contain 28 and 29 lines to a page and the page from head line to *catch-word* measures 5*in.* and crosswise 2⅝*in.*—Title Page displaying in fancy border: | A PRO- | LOGE IN TO THE | thirde boke of Mofes | called Leuiticus. | Recto of signature A.i. not marked. Verso: | W T | ℭ Aprologe in to the thirde boke of Mofes, | called Leuiticus. | "The ceremonies which, &c.," to "with his honoure?" (concluding the Prologe) one signature of 8 ff., followed by Title Page displaying in fancy border: | ℭ The | Thyrde Bo- | ke of Mofes. Cal- | led Leuiti- | cus. | on recto of first folio of signature A; verso, blank. | 1. Chapter. Fo. II. | ℭ The thirde boke of Mofes, cal- | led Leuiticus. | ℭ The firfte Chapter. | recto of signature A.ij, to | ℭ The ende of the thyrde boke | of Mofes. | on verso of fourth folio of signature G., in all 52 ff. The Prologe and the boke of Leuiticus are in Dutch or German Latin Letter, contain 29 lines to a page, and each page measures from head line to catchword 5*in.* and crosswise 2⅝*in.* approximately.—Title Page displaying in fancy border: | ℭ A prolo | ge in to the fourth boke of | Mofes, called Numeri. | on recto of first folio of signature A; verso: | W T | ℭ A Prologe in to the fourth boke of Mo- | fes, called Numeri. | "In the feconde ād thirde boke, &c.," to "fhall teach the all thynges," 10 ff. of one signature A in tens, in Dutch or German Black Letter.—Title Page displaying in fancy border: | The four | the boke of Mofes called | Numeri. | ; verso, blank. | 1. Chapter. Fo. ij. | ℭ The .iiij. boke of Mofes, called Numeri. | on signature B.ij to | ℭ The ende of the .iiij. boke of Mofes. | on verso of f. lxvij., being the third folio of signature K in eights, in all 67 ff., in Dutch or German Black Letter, part of the verso of the last folio being blank; this book, like Genesis, is without catchwords, and the page from head line to signature measures 5¼*in.* and crosswise 2⅝*in.* approximately; the Prologe and the Boke of Numbers contain 32 lines to a page.—One blank leaf; Title Page displaying in fancy border: | A PRO | LOGE IN TO THE | fyſte boke of Moſes, cal- | led Deuteronomye. | verso: | W T | From | "This is a boke worthye to be rede, &c.," to "loke ĩ the ſcripture, foũde but ful of foliſhneſſe." 4 ff., in Dutch or German Latin Letter, on the fourth folio of sign. A.— | The firſt Chapter of Deuteronomye. Fo. I. | on signature B. to | ❡ The ende of the fifth boke of Moſes. | on verso of Fo. LXIII., in the middle of the page, followed by: "Avims, A kinde of geauntes" to "imaginĩge," ending line 9 of recto of the last folio (not marked) of signature I, in tens, in Dutch or German Latin Letter, in all 64 ff., the last, nine lines excepted, blank. Each page of the Prologe and the Boke of Deuteronomye measures from head line to catchword 5*in.* and crosswise 2⅝*in.* approximately, and contains 30 lines.—The dimensions vary occasionally ⅛*in.* in both directions, the margins vary from ½*in.* to ⅝*in.* and the pages also sometimes contain a line less or more than here indicated, the number of lines including both the head line and that of the catchword or signature.—"W. T. To the Reader" and "Aprologe ſhewinge the vſe of the ſcripture" are without head lines. The Prologues to Exodus, Leviticus, Numbers and Deuteronomy have the head line W. T. on every page. The several books themselves generally give on *every* page the Chapter only, and generally the folio number on the recto. An example will illustrate this. In the book of Genesis: Recto, i Chapter. Fo. i. Verso, i Chapter. Sometimes the order is reversed, *e. g.*, Recto, Chapter .xix. Fo. xxiij. Verso, Chapter .xix; sometimes the head line reads, The .xliii. Chapter; and sometimes it is entirely omitted, as on verso of ff. xxxiii., .xxxv., .lxx.; the numeration also is very faulty.

Recapitulation.

The fyrst boke of Moses, called Genesis.		
Two Prologes	8	folios.
Text	79	"
Blank	1	"
The seconde boke of Moses, called Exodus.		
Prologe	8	"
Text	76	"
The thirde boke of Moses, called Leuiticus.		
Prologe	8	"
Text	52	"
The fourth boke of Moses, called Numeri.		
Prologe	10	"
Text	67	"
Blank	1	"
The fyfte boke of Moses, called Deuteronomye.		
Prologe	4	"
Text	64	"
Total	378	folios.

The same fancy border (compare illustration, page 1) is used seven times (Genesis once, Exodus once, Leviticus twice, Numbers twice, Deuteronomy once). The volume contains eleven woodcuts:

1. The forme of the arke of wittnesse &c.	Exod. XXV.	Fo. XLIII.
2. The table of shewbreed &c.	" "	" "
3. The facion of the cādelsticke &c. [F. S. by H.]	" "	" XLIIII.
4. The forme of the ten cortaynes [F. S. by H.]	" XXVI.	" not marked.
5. The facion of the bordes of the tabernacle &c.	" "	" XLVI. verso.
6. The facion of the corner bordes &c.	" "	" XLVII.
7. The forme of the alter of the burntoffrynge &c.	" XXVII.	" XLVIII. verso.
8. The figure of the orderinge of all the ornamētes &c.	" "	" XLIX. verso.
9. The forme of Aaron with all his apparell.	" XXVIII.	" L. verso.
10. The forme of the altare of incense &c.	" XXX.	" LVI.
11. The figure of the lauer of brasse &c.	" "	" LVII. verso.

The cuts measure $4\frac{1}{4}$*in.* × $3\frac{1}{4}$*in.* and are doubtless made from the same blocks which were used in Vorsterman's: | Dey Bibel. | Tgeheele Oude ende Nieu | we Testament met grooter naersticheyt | naden Latijnschen text gecorigeert, eñ opten | cant des boecks die alteratie die hebreeusche | veranderinge, naerder hebreeuscer waerheyt | der boeckē die int hebreus zijn, eñ die griecsce | der boeckē die int griecs zijn, ēdinhout voor | die capittelen gestelt, Met schoonen figueren | ghedruct, eñ naerstelijc weder ouersien. | Cum Gratia et Priuilegio. | —Colophon: | ℭ Ghedruct Thantwerpen in die Cammer- |

ſtrate, inden ghulden Eenhoren, Bimi | Willem Vorſterman, Voleyndt op | Sinte Simons ende Iudas | auontdey .xxviii. dach | van October Int Iaer | nae die gebuerte Christi ons | ſalichmakers .M.ccccc.xxviij. |

Comparison shows that with the sole exception of some of the cuts in Tyndale's Pentateuch having been either slightly trimmed or enlarged at the sides, they are identical with those in Vorsterman's Bible, in–folio.

The same cuts however had been used in Lotter's edition of Luther's Translation of the Pentateuch in larger size, viz., *9in.* × *5⅝in. circa*, and since that folio was printed in 1523, Vorsterman either had them reduced for his Bible, or the cuts were prepared and sold in different sizes by the engraver in wood who made them. They are identical in all respects except in figure 4, where Lotter's illustration gives some houses on the right side of the cut which in the corresponding cut in Vorsterman and Tyndale appear on the left side.

2. *The Present Edition.*

In the preparation of my *Hand Book of the English Versions* the necessity of consulting the original copy of Tyndale's Pentateuch was often very pressing, and although sundry extracts contained in that volume were courteously supplied, the want of accurate information on the subject in print, and the singular excellence of Tyndale's translation appeared to me to call imperatively for a reprint of the work as it came from his hands. The book of Genesis was revised by Tyndale in 1534, but copies of that edition appear to be even more rare than those of 1530. Matthew's Bible, published in 1537, contains the text of Tyndale's Pentateuch of 1530 with numerous variations. There is also a London edition by Ihon Day, printed in 1551, exceedingly scarce, containing the entire Pentateuch in a text of which an example will be presented on a subsequent page. The prologues, finally, to the different books of Tyndale's Pentateuch and certain Tables were printed in Daye's folio edition of Tyndale's Works published in 1573. A reprint of the last, adapted to the modern spelling, has been issued by the Parker Society. This completes the list and proves that an exact reproduction of the text of the edition of 1530 has never been printed. It seemed to me a burning shame that one of the noblest monuments of English Literature should continue to lie in undeserved oblivion, especially because its author, who had consecrated his life to the work of evangelizing the world by the translation of the Scriptures into the vernacular, had earned for it, the Martyr's crown.[1]

Tyndale's Pentateuch is the first English translation of the Hebrew original, and on that account, if on no other, deserves to be made accessible not only to scholars, but to every lover of the English Bible. His translation was intended for the *people*, and the Martyr's design has been attempted to be carried out in the present issue, which gives to the people not only everything he translated in the original volume, but presents it also in the very form in which he wrote it. To the *scholar* this minute accuracy will be peculiarly valuable, and he moreover may reap a rich harvest of instruction from the notes which owe their origin to the wide-spread slander that Tyndale translated from the Latin and the German versions. This calumny thoughtlessly repeated by numerous writers is disproved on every page of this volume. I deem it unnecessary to name here any of the authors in question, and to transcribe their statements.

[1] There is reason for believing that the marginal notes in the Pentateuch were used, with other of his printed opinions, as evidence of his heresy. An instance may be seen in the marginal note on Deuter. I, 43, which reads

In the edition of 1530:	*In Matthew's Bible, 1537:*
"Here thou feift the verey image of the papiftes. For *thei* like wife where Gods worde is, *there they* beleue not ād where it is not there *they* be bold."	"Here thou feyft the vereye Image of *vs that lyue* ĩ *this moft perilous tyme*, for *euen we* lykewyfe, where goddes worde is, *here* beleue *we* not: and where it is not, there be *we* bolde."

In 1536 Tyndale was martyred; the memory of the scene at Vilvorde was indelibly stamped on the mind of John Rogers and doubtless prompted the change in the note, which contains a chapter of history.

As a matter of fact Tyndale's version of the Pentateuch, as it came from his hand, is known only to an infinitesimally small fraction of the English speaking nations of the earth, and its text, identified as Tyndale's, except in a few isolated passages, not known at all; indeed, as no actual critical collation of this Pentateuch has ever been published,[1] we cannot even tell how far and how truly the actual text of Tyndale has been transmitted. This is the more remarkable on account of its indisputably great critical value in fixing the character of the first *English* text of the Pentateuch in the ancestral line of the Common Version, a point of considerable importance just now in view of the *general principles* to be followed by the Companies for the Revision of the Authorized Version, the first two of which read as follows:

"1. To introduce as few alterations as possible into the text of the Authorized Version consistently with faithfulness.

"2. To limit as far as possible the expression of such alterations to the language of the Authorized and earlier English versions."

This, as far as the Pentateuch is concerned, must apply pre-eminently to Tyndale's version as the *only English* version, which, without leaning on any other that had gone before, was made directly from the original, and, changes in the spelling and *occasionally* in language and expression excepted, has been substantially preserved in the Authorized Version.

The reasons which have moved me to make the present issue are these:

It is designed, to be a grateful tribute to the memory of the martyr-translator; to make this noble version, which as a first translation is not excelled by any other with which I am acquainted, generally accessible to Bible readers; to *fix* its text by actual collation with different editions, to establish its relation to

[1] There is a MS. collation of the Pentateuch with Taverner's edition of 1539, which I have not seen.

the Latin and German Versions; to furnish a contemporary Commentary in the Notes of Luther and Rogers, and to enrich the Philology of the Language with a copious vocabulary.

3. *Form and Size of this Edition.*

Reference to the *Bibliographical Notice* and to the specimen pages presented in this volume will show that the original copy contains 378 ff., or 756 pages of rather small dimensions, viz., $5\frac{1}{2}$ *in.* × $2\frac{5}{8}$ *in. circa*, the full page ranging from 29 to 33 lines, and that the books of Genesis and Numbers are printed in Black Letter and the remaining three books in Latin Letter. The first intention of reproducing the Original page for page, and line for line, in the same type, had to be abandoned as incompatible with the ends to be served by the present issue. The matter contained in the notes and margins may be approximately estimated at about one-third of the contents of the text, which with the introductory matter would have made a very thick and unhandy duodecimo, even if the type used had been correspondingly small. The reproduction of the same type, would have necessitated the casting of two distinct founts of letter, for which, in America at least, the printer would have had no other use. Tyndale himself printed his Genesis of 1534 in Latin Letter, and this fact, as well as the further consideration that the reading of Black Letter with various contractions would have interfered with the ready use of the volume by a large number of readers, suggested the propriety of adopting a Letter familiar to all and capable of presenting all the peculiarities of the edition; the edition of 1534, that of 1551, Matthew's Bible of 1537, Daye's folio of 1573 and the Parker Society's reprint of the Prologues, moreover, do not conform to the page for page and line for line plan. On these grounds an octavo page has been selected as the most convenient size for the purposes to be served by this edition, which carefully marks the beginning of the recto and verso of every folio, and aims to adhere with diplomatic fidelity to every, even the minutest, detail of the original copy. The omission of the strictly *facsimile* plan has also had the additional advantage of enabling me to correct palpable misprints, which in every instance have been removed by analogy drawn from Tyndale's own page, or, where that failed, by reference to Matthew's Bible. An accurate list of these changes is furnished at the end of the Prolegomena; in all doubtful cases the text is given unchanged, but every case, (broken, defaced, or blurred letters excepted) has been carefully noted. In the edition of 1530 different numerals have been employed; to avoid confusion and inconsistency only one kind of numerals has been used in this edition. It is necessary to add that the running head lines in Black Letter are not in the edition of 1530, which gives only the folio and chapter; that edition, and all the other editions used in the preparation of this volume, are without verse-division, which for convenience of reference had to be adopted and conformed to that observed in the Authorized Version.

This feature of course increases the value, and facilitates the use of this book without in any way interfering with the integrity of Tyndale's text, which stands *exactly* as in the edition of 1530. For the same reason the Chapter Summaries from Matthew's Bible, marked *M. C. S.* have not been placed before the chapter, but in the Margin, which has also been used for the explanation of a few archaic terms. The Various Readings, and parallel places in other Versions, are given in the lower margin. The collation with Genesis 1534, being an independent work, chiefly due to the careful scholarship of Dr. Culross, who has compared the text of this edition with that of the copy in the Museum of the Baptist College at Bristol, is given in a separate section; the collation of the Prologues of 1530 with the Prologues in Daye's folio of 1573, due (in Genesis and Exodus) to Dr. Culross, appears immediately after it, while a list of marginal notes in the same volume gives an analysis of that interesting part of Tyndale's Pentateuch.

4. *Means adopted for Securing an accurate Text.*

The whole of Tyndale's Pentateuch, the Prologues to Genesis and Exodus excepted, has been transcribed by me from the copy in the Lenox Library. The transcript thus secured, upon careful revision, and the original copy by its side, was then compared with the text of Matthew's Bible, and the variant readings and renderings duly recorded. In this difficult work I had the benefit of the assistance of Dr. S. Austin Allibone, whose quick and experienced perception enabled me to note the differences as they occurred. He either read to me, or I read to him, the entire Pentateuch in Matthew's version. Then I compared Tyndale's text, first, with that of the Latin Bible, and afterwards with Luther's *first* edition of the Pentateuch. The Manuscript then was sent to the printer, and at my express request not returned. The first proofs were twice read at the printer's by the MS. and twice in succession compared with the original printed copy. Here also Dr. Allibone afforded me valuable aid. Second or revised proofs were then procured, and again read very carefully by the original. Third or plate proofs followed, of which one copy was sent to Dr. Culross, and another, retained by me, was again compared with the original. In the book of Genesis all the variant readings in the edition of 1534 were marked by Dr. Culross on the plate proofs, and in this way was obtained the valuable and interesting collation at the end of the Prolegomena. A number of test passages in the remaining four books transcribed by Dr. Culross from the Bristol copy, and another set copied by me from the Lenox copy, were compared by us with the respective copies, and their minute agreement in text, even to misprints and inaccuracies, led to the discovery that both copies were made from the same forms of the edition of 1530. The *uncorrected* plate proofs were then compared by Dr. Culross with the text of the Bristol copy, and by me with that of the Lenox copy; at this stage, a clean set of plate proofs was also compared with the original by Dr. Allibone; then I attended to the final comparisons of corrections made by my kind friends and myself, with the result, that every correction noted and verified, was made by me in the proofs, and the constant agreement of our corrections, frequently extending to such minute points as the appearance of a faulty letter, the use or non-use of a mark of punctuation, bears testimony to the rare and scrupulous fidelity with which Drs. Culross and Allibone have performed their labor of love. Occasional differences, chiefly of this or that little matter omitted by one of the correctors, I have duly noted, and in every instance, corrected by the Lenox copy. Then the plates were corrected and the first plate proofs accompanied by clean proofs were again examined, and, upon evidence that all the corrections had been made, the order to print was given. The text, thus obtained, is that furnished in this volume. It is proper to add that all the notes also have been repeatedly compared with the originals from which they are taken.

5. *Helps used by Tyndale.*

On this point it is difficult, if not impossible, to speak with any degree of certainty. The material to be had, was not by any means so scant as is generally thought, but in the absence of all data, except those contained in Tyndale's letter written in prison, (see page li.) and those derived from the study of his text, the subject cannot be discussed in detail.

Of Hebrew *Grammars* he might have used any of the following:

D. KIMCHI: *Michlol* (perfectio), embracing Grammar and Lexicon, Constantinople 273 (1513), 290 (1530). Venice, Bomberg, 289 (1529).—ABRAHAM DE BALMIS: *peculium Abræ. Grammatica hebr. una cum latino.* Venice, Bomberg, 1523, in–4.—KR. PELLICAN: *de modo legendi et intelligendi hebræa.* Basel, 1503, in–4.—ELIAS LEVITA: *Sepher Habbachur* (liber electus). Cracow, 277 (1517); also, cum SB. MUNSTERI *vers. lat. et scholiis*, Basel, 285 (1525), in–8.—I. REUCHLIN: *ad Dionysium fratrum suum germanum de rudimentis hebraicis libri 3.* (l. 1. 2. Lexicon. l. 3 Grammar) s. l. 1506, in–4.—SCT. PAGNINUS: *hebr. institutiones in quibus quicquid est grammatices hebraicæ facultatis edocetur ad amussim.* Lyons, 1526, in–4.

Of *Lexica:*

SB. MÜNSTER: *lex. hebr.–chald.* Basel, 1508, 23, 25, in–8.—SCT. PAGNINUS: *thesaurus linguæ sanctæ sive lex. hebr.* Lyons, 1529, in–folio.

Of *Hebrew Bibles:*

Biblia hebr. integra cum punctis et accentibus, auctoritate et consilio Josuæ Salomonis fil. Israelis Nathanis per Abraham fil. Chajim finita Soncini die 11. mensio Jiar a. 248 (1488), in–folio.—*Biblia hebr. integra cum punctis et accentibus.* Brescia, Gersom fil. Mosis, 295 (1494) in–8.—*Biblia Sacra Hebræa cum Masora et Targum Onkelosi in Pentateuchum,* &c. Venetiis, typis Dan. Bomberg. 5278 (1517) 4vv. in–folio., 2d ed. with *Abenesra in Pent.*, &c. Venet. 5285, 86 (1525. 26), 4vv. in–folio.—*Pentateuchus hebraicus c. Targum Onkel. et Comment. R. Sal. Jarchi.* In fine subscriptio R. Ioseph Cajim correctoris: Absolutum opus hoc perfectum feria VI. die V. mensis Adar primi anno 242. a creatone mundi (1482) ibi Bononiæ per Abraham Ben Chaiim Pisaurensem, impensis Ios. Chaiim Ben Aaron Argentoratensis. Char. textus quadratus cum punctis et accentibus, Targum et Comment. char. rabb minore.—*Pentateuchus hebraicus absque punctis cum Chaldaica paraphrasi Onkelosi et commentario Iarchi* באי״שאר, *videlicet, uti creditur in Insula Soræ anno* CCL. *Christi* MCCCCXC, in–folio.—*Biblia Sacra Polyglotta,* &c., *studio, opera, et Impensis Cardinali Francisci Ximenes de Cisneros.* Compluti, 1514, 15, 17, 6vv. in–folio.—*Biblia Hebraica Pisauri* MCCCCXCIV *sine punctis* in–folio and 4. et cum punctis in–8.

To these should still be added Vorsterman's Dutch Bible in–folio (See Title, p. lxiii.), which though made from the Vulgate, contains numerous references to the Hebrew; it was doubtless known to Tyndale, but as the volume was sent to me after the present edition was in type, I have not been able to use it in the preparation of my notes; it is not improbable that Tyndale used it for reference.

Besides the Greek Text of the Old Testament contained in the Complutensian Polyglot, the Aldine edition of 1518 (*Sacræ Scripturæ Veteris Novæque omnia*, Venetiis, 1518, in–folio), and the Strassburg edition of 1526 (*Divinæ Scripturæ Veteris Novæque omnia*, Argentorati, apud Wolphium Cephalæum, 1526, 4vv. in–8) were also available to Tyndale.

Most, perhaps all, the works here enumerated might have been procured at Antwerp, Hamburg, and Wittenberg.

Of other versions we have to name first, the Vulgate, which must have been as familiar to Tyndale as the Authorized Version is to every English divine of the present century, secondly, the Wiclifite Versions and lastly, Luther's translation.

A brief account of these versions is now in place. Beginning with the Vulgate, it may be accepted as a fact, that the Apostles and first Christian missionaries used the Greek version in planting the Church. Greek was the language of civilization, understood especially by people of higher culture. At Rome and throughout Italy, however, the masses of the people clung tenaciously to the Old Latin. In order to reach them, the necessity of a Latin version was universally felt, and oral translations of the Scriptures were speedily followed by written ones, the oldest of which were made from the Greek. They multiplied so rapidly that in the fourth century it was affirmed by the highest authorities that there were almost as many versions as copies. This was a great and crying evil, for not only were those versions very faulty and corrupt, but they presented a text which differed in almost every version. To remedy the evil Jerome undertook a *revision*, which proved generally acceptable, and speedily entered into almost universal circulation. But that remarkable scholar was not satisfied with his revision, and engaged upon the Herculean enterprise of translating the Scriptures from the original Hebrew into Latin.

This new Version encountered bitter opposition, and could not displace for centuries the old version made from the Greek, or, more correctly, it never displaced it entirely, for to this day parts of the Old Latin version are embedded in the official version of the Roman Catholic Church known as the Vulgate. In course of time, however, the unquestionable superiority of Jerome's version led to its partial adoption, with the result, that it was either *adapted* to the old version or *mixed up* with it, and produced an uncertain text, which, through careless transcribers or ignorant correctors and emendators, had become so corrupt as to necessitate a new Revision by Alcuin. This Alcuinian recension, patronized by Charlemagne, was the best text in use during the Middle Ages, and held its ground until the invention of printing, and the time of the Reformation. Guttenberg's Bible, the first Bible and first book printed with movable type, presents that text which, with but few exceptions, has been copied in subsequent editions of the Latin Bible. From that text were made numerous versions into the vernacular tongues of Europe *before the Reformation*.

A copy of the Bible containing the text of the Alcuinian Recension was used by Tyndale. The edition used in the preparation of the Notes in this Volume is that of Stephanus, published in 1528. Its *text*, like that of most of the Latin Bibles printed before that date, may be said to be identical with that used by Tyndale and Luther, but it contains also references to MSS. and to the Hebrew. It is printed with great accuracy in beautiful type. A brief description of the volume may be useful:

Title Page: BIBLIA. Cut of grafted olive tree with motto: Noli altum sapere, ſed time.—Pariſiis Ex officina Roberti Stephani, eregione Scholæ Decretorum M.D.XXVIII.—CVM PRIVILEGIO REGIS.—Verso: Hoc bibliorum opus, cum reſtituta hebraicorum nominum interpretatione, et duobus indicibus, regiis literis, ne quis alius in hoc regno impune imprimat, aut vendat intra quadriennium, cautum est.—Lectori. *ij; verso: Ex Sacris Literis Exhortatio ad Lectores.—Index Teſtimoniorum &c. 2 ff. *iij. iiij.—Præter ea quæ caſtigata &c. recto of *.v; verso: Ordo.—Hieronymi Prologus Galeatus 1 f.; Hieron. Paulino 3 ff.—Præfatio &c. recto of 1 f., verso blank; in all 5 ff. without signature and pagination.—Liber Geneſis f. 1, signature a.j. to f. 394 (misprinted 390), on last folio of signature D.d.—Colophon: Pariſiis excudebat in ſua officina Robertus Stephanus, iiii Cal. Decemb. Anno M.D.xxvii.—Errata.—Then follows: Lectori, a.ij; verso: Interpretatio Nominum &c. to ende of ee and 2 ff. over; verso of last folio blank.—Index Rerum &c. signature aaa.j. to end of signature fff., verso of last folio, containing: *Le Priuilege*, ending with DES LANDES.

The volume is in-folio, margins ruled in carmine, the signatures are in eights, the first four folios marked, the last four unmarked, and a full page numbers 61 lines.

The subjoined readings of places in the Pentateuch, taken from this volume with the note introducing them, are very interesting since not a few of them were adopted by the Sixtine-Clementine editors of the Vulgate.

Præter ea quæ caſtigata ſunt in hac bibliorum emiſſione, hæc quoque reſtituenda annotat Lyranus & Paulus ex antiquis Latinis exemplaribus, quibus & Hebræa conſentiunt: quæ partim corrupte leguntur in noſtris illis veteribus exemplaribus, partim emendate, cæterum a nobis non fuerunt inter imprimendum deprehenſa.

Gen. 5, 3 genuit ad[1] 6, 16 ſic diſtingue, ex latere: deorſum cœnacula 7, 9 præceperat deus 7, 13 & tres vxores 8, 15 autem deus ad 9, 26 ſeruus eis. 15, 6 Abram domino, 17, 1 apparuit ei deus: 17, 16 orientur ex ea, ſ. Sara 18, 28 propter quinque vniuerſam 22, 14 Dominus videbit. Vnde 23, 12 coram populo 24, 29 hominem foras vbi 24, 32 pedes eius, & 44, 28 dixi, Beſtia

Exod. 3, 12 populum de 12, 25 dominus daturus 13, 17 duxit deus per 18, 26 plebem omni 20, 11 fecit dominus cælum 22, 6 inuenerit ſpinas, 22, 29 tardabis reddere 23, 20 angelum, qui 24, 4 altare ad radices 27, 21 collocabunt eum Aaron 28, 2 fratri tuo. Et loqueris 28, 4 tunicam lineam, 29, 5 linea tunica 31, 14, ſabbathum, ſanctum 33, 1 populus quem 33, 13 mihi viam tuam, 35, 25 quæ neuerant,

Leuit. 3, 2 ſacerdotes, 8, 26 fermento vnum, & 13, 31 capillum

[1] The Sixtine-Clementine editors have struck *filium* from the text.

non nigrum: 19, 3 Vnuſquiſque matrem ſuam & patrem ſuum timeat.

Num. 11, 4 deſyderio ſedens, 34, 11 fontem, inde

Deut. 1, 18 Præcepique vobis omnia 4, 35 præter eum. De 6, 4 noſter, dominus vnus 9, 9 vobiſcum dominus: & 12, 10 hoſtibus veſtris per 25, 3 abeat frater 29, 11 aduenæ qui tecum morantur in caſtris, ex 29, 23 ſalis ardore 32, 15 directus, &

The *Wiclifite Versions*, of course, were made from Manuscript copies of the Latin Bible,[1] and circulated in Tyndale's time in MS. I fully concur in the statement of the learned editors of the superb edition of Wiclif's Bible[2] that "the versions of Wycliffe and his followers . . . . contributed largely to the religious knowledge which prevailed at the commencement of the Reformation; and at that period they supplied an example and a model to those excellent men, who in like manner devoted themselves at the hazard of their lives to the translation of Scripture, and to its publication among the people of the land" (Preface, p. xxxiv.). The comparison of Exodus xx. in Purvey's revision, Forshall and Madden's edition, with the text of Tyndale appears to justify this statement, the ring and language of that ancient version resound distinctly in Tyndale's translation.

EXODUS XX.

1 And the Lord spak all these wordis, 2 Y am thi Lord God, that
ladde thee out of the lond of Egipt, fro the house of seruage. 3 Thou
schalt not haue alien goddis bifore me. 4 Thou schalt not make to
thee a grauun ymage, nethir ony licnesse *of thing* which is in heuene
aboue, and which is in erthe bynethe, nether of tho thingis, that ben
in watris vndur erthe; 5 thou schalt not herie tho, nether thou schalt
worschipe; for Y am thi Lord God, a stronge gelouse louyere: and
Y visite the wickidnesse of fadris in to the thridde and the fourthe
generacioun of hem that haten me, 6 and Y do mercy in to a thou-
synde, to hem that louen me, and kepen myn heestis. 7 Thou
schalt not take in veyn the name of thi Lord God, for the Lord schal

[1] See *Hand Book of the English Versions*, pp. 40–76.

[2] *The Holy Bible*, &c., *in the earliest English Versions made from the Latin Vulgate by John Wycliffe and his followers;* edited by Rev. Josiah Forshall, F. R. S., &c., and Sir Frederic Madden, K. H. F. R. S., &c., Oxford, 1850, 3vv. in-4.

not haue hym giltles, that takith in veyn the name of his Lord God.
8 Haue thou mynde, that thou halowe the dai of the sabat; 9 in sixe
daies thou schalt worche and schalt do all thi werkis; 10 forsothe in
the seuenthe day is the sabat of thi Lord God; thou schalt not do ony
werk, thou, and thi sone and thi douȝtir, and thy seruaunt, and thin
handmaide, thi werk beeste, and the comelyng which is withynne
thi ȝatis; 11 for in sixe dayes God made heuene and erthe, the see,
and alle thingis that ben in tho, and restide in the seuenthe dai;
herfor the Lord blesside the dai of the sabat, and halewide it. 12 On-
oure thi fadir and thi moder, that thou be long lyuyng on the lond,
which thi Lord God schal ȝyue to thee. 13 Thou schalt not sle. 14
Thou schalt do no letcherie. 15 Thou schalt do no theft. 16 Thou
schalt not speke fals witnessyng aȝens thi neiȝbore. 17 Thou schalt
not coueyte the hous of thi neiȝbore, nether thou schalt desyre his
wijf, not seruaunt, not handmaide, not oxe, not asse, nether alle
thingis that ben hise. 18 Forsothe al the puple herde voices, and
siȝ laumpis, and the sowne of a clarioun, and the hil smokynge; and
thei weren afeerd, and schakun with inward drede, and stoden a
fer, and seiden to Moises, 19 Speke thou to vs, and we schulen here;
the Lorde speke not to vs, lest peraduenture we dien. 20 And
Moises seide to the puple, Nyle ȝe drede, for God cam to proue
ȝou, and that his drede schulde be in ȝou, and that ȝe schulden not
do synne. 21 And the puple stood a fer, forsothe Moises neiȝede to
the derknesse, wherynne God was. 22 And the Lord seid ferther-
more to Moises, Thou schalt seie these thingis to the sones of Israel,
Ȝe seiȝen that fro heuene Y spak to ȝou; 23 ȝe schulen not make
goddis of silver, nethir ȝe schulen make to ȝou goddis of gold.
24 Ȝe schulen make an auter of erthe to me, and ȝe schulen offre
theronne ȝoure brent sacrifices, and pesible sacrifices, ȝoure scheep,
and oxun, in ech place in which the mynde of my name schal be; Y
schal come to thee, and Y schal blesse the. 25 That if thou schalt
make an auter of stoon to me, thou schalt not bilde it of stoonys
hewun; for if thou schalt reise thi knyif theronne, it schal be polluted,
ether defoulid. 26 Thou schalt not stye by grees to myn auter, lest
thi filthe be schewid.

EXODUS XX.

1 Places where Tyndale agrees with Hebrew against all the authorities used: 3 in my ſyght 12 geueth the 18 noyſe of the horne 21 thicke clowde 23 with me

2 Places where Tyndale agrees with Wiclif verbally: 4 grauen ymage . . heauen aboue . . erth beneth 5 viſet . . . generacion 7 take . . . in vayne . . giltleſſe 16 falſe witneſſe 17 couet 20 proue 24 alter of erth . . there on offer (*transposed*) 25 alter off ſtone . . hewed (Wiclif, *hewun*) ſtone . . polute.

3 Places where Tyndale agrees with, or has been influenced by Luther: 14 Thou ſhalt not breake wedlocke 18 thunder . . lyghtenynge 24 burntofferinges . . peaceoffringes 26 nakedneſſe

4 Places where Tyndale agrees with, or has been influenced by the LXX.; 5 gelouſe God [Θεος ζηλωτης] 12 geueth [διδωσι] 21 where God was [ου ην ο Θεος] 25 tool [εγχειριδιον] 26 nakedneſſe.

5 Places where Tyndale agrees with, and has been influenced by the Latin: 1 God [Compl. *deus*, Steph. *dominus*] 24 remēbraunce [*memoria*, cf. however Luther's *Gedechtnis*].

While the Wiclifite versions were the only English translations and circulated only in *manuscript*, Germany as early as 1522 could point to not less than fourteen *printed* editions of the Scriptures in High German and three in Low German: they were all made from the Latin, but too literal to be intelligible.[1]

The first vernacular version made direct from the original is Luther's. It is in every respect remarkable, but in none more than in its lucidity, terseness, and strength. Made for the people, it attained from the start a popularity, which continues to this hour, and although subjected to successive revisions, the changes introduced into it, are mainly the substitution of modern for archaic terms, the assimilation of the verbs to modern flexions, and the introduction of the prevailing system of spelling. The changes in the rendering are comparatively few, and only such as the superior knowledge of the ancient languages and the discovery of important manuscripts of the original Scriptures have made indispensable.

The precise relation of Luther's Version to the Older German versions may be seen in the following example,

[1] German Bibles before the Reformation:—*High German:* 1 Eggesteyn, Henr, Strassb., 1466; 2 Mentelin, Jo., Strassb., 1466; 3 Jod. Pflantzmann, Augsb., 1470 or 73; 4 Sensenschmidt and Frisner, Nürnb., 1470, 73; 5 Zainer, Günther, Augsb., 1473, 75; 6 *Ibid.*, 1477; 7 Ant. Sorg., Augsb., 1477; 8 *Ibid.*, 1480; 6 Ant. Koburger, Nüremb., 1483; 10 no name, Strassbg, 1485; 11 Hanns Sehönsperser, Augsbg., 1487; 12 *Ibid.*, 1490; 13 *Ibid.*, 1507; 14 Silv. Otmar, Augsbg., 1518, 14th and last H. G. edition before Luther. *Low German:* 1 Quentel, Cologne, 1480; 2 Steffen Arndes, Lubeck, 1494; 3 Halberstadh, *reprint*, 1522.

which gives the text of Exodus xx. in the first printed edition and in the first edition of Luther's Translation.

EXOD. XX.

From the first German Bible printed by Henry Eggeſteyn, Straſſburg, circa 1466. folio.

1 Vnd d. herr redt alle diſe
wort.
2 Ich bins d. herr deī got ich
dich aus fürt von dē land egipt:
vnd von dē haus des dienſtes.
3 Nit hab frembd göt vor mir.
4 Nit mach dir bild noch ein
iegklich gleichſam die do iſt
in dē hymel oben vnd die ding
die do ſint auff d. erd nidē:
noch d. die do ſint ī den waſ-
5 ſern vnder d. erd. Nit ambecht ſy noch ere ſy. Wan̄
ich bins d. herr dein got
ſtarcker recher: heimſuchent
die vngangkeit d. vetter in die
ſun. in dz drit vnd in dz vierd
geſchlecht d. die mich haſſent:
6 vnd thun derbermbde in tau-
ſenten den die mich lieb habent. vnd behüten meine ge-
bot.
7 Nichten nym dē namē deins
herrn gotz ī vppig. Wan̄ der
herr laſt es nit on ſchaden. dem
d. do nimpt dē namen ſeins
herrn gotz ī vppig.
8 Gedenck das du geheiligeſt
9 dē tag d. feyr. Sechs tag
werck vnd thu alle deine
10 werck. Wann an dē ſybendē
tag iſt die feyr deins herren
gotz. Nit thu alles werck ī
im: du vnd dein ſun. vnd deī
tochter. deī knecht vnd deī
diern. deī vich vnd d. frembd
d. do iſt inwendig deiner tor.

From Luther's ALTES TESTAMENT, *Wittemberg, Melchior Lotter, 1523. folio.*

Vnd der Herr redte all diſe 1
wort.
Ich byn der Herr deyn Gott, 2
der dich aus Egypten land aus
dem dienſthaus gefurt habe.
Du ſolt keyn ander Gotter 3
neben mir haben, du ſolt dyr 4
keyn bildnis noch yrgent eyn
gleychnis machen, widder des
das oben ym hymel, noch des
das vnden auff erden, oder des
das ym waſſer vnter der erden
iſt. Bete ſie nicht an, vnd diene 5
yhn nicht, Denn ich der Herr
deyn Gott, byn eyn ſtarcker
eyfferer, der do heymſucht der
veter miſſethat an den kindern
bis ynn das dritte and vierde
gelidt, die mich haſſen, Vnd 6
thu barmhertzickeyt an viel
thauſent, di mich lieb haben
vnd meine gepot halten.
Du ſolt den namen des Herrn 7
deyns Gottis nit vergeblich furen, denn der Herr wirt den
nicht vnſchuldig halten, der
ſeynen namen vergeblich furet.
Gedenck des Sabbathstags, 8
das du yhn heyligiſt, Sechs 9
tage ſoltu erbeyten vnd alle
deyne werck ſchaffen, Aber 10
am ſiebenden tag iſt der Sabbath des Herrn deyns Gottis,
da ſoltu keyn geſchefft thun,
noch deyn ſon noch deyn tochter, noch deyn knecht, noch
deyn magd, noch deyn viech,

11 In ſechs tagē macht d. herr dē
hymel vnd die erd vnd dz mer
vnd alle ding die do ſint in in:
vnd ruet an dem ſybenden tag.
Dorum geſegent d. herr dē tag
d. feir vnd geheiliget in

12 Ere deī vatter vnd dein mutter: dz du ſeyeſt langes lebens
auff d. erd dz dir gibt dein
herre gott.
13 Nicht derſchlag.
14 Nicht brich dein ee.
15 Nit thu diepheit.
16 Nit rede valſche gezeugk-
nuſſe wider dein nechſten.

17 Nit begeitig das haus deins
nechſten. Nit beger ſeins
weybs: nit dē Knecht nitt die
diern nit dē ochſſen nitt dē
eſeln: noch aller der ding die
ſeī ſint.

18 Wann alles dz volck ſach
die ſtymmen. vnd die glaſz-
uaſz. vnd den done dz horns:
vnd den berg riechen: vnd ſy
derſchrackē vnd wurdē ge-
ſchlagen mit vorcht ſy ſtunden
19 von im verr: vnd ſprachē zu
moyſes. Du rede mit vns: vnd
wir hörn es Der herre rede
nit mit vns: das wir villeicht
20 icht ſterbē. Vnd moyſes ſprach
zu dem volcke. Nichten welt
euch ſurchten. Wann d. herr
iſt kummen das er euch bewert: vnd das ſein vorcht wer
in euch: vnd das ir nichten ſin-
21 deten. Vnd daz volck ſtund vō
verr: wann moyſes genacht ſich
zu der dunckel ī der gott was.

noch deyn frembdlinger, der
ynn deyner ſtadt thor iſt, Denn 11
ſechs tage hat der Herr hymel
vnd erden gemacht vnd das
meer vnd alles was drynnen
iſt, vnd ruget am ſiebenden
tage, Darumb ſegnet der Herr
den Sabbathtag vnd heyliget
yhn.

Du ſolt deyn vater vnd deyn 12
mutter ehren, auff das du lange
lebiſt ym land das dyr der Herr
deyn Gott geben wirt.
Du ſolt nicht todten. 13
Du ſolt nicht ehebrechen. 14
Du ſolt nicht ſtelen. 15
Du ſolt keyn falsch getzeug- 16
nis geben widder deynen nehiſten.

Du ſolt dich nicht laſſen ge- 17
luſten deyns nehiſten haus. Du
ſolt dich nicht laſſen geluſten
deyns nehiſten weybis, noch
ſeynes knechts, noch ſeyner
magd, noch ſeynes ochſen,
noch ſeyns eſels, noch alles
das deyn nehiſter hat.

Vnd alles volck ſahe den 18
donner vnd blix vnd den dohn
der poſaunen vnd den berg rauchen, vnd furcht ſich, vnd
wancketen vnd tratten von
ferne, vnd ſprachen zu Moſe, 19
Rede du mit vns, wyr wollen
gehorchen, vnd las Gott nicht
mit vns reden, wyr mochten
ſonſt ſterben.

Moſe aber ſprach zum volck, 20
furcht euch nicht, denn Gott
iſt komen, das er euch verſuchte, vnd das ſeyn furcht
euch fur augen were, das yhr
nicht ſundiget.

Vnd das volck trat von ferne, 21
aber Moſe macht ſich hyntzu
yns tunckel, da Gott ynnen

22 Vnd dorumb d. herr ſprach zu
moyſes. Diſe ding ſag den
ſunen iſrahel. Ir habt gehort
dz ich redt zu euch vom himel
23 Nichten macht euch ſilbrin
götl noch macht euch guldin
götl.

24 Macht mir ein altar von der
erd: vnd opffert auff in die
gantzen opffer vnd euwer ge-
fridſam. euwer ſchaff vnd die
ochſſẽ an einer iegklichen ſtatt
in der do wirt die gedenckung
meins namẽ. Ich kum zu dir:
25 vnd geſegen dir Vnd ob du
mir machſt ein ſteinin altar nit
mach in von gehauwen ſtei-
nen. Wann ob du authebeſt
dem waffen vber in. er wirt
26 entzeubert. Nicht ſteig auff
durch die ſtaffeln zu meim
altar dz dein entzeuberkeit
nit werd deroffent.

war, vnd der Herr ſprach zu 22
yhm, Alſo ſoltu den kindern
Iſrael ſagen, yhr habt geſehen
das ich mit euch vom hymel
geredt hab, darumb ſolt yhr 23
nichts neben myr machen,
ſylbern vnd guldenen Gotter
ſolt yhr euch nicht machen.

Eyn altar von erden mache 24
myr, darauff du deyn brandopffer vnd fridopffer, deyn ſchaff
vnd rinder opfferſt. Denn an
wilchem ort ich meynes namens gedechtnis mache, da
wil ich zu dyr komen vnd dich
ſegenen.

Vnd ſo du myr eynen ſteyn- 25
ern altar wilt machen, ſoltu
yhn nicht von gehawen ſteynen bawen, denn wo do mit
deym meſſer drauff fereſt, ſo
wirſtu yhn entweyhen, Du ſolt 26
auch nicht auff ſtuffen zu meynem altar ſteygen, das nicht
deyne ſchame auff deckt werde
fur yhm.

Examination yields the following results:

EXODUS XX.

Luther agrees with Old German Version: vv. 1, 2, 3, 4, 5, 6, 7, 8, 9, 10, 11, 12, 13, 14, 15, 16, 17, 18, 19, 20, 21, 22, 23, 24, 25, 26.

Differs from Old German Version: in renderings other than archaic and linguistic forms, v. 5. diene, eyfferer, miſſethat 6 viel thauſent, halten 7 vergeblich, vnſchuldig, furet 8 Sabbathstags 10 Sabbath, deiner ſtadt thor 11 Sabbathtag 12 land, geben wirt 18 blix, poſaunen, vnd wancketen 19 gehorchen, wyr mochten ſonſt ſterben 20 verſuchte, fur augen were 21 macht ſich hintzu, . . . ynnen war 22 Und der Herr,. alſo,. kindern,. geſehen, 23 darumb ſollt yhr nichts neben myr machen 24 brandopffer, fridopffer, rinder . . Denn an wilchem Ort ich meyns namens gedechtnis mache 25 bawen . . meſſer drauff fereſt . . entweyhen 26 nicht deyne ſchame auffgedeckt werde fur yhm.

Of these, the following agree with the Vulgate: 5 coles, zelotes, iniquitatem 7 in vanum, inſontem 8 ſabbati 10 ſabbatum 11 ſabbati

12 terram, dabit 18 lampades . . buccinæ . . . perterriti ac pauore percuſſi 19 ne forte moriamur. 20 probaret 21 acceſſit . . in qua erat . . . 22 vidiſtis 25 ædificabis . . . cultrum (ʾεγχειρίδιον) 24 holoc. et pacif.

With the Hebrew: 21 al penechem 22 vajōmer . . ko tōmar . . 23 lo taaſun itti 24 aſher aſeccir 26 lo thiggaleh ervathecha

The old renderings appear preferable: 5 ere 7 nimpt den namen 10 inwendig deiner tor 12 dir gibt 20 bewert 21 genacht 25 dem waffen

Supplemental renderings: 6 viel; a mistaken rendering: 25 meſſer drauff ferezt

This analysis shows that the old German was the basis of Luther's version, that the variations not noted were either linguistic or required by the change the language had undergone, that of those noted, eighteen were due to the Latin, seven apparently original renderings and not less than seven very doubtful improvements.

The edition of Luther used by Tyndale and in the preparation of this volume is the following:

Lotter's edition of Luther's Old Testament.

Two parts in one vol., in-folio, hog's skin, entitled on back of volume: Das Alte | Testament | I. u. II Theil | Wittenberg | 1523 | Cum Signo M. Lutheri | .—Ornamented frontispiece with title: Das All | te Teſta | ment | deutſch. | M. Luther. | Vvittemberg. | Verso: Die bucher des alten teſtaments XXIIII. Vorrede Martini Luther, Aij 5 ff. Das erſt buch Moſe, recto fo. I, sign. A., 36 ff. to recto of fo. XXXVI, verso: blank. Das Ander buch Moſe fo. XXXVII, r. sig. G to r. fo. LXV. Verso: Das Dritte buch, to r. fo. LXXXVI, sig. Pij Verso: Das vierde buch Moſı to r. fo. CXIIII, verso: blank. Das Funffte buch Moſe, r. fo. CXV, sig. V to verso fo. CXXXX: Das ende der bucher Moſe. 1 f., sign. ciij (corrections). 1 f. blank. Title Page: Joshua in coat of mail: Title: Das Ander | teyl des alten | testaments. | Verso: Das regiſter, &c. Fo. I, sig. Aij. Das Buch Ioſua to r. fo. XX, Diij, verso and leaf blank.—R. fo. XXI, E, Das Buch der Richter, to verso of fo. XLII. R. fo. XLIII, I, Ruth to r. fo. XLV. Verso:

blank. R. fo. XLVI, Iiiij, Das erſte teyl des Buchs Samuel. to v. fo. LXXII. R. fo. LXXIII, O to r. fo. XCIIII, v. blank.—R. fo. XCV, S, Das Erſte teyl des buchs von den konigen. to v. fo. CXX.—R. fo. CXXI, Yiij, Das ander teyl des buchs von den konigen. to r. fo. CXLIII, Cc.—V. Das erſte Teyl. Die Chronica. R. fo. CXLIIII, Ccij to v. fo. CLXIIII.—R. fo. CLXV, Gg, Das Ander Teyl der Chronica to r. fo. CXC, Lliij Verso: blank.—R. fo. CXCI, Das Buch Esra. to r. fo. CXCVIII, Nn. Verso: blank.—R. fo. CXCIX, Nnij Das Buch Nehemia. to r. fo. CCX.—Verso: Das Buch Esther to recto fo. CCXVI. | Ende des buchs | Esther. | Ende des ander teyls des | Allten teſtaments. | Corrections, 6 lines. Then follows Luther's emblems of the Lamb, and the Rose with a heart and a cross, and the subscription:

Dis zeichen ſey zeuge, das ſolche bucher durch meine hand gangen sind, deñ des falſchen druckēs vnd bucher verderbens, vleyſſigen ſich ytzt viel
Gedruckt zu Wittemberg.

The date 1523 has been added in modern handwriting.

The selection of that edition, and the retention of its archaic language, were necessary in order to present the material precisely as Tyndale found it. The original renderings illustrate the scholarship of Luther, as compared with Tyndale's, and mark the changes introduced in subsequent editions of the German version; their linguistic character also is highly instructive for it sheds light not only on the pronunciation of German in the second decade of the sixteenth century, but also on the remarkable changes in the spelling and flexions of the language. On almost every page of this volume may be found examples of words and flexions banished from the written language but still current in the familiar, and especially, the dialectic speech of Germany.

I call attention to the following words in the text of Eggesteyn: 5 *ambecht*, bete an, pray to; *vngangkeit*, bosheit, wickedness; 6 *derbermde*, erbarmen, compassion; 7 *vppig*, umsonst, in vain; 9 *werck*, imper., wirk, work; 15 *diepheit*, theft; 17 *begeitig*, imp., begeizen, to desire from envy; 18 *riechen*, rauchen, to smoke; 19 *im verr*, 21 *von verr*, in der ferne, von ferne, afar, from afar; 20 *bewert*, bewähren, to put to proof; 21 *genacht*, nahen, nähern, to draw near; 26 *entzeubert*, *entzeuberkeit*, unsaubern, verunsaubern, to make unclean, to pollute.

6. *The Notes in the present Issue.*

The notes are taken from Matthew's Bible, the Vulgate, and Luther's version. A brief description of the first is now in place.

Matthew's Bible, in–folio.

Frontispiece: Cut with allegorical representations of Biblical dogmas $10\frac{5}{8}$*in.* × $7\frac{13}{16}$*in.*, showing in the centre a panel 4*in.* × $1\frac{3}{4}$*in.* with the title: ¶ *The Byble*, | *which is* all the holy *Scrip-* | *ture:* In whych *are contayned* the | Olde *and Newe* Teſtament *truly* | *and* purely *tranſlated* into En- | glyſh *by Thomas* | Matthew. | Three leaf-shaped emblems, two black, one red. | ¶. Eſaye .I. I | ☞ *Hearcken to* ye heauens *and* | *thou* erth *geaue eare:* For the | *Lorde* ſpeaketh. | *M*.D.*XXXVII.* [The italicized portions are printed in red. The type used is German Black Letter.] Underneath the cut in large Black Letter: Set forth with the Kinges moſt gracyous lycẽce.—Verso: Theſe thynges enſuyned are ioyned with thys preſent volume of the Byble.—A Calendar with an Almanack.—An exhortacyon to the ſtudye of the holy Scrypture gathered oute of the Byble.—The ſumme and content of all the holy Scrypture both of the Olde and New Teſtament.—A table for to fynde many of the cheafe and pryncipall matters conteyned in the Byble.—The names of all the bokes of the Byble, wyth the content of the Chapters, and in what leafe euery boke begynneth.—A bref reherſall declarynge how longe the worlde hath endured from the creacyon of Adam vnto thys present yeare of oure Lorde M.D.xxxvii.—And in the Margēt of the boke are there added many playne exposycyons of soch places as vnto the symple and vnlearned seame harde to vnderstande. Then follows: The Kalender, rubricated beginning on f. *ii.—2 ff. ☾ An exhortacyon, &c., recto of *iiii. ending with IR in the ornamental floriated letter known as German *Fractur*. Verso: ☾ The summe & content, &c., 2 pages.—Verso of unnumbered folio: ☾ To the moost noble and gracyous Prynce Kyng Henry the eygt, &c., 3 pages. The dedication ends: Youre graces faythfull & true subiect Thomas Matthew, followed by three leaf-shaped emblems and the letters HR in German *Fractur*.—☾ "To the Chrysten Readers," a note introducing: A table of the pryncypall matters conteyned in the Byble, in whych the readers may fynde and practyse many commune places. 13 ff. from ** to verso of *** .v. unnumbered.—☾The names of all the bokes of the Byble, &c.; then, ☾ A brief rehersall of the yeares, &c., one page recto of unnumbered leaf, verso, a full-page cut of Adam and Eve in Paradise.—☾ The fyrst boke of Moses called Genesis, &c. fo. .i. not marked, sig. a to fo. .ccclvii. —The subscription: "☾ The ende of the Ballet of Ballettes of Salomon, called in Latyne Canticum Canticorum" ends the first volume on signature Hh leaf vii not marked. The signatures run in eights, the first five leaves being numbered, except when the fifth leaf coincides with the beginning or ending of a book.—The type is a large and handsome German Black Letter; a full page measures $11\frac{7}{8}$*in.* × 8*in.* margins included, arranged in double columns, and contains 60 lines.—A blank page.—Followed by ornamented Frontispiece, $12\frac{1}{4}$*in.* × $8\frac{5}{16}$*in.*, divided into seventeen panels, sixteen giving cuts of Scriptural subjects, the seventeenth and central panel with the title: | The *Prophetes* | *in* Englysh, | Esay. *Ionas.* | *Ieremy.* Micheas. | Ezechiel. *Naum.* | *Daniel.* Abacuc. | Oseas. *Sophony.* | *Ioel.* Aggeus. | Amos. *Zachary.* | *Abdy.* Malachy. | —[The italicized words are printed in red.] Followed by three leaves, two black, one red. Verso:

R | The Prophete | Esaye | G
Three leaves
Cut illustrating Es. vi. b.
E | The worde of the Lorde | W
| endureth for euer. |
Esay .XL. a.

❡ The boke of the | prophete Esay, &c. fo. .i. sig. A. A., to verso of fo. .xciiij. | The subscription: ❡ The ende of the prophecy of Malachy: and consequently of all the Prophetes," followed by the customary three leaves, and then by the floriated letters W T, ends this volume on signature M.M.vi, fo. not marked. Signatures and dimensions those of the first volume. Then follows an ornamented frontispiece divided into sixteen panels, fifteen giving most of the cuts of the frontispiece to the Prophets, the sixteenth panel with the title: | ❡ *The Volume* of | *the bokes called* Apocripha: | Contayned in the *comen Transl.* | *in Latyne*, whych are not | founde in the *Hebrue* | *nor* in the | *Chalde.* | — Three leaves, two red, one black, and two hands.—❡ *The Regestre therof. The* thyrde boke of Esdras. *The fourth boke of Esdras.* The boke of Tobiah. *The boke of Iudith.* The reast of the boke of Hester. *The boke of Wysdome.* Ecclesiasticus. *Baruch the Prophete.* The songe of the .iij. Chyldrē in the ouē. *The storye of Susanna.* The storye of Bel and of the Dragon. *The prayer of Manasseh.* The fyrst boke of the Machabees. *The second boke of the Machabees.* [The italicized words are printed in red.] Verso, ❡ To the Reader, 1 page. ❡ The thyrde boke of Esdras., fo. .ij. sig. Aaa.ij. to ❡ The ende of the seconde boke Machabees. verso f. LXXXI. sig. Kkk. supernumerary unmarked leaf, being the ninth of Kkk. —Then follows the same full-page illustrated frontispiece described in the opening lines of this collation, the central panel with the title: | Emblem. *The* newe | *Testament* of | oure sauyour *Iesu Christ* | *newly and* dylygently translated | into Englyshe with *Annotacions* | *in the* Mergent to helpe the | Reader to *the vnderſtan-* | dynge of the | *Texte.* | ❡ *Prynted* in the yere *of* | oure *Lorde* God. | M.D.xxxvii. | —The Goſpell of S. Matthew, &c., fo. ij. sig. A.ij. to end of Reuelacion, and ❡ The ende of the newe Teſtament, emblems as before. recto f. CIX, not marked, sig. O.v; [A duplicate of f. CIX. in facsimile is bound up with this volume; it is very poorly done and disfigured by many errors, *e. g.*, line 3, col. 1, it has Cryſopra*g*os, line 4, Iacyn*e*te; line 13, col. 2, has incha*u*ters.]—to the end of: This is the Table wherin ye ſhall fynde the Epiſtles and the Goſpels, after the vſe of Salſbury., 5 pages, ending with: ❡ The ende of this Table. verſo f. CXI. sig. O.vij. not marked. |

The relation of these works to Tyndale's version suggested the arrangement, that the Chapter Summaries, supplied by Rogers, should appear in the margin at the beginning of every chapter, and the variant readings of his text immediately under the text of Tyndale. The Notes from the Vulgate, the older of the versions used, come next, and are followed by those from Luther's translation.

The marginal notes of Matthew and Luther conclude the Apparatus.

Matthew's Bible being the first English Bible with Tyndale's translation, it seemed a fitting tribute to the memory of John Rogers and a recognition of his valuable labors and near relations to Tyndale, to embody his additions and notes in the present edition, which, in this respect, enables the reader to construct the whole text as to various readings, but of course not as to the variant orthography of the Pentateuch, as it stands in Matthew's Bible, copies of which are but rarely met with.

7. *Examples of the Notes.*

The first and chief design of these notes being to demonstrate the independence of Tyndale's translation, I have compared the *whole* of Tyndale's text with the *whole* of the Latin and German versions, and confined the selection to passages which upon comparison with the Hebrew supply that proof. The parallels not less than the variants furnish valuable material for the study of the Pentateuch; they illustrate the merits and demerits of the collated versions and establish the indisputable fact that the first English version conforms more to the original than the Latin and German translations. The scholarly tact and judgment of Tyndale will be recognized in numerous passages, especially in those where Luther allowed himself to be influenced by the Vulgate. The notes, though numerous, are only specimens and may be almost indefinitely increased. The marginal notes of Luther and Rogers may be regarded as a contemporary commentary on difficult passages designed to supplement the translation and to make the people understand the Scriptures; they afford a lively view of the spirit of the age and a true picture of the scholarship of the translators. A few illustrations are now in order.

Instances of Places in the Vulgate containing readings not found in the Hebrew:

Gen. iv. 8 Egrediamur foras

Ex. ii. 22 Alterum vero peperit: quem vocauit Eliezer, dicens, Deus enim patris mei adiutor Meus, & eripuit me de manu Pharaonis. Compare Ex. xviii. 4 and the variation.

Lev. xviii. 15 Et vxorem fratris ſui nullus accipiat.

Num. viii. 2 candelabrum in auſtrale parte erigatur. Hoc igitur præcipe vt lucernæ contra boream eregione reſpiciant ad menſam panum propoſitionis:

Num. xx. 6 clamaueruntque ad dominum, atque dixerunt, Domine deus audi clamorem huius populi, & aperi eis theſaurum tuum fontem aquæ viuæ, vt ſatiati ceſſet murmuratio eorum.

Instances of places in the Vulgate redundant, free, or paraphrastic:

Gen. xxi. 9 cum Iſaac filio ſuo

Num. vi. 2 vt ſanctificentur, & ſe voluerint domino conſecrare:

" " 3 a vino, & omni quod inebriare poteſt

" vii. 89 vt conſuleret oraculum

" viii. 25 annum ætatis impleuerint

" " 26 vt cuſtodiant quæ ſibi fuerint commendata

Num. ix. 5 Qui fecerunt tempore ſuo
" " 7 quare fraudamur, vt non valeamus
" x. 32 quicquid optimum fuerit ex opibus

Instance of a rendering by Luther and Tyndale found in the LXX. and the Vulgate, but not in the Hebrew:

Ex. ii. 22 (See the passage on p. 125 in Tyndale and in any copy of Luther's version.)

Instances showing the influence of the Vulgate on Luther and Tyndale:

	Vulgate.	*Luther.*	*Tyndale.*
Num. viii. 9	omni multitudine	gantze gemeyne	hole multitude
" " 19	dono Aaron	zum Geschencke Aaron	
" xii. 1	vxorem eius Æthiopiſſam	eyne morynne zum weybe	wife of Inde
Deut. xvii. 3	omnem militiam cæli	irgent eyn heer des hymels	
" " 7,12	vt auferas malum	das du den böſen von dir thuest	
Deut. xxxii. 41	Si acuero vt fulgur gladium meum	wenn ich den blitz meyns ſchwerds wetzen werde	Yf I whett the lyghtenynge of my ſwerde

The last example affords a curious illustration of the influence of one version on others. Tyndale's rendering conforms literally to the Hebrew but the figure of lightning applied to a sharpened and highly polished sword is rather German than English; Luther's rendering is idiomatic but suggested by the Latin and an improvement: the Latin in its turn is a literal translation of the LXX. and *si* appears to us a truer rendering of the Hebrew *im* than the Greek *hoti*, while the Chaldee version has the remarkable amplification: *si in duplum pluſquam fulgur apparet a ſummitate celi & vſque ad ſummitatem eius reuelabitur gladius meus.*

Instances of renderings by Tyndale, in close agreement with the Hebrew where the LXX., the Vulgate and Luther depart from it:

Num. xxii. 34 stands in the LXX.: *and now if it displease thee,* a rendering literally reproduced by *ſi displicet tibi* (Vulg.) and *ſo dyrs nicht gefällt* (Luther); all these versions fail to bring out the force of the Hebrew phrase *evil in the sight* or *eyes of any one, i. e., displeasing to him;* Tyndale with excellent judgment retained *displease* but added the Hebraism *thyne eyes.*

The following is a longer example presented in English:

GEN. XXII. 19.

Hebr.	And Abraham returned to his young men,* and they
LXX.	And Abraham returned to his young men,* and
Vulg.	Abraham returned to his young men,*
Luther	Thus Abraham returned to his young men,* and they
Tynd.	So turned Abraham agayne vnto his yonge men, and they
Hebr.	arose, and they went together unto Beer Shava,
LXX.	rising they went together unto the well of the oath,
Vulg.	and they went to Berſabee together,
Luther	arose, and went together to Bersaba,
Tynd.	roſe vp and went to gether to Berſeba.
Hebr.	and Abraham dwelt at (*or* in) Beer Shava.
LXX.	and Abraham dwelt at the well of the oath.
Vulg.	and dwelt there.
Luther	and he dwelt there.
Tynd.	And Abraham dwelt at Berſeba.

Comparing these renderings with the Hebrew, we find that the LXX. are very close except in the proper name, whose translation into common speech obliterates the geography; the Vulgate restores the geography, but fails to translate *and they arose* and condenses *And Abraham dwelt at Beer Shava* into *and dwelt there*; Luther restores *and they arose*, omitted by the Vulgate, but forsakes the Hebrew for the Vulgate in the *last clause*; Tyndale adheres throughout to the Hebrew, and impartial critics will concede that his version is superior to the others.

The marginal notes of Tyndale in the present issue are those of the edition of 1530 and differ materially from those in the corrected edition of Genesis of 1534 as well as those of Rogers of 1537. *All* the notes of Genesis 1534 are given in the collation in No. 8 of this Chapter; the marginal notes of Luther (L. M. N.) and Rogers (M. M. N.) appear in the lower margin of this edition.

* To avoid variants I have rendered *naar*, *pais*, *puer*, and *knabe* as above.

All the marginal notes of the edition of 1530 except those at xxiiii, 35, 60 and xxxii, 9 are omitted in that of 1534; with these exceptions the marginal notes of 1534 are *new.* The omitted notes are strongly anti-papal, viz.. Gen. iv, 15; ix, 5; xlvii, 22, Tyndale's own example in Genesis doubtless led Rogers to pursue a similar course with the notes in the other books of the Pentateuch; *e. g.*, the note (1530) Ex. xii, 26. "The lambe was called paſſeouer that the very name it ſelf ſhuld *put them in remembraunce what it ſignified, for the signes that god ordined ether ſignified the benefits done, or promyſes to come, and were not domme as are the ſignes of our domme God the Pope,*" appears in Matthew's Bible (1537) thus: "The lambe was called *the* paſſeouer: that the very name it ſelfe ſhulde *kepe in memorye what was ſignyfyed therby, which phraſe & maner of ſpeakynge the ſcripture vſeth often, callynge the ſigne by the name of the thynge that it sygnyfieth, as Gen. xvi, b.*" Again the note to Deut. xxiii, 18 (1540) *The hyre &c.* reads: "The *pope* wil take *tribute* of them yet and *biſſhopes* and *abbotes* deſire no better *tenauntes*," stands in Matthew: "There be now *many* that desyre no beter *rentes.*" Sometimes the anti-papal note is entirely omitted, or makes room for another: *e. g.*, Deut. xix, 4 (1530): "The popis ſentuariese are of an other purpoſe. For he had lever haue the frenſhep of the euel, then to ſaue them that are good," disappears in Matthew, which gives in its place "Here are ſhewed .ii. maner of manquellyng, &c., &c."

The notes of Luther are often anti-papal, but not as bitter as Tyndale's; their characteristic is his allegorical and typological treatment of things, persons, events and institutions with a degree of dogmatism illustrative both of the man and of the spirit of the time. A few examples in English may prove interesting:

Gen. ix, 22. "Many draw from this story an argument that the vices of prelates should not be denounced, although Christ and all the apostles denounced them. But see that thou give it the right sense, viz. that Noe is Christ and all believers; drunkenness is love and faith in the Holy Spirit; and nudity the cross and sufferings before the world; Ham, to practise false works, and hypocrites who despise Christ and His people and delight in their sufferings; Sem and Iapheth are pious christians who praise and honor such sufferings."

Gen. xxx, 32: "This story signifies that the Gospel leads the souls of men away from the law-mongers and work-saints, wherein they are party-colored, spotted and streaked, that is, adorned with the manifold gifts of the Spirit, Rom. xii and 1 Cor. xii, and that incompetents only remain under the Law, and works, for Laban signifies white or glittering and imports hypocrites even in the fair works of the divine law."

The German word *gleyſſner*, hypocrite, is derived from gleiſſen, to glitter, or *appear* white or resplendent.

Gen. xxxviii, 29: "*Perez* a tearer, *Sorah* means rising. This denotes that the work-saints affect outwardly to thrust themselves forward and aspire to be the first, but become the last, on which account there rises a great tearing among the people of God. But the red thread about the hand shows that they work carnal holiness and persecute the true saints."

Ex. xiii, 6: "Leaven is so strongly prohibited, that we are to preach the pure Gospel and the grace of God, and not our works and the law, after the resurrection of Christ, as Paul shows 1 Cor. v. and such eating is nothing else than faith in Christ."

Num. xxiii, 21: *The trumpets of the king, &c.* "That is, the bodily trumpets of God their king, who ordered them to be made, because they were invincible in battle. But it means the Gospel in Christendom."

The notes of Rogers are often didactic, but not as dogmatical as those of Luther; they are frequently thoughtful and suggestive; *e. g.*,

Lev. xxi, 1: "The preaſtes be warned that they ſhall not come at the commen waylynges & lamentacyons of the deed leſt they ſhuld therby be the moare vnapte to do their ſacryfyces wherunto they were properly appoynted, and leſt they ſhulde by theire wepyng geue an occaſion to deſtroye the beleuve of the reſurreccion of the dead."

Lev. ii, 13: "All offringes muſt be ſalted with ſalt, whiche signyfieth that all our good workes muſt be directed after the doctryne of the Apoſtles & prophetes, for then ſhall they be acceptable in the ſyghte of the Lorde, yf they ſauer of the ſalt therof, & elles not."

Occasionally the notes of Rogers have been taken from Luther.

Many of the notes of Luther, Tyndale and Rogers are etymological and display the familiarity of the translators with the original scriptures, and not unfrequently the embarrassments of Hebrew lexicography in the first third of the sixteenth century. The Tables, &c., of Tyndale are very interesting on this account, and require no comment; this applies also to the etymological notes of Rogers. A few examples from Luther are the following.

Gen. xvii, 5: "Abram means high father, but Abraham denotes father of multitudes, although the same multitudes are indicated in his name by only one letter, not without cause;" xxi, 31: "Berfaba denotes in German, oath-well, or earth-well, but perhaps also seven wells;" xxiii, 2: "Hebron is Kiriath Arba, sayth Mofes, that is, four-town, for all the great capitals were of old Arba, that is, divided into four quarters, as Rome, Jerufalem and Babylon, also Gen. x."*

Rogers has but few etymological notes, but many explanatory ones; *e. g.*,

Gen. xxxv, 18: "Ben Iamin: that is the fonne of the ryghthand. And righthande is taken for good fortune;" xlix, 27: Wolfe is here taken in a good fence, and fignifieth a feruent preacher of godes worde as was Paule in whome this text is verified;" Ex. xxv, 30: "Shewbreed, becaufe it was alwaye in the prefence and fyghte of the Lorde;" Lev. l. 9: "This fwete odoure is: the facryfyce of fayth & of pure affeccyon in which God is delited, as a man is delited in the good fauoure of meates, as it is fayd of Noe, Gen. viii, d;" xxv, 10: "Iubelye, of this Hebrewe woorde iobeli, which in Englyfhe fygnifieth a trumpet. A yere of fynguler myrth and ioye and of mocke reft, wher in their corne and all their frutes cam forth wythout fowynge, tyllynge or any other laboures." 15 "By this iubelye is fygnified the reftorynge of all thynge to his perfeccion, which fhal be after the generall iudgement in that floryfſhynge worlde, when the chofen fhal be admytted in to lybertye from all wretchednes, pouertye, anguyfhe & oppreffion, when all fhalbe fully reftored agaiae in Christ, that thorow the fynne of the fyrst man was taken awaye."

* Rogers has this note on Gen. xiii, 18: "Ebron is the name of a citie where Adam, Abraham and his wyfe with Ifaac &c. were buryed, as in Gen. xxiii, d."

A few explanatory notes of archaic and obsolete words have been given in the margin, but a much fuller list will be found in No. 12 of this Chapter.

8. *The Collations.*

Three distinct collations have been made: 1. one of the book of Genesis of the edition of 1530 with that of 1534, from the careful notes, in the margin of a duplicate set of plate proofs, furnished by Dr. Culross; 2. another of the Prologues of the edition of 1530 (1534) with the text in Daye's folio of 1573, in those to Genesis and Exodus, also by Dr. Culross; 3. and a third of the text of the Pentateuch of 1530 with that of the Pentateuch in Matthew's Bible of 1537. The last is given immediately under Tyndale's text marked 𝔐. These collations are presented in parallel columns in order to mark the variations and to illustrate the nature of the changes introduced. The first intention of extending the variants to orthography had to be abandoned as impracticable, for they are so numerous that their production would have required a volume fully twice as large as this; besides the practice of Tyndale and Rogers of spelling the same word in constantly differing forms and the variations caused by the arbitrary use of contractions seemed to be imperative reasons for limiting the comparisons to different readings and renderings. To make this clear to the eye is the design of the subjoined passage showing all the variations in the editions of 1530, 1534 and 1537.

EXAMPLE SHOWING THE VARIATIONS IN THE ORTHOGRAPHY AND PUNCTUATION OF THE EDITIONS OF 1530, 1534, AND 1537.

GENESIS I, 14–19.

1530.

Than ſayd God: let ther*e* be lyghtes in yᵉ firmament of heaven to devyde the daye frō the nyght*e*, that they may be vnto ſygnes, ſeaſons, days & yeares. And let them be lyghtes in the ſyrmament of heavē, to ſhyne vpon the erth. & ſo it was. And God made two great lyghtes A greater lyghte to rule the daye, & a leſſe lyght*e* to rule the nyght*e*, and he made ſterres alſo. And God put them in the ſyrmament of heaven to ſhyne vpon the erth, and to rule the daye & the nyght*e*, ād to devyde the lyght*e* from darckneſſe. And God ſawe yᵗ it was good: and ſo of the evenynge ād mornynge was made the fourth daye.

1534.

Th*e*n ſayd *g*od: let *ther* be l*i*ghtes in *the* firmament of hea*u*ē to de*u*yde the daye frō the *night*, that they may be vnto ſ*i*gnes, ſeaſons, day*es* & yeares. And let them be l*i*ghtes in the f*i*rmament of hea*uen*, to ſhyne vpon the erth: & ſo it was. And God made two great l*i*ghtes: *a* greater lyghte to rule the daye, *and* a leſſe lyghte to rule the n*i*ghte, and he made ſterres alſo. And *g*od put them in the f*i*rmament of hea*u*en to ſhyne vpon the erth, and to rule the daye *and* the n*i*ghte, *and* to de*u*yde the lyghte from*e* darckneſſe. And *g*od ſawe *that* it was good: and ſo of the e*u*enynge *and* morn*i*nge was made the fourth daye.

1537.

Than ſayd*e* God: let there be l*i*ghtes in yᵉ ſyrmamēt of hea*u*ē, to de*u*yde the daye fro*m* the *nyght*, that they may be vnto ſygnes, ſeaſons, day*es* & yeares. And let *thē* be lyghtes in yᵉ ſyrmamē*t* of hea*u*ē, to ſhyne vpō the erth: *And* ſo it was. And God made two great*e* lyghtes: A greater lyghte to rule the daye, & a leſſe *lyght* to rule the *nyght:* and he made ſterres alſo. And God put them in the ſyrmamēt of hea*u*en to ſhyne vpon the erth, and to rule the daye & the *nyght: &* to de*u*yde the *lyght* from darckneſſe. And God ſawe *that* it was good: and ſo of the e*u*enynge ād mornynge was made the fourth daye.

In these five verses 1534 differs from 1530 in 29 places in the spelling and in 2 places in the punctuation; 1537 differs from 1530 in 26 places in the spelling and in 5 places in the punctuation. These numerous differences are mainly due to the indiscriminate use of double or triple forms of the same word by the same writer and the employment of contract forms introduced on purely technical grounds to bring a given number of words or letters into a line; if the available space was ample the printer used the full form, if it was scant he chose the contract form. Of the former we meet with, *light*, *lighte*, *lyght*, *lyghte; hand*, *hande*, *hond*, *honde;* of both, *and*, *ād*, *&;* *hande*, *honde*, *hāde*, *hōde; lambe*, *lābe; heaven*, *heauen*, *heauē*, *hevē; fyrmament*, *firmament*, *fyrmamēt*, *firmamēt; kynde*, *kinde*, *kȳde*, *kīde*. The contractions are mostly simple and besides ı for *the*, ẏ for *that*, *&* for *and*, are made over the vowel, the presence of a long accent indicating that *m* or *n* has to be supplied, *e. g.*, *nothīge* stands for *nothinge*, *cā* for *can*, *Adā* for *Adam*, *thē* for *them;* unusual forms such as *whō me* for *whome*, *ẏ ſe* for *these* are very rare. The contractions in German are complicated, for they are introduced over vowels and consonants, but as the latter have not been used in this volume, it is unnecessary to discuss the matter.

The subjoined photo-engravings of the same portion of the book of Genesis in the editions of 1530 and 1534, and of a page in Latin Letter of the former, afford a true picture of their typographical characteristics, and may have the effect of solving the question where they were printed. Antiquarian students in Germany, Belgium, and Holland, having access to books printed at Wittenberg, Hamburg and Antwerp, between 1530 and 1534, will doubtless be able to shed light on this interesting point.⁂ They illustrate also, but only feebly, the difference in the orthography and punctuation followed in the editions of Genesis of 1530 and 1534.

⁂ *I shall feel grateful for the communication of any facts bearing on this subject, and beg that correspondence may be forwarded to me through the London or New York publishers.*

The transcripts from Matthew's Bible and Daye's edition of Tyndale's Pentateuch of 1551 * giving the same passage complete the picture of orthographical variety, suggestive of valuable hints on the phonetic power of the language.

* For this transcript I am indebted to the courtesy of Edward Augustus Bond, Esq., LL.D., Principal Librarian, and George Bullen, Esq., Keeper of Printed Books, British Museum. It gives also the following description of the copy of this rare volume in the British Museum.

"[*Title*]. ¶ The fyrſte | parte of the Bible | called the .v. bookes of | Moſes tranſlated by W | T. wyth all his prologes | before euery boke, and cer | teine learned notes vpon | many harde wordes. | Geneſis. | Exodus. | Leuiticus. | Numeri. | Deuteronomium. | Anno Dom. M. | D.L.I. |

"[*Colophon.*] Imprinted at | London by Ihon | Day dwellyng ouer | Alderſgate. | beneth Saint Martins. | Anno Domi. M.D. | (.·.) L.I. (·.·) Cum priuilegio ad impri | mendum ſolum. |

"[Note. Printed in Black Letter, 335 leaves, 33 lines to a full page. The title is surrounded by a woodcut border.]" The volume is in–8. From the notice in Cotton, List of Editions of the Bible, &c., Oxford, 1821, in–8; Appendix, p. iii, are drawn these additional particulars: "On the reverse [of the Title Page] is an address to the Reader by John Daye, announcing that for the convenience of the poor he had printed the Bible in four separate parts." "The leaves of the volume are not numbered. The signatures run in eights. It has all the prologues, heads of chapters, marginal notes and references: all these are printed in smaller letter. It contains sign. A—Y. Aa—Vu. A full page contains 33 lines." Cotton calls it a 12mo.

Photo-Engraving, showing the Latin Letter used in Exodus, Leuiticus, and Deuteronomye, of Tyndale's Pentateuch of 1530.

The firſt Chapter of Deuteronomye. Fo:I.

THeſe be the wordes which Moſes ſpake vnto all Iſrael, on the other ſyde Iordayne in the wilderneſſe and in the feldes by the red ſee: betwene Pharã ãd Tophel, Laban, Hazeroth and Diſahab.xij.dayes iurney from Horeb vnto Cades bernea, by the waye that leadeth vnto mount Seir. And it fortuned the firſt daye of the.xi.moneth in the fortieth yere, that Moſes ſpake vnto the childern of Iſrael acordinge vnto all that the Lorde had geuen him in commaundment vnto them, after that he had ſmote Sihon the kynge of the Amorites which dwelt in Heſbon, and Og kinge of Baſan which dwelt at Aſtaroth in Edrei.

On the other ſyde Iordayne in the londe of Moab, Moſes begane to declare this lawe ſayinge: the Lorde oure God ſpake vnto us in Horeb ſayenge: Ye haue dwelt longe ynough in this mount: departe therfore and take youre iurney and goo vnto the hilles of the Amorites and vnto all places nye there vnto: both feldes, hilles and dales: and vnto the ſouth and vnto the ſees ſyde in the londe of Canaan. and vnto Libanon: euen vnto the greate ryuer Eu-

B phrates

Photo-Engraving of Gen. xxxv, 23 to xxxvi, 16, showing the Black Letter used in Genesis, and Numbers, of Tyndale's Pentateuch of 1530.

xxxv. Chapter Fo. li.

The sonnes of Jacob were. xij. in nombre.
The sonnes of Lea. Ruben Jacobs eldest son-
ne/ & Simeō/ Leui/ Juda/ Jsachar/ & Zabulon
The sonnes of Rahel: Joseph & Ben Jamin.
The sonnes of Bilha Rahels mayde: Dan &
Nepthali. The sonnes of Zilpha Leas mayde
Gad & Aser. Thes are the sōnes of Jacob wh-
ich were borne him in Mesopotamia.

Then Jacob went vnto Jsaac his father to
Mamre a prīcipall cyte/ otherwise called Hebron: where Abrahā & Jsaac sogeorned as straungers. And the dayes of Jsaac were an hundred & lxxx. yeres: & than fell he secke & dyed/ ād
was put vnto his people: beynge olde and full
of dayes. And his sonnes Esau ād Jacob buried him.

The. xxxvi. Chapter.

THese are the generacions of Esau
which is called Edō. Esau toke his
wyues of the doughters of Canaan
Ada the doughter of Elon an Hethite/ & Ahalibama the doughter of Ana/ which Ana was
the sonne of Zibeon an heuyte/ And Basmath
Jsmaels doughter & sister of Nebaioth. And
Ada bare vnto Esau/ Eliphas: and Basmath
bare Reguel: And Ahalibama bare Jeus/ Jaa-
lam and Korah. These are the sonnes of Esau
which were borne him in the lande of Canaan.

And Esau toke his wyues/ his sonnes and
doughters and all the soules of his house: his

Photo-Engraving of Gen. xxxv, 23 to xxxvi, 16, showing the Latin Letter used in Genesis, Newly correctyd and amendyd by W. T. M.D.XXXIIII.

Genesis.

Iacobs eldest sonne, and Simeon, Leui, Iu
da, Isachar, and Zabulō. The sonnes of Ra
hel: Ioseph and Ben Iamin. The sonnes of
Bilha Rahels mayde: Dan and Nepthali.
Thē sonnes of Zilpha Leas mayde: Gad &
Aser. Thes are the sonnes of Iacob which
were borne him in Mesopotamia.

The deith of Isaac

Then Iacob went vnto Isaac his father
to Mamre the cyte of Arbe otherwise cal
led Hebron: where Abraham and Isaac so
georned as straūgers. And the dayes of Isa
ac were an huudred and .lxxx. yeres: and
than fell he seke & dyed, and was put vnto
his people: beynge olde and full of dayes.
And his sonnes Esau & Iacob buried him.

The .xxxvi. Chapter.

THese are the generations of Esau wh
ich is called Edom: Esau toke his wy
ues of the doughters of Canaan. Ada
the doughter of Elon an Hethite; and Aha
libama the doughter of Ana, which Ana
was the sonne of Zibeon an heuyte, and
Basmath Ismaels doughter and sister of Ne
baioth, And Ada bare vnto Esau Eliphas:
and Basmath bare Reguel: And Ahaliba
ma bare Ieus, Iaelam and korah, These are
the sonnes of Esau which were borne him
in the lande of Canaan.

And Esau toke his wyues, his sones ād
doughters ād all the soules of his house: his
goo-

Matthew's Bible, 1537.

Genefis xxxv, 22 to xxxvi, 16.

. . . . . The D.
fonnes of Iacob were .xii. in nōbre. The fonnes of Lea. Ruben Iacobs eldeft fonne, and Simeon, Leui, Iuda, Ifachar, & Zabulon. The fonnes of Rahel: Iofeph & Ben Iamin. The fonnes of Bilha Rahels mayde: Dan & Nepthali. The fonnes of Zilpha Leas mayd Gad & Afer. Thefe are the fonnes of Iacob which were borne him in Mefopotamia.

Then Iacob went vnto Ifaac hys father to Māre a principall cyte, otherwyfe called Hebron: where Abraham & Ifaac fogeorned as ftraungers. And the dayes of Ifaac were an hundred & .lxxx. yeres: & than fell he feke & dyed, and [c] was put vnto his people beyng olde and full of dayes. And his fonnes Efau and Iacob buried hym.

c. To be put vnto his people looke in Gene. xxv. a.

¶ The wiues of Efau. Iacob & Efau are ryche. The genealogie of Efau. Efau dwelleth in the hill Seir.

¶ The .XXXVI. Chapter.

THefe are the generacions of Efau which is called Edō. Efau toke his wyues of the daughters of Canaā Ada the daughter of Elon an Hethite, and Ahalibama the daughter of Ana, which Ana was the fonne of Zibeon an He uyte, and Bafmath Ifmaels * daughter and fifter of Nebaioth. And Ada bare vnto Efau, Eliphas: and [a] Bafmath bare Reguel: And Ahalibama bare Ieus, Iaelam and Korah. Thefe are the fonnes of Efau whych were borne him in the lande of Canaan. A.

** Gen. xxviii. a.*

a. Bafmath, otherwyfe called Maheleth, and fo in other places is there dyuers names geuē to one perfon.

And Efau toke hys wyues, hys fonnes & daughters & all the foules of hys houfe: hys

Genefis xxxv, 23 to xxxvi, 16 transcribed from *The fyrfte parte of the Bible called the .V. bookes of Mofes*, &c., &c. London: Ihon Day, M.D.L.I. (See p. lxiv.)

. . . . . Ia cobs eldeft fonne, and Symeon, Leui, Iu- da: Ifachar, and zabulon. The Sonnes of Rachell: Iofeph & Ben Iamyn, The fons of Bilha Rachels mayde: Dan and Neph thali, The fons of zilpha Leas mayd, Gad & Afar. Thefe are the fõnes of Iacob whi- che were borne him in Mefopotamia.

[Genefis. Cap. xxxv.] [fol. Hj recto.] Iacob.

Thẽ Iacob went vnto Ifaac his father o Mamre a principal citi, otherwife called Hebron, wher Abraham and Ifaac foiour ned as ftraungers. And the dayes of Ifaac were an .c: and .lxxx. yeares: and thẽ fel he ficke & dyed, & was put unto hys people be ing old and ful of daies. And his fonnes E fau and Iacob buryed hym.

Ifaac dieth

The .XXXVI. Chapter,

The wiues of Efau. Iacob and Efau are ryche. The genealogy of Efau. Efau dwel leth in the hyl Seir.

A. *[fol. Hj verso.]*

Thefe ar the generations of Efau whi che is called Edom. Efau toke his wi ues of the doughters of Canaan, A- da the Daughter of Elon an Hethite, and Ahalibama the Doughter of Ana, whyche Ana was the fonne of zibeon an Heuite. And Bafmath Ifmaels * doughter and fy fter of Nebaioth. And Ada bare vnto Efau Eliphas: and * Bafmathe bare Reguell: And Ahalibama bare Ieus, Iaelam and Korah. Theefe are the Sonnes of E fau whyche were borne hym in the Lande of Canaan.

Ge. xxviii. a.

Bafmah o- therwyfe called Ma- heleth.

And Efau tooke his wiues, hys Sonnes and Doughters, and all the foules of hys houfe: hys

The punctuation calls for a few words of explanation. In the edition of 1530 the marks used are the comma, the colon, the interrogation point, the period, and occasionally, parentheses. Very often no mark whatever is used where modern usage requires one, especially at the end of a sentence, of a line, a paragraph and even a chapter. This peculiarity I have tried to preserve in all cases where the sense is clear; where the absence of a mark appeared to me to obscure the sense, a mark has been supplied on the authority of Matthew's Bible which is generally very accurate and conforms in this respect, as well as in the matter of orthography, much more to modern usage. The punctuation in the edition of 1534 is more consistent than in that of 1530. In very few instances the punctuation has been supplied by consequence. The absence of hyphens in the division of words has also been preserved wherever it could be done without obscuring the sense. The treatment of numerals introduced in the text is that more or less common in old MSS. and in the earliest specimens of printed books; a period generally precedes and follows a numeral, *e. g.*, The .V. chapter, at the end of a line the period following the numeral, or at the beginning of a line the period preceding the numeral are omitted, as .V (end of a line) and V. (beginning of a line); the j instead of i in Roman numerals has not been reproduced except in particular citations, where the exact appearance of a title, &c., &c., was intended to be given. This seemed to be consistent with the general typographical arrangement of this edition which does not give the *letter* in facsimile. Letters belonging to Black Letter type are of constant occurrence in the body of words printed in Latin Letter, and occasionally the comma of the former / is used instead of the ordinary comma; these features also have not been reproduced.

I.

COLLATION OF THE BOOK OF GENESIS, SHOWING THE DIFFERENT READINGS IN THE EDITIONS OF 1530 AND 1534, DRAWN UP FROM THE NOTES ON THE MARGINS OF DUPLICATE PROOF SHEETS OF THIS REPRINT, MADE BY DR. CULROSS.*

1530.		*1534.*
W. T. To the Reader pp. 2–6.†		Wanting.
Aprologe ſhewinge the vſe of the ſcripture	p. 7	Vnto the reader W. T.
"Paule, in ye thyrde &c."	7 l. 19	See the variants, footnote p. 7.
to "ventyons."	8 8	
"Seke therefore &c."	8 24	See the variants, footnote, pp. 8–10.
to "a new."	11 2	
This comforte	11 3	And this lerninge and comforte

Geneſis.

flee over	1 : 20	flee above
had make	2 : 19	had made
once bone	23	one bone
Cherubin with a naked ſwerde	3 : 24	Cherubes with naked ſwerdes
haue gotten	4 : 1	haue obteyned
Abell (vv. 4, 8, 9)	2	Abel (vv. 4, 8, 9)
yf thou doſt . . yf thou doſt	7	yf thou do . . yf thou do
the the name	17	the name
Lamech vnto	23	Lamech to
a nother	25	another
and begat	5 : 4	and he begat
yeres and dyed.	8	yere and then he dyed.
Mahalalyell	16	Mahalalyel
and then Henoch lyved a godly lyfe	24	And Henoch walked with god
Mathuſala (vv. 21, 26, 27)	25	Mathuſalah (vv. 21, 26, 27)
had begot	30	hath begot
.v. hundred	30	.v. anhundred
And ſayd	6 : 7	And the lorde ſayd
vnto the	21	v̄to the
in to (vv. 9, 13)	7 : 7	into (vv. 9, 13)
Iapheth	13	Iaphet
and all maner	8 : 20	and of all maner
bōd	9 : 10	couenaunte
bonde	11	couenaunte
bōde	12	couenaunte
waters	15	water
Iapheth. (v. 23)	18	Iaphet. (v. 23)

* An Article of "Francis Fry on Tyndale's two editions of Genesis," reprinted from "Notes and Queries," Feb. 10 and 24, 1883, kindly sent to me by the author, came too late to be of use.

† Of this volume.

Iapheth	10 : 1	Iaphet
Dodanim	4	Sodanim
Where of came	9	And therot came
the begynnynge	10	the cheffe
Enanum	13	Enamim
whence came the Philyſtyns and the Caphtherynes.	14	whence the Philiſtins and the Capththorynes came.
Gerera	19	Gerara
Iapheth	21	Iaphet
eaſte lande	30	eaſtelande
ſhall be	11 : 4	ſhalbe
Babell	9	Babel
becauſe that	9	becauſe of that
Canaanytes	12 : 6	Cananytes
Egipte (v. 11)	10	Egypte (v. 11)
Egiptians	12	Egyptians
Pharaos lordes	15	Pharaos lorde
So that ſhe . . . in to Pharaos houſe	16	And ſhe . . . into the houſe of Pharao
the wife	19	thy wife
frō	13 : 9	fro
ſo departed the one brother	11	ſo the one brother departed
Thydeall	14 . 1	Thydeal
ſubiecte	4	ſubiectes
Raphayms . . Karnaim . . Suſims . . Emyms . . Kariathaim	5	Raphaites . . Rarnaim . . Suſites . . Emites . . Rariathaim
Horyms . . . Seir	6	Horytes . . . Seyr
Eſcholl	24	Eſcoll
Abram . . ſe to me	15 : 3	Abraham . . ſe unto me
bodye ſhalbe	4	bodye, he ſhalbe
And ſayde	5	And he ſayde
a thre yere olde ram	9	a ram off thre yere olde
Amorites	16	Amorytes
made covenaunte	18	made a couenante
Pherezites. Raphaims	20	Pherezytes. Raphaites
Canaanites	21	Cananites
Egyptian (v. 3)	16 : 1	Egyptian (v. 3)
by meanes of her	2	by her
Thou doſt me vnrighte,	5	the wronge I ſofre, be on thine heed,
fared foule	6	was to cruell
And yet ſhall he	12	And he ſhall
Iſmaell	15	Iſmael.
bonde	17 : 2	couenaunt
teſtamēt	4	couenaunt
bonde	7	couenaunt
tymes to be an everlaſtynge teſtamente, So that	7	tymes euen an everlaſtynge couenaunt, that
my teſtamente	9	myne appoyntmente
teſtamente	10	couenaunt
bond betwixte me and you.	11	couenaunt betwene me you.
all ſervauntes	12	all the ſervauntes
teſtament . . . bonde	13	couenaunt . . . couenaunt
teſtamēt.	14	couenaunt.
bonde . . . bonde	19	couenaunte . . . couenaunte
And as concernynge	20	And concernynge

bonde	17 : 21	couenaunte
left of talkyng	22	left talkyng
Ifmaell	23	Ifmael
for even therfore ar ye	18 : 5	feinge ye be
and they ate.	8	and they fate.
That herde Sara	10	And Sara hearked
doore which was behind	10	doore behind
ftode vp from thence	16	ftode vp to departe thence
and all	18	and that all
Sodom	20	Sodome
foũde .xxx. there?	30	foũde .xxx?
with his face.	19 : 1	vpon his face.
at doores	6	at the doores
for therfore came they	7	for as moch as they are come
Wherfore	13	And therfore
this	21	the
fone was vppon	23	fone was vp vppon
Ammi	38	Ammy
therfore fayde	20 : 4	therfore he fayde
innocent handes haue	5	innocent haue
in pureneffe	6	in the pureneffe
men and an excufe	16	men an excufe
Egiptian	21 : 9	Egyptian
a mockynge.	9	a mocker.
Egypte.	21	Eghypte.
Phicoll . . . Philiftines	32	Phycoll . . . Phyliftines.
Pheliftinlãde	34	Philiftinflande
Ifaac whome	22 : 2	Ifaac whõ me
hande and a knyfe	16	hande ana knyfe
Milcha (v. 23)	20	Mylcha (v. 23)
Kemuell . . . Sirians	21	Remuell . . . Syrians
an hundred and .xxvii.	23 : 1	an hundred and .xxii.
in a heade cyte called	1	at kyriat arba which is
And made	24 : 11	And he made
to whom	14	tho whom
ftoupe	14	boue
yᵉ	14	that
Milcha	24	Mylcha
And	43	Now
Bathuell	47	Bethuell
Bathuel	50	Bethuel
Rebecca	67	Rcbecca
Ketura	25 : 1	Retura
Iackfam	2	Iacfam
Letufim	3	Letufym
Kethura	4	Rethura
ynough	8	a full age,
Ifmael	12	Ifmaell
Kedar . . . Abdeel	13	Redar . . . Abeel
Kedma	15	Redma
Sirian	20	Syrian
Sirien.	20	Syrien.
a tyllman	27	atyllman
yᵉ	30	that
fe	26 : 9	beholde
yᵗ	9	the (*misprint.*)
yᵉ	10	that

Abimelech	26 : 11	Abymelech
yͤ	12	that
an	12	and
another	21	a nother
& Ahuſath . . . Phicol	26	& a certene of Ahuſath . . . Phicoll
When	34	And when
vnto	27 : 1	to
voyce goo	13	voyce and goo
and plētie	28	with plētie
Sirien	28 : 5	Syrien
And toke	11	And he toke
When	30 : 1	And when
Nepthali.	8	Nepthaly.
an other	12	another
And called	13	And ſhe called
Rahel, herde	22	Rahel, and herde
But he	29	And he
all the gootes	35	all the ſhe gootes
And he put the ſtaues	38	*omitted.*
brode	42	lamyng
ſolde vs, and hath	31 : 15	*omitted.*
vp vpon	17	vpon
catell and all	18	*omitted.*
Siriē	20	Syriē
ryuers	21	ryuer
Siriā	24	Syriā
wenteſt	27	fleyſt
to .ii.	33	to the .ii.
awaye now	42	now awaye
a bonde	44	appoyntemāt
ſtoones	46	ſtoone
Gylead	48	Gilead
And they ate breed	54	*omitted.*
ſaue it ſelfe	32 : 8	eſſcape.
de all	9	deall
foorde Iabok.	22	foorde of Iabot.
Iſraell.	28	Iſrael.
vntil	33 : 3	yer
yͤ	16	that
Salem to yͤ	18	Salem yͤ
Iſraell.	20	Iſrael.
yͤ	34 : 4	that
Iſraell	7	Iſrael
Sichem	13	Sychem
they	22	thy
Iſraell.	35 : 10	Iſrael.
thy	11	they
Iſraell	21	Iſrael
a prīcipall cyte	27	the cyte of Arbe
Hethite	36 : 2	Aethite
Eſau	8	Fſau (*misprint.*)
in mounte	9	in the mounte
Amalech.	12	Amalek.
Amalech	16	Amalek
of yͤ horites	21	of horites
Maſreka	36	Maſteka

the doughter of matred	36 : 39	*omitted.*
Iram.	42	Iam.
they hated	37 : 5	thy hated
Ifraell	13	Ifrael
wiked	20	cruell
to	26	unto
Egipte	28	Egypte
wicked	33	cruell
Canaanyte	38 : 2	Canaanite
hem	5	him
Thimnath	14	Thymnath
And turned	16	And he turned
rent a rent	29	made a rent
Egiptian	39 : 2	Egyptian
	2	the houfe of his mafter the Egyptian, (*repeated*)
Egiptians	5	Egyptians
& well	6	& a well
And	12	and And
Hebrues	17	Hebruifhe
tel me	40 : 8	tel it me
in good	14	in a good
fervauntes. And reftored	20, 21	fervauntes; reftored
dreamed	41 : 1	dreameded
ryuers fyde	1	lakesfyde
ryuer	2	lake
ryuer (*twice*)	3	lake (*twice*)
he awoke their with.	4	ther with Pharao awoke
in to	14	into
ryuers	17	lakes
ryuer	18	lake
Egipte	30	Egypte
afene	31	perceaued
Egipte (vv. 34, 36, 41, 43, 44, 56)	33	Egypte (vv. 34, 36, 41, 43, 44, 56)
nor	39	or
becaufe that the	57	becaufe the
Egipte (v. 3)	42 : 1	Egypte (v. 3)
Ifraell	5	Ifrael
aftoynyed and	28	aftoynyed amõge them felues and
one to a nother	28	*omitted.*
Ifraell (v. 8)	43 : 6	Ifrael (v. 8)
Egipte	15	Egypte
Egiptians	32	Egyptians
vnto	34	to
not yet	44 : 4	yet not
vnto (v.. 16)	6	to (v. 16)
oh my lorde, let	18	oh my, let
vnto (v. 32)	31	to (v. 32)
Egipte	45 : 13	Egypte
Ben Iamins	14	Ben Iamyns
Iofephes	16	Iofephs
vnto (v. 22)	17	to (v. 22)
Ifraell	21	Ifrael
he affes	23	affes
fhe affes	23	affes

Kahath	46 : 11	Rahath
Pharez . . . Zerak	12	Phares . . . Zerai
.xvi. ſoules	18	.xxi. ſoules
Nepthali	24	Nephtali
vnto (*twice*, 29 *twice*, 30, 31 *three times*, 34 *twice*)	28	to (*twice*, 29 *twice*, 30, 31 *three times*, 34 *twice*)
Iſraell	29	Iſrael
in ſo moch	30	in as moch
vnto	47 : 5	to
ſeed	19	food
vnto (*twice*, 22, 23, 26 *twice*, 31 *three times*)	21	to (*twice*, 22, 23, 26 *twice*, 31 *three times*)
were	48 : 1	was
vnto (2 *three times*, 3 *twice*, 4 *three times*, 5 *twice*, 11, 17, 18, 21, *twice*, 22)	1	to (2 *three times*, 3 *twice*, 4 *three times*, 5 *twice*, 11 17, 18, 21, *twice*, 22)
Egipte	5	Egigte
Ioſephes	8	Ioſephs
Iſraell	10	Iſrael
vnto (6, 8, 10, 11, 15, 28, 29)	49 : 2	to (6, 8, 10, 11, 15, 28, 29)
heles, ſo y^t	17	heles, y^t
The ſhoters haue envyed	23	Though the ſhoters angred
and yet	24	yet
come an herde mā a ſtone	24	come herdemen as ſtones
Hethyte	29	Hethite
vnto (*twice*, 12, 19, 20 *twice*, 21, 23, 24 *three times*)	50 : 4	to (*twice*, 12, 19, 20 *twice*, 21, 23, 24 *three times*)
Atad	10	Arad
Cananytes	11	Cananites
vnto them	19	to hī
and for youre	21	and youre
Egipte.	26	Egypte.
Moſes.		Moſes, called Geneſis.

A TABLE EXPOUNDINGE CERTEYNE WORDES, P. 153 sqq., OMITTED IN EDITION OF 1534, BUT FOUND IN DAYE'S FOLIO OF 1573.

1530.	P.*	L.	*1573.*
or a coſer.	153	3	or coſer.
it is		22	is it
Ihonn		25	Iohn
hāce		26	Haunce
laten		27, 29	latine
ſkyes	154	9	ſky
ſaye favoure		35	ſaye found favoure
hebrewe	155	2	hebrue
hebreue		4	hebrue
that me		9	that I
as is		13	as it were
.xi. Chapter		15	chap. xi.
.xiv. chapter		16	chap. 4.
oſed		17	iſſued
Meſias		20	Meſſias
y^t all y^e		23	all y^e

* Of this volume.

	P.	L.	
of tribe	155	28	of the tribe
Teſtamēt here is an appoyntemēt betwene		30	Teſtamēt that is an appoymente made betwene
ſoch an		32	ſoch
fathers	156	8	father
that is		16	*omitted.*
Egipte		21	Egipt
ſoch ſubiec-		25	ſoch a ſubiec-
Abel, Iſmael	157	3	Abell, Iſmaell
Pharez		5	Phares

II.

LIST OF MARGINAL NOTES IN *Genesis. Newly correctyd and amendyd*, 1534, FURNISHED BY DR. CULROSS.

1 : 3 The .i. daye.
6 The .ij. daye.
9 The .iij. daye.
14 The .iiij. daye.
20 The .v. daye.
24 The .vi. daye.
2 : 3 Bleſſed and ſanctified: dedicated and appoynted it to preach the worde of God in to prayer ād to doo all maner workes of mercye in.
8 Eden. ✦
11 Heuila.
19 Adā named all creatures.
24 Wedlocke.
3 : 1 The ſerpent.
14 A couenaūt that chriſt whch came of eue & was hir ſeed, ſhuld ouer come the power of the deuell & deliuer all true beleuers ī Chriſt and haters of the deuels workes, frō all daūger of ſatā, of ſinne and of hell. The womās curſe is, to beare hir childern with paine ād to be vnder the geuernaūce of hir huſbād.
4 : 1 Cain.
2 Abel.
3,4 offeringes.
25 Seth.
26 Enos.
5 : 21 henoch.
6 : 9 To walke withe God: is to lyue godlye to kepe his lawes and to truſte in him.
8 : 20 The rightwyſe will thāke god ād god doth alowe the harte of him.
9 : 13 The rayne bowe is a ſacrament, a ſigne, a witneſſe and a ſure erneſt of the couenaūt made betwene vs & god.
10 : 8 Nērod.
11 : 1 The wiſdome of man is ſore punyſhed of god with the diuiſiō off tongis.
9 Babel.
12 : 1 Abram
2 A promyſe.
7 A promyſe.
10 Abram goeth to Egipte.
14 : 18 Melchiſedech
22 See the anſwer of Abrā to the kynge of Sodome as touchinge the ſpole.
15 : 1 A promyſe to Abram.
6 Rightwiſenes.
13 The electe muſt ſoffer of the wicked for a tyme but god will deliuer hī.
18 Couenaunte.
16 : 1 Hagar
15 Iſmael.
17 : 5 Abrahā.
12 Circumcyſion

17 : 15 Sara
18 : 2 Hoſpitalyte.
19 : 33 lot was dronk ād laye with his two doughters
20 : 6 god deliuer his from evyll.
12 Sara was Abrahās ſiſter by the father.
17 The praier of Abraham
21 : 4 Iſaac.
31 Abrahā and abimelech. ded ſwere togeter.
22 : 9 godly loue putteth awaye all fleſhly loue.
17 promiſe
23 : 2 the deythe of Sarai.
24 : 3 Othe geyuen bi Abraham to his ſeruant.
12 note the gret fayth of the ſeruaunt.
15 Rebecca.
35 * God bleſſeth vs whē he geueth vs his benefites, ād curſeth vs, whē he taketh thē a waye.
51 who wonder fully god prouide for his fethfull
60 To bleſſe &c. (as in edition of 1530.)
25 : 34 Eſau ſolde his herytage.
26 : 4 promiſe to Iſaac.
6,7 Iſaac called rebecca his ſiſter.
13 the bliſſinge of god.
24 a promyſe,
32 the bliſſinge of god.
27 : 6 the coūcell of rebecca.
28 the bliſſing of Iacob.
40 a propheſi of the callyng of the gentylls.
28 : 5 Iacob gooth into meſopotamia.
12 the dreme of Iacob
14 promiſe
15 god fulfill hys promiſe
17 god ys wyth his choſyn in eueri place.
20 ſe Iacbos vowe what it was
22 the ſtone was a wytneſſe of the goodneſſe of god ſhowde to Iacob.
29 : 6 Rahel:
10 Aſſone.
32 Ruben.
33 Simeon
35 Iuda.
30 : 2 The āſwere of Iacob to Rahel.
30 : 6 Dan.
8 Nephtali.
11 Gad,
13 Aſſer.
18 Iſachar
20 Zabulō
24 Ioſeph.
30 the bleſſinge of the lorde.
31 : 19 Labans ymages or his goddes.
21 Ryuer Euphrates.
46 the heape of ſtonys was a ſyng betwixt Iacob & Laban.
32 : 1 the angell of God.
4 *sq.* Trobill make vs to call to God wyth prayer.
9 *Prayer is, &c., (as in edition of 1530)
24 the wraſtelyng of iacob
29 yᵉ electe ouercome all yᵉ world wyth . the tentations of it
33 : 11 preſent.
34 : 1 Dina was defiled bi Sichem.
35 : 6 Bethell
8 the ooke of lamentacyon.
10 Iſrael.
11 promiſe to iſrael
18 Beniamin.
19 the dethe of Rahel
22 the ſynne of ruben.
29 yᵉ deith of Iſaac
36 : 8 Edom.
12 amalek
20 Seir.
31 *sq.* Edom.
37 : 6 Ioſeph dreamyd.
21 *sq.* where be now ſuch rubens.
26 *sq.* the wōder prouiſiō of god for his electe.
28 Madianytes
38 : 1 Iudas.
6 thamar
9 the wyckidneſſe of Onā
26 the iugement of Iudas.
39 : 2 Ioſeph was luckie.
9 the goodneſſe of Ioſeph.
17 *sq.* the accuſation of Ioſeph.
23 The prouiſion of god for his.
40 : 12 the interpretation of yᵉ buttlars dreme
18 of the baker.
41 : 5 the dreame of pharao
25 Ioſeph interprete Pharaos dreme.

41 : 39 *sq.* god delyuer his elect to hys honor.
43 Abrech ys as moche to ſay as tender father.
51 Manaſſe.
52 Ephraī
42 : 1 *sq.* all turne to good for the electe.
5 *sq.* rede this ſtori in thi harte.
9 the dreme Ioſeph ys fulfilled.
21 *sq.* Conſcience beginneth to awake out of hir dreame in tyme of tribulacion.
36 *sq.* fatherli loue off Iacob.
43 : 11 *sq.* the rythwyſe doyng of Iſraell
18 *sq.* Lacke of feythe maketh to diſtruſt all thīg
43 : 32 the egiptiās might not eat with the Hebrues.
45 : 1 Low [Loue] muſt vtter
5 They y^{t} know god, know y^{t} al thinges are his workinge & prouidence
26 *sq.* Loue muſt breke out in workis
46 : 3 promiſe.
32 ſhepardys.
47 : 9 pilgremage
48 : 14 *sq.* the blyſſing of ephraī and manaſſes.
21 Iſrael was certayne of godes promiſe.
49 : 33 the dethe of iacob.
50 : 19 the anſwer off Ioſeph to hys brethrē
24 the faith of Ioſeph,
26 The dethe off Ioſeph.

III.

COLLATION OF THE PENTATEUCH SHOWING THE DIFFERENT READINGS IN THE EDITION OF 1530 AND MATTHEW'S BIBLE OF 1537.

Genesis.

1530.		*1537.*
rule	1 : 26	domynion
ſurely dye.	2 : 17	dye the dethe.
Ah ſyr, that God hath sayd	3 : 1	ye, hath God sayd in dede
for to make wyſe.	6	for to geue vnderſtondynge.
cryeth	4 : 10	cryed
beſte	9 : 10	beſtes
the wife	12 : 19	thy wyfe
Sodome agaynſt him vnto the vale	14 : 17	Sodome to mete him in the vale
out at the doores	15 : 5	out of the dores
one over agenſt a nother	10	one agaynſt another
parties	16 : 13	partes
God: na, Sara . . . a ſonne, ād	17 : 19	God: Sarah . . . a ſonne in dede &
ran agenſt them	18 : 2	ran to mete them
vp agaynſt them	19 : 1	vp to mete them
beholde he . . . men and an excuſe	20 : 16	beholde this thinge . . . men an excuſe
bare.	17	bare chyldrē.
had ſpoken.	21 : 1	promyſed.
lande of Moria	22 : 2	lāde Moria
ſyppe	24 : 17	ſuppe
an earynge	22	a golden earyng

Than they broughte Rebecca their ſiſter on the waye and her norſe	24 : 59	So they let Rebecca their ſyſter go with her norſe
ſyppe	25 : 30	ſuppe
y^{e}	26 : 12	that
ſpringynge water.	19	lyuyng water.
y^{e}	32	that
bleſſige, Iacob & Iacob	27 : 30	bleſſyng, Iacob
ranne agaynſt him . . . in to his houſe.	29 : 13	rāne to mete him . . to his houſe.
ſhall I geue the ?	30 : 31	ſhal I then geue the ?
the partie and ſpotted	32	the partye, and the ſpotted
And then ſuch ſhalbe	33	& the ſame ſhalbe
And Iacob went awaye vnknowynge to Laban . . , & tolde him	31 : 20	And Iacob ſtale awaye the hart of Laban . . in y^{t} he tolde hym
was fled.	22	fled
y^{t} (that)	25	y^{e} (the)
done vnknowynge to me? and haſt caried awaye . . . with ſwerde ?	26	done to ſteale awaye my hert, and carye awaye . . . with the ſwerde ?
de all wel	32 : 9	do all well
God and with men ād haſt	28	God & haſt
ranne agaynſt him	33 : 4	ranne to mete him
me frely. And	11	me. And
And Iacob went to Salem to ye citie of Sichem	18	And Iacob came peaſably in to the cite of Sichem
vnto Dina	34 : 3	vn Dina
place Elbethell	35 : 7	place Bethell
ſygnett, thy necke lace, and	38 : 18	ſygnett, thy bracelet, and
ſeall, necklace, and	25	ſeall, bracelet, and
and is	41 : 26	and it is
are .vii. yeres	27	are .vii. eares
nor of	39	or of
agayne with you in youre handes, peraduenture	43 : 12	agayne wyth you, peraduenture
ſoughte for to wepe	30	ſought where to wepe
lordes audyence	44 : 18	lordes eare
.x. he aſſes	45 : 23	.x. aſſes
Semnon	46 : 13	Semſon
xxx. and .vi.	15	.xxx. and .iii.
went agaynſt Iſraell	29	wēt to mete Iſrael
For an abhominacyon vnto the Egiptians are all that feade ſhepe.	34	For the Egyptiās abhore all ſheppardes:
Pharao: feaders of ſhepe	47 : 3	Pharao: ſheppardes are
the doughters come forth to bere rule.	49 : 22	the daughters ran vpon the walle.
wombes.	25	wombe.
charged before	50 : 16	charged vs before

Exodus.

the ſoules	1 : 5	theſe ſoules
whē ye mydwiue the women	16	when ye do ye office of a mydwife to the womē
and alſo drewe	2 : 19	& ſo drewe

cometh out agaynſt the	4 : 14	cometh to mete the
Egipte dyd	7 : 12	Egypte: and they dyd
wolde not	8 : 29	wille not
ſende out my people that	9 : 1	let my people goo that
Moſes, by the reaſon of botches on the	11	Moſes, for there were botches vpon the
ſhall this felowe thus plage vs? . . . God, or els wilt thou ſee Egipte firſt deſtroyed?	10 : 7	ſhall we be thus euell intreated? . . God: wilt thou not yet knowe that Egypt is deſtroyed?
muſt goo	9	wyll go
ſhall it be ſoo?	10	let it be ſo?
one greſhopper left in	19	one greſhopper in
a darke myſt vppō	22	a thicke darcknes vpō
And all theſe	11 : 8	And theſe
euē the fyrſt moneth	12 : 2	euen of the fyrſt moneth
him in warde, vntyll	12 : 6	hym in, vntyll
therof ſodē . . . both head	9	therof rawe ner ſoden . . . both the head
hande and a remembraunce	13 : 9	hande a remembraūce
matrice, and all	12	matryce, all
made for the to dweld in	15 : 17	made for to dwell in,
water	25	waters
of this diſeaſes	26	of theſe diſeaſes
at euen he ſhall	16 : 6	at euen ye ſhall
Sixte	26	Sixe
al moſt	17 : 4	all moſt
with ſwerde	22 : 24	with y[e] ſwerde
And as I haue ſhewed	25 : 9	And I ſhall ſhewe
And hundred	39	And an hundred
ſhalle brynge	26 : 33	ſhalt brynge
braſſe after the faſcyon of a net, ād put apon the nette .iiii rynges: euen in .iiii. corners of it, and put it beneth vnder the compaſſe of the altare, and let the net reache vnto the one half of the altare, And make ſtaues	27 : 4–7	and thou ſhalt make a gredyern alſo lyke a net of braſſe, vpon whoſe .iiii. corners ſhalbe .iiii. braſen rynges: and the gredyern ſhall reache vnto the myddes of the altare. And thou ſhalt make ſtaues
ſhall Aaron ād his ſonnes dreſſe	27 : 21	& Aaron & hys ſonnes ſhall dreſſe
breſtlappe of enſample	28 : 15	breſtlappe of iudgemēt
brodered	27	bordered
breſtlappe of enſāple; ſo v. 30	29	breſtlappe of iudgement; ſo v. 30
lighte and perfectneſſe	30	Vrim and Thumin
maunde with the oyle	29 : 3	maunde with the oxe
reconcyle his hornes	30 : 10	reconcyle vpon the hornes of it
after the holye ſycle	13	after the ſycle of the ſanctuarye
make attonement	16	make an attonement
Bezabeel	35 : 30	Bezaleel
forboden	36 : 6	forbidden
vp the firſt moneth	40 : 17	vp the fyrſt daye in the fyrſt moneth
they iornayed.	36	they had iorneyed.

Leviticus.

then take of that	2 : 14	then take that
Lorde talked with	4 : 1	Lorde ſpake vnto
apon the oxes heade	4	vpon the oxe heade
the oxes bloude	5	the oxe bloude
ſhepe . . . bringe a yewe	32	lambe . . . bringe a female
that wherein that he hath	5 : 5	that wherin he hath
an yewe	6	a lambe
ſycles after the holy ſycle	15	ſycles after the ſycle of the ſanctuary
fifte parte moare there to	16	fyſte parte more to
ſcoured and plunged	6 : 28	ſcoured and ryneſed
amonge the childern of Aarō ſhall	29	amonge the Preaſtes ſhall
lighte ād perfectneſſe.	8 : 8	Vrim and Thumim.
Soleam . . . kynde, ād the Hagab	11 : 22	Selaam . . . kynde, the Hagab
on all foure	27	on all foure fete
Make not youre ſoules abhominable	42	*omitted*
make hym (or him, it) vnclene (or cleane) (so vv. 11, 15, 20, 22, 23, 25, 27, 30, 34, 35, 37, 44, 59)	13 : 3	iudge hym (or him, it) vnclene (or clene) (so vv. 11, 15, 20, 22, 23, 25, 27, 30, 34, 35, 37, 44, 59)
make the diſeaſe (so v. 17)	13	iudge the diſeaſe (so v. 17)
fretē	55	freat
cipreſſe or cypreſſe (so vv. 6, 49, 51, 52)	14 : 4	cedar (so vv. 6, 49, 51, 52)
ouer an erthē	5	in an erthen
put of the oyle	28	put on the oyle
byrdes ouer	50	byrdes in
renſed in the water.	15 : 12	ryneſed in water.
lyeth apō as longe as	20	lyeth or ſytteth vpō as longe as
aparte as well	24	aparte was well
tyme: whether out	25	tyme: out
And when ſhe is clenſed of	28	But yf ſhe be cleane of
with a yonge oxe	16 : 3	with a bullock
oxe (so vv. 11, 14, 15, 18, 27)	6	bullock (so vv. 11, 14, 15, 18, 27)
Iſraell, and all their	21	Iſraell, and their
offerynges they offer . . . thē for peaſeofferynges	17 : 5	offerynges yᵗ they offer . . . the peace offerynges
nexte kyn. (v. 13)	18 : 12	nexte kynſwoman. (v. 13)
open	14	vncouer
apon his houſſholde	20 : 5	vpon hys generacion
turne vnto them that worke with ſpirites or makers of dyſemall dayes	6	turne him to enchaũters or expounders of tokens
his bloude on his heed	9	his bloud on his head
with the mankynde . . . heed.	13	with mankynde . . . heades.
vnheale hir ſecrettes and vncouer	18	vncouer her ſecrettes and open
fathers ſyſters	19	father ſyſter
or a maker of dyſemall dayes	27	or that expoundeth tokens
preſe	21 : 17	preace

any monſtrous mēbre	21 : 18	any myſſhapē mēbre
preſe	21	preace
that hath twyched any ſoch	22 : 6	that hath any ſoch
that which hath his ſtones brooſed brokē, plucked out	24	that which is brooſed, broken, plucked
vayle of teſtimonye	24 : 3	vayle of wytneſſe
him that curſed	14	hym that blaſphemed
a yere of hornes blowynge (so vv. 11, 12, 13)	25 : 10	a yere of iubilee (or iubelye) (vv. 11, 12, 13)
the trompett yere	15	iubelye yere
the horneyere (*bis*)	28	the yere of iubelye (*bis*)
the trompet yere (so vv. 31, 33, 40, 50, 52, 54)	30	the yere of iubelye (so vv. 31, 33, 40, 50, 52, 54)
londe of their enemyes	26 : 44	lande of their enemye
trompet yere (so vv. 21, 23, 24)	27 : 17	yere of iubely *or* iubelye (vv. 21, 23, 24)

Numbers.

ſtōde . . . in Rubē	1 : 5	ſtande . . . of Ruben
In Simeon	6	of Simeon
In . . . of Iuda	7	of . . of Iuda
In Iſachar	8	of Iſachar
In Sebulō	9	of Zabulon
In Ephraī . . . In Manaſſe	10	of Ephraim . . . of Manaſſe
In Bē Iamin	11	of Ben Iamin
In Dan	12	of Dan
In Aſſer	13	of Aſer
In Naphtaly	15	of Nephthali
.Liii.	43	thrye and fyſtye
ſyxe hundred thouſande	46	ſyxe hundred and thre thouſande
was the habitacion	3 : 25	was to kepe the habitacyon
was: the arcke	31	was to kepe the arcke
was: the bordes	36	was to kepe y[e] bordes
witneſſe: Tyndale omits from *This ſhall &c.* to *moſt holy*.	4 : 4	witneſſe. This ſhalbe the office of the chyldrē of Kahath in the tabernacle of witneſſe which is mooſt holy.
amōge which I dwell.	5 : 3	amōge which ye dwell.
& an oxe	7 : 15	& an bullock
omitted	19	and both full of fyne floure myngled with oyle for a meatofferynge:
oxe (so vv. 33, 39, 51, 57, 63, 69, 75, 81)	21	bullock (so vv. 33, 39, 51, 57, 63, 69, 75, 81)
harde ſyluer	10 : 2	beaten ſyluer
y[e] firſt	13	they firſt
Selumiel the ſonne (Tyndale omits from *of Suri &c. &c.* to *the ſonne*)	19	Salamiel y[e] ſonne of Suri ſaddai. And ouer the hoſte of the tribe of the chyldren of Gad was Eliaſaph the ſonne of Deguel.
Samaleel	10 : 23	Gamaliel

father lawe	10:29	father in lawe
waxed vnpacient	11: 1	complayned
boke . . . cakes	8	baked . . . kakes
put apon them	17	put apon the and apon them
ſtode vpp all that nyghte and on the morowe	32	ſtode vp all that daye & all that nyghte
place, the graues of luſt	34	place kibrath hathauah
graues of luſt	35	kibraſh hathauah
Ioſeph: In the trybe of Manaſſe, Gaddi	13:11	Ioſeph: that was of Manaſſe, Gaddi
Eſcol	24	Nehel Eſcol
Egipte, to be youre God.	15:41	Egipte, for to be youre God
from amonge childern	18: 6	from amonge the chyldren
cipreſſe wodd	19: 6	Cedar wood
Whoſoeuer twicheth	13	Whoſouer toucheth
omitted.	20	holy place of ye Lorde, & is not ſprynkled with ſprinklyng water therfore is he vncleane. And this ſhalbe a perpetual lawe vnto thē.
Piſga . . . the wilderneſſe.	21:20	Phaſgah . . . Ieſimon.
Chemos ye are forloren.	29	Chamos ye are vndone.
lye	22: 5	lyeth
to	20	vnto
this .iii. tymes?	28	thus .iii. tymes?
this .iii. tymes?	33	thus .iii. tymes?
vnto the cytie of Huzoth.	39	vnto the large cytie.
oxen	23: 1	bullockes
alter an oxe	2	alter a bullock
alter, an oxe	4	alter, a bullock
thine habitacions	24: 5	thyne habitacion
Egipte is as the ſtrength	8	Egypt his ſtrenght is as the ſtrenght
Cittim	24	Chittim
Zur and heed	25:15	Zur a heed
Tola . . . Tolaites	26:23	Thola . . . Tholaites
Aabrim	27:12	Abarim
ye maner of the lighte	21	the iudgemēt of Vrim
offer vnto me ye offryng	28: 2	offer vnto the offeryng
.ii. bollockes	19	two younge bullockes
yerelynges & pure	29:23	yerelynges pure
acordynge to their nūbre	24	accordyng to the nombre of them
.xiiii. lambes	32	.xiii. lambes
Ataroth Dibo & Beon, whiche	32: 3	Ataroth & Dibō & Iazer, and Nemrah & Heſbon & Elealeh & Sabam & Nebo & Beon, which
ſtede, the encreaſe . . . , to augmente	14	ſteade, to ye encreaſe . . . & to augmēte
ſtronge cities	17	fenced cyties
Betharan ſtronge cities	36	Betharan fencend cyties
ſmoten	33: 4	ſmyttē
.Lxx. datetrees	9	.Lxx. paulmetrees
pitched amonge the childern of Iaecon.	31	pytched in Bane Iakan.

from the childern of Iaecon . . . Hor gidgad . . . Hor gidgad	33 : 32	from Bane Iakan . . . Hor gad-gad . . . Hor gadgad
londe of Moab.	37	land of Edom.
Igim Abarim (v. 46)	44	Iehabarim (v. 46)
playne of Sitim	49	Abelſatim
their Ymaginacions	52	their chappelles
theſe which	55	thoſe which
Demuel	34 : 20	Semuel
Iordayne Iericho	35 : 1	Iordan ouer againſt Iericho
iudge of bloude	19	iuſtice of bloude
the bloudvenger	26	the auẽger of bloud
bloude of it	33	bloude of hym
I alſo dwell, for I am ye Lorde which dwell amonge the childern	34	I alſo dwell amonge the chyl-dren
when the fre yere . . . where they are in	36 : 4	when the yere of iubelye . . . wherin they are

Deuteronomy.

.xii. dayes . . . bernea	1 : 2	.xi. dayes . . . barne
Sihon . . . Edrei.	4	Sehon . . . Edrai.
for the lawe	17	for the iudgement
bernea.	20	barne.
Bolde	38	Boldē
acordinge vnto the tyme that ye there dwelt.	46	*omitted.*
Emymes.	2 : 11	Emims.
Horimes	12	Horims
bernea	14	barne
Zamzumyms.	20	Zamzumims.
Enakyms.	21	Enakims.
Sihō	24	Sehon
wilderneſſe of Kedemoth . . . Syhon	26	wilderneſſe of the eaſte . . . Sehon
Iordayne	29	Iordan
Sihon (31)	30	Sehon (31)
Sihon . . . Iahab.	32	Sehon . . . Iahaza.
Gilead	36	Galaad
Edrey	3 : 1	Edrai
Sihon	2	Sehon
Sihon	6	Sehon
Gilead . . . Salcha . . . Edrei	10	Galaad . . . Salecha . . . Edrai
Gilead	12	Galad
Gilead (vv. 15, 16)	13	Galaad (vv. 15, 16)
and called the townes of Ba-ſan after his owne name: the townes of Iair	14	& called them after his owne name: Baſan Hauoth Iair
Cenereth . . . Piſga	17	Ceneroth . . . Phaſgah
O lorde Iehoua	24	O lorde God
Piſga	27	Phaſgah
thine life	4 : 9	thy lyfe
geueth the for euer.	40	geueth the thy lyfe longe.
Gilead	43	Galaad
witneſſe	45	witneſſes
Sihō	46	Sehon
Piſga.	49	Phaſgah.

in the erth beneth	5: 8	in erth benethe
Girgoſites	7: 1	Gergeſites
nor haue compaſſion	2	not haue compaſſyon
thy oyle	13	thyne oyle
ād thurſte	8:15	and drouth
caſt them out, and brynge them to noughte	9: 3	caſt thē out, and brynge them out, and brynge them to noughte
Thabeera	22	Thaberah
Bernea	23	Barne
in the table	10: 2	in ye tables
mount out of the fire . . . people were gathered	4	mount of the fire . . . people gethered together
Beroth Bē Iakē	6	Beroth of the childrē of Iakan
Gudgod (*bis*)	7	Gadgad (*bis*)
all theſe nacions both greatter	11:23	all theſe nacions & ye ſhall conquere thē which are both greatter
Griſim	29	Garizim
Gilgal beſyde moregroue.	30	Galgal beſyde the groue of Moreh.
thy fyrſt borne	12: 6	the fyrſt borne
deſtroye it	13:15	deſtroye hit
ſpoyle of it	16	ſpoyle of hit
hertgoote	14: 5	wyldegoote,
luſteth after: on oxen	26	luſteth after: of oxen
axe	15: 2	aſke
an heritaunce	4	enheritaũce
handes, and thou ſhalt be aii together gladneſſe.	16:15	handes, & therfore ſhalt thou be glad.
booth feaſt.	16	feaſt of tabernacles
thi cities	17: 2	the cytyes
vnto thi gates	5	vnto the gates
dayes, and axe	9	dayes, and aſke
ſeten	17:18	ſett
all thy trybes	18: 5	all the trybes
doughter go thorow fyre, ether a bruterar or a maker of diſmale dayes or that vſeth witchcraft or a ſorcerar	10	daughter to go thorow the fyre, or that uſeth withcraft, or a choſer oute of dayes or that regardeth the flyẽg of foules, or a ſorcerar
or a charmar or that ſpeaketh with a ſpirite or a ſothſayer or that talketh with them that are deed.	11	or a charmar, or that counceleth with ſpretes, or a propheciar or that aſketh the aduyſe of the deed.
herken vnto makers of dyſemall dayes and bruterars.	14	herken vnto choſers oute of dayes and prophecyars.
commaunded him not	20	commaunded not
And ſo thou ſhalt	21:21	And thou ſhalt
axe	22: 2	aſke
in- the congregacyō	23: 2	in to the congregacyō
When there is	25: 1	If there be
vngodly	3	vngoodly
ſyſterlawe (v. 8)	7	ſyſter in lawe (v. 8)
maner weyghtes	13	maner of weyghtes
Griſim	27:12	Garizim
at none daye . . . the right waye.	28:29	at none dayes . . . ye ryght awaye.

betrothed	28 : 30	betrawthed
for the locuſtes	38	for the greſhoppers
fleeth	49	flyeth
kepe the in all thy cities . . . thorow all thy londe.	52	kepe the in, in all thy cities . . . thorow all the lande
auenture	56	aduēture
worde	29 : 9	wordes
ſayenge: I feare it not, I will ther fore walke . . . that the drounken deſtroye the thurſtie.	19	ſayinge. I ſhall haue peace. I will therfore worcke . . . that the dronckē may peryſh with the thryſtye.
ſalt, that it is	23	ſalt, & yt it is
And than all	24	And then ſhall all
The ſecrettes perteyne vnto the Lorde oure God and the thinges that are opened perteyne vnto us and oure	29	The ſecrettes of the Lorde oure God are opened vnto vs and oure
for us in to heauen	30 : 12	for vs to heauen
yere olde this daye	31 : 2	yere this daye
Sihon	4	Sehon
ād Iſrael is	32 : 9	and Iacob is
whett the lyghtenynge of my ſwerde	41	whett the edge of my ſwerde
Reioyſe hethen wyth hys	43	Prayſe ye hethen his
Paran	33 : 2	Pharan
tempteſt at Maſa ād with whom thou ſtriuedſt	8	tēptedeſt at Maſah wyth whom thou ſtryuedſt
hate them: that they ryſe	11	hate them: they ryſe
Manaſſe.	17	Manaſſes.
a parte of the teachers were . . . ād come	21	a parte of the teacher was . . . and came
vnto the God of the off Iſrael	26	vnto the God of Iſrael
Piſga . . . Gilead	34 : 1	Phaſgah . . . Galaad
datetrees	3	paulmetrees

IV.

LIST OF MARGINAL NOTES IN THE PROLOGUES TO THE SEVERAL BOOKS OF THE PENTATEUCH GIVEN IN DAYE'S FOLIO OF 1573, AND ATTRIBUTED TO JOHN FOXE,* WITH REFERENCE TO THE PLACES IN THIS EDITION TO WHICH THEY BELONG.

Notes on *W. T. to the Reader*.†

	P.	L.
The reafon that the papiftes make agaynft the tranflation of the fcripture into Englifh.	2	5
A fubtle fhift of the popes clergy to couer their euill.		13
How the Papiftes were vexed with Tindals tranflation of the new teftament.		24
The Papiftes fhamed not to wreft the fcriptures.	3	4
The Papiftes haue wrought wonderfully to haue fuppreffed ye fcripture.	3	18
As owles abide not the brightnes of the day, fo cannot the papiftes abide the lyght of the gofpell.		32
What firft moued W. Tyndale to tranflate ye Scripture into englifh.		35
This bifhop of Lōdon was Tunftall, which afterward was bifhop of Durham.	4	9
The popes chaplens pulpet, is the alehoufe.		29
Chriftes apoftles dyd mekely admonifh, but the Popes fectaryes dyd braule and fkold.		34
Parcialitie fometyme in men of great learnyng.		41
How Tindale was deceaued.	5	17
Roome enough in my Lordes houfe for belly chere, but none to tranflate the new teftament.		35
Tindale could get no place in the bifhop of Londōs houfe.		39
Tyndals fubmiffion is to all fuch as fubmit them felues to God.	6	20

Notes on *A Prologe fhewinge the vfe of the fcripture.*

Not the toung but the life proueth a true Gofpeller.	7	8
The trueft touchestone of Religion is Chriftes Gofpell.		19
The fcripture of god is ye fworde of the Spirite.	8	9
Tribulatiō is the gifte of God.	9	4
What we ought to feeke in the fcriptures.	10	2

---

* The Whole | workes of W. Tyndall, Iohn | Frith, and Doct. Barnes, three | worthy Martyrs, and principall | teachers of this Churche of England, | collected and compiled in one Tome to- | gither, beyng before fcattered, & now in | Print here exhibited to the Church. | To the prayfe of God, and | profite of all good Chri- | ftian Readers | *Mortui refurgent.* | At London | Printed by Iohn Daye, | and are to be fold at his fhop | vnder Alderfgate . . | An. 1573. | ¶ *Cum gratia & Priuilegio* | *Regiæ Maieftatis* | . IN FOLIO.

† The Titles are given in the spelling of Tyndale, not of Foxe.

Notes on *A Prologe in to the ſeconde boke of Moſes, called Exodus.*

* Misprinted brea*d*eth

Notes on *A Prologe in to the thirde boke of Moſes, called Leuiticus.*

* The letters *t* and *r* are transposed in the Original.

	P.	L.
Baptiſme teacheth vs repentaunce of ſinne.	295	3
The bare waſhyng helpeth not but through the worde of fayth it purifieth vs.		9
How chriſt boroweth figures of the old Teſtament, to make plain the textes of the new teſtament.		24
Our duety is to do good dedes but ſaluation we cannot chalēge therby.	296	16
A good example taken of the Lepers.		22
The true preachyng of Gods word, doth bynde and loſe conſciences.		34
In allegories is both hony & gall, that is to ſay, both good & euil.	297	5
All good dedes are gods workmanſhip, & wee hys inſtrumētes wherby he doth them.		22

Notes on *A Prologe in to the fourth boke of Moſes, called Numeri.*

Freewill and vnbeliefe were the ouerthrow of oure forefathers.	385	5
Then cannot they be the childrē of God, which put more truſt in their owne workes, then in ye bloud of Ieſus Chriſt.		16
Faithleſſe workes.	386	1
The Phariſes by their freewill excluded them ſelues from the ſaluatiō in Chriſt.		7
Blaſphemy to chriſtes death.		23
O ſubtle Foxes thorow pouerte made themſelues Lordes of all.		28
Wilfull chaſtitie is wilful wickednes.		40
The Papiſtes wilful obedience, is cōmon diſobedience to all princes.	387	5
Our righteouſnes commeth not by our merites, but thorow fayth, by the bloud of our ſauiour Ieſus Chriſt.		13
Fayth only bringeth vs to chriſt and vnbelief driueth vs from Chriſt.		21
Chriſt rebuked the Phariſes for their holy and hipocritical dedes.		29
The phariſes aſcribe righteouſneſſe to workes, & therfore were condemned of Chriſt.		39
The iuſtifying of our ſelues maketh the diuell more buſier then he wold be.	388	9
What is meant in the ſcripture by this word vii. tymes.		16
Meritmōgers ye more their blindnes is rebuked, the more they rebell againſt Chriſt and his goſpell.		24
The doctrine of the phariſes, and the doctrine of our papiſts do well agree.		34
The Papiſtes cannot away with iustification by fayth.	389	13
Of vowes.		16
God accepteth for vs none other ſacrifice, but onely Ieſu chriſt his ſonne.		28
All holines in our own imaginatiō is a robbing of chriſtes honor.		37
Faith foloweth repentaunce of ſinne.	390	22
Repentāce goeth before fayth, and prepareth the way vnto Chriſt.		30

	P.	L.
How our workes are good in the ſight of God.	390	39
The work ſaueth not, but the word, that is to ſay, the promiſe.	391	6
An apt ſimilitude for reward of good workes.		17
All vowes muſt be made for yͤ mortifying or tamyng of our members or the edifying of our neighbours, oɪ els they are wicked.		24
How we ought to vowe wilfull pouertie.		32
Whether fiſhed the Popes prelates with this net or no?	392	2
Our workes do not ſtand in the wiſedome of mā but in the power of God.		24
Deſert, and fre gift are contraries.	393	2
The ſight of riches, is rather a cauſe of couetouſnes then a meane to honor God.		14
Whether dyd the papiſt ſo or no		30
Yet yͤ ſpiritualties pilage was more then theyr ſtanding ſtipēd.		41
A good vowe is to kepe Gods commaundementes.	394	6
How thou mayſt lawfully goe on pilgrimage.		17
God heareth all that call vppon him in all tymes and at al places alyke.		30
God dwelleth not in temples made with mannes handes.		34
God regardeth the hart & not yͤ place where wee pray.	395	4
Wilfull chaſtitie is not mete for all perſons to vow.		11
Falſe fayned chaſtitie.		24
The Pope reſtrayned that which God permitted and ſetteth at liberty that which God forbiddeth.		35
A good adminition to ſuch as wil make vowes.	396	6
Wherunto and howe we ſhould apply our vowes.		17
How a vow is to be made.		22
He that faſteth to any other ende thā to tame his body, that it may wayte vpon God, deceiueth hym ſelfe.		32
All our doynges muſt tende to the honour of God, and loue of our neighbour.	397	2

Notes to *A Prologe in to the fyfte boke of Moſes, called Deuteronomye.*

	P.	L.
This boke is a preachyng of fayth and loue.		4
Here thou mayeſt learne a right meditation or contemplation.		8
The workes of God are ſupernatural.		17
We muſt abſtaine frō outward euill though not for loue yet for feare of the vengeance of God.		27
Vnto the law of god, we may neither add nor miniſh.		31
We are cōmaunded to abſtayne from Images.	518	4
God is mercyful to them that repent.		12
Chriſt hath deliuered vs, & therfore we ought to ſerue him & our neyghbour for his ſake.		20
Loue onely is the fulfillyng of the lawes of God.		29
We muſt truſt onely in God, & not in our ſelues.		37
How a mā may trye & examine hym ſelfe, how much he loueth God, and his neighbour.	519	6
God ſtyrreth vp his people vnto fayth.		13
A right of way of prayer.		17
The pith & effect of all yͤ lawes of God.		20

	P.	L.
And if wee firſt loue God, then out of that loue, we muſt nedes loue our neighbour.	519	27
What it is to loue and feare God, and what it is to deſpiſe him.		36
The word of god may not be altered.	520	1
Let no man draw vs from gods worde.		4
Of maters of the common weale.		14
None may be condemned vnder two witneſſes.		22
Chriſt our ſauiour declared in the old teſtament.		35
The curſe and wrath of God ouer al thoſe that break his lawes.	521	1
We may not be to curious in the ſearchyng of Gods ſecretes, but rather ſtudy to vnderſtand & to do our duety toward god and our neighbour.		9

V.

COLLATION OF THE PROLOGUES TO THE SEVERAL BOOKS OF THE PENTATEUCH SHOWING THE DIFFERENT READINGS IN TYNDALE'S PENTATEUCH OF 1530, AND IN DAYE'S FOLIO OF 1573.

1530.	P.	L.	*1573.*
W. T. To the Reader.			¶ The Preface of maſter William Tyndall, | that he made before the fiue bookes of | Moſes, called *Geneſis. An. 1530, Ianua. 17.*
their both	2	9	both their
wiſdom.	3	25	wiſdom:
vttmoſt		27	vttermoſt
biſſhope	4	9	Byſhops
tended		10	tented
accuſe		34	accuſed
yt		41	the
litle	5	2	litles
piſtle		14	epiſtle
piſtle		15	epiſtle
the	6	7	them
it full		17	it a full
other		21	either
Aprologe ſhewinge the vſe of the ſcripture			A prologue by Williã Tyn- | dall, ſhewyng the vſe of the Scrip- | ture, which he wrote before the fiue | bookes of Moſes.
other for	7	17	other in
invencyon		18	invencyons.
ye		19	*omitted.*

	P.	L.	
enſamples	8	11	examples
hope.		21	hope for.
enſamples	9	4	examples
enſamples	10	1	example
haunſed them	11	22	chaunſed
enſample:		24	example:
enſamples,		35	examples,
of the harte	12	1	of harte
the		19	yt
countre		23	countey
that he		24	that
bleſſe		25	bleſſe,
behaue		30	behaued
vttmoſte		40	vttermoſte
out but with	13	13	out with
ſynners.		18	ſynnes.
enſamples		28	examples
to kepe		31	*omitted.*
enſample		37	example
at the laſte.		39	at laſte.
there		41	there there
folowed ?	14	7	foloweth ?
enſamples		9	examples
Thoſe		14	Theſe
enſamples		18	examples
for theyr		22	for
A PROLO | GE IN TO THE SECON- | de boke of Moſes called | Exodus.			The Prologue to the ſe- | cond booke of Moſes | called Exodus.
Of	161	1	By
promiſes		21	promiſe
all captiuite		33	all the captiuite
vntill		35	till
pope	162	7	people
becauſe that whē		12	*omits* that
they fight		19	they do fight
neyghbours		29	owne
of goddes worde		34, 35	*omitted.*
Where		40	When
as	163	9	an
ād to		11	*omits* to
which		13	that
god had		14	god hath
nought		16	ought
nought therfro		17	ought from it
to do only that which		17	cōmaundyng to do that only that
muſt		29	ſhould
his		36	the
vs care		40	vs to care
evell	164	2	ill
wedowe		14	wedowes
all		19	*omitted.*
ſhall		24	ſhould
the mouth of		30	*omitted.*
not grudge		33	*omitted.*
no		34	none

	P.	L.	
ſhadowes of Moſes	165	1	ſhadowe of Moyſes
namely of the		8	namely the
thīge		10	thīges
pertayned		13	pertayning
ſo bewtifull		13	*omitted.*
ſe more		14	ſe things more
ād wonderfull		15	*omitted.*
of the ſacrifices		17	of ſacrifices
be by		22	be there by
places		36	bookes
of thē		40	of
this	166	3	his
puniſhment		6	puniſhments
with		6	and
euen		7	*omitted.*
yere		10	yeres
ſaye		13	haue ſayd
but hath		15	but God hath
the		17	them
ād to make		21	ād make
dryve vnto		32	dryve vs vnto
So		37	*omitted.*
alepope		41	ale pole
on	167	19	in
which		22	that
euerlaſtinge lyfe		23	lyfe euerlaſtinge
geueth her		26	geueth it
or		37	nor
hilles or	168	5	*omitted.*
bleſſynge		20	bleſſynges
naturall		23	*omitted.*
curſes		24	curſe
ceaſon		40	tyme
theſe		41	thoſe
this	169	6	theſe
this		8	theſe
			A Table expounding cer- | tayne wordes of the ſec- ond | booke of Geneſis (*ſic*).
oure ſhrynes		14	ours
offerīges		31	offerīge
be	170	7	was
or the newe		8	or newe

Daye (1573) adds:

Of this word ***I will be***, commeth the name of God ***Iehouah***, which we interprete Lord, and is as much to ſaye, as I am that I am. 3. Chap.

That I here call a ſhepe in Hebrue is a worde indifferent to a ſhepe, and a goate both. 12. Chap.

The Lambe was called Paſſeouer, that the very name its ſelfe, ſhould put them in remembraunce, what it ſignified, for the ſignes that God ordained, either ſignified the benefites done, or promſſes to come, and were not done, as the ſignes of our domme God the Pope.

Iehouah Niſſi, the Lord is he that exalteth me. Chap. 17.

Ephod, is a garment like an amice. Chap. 25.

Shewbread, becauſe it was alway in the ſighte and preſence of the Lord. Chap. 25.

1530.	P.	L.	1573.
A PRO- | LOGE IN TO THE | thirde boke of Mofes | called Leuiticus.			A Prologue into the thirde | booke of Mofes called Le- | uiticus.
boke	289	2	booke
heed		10	head
childers	290	7	childerns
faythes		38	faythe
vnto		41	vntil
faythes	292	3	faithe
Iohan		14	Iohn
Paule fayenge		25	Pauls fayenge
baptim		27	Baptifme
apon the croffe		40, 41	vpon croffe
hote	293	24	hoate
my fynnes.		29, 30	fynnes.
axed off God		33	afked God
envieth me Chrifte		35	envieth Chrifte
wyle	294	1	wyld
invifible		11	inuifibles
baptim		15, 16	baptifm
vnderftonde.		26	vnderftand.
baptim.		29	baptifme.
bagge		30, 34	badge
fodiars		31	fouldiers
baptim		33	baptifm
baptim		39	baptifme
baptim	295	3, 9	Baptifme
baptim		10, 13, 17	Baptifme
chrift fayenge		25	Chrifts faying
boke		41	booke
fett	296	37	fetch.
apte a thinge	297	6	apte thinge
vnderftond		17	vnderftand
nurteringe		28	nurtering

Daye's folio of 1573 has also the following table drawn up from the marginal notes in *Deuteronomy*, and erroneously inserted before *Numbers*.

An expofition of certayne | wordes of the fourth booke | of Mofes, called Numeri.

Avims, a kynde of Giauntes, and the worde fignifieth crooked, vnright, or weaked.

Beliall, weaked, or weakeneffe, hee that hath caft the yoke of God of his necke, and will not obey God.

Bruterer, prophefies or fouthfayers.

Emims, a kynde of gyauntes fo called becaufe they were terrible and cruell, for *Emim* fignifieth terriblenes.

Enacke, a kinde of Giauntes fo called happly, becaufe they ware chaynes about their neckes.

Horims, a kynde of Giauntes, and fignifieth noble, becaufe that of pride they called themfelues nobles, or gentles.

Rocke, God is called a rocke, becaufe both he and hys word lafteth for euer.

Whet them on thy children, that is, exercife thy children in them, and put them in vre.

Zamzumims, a kynde of Gyauntes, and fignifieth mifcheuous, or that be alway imagining.

1530.	P.	L.	*1573.*
ℂ A prolo | ge in to the fourth boke of | Mofes, called Nu- | meri.			The Prologue into the | fourth boke of Mofes | called Numeri.
lowfeth	386	5	loofeth
vnlithed	387	34	untithed
hijfh	388	32	hifh
axe	389	36	afke
baptyme	390	11	Baptifme
haue to god		40	haue God
promeffe me to	391	11	promife to
enfample		40	example
no nother	392	34	no other
a nother		36	an other
Thou wilt	393	10	But thou peraduenture wilt
a nother		19	another
a nother	394	24, 25, 26, 30	another
axe	395	1	afke
fonne		6	fonnes
fame		20	fome
vfe the remeadye		24	vfe remedy
A nother		25	An other
boke		28	booke
other	396	6	either
as wife god		6	as God
nother		7	neither
requyreth not nor forfwere that which god		8	*omitted.*
nother		41	neither
a nother	397	8	an other
A PRO | LOGE IN TO THE | fyfte boke of Mofes, cal- | led Deuteronomye.			A Prologue into the fifte | booke of Mofes called Deu- | teronomy.
boke	517	1	booke
wete		5	wit
boke		14	booke
power and beyonde all naturall		17	*omitted.*
them	520	22	then
appoffe		27	oppofe
curfes	521	6	curfe

VI.

LIST OF PLACES IN THIS EDITION OF THE PENTATEUCH EXPLAINED OR ILLUSTRATED BY LUTHER, TYNDALE, AND ROGERS.

(L denotes Luther; T, Tyndale; and M, Matthew's Bible.)

Gen. 1 : 2 M
7 M
22 M
26 M
2 : 1 M
3 M
7 M
10 M
11 L
17 M
3 : 6 M
8 L M
15 L M
20 L
22 M
4 : 1 L
4 M
10 M
15 T
26 M
5 : 22 M
6 : 2 L M
12 M
13 M
7 : 1 M
2 M
11 M
8 : 7 L
11 L
21 M
9 : 5 T M
6 L
22 L
27 M
10 : 25 L
11 : 5 M
9 L
12 M
12 : 2 M
5 M
13 : 8 M
15 M
18 M
14 : 2 M
5 M
18 L M
19 M
21 M

Gen. 15 : 1 M
6 M
11 L
14 M
16 M
17 M
16 : 2 M
5 M
11 L
13 M
17 : 5 L
13 M
18 : 1 M
2 L
5 M
19 : 5 M
15 M
20 L
20 : 11 M
16 M
21 : 9 L
31 L
22 : 2 L M
5 M
12 M
23 : 2 L
15 L
24 : 2 M
22 M
23 M
33 T M
49 M
60 T M
63 M
25 : 6 M
8 M
23 M
27 M
26 : 20 L
21 L
22 L M
33 L
27 : 4 M
13 M
28 M
36 L
28 : 14 L
17 M

Gen. 28 : 19 M
21 L
22 M
29 : 32–35 L
30 : 8 L
11 L
13 L
14 M
18 L
20 L
21 L
24 L
32 L
33 M
31 : 20 L
42 L M
48 L
32 : 9 T
10 M
28 L
30, 31 L M
33 : 14 L
34 : 1 L
2 M
35 : 2 M
14 L
18 L M
29 M
36 : 4 M
37 : 3 L
34 M
35 L
38 : 7 M
29 L
41 : 43 M
45 L M
46 M
51, 52 L
42 : 22 M
38 M
43 : 11 L
32 M
45 : 4 L
46 : 3, 4 M
47 : 9, 10 M
20 M
22 T
29 M

Gen. 47 : 31 L
48 : 14 M
22 L
49 : 3 L
6 M
10 L M
16 L
19 L
20 L M
21 L
22 L
27 L M
50 : 24 M

**** For the marginal notes in Genesis, 1534, see Table, page cix.*

Ex. 1 : 21 M
2 : 10 L M
12 M
17 M
22 L
25 M
3 : 1 M
5 M
8 M
14 L T M
22 M
4 : 16 M
25 L
31 M
5 : 2 M
21 M
6 : 3 L M
5 M
6 T M
8 M
9 T
12 M
7 : 1 M
11 T
23 M
8 : 19 M
9 : 6 M
27 M
10 : 11 L
26 M
11 : 5 M
8 M
12 : 3 T M
6 L
12 T M
14 M
23 M
26 T
43 L
49 M
13 : 2 M

Ex. 13 : 4 L M
6 L
8 T
9 M
14 T
18 L
14 : 9 M
14 M
15 L M
15 : 16 M
18 M
23 L
26 T M
16 : 7 M
15 L
32 T
17 : 3 M
7 L
12 L
15, 16 L T M
18 : 21 T M
22 M
24 L
19 : 10 M
15 M
20 : 5 M
12 M
18 T
21 : 6 T M
12 T
14 T
28 T M
32 M
22 : 8 L
11 M
18 T
22 T M
25 T
26 T
28 T
29 L M
23 : 8 T M
9 T
14 L
18 L
19 L M
28 M
31 T
24 : 3 L
5 M
10 M
16 M
25 : 7 T M
22 L
30 T M
26 : 1 M
4 L M

Ex. 26 : 33 M
27 : 9 M
21 M
28 : 1 T
4 M
15 L
17 M
18 M
30 L T M
36 T M
38 M
41 L
43 M
29 : 4 T
18 M
33 M
36 L
38 T
30 : 25 M
31 : 13 T M
18 M
32 : 4 L
11 T
25 L
28 T
32 T M
34 M
33 : 8 L
11 M
14 T
19 L
20 M
34 : 19 M
20 T
30 M
34 T
35 : 6 M
22 L
23 M
36 : 7 T
37 : 6 M
19 L
38 : 8 L
39 : 10 M
11 M
40 : 9 T

Lev. 1 : 9 M
2 : 2 M
13 M
3 : 1 L
4 M
5 : 24 T M
6 : 5 T M
27 M
7 : 1 M
16 M
8 : 1 *sqq.* T

Lev. 8: 8 M
36 M
9:22 *sqq.* T
10: 1 T M
3 T M
4 M
8 T
9 M
19 T M
11:22 L M
12: 2 M
13: 1 *sqq.* T
2 M
4 L
13 M
47 M
14:10 L
15 M
21 L
37 M
16: 2 T M
29 M
34 M
17: 7 M
18:21 L M
19:10 M
16 T
19 M
20 L
20: 1 *sqq.* T
2 M
20, 21 T M
21: 1 M
5 T
8 T
12 T
16, 17 T
22:29 M
23:10 M
27 M
32 M
36 L
24: 5 M
11 M
15 M
25: 8 M
9 T
10 M
15 M
26: 2 M
14 T
18 T M
21 M
26 M
42 T M
27:16 M
25 M

Num. 1:13 M
20 M
22 M
24 M
26 M
28 M
30 M
32 M
34 M
36 M
38 M
40 M
42 M
2: 3 M
10 M
17 M
18 M
25 M
3:12 M
21 M
27 M
33 M
38 M
39 M
5: 6 T M
14 M
22 M
6: 2 L M
7 M
24 *sqq.* T
25 M
7:12 M
18 M
24 M
30 M
36 M
42 M
48 M
54 M
60 M
66 M
72 M
78 M
8: 7 L
9:13 M
22 M
10: 4 M
7 M
9 M
10 T
26 M
29 M
31 M
11: 1 M
3 M
17 M
20 M

Num. 11:23 M
25 M
29 T
35 M
12: 5 M
8 M
14 M
13:16 M
22 M
24 L M
27 M
32 M
14: 6 M
13 T
21 M
30 M
33 M
40 T M
15:15 M
32 M
38 T M
16: 1 M
15 T
29 M
30 M
38 M
48 M
18: 1 M
19 L M
24 T
19: 9 T
10 M
13 M
20:12 M
21: 1 T
3 L
5 M
6 M
14 M
20 M
29 M
32 L
22:39 M
23: 8 T
9 M
21 L M
24: 1 L
5 M
17 L
20 L
24 M
25: 4 M
8 M
26: 5 M
12 M
15 M
19 M

Num. 26 : 23 M
26 M
28 M
35 M
38 M
42 M
44 M
48 M
57 M
27 : 15 T
17 M
20 L
21 L T M
23 T
28 : 2 T
29 : 35 L T
30 : 2 M
3 L
31 : 43 M
33 : 52 M
55 M
35 : 11 T M
30 M
Deut. 1 : 6 M
16 T M
21 M
26 M
27 M
43 T M
2 : 10 M
12 M
20 M
24 M
32 M
3 : 5 M
14 M
17 M
4 : 2 T M
9 T M
12 T M
20 M
24 M
5 : 4 M
8 T M
15 T
32 T M
6 : 2 M
7 T M
13 M

Deut. 6 : 15 M
16 M
18 T M
20 T M
25 T M
7 : 7 T M
10 T M
18 T
20 M
25 M
26 M
8 : 3 T M
4 M
17 M
18 T
9 : 1 M
4 T M
25 T M
10 : 7 M
20 M
11 : 6 M
10 M
14 M
19 T
12 : 15 T M
21 L
22 M
32 T M
13 : 3 T M
13 M
14 : 1 M
21 M
15 : 9 M
17 M
22 M
16 : 1 M
11 M
12 T
16 M
18 M
17 : 5 T M
14 T M
18 : 2 T
10 M
11 M
15 L T M
19 : 4 T M
6 T
15 T

Deut. 20 : 5 T M
6 T M
21 : 9 T M
11 M
14 M
22 : 5 M
6 M
8 T M
9 M
10 M
29 M
23 : 1 M
13 M
18 T M
24 : 6 M
8 T
25 : 3 M
25 : 5 T
6 M
11 M
26 : 5 M
17 M
27 : 15 T
28 : 5 L
14 M
20 L
42 M
46 M
29 : 19 L M
29 L M
31 : 2 M
17 M
32 : 1 M
4 L M
9 M
11 M
14 M
20 M
42 L M
46 M
33 : 3 M
5 L
8 L M
13 L
19 M
20 L M
21 M
26 M
28 M

VII.

LIST OF OBSOLETE OR OBSOLESCENT WORDS AND PHRASES, AND OF WORDS STILL CURRENT, BUT DIFFERING IN THE MEANING AND THE SPELLING; ALSO OF ALLUSIONS IN THE PROLOGUES, ETC.

⁂ The list might be considerably enlarged. The etymology of the words has not been attempted. The references to Wiclif are due to the Glossary in Vol. IV. of Forshall and Madden's edition. Many of the illustrations are drawn from Halliwell and Wright's edition of Nares' *Glossary*, London, 1872, in-8, and marked *H. W.* Those from miscellaneous sources are not marked. Abbreviations: *s.* denotes substantive; *v.*, verb; *pr.*, present tense; *p. t.*, past tense; *p. p.*, past participle; *v. t.*, transitive verb; *v. i.*, verb intransitive; *imperat.*, imperative; *adj.*, adjective; *adv.*, adverb.

A.

a dreade, *afraid;* adrad, or adredd, *p. p.*, *frighted*, Spenser, *F. Q.*, vi. 16, Deut. 20:3.
a farr of, *afar off*, Gen. 22:4.
a frayde, *afraid*, Gen. 20:8.
a fyre, a fire, *adv.*, *on fire*, p. 397, l. 13; Deut. 32:22.
a good, *adv.*, *thoroughly*, Deut. 9:21. Shakesp., *Two Gentl.*, iv. 3, *in good earnest*, *heartily.*
a lyue, *alive*, p. 293, l. 7.
a newe, *anew*, p. 297, l. 25.
a nother, *another*, very often.
a noyntynge, *adj.*, *anointing*, Ex. 25:6.
a sondre, a sundre, *asunder*, Lev. 5:8; often, p. 293, l. 37.
a straye, *adj.*, *astray*, p. 590, margin.
a waye, *adv.*, *away*, Num. 2:2.
accoyntaunce, *acquaintance*, p. 5, l. 8.
acoynted, *acquainted*, Lev. 16:22.
actiuyte, men of, *able*, *competent men*, Gen. 47:6.
admyt, *p. p.*, *admitted*, p. 594, margin.
aduenge, *avenge*, ed. 1534, p. 9, note.
aferde, *afraid*, Deut. 28:10; afear'd, *affear'd*, common in Shakespeare.
afflyct, *p. p.*, *afflicted*, p. 589, note.
agenst, cometh, *comes to meet*, Gen. 24:65; 33:4.
ah syr, *ah surely*, Gen. 3:1; sur, Will. of Palerne, 973; seur, *Seven Sages*, ed. Web. 2033; Skeat.*
Albertus, *i. e.*, Albertus Magnus, bishop of Ratisbon, whose book, *De secretis mulierum opus* (1. ed. 1428 pro 1478) in–4, has often been reprinted in the fifteenth century, and since, p. 4, l. 18.
ale pole, *so* Daye, 1573, *the pole set up before a tavern, or ale house.*
ale pope, *probably misprint for ale pole*, p. 166, l. 41.
all be it, *albeit*, p. 290, l. 6.
all to geder, all togedder, al to gether, all to gether, *altogether*, often.
almery, *cupboard*, *store-room*, Deut. 28:5; store-chest, Wic.; also spelled almerie, from Low Latin *almariolum*, a cupboard; Heywood, *Spider and Flie*, 1556.
alowe, *adv.*, *alow*, *low-down*, Deut. 28:43; *used also by* Foxe.
an hye, *adv.*, *on high*, Deut. 28:43, quite common.
apoynte, appoynte, *v.*, 1, *to name*, *indicate*, *tell*, Gen. 34:11; 2, *assign*, *separate*, p. 169, ll. 19. 36; Ex. 13:12.
apoyntement, apoyntemente, apoyntment, *covenant*, often, p. 6, l. 5; Ex. 24:6.

* *An Etymological Dictionary, &c.*, Oxford, 1882.

apparell, *the heavenly bodies*, Gen. 2:1.
appoſſe, *v.*, *to examine by questions*, p. 520, l. 27; appose, *to dispute with, or object to*, H. W.
appoynte, *to adjudge*, Ex. 21:22; *to assign, separate*, Ex. 13:12.
aſene, *p. p.*, *seen, known*, Gen. 41:31.
as farforth . . . ſo farforth, *as far as*, p. 291, ll. 13, 14.
aſſone, aſſoone, *as soon*, often, Ex. 9:29.
at, *to*, Gen. 14:14.
atall, *at all*, p. 2, l. 8.
atonce, attonce, *at once, immediately, once for all*, often, p. 13, l. 29; Deut. 9:16.

"And all *attonce* her beastly body rais'd
With double forces high above the ground."
Sp. *F. Q.*, II, i. 42. H.W.

at the leſt waye, *at least*, p. 164, l. 17; p. 517, l. 26.
awaye, *s.*, *a way*, p. 161, l. 32.

B.

bagge, *badge*, p. 294, ll. 30, 34.
bakemeates, *cakes, pies*, Gen. 40:17; also bak'd meat, see Sherwood's definition (in Cotgrave's *Dict.*) of *pastisserie:* all kinds of pies or bak'd meat, H. W.
baptim, *baptism*, often, p. 294, ll. 15, 16, &c.; also baptime, baptyme, baptem, bapteme, baptyme, *pl.* baptyms, baptimys, Wic.
be fore, *before*, Gen. 2:4.
be gile, *beguile*, p. 297, l. 6.
Belial, poynte of, *wickedness*, Deut. 15:9, see note.
beeſſe, *beasts*, Num. 20:8.
bewepe, bewepte, *to weep over*, or *for*, cf. Germ. *beweinen*, Lev. 10:6.
blaynes, *pimples, pustules*, Ex. 9:9.
bloudvenger, *avenger of blood*, Num. 35:27.
blynded, *darkened as to the mind*, Num. 14:44.
boke, *book*, almost constant; boke, *book*, Wic.
boket, *bucket*, Num. 24:7; boket, bokat, Wic.
bolde, *v.t.*, *to encourage, strengthen*, Deut. 3:28; to bolden, *render bold*, Lear, v. 1, H. W.
boldlye, *firmly*, p. 518, l. 40.
bond, bonde, *covenant*, Gen. 9:9.
bonde, *band*, Ex. 28:32.
boogges, bugges, p. 167, l. 38; *objects of terror;* bugbear, terrifying spectre, Skeat.

Ps. 91:5: "Thou ſhalt not nede to be afrayed for eny *bugges* by night."—*Matthew's Bible.*

borne, *burn*, p. 6, l. 18.
bothe two, *both*, Lev. 9:3.
boulled, *grown into buds*, Ex. 9:32.
boundes, *ties, obligations*, Num. 30:14.
bowe from, *decline from, turn aside*, Deut. 28:14.
brede, *breadth*, Gen. 48:7.
breche, *sing. of breeches*, Lev. 16:4; see Richardson, who cites Chaucer, *Cant. Tales*, &c. The word appears to have denoted any kind of garment to cover the loins. It is used by Wiclif and Purvey in Gen. 3:7, and in *Gold. Leg.* (Caxton's ed. 1484).
brente, *burnt*, Gen. 38:24; brenne, *p. t.* brente, *p. p.* brent, Wic.
bretren, *brethren*, Gen. 42:32.
broke, *s.*, *breach*, Lev. 24:20.
brothren, *brethren*, often, p. 13, l. 33; p. 162, l. 24.
bruterar, *murmurer*, Deut. 18:10.
bugle, *buffalo*, Deut. 14:5; so Wic.
buſſhe, *hair, beard*, p. 420, note; bush of haire, Holland, *Plinie*, ii, 25.
by cauſe, *because*, p. 8, l. 6.
byele, *s.*, *boil*, often; biel, byil, *pl.* biles, bilis, bylis, Wic.

C.

candelſticke ſelfe (*itself*), Ex. 37:20.
caren leane, *carrion lean*, p. 297, l. 23.
Caimes, misprint for Caines, *pl.* of Cain, Gen. 9:5, marg.
cauellacions, *overreaching, fraud*, Lev. 19:13.
cheſt, *coffin*, Gen. 50:26.
cheueſaunce, *bargain*, Deut. 21:14; enterprise, achievement, see H. W., *s. v.*, *chevisance*, al-

so Blackwood, and Old French Dictionaries.
childers, p. 290, l. 7.
chofe, *p. p.*, p. 163, l. 11.
chriften, *sing.*, p. 168, l. 35; *pl.* p. 162, l. 41, *christian*, often.
chriftenlye, *adv.*, p. 162, l. 32.
clarkes, *clerks*, p. 11, l. 8.
cleane, p. 392, l. 26, clene, p. 5, l. 33, *quite.*
cloke, p. 2, l. 29; make a cloke, p. 161, l. 26; other clokes, p. 2, l. 17; *cloak*, &c., *disguise*, *pretext*, or *pretence.*
clofed to, *closed*, Gen. 20:18.
clouden piler, Ex. 33:9,10.
colore, *collar*, Ex. 28:32.
comened, Lev. 22:1; comentye, *congregation*, Lev. 8:3; comenynge, Gen. 18:33, 23:8; comon, comoned, (often,) comyned, *to commune*, *converse*, *speak*, Ex. 25:22; Lev. 5:14; comyne, comunen, comenynge, comynynge, Wic.
comynalte, Lev. 4:13.
corage, *v.*, *to encourage*, Ex. 35:21, Deut. 3:28.
corofye, corefyes, *corrosive*, p. 166, ll. 20, 39; see H. W.

"Whereas he meant his *córrofives* to apply,
And with streight diet tame his stubborne malady."—Sp. *F. Q.*, I, x. 25.

coniure, *adjure*, Num. 5:19.
coorfe, *corpse*, Gen. 23:3; cors, Wic.
coude, cowd, cowde, *could*, often.
couerynge, *screening from observation*, Gen. 20:16.
courage, *s.*, *the heart, as the seat of the affections;* cf. Low Latin *coragium*, p. 167, l. 39.
curtefie, *kindness*, p. 164, l. 28.
curtefie, *a small quantity*, Gen. 43:11.

D.

dayefmen, *judges*, Ex. 21:22; daysman, an umpire, or arbitrator, from his fixing a day for decision; *day*, according to Todd, sometimes means judgment, H. W.
dead, deade, *pl.* deades, *deed*, p. 11, l. 40; p. 12, ll. 12,15.
deale, *s.*, *part*, *portion*, cf. German *Theil.*
dealeth, *divideth*, cf. Germ. *theilen*, Deut. 21:16.
dethe, 1534, Gen. 23:2; deith, 1534: Gen. 35:29; dethe, 1534: Gen. 50:26; *death*, margin.
difmale dayes, *unlucky days:* Trench, *Sel. Gloss*, Deut. 18:10.
difmall, same as difmale, Lev. 19:26.
difcouer, *uncover*, Lev. 18:7,8.
dome, domme, *dumb*, often, p. 292, l. 30; p. 296, l. 32.
dowry, *gift*, Gen. 30:20; *present*, Gen. 34:12.
drewe vnto, *amounted to*, Numb. 3:34.
duns, *the works of John Duns Scotus*, schoolman, died A. D. 1308.
dutye, *s.*, *due*, often, Ex. 29:28; *law*, Lev. 7:36.
dweld, *v.*, *infin.*, *to dwell*, Ex. 15:17.

E.

earynge, *ploughing*, Ex. 34:21.
emperies, *empires*, p. 460, margin.
enceadinge, *exceeding*, Ex. 1:7.
ende, vp an, *upright*, Gen. 28:18.
endote, *endow*, Ex. 22:16.
enfample, *example*, Wic., often, p. 13, ll. 28,37; at the enfample, *according to the example*, Gen. 48:20.
ere, *v.*, *to plough*, p. 12, l. 35; ere, eren, eeren, Wic.
erthy, *adj.*, *earthly*, p. 295, l. 24.
ether, *both*, Gen. 2:25; etherother, *both*, p. 292, l. 11; Deut. 22:22.

F.

facion, *pattern*, Ex. 25:9.
facyon, *appearance*, Ex. 24:10.
faintie, *faint*, Gen. 25:30.
faith, 1534, Gen. 50:24, margin.
famefhment, *famine*, Gen. 47:4.
fantafye, *liking*, *fondness*, Deut. 21:11.
faft, *adv.*, *near to*, Ex. 14:9; Num. 2:27.
faul, *v.*, *to fall*, p. 395, l. 33.
faute, *fault*, p. 392, l. 18.
fayre, *adv.*, *gently*, *quietly*, Gen. 33:14.

"Go *faire* and softlie."
Holland, *Livy*, p. 83.

faytes, *feats, works well done*, Ex. 31:4.
faythes, *pl.* of *faith*, often, p. 290, l. 38; p. 291, l. 38; p. 392, l. 8.
feare, *v. t.*, *to make afraid*, often, p. 8, ll. 16, 23.
feders, *feathers*, Gen. 7:14.
felaſhippe, a, Num. 22:6.
feldedeuels, *satyrs*, Deut. 32:17.
felowſhipe, a good, *peaceably*, Num. 20:17; comp. citation from Shakesp. in Webster's *Dict.*, 1883, Unab. Ed., *s.v.*, fellowship.
fett, *v.*, *to fetch*, often.
feythe, *faith*, 1534, Gen. 43:18; margin.
fifte, fyfte, *fifth*, often.
finde, *to support*, p. 5, l. 22.
firſtborneſhipp, Deut. 21:17.
fleth, *flieth*, Deut. 4:17.
folk, folke, *nation*, cf. German *volk*, Gen. 47:23; Num. 32:15; Deut. 3:3.
for as moch, often.
forboden, *forbidden*, p. 164, l. 38.
forcaſt, *s.*, *prognostication*, Deut. 32:28.

"In thinges pertaining to this presente lyfe ye haue a witte and a *forecaste*."—Udal, Luke xii., Richardson.

forgeten, forgetten, *forgotten*, cf. German *vergessen*, *p. p.*, Gen. 41:30; Deut. 31:21.
forloren, *lost, undone*, cf. German *verloren*, *p. p.* of *verlieren*, Num. 21:29.
freat, freten, fretynge, *eaten away*, cf. German *fressen*, and note, Lev. 13:51.
for ſoke, *forsook*, p. 14, l. 16.
ful onlike, *very unlike*, Num. 27:16, margin; ful, *very*, Wic. often.
furmentye, *pottage made of wheat*, Minshew, Lev. 23:14.

"In Fraunce and Spaine, bruers steep their wheat or *frument* in water," Holland, *Plin.*, xviii. 7; "*Frument* with venyson," Fabyan, v. II, an.-1530.—Richardson.

furiouſſer, p. 388, l. 28.
furres, *skins*, Lev. 15:16.

G.

gardes, *fringes*, Num. 15:38.
gate, *p. p.* of *to get*, p. 5, l. 20.
geſte, *acts*, p. 11, l. 9; gestis, *pl.*, *deeds*, Wic.
geſtyngeſtocke, *laughing stock*, Deut. 28:37.
geuernaũce, 1534, note, Gen. 3:14.
gile, *guile*, so Wic. Ex. 21:14.
goddes, *judges*, Ex. 21:6; 22:8,9.
Godwarde, to, Ex. 18:19.
goo a warrefare, Deut. 24:5.
goodman, *master of the house*, Ex. 22:8.
goten, *acquired*, Ex. 15:16.
gott, *procured*, Gen. 21:21; gott him, *went*, Gen. 22:3.
greteth, *grateth*, acts harshly upon the thoughts or feelings, p. 297, l. 17.

Richardson: "His gall did *grate* for griefe and high disdaine."—Sp., *F. Q.*, I, 1.

grounded, *established, founded*, Ex. 9:18.

H.

hande brede, Ex. 37:12; handibreede, Wic.
hanfaſted, *p. p.* of hanfaſt, A. S., *handfæstan*, to betroth, Deut. 22:23.

"A gentleman, being *handfasted* to a gentlewoman."—Wilson, *Arte of Rhetorique*, p. 144, Richardson; see also Todd's *Johnson's Dict.*

harde, *heard*, Gen. 39:15.
harde vnder, *immediately under*, Ex. 25:27.
happe, *v.*, *to happen*, Deut. 23:1, margin.
hare, *v.*, *to hear*, p. 520, l. 29.
harneſſe, *s.*, *armor*, Num. 32:20, 21; *ordinary clothes*, p. 591, note.
harneſſed, *armed*, often, Ex. 13:18.
harte, hert, herte, *s.*, *the heart*, often; phrase, "His harte laye," Gen. 34:3.
heares, *heirs*, p. 416, note.
herde fauored nacion, *adj.*, *Bishops' Bible: a nation of ſhameleſſe and cruel countenance; A. V.*, 1611: *a nation of fierce countenance*, Deut. 28:50.
himward, to, Deut. 32:5.
hijſh, *v.*, to hiss, *to express contempt*, p. 388, l. 32.
hit, *it*, Gen. 3:15.
hole, *a.*, *whole*, often, Lev. 4:13; in the hole, *in the whole, i. e.*, *the principal*, Num. 5:7; hol, hoel, hool, hoole, *wholly altogether*, Wic.

holowenge, *p. p.*, *to hallow, consecrate*, p. 318, margin.
hoorehed, *hoary head*, Lev. 19:32.
houſes, *families*, Ex. 1:21.

I.

iacyncte, *hyacinth*, *blue*, often, Ex. 25:4; iacynt, iacynkt, Wic.
idolatryſſe, *idolatrous*, p. 143, margin.
imagerye, *figures*, *statues*, *or effigies*, p. 518, l. 5.
"An altar, carv'd with cunning *imagery*." Sp., *F. Q.*, I, 8.
incloſers, *settings*, Ex. 39:14.
in deade, Deut. 21:16.
inſtruct, *instructed*, *p. p.*, p. 589, note.
inleſſe, *unless*, p. 7, l. 13.
interpretate, *v. infin*,, and *p. p.*, *to interpret*, Gen. 40:16; 41:15; *p. p.*, p. 303, note.
in to, *into*, often.
iolye, *spirited*, *in good case*, Ex. 15:4.
"Full *jolly* knight he seemed."—Spencer.
iolif, iolyf, ioly, *wanton*, Wic.

K.

karen, *carrion*, p. 348, margin.
kepte, *imperative*, 3 p., *pl.*, Gen. 41:35.
knowleage, knowlege, *v.*, *to acknowledge*, often, Ex. 22:29, note; p. 291, l. 41; knouleche, knowleche, knowliche, *to confess*, *acknowledge*, Wic.

L.

leafull, *lawful*, p. 416, note.
lefully, *lawfully*, p. 29, note.
lenger, *longer*, p. 4, l. 11.
let, *hinder*, often.
lift, *p. t.*, p. 421, margin.
lightely, *easily*, *readily*, Gen. 26:10.
linwod, *i. e.*, the work of William Lindewood, Lindwood, or Lyndewood, Divinity Professor at Oxford and bishop of St. Davids († 1446), called *Constitutiones Provinciales Ecclesiæ Anglicanæ*, Oxon., 1466, p. 4, l. 21.
liſte, *v.*, *to like*, *please*, p. 25, margin.
loke of, to, *v.*, *to look at*, p. 545, margin.
longe, longeth, longinge, *belong*, *belongeth*, *belonging*, often, Num. 1:50; 6:15; Lev. 23:18.
loured, loureſte, *lowered*, *looked sullen*, Gen. 4:5,6.
loueday, *s.*, *a day of amity or reconciliation*. Todd's *Illustr. of Chaucer*, Glossary. "Love-days: days anciently so called, on which arbitrations were made, and controversies ended between neighbours and acquaintance." N. Bailey, *Univ. Etymol. Engl. Dict.*, Lond., 1755, p. 397, l. 7.
luckie, *prosperous*, Gen. 39:2.
luſt, *s.*, luſtie, *adj.*, *delight*, *affording pleasure*, Gen. 3:6; *earnest desire*, Deut. 18:6; *adj.*, *strong*, *hale*, *good*.
lyfte, *p. t.*, *lifted*, Gen. 18:2; 21:16; lyfte, *imperat.*, Gen. 21:18.
lyne, *lain*, *p. p.* of *to lie*, *v. i.*, Gen. 26:10.
lyuehode, *s.*, *livelihood*, *means of supporting life*, p. 416, note; lijflode, liflode, lyuelod, *pl.* lyuelodis, *a living sustenance*. Wic.

M.

maliciouſſer, p. 388, l. 28.
maner, *custom*, *law*, Num. 15:24.
maner, with the; phrase; *in the very act*, see *Law Dictionary* under *mainour*, H. W. Num. 5:14.
manquellyng, *man killing*, *murder*, p. 565, note, p. 583, note.
manquellare, manquellere, *mankiller*, *man slayer*, (manſlear) p. 583, note; Wic. *murderer*, *executioner*.
marre, *v.*, *to hurt*, *injure*, *damage*, Deut. 4:16; marred, *p. p.*, Deut. 9:12.
marye, *marrow;* p. 290, l. 23; mary, merow, and seven different forms, Wic.
maunde, *hand basket*, cf. German *mande*.
maſtreſs, *mistress*, Gen. 16:4,8,9.
meet, *v.*, *to measure*, Deut. 21:2.
merſed, *amerced*, Ex. 21:22.

mercyſeate warde, *toward the mercy seat*, Ex. 25:20; 37:9.
mercyleſſe, *adv.*, Deut. 13:15.
meritmongers, Daye's Note, p. 388, l. 24; p. cxxiii.
meſellynge, *small rain, drizzle*, Deut. 32:2.
me thinke, *it seems to me*, Lev. 14:35; see Skeat, *s. v.*, methinks.
meyny, *s.*, Gen. 22:3, *men of his household:* meine, meyne, meynee, *pl.* meynes, meynees, *household, family*, Wic.
miſchefe, for a; phrase; *for evil*, Ex. 13:12; compare: *Abi in malam rem*, go hense with a mischiefe; Eliote's *Dict.*, 1559, H. W.; and *to cheve* or *achieve*, to bring to an end, to finish; also Trench, *meschef, bonchef*. Richardson.
moare, *more*, often; moare lower, Lev. 13:34.
moo, *more*, often.
moo, *else, besides*, Deut. 4:39.
moren, *murrain*, p. 168, l. 25.
more ſtronger, p. 290, l. 11.
more ouer, Num. 20:2.
moulte, *p. p.* of *to melt*, Ex. 16:22.

N.

naked, *bareheaded*, Ex. 32:25; see margin, and L. M. N.
namely, *especially*, Ex. 4:10; nameli, same meaning, Wic.
naule, *s.*, *an awl*; Ex. 21:6; nal, *an awl*, Wic.
necke verſes, p. 34, margin. A neck verse was the verse read by a malefactor, to entitle him to benefit of clergy, and therefore eventually to save his life; generally Ps. 51:1, H. W.
nether . . nether, *neither . . nor*, Gen. 19:35.
neuerthelater, neuer the later, neuer the lather, *nevertheless, yet*, Lev. 11:36; Num. 14:44; Deut. 4:29.
no . . nor, *not . . or*, p. 292, l. 30.
no nother, *none other*, p. 389, l. 1; p. 392, l. 34; p. 396, l. 41.
nother, *neither*, often; nother, nothir, nouthir, *neither*, Wic.
nother . . nor, *neither . . nor*, p. 7, ll. 3,4.
not withſtondynge, Deut. 12:15.
nurter, *v. t.*, *to bring up, educate*, Deut. 4:36.
nurter, *s.*, *discipline*, p. 517, l. 30.

O.

obedience, the, *i. e.*, Tyndale's *Obedience of a Chriſten man*, &c.; see p. liii., l. 5; p. 161, l. 9.
occupie, *v. i.*, *to trade, traffic*, Gen. 42:34.
once, *adv.*, *now*, Gen. 2:23.
ons, *once*, Ex. 33:5; oons, ones, onys, onus, *once*, Wic.
optayne, Lev. 7:18; opteine, p. 547, margin.
or, *before*, p. 344, note.
other . . nother, *either . . neither*, p. 396, ll. 6, 7.
ouerſcaped, *overlooked*, Lev. 19:10.
ouerſe, *v. refl.*, *to err through ignorance, or inadvertence*, Num. 15:22.
ouerthwarte, *adj.*, *opposite, perverse*, Deut. 32:5; see examples in H. W.; ouerthwart, ouerthewert, ouerthwert, ouerwhert, *perverse, froward*, Wic.
out, to be, *to be finished, ended*, Lev. 12:4,6.
out at doors, Gen. 19:6.

P.

pagiantes, *feats, exploits*, Ex. 10:2.
parelles, *perils*, p. 12, l. 26.
partie coloured, *colored part by part; of diverse tints*, Gen 30:34.
parties, *parts*, *s.*, Gen. 16:13.
partlet, *s.*, *a band or collar for the neck.*
payne, *s.*, *punishment*, Lev. 19:20
paynte a . . cauſe, *to favour a cause, to be partial*, Ex. 23:3
perlouſe, *perilous*, p. 529, note.
piſtle, *epistle*, often.
pither, pyther, *pitcher*, Gen. 24:17
plecke, *speck*, Lev. 13:4; cf. German *flecken;* ſpleckid, *specked*, Wic.
pollar, *s.*, *plunderer, robber*, p. 293, l. 21.
polled, *plundered, robbed*, Deut. 28:29.
pope holyneſſe, p. 387, l. 24.
porteſſes, *s.*, *pl.* of porteſſe, *a por-*

tasse, a portable prayer book or breviary, p. 4, l. 16; the word is also spelt *portise*, *porthose*, *portos*, *portals*, all corruptions of the French *porte-hors*, a literal rendering of the Low Latin *portiforium*, from *portare foras*, to carry out of doors, abroad; see Richardson and H. W. for examples.

poynte of Belial, Deut. 15:9.

Bishops' Bible, 1572: "a wicked thought in thyne heart"; *A.V.*, 1611: "a thought in thy wicked heart."

poyntment, *covenant*, *A. V.*, Deut. 7:9.

preaſe, preſe, preaſed, *v.*, *to press*; Wic. *to press*, Gen. 19:9; *to approach*, Lev. 21:17,21; *Bishops' Bible*, 1568: *preaſe, come neare, come nye*; 1572: *preſſe, comme neare, preſſe*; *A. V.*, 1611: *approche, approche, come nigh*.

propheſie, *v.*, *to divine*, *A. V.*, Gen. 44:5; Wic. *wonte to dyuyne*; *Bishops'*, 1572: *conſulteth with the propheciers*, *A. V.*, 1611: *diuineth*, or *maketh triall*.

pyke, *v. t.*, *to pick*, Gen. 43:18.

Q.

quarters, *corners*, Num. 15:38.

quyte, *quit free*, Ex. 21:19; Wic. *ynnocent*.

R.

raſcall people, *rabble*, Num. 11:4; raſkeyl, *common people*, I. K. 6:19, Wic.; cf. French *racaille* and *racler*, to scrape together.

raueſhynge, *taking away by violence*, Gen. 49:27; Wic. *raumpynge*; Purvey, *rauyschynge*; *Bishops'*, 1568, 72: *rauiſhe*; *A. V.*, 1611: *rauine*.

rebellyons, *s. pl.*, *rebels*; so *Matthew*; *Bishops'*, 1568, '72: *rebelles*; *A. V.*, 1611: *rebels*; Wic. *rebells*, *rebel*, Num. 20:10; *rebeller*, p. 577, margin.

renne, *v.*, *to run*, p. 417, note.

rennegate, runnagate, *renegade*, *i. e.*, *wanderer*, *fugitive*, *vagabond*, Gen. 4:12; Wic. *vagaunt*, *i. e.*, wandering; *Bishops'*, 1568: *vacabounde*.

rightwyſe, *righteous*; often in different spelling; Wic. *rightwis*, *ryghtwisness*, wis and wisness, denoting *wise* and *wiseness*, or *wisdom*.

robenhode, a tale of, p. 11, l. 10, in allusion to the fictitious nature of many of the alleged adventures of Robin Hood, the famous outlaw.

Rocheſtre, *i. e.*, Fisher, bishop of Rochester, p. 162, l. 27. Professor Walter, *Doctrinal Treatises*, &c., pp. 208, 209, note, cites:

"But Moyses and Aaron which were the heads of that people, whereof then be they shadow? Without doubt they must be the shadow of Christ and of his vicar, St. Peter, which under Christ was also the head of christian people." "The third likeness is this. Moyses ascended unto the mount to speak with Almighty God, and Aaron remained behind to instruct the people. Did not Christ likewise ascend unto his Father, unto the great mount of heaven? and to what intent, I pray you? St. Paul telleth: *Ut appareat vultui Dei pro nobis*: To appear before the face of Almighty God for us, and there to be our advocate, as saith St. John. And did not Peter remain behind to teach the people, the which our Saviour committed to his charge, like as Aaron was left for to do the people of the Jews, when Moses was alone in the mount with God? Thus every man may see how that shadow, and this thing, agreeth and answereth one to another, fully and clearly." Fisher's *Sermon*, verso of Avij, and verso of Bj.

roudier, *ruddier*, *redder*, Gen. 49:12.

royalme, *realm*, p. 391, l. 12; the form *roialme* occurs in Gower, *C.A.* iii. 199, l. 3, Skeat.

ryd, *p. t.*, of *to ride*, Num. 22:22; cf. German *ritt*.

S.

ſacrifie, *to sacrifice*, Ex. 30:29; so Wic.

ſaffe, *safe*, p. 293, l. 9.

ſaint thomas ſhryne, *the shrine of Thomas à Becket in Christ Church, Canterbury*; see Erasmi *Colloquia*, Lugd. Bat., 1655, pp. 368, 387; and 'walſingham' in this list, and p. 393, l. 14.

ſcrale, ſcraule, *to crawl, creep*, see Lev. 11:41,42; Ex. 8:3.

ſeer bowes, *withered boughs*, p. 143, margin.

ſees ſyde, *sea side*, Deut. 1:7.

ſeten, *p. p.* of *to sit*, Lev. 15:23;

Deut. 17:18; the same form occurs in Chaucer, *C. T.;* see Skeat.
ſette to, *fined in*, Ex. 21:30; Wic. *if pryis be set to him; Bishops' B.: set to; A. V.*, 1611: *layed on.*
ſeuerall, *separate, separated*, often, Deut. 7:6; 26:18.
ſewer, *sure*, p. 418, note.
ſhetto, *shut to, close*, Deut. 15:7.
ſheyppe, *ship*, p. 295, 11.
ſhope, *created, made*, cf. German *schaffen* and deriv., Gen. 2:7.
ſhorte, *v. t.*; phrase: to prolonge the tale, to ſhorte the tyme with all, p. 4, l. 33.
ſhrode, *evil*, Ex. 5:19; Wic. *yuel; Bishops'*, 1568, '72: *worse.*
ſmoten, *p. p.* of *to smite*, Num. 33:4; Wiclif has *smoten*, as *pl. p. t.*
Sodomeward, to, Gen. 18:22.
ſo far forth as, *as far as*, p. 396, l. 34.
ſoftly, *adv., at a gentle pace*, Gen. 33:14.
ſondrie, *adj., distinct, separate*, Gen. 40:5.
ſoule health, p. 293, l. 17.
ſowre, *bitter*, Ex. 12:8; Purvey, margin, *in Ebrew it is with bitternessis; A. V.*, 1611: *bitter.*
ſprete, ſprite, ſprites, *spirit, spirits*, often.
ſtampe, *p. t.*, Deut. 9:21.
ſtiffe, *solid, beaten*, Num. 8:4; Wic. *beten out;* Purvey: *betun out with hameris.*
ſtoppe, *p. p.*, Gen. 26:18.
ſtoukes, *ſtacks*, Ex. 22, 6; *Bishops'*, 1568: *ſtackes.*
ſtrayned, *p. t., tied, bound*, Ex. 39:21; Wic. ſtreyne, ſtreynede, ſtreyned, *to draw tight, bind.*
ſtrenght, *strength*, often.
ſtrypes, *s., wounds*, Gen. 4:23; Ascham, *Toxophilus, b.* II.: "The ſhaftes of Inde . . gave the greater *ſtrype.*" Richardson.
ſurgione, *physician, healer*, Ex. 15:26; *Bishops'*, 1568: I am the Lord that *healeth* thee.
ſuſpect, *s., suspicion*, p. 417, note, see H. W. and Richardson for examples.
ſymnell, *s., a kind of cake*, cf. German *Semmel*, Ex. 29:23; Wic. *cake of a loof;* Purvey: *tendur cake of o loof;* see *wastell.*

T.

tached, *p. p., arrested, apprehended, taken*, p. 13, l. 33; cf. *attached*, in Skeat, who gives under *tache*, Mineu's '*to tache* or *tacke*'.
take, was, Gen. 2:23; Num. 10:11.
tale, *s., number*, Ex. 5:18; Num. 1:36.
tent, *v., to pitch a tent*, Gen. 13:12; *Bishops'*, 1568, '72: *pitched his tent.*
tenthdeale, *v., tenth part*, cf. German *Theil*, and *Zehntheil, Zehntel*, often.
teſtament, *covenant*, often.
than, *then*, often.
them ſelfe, Gen. 43:15.
then, *than*, often.
ther of, *thereof*, Gen. 2:21.
theſe are that Aaron and **Moſes**, Ex. 6:26,27.
they them ſilfe, Num. 36:6.
this **is** that Dathan and **Abi**ram, Num. 26:9.
thriſt, thruſt, *thirst*, p. 616, note, Deut. 28: 48; thriſye, thryſtye, thirsty, p. 616, notes.
thryd, *third*, Gen. 42:18; thryde, Num. 2:24.
thyn, *thin*, Num. 16:38.
to daſh, *to thrust through*, Ex. 15:6.
to gedder, *together*, p. 4, l. 29; Wic. to-gider, to-gidre, to-gideres, to-giderys, &c., *together.*
tole, *tool, chisel, knife*, Ex. 20:25.
too, *s. pl.*, tooes, *toe, toes*, Lev. 8:23,24.
totehill, *watch tower, or beacon*, Gen. 31:49; Wic. toothil, tote-hil, tute-hil, *a citadel, a watchplace.*
trompe, *v., to sound with a trump*, Num. 10:5,6. Wic. Num. 10:3; sownest with thi trompes, *soundest with thy trompes;* v. 5 lenger and

stowndmeel trompynge sowne; *prolonged, and successive tromping sound;* v. 6. sownynge and euen ȝollynge of the trompe, *sounding and even velling of the trompe; Bishops'*, 1568, '72: v. 4, *blowe . . . trumpet;* v. 5, *blowe, an alarm.*

trouth, *s.*, truth, p. 6, l. 18; Wic. trouthe, truth.

turtels, *s., pl., turtle-doves*, Num. 6:10; Wic. turtil, turtle, turtur, *a turtle-dove.*

twych, twytche, *v., to touch*, often.

tyllman, *s., a farmer, i. e., a tiller of the ground*, Gen. 25:27; Wic. a man erthe tilier; tyllman, Udal, Matthew, *c. 7.* Rich.

tytle, *tittle*, the dot over the letter *i.*, p. 3, l. 7.

U. V.

vehementer, *compar. of vehement, adj.*, p. 297, l. 10.

vnderſtande, *p. p., understood*, p. 316, note; vnderſtande, p. 576, note; vnderſtonde, p. 294, l. 26; 297, l. 17.

vnderſtonge, *s.*, underſtanding, Deut. 32:29.

vnheale, *uncover*, Lev. 18:7; Wic. vnhile, *to uncover.*

vnrighte, *not right, wrong*, cf. Germ. *Unrecht*, Gen. 16:5; Wic. vnriȝt, *unjust, also* vnriȝtfulli, vnriȝtfulnesse, &c.

vn to, *unto*, very often.

vnwares, *not aware, not heeding, not knowing*, Num. 35:15; Deut. 4:42; Wic. not wilnynge, not willynge; Purvey, not wilfuli. See *ware.*

vre, to put in, *to put to use*, p. 545, note. See H. W., under Vre.

uſe, to, one's self, *to behave toward, deal with*, p. 161, ll. 11, 13; Wic. vsen, *to deal with.*

W.

walſingham, p. 393, l. 14. *Walſingham Priory in Norfolk.* See Erasmi *Colloquia*, Lugd. Bat. 1655, pp. 368, 387 for an imaginary pilgrimage to this shrine, and that of Thomas à Becket, and for a description.

ward, in, *in separate confinement*, Ex. 12:6; Wic. warde keeping, custody.

ware, was not, *knew not* (wist not) Lev. 5:18; warre of, *aware of, i. e.*, to be conscious, Lev. 5:2; Wic. war, ware, *wary, prudent, aware.*

ware, *were*, p. 11, l. 21.

waſtell, *fine bread, cake*, Lev. 24:5; "The *simnel* bread and *wastel* cakes, which were only used at the tables of the highest nobility." Sir W. Scott.

wayte, *s., watch, service, charge*, cf. German *Hut*, Num. 4:28; Wic. waiten, *v., to keep watch;* wayte *s., a spy;* waitere, weyter, *a spy, a watcher.*

welth, *prosperity, happiness, weal, welfare*, Deut. 6:24; 10:13.

wenſt, *wentest*, Gen. 49:4.

wete, *v., to know*, often. Wic. wite, *to know.*

where to fore, *where before*, Deut. 28:62.

whether, *whither*, Ex. 21:13.

whett on, *v., to sharpen, discipline, stimulate*, Deut. 6:7.

whitter, *whiter*, Gen. 49:12.

whone, *one*, Lev. 15:18.

whope, whoope, *s., hoop*, Ex. 38:10,11; whoped, *hooped*, vv. 17,19.

whote, *hot*, often, Num. 11:10,33.

whyned, *wept*, cf. German *weinen*, to weep, Num. 11:18; this word retained as late as in the Bishops' Bible of 1572 'your whynyng is in the eares of the Lorde,' is rendered in A. V. 1611: 'you haue wept in the eares, &c.'; the Latin version of the Chaldee in *Complut.* has *plorastis.*

wife, wyfe, wyves, *woman, women*, Gen. 18:11; Num. 5:18, often; wife, *consort*, Gen. 24:39, also common.

with, *besides*, Ex. 20:23.

with all, *withal*, often, p. 389, l. 36.

without forth, *adv.*, *without*, Deut. 32:25; Wic. without-forth, withoute-forth, *outwardly*, *without*; he also has withinnen-forth, withynneforth, withyn-forth, *adv.*, *within*.

witneſſe, *pl.*, probably a misprint for *witnesses* (Matthew) Deut. 4:45.

wolfe, *s.*, *woof*, often, Lev. 13:48.

wolward, *woolward*, dressed in wool only without linen; a well known and ancient act of penance; 'nudis pedibus et *absque linteis circumire*.' H. W. Stratmann: '*wolwarde*, cutis lanam uersu'; Skeat: 'with the skin against the wool'; Fisher, *Seuen Psalmes*, Ps. 143. pt. II. 'in colde going *wolward*.'

wot, *p. t.*, Gen. 20:6, wott, *pres. indic.*, p. 11, l. 8, woteſt, 2 p., *s.*, *pres. indic.* of wite, *to know;* Wiclif has wost, woost, wotist, all, 2 p., *s.*, *pres. ind.*

wrenſhed, *p. t.*, of to wrenſh, wrench, *to turn suddenly*, *push*, *thrust;* cf. Cerm. *renken*, *verrenken*, Num. 22:25.

wylde, *not domesticated*, Gen. 16:12.

wylde, *open*, Lev. 14:53, cf. wyde, 17:5.

wyle, *wild*, *immature*, *reckless*, *thoughtless*, p. 294, l. 1.

wyſt, *p. t.* of wite, *to know*, Gen. 9:24; 21:26; Wic. wiste, 2 p. wistest, *pl.* wisten.

Y.

yer, *ere*, *before*, often, p. 10, note, l. 12.

yerlee, early, Num. 14:40.

yerwhile, *before*, p. 447, margin.

ymaginacions, *columnar images*, Num. 33:52.

ynowe, *enough*, p. 163, l. 3; Wic. ynow, ynowȝ, ynewȝ, *enough*.

y[e] ſe, contraction of *theſe*, Num. 3:18.

VIII.

LIST OF MISPRINTS IN TYNDALE'S PENTATEUCH OF 1530, CORRECTED IN THIS EDITION, EITHER BY ANALOGY OF TYNDALE'S TEXT, OR BY THE TEXT OF MATTHEW'S BIBLE.

	1530.	*1884.*
	Prologe to Genesis.	
P. L.		
11, 14	bett*t*er	better
11, 21	ſ*t*ripture	ſcripture
	Genesis.	
C. V		
1 : 27	femal*c*	female
4 : 4	off*e*ynge	offrynge
6 : 4	*c*he	the
15	lenth	len*g*th
15	h*c*yth	heyth
7 : 18	pr*c*vayled	prevayled
10 : 31	o	o*f*
11 : 10	Ar*c*phach-ſad	Arphachſad

	1530.	*1884.*
C. V.		
11 : 11	an	an*d*
12 : 20	wyf*c*	wyfe
13 : 4	rec eaue,	receaue
14 : 2	Sodō*h*	Sodome
9	Syn*c*ar	Synear
20 : 17	Abimeleh	Abimele*c*h
22 : 17	th	th*e*
23 : 17	Fo.XXIIII.	Fo.XXX.
24 : 14	th*e*y	thy
14	ye*c*	yee
35	Fo. XXXI.	Fo. XXXII.
60	e*mn*ies	enimies
25 : 20	*I*aban	Laban
27 : 29	leſſed	*b*leſſed
36	XXX imp.	XXXX.

C. V.	*1530.*	*1884.*
31 : 29	tha	tha*t*
32 : 1	m*e*eſſengers	meſſengers
11	childer*u*	childern
35 : 4	*c*arynges	earynges
11	th*e*y	thy
36 : 5	Ia*c*lam	Iaelam
41 : 3	though	though*t*
42 : 30	coun*t*te	countre
43 : 15	Ben Iami*m*	Ben Iamin
16	redi*c*	redie
46 : 30	*C* am	I am

Prologe to Exodus.

P. L.		
161, 25	doctine	doct*r*ine
162, 9	what*h*	what
38	con*ſ*ermeth	confermeth
165, 34	Deuteromii	Deutero*no*mii

Exodus.

C. V.		
1 : 11	byl-	byl*te*
2 : 7	the *the*	the
14	aiudge	a iudge
15	bya	by a
4 : *title*	Chaptre.	Chapter.
20	E.gipte	Egipte
8 : *title*	Chaptre	The . . Chapter
10	in *in*	in
28	ferr*r*e	ferre
12 : 5	y*c*re	yere
39	thy	th*e*y
14 : 10	Iſreal	Iſrael
28	ho*u*ſemē	horſemē
15 : 8	*ſ*yll	ſtyll
16 : 6	childer*c̄*	childerē
10	wilder*u*eſſe	wilderneſſe
12	murm*n*rīg	murmurīg
35	inha*h*ited	inhabited
18 : 6	a*ſ*ſo	alſo
10	Fo. XXXI.	Fo. XXXII.
13	chaunc*h*ed	chaunced
18	greuo*ns*	greuous
22 *mar.*	rece*an*ed	receaued
19 : *title*	Chaptre.	Chapter.
6	and an*d*	and an
7	I*ſ*rael	Iſrael
21 : 4	Fo. XXAV.	Fo. XXXVI.
22 : 1	ſtea*k*e	ſteale
21	vexe	Vexe
25	v*ſ*erye	vſerye
23 : 3	a ſyde-	a ſyde
25	ouertrowe	ouert*h*rowe

C. V.	*1530.*	*1884.*
24 : 2	peopl*c*	people
10	wor*d*e	worke
25 : 28	wo*re*	wod
26 : 5	ſyfti*c*	ſyftie
5	loupp*c*s	louppes
25	ſo*l*ettes	ſokettes
27 : *cut*	orname*t*es	ornamētes
28 : 34	golde*m*	golden
35	*ſecond* in	*omitted*
29 : 41	ſhal*l*	ſhalt
30 : 13	Fo. LIVII.	Fo. LVII.
23	cynamo*m*e	cynamone
32	aft*c*r	after
32 : 20	Fo. XLI.	Fo. LXI.
33 : 11	whe*m*	when
16	known*c*	knowne
16	Fo. XLIII.	Fo. LXIII.
34 : 9	Fo. XLIIII.	Fo. LXIIII.
11	th*c*	the
20	neck*c*	necke
25	bloud*c*	bloude
35 : 27	Epod	Ep*h*od
28	Fo.XLVII.	Fo. LXVII.
36 : 2	a*b*	as
8	Fo.XLVIII.	Fo.LXVIII.
40 : 36	I*ſ*rael	Iſrael

Prologe to Leviticus.

P. L.		
289, 23	ceremoni*c*s	ceremonies
293, 9	*ſ*affe	ſaffe
29	forgeueſſe	forgeue*ne*ſſe
294, 38	ſinner	ſynnes
295 : 3	ſignyf*g*eth	ſignyfyeth
26	lyſtedvpp	lyſted vpp
296 : 10	wordly	wor*l*dly
13	wordly	wor*l*dly

Leviticus.

C. V.		
6 : 2	treſpa*e*eth	treſpaceth
7	preſt	pre*a*ſt
7 : 7	peo*o*le	people
11 : 10	Fo. XVII.	Fo. XVIII.
12 : 5	maydehilde	mayde*c*hilde
14 : 43	noʍ	now
48	futher	fu*r*ther
15 : 10	bat*b*e	bathe
18 : 28	w*h*ere	were
19 : 30	ſa*u*ctuary	ſanctuary
33	ſoioure	ſoiour*ne*
20 : 4 *mar.*	wordlye	wor*l*dlye
6	wil*t*	will
13	man*c*r	maner

C. V.	*1530.*	*1884.*
22 : 25	a*d*d	and
23	not accepted	not *be* accepted
23 : 5	Paſſ*c*ou*c*r	Paſſeouer
24	ſ*ue*nth	ſeuenth
27	*o*n	an
25 : 11	y*c*re	yere
18	*ſ*aftie	ſaftie
26 : 5	plenteouſ*ue*s	plenteouſnes
9	multipye	multip*l*ye
15	commaund*n*entes	commaundmentes
27 : 17	i*n*m*c*diatly	immediatly

Prologe to Numbers.

P. L.	*1530.*	*1884.*
387, 34	vn*l*ithed	vntithed
388, 34	ſcriptu	ſcriptu*re*
391, 40	edefynge	edefy*i*nge

Numbers.

C. V.	*1530.*	*1884.*
1 : 22	*ſ*rom	from
32	gen*c*racion	generacion
2 : 3	*c*aſt	eaſt
3	Amina*b*ab	Aminadab
14	o*n*er	ouer
3 : 38	ſõnes	ſonnes
4 : 15	ſantuary	ſan*c*tuary
27	ſ*c*ruyce	ſeruyce
5 : 27	water*r*	water:
7 : 11	prīc*h*es	prīces
17	lamb*c*s	lambes
87	ſynne-*yr* offrynges	ſynne offrynges
9 : 20	chaunc*h*ed	chaunced
15 : 6	myngl*c*d	myngled
7	thyrd*c*	thyrde
19 : 20	cloth*c*s	clothes
21 : 28	ci*it*e	citie
26 : 8	an	an*d*
23	kyndes	kyn*re*des
48	G*im*ites	Gunites
29 : 2	burnt oferyge	burnt offery*n*ge
11	burnt off*c*rynge	burnt offerynge
31 : 30	fy*ſ*tye	fyſtye
32 : 29	ſyghte	*ſ*yghte
33 : 55	dry*ne*	dryue
34 : 13	Iſra*c*l	Iſrael
35 : 29	aft*c*r	after

Prologe to Deuteronomye.

P. L.	*1530.*	*1884.*
519, 4	eth*c*r	ether
9	pe*a*ceaue	perceaue
520, 22	the*m*	then

Deuteronomye.

C. V.	*1530.*	*1884.*
1 : 16	ſtraunge*s*	ſtraunger
28	wal*k*ed	walled
37	thiter	thit*h*er
2 : 9	nethe*t*	nether
20	theri*m*	therin
37	Fo. XIIII.	Fo. VI.
3 : 16	Fo. TII.	Fo. VII.
4 : 2	Fo. XVI.	Fo. VIII.
44	Fo. II.	Fo. XI.
5 : 2	Loode	Lorde
21	ſhat	ſha*l*t
24	ſ*n*ewed	ſhewed
6 : 10	b*oru*ght	brought
8 : 14	fo*t*gett	forgett
9 : 1	Io*a*dayne	Iordayne
4	in to the	in to
6	ſti*ſſ*enecked	ſtiffenecked
10 : 16	ſ*c*iffnecked	ſtiffnecked
11 : 22	comaundmentes	cōmaundmentes
26	ſe*c*t, õr ſe*e*t	ſett
12 : 17	of *of*	of
14 : *title*	VI.	XIIII.
27	for*ſ*ake	forſake
27	*c*nheritaunce	enheritaunce
28	w*h*itin	wit*h*in
29	ha*r*h	hath
16 : 1	paſſ*c*over	paſſeover
17 : 17	go*d*lde	golde
18 : 19	*k*erken	herken
19 : 1	Ga*d*	God
19	tought	t*h*ought
24 : 8	t*h*each	teach
25 : 3	ſt*ir*pes	ſtripes
28 : 52	in *in*	in
63	ſhabe	ſha*l*be
29 : 12	ſhul*d*deſt	ſhuldeſt
23	ouertrowenge	ouert*h*rowenge
30 : 16	multipye	multip*l*ye
16	ma*n*	maye
31 : 29	we*l*kedneſſe	wekedneſſe
32 : 31	thugh	th*o*ugh
33 : 7	*h*e	be
23	Nephali	Nep*t*hali
34 : 2	period(.) before, Dan	*omitted*

CHAPTER IV.

BIBLIOGRAPHICAL NOTICE OF THE COPY OF TYNDALE'S PENTATEUCH IN THE BAPTIST COLLEGE, BRISTOL.

This volume contains the books of Exodus, Leviticus, Numbers, and Deuteronomy of the first edition of 1530, and the book of Genesis of the edition of 1534. All the books are separate, and the general description of the Pentateuch of 1530, p. lx. *sqq.*, applies also to the books of Exodus, Leviticus, Numbers, and Deuteronomy of this copy.

The book of Genesis in the Bristol copy bears the title: *The firſte | Boke of Moſes called | Geneſis. Newly | correctyd | and | amendyd by | W. T. | M.D.XXXIIII.*, in an ornamented border with woodcuts of Moses and the Tables of the Law, the Brazen Serpent, Abraham offering up Isaac, and the Passage of the Red Sea. (See Photo-engraving facing this page.) The dimensions of a page covered by type are 5 inches by 2½ inches *circa*, the margin included, 3 inches, and a full page contains 31 lines, the headlines included. The type is German Latin Letter. (See Photo-engraving of a page of the text, p. xcix.)

The volume contains: Frontispiece, verso blank. 1 fo. Vnto the reader | W. T. beginning on recto of A ij and ending on A vij (unmarked) 6 ff. "The firſt Boke of Moſes called Geneſis" begins on recto of A viij (unmarked) and is fo. 1, and ends on verso of L viij (unmarked) fo. 81. "*The end of the firſt boke off | Moſes, called Geneſis.*" The signatures are in eights. Whole number of folios 88. The headline of the verso of each folio is "Geneſis," and of the recto "Chapter" and the number. Catchwords are employed throughout; the first catchword is *lande*, recto fo. 1, the last *der*, recto fo. 81. For further details see the collations.

INTRODUCTION

By F. F. Bruce, D.D.

Rylands Professor of Biblical Criticism and Exegesis in the University of Manchester

When William Tyndale published his English translation of the first five books of the Bible in 1530, it was the first time that any part of the Old Testament had been translated into English from the Hebrew original. English renderings of the Old Testament in part or in whole had appeared from time to time over the centuries—versifications of some of the narrative books, several translations of the Psalter, and the two complete Wycliffite versions of the fourteenth century—but these were all based on the Latin Vulgate. It would have been honour enough for Tyndale to have been remembered as the man who first translated the New Testament into English from the original Greek, but to have added to that record by being the first man to translate part of the Hebrew scriptures into English as well makes him worthy of double honour. It is certain that, but for his imprisonment and death, he would have completed the work so well begun; as it was, he not only published his English Pentateuch in 1530 but followed it up the following year by a translation of the Book of Jonah. In 1534 he produced a revision of Genesis, and his revised New Testament, published later in the same year, included as an appendix his translation from the Hebrew of the Old Testament "Epistles" prescribed for church reading according to the use of Sarum. In addition, he left in manuscript a translation of most of the historical books of the Old Testament.

* * * *

James Isidor Mombert, whom we have to thank for this edition, was born at Cassel, Germany, in 1829. He came to England at the age of twelve, and was ordained deacon in the Church of England in 1857. He then went to Canada, where he was ordained priest the following year. He was Rector successively of St. James's Church, Lancaster, Pennsylvania (1859–70), St. John's, Dresden, Germany (1870–76), Christ Church, Jersey City, New Jersey (1877–78), and St. John's, Passaic, New Jersey (1879–82). He spent the remaining years of his life in Paterson, New Jersey, engaged in literary work, and died in 1913.

He translated some important theological works from German into English, while his own works were mainly historical studies, including one on Charlemagne and one on the Crusades. But the work of his that comes closest to our present interest is his *English Versions of the Bible,* which appeared in three editions (1883, 1890 and 1906), and traced the history of the English Bible from the Old English renderings to the British and American revisions of 1881, 1885 and 1901. It was while he was engaged on this study that he felt the need to produce a new edition of Tyndale's Pentateuch, a work of which not many copies were extant, and only one of them perfect. He based his edition mainly on the copy of Tyndale's 1530 edition in the Lenox Library, New York, and partly on the copy in the Baptist College, Bristol, which embodies the 1534 edition of Genesis and the 1530 edition of the other four books.

* * * *

William Tyndale—or William Hutchins, as he sometimes called himself, using an alternative family name (there is no fixed spelling of either surname)—was born in Gloucestershire in 1494 or 1495. In his middle teens he went to Magdalen Hall, Oxford, where he took his B.A. in 1512 and his M.A. three years later. A year or two after that he went to Cambridge, which was in advance of Oxford as a school of the new learning; in particular, he was able to study Greek under Richard Croke, who returned to Cambridge in 1518 after occupying the Chair of Greek in Leipzig. From Cambridge in 1522 Tyndale went back to his native Gloucestershire to be tutor in the household of Sir John Walsh at Little Sodbury. While he was there he conceived the firm ambition to give his fellow-countrymen a trustworthy version of the New Testament, based on the Greek text.

Finding it impossible to procure the necessary leisure and financial backing to carry out this work in England,

Tyndale sailed for the Continent in 1524. By August 1525 his translation of the New Testament was practically complete, and he arranged to have it printed in Cologne. Ten sheets had been printed when the city senate received information about the work, and the printer was forbidden to proceed with it. Eight sheets (64 pages) of one copy of this " Cologne Quarto " have survived, and are included in the Grenville collection in the British Museum; a facsimile edition was published in 1871. Tyndale left Cologne for Worms, farther up the Rhine, and here the work of printing his New Testament was started afresh, and completed without further hitch. This edition, the "Worms Octavo," was published in February 1526. It has a twofold claim to fame, being not only the first complete English New Testament to be printed, but also the first translation of the English New Testament from Greek instead of Latin. Two copies of this edition are known to survive—one in the Baptist College, Bristol, and one in the library of St. Paul's Cathedral, London.

Tyndale was encouraged to undertake this work not only by his personal conviction that the state of religion and learning in England required it, but also by the publication a few years previously of Erasmus's printed edition of the Greek New Testament (1516) and of Luther's German New Testament (1522). Tyndale, like Luther, translated from Erasmus's Greek text. He also had Luther's version before him, but while he was undoubtedly influenced by Luther's work, his own version is no mere English imitation of Luther. Tyndale was the better Greek scholar of the two, and he turns the original Greek into racy and idiomatic English, which has made its own contribution to the subsequent development of our language.

In 1534 and again in 1535 Tyndale produced revised editions of his New Testament.

* * * *

It is, however, with his Old Testament work, and more especially with his Pentateuch, that we are concerned here. Here too he had been anticipated by Luther, whose German translation of the Pentateuch from Hebrew appeared in 1523, followed by other instalments of the Old Testament, until the whole work was published in

1534. But in the Old Testament, as in the New, Tyndale, while obviously influenced by Luther, shows his independent qualities as scholar and translator.

By the time that Tyndale came to translate the Pentateuch, there were several useful printed editions of the Hebrew Bible with which he could work. The Hebrew Pentateuch was first printed at Bologna, Italy, in 1482; six years later appeared the first complete Hebrew Bible in print, at Soncino, near Cremona. Further printed editions of the Hebrew Bible appeared at Brescia (1494) and Venice (1517); the Hebrew text was also included in the great Complutensian Polyglot, printed at Alcala in Spain between 1514 and 1517, and published in 1520. An edition prepared by the Tunisian Jew Jacob ben Chayyim, printed and published at Venice in 1524–25, became the basis for all subsequent printed editions of the Hebrew Bible until our own day. Hebrew grammars were also available—those by Pellican (1503), Reuchlin (1506) and Sebastian Münster (1525)—while Reuchlin (1506) and Pagninus (1529) compiled Hebrew dictionaries. The Complutensian Polyglot also included a Hebrew grammar and lexicon. Thus, although Tyndale had no facilities for Hebrew instruction in the curricula at Oxford and Cambridge, a man with such an appetite for learning had no lack of helps to the private study of Hebrew. It is easy in the light of the ampler knowledge of later days to see the gaps in Tyndale's knowledge of Hebrew. Tyndale was a pioneer, and the real wonder is that he did his pioneer work so well. To the end of his days he endeavoured to perfect his Hebrew learning; the last piece of writing to come from his pen, so far as we know, is the letter reproduced on pages li–lii of Mombert's Prolegomena, in which he begs the influential person to whom he writes (perhaps the Marquis of Bergen) to direct the prison governor to let him have his Hebrew Bible, grammar and dictionary, "that I may pass the time in that study." Evidently, even in prison, he was anxious to continue and, if possible, complete his translation of the Hebrew Bible. It would be pleasant if we could think that his request was granted. But the conditions of his prison life must have been strict indeed if he found it necessary to write to such an exalted personage in order to have the use of his own warmer clothes, not to mention his Hebrew books. The authorities may well have decided that he could not be allowed access to literature which would only encourage him in further heretical activity.

At the time of his execution on October 6, 1536, Tyndale left in manuscript an English version of the Old Testament books from Joshua to II Chronicles. This work, fortunately, was preserved by John Rogers, one of his associates, who incorporated it in the English Bible which he edited in 1537, under the pen-name of Thomas Matthew. "Matthew's Bible" included all that was available of Tyndale's version—his New Testament of 1535 and all that he had completed of the Old Testament—while the remainder of the Old Testament was supplied from Coverdale's Bible of 1535. "Matthew's Bible" was also the first English Bible to be published by royal permission—"set forth with the king's most gracious licence"—and it may be regarded as a signal act of justice (ordinary justice and poetic justice too) that the first English Bible to receive the royal licence should be Tyndale's Bible (so far as Tyndale had been able to go), even if it was not yet politic to have Tyndale's name publicly associated with it. The initials "W.T." at the end of Malachi were perhaps intended to be a discreet indication to the discerning reader that Tyndale was the principal, though not the sole, translator of the Old Testament books in this edition.

* * * *

Pen-names were much in use in the conditions of those times, not only by translators but by printers too. Tyndale's Pentateuch (together with some of his other writings) bears the imprint of one Hans Luft at Malborow (i.e. Marburg) in Hesse. Now there *was* a printer by the name of Hans Luft, who printed Luther's works at Wittenberg. He was not known to have a branch of his business at Marburg, but it was quite conceivable that he had, and it is highly likely that Tyndale visited Marburg not long before the publication of his Pentateuch. However, it has now been established that the Hans Luft who printed Tyndale's Pentateuch was not Luther's printer, but one Johann Hoochstraten at Antwerp. The printer's name and the place-name were alike pen-names! At times during Hoochstraten's career as a printer he used his own name; between 1526 and 1530 and again between 1535 and 1540 he assumed the guise of Hans Luft of Marburg; at other times he used yet other pen-names. The printing of works tainted with the Lutheran heresy was fraught with danger at certain times and places, and Hoochstraten judged it politic on occasion to conceal his true identity, not realizing how much trouble he was giving to bibliographers of later centuries! The credit for establishing Hoochstraten's part in the production of Tyndale's work lies chiefly with a Dutch scholar, Miss M. E. Kronenberg.

The Book of Exodus in Tyndale's Pentateuch was embellished with eleven woodcuts illustrating the descriptions of the Tabernacle and its furniture and the high-priestly vestments in chapters 25 to 30. These woodcuts, along with others illustrating other parts of the Pentateuch, had been used by another Antwerp printer, Vostermann by name, for two Dutch editions of the Bible published in 1528, and by Peter Quentel of Cologne (printer of Tyndale's quarto New Testament of 1525) for two Latin Bibles in 1527 and 1529. Robert Demaus, in his biography of Tyndale (1871), suggested that Tyndale bought the blocks from Vostermann with the money which the Bishop of London, in the well-known story, paid to buy up copies of Tyndale's New Testament for burning. But, apart from the question why only eleven of Vostermann's blocks were used for Tyndale's Pentateuch, it is no longer necessary to suppose, as Demaus did, that the blocks were taken from Antwerp to Marburg. One Antwerp printer might easily place them, or as many of them as were desired, at the disposal of another Antwerp printer without formality. Demaus thought that Vostermann no longer had them in his possession in 1532, since a further edition of the Dutch Bible which he printed in that year has a different set of woodcuts; but that might be due simply to the fact that the 1532 Bible has a smaller page than its predecessors of 1528.

* * * *

The quality of Tyndale's English may be savoured by the reader of this volume for himself. To Tyndale's own annotations Mombert has added some of his own, largely explanatory of some obsolete words and phrases used by

Tyndale, together with an apparatus giving parallel renderings from the Latin Vulgate, Luther's Pentateuch, and "Matthew's Bible." The renderings adduced from the Vulgate and Luther are intended to illustrate the nature of Tyndale's dependence on these versions, but it must be said that Tyndale was more independent of them, and more directly dependent on the Hebrew text, than Mombert gives him credit for.

One place where he cannot make anything intelligible of the Hebrew, and follows Luther into the same ditch, is in Genesis 49: 22, where the clause which we know as "the branches run over the wall" appears as "the daughters come forth to bear rule." Even Jerome had some difficulty here, rendering "the daughters ran over the wall"; the point which they all missed is the figurative use of the Hebrew word for daughters in the sense of branches. But such unintelligible renderings are rarer than might have been looked for in a pioneer work; they are more than offset by such pithy translations as Pharaoh's "jolly captains" (i.e. his valiant captains) being drowned in the Red Sea (Exodus 15: 4) and "I am the Lord thy surgeon" (Exodus 15: 26).

* * * *

The salty marginalia of Tyndale's Pentateuch, with their anti-papal satire, have become famous. Our detachment from the situation enables us to appreciate such remarks as "The Pope's bull slayeth more than Aaron's calf" (on Exodus 32: 28) without regard to our ecclesiastical affiliation; but at the time the delight they gave to readers likeminded with Tyndale was more than matched by the sense of insult felt by those who disagreed with him. Tyndale was wholeheartedly and passionately committed to the Protestant cause, and wears his heart on his sleeve, or on his margin; but such notes remind us that any Bible intended for general circulation must be completely free from features reflecting a partisan view, or calculated to give offence to potential readers. Tyndale's Bible was violently attacked, but in spite of all his opponents' attempts to prove that it was a poor translation it is plain that what really irked them was not the translation but the translator.

Yet some of his marginal notes have still power to warm

the heart because of the passion for social justice which they evince. One may think, for example, of the note on Exodus 22: 22, forbidding the affliction of the helpless: "Let all oppressors of the poor take heed to this text." Repeatedly he shows his dislike of the custom by which criminals might avoid being brought to justice by seeking religious protection, as in the notes on Genesis 4: 15; 9: 4; Exodus 21: 14 (where the wilful murderer cannot claim sanctuary at the altar). And the inwardness of true religion is expressed unmistakably in his note on Jacob's prayer in Genesis 32: 9: "Prayer is to cleave unto the promises of God with a strong faith and to beseech God with a fervent desire that he will fulfil them for his mercy and truth only, as Jacob here doth."

Lastly, mention must be made of Tyndale's sound grasp of the principles of Biblical interpretation. This appears in his prologues to the five books of the Pentateuch, and especially in his recurrent warnings against allegorization. The stories of Genesis, for example, were not intended to be allegorized so as to signify something quite different from their obvious meaning; they are recorded of men and women of old "for our consolation and comfort, that we despair not if such like things happen to us." By applying the examples set out in them the reader may "suck out the pith of the scripture." Allegories, he says in his prologue to Leviticus, prove nothing; they can only serve to illustrate truths plainly taught elsewhere. Even the ritual prescriptions of the sacrificial law must not be allegorized; they are to be regarded as an object lesson or ABC for the people of God in the earlier phase of their religious experience. And if they cannot be applied literally today, this is not to say that they must be interpreted allegorically; their language should rather be taken as pictorial, like the language of common proverbs: thus, says Tyndale, "Put salt to all your sacrifices" is a pithier way of saying "Do all your deeds with discretion"; and this proverbial way of phrasing it "greteth and biteth (if it be understand) more than plain words."

It is a pleasure to greet this fresh edition of a great work, which will thus become more widely known and appreciated, as it is an honour to introduce it.

November, 1966

The firſte

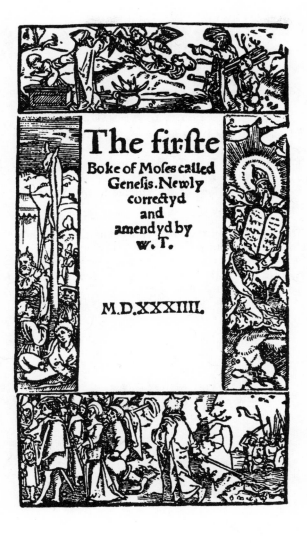

Boke of Moſes called Geneſis. Newly correctyd and amendyd by W. T.

M.D.XXXIIII.

ABBREVIATIONS.

ON THE SIDE MARGIN.

𝔐. ℭ. 𝔖. denotes the Chapter Summaries in *Matthew's Bible*

IN THE LOWER MARGIN.

𝔐. denotes the Text, 𝔐. 𝔐. 𝔑. the Marginal Notes, in *Matthew's Bible*, 1537.

𝔏. denotes the Text, 𝔏. 𝔐. 𝔑. the Marginal Notes, in Luther's *Das Alte Teſtament*, 1523.

𝔙. denotes the Text of the Vulgate in the *Biblia* of Stephanus, 1528.

The beginning of the *recto* of Tyndale's folio is indicated thus: [Fo. I.], the beginning of the *verso* by the mark .❡.

A dash over a vowel denotes that *n* or *m* should be supplied; *e. g.*, ī, is the contraction of *in*, ād, of *and*, Adā, of *Adam*, &c.; yͤ denotes *the*, and yͭ, that.

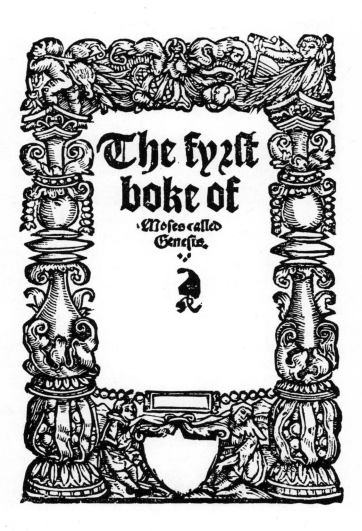

The fyrst boke of Moses called Genesis.

* W. T. To the Reader.

WHEN I had tranſlated the newe teſtament, I added a piſtle vnto the latter ende, In which I deſyred them ẏ were learned to amend if ought were founde amyſſe. But oure malicious and wylye hypocrytes which are ſo ſtubburne and hard herted in their weked abhominaciōs that it is not poſſible for them to amend any thinge atall (as we ſee by dayly experience, when their both lyvinges and doinges are rebuked with the trouth) ſaye, ſome of them that it is impoſſible to tranſlate the ſcripture in to Engliſh, ſome that it is not lawfull for the laye people to haue it in their mother tonge, ſome, that it wold make them all heretykes, as it wold no doute from many thinges which they of longe tyme haue falſly taught, ād that is the whole cauſe wherfore they forbyd it, though they other clokes pretende. And ſome or rather every one, ſaye that it wold make them ryſe ageynſt the kinge, whom they them ſelves (vnto their damnatyō) never yet obeyed. And leſte the temporall rulars ſhuld ſee their falſehod, if the ſcripture cam to light, cauſeth them ſo to lye.

And as for my tranſlatiō in which they afferme vnto the laye people (as I haue hearde ſaye .P. to be I wotte not how many thouſande hereſyes, ſo that it cā not be mēded or correcte, they haue yet taken ſo greate payne to examyne it, & to compare it vnto that they wold fayne haue it and to their awne imaginations and iugglinge termes, and to haue ſome what to rayle at, and vnder that cloke to blaſpheme

* This entire prologe "W. T. To the Reader," is not in the Bristol copy of the edition of 1534.

the treuth, that they myght with as litle laboure (as I ſuppoſe) haue tranſlated the moſte parte of the bible. For they which in tymes paſte were wont to loke on no more ſcripture then they founde in their duns or ſoch like develyſh doctryne, haue yet now ſo narowlye loked on my tranſlatyon, that there is not ſo moch as one I therin if it lacke a tytle over his hed, but they haue noted it, and nombre it vnto the ignorant people for an hereſy. Finallye in this they be all agreed, to dryve you from the knowlege of the ſcripture, & that ye ſhall not haue the texte therof in the mother tonge, and to kepe the world ſtyll in darkeneſſe, to thentent they might ſitt in the conſciences of the people, thorow vayne ſuperſtition and falſe doctrine, to ſatiſfye their fylthy luſtes, their proude ambition, and vnſatiable covetuouſnes, and to exalte their awne honoure aboue kinge & emperoure, yee & aboue god him ſilfe

¶ A thouſand bokes had they lever to be put forth agenſte their abhominable doynges and doctrine, then that the ſcripture ſhulde come to light. For as longe as they maye kepe that doune, they will ſo darken the ryght way with the .P. miſte of their ſophiſtrye, and ſo tangle thē that ether rebuke or deſpyſe their abhominations with argumentes of philoſophye & with wordly ſymylitudes and apparent reaſons of naturall wiſdom. And with wreſtinge the ſcripture unto their awne purpoſe clene contrarye unto ỳ proceſſe, order and meaninge of the texte, and ſo delude them in deſcantynge vppon it with alligoryes, and amaſe thē expoundinge it in manye ſenſes before the vnlerned laye people, (when it hath but one ſymple litterall ſenſe whoſe light the owles cā not abyde) that though thou feale in thyne harte and arte ſure how that all is falſe ỳ they ſaye, yet coudeſte thou not ſolve their ſotle rydles.

¶ Which thinge onlye moved me to tranſlate the new teſtament. Becauſe I had perceaved by experyence, how that it was impoſſible to ſtablyſh the laye people in any truth, excepte ỳ ſcripture were playnly layde before their eyes in their mother tonge, that they might ſe the proceſſe, ordre and meaninge of the texte: for els what ſo ever truth is taught them, theſe ennymyes of all truth qwench it ageyne, partly with the ſmoke of their bottomleſſe pytte wherof thou readeſt apocalipſis ix. that is, with apparent reaſons of ſophiſtrye & traditions of their awne makynge, founded with out grounde of ſcripture, and partely in iugglinge with the texte, expoundinge it in ſoch a ſenſe as is impoſſi- .P. ble to gether of the texte, if thou ſee the proceſſe ordre and meaninge therof.

¶ And even in the biſſhope of londons houſe I entended to have done it. For when I was ſo turmoyled in the contre where I was that I coude no lenger there dwell (the proceſſe wherof were to longe here to reherce) I this wyſe thought in my ſilfe, this I ſuffre becauſe the preſtes of the contre be vnlerned, as god it knoweth there are a full ignorant ſorte which haue ſene no more latyn then that they read in their porteſſes and miſſales which yet many of them can ſcacely read, (excepte it be Albertus de ſecretis mulierū in which yet, though they be never ſo ſoryly lerned, they pore day and night and make notes therin and all to teach the mydwyves as they ſay, and linwod a boke of conſtitutions to gether tithes, mortuaryes, offeringes, cuſtoms, and other pillage, which they calle, not theirs, but godes parte and the deuty of holye chirch, to diſcharge their conſciences with all: for they are bound that they ſhall not dimynyſh, but encreace all thinge vnto the vttmoſt of their powers) and therfore (becauſe they are thus vnlerned thought I) when they come to gedder to the ale houſe, which is their preachinge place, they afferme that my ſainges are hereſy. And beſydes ỷ they adde to of thir awne heddes which I never ſpake, as the maner is to prolonge the tale to ſhorte .P. the tyme with all, and accuſe me ſecretly to the chauncelare and other the biſhopes officers, And in deade, when I cam before the chauncelare, he thretened me grevouſly, and revyled me and rated me as though I had bene a dogge, and layd to my charge wherof there coude be none accuſer brought forth, (as their maner is not to bringe forth the accuſer) and yet all the preſtes of ỷ contre were ỷ ſame daye there. As I this thought the biſhope of london came to my remembrance whom Eraſmus (whoſe tonge maketh of litle gnattes greate elephātes and lifteth upp aboue the ſtarres whoſoever geveth him a litle exhibition) prayſeth excedingly amonge other in his annotatyons on the new teſtament for his great learninge. Then thought I, if I might come to this mannes ſervice, I were happye. And ſo I gate me to london, & thorow the accoyntaunce of my maſter came to ſir harry gilford the kinges graces countroller, ād brought him an oration of Iſocrates which I had tranſlated out of greke in to Engliſh, and deſyred him to ſpeake vnto my lorde of london for me, which he alſo did as he ſhewed me, ād willed me to write a piſtle to my lorde, and to goo to him my ſilf which I alſo did, and delivered my piſtle to a ſervaunt of his awne, one wyllyam hebilthwayte, a mā of myne old accoyntaūce. But god which knoweth what is within hypocrites, ſawe that I was begyled, ād that that councell was not the nexte way vnto .P. my purpoſe. And therfore he gate me no favoure in my lordes ſight ❨ Wheruppō my lorde anſwered me, his houſe was full, he had mo thē he coude well finde, and adviſed me to ſeke in london, wher he ſayd I coude not lacke a ſervice, And ſo in london I abode almoſte an yere, and marked the courſe of the worlde, and herde oure pratars, I wold ſay oure preachers how they boſted them ſelves and their hye authorite, and beheld the pompe of oure prelates and how beſyed they were as they yet are, to ſet peace and vnite in the worlde (though it be not poſſible for them that walke in darkeneſſe to cōtinue longe in peace, for they can not but ether ſtōble or daſh them ſelves at one thinge or a nother that ſhall cleane vnquyet all togedder) & ſawe thinges wherof I deferre to ſpeake at this tyme and underſtode at the laſte not only that there was no rowme in my lorde of londons palace to tranſlate the new teſtament, but alſo that there was no place to do it in all englonde, as experience doth now openly declare.

❨ Vnder what maner therfore ſhuld I now ſubmitte this boke to be corrected and amended of them, which can ſuffer nothinge to be well? Or what proteſtacyon ſhuld I make in ſoch a matter vnto oure prelates thoſe ſtubburne Nimrothes which ſo mightely fight agenſte god and reſiſte his holy ſpirite, enforceynge with all crafte and ſotelte to qwench the light of the everlaſtinge teſtament, promyſes, and a-.P. poyntemente made betwene god & vs: and heapinge the firce wrath of god vppon all princes and rulars, mockinge thē with falſe fayned names of hypocryſye, and ſervinge their luſtes at all poyntes, & diſpenſinge with thē even of the very lawes of god, of which Chriſte him ſilf teſtifieth Mathew v. ẏ not ſo moch as one tittle therof maye periſh, or be brokē. And of which the prophete ſayth Pſalme .cxviii. Thou haſte cōmaunded thy lawes to be kepte **meod**, ẏ is in hebrew excedingly, with all diligēce, might & power, and haue made thē ſo mad with their iugglinge charmes and crafty perſuaſiōs that they thinke it full ſatiſfaction for all their weked lyvinge, to tormēt ſoch as tell thē trouth, & to borne the worde of their ſoules helth, & ſle whoſoever beleve theron.

❡ Not withſtōdinge yet I ſubmytte this boke and all other that I haue other made or trāſlated, or ſhall in tyme to come, (if it be goddes will that I ſhall further laboure in his herveſt) unto all them that ſubmytte thē ſelves vnto the worde of god, to be corrected of thē, yee and moreover to be diſalowed & alſo burnte, if it ſeme worthy when they have examyned it wyth the hebrue, ſo that they firſt put forth of their awne tranſlatinge a nother that is more correcte.

.P.

¶ *Aprologe

ſhewinge the vſe of the ſcripture

THOUGH a man had a precious iuell and a rich, yet if he wiſte not the value therof nor wherfore it ſerved, he were nother the better nor rycher of a ſtraw. Even ſo though we read the ſcripture & bable of it never ſo moch, yet if we know not the uſe of it, and wherfore it was geven, and what is therin to be ſought, it profitteth vs nothinge at all. It is not ynough therfore to read and talke of it only, but we muſt alſo deſyre god daye and night inſtantly to open oure eyes, ād to make vs vnderſtond and feale wherfore the ſcripture was geuen, that we maye applye the medicyne of the ſcripture, every mā to his awne ſores, inleſſe then we entend to be ydle diſputers, and braulers aboute vayne wordes, ever gnawenge vppon the bitter barcke with out and never attayninge unto the ſwete pith with in, and perſequutinge one an other for defendinge of lewde imaginacions and phantaſyes of oure awne invencyon

** ¶ Paule, in ỹ thyrde of ỹ ſecōde epiſtle to Tymothe

---

* The Bristol copy of the edition of 1534 gives instead of the title "Aprologe ſhewinge," etc., the title:

Vnto the reader W. T.

** Lines 19 *sqq.* above stand in the Bristol copy thus: Page Signature Aij.

Paule in the third of the ſeconde epiſtle to Timothe ſaith, that the ſcripture is good to teache (for that ought men to teache] and not dreames of their awne makinge, as the pope doth,) and alſo to improue, for that ſcripture is the twichſtone that tryeth al doctrines, and by that we know the falſe from the true. And in the .vi. to the Ephesians he calleth in the ſwerde of the ſpirite by cauſe it killeth hypocrites and vttereth and improueth their falſe inuentions

The ſcri pture w herfore it is good.

ſayth, ẏ the ſcripture is good to teache (for ẏ ought mē to teach & not dreames of their awne makīge, as ẏ pope doth) & alſo to improve, for ẏ ſcripture is ẏ twichſtone ẏ tryeth all doctrynes, ād by ẏ we know the falſe from ẏ true. .¶. And in the .vi. to the epheſians he calleth it the ſwerd of the ſpirite, by cauſe it killeth hyppocrites, and vttereth ād improveth their falſe inventyons. And in the .xv. to the Romayns he ſayth all that are wryten, are wryten for oure learninge, that we thorow pacyence and cōforte of the ſcripture myght have hope. That is, the enſamples that are in the ſcripture comforte vs in all oure tribulacyons, and make vs to put oure truſte in god, and pacyently to abyde his leyſure.

And in the .x. of the firſte to the Corinthyans he bringeth in examples of the ſcripture to feare vs and to bridle the fleſhe, that we caſte not the yoke of the lawe of god from of oure neckes, and fall to luſtynge and doinge of evill.

¶ So now the ſcripture is a light and ſheweth vs the true waye, both what to do, and what to hope. And a defence from all erroure, and a comforte in adverſyte that we deſpayre not. and feareth vs in proſperyte that we ſynne not *Seke therfore in the ſcripture

---

* The passage "Seke therfore" to "world a new." is not in the Bristol copy of the edition of 1534, which has instead:

Seke therfore in the
ſcripture as thou readeſt it, chefely and abo
ue all, the conuenaūtes made betwene god
and vs. That is to ſaye; the lawe and cōma]
undementes which God commaūdeth vs
to do. And then the mercie promyſed vnto
all them that ſubmite them ſelues vnto the
lawe. For all the promyſes thorow out the
hole ſcripture do include a couenaūt. That
is: god byndeth him ſelfe to fulfil that mer
cie vnto the, onlye if thou wilt endeuoure
thy ſelfe to kepe his lawes: ſo that no man
hath his parte in the mercie of god, ſaue he
onlye that loueth his lawe and conſenteth
that it is righteous and good, & fayne wol
de do it, ād euer mourneth becauſe he now
and then breaketh it thorow infirmite, or
dothe it not ſo perfectly as his harte wolde
And let loue interprete the lawe: that th
ou vnderſtōde this to be the finall ende of

as thou readeſt it firſt the law, what god cōmaundeth vs to doo. And ſecundarylye the promyſes, which god promyſeth us ageyne, namely in Chriſte Ieſu oure lorde. Then ſeke enſamples, firſte of comforte, how god purgeth all them that ſubmitte them ſelves to walke in his wayes, in the purgatorye of tribulatyon, delyveringe them yet at the latter ende, and never ſoferinge any of them to peryſh, that cleave faſte to his promyſes.

---

the lawe, and the hole cauſe why the lawe
was geuen: euen to bringe the to the kno
ledge of god, how that he hath done all th
inge for the, that thou mighteſt loue hym
agayne with al thine harte and thy neyb
oure for his ſake as thy ſilfe and as Chriſt
loued the. Becauſe thy neyboure is the ſon
ne of god alſo and created vnto his lykenes
as thou arte, and bought with as dere blo
ude as arte thou. Whoſoeuer feleth in his
herte that euery man ought to loue his ney
boure as Chriſt loued him, and conſenteth
therto, and enforſeth to come therto: the ſa
me onlye vnderſtondeth the lawe aryght
and can interprete it. And he that ſubmyt-
A iij.]
teth not hī ſelfe in the degre he is in, to ſeke
his neyboures proffite as Chriſt did his, cā
neuer vnderſtonde the lawe, though it be
interprete to him. For that loue is the light
of the lawe, to vnderſtonde it bye.

And beholde how righteous, howe honeſt and howe due a thinge it is by nature,
that euery man loue his brother vnſayned
ly euē as him ſelfe, for his fathers ſake. For
it is the fathers great ſhame and his hie diſpleaſure, if one brother hurte another, Yf
one brother be hurte of another, he maye
not aduēge him ſelfe, but muſt complayne
to his father or to them that haue auctorite
of his father to rule in his abſence. Euen ſo
if any of godes children be hurt by any of
his brethren, he maye not aduenge him ſel
ſe with hande or herte. God muſt aduenge.
And the gouerners and miniſters of the lawe that God hath ordeyned to rule vs by
concerninge oure outwarde conuerſacion
of one with another, they muſt aduenge.
If they will not auenge, but rather maynte
ne wronge, and be oppreſſers them ſelues,
then muſt we tarye paciently tyll God co
me which is euer readie to reape tiraūntes
from of the face of the erth, aſſone as theyr
ſinnes are rype.

Conſidre alſo what wrath, vengeaunce

And fynallye, note the enſamples which are w- .P. riten to feare the fleſh that we ſynne not. That is, how god ſuffereth the vngodlye and weked ſynners that reſiſte god and refuſe to folow him, to contynue in their wekedneſſe, ever waxinge worſe and worſe vntyll their ſynne be ſo ſore encreaſed and ſo abhomynable, that if they ſhuld longer endure they wold corrupte the very electe. But for the electes ſake god ſendeth thē preachers. Nevertheleſſe they harden their hartes agenſte

---

and plages god threateneth to them that ar
rebellious and diſobedient.]
Thē go to & reade the ſtoryes of the by-
ble for thy lerninge & comforte, & ſe euery thinge practyſed before thyne eyes: for
accordinge to thoſe enſamples ſhall it goo
with the & all mē vntill the worldes ende.
So that into whatſoeuer caſe or ſtate a mā be
brought, accordīge to whatſoeuer ēſāple of
the bible it be, his ende ſhalbe accordīge as
he there ſeith and readeth. As god there w
arneth yer he ſmyte, & ſoffreth lōge yer he
take extreme vēgeaūce, ſo ſhall he do with
vs. As they that turne, are there receaued to
mercie, & they that maliciouſly reſiſt, periſſhe vtterlye, ſo ſhall it be with vs. As they
that refuſe the coūſel of God periſſhe thorow their awne coūcel, ſo ſhall it be with vs
vntill the worldes ende. As it wēt with the
ir kinges & rulers, ſo ſhall it go with oures
As it was with their comē people, ſo ſhall
it be with oures. As it was with theyr ſpirituall officers, ſo ſhall it be with oures. As it w-
as wyth theyr true prophetes, ſo ſhall it be
with oures vntill the worldes ēde. As they
had euer amōge thē falſe prophetes & true:
& as their falſe *perſecuted the true, & moued
the prynces to ſle thē, ſo ſhall it be with vs
vntyll the ende of the worlde. As there was
amōge thē but a fewe true herted to god, ſo
ſhall it be amōge vs: & as their ydolatry was
ſo ſhall ours be vntyll the ende of the worl
de. All mercy that was ſhewed there, is a *pro-]
A iiij.
myſe vnto the, if thou turne to god. And
all vengeaunce and wrath ſhewed there, is
threatened to the, if thou be ſtoubourne ād
reſiſte &c.

Then follows:

And this lerninge and comforte ſhalt th
ou euermore finde, etc.

* *per* and *pro*, instead of abbreviated letters not in our fonts.

the truth, and god deſtroyeth thē vtterlye and begynneth the world a new.

❡ This comforte ſhalt thou evermore finde in the playne texte and literall ſenſe. Nether is there any ſtorye ſo homely, ſo rude, yee or ſo vyle (as it ſemeth outwarde) wherin is not exceadinge greate comforte. And when ſome which ſeme to them ſelves great clarkes ſaye: they wott not what moare profite is in many geſtes of the ſcripture if they be read with out an allegorye, then in a tale of robenhode, ſaye thou: that they were wryten for oure conſolacyon and comforte, that we deſpayre not, if ſoch like happen vnto vs. We be not holyer then Noe, though he were once dronke. Nether better beloved then Iacob, though his awne ſonne defyled his bedde. We be not holyer than lot, though his doughters thorow ignorance deceaved him, nor peradventure holyer then thoſe doughters. Nether are we holyer then David, though he brake wedlocke and uppon the ſame commytted abhomynable murther. All thoſe men have witne- .P. ſſe of the ſcripture that they pleaſed god and ware good men both before that thoſe thinges chaunſed them and alſo after. Nevertheleſſe ſoch thinges happened them for oure enſample: not that we ſhuld contraſayte their evill, but if whyle we fight with oure ſelves enforſynge to walke in the law of god (as they did) we yet fall likewiſe, that we deſpayre not, but come agayne to the lawes of god and take better holde

❡ We read ſens the tyme of Chriſtes deeth of virgins that have bene brought vnto the comē ſtues, and there deſyled, and of martyrs that haue bene bounde and hores haue abvſed their bodyes. Why? The iudgemētes of god are bottōleſſe. Soch thinges chaunced partely for enſamples, partely God thorow ſynne healeth ſynne Pryde can nether be healed nor yet appere but thorow ſoch horrible deades. Paraduenture they were of ẏ popes ſecte ād reioyſed fleſhly, thinkinge that heaven came by deades and not by Chriſt, and that the outwarde dead iuſtyſyed them & made them holy and not the inward ſpirite receaved by fayth and the conſent of the harte vnto the law of god.

¶ As thou readeſte therfore thinke that every ſillable pertayneth to thyne awne ſilf, and ſucke out the pithe of the ſcripture, and arm thy ſilf ageynſt all aſſaultes. Firſte note with ſtronge faith the power of god in creatinge all of nought Then marke the grevous fall of Adam and of vs all in him, thorow the lightregardĩge of the .¶. commaundement of god. In the .iiii. Chapitre god turneth him vnto Abel and then to his offeringe, but not to Cain and his offeringe. Where thou ſeeſt that though the deades of the evel apere outwardly as gloryous as the deades of the good: yet in the ſight of god which loketh on the harte, the deade is good becauſe of the man, and not the man good becauſe of his deade. In the .vi. God ſendeth Noe to preach to the weked and geveth them ſpace to repent: they wax hard herted, God bringeth them to nought And yet ſaveth Noe: even by the ſame water by which he deſtroyed them. Marke alſo what folowed the pryde of the buyldinge of the toure of Babel

Conſydre how God ſendeth forth Abrahã out of his awne countre in to a ſtrange lande full of weked people, and gave him but a bare promeſſe with him that he wold bleſſe him and defende him. Abraham beleved: and that worde ſaued and delyuered him in all parelles: ſo that we ſe, how that mannes life is not mayntayned by bred onlye (as Chriſte ſayeth) but moch rather by belevinge the promyſes of god. Behold how ſoberly and how circũſpectly both Abraham and alſo Iſaac behaue them ſelves amõge the infideles. Abraham byeth that which might have ben geven him for nought, to cutte of occaſions. Iſaac when his welles which he had digged were taken from him, geveth rowme and reſiſteth not. More over they ere and ſo- .¶. we and ſede their catell, and make confederacyons, ãd take perpetuall truce, and do all outward thinges: Even as they do which have no faith, for god hath not made vs to be ydle in this world. Every man muſt worke godly and truly to the vttmoſte of the power that god hath geven him: and yet not truſte therin: but in goddes worde or promeſſe: and god will worke with vs and bringe that we do to good effecte. And thē when oure power will extend no further, goddes promeſſes wyll worke all alone

¶ How many thinges alſo reſiſted the promeſſes of god to Iacob? And yet Iacob coniureth god with his awne promeſſes ſayenge? O god of my father Abraham: and god of my father Iſaac, O Lorde which ſaydeſte vnto me returne vnto thyne awne contre, and vnto the place were thou waſte borne and I wil do the good I am not worthy of the leſte of thoſe mercyes, nor of that trouth which thou haſte done to thy ſeruant I went out but with a ſtaffe, and come home with .ii droves, delyver me out of the handes of my brother Eſau, for I feare him greatly &c. And god delyvered him, and will likewyſe all that call unto his promeſſes with a repentinge herte, were they never ſo great ſynners. Marke alſo the weake infirmites of the mā He loveth one wife more than a nother, one ſonne more than a nother. And ſe how god purgeth him. Eſau threteneth him: Laban begyleth him. The beloued wife is longe baren: his .¶. doughter is ravyſhed: his wife is defyled, and that of his awne ſonne. Rahel dieth, Ioſeph is taken a way, yee and as he ſuppoſed rent of wild beaſtes And yet how gloryous was hys ende? Note the wekeneſſe of his Children, yee and the ſynne of them, and how god thorow their awne wekednes ſaved them. Theſe enſamples teach vs that a man is not attonce parfecte the firſte daye he beginneth to lyve wel They that be ſtronge therfore muſte ſuffre with the weake, and helpe to kepe them in vnite & peace one with a nother vntill they beſtrōger

Note what the brothren ſayde when they were tached in Egipte, we haue verelye ſynned (ſayde they) ageynſte oure brother in ẏ we ſawe the anguyſh of his ſoule when he beſought vs, and wold not heare him: ād therfore is this tribulation come vppon vs. By which enſample thou ſeiſte, how that conſcience of evyll doenges findeth men out at the laſte. But namely in tribulacyon and adverſyte: there temptacyon and alſo deſperacyon: yee and the verye paynes of hell find vs out: there the ſoule feleth the ferſe wrath of god and wyſſheth mountaynes to falle on her and to hyde her (yf it were poſſible) frō the angrye face of god.

Marke alſo how greate evelles folow of how litle an occaſion Dinah goeth but forth alone to ſe the doughters of the contre, and how greate myſcheve and troble folowed? Iacob loved but one ſonne more then a nother, ād how grevous .ꝑ. murther folowed in their hartes? Theſe are enſamples for oure learninge to teach us to walke warely and circūſpectlye in the worlde of weake people, that we geve no mā occaſions of evyll

❡ Finally, ſe what god promyſed Ioſeph in his dreames. Thoſe promeſſes accōpanyed him all ways, and went doune wyth him even in to the depe dongeon, And brought him vppe agayne, And never for ſoke him till all that was promyſed was fulfilled. Theſe are enſamples wrytē for oure learnīge (as paule ſayth) to teach vs to truſte in god in yͤ ſtrōge fyre of tribulation and purgatorye of oure fleſh. And that they which ſubmytte them ſelves to folow god ſhuld note and marke ſoch thinges, for theyr lerninge and comforte, is the frute of the ſcripture and cauſe why it was wryten: And with ſoch a purpoſe to read it, is the waye to everlaſtynge life, and to thoſe ioyfull blyſſinges that are promyſed vnto all nacyons in the ſeade of Abraham, which ſeade is Ieſus Chriſte oure lorde, to whom be honoure and prayſe for ever and unto god oure father thorow him.

A M E N .

THE FYRST BOKE
OF MOSES CALLED GENESIS

I. 1–9.

The fyrſt Chapiter.

1 IN the begynnynge God created
2 heaven and erth. The erth was
voyde and emptie, ād darckneſſe was vpon the depe, and
the ſpirite of god moved vpon the water
3 Than God ſayd: let there be lyghte and
4 there was lyghte. And God ſawe the
lyghte that it was good: & devyded
5 the lyghte from the darckneſſe, and
called the lyghte daye, and the darckneſſe nyghte: and ſo of the evenynge and
mornynge was made the fyrſt daye

M.C.S. How heauen & erth, the lyght, the fyrmament, the ſonne, the mone, the ſterres, and all beaſtes, foules & fyſſhes in the ſee were made by the worde of God. And how man alſo was creat.

6 And God ſayd: let there be a fyrmament betwene
7 the waters, ād let it devyde the waters a ſonder. Than
God made the fyrmament and parted the waters which
were vnder the fyrmament, from the waters that were
8 above the fyrmament: And it was ſo. And God called
the fyrmament heaven, And ſo of the evenynge and
morninge was made the ſeconde daye
9 And God ſayd, let the waters that are vnder heaven
gether them ſelves vnto one place, that the drye londe

M. 1 beginnyng. God, throughout with capital G. 3 ſayde, and ſo throughout the chapter. lyght, *bis* 4 lyght, nyght, and often. 5 the day, the night. 7 mornyng 9 lande

V. 2 ferebatur 5 tenebris. appellauitque. factumque eſt veſpere· & mane dies vnus (cf. vv. 8, 13, 19, 24, 31) 7 et factum eſt ita (ſo vv. 9, 15, 24, 30).

L. 2 tieffe. auf dem Waſſer 3 es ward liecht 5 da ward aus abend und morgen der erſte tag.

M. M. N. 2 *moued*, brethed or ſtyred 7 *fyrmamēt*, or heauen, Ps. cxxxv a. v. b. It is an Hebrew worde and ſygnyfyeth thruſting forth or ſpredynge abrode.

10 may appere: And it came ſo to paſſe. And god called
the drye lande the erth and the gatheringe togyther
of waters called he the ſee, And God ſawe that it was
good
11 .P. And God ſayd: let the erth bringe forth herbe
and graſſe that ſowe ſeed, and frutefull trees that bere
frute every one in his kynde, havynge their ſeed in
them ſelves vpon the erth. And it came ſo to paſſe:
12 ād the erth brought forth herbe and graſſe ſowenge
ſeed every one in his kynde & trees berynge frute &
havynge their ſeed in thē ſelves, every one in his kynde.
13 And God ſawe that it was good: and thē of the evenynge
and mornynge was made the thyrde daye.
14 Than ſayd God: let there be lyghtes in ŷ firmament
of heaven to devyde the daye frō the nyghte, that they
15 may be vnto ſygnes, ſeaſons, days & yeares. And let
them be lyghtes in the fyrmament of heavē, to ſhyne
16 vpon the erth. & ſo it was. And God made two great
lyghtes A greater lyghte to rule the daye, & a leſſe
17 lyghte to rule the nyghte, and he made ſterres alſo. And
God put them in the fyrmament of heaven to ſhyne
18 vpon the erth, and to rule the daye & the nyghte,
19 ād to devyde the lyghte from darckneſſe. And God
ſawe ŷ it was good: and ſo of the evenynge ād mornynge
was made the fourth daye.
20 And God ſayd, let the water bryng forth creatures
that move & have lyfe, & foules for to flee over the
21 erth vnder the fyrmament of heaven. And God created
greate whalles and all maner of creatures that lyve
and moue, which the waters brought forth in their
kindes, ād all maner of federed foules in their kyndes.
22 And [Fo. II] God ſawe that it was good: and God
bleſſed them ſaynge. Growe and multiplye ād fyll the

M. 14 lightes 22 ſayinge

V. 10 maria 12 habens vnumquodque ſementem 14 et diuidant diem ac noctem 16 vt præeſſet. nocti: & ſtellas. & poſuit 21 omne volatile 22 benedixitque eis

L. 10 Meere 12 vnd yhren eygen ſamen bey ſich ſelbs hatten 16 furſtunde 21 allerley geſidderts geuogel

M. M. N. 22 *Bleſſed*, here is bleſſynge takē for encreaſynge & multiplyenge.

waters of the fees, & let the foules multiplye vpō the
23 erth. And fo of the evenynge & morninge was made
the fyfth daye.

24 And God fayd: let the erth bring forth lyvynge
creatures in thir kyndes: catell & wormes & beaftes
25 of the erth in their kyndes, & fo it came to paffe. And
god made the beaftes of the erth in their kyndes, &
catell in their kyndes, ād all maner wormes of the erth
in their kyndes: and God fawe that it was good.

26 And God fayd: let vs make man in oure fymilitude
ād after oure lyckneffe: that he may have rule over
the fyfh of the fee, and over the foules of the ayre,
and over catell, and over all the erth, and over all
27 wormes that crepe on the erth. And God created man
after hys lyckneffe, after the lyckneffe of god created
he him: male & female created he them.

28 And God bleffed them, and God fayd vnto them.
Growe and multiplye and fyll the erth and fubdue it,
and have domynyon over the fyfh of the fee, and over
the foules of the ayre, and over all the beaftes that
move on the erth.

29 And God fayd: fe, I have geven yow all herbes that
fowe feed which are on all the erth, and all maner
trees that haue frute in them and fowe feed: to be
30 meate for yow & for all .P. beaftes of the erth, and
vnto all foules of the ayre, and vnto all that crepeth
on the erth where in is lyfe, that they may haue all
maner herbes and graffe for to eate, and even fo it
31 was. And God behelde all that he had made, ād loo
they were exceadynge good: and fo of the evenynge
and mornynge was made the fyxth daye

M. 26 domynion. fyfhes 29 fee. whyche. 31 fyxte.
V. 24 reptilia 25 omnique reptili 26 ad imaginem et fimilitudinem 29 Ecce. in efcam.
L. 24 gewurm 26 eyn bild das uns gleych sey 29 fehet da. zu ewr fpeyfe.
M. M. N. 26 *Lyckneffe of God*, that is after the fhape and ymage whyche was before appoynted for the fonne of God: The chefepart of man alfo, whyche is the foule is made lyke vnto God in a certen proporcyon of nature, of power workynge, fo that in that we are made lyke vnto God.

The Seconde Chapter.

1 THUS was heavē & erth fynished
2 wyth all their apparell: ād ī ẏ
seuēth daye god ended hys
worke which he had made &
rested in ẏ seventh daye frō all his workes
3 which he had made. And God blessed ẏ
seventh daye, and sanctyfyed it, for in it
he rested from all his workes which he
had created and made.
4 ¶ These are the generations of heaven
& erth when they were created, in the
tyme when the LORde God created heaven
and erth and all the shrubbes of the felde
5 be fore they were in the erthe. And all
the herbes of the felde before they sprange:
for the LORde God had yet sent no rayne
vpon the erth, nether was there yet any
6 man to tylle the erth. But there arose a
myste out of the ground and watered all the face of
7 the erth: Then the LORde God shope
man, even of the moulde of the erth and
brethed into his face the breth of lyfe. So man was
made a lyvynge soule.
8 ¶ The LORde God also planted a garden in Eden
from the begynnynge, and there he sette [Fo. III.] man
9 whom he had formed. And the LORde God made to
sprynge out of the erth, all maner trees bewtyfull to

𝔐.𝔆.𝔖. *The Chapter that went before is here repeted agayne: the halowing of the Saboth daye: the foure floudes of paradyse: The settynge in of man in paradyse: the tree of knowledge is forbydden hym: how Adam named all creatures: the creacyon of Eua: the institutyon of maryage.*

apparell, *the heavenly bodies*

shope, *created*

moulde, *earth*

𝔙. 1 perfecti 5 non enim pluerat dominus deus 6 sed fons ascendebat e terra 7 de limo terræ, & inspirauit in faciem eius 8 paradisum voluptatis a principio

𝔏. 4 Gepurt 7 vnd blies ynn seyn angesicht eyn lebendigen odem, vnd also wart der mensch eyn lebendige seele. 8 Eden, gegen dem morgen

𝔐. 𝔐. 𝔑. 1 *apparell*, The apparell of heauē is the sterres and planettes, etc., 3 *blessed*, Blesse here is taken for magnifyenge and praysynge, as it is in Ps. xxxiii, a. *sanctyfyed*, Sanctifyēg in this place is as moche to saye as to dedicate & ordayne a thing to his awne use as Ex. xiii, a and .xx, b. 7 *moulde*, Slyme: dust or claye.

the ſyghte and pleaſant to eate, and the tree of lyfe
in the middes of the garden: and alſo the tree of
knowledge of good and euell.
10 ¶ And there ſpronge a rever out of Eden to water the
garden, and thence devided it ſelfe, and grewe in to
11 foure principall waters. The name of the one is Phiſon,
he it is that compaſſeth all the lande of heuila, where
12 gold groweth. And the gold of that contre ys precious,
13 there is found bedellion and a ſtone called Onix. The
name of the ſeconde ryver is Gihon, which compaſſyth
14 all the lande of Inde. And the name of the thyrde
river is Hidekell, which runneth on the eaſte ſyde of
the aſſyryans. And the fourth river is Euphrates.
15 ¶ And the LORde God toke Adam and put him in
16 the garden of Eden, to dreſſe it and to kepe it: and
the LORde God cõmaunded Adã ſaynge: of all the
17 trees of the gardẽ ſe thou eate. But of the tre of
knowlege of good and badd ſe that thou eate not:
for even ỹ ſame daye thou eateſt of it, thou ſhalt
ſurely dye.
18 ¶ And the LORde God ſayd: it is not good that
man ſhulde be alone, I will make hym an helper to
19 beare him company: And after ỹ the LORde God had
make of the erth all maner beaſtes of the felde, and all
maner foules of the ayre, he brought them vnto Adam
to ſee what .P. he wold call them. And as Adã called
all maner livynge beaſtes: evẽ ſo are their names.
20 And Adam gave names vnto all maner catell, and
vnto the foules of the ayre, and vnto all maner beaſtes

M. 10 ſprange 16 ſayinge 17 dye the dethe. 19 made

V. 13 omnem terram Æthiopiæ 14 Tigris 17 morte morîeris. 18 faciamus

L. 10 es gieng aus . . . teylet ſich daſelbs ynn vier hewbtwaſſer 12 koſtlich 17 wirſtu des tods ſterben.

M.M.N. 10 *Eden;* Eden ſygnifieth pleaſures 17 *dye the dethe;* Soche reherſalls of wordes dothe ſygnifye ſomtyme an haſtynes or vehemẽce, ſomtyme an aſſewrance that the thinge ſhalbe performed that is promyſed, as it is Ps. cxvii, c.

L.M.N. 11 *Piſon* iſt das groſſe waſſer ynn India, das man Ganges heyſt, denn *Heuila* iſt Indienland, *Gihon* iſt das waſſer ynn Egypten das man Nilus heyſt, *Hydekel* iſt das waſſer in Aſſyria das man Tygris heyſt. *Phrato* aber iſt das nehiſt waſſer ynn Syria das man Euphrates heyſt.

of the felde. But there was no helpe founde vnto Adam
to beare him companye
21 Then the LORde God caſt a ſlomber on Adam, and
he ſlepte. And then he toke out one of his rybbes,
and in ſtede ther of he fylled vp the place with fleſh.
22 And the LORde God made of the rybbe which he toke
out of Adam, a womā and brought her vnto Adam.
23 Then ſayd Adā this is once bone of my
boones, and fleſh of my fleſh. This ſhall
be called woman: becauſe ſhe was take of the man.
24 For this cauſe ſhall a man leve father and mother &
25 cleve vnto his wyfe, & they ſhall be one fleſh. And
they were ether of them naked, both Adam and hys
wyfe, ād were not aſhamed:

once, *now* (*a Saxon idiom*).

The .III. Chapter.

1 BUT the ſerpent was ſotyller than
all the beaſtes of the felde
which ỳ LORde God had
made, and ſayd vnto the woman. Ah ſyr, that God hath ſayd, ye
ſhall not eate of all maner trees in the
2 garden. And the woman ſayd vnto the
ſerpent, of the frute of the trees in the gar-
3 den we may eate, but of the frute of the
tree ỳ is in the myddes of the garden
(ſayd God) ſe that ye eate not, and ſe that ye touch
it not: leſt ye dye.
4 [Fo. IIII.] Then ſayd the ſerpent vnto the woman:
5 tuſh ye ſhall not dye: But God doth knowe, that
whenſoever ye ſhulde eate of it, youre eyes ſhuld be

M. C. S. *The ſerpent deceaueth the woman. The ſerpēt the woman & the man are curſed, and dryuen out of Paradiſe. Chriſt oure ſauyour is promyſed.*

Ah ſyr, *ah ſurely*

M. 1 ye, hath God ſayd in dede
V. 1 callidior. Cur præcepit 4 nequaquam morte moriemini.
L. 21 ein tieffen ſchlaff fallen 23 das were eynmal beyn iii. 1 Ja, ſollt Gott geſagt haben 4 yhr werdet mit nicht des tods ſterben 5 ſo werden ewer augen wacker

opened and ye ſhulde be as, God and knowe both good
6 and evell. And the woman ſawe that it was a good
tree to eate of and luſtie unto the eyes and
a pleaſant tre for to make wyſe. And
toke of the frute of it and ate, and gaue vnto hir huſ-
7 band alſo with her, and he ate. And the eyes of both
of them were opened, that they vnderſtode how that
they were naked. Than they ſowed fygge leves togedder and made them apurns.

luſtie, *affording pleaſure*

8 And they herd the voyce of the LORde God as
he walked in the gardē in the coole of the daye.
And Adam hyd hymſelfe and his wyfe alſo from the
face of the LORde God, amonge the trees of the
9 garden. And the LORde God called Adam and ſayd
10 vnto him where art thou? And he anſwered. Thy
voyce I harde in the garden, but I was afrayd becauſe
11 I was naked, and therſore hyd myſelfe. And he ſayd:
who told the that thou waſt naked? haſt thou eaten
of the tree, of which I bade the that thou ſhuldeſt not
12 eate? And Adam anſwered. The woman which thou
gaveſt to bere me company ſhe toke me of the tree, ād
13 I ate. And the LORde God ſayd vnto the woman:
wherfore dideſt thou ſo? And the woman anſwered,
the ſerpent deceaved me and I ate.
14 ¶ .P. And the LORde God ſayd vnto the ſerpēt
becauſe thou haſte ſo done moſte curſed be thou of
all catell and of all beaſtes of the feld: vppō thy
bely ſhalt thou goo: and erth ſhalt thou eate all dayes
15 of thy lyfe. Morover I will put hatred betwene the
and the woman, and betwene thy ſeed and hyr ſeed.

M. 6 for to geue vnderſtondynge
V. 8 ad auram poſt meridiem
L. 7 wurden yhr beyder augen wacker
M. M. N. 6 *eyes ſhuide be opened*, To haue their eyes opened is to knowe or vnderſtonde 8 *from the face*, That is from hys preſence

L M. N. 8 *Adam verſteckt*, Adam heyſt auff Ebreiſch, Menſch, darumb mag man menſch ſagen, wo Adam ſteht vnd widderumb. *tag kuele war*, Das war vmb den abent, wenn die hitze vergangen iſt, bedeut, das nach gethaner ſund, das gewiſſen angſt leydet, bis das Gottis gnedige ſtym kome vnd wider kule vn erquicke das hertz, wie wol ſich auch die blode natur entſetzt vnd fleucht fur dem Euangelio, weyl es das creutz vnd ſterben leret.

And that ſeed ſhall tread the on the heed, ād thou
ſhalt tread hit on the hele.
16 And vnto the woman he ſayd: I will ſuerly encreaſe
thy ſorow ād make the oft with child, and with payne
ſhalt thou be deleverd: And thy luſtes ſhall pertayne
vnto thy huſbond and he ſhall rule the.
17 And vnto Adā he ſayd: for as moch as thou haſt
obeyed the voyce of thy wyfe, and haſt eaten of the
tree of which I commaunded the ſaynge: ſe thou eate
not therof: curſed be the erth for thy ſake. In ſorow
18 ſhalt thou eate therof all dayes of thy life, And
it ſhall beare thornes ād thyſtels vnto the. And thou
19 ſhalt eate the herbes of ÿ feld: In the ſwete of thy
face ſhalt thou eate brede, vntill thou returne vnto the
erth whēce thou waſt takē: for erth thou art, ād vnto
erth ſhalt thou returne.
20 And Adam called his wyfe Heua, becauſe ſhe was
21 the mother of all that lyveth And the LORde God
made Adam and hys wyfe garmentes of ſkynnes, and
22 put them on them. And the LORde God ſayd: loo,
Adam is become as it were one of vs, in knowlege of
good and evell. But now leſt he ſtrech forth his hand
[Fo. V.] and take alſo of the tree of lyfe and eate and
lyve ever.
23 And the LORde God caſt him out of the garden of
24 Eden, to tylle the erth whēce he was taken. And he

M. 15 treade it on the hele

V. 15 ipſa conteret 16 erūnas tuas—in dolore paries filios, & ſub viri poteſtate eris & ipſe dominabitur tui 17 maledicta terra in opere tuo 19 puluis. puluerem

L. 15 ynn die verſen beyſſen

M. M. N. 15 *on thy heed,* The heed of the ſerpent ſygnifyeth the power and tyranny of the deuell whych Chriſt the ſeede of the womā ouercame. The hele is Chriſtes māhod which was tēpted wyth oure ſynnes. 22 *Loo.* Here thys worde *lo* is taken as a mocke as it is in iii Regu. xviii, c.

L. M. X. 15 *Derſelb,* Dis iſt das erſt Euangelion vnd verheyſſung von Chriſto geſchehen auff erden, Das er ſolt, ſund, tod vnd helle vber winden, vnd vns von der ſchlangē gewalt ſelig machen. Daran Adam glawbt mit allen ſeynen nach komē, dauon er Chriſten vnd ſelig worden iſt von ſeynem fall. 20 *Heua,* Hai heyſt lebē, Daher kompt Heua oder Haua, Leben oder lebendige.

cast Adā out, and sette at ẏ enteringe of the garden Eden, Cherubin with a naked swerde movinge in and out, to kepe the way to the tree of lyfe.

swerd, *sword*

The .IIII. Chapter.

.M.C.S. Cayn kylleth hys ryghteous brother Abell. Cayn dispayreth & is cursed. The generacyō of Enoch, Mathusael, Tuball, Lamech, Seth and Enos.

1 AND Adam lay wyth Heua ys
wyfe, which conceaved and
bare Cain, and sayd: I haue
gotten a mā of the LORde.
2 And she proceded forth and bare hys
brother Abell: And Abell became a
sheperde, and Cain became a ploweman.
3 And it fortuned in processe of tyme,
that Cain brought of the frute of the erth:
4 an offerynge vnto the LORde. And Abell, he brought
also of the fyrstlynges of hys shepe and of the fatt of
them. And the LORde loked vnto Abell and to his
5 offrynge: but vnto Cain and vnto hys offrynge,
looked he not. And Cain was wroth exceadingly,
6 and loured. And the LORde sayd vnto
Cain: why art thou angry, and why
7 lourește thou? Wotest thou not yf thou
dost well thou shalt receave it? But & yf thou dost
evell, by & by thy synne lyeth open in the dore. Not
withston-.¶.dyng let it be subdued vnto the, ād see thou
8 rule it. And Cain talked with Abell his brother.

loured, lourest, *looked sullen*

V. 24 flammeum gladium atque versatilem. iiii. 5 et concidit vultus eius 8 Dixitque Cain ad Abel fratrē suū, Egrediamur foras

L. 24 vnd eyn glentzendes fewrigs schwerd. iiii. 1 ich hab vberkomen den man des Herren

M.M.X. 4 *loked vnto Abell*, The Lorde looked vnto Abel & to hys offerynge: that is he was pleased with Abell & his offeringe, but with Cayn nor his offering was he not pleased: & therfore he saith that he loked not therto, the same vse of spekynge is also in the .ii. of kynges in the .xvi. Chapter.c. Ps. xxx. b.

L.M.N. 1 *vberkomen*, Kain heyst, das man kriegt odder vberkompt, Heua aber meynet, er solt der same seyn, da der herr vō gesagt hatte, das er der schlangen kopff zutretten wurde.

And as ſoone as they were in the feldes, Cain fell
9 vppon Abell his brother and ſlewe hym. And ỷ LORde
ſayd vnto Cain: where is Abell thy brother? And he
10 ſayd: I cannot tell, am I my brothers keper? And
he ſayd: What haſt thou done? the voyce of thy
11 brothers bloud cryeth vnto me out of the erth. And
now curſed be thou as pertaynyng to the erth, which
opened hyr mouth to receaue thy brothers bloud of
12 thyne hande. For when thou tylleſt the grounde ſhe
ſhall hẽceforth not geve hyr power vnto
the. A vagabunde and a rennagate ſhalt
thou be vpon the erth.

rennagate, *renegade, i. e. wanderer, fugitive.*

13 And Cain ſayd vnto the LORde: my ſynne is greater,
14 than that it may be forgeven. Beholde thou caſteſt
me out thys day from of the face of the erth, and frõ thy
ſyghte muſt I hyde myſelfe ãd I muſt be wandrynge
and a vagabunde vpon the erth: Morover whoſoever
15 fyndeth me, wyll kyll me. And the LORde ſayd vnto
hĩ Not so, but who ſo ever ſleyth Cain ſhalbe punyſhed
vii. folde. And the LORde put * a marke
vpõ Cain that no mã ỷ founde hym ſhulde
16 kyll hym. [Fo. VI.] And Cain went out
frõ the face of the LORde and dwelt in
the lande Nod, on the eaſt ſyde of Eden.
17 And Cain laye wyth hys wyfe, which
conceaved and bare Henoch. And he
was buyldinge a cyte and called the
the name of it after the name of hys
18 ſonne, Henoch. And Henoch begat Irad.
And Irad begat Mahuiael. And Mahuiael
begat Mathuſael. And Mathuſael begat
Lamech.
19 And Lamech toke hym two wyves,

** Of this place no doute ỷ pope which in all thinges maketh hĩſelf equal with god, toke an occaſion to marke all his creatures: and to forbid vnder payne of excõmunicatiõ ỷ no mã (whether he were kĩge or emperoure) be ſo hardy to puniſhe them for what ſo ever*

M. 10 bloud cryed vnto me

V. 13 quam ut ueniam merear 16 habitauit profugus in terra ad orientalem plagam Eden

L. 12 Soll'er dyr fort ſeyn vermugen nicht geben 16 jenſyd Eden gegen den morgen.

M. M. N. 10 *cryed*, Cryeth: that is aſketh vengeaunce, as ye haue Geneſis xix. c.

the one was called Ada, and the other
20 Zilla. And Ada bare Iabal, of whome
came they that dwell in tentes ād possesse
21 catell. And hys brothers name was Iubal:
of hym came all that exercyse them selves
22 on the harpe and on the organs. And
Zilla she also bare Tubalcain a worker in
metall and a father of all that grave in brasse and
yeron. And Tubalcains syster was called Naema.
23 Then sayd Lamech vnto hys wyves Ada ād Zilla:
heare my voyce ye wyves of Lamech and herken vnto
my wordes, for I haue slayne a man and wounded my
selfe, and have slayn a yongman, and gotte my selfe
24 strypes: .P. For Cain shall be avenged
sevenfolde: but Lamech seventie tymes sevenfolde.
25 ¶ Adam also laye with hys wyfe yet agayne, and
she bare a sonne ād called hys name Seth for god
(sayd she) hath geven me a nother sonne for Abell
26 whom Cain slewe. And Seth begat a sonne and called
hys name Enos. And in that tyme began men to call
on the name of the LORde.

myschef they doo. The crowne is to thē a licence to do what they liste a protectiō & a sure sentuarye. =sentuary, *protection*

strypes, *wounds*

The .V. Chapter.

1 THYS is the boke of the generacion of man, In the daye
when God created man and
made hym after the symilytude of god.
2 Male and female made he thē and called their names
3 man, in the daye when they were created. And when
Adam was an hundred and thirty yere old, he begat a
sonne after his lycknesse and symilytude: and called

M. C. S. *The genealogye of Adam vnto Noe.*

V. 21 cithara & organo 25 semen aliud 26 Enos. iste cœpit inuocare nomen domini .v, 1 Adam. hominem

M. M. N. 26 *To call on the name of the Lorde* is to requyer all thynges of hym and to trust in him, geuing hym the honour and worshyp that belongeth to hym, as in Gen. xii b.

4 hys name Seth. And the dayes of Adam after he
begat Seth, were eyght hundred yere, and begat
5 ſonnes and doughters, and all the dayes of Adam
which he lyved, were .ix. hundred and .xxx. yere,
and then he dyed.

6 And Seth lyved an hundred and .v. yeres, and
7 begat Enos. And after he had begot Enos he lyved
viii. hundred and .vii. yere, and begat ſonnes and
8 doughters. And all the dayes of Seth were .ix. hundred and .xii. yeres and dyed.

9 And Enos lyved .Lxxxx. yere and begat [Fo. VII.]
10 kenan. And Enos after he begat kenan, lyved .viii
hundred and .xv. yere, and begat ſonnes and dough-
11 ters: and all the dayes of Enos were .ix. hundred and
v. yere, and than he dyed.

12 And kenan lyved .Lxx. yere and begat Mahalaliel.
13 And kenan after he had begot Mahalaliel, lyved .viii
hundred and .xl. yere and begat ſonnes and doughters:
14 and al the dayes of kenan were .ix. hundred and .x
yere, and than he dyed.

15 And Mahalaliel lyued .Lxv. yere, and begat Iared.
16 And Mahalaliel after he had begot Iared lyved .viii
hundred and .xxx. yere and begat ſonnes and dough-
17 ters: and all the dayes of Mahalalyell were .viii. hun-
18 dred nynetye and .v. yeare, and than he dyed And
Iared lyved an hundred and .Lxii. yere and begat He-
19 noch: and Iared lyved after he begat Henoch, .viii
20 hundred yere and begat ſonnes and doughters. And
all the dayes of Iared were .ix. hundred and .Lxii
yere, and than he dyed.

21 And Henoch lyved .Lxv. yere ād begat Mathuſala.
22 And Henoch walked wyth god after he had begot
Mathuſalah .iii. hundred yere, and begat ſonnes and
23 doughters. And all the dayes of Henoch were .iii
24 hundred and .Lxv. yere. and than Henoch lyved a

M. 4 daughters
V. 9 Enos nonaginta annis 22 Et ambulauit Enoch cū deo
M. M. N. 22 *And Henoch walked with God,* To walke wyth God, is to do hys will & leade a lyfe accordynge to hys worde.

godly lyſe, and was no more ſene, for God toke him
away.
25 And Mathuſala lyved an hundred and .Lxxxvii
26 yere and begat Lamech: and Mathuſala .P. after he
had begot Lamech, lyved .vii. hundred and .Lxxxii
27 yere: ãd begat ſonnes and doughters. And all the
dayes of Methuſala were .ix. hundred .Lxix. yere,
and than he dyed.
28 And Lamech lyved an hundred .Lxxxii. yere and
29 begat a ſonne and called hym Noe sayng. This
ſame ſhall comforte vs: as concernynge oure worke and
ſorowe of oure handes which we haue aboute the erthe
30 that the LORde hath curſed. And Lamech lyved
after he had begot Noe .v. hundred, nynetie and .v
31 yere, and begat ſonnes and doughters. And all the
dayes of Lamech were .vii. hundred .Lxxvii. yere,
32 and than he dyed. And when Noe was .v. hundred
yere olde, he begat Sem, Ham and Iaphet.

ℭ The .VI. Chapter.

1 AND it came to paſſe whã men
begã to multiplye apõ the erth
ãd had begot them doughters,
2 the ſonnes of God ſawe the
doughters of men that they were fayre,
and toke vnto them wyves, which they
3 beſt liked amõge thẽ all. And the LORd ſayd: My
ſpirite ſhall not all waye ſtryve withe man, for they are

M. C. S. *The cause of the floude. God warneth Noe of the cõmyng of the floud: The preparing of the arcke.*

V. 24 ambulavitque cũ deo, & nõ apparuit: quia tulit eũ deus.
vi. 3 non permanebit ſpiritus meus in homine

L. 2 Kinder Gottis

M. M. N. 2 *The ſonnes of God* are the ſonnes of Seth which had inſtruct & noriſhed thẽ in the feare of God. The ſonnes of men are the ſonnes of Cayn inſtruct of him to all wyckednes.

L. M. N. 2 *kinder Gottis,* Das waren der heyligen vetter kinder, Die ynn Gottiſſurcht auferzogen, darnach erger, den die ander worden, vnter dem namen Gottis, wie altzeyt die geyſtlichen, die ergiſten tyrannen vnd verkeritiſten zu letzt worden ſind.

fleſh. Nevertheles I wyll geue them yet ſpace, and
hundred and .xx. yeres
4 There were tirantes in the world in thos dayes.
For after that the children of God had gone in vnto
the doughters of men and had begotten them childern,
the ſame childern were the mightieſt of the world and
men of renowne. [Fo. VIII. miſplaced in the original]
5 And whan the LORde ſawe ẏ the wekedneſſe of man
was encreaſed apon the erth, and that all the ym-
aginacion and toughtes of his hert was
6 only evell continually, he repented that
he had made man apon the erth and
7 ſorowed in his hert. And ſayd: I wyll deſtroy mankynde which I haue made, frō of the face of the erth:
both man, beaſt, worme and foule of the ayre, for it
8 repēteth me that I haue made them. But yet Noe
found grace in the ſyghte of the LORde.
9 Theſe are the generatiōs of Noe. Noe was a
righteous man and vncorrupte in his tyme, &
10 walked wyth god. And Noe begat .iii. ſonnes: Sem,
11 Ham and Iapheth. And the erth was corrupte in the
12 ſyghte of god, and was full of miſchefe. And God
loked vpon the erth, ād loo it was corrupte: for all
fleſh had corrupte his way vppon the erth.
13 Than ſayd God to Noe: the end of all fleſh is come
before me, for the erth is full of there myſchefe. And
14 loo, I wyll deſtroy them with the erth. Make the
an arcke of pyne tree, and make chaumbers in the
arcke, and pytch it wythin and wythout wyth pytch.
15 And of this facion ſhalt thou make it.
The lenth of the arcke ſhall be .iii. hundred cubytes,
ād the bredth of it .L. cubytes, and the heyth of it
16 xxx. cubytes. A wyndow ſhalt thou make aboue in

toughtes, *ſhould be*, *thoughtes*

M. 5 thoughtes

V. 4 gigantes autem 9 Noe vir iuſtus atque perfectus fuit 14 arca de lignis leuigatis

L. 4 tyrannen 12 alles fleyſch hatte ſeyn weg verterbet auff erden 14 thennen holtz

M.M.N. 12 *All fleſh.* All fleſſhe that is all men that lyue fleſhly, as in the .viii. of the Roma. 13 *The ende of all fleſh.* The ende of all fleſſhe: that is, the ende of all men is come before me.

the arcke. And wythin a cubyte compaſſe ſhalt thou
finyſh it. .¶. And the dore of the arcke ſhalt thou ſette
in ỹ ſyde of it: and thou ſhalt make it with .iii. loftes
17 one aboue an other. For behold I will bringe in a
floud of water apon the erth to deſtroy all fleſh from
vnder heaven, wherin breth of life is ſo that all that
18 is in the erth ſhall periſh. But I will make myne
apoyntement with the, that both thou
ſhalt come in to ỹ arcke and thy ſonnes,
thy wyfe and thy ſonnes wyves with the.

apoyntement, *covenant*

19 And of all that lyveth what ſoever fleſh it be,
ſhalt thou brynge in to the arcke, of every thynge
a payre, to kepe them a lyve wyth the. And male
20 and female ſe that they be, of byrdes in their kynde,
and of beaſtes in their kynde, and of all maner of
wormes of the erth in their kinde: a payre of every
thinge ſhall come vnto the to kepe them a lyve.
21 And take vnto the of all maner of meate ỹ may be
eaten & laye it vp in ſtoore by the, that it may be
22 meate both for ỹ and for thē: and Noe dyd acordynge
to all that God commaunded hym.

The .VII. Chapter.

1 AND the LORde ſayd vnto Noe:
goo into the arcke both thou
and all thy houſſold. For the
haue I ſene rightuous before
2 me in thys generacion. Of all clene beaſtes

M. C. S. *The entraunce of Noe & them that were with him into the arcke. The ryſynge*

M. 16 aboue a nother

V. 18 ponamque fœdus meũ tecum 20 ut poſſint viuere vii. 1 dominus ad eum

L. 18 bund auffrichten .vii. 1 rechtfertig erſehen fur myr zu diſer zeit

M. M. N. 1 *For the haue I ſene ryghteous*, They are ryghteous before God that loue their neybours for gods ſake, vnſaynedly: hauynge the ſpirite of god whych maketh thē the ſonnes of God & therfore are accepted of God as iuſt and ryghteous as it is in Gen. xviii. c. 2 *and of clene beaſtes*, cleane beaſtes is ſoche as they myght lefully eate, and the vncleane are thoſe that they might not eate, as it apereth in Leuit. ii. a & Deut. xiiii.

take vnto the .vii. of every kynde the male
and hys female [Fo. IX.] And of vnclene
beaſtes a payre, the male and hys female:
3 lykewyſe of the byrdes of the ayre .vii. of every kynde,
4 male and female to ſave ſeed vppon all the erth. For
vii. days hence wyll I ſend rayne vppō the erth .XL
dayes. & .XL. nyghtes and wyll dyſtroy all maner of
thynges that I haue made, from of the face of the
erth.

of the floude wherwith all thynges dyd peryſhe.

5 And Noe dyd acordynge to all ẏ the lorde cō-
6 maunded hym: and Noe was .vi. hundred yere olde, when
7 the floud of water came vppon the erth: and Noe went
and his ſonnes and his wyfe and his ſonnes wyves wyth
8 hym, in to the arke from the waters of the floud. And
of clene beaſtes and of beaſtes that ware vnclene and
9 of byrdes and of all that crepeth vppō the erth, came
in by cooples of every kynde vnto Noe in to the arke:
a male and a female: even as God commaunded Noe.
10 And the ſeventh daye the waters of the floud came
vppon the erth.

11 In the .vi. hundred yere of Noes lyfe, in the ſecōde
moneth, in the .xvii. daye of the moneth, ẏ ſame daye
were all the founteynes of the grete depe broken vp,
12 & the wyndowes of heavē were opened, ād there fell
a rayne vpon the erth .XL. dayes and .XL. nyghtes.

13 And the ſelfe ſame daye went Noe, Sem, Ham and
Iapheth, Noes ſonnes, and Noes wyfe and the .iii. wyves
14 of his ſonnes wyth them in to the arke: both they and
all maner of beaſtes in their kīde, & all maner of
catell in their kynde & all maner of wormes that crepe
vppon .P. the erth in their kynde, and all maner of
byrdes in there kynde. and all maner off foules what

V. 11 omnes fontes abyſſi magnæ & cataractæ cæli 13 In articulo diei illius

L. 11 da auff brachen alle brunne der groſſen tieffen, vnd theten ſich auff die fenſter des hymels

M. M. N. 11 *Founteynes*, The fountaynes of the great depe etc. that is, all the waters that were on the erth ſprāge vp, encreaſed & multyplyed. *Wyndowes of heaven*, The wyndowes of heuē opened &c. that is, all waters aboue the erth deſcended and increaſed the floude.

15 ſoever had feders. And they came vnto Noe in to the
arke by cooples, of all fleſh ỷ had breth of lyfe in it.
16 And they that came, came male ād female of every
fleſh accordīge as God cōmaunded hym: & ỷ LORde
ſhytt the dore vppō him
17 And the floud came .XL. dayes & .XL. nyghtes
vppon the erth, & the water increaſed and bare vp
18 the arcke ād it was lifte up from of the erth And
the water prevayled and increaſed exceadingly vppon
the erth: and the arke went vppō the toppe of the
waters.
19 And the waters prevayled excedingly above meſure
vppō the erth, ſo that all the hye hylles which are vnder
20 all the partes of heaven, were covered: evē .xv. cubytes
hye prevayled the waters, ſo that the hylles were
covered.
21 And all fleſhe that moved on the erth, bothe birdes
catell and beaſtes periſſhed, with al that crepte on the
22 erth and all men: ſo that all that had the breth of liffe
in the noſtrels of it thorow out all that was on drye
lond dyed.
23 Thus was deſtroyed all that was vppō the erth, both
man, beaſtes, wormes and foules of the ayre: ſo that
they were deſtroyed from the erth: ſave Noe was
reſerved only and they that were wyth hym in the
24 arke. And the waters prevayled vppon the erth, an
hundred and fyſtye dayes.

L. 22 Alles was eyn lebendigen oden hatte ym trocken, das ſtarb.

The .VIII. Chapter.

The .VIII. Chapter. [Fo. X.]

1 AND god remēbred Noe & all ŷ
beaſtes & all ŷ catell ŷ were
with hī in ŷ arke And god
made a wynde to blow vppō
2 ŷ erth, & ŷ waters ceaſed: ād ŷ fountaynes
of the depe ād the wyndowes of heavē
were ſtopte and the rayne of heaven was
3 forbiddē, and the waters returned from of
ŷ erth ād abated after the ende of an hundred and .L
dayes.

M.C.S. After the ſendyng forth of the rauē & the doue Noe went forth of the arcke. He offreth ſacrifice. The malyce of mannes heart.

4 And the arke reſted vppō the mountayns of Ararat,
5 the .xvii. daye of the .vii. moneth. And the waters
went away ād decreaſed vntyll the .x. moneth. And
the fyrſt daye of the tenth moneth, the toppes of the
mounteyns appered.

6 And after the ende of .XL. dayes. Noe opened the
7 wyndow of the arke which he had made, ād ſent forth
a raven, which went out, ever goinge and cominge
agayne, vntyll the waters were dreyed vpp vppon the
erth

8 Then ſent he forth a doue from hym,
to wete whether the waters were fallen
9 from of the erth. And when the doue coude fynde
no reſtinge place for hyr fote, ſhe returned to him
agayne vnto the arke, for the waters were vppon the
face of all the erth. And he put out hys honde and
toke her and pulled hyr to hym in to the arke

wete, *know*

10 And he abode yet .vii. dayes mo, and ſent out the
11 doue agayne out of the arke, And the doue came to
hym agayne aboute eventyde, and beholde: There

M. 10 more

V. 1 adduxit ſpiritum ſuper terram 2 & prohibitæ ſunt 4 viceſimoſeptimo die—montes Armeniæ 7 et non reuertebatur

L. 1 waſſer fielen 2 ward gewehret

L. M. V. 7 *vnd kam widder*, Das iſt, er machts ſo lange mit ſeym widder komen bis das alles trocken wart, das iſt ſo viel geſagt, Er ſoll noch widder komē.

was in hyr mouth a lefe of an olyve tre which ſhe had
plucked .P. wherby Noe perceaved that the waters were
12 abated vppon the erth. And he taried yet .vii. other
dayes, and ſent forth the doue, which from thence
forth came no more agayne to him.
13 And it came to paſſe, the ſyxte hundred and one
yere and the fyrſt daye of the fyrſt moneth, that the
waters were dryed vpp apon the erth. And Noe toke
off the hatches of the arke and loked: And beholde,
14 the face of the erth was drye. So by the .xxvii. daye
of the ſeconde moneth the erth was drye.
15, 16 And God ſpake vnto Noe ſaynge: come out of
the arcke, both thou and thy wyfe ād thy ſonnes and
17 thy ſonnes wyues with the. And all the beaſtes that
are with the whatſoever fleſh it be, both foule and catell
and all manner wormes that crepe on the erth, brynge
out with the, and let them moue, growe ād multiplye
18 vppon the erth. And Noe came out, ād his ſonnes
19 and his wyfe and his ſonnes wyues with hym. And all
the beaſtes, and all the wormes, and all the foules,
and all that moved vppon the erth, came alſo out of
the arke, all of one kynde together.
20 And Noe made an aulter vnto the LORDE, and
toke of all maner of clene beaſtes and all maner of
clene foules, and offred ſacrifyce vppon the aulter.
21 And the LORDE ſmellyd a ſwete ſavoure and ſayd in
his hert: I wyll henceforth no more curſe the erth for
mannes ſake, for the imagynacion of mannes hert is
[Fo. XI.] evell even from the very youth of hym.
Moreouer I wyll not deſtroy from henceforth all that
22 lyveth as I haue done. Nether ſhall ſowynge tyme
and harveſt, colde, and hete, ſomere & wynter, daye
and nyghte ceaſſe, as longe as the erth endureth.

F. 11 ramum oliuæ virentibus foliis 20 Ædificauit . . obtulit holocauſta

L. 11 eyn oleblat 13 Ym ſechs hunderſten und eynem iar 19 eyn iglichs zu ſeyns gleychen 20 bawet . . brandopfter 21 hinfurt nicht mehr ſchlahen

M. M. N. 21 The Lordes ſmellynge of ſauoure: is the alowāce of the workes of the faythfull, as in Ex. xxix. Lev. i. iii. iv.

L. M. N. 11 *oleblat;* Das Blat bedeut das Euangelion, dz der heylig geyſt ynn die Chriſtenheyt hat predigen laſſen, Denn ole bedeutt barmherzickeyt vnnd fride, dauon das Evangelion leret

ℭ The .IX. Chapter.

1 AND God blessed Noe and his
sonnes, and sayd vnto them:
Increase and multiplye and fyll
the erth.
2 The feare also and drede of yow be
vppon all beasts of the erth, and vppon
all foules of the ayre, ād vppon all that
crepeth on the erth, and vppon all fyshes
of the see, which are geuen vnto youre
3 handes And all that moveth vppon the
erth havynge lyfe, shall be youre meate:
Euen as ẙ grene herbes, so geue I yow
4 all thynge. Only the flesh with his life
which is his bloud, se that ye eate not.
5 * For verely the bloude
of yow wherein youre lyves
are wyll I requyre. Euē of
the hande of all beastes wyll
I require it, And of the hande
of man and of the hand off
euery mannes brother, wyll I requyre the
6 lyfe of man: so ẙ he which shedeth mannes
bloude, shall haue hys bloud shed by man
agayne: for God made man after hys awne
7 lycknesse. See that ye encrease, and waxe,
and be occupyde vppon the erth, & multiplye therein.
8 Farthermore God spake vnto Noe &
9 to hys sonnes with hym sayinge: see,

M.C.S. God blesseth Noe and hys sonnes. He forbyddeth to eate the bloude of beastes and forbyddeth the sheding of mānes bloude. The lawe of the swerde. He maketh a couenaunt that he wyll destroye the world no more by water, and geueth the raynebowe as a token & confirmacyon of the same. Noe is droncken, and Ham vncouereth hym, and getteth his curse.

** This lawe and soch like to exequute, were kinges and rulars ordeyned of God wherfore they ought not to suffre the popes Caimes thus to shede bloud theirs not shed ageyne, nether yet to sett vpp their abhominable setuaryes & necke verses cleane agenste the ordinaunce of*

V. 5 Sanguinem enim animarum vestrarum 7 et ingredimini
L. 2 vnd alle fisch ym meer seyen ynn ewer hend geben
4 Alleyne . . darynn die seele ist 8 vnd reget euch auff erden
M. M. N. 5 *the bloude of you;* Here is all cruelnes forbydden mā: so that he will not let it be vnauēged in bestes, moche lesse in oure neybour.
L. M. N. 6 *durch menschen;* Hie ist das welltlich schwerd eyngesetzt, das man die morder todten sal.

god, but vntō their dāna-cyon.

I make my bōd .P. wyth you
10 and youre ſeed after you, and
wyth all lyvynge thinge that is wyth you:
both foule and catell, and all maner beſte of the erth
that is wyth yow, of all that commeth out of the arke
what ſoeuer beſte of the erth it be.

bond, *covenant*

11 I make my bonde wyth yow, that henceforth all
fleſh ſhall not be deſtroyed wyth ẏ waters of any floud,
ād ẏ henceforth there ſhall not be a floud to deſtroy
the erth.
12 And God ſayd. This is the token of my bōde
which I make betwene me and yow, ād betwene all
13 lyvynge thyng that is with yow for ever: I wyll ſette
my bowe in the cloudes, and it ſhall be a ſygne of
the appoyntment made betwene me and
14 the erth: So that when I brynge in cloudes
vpō ẏ erth, the bowe ſhall appere in ẏ cloudes.

appoyntment *covenant*

15 And than wyll I thynke vppon my
teſtament which I haue made betwene
me and yow, and all that lyveth what ſoeuer fleſh it
be. So that henceforth there ſhall be no more waters
to make a floud to deſtroy all fleſh.

teſtament, *covenant*

16 The bowe ſhalbe in the cloudes, and I wyll loke
vpon it, to remembre the euerlaſtynge teſtament betwene God and all that lyveth vppon the erth, what
17 ſoeuer fleſh it be. And God ſayd vnto Noe: This is
the ſygne of the teſtament which I have made betwene
me and all fleſh ẏ is on the erth.
18 The ſonnes of Noe that came out of the arcke were:
Sem, Ham, and Iapheth. And Ham [Fo. XII.] he is
19 the father of Canaā. Theſe are the .iii. ſonnes of Noe,
and of theſe was all the world overſpred.
20 And Noe beynge an huſbād man, went furth and

M. 10 all maner beſtes 20 forth

V. 9 Statuam pactum meum 12 hoc eſt ſignum fœderis 14 nubibus cælum 15 anima viuente quæ carnem vegetat 20 cœpitque Noe

L. 9 Sihe ich richte mit euch eyn bund auff 14 ſoll das zeychen ſeyn meyns bunds—wolken vber die erden fure 16 Darumb ſoll meyn bogen . . . allem lebendigen thier ynn allem fleyſch, das auff erden iſt 19 alle land beſetzt 20 Noah aber fieng an

21 planted a vyneyarde and drancke of the wyne and was
droncke, and laye vncouered in the myddeſt of his
22 tēt. And Ham the father of Canaan ſawe his fathers
prevytees, & tolde his .ii. brethren that were wythout.
23 And Sem and Iapheth toke a mantell and put it on
both there ſhulders ād went backward, ād covered there
fathers ſecrets, but there faces were backward So
24 that they ſawe not there fathers nakydnes. As ſoone
as Noe was awaked frō his wyne and wyſt what his
25 yongeſt ſonne had done vnto hym, he ſayd: curſed be
Canaan, ād a ſeruante of all ſeruantes be he to his
26 brethren. An he ſayd: Bleſſed be the LORde God of
27 Sē, and Canaan be his ſeruante. God increaſe Iapheth
that he may dwelle in the tentes of Sem. And Canaan
be their ſeruante.

28 And Noe lyved after the floude .iii. hundred and .L
29 yere: So that all the dayes of Noe were .IX. hundred
and .L. yere, ād than he dyed.

The .X. Chapter.

M.C.S. *The genealogye of Iaphet, Sem and Ham.*

1 THESE are the generations of
the ſonnes of Noe: of Sem,
Ham and Iapheth, which be-
2 gat them children after the floude. .P. The
ſonnes of Iapheth were: Gomyr, Magog, Madai, Iauan,
3 Tuball, Meſech and Thyras. And the ſonnes of Gomyr
4 were: Aſcenas Riphat and Togarma. And the ſonnes

M. 21 wus 23 their

M. M. N. 27 *God increaſe;* To encreaſe, that is: to reioyſe or to be in peace & of good comfort, as it is in Gen. xxvi. c & Ps. iiii. a.

L. M. N. 22 *Vatters ſcham,* Dis geſchicht deuten viel dahyn man ſolle der prælatō laſter nit ſtraffen wilchs doch Chriſtus vnd alle Apoſtel thatten, Aber deute du es recht, das Noe ſey Chriſtus vnd alle glewbigen, die trunkenheyt ſey die lieb vnd glawbe ym heyligen geyſt die bloſſe ſey das creutz vnd leyden fur der wellt Ham ſey, die falſchen werck beylegen vnd gleyſſener, die Chriſtum vnd die ſeynen verſpotten vnd luſt haben ynn yhrem leyden. Sem vnd Iaphet ſeyen die fromen Chriſten die ſolch leyden preyſen vn ehren.

of Iauan were: Elisa, Tharsis, Cithim, and Dodanim.
5 Of these came the Iles of the gentylls in there contres,
every man in his speach, kynred and nation.
6 The sonnes of Ham were: Chus Misraim Phut and
7 Canaan. The sonnes of Chus: were Seba, Heuila,
Sabta, Rayma and Sabtema. And the sones of Rayma
8 were: Sheba, & Dedan. Chus also begot Nemrod,
9 which begã to be myghtye in the erth. He was a
myghtie hunter in the syghte of the LORde: Where
of came the proverbe: he is as Nemrod that myghtie
10 hunter in the syghte of the LORde. And the begynnynge of hys kyngdome was Babell, Erech, Achad
11 and Chalne in the lande of Synear: Out of that lande
came Assur and buylded Ninyue, and the cyte reho
12 both, and Calah. And Ressen betwene Ninyue ãd
13 Chalah That is a grete cyte. And Mizraim begat
14 ludim, Enanum, Leabim, Naphtuhim, Pathrusim &
Casluhim: from whence came the Philystyns, and the
Capththerynes.
15 Canaan also begat zidon his eldest sonne & Heth,
16, 17, 18 Iebusi, Emori, Girgosi, Hiui, Arki, Sini, Aruadi,
Zemari and hamati. And afterward sprange the
19 kynreds of the Canaanytes And the costes of the
Canaanytes were frõ Sy- [Fo. XIII.] don tyll thou come
to Gerera & to Asa, & tyll thou come to Sodoma,
20 Gomorra, Adama Zeboim: evẽ vnto Lasa. These were
the chyldrẽ of Ham in there kynreddes, tonges, landes
and nations.
21 And Sem the father of all ẏ childrẽ of Eber and the
22 eldest brother of Iapheth, begat children also. And
his sonnes were: Elam Assur, Arphachsad, Lud ãd
23 Aram. And ẏ children of Aram were: Vz, Hul,
24 Gether & Mas And Arphachsad begat Sala, and
25 Sala begat Eber. And Eber begat. ii. sonnes. The

M. 13 Mizrim 18 Harmati

L. 5 secundum linguam suam & familias in nationibus suis. 11 Niniuen, & plateas ciuitatis 18 per hos disseminati sunt populi chananæorum 20 filii cham in cognationibus (cf. v 31.)

V. 5 sprach geschlecht vnd leuten 11 Niniue vnd der stat gassen 18 daher sind aufgebreyt

name of the one was Peleg, for in his tyme the erth
was devyded. And the name of his brother was
Iaketan.
26 Iaketan begat Almodad, Saleph, Hyzarmoneth,
27, 28 Iarah, Hadoram, Vſal, Dikela, Obal, Abimael, Seba,
29 Ophir, Heuila & Iobab. All theſe are the ſonnes of
30 Iaketan. And the dwellynge of them was from Meſa
vntill thou come vnto Sephara a mountayne of the
31 eaſte lande. Theſe are the ſonnes of Sem in their
kynreddes, languages, contrees and nations.
32 Theſe are the kynreddes of the ſonnes of Noe,
in their generations and nations. And of theſe
came the people that were in the world after the
floude.

¶ The .XI. Chapter.

1 AND all the world was of one
2 tonge and one language. And
as they came from the eaſt,
they founde a play-.P.ne in the
lande of Synear, and there they dwelled.
3 And they ſayd one to a nother: come on,
let us make brycke ād burne it wyth fyre.
So brycke was there ſtone and ſlyme was
4 there morter And they ſayd: Come on,
let vs buylde us a cyte and a toure, that the toppe
may reach vnto heauen. And let vs make us a name,
for perauenture we ſhall be scatered abrode over all
the erth.

M.C.S. *The buylding of the tower of Babel. The confuſyon of tonges. The generacyon of Sem the ſonne of Noe vntyll Abrā which goeth with Lot vnto Haran.*

V. 30 Sephar montem orientalem 32 Hæ familiæ Noe. xv. 1 ſermonum eorundem 4 antequam diuidamur in vniuerſas terras

L. 30 gen Sephara, an den berg gegen dem morgen. xi. 2 eyn plan ym land Sinear 4 denn wyr werden villeicht zurſtrewet ynn alle lender

L. M. N. 25 *Peleg;* auff deutſch, Eyn zuteylung.

5 And the LORde came downe to see the cyte and
the toure which the childern of Adã had buylded.
6 And the LORde ſayd: See, the people is one and haue
one tonge amonge them all. And thys haue they
begon to do, and wyll not leaue of from all that they
7 haue purpoſed to do. Come on, let vs deſcende and
myngell theire tonge even there, that one vnderſtonde
8 not what a nother ſayeth. Thus ŷ LORde ſkatered
them from thence vppon all the erth. And they left
9 of to buylde the cyte. Wherfore the name of it is
called Babell, becauſe that the LORDE there con-
founded the tonge of all the world. And becauſe that
the LORde from thence, ſkatered them abrode vppon
all the erth.

10 Theſe are the generations of Sem: Sẽ was an hundred yere olde and begat Arphachſad .ii. yere after the
11 floude. And Sẽ lyved after he had begot Arphachſad
v. hundred yere and begat ſonnes and doughters

12 And Arphachſad lyued .xxxv. yere and be- [Fo.
13 XIIII.] gat Sala, and lyved after he had begot Sala .iiii
hũdred yere & .iii. & begat ſonnes and doughters.
14 And Sala was .xxx. yere old and begat Eber,
15 ãd lyved after he had begot Eber .iiii. hũdred and
thre yere, ãd begat ſonnes and doughters.

16 When Eber was .xxxiiii. yere olde, he begat Peleg,
17 and lyued after he had begot Peleg, foure hundred
and .xxx. yere, and begat ſonnes and doughters.

18 And Peleg when he was .xxx. yere olde begat

V. 7 vnusquiſque vocem proximi ſui

L. 7 daſelbs verwyrren

M. M. N. 5 *came downe;* God is counted to come downe, whẽ he dothe any thing in the erthe amõge men that is not accustomed to be done: in maner ſhewynge hymſelfe preſent amonge men by his wonderfull worke, as it is in Ps. xvii. b. and .cxliii. a. *To ſe the cyte;* not that god ſeeth not at all tymes, but only that he maketh hym ſelfe both to be ſene and knowen in his wonderfull workes amõge vs. 12 *Arphachſad;* Here the ſeuentie Interpreters leaue oute the generacion of Caynan, the which after the reconynge of the Ebrues begat Sala, when he was .xxx. yere of age. Luke .iii. g.

L. M. N. 9 *Babel;* auff deutſch Eyn vermiſſchung oder verwyrrung

19 Regu, and lyued after he had begot Regu .ii. hundred
and .ix. yere, and begat ſonnes and doughters.
20 And Regu when he had lyued .xxxii. yere begat
21 Serug, and lyued after he had begot Serug .ii. hundred
and .vii. yere, and begat ſonnes and doughters.
22 And when Serug was .xxx. yere olde, he begat
23 Nahor, and lyued after he had begot Nahor .ii. hundred
yere, and begat ſonnes & doughters.
24 And Nahor when he was .xxix. yere olde, begat
25 Terah, and lyved after he had begot Terah, an hundred and .xix. yere, .¶. and begat ſonnes and doughters.
26 And when Terah was .Lxx. yere olde, he begat
Abram, Nahor and Haran.
27 And theſe are the generations of Terah. Terah
begat Abram, Nahor and Haran. And Haran begat
28 Lot. And Haran dyed before Terah his father in the
29 londe where he was borne, at Vr in Chaldea. And
Abram and Nahor toke them wyves. Abrās wyfe was
called Sarai. And Nahors wyfe Mylca the doughter
30 of Haran which was father of Milca ād of Iiſca. But
Sarai was baren and had no childe.
31 Then toke Terah Abram his ſonne and Lot his
ſonne Harans ſonne, & Sarai his doughter in lawe his
ſone Abrams wyfe. And they went wyth hym from
Vr in Chaldea, to go in to the lāde of Chanaan. And
32 they came to Haran and dwelled there. And when Terah was .ii. hundred yere old and .v. he dyed in Haran.

¶ The .XII. Chapter.

1 THEN the LORde ſayd vnto Abrā Gett the out of thy contre and from thy kynred, and out of thy fathers houſe, into a londe which I wyll ſhewe the.

M.C.S. Abram is bleſſed of God, and goeth with Lot into a ſtraunge lande that apered

M. 29 Ieſca.

to hym in Canaan. And God promyſeth to geue the ſame lande to hym and to his ſede. And afterwarde goeth Abram into Egypt & cauſeth Sarai his wyfe to ſaye that ſhe is his ſiſter. And ſhe was rauyſſhed of Pharao, for whyche the Lorde plageth hym.

2 And I wyll make of the a myghtie people, and wyll bleſſe the, and make thy
name grete, that thou mayſt be a bleſſ-
3 inge. And I wyll bleſſe thē that bleſſe
the, ād curſe thē that curſe the. And
in the ſhall be bleſſed all the generations
of the erth.
4 And Abram wēt as the LORde badd
hym, [Fo. XV.] and Lot went wyth him.
Abram was .Lxxv. yere olde, when he
5 went out of Haran. And Abram toke
Sarai his wyfe ād Lot his brothers ſonne,
wyth all their goodes which they had
goten and ſoulles which they had be-
goten in Haran. And they departed to goo in to
the lāde of Chanaan. And when they were come in
6 to the lande of Chanaan, Abram went furth in to
the lāde tyll he came vnto a place called Sychem,
and vnto the oke of More. And the Canaanytes
dwelled then in the lande.
7 Then the LORde apeared vnto Abram ād ſayd:
vnto thy ſeed wyll I geue thys lāde. And he buylded
an aultere there vnto the LORDE which apeared to
8 hym. Then departed he thence vnto a mountayne
that lyeth on the eaſt ſyde of BETHEL and pytched
hys tente: BETHEL beynge on the weſt ſyde, and
Ay on the eaſt: And he buylded there an aulter vnto
the LORde & called on the name of yͤ LORde.
9 And than Abram departed and toke his iourney
ſouthwarde
10 After thys there came a derth in the lande. And
Abram went doune in to Egipte to ſoiourne there, for

M. 6 forth
V. 6 pertranſiuit . . Sichem, & vſque ad conuallem illuſtrem 10 fames
L. 6 Zoch er durch . . an den hayn More 10 eyn tewere zeyt
M. M. N. 2 *Bleſſe the;* To bleſſe, is here to be made happye and fortunate. And to make great his name, is to aduaunce and extolle hym and aboue other people. 5 *Soules;* Soules here are taken for his ſeruauntes and maydens, which were very many as ye maye ſe in Gen. xiv, c.

11 the derth was ſore in the lande. And when he was
come nye for to entre in to Egipte, he ſayd vnto
Sarai his wife. Beholde, I knowe that thou art a
12 fayre woman to loke apō. It wyll come to paſſe
therfore whē the Egiptians ſee the, that they wyll
ſay: ſhe is his wyfe. And ſo ſhall they ſley me and
13 ſave the. .P. Saye I praye the therfore that thou art
my ſiſter, that I maye fare the better by reaſon of the
and that my ſoule maye lyue for thy ſake.

14 As ſoon as he came in to Egipte, the Egiptiās ſawe
15 the woman that ſhe was very fayre. And Pharaos
lordes ſawe hir alſo, and prayſed hir vnto Pharao: So
16 that ſhe was taken in to Pharaos houſe, which entreated Abram well for hir ſake, ſo that he had ſhepe,
oxſen ād he aſſes, men ſeruantes, mayde ſeruātes, ſhe
aſſes and camels.

17 But God plaged Pharao and his houſe wyth grete
18 plages, becauſe of Sarai Abrams wyfe. Then Pharao
called Abram and ſayd: why haſt thou thus dealt with
me? Wherfore toldeſt thou me not that ſhe was thy
19 wife? Why ſaydeſt thou that ſhe was thy ſiſter, and
cauſedeſt me to take hyr to my wyfe? But now loo,
20 there is the wife, take hir ād be walkynge. Pharao
alſo gaue a charge vnto his men over Abram, to leade
hym out, wyth his wyfe and all that he had.

M. 19 there is thy wyfe

V. 12 et te reſeruabunt 15 principes Pharaoni 16 Abram vero bene vſi ſunt 17 Flagellauit autem dominus 19 vt tollerem eam mihi in uxorem

L. 12 vnd dich behalten 14 das ſie faſt ſchon war 15 und die furſten des Pharao 17 Aber der Herr 19 derhalben ich ſie myr zum weybe nam

The .XIII. Chapter.

M.C.S. Abram & Loth departe oute of Egypt. And Abram deuyded his lande & catell with his brother Lot. Here agayne is promysed to Abram the lande of Canaan.

1 THAN Abram departed out of
Egipte, both he and his wyfe
and all that he had, and Lot
wyth hym vnto the [Fo. XVI.]
2 ſouth. Abram was very rich in catell,
3 ſyluer & gold. And he went on his iourney frō the ſouth even vnto BETHEL,
ād vnto the place where his tente was at
the fyrſt tyme betwene BETHEL and
4 Ay, and vnto the place of the aulter
which he made before. And there called Abram vpon
the name of the LORde.

5 Lot alſo which went wyth him had ſhepe, catell
6 and tentes: ſo that the londe was not abill to receaue
them that they myght dwell to gether, for the ſubſtance of their riches was ſo greate, that they coude
7 not dwell to gether And there fell a ſtryfe betwene
the herdmen of Abrams catell, and the herdmen of
Lots catell. Moreouer the Cananytes and the Phery-
ſites dwelled at that tyme in the lande.

8 Than ſayd Abram vnto Lot: let there be no ſtryfe
I praye the betwene the and me and betwene my
9 herdmen and thyne, for we be brethren. Ys not all
the hole lande before the? Departe I praye the frō
me. Yf thou wylt take the lefte hande, I wyll take
the right: Or yf thou take the right hande I wyll take
10 the left. And Lot lyſt vp his eyes and beheld all the
contre aboute Iordane, which was a plenteous contre
of water every where, before the LORde deſtroyed
Sodoma and Gomorra. .P. Even as the garden of the

M. 3 to the place
V. 1 Aſcendit . . . auſtralem plagam 3 Reuerſuſque 4 quod feceret prius 6 habitarent ſimul . . communiter
L. 7 vnd war ymer zank
M. M. N. 8 *brethren;* The Hebrues vnderſtonde by this worde brother al nevews, coſſyns & neyboures, & all that be of one ſtocke. Rom. ix, a; Ino. vii, a.

LORde, & as the lande of Egipte tyll thou come to
Zoar.
11 Than Lot chofe all the coftes of Iordane ād toke
hys iourney from the eaft. And fo departed the one
brother from the other.
12 Abram dwelled in the lande of Canaan. And lot
in the cytes of the playne, & tented tyll he came to
13 Sodome. But the men of fodome were wyked and
fynned exceadyngly agenft the LORde.
14 And the LORde fayed vnto Abram, after that Lot
was departed from hym: lyfte vp thyne eyes & loke
from ŷ place where thou art, northward, fouthward,
15 eaftward and weftward, for all the lande which thou
feifte wyll I gyue vnto the & to thy feed for ever.
16 And I wyll make thy feed, as the duft of the erth;
fo that yf a mā can nombre the duft of the erth, than
17 fhall thy feed alfo be nombred. Aryfe and walke
aboute in the lande, in the length of it ād in the
bredth for I wyll geue it vnto the.
18 Than Abrā toke downe hys tente, & went and
dwelled in the okegrove of Mamre which is in Ebron
and buylded there an altar to the LORde.

The .XIIII. Chapter.

1 AND it chaunfed within a while,
that Amraphel kynge of Synear, Arioch kynge of Ellafar,
Kedorlaomer kynge of Elam
2 and Thydeall kynge of the nations: made
warre wyth Bera kynge of Sodōe and

M.C.S. *Lot is taken pryfoner. The victory of Abrā of the Sodomytes. Lot is delyuered by Abram.*

M. 1 Kedorlaomor cf. vv. 4. 9
V. 18 iuxta conuallem
L. 14 heb deyn augen auff
M. M. X. 15 *for ever;* Euer is not here taken for tyme wythoute ende; but for a longe ceafon that hath not his ende apoynted. 18 *Ebron* is the name of a citie where Adam Abraham and his wyfe with Ifaac etc. were buryed, as in Gen. xxiii, d.

with Birſa kynge of Gomorra. And wyt-
[Fo. XVII.] he Sineab kynge of Adama,
& with Semeaber kynge of Zeboim, and
wyth the kynge of Bela Which Bela is
3 called Zoar. All theſe came together
vnto the vale of ſiddim which is now the
4 ſalt ſee Twelve yere were they ſubiecte
to kinge kedorlaomer, and in the .xiii
yere rebelled.

5 Therefore in the .xiiii. yere came kedorlaomer and
the kynges that were wyth hym, and ſmote the
Raphayms in Aſtarath Karnaim, and the Suſims in
6 Ham, ād the Emyms in Sabe Kariathaim, and the
Horyms in their awne mounte Seir vnto the playne
7 of Pharan, which bordreth vpon the wylderneſſe. And
then turned they and came to the well of iugmente
which is Cades, and ſmote all the contre of the Amalechites, and alſo the amorytes that dwell in Hazezon
Thamar.

8 Than went out the kynge of Sodome, and the
kynge of Gomorra, and the kynge of Adama and the
kynge of Zeboijm, and the kynge of Bela now called
Zoar. And sette their men in aray to fyghte wyth
9 them in the vale of ſiddim, that is to ſay, wyth
kedorlaomer the kynge of Elam and with Thydeall
kynge of the Nations, and wyth Amraphel kynge of
Synear. And with Arioch kynge of Ellaſar: foure
10 kynges agenſte v. And that vale of ſiddim was full of
ſlyme pyttes.

And the kynges of Sodome and Gomorra fled,
and fell there. And the reſydue fled to the moun-
11 taynes. And they toke all the goodes .⁋. of Sodome and Gomorra and all their vitalles, ād went

Melchiſedech offreth gyftes vnto Abram. Abram payeth tythes vnto Melchiſedech. Abram holdeth nothynge of the kynge of Sodomes goodes.

M. 2 Semeabar

V. 3 conuenerunt in vallem ſylueſtrem 6 campeſtria Pharan quæ eſt in ſolitudine

L. 3 das breytte tall cf. vv. 8, 10 5 die Ryſen zu Aſtaroth 6 bis an die breyte Pharan, wilch an die wuſten ſtoſt 7 an den Rechtborn

M. M. T. 2 *kynge of Bela;* Bela is the citie that Lot deſyred for his refuge when he came oute of Sodome as in Gen. xix, c. 5 *Raphaim*, are counted in the ſcripture for gyauntes as in .ii Reg. v, b. Es. xvii. which lyued by theft and robberye.

12 their waye. And they toke Lot alſo Abrams brothers
ſonne and his good (for he dwelled at Sodome) and
departed.
13 Than came one that had eſcaped, and tolde Abram
the hebrue which dwelt in the okegrove of Mamre the
Amoryte brother of Eſchol and Aner: which were
14 confederate wyth Abram. When Abram herde that
his brother was taken, he harneſſed his harneſſed,
ſeruantes borne in his owne houſe .iii *armed*
hundred & .xviii. ād folowed tyll they came at Dan.
15 And ſette hymſelfe ād his ſeruantes in aray, & fell
vpon them by nyght, & ſmote them, & chaſed them
awaye vnto Hoba: which lyeth on the lefte hande of
16 Damaſcos, and broughte agayne all the goodes & alſo
his brother Lot, ād his goodes, the wemē alſo and
the people.
17 And as he retourned agayne from the ſlaughter of
kedorlaomer and of the kynges that were with hym,
than came the kynge of Sodome agaynſt hym vnto
the vale of Saue whīch now is called kynges dale.
18 Than Melchiſedech kinge of Salem brought forth
breed and wyne. And he beynge the preſt of the
19 moſt hygheſt God, bleſſed hym ſaynge. Bleſſed be
Abram vnto the moſt hygheſt God, poſſeſſor of heaven
20 and erth. And bleſſed be God the moſt hygheſt,
which hath delyvered thyne enimies in to thy handes.
And Abrā gaue hym tythes of all.
21 [Fo. XVIII.] Than ſayd the kynge of Sodome vnto

M. 13 Abram the Hebrew 16 women alſo 17 returned . . Sodome to mete him in the vale of Saue 18 Preſte.

V. 15 Et diuiſis ſociis, irruet ſuper eos nocte: 17 a cæde Chodorlaomor 18 proferens panem et vinum 20 quo protegente

L 12 und ſeyn habe 13 dem Auſländer 15 vnd teylet ſich 17 von der ſchlacht des Kedorlaomor 18 trug brot vnd weyn erfur

M. M. N. 18 *Melchiſedech;* The Jewes ſuppoſed Mechiſedek to be Sem the ſonne of Noe becauſe he lyued after the floude .v hūdred yere, & after the death of Abraham (by godes prouidence) was kynge of Salem 19 *Bleſſed* be Abram, that is prayſed be Abrā. And prayſed be the mooſt hygheſt God as it is in Genes. xlvii, b.

L. M. N. 18 *Trug brod;* Nicht das ers opferte, ſondern das er die geſte ſpeyſet vnd ehret da durch Chriſtus bedeut iſt, der die wellt mit dem Euangelio ſpeyſet.

Abram: gyue me the ſoulles, and take the goodes
22 to thy ſelfe. And Abram anſwered the Kynge of
Sodome: I lyſte vpp my hande vnto the LORde God
23 moſt hygh poſſeſſor of heaven ād erth, that I will not
take of all ỳ is thyne, ſo moch as a thred or a
ſhoulachet, leſt thou ſhuldeſt ſaye I haue made Abrā
24 ryche. Saue only that which the yonge men haue
eaten ād the partes of the men which went wyth me.
Aner, Eſcholl & Mamre. Let them take their partes.

XV. Chapter.

1 AFTER theſe deades, ỳ worde of
God came vnto Abram in a
viſion ſaynge feare not Abram,
I am thy ſhilde, and thy re-
2 warde ſhalbe exceadynge greate. And
Abram anſwered: LORde Iehouah what
wilt thou geue me: I goo childleſſe, and
the cater of myne houſſe, this Eleaſar
3 of Damaſco hath a ſonne. And Abram
ſayd: ſe, to me haſt thou geven no ſeed:
lo, a lad borne in my houſſe ſhal be myne
heyre.
4 And beholde, the worde of the LORde
ſpake vnto Abram ſayenge: He ſhall not
be thyne heyre, but one that ſhall come out of thyne
5 awne bodye ſhalbe thyne heyre. .P. And he brought
him out at the doores ād ſayde. Loke vpp vnto

M.C.S. *The lande of Canaan is yet agayne promyſed to Abram. God promyſeth hym ſeed. He beleueth & is iuſtifyed. The prophecye of the bondage wherin the chyldren of Iſrael ſhuld be vnder Pharao, & of their delyuerance from the ſame.*

M. 1 ſaying 5 out of the dores

V. 21 animas 22 poſſeſſorem. xv, 2 filius procuratoris domus meæ

L. 21 die ſeelen 22 beſitzt. xv, 1 ſchilt 2 Herr Herr cf. v. 8. 4 der von deynem leyb komen wirt

M. M. N. 21 *Gyue me the ſoules;* Soules are men & women, as Gen. xlvi, c & Deut. x, b. xv, 1 *The worde of God;* The word of the Lorde cometh when he ſheweth any thynge vnto vs by reuelacyon as it is vſed in diuers places of the Scripture, and ſpecially in the Prophetes & is a maner of ſpeache of the Hebrewes.

heaven and tell the ſtarres, yf thou be able to nōbre
them. And ſayde vnto him Even ſo ſhall thy ſeed be.
6 And Abram beleved the LORde, and it was counted
7 to hym for rightweſnes. And he ſayde vnto hym: I
am the LORde that brought the out of Vr in Chaldea
to geue the this lande to poſſeſſe it.

8 And he ſayde: LORde God, whereby ſhall I knowe
9 that I ſhall poſſeſſe it? And he ſayd vnto him: take
an heyfer of .iii. yere olde, and a ſhe gotte of thre yeres
olde, and a thre yere olde ram, a turtill doue and a
10 yonge pigeon. And he toke all theſe and devyded
them in the myddes, and layde euery pece, one over
11 agenſt a nother. But the foules devyded he not. And
the byrdes fell on the carcaſes, but Abrā droue thē
12 awaye. And when the ſonne was doune, there fell
a ſlomber apon Abram. And loo, feare and greate
darkneſſe came apon hym.

13 And he ſayde vnto Abram: knowe this of a ſuertie,
that thi ſeed ſhalbe a ſtraunger in a lande that perteyneth
not vnto thē. And they ſhall make bondmen of them
14 and entreate them evell .iiii. hundred yeares. But the
nation whom they ſhall ſerue, wyll I iudge. And
afterwarde ſhall they come out wyth greate ſubſtāce.
15 Neuertheleſſe thou ſhalt goo vnto thi fathers in peace,
16 ād ſhalt be buried when thou art of a good age: ād in
the fourth generation they ſhall come hyther [Fo.

M. 10 pece, one agaynſt another 12 vpon- vpon

V. 10 diuiſit ea per medium 12 horror magnus & tenebroſus inuaſit eum 13 Scito praenoſcens

L. 5 zele die ſterne . . kanſtu ſic zelen 10 zuteylet es mitten von ander 11 das gevogel fiel 12 ſchrecken vnd groſſe finſternifs

M. M.X. 6 *And Abram beleued;* To beleue is to haue a ſure truſt & confydence to obtayne the thing promyſed and not to haue any doute in hym that promyſeth as Rom. iiii, a, Gal. iii, a .ii, d. 14 *ſerue wyll I iudge;* To iudge is here to take vēgeaunce, Ps. xxxiiii, a. 16 *Fourth generation*, a generacyō or an age is here taken for an hundred yere, as Gen. vi, d.

L. M. X. 11 *Gevogel fiel;* Das gevogel vnd der rauchend offen vnd der feuriger brand, bedeuten die Egypter, die Abrahams Kinder verfolgen ſollten Aber Abraham ſcheucht ſie davon, das iſt, Got erloſet ſie vmb der verheyſſung willen Abraham verſprochen, Das aber er nach der ſonnen vntergang erſchrickt, bedeut, das Got ſeyn Samen eyn zeyt verlaſſen wollt, das ſie verfolget wurden, wie der herr ſelbs hie deut. Alſo gehet es auch allen glewbigen, das ſie verlaſſen vnd doch erloſet werden.

XIX.] agayne, for the wekedneſſe of the Amorites ys
not yet full.
17 When the ſonne was doune and it was waxed darcke:
beholde, there was a ſmokynge furneſſe and a fyre brand
that went betwene the ſayde peces.
18 And that ſame daye the LORde made a covenaunte
with Abram ſaynge: vnto thy ſeed wyll I geue thys
londe, frõ the ryver of Egypte, even vnto the greate
19 ryver euphrates: the kenytes, the kenizites, the Cad-
20 monites, the Hethites, the Pherezites, the Raphaims,
21 the Amorytes, the Canaanites, the Gergeſites and the
Iebuſites.

The .XVI. Chapter.

1 SARAI Abrams wyfe bare him
no childerne. But ſhe had an
hand mayde an Egiptian, whoſe
2 name was Hagar. Wherfore
ſhe ſayde vnto Abram. Beholde the
LORde hath cloſed me, that I cannot
bere. I praye thee goo in vnto my mayde,
peraduẽture I ſhall be multiplyed by
meanes of her. And Abram herde the
voyce of Sarai.
3 Than Sarai Abrams wife toke Hagar
hyr mayde the Egiptian (after Abram had
dwelled .x. yere in the lande of Canaan)

M.C.S. *Sarai geueth Abram leaue to take Agar hyr mayde to wyfe. Agar deſpyſed hyr mayſtres: for which ſhe was euyll intreated of Sarai, and therfore runneth awaye. The angell metynge hyr commaundeth hyr to turne agayne and doth*

M. 1 chyldren 3 Hagar

V. 17 & lampas ignis xvi, 2 concluſit 3 ancillam ſuam poſt annos decem quam habitare cœperant

L. 17 und eyn fewriger brand. xvi, 2 verſchloſſen . . Lieber leg dich . . aus yhr mich bawen muge mehr denn aus mir 3 nachdem ſie—gewonet hatten

M.M.N. 17 *That went betwene:* This worde went betwene: is taken for burning or conſumynge. xvi, 2 To go in vnto hyr mayde is to haue carnall copulacion with hyr as theſe wordes knowe & ſlepe do alſo ſignifye as Gen. iiii. a and .xxix. c.

and gaue her to hyr huſbonde Abram, to
be his wyfe.
4 And he wente in vnto Hagar, & ſhe
conceaved. And when ſhe ſawe that ſhe

promyſe hyr ſede. And nameth hyr fyrſt chylde Iſmael.

had conceyved .P. hyr maſtreſſe was deſpiſed in hyr
ſyghte.
5 Than ſayd Sarai vnto Abram: Thou doſt
me vnrighte, for I haue geuen my mayde

vnrighte, *wrong*

in to thy boſome: & now becauſe ſhe ſeyth that ſhe hath
cõceaved, I am deſpyſed in her ſyghte: the LORde iudge
6 betwene the and me. Than ſayd Abrã to Sarai: beholde,
thy mayde is in thy hande, do with hyr as it pleaſeth the.
And becauſe Sarai fared foule with her, ſhe fled from
7 her. And the angell of the Lorde founde her beſyde
a fountayne of water in the wyldernes: euen by a well
8 in the way to Sur. And he ſayde: Hagar Sarais
mayde, whence comeſt thou and whether wylt thou
goo? And ſhe anſwered: I flee from my maſtreſſe
9 Sarai. And the angell of the LORde ſayde vnto
her: returne to thy maſtreſſe agayne, & ſubmytte thy
ſelfe vnder her handes.
10 And the angell of ỷ LORde ſayde vnto her: I will
ſo encreaſe thy ſeed, that it ſhall not be numbred for
11 multitude. And the LORdes angell ſayd further
vnto her: ſe, thou art wyth childe and ſhalt bere a
ſonne, and ſhalt call his name Iſmael: becauſe the
12 LORDE hath herde thy tribulation. He will be a
wylde man, and his hande will be agenſt
every man, & euery mans hande agenſt

wylde, *not domeſticated*

him. And yet ſhall he dwell faſte by all his brothren.
13 [Fo. XX.] And ſhe called the name of the LORde
that ſpake vnto her: thou art the God that lokeſt

M. 4 Agar 5 ſeeth 12 brethren

V. 9 humiliare ſub manu illius. 12 ferus homo . . et eregione vniverſorum fratrum ſuorum figet tabernacula.

L. 5 ich muſs vnrecht leyden . . vnter deyner gewallt 6 Da ſie nu Sarai wolt demutigen 9 vnd demutige dich 11 armſelickeyt 12 ein wilder Menſch.

M. M. N. 5 *Boſome:* Boſome after the maner of the Hebrewes is taken for companyeng wyth a woman, & is alſo takẽ for fayth as in Luc. xvi. f. of Lazarus.

L. M. N. 11 Iſmael, heyſt Gott erhoret.

on me, ſor ſhe ſayde: I haue of a ſuertie ſene here
14 the backe parties of him that ſeith me. Wherfore
ſhe called the well, the well of the lyuynge that ſeith
me which well is betwene Cades & Bared.
15 And Hagar bare Abram a ſonne, and Abram called
16 his ſons name which Hagar bare Iſmaell. And Abram
was .lxxxvi. yere olde, when Hagar bare him Iſmael.

¶ The .XVII. Chapter.

1 WHEN Abram was nynetye yere
old & .ix. the LORde apeared
to hym ſayenge: I am the
almyghtie God: walke before
2 me ād be vncorrupte. And I wyll make
my bonde betwene the and
me, and wyll multiplye the
excedyngly.

bonde, *covenant*

3 And Abrā fell on his face. And God
4 talked moreover with hym ſaynge: I am,
beholde my teſtamēt is with
the, that thou ſhalt be a fa-
5 ther of many natiōs. Therfore ſhalt thou no more be
called Abram, but thy name ſhalbe Abraham: for a
6 father of many nations haue I made the, and I will
multiplye the excedyngly, and wyll make nations of
the: yee and kynges ſhall ſprynge out of the.

teſtament, *covenant*

M.C.S. *Abram is called Abrahā, & Sarai is named Sara. The lande of Canaan is here the fourth tyme promyſed. Circumſyſion is here inſtitute. Iſaac is promyſed. Abraham prayeth for Iſmael.*

7 Moreover I will make my bonde betwene me and
the, and thy ſeed after the, in their tymes .P. to be an
everlaſtynge teſtament, So that I wyll be God vnto
8 the and to thy ſeed after the. And I will geue vnto

M. 13 partes

V. 13 poſteriora videntis me. xvii, 3 Cecidit Abram pronus in faciē.

L. 1 vnd ſey on wandel 2 faſt ſeer mehren 4 Sihe ich byns 6 faſt ſeer fruchtbar machen

M. M. N. 13 They ſe the backe partes of God that by reuelaciō or any other wyſe haue perſeuerāce or knowledge of God.

L. M. N. 5 *Abram* heyſt hoher vatter, *Abraham* aber der haufen vater, wie wol die ſelben hauffen nur mit eynen buchſtaben antzeygt werden yn ſeynem namen, nicht on vrſach.

the ād to thy ſeed after the, the lande where in thou
arte a ſtraunger: Euen all the lande of Canaan, for an
everlaſtynge poſſeſſion, and will be their God.
9 And God ſayde vnto Abrahā: Se thou kepe my
teſtamente, both thou & thy ſeed after the in their
10 tymes: This is my teſtamente which ye ſhall kepe
betwene me and you and thy ſeed after the, that ye
11 circūſyſe all youre men childern Ye ſhall circumcyſe
the foreſkynne of youre fleſh, ād it ſhal be a token of
12 the bond betwixte me and you. And euery manchilde when it is .viii. dayes olde, ſhall be circūſyſed
amonge you in youre generations, and all ſervauntes
alſo borne at home or boughte with money though they
13 be ſtraungers and not of thy ſeed. The ſeruaunte
borne in thy houſſe, ād he alſo that is bought with
money, muſt needes be circumcyſed, that my teſtament may be in youre fleſh, for an everlaſtinge bonde.
14 Yf there be any vncircuncyſed manchilde, that hath
not the forſkynne of his fleſh cutt of, his ſoule ſhall
periſh from his people: because he hath brokē my
teſtamēt
15 And God ſayde vnto Abraham. Sarai thy wyfe
ſhall nomore be called Sarai: but Sara ſhall hir name
16 be. For I will bleſſe her & geue the a ſonne of
her and will bleſſe her: ſo that people, ye and kynges
17 of people ſhall ſpringe of her. And Abraham fell vpon
his face ād [Fo. XXI.] laughte, and ſayde in his harte:
ſhall a childe be borne vnto hym that is an hundred
yere olde, ād ſhall Sara that is nynetie yere old, bere?
18 And Abrahā ſayde vnto God. O that Iſmaell myghte
lyve in thy ſyghte.
19 Thē ſayde God: na, Sara thy wife ſhall bere the a

M. 19 God: Sarah thy wife . . . a ſonne in dede

V. 8 terrā peregrinationis tuæ 14 pactum meum irritū fecit. 19 Sara vxor tua pariet tibi filium . . . & conſtituam pactum meum illi in fœdus ſempiternum

L. 19 ia, Sara deyn weyb ſoll dyr eynen ſon geperen

M. M. N. 13 *Bōde:* The ſcripture vſeth to call the ſigne of a thynge by the name of the thīge it ſelfe only to kepe the thynge ſygnifyed, the better in memory as here he calleth circumciſyon his bonde which is but a token therof, and as Peter calleth baptyme Chriſt. 1 Pet. iii d.

ſonne, ād thou ſhalt call his name Iſaac. And I will
make my bonde with him, that it ſhall be an ever-
20 laſtynge bonde vnto his ſeed after him. And as
concernynge Iſmaell alſo, I haue herde thy requeſt:
loo, I will bleſſe him and encreaſe him, and multiplye
him excedyngly. Twelve prynces ſhall he begete, and I
21 will make a great nation of him. But my bonde will
I make with Iſaac, which Sara ſhall bere vnto the:
euen this tyme twelue moneth.
22 And God left of talkyng with him, and departed vp
23 from Abraham. And Abraham toke Iſmaell his ſonne
& all the ſervauntes borne in his houſſe and all that
was bought with money as many as were men children
amonge the mē of Abrahās houſſe, and circumcyſed
the foreſkynne of their fleſh, even the ſelfe ſame daye,
24 as God had ſayde vnto him. Abraham was nynetie
yere olde and .ix. when he cutt of the foreſkynne of
25 his fleſh. And Iſmaell his ſonne was .xiii. yere olde,
when the foreſkynne of hys fleſh was circumcyſed.
26 The ſelfe ſame daye was Abrahā circūciſed & Iſmael
27 his ſonne. And all the men in his houſſe, whether
thy were borne in his houſſe or bought wyth .P. money
(though they were ſtraungers) were circumcyſed with
him.

¶ The .XVIII. Chapter.

1 AND the LORde apeared vnto him
in the okegrove of Mamre as
he ſat in his tent dore in the
2 heate of the daye. And he
lyfte vp his eyes and looked: ād lo, thre
men ſtode not farr from hym. And whē

M.C.S. There apered thre men vnto Abraham. Iſaac is promyſed to hym agayne, at whych Sara

T. 1 conualle
L. 1 hayn Mamre 2 drey menner gegen yhm
M. M. N. 1 *The heate of the daye* is taken for none.

he ſawe them, he ran agenſt them from
the tent dore, and fell to the grounde
3 and ſayde: LORde yf I haue founde
fauoure in thy ſyght, goo not by thi
4 ſeruaunte. Let a litle water be fett,
& waſh youre fete, and reſt youre ſelves
5 vnder the tree: And I will fett a morſell
of breed, to comforte youre harts wythall. And thā
goo youre wayes, for even therfore ar ye come to youre
ſeruaunte. And they anſwered: Do even ſo as thou
haſt ſayde.

laughed. The deſtruccion of the Sodomites is declared vnto Abraham. Abraham prayeth for them.

fett, *fetch*

6 And Abrahā went a pace in to his tent vnto Sara
ād ſayde: make redy att once thre peckes of fyne meale,
7 kneade it, and make cakes. And Abraham ran vnto
his beaſtes and fett a calfe that was tendre and good,
and gaue it vn to a yonge man which made it redy
8 attonce. And he toke butter & mylcke and the calfe
which he had prepared, and ſett it before them, and
ſtode hymſelfe by them vnder the tre: and they ate.
9 [Fo. XXII.] And they ſayde vnto him: Where is
10 Sara thy wife? And he ſayde: in the tent. And he
ſayde: I will come agayne vnto the as soone as the
frute can lyue. And loo: Sara thy wife
ſhall haue a ſonne. That herde Sara,
out of the tent doore which was behind
11 his backe. Abraham and Sara were both olde and
well ſtryken in age, and it ceaſed to be with Sara after
12 the maner as it is wyth wyves. And Sara
laughed in hir ſelfe ſaynge: Now I am waxed olde,
ſhall I geue my ſelfe to luſt, and my lorde olde alſo?

frute, *either the child, or the ſeaſon of the year.*

wyves, *women*

M. 2 ran to mete them

V. 2 cucurrit in occurſum eorum de oſtio . . et adorauit in terra 5 Ponamque buccellam panis 6 tria ſata ſimilæ . . ſubcinericios panes 7 vitulum tenerrimum & optimum 10 vita comite 12 voluptati operam dabo

L. 6 drey mas ſemel meel 8 vnd von dem kalbe 10 nach der zeyt die frucht leben kan 12 mit wolluſt vmbgehen

M. M. X. 5 *Brede:* By Brede in the ſcripture is vnderſtonde all maner of fode, mete for mānes eatynge as in 1 Regū. xxviii, d.

L. M. X. 2 *fur yhm nydder:* fur eynem fellt er nydder vnd redet auch als mit eynem vnd mit dreyen, da iſt die dreyfelltickeyt ynn Gott antzeyget.

13 Than ſayde the LORde vnto Abrahã: wherſore doth
Sara laughe ſaynge: ſhall I of a ſuertie bere a childe,
14 now when I am olde? is the thinge to harde for the
LORde to do? In the tyme appoynted will I returne
vnto the, as ſoone as the frute can haue lyfe, And Sara
15 ſhall haue a ſonne. Than Sara denyed it ſaynge: I
laughed not, for ſhe was afrayde. But he ſayde: yes
thou laughteſt.
16 Than the men ſtode vp from thence ãd loked
towarde Sodome. And Abraham went with them
17 to brynge them on the waye. And the LORde ſayde:
Can I hyde from Abraham that thinge which I am
18 aboute to do, ſeynge that Abraham ſhall be a great ãd
a myghtie people, and all the nations of the erth ſhalbe
19 bleſſed in him? For I knowe him that he will commaunde his childern and .P. his houſholde after him, ÿ
they kepe the waye of the LORde, to do after righte
and conſcyence, that the LORde may brynge vppon
Abraham that he hath promyſed him.
20 And the LORde ſayde: The crie of Sodome and
Gomorra is great, and there ſynne is excedynge
21 grevous. I will go downe and ſee whether they haue
done all to gedder acordynge to that crye which is
22 come vnto me or not, that I may knowe. And the
mẽ departed thẽce and went to Sodomeward. But
23 Abraham ſtode yet before ÿ LORde, and drewe nere
& ſayde Wylt thou deſtroy the rightwes with the
24 wyked? Yf there be .L. rightwes within the cyte, wilt
thou deſtroy it and not ſpare the place for the ſake of
25 L. rightwes that are therin? That be farre from the,
that thou ſhuldeſt do after thys maner, to ſley the
rightwes with the weked, ãd that the rightwes ſhulde
be as the weked: that be farre from the. Shulde not
26 the iudge of all ÿ worlde do acordynge to righte? And

M. 21 together
V. 14 vita comite 19 & faciant iudicium & iuſtitiam; vt adducat 21 venit ad me, opere compleuerint 25 Abſit a te . . ſiatque iuſtus ſicut impius . . nequaquam facias iudicium hoc.
L. 14 nach der zeyt die frucht leben kan 19 was recht vnd redlich iſt 24 dem ort nicht vergeben

the LORde ſayde: Yf I fynde in Sodome .L. rightwes
within the cyte, I will ſpare all the place for their
ſakes.
27 And Abraham anſwered and ſayde: beholde I haue
taken vppon me to ſpeake vnto ẏ LORde, ād yet am
28 but duſt ād aſhes. What though there lacke .v. of
L. rightwes, wylt thou deſtroy all the cyte for lacke
of .v.? And he ſayde: Yf I fynde there .xl. and .v
I will not deſtroy them.
29 And he ſpake vnto him yet agayne and ſay-[Fo.
XXIII.] de: what yf there be .xl. foũde there: And he
30 ſayde: I wyll not do it for forties ſake. And he ſayde:
O let not my LORde be angrye, that I ſpeake. What
yf there he foũde .xxx. there? And he ſayde: I will
31 not do it, yf I finde .xxx. there. And he ſayde: Oh,
ſe, I haue begonne to ſpeak vnto my LORde, what yf
there be .xx. founde there ? And he ſayde: I will not
32 diſtroy thē for twēties ſake. And he ſayde: O let not
my LORde be angrye, that I ſpeake yet, but euē once
more only. What yf ten be founde there ? And he
ſayde: I will not deſtroy thē for .x. ſake.
33 And the LORde wēt his waye as ſoone as he had
lefte comenynge with Abrahā. And
Abraham returned vnto his place

comenynge, *communing*

The .XIX. Chapter.

1 AND there came .ii. angells to
Sodome at euen. And Lot
ſatt at the gate of the cyte.
And Lot ſawe thē, and roſe
vp agaynſt them, and he bowed hym ſelfe
2 to the grounde with his face. And he

M.C.S. *Lot receaued two Angelles into hys houſe. The fylthy luſtes of the Sodomytes. Lot is delyuer-*

M. 1 vp to mete them
V. 26 in medio ciuitatis, dimittam omni loco propter eos. 31 Quia ſemel, ait cœpi 32 Obſecro, inquit, ne iraſcaris
L. 26 alle den ortten. xix, 1 buckt ſich mit ſeym angeſicht auff die erden

ſayde: Se lordes, turne in I praye you in
to youre ſeruauntes houſe and tary all
nyghte & waſh youre fete, & ryſe up
early and go on youre wayes. And they
ſayde: nay, but we will byde in the
3 ſtreates all nyghte. And he cōpelled
them excedyngly. And they turned in
vnto hym and entred in to his houſe, and
he made them a feaſte and dyd bake
ſwete cakes, and they ate.

ed & deſyreth to dwell in the cytie Zoar. Lottes wyfe is torned into a pyler of ſalt, Sodome is deſtroyed. Lot is dronken & lyeth with his daughters whych conceaued chyldren by hym.

4 But before they went to reſt, the men of the cyte
of Sodome compaſſed the houſe rownde .P. aboute
both olde and yonge, all the people from all quarters.
5 And they called vnto Lot and ſayde vnto him: where
are the men which came in to thy houſe to nyghte?
brynge thē out vnto vs that we may do oure luſt with
them.

6 And Lot went out at doores vnto them and ſhote
7 the dore after him and ſayde: nay for goddes ſake
8 brethren, do not ſo wekedly. Beholde I have two
doughters which haue knowne no man, thē will I
brynge out vnto you: do with them as it ſemeth you
good: Only vnto theſe men do nothynge, for therfore
9 came they vnder the ſhadow of my rofe. And they
ſayde: come hither. And they ſayde: cameſt thou
not in to ſogeorne, and wilt thou be now a iudge? we
will ſuerly deale worſe with the than with them
And as they preaſed ſore vppon Lot and
10 beganne to breake vp the doore, the men
put forth their handes and pulled Lot in to the houſe
to them and ſhott to the doore. And the men that
11 were at the doore of the houſe, they ſmote with

preaſed, *preſſed*

F. 2 & manete ibi . . in platea manebimus 3 Compulit illos oppido vt diuerterent ad eum . . azyma 7 Nolite-nolite 8 et abutimini eis . . . ſub vmbra culminis mei 9 Recede illuc 13 coram domino, qui miſit nos

L. 2 Sihe, meyne Herr, keret eyn . . bleybt vbernacht . . vber nacht auff der gaſſen bleyben 3 buch vngeſeurt kuchen 4 aus allen enden 8 diſen mennern Gottis

M. M. N. 5 *Nyght:* The nyght is here taken for the euenyng which is the begynnyng of the nyght as in the Prou. vii, b.

blyndneſſe both ſmall and greate: ſo that they coude
not fynde the doore.
12 And the men ſayde moreover vnto Lot: Yf thou
have yet here any ſonne in lawe or ſonnes or doughters or what ſo euer thou haſt in the cyte, brynge it
13 out of this place: for we muſt deſtroy this place,
becauſe the crye of thē is great before the LORde.
Wherfore he hath ſent vs to deſtroy it.
14 And Lot went out and ſpake vnto his ſonnes [Fo.
XXIIII.) in lawe which ſhulde have maried his doughters, and ſayde: ſtonde vpp and get yow out of this
place, for the LORde will deſtroy the cite. But he
ſemed as though he had mocked, vnto his ſonnes in
law.
15 And as the mornynge aroſe the angells cauſed Lot
to ſpede him ſaynge. Stonde vp, take thy wyfe and
thy two doughters and that that is at hande, leſt thou
16 periſh in the ſynne of the cyte. And as he prolonged
the tyme, the men caught both him, his wife ād his
two doughters by the handes, becauſe the LORde was
mercyfull vnto him, ād they brought him forth and
ſette him without the cyte.
17 When they had brought them out, they ſayde: Saue
thy lyfe and loke not behynde the nether tary thou in
any place of the contre, but ſaue thy ſelfe in the
18 mountayne, leſt thou periſſhe. Than ſayde Lot vnto
19 them: Oh nay my lorde: beholde, in as moch as thy
ſeruaunte hath fownde grace in thy ſyghte, now make
thi mercy great which thou ſheweſt vnto me in ſavinge
my lyfe. For I can not ſaue my ſelfe in the mountayns, leſt ſome miſſortune fall vpon me and I dye.
20 Beholde, here is a cyte by, to flee vnto, and it is a

V. 15 vxorem tuam & duas filias quas habes: 16 Diſſimulante illo . . . parceret dominus illi 17 Salua animam tuam . . ne & tu ſimul pereas. 19 ſaluares animam meam

L. 13 verderben 14 Aber es war yhn lecherlich. 15 deyn weyb vnd deyn zwoo tochter, die fur handen ſind, 17 Erredte deyn ſeele 19 meyn ſeel bey dem leben erhielteſt

M. M. N. 15 *Synne:* The ſynne is taken for the ſynner, as malyce is for the wicked, & righteouſnes for ryghteous, as Paul to Tytus the fyrſt .c.

lytle one, let me ſaue my ſelfe therein: is it not a litle
one, that my ſoule may lyve?
21 And he ſayde to him: ſe I haue receaved thy requeſt as concernynge this thynge, that I will nott
overthrowe this cytie for the .P. which thou haſt ſpoken.
22 Haſte the, ād ſaue thy ſelfe there, for I can do
nothynge tyll thou be come in thyder. And therfore
23 the name of the cyte is called Zoar. And the ſone
was vppon the erth when Lot was entred into Zoar.
24 Than the LORde rayned vpon Sodome and Gomorra, brymſtone and fyre from the LORde out of
25 heaven, and overthrewe thoſe cyteis and all the region,
and all that dwelled in the cytes, and that that grewe
26 vpon the erth. And lots wyfe loked behynde her, ād
was turned in to a pillare of ſalte.
27 Abraham roſe vp early and got him to the place
28 where he ſtode before the LORde, and loked toward
Sodome and Gomorra and toward all the londe of
that contre. And as he loked: beholde, the ſmoke of
the contre aroſe as it had bene the ſmoke of a fornace.
29 But yet whē God deſtroyed the cities of ẏ region, he
thought apon Abrahā: and ſent Lot out from the
dāger of the overthrowenge, when he overthrewe the
cyties where Lot dwelled.
30 And Lot departed out of Zoar and dwelled in the
mountayns ād his .ii. doughters with him for he feared
to tary in Zoar: he dwelled therefore in a caue, both
he and his .ii. doughters alſo.
31 Than ſayde the elder vnto the yonger oure father
is olde, and there are no moo men in the erth to come
32 in vnto vs after the maner of all the world. Come
therfore, let vs geue oure father wyne to dryncke, and
let vs lye with him [Fo. XXV.] that we may ſaue ſeed

M. 22 thither

V. 20 Eſt ciuitas hæc iuxta 21 ſubuertam 22 Idcirco 25 & cuncta terræ virētia 28 fauillam de terra quaſi fornacis fumum 29 vrbium, in quibus 31 iuxta morem vniuerſæ terræ.

L. 25 vnd was auff dem land gewachſen war 31 nach aller welt weyſe 32 trincken geben, vnd mit yhm truncken werden

L. M. N. 20 *kleyn:* Zoar heyſt kleyn.

33 of oure father. And they gaue their father wyne to
drynke that ſame nyghte. And the elder doughter
went and laye with her father. And he perceaued it
not, nether when ſhe laye downe, nether when ſhe
roſe vp.
34 And on the morowe the elder ſayde vnto the
yonger: beholde, yeſternyghte lay I with my father.
Let us geue hym wyne to drinke this nyghte alſo, and
goo thou and lye with him, and let us ſaue ſeed of
35 oure father. And they gaue their father wyne to
drincke that nyghte alſo. And the yonger aroſe and
laye with him. And he perceaved it not: nether
when ſhe laye down, nether when ſhe roſe vp.
36 Thus were both the doughters of lot with childe by
their father
37 And the elder bare a ſone and called hym Moab,
which is the father of the Moabytes vnto this daye.
38 And the yonger bare a ſonne and called hym Ben
Ammi, which is the father of the childern of Ammon
vnto this daye.

The .XX. Chapter.

1 AND Abraham departed thence
towarde the ſouthcontre and
dwelled betwene Cades and
Sur ād ſogeorned in Gerar.
2 And Abraham ſayde of Sara his wyfe,
that she was his ſiſter. Than Abimelech
kynge of Gerar ſent and fett Sara awaye.

M.C.S. Abraham went as a ſtranger into the lande of Gerar. The kynge of Gerar taketh awaye his wyfe.

3 And God came to Abimelech by nyghte in a
dreame and ſayde to him: Se, thou art but a .P. deed
man for the womās ſake which thou haſt taken awaye,

V. 33 dormiuitque . . accubuit filia 34 nocte, & dormies cum eo 38 Ammon (marg. Heb. Ben ammi.) id eſt filius populi mei xx. 3 En morieris

L. 3 Sihe da

4 for ſhe is a mans wyfe. But Abimelech had not yet
come nye her, and therfore ſayde: lorde wilt thou ſley
5 rightewes people? ſayde not he vnto me, that ſhe was
hys ſiſter? yee and ſayde not ſhe herſelf that he was
hir brother? wyth a pure herte and innocent handes
haue I done this.

6 And God ſayde vnto him in a dreame. I wot it
well that thou dydeſt it in pureneſſe of thi herte: And
therfore I kepte ẏ that thou ſhuldeſt not ſynne agenſt
7 me, nether ſuffred I the to come nygh her. Now
therfore delyuer the mā his wyfe ageyne, for he is a
prophete. And let him praye for the that thou mayſt
lyue. But and yf thou delyuer her not agayne, be
ſure that thou ſhalt dye the deth, with all that thou
haſt.

8 Than Abimelech roſe vp be tymes in the mornynge
and called all his ſervauntes, and tolde all theſe thinges
9 in their eares, and the men were ſore a frayde. And
Abimelech called Abraham and ſayde vnto him: What
haſt thou done vnto vs, & what haue I offended the,
that thou ſhuldeſt brynge on me and on my kyngdome
ſo greate a ſynne? thou haſt done dedes vnto me that
10 ought not to be done. And Abimelech ſayde morouer
vnto Abraham: What ſaweſt thou that moved the to
do this thinge?

11 And Abraham Anſwered. I thought that perad-
vēture the feare of God was not in this [Fo. XXVI.]
place, and that they ſhulde ſley me for my wyfes ſake;
12 yet in very dede ſhe is my ſiſter, the doughter of my
father, but not of my mother: and became my wyfe.
13 And after God cauſed me to wandre out of my fathers
houſe, I ſayde vnto her: This kyndneſſe ſhalt thou
ſhewe vnto me in all places where we come, that thou
ſaye of me, how that I am thy brother.

V. 4 gentem ignorantem & iuſtam 7 redde viro ſuo vxorem 8 Statimque de nocte . . in auribus eorum 9 quæ non debuiſti facere 10 Quid vidiſti

L. 4 eyn gerecht volck 7 des tods ſterben 8 fur yhr oren

M. M. N. 11 *The feare of God* amōge the Hebrewes is princypally takē for the honour and faith that we owe vnto god, & that wyth ſoche a loue as the childe hathe to the father.

14 Than toke Abimelech ſhepe and oxen, menſervauntes and wemenſeruauntes and gaue them vnto
Abraham, and delyvered him Sara his wyfe agayne.
15 And Abimelech ſayde: beholde the lande lyeth be fore
16 the, dwell where it pleaſeth ẏ beſt. And vnto Sara he
ſayde: Se I haue geuen thy brother a thouſande peeces
of ſyluer, beholde he ſhall be a couerynge
to thyne eyes vnto all that ar with the
and vnto all men and an excuſe.
17 And ſo Abraham prayde vnto God,
and God healed Abimelech and his wyfe
18 and hys maydens, ſo that they bare. For the LORde
had cloſed to, all the matryces of the houſe of Abimelech, becauſe of Sara Abrahams wyfe.

couerynge, *ſcreening from obſervation;* excuſe, *a doubtful rendering*

The .XXI. Chapter.

1 THE lorde viſyted Sara as he
had ſayde and dyd vnto her
acordynge as he had ſpoken.
2 And Sara was with childe and
bare Abrahā a ſonne in his olde age .¶
euen the ſame ſeaſon which the LORde
3 had appoynted. And Abraham called
his ſonnes name that was borne vnto him
4 which Sara bare him Iſaac: & Abrā circūcyſed Iſaac his ſōne whē he was .viii. dayes olde, as
5 God commaunded him And Abrahā was an hundred
yere olde, when his ſonne Iſaac was borne vnto him.

M.C.S. *Iſaac is borne. Agar is caſt oute wyth hyr younge ſonne Iſmael. The Angell comforteth Agar. The couenaunt betwene Abimelech and Abraham.*

M. 16 beholde this thinge ſhall be . . all men an excuſe 17 maydēs . . ſo that they bare chyldrē. xxi, 1 promyſed

V. 14 reddiditque illi Saram vxorem ſuam 16 & quoc. . perrexeris, memento te deprehenſam. xxi, 5 hac quippe ætate patris, natus eſt Iſaac.

L. 16 Sihe da, ich hab . . vnd allenthalben, vnd eyn verantwortter 17 das ſie kinder geporen 18 zuuor hart verſchloſſen xxi, 1 vnd thet mit yhr

M. M. N. 16 Couerynge & excuſe is all one.

6 And Sara ſayde: God hath made me a laughinge
7 ſtocke: for all ỳ heare, will laugh at me She ſayde
alſo: who wolde haue ſayde vnto Abraham, that Sara
ſhulde haue geuen childern ſucke, or ỳ I ſhulde haue
8 borne him a ſonne in his old age: The childe grewe
and was wened, and Abraham made a great feaſt, the
ſame daye that Iſaac was wened.

9 Sara ſawe the ſonne of Hagar the Egiptian which
10 ſhe had borne vnto Abraham, a mockynge. Then ſhe
ſayde vnto Abraham: put awaye this bondemayde and
hyr ſonne: for the ſonne of this bondwoman ſhall not
11 be heyre with my ſonne Iſaac: But the wordes ſemed
verey greavous in Abrahams ſyghte, becauſe of his
12 ſonne. Than the LORde ſayde vnto Abraham: let it
not be greavous vnto the, becauſe of the ladd and of
thy bondmayde: But in all that Sara hath ſaide vnto
the, heare hir voyce, for in Iſaac ſhall thy ſeed be
13 called. Moreouer of the ſonne of the Bondwoman will
I make a nation, becauſe he is thy ſeed.

14 And Abraham roſe vp early in the mornyng and
toke brede and a bottell with water, and ga- [Fo.
XXVII.] ue it vnto Hagar, puttynge it on hir ſhulders
wyth the lad alſo, and ſent her awaye. And ſhe departed and wãdred vpp and doune in the wyldernes
15 of Berſeba. When the water was ſpent that was in
16 the botell, ſhe caſt the lad vnder a buſh and went &
ſatt her out of ſyghte a great waye, as it were a bow-
ſhote off: For ſhe ſayde: I will not ſe the lad dye.
And ſhe ſatt doune out of ſyghte, and lyfte vp hyr
17 voyce and wepte. And God herde the voyce of the
childe. And the angell of God called Hagar out of

V. 9 ludentem cum Iſaac 11 Dure accepit 12 Non tibi videatur aſperum . . in Iſaac vocabitur tibi ſemen 14 ſcapulæ eius, traditque puerum . . errabat in ſolitudine Berſabee 15 abiecit puerum

L. 7 das Sara kinder ſeuget 9 das er eyn ſpotter war 10 treybe . . . aus 12 dyr der ſame genennet werden 14 auff yre ſhulder, vnd den knaben mit, vnd lies ſie aus . . vnd gieng ynn der wüſten yrre bey Berſaba 15 warff ſie den knaben 16 eyn ambruſt ſchos weit

L. M. N. 9 *Hagar*, Merck hie auff Hagar, wie die des Geſetzs vnd glaubloſer werck figur iſt, Gal. iiii. vnd dennoch ſie Gott zeitlich belonet vnd groſs macht auff erden.

heaven and ſayde vnto her: What ayleth the Hagar?
Feare not, for God hath herde the voyce of the childe
18 where he lyeth. Aryſe and lyfte vp the lad, and take
hym in thy hande, for I will make off him a greate
19 people. And God opened hir eyes and ſhe ſawe a well
of water. And ſhe went and fylled the bottell with
20 water, and gaue the boye drynke. And God was
21 wyth the lad, and he grewe and dweld in the wilderneſſe, and became an archer. And he dweld in the
wylderneſſe of Pharan. And hys mother gott him a
wyfe out of the land of Egypte.

22 And it chaunced the ſame ſeaſon, that Abimelech
and Phicoll his chefe captayne ſpake vnto Abraham
23 ſaynge: God is wyth the in all that thou doiſt. Now
therfore ſwere vnto me even here by God, that thou
wylt not hurt me nor my childern, nor my childerns
childern .P. But that thou ſhalt deale with me and the
contre where thou art a ſtraunger, acordynge vnto
24 the kyndneſſe that I haue ſhewed the. Then ſayde
Abraham: I wyll ſwere.

25 And Abraham rebuked Abimelech for a well of
water, which Abimelech ſervauntes had taken awaye.
26 And Abimelech anſwered I wyſt not who dyd it:
Alſo thou toldeſt me not, nether herde I of it, but this
daye.

27 And Abraham toke ſhepe and oxen and gaue them
vnto Abimelech. And they made both of them a
28 bonde together And Abraham ſett .vii. lambes by
29 them ſelues. And Abimelech ſayde vnto Abraham:
what meane theſe .vii. lambes which thou haſt ſett by
30 them ſelues. And he anſwered: vii. lambes ſhalt thou
take of my hande, that it maye be a wytneſſe vnto
31 me, that I haue dygged this well: Wherfore the place

M. 25 Abimelechs ſeruauntes

V. 18 tolle puerum, et tene manum illius 20 ſolitudine, factusque eſt iuuenis ſagittarius 25 quem vi abſtulerant 27 percuſſeruntque ambo fœdus.

L. 17 des knabens da, er ligt 18 füre ynn an deyner hand 25 hatten mit gewalt genomen 27 machte beide einen bund mit einander

is called Berſeba, becauſe they ſware both of them.
32 Thus made they a bonde to gether at Berſeba.
Than Abimelech and Phicoll his chefe captayne
roſe vp and turned agayne vnto the lande of the
33 Philiſtines. And Abraham planted a wodd in Berſeba, and called there, on the name of the LORde the
34 everlaſtynge God: and dwelt in the Pheliſtinlāde a
longe ſeaſon

❡ The .XXII. Chapter.

[Fo. XXVIII.] The .XXII. Chapter.

1 AFTER theſe dedes, God dyd
proue Abraham & ſayde vnto
him: Abraham. And he an-
2 ſwered: here am I. And he
ſayde: take thy only ſonne Iſaac whome
thou loueſt, & get the vnto the lande of
Moria, and ſacrifyce him there for a ſacrifyce vpon one of the mountayns which I
3 will ſhewe the Than Abraham roſe vp
early in the mornynge and ſadled his
aſſe, and toke two of his meyny wyth him, and Iſaac
his ſonne: ād clove wod for the ſacrifyce, and roſe vp
and gott him to the place which God had appoynted
4 him. The thirde daye Abraham lyfte vp his eyes
5 and ſawe the place a farr of, and ſayde vnto his yong
men: byde here with the aſſe. I and the lad will goo

M.C.S. *The fayth of Abraham is proued in offrynge hys ſonne Iſaac. Chriſt our ſauyour is promyſed. The generacyon of Nachor Abrahams brother.*

M. 34 Philiſtin lande. xxii, 2 lāde Moria

V. 32 pro puteo iuramēti 33 inuocauit ibi nomen 34 colonus terræ Paleſt. xxii, 2 in terram Viſionis . . holocauſtum 3 ſtrauit aſinum

L. 33 Berſaba, vnnd predigt daſelbſt von den namen 34 im lang zeit. xxii, 2 brand opffer 3 gürtet 5 ich vnnd du knabe

M. M. N. 2 *Only ſonne* for only beloued or mooſt chefly beloued aboue other, after the Ebrew phraſe as in the Prouer. iiii, a.

L. M. N. 31 *Berſaba*, heiſt auff deudſch ſchweer brun, oder erdbrun, möcht auch wol ſieben brun heiſſen. xxii, 2 *Moria* heiſt ſchauung, vnnd iſt der berg, da Salomon hernac zu Iieruſalem den Tempel auff bowet, vnnd heiſt der ſchawen berg, das Gott da ſilbſt hinſchawd.

yonder and worſhippe and come agayne vnto you
6 And Abraham toke the wodd of the ſacrifyce and
layde it vpon Iſaac his ſonne, and toke fyre in his
hande and a knyfe. And they went both of them
together.
7 Than ſpake Iſaac vnto Abraham his father & ſayde:
My father? And he anſwered here am I my ſonne.
And he ſayde: Se here is fyre and wodd, but where is
8 the ſhepe for ſacrifyce? And Abraham ſayde: my
ſonne, God wyll prouyde him a ſhepe for ſacrifyce. So
went they both together.
9 And when they came vnto the place which God
ſhewed him, Abrahā made an aulter there and dreſſed
the wodd, ād bownde Iſaac his .P. ſonne and layde him
10 on the aulter, aboue apon the wodd. And Abraham
ſtretched forth his hande, and toke the knyfe to haue
kylled his ſonne.
11 Than the angell of the LORde called vnto him
from heauen ſaynge: Abraham, Abraham. And he
12 anſwered: here am I. And he ſayde: laye not thy
handes apon the childe nether do any thinge at all
vnto him, for now I knowe that thou feareſt God, in
13 ẏ thou haſte not kepte thine only ſonne frō me. And
Abraham lyfted vp his eyes and loked aboute: and
beholde, there was a ram caught by the hornes in a
thykette. And he went and toke the ram and offred
14 him vp for a ſacrifyce in the ſteade of his ſonne And
Abraham called the name of the place, the LORde
will ſee: wherfore it is a comē ſaynge this daye: in the
mounte will the LORde be ſene.
15 And the Angell of the LORde cryed vnto Abra-
16 ham from heaven the ſeconde tyme ſaynge: by my
ſelfe haue I ſworne (ſayth the LORde) becauſe thou

V. 7 victima holocauſti 9 in altare ſuper ſtruem lignorum 10 vt immolaret 12 nunc cognoui 14 Dominus videt . . . In monte Dominus videbit

L. 7 Sihe hie iſt . . ſchaff zum brandopffer 9 oben auff das holtz 10 ſchlachtet 12 Denn nu weis ich 14 Der Herrn ſchawet . . der Herr geſchawet wird

M. M. N. 5 *To worſhyp* is here to do ſacryfyce. 12 *I knowe;* that is, I haue experiēce that thou feareſt God, as in Philippē. iiii, c.

hast done this thinge and hast not spared thy only
17 sonne, that I will blesse the and multiplye thy seed as
the starres of heaven and as the sonde vpō the see syde
And thy seed shall possesse the gates of hys enymies.
18 And in thy seed shall all the nations of the erth be
blessed, because thou hast obeyed my voyce
19 So turned Abraham agayne vnto his yonge men,
and they rose vp and wēt to gether to Ber- [Fo.
XXIX.] seba. And Abraham dwelt at Berseba
20 And it chaũsed after these thĩges, that one tolde
Abraham saynge: Behold, Milcha she hath also borne
21 childern vnto thy brother Nachor: Hus his eldest sonne
and Bus his brother, and Kemuell the father of the
22 Sirians, and Cesed, and Haso, and Pildas, and Iedlaph,
23 and Bethuel. And Bethuel begat Rebecca. These
viii. dyd Milcha bere to Nachor Abrahams brother.
24 And his concubyne called Rheuma she bare also Tebah,
Gaham, Thahas and Maacha.

¶ The .XXIII. Chapter.

1 SARA was an hundred and .xxvii
yere olde (for so longe lyued
2 she) and than dyed in a heade
cyte called Hebron in the
londe of Canaan. Than Abraham came
3 to morne Sara and to wepe for her. And
Abraham stode vp from the coorse and
talked with the sonnes of heth saynge:
4 I am a straunger ād a foryner amonge
yow, geue me a possession to bury in with you, that I
may bury my dead oute of my sighte.

M.C.S. *Sarah dyeth & is buried in the felde that Abraham bought of Ephron the Hethite.*

heade cyte, *chief cyte, capital*

coorse, *corpse, body*

F. 17 inimicorum suorum 18 quia obedisti voci meæ. xxiii, 2 in ciuitate Arbee 3 ab officio funeris 4 date mihi ius sepulchri

L. 18 vnnd durch deinen samen. xxiii, 2 heubstad 3 von seyner leych 4 eyn erb begrebnis . . . der fur myr liegt

L. M. N. 2 *Hebron* ist Kiriath Arba (spricht Mose) das ist, die vierstad, denn die hohen heubt stede, waren vertzeytten alle Arba, das ist, ynn vier teyl geteylet, wie Rom, Jerusalem vnd Babylon auch Gen. x.

5 And the children of heth anſwered Abraham ſaynge
6 vnto him: heare vs lorde, thou arte a prynce of God
amonge vs. In the cheſeſt of our ſepulchres bury thy
dead: None of vs ſhall forbydd yͤ his ſepulchre, yͭ thou
7 ſhuldeſt not bury thy deade therein. Abrahā ſtode vp
& bowed hī ſelfe before yͤ people of yͤ lāde yͤ childrē of
8 heth. And he comoned with them ſaynge: comoned, *com-*
Yf it .P. be youre myndes yͭ I ſhall bury my *muned*
deade oute of my ſighte, heare me ād ſpeke for me tc
9 Ephron the ſonne of Zoar: and let him geue me the
dubill caue which he hath in the end of his felde, for
as moch money as it is worth, let him geue it me in
10 the preſence of you, for a poſſeſſion to bury in. For
Hephron dwelled amōge yͤ childern of heth.
Than Ephron the Hethite anſwered Abraham in the
audyēcē of the childern of Heth and of all that went in at
11 the gates of his cyte, ſaynge: Not ſo, my lorde, but heare
me: The felde geue I the, and the caue that therein
is, geue I the alſo, And even in the preſence of the
ſonnes of my people geve I it the to bnry thy deede in.
12 Than Abraham bowed himſelfe before the people of
13 the lāde and ſpake vnto Ephrō in the audyence of the
people of the contre ſaynge: I praye the heare me, I
will geue ſylver for the felde, take it of me, ād ſo will
I bury my deed there.
14, 15 Ephron anſwered Abrahā ſaynge vnto him My
lorde, harken vnto me. The lande is worth .iiii. hun-
dreth ſycles of ſylver: But what is that betwixte the
16 and me? bury thy deede. And Abraham harkened
vnto Ephron and weyde him the ſylver which he had

M. 10 Ephron.

V. 6 in electis ſepulchris noſtris ſepeli 7 Heth: 8 dixitque ad eos: Si placet animæ veſtræ 9 ſpeluncam duplicem 10 cunctis audientibus qui ingrediebantur portam 12 Adorauit Abraham coram domino & populo terræ 13 Dabo pecuniam pro agro 15 iſtud eſt pretium inter me et te, ſed quantum eſt hoc?

L. 6 ynn vnſern koſtlichen grebern 8 Iſts ewr gemuete . . . todten fur myr begrabe 12 nym von myr des ackers gellt 15 was iſt das aber zwiſchen myr vnd dyr

L. M. N. 15 *Sekel* iſt eyn gewichte, an der muntze, eyn orttis gulden, Denn vertzeytten man das gellt ſo wug, wie man itzt mit gollt thut.

ſayde in the audyence of the ſonnes of Heth. Euen
iiii. hūdred ſyluer ſycles of currant money amonge
marchauntes

17 Thus was the felde of Ephron where in the dubbill
caue is before Mamre: euen the felde & [Fo. XXIIII.]
the caue that is therein and all the trees of the felde
which growe in all the borders rounde aboute, made
18 ſure vnto Abraham for a poſſeſſion, in the ſyghte of the
childern of Heth and of all that went in at the gates
of the cyte.

19 And then Abraham buried Sara his wyfe in the double
caue of the felde that lyeth before Māre, otherwiſe
20 called Ebron in the lande of Canaan. And ſo both the
felde ād the caue that is therein, was made vnto Abraham, a ſure poſſeſſion to bury in, of the ſonnes of Heth.

ℭ The .XXIIII. Chapter.

M.C.S. *Abraham maketh hys ſeruant to ſwere, & ſendeth him to ſeke a wyfe for Iſaac his ſonne. The ſeruaunt was faythfull and brought Rebecca, whych Iſaac toke to his wyfe.*

1 ABRAHAM was olde and ſtryken
in dayes, and the LORde had
2 bleſſed him in all thinges. And
he ſayde vnto his eldeſt ſervaunte of his houſe which had the rule
over all that he had: Put thy hande vnder
3 my thye that I maye make the ſwere by
the LORde that is God of heauen and
God of the erth, that thou ſhalt not take
a wyfe vnto my ſonne, of the doughters
4 of the canaanytes, amonge which I dwell. But ſhalt
goo vnto my contre and to my kynred, and there take
a wyfe vnto my ſonne Iſaac.

5 Thā ſayde the ſeruaunte vnto him: what ād yf

V. 16 probatæ monetæ publicæ 20 ager & antrum quod erat in eo. xxiv, 2 præerat omnibus

L. 16 Sekel ſylbers das ym kauff geng vnd gebe war. xxiv, 4 ynn meyn vatterland

M. M. N. 2 *Put thy hande:* To put the hand under the thyghe was an othe which the Hebreues vſed in ſoch thīges as perteyned to the teſtament & promeſſe of god as in Gen. xlvii, g.

the womā wyll not agree to come with me vnto
this lāde, ſhall I brynge thy ſonne agayne vnto
6 the land which thou cameſt out of? And Abrahā
ſayde vnto him: bewarre of that, that thou brīge
7 not my ſonne thither. The LORde God of heauen
which toke me from my fathers .P. houſe and from
the lande where I was borne, and which ſpake vnto
me and ſware vnto me ſaynge: vnto thy ſeed wyll I
geue this lande, he ſhall ſende his angell before the,
ỷ thou mayſt take a wife vnto my ſonne from thence.
8 Neuertheleſſe yf the womā will not agree to come
with the than ſhalt thou be without daunger of this ooth. But aboue all thinge
bringe not my ſonne thyther agayne.
9 And the ſeruaunte put his hand vnder
the thye of Abraham and ſware to him as concernynge that matter.

without danger of this ooth, *i. e. abſolved from its obligation*

10 And the ſeruaunte toke .x. camels of the camels of
his maſter and departed, and had of all maner goodes
of his maſter with him, and ſtode vp and went to
11 Meſopotamia, vnto the cytie of Nahor. And made
his camels to lye doune without the cytie by a wels
ſyde of water, at euen: aboute the tyme that women
come out to drawe water, and he ſayde.
12 LORde God of my maſter Abrahā, ſend me good ſpede
13 this daye, & ſhewe mercy vnto my maſter Abraham. Lo
I ſtonde here by the well of water and the doughters of
14 the men of this citie will come out to drawe water: Now
the damſell to whom I ſaye, ſtoupe doune thy pytcher
and let me drynke. Yf ſhe ſaye, drynke, and I will geue
thy camels drynke alſo, ỷ ſame is ſhe that thou haſt ordened for thy ſervaunte Iſaac: yee & therby ſhall I
knowe that thou haſt ſhewed mercy on my maſter.
15 And it came to paſſe yer he had leeft ſpakyn- [Fo.
XXXI.] ge, that Rebecca came out, the doughter of
Bethuell, ſonne to Melcha the wife of Nahor Abrahams
16 brother, and hir pytcher apon hir ſhulder: The damſell

V. 8 non teneberis iuramento
L. 7 von dem land meyner freuntſchafft 10 vnd macht ſich auff vnd zoch

was very fayre to loke apon, and yet a mayde and
vnknowen of man.
And ſhe went doune to the well and fylled hyr
17 pytcher and came vp agayne. Then the ſeruaunte
ranne vnto her and ſayde: let me ſyppe a litle water
18 of thi pither. And ſhe ſayde: drynke my lorde.
And ſhe haſted and late downe her pytcher apon
19 hyr arme and gaue him drinke. And whē ſhe had
geven hym drynke, ſhe ſayde: I will drawe water for
20 thy camels alſo, vntill they haue dronke ynough. And
ſhe poured out hyr pitcher in to the trough haſtely
and ranne agayne vnto the well, to fett water: and
drewe for all his camels.
21 And the felowe wondred at her. But felowe, *man*
helde his peace, to wete whether the LORde had made
22 his iourney proſperous or not. And as the camels
had lefte dryncкynge, he toke an earynge of halfe a
ſicle weght and .ii. golden bracelettes for hyr hādes,
23 of .x. ſycles weyght of gold and ſayde vnto her: whoſe
doughter art thou? tell me: ys there rowme in thy
24 fathers houſe, for vs to lodge in? And ſhe ſayde vnto
him: I am the doughter of Bethuell the ſonne of Milcha
25 which ſhe bare vnto Nahor: and ſayde moreouer vnto
him: we haue litter and prauonder ynough and alſo
26 rowme to lodge in .P. And the man bowed himſelfe
27 and worſhipped the LORde and ſayde: bleſſed be the
LORde God of my maſter Abraham which ceaſſeth
not to deale mercyfulle and truly with my maſter, And
hath brought me the waye to my maſters brothers houſe.
28 And the damſell ranne & tolde them of her mothers
29 houſe theſe thinges. And Rebecca had a brother
called Laban.

M. 17 ſuppe 22 a golden earyng
V. 17 mihi ad ſorbendum præbe . . Celeriterque depoſuit hydriam ſuper vlnam ſuam 22 inaures aureas 23 Cuius es filia
L. 17 aus deynem krug trincken 18 vnnd eylent lies ſie den krug ernydder uaff yhre hand 22 eyn gulden ſtyrnſpangel 23 Meyn tochter, wen gehorſtu an?
M. M. N. 22 *Earyng;* Earynges are deckynges, ether to apparell the face & forhed of the woman, or the eares. And bracelettes is to decke the armes or hādes. 23 *Worſhypped;* To worſhyp is here to geue thankes, as in the .xxiii. afore at this letter B.

And Laban ranne out vnto the man, to the well:
30 for as ſoone as he had ſene the earynges and the bracelettes apon his ſiſters handes, ād herde the words of
Rebecca his ſiſter ſaynge thus ſayde the man vnto me,
than he went out vnto the man. And loo, he ſtode
31 yet with the camels by the well ſyde. And Laban
ſayde: come in thou bleſſed of the LORde. Wherfore
ſtondeſt thou without? I haue dreſſed the houſe and
32 made rowme for the camels. And than the mā came in
to the houſe. And he vnbrydeld the camels: and
brought litter and prauonder for the camels, and
water to weſhe his fete and their fete that were
33 with him, and there was meate ſett before him to
eate.

But he ſayde: I will not eate, vntill I haue ſayde
34 myne earēde: And he ſayde, ſaye on, And he
35 ſayde: I am Abrahās ſervaunte, & the LORDE hath
*bleſſed my maſter out of meaſure that he
is become greate and hath geven him ſhepe
oxen, ſyluer and golde, menſervauntes,
[Fo. XXXI.] maydeſervauntes, camels ād
36 aſſes. And Sara my maſters wyfe bare
him a ſonne, whē ſhe was olde: and vnto
him hath he geven all that he hath.

** God bleſſeth vs whē he geveth vs his benefites: and curſeth vs, when he taketh them awaye.*

37 And my maſter made me ſwere ſaynge: Thou ſhalt
not take a wyfe to my ſonne, amonge the doughters of
38 the cananytes in whoſe lāde I dwell. But thou ſhalt
goo vnto my fathers houſe and to my kynred, and
39 there take a wyfe vnto my ſonne. And I ſayde vnto
my maſter. What yf the wyfe will not folowe me?
40 And he ſayde vnto me: The LORde before whom I
walke, wyll ſende his angell with the and proſper
thy iourney that thou ſhalt take a wyfe for my
ſonne, of my kynred and of my fathers houſe. But
and yf (when thou comeſt vnto my kynred) they will

V. 32 aquam ad lauandos pedes camelorum, & virorum 33 donec loquar ſermones meos . . Loquere.

L. 33 bis das ich zuuor meyn ſach geworben habe . . ſage her 38 vatters haus vnd zu meynem geſchlecht

M. M. N. 33 The ſame note as in Tyndale.

41 not geue the one, thā ſhalt thou bere no perell of
myne oothe.
42 And I came this daye vnto the well and ſayed: O
LORde, the God of my maſter Abrahā, yf it be ſo that
43 thou makeſt my iourney which I go, proſperous: beholde, I ſtōde by this well of water, And when a virgyn
cometh forth to drawe water, and I ſaye to her: geue
44 me a litle water of thi pitcher to drynke, and ſhe ſaye
agayne to me: dryncke thou, and I will alſo drawe
water for thy camels: that ſame is the wife, whom the
LORde hath prepared for my maſters ſonne .¶.
45 And before I had made an ende of ſpeakynge in myne
harte: beholde Rebecca came forth, and hir pitcher on hir
ſhulder, and ſhe went doune vnto the well and drewe.
46 And I ſayde vnto her geue me dryncke. And ſhe
made haſt and toke doune hir pitcher from of hir, ād
ſayd: drinke, and I will geue thy camels drynke alſo.
And I dranke, and ſhe gaue the camels drynke alſo. And
47 I aſked her ſaynge: whoſe doughter art thou? And
ſhe anſwered: the doughter of Bathuell Nahors ſonne
whome Milca bare vnto him.
And I put the earynge vpon hir face and the brace-
48 lettes apon hir hondes. And I bowed my ſelfe and
worſhepped the LORde and bleſſed the LORde God
of my maſter Abrahā which had brought me the right
waye, to take my maſters brothers doughter vnto his
49 ſonne. Now therfore yf ye will deall mercyfully and
truly with my maſter, tell me. And yf not, tell me
alſo: that I maye turne me to the right hande or to
the left.
50 Than anſwered Laban and Bathuel ſaynge: The
thinge is proceded even out of the lorde, we can not

V. 41 Innocens eris a maledictione mea 49 vt vadam ad dexterā, ſiue ad ſiniſtrā 50 A domino egreſſus eſt ſermo

L. 41 ſo biſtu meyns eydes quyd. 44 das der Herr meyns herrn ſon beſcheret hat 49 das ich mich wende zur rechten odder zur lincken. 50 von dem Herrn auſzgangen

M. M. N. 49 *Mercyfully and truly* is as moche to ſaye in this place as to ſhewe pleaſure, gētlynes or kyndnes, as .iiii Reg. xx, d. 49 *The ryght hād or the left* is no more to ſaye, but tel me one thing or a nother, that I may knowe wherevnto to ſtycke, and is a phraſe of the Hebrew.

51 therfore ſaye vnto the, ether good or bad: Beholde
Rebecca before thy face, take her and goo, and let
her be thy maſters ſonnes wife, euen as the LORde
52 hath ſayde. And whē Abrahams ſervaunte herde their
wordes, he bowed him ſelfe vnto the LORde, flatt vpon
53 the erth. And the ſervaunte toke forth iewells [Fo.
XXXIII. *ſic.*] of ſyluer and iewelles of gold and rayment,
and gaue them to Rebecca: But vnto hir brother &
54 to hir mother, he gaue ſpyces. And then they ate and
dranke, both he and the men that were with him, and
taried all nyghte and roſe vp in the mornynge.
55 And he ſayde: let me departe vnto my maſter. But
hir brother and hir mother ſayde: let the damſell abyde
with vs a while, ād it be but even .x. dayes, and than
56 goo thy wayes. And he ſayde vnto them, hinder me
not: for the lorde hath proſpered my iourney. Sende
57 me awaye ŷ I maye goo vnto my maſter. And they
ſayde: let vs call the damſell, and witt what ſhe ſayth
58 to the matter. And they called forth Rebecca ād
ſayde vnto her: wilt thou goo with this mā? And
59 ſhe ſayde: Yee. Than they broughte Rebecca their
ſiſter on the waye and her norſe and Abrahās ſer-
60 vaunte, and the men that were wyth him. And they
* bleſſed Rebecca & ſayde vnto her: Thou
art oure ſiſter, growe in to thouſande thouſandes, & thy ſeed poſſeſſe ŷ gates of
61 their enimies. And Rebecca aroſe & hir
damſels, & ſatt thē vp apō the camels &
went their waye after the man. And ŷ
ſervaunte toke Rebecca & went his waye
62 And Iſaac was a comīge from the well of
ŷ lyvynge & ſeynge, for he dwelt in the
63 ſouth cōtre, & was gone out to walke in his
meditatiōs before ŷ euē tyde. And he lyfte vp his eyes

* *To bleſſe a mās neyboure is to praye for hī, ād to wiſſh him good: and not to wagge ii figers ouer him.* =wagge ii. fingers ouer him, *alluſion to ſacerdotal bleſſing in the Church of Rome*

M. 59 So they let Rebecca their ſyſter go with her norſe

V. 53 vaſis argenteis . . matri dona obtulit 55 ſaltem decem dies 58 Vadam 61 ſunt virum: qui feſtinus reuertebatur

L. 55 eyn tag odder zehen 58 Ya, ich will mit yhm. 61 nam Rebecca an

M. M. N. 60 *And they bleſſed Rebecca.* The ſame note as in Tyndale. 63 *Meditacyons* is the exercise of the ſpirite and lyftynge vp the mynde to God.

64 & loked, & beholde y͛ camels were cominge. And .P. Rebecca lyfte vp hir eyes, & whē ſhe ſawe Iſaac, ſhe lyghted
65 of the camel ād ſayde vnto the ſervaunte: what mā is
this y͛ cometh agenſt vs in the feld? And the ſervaūte
ſayde: it is my maſter. And then ſhe toke hir mantell
66 ād put it aboute her. And the ſervaūte tolde Iſaac all
67 that he had done. Thē Iſaac broughte her in to his
mother Saras tente, ād toke Rebecca & ſhe became
his wife, & he loved her: & ſo was Iſaac cōforted over
his mother.

The .XXV. Chapter.

M.C.S. Abraham taketh Kethura to his wyfe & begetteth many chyldren. Abrahā dyeth & geueth all his goodes to Iſaac. The genealogie of Iſmael. The byrth of Iacob and Eſau. Eſau ſelleth his byrthright for a meſſe of potage.

1 ABRAHĀ toke hī another wyfe
2 cald Ketura, which bare
hī Simram, Iackſam, Medan,
3 Midiā Ieſback & Suah. And
Iackſan begat Seba & Dedan. And the
ſonnes of Dedan were Aſſurim, Letuſim
4 & Leumim. And the ſonnes of Midian
were Epha, Epher, Hanoch, Abida &
Elda. All theſe were the childern of
5 Kethura. But Abrahā gaue all that he
6 had vnto Iſaac. And vnto the ſonnes of
his concubines he gaue giftes, and ſent
them awaye from Iſaac his ſonne (while
he yet lyved) eaſt ward, vnto the eaſt contre.
7 Theſe are the dayes of the life of Abrahā which he
8 lyved: an hūdred & .Lxxv. yere and than fell ſeke ād
dyed, in a luſtie age (whē he had lvved

luſtie, *good*

M. 2 Ieckſan 4 Ketura
V. 65 pallium ſuum, operuit ſe. xxv, 6 ſeparauit eos . . ad plagam orientalem 8 Et deficiens mortuus eſt
L. 65 den ſchleyer vnd verhullet ſich. xxv, 6 vnd lies ſie . . . zihen 8 vnd ward krank vnd ſtarb, ynn eynem rugigem allter, da er allt vnd lebens ſatt war . . zu ſeynem volck geſamlet,
M. M. N. 6 *Concubynes* in the ſcripture are not harlottes, but wyues: yet bare they no rule in the houſe, but were ſubiectes as ſeruauntes. As Agar was vnto Sara. Geneſis vi, a. Bylha Gen. xxx, a.

9 ynough) ād was put vnto his people. And his ſonnes
Iſaac ād Iſmael buried hī in the duble caue in the feld
of Ephrō ſōne of Zoar the Hethite before Mamre.
10 Which felde abrahā boughte of the ſonnes of Heth:
11 There was Abrahā buried and Sara hys wyfe. And
after ẏ deeth of Abrahā god bleſſed Iſaac his ſonne [Fo.
XXXIIII.] which dweld by the well of the lyvīge & ſeīge
12 Theſe are the generatiōs of Iſmael Abrahās ſonne,
which Hagar the Egiptiā Saras handmayde bare vnto
13 Abraham. And theſe are the names of the ſōnes of
Iſmaell, with their names in their kīreddes. The eldeſt ſōne of Iſmael Neuaioth, thē Kedar, Abdeel, Mib-
14, 15 ſā, Miſma, Duma, Maſa, Hadar, Thema, Ietur,
16 Naphis & Kedma. Theſe are the ſōnes of Iſmael, and
theſe are their names, in their townes and caſtels .xii
17 princes of natiōs. And theſe are the yeres of the lyfe
of Iſmael: an hūdred and .xxxvii. yere, & than he fell
18 ſeke & dyed & was layde vnto his people. And he
dweld from Euila vnto Sur ẏ is before Egypte, as men
go toward the Aſſiriās. And he dyed in the preſence
of all his brethren.

19 And theſe are the generatiōs of Iſaac Abrahās
20 ſonne: Abrahā begat Iſaac. And Iſaac was .XL. yere
olde whē he toke Rebecca to wyfe the doughter of
Bethuel the Sirian of Mesopotamia & ſiſter to Laban
the Sirien.

21 And Iſaac made interceſſiō vnto ẏ LORde for his
wife: becauſe ſhe was barē: and ẏ LORde was ītreated
22 of hī, & Rebecca his wife cōceaued: and ẏ childern
ſtroue together withī her. thē ſhe ſayde: yf it ſhulde
goo ſo to paſſe, what helpeth it ẏ I am with childe?

M. 13 Cedar

V. 16 & hæc nomina per caſtella & oppida eorū, . . . tribuum ſuarum. 18 introeuntibus Aſſyrios. 20 ſororem Laban. 21 Deprecatuſque 22 Sed collidebantur

L. 9 zwiffachen hole 16 ynn yhren hoffen vnd ſtedten 18 Aſſyrian gehet, Vnd vberfiel alle ſeyne bruder. 22 Kinder ſtieſſen ſich miteynander . . da myrs alſo ſollt gehen

M. M. N. 8 *And was put unto his people;* To be put amōge hys people, is not only to be put in a goodly place of buryall, but to be put with the cōpany of the auncyent fathers that dyed in the ſame fayth that he dyd.

23 And ſhe went & axed ẏ LORde. And ẏ LORde
ſayde vnto her there are .ii. maner of people in thi
wombe and .ii. nations ſhall ſpringe out of thy bowels,
P. and the one nation ſhalbe myghtier than the other.
and the eldeſt ſhalbe servaunte vnto the yonger.
24 And whē hir tyme was come to be delyuered be-
25 holde: there were .ii. twyns in hir wōbe. And he that
came out firſt, was redde & rough ouer all as it were
26 an hyde: and they called his name Eſau. And after
ward his brother came out & his hande holdynge
Eſau by the hele. Wherfore his name was called
Iacob And Iſaac was .LX. yere olde whē ſhe bare
27 thē: and the boyes grewe, and Eſau became a conynge
hunter & a tyllman. But Iacob was a tyllman,*farmer*
28 ſimple man & dwelled in the tentes. Iſaac loved Eſau
becauſe he dyd eate of his venyſō, but Rebecca loued
29 Iacob. Iacob ſod potage & Eſau came from the feld
30 & was faītie, & ſayd to Iacob: let me ſyppe of ẏ redde
potage, for I am fayntie. And therfore was his name
31 called Edom. And Iacob ſayde: ſell me this daye thy
32 byrthrighte. And Eſau anſwered: Loo I am at the
poynte to dye, & what profit ſhall this byrthrighte do
33 me? And Iacob ſayde, ſwere to me then this daye.
And he ſwore to him & ſold his byrthrighte vnto
Iacob.

34 Than Iacob gaue Eſau brede and potage of redde
ryſe. And he ate & dronke & roſe vp and went his
waye. And ſo Eſau regarded not his byrthrighte.

M. 29, 30 fayntye . ſuppe

V. 23 ex vētre tuo diuidentur 25 & totus in morem pellis hispidus . . plantam fratris tenebat manu 27 vir ſimplex 28 Iſaac amabat . . Rebecca diligebat 29 Coxit . . . pulmētum 30 quia oppido laſſus ſum 34 Et ſic accepto pane & lentis edulio comedit, & bibit, & abijt, paruipendens quod primogenita vendidiſſet.

L. 23 werden ſich ſcheyden 25 gantz rauch wie eyn fell 27 eyn bydder man 31 verkauff myr heutte 33 ſchwere myr heut 34 linſen gericht . . . vnd ſtund auff vnd gieng dauon vnd alſo verachtet Eſau

M. M. N. 23 *Two maner of people;* By this .ii. people is ſignifyed vnto vs the lawe & the goſpell as ye maye rede in Gal. iii, d. 27 *A ſymple;* He is ſimple that is without craft & decept & contynueth in beleuyng & executynge of godes wyll.

The .XXVI. Chapter.

1 AND there fell a derth in ẏ lande,
paſſinge the firſt derth ẏ fell
in the dayes of Abraham.
Wherfore Iſaac [Fo. XXXV.]
went vnto Abimelech kinge of ẏ Phil-
2 iſtiãs vnto Gerar. Thē the LORde a-
peared vnto him & ſayde: goo not doune
in to Egipte, but byde in ẏ land which I
3 ſaye vnto ẏ: Sogeorne in this lãde, & I
wyll be with ẏ & wyll bleſſe ẏ: for vnto
the & vnto thy ſede I wyll geue all theſe
cõtreis And I will performe the oothe
which I ſwore vnto Abrahã thy father,
4 & will multiplye thy ſeed as ẏ ſtarres of
heavē, & will geue vnto thy ſeed all theſe
contreis. And thorow thy ſeed ſhall all the natiõs of
5 the erth be bleſſed, becauſe ẏ Abrahã harkened vnto
mi voyce & kepte mine ordinaũces, cõmaundmētes,
ſtatutes & lawes

M.C.S. The iorneye of Iſaac toward Abimelech. The promes made vnto Iſaac & his ſeede. Iſaac is rebuked of Abimelech for callyng his wyfe his ſyſter. The chydyng of the ſhepardes for the welles. Isaac is comforted. The atonemēt betwene Abimelech & Iſaac.

6, 7 And Iſaac dwelled in Gerar. And ẏ mē of the
place aſked hĩ of his wife, & he ſayde ẏ ſhe was his
ſiſter: for he feared to calle her his wife leſt the mē of
the place ſhulde haue kylled him for hir ſake, becauſe
8 ſhe was bewtyfull to ẏ eye. And it happened after he
had bene there longe tyme, ẏ Abimelech kinge of ẏ
Philiſtiãs loked out at a wyndow & ſawe Iſaac ſport-
9 inge with Rebecca his wife. And Abimelech ſende
for Iſaac & ſayde: ſe, ſhe is of a ſuertie thi wife, and
why ſaydeſt thou ẏ ſhe was thi ſiſter? And Iſaac ſaide
vnto hĩ: I thoughte ẏ I mighte peradventure haue
10 dyed for hir ſake. Thē ſayde Abimelech: whi haſt

V. 1 poſt eam ſterilitatem 3 Et peregrinare 4 benedicentur in ſemine 7 propter illius pulchritudinem. 8 iocantem c. Reb. 9 cur mentitus es eam ſororem

L. 3 dis land geben 4 dis land geben . . vnd durch deynen ſamen. 8 Yſaac ſchertzet mit ſeynem weyb Rebeca.

thou done this vnto vs? one of ẏ people myght
lightely haue lyne by thy wife & ſo ſhuldeſt thou haue
11 broughte ſynne vpon vs Thā Abimelech charged all
his people ſaynge: he ẏ toucheth this man or his wife,
ſhall ſurely dye for it.
12 .P. And Iſaac ſowed in ẏ lāde, & founde in ẏ ſame
13 yere an hūdred buſhels: for ẏ LORde bleſſed hī, & the
man waxed mightye, & wēt forth & grewe till he was
14 exceadinge great, ẏ he had poſſeſſiō of ſhepe, of oxē
& a myghtie houſholde: ſo ẏ the Phileſtians had envy
15 at him: In so moch ẏ they ſtopped & ſylled vp
with erth, all the welles which his fathers ſervauntes
16 dygged in his father Abrahams tyme. Than ſayde
Abimelech vnto Iſaac: gett the frō me, for thou art
myghtier then we a greate deale.
17 Than Iſaac departed thenſe & pitched his tente in
18 the valey Gerar & dwelt there. And Iſaac digged
agayne, the welles of water which they dygged in the
dayes of Abrahā his father which the Phileſtiās had
ſtoppe after ẏ deth of Abrahā & gaue thē the ſame
19 names which hys father gaue thē. As Iſaacs ſeruaūtes
dygged in the valey, they founde a well of ſpringynge
20 water. And the herdmē of Gerar dyd ſtryue with
Iſaacs herdmē ſaynge: the water is oures Than called
he the well Eſeck becauſe they ſtroue with hym.
21 Than dygged they another well, & they ſtroue for
22 ẏ alſo. Therfore called he it Sitena. And than he
departed thēſe & dygged a nother well for the which
they ſtroue not: therfore called he it Rehoboth ſaīge:
ẏ LORde hath now made vs rowme & we are en-

M. 12 ſowed in that lande 19 lyuyng water 20 Eſeck

V. 11 morte morietur 12 in ipſo anno centuplum 14 Ob hoc inuidentes 16 in tantum vt ipſe Abim. 17 torrentem Geraræ 18 quos foderant ſerui patris ſui Abraham, & quos illo mortuo olim obſtruxerāt Philiſthijm: 19 repererunt aquam viuam. 20 ex eo quod acciderat, vocauit Calumniam. 21 appellauitque eum Inimicitias. 22 Latitudo:

L. 11 des tods ſterben 12 hundert ſcheffel 20 das ſie yhn da verhonet hatten

L. M. N. 20 *Eſek* heyſt, Hon, wenn man yemannt gewallt vnd vnrecht thut. 21 *Sitena*, heyſt widderſtand, daher der teuffel Satan heyſt eyn widder wertiger. 22 *Rehoboth* heyſt, raum odder breytte, das nicht enge iſt.

23 creased vpō the erth. Afterward departed he thēce
& came to Bersseba
24 And the LORde apered vnto hī the same nyghte
& sayde. I am the God of Abrahā thy father, feare
not for I am with the & will blesse [Fo. .XXXVI.] the
& multiplye thy sede for my seruaūte Abrahams sake.
25 And than he buylded an aulter there and called vpō
the name of the LORde, & there pitched his tente.
And there Isaacs servauntes dygged a well.
26 Than came Abimelech to him frō Gerar & Ahusath
27 his frende and Phicol his chefe captayne. And Isaac
sayde vnto thē: wherefore come ye to me, seīge ye
28 hate me & haue put me awaye frō you? Than sayde
they: we sawe that the LORde was with the, and
therfore we sayde that there shulde be an oothe betwixte vs ād the, & that we wolde make a bonde with
29 the: ỷ thou shuldeste do vs no hurte, as we haue not
touched the and haue done vnto the nothinge but
good, and sēd the away in peace: for thou art now
30 the blessed of the LORde. And he made thē a feast,
31 and they ate ād drōke. And they rose vp by tymes in
the mornynge and sware one to another. And Isaac
sent thē awaye. And they departed from him in peace.
32 And ỷ same daye came Isaacs servaūtes & tolde hī
of a well which they had dygged: & sayde vnto hī, that
33 thei had founde water. And he called it Seba, wherfore
the name of the cyte is called Berseba vnto this daye.

M. 32 that same daye

V. 29 nec fecimus quod te læderet 33 Vnde appellauit eum Abundantiam:

L. 28 Wyr sehen mit sehenden augen 29 vnd wie wyr dyr nichts denn alles gutt than haben.

M. M. N. 22 *Encreased:* as yf he shulde saye, after so great paynes & laboures, God hath geuen vs peace & quyetnes. For quyetnes doth open & increase the hert, & sadnes restrayneth it: as in Gen. ix, d. Ps. iiii, a.

L. M. N. 33 *Seba* heyst eyn, Eyd, oder schwur *Ber* aber heyst eyn brun.

The .XXVII. Chapter.

34 WHEN Eſau was .XL. yere olde, he toke to
wyfe Iudith the doughter of Bery an Hethite, and Baſmath the doughter of Elon an
35 Hethite alſo, which were diſhobedient vnto
Iſaac and Rebecca.

1 .P. And it came to paſſe that Iſaac
wexed olde & his eyes were dymme, ſo
that he coude nat ſee. Thã called he
Eſau his eldeſt ſonne & ſayde vnto him:
mi ſonne. And he ſayde vnto hym: heare
2 am I. And he ſayde: beholde, I am olde
3 ãd knowe not the daye of mi deth: Now
therfore take thi weapẽs, thy quiver & thi
bowe, & gett the to the feldes & take me
4 ſome venyſon & make me meate ſuch as I loue, &
brynge it me & let me eat that my ſoull may bleſſe
the before that I dye:

M.C.S. *Iacob ſtealeth the bleſſynge from Eſau by his mothers council. Iſaac is ſad. Eſau is comforted. The hatred of Eſau toward Iacob.*

5 But Rebecca hard whẽ Iſaac ſpoke to Eſau his
ſonne. And as ſoone as Eſau was gone to the felde
6 to catche venyſon & to brĩge it, ſhe ſpake vnto Iacob
hir ſonne ſainge? Behold I haue herde thi father talk-
7 inge with Eſau thy brother & ſaynge: bringe me
venyſon & make me meate that I maye eate & bleſſe
8 the before the LORde yer I dye. Now therfore my
ſonne heare my voyce in that which I cõmaunde the:
9 gett the to the flocke, & bringe me thẽce .ii. good
kiddes, & I will make meate of thẽ for thi father, ſoch
10 as he loueth. And thou ſhalt brĩge it to thi father &
he ſhal eate, ỷ he maye blyſſe the before his deth
11 Than ſayde Iacob to Rebecca his mother. Beholde
12 Eſau mi brother is rugh & I am ſmooth. Mi father ſhal
peraduẽture fele me, ãd I ſhal ſeme vnto hĩ as though

V. 4 pulmentum, ſicut velle me noſti 8 eſcas . . quibus libenter veſcitur

L. 4 wie ichs gern hab

M. M. N. 4 *Bleſſe;* that is that my ſoule may wyſhe the good and praye to God for the.

I wēt aboute to begyle hī, & ſo ſhall he brīge a curſe
13 vpō me & not a bleſſīge: & his mother ſaide vnto him.
Vppō me be thi curſe my ſonne, only heare my voyce,
14 & goo and fetch me them. And Iacob went ād [Fo.
XXXIX.] fett them and brought them to his mother.
And his mother made meate of them accordinge as
15 his father loued. And ſhe went and fett *fett, fetched.*
goodly rayment of hir eldeſt ſonne Eſau which ſhe had
in the houſe with hir, and put them vpon Iacob hir yong-
16 eſt ſonne, ād ſhe put the ſkynnes vpon his hādes & apon
17 the ſmooth of his necke. And ſhe put ẏ meate & brede
which ſhe had made in the hōde of hir ſonne Iacob
18 And he went in to his father ſaynge: my father,
And he āſwered: here am I, who art thou my ſonne?
19 And Iacob ſayde vnto his father: I am Eſau thy eldeſt
ſonne, I haue done acordinge as thou baddeſt me, vp
and ſytt and eate of my venyſon, that thi ſoule maye
20 bleſſe me. But Iſaac ſayde vnto his ſonne. How
cōmeth it that thou haſt fownde it ſo quicly my
ſonne? He anſwered: The LORde thy god brought
21 it to my hande. Than ſayde Iſaac vnto Iacob: come
nere and let me fele the my ſonne, whether thou be
22 my ſonne Eſau or not. Than went Iacob to Iſaac his
father, & he felt him & ſayde the voyce is Iacobs
23 voyce, but the hādes ar ẏ hādes of Eſau. And he
knewe him not, becauſe his handes were rough as his
brother Eſaus handes? And ſo he bleſſed him.
24 And he axed him, art thou my ſonne Eſau? And
25 he ſayde: that I am. Than ſayde he: brynge me and
let me eate of my ſonnes venyſon, that my ſoule maye
bleſſe the. And he broughte him, & he ate. And he
26 broughte him wyne .P. alſo, and he dranke. And his
father Iſaac ſayde vnto him: come nere and kyſſe me
27 my ſonne. And he wēt to him & kiſſed him. And

V. 20 Voluntas dei fuit vt cito occurreret mihi quod volebā
L. 20 der Herr deyn Gott beſcheret myrs
M. M. N. 13 *Curſe:* There are two maner of curſes vſed in the ſcripture. The one is in the ſoule, that pertayneth to the ſoule, & ſynne & wyckednes. And the other to the bodye, as all tēporall miſery and wretchednes, as in Gen. iii, c. & Deut. xxiii, a.

he ſmelled ỷ ſauoure of his raymēt & bleſſed hī &
ſayde See, ỷ ſmell of my ſōne is as ỷ ſmell of a feld
28 which the lorde hath bleſſed. God geue the of ỷ dewe
of heavē & of the fatneſſe of the erth and plētie of
29 corne & wyne. People be thy ſervauntes & natiōs
bowe vnto the. Be lorde ouer thy brethrē, and thy
mothers children ſtoupe vnto the. Curſed be he ỷ
curſeth the, & bleſſed be he that bleſſeth the.
30 As ſoone as Iſaac had made an end of bleſſīg,
Iacob & Iacob was ſcace gone out frō the preasence
of Iſaac his father: then came Eſau his brother frō his
31 huntynge: And had made alſo meate, and brought it
in vnto his father & ſayde vnto him: Aryſe my father
& eate of thy ſonnes venyſon, that thy ſoule maye
32 bleſſe me. Thā his father Iſaac ſayde vnto him. Who
art thou? he anſwered I am thy eldeſt ſonne Eſau.
33 And Iſaac was greatly aſtoyned out of
meſure and ſayde: Where is he then that
hath hūted venyſon and broughte it me,
and I haue eaten of all before thou cameſt, and haue
34 bleſſed him, ād he ſhall be bleſſed ſtyll. Whē Eſau
herde the wordes of his father, he cryed out greatly
& bitterly aboue meſure, and ſayde vnto his father:
35 bleſſe me alſo my father. And he ſayde thy brother
came with ſubtilte, ād hath takē awaye thy bleſſynge.
36 Than ſayde he: He maye [Fo. XXXX.] well be called
Iacob, for he hath vndermyned me now .ii. tymes, fyrſt

aſtoyned, *amazed, ſtruck with amazement.*

M. 30 bleſſyng, Iacob was 31 brought it vnto hys

V. 27 ſenſit veſtimentorum illius fragrantiam 33 Expauit Iſaac ſtupore vehementi: & vltra quam credi poteſt admirans

L. 29 Sey eyn herr vber deyne bruder, vnd deiner mutter kinder 33 Da entſatzt ſich Yſaac vber die mas ſeer .... Wer? wo iſt denn der ieger

M. M. N. 28 *Dewe;* By this worde dewe is vnderſtond of the Hebrews al that is in the fyrmament, that cōforteth the erth, as the ſonne, the mone, rayne, & temperatnes of wether, as by the fatnes of the erth they vnderſtonde all that is brought forthe benethe in the erth, as Ex. xvi, d, and Numeri xi, b. *Corne;* By corne and wyne is vnderſtonde aboundance of all tēporall thynges.

L. M. N. 36 *Vntertretten;* Ekeb heyſſt eyn fuſz ſoll, da her kompt Iakob oder Iacob eyn vntertreter odder der mit fuſſen tritt, vnd bedeut alle gleubigen, die durch das Euangelion die wellt vnd das fleyſch vnd den teuffel mit ſund und todt vnter ſich tretten.

he toke awaye my byrthrighte: and ſe, now hath he
taken awaye my bleſſynge alſo. And he ſayde, haſt
thou kepte neuer a bleſſynge for me?
37 Iſaac anſwered and ſayde vnto Eſau: beholde I
haue made him thi LORde & all his mothers childern haue I made his ſeruantes. Moreouer wyth corne
ād wyne haue I ſtableſſhed him, what cā I do vnto the
38 now my ſonne? And Eſau ſayde vnto his father: haſt
thou but ẏ one bleſſynge my father? bleſſe me alſo my
39 father: ſo lyfted vp Eſau his voyce & wepte Thā
Iſaac his father anſwered & ſayde vnto him
Beholde thy dwellynge place ſhall haue of the fat-
40 neſſe of the erth, & of the dewe of heauen frō aboue. And
wyth thy ſwerde ſhalt thou lyue and ſhalt be thy brothers ſeruaunte But the tyme will come, when thou ſhalt
gett the maſtrye, and lowſe his yocke from of thy necke.
41 And Eſau hated Iacob becauſe of the bleſſynge ẏ
his father bleſſed him with all, & ſayde in his harte:
The dayes of my fathers ſorowe are at hāde, for I will
42 ſley my brother Iacob. And theſe wordes of Eſau hir
eldeſt ſonne, were told to Rebecca. And ſhe ſente ād
called Iacob hir yongeſt ſonne, and ſayde vnto hī: be-
43 holde thy brother Eſau threatneth to kyll the: Now
therfore my ſōne heare my voyce, make the redie &
44 flee to Labā my brother at Haran. And tarie with
him a while, vntill thy .P. brothers fearſnes be ſwaged,
45 and vntill thy brothers wrath turne awaye from the,
and he forgett that which thou haſt done to him. Thā
will I ſende and fett the awaye from thence. Why
ſhulde I loſe you both in one daye.
46 And Rebecca ſpake to Iſaac: I am wery of my life,
for feare of the doughters of Heth. Yf Iacob take a wife
of the doughters of Heth, ſoch one as theſe are, or of the
doughters of the lande, what luſt ſhuld I haue to lyue.

V. 37 et omnes fratres eius 38 Cumque eiulato magno fleret, 39 motus Iſaac dixit . . In ping. terræ, & in rore cæli deſuper erit benedictio tua 40 eum excutias et ſoluas . . . de ceruicibus tuis 41 dies luctus 46 nolo viuere.

L. 40 Vnd es wirt geſchehen daſs du ſeyn ioch ablegiſt vnd von deynem halſze reyſſiſt. 41 das mein vater leyde tragen mus 45 ſeyn zorn wydder dich von dyr wende 46 waſſol myr das leben?

The .XXVIII. Chapter.

M.C.S. Iacob is ſent into Meſopotamia to Laban for a wyfe. Eſau marieth an Iſmaelyte. Iacob dreameth a dreame. Chriſt is promyſed. Iacob maketh a vowe.

1 THAN Iſaac called Iacob his
ſonne and bleſſed him, ād
charged him and ſayde vnto
him: ſe thou take not a wife
2 of the doughters of Canaan, but aryse
ād gett the to Meſopotamia to the houſe
of Bethuel thy mothers father: and there
take the a wife of the doughters of Laban
3 thi mothers brother. And God allmightie
bleſſe the, increaſe the and multiplie the that thou
4 mayſt be a nombre of people, and geue the the bleſſynge of Abraham: both to the and to thy ſeed with
the that thou mayſt poſſeſſe the lāde (wherein thou art
5 a ſtrangere) which God gaue vnto Abraham. Thus
Iſaac ſent forth Iacob, to goo to Meſopotamia vnto
Laban, ſonne of Bethuel the Sirien, and brother to
Rebecca Iacobs & Esaus mother.

6 When Eſau ſawe that Iſaac had bleſſed Iacob, and
ſent him to Meſopotamia, to fett him a wife thence,
and that, as he bleſſed him [Fo. XLI.] he gaue him a
charge ſaynge: ſe thou take not a wife of the
7 doughters of Canaan: and that Iacob had obeyed
his father and mother, & was gone vnto Meſopo-
8 tomia: and ſeynge alſo that the doughters of Canaan
9 pleaſed not Iſaac his father: Then went he vnto
Iſmael, and toke vnto the wiues which he had, Mahala
the doughter of Iſmael Abrahams ſonne, the ſiſter of
Nabaioth to be his wife.

10 Iacob departed from Berſeba and went toward
11 Haran, and came vnto a place and taried there all
nyghte, becauſe the ſonne was downe. And toke a
ſtone of the place, and put it vnder his heade, and

V. 2 Laban auunculi tui 4 terram peregrinationis tuæ, quam pollicitus eſt auo tuo. 6 quod poſt benedictionem præcep. 11 tulit de lapidibus qui iacebant

L. 2 deyner mutter bruder 3 eyn hauffen volcker 5 ſeyner vnd Eſau mutter 6 ynn dem er yhn ſegenet, yhm gepot 9 nam vber die weyber, die er zuuor hatte 11 eynen ſteyn des orts

12 layde him down in the ſame place to ſlepe. And
he dreamed: and beholde there ſtode a ladder apon
the erth, and the topp of it reached vpp to heauē.
And ſe, the angells of God went vpp and downe apon
13 it, yee ād the LORde ſtode apon it and ſayde.
I am the LORde God of Abraham thi father and
the God of Iſaac: The londe which thou ſlepeſt apon
14 will I geue the and thy ſeed. And thy ſeed ſhalbe as
the duſt of the erth: And thou ſhalt ſpreade abrode:
weſt, eaſt, north and ſouth. And thorow the and thy
ſeed ſhall all the kynreddes of the erth be bleſſed.
15 And ſe I am with the, and wylbe thy keper in all
places whother thou gooſt, and will brynge yͤ agayne
in to this lande: Nether will I leaue the vntill I haue
made good, all that I haue promyſed the .¶.
16 When Iacob was awaked out of his ſlepe, he ſayde:
ſurely the LORde is in this place, ād I was not aware.
17 And he was afrayde & ſayde how fearfull is this place?
it is none other, but euen the houſe of God and the
18 gate of heauē. And Iacob ſtode vp early in the mornynge and toke the ſtone that he had layde vnder his
heade, and pitched it vp an ende and — vp an ende, *upright*
19 poured oyle on the topp of it. And he
called the name of the place Bethell, for in dede the
name of the citie was called Lus before tyme.
20 And Iacob vowed a vowe ſaynge: Yf God will be
with me and wyl kepe me in this iourney which I goo
and will geue me bread to eate and cloothes to put on,

M. 15 whether

V. 13 dominum innixum ſcalæ 14 quaſi puluis terræ: dilataberis 18 & erexit in titulum, fundens

L. 14 auszbreyttet werden . . Vnd durch dich 16 gewiſlich iſt der herr 18 vnd richtet yhn auff

M. M. N. 17 *Houſe of God;* He calleth it the houſe of god becauſe of the houſholde of angells that he there ſawe: we in lyke maner call the church of lyme and ſtone the houſe of God, becauſe the people come thether, whych are the church of God. As ſaynt Paul teacheth 1 Cor. iii. 2 Cor. vi. Eph. xii. (?). 19 *Bethel* ſygnifyeth the houſe of God

L. M. N. 14 *Deynen Samen;* Hie wirt dem dritten Patriarchen, Chriſtus verheyſſen der heyland aller wellt, vnd das kunfftige Euangelion von Chriſto ynn allen landen zu predigen durch die engel auff der leytter fürgebildet.

21 so that I come agayne vnto my fathers house in saftie:
22 then shall the LORde be my God, and this stone which
I haue sett vp an ende, shalbe godes house, And of all
that thou shalt geue me, will I geue the tenth vnto the.

The .XXIX. Chapter.

M.C.S. Iacob cometh to Laban & serueth seuē yere for Rachel. Lea was brought to his bed in stede of Rachel. He maryeth them bothe, and serueth yet .vii yere more for Rachel. Lea conceaueth.

1 THEN Iacob lyfte vp his fete &
wēt toward the east countre.
2 And as he loked aboute, beholde there was a well in the
feld, and .iii. flockes of shepe laye therby
(for at that well were the flockes watered)
& there laye a great stone at the well
3 mouth And the maner was to brynge
the flockes thyther, & to roull the stone
frō the welles mouth and to water the
shepe, and to put the stone a- [Fo. XLII.]
gayne vppon the wells mouth vnto his place.
4 And Iacob sayde vnto thē: brethern, whēce be ye?
5 and they sayde: of Haran ar we. And he sayde vnto
thē: Knowe ye Laban the sonne of Nahor. And they
6 sayde: We knowe him. And he sayde vnto thē: is he
in good health? And they sayde: he is in good health:
and boholde, his doughter Rahel cometh with ỹ shepe.
7 And he sayde: lo, it is yet a great whyle to nyghte,
nether is it tyme ỹ the catell shulde be gathered
together: water the shepe and goo and fede thē.

V. 3 Morisque erat . . . deuoluerent lapidem, & refectis 7 vt reducantur ad caulas greges . . . & sic eas ad pastum reducite

L. 3 vnd sie pflegten . . an seyne stett 7 es ist noch viel tages (corrected into: hoch tag)

M. M. N. 22 *Tythes:* By tythes the auncyent fathers meāt all great rewardes as in Gen. xiiii, d.

L. M. N. 21 *Mein Gott seyn;* Nicht das er vorhyn nicht seyn Got gewesen sey, sondern er gelobd eyn gottis dienst auff zu richten, do man predigen vnd betten sollt, Da will er den zehenden zugeben, den predigern, wie Abraham dem Melchisedek den zehenden gab.

8 And they ſayde: we may not, vntill all ẏ flockes be
brought together & the ſtone be roulled frō the wells
mouth, and ſo we water oure ſhepe.

9 Whyle he yet talked with thē, Rahel came with
10 hir fathers ſhepe, for ſhe kepte them. As ſoone As
Iacob ſawe Rahel, the doughter of Laban his mothers
brother, and the ſhepe of Laban his mothers brother,
he went and rowled the ſtone frō the wells mouth, and
11 watered the ſhepe of Labā his mothers brother And
Iacob kyſſed Rahel, and lyfte vp his voyce and wepte:
12 and tolde her alſo ẏ he was hir fathers brother and
Rebeccas ſonne. Thē Rahel ranne and tolde hir
13 father. When Laban herd tell of Iacob his ſiſters
ſonne, he ranne agaynſt him and embraced hī & kyſſed
him ād broughte him in to his houſe. And thē Iacob
14 told Laban all ẏ matter. And thē Labā ſayde: well,
thou art my bone & my fleſh .P. Abyde with me the
15 ſpace of a moneth. And afterward Laban ſayd vnto
Iacob: though thou be my brother, ſhuldeſt thou therfore ſerue me for nought? tell me what ſhall thi wages
16 be? And Laban had .ii. doughters, the eldeſt called
17 Lea and the yongeſt Rahel. Lea was tender eyed:
18 But Rahel was bewtifull ād well fauored. And Iacob
loued her well, and ſayde: I will ſerue the .vii. yere for
19 Rahel thy yongeſt doughter. And Laban anſwered:
it is better ẏ I geue her the, than to another man?
byde therfore with me.

20 And Iacob ſerued .vii. yeres for Rahel, and they
ſemed vnto him but a fewe dayes, for the loue he had
21 to her. And Iacob ſayde vnto Laban, geue me my
wife, that I maye lye with hir For the tyme appoynted
me is come.

M. 9 for ſhe kepte thē 13 he rāne to mete him . . . brought him to his houſe.

V. 10 Quam cum vid. Iac. & ſciret conſobrinam ſuam 13 Auditis autem cauſis itineris 17 Lia, lippis erat oculis: Rachel decora facie & venuſto aspectu. 18 præ amoris magnitudine

L. 8 zu ſammen bracht werden . . vnd alſzo die ſchaff 10 die ſchaff . . ſeyner muter bruder. 13 all dis geſchicht 14 Wolan du biſt 17 eyn blode geſicht 20 vnd dauchten yhn als werens eyntzele tage 21 denn die zeyt iſt hie, das ich bei lige

22 Than Laban bade all the men of that place, and
23 made a feaſt. And when euē was come, he toke Lea
his doughter and broughte her to him and he went in
24 vnto her. And Laban gaue vnto his doughter Lea,
Zilpha his mayde, to be hir ſeruaunte.
25 And when the mornynge was come, beholde it was
Lea. Than ſayde he to Laban: wherfore haſt thou
played thus with me? dyd not I ſerue the for Rahel,
26 wherfore than haſt thou begyled me? Laban anſwered:
it is not the maner of this place, to marie the yongeſt
27 before the eldeſt. Paſſe out this weke, & thā ſhall this
alſo be geven the for ẏ ſeruyce which thou ſhalt [Fo.
28 XLI.] ſerue me yet .vii. yeres more. And Iacob dyd
euē ſo, and paſſed out that weke, & than he gaue hī
29 Rahel his doughter to wyfe alſo. And Laban gaue to
Rahel his doughter, Bilha his handmayde to be hir
30 ſervaūte. So laye he by Rahel alſo, and loved Rahel
more than Lea, and ſerued him yet .vii. yeres more.
31 When the LORde ſawe that Lea was deſpiſed, he
32 made her frutefull: but Rahel was baren. And Lea
conceaued and bare a ſonne, ād called his name Rubē,
for ſhe ſayde :: the LORde hath loked apon my tribula-
33 tion. And now my huſbonde will loue me. And ſhe
conceaued agayne and bare a ſonne, and ſayde: the
LORde hath herde that I am deſpiſed, ād hath therfore
geuen me this ſonne alſo, and ſhe called him Simeon.
34 And ſhe conceaued yet and bare a ſonne, ād ſayde: now
this once will my huſbonde kepe me company, becauſe
I haue borne him .iii. ſonnes: and therfore ſhe called
35 his name Levi. And ſhe conceaued yet agayne, and
bare a ſonne ſaynge: Now will I prayſe the LORde:
therfore ſhe called his name Iuda, and left bearynge.

V. 24 Ad quam cum ex more, Iac. f. ingreſſus 27 Imple hebdomadam dierum huius copulæ 30 Tandemque potitus optatis nuptijs, amorem ſequentis priori prætulit 32 humilitatem meam

L. 25 denn betrogen 26 die iungſt aufgebe 27 hallt diſe wochen aus 27 Rahel ſeyne tochter zum weybe 30 lag er auch bey mit R. 31 macht er . . . vnd R. vnfruchtbar 33 hat gehoret, das ich gehaſſet 34 nu . . . . widder zu myr thun

L. M. N. 32 *Ruben* heyſt eyn ſeheſon. 33 *Simeon* heyſt eyn horer. 34 *Leui* heyſt zuthat. 35 *Iuda* heyſt eyn bekenner odder danck ſager. *Dan* heyſt eyn richter. [xxx, 6]

☙ The .XXX. Chapter.

1 WHEN Rahel ſawe that ſhe bare
Iacob no childern, ſhe enuied
hir ſiſter & ſayde vnto Iacob:
geue me childern, or ells I am
2 but deed. Than was Iacob wrooth with
Rahel ſaynge: Am I in godes ſteade which
3 kepeth frō the the frute of thi wōbe? Then
ſhe ſayde: here is my mayde Bilha: go in
vnto .P. her, that ſhe maye beare vpō my
lappe, that I maye be encreaſed by her.
4 And ſhe gaue him Bilha hir hādmayde to
5 wife. And Iacob wēt in vnto her, And
6 Bilha conceaued and bare Iacob a ſonne. Than ſayde
Rahel. God hath geuen ſentēce on my ſyde, and hath
alſo herde my voyce, and hath geuen me a ſonne.
7 Therfore called ſhe him Dan. And Bilha Rahels
mayde cōceaued agayne and bare Iacob a nother
8 ſonne. And Rahel ſayde. God is turned, and I haue
made a chaunge with my ſiſter, & haue gotē ẏ vpper
hāde. And ſhe called his nam: Nepthali.

M.C.S. Rachel and Lea being bothe baren geue their maydēs vnto their huſbande & they bare him chyldren. Iacob deceaueth Laban in the conceyuinge of the ſhepe and kyddes. Iacobs rewarde for hys ſerues.

9 Whē Lea ſawe that ſhe had left bearinge, ſhe toke
10 Silpha hir mayde and gaue her Iacob to wiffe. And
11 Silpha Leas made bare Iacob a ſonne. Than ſayde
12 Lea: good lucke: and called his name Gad. And
13 Silpha Leas mayde bare Iacob an other ſonne. Thā
ſayd Lea: happy am I, for the doughters will call me
bleſſed. And called his name Aſſer.

14 And Rubē wēt out in the wheatharueſt & foūde

V. 2 qui priuauit te fructu ventris 3 ſuper genua mea 6 Iudicauit mihi dom. 13 Hoc pro beatudine mea

L. 1 nichts gepar 3 auff meynen ſchos .. durch ſie erbawet werde.

L. M. N. 8 *Naphthali* heyſt verwechſelt, vmbgewand, vmbgekert, wenn man dz widderſpiel thut. Ps. 17. mit dem verkere. en verkeriſtu dich. 11 *Gad,* heyſt ruſtig zum ſtreyt 13 *Aſſer* heyſt ſelig.

mandragoras in the feldes, and brought thē vnto his
mother Lea. Than ſayde Rahel to Lea geue me of
15 thy ſonnes mādragoras. And Lea anſwered: is it not
ynough, ỷ thou haſt takē awaye my houſbōde, but
woldeſt take awaye my ſons mandragoras alſo? Than
ſayde Rahel well, let him ſlepe with the this nyghte,
16 for thy ſonnes mandragoras And whē Iacob came
from the feldes at euen, Lea went out to mete him, &
ſayde: come in to me, for I haue bought [Fo. XLII.]
the with my ſonnes mandragoras.
17 And he ſlepte with her that nyghte. And God
herde Lea, ỷ ſhe cōceaued and bare vnto Iacob ỷ .v
18 ſonne. Than ſayde Lea. God hath geuē me my rewarde, becauſe I gaue my maydē to my houſbōd, and
19 ſhe called him Iſachar. And Lea cōceaued yet agayne
20 and bare Iacob the ſexte ſonne. Than ſayde ſhe: God
hath endewed me with a good dowry. dowry, *gift*
Now will my houſbond dwell with me, becauſe I haue
borne him .vi. ſonnes: and called his name Zabulō.
21 After that ſhe bare a doughter and called her Dina.
22 And God remēbred Rahel, herde her, and made
23 her frutefull: ſo that ſhe cōceaued and bare a ſonne
24 and ſayde God hath takē awaye my rebuke. And ſhe
called his name Ioſeph ſaynge The lorde geue me
25 yet a nother ſonne. As ſoone as Rahel had borne
Ioſeph, Iacob ſayde to Laban: Sēde me awaye ỷ I
26 may goo vnto myne awne place and cūtre, geue me
my wives and my childern for whom I haue ſerued
the, and let me goo: for thou knoweſt what ſeruyce I

M. 15 houſband (alſo vv. 19, 20.)

V. 15 quod præripueris 16 mercede cōnduxi te pro mandragoris 20 Dotauit me deus dote bona 25 Nato autem Ioſeph

V. 14 der alrun deyns ſons eyn teyl 15 wohlan, laſs yhn

M. M. N. 14 *Mandragoras;* The Hebrews call it an erbe or rather a rote that beareth the ſimylitude of mānes bodye. Other call it an apple whych being eatē wyth meate cauſeth concepciō. Saynt Auſten thynketh that it pleaſeth women becauſe it hath a pleaſant ſauoure, or rather for dayntines, becauſe there was not many of them to get.

L. M. N. 18 *Iſachar* heyſt lohn. 20 *Sebulon*, heyſt beywonung 21 *Dina* heyſt eyn ſach oder gericht 24 *Ioſeph* heyſt, zuthun, odder fort mehr thun.

27 haue done the. Than ſayde Laban vnto hī: If I haue
fownde fauoure in thy ſyghte (for I ſuppoſe ẏ the
28 LORde hath bleſſed me for thy ſake) appoynte what
29 thy rewarde ſhalbe and I will geue it ẏ. But he ſayde
vnto hym, thou knoweſt what ſeruyce I haue done ẏ
& in what takynge thy catell haue bene vnder me:
30 For it was but litle that thou haddeſt before I came,
and now it is encreaſed in to a multitude, and the
LORDE hath bleſſed the for my ſake .¶. But now
when ſhall I make provyſion for myne awne houſe
31 alſo? And he ſayde: what ſhall I geue the? And
Iacob anſwerd: thou ſhalt geue me nothinge at all,
yf thou wilt do this one thinge for me: And then will
I turne agayne & fede thy ſhepe and kepe them.
32 I will go aboute all thy ſhepe this daye, and ſeparate frō thē all the ſhepe that are ſpotted and of dy-
verſe coloures, and all blacke ſhepe amonge the lambes
33 and the partie and ſpotted amonge the kyddes: And
then ſuch ſhalbe my rewarde. So ſhall my rightwes-
nes anſwere for me: when the tyme commeth that
I ſhall receaue my rewarde of the: So that what
ſoeuer is not ſpeckeld and partie amonge the gootes

M. 31 ſhal I then geue the? 32 and the ſpotted 33 & the ſame ſhalbe

V. 27 experimēto didici quia bened. 30 nūc diues effectus es . . deus ad introitū meū 33 Reſpondebitque mihi cras iuſtitia mea . . furti me argues

L. 29 was fur eynen dienſt ich dyr gethan habe

M. M. N. 33 Ryghteouſnes ſygnifyeth here true and faythfull ſeruyce.

L. M. N. 32 *Zigen.* Du muſt hie dich nicht yrren, das Moſes, das kleyne viech, itzt zigē, itzt lemmer, itzt bocke heyſt, wie diſer ſprach art iſt, Denn er will ſo viel ſagen, dz Iacob hab alles weys einferbig viehe behalten vnnd alles bundte vnd ſchwartz Laban gethan, was nu bund von dem einferbigen viech keme, das ſollte ſeyn lohn ſeyn, des wart Laban froh, vnd hatte die natur fur ſich, das vō eynferbigen nicht viel bundte naturlich komen, Aber Iacob halff der natur mit kunſt, das die eynferbigen viel bundte trugen.

Durch dis geſchichte iſt bedeut, das durchs Euangelion werdē die ſeelē von den geſetz treybern vnd werck heyligen abgefurt, darynnen ſie bund, ſprincklicht vnd flecket, dz iſt, mit mancherley gaben des geyſt getziert werden Rom. 12. vnd 1 Cor. 12. das vnter dem geſetz vnd wercken nur die vntuchtigen bleyben, denn Laban heyſt, weys odder gleyſend, vnd bedeut, der gleyſſener hauffen ynn den ſchonen wercken auch gottlichs geſetzs.

and blacke amonge the lambes, let that be theft
with me.
34 Than ſayde Laban: loo, I am contēte, that it be
35 acordinge as thou haſt ſayde. And he toke out that
ſame daye the he gootes that were partie & of dyuerſe
coloures, & all the gootes that were ſpotted and partie
coloured, & all that had whyte in thē, & all the blacke
amonge the lambes: ād put thē in the kepinge of his
36 ſonnes, & ſett thre dayes iourney betwixte hīſelfe &
Iacob. And ſo Iacob kepte ẏ reſt of Labās ſhepe.
37 Iacob toke roddes of grene popular, haſell, & of
cheſtnottrees, & pilled whyte ſtrakes in thē & made
38 the white apere in the ſtaues: And he put the ſtaues
which he had pilled, euē before ẏ ſhe- [Fo. XLIII.] pe,
in the gutters & watrynge troughes, whē the ſhepe
came to drynke: ẏ they ſhulde cōceaue whē they came
39 to drynke. And the ſhepe cōceaued before the ſtaues
40 & brought forth ſtraked, ſpotted & partie. Thē Iacob
parted the lābes, & turned the faces of the ſhepe toward ſpotted thinges, & toward all maner of blacke
thinges thorow out the flockes of Labā. And he
made him flockes of his owne by thē ſelfe, which he
41 put not vnto the flockes of Labā. And allwaye in
the firſt buckinge tyme of the ſhepe, Iacob put the
ſtaues before the ſhepe in the gutters, ẏ they myghte
42 conceaue before the ſtaues, But in the latter buckynge tyme, he put them not there: ſo the laſt brode
43 was Labās and the firſt Iacobs. And the man became excedynge ryche & had many ſhepe, mayde-
ſeruauntes, menſeruauntes, camels & aſſes.

V. 37 ex parte decorticauit eas: detractiſque corticibus in his quæ ſpoliata fuerant, cādor apparuit: illa vero quæ integra fuerant viridia permanſerunt: atque in hunc modum color effectus eſt varius. 42 Quādo vero ſerotina admiſura erat, & cōceptus extremus

L. 33 das ſey eyn diebſtal bey myr. 36 vnd macht rawm

ℭ The .XXXI. Chapter.

𝔐.ℭ.𝔖. At the cōmaundement of God, Iacob departed frō Laban, & toke hys goodes with hym. Rachel ſtealeth hyr fathers ymages. Laban foloweth Iacob. The couenaunt betwene Laban and Iacob.

1 AND Iacob herde the wordes of
Labās ſonnes how they ſayde:
Iacob hath takē awaye all that
was oure fathers, and of oure
fathers goodes, hath he gotē all this
2 honoure. And Iacob behelde the countenaūce of Laban, that it was not toward
him as it was in tymes paſt.
3 And the LORde ſayde vnto Iacob:
turne agayne in to the lāde of thy fathers
4 & to thy kynred, & I wilbe with ỷ. Thā
Iacob ſent & called Rahel & Lea to the
5 felde vnto his ſhepe & ſayde vnto thē: I ſe youre
fathers countenaūce ỷ it is not toward me as in tymes
paſt. Morouer .P.· ỷ God of my father hath bene with
6 me. And ye knowe how that I haue ſerued youre
7 father with all my myghte. And youre father hath
diſceaued me & chaunged my wages .x. tymes: But
8 God ſuffred him not to hurte me. When he ſayde
the ſpotted ſhalbe thy wages, thā all the ſhepe bare
ſpotted. Yf he ſayde the ſtraked ſhalbe thi rewarde,
9 thā bare all the ſhepe ſtraked: thus hath God takē
10 awaye youre fathers catell & geuē thē me. For in
buckynge tyme, I lifted vp myne eyes and ſawe in a
dreame: and beholde, the rammes that bucked the
11 ſhepe were ſtraked, ſpotted and partie. And the
angell of God ſpake vnto me in a dreame ſaynge:
12 Iacob. And I anſwered: here am I. And he ſayde:
lyfte vp thyne eyes ād ſee how all the rāmes that
leape vpon the ſhepe are ſtraked, ſpotted and partie:
13 for I haue ſene all that Laban doth vnto ỷ. I am ỷ
god of Bethell where thou anoynteddeſt the ſtone ād
where thou vowdeſt a vowe vnto me. Now aryſe and

𝔙. 1 ditatus, factus eſt inclytus 2 heri & nudiuſtertius [ſo v. 5]. 6 totis viribus meis

𝔏. 2 wie giſtern and ehigſtern (and v. 5).

gett the out of this countre, ād returne vnto the lāde
14 where thou waſt borne. Than anſwered Rahel & Lea
& ſayde vnto him: we haue no parte nor enheritaunce
15 in oure fathers houſe he cownteth vs euē as ſtraungers,
for he hath ſolde vs, and hath euen eaten vp the price
16 of vs. Moreouer all the riches which God hath takē
from oure father, that is oures and oure childerns.
Now therfore what ſoeuer God hath ſayde vnto the,
17 that doo. Thā Iacob roſe vp & ſett his ſōnes and wiues
18 vp vpon camels, & caried away all [Fo. XLIIII.] his
catell & all his ſubſtāce which he had gottē in Meſopotamia, for to goo to Iſaac his father vnto the lāde
19 of Canaan. Labā was gone to ſhere his ſhepe, &
20 Rahel had ſtollē hir fathers ymages. And Iacob went
awaye vnknowynge to Laban the Siriē, & tolde him
21 not ẏ he fled. So fled he & all ẏ he had, & made him
ſelf redy, & paſſed ouer the ryuers, and ſett his face
ſtreyght towarde the mounte Gilead.

22 Apō the thirde day after, was it tolde Labā ẏ Iacob
23 was fled. Thā he toke his brethrē with him and folowed after him .vii. dayes iourney and ouer toke him
at the mounte Gilead.

24 And God came to Labā the Siriā in a dreame by
nyghte, and ſayde unto him: take hede to thi ſelfe,
that thou ſpeake not to Iacob oughte ſave good.
25 And Labā ouer toke Iacob: and Iacob had pitched
his tēte in ẏ mounte. And Laban with his brethern
26 pitched their tēte alſo apon the mounte Gilead. Than
ſayde Labā to Iacob: why haſt thou this done vnknowynge to me? and haſt caried awaye my doughters

M. 20 And Iacod ſtale awaye the hert of Laban the Syrien, in ẏ[t] he tolde hym 22 ẏ[t] Iacob fled 25 tēte in ẏ[e] moūte. 26 done to ſteale awaye my hert, and carye awaye . . the ſwerde ?

V. 14 in facultatibus & haereditate 15 & vendidit, comeditque pretium noſtrum 21 amne tranſmiſſo pergeret 24 contra Iacob. 25 Iamque Iacob extenderat 26 clam me abigeres

L. 13 zeuch widder ynn das landt deyner fruntſchafft 15 vnſer lohn vertzehret 20 alſo ſtal Iacob dem Laban zu Syrien das hertz (v. 28) 21 fur vber das waſſer 23 erwiſſcht yhn

L. M. N. 20 *Stal das hertz;* hertz ſtelen iſt Ebreiſch geredt, ſo viel, als etwas thun hynder eyns andern wiſſen, bedeut aber, das die gleubigen den rechten kern Gottis wort faſſen, des die werck heyligen nymer gewar worden.

as though they had bene takē captyue with ſwerde?
27 Wherfore wenteſt thou awaye ſecretly vnknowne to
me & dideſt not tell me, yͭ I myghte haue broughte
yͤ on the waye with myrth, ſyngynge, tymrells and
28 harppes, and haſt not ſuffred me to kyſſe my childern
29 & my doughters. Thou waſt a fole to do it, for I am
able to do you evell. But the God of youre father
ſpake vnto me yeſterdaye ſaynge take hede that .P.
30 thou ſpeake not to Iacob oughte ſaue goode. And
now though thou wēteſt thi waye becauſe thou lōgeſt
after thi fathers houſe, yet wherfore haſt thou ſtollen
my goddes?

31 Iacob anſwered & ſayde to Labā: becauſe I was
afrayed, & thought that thou woldeſt haue takē awaye
32 thy doughters frō me. But with whome ſoeuer thou
ſyndeſt thy goddes, let him dye here before oure
brethrē. Seke that thine is by me, & take it to the:
33 for Iacob wiſt not that Rahel had ſtollē thē. Thā
wēt Labā in to Iacob's tēte, & in to Leas tēte, & in
to .ii. maydens tentes: but fownde thē not. Thā wēt
34 he out of Leas tēte, & entred in to Rahels tēte. And
Rahel toke the ymages, & put them in the camels
ſtrawe & ſate doune apō thē. And Labā ſerched all
35 the tēte: but fownde thē not. Thā ſayde ſhe to hir
father: my lorde, be not angrye yͭ I cā not ryſe vp
before the, for the diſeaſe of wemē is come apon me.
So ſearched he, but foūde thē not.

36 Iacob was wrooth & chode with Labā: Iacob alſo
anſwered and ſayde to him: what haue I treſpaced or
what haue I offended, that thou foloweddeſt after me?
37 Thou haſt ſearched all my ſtuffe, and what haſt thou
founde of all thy houſholde stuffe? put it here before
thi brethern & myne, & let thē iudge betwyxte vs
38 both. This .xx. yere yͭ I haue bene wyth the, thy
ſhepe and thy gootes haue not bene baren, and the

V. 28 ſtulte operatus es 31 Quod inſcio te profectus ſum 32 Quod autem furti me arguis 33 Cumque intraſſet t. Rachelis 35 ſic deluſa ſolicitudo quærentis eſt. 37 ſuppellectilem

L. 29 vnd ich hette, gottlob, woll ſo viel macht das ich euch kund vbels thun 35 vnd ſand die bilder nicht

39 rammes of thi flocke haue I not eatē. What ſoeuer
was torne of beaſtes I broughte it not vnto ẏͤ, [Fo.
XLV.] but made it good my ſilf: of my hāde dydeſt
thou requyre it, whether it was ſtollen by daye or
40 nyghte Moreouer by daye the hete conſumed me,
and the colde by nyghte, and my ſlepe departed frō
41 myne eyes. Thus haue I bene .xx. yere in thi houſe,
and ſerued the .xiiii. yeres for thy .ii. doughters, and
vi. yere for thi ſhepe, and thou haſt changed my re-
42 warde .x. tymes. And excepte the God of my father,
the God of Abrahā and the God whome Iſaac feareth,
had bene with me: ſurely thou haddeſt ſent me awaye
now all emptie. But God behelde my tribulation, and
the laboure of my handes: and rebuked the yeſter daye.
43 Laban anſwered ād ſayde vnto Iacob: the doughters are my doughters, and the childern are my childern, and the ſhepe are my ſhepe, ād all that thou
ſeiſt is myne. And what can I do this daye vnto
theſe my doughters, or vnto their childern which they
44 haue borne? Now therfore come on, let us make a
bonde, I and thou together, and let it be a wytneſſe be-
45 twene the & me. Than toke Iacob a ſtone and ſett it vp
46 an ende, ād ſayde vnto his brethern, gather
ſtoones And they toke ſtoones ād made
47 an heape, and they ate there, vpō the heape. And Labā
called it Zegar Sahadutha, but Jacob called it Gylead.
48 Than ſayde Laban: this heape be witneſſe betwene
the and me this daye (therefore is it called Gylead)
49 and this totehill which the lorde .P. ſeeth
(ſayde he) be wytneſſe betwene me and
the when we are departed one from a

vp an ende, *upright*

totehill, *watch tower or beacon*

V. 40 fugiebatque ſomnus ab oculis meis 42 Abraham & timor Iſaac 45 erexit illum in titulum 47 Laban Tumulum teſtis: & Iacob Aceruum teſtimonii, vterque iuxta proprietatem linguæ ſuæ . . 48 Galaad, id eſt tumulus teſtis. 49 Intueatur & iudicet

L. 42 meyn elend vnd erbeyt angeſehen 45 zu eynem mal 49 vnd ſey eyn wartte

M. M. N. 42 Feare is taken for honoure as a fore in Gen. xx, c.

L. M. N. 42 *Furcht;* Iacob nennet hie Gott, Iſaac furcht darumb das Iſaac Gott furchtig war and Gottis diener. 48 *Gilead;* Gilead heyſt eyn zeuge hauffe, vnnd bedeut die ſchrifft, da viel zeugnis von Gott heuffig ynnen ſind.

50 nother: that thou ſhalt not vexe my doughters nether ſhalt take other wyves vnto them. Here is no
man with vs: beholde, God is wytneſſe betwixte the
51 and me. And Laban ſayde moreouer to Iacob: beholde, this heape & this marke which I haue ſett
52 here, betwyxte me and the: this heape be wytneſſe
and alſo this marcke, that I will not come ouer this
heape to the, ād thou ſhalt not come ouer this heape
53 ād this marke, to do any harme. The God of Abraham, the God of Nahor and the God of theyr fathers,
be iudge betwixte vs.
And Iacob ſware by him that his father Iſaac feared.
54 Then Iacob dyd ſacrifyce vpon the mounte, and called
his brethern to eate breed. And they ate breed and
55 taried all nyghte in the hyll. And early in the mornynge Laban roſe vp and kyſſed his childern and his
doughters, and bleſſed thē and departed and wēt vnto
XXXII, 1 his place agayne. But Iacob went forth on
his iourney. And the angells of God came & mett
2 him. And when Iacob ſawe them, he ſayde: this is
godes hooſt: and called the name of that ſame place
Mahanaim.

The .XXXII. Chapter.

3 IACOB ſente meſſengers before
him to Eſau his brother, vnto
the lande of Seir and the felde
4 of Edom. And he cōmaunded
them ſaynge: ſe that ye ſpeake after [Fo.
XLVI.] this maner to my lorde Eſau:
thy ſeruaunte Iacob ſayth thus. I haue

M.C.S. *The viſion of the Angells. Iacob ſendeth preſents vnto hys brother Eſau. How he wreſtled with the angell which*

V. 52 aut ego tranſiero illum pergens ad te: aut tu præterieris, malum mihi cogitans. 53 per timorem patris ſui Iſaac. 55 in locum ſuum. xxxii, 3 Miſit autem & nuntios 4 domino meo (v. 5, 18)

L. 50 Es iſt hie keyn menſch mit uns 51, 52 das mal .xxxii, 2 heer lager, corrected into Mahanaim.

chaunged his name and called him Israel.

ſogerned ād bene a ſtraunger with La-
5 ban vnto this tyme: & haue gotten oxen,
aſſes and ſhepe, menſervauntes & wemanſeruauntes,
& haue ſent to ſhewe it mi lorde, that I may fynde
grace in thy ſyghte.

6 And the meſſengers came agayne to Iacob ſainge:
we came vnto thi brother Eſau, and he cometh ageynſt
7 the and .iiii. hundred men with hī. Than was Iacob
greatlye afrayde, and wiſt not which waye to turne
him ſelfe, and devyded the people that was with him
& the ſhepe, oxen and camels, in to .ii. companies,
8 and ſayde: yf Eſau come to the one parte and ſmyte it,
the other may ſaue it ſelfe.

9 * And Iacob ſayde: O god of my father Abraham, and God of my father
Iſaac: LORde which ſaydeſt vnto me, returne vnto thy cuntre and to thy kynrede,
10 and I will de all wel with the. I am
not worthy of the leaſte of all the mercyes
and treuth which thou haſt ſhewed vnto
thy ſeruaunte. For with my ſtaf came I
over this Iordane, and now haue I goten
11 ii. droves Delyver me from the handes
of my brother Eſau, for I feare him: leſt
he will come and ſmyte the mother with the childern.
12 Thou ſaydeſt that thou woldeſt ſurely do me good, and
woldeſt make mi ſeed as the ſonde of the ſee which
can not be nombred for multitude.

** Prayer is to cleave vnto the promyſes of god with a ſtrōge fayth and to beſech god with a fervent deſyre that he will fulfyll them for his mercye & truth onlye. As Iacob here doth.*

13 And he taried there that ſame nyghte, & toke of
that which came to hande, a preaſent, .¶. vnto Eſau his
14 brother: .ii. hundred ſhe gootes ād .xx. he gootes: .ii
15 hundred ſhepe and .xx. rammes: thyrtye mylch camels
with their coltes: .xl. kyne ād .x. bulles: .xx. ſhe aſſes

M. 9 do all well

V. 6 properat in occurſum tibi 7 & perterritus 8 et percuſſerit 10 minor ſum 11 percutiat matrem cum filiis 12 dilatares ſemen meum 15 camelos fœtas

L. 6 zeucht dyr auch entgegen 10 ich byn zu geringe

M. M. N. 10 To go with a ſtaffe is a maner of ſpeakīg of the Hebrews which ſygnifyeth nothing els but to go ſymply, barely and without any riches or ſtrēght as in Marc vi, b.

16 ād .x. foles and delyuered them vnto his ſeruauntes,
euery drooue by them ſelues, ād ſayde vnto them: goo
forth before me and put a ſpace betwyxte euery drooue.
17 And he cōmaunded the formeſt ſaynge Whē Eſau my
brother meteth the ād axeth the ſaynge: whoſe ſeruaūte
art thou & whither gooſt thou, & whoſe ar theſe that
18 goo before ỹ: thou ſhalt ſay, they be thy ſeruaunte
Iacobs, & ar a preſent ſent vnto my lorde Eſau, and
19 beholde, he him ſelfe cometh after vs. And ſo cōmaunded he the ſeconde, ād euen ſo the thirde, and
lykewyſe all that folowed the drooues ſainge, of this
maner ſe that ye ſpeake vnto Eſau whē ye mete him,
20 ād ſaye more ouer. Beholde thy ſeruaunte Iacob cometh after vs, for he ſayde. I will peaſe his wrath with
the preſent ỹ goth before me and afterward I will ſee
him myſelf, ſo peradventure he will receaue me to grace.
21 So went the preſēt before him ād he taried all that
22 nyghte in the tente, ād roſe vp the ſame nyghte ād
toke his .ii. wyves and his .ii. maydens & his .xi. ſonnes,
23 & went ouer the foorde Iabok. And he toke them ād
24 ſent thē ouer the ryuer, ād ſent ouer that he had ād
taried behinde him ſelfe alone.

And there wraſtled a man with him vnto the [Fo.
25 XLVII.] breakynge of the daye. And when he ſawe
that he coude not prevayle agaynſt him, he ſmote hī
vnder the thye, and the ſenowe of Iacobs thy ſhranke
26 as he wraſtled with him. And he ſayde: let me goo,
for the daye breaketh. And he ſayde: I will not lett
27 the goo, excepte thou bleſſe me. And he ſayde vnto
28 him: what is thy name? He anſwered: Iacob. And he
ſayde: thou ſhalt be called Iacob nomore, but Iſraell.

V. 17 iſta quæ ſequeris? 20 forſitan propitiabitur mihi 23 Transductiſque omnibus quæ ad ſe pertinebāt, manſit 25 tetigit neruum femoris . . . emarcuit. 26 aſcendit aurora.

L. 20 Ich will yhn verſunen mit dem geſchenck . . . villeicht wirt er mich annehmen. 21 ym lager 25 ruret er das gelenck ſeyner hufft an

L. M. N. 28 *Iſrael* kompt von Sara, das heyſt kempffen oder vber weldigen, da her auch Sar eyn fürſt oder herr, vnd Sara eyn fürſtyn oder fraw heyſt, vnd Iſrael eyn fürſt oder kempffer Gottis, das iſt, der mit Gott ringet vnd angewynnet, wilchs geſchicht durch den glauben, der ſo feſt an Gottis wort helt bis Gottis zorn vber windet vnd Gott zu eygen erlanget zum gnedigen vatter.

For thou hast wrastled with God and with men ād hast
preuayled.
29 And Iacob asked him sainge, tell me thi name.
And he sayde, wherfore dost thou aske after my name?
30 and he blessed him there. And Iacob called the name
of the place Peniel, for I haue sene God face to face,
31 and yet is my lyfe reserved. And as he went ouer
Peniel, the sonne rose vpon him, and he halted vpon
32 his thye: wherefore the childern of Israell eate not of
the senow that shrancke vnder the thye, vnto this daye:
because that he smote Iacob vnder the thye in the
senow that shroncke.

The .XXXIII. Chapter.

M.C.S. Esau & Iacob are agreed, & Iacob came into Sichē.

1 IACOB lyfte vp his eyes and
sawe his brother Esau come,
& with him .iiii. hundred men.
And he deuyded the childern
vnto Lea and vnto Rahel and vnto ẏ .ii. maydens.
2 And he put the maydens ād their childern formest,
ād Lea and hir childern after, and Rahel ād Joseph
3 hindermost. And he went before them and fell on the
grownde .vii. .[illegible]. tymes, vntill he came vnto his brother.
4 Esau ranne agaynst him and enbraced hym and fell on
5 his necke and kyssed him, and they wepte. And he
lifte vp his eyes and sawe the wyves and their childern,

M. 28 hast wrastled wyth God & hast preuayled. 30 Pheniel (v. 31). xxxiii, 4 Esau ranne to mete him

V. 28 quoniam si contra deum fortis fuisti, quanto magis cōtra homines prævalebis? 29 nomen meū—quod est mirabile? .. in eodem loco. 30 & salua facta est anima mea. 31 claudicabat pede. 32 femoris eius, & obstupuerit. xxxiii, 1 Rachel, ambarumque 3 donec appropinquaret frater eius. 4 & osculans fleuit.

L. 28 mit Gott vnd mit menschen 30 vnd meyn seel ist genesen 32 hoh ader auff dem gelenck der hufft. xxxiii, 3 vnd buckt sich .. auff die erden (and v. 7)

M. M. N. 30 To se God face to face is to haue a certē and sure knowledge of him as in Ex .xxxiii, b.

L. M. N. 30, 31 *Pniel* oder *Pnuel* heyst Gottis angesicht odder erkentnis, denn durch den glauben ym streyt des creutzs lernt man Gott recht erkennen, vnd erfaren, so hats denn keyn nott mehr, so geht die Sonne auff.

and ſayde: what are theſe which thou there haſt? And
he ſayde: they are the childern which God hath geuen
6 thy ſeruaunte. Than came the maydens forth, ād dyd
7 their obayſaunce. Lea alſo and hir childern came and
dyd their obayſaunce. And laſt of all came Ioſeph
and Rahel and dyd theyr obayſaunce.
8 And he ſayde: what meanyſt thou with all ẏ drooues
which I mett. And he anſwered: to fynde grace in the
9 ſyghte of my lorde. And Eſau ſayde: I haue ynough
10 my brother, kepe that thou haſt vnto thy ſilf. Iacob
anſwered: oh nay but yf I haue founde grace in thy
ſyghte, receaue my preaſēt of my hāde: for I haue ſene
thy face as though I had ſene ẏ face of God: wherfore
11 receaue me to grace and take my bleſſynge that I haue
brought the, for God hath geuen it me frely. And I
haue ynough of all thynges. And ſo he compelled
him to take it.
12 And he ſayde: let vs take our iourney and goo, and
13 I will goo in thy cōpany. And he ſayde vnto him: my
lorde knoweth that I haue tendre childern, ewes and
kyne with yonge vnder myne hande, which yf men
ſhulde ouerdryue but euen one daye, the hole flocke
wolde dye. [Fo. XLVIII.].
14 Let my lorde therfore goo before his ſervaunte and
I will dryue fayre and ſoftly, accordynge
as the catell that goth before me and the
childern, be able to endure: vntil I come to mi lorde
vnto Seir.

ſoftly, *at a gentle pace*

15 And Eſau ſayde: let me yet leaue ſome of my folke
with the. And he ſayde: what neadeth it? let me

M. 11 geuē it me. And

V. 6 incuruati 7 adoraſſent . . adorauerunt. 8 Dixitque Eſau . . domino 9 At ille 10 Noli ita obſecro . . munuſculū 11 & quā donauit . . tribuēs omnia. Vix fratre 13 domine . . paruulos teneros 14 dominus 15 Non eſt . neceſſe: hoc vno tantum indigeo, vt inueniam

L. 11 Nym den ſegen an, den ich dyr zubracht hab 13 zarte kinder . . vbertryben 14 meylich hynnach treyben

L. M. N. 14 *Meylich;* Merck, das rechtgleubigen vnd werck heyligen nicht konnen mit eynander wandeln, denn die gleubigen faren ſeuberlich mit ſtyllem geyſt, aber die werckheyligen faren ſtarck mit vermeſſenheyt yhrer werck ynn gottis geſetzen.

16 fynde grace in the ſyghte of my lorde So Eſau went
his waye agayne ỹ ſame day vnto Seir.
17 And Iacob toke his iourney toward Sucoth, and
bylt him an houſe, and made boothes for his catell:
wherof the name of the place is called Sucoth.
18 And Iacob went to Salem to ỹ citie of Sichem in
the lande of Canaã, after that he was come from Meſ-
19 opotamia, and pitched before the cyte, and bought a
parcell of ground where he pitched his tent, of the
childern of Hemor Sichems father, for an hundred
20 lambes. And he made there an aulter, and there
called vpon the myghtie God of Iſraell.

The .XXXIIII. Chapter.

M.C.S. The rauesſhyng of Dyna Iacobs daughter by the men of Syche̅. And of the gret bloude ſhedynge done by the ſonnes of Iacob.

1 DINA the doughter of Lea which
ſhe bare vnto Iacob, went out
to ſee the doughters of the
2 lande. And Siche̅ the ſonne
of Hemor the Heuite lorde of the countre, ſawe her, & toke her, and laye with
3 her, and forced her: & his harte laye
vnto Dina ỹ doughter of Iacob. And
4 he loued ỹ damſell & ſpake ki̅dly vnto her, & ſpake
vnto his father Hemor ſaynge, gett me this mayde̅
vnto my wyfe.

M. 18 And Iacob came peaſably in to the cite of Sichem. xxxiv, 3 laye vn Dina

V. 17 Socoth, id eſt tabernacula 20 inuocauit ſuper illud fortiſſimum deum Iſrael. xxxiv, 1 Dina filia Liæ, vt videret 2 adamauit eam: & rapuit . . . vi opprime̅s virginem. 3 Et conglutinata eſt anima eius cum ea, triſtemque deliniuit blanditiis.

L. 19 Sichem, vmb hundert groſſchen, Da ſelb richtet er ſeyne hutten auff, 20 vnd richtet daſſelbs eyn alltar zu. xxxiv, 2 ſchwecht ſie, 3 vnd ſeyn hertz hieng an yhr, vnd hatte die dyrne lieb, vnd redet freuntlich mit yhr

M. M. N. 2 To lye with hyr, looke in Gen. xix, g.

L. M. N. 1 *Tochter des lands;* was man auſſer Gottis wort, bey der vernunfft vnd menſchlicher weyſheyt ſucht, das verterbet gewiſlich den geyſt and glauben, darumb ſoll keyn zuſatz menſchlicher lere vnd werck zu Gottis wort gethan werden.

5 .T. And Iacob herde that he had defyled Dina his
doughter, but his ſonnes were with the catell in the
felde, and therfore he helde his peace, vntill they
6 were come. Then Hemor the father of Sichem went
7 out vnto Iacob, to comē with him. And the ſonnes
of Iacob came out of the felde as ſoone as they herde
it, for it greued them, and they were not a litle
wrooth, becauſe he had wrought folie in Iſraell, in
that he had lyen with Iacobs doughter, which thinge
oughte not to be done.

8 And Hemor comened with thē ſainge? the ſoule of
my ſonne Sichē lōgeth for youre doughter geue her
9 him to wyfe, and make mariages with vs: geue youre
doughters vnto vs, ād take oure doughters vnto you,
10 and dwell with vs, & the lande ſhall be at your pleaſure, dwell and do youre buſynes, and haue youre
11 poſſeſſions there in. And Sichem ſayde vnto hyr
father and hir brethern: let me fynde grace in youre
eyes, and what ſoeuer ye apoynte me,
12 that will I geue. Axe frely of me both
the dowry & gyſtes, and I will geue
acordynge as ye ſaye vnto me, and geue
me the damſell to wyfe.

apoynte, *name or indicate, tell*

dowry, *the preſent made by Shechem*

13 Then the ſonnes of Iacob anſwered to Sichem ād
Hemor his father deceytefully, becauſe he had defyled
14 Dina their ſyſter. And they ſayde vnto them, we can
not do this thinge, ẏ we ſhulde geue oure ſyſter to one
that is vncircumcyſed, for that were a ſhame vnto vs.
15 Only in this will we conſent unto you? Yf ye will
[Fo. XLIX.] be as we be, that all the men childern
16 amonge you be circumcyſed, thā will we geue oure
doughter to you and take youres to vs, and will dwell
17 with you and be one people. But and yf ye will not
harken vnto vs to be circumcyſed, than will we take
oure doughter and goo oure wayes.

T. 7 fœdam rem operatus . . . rem illicitam perpetraſſet. 11 dabo: 12 augete dotē 13 ſæuientes ob ſtuprum ſororis, 14 Non poſſumus . . . quod illicitum & nepharium

L. 7 das er eyn narreyt ynn Iſrael begangen 10 wonet vnd werbet vnd erbet drynnen 12 foddert nur getroſt yon mvr morgengab vnd geſchenck

18 And their wordes pleaſed Hemor and Sichem his
19 ſonne. And the yonge man deferde not for to do the
thinge, becauſe he had a luſt to Iacobs doughter: he
was alſo moſt ſett by of all that were in his fathers houſe.
20 Thā Hemor and Sichem went vnto the gate of their
cyte, and comened with the men of their cyte ſaynge.
21 Theſe men ar peaſable with vs, & will dwell in the
lāde and do their occupatiō therin And in the land
is rowme ynough for thē, let vs take their doughters
22 to wyues and geue them oures: only herin will they
conſent vnto vs for to dwell with vs and to be one
people: yf all the men childern that are amonge
23 vs be circumcyſed as they are. Their goodes &
their ſubſtance and all their catell are oures, only
let vs conſente vnto them, that they maye dwell
with vs.

24 And vnto Hemor and Sichem his ſonne harkened
all that went out at the gate of his cyte. And all the
men childern were circumcyſed what ſo euer went out
25 at the gates of his cyte. And the third daye when
it was paynefull to them, .ii. of the ſonnes of Iacob
Simeon & Leui .ꝑ. Dinas brethren, toke ether of them
his ſwerde & went in to the cyte boldly, and ſlewe
26 all ẏ was male, and ſlewe alſo Hemor and Sichem
his ſonne with the edge of the ſwerde, ād toke
Dina their ſiſter out of Sichems houſe, and went
their waye.

27 Than came the ſonnes of Iacob vpon the deede,
and ſpoyled the cyte, becauſe they had defyled their
28 ſiſter: and toke their ſhepe, oxen, aſſes and what ſo
29 euer was in the cyte and alſo in ẏ feldes. And all
their goodes, all their childern and their wyues toke
they captyue, and made havock of all that was in the
houſes.

V. 18 Placuit oblatio eorum 19 quin ſtatim quod petebatur expleret . . . inclytus 21 quæ ſpatioſa et lata cultoribus indiget 22 Vnum eſt, quo differtur tantum bonum, Si circuncidamus 23 & habitantes ſimul, vnum efficiamus populum. 27 in vltionem ſtupri. 29 duxerunt captiuas.

L. 21 diſe leut ſind fridſam bey vns 24 zu ſeiner ſtad thor aus vnd eyn giengen (So v. 25)

30 And Iacob ſayde to Simeon and Leui: ye haue
troubled me ād made me ſtyncke vnto the inhabita-
tours of the lande, both to the Canaanytes and alſo
vnto the Pherezites. And I am fewe in nombre.
Wherfore they ſhall gather them ſelves together
agaynſt me & ſley me, and ſo ſhall I and my houſe
31 be dyſtroyed. And they anſwered: ſhuld they deall
with oure ſiſter as wyth an whoore?

The .XXXV. Chapter.

1 AND God ſayd vnto Iacob, aryſe
ād get the vp to Bethell, &
dwell there. And make there
an aulter vnto God that ap-
eared vnto the, when thou fleddeſt from
2 Eſau thy brother. Than ſayd Iacob vnto
his [Fo. L.] houſholde & to all ÿ were
with him, put away the ſtraūge goddes
that are amonge you & make youre ſelues
3 cleane, & chaunge youre garmētes, & let
vs aryſe & goo vp to Bethell, ÿ I maye
make an aulter there, vnto God which
herde me in the daye of my tribulatiō &
was wyth me in the waye which I went.

M.C.S. *Iacob goeth vp vnto Bethel, & buryeth his ymages vnder an oke. Debora dyeth. Iacob is called Iſrael. The lande of Canaā is promyſed hym. Rachel dyeth in laboure: Ruben laye with his fathers concubyne. The death of Iſaac.*

4 And they gaue vnto Iacob all the ſtraunge goddes
which were vnder their handes, ād all their earynges
which were in their eares, and Iacob hyd them vnder
an ooke at Sichem.
5 And they departed. And the feare of God fell

V. 30 Quibus perpetratis audacter, Iacob dixit...... odioſū.. Nos pauci ſumus 31 vt ſcorto abuti. ſorore noſtra? xxxv, 3 Surgite, & aſcendamus 4 infodit eas ſubter terebinthum.. poſt vrbem

L. 30 das ich ſtincke fur den eynwonern 31 mit vnſer ſchweſter... handelln? xxxv, 2 endert ewr kleyder 4 vergrub ſie vnter eyne eyche

M. M. N. 2 *Straunge goddes;* The ſcripture calleth all maner of ydolles or ymages ſtraunge goddes, becauſe the worſhyppers of them eſteme them as goddes.

vpon the cyties that were rounde aboute them, that
6 they durſt not folowe after the ſonnes of Iacob. So
came Iacob to Lus in the lande of Canaan, otherwiſe
called Bethell, with all the people that was with him.
7 And he buylded there an aulter, and called the place
Elbethell: becauſe that God appered vnto him there,
when he fled from his brother.

8 Than dyed Debora Rebeccas norſe, and was buryed
benethe Bethell vnder an ooke. And the name of
it was called the ooke of lamentation.

9 And God appeared vnto Iacob agayne after he
10 came out of Meſopotamia, & bleſſed him and ſayde
vnto him: thy name is Iacob. Notwithſtondynge thou
ſhalt be no more called Iacob, but Iſrael ſhalbe thy
name. And ſo was his name called Iſraell.

11 .P. And God ſayde vnto him: I am God allmightie,
growe and multiplye: for people and a multitude of
people ſhall ſprynge of the, yee ād kynges ſhall come
12 out of thy loynes. And the lande which I gaue Abrahā & Iſaac, will I geue vnto the & vnto thi ſeed after
13 the will I geue it alſo. And god departed frō him
14 in the place where he talked with him. And Iacob
ſet vp a marke in the place where he talked with him:
euen a pilloure of ſtone, & powred drynkeoffringe
15 theron & powred alſo oyle theron, and called the
name of the place where God ſpake with him, Bethell.

16 And they departed from Bethel, & when he was
but a feld brede from Ephrath, Rahel began to trauell.
17 And in travelynge ſhe was in perell. And as ſhe was
in paynes of hir laboure, the mydwyfe ſayde vnto her:
18 feare not, for thou ſhalt haue this ſonne alſo. Then
as hir ſoule was a departinge, that ſhe muſt dye: ſhe

M. 7 place Bethell

V. 7 Domus dei 8 ad radices Bethel ſubter quercum 13 Et receſſit ab eo: 14 titulū lapideum 16 verno tempore 17 periclitari cœpit 18 Egrediente autem anima præ dolore, & imminente iam morte, . . .

L. 14 eyn ſteynernmal 16 eyn feldwegs 18 Da yhr aber die ſeel ausgieng, das ſie ſterben muſte

L. M. N. 14 *Tranckopffer;* Das war weyn, wie das ynn den folgenden buchern gnugſam geſehen wirt.

called his name Ben Oni. But his father called him
19 Ben Iamin. And thus dyed Rahel ād was buryed in
the waye to Ephrath which now is called Bethlehem.
20 And Iacob ſett vp a piller apon hir graue, which is
21 called Rahels graue piller vnto this daye. And Iſraell
went thēce and pitched vp his tent beyonde the toure
of Eder.

22 And it chaunced as Iſrael dwelt in that lande, that
Ruben went & laye with Bilha his fathers concubyne,
& it came to Iſraels eare. [Fo. LI.].

The ſonnes of Iacob were .xii. in nombre.

23 The ſonnes of Lea. Ruben, Iacobs eldeſt ſonne,
24 & Simeō, Leui, Iuda, Iſachar, & Zabulon. The ſonnes
25 of Rahel: Ioſeph & Ben Iamin. The ſonnes of Bilha
26 Rahels mayde: Dan & Nepthali. The ſonnes of Zilpha
Leas mayde Gad & Aſer. Thes are the ſōnes of Iacob
which were borne him in Meſopotamia.

27 Then Iacob went vnto Iſaac his father to Mamre a
prīcipall cyte, otherwiſe called Hebron: where Abrahā
28 & Iſaac ſogeorned as ſtraungers. And the dayes of
29 Iſaac were an hundred & .lxxx. yeres: & than felle
he ſeke & dyed, ād was put vnto his people: beynge
olde and full of dayes. And his ſonnes Eſau ād Iacob
buried him.

V. 18 Ben-oni, id eſt filius doloris mei . . . Beniamin, id eſt filius dextræ. 20 hic eſt titulus monumenti Rachel, vſque 21 trans turrem gregis. 22 quod illū minime latuit. 26 Meſopotamia Syriæ. 27 Mambre ciuitatem Arbee 29 Conſumptuſque ætate . . appoſitus

L. 21 richtet eyne hutten auff ienſyddem turn Eder. 27 Mamre ynn die hewbt ſtad, 29 ward krank . . . alt vnd des lebens ſatt

M. M. X. 18 *Ben Iamin;* that is the ſonne of the ryght hād, And right hande is taken for good fortune. 29 To be put vnto his people looke in Gen. xxv, a.

L. M. X. 18 Ben Oni heyſt meyns schmertzen ſon Ben Iamin heyſt, der rechten ſon.

The .XXXVI. Chapter.

1 THESE are the generations of
Esau which is called Edō.
2 Esau toke his wyues of the
doughters of Canaan Ada the
doughter of Elon an Hethite, and Ahalibama the doughter of Ana, which Ana
3 was the sonne of Zibeon an heuyte, And
4 Basmath Ismaels doughter & sister of Nebaioth. And
Ada bare vnto Esau, Eliphas: and Basmath bare Reguel:
5 And Ahalibama bare Ieus, Iaelam and Korah. These
are the sonnes of Esau which were borne him in the
lande of Canaan.

M.C.S. The wiues of Esau. Iacob & Esau are ryche. The genealogie of Esau. Esau dwelleth in the hill Seir.

6 And Esau toke his wyues, his sonnes and doughters
and all the soules of his house: his .P. goodes and all
his catell and all his substance which he had gott in the
land of Canaan, ād went in to a countre awaye from his
7 brother Iacob: for their ryches was so moch, that they
coude not dwell together, and that the land where in
they were straungers, coude not receaue thē: because
of their catell.

8 Thus dwelt Esau in moūte Seir, which Esau is
called Edō

9 These are the generations of Esau father of the
10 Edomytes in mounte Seir, & these are the names of
Esaus sonnes: Eliphas the sonne of Ada the wife of
Esau, ād Reguel the sonne of Basmath the wife of Esau
11 also. And the sonnes of Eliphas were. Theman, Omar,
12 Zepho, Gaetham and kenas. And thimna was concubyne to Eliphas Esaus sonne, and bare vnto Eliphas,
Amalech. And these be the sonnes of Ada Esaus wyfe.
13 And these are the sonnes of Reguel: Nahath, Serah,

M. 6 catell and all his

V. 6 & cūcta quæ habere poterat . . abiit in alteram regionem, recessitque 8 mōte Seir, ipse est Edom.

L. 2 Ana die neff Zib. 6 ynn eyn land von seynem bruder 7 nicht ertragen fur yhren guttern

M. M. N. 4 *Basmath*, other wyse called Maheleth and so in other places is there dyuers names geuē to one person.

Samma and Miſa: theſe were the ſonnes of Baſmath
14 Eſaus wyfe. And theſe were the ſonnes of Ahalibama
Eſaus wyfe the doughter of Ana ſonne of Zebeō, which
ſhe bare vnto Eſau: Ieus, Iealam and Korah.
15 Theſe were dukes of the ſonnes of Eſau. The childern of Eliphas the firſt ſōne of Eſau were theſe: duke
16 Theman, duke Omar, duke Zepho, duke Kenas, duke
Korah, duke Gaetham & duke Amalech: theſe are yͤ
dukes that came of Eliphas in the lande of Edom, ād
theſe were the ſonnes of Ada. [Fo. LII.]
17 Theſe were the childern of Reguel Eſaus ſonne: duke
Nahath, duke Serah, duke Samma, duke Miſa. Theſe
are the dukes that came of Reguel in the lande of
Edom, ād theſe were the ſonnes of Baſmath Eſaus wyfe.
18 Theſe were the childern of Ahalibama Eſaus wife:
duke Ieus, duke Iaelam, duke Korah theſe dukes came
19 of Ahalibama yͤ doughter of Ana Eſaus wife. Theſe
are the childern of Eſau, and theſe are the dukes of
them: which Eſau is called Edom:
20 Theſe are the childern of Seir the Horite, the in-
habitoure of the lande: Lothan, Sobal, Zibeon, Ana,
21 Diſon, Eſer and Diſan. Theſe are the dukes of yͤ horites
22 the childern of Seir in the lande of Edom. And the
childern of Lothan were: Hori and Hemam. And
Lothans ſiſter was called Thimna.
23 The childern of Sobal were theſe: Alvan, Manahath,
24 Ebal, Sepho & Onam. Theſe were the childern of
Zibeō. Aia & ana, this was yͤ Ana yͤ foūde yͤ mules in
25 yͤ wildernes, as he fed his father Zibeons aſſes. The
childern of Ana were theſe. Diſon and Ahalibama yͤ
doughter of Ana.
26 Theſe are the childern of Diſon. Hemdan Eſban,
27 Iethran, & Cherā. The childern of Ezer were theſe,
28 Bilhan, Seavan & Akan. The childern of Diſan were:
Vz and Aran.

M. 14 Iealam and Roah 17 Miſſa
V. 16 Amalec. hi filii Eliphaz 19 eorū: ipſe eſt Edom. 24 inuenit aquas calidas in ſolitudine, cū paſceret aſinas Sebeon 25 Habuitque filium Diſon, & filiam Oolibama.
L. 14 Ana der neffe 15 furſten [and ſo throughout this chapter]

29 Theſe are the dukes that came of Hori: duke Lothan,
30 duke Sobal, duke Zibeō, duke Ana .P. duke Diſon, duke
Ezer, duke Diſan. Theſe be the dukes that came of
Hory in their dukedōs in the lande of Seir.
31 Theſe are the kynges that reigned in the lande of
Edom before there reigned any kynge amonge the
32 childern of Iſrael. Bela the ſonne of Beor reigned in
33 Edomea, and the name of his cyte was Dinhaba. And
when Bela dyed, Iobab the ſonne of Serah out of Be-
34 zara, reigned in his ſteade. When Iobab was dead,
Huſam of the lande of Themany reigned in his ſteade.
35 And after the deth of Huſam, Hadad the ſonne of
Bedad which ſlewe the Madianytes in the feld of the
Moabytes, reigned in his ſteade, and the name of his
cyte was Avith.
36 Whē Hadad was dead, Samla of Maſreka reigned in
37 his ſteade. Whē Samla was dead, Saul of the ryver
38 Rehoboth reigned in his ſteade. When Saul was dead,
Baal hanan the ſonne of Achbor reigned in his ſteade.
39 And after the deth of Baal Hanan the ſonne of Achbor, Hadad reigned in his ſteade, and the name of his
cyte was Pagu.

And his wifes name Mehetabeel the doughter of
matred the doughter of Meſaab.

40 Theſe are the names of the dukes that came of Eſau,
in their kynredds, places and names: Duke Thimma,
41 duke Alua, duke Ietheth, duke Ahalibama, duke Ela,
42 duke Pinon, duke Kenas, duke Theman, duke Mibzar
43 duke Magdiel, duke Iram. Theſe be the dukes of
[Fo. LIII.] Edomea in their habitations, in the lande
of their poſſeſſions. This Eſau is the father of the
Edomytes.

M. 29 Sabal
V. 30 Horræorum qui imperauerunt in terra 35 Hoc quoque mortuo . . percuſſit Madian in regione Moab 36 Semla de Maſreca. 38 Cumque et hic 39 Iſto quoque mortuo
L. 35 Madianiter . . auff der Moabiter feld 36 Maſrek

The .XXXVII. Chapter.

M.C.S. Ioseph accuseth his brethren. Ioseph dreameth & is hated of hys brethren & is solde to the Ismaelites. Iacob bewayleth Ioseph.

1 AND Iacob dwelt in the lande
wherein his father was a
straunger, ẏ is to saye in
the lande of Canaan.
2 And these are the generations of
Iacob: when Ioseph was .xvii. yere olde,
he kepte shepe with his brethren, and
the lad was with the sonnes of Bilha &
of Zilpha his fathers wyues. And he brought vnto
3 their father an euyll saynge ẏ was of them. And
Israel loued Ioseph more than all his childern, because
he begat hym in his olde age, and he made him a
coote of many coloures.
4 When his brothren sawe that their father loued
him more than all his brethern, they hated him and
5 coude not speke one kynde worde vnto him. Moreouer Ioseph dreamed a dreame and tolde it his breth-
6 ren: wherfore they hated him yet the more. And he
sayde vnto them heare I praye yow this dreame which
7 I haue dreamed: Beholde we were makynge sheues in
the felde: and loo, my shefe arose and stode vp right,
and youres stode rounde aboute and made obeysaunce
8 to my shefe. Than sayde his brethren vnto him:
what, shalt thou be oure kynge or shalt thou reigne
ouer us? And they hated hī yet the more, because
9 of his dreame and of his wordes. ¶.
And he dreamed yet another dreame & told it his
brethren saynge: behold, I haue had one dreame more:
me thought the sonne and the moone and .xi. starres made
10 obaysaunce to me. And when he had told it vnto his father and his brethern, his father rebuked him and sayde

V. 2 sedecim . . suis adhuc puer: & erat 3 polymitam 4 quicquam pacifice loqui. 5 maioris odii seminarium 8 subiiciemur ditioni tuæ? Hæc ergo causa somniorum atque sermonum, inuidiæ & odii fomitem ministrauit.

L. 4 keyn freuntlich wort zusprechen

L. M. N. 3 *Der bundte rock* Iosephs war von mancherley farben faden gewebt, vnd bedeut die mancherley gnade vnd gaben des eynigen geysts ynn Christo vnd seynen Christen.

vnto him: what meaneth this dreame which thou haſt
dreamed: ſhall I and thy mother and thy brethren
11 come and fall on the grounde before the? And his
brethern hated him, but his father noted the ſaynge.
12 His brethren went to kepe their fathers ſhepe in Si-
13 chem, and Iſraell ſayde vnto Ioſeph: do not thy brethern kepe in Sichem? come that I may ſend ỹ to thē.
14 And he anſwered here am I And he ſayde vnto him:
goo and ſee whether it be well with thy brethren and
the ſhepe, and brynge me worde agayne: And ſent
him out of the vale of Hebron, for to go to Sichem.
15 And a certayne man founde him wandrynge out of
his waye in the felde, ād axed him what he ſoughte.
16 And he anſwered: I ſeke my brethren, tell me I praye
17 the where they kepe ſhepe And the man ſayde, they
are departed hēce, for I herde them ſay, let vs goo
vnto Dothan. Thus went Ioſeph after his brethren,
and founde them in Dothan.
18 And whē they ſawe him a farr of before he came
at them, they toke councell agaynst him, for to ſley
19 him, and ſayde one to another, Beholde this dreamer
20 cometh, come now and let [Fo. LIIII.] us ſley him
and caſt him in to ſome pytt, and let vs ſaye that
ſome wiked beaſt hath deuoured him, and let us ſee
what his dreames wyll come to.
21 When Ruben herde that, he wēt aboute to ryd him out
22 of their handes and ſayde, let vs not kyll him. And Ruben ſayde moreouer vnto them, ſhed not his bloude, but
caſt him in to this pytt that is in the wildernes, and laye
no handes vpon him: for he wolde haue rydd him out of
their handes and delyuered him to his father agayne.
23 And as ſoone as Ioſeph was come vnto his brethren, they ſtrypte him out of his gay coote that was
24 vpon him, and they toke him and caſt him in to a
pytt. But the pytt was emptie and had no water

V. 11 Inuidebant ei igitur . . . rem tacitus conyderabat. 14 renuntia mihi quid agatur. 18 antequam accederet ad eos 20 ciſternam veterem 22 animam eius . . manuſque veſtras ſeruate innoxias. 23 nudauerunt eum tunica talari & polymita 24 ciſternam veterem, quæ non habebat aquam.

L. 11 neydeten yhn 14 ſage mir widder wie ſichs hellt

25 therein. And they ſatt them doune to eate brede.
And as they lyft vp their eyes and loked aboute, there
came a companye of Iſmaelites from Gilead, and their
camels ladē with ſpicery, baulme, and myrre, and were
goynge doune in to Egipte.
26 Than ſayde Iuda to his brethrē, what avayleth it
that we ſley oure brother, and kepe his bloude ſecrett?
27 come on, let vs ſell him to the Iſmaelites, and let not
oure handes be defyled vpon him: for he is oure brother
28 and oure fleſh. And his brethren were content. Than
as the Madianites marchaunt men paſſed by, they
drewe Ioſeph out of the pytt and ſold him vnto the
Iſmaelites for .xx. peces of ſyluer.
.P. And they brought him into Egipte.
29 And when Ruben came agayne vnto the pytt and
30 founde not Ioſeph there, he rent his cloothes and went
agayne vnto his brethern ſaynge: the lad is not yon-
31 der, and whether ſhall I goo? And they toke Ioſephs
coote ād kylled a goote, & dypped the coote in the
32 bloud. And they ſent that gay coote & cauſed it to
be brought vnto their father and ſayd: This haue we
33 founde: ſe, whether it be thy ſōnes coote or no. And
he knewe it ſaynge: it is my ſonnes coote a wicked
beaſt hath deuoured him, and Ioſeph is rent in peces.
34 And Iacob rent his cloothes, ād put ſacke clothe aboute
his loynes, and ſorowed for his ſonne a longe ſeaſon.
35 Than came all his ſonnes ād all his doughters to
comforte him. And he wold not be comforted, but
ſayde: I will go doune in to ẏ grave vnto my ſonne,
36 mornynge. And thus his father wepte for him. And
the Madianytes ſolde him in Egipte vnto Putiphar a
lorde of Pharaos: and his cheſe marſhall.

V. 30 Puer non cōparet 33 fera peſſima . . beſtia deuorauit 35 vt lenirent dolorem patris, noluit conſolationem accipere . . lugens in infernum. 36 Phutiphari eunucho Pharaonis magiſtro militum.

L. 33 Eyn boſes thier hat yhn freſſen, Eyn reyſſend thier . . . Ioſeph zuriſſen 34 ſack vmb ſeyne lenden . . lange zeyt. 35 ynn die helle, 36 Pharao hoffemeyſter.

M. M. N. 34 *Rent hys clothes:* it was ſpecially vſed amonge the hebrewes to rent their clothes whē the glorie of God was cō-tēpned as here, where they feared God ſo lytle as to kyll their awne brother.

L. M. N. 35 *Vatter,* das war Iſaac.

The .XXXVIII. Chapter.

M.C.S. *The maryage of Iuda. The trespace of her and Onan and the vengeaunce of god that came ther vpō. Iuda laye wyth hys daughter Thamar. The byrthe of Pharez and Zarah.*

1 AND it fortuned at that tyme
that Iudas went from his
brethren & gatt him to a
man called Hira of Odollam,
2 and there he sawe the doughter of a man
called Sua a Canaanyte. And he toke
3 her ād went in vnto her. And she conceaued and bare a sonne and called his
4 name Er. And she conceaued agayne
and bare a sonne and called him [Fo.
5 LV.] Onan. And she conceaued the
thyrde tyme & bare a sonne, whom she called Sela:
& he was at Chesyb when she bare hem.
6 And Iudas gaue Er his eldest sonne, a wife whose
7 name was Thamar. But this Er Iudas eldest sonne
was wicked in the syghte of the LORde, wherfore the
8 LORde slewe him. Then sayde Iudas vnto Onan: goo
in to thi brothers wyfe and Marie her, and styrre vp
9 seed vnto thy brother. And when Onan perceaued
that the seed shulde not be his: therfore when he went
in to his brothers wife, he spylled it on the grounde,
10 because he wold not geue seed vnto his brother. And
the thinge whoch he dyd, displeased the LORde, wher-
11 fore he slew him also. Than sayde Iudas to Thamar
his doughter in lawe: remayne a wydow at thi fathers
house, tyll Sela my sonne be growne: for he feared lest
he shulde haue dyed also, as his brethren did. Thus
went Thamar & dwelt in hir fathers house.
12 And in processe of tyme, the doughter of Sua Iudas
wife dyed. Than Iudas when he had left mornynge,
went vnto his shepe sherers to Thimnath with his

V. 2 & accepta vxore 5 Sela . quo nato, parere vltra cessauit. 9 non sibi nasci filios 10 et idcirco percussit eum dominus, eo quod rem detestabilem faceret. 12 Euolutis autem multis diebus

L. 8 samen erweckist 10 gefiel dem Herrn vbel

M. M. N. 7 *To be wycked in the sight of the lorde*, is to walke in wyckednes: knowinge that the lorde seeth vs and yet we wyll not repēt.

13 frende Hira of Odollam. And one told Thamar ſaynge: beholde, thy father in lawe goth vp to Thimnath,
14 to ſhere his ſhepe. And ſhe put hyr wydows garmētes
of from her and couered her with a clooke, and dis-
gyſſed herſelf: And ſat her downe at the entrynge of
Enaim which is by the hye- .P. wayes ſyde to Thimnath, for becauſe ſhe ſawe that Sela was growne, and
ſhe was not geūe vnto him to wife.

15 When Iuda ſawe her he thought it had bene an
16 hoore, becauſe ſhe had couered hyr face. And turned
to her vnto the waye and ſayde, come I praye the,
let me lye with the, for he knewe not that it was his
doughter in lawe. And ſhe ſayde what wylt thou
17 gyue me, for to lye with me? Thā ſayde he, I will
ſende the a kydd frō the flocke. She anſwered, Than
18 geue me a pledge till thou ſende it. Than ſayd he,
what pledge ſhall I geue the? And ſhe ſayde: thy
ſygnett, thy necke lace, and thy ſtaffe that is in thy
hande. And he gaue it her and lay by her, and ſhe
19 was with child by him. And ſhe gatt her vp and
went and put her mantell from her, ād put on hir
widowes rayment agayne.

20 And Iudas ſent the kydd by his neybure of Odollam, for to fetch out his pledge agayne from the wifes
21 hande. But he fownde her not. Than aſked he the
men of the ſame place ſaynge: where is the whoore
that ſatt at Enaim in the waye? And they ſayde:
22 there was no whoore here. And he came to Iuda
agayne ſaynge: I can not fynde her, and alſo the men
of the place ſayde: that there was no whoore there.
23 And Iuda ſayde: let her take it to her, leſt we be
ſhamed: for I ſent the kydd & thou coudeſt not
fynde her.

24 And it came to paſſe that after .iii. mone- [Fo.

M. 18 thy ſygnett, thy bracelet, and

V. 12 Hiras opilio gregis Odollamites 14 aſſumpſit theriſtrum . . in biuio itineris 15 vultum ſuum ne agnoſceretur. 17 Patiar quod vis, ſi dederis mihi arabonē 20 per paſtorem ſuum Odoll. 23 certe mendacii arguere nos non poterit

L. 12 mit ſeynem hirtten Hira von Odollam. 14 fur die thur eraus an dem wege gen Thimn. 18 deyn ſechel 23 Sie habs yhr, das wyr nicht villeicht zu ſchanden werden

LVI.] thes one tolde Iuda ſaynge: Thamar thy doughter in lawe hath played the whoore, and with playnge
the whoore is become great with childe. And Iuda
25 ſayde: brynge her forth ād let her be brente. And
when they brought her forth, ſhe ſent to her father
in lawe ſaynge: by the mā vnto whome theſe thinges
pertayne, am I with childe. And ſayd alſo: loke whoſe
26 are this ſeall necklace, and ſtaffe. And Iuda knewe them
ſaynge: ſhe is more rightwes thā I, becauſe I gaue her
not to Sela my ſōne. But he laye with her no more.
27 When tyme was come that ſhe ſhulde be delyuered,
28 beholde there was .ii. twynnes in hyr wōbe. And as ſhe
traveled, the one put out his hande and the mydwife toke
and bownde a reed threde aboute it ſaynge: this wyll
29 come out fyrſt. But he plucked his hande backe agayne,
and his brother came out. And ſhe ſayde: wherfore
haſt thou rent a rent vppon the? and called him Pharez.
30 And afterward came out his brother that had the reade
threde about his hāde, which was called Zarah.

¶ The .XXXIX. Chapter.

M.C.S. God proſpereth Ioſeph. Pharaos [ſic] wyfe tempteth hym. He is accuſed & caſt in pryſon. God hath mercye vpon hym.

1 IOSEPH was broughte vnto
Egipte, ād Putiphar a lorde
of Pharaos: ād his chefe marſhall an Egiptian, bought him
of ỹ Iſmaelites which brought hī thither
2 .P. And the LORde was with Ioſeph,
and he was a luckie felowe
and continued in the houſe

luckie, *proſperous*

M. 25 ſeall, bracelet, and ſtaffe.

V. 24 vid. vterus illius intumeſcere. 26 duceretur ad pœnam 27 ipſa effuſione infantium 29 diuiſa . . maceria? xxxix, 1 eunuchus . . princeps exercitus

L. 29 umb deynen willen eyn ſach geriſſen? xxxix, 2 gluck ſeliger man wart, vnd war

L. M. N. 29 *Perez* eyn zureyſer, Sorah heyſt aufgang. Hie iſt bedeut, das die werck heyligen ſich euſerlich ſtellen als wolten ſie erfur vnd die erſten ſeyn, vnd werden die letzten, darvber ſich eyn groſs reyſſen hebt vnter dem volck Gottis. Aber der rod faden vmb die hand iſt daſz ſie fleyſchlich heylickeyt wircken vnd die rechten heyligē verfolgen.

3 of his maſter the Egiptian. And his maſter ſawe that
the LORde was with him and that the LORde made all
4 that he dyd proſper in his hande: Wherfore he founde
grace in his maſters ſyghte, and ſerued him. And his
maſter made him ruelar of his houſe, and put all that
5 he had in his hande. And as ſoone as he had made
him ruelar ouer his houſe ād ouer all that he had, the
LORde bleſſed this Egiptians houſe for Ioſephs ſake,
and the bleſſynge of the LORde was vpon all that he
6 had: both in the houſe and alſo in the feldes. And
therfore he left all that he had in Ioſephs hande, and
loked vpon nothinge that was with him, ſaue only on
the bread which he ate. And Ioſeph was a goodly
perſone & well favored

7 And it fortuned after this, that his maſters wife caſt
hir eyes vpon Ioſeph and ſayde come lye with me.
8 But he denyed and ſayde to her: Beholde, my maſter
woteth not what he hath in the houſe with me, but
9 hath commytted all that he hath to my hande He
him ſelfe is not greatter in the houſe than I, ād hath
kepte nothīge frō me, but only the becauſe thou art
his wife. How than can I do this great wykydnes,
10 for to ſynne agaynſt God? And after this maner
ſpake ſhe to Ioſeph daye by daye: but he harkened
not vnto her, to ſlepe nere her or to be in her com-
11 pany. [Fo. LVII.] And it fortuned aboute the ſame
ſeaſon, that Ioſeph entred in to the houſe, to do his
buſynes: and there was none of the houſhold by, in
12 the houſe. And ſhe caught him by the garment ſaynge: come ſlepe with me. And he left his garment
13 in hir hande ād fled and gott him out When ſhe
ſawe that he had left his garmēt in hir hande, and
14 was fled out, ſhe called vnto the men of the houſe,
and tolde them ſaynge: Se, he hath brought in an
Hebrewe vnto vs to do vs ſhame. for he came in to

V. 8 nequaquā acquieſcens operi nephario 10 et mulier moleſta erat adoleſcenti . . . recuſabat ſtuprum. 11 operis quippiam abſque arbitris 12 lacinia veſtimenti 13 & ſe eſſe cōtemptam 14 vt illuderet nobis

L. 9 Vnd hat nichts ſo gros ynn dem haus 10 das er neben yhr ſchlieff, noch vmb ſie were. 12 erwiſſcht yhn bey ſeynem kleid 14 das er vns zu ſchanden mache (v. 17)

me, for to haue ſlept wyth me. But I cried with a
lowde voyce.
15 And when he harde, that I lyſte vp my voyce and
cryed, he left his garment with me and fled awaye and
got him out.
16 And ſhe layed vp his garment by her, vntill hir
17 lorde came home. And ſhe told him acordynge to
theſe wordes ſaynge. This Hebrues ſervaunte which
18 thou haſt brought vnto vs came in to me to do me ſhame.
But as ſoone as I lyft vp my voyce and cryed, he left
19 his garment with me and fled out. When his maſter
herde the woordes of his wyfe which ſhe told him
ſaynge: after this maner dyd thy ſervaunte to me, he
waxed wrooth.
20 And he toke Ioſeph and put him in pryſon: euen
in the place where the kynges priſoners laye bounde.
21 And there contynued he in preſon. But the LORde
was with Ioſeph ād ſhewed him mercie, and gott him
22 fauoure in the ſyghte of the keper of yͤ preſon which
com- .P. mytted to Ioſephs hāde all the preſoners that
were in the preſon houſſe. And what ſoeuer was done
23 there, yͤ dyd he. And the keper of the preſõ loked
vnto nothinge that was vnder his hande, becauſe the
LORde was with him, & becauſe that what ſoeuer he
dyd, the LORde made it come luckely to paſſe.

The .XL. Chapter.

1 AND it chaunced after this, that
the chefe butlar of the kynge
of Egipte and his chefe baker
had offended there lord the
2 kynge of Egypte. And Pharao was angrie with them
3 and put thē in warde in his chefe marſhals houſe: euen

M.C.S. *Ioſeph expoundeth the dreames of the two pryſoners.*

V. 16 In argumentū ergo fidei retentum pallium 19 & nimium credulus verbis coni. 20 cuſtodiebantur 23 & omnia opera eius dirigebat. xl. 1 vt peccarent duo eunuchi 2 Pharao (nam alter pincernis præerat, alter piſtoribus)

L. 15 floch vnd lieff hynaus. 17 deyn Ebreiſcher knecht 22 auff das alles was da geſchach, durch yhn geſchehen muſte 23 glucklich abgehen lies

4 in ỹ preſon where Ioſeph was bownd. And the chefe
marſhall gaue Ioſeph a charge with them, & he ſerued
them. And they contynued a ſeaſon in warde.
5 And they dreamed ether of them in one nyghte:
both the butlar and the baker of the kynge of Egipte
which were bownde in the preſon houſe, ether of
them his dreame, and eche mãnes dreame of a ſon-
6 drie interpretation When Ioſeph came ſondrie, *diſ-*
in vnto them in the mornynge, and loked *tinct, ſeparate*
7 apon them: beholde, they were ſadd. And he aſked
8 them ſaynge, wherfore loke ye ſo ſadly to daye? They
anſwered him, we haue dreamed a dreame, and haue no
man to declare it. And Ioſeph ſay- [Fo. LVIII.] de vnto
thẽ. Interpretynge belongeth to God but tel me yet.
9 And the chefe butlar tolde his dreame to Ioſeph
and ſayde vnto him: In my dreame me thought there
10 ſtode a vyne before me, and in the vyne were .iii
braunches, and it was as though it budded, & her
11 bloſſõs ſhott forth: & ỹ grapes there of waxed rype.
And I had Pharaos cuppe in my hande, and toke of
the grapes and wronge them in to Pharaos cuppe,
& delyvered Pharaos cuppe in to his hande.
12 And Ioſeph ſayde vnto him, this is the interpreta-
13 tion of it. The .iii. braũches ar thre dayes: for within
thre dayes ſhall Pharao lyft vp thine heade, and reſtore
the vnto thyne office agayne, and thou ſhalt delyuer
Pharaos cuppe in to his hãde, after the old maner,
14 even as thou dydeſt when thou waſt his butlar. But
thinke on me with the, when thou art in good caſe,
and ſhewe mercie vnto me. And make mencion of
me to Pharao, and helpe to brynge me out of this
15 houſe: for I was ſtollen out of the lande of the Hebrues,
& here alſo haue I done nothĩge at all wherfore they
ſhulde haue put me in to this dongeon.

V. 5 iuxta interpretationem congruam ſibi. 7 triſtior . . hodie ſolito facies 8 referte mihi quid videritis. 13 recordabitur Pharao miniſterii tui . . iuxta officium tuum, ſicut ante

L. 5 hatte ſeyne bedeutung 8 Auslegen gehoret Gott zu, ertzelet myrs doch. 11 zudruckt ſie ynn den becher 13 deyn heubt erheben . . nach der vorigen weyſze 15 das ſie mich eyngeſetzt haben.

16 When the chefe baker ſawe that he had well interpretate it, he ſayde vnto Ioſeph, me thought alſo in
my dreame, ẏ I had .iii. wyker baſkettes on my heade:
17 And in ẏ vppermoſt baſket, of all maner bakemeates
for Pharao .P. And the byrdes ate them out of the
baſket apon my heade
18 Ioſeph anſwered and ſayde: this is the interpreta-
19 tion therof. The .iii. baſkettes are .iii. dayes, for this
daye .iii. dayes ſhall Pharao take thy heade from the,
and ſhall hange the on a tree, and the byrdes ſhall
eate thy fleſh from of the.
20 And it came to paſſe the thyrde daye which was
Pharaos byrth daye, that he made a feaſt vnto all his
ſervauntes. And he lyſted vpp the head of the chefe
buttelar and of the chefe baker amonge his ſervauntes.
21 And reſtored the chefe buttelar vnto his buttelarſhipe
agayne, and he reched the cuppe in to Pharaos hande,
22 ād hanged the chefe baker: euē as Ioſeph had inter-
23 pretated vnto thē. Notwithſtonding the chefe buttelar
remembred not Ioſeph, but forgat hym.

The .XLI. Chapter.

1 AND it fortuned at .ii. yeres
end, that Pharao dreamed,
and thought that he ſtode
2 by a ryuers ſyde, and that
there came out of the ryuer .vii. goodly
kyne and fatt fleſhed, and fedd in a med-
3 owe. And him thought that .vii. other
kyne came vp after them out of the ryver
evelfauored and leane fleſhed and ſtode

M.C.S. Pharaos dreames are expounded by Ioſeph. He is made ruler ouer all Egypt. He hath two ſonnes, Manaſſes and Ephraim. The derth begynneth in Egypt.

V. 16 prudenter ſomnium diſſoluiſſet . . . caniſtra farinæ 19 auferet Pharao caput tuū . . in cruce 20 pueris ſuis, recordatus eſt inter epulas magiſtri pinc. & piſtor . prin. 22 ſuſpendit in patibulo, vt coniectoris veritas probaretur. 23 Et tamen ſuccedentibus proſperis, præp. pinc. oblitus eſt interpretis ſui. xli, 2 & paſcebantur in ipſa amnis ripa in locis virentibus.

L. 19 deynen kopff erheben 20 vnd erhub das hewbt (*bis*). 23 gedacht nicht . . . vergaſs

by the other vpon the brynke [Fo. LIX.] of the ryuer.
4 And the evill favored and lenefleshed kyne ate vp
the .vii. welfauored and fatt kyne: and he awoke
their with.

5 And he slepte agayne and dreamed the second
tyme, that .vii. eares of corne grewe apon one stalke
6 rancke and goodly. And that .vii. thynne eares blasted
7 with the wynde, spronge vp after them: and that the
vii. thynne eares deuowrerd the .vii. rancke and full
eares. And then Pharao awaked: and se, here is his
8 dreame. When the mornynge came, his sprete was
troubled And he sent and called for all the soyth-
sayers of Egypte and all the wyse men there of, and
told them his dreame: but there was none of them
that coude interpretate it vnto Pharao.

9 Than spake the chefe buttelar vnto Pharao saynge.
10 I do remembre my fawte this daye. Pharao was angrie with his servauntes, and put in warde in the chefe
11 marshals house both me and the chefe baker. And
we dreamed both of vs in one nyght and ech mannes
dreame of a sondrye interpretation.

12 And there was with vs a yonge man, an Hebrue
borne, servaunte vnto the chefe marshall. And we
told him, and he declared oure dreames to vs acord-
13 ynge to ether of oure dreames. And as he declared
them vnto vs, euen so it came to passe. I was restored
to myne office agayne, and he was hanged.

14 .P. Than Pharao sent and called Ioseph. And they
made him haste out of preson. And he shaued him
self and chaunged his rayment, & went in to Pharao.
15 And Pharao sayde vnto Ioseph: I haue dreamed a
dreame and no man cā interpretate it, but I haue
herde saye of the ỹ as soone as thou hearest a dreame,
16 thou dost interpretate it. And Ioseph answered Pharao

V. 6 percussæ vredine 7 omnem priorum pulchritudinem. . . post quietem 8 cōiectores 9 Tunc demum reminiscens pincernarū magister, ait, Confiteor 11 somniū, præsagium futurorū. 13 audiu. quicquid postea rei probauit euentus. 14 Ioseph totonderunt

L. 8 der sie . . . deutten kund. 9 Ich gedencke heut an meyn sunde 11 des deuttung yhn betraff 14 vnd liessen yhn aus dem loch, . . . lies sich bescheren

ſaynge: God ſhall geue Pharao an anſwere of peace
without me.
17 Pharao ſayde vnto Ioſeph: in my dreame me thought
18 I ſtode by a ryvers ſyde, and there came out of the
ryver .vii. fatt fleſhed ād well fauored kyne, and fedd
19 in the medowe. And then .vii. other kyne came vp
after them, poore and very euell fauored ād leane
fleſhed: ſo that I neuer ſawe their lyke in all the lande
20 of Egipte in euell fauordneſſe. And the .vii. leane and
21 euell fauored kyne ate vpp the firſt .vii. fatt kyne And
when they had eaten them vp, a man cowde not perceaue that they had eatē them: for they were ſtill as
evyll fauored as they were at the begynnynge. And
I awoke.
22 And I ſawe agayne in my dreame .vii. eares ſprynge
23 out of one ſtalk full and good, and .vii. other eares
wytherd, thinne and blaſted with wynde, ſprynge vp
24 after them. And the thynne eares deuowred the .vii
good eares. And I haue tolde it vnto the ſoth- [Fo.
LX.] ſayers, but no man can tell me what it meaneth.
25 Then Ioſeph ſayde vnto Pharao: both Pharaos
dreames are one. And god doth ſhewe Pharao what
26 he is aboute to do. The .vii. good kyne are .vii
yeres: & the .vii. good eares are .vii. yere alſo, and
27 is but one dreame. Lykewyſe, the .vii. thynne and
euell fauored kyne that came out after them, are .vii
yeares: and the .vii. emptie and blaſted eares ſhalbe
28 vii. yeares of hunger. This is that which I ſayde vnto
Pharao, that God doth ſhewe Pharao what he is aboute
to doo.
29 Beholde there ſhall come .vii. yere of great plen-
30 teouſnes through out all the lande of Egypte. And
there ſhall aryſe after them .vii. yeres of hunger. So

M. 26 and it is 27 are .vii. eares

V. 16 reſpondebit proſpera 17 Putabā me ſtare 21 nullum ſaturitatis dedere veſtigium 25 Somnium regis vnum eſt 26 Septem boues pulchræ, & ſeptem ſpicæ plenæ . . ſeptem vbertatis anni ſunt, eandemque vim ſomnii comprehendunt.

L. 16 gluck ſagen laſſen 19 Ich hab . . . nicht ſolch vngeſtallte 21 merckt man nicht an yhn, das ſie freſſen hatten 25 das Got Pharao zeyget was er thut.

that all the plenteousnes shalbe forgeten in the
lande of Egipte. And the hunger shall consume
31 the lande: so that the plenteousnes shal not be once
asene in the land by reason of that hun- asene, *sene*, *i. e. known*
ger that shall come after, for it shalbe
32 exceading great And as concernynge that the dreame
was dubled vnto Pharao the second tyme, it betoken-
eth that the thynge is certanly prepared of God, ād
that God will shortly brynge it to passe.
33 Now therfore let Pharao provyde for a man of vn-
derstondynge and wysdome, and sett him over the
34 lande of Egipte. And let .P. Pharao make officers
ouer the lande, and take vp the fyste parte of the land
35 of Egipte in the .vii. plenteous yeres and let them
gather all the foode of these good yeres that come,
ād lay vp corne vnder the power of Pharo: that there
may be foode in the cities, and there let them kepte
36 it: that there may be foode in stoore in the lande,
agaynst the .vii. yeres of hunger which shall come in
the lande of Egipte, and that the lande perishe not
thorow hunger.
37 And the saynge pleased Pharao ād all his seruauntes.
38 Than sayde Pharao vnto his servauntes: where shall
we fynde soch a mā as this is, that hath the sprete of
39 God in him? wherfore Pharao sayde vnto Joseph: for
as moch as God hath shewed the all this, there is no
man of vnderstondyng nor of wysdome lyke vnto the
40 Thou therfore shalt be ouer my house, and acordinge
to thy worde shall all my people obey: only in the
41 kynges seate will I be aboue the. And he sayde vnto
Ioseph: beholde, I haue sett the ouer all the lande of
42 Egipte. And he toke off his rynge from his fyngre,
and put it vpon Iosephs fingre, and arayed him in raymēt of bisse, and put a golden cheyne aboute his

M. 39 or of wysdome
V. 30 vt obliuioni tractatur 31 & vbertatis magnitudinem perditura est inopiæ magnitudo. 32 firmitatis indicium . . sermo dei, & velocius impleatur. 35 sub Phar. potestate condatur 39 sapientiorem & similē tui inuenire potero? 41 rursum 22 stola byssina
L. 32 solch ding von Gott gefertiget . . dasselbs eylend thun

43 necke and ſet him vpon the beſt charett that he had
ſaue one. And they cryed before him Abrech, ād that
Pharao had made him ruelar ouer all the lande of Egipte.
44 And Pharao ſayde vnto Ioſeph: I am Pharao, without thi will, ſhall no man lifte vp e- [Fo. LXI.] ther
45 his hande or fote in all the lande of Egipte. And he
called Ioſephs name Zaphnath Paenea. And he gaue
him to wyfe Aſnath the doughter of Potiphara preaſt
of On. Than went Ioſeph abrode in the lāde of Egipte.
46 And he was .xxx. yere olde whē he ſtode before Pharao
kynge of Egipte. And than Ioſeph departed from
Pharao, and went thorow out all the lande of Egipte.
47 And in the .vii. plēteous yeres they made ſheves
48 and gathered vp all the fode of the .vii. plenteous
yeres which were in the lande of Egipte and put it
in to the cities. And he put the food of the feldes
that grewe rounde aboute euery cyte: euen in the
49 ſame. And Ioſeph layde vp corne in ſtoore, lyke vnto
the ſande of the ſee in multitude out of meſure, vntyll
he left nombrynge: For it was with out nombre.
50 And vnto Ioſeph were borne .ii. ſonnes before the
yeres of hunger came, which Aſnath the doughter of
51 Potiphara preaſt of On, bare vnto him. And he called
the name of the firſt ſonne Manaſſe, for God (ſayde he)
hath made me forgett all my laboure & all my fathers
52 huſholde. The ſeconde called he Ephraim, for God
(ſayde he) hath cauſed me to growe in the lande of
my trouble.

V. 43 currum ſuum ſecundum . . genu flecterent 44 non mouebit quiſquam manu aut ped. 45 & vocauit eum lingua Ægypt. Saluatorem mundi . . . . ſacerd. Heliopoleos. 47 in manipulos . . . congr. in horrea Ægypti. 49 arenæ maris coæquaretur, & copia menſuram excederet. 52 terra paupertatis

L. 43 auff dem andern wagen faren, . . knye fur yhm beugen 49 alſo das er auffhoret zu zelen, denn man kunds nicht zelen.

M. M. N. 43 *Abrech:* that is tender father or as ſome will bowe the knee. 45 *zaphnath paena;* they are wordes of Egypt, and as moch to ſaye: As a man to whome ſecret thynges are opened. 46 *When he ſtode before Pharao:* that is whē he was admytted of Pharao into hys office, as in 1 Reg. xvi, d.

L. M. N. 45 *Zaphnath paenea* iſt Egyptiſch geredt, vnd noch vnbewuſt was es ſey, on das ſo viel man ſpuren kan, heyſt es wie man auff deutſch ſpricht, der heymliche nehiſter radt. 51 *Manaſſe* heyſt vergeſſen. 52 *Ephraim* heyſt, die gewachſen.

53 And when the .vii. yeres of plenteouſnes that
54 was in the lande of Egypte were ended, than came
the .vii. yeres of derth, acordynge as .P. Ioſeph had
ſayde. And the derth was in all landes: but in the
55 lãde of Egipte was there yet foode. When now all
the lande of Egipte began to hunger, than cried
the people to Pharao for bread. And Pharao ſayde
vnto all Egipte: goo vnto Ioſeph, and what he ſayth
56 to you that doo And when the derth was thorow
out all the lande, Ioſeph opened all that was in the
cities, and ſolde vnto the Egiptiãs And hunger waxed
57 ſore in the land of Egipte. And all countrees came
to Egipte to Ioſeph for to bye corne: becauſe that the
hunger was ſo ſore in all landes.

ℂ The .XLII. Chapter.

1 WHEN Iacob ſawe that there was
corne to be ſolde in Egipte,
he ſayde vnto his ſõnes: why
2 are ye negligent? beholde, I
haue hearde that there is corne to be
ſolde in Egipte. Gete you thither and
bye vs corne frõ thẽce, that we maye
3 lyue and not dye. So went Ioſephs ten
brethern doune to bye corne in Egipte,
4 for Ben Iamin Ioſephs brother wold not
Iacob ſende with his other brethren: for
he ſayde: ſome myſſortune myght happen
him
5 And the ſonnes of Iſraell came to bye
corne amonge other that came, for there was derth
6 alſo in the lande of Canaan. And Io- [Fo. LXII.]
ſeph was gouerner in the londe, and ſolde corne to all
the people of the londe. And his brethren came, and

M.C.S. *Ioſephs brethren come into Egypte to bye corne. And he knoweth them and tryeth them. Symeon is put in pryſon, the other retorne to their father to fetche Ben Iamin. His father is lothe to let hym go, but at the laſt he graunted it.*

V. 56 vniuerſa horrea & vendeb . . . . nam & illos oppreſſerat fames. 57 & malum inopiæ temperarent. xlii, 1 Quare negligitis? 2 triticum. . . & non conſumamur inopia.

7 fell flatt on the grounde before him. When Iofeph fawe
his brethern, he knewe them: But made ftraunge vnto
them, and fpake rughly vnto them faynge: Whence
come ye? and they fayde: out of the lande of Canaan,
8 to bye vitayle. Iofeph knewe his brethern, but they
knewe not him.

9 And Iofeph remembred his dreames which he
dreamed of them, and fayde vnto them: ye are fpies,
and to fe where the lande is weake is your comynge.
10 And they fayde vnto him: nay, my lorde: but to bye
11 vitayle thy feruauntes are come. We are all one mans
fonnes, and meane truely, and thy feruauntes are no
fpies.

12 And he fayde vnto them: nay verely, but euen to
13 fe where the land is weake is youre comynge. And
they fayde: we thi feruauntes are .xii. brethern, the
fonnes of one man in the lande of Canaan. The
youngeft is yet with oure father, and one no man
woteth where he is.

14 Iofeph fayde vnto them, that is it that I fayde vnto
15 you, that ye are furelye fpies. Here by ye fhall be
proued. For by the lyfe of Pharao, ye fhall not goo
hence, vntyll youre yongeft brother be come hither.
16 Sende therefore one off you and lett him fette youre
.P. brother, and ye fhalbe in preafon in the meane
feafon. And thereby fhall youre wordes be proued,
whether there be any trueth in you: or els by the lyfe
17 of Pharao, ye are but fpies. And he put them in
warde thre dayes.

18 And Iofeph fayde vnto thē the thryd daye: This
19 doo and lyue, for I feare God Yf ye meane no hurte,
let one of youre brethern be bounde in the preafon,
and goo ye and brynge the neceffarie foode vnto youre

V. 6 atque ad eius nutum 7 durius loquebatur . . victui necessaria. 8 infirmiora terræ 11 pacifici venimus, nec quicquam famuli tui machinantur mali. 12 immunita terræ 13 alius non eft fuper. 15 per falutem Phar. 16 eritis in vinculis 19 Si pacifici eftis

L. 6 nydder zur erden auff ihr antlitz 7 redet hart 13 nicht mehr furhanden. 16 Bey dem leben Phar. 17 ynn eyn verwarung drey tag lang.

20 housholdes, and brynge youre yongest brother vnto
me: that youre wordes maye be beleved, ād that ye
dye not. And they did so.
21 Than they sayde one to a nother: we haue verely
synned agaynst oure brother, in that we sawe the
anguysh of his soull when he besought vs, & wold not
heare him: therfore is this troubyll come apon vs.
22 Ruben answered thē sayinge: sayde I not vnto you
that ye shuld not synne agaynst the lad: but ye wolde
not heare And now verely see, his bloude is requyred.
23 They were not aware that Ioseph vnderstode them, for
24 he spake vnto them by an interpreter. And he turned
from them and wepte, and than turned to them agayne
ād comened with them, and toke out Simeon from
25 amonge thē and bownde him before their eyes, ād
commaunded to fyll their sackes wyth corne, and to
put euery mans money in his sacke, and to geue them
vitayle to spende by the waye. And so it was done
to them.
26 [Fo. LXIII.] And they laded their asses with the
27 corne and departed thence. And as one of them
opened his sacke, for to geue his asse prauender in the
28 Inne, he spied his money in his sacks mouth And he
sayde vnto his brethren: my money is restored me
agayne, & is euē in my sackes mouth Than their
hartes fayled them, and were astoynyed and sayde
one to a nother: how cometh it that God dealeth thus
with vs?
29 And they came vnto Iacob their father vnto the
lande of Canaan, and tolde him all that had happened
30 them sayinge. The lorde of the lāde spake rughly to
31 vs, and toke us for spyes to serche the countre. And
we sayde vnto him: we meane truely and are no spies.

V. 20 vestros probare sermones et non moriamini. 21 Merito hæc patimur . . angustias animæ . . . ista tribulatio. 22 en sanguis eius exquiritur. 25 saccos tritico 31 Pacifici sumus, nec vllas molimur insidias.

L. 20 glewben, das yhr nicht sterben musset 21 angst seyner seelen 22 blut gefoddert. 28 da entpfiel yhn yhr hertz

M. M. N. 22 *To requyer the bloude of the hāde of another*, is to take vengeaunce of the euell done vnto him, as in Gen. ix, a. Psal. ix. b, and Ezech iii, c.

32 We be .xii. bretren sõnes of oure father, one is awaye,
and the yongest is now with oure father in the lande
of Canaan.
33 And the lorde of the countre sayde vnto us: here
by shall I knowe yf ye meane truely: leaue one of
youre brethern here with me, and take foode necessary
34 for youre houšholdes and get you awaye, and brynge
youre yongest brother vnto me And thereby shall I
knowe that ye are no spyes, but meane truely: So will
I delyuer you youre brother agayne, and ye shall occupie in the lande.
35 And as they emptied their sackes, beholde: euery-
mans bundell of money was in his sacke And when
both they and their father sawe the bundells of money,
they were afrayde.
36 .P. And Iacob their father sayde vnto them: Me
haue ye robbed of my childern: Ioseph is away, and
Simeon is awaye, and ye will take Ben Iamin awaye.
37 All these thinges fall vpon me. Ruben answered his
father saynge: Slee my two sonnes, yf I bringe him
not to the agayne. Delyuer him therfore to my honde,
38 and I will brynge him to the agayne: And he sayde:
my sonne shall not go downe with you. For his brother is dead, and he is left alone Moreouer some mys-
fortune myght happen vpon him by the waye which
ye goo. And so shuld ye brynge my gray head with
sorowe vnto the graue.

V. 32 vnus non est super 34 qui tenetur in vinculis . . . emendi habeatis licẽtiam. 35 His dictis cum frumenta . . ligatas pecunias 36 non est super, Simeon tenetur in vinculis . . in me . . . reciderunt. 38 ipse solus remansit . . cum dolore ad inferos.

L. 32 ist nicht mehr furhanden 34 im land werben. 36 Ioseph ist nit mehr furhanden 38 alleyn vberblieben . . mit schmertzen zur helle

M. M. N. 38 *Brynge me to my graue;* that is, ye shall brynge me to my death, as in Esa. xxxviii.

ℭ The .XLIII. Chapter.

M.C.S. When Bē Iamin was brought, they retorned with gyftes. Symeon is delyuered out of pryson. Ioseph goeth aſyde and wepeth. They feaſt together.

1 AND the derth waxed ſore in the
2 lande. And when they had
eatē vp that corne which they
brought out of the lande of
Egipte, their father ſayde vnto them: goo
3 agayne and by vs a litle food. Than
ſayde Iuda vnto him: the man dyd teſti-
fie unto vs ſaynge: loke that ye ſee not
my face excepte youre brother be with
4 you. Therfore yf thou wilt ſende oure brother with
5 vs, we wyll goo and bye the food. But yf thou wylt
not ſende him, we wyl! not goo: for the man ſayde
vnto vs: loke that ye ſee not my face, excepte youre
brother be with you.
6 And Iſraell ſayde: wherfore delt ye ſo cruelly with
me, as to tell the man that ye had yet [Fo. LXIIII.]
7 another brother? And they ſayde: The man aſked vs
of oure kynred ſaynge: is youre father yet alyue? haue
ye not another brother? And we tolde him acordynge
to theſe wordes. How cowd we knowe that he wolde
8 byd vs brynge oure brother downe with vs? Than ſayde
Iuda vnto Iſraell his father: Send the lad with me, and
we wyll ryſe and goo, that we maye lyue and not dye:
9 both we, thou and alſo oure childern. I wilbe ſuertie
for him, and of my handes requyre him. Yf I brynge
h:m not to the and ſett him before thine eyes, than let
10 me bere the blame for euer. For excepte we had made
this tariēg: by this we had bene there twyſe and come
agayne.
11 Than their father Iſrael ſayde vnto thē: Yf it muſt
nedes be ſo now: than do thus, take of the beſt frutes

V. 2 pauxillum eſcarum. 3 Denūtiauit nobis . . . ſub atteſtatione iuriſiurandi 4 ememus tibi neceſſaria. 6 miſeriam vt indicaretis 7 per ordinem noſtram progeniē . . iuxta id quod fuerat ſciſcitatus 8 ne moriamur nos et paruuli noſtri. 9 ſuſcipio puerum: . . require illum . . ero peccati reus

L. 6 dem man anſaget 8 wir vnd du vnd vnſer kindle 9 burge fur yhn ſeyn

of the lande in youre veſſeles, and brynge the man a
preſent, a curteſie bawlme, and a curteſie curteſie, *a*
of hony, ſpyces and myrre, dates and al- *ſmall quantity*
12 mondes. And take as moch money more with you.
And the money that was brought agayne in youre
ſackes, take it agayne with you in youre handes, peraduenture it was ſome ouerſyghte.
13 Take alſo youre brother with you, and aryſe and
14 goo agayne to the man. And God almightie geue
you mercie in the ſighte of the man and ſend you youre
other brother .P. and alſo Bē Iamin, and I wilbe as a
mā robbed of his childern.
15 Thus toke they the preſent and twiſe ſo much more
money with them, and Ben Iamin. And roſe vp, went
downe to Egipte, and preſented them ſelfe to Ioſeph.
16 When Ioſeph ſawe Ben Iamin with them, he ſayde to
the ruelar of his houſe: brynge theſe men home, and
ſley and make redie: for they ſhall dyne with me at
17 none. And the man dyd as Ioſeph bad, and brought
them in to Ioſephs houſe.
18 When they were brought to Ioſephs houſe, they
were afrayde ād ſayde: becauſe of the money ẏ came
in our ſackes mouthes at the firſt tyme, are we brought,
to pyke a quarell with vs & to laye ſome thinge to
oure charge: to brynge vs in bondage and oure aſſes
19 alſo. Therfore came they to the man that was the
ruelar ouer Ioſephs houſe, and comened with him at
20 the doore and ſayde:
Sir, we came hither at the firſt tyme to bye foode,
21 and as we came to an Inne and opened oure ſackes:
beholde, euery mannes money was in his ſacke with
full weghte: But we haue broght it agene with us,
22 & other mony haue we brought alſo in our handes, to

M. 12 agayne with you, peraduenture

V. 14 vobis eū placabilem: . quē tenet in vinculis, & hunc Beniamin 16 occide victimas, & inſtrue conuiuium 18 vt deuoluat in nos calumniā 20 Oramus domine, vt audias nos 21 eodem pondere reportauimus.

L. 14 euch laſſe ewrn andern bruder 18 das ers auff vns brenge 21 mit volligem gewicht

L. M. N. 11 Dieſe namen der fruchten ſind noch biſzher vngewiſs auch bey den Iuden ſelbs.

bye foode, but we can not tell who put oure money
in oure ſackes.
23 And he ſayde: be of good chere, feare not: Youre
God and the God of youre ſathers hath put you that
treaſure in youre ſackes, for I had [Fo. LXV.] youre
24 money. And he brought Simeon out to them ād led
thē in to Ioſephs houſe, & gaue them water to waſhe
25 their fete, and gaue their aſſes prauender: And they
made redie their preſent agaynſt Ioſeph came at none,
for they herde ſaye that they ſhulde dyne there.
26 When Ioſeph came home, they brought the preſent
in to the houſe to him, which they had in their handes,
ād fell flat on the grounde befor him.
27 And he welcomed thē curteouſly ſainge: is youre
father that old man which ye tolde me of, in good
28 health? and is he yet alyue? they anſwered: thy
ſervaunte oure father is in good health, ād is yet
alyue. And they bowed them ſelues and fell to
the grounde.
29 And he lyfte vp his eyes & behelde his brother Ben
Iamin his mothers ſonne, & ſayde: is this youre yongeſt
brother of whome ye ſayde vnto me? And ſayde: God
30 be mercyfull vnto ỹ my ſonne. And Ioſeph made haſt
(for his hert dyd melt apon his brother) and ſoughte for
to wepe, & entred in to his chambre, for to wepe there.
31 And he waſſhed his face and came out & refrayned
him ſelſe, & bad ſett bread on the table
32 And they prepared for him by himſelſe, and for them
by them ſelues, and for the Egiptians which ate with
him by them ſelues, becauſe the Egyptians may not
eate bread with the Hebrues, for that is an abhomyna-
33 cyon vnto the Egiptians. And they ſatt before him:

M. 30 ſought where to wepe

V. 22 in marſupiis noſtris. 23 Pax vobiſcum . . probatam ego habeo. 25 comeſturi eſſent panem. 26 adorauerunt proni in terram. 27 clementer reſalutatis eis 28 Soſpes eſt . . incuruati ador. 29 fratrem ſuum vterinum 30 commota fuerant viſcera . . et erumpebāt lachrymæ 31 continuit ſe 32 prophanum putant

L. 25 das brod eſſen ſollten. 27 Er aber gruſſet ſie freuntlich 30 ſeyns hertzen grund entbrand yhm 31 hielt ſich feſt

M. M. N. 32 *Abhominacion*, that is, it was abhorred of the Egypcians that an Hebrew ſhuld eate with thē.

the eldeſt acordynge vnto his .P. age, and the yongeſt
acordyng vnto his youth. And the men marveled
34 amonge them ſelves. And they broughte rewardes
vnto them from before him: but Ben Iamins parte was
fyue tymes ſo moch as any of theirs. And they ate
and they dronke, and were dronke wyth him

The .XLIIII. Chapter.

M.C.S. Ioſeph accuſeth his brother of theft. Iuda becommeth ſurety for Ben Iamin.

1 AND he commaunded the rueler
of his houſe ſaynge: fyll the
mens ſackes with food, as
moch as they can carie, and
put euery mans money in his bagge
2 mouth, and put my ſyluer cuppe in the ſackes mouth
of the yongeſt and his corne money alſo. And he
3 dyd as Ioſeph had ſayde. And in ẏ mornynge as
ſoone as it was lighte, the mē were let goo with
their aſſes.

4 And when they were out of the cytie and not yet
ferre awaye, Ioſeph ſayde vnto the ruelar of his houſe:
vp and folowe after the men and ouertake them, and
ſaye vnto them: wherefore haue ye rewarded euell for
5 good? is that not the cuppe of which my lorde drynketh, ād doth he not propheſie therin?
ye haue euell done that ye haue done.

prophesie, *divine*

6 And he ouertoke them and ſayde the ſame wordes
7 vnto them. And they anſwered him: wherfore ſayth
my lorde ſoch wordes? God forbydd that thy ſer-
8 uauntes ſhulde doo ſo. Beholde, the money which we
founde in oure ſackes mouthes, we brought agayne
vnto the, out of the land of Canaā: how then ſhulde

V. 33 primogenita ſua . . . ætatem ſuam. 34 ſumptis partibus quas ab eo acceperant: . et inebriati ſunt cum eo. xliiii, 1 ſummitate ſacci. 2 tritici 5 Scyphus quē furati eſtis 6 apprehenſis per ordinem 8 quomodo conſequens eſt vt furati ſimus

L. 33 gepurt . . . iugent 34 vnd wurden truncken mit yhm. xliiii, 1 oben ynn ſeynen ſack 6 Vnd als er ſie ergreiff

we ſteale [Fo. LXVI.] out of my lordes houſe, ether
9 ſyluer or golde? with whoſoeuer of thy ſeruauntes it
be founde let him dye, and let vs alſo be my lordes
10 bondmen. And he ſayde: Now therfore acordynge
vnto youre woordes, he with whom it is found, ſhalbe
my ſeruaunte: but ye, ſhalbe harmleſſe.

11 And attonce euery man toke downe his ſacke to
12 the grounde, ād every man opened his ſacke. And he
ſerched, and began at the eldeſt & left at the yongeſt.
13 And the cuppe was founde in Ben Iamins ſacke. Then
they rent their clothes, and laded euery man his aſſe
14 and went agayne vnto the cytie. And Iuda and his
brethrē came to Ioſephs houſe, for he was yet there,
15 ād they fell before him on the grounde. And Ioſeph
ſayde vnto thē: what dede is this which ye haue done?
wiſt ye not that ſoch a man as I can propheſie?

16 Then ſayde Iuda: what ſhall we ſaye vnto my lorde,
what ſhall we ſpeake or what excuſe can we make?
God hath founde out ẏ wekedneſſe of thy ſeruauntes.
Beholde, both we and he with whom the cuppe is
17 founde, are thy ſeruauntes. And he anſwered: God
forbyd ẏ I ſhulde do ſo, the man with whom the cuppe
is founde, he ſhalbe my ſeruaunte: but goo ye in peace
vn to youre father.

18 Then Iuda went vnto him and ſayde: oh my lorde,
let thy ſervaunte ſpeake a worde in my lordes audyence, and be not wrooth with .P. thi ſervaunte: for
19 thou art euen as Pharao. My lorde axed his ſeruaunte
20 ſainge: haue ye a father or a brother? And we anſwered my lord, we haue a father that is old, and a
yonge lad which he begat in his age: ād the brother
of the ſayde lad is dead, & he is all that is left of that
mother. And his father loueth him.

M. 18 my lordes eare, and

T. 14 Primuſque Iudas cum fratribus . . . omneſque . . . pariter in terram corruerunt. 15 ſimilis mei in augur. ſcientia? 16 aut iuſte poterimus obtendere? 17 Abſit a me . . . abite liberi 18 propius Iudas . . tu es enim poſt Pharaonem dominus meus. 20 ipſum ſolum habet mater ſua

L. 15 erradten kunde? 16 fur wenden 17 mit friden 18 fur deinen oren 20 alleyn vberblieben von ſeyner mutter

21 Then ſayde my lorde vnto his ſeruauntes brynge
him vnto me, that I maye ſett myne eyes apon him.
22 And we anſwered my lorde, that the lad coude not
goo from his father, for if he ſhulde leaue his father, he
23 were but a deed man. Then ſaydeſt thou vnto thy
ſervauntes: excepte youre yongeſt brother come with
you, loke that ye ſe my face no moare.

24 And when we came vnto thy ſeruaunt oure father,
25 we ſhewed him what my lorde had ſayde. And when
oure father ſayde vnto vs, goo agayne and bye vs a
26 litle fode: we ſayd, ẏ we coude not goo. Neverthèleſſe
if oure yoūgeſte brother go with vs then will we goo,
for we maye not ſee the mannes face, excepte oure
27 yongeſt brother be with vs. Then ſayde thy ſervaunt
oure father vnto vs. Ye knowe that my wyfe bare me
28 ii. ſonnes. And the one went out from me and it is
ſayde of a ſuertie that he is torne in peaces of wyld
29 beaſtes, and I ſawe him not ſence. Yf ye ſhall take
this alſo awaye frō me and ſome myſſortune happen
apon him, then ſhall ye brynge my gray heed with
ſorow vnto the grave.

30 [Fo. LXVII.] Now therfore whē I come to thy ſervaunt my father, yf the lad be not with me: ſeinge that
31 his lyfe hāgeth by the laddes lyfe, then as ſoone as he
ſeeth that the lad is not come, he will dye. So ſhall
we thy ſervaūtes brynge the gray hedde of thy ſer-
32 vaunt oure father with ſorow vnto the grave. For I
thy ſervaunt became ſuertie for the lad vnto my father
& ſayde: yf I bringe him not vnto the agayne. I will
33 bere the blame all my life lōge. Now therfore let me thy
ſervaunt byde here for ẏ lad, & be my lordes bondman: &
34 let the lad goo home with his brethern. For how can
I goo vnto my father, and the lad not wyth me: leſt I
ſhulde ſee the wretchednes that ſhall come on my father.

V. 21 ponam oculos 26 non audemus videre 28 Egreſſus eſt vnus 29 cum mœrore ad inferos. 30 anima illius ex huius anima dependeat 32 recepi fidem, & ſpopondi 34 Non enim poſſum . . . ne calamitatis . . . teſtis aſſiſtam.

L. 28 Eyner gieng hynaus von myr 29 hynunter in die hell 30 weyl ſeyn ſeel an diſes ſeel hanget 32 burge worden 34 iamer ſehen, der meynem vatter begegen wurde.

The .XLV. Chapter.

M.C.S. Ioſeph maketh hym ſelfe knowen vnto his brethren, and ſendeth for his father.

1 AND Ioſeph coude no longer refrayne before all them that ſtode aboute him, but commaunded that they ſhuld goo all out from him, and that there ſhuld be
no man with him, whyle he vttred him ſelfe vnto his
2 brethern. And he wepte alowde, ſo that the Egip-
3 tians and the houſe of Pharao herde it. And he ſayde
vnto his brethern: I am Ioſeph: doth my father yet
lyue? But his brethern coude not anſwere him, for
they were abaſſhed at his preſence.
4 And Ioſeph ſayde vnto his brethern: come nere to
me, and they came nere. And he .¶. ſayde: I am
5 Ioſeph youre brother whom ye ſold in to Egipte. And
now be not greued therwith, nether let it ſeme a cruel
thinge in youre eyes, that ye ſolde me hither. For God
6 dyd ſend me before you to ſaue lyfe. For this is the
ſeconde yere of derth in the lande, and fyue moo are
behynde in which there ſhall nether be earynge nor
herveſt.
7 Wherfore God ſent me before you to make prouiſion,
that ye myghte continue in the erth and to ſave youre
8 lyues by a greate delyuerance. So now it was not ye
that ſent me hither, but God: and he hath made me
father vnto Pharao and lord ouer all his houſe, and
9 rueler in all the land of Egipte. Haſt you ād goo to
my father and tell him, this ſayeth thy ſonne Ioſeph:
God hath made me lorde ouer all Egipte. Come downe
10 vnto me and tarye not, And thou ſhalt dwell in the
londe of Goſan & be by me: both thou and thi chil-

T. 1 intereſſet . . agnitioni mutuæ. 3 nimio terrore perterriti. 5 pro ſalute enim veſtra 6 nec arari . . nec meti 7 & eſcas ad viuẽdum habere poſſitis.

L. 1 mit ſeynen brudern bekennete 5 vnd denckt nicht das zorn ſey . . vmb ewers lebens willen 6 pflugen . . . erndten 7 durch eyn groſſe errettunge

L. M. N. 4 *zu myr:* Das ſind die ſuſſen wort des Euangelii, alſo redet Chriſtus mit der ſeelen im glawben, nach dem ſie durchs geſetz vnd gewiſſen der ſund, woll gedemutiget vnd geengſtet iſt.

dern, and thi childerns childern: and thy ſhepe, and
11 beaſtes and all that thou haſt. There will I make
proviſion for the: for there remayne yet .v. yeres of
derth, leſt thou and thi houſholde and all that thou
haſt periſh.
12 Beholde, youre eyes do ſe, and the eyes alſo of my
brother Ben Iamin, that I ſpeake to you by mouth.
13 Therfore tell my father of all my honoure which I
haue in Egipte and of all that ye haue ſene, ād make
haſt and brynge mi [Fo. LXVIII.] father hither.
14 ¶ And he fell on his brother Ben Iamins necke &
15 wepte, & Ben Iamin wepte on his necke. Moreouer
he kyſſed all his brethern and wepte apon them. And
16 after that, his brethern talked with him. And when
the tidynges was come vnto Pharaos houſſe that Io-
ſephes brethern were come, it pleaſed Pharao well and
all his ſeruauntes.
17 And Pharao ſpake vnto Ioſeph: ſaye vnto thy brethern, this do ye: lade youre beeſtes ād get you hence,
18 And when ye be come vnto the londe of Canaan, take
youre father and youre houſholdes and come vnto me,
and I will geue you the beſte of the lande of Egipte,
and ye ſhall eate the fatt of the londe.
19 And commaunded alſo. This do ye: take charettes
with you out of the lande of Egipte, for youre childern
and for youre wyues: and brynge youre father and come.
20 Alſo, regarde not youre ſtuff, for the goodes of all the
londe of Egipte ſhalbe youres.
21 And the childern of Iſraell dyd euen ſo, And Ioſeph
gaue them charettes at the commaundment of Pharao,
and gaue them vitayle alſo to ſpende by the waye.
22 And he gaue vnto eche of them chaunge of rayment:
but vnto Ben Iamin he gaue .iii. hundred peces of
23 ſyluer and .v. chaunge of rayment. And vnto his father he ſent after the ſame maner: x. he aſſes laden

M. 23 maner .x. aſſes

V. 11 Ibique te paſcam 16 omnis familia eius. 18 medullam terræ. 19 ac coniugū: et dicito, Tollite patrem veſtrum & properate quantocyus venientes 22 ſtolis optimis 23 tantūdem pecuniæ & veſtium

L. 12 mundlich mit euch rede 20 ſchonet nicht ewrs hauſzradts

with good out of Egipte, and .x. ſhe aſſes laden with
corne, bred and meate: to ſerue his .P. father by the
24 waye. So ſent he his brethern awaye, and they departed. And he ſayde vnto them: ſe that ye fall not
out by the waye.
25 And they departed from Egipte and came in to the
26 land of Canaan vnto Iacob their father, and told him
ſaynge. Ioſeph is yet a lyue and is gouerner ouer all the
land of Egipte. And Iacobs hert wauered, for he be-
27 leued thē not. And they tolde him all the wordes of
Ioſeph which he had ſayde vnto them. But when he
ſawe the charettes which Ioſeph had ſent to carie him,
28 then his ſprites reuiued. And Iſrael ſayde. ſprites, *ſpirits*
I haue ynough, yf Ioſeph my ſonne be yet alyue: I
will goo and ſe him, yer that I dye. yer, *before*

The .XLVI. Chapter.

M.C.S. Iacob with all his houſholde goeth to Ioſeph in to Egypt. The genealogie of Iacob. Ioſeph meteth hys father.

1 ISRAEL toke his iourney with
all that he had, and came
vnto Berſeba and offred offrynges vnto the God of his
2 father Iſaac. And God ſayde vnto Iſrael
in a viſion by nyghte, and called vnto
him: Iacob Iacob. And he anſwered:
3 here am I. And he ſayde; I am that mightie God of
thy father, feare not to goo downe in to Egipte. For
4 I will make of the there a great people. I will go
downe with ẏ in to Egipte, & I will alſo bringe the vp
agayne, & Ioſeph ſhall put his hand apon thine eyes.

V. 23 . . . addens . . triticum in itinere, paneſque portātes. 24 Ne iraſcamini in via. 26 Quo audito Iacob, quaſi de graui ſomno euigilans 27 reuixit ſpiritus eius, & ait xlvi, 1 puteum iuramenti (v. 5) . . mactatis ibi victimis 2 audiuit eum

L. 24 zancket nicht auff dem wege. 26 ſeyn hertz ſchlugs ynn wind 28 Ich hab gnug. xlvi, 1 opffert er opffer

M. M. N. 3 *I will make the a great people:* that is I wyll multiplye thy ſeede, that many people ſhall come therof 4 *To put hys hande vpon his eyes* is to be preſent at hys death and to burye him, as in Tob. xiiii, d.

5 And Iacob rose vp from Berseba. And ỹ sonnes of
Israel caried Iacob their father, ād [Fo. LXIX.] their
childern and their wyues in the charettes which Pharao
6 had sent to carie him. And they toke their catell ād
the goodes which they had gotten in the land of Canaan, and came in to Egipte: both Iacob and all his
7 seed with him, his sonnes and his sonnes sonnes with
him: his doughters and his sonnes doughters and all
his seed brought he with him in to Egipte.·

8 These are the names of the childern of Israel which
came in to Egipte, both Iacob and his sonnes: Rubē
9 Iacobs first sonne. The childern of Ruben: Hanoch,
10 Pallu, Hezron and Charmi. The childern of Simeon:
Iemuel, Iamin, Ohad, Iachin, Zohar and Saul the sonne
11 of a Cananitish woman The childern of Leui: Gerson,
12 Kahath and Merari. The childern of Iuda: Er, Onan,
Sela, Pharez and Zerah, but Er and Onan dyed in the
lande of Canaan. The childern of Pharez, Hezrō, &
13 Hamul. The childern of Isachar: Tola, Phuva Iob
14 and Semnon. The childern of Sebulon: Sered, Elon
15 and Iaheleel. These be the children of Lea which she
bare vnto Iacob in Mesopotamia with his doughter
Dina. All these soulles of his sonnes and doughters
make .xxx. and .vi.

16 The childern of Gad: Ziphion, Haggi, Suni, Ezbon,
17 Eri, Arodi and Areli. The childern of Asser: Iemna,
Iesua, Iesui, Brya and Se- .P. rah their sister. And
18 the childern of Brya were Heber and Malchiel. These
are the childern of Silpha whom Labā gaue to Lea his
doughter. And these she bare vnto Iacob in nombre
xvi. soules.

19 The childern of Rahel Iacobs wife: Ioseph and ben
20 Iamin. And vnto Ioseph in the lōde of Egipte were
borne: Manasses and Ephraim which Asnath the dough-
21 ter of Potiphara preast of On bare vnto him. The chil-

M. 13 Semson 15 make .xxx. and .iii.
V. 5 ad portandum senem [The whole passage 1–7 is very free.]
15 triginta tres. 20 sacerdot. Heliopoleos
L. 6 erworben hatten 11 Gerson, Cuhuz vnd M., 12 Hezron vnd Thamul 14 Semron 15 drey vnd dreyzg zeelen 16 Arobi 20 Priesters zu On

dern of Ben Iamin: Bela, Becher, Aſbel, Gera, Nae-
22 man, Ehi Ros Mupim, Hupim and Ard. Theſe are
the childern of Rahel which were borne vnto Iacob:
xiiii. ſoules all to gether.
23, 24 The childern of Dan: Huſim. The childern of
25 Nepthali: Iahezeel, Guni, Iezer and Sillem. Theſe
are the ſonnes of Bilha which Laban gaue vnto Rahel
his doughter, and ſhe bare theſe vnto Iacob, all to-
26 gether .vii. ſoulles All the ſoulles that came with
Iacob in to Egipte which came out of his loyns (beſyde his ſonnes wifes) were all togither .Lx. and .vi
27 ſoulles. And the ſonnes of Ioſeph, which were borne
him in egipte were: .ii. ſoules. So that all the ſoulles
of the houſe of Iacob which came in to Egipte are .Lxx
28 And he ſent Iuda before him vnto Ioſeph that the
waye myghte be ſhewed him vnto Goſan,and they came
29 in to the lande of Goſan And Ioſeph made redie his
charett and went agaynſt Iſraell his father vnto Goſan,
ãd pre- [Fo. LXX.] ſented him ſelfe vnto him, and fell
on his necke and wepte vpon his necke a goode whyle.
30 And Iſrael ſayd vnto Ioſeph: Now I am cõtẽt to dye,
in ſo moch I haue ſene the, that thou art yet alyue.
31 And Ioſeph ſayde vnto his brethrẽ and vnto his fathers
houſe: I will goo & ſhewe Pharao and tell him: that my
brethern and my fathers houſe which were in the lãde of
32 Canaan are come vnto me, and how they are ſhepardes
(for they were men of catell) and they haue brought their
ſhepe and their oxen and all that they haue with them.
33 Yf Pharao call you and axe you what youre occupa-
34 tion is, ſaye: thi ſeruauntes haue bene occupyed aboute
catell, frõ oure chilhode vnto this tyme: both we and oure
fathers, that ye maye dwell in the lande of Goſan. Fo: an
abhominacyon vnto the Egiptians are all that feade ſhepe.

M. 29 and wẽt to mete Iſrael 34 For the Egyptiãs abhore all ſheppardes.

V. 27 *in Aegyptum* 28 vt nuntiaret ei, et ille occurreret in Geſſen. 29 ad eũdem locum . . . & inter amplexus fleuit. 32 curamque habent alendorum gregum: . omnia quae habere petuerunt 34 reſpondebitis, Viri paſtores ſumus . . . Hæc autum dicetis

L. 26 die aus ſeynen landen komen waren 29 Vnd da er yn ſahe 32 leute die mit vieh vmbgehen (v. 34) 34 Denn was vieh hirten ſind, das iſt den Egyptern ein grewel.

The .XLVII. Chapter.

M.C.S *Iacob cometh before Pharao, & vnto hym is geuē the lande of Goſan. He ſwereth his ſonne for his buryall.*

1 AND Ioſeph wēt and told Pharao
and ſayde: my father and my
brethern their ſhepe and their
beaſtes and all that they haue,
are come out of the lāde of Canaan and
2 are in the lande of Goſan. And Ioſeph
toke a parte of his brethern: euen fyue of
3 them, and preſented them vnto Pharao. And Pharao
ſayde vnto his brethern: what is your occupation?
And they ſayde vnto Pharao: feaders of ſhepe are thi
4 ſeruauntes, both we ād alſo oure fathers. They ſayde
moreouer vnto Pha- .P. rao: for to ſogeorne in the
lande are we come, for thy ſeruauntes haue no paſture
for their ſhepe ſo ſore is the fameſhment in the lande
of Canaan. Now therefore let thy ſeruauntes dwell
in the lande of Goſan.

5 And Pharao ſayde vnto Ioſeph: thy father and thy
6 brethren are come vnto the. The londe of Egipte is
open before the: In the beſt place of the lande make
both thy father and thy brothren dwell. And euen in
the lond of Goſan let them dwell. Moreouer yf thou
knowe any men of actiuyte amonge them,
7 make them ruelars ouer my catell. And
Ioſeph brought in Iacob his father and ſett him be-
8 fore Pharao. And Iacob bleſſed Pharao. And Pharao
9 axed Iacob, how old art thou? And Iacob ſayde vnto
Pharao: the dayes of my pilgremage are an hundred
and: .xxx. yeres. Few and euell haue the dayes of
my lyfe bene, and haue not attayned vnto the yeres
of the lyfe of my fathers in the dayes of their pilgrem-
10 ages. And Iacob bleſſed Pharao and went out from

men of actiuyte, *able men*

M. 3 Pharao: ſheppardes are

V. 2 Extremos quoque fratrum 6 viros induſtrios 7 ſtatuit eum coram eo [7–12 is very free with repeated omiſſions.]

L. 3 Wes nehret jr euch? 6 offen, las ſie . . die tüchtig ſind 7 ſtellet im fur Pharao 9 die zeit meiner walfart (3 times)

M. M. N. 9 *The dayes of hys pilgremage* was all the tyme that he lyued, as in Iob .xiiii, c, and Psal. cxviii, c. 10 *To bleſſe*, is here to prayſe & geue thankes as a fore in the .xiiii. of Gene. d. and 1 Co. x, d.

11 him. And Ioſeph prepared dwellinges for his father
and his brethern, and gaue them poſſeſſions in the
londe of Egipte, in the beſt of the londe: euẽ in the
12 lande of Raemſes, as Pharao commaunded. And Ioſeph made prouyſion for his father, his brethern and
all his fathers houſholde, as yonge children are fedd
with bread.
13 There was no bread in all the londe, for the derth
was exceadĩge ſore: ſo yͭ yͤ lõde of Egipte & yͤ lõde
of Canaan, were fameſhyd by yͤ reaſon [Fo. LXXI.]
14 of yͤ derth. And Ioſeph brought together all yͤ money
yͭ was founde in yͤ lãde of Egipte and of Canaan, for
yͤ corne which they boughte: & he layde vp the money
in Pharaos houſſe.
15 When money fayled in the lãde of Egipte & of
Canaan, all the Egiptians came vnto Ioſeph and ſayde:
geue us ſuſtenaunce: wherfore ſuffreſt thou vs to dye
16 before the, for oure money is ſpent. Then ſayde Ioſeph: brynge youre catell, and I will geue yow for
17 youre catell, yf ye be without money. And they
brought their catell vnto Ioſeph. And he gaue them
bread for horſes and ſhepe, and oxen and aſſes: ſo he
fed them with bread for all their catell that yere.
18 When that yere was ended, they came vnto him
the nexte yere and ſayde vnto him: we will not hyde
it from my lorde, how that we haue nether money nor
catell for my lorde: there is no moare left for my lorde,
19 but euen oure bodies and oure londes. Wherfore lateſt
thou vs dye before thyne eyes, and the londe to goo
to noughte? bye vs and oure landes for bread: and let
both vs and oure londes be bonde to Pharao. Geue
vs ſeed, that we may lyue & not dye, & that the londe
goo not to waſt.
20 And Ioſeph boughte all the lande of Egipte for

V. 17 pro commutatione pecorũ 19 redigatur terra in ſoli-
tudinem.

L. 12 einem jglichen ſein theil brod, von alten bis auff die
jungen kinder. 13 jn allen landen . . verſchmachten 14 bracht alles
geld zu zamen 18 vnſern herrn nicht verbergen . . auch alles vieh
. . . beide vns ſterben vnd vnſer feld? 19 leibeigen ſeien . . nicht
verwüſte.

Pharao. For the Egiptians ſolde euery man his londe
becauſe the derth was ſore apō them: and ſo the londe
21 became Pharaos. And he appoynted the people vnto
the cities, from one ſyde of Egipte vnto the other:
22 only the londe of the Preſtes bought he not. For
there .P. was an ordinaũce made by Pharao for
ỹ * preaſtes, that they ſhulde eate that
which was appoynted vnto them: which
Pharao had geuen them wherfore they
ſolde not their londes.
23 Then Ioſeph ſayde vnto the folke: beholde I haue boughte you this daye ād
your landes for Pharao. Take there ſeed
24 and goo ſowe the londe. And of the
encreaſe, ye ſhall geue the fyſte parte
vnto Pharao, and .iiii. partes ſhalbe youre
awne, for ſeed to ſowe the feld: and for
you, and them of youre houſholdes, and
25 for youre childern, to eate. And they
anſwered: Thou haſt ſaued oure lyves
Let vs fynde grace in the ſyghte of my
lorde, and let us be Pharaos ſervaũtes.
26 And Ioſeph made it a lawe ouer the lāde
of Egipte vnto this daye: that men muſt
geue Pharao the fyſte part, excepte the
londe of the preaſtes only, which was not
bond vnto Pharao.
27 And Iſrael dwelt in Egipte: euen in
the countre of Goſan. And they had
their poſſeſſions therein, and they grewe and multi-
28 plyed exceadingly. Moreouer Iacob lyued in the
lande of Egipte .xvii. yeres, ſo that the hole age of
Iacob was an hundred and .xlvii. yere.

** The blīde gydes gett previleges frō bearīge with their brethrē contrarye to Chriſtes lawe of love. And of theſe preſtes of idolles did our cōpaſſīge yvetrees lerne to crepe vp by litle & litle & to cōpaſſe ỹ greate trees of ỹ world with hypocriſye, ād to thruſt ỹ rotes of idolatryſſe ſuperſtition in to thē & to ſucke out ỹ iuce of thē with their poetrye, till all be ſeer bowes and no thinge grene ſave their awne cōmewelth.*

V. 20 Subiecitque eā Pharaoni 22 quibus & ſtatuta cibaria ex horreis publicis præbebantur, & idcirco non ſunt compulſi vendere poſſ. ſuas. 25 reſpiciat nos tantum dom. noſter, et læti ſeruiemus regi. 26 quæ libera ab hac conditione fuit. 28 vixit in ea

L. 20 tewrung 21 ſtedten aus vnd einging 22 was jnen benant war . . durfften . . nicht verkauffen. 23 Sihe, da habt jr ſamen 25 las vns nur leben 26 nicht eigen Pharao.

M. M. N. 20 This name Pharao was a generall name to all the kynges of Egypte. As abimelech was a cōmen name to all the kynges of the gentiles, as in Exod. xvi.

29 When the tyme drewe nye, that Israel must dye:
he sent for his sonne Ioseph and sayde vnto him: Yf
I haue founde grace in thy syghte, put thy hande
vnder my thye and deale mercifully ād truely with me,
30 that thou burie me not in Egipte: but let me lye by
my fathers, and ca- [Fo. LXXII.] rie me out of Egipte,
and burie me in their buryall. And he answered: I
31 will do as thou hast sayde. And he sayde: swere vnto
me: ād he sware vnto him. And than Israel bowed
him vnto the beddes head.

The .XLVIII. Chapter.

1 AFTER these deades, tydīges were
brought vnto Ioseph, that his
father was seke. And he toke
with him his .ii. sōnes, Manas-
2 ses and Ephraim. Then was it sayde vnto
Iacob: beholde, thy sonne Ioseph commeth
vnto the. And Israel toke his strength vnto him, and
3 satt vp on the bedd, and sayde vnto Ioseph: God all
mightie appeared vnto me at lus in the lande of Ca-
4 naan, ād blessed me, and sayde vnto me: beholde, I
will make the growe and will multiplye the, and will
make a great nombre of people of the, and will geue
this lande vnto the and vnto thy seed after ỹ vnto an
5 euerlastinge possession. Now therfore thy .ii. sōnes
Manasses ād Ephraim which were borne vnto the before I came to the, in to Egipte, shalbe myne: euen
6 as Ruben and Simeō shall they be vnto me. And the

M.C.S. *Iacob lyeth sycke. He desyreth Ephraim and Manasses for hys sonnes and blesseth them.*

V. 29 cerneret diem . . & facies mihi misericordiam & veritatem . . auferas me de terra hac, condasque in sepulchro maior. 31 Quo iurante, adorauit Isr. dom., conuersus ad lectuli caput. xlviii, 2 Dictumque est seni . . Qui confortatus sedit in lectulo.

L. 29 liebe vnd trewe an mir thust . . jm jrem begrebnis begraben 31 jnn dem bette zum heubten. xlviii, 2 vnd Israel macht sich stark

M. M. N. 29 To put his hand vnder his thye, loke in Gen. xxiiii, a.

L. M. N. 31 *Nieget:* Er lag im bette kranck, richtet sich doch auff, nieget sich zum heubten, vnd bettet, die weil thut Ioseph den eid.

childern which thou getest after them, shalbe thyne
awne: but shalbe called with the names of their brethern in their enheritaunces.
7 And after I came from Mesopotamia, Rahel dyed
apon my hande in the lande of Canaã, by the waye:
when I had but a feldes bre- .P. de to goo vnto Ephrat. And I buried her there in ẏ waye to Ephrat
which is now called Bethlehem.
8 And Israel behelde Iosephes sonnes & sayde: what
9 are these? And Ioseph sayde vnto his father: they
are my sonnes, which God hath geuen me here. And
he sayde: brynge them to me, and let me blesse them.
10 And the eyes of Israell were dymme for age, so that he
coude not see. And he brought them to him, ād he
11 kyssed thē and embraced them. And Israel sayde vnto
Ioseph: I had not thoughte to haue sene thy face, and
yet loo, God hath shewed it me and also thy seed.
12 And Ioseph toke them awaye from his lappe, and they
fell on the grounde before him.
13 Than toke Ioseph them both: Ephraim in his ryghte
hande towarde Israels left hande ād Manasses in his
left hande, towarde Israels ryghte hande, and brought
14 them vnto him. And Israel stretched out his righte
hande and layde it apon Ephraims head which was
the yonger, and his lyft hāde apon Manasses heed,
15 crossinge his handes, for Manasses was the elder. And
he blessed Ioseph saynge: God before whome my fathers
Abraham and Isaac dyd walke, and the God which hath
16 fedd me all my life longe vnto this daye, And the
angell which hath delyuered me frō all euyll, blesse
these laddes: ẏ they maye be called after my name,

V. 7 ipso itinere, eratque vernum tempus: & ingred. 12 de gremio patris, adorauit 14 commutans manus. 15 Benedixitque Iac. filiis Ios., & ait, Deus . . . qui pascit me 16 et inuocetur super eos nomen

L. 6 sollen generet sein mit jrer brüder namen 7 Ephrath, die jm Bethelehem heist. 8 Wer sind die? 10 tunkel . für alter . . wol sehen . . hertzet sie, 11 vnd sprach 12 von seinem schos, vnd er nieget sich 14 Vnd thet wissend also mit seinen henden 15 erneeret hat . . diesen tag, 16 das sie nach meinem

M. M. N. 14 The puttyng on of hādes was comenly vsed of the Hebrews, whē they cōmended or offred any thyng to God, as Leuit. i, b.

and after my father Abraham and Iſaac, and that they
maye growe ād multiplie apō [Fo. LXXIII.] the erth.
17 When Ioſeph ſawe that his father layd his ryghte
hande apon the heade of Ephraim, it diſpleaſed him.
And he lifte vpp his fathers hāde, to haue removed it
18 from Ephraims head vnto Manaſſes head, and ſayde
vnto his father: Not ſo my father, for this is the eldeſt.
19 Put thy right hand apon his head. And his father
wold not, but ſayde: I knowe it well my ſonne, I
knowe it well. He ſhalbe alſo a people ād ſhalbe
great. But of a troth his yonger brother ſhalbe great-
20 ter than he, and his ſeed ſhall be full of people. And
he bleſſed them ſainge. At the enſample
of theſe, the Iſraelites ſhall bleſſe and ſaye:
God make the as Ephraim and as Manaſſes.
Thus ſett he Ephraim before Manaſſes.

At the enſample, *according to*

21 And Iſrael ſayde vnto Ioſeph: beholde, I dye. And god
ſhalbe with you and bringe you agayne vnto the land of
22 youre fathers. Moreouer I geue vnto the, a porcyon of
lande aboue thy brethern, which I gatt out of the handes
of the Amorites wyth my ſwerde and with my bowe.

The .XLIX. Chapter.

1 AND Iacob called for his ſonnes
ād ſayde: come together, that
I maye tell you what ſhall
happē you in the laſt dayes.
2 Gather you together and heare ye ſones
of Iacob, and herken vnto Iſrael youre
father.

M.C.S. *Iacob bleſſeth all his awne ſonnes and ſheweth thē what is to come. He apoynteth where he wyl be buryed: and dyeth.*

V. 17 Ephraim, grauiter accepit 20 in tempore illo . . In te benedicentur Iſrael 22 vnam partem extra fratres

L. 16 . . das ſie waſchen * 17 gefiel es jm vbel 18 Nicht ſo 19 Ich weis wol (*bis*) 20 geſegnet er ſie des tages . . Nach deiner weiſe werde Iſrael geſ. . . ſetze dich . ſetzt. . fur 22 ein ſtück lands

L. M. N. 22 *Stück:* heiſt im Ebreſchen Sichem, vnd die ſelbe ſtat meinet er hie.

---

* A curious typographical error, *waſchen* (to wash) being put for *wachſen* (to grow).

3 .P. Ruben, thou art myne eldeſt ſonne, my myghte
and the begynnynge of my ſtrength, chefe in receau-
4 ynge and chefe in power. As unſtable as water waſt
thou: thou ſhalt therfore not be the cheſeſt, for thou
wenſt vp vpō thy fathers bedd, and than deſyledeſt thou
my couche with goynge vppe.
5 The brethern Simeon and Leui, weked inſtrumentes
6 are their wepōs. In to their ſecrettes come not my
ſoule, and vnto their congregation be my honoure
not coupled: for in their wrath they ſlewe a man, and
7 in their ſelfewill they houghed an oxe. Curſed be
their wrath for it was ſtronge, and their fearſnes for it
was cruell. I will therfore deuyde them in Iacob, &
ſcater them in Iſrael.
8 Iuda, thy brethern ſhall prayſe the, & and thine
hande ſhalbe in the necke of thyne enimies, & thy
9 fathers childern ſhall ſtoupe vnto the. Iuda is a lions
whelpe. Frō ſpoyle my ſonne thou art come an hye:
he layde him downe and couched himſelfe as a lion,
10 and as a lioneſſe. Who dare ſtere him vp? The
ſceptre ſhall not departe from Iuda, nor a ruelar from

V. 3 principium doloris mei 4 effuſus es ſicut aqua 6 & in voluntate ſua ſuffoderunt murum 9 quis ſuſcitabit eum

L. 3 öberſt jm opffer . . jm reich 5 Vnrecht haben ſie gehandelt 6 den ochſen verderbt 9 du biſt hoch komen . . widder yhn auff lehnen?

M. M. N. 6 That is, cut the ſenowes on the inſyde the knee, or as ſome call it the hamme, ſo that he coulde not goo. 10 *Sceptre* is here taken for power royall & dignytie. Here is alſo prophecied the cōminge of Chriſt, as in Eſaye. ix, a. *Judge hys people*, that is, he ſhall rule & gouerne them, as Exo. xviii, d.

L. M. N. 3 *Reuben* ſolt der erſte geburte wurde haben, nemlich, das Prieſterthum vnd königreich, Nu aber wirds beides von jm genomē vnd Leui das Prieſterthum, vnd Iuda das königreich gebē, Hie iſt bedeut, die Syund Nagaga, die das bette Iacob, das iſt der Schrifft beſuddelt mit falſche lere darüber ſie verloren hat Prieſterthum & ynn königreich Iſrael. 10 *Scepter;* Hie ſehet an der ſegen von Chriſto, der von Iuda geporn ſollt werden, vnd heyſt yhn Silo, das iſt der gluck ſelig ſeyn vnd friſch durch dringen ſolt, mit geyſt vnnd glauben, das zuuor durch werck ſaur vnd vnſelig ding war, darumb nenn wyr, Silo, eyn helt, denn das vorige teyl dis ſegens betrifft den konig Dauid, vnd iſt ſonſt ynn allen ſegen nichts mehr von Chriſto Sondern alles ander iſt von zeytlichem heyl, das den kindern Iſrael geben iſt, als das *Sebulon* am meer wonen bis gen Sidon, vnd Iſſachar mitten ym land vom meer wonen, vnd doch zinſsbar geweſen iſt den konigen von Aſſyrien,

betwene his legges, vntill Silo come, vnto whome the
11 people ſhall herken. He ſhall bynde his fole vnto the
vine, and his aſſes colt vnto the vyne braunche, ād
ſhall waſh his garment in wyne and his mantell in the
12 bloud of grapes, his eyes are roudier than roudier, *rud-*
wyne, ād his teeth whitter then mylke. *dier, redder*
13 [Fo. LXXIIII.] Zabulon ſhall dwell in the hauen of the
ſee and in the porte of ſhippes, & ſhall reache vnto Sidon.
14 Iſachar is a ſtronge aſſe, he couched him doune
15 betwene .ii. borders, and ſawe that reſt was good and
the lande that it was pleaſant, and bowed his ſhulder
to beare, and became a ſervaunte vnto trybute.
16 Dan ſhall iudge his people, as one of the trybes of
17 Iſrael. Dan ſhalbe a ſerpent in the waye, and an edder
in the path, and byte the horſe heles, ſo ẏ his ryder
18 ſhall fall backwarde. After thy ſauynge loke I LORde.
19 Gad, men of warre ſhall invade him. And he ſhall
turne them to flyght.
20 Off Aſſer cometh fatt breed, and he ſhall geue pleaſures for a kynge.
21 Nepthali is a ſwyft hynde, ād geueth goodly wordes.
22 That floriſhynge childe Ioſeph, that floriſhing childe
and goodly vn to the eye: the doughters come forth

M. 22 the daughters ran vpon the walle.

V. 10 qui mittendus eſt, et ipſe erit expectatio gentium. 11 et ad vitem o fili mi, aſinam 12 Pulchriores ſunt oculi 17 mordens ungulas equi, vt cadat aſc. eius retro. 18 Salutare tuum expectabo 19 accinctus præliabitur 20 præbebit delicias regibus. 21 dans eloquia pulchritudinis. 22 filiæ diſcurrerunt ſuper murum.

L. 10 noch eyn meyſter von ſeynen fuſſen, bis das der Hellt komme 14 beynern eſel 17 reutter zu ruck falle 18 ich wartte auff deyn heyl 19 vnd widder erumb furen. 20 konigen niedliche ſpeyſe 22 holdſelige kind . . die tochter tretten eynher im regiment

M. M. N. 20 Fat brede, is plenteouſnes of the erth: as encreaſe of corne and other. &c. therwith ſhall fede kinges, & all the mē of the erth, as .ii. Eſd. ix, c.

L. M. N. 16 Den Segen *Dan* hat Sampſon erfullet, Iudic. xii. 19 *Gad* hat ſeyn ſegen auſzgericht, do ſie fur Iſrael her zogē Ios. i. 20 *Aſſer* hat gut getreyde land ynnen gehabt. 21 *Naphthali* ſegen iſt erfüllet durch Debora vnnd Barac Iud. v. 22 Der ſegen *Ioſeph* gehet auff das konigreych Iſrael vnnd iſt ganz von leyblichem regiment geſagt, das die tochter (das iſt die ſtedte ym land) wol regirt worden zeytlich, vnd viel propheten vnd gros leut zu eckſteyn hatten, vnd wie wol ſie offt angefochtē worden, gewonnen ſie doch, vnd dis konigreich war im geſchlecht *Ephraim*, alſzo bleybt der geyſtlich ſegen vnd reich auff Iuda, vnd das leyplich reich auff Ephraim.

23 to bere ruele. The ſhoters haue envyed him and chyde
24 with him ād hated him, and yet his bowe bode faſt, &
his armes and his handes were ſtronge, by the handes
of the myghtye God of Iacob: out of him ſhall come
25 an herde mā a ſtone in Iſrael. Thi fathers God ſhall
helpe the, & the almightie ſhall bleſſe the with bleſſinges
from heaven aboue, and with bleſſinges of the water
that lieth vnder, & with bleſſinges of the breſtes & of
26 the wombes .P. The bleſſinges of thy father were
ſtronge: euen as the bleſſinges of my elders, after the
deſyre of the hieſt in the worlde, and theſe bleſſinges
ſhall fall on the head of Ioſeph, and on the toppe of
the head of him ẏ was ſeparat from his brethern.
27 Ben Iamin is a raueſhynge wolfe. In the mornynge
he ſhall deuoure his praye, ād at nyghte he ſhall deuyde his ſpoyle.
28 All theſe are the .xii. tribes of Iſrael, & this is that
which their father ſpake vnto them whē he bleſſed
29 them, euery man with a ſeverall bleſſinge. And he
charged them and ſayde vnto them. I ſhall be put
vnto my people: ſe that ye burye me with my fathers,
in the caue that is in the felde of Ephron the Hethyte,
30 in the double caue that is in the felde before Mamre
in the lande of Canaan. Which felde Abraham boughte
31 of Ephron the Hethite for a poſſeſſiō to burye in. There
they buryed Abrahā and Sara his wyfe, there they
buryed Iſaac and Rebecca his wyfe. And there I
32 buryed Lea: which felde & the caue that is therin,
was bought of the childern of Heth.

M. 25 wombe.

V. 24 diſſoluta ſunt vincula brach. & man. illius per . . inde paſtor egreſſus eſt lapis Iſrael. 26 patris tui confortatæ ſunt . . . patrum eius: donec ven. deſyderium collium ætern., . . et in vertice Nazaræi 29 ego congregor ad pop. 31 eum, et Saram [v. 32 wanting in Latin]

L. 24 die arm ſeyner hende . . ſind komen hirtten vnd ſteyn 25 ſegen von der tieffe . . an bruſten vnd beuchen. 26 nach wundſch der hohen in der welt . . aus Ioſeph ſollen hewbter werden, vnd vberſte Naſerer 32 ynn dem gut des ackers vnd der hole drynnen

M. M. N. 27 Wolfe is here taken in a good ſence, and ſignifieth a feruent preacher of godes worde as was Paule in whome this text is verified.

L. M. N. 27 *Ben Iamin* ſegen hat S. Paullus erfullet, oder der Konig Saul vnd die burger zu Gaba. Iudic. xx.

33 When Iacob had commaunded all that he wold
vnto his ſonnes, he plucked vp his fete apon the bedd
L, 1 and dyed, and was put vnto his people. And Ioſeph fell apon his fathers face, and wepte apon him,
and kyſſed him.

[Fo. LXXV.] The .L. Chapter.

M.C.S. Iacob is buryed. Ioſeph forgeueth hys brethrē the Iniury that they dyd to hym. And he dyeth.

2 AND Ioſeph commaunded his ſeruauntes that were Phiſicions,
to embawme his father, and
the Phiſiciōs ēbawmed Iſrael
3 xl. dayes lōge, for ſo lōge doth ỹ em-
bawminge laſt, & the Egiptians bewepte
him .Lxx. dayes.
4 And when the dayes of wepynge were ended, Ioſeph ſpake vnto ỹ houſe of Pharao ſaynge: Yf I haue
founde fauoure in youre eyes, ſpeake vnto Pharao and
5 tell him, how that my father made me ſwere and ſayde:
loo, I dye, ſe that thou burye me in my graue which I
haue made me in the lande of Canaan. Now therfor
let me goo and burye my father, ād thā will I come
6 agayne. And Pharao ſayde, goo and burye thy father,
acordynge as he made the ſwere.
7 And Ioſeph went vp to burie his father, and with
him went all the ſeruauntes of Pharao that were the
8 elders of his houſe, ād all ỹ elders of Egipte, and all
the houſe of Ioſeph ād his brethern & his fathers houſe:
only their childern & their ſhepe and their catell lefte
9 they behinde them in the lande of Goſan. And there
went with him alſo Charettes and horſemen: ſo that
they were an exceadynge great companye.

V. 33 appoſituſque eſt . . . l, 1 quod cernens . . . patrem. 2 Quibus iuſſa 3 explentibus . . . cadauerum conditorum 5 in ſepulchro meo quod fodi mihi 7 ſenes domus Phar., cunctique maiores natu terræ 9 turba non modica.

L. 33 bette, nam ab. l, 2 **erzten** (*bis*) 5 begrabe . . . **grabe** . . . graben hab 10 ſeer groſſe vnd bittere klag

10 And when they came to ỹ felde of Atad beyonde Iordane, there they made great & excea- .P. dinge sore
lamentaciō. And he morned for his father .vii. dayes.
11 When the enhabiters of the lande the Cananytes sawe
the moornynge in ỹ felde of Atad, they saide: this
is a greate moornynge which the Egiptians make.
Wherfore ỹ name of the place is called Abel mizraim, which place lyeth beyonde Iordane. And his
12 sonnes dyd vnto him acordynge as he had commaunded them.
13 And his sonnes caried him in to the land of Canaan
and buryed him in the double caue which Abrahā had
boughte with the felde to be a place to burye in, of
14 Ephron the Hethite before Mamre. And Ioseph returned to Egipte agayne and his brethern, and all that
went vp with him to burye his father, assone as he had
buryed him.
15 Whē Iosephs brethern sawe that their father was
deade, they sayde: Ioseph myght fortune to hate us
and rewarde us agayne all the euell which we dyd
16 vnto him. They dyd therfore a commaundment vnto
Ioseph saynge: thy father charged before his deth sa-
17 ynge. This wise say vnto Ioseph, forgeue I praye the
the trespace of thy brethern & their synne, for they
rewarded the euell. Now therfore we praye the, forgeue the trespace of the servauntes of thy fathers God.
And Ioseph wepte when they spake vnto him.
18 And his brethern came ād fell before him and sayde:
19 beholde we be thy servauntes. And [Fo. LXXVI.]
Ioseph sayde vnto them: feare not, for am not I vnder
20 god? Ye thoughte euell vnto me: but God turned it
vnto good to bringe to passe, as it is this daye, euen to
21 saue moch people a lyue Feare not therfore, for I will

M. 16 charged vs

V. 11 loci illius, Planctus Ægypti. 15 & mutuo colloquentes 16 mandauerunt ei dicentes . . præcepit nobis 17 Obsecro vt obliuiscaris . . malitiæ quam exercuerūt 19 nū dei possumus resistere uoluntati? 20 saluos faceret

L. 11 den ort, der Egypter leyde 14 sie yhn begraben 16 darumb liessen sie yhm sagen 17 das sie so vbel an dyr than haben 19 ich byn vnter Gott 20 gedachtet boses vber mich . . zum gutten gewand

care for you and for youre childern, and he ſpake
kyndly vnto them.
22 Ioſeph dwelt in Egipte and his fathers houſe alſo,
23 ãd lyved an hundred & .x. yere. And Ioſeph ſawe
Ephraims childern, euẽ vnto the thyrde generation.
And vnto Machir the ſonne of Manaſſes were childern
borne, and ſatt on Ioſephs knees.
24 And Ioſeph ſayde vnto his brethern: I die And
God will ſuerlie vyſett you and bringe you out of this
lande, vnto the lande which he ſware vnto Abraham,
25 Iſaac and Iacob. And Ioſeph toke an ooth of the
childern of Iſrael ãd ſayde:
God will not fayle but vyſett you, ſe ther-
26 fore that ye carye my boones hence. And
ſo Ioſeph dyed, when he was an
hundred and .x. yere olde.
And they emba-
wmed him
and
put him in a cheſt in Egipte. cheſ. coffin

The end of the firſt boke of Moſes.

F. 21 cõſolatuſque eſt eos, & blande ac leniter eſt locutus. 23 nati ſunt in genibus Ioſeph. 25 dixiſſet, Deus viſitabit . . de loco iſto. 26 repoſitus eſt in loculo . .

L. 21 euch verſorgen . . vnd er troſtet ſie vnd redet freuntlich mit yhn. 23 zeucheten auch kinder auff Ios. ſchos. 26 eyn lade.

M. M. N. 24 God wyll vyſet you, that is, he wyll remember you and delyuer you oute of bõdage that ye ſhalbe in vnder Pharao.

.P. ❡ A table expoundinge certeyne wordes

Abrech, tender father, or, as ſome will, bowe the knee.

Arcke, a ſhippe made flatte as it were a cheſt or a cofer.

Biſſe: fyne whyte, whether it be ſilke or linen.

Bleſſe: godes bleſſinges are his giftes, as in the firſte chaptre he bleſſed them, ſayng: growe & multiplye & haue dominion &c. And in the .ix. chaptre he bleſſed Noe and his ſonnes, & gaue thē dominiō over all beeſtes & authoryte to eate thē. And god bleſſed Abrahā with catell ād other ryches. And Iacob deſyred Eſau to receaue ỹ bleſſinge which he brought him, ỹ is, the preaſent & gifte. God bleſſed the .vii. daye, ỹ is, gaue it a prehemynence ỹ men ſhuld reſt therein from bodely laboure & lerne to know the will of god & his lawes & how to worke their workes godly all the weke after. God alſo bleſſeth all nations in Abrahams ſeed, that is, he turneth his loue & favoure unto thē and geveth thē his ſpirite and knowledge of the true waye, ād luſt and power to walke therin, and all for chriſtes ſake Abrahams ſonne.

Cain, ſo it is writen in Hebrue. Notwitſtōdinge whether we call him Cain or caim it maketh no matter, ſo we vnderſtond the meaninge. Euery lande hath his maner, that we call Ihonn the welchemen call Evan: the douch hāce. Soch differēce is betwene the Ebrue, greke and laten: and that maketh them that tranſlate out of the ebrue varye in names from them that tranſlate out of laten or greke.

Curſe: Godes curſe is the takynge awaye of his benefytes. As god curſed the erth and made it baren. So now hunger, derth, warre, peſtilence and ſoch like are yet ryght curſes and ſignes of the wrath of God vnto the vnbeleuers: but vnto them that knowe Chriſt, they are very bleſſinges and that wholſome croſſe & true purgatorye of oure fleſh, thorow which all muſt go that will lyue godly ād be ſaued: as thou readeſt Matt. v. Bleſſed are they that ſuffre perſecution for rightewesnes ſake. &c. And hebrewes .xi. The lorde chaſtyſeth whom he loveth and ſcorgeth all the children that he receaveth.

Eden: pleaſure

Firmament: The ſkyes

Fayth is the belevinge of goddes promeſſes & a ſure truſt in the goodneſſe and truth of god. Which faith iuſtifyeth Abrahā gen. xv. and was the mother of all his good workes which he afterward did. For faith is the goodneſſe of all workes in the ſight of God. Good workes .⁋. are thinges of godes commaundemēt, wrought in faith. And to ſow a ſhowe at the commaundement of god to do thy neyghboure ſervice withal, with faith to be ſaved by Chriſt (as god promyſeth vs.) is moch better thē to bild an abbay of thyne awne imagination, truſtinge to be ſaved by the fayned workes of hypocrites. Iacob robbed Laban his vncle: Moſes robbed the Egiptians: And Abrahā is aboute to ſlee and burne his awne ſonne: And all are holye workes, becauſe they were wrought in fayth at goddes commaundement. To ſtele, robbe and murther are no holye workes before worldly people: but vnto them that haue their truſte in god: they are holye when god commaundeth them. What god commaundeth not getteth no reward with god. Holy workes of mens imagination receave their rewarde here, as Chriſt teſtyfyeth Matt. .vi. How be it of fayth & workes I haue ſpoken abundantly in mammon. Let him that deſyreth more ſeke there.

Grace: fauoure, As Noe founde grace, that is to ſaye favoure and love.

Ham and Cam all one.

Iehovah is goddes name, nether is any creature ſo called. And it is as moch to ſaye as one that is of him ſelf, and dependeth of nothinge. Moreouer as oft as thou ſeiſt LORde in gre-.P.at letters (excepte there be any erroure in the prētinge) it is in hebrewe Iehovah, thou that arte or he that is.

Marſhall, In hebreue he is called Sar tabaim, as thou woldeſt ſaye, lorde of the ſlaughtermen And though that Tabaim be takē for cokes in many places, for the cokes did ſle the beaſtes thē ſelues in thoſe dayes: yet it may be taken for them that put men to execution alſo. And that me thought it ſhould here beſt ſignifye in as moch as he had the overſight of the kinges preſon and the kinges preſoners were they neuer ſo great mē were vnder his custodye. And therfore I call him cheffe marſhall an officer as is the lefetenaunte of the toure, or maſter of the marſhalſye.

Slyme was their morter .xi. Chapter, and ſlyme pittes .xiv. chapter: that ſlyme was a fatteneſſe that oſed out of the erth lyke vnto tarre, And thou mayſt call it cement, if thou wilt.

Siloh after ſome is as moch to ſaye as ſent, & after ſome, happie, and after ſome it ſignifieth Meſias, ỷ is to ſaye annoynted, and that we call Chriſte after the greke worde. And it is a propheſie of Chriſt: For after ỷ all ỷ other tribes were in captiuite & their kyngdom deſtroyed, yet the tribe of Iuda had a ruler of the ſamebloud, even vnto the comynge of Chriſt.

.P. And aboute the comīge of Chriſt the Romayns conquered them, and the Emperoure gaue the kyngdom of tribe Iuda unto Herode which was a ſtraunger, even an Edomite of the generacyon of Eſau.

Teſtamēt here, is an appoyntemēt betwene god and mā, and goddes promyſes. And ſacramēt is a ſigne repreſentinge ſoch an appoyntement and promeſes: as the raynebowe repreſenteth the promyſe made to Noe, that god will no more drowne the worlde. And circumciſion repreſenteth the promyſes of god to Abraham on the one ſyde, and that Abrahā and his ſeed ſhuld circumcyſe and cut off the luſtes of their fleſhe, on the other ſyde, to walke in the wayes of the lorde: As baptyme which is come in the roume therof, now ſignifieth on the one ſyde, how that all that repent and beleve are waſhed in Chriſtes bloud: And on the other ſyde, how that the ſame muſt quench ād droune the luſtes of the fleſh, to folow the ſteppes of Chriſt.

There were tyrantes in the erth in thoſe dayes, for the ſonnes of god ſaw the doughters of men. &c. The ſonnes of god were the prophetes childerne, which (though they ſucceded there fathers) fell yet from the right waye, and thorow falſehod of hypocryſye ſubdued the world vnder them, and became tyrantes, As the ſucceſ- .P. ours of the apoſtles haue played with vs.

Vapor, a dewy miſte, as the ſmoke of a ſethynge pott.

To walke with god is to lyve godly and to walke in his commaundementes.

Enos walked with god, and was no moare ſene: that is, he lyved godly and dyed, God toke him a waye: that is, god hyd his bodye, as he did Moſes ād Aarons: leſt haplye they ſhuld haue made an Idoll of him, for he was a great preacher and an holye man.

Zaphnath paenea, wordes of Egipte are they (as I ſuppoſe) and as moch to ſaye: as a man to whom ſecrete thinges be opened, or an expounder of ſecrete thinges as ſome enterprete it.

That Ioſeph brought the egiptians in to ſoch ſubiection wold ſeme vnto ſome a very cruell deade: how be it it was a very equal waye. For they payde but the fifte part of that that grewe on the grounde. And therwith were they qwytt of all duetyes, both of rent, cuſtome, tribute & toll. And the kinge therwith founde them lordes and all miniſtres and defended them. We now paye half ſo moch vnto the preſtes only, beſyde their other craftye exactions. Then paye we rent yerely, though there grow never ſo litle on the grounde, And yet, when the kinge cal- .¶. leth paye we neuer the leſſe. So that if we loke indifferently, their condition was eaſyar thē oures, and but even, a very indifferēt waye, both for the comen people and the kynge alſo.

Se therfore that thou loke not on the enſamples of the ſcripture with worldly eyes: leſt thou preferre Cain before Abel, Iſmael before Iſaac, Eſau before Iacob, Ruben before Iuda, Sarah before Pharez, Manaſes before Ephraim. And euen the worſt before the beſt, as the maner of the worlde is.

¶ Emprented at Malborow in the lande of Heſſe, by me Hans Luft, the yere of oure Lorde, M.CCCCC.xxx. the xvii. dayes of Ianuarij.

A PROLO
GE IN TO THE SECON=
de boke of Moſes called
Exodus.

W T

OF the preface vppō Geneſis mayſt thou vnderſtonde how to behaue thi ſilf in this boke alſo ād ī all other bokes of the ſcripture. Cleaue vnto the texte and playne ſtorye and endevoure thi ſilf to ſerch out the meaninge of all that is deſcribed therin and the true ſenſe of all maner of ſpeakynges of the ſcripture, of proverbes, ſimilitudes ād borowed ſpeach, wherof I entreated in the ende of the obedience, and beware of ſotle allegoryes. And note euery thinge erneſtly as thinges partayninge vnto thine awne herte and ſoule. For as god vſed hym ſylf vnto them of the old teſtament, even ſo ſhall he vnto the worldes ende vſe him ſilf vnto vs which haue receaved his holye ſcripture ād the teſtimonye of his ſonne Ieſus. As god doeth all thinges here for them that beleve his promiſes and herken vnto his commaundmentes and with pacience cleaue vnto him and walke with him: euen ſo ſhall he do for vs, yf we receaue the witneſſe of Chriſt with a ſtronge faith and endure paciently folowinge his ſteppes. And on the otherſyde, as they that fell from the promises of god thorow vnbeleffe and from his lawe and ordinaunces thorow impaciencie of their awne luſtes, were for ſaken of god ād ſo peryſhed: even ſo ſhall we as many as do lykewyſe and as.¶.manye as mock with the doctrine of chriſt and make a cloke of it to lyue fleſhlye ād to folow oure luſtes.

Note therto how god is founde true at the laſt, and how when all is paſt remedye ād brought into deſperacion, he then fulfilleth his promiſes, and that by an abiecte and a caſtawaye, a deſpiſed and a refuſed perſon: ye and by awaye impoſſible to beleue.

The cauſe of all captiuite of goddes people is this. The worlde ever hateth them for their fayth and truſt which they haue in god: but ī vayne vntill they falle frō the fayth of the promyſes ād love of the lawe ād ordinaunces of god, and put their truſt in holy deades of their awne findinge and live all to gether at their awne luſt and pleaſure without regard of god or reſpecte of their neygboure. Then god forſăketh vs and ſendeth vs in to captiuite for oure diſhonouringe of his name and deſpiſinge of oure neghboure. But the world perſecuteth vs for oure faith in chriſt only (as the pope now doeth) ād not for oure weked livinge For in his kīgdome thou maiſt quietly ād with licēce ād vnder a protectiō doo what ſo euer abhominatiō thi herte luſteth: but god perſecuteth us becauſe we abuſe his holye teſtamēt, ād becauſe that whē we knowe the truth we folowe it not.

.P. Note alſo the mightye hand of the Lorde, how he playeth with his aduerſaries ād provoketh thē ād ſturreth thē upp a litle ād a litle, ād deliuereth not his people in an houre: that both the paciēce of his electe ād alſo the worldly witte ād wilye policye of the weked wherwith they fight agaynſt god, might appeare.

Marke the longeſoferinge and ſofte paciēce of Moſes and how he loveth the people ād is euer betwene the wrath of god ād thē ād is readye to lyue ād dye with thē ād to be put out of the boke that god had written for their ſakes (as Paule for his brothren Roma. ix.) and how he taketh his awne wrōges pacientlie ād never avengeth him ſilf. And make not Moſes a figure of Chriſt with Rocheſtre: but an enſample vnto all princes ād to all that are in authorite, how to rule vnto goddes pleaſure ād vnto their neyghbours profette. For there is not a perfecter lyffe in this world both to the honoure of god and profytte of his neygboure nor yet a greatter croſſe, thē to rule chriſtenlye. And of Aaron alſo ſe that thou make no figure of chriſt vntill he come vnto his ſacrifiſinge, but an enſample vnto all preachers of goddes worde, that they adde nothing vnto goddes worde or take ought therfro.

Note alſo how god ſendeth his promiſſe to .P. the people ād Moſes confermeth it with miracles ād the people beleve. But whē tēptacion cometh they falle into vnbeleffe ād few byde ſtōdinge. Where thou ſeeſt that all be not chriſtē that wilbe ſo called, ād that the croſſe trieth the true frō the fayned: for yf the croſſe were not Chriſt ſhuld haue diſſiples ynowe. Wherof alſo thou ſeeſt what an excellent gifte off god true fayth is, ād impoſſible to be had without the ſprete of god. For it is aboue all naturall power that a man in tyme of tēptation when god ſcorgeth him ſhuld beleue then ſtedfaſtlye how that god loveth him ād careth for hī ād hath prepared all good thinges for him, ād that that ſcorginge is as erneſt that god hath electe and choſe him.

Note how oft Moſes ſturreth thē vpp to beleve ād to truſt in god, puttinge thē in remembraunce alwaye in tyme of temptation of the miracles and wonders which god had wrought before tyme in their eyſight. How diligently alſo forbiddeth he al that might withdrawe their hartes from god? to put nought to goddes word: to take nought therfro: to do only that which is right in the ſyght of the Lorde: that they ſhuld make no maner image to knele doune before it: ye that they ſhuld make none altar of hewed ſtone for feare off images: .¶. to ſlee the hethen Idolatres vtterly ād to deſtroye their Idolles ād cutte doune their groves where they worſhupped: And that they ſhulde not take the doughters of them vnto their ſonnes, nor geue their doughters to the ſonnes of them. And that whoſoeuer moued any of thē to worſhuppe falſe goddes, how ſo euer nye of kynne he were, they muſt accuſe him ād bryng him to deth, ye and whereſoeuer they hard of mā, womā or citye that worſhupped falſe goddes, they muſt ſlee thē ād deſtroye the citie for ever ād not bild it agayne. And all becauſe they ſhuld worſhuppe nothinge but God, nor put confidence in any thinge ſaue in his word Yee and how warneth he to beware of witchcraft, ſorcery, inchauntment, negromātie ād all craftes of the devell, ād of dreamers, ſothſayers and of myracledoers to deſtroye his worde, and that they ſhulde ſuffer none ſoch to lyue,

Thou wilt happlye ſaye, They tell a man the truthe. What then? God will that we care not to knowe what ſhall come. He will haue vs care only to kepe his commaundmētes and to commytte all chaunſes vnto him

He hath promyſed to care for vs and to kepe vs from all evell. All thinges are in his hande, he can remedye all thinges and wil for his truthes ſake, yf we praye him. In his promyſes only will he haue vs truſt ād there reſt ād to ſeke .¶. no farther.

How alſo doth he prouoke them to loue, euer reherſynge the benefites of God done to them allready and the godly promyſes that were to come? And how goodly lawes of loue geveth he? to helpe one another: and that a man ſhuld not hate his neyghboure in his harte, but loue him as him ſilf, Leuitici .xix. And what a charge geueth he in euery place over the poore and neadye: over the ſtraunger frendleſſe ād wedowe? And when he deſyreth to ſhew mercye, he reherſeth with all, the benefites of God done to them at their neade, that they myght ſe a cauſe at the left waye in God to ſhew mercye of very loue vnto their neyghboures at their neade. Alſo there is no lawe ſo ſimple in apperaunce thorow out all the fiue bokes of Moſes, but that there is a greate reaſon of the makynge therof if a man ſerch diligently. As that a man is forbyd to ſeth a kyd in hys mothers milke, moueth vs unto compaſſyon and to be pytyefull, As doth alſo that a man ſhall not offer the ſyre or dame and the yonge both in one daye Leuitici .xxii. For it myght ſeme a cruell thing in as moch as his mothers milke is as it were his bloude, wherfore god will not haue him ſod therin: but will haue a man ſhewe cur-.¶.teſye vppon the very beaſtes: As in another place he commaundeth that we moſell not the mouth of the oxe that treadeth oute the corne (which maner of threſſhinge is vſed in hote contrees) and that becauſe we ſhuld moch rather not grudge to be liberall and kynde vnto mē that do vs ſervice. Or happlye God wold have no ſoch wanton meate vſed among hys people. For the kyd of it ſelf is noryſhinge and the gotes milke is reſtauretyue, and both together myght be to rancke and therfore forbodē or ſome other like cauſe therewas.

Of the ceremonies, ſacrifices and tabernacle with all his glorye ād pompe vnderſtōde, that they were not permitted only, but alſo commaunded of God to lead the people in the ſhadowes of Moſes ād night of the old teſtamēt, vntyll the light of chriſt ād daye of the new teſtamēt were come: As childern are ledde in the phantaſies of youth, vntyll the diſcretiō of mās age become vppon them. And all was done to kepe them from idolatrye. The tabernacle was ordened to the entent they might haue a place appoynted them to do their ſacrifices openly in the ſyght of the people ād namelye of the preaſtes which wayted therō: that it might be ſene that they dyd all thīge accordīg to gods word, and not after the Idolatrie of their awne .P. imaginacion. And the coſtlineſſe of the tabernacle ād the bewtye alſo pertayned therevnto, that they ſhuld ſe nothinge ſo bewtifull amonge the hethē, but that they ſhuld ſe more bewtifull ād wonderfull at home: becauſe they ſhuld not be moued to folowe them. And in like maner the diuers facions of the ſacrifices and ceremonies was to occupye their mindes that they ſhuld haue no luſt to folow the hethē: ād the multitude of them was, that they ſhuld haue ſo moch to do in kepinge thē that thei ſhuld haue no leyſure to ymagine other of their awne: yee and that gods word might be by in all that they dyd, that they might have their fayth and truſt in God, which he can not haue, that ether foloweth his awne invencyons, or tradicyons of mēnes makynge wyth out Gods word.

Finally God hath two teſtamentes: the old and the newe. The old teſtament is thoſe temporall promyſes which God made the childrē of Iſrael of a good londe and that he wolde defende them, and of welth and proſperyte ād of temporall bleſſynges of whiche thou readeſt ouer all the lawe of Moſes, But namelye Leuitici xxvi. And Deuteronomii .xxviii. ād the avoydynge of all threateninges and curſes off which thou readeſt lykewyſe everye where, but ſpecyallye in the two places aboue reherſed, .P. and the avoydinge of all punyſhmēt ordened for the tranſgreſſers of the lawe.

And the old teſtamēt was bilt all to gether vppō the kepinge of the lawe ād ceremonyes and was the reward of kepinge of thē in this liffe only, ād reached no further than this liffe and this world, as thou readeſt leu. xviii. a mā that doth them ſhall live there in which texte Paule reherſeth Rom. x. and Gala. iii. That is, he that kepeth them ſhall haue this liffe growe glorioſe accordinge to all the promiſes and bleſſinges of the lawe, and ſhall avoyde both all temporall puniſhment of the lawe, with al the threateninges and curſinges alſo. For nether the lawe, euen of the .x. cōmaundmentes nor yet the ceremonies iuſtifyed in the herte before god, or purifyed vnto the life to come. Inſomoch that Moſes at his deeth euen. xl. yere after the lawe and ceremonyes were geuen complayneth ſayenge: God hath not geven you an hart to vnderſtonde, nor eyes to ſe, nor eares to heare vnto this daye. As who ſhuld ſaye, god hath geuen you ceremonies, but ye know not the vſe of them, and hath geuē you a lawe, but hath not wryten it in youre hartes.

Wherfore ſerveth the lawe then, yf it geue vs no power to do the lawe? Paule anſwereth the, that it was geuen to vtter ſynne onlye and .P. to make it appere. As a coroſye is layde vnto an old ſore, not to heale it, but to ſtere it vp ād to make the diſeaſe a lyve, that a mā might feale in what ioperdye he is ād how nye deeth ād not aware, ād to make awaye vnto the healinge playſter. Euē ſo ſayth Paule Gala. iii. The lawe was geven becauſe of tranſgreſſiō (that is, to make the ſynne alyve that it might be felt and ſene) untill the ſeed came vnto whom it was promiſed: that is to ſaie, vntil the childern of ſayth came, or vntill Chriſt that ſeed in whom god promiſed Abrahā that all nations of the worlde ſhuld be bleſſed, came. That is, the lawe was geuē to vtter ſynne, deeth damnatiō and curſe, ād to dryve vnto Chriſt in whō forgeueneſſe, life, iuſtifyinge ād bleſſinges were promiſed, that we might ſe ſo greate love of god to vs ward in chriſt, that we hēceforth ouercome with kindneſſe might love againe ād of love kepe the cōmaūdmētes. So now he that goeth aboute to quiette his cōſciēce ād to iuſtifye him ſilf with the lawe, doth but heale his wondes with freatīge coreſyes. And he that goeth aboute to purchaſe grace with ceremonies, doth but ſucke the alepope to qwēch his thirſt, in as moch as the ceremonies were not gevē to iuſtifie the herte, but to ſignifie the iuſtifiynge: and forgeueneſſe that is in chriſtes bloude

.¶. Of the ceremonies that they iustifie not, thou readeſt. Ebrues .x. It is impoſſible that ſynne ſhuld be done awaye with the bloud of oxē ād gootes. And of the law thou readeſt .Gala. iii. Yf there had bene a lawe geuē that coude haue quykened or geuē liffe, then had rightuouſneſſe or iuſtifyinge come by the lawe in dede. Now the lawe not only quyckeneth not the harte, but alſo woundeth it with conſcience of ſynne and miniſtreth deeth ād damnaciō vnto her: ii. Corin. iii. ſo that ſhe muſt neades dye ād be damned excepte ſhe finde other remedy, ſo farre it is of that ſhe is iuſtified or holpe by the lawe.

The newe teſtament is thoſe euerlaſtinge promyſes which are made vs in chriſt the Lorde thorow out all the ſcripture. And that teſtamēt is bylt on faith ād not on workes. For it is not ſayde of that teſtament he that worketh ſhall lyue: But he that beleveth ſhall lyue, as thou readeſt .Ioan. iii. God ſo loued the worlde that he gaue his only begotē ſonne that none which beleue in hī ſhuld periſh but haue euerlaſtinge lyſe.

And when this teſtament is preached and beleued, the ſprete entreth the hart and quyckeneth it, and geueth her lyfe and iuſtifieth her. The ſprete alſo maketh the lawe a lyuely thing .¶. in the herte, ſo that a man bringeth forth good workes of his awne acord without compulſiō of the lawe, without feare of threateninges or curſinges: yee and with out all maner reſpecte or loue vnto any temporal pleaſure, But of the very power of the ſprete receaved thorow faith, As thou readeſt .Ioan .i. He gaue them power to be the ſonnes of God in that they beleued on his name. And of that power they worke: ſo that he which hath the ſprete of chriſt is now no moare a childe: he nether learneth or worketh now any longer for payne of the rodde or for feare of boogges or pleaſure of apples, But doth althinges of his awne courage As chriſt ſayeth .Ioan. vii. He that beleueth on me ſhall haue riuers of lyuinge water flowinge out of his belye.

That is, All good workes ād all giftes of grace ſpringe out of him naturallye and by their awne accorde. Thou neadeſt not to wreſt good workes out of him as a mā wold wringe veriuce out of crabbes: Nay thei flow naturally out of him as ſpringes out off hilles or rockes.

The newe teſtament was euer, euē from the beginning of the world. For there were alwaye promyſes of Chriſt to come by faith in whiche promyſes the electe were then iuſtified .P̄. inwardly before God, as outwardly before the world by kepynge of the lawe and ceremonies

And in concluſyon as thou ſeyſt bleſſinges or curſynges folow the kepinge or breakynge of the lawe of Moſes: euē ſo naturally do bleſſynges or curſynges folow the breakyng or kepynge of the lawe of nature, out of which ſprīge all oure temporall lawes. So that whē the people kepe the temporall lawes of their lond temporall proſperite and all maner of ſoch tēporall bleſſynge as thou readest of in Moſes doo accompanye them and fall vppon them.

And contraryewyſe when they ſynne vnpuniſhed, ād whē the rulars haue no reſpecte vnto naturall equyte or honeſtye, thē God ſendeth his curſes amonge thē, as hungre, derth, moren banynge, peſtilēce, warre, oppreſſyon with ſtraunge ād wonderfull diſeaſes ād newekyndes of miſſortune ād evell lucke,

Yf any mā axe me, ſeyng that faith iuſtifieth me why I worke? I anſwere loue cōpelleth me For as lōge as my ſoule fealeth what loue god hath ſhewed me in Chriſte, I can not but loue god agayne ād his will ād cōmaūdmētes and of loue worke them, nor cā they ſeme hard vnto me. I thinke not my ſelf better for my workynge, nor ſeke heuē nor an hyer place in heuē becauſe of it. For a chriſtē worketh to ma- .P̄. ke his weake brother perfecter, ād not to ſeke an hier place in heuē. I cōpare not my ſilf vnto him that worketh not: No, he that worketh not to daye ſhall haue grace to turne ād to worke tomorow, ād in the meane ceaſon I pytye hym ād praye for him. Yf I had wrought the wil of god theſe thouſande yeres, ād another had wrought the will of the devell as long ād this daye turne ād be as well willynge to ſuffre wyth Chriſt as I, he hath this daye ouertakē me ād is as farre come as I, and ſhall haue as moche rewarde as I. And I envye him not, but reioyce moſt of all as of loſte treſure founde. For yf I be of god, I haue this thouſand yere ſofred to wynne him for to come ād prayſe the name of God with me: this .M. yeres I haue prayed ſorowed, longed, ſyghed ād ſought for that whiche I haue this daye founde, ād therfore reioyſe with all my myght and prayſe God for hys grace and mercy.

ALBE, a longe garment of white lynen.

Arcke, a cofer or cheſte as oure ſhrynes ſaue it was flatte, ād the ſample of oure ſhrynes was taken thereof.

Boothe, an houſſe made of bowes.

Breſtlappe or breſtflappe, is ſoche a flappe as thou ſeiſt in the breſt of a cope.

Conſecrate, to apoynte a thinge to holy vſes.

Dedicate, purifie or ſanctifie.

.P. Ephod, is a garment ſomwhat like an amyce, ſaue the armes came thorow ād it was gird to.

Geeras, in weyght as it were an englyſh halffpenye or ſomwhat more.

Heveoffringe, becauſe they were hoven vp before the Lorde.

Houſe, he made thē houſes: that is, he made a kynred or a multitude of people to ſpringe out of them: as we ſaye the houſe of Dauid for the kinred of Dauid.

Peaceoffrīge: offerīges of thākesgeuīge of deuotiō, ād not for cōſciēce of ſinne ād treſpace.

Polute, defyle.

❡ Reconcyle, to make at one and to bringe in grace or fauoure.

Sanctefie, to clēſe ād purifie, to apointe a thinge vnto holie vſes and to ſeperate frō vnclene ād unholye vſes.

❡ Sanctuarie, a place halowed and dedicate vnto god.

❡ Tabernacle, an houſe made tentwiſe, or as a pauelion.

Tunicle, moch like the vppermoſt garmēt of the deakē.

❡ Waueoffringe, becauſe they were wauē in the preaſtes hādes to diuers quarters.

Worſhuppe: by worſhuppinge whether it be in the old teſtamēt or the newe, vnderſtōd the bowenge of a mans ſelf vppon the grounde: As wee oftymes as we knele in oure prayers bowe oure ſelves ād lye on oure armes ād handes with oure face to the grounde.

The ſecon
de boke of Moſes, cal=
led Exodus.

¶ THE SECONDE BOKE
OF MOSES CALLED EXODUS.

¶ The firſt Chapter.

𝔐.𝔆.𝔖. The children of Iacob are nōbred. The new Pharao oppreſſeth thē. The acte of the godly mydwiues.

1 THESE are the names of the
children of Iſrael, which came
to Egipte with Iacob, euery
2 man with his houſholde: Ru-
3 bē, Simeon, Leui, Iuda, Iſachar, Zabulon,
4 Beniamin, Dan, Neptali, Gad ād Aſer.
5 All the ſoules that came out of the loynes
of Iacob, were .Lxx. and Ioſeph was in Egipte all redie.
6 when Ioſeph was dead and all his brethern and all
7 that generation: the children of Iſrael grewe, encreaſed,
multiplied and waxed enceadinge myghtie: ſo that
the londe was full of them.
8 Then there roſe vp a new kynge in Egipte which
9 knewe not Ioſeph. And he ſayde vnto his folke: beholde the people of the childrē of Iſrael are moo ād
10 mightier than we. Come on, let vs playe wiſely with
them: leſt they multiplie, and then (yf there chaunce
any warre) they ioyne them ſelues vnto oure enimies
and fyghte ageynſt vs, and ſo gete them out of the lande.
11 .P. And he ſette taſkemaſters ouer them, to kepe
them vnder with burthens. And they bylte vnto
12 Pharao treaſurecities: Phiton and Raamſes. But the
more they vexed thē, the moare they multiplied and
grewe: ſo that they abhorred the childrē of Iſrael.

𝔐. 4 Nephtali 5 All theſe ſoules 6 all his brether 11 Rameſes
V 7 & quaſi germinātes multiplicati ſunt 10 ſapienter opprimamus eum 11 vrbes tabernaculorum
𝔏. 5 zuuor 7 vnd wymmelten vnd mehrten 10 vnd vns überwinden 11 ſchatzhewſern 12 den kindern Iſrael gram

13 And the Egiptiās helde the childern of Israel in bond-
14 age without mercie, and made their lyues bitter vnto
them with cruell laboure in claye and bricke, and all
maner worke in the feldes, and in all maner of service,
which they caused thē to worke cruelly

15 And the kynge of Egipte sayde vnto the mydwiues
of the Ebrueswomen, of which the ones name was
16 Ziphra ād the other Pua: whē ye mydwiue the women
of the Ebrues and se in the byrth tyme that it is a
17 boye, kyll it. But yf it be a mayde, let it lyue. Not-
withstonding the mydwiues feared God, and dyd not as
the kinge of Egipte commaūded them: but saued the
menchildern.

18 Thē the kinge of Egipte called for the midwiues ād
sayde vnto thē: why haue ye delt on this maner and
19 haue saued the menchildern? And the mydwiues
answered Pharao, that the Ebrues wemen were not
as the wemen of Egipte: but were sturdie women,
and were delyuered yer the midwyues came at them.
20 And God therfore delt well with the midwyues. [Fo.
III.] And the people multiplied and waxed very
21 mightie. And because the mydwiues feared God, he
made them houses. houses, *families*

22 Than Pharao charged all his pepple
sayng All the menchildern that are borne, cast in to
the ryuer and save the maydchildern a lyue.

M. 15 Sephora . . Phua: 16 when ye do ẏ office of a mydwife to the womē 22 people

V. 13 & affligebant illudentes eis & inuidētes. 18 Quibus accersitis ad se rex 19 ipsæ enim obstetricandi habent scientiam 21 ædificauit illis domos. 22 fœminini, reseruate.

L. 13 vnbarmhertzickeyt (v. 14) 14 thon vnd zigelln 16 den Ebr. weyb. helfft, vnd auff dem stuel sehet das 18 die kinder leben 19 hartte weyber 21 machet er jn heuser.

M. M. N. 21 *He made them houses:* that is, he encreased and multiplyed them, & made housholdes of them: geuynge thē both husbandes and chyldrē, as in Gen. vii, a.

¶ The Seconde Chapter.

M.C.S. Moses is borne and cast into the flagges. He is takē vp of Pharaos daughter. He kylleth the Egypcian. He flyeth & maryeth a wyfe. The Israelites crye vnto the Lorde.

1 AND there wēt a mā of the house
of Leui ād toke a doughter of
2 Leui. And the wife cōceaued
ād bare a sonne. And whē she
sawe that it was a propre childe, she hyd
3 him thre monethes longe. And whē she
coude no longer hyde him, she toke a
basket of bulrusshes ād dawbed it with
slyme ād pytche, ād layde the childe
therin, ād put it in the flagges by the
4 riuers brynke. And his sister stode a ferre of, to
wete what wold come of it.

wete, *know*

5 And the doughter of Pharao came doune to the
riuer to washe her selfe, and hir maydens walked a
longe by the riuers syde. And when she sawe the
basket amōge the flagges, she sent one of hir maydes
6 and caused it to be fet. And whē she had opened it
she sawe the childe, and behold, the babe wepte.
And she had cōpassiō on it ād sayde: it is one of the
Ebrues childern

7 Then sayde his sister vnto Pharaos doughter: shall
I goo and call vnto the a nurse of the Ebrues wemen,
8 to nurse the childe? .P. And the mayde ranne and
9 called the childes mother. Thē Pharaos doughter
saide vnto her, Take this childe awaye ād nurse it for
me, ād I will rewarde the for thi laboure. And the
woman toke the childe and nursed it vp.

10 And whē the childe was growne, she brought it
vnto Pharaos doughter, and it was made hir sonne,
and she called it Moses, because (sayde she) I toke
him out of the water.

V. 1 vxorem stirpis suæ 3 fiscellam scirpeam . . carecto ripæ fluminis 5 vt lauaretur in flumine . . . fiscellam in papyrione 6 paruulum vagientem 10 adoptauit in locum filii, . . Quia de aqua tuli eum.

L. 3 rhor . . schilff 6 das kneblin weynet 10 vnd es ward jr son

M. M. N. 10 *Moses* is an Egipt name & it signifieth drawen out of the water.

L. M. N. 10 *Masa* heyst zihen daher heyst Mose getzogen, nemlich aufs dem wasser.

11 And it happened in these dayes when Moses was
waxte great, that he went out vnto his brethern ād
loked on their burthens, and spied an Egiptian smyt-
12 ynge one of his brethern an Ebrue. And he loked
round aboute: and when he sawe that there was no
man by, he slewe the Egiptian and hyd hī in the sonde.
13 And he went out a nother daye: and beholde, two
Ebrues stroue to gether. And he sayde vnto him that
dyd the wronge: wherfore smytest thou thine neygh-
14 boure? And he answered: who hath made the a ruelar
or a iudge ouer vs? intendest thou to kill me, as thou
killedst the Egiptian? Then Moses feared and sayde:
15 of a suertie the thinge is knowne. And Pharao herde
of it and went aboute to slee Moses: but he fled from
Pharao ād dwelt in the lāde of Madian, and he satt
doune by a welles syde.
16 The preast of Madian had .vii. doughters [Fo. IIII.]
which came ād drew water and fylled the troughes,
17 for to water their fathers shepe. And the shepardes
came and drove them awaye: But Moses stode vp and
18 helped them and waterd their shepe. And when they
came to Raguel their father, he sayde: how happeneth
19 it that ye are come so soone to daye? And they an-
swerede there was an Egiptiā that delyuered vs frō
the shepardes, and also drewe vs water & waterd the
20 shepe. And he sayde vnto his doughters: where is he?
why haue ye lefte the man? Goo call him that he
maye eate bread.
21 And Moses was content to dwell with the man.

M. 19 shepardes, & so drewe

V. 12 circunspexisset huc atque illuc 13 ei qui faciebat iniuriam 14 constituit te in princ. 15 iuxta puteū. 21 Iurauit ergo Moyses

L. 13 sprach zu dem gottlosen 14 vbirsten odder richter 15 bei eynen brunnen. 20 das jr jn nicht ludet

M. M. N. 12 *He slew the Egypcyā:* that is, he declared hī selfe to haue suche loue unto hys brethrē the Israelytes that were the people of god: that he wolde rather slaye or be slayne then that hys brother shulde suffer wrōg of the enemy of the lord. In which acte also, he shewed hym selfe to be predestinate of the lorde, to be a defence and sauer of the Israelytes. 17 *Raguel:* This Raguel is not Iethro, but is the father of Iethro and the graundfather of zephora, and was also the preste of Madian. For it was a lyke order with them as it was with the Iewes, that the sonne possessed the office of his father.

22 And he gaue Mofes Zipora his doughter which bare a
sonne, ād he called him Gerson: for he sayde. I haue
bene a straunger in a straunge lande. And she bare
yet another sonne, whom he called Eliefer sayng: the
God of my father is myne helper, and hath rid me out
of the handes of Pharao.
23 And it chaunced in processe of tyme, that the kinge
of Egipte dyed, and the childern of Israel syghed by
the reason of laboure and cryed. And their complaynt
24 came vp vnto God from the laboure. And God remem-
25 bred his promise with Abraham, Isaac ād Iacob. And
God loked apon the children of Israel and knewe them.

P. ¶ The thyrde Chapter.

1 MOSES kepte the shepe of Iethro
his father in law preast of
Madian, and he droue the
flocke to the backesyde of the
deserte, ād came to the moūtayne of
2 God, Horeb. And the angell of the
Lorde apeared vnto hī in a flame of
fyre out of a bush. And he perceaued
that the bush burned with fyre and consumed not.
3 Than Moses sayde: I will goo hēce and see this grete
syghte, howe it cometh that the bushe burneth not.
4 And whē the Lorde sawe that he came for to see,
he called vnto him out of the bush and sayde: Moses

M.C.S. *Moses kepeth shepe. God appereth vnto hym in a bush, & sendeth hym to the chyldren of Israel, and to Pharao that tyrant.*

M. 22 Zephora

V. 22 Accepitque Sephoram . . *Alterum vero peperit: quem vocauit Eliezer, dicens, Deus enim patris mei adiutor Meus, & eripuit me de manu Pharaonis.* 23 ad deum ab operibus. . . Et audiuit gemitum . . 24 fœderis quod pepigerat 25 respexit . . . et cognouit eos. iii, 1 ad interiora deserti 3 videbo visionem hanc magn.

L. 22 bewilligete . . vnd er gab 23 Gott erhöret jr wehklagen 24 . . seynen bund 25 sahe sie an vnd erkennet es. iii, 1 treib . . enhindern 3 besehen disz gros gesicht

M. M. N. 25 *Looked vpō thē:* that is he had pitie & compassyon ouer their soore labours, as Deut. xxvi, d.—iii, 1 *Desert:* that is in the wyldernes, a place not inhabited.

L. M. N. 22 *Gerson,* heyst ein frembder oder auszlender. *Eliefer,* heyst Gott meyn hylffe.

5 Mofes And he anfwered: here am I. And he fayde:
come not hither, but put thy fhooes off thi fete: for the
6 place whereon thou ftondeft is holy grounde. And he
fayde: I am the God of thy father, the God of Abraham, the God of Ifaac and the God of Iacob. And
Mofes hyd his face, for he was afrayde to loke vpon
God.
7 Than the Lorde fayde: I haue furely fene the trouble
of my people which are in Egipte and haue herde their
crye which they haue of their tafkemafters. For I
8 knowe theire forowe and am come downe to delyuer
them out of the handes of the Egiptians, and to brynge
thē out of that londe vnto a good londe and a lar-[Fo.
V.] ge and vnto a londe that floweth with mylke and
hony: euen vnto the place of the Canaanites, Hethites,
Amorites, Pherezites, Heuites, and of the Iebufites.
9 Now therfore beholde, the complaynt of the children
of Ifrael is come vnto me and I haue alfo fene the
oppreffion, wherwith the Egiptians oppreffe them.
10 But come, I will fende the vnto Pharao, that thou
mayft brynge my people the childern of Ifrael out of
Egipte.
11 And Mofes fayde vnto God: what am I to goo to
Pharao and to brynge the childern of Ifraell out of
12 Egipte? And he fayde: I wilbe with the. And this
fhalbe a token vnto the that I haue fent the: after that
thou haft broughte the people out of Egipte, ye fhall
13 ferue God vppon this mountayne.
Than fayde Mofes vnto God: when I come vnto the
childern of Ifraell and faye vnto them, the God of youre
fathers hath fent me vnto you, ād they faye vnto me,
14 what ys his name, what anfwere fhall I geuethem?

M. 11 vnto Pharao

V. 5 folue calceamentum . . terra fancta 6 non enim audebat afpicere contra 12 immolabis deo

L. 5 zeuch deine fchuch aus . . ein heylig land 7 die, fo fie treyben 9 befchwerung . . . befchweren. 12 Gotte eyn dienft thun

M. M. N. 5 The fcripture vfeth to call that holy whyche ether the Lorde chofeth vnto hym felfe: or is dedicate vnto the Lorde as Ex. xxii, d. 8 By *mylcke and hony* is vnderftonde aboūdaunce & plenteoufnes of all thynges that pertayne to the comfort of mā.

Then ſayde God vnto Moſes: I wilbe what
I wilbe: ād he ſayde, this ſhalt thou ſaye
vnto the children of Iſrael: I wilbe dyd
ſend me to you.
15 And God ſpake further vnto Moſes:
thus ſhalt thou ſaye vnto the children of
Iſraell: .I. the Lorde God of youre fathers, the God of Abraham, the God of
Iſaac, and the God of Iacob hath ſent me vnto you:
this is my name for euer, and this is my memoriall
16 thorow out all generacyons. Goo therfore and gather
the elders of Iſrael to gether and ſaye vnto them: the
Lorde God of youre fathers, the God of Abraham, the
God of Iſaac and the God of Iacob, appeared vnto me
and ſayde: I haue bene and ſene both you and that
17 whiche is done to you in Egipte. And I haue ſayde it,
that I will bringe you out of the tribulaciō of Egipte
vnto the londe of the Canaanites, Hethites, Amorites,
Pherezites, Heuites and Iebuſites: euen a londe that
floweth wyth mylke ād hony.
18 Yf it come to paſſe that they heare thy voyce, then
goo, both thou ād the elders of Iſrael vnto the kinge
of Egipte and ſaye vnto him: The Lord God of the
Ebrues hath mett with vs: Let vs goo therfore .iii. dayes
iourney in to the wilderneſſe, that we maye ſacrifice vnto
19 the Lorde oure God. Notwithſtondinge I am ſure that
the kinge of Egipte will not lett you goo, excepte it be
20 with a mightie hande: ye ād I will therfore ſtretche out
myne honde, and ſmyte Egipte with all my wōders which
I wil do therin. And after that he will let you goo.

Of this vvord, I vvilbe cometh the name of God Iehovah vvhich vve interprete, Lorde, and is as moch to ſaye as I that am.

M. 14 vnto you

V. 14 Ego ſum qui ſum . . Qui eſt, miſit me 15 hoc memoriale meum 16 Viſitans viſitaui 18 vt immolemus 20 in medio eorum

L. 14 Ich werde ſeyn, der ich ſeyn werde . . Ich werds ſeyn, . . . geſandt 16 heymgeſucht vnd geſehen 18 das wyr opffern 20 wunder die ich drynnen thun werde

M. M. N. 14 *I wyll be that I wyll be:* that is I am as ſome interprete it: which is, I am the begynnyng & endynge: by me haue you all thinges & with out me haue you nothynge that good is, Iohn i, a.

L. M. N. 14 *Ich werds ſeyn.* Der name Gottis ich werds ſeyn zeygt an, wie man mit glawben zu Gott, vnd er zu vns komen muſz, denn der glawbe ſagt, was God ſeyn vnd thun wirt mit vns nemlich gnade vnd hulffe.

21 And I will gett this people fauoure in the [Fo. VI.]
ſyghte of the Egiptians: ſo that when ye goo, ye ſhall
22 not goo emptie: but euery wife ſhall borow of hir
neyghboureſſe and of her that ſogeorneth in hir houſe,
iewels of ſyluer ād of gold and rayment. And ye ſhall
put them on youre ſonnes and doughters, and ſhall
robbe the Egiptians.

ℂ The .IIII. Chaptre.

1 MOSES anſwered and ſayde: Se,
they wil not beleue me nor
herkē vnto my voyce: but
wil ſaye, the Lorde hath not
2 apeared vnto the. Then the Lorde ſaide
vnto him: what is that in thine hande?
3 and he ſayde, a rodd. And he ſayde,
caſt it on the grounde, and it turned
vnto a ſerpent. And Moſes rā awaye
4 from it. And the Lorde ſayde vnto
Moſes: put forth thine hande ād take
it by the tayle. And he put forth his hande and
caught it, and it became a rodd agayne in his hand,
5 that they may beleue that the Lorde God of their
fathers, the God of Abraham, the God of Iſaac ād the
God of Iacob hath appeared vnto the.

M.C.S. *Moſes receaueth ſignes of his callynge and was ſent into Egypte. His wyfe zephora circumciſeth hir ſonne. Aaron meteth with Moſes. Moſes taketh his leaue of his father in lawe.*

6 And the Lorde ſayde forther more vnto him: thruſt
thine hande in to thy boſome. And he thruſt his
hande in to his boſome and toke it out. And beholde, his hand was leporous euen as ſnowe. And he

V. 22 poſtulabit mulier a vicina ſua & ab hoſpita ſua vaſa . . ſpoliabitis. iiii, 4 apprehende caudam eius. 5 Vt credant, inquit

L. 22 foddern ſilberen vnd gulden geſeſz . . . entwenden. iiii, 4 erhaſche ſie bey dem ſchwantz.

M. M. N. 22 *Robbe the Egypcians:* here ye maye not note that they ſtale and therfore ye maye ſteale: but note that it was done at godes cōmaundement & therfore was it a Iuſt & a righteous thing to be done. For he is not the auctor of euell &c.

7 ſaide: put thine hande in .P. to thy boſome agayne.
And he put his hande in to his boſome agayne, and
plucked it out of his boſome, and beholde, it was
8 turned agayn as his other fleſh. Yf they will not
beleue the nether heare the voyce of the firſt token:
yet will they beleue the voyce of the ſeconde tokē
9 But and yf they will not beleue the two ſignes nether
herken vnto thy voyce, then take of the water of the
riuer and poure it vpon the drye lond. And the water
which thou takeſt out of the riuer ſhall turne to bloude
vpon the drie londe.

10 And Moſes ſayde vnto the Lorde: oh my Lorde. I
am not eloquēt, no not in tymes paſt and namely ſence
thou haſt ſpoken vnto thy ſeruaunte: but I am ſlowe
11 mouthed and ſlowe tongued. And the Lorde ſayde unto
hī: who hath made mās mouth, or who hath made the
domme or the deaff, the ſeynge or the blynde? haue
12 not I the Lorde? Go therfore and I wilbe with thy
mouth and teach the what thou ſhalt ſaye.

13 And he ſayde: oh my Lorde, ſend I pray the
14 whome thou wilt. And the Lorde was angrie with
Moſes and ſayde: I knowe Aarō thy brother the leuite
that he can ſpeake. And morouer behold, he cometh
out agaynſt the, ād whē he ſeyth the, he wilbe glad
15 ī his hert. And thou [Fo. VII.] ſhalt ſpeake vnto hī
and put the wordes in his mouth, ād I wilbe with thy
mouth ād with his mouth, ād will teach you what ye
16 ſhal do. And he ſhalbe thy ſpokesmā vnto the people: he ſhall be thy mouth, ād thou ſhalt be his God.
17 and take this rodd in thy hāde, wherwith thou ſhalt do
myracles.

M. 14 he cometh to mete the

V. 7 retrahe . . ſinum tuum . . . . et erat ſimilis 8 audier. ſermonem . . . credēt verbo 10 obſecro domine, non ſum eloquens ab heri & nudiuſtertius 12 ero in ore tuo 15 pone verba mea . . quid agere debeatis. 16 tu autem eris in his quæ ad deum pertinent. 17 facturus es ſigna.

L. 7 vnd er thet ſie wieder 8 horen die ſtim . . . glawben der ſtim 10 von giſtern vnd ehegiſtern her 12 mit deynem mund 14 ſeer zornig 15 was jr thun ſolet 16 ſolet ſeyn Got ſeyn 17 zeychen thun ſolt.

M. M. N. 16 *He ſhalbe thy mouth:* that is, he ſhall ſpeake for the as in Iob xxix, c.

18 And Moses went ād returned to Iethro his father in
lawe agayne ād seyde vnto hī: let me goo (I praye
the) ād turne agayne vnto my brethern which are in
Egipte, that I may se whether they be yet alyue.
19 And Iethro sayde to Moses: goo in peace. And the
Lorde sayde vnto Moses in Madiā: returne agayne in
to Egipte for they are dead which wēt aboute to kyll
20 the And Moses toke his wife and his sonnes and put
them on an asse, and went agayne to Egipte, and toke
the rodd of God in his hande.
21 And the Lorde sayde vnto Moses: when thou art
come in to Egipte agayne, se that thou doo all the
wondres before Pharao which I haue put in thy hande:
but I will harden his herte, so that he shall not let the
people goo.
22 And tell Pharao, thus sayth the Lorde: Israel is
23 mine eldest sonne, and therfore sayth vnto the: let my
sonne goo, that he may serue me. Yf thou wilt not
let hī goo: beholde, I will slee thi-.ne eldest sonne.
24 And it chaunced by the waye in the ynne, that the
25 Lorde mett him and wolde haue kylled him. Than
Zepora toke a stone ād circumcised hyr sonne, and fell
at hys fette, and sayde: a bloudy husband art thou
26 vnto me. And he lett him goo. She sayde a bloudy
husbonde, because of the circumcision.
27 Than sayde the Lorde vnto Aaron: go mete Moses
in the wildernesse. And he went and mett him in the
28 mounte of God and kissed hī And Moses told Aaron
all the wordes of the Lorde which he had sent by him,
ād all the tokens which he had charged him with all.
29 So went Moses and Aaron and gatherd all the elders
30 of the childern of Israel. And Aarō told all the wordes

V. 19 quærebant animam tuam. 25 tetigitque pedes eius 26 postquam dixerat, Sponsus 28 pro quibus miserat eum 29 & fecit signa

L. 19 nach deynem leben stunden. 25 ruret jhm seyn fusse an 28 zeychen . . befolhen hatte

L. M. N. 25 *Blutbreutgam*, das ist sie ward zornig vnd sprache, Es kost blut, das du mein man bist vnd mus mein kind beschneytten, wilches sie vngerne thet, als das ein schant war vnter dē heydē. Bedeut aber des gesetz volck wilchs gern wollt Got haben, aber es will dz creutz nicht leyden noch den alten Adam beschneytten lassen bisz es thun mus.

which the Lorde had ſpokē vnto Moſes, and dyd the
31 myracles in the ſyght of the people, and the people
beleued. And whē they herde that the Lord had
viſited the children of Iſrael and had loked vpon their
tribulacion, they bowed them ſelues, and worſhipped

¶ The .V. Chapter.

1 THEN Moſes ād Aarō wēt and
told Pharao, thus ſayth the
Lorde God of Iſrael. Let my
people goo, that they may
kepe holye [Fo. VIII.] daye vnto me in
2 the wilderneſſe. And Pharao anſwered:
what felowe is the Lord, that I ſhulde heare
his voyce for to let Iſrael goo? I knowe
not the Lorde, nether will let Iſrael goo.

M.C.S. *Moſes & Aaron goeth vnto Pharao. The people of Iſrael are oppreſſed more and more, and they crye out vpon Moſes & Aaron therfore.*

3 And they ſayde: the God of the Ebrues hath mett
with vs: let vs goo (we praye the) .iii. dayes iourney
in to the deſerte, that we maye ſacrifice vnto the
Lorde oure God: leſt he ſmyte vs ether with peſtilence
4 or with ſwerde. Then ſayde the kinge of Egipte vnto
them: wherfore do ye, Moſes and Aaron, let the people frō their worke, gett you vnto youre laboure.
5 And Pharao ſayde further more: beholde, there is
moch people in the londe, and ye make them playe
and let their worke ſtonde.

V. 2 neſcio dominum 3 Deus Hebr. vocauit nos . . accidat nobis peſtis aut gladius. 5 videtis quod turba ſuccreuerit

*** NOTE—*The German notes in this Chapter and in Chapters VI., VII., VIII., and IX. were taken from a copy of Luther in the Lenox Library which is made up from different editions; the text of these chapters belongs to later editions.* A PERFECT *copy of the edition of 1523 having come into my use since the notes were prepared and set up in type, they have been carefully compared with that copy and agree with the former text in all particulars except the spelling, which being materially different from that in the edition of 1523, has been retained as illustrating the changes introduced. The precise date of the later editions I have not been able to verify.*

L. 1 feyre in der wüſten 2 weyſz nichts von dem H. 3 der Ebräer Got hat vns geruffen . . widerfare peſtilentz oder ſchwerd.

M. M. N. 31 *They bowed thē selues*, that is, gaue thāckes & prayſed the Lorde. v, 2 *I knowe not the Lorde*, that is: I feare him not, I beleue not in him: nether haue I any thyng to do with him. And euen thus ſaye all hardened hartes that haue not the feare of the Lorde before their eyes.

6 And Pharao commaunded the ſame daye vnto the
taſkemaſters ouer the people and vnto the officers ſa-
7 ynge: ſe that ye geue the people no moare ſtrawe to
make brycke with all as ye dyd in tyme paſſed: let
8 them goo and gather them ſtrawe them ſelues, and
the nombre of bricke which they were wont to make
in tyme paſſed, laye vnto their charges alſo, and minyſh nothinge therof. For they be ydill ād therfore
crye ſaynge: let vs goo and do ſacrifice vnto oure
9 God. They muſt haue more worke layed vpon them,
that they maye laboure theryn, and than will they
not turne them ſelues to fal-.P.ſe wordes.
10 Than went the taſkemaſters of the people and the
officers out and tolde the people ſaynge: thus ſayeth
11 Pharao: I will geue you no moare ſtrawe, but goo
youre ſelues ād gather you ſtrawe where ye can fynde
12 it, yet ſhall none of youre laboure be minyſhed. Than
the people ſcatered abrode thorowe out all the lande of
Egipte for to gather them ſtubyll to be in ſtead of ſtrawe.
13 And the taſkemaſters haſtied thē forward ſayng: fulfill youre werke daye by daye, euē as when ſtrawe
14 was geuen you. And the officers of the childern of
Iſrael which Pharaos taſkmaſters had ſett ouer them,
were beaten. And it was ſayde vnto them: wherfore
haue ye not fulfilled youre taſke in makinge brycke,
both yeſterdaye and to daye, as well as in tymes paſt.
15 Than went the officers of the childern of Iſrael ād
complayned vnto Pharao ſaynge: wherfore dealeſt thou
thus with thy ſervauntes? there is no ſtrawe geuen
16 vnto thy ſervauntes, and yet they ſaye vnto vs: make
brycke. And loo, thy ſervauntes ar beaten, and thy
17 people is foule intreated. And he anſwered: ydill ar
ye ydill and therfore ye ſaye: let vs goo ād do ſac-

V. 8 imponetis ſuper eos, nec minuetis quicquam 9 Opprimantur oper., & expleant ea 12 colligendas paleas. 13 Præfecti 14 Flagellatique ſunt . . ab exactoribus Pharaonis . . . ſicut prius, nec heri nec hodie? 16 lateres ſimiliter imperantur . . iniuſte agitur 17 Vacatis otio

L. 7 ſamlen vnd geben 8 aufflegen vnd nichts myndern 14 wurden geſchlagen . . heut noch geſtern . . wie geſtern vnd ehegeſtern? 16 man ſündiget an deynem volck. 17 Ir ſeit müſſig, müſſig ſeit jr

18 rifice vnto the Lorde. Goo therfore and worke, for
[Fo. IX.] there ſhall no ſtrawe be geuen you, and
yet ſee that ye delyuer the hole tale of brycke. (tale, *number* cf. German *Zahl*)
19 when the officers of the childern of Iſrael ſawe
them ſilfe in ſhrode caſe (in that he ſayde (ſhrode. *evil*)
ye ſhall minyſh nothinge of youre dalye makĩge of
20 brycke) than they mett Moſes and Aarõ ſtondinge in
21 there waye as they came out frõ Pharao, and ſayde
vnto them: The Lorde loke vnto you and iudge, for
ye haue made the ſauoure of vs ſtincke in the ſighte
of Pharao and of his ſervauntes, and haue put a ſwerde
in to their handes to ſlee vs.
22 Moſes returned vnto the Lorde and ſayde: Lorde
wherfore dealeſt thou cruelly with this people: and
23 wherfore haſt thou ſent me? For ſence I came to
Pharao to ſpeke in thy name, he hath fared foull with
this folke, ãd yet thou haſt not delyuered thy people
VI, 1 at all. Then the Lorde ſayde vnto Moſes. Now
ſhalt thou ſee what I will doo vnto Pharao, for with
a myghtie hande ſhall he let them goo, and with a
mightye hande ſhall he dryue them out of hys lande.

ℭ The .VI. Chapter

2 AND God ſpake vnto Moſes ſayng vnto him: I am the Lorde,
3 and I appeared vnto Abraham
Iſaac and Iacob an allmightie
God: but in my name Iehouah was I not

(M.C.S. *God promyſeth delyueraunce of the Iſraelites, & the lande of Canaan. The genealo-*)

V. 19 Videbantque ſe . . . in malum 20 Occurreruntque Moyſi et Aaron, qui ſtabant ex aduerſo 21 coram Pharaone . . ei gladium 23 afflixit populum tuum & non liberaſti eos. vi, 1 eiiciet illos 3 in deo omnipotente . . nomen meum Adonai

L. 19 das nicht beſſer ward 20 traten ſie dahin, das ſie in begegneten 21 vor Pharao. vi, 1 von ſich treiben 3 zum almechtigen got . . . meinen namẽ HERRE

M. M. N. 21 *Ye haue made vs ſtincke in the ſyght of Pharao,* that is, by your wordes & meanes: all the wrath & dyſpleaſure of Pharao is brought vpon vs, that he vtterly hateth & abhorreth vs. vi, 3 *Iehouah* is the name of god, wherwith no creature is named, & is as moch to ſaye as one that is of hym ſelfe & dependeth of no thing.

4 kno-.P. wne vnto them. Moreouer I made *gie of Ruben, Simeon and Leui.*
appoyntment, an appoyntment with them
covenant to geue them the londe of Canaã: the
londe of their pilgremage wherin they were ſtraungers.
5 And I haue alſo herde the gronyng of the childern of
Iſrael, becauſe the Egiptians kepe them in bondage,
ãd haue remembred my promyſſe *A promyſe,*
6 wherfore ſaye vnto the childern of *or a teſtamẽt*
Iſrael: I am the Lorde, and will brynge you out from
vnder the burdens of the Egiptians, and wyll rydd you
out of their bondage, and wyll delyuer you wyth a
7 ſtretched out arme and wythe great iudgementes. And
I wil take you for my people and wilbe to you a God.
And ye ſhall knowe that I am the Lorde youre God
which bringe you out from vnder the burthens of the
8 Egiptians. And I wyll brynge you vnto the londe
ouer the which I dyd lyfte vpp my hande to geue it
vnto Abraham, Iſaac and Iacob, and will geue it vnto
9 you for a poſſeſſyon: euẽ I the Lorde, And Moſes
tolde the children of Iſrael euen ſo: But they harkened
not vnto Moſes for anguyſhe of ſprete and ſprete, *ſpirit*
for cruell bondage. *Temptacyon trieth faith.*
10, 11 And the Lorde ſpake vnto Moſes ſaynge Goo and
bydd Pharao kynge of Egipte, that he let the childern
12 of Iſrael goo out of his londe. And Moſes ſpake before
the Lorde ſa-[Fo. X.] ynge: beholde, the childern of
Iſraell herken not vnto me, how than ſhall Pharao
heare me: ſeynge that I haue vncircumciſed lippes.

V. 4 Pepigique fœdus 5 audiui gemitum . . pacti mei. 6 ergaſtulo Ægyyt., . . iudiciis magnis. 8 ſuper quam leuaui manum meã 9 propter anguſtiam ſpiritus, & opus duriſſimum.

L. 4 bund . . auffgericht 5 die wehklage . . bund gedacht. 6 laſten in Eg. . groſſe gerichte 8 darüber ich habe meine hand gehaben 9 vor keychen des geyſts vnd vor harter arbeyt.

M. M. N. 5 A promyſe or a teſtament. 6 *Iudgemẽtes* are taken for the wõderfull dedes of God: as here for his wõderfull plages as Pſal. xxx, d. & cxviii. 8 *To lyfte vp the hande* is to promyſe by an othe, as in Gen. xiiii, d. of Abraham.—12 *To be of vncircumciſed lippes,* is to haue a tonge that lacketh good vtterance & lacketh eloquence to ſet out his matter with all.

L. M. N. 3 *Nicht kundt gethan:* Die Patriarchen haben Gott wol erkand, aber ein ſolche offentliche gemeyne predig war zu der zeyte von Gott noch nicht auff gangen, wie durch Moſe vnd Chriſtũ geſchehen iſt.

13 And the Lorde ſpake vnto Moſes and Aaron and
gaue them a charge vnto the childern of Iſrael ād vnto
Pharao kyng of Egipte: to brynge the childern of Iſrael
out of the londe of Egipte.

14 Theſe be the heedes of their fathers houſſes. The
childern of Ruben the eldeſt ſonne of Iſrael are theſe:
Hanoh, Pallu, Hezron, Charmi, theſe be the houſholders
15 of Ruben. The childern of Symeon ar theſe: Gemuel,
Iamin, Ohad, Iachin. Zohar, and Saul the ſonne of a
Cananyteſh wiſe: theſe are the kynreddes of Symeon

16 Theſe are the names of the childern of Leui in
their generations: Gerſon, Kahath and Merari. And
17 Leui lyued an hundred and .xxxvii. yere. The
ſonnes of Gerſon: Libni ād Semei in their kinreddes.
18 The childern of Kahath: Amram, Ieſear, Hebron and
Vſiel. And Kahath lyued an hundred and .xxxiii. yere.
19 The children of Merari are theſe: Mahely and Muſi:
theſe are the kynreddes of Leui in their generations.

20 And Amram toke Iochebed his nece to wyfe which
bare him Aaron and Moſes. And Amram lyued an
21 hundred and .xxxvii. yere. .¶. The childern of Iezear:
22 Korah, Nepheg and Sichri. The childern of Vſiel:
Miſael, Elzaphan and Sithri.

23 And Aaron toke Elizaba doughter of Aminadab ād
ſiſter of Nahaſon, to wife: which bare him Nadab,
24 Abehu, Eleazar and Ithamar. The childern of Korah:
Aſſir, Elkana ād Abiaſſaph: theſe are the kynreddes
25 of the Korahites. And Eleazar Aarons ſonne toke
him one of the doughters of Putuel to wife: which bare
him Pinehas: theſe be the principall fathers of the
Leuites in their kynreddes.

26 Theſe are that Aaron and Moſes to whom the Lorde
ſayde: carie the childern of Iſrael out of the lond of
27 Egipte, with their armyes. Theſe are that Moſes and
Aaron whiche ſpake to Pharao kynge of Egipte, that
they myghte brīge the childern of Iſrael out of Egipte.

V. 14 hæ cognationes Ruben. 20 Moyſen & *Mariam* 25 principes familiarum Leuit. 27 Hi ſunt . . Iſrael de Ægypto: iſte eſt Moyſes & Aaron

L. 27 Sie ſinds

28 And in the daye whē the Lorde ſpake vnto Moſes in
29 the londe of Egipte, he ſpake vnto him ſaynge, I am
the Lorde, ſe that thou ſpeake vnto Pharao the kinge
30 of Egipte all that I ſaye vnto the. And Moſes
anſwered before the Lorde: I am of vncircumciſed
lippes, howe ſhall Pharao than geue me audience?

ℭ The .VII. Chaptre.

1 AND the Lorde ſaide vnto Moſes: beholde, I haue made the
Pharaos God, and [Fo. XI.]
Aaron thy brother ſhal be
2 thy prophete. Thou ſhalt ſpeake all that
I commaunde the and Aaron thy brother
ſhall ſpeake vnto Pharao: that he ſende
the childern of Iſrael out of his londe.
3 But I will harden Pharaos hert, that I

M.C.S. *The tokens to knowe God. The rodde of Moſes is torned to a ſerpēt. The ſorcerars do euē the ſame. The waters are tourned into bloude.*

may multiplie my myracles and my wondres in the
4 land of Egipte. And yet Pharao ſhall not herken
vnto you, that I maye ſett myne honde vpon Egipte
and brynge out myne armyes, euē my people the childern of Iſrael out of the lāde of Egipte, with great
5 iudgementes. And the Egiptians ſhall knowe that I
am the Lorde when I haue ſtretched forth my hande
vpō Egipte, and haue brought out the childern of
Iſrael from amonge thē.
6 Moſes and Aaron dyd as the Lorde commaunded
7 them. And Moſes was .Lxxx. yere olde and Aaron
8 Lxxxiii. when they ſpake vnto Pharao. And the

V. 28 in die qua locutus eſt dominus ... in terra Æg. vii. 1 conſtitui te deum Phar. 3 ſigna & oſtenta 4 exercitum & populum meum . . . iudicia maxima. 5 de medio eorum.

L. 1 eynen Gott geſetzt vber Phar. 3 zeychen vnd wunder 4 füre meyn heer, meyn volck . . groſſe gerichte 5 mitten auſz ynen

M. M. N. 1 *I haue made the Pharaos God,* that is: I haue made the Pharaos iudge as in Ex. xxii, d.

9 Lorde ſpake vnto Moſes and Aaron ſaynge: when
Pharao ſpeaketh vnto you and ſayth: ſhewe a wondre,
than ſhalt thou ſaye vnto Aaron, take the rodd and
caſt it before Pharao, and it ſhall turne to a ſerpent
10 Than went Moſes and Aarō in vnto Pharao, and
dyd euen as the Lorde had commaunded. And Aaron
caſt forth his rodd before Pharao and before his ſer-
11 vauntes, and it turned to a ſerpente. Than Pharao
called for the .P. wyſe men and enchaunters of Egipte
12 dyd yn lyke maner with there ſorcery.
And they caſt doune euery mā his rodd,
ād they turned to ſerpētes: but Aarons
13 rodd ate vp their roddes: ād yet for all
that Pharaos herte was hardened, ſo that
he herkened not vnto thē, euen as the
Lorde had ſayde.
14 Than ſayde the Lorde vnto Moſes.
Pharaos herte is hardened, and he re-
15 fuſeth to let the people goo. Get the

Euē ſo do ourecharmars novv deceaue all princes vvith theire ſophiſtrie: ād turne thēclene from repētaūce tovvarde the lavve of god: ād frō the fayth that is in Chriſt.

vnto Pharao in the mornynge, for he will come vnto
the water, and ſtōde thou apon the ryuers brynke
agenſt he come, and the rodd whiche turned to a
16 ſerpente take in thine hande. And ſaye vnto him:
the Lorde God of the Hebrues hath ſente me vnto the
ſaynge: let my people goo, that they maye ſerue me
in the wildernes: but hither to thou woldeſt not heare.
17 wherfore thus ſayth the Lorde: hereby thou ſhalt
knowe that I am the Lord. Behold, I will ſmyte with
the ſtaffe that is in myne hand apon the waters that
18 are in the ryuer, and they ſhall turne to bloude. And
the fiſhe that is in the riuer ſhall dye, and the riuer
ſhall ſtinke: ſo that it ſhall greue the Egiptiās to
drinke of the water of the ryuer.
19 And the Lorde ſpake vnto Moſes, ſaye vnto Aaron:
take thy ſtaffe and ſtretch out thyne hande ouer the
waters of Egipte, ouer the- [Fo. XII.] ir ſtreames,

M. 11 Egypte: and they dyd

V. 9 Oſtendite ſigna 12 dracones 14 Ingrauatum 16 vt ſacrificet mihi in deſerto

L. 9 beweyſet ewre wunder 11 ſchwarzkünſtigen 13 verſtockt 16 diene in der wüſten.

ryuers, pondes and all pooles off water, that they maye
be bloude, and that there may be bloude in all the lande
of Egipte: both in veſſells of wodd and alſo of ſtone.
20 And Moſes and Aaron dyd euen as the Lorde commaunded. And he liſte vp the ſtaffe and ſmote the
waters that were in the riuer, in the ſyghte of Pharao
and in the ſyghte of his ſervauntes, and all the water
21 that was in the ryuer, turned in to bloude. And the
fiſh that was in the riuer dyed, and the ryuer ſtanke:
ſo that the Egiptians coude not drinke of the water of
the ryuer. And there was bloude thorowe out all the
lande of Egipte.
22 And the Enchaunters of Egipte dyd lyke wyſe with
their enchauntmentes, ſo that Pharaos herte was hardened and dyd not regarde them as the Lorde had ſayde.
23 And Pharao turned him ſelfe and went in to his houſſe,
24 and ſet not his herte there vnto. And the Egiptians
dygged round aboute the ryuer for water to drynke,
for they coude not drynke of the water of the ryuer.
25 And it continued a weke after that the Lorde had
ſmote the ryuer.

The .VIII. Chapter.

.P.

1 THE Lorde ſpake vnto Moſes:
Goo vnto Pharao and tell
him, thus ſayeth the Lorde:
let my people goo, that they
2 maye ſerue me. Yf thou wilt not let
them goo: beholde I will ſmyte all thy londe with
3 frogges. And the ryuer ſhall ſcrale with
frogges, ād they ſhall come vp and goo
in to thine houſſe and in to thy chaumbre

M.C.S. *The plage of frogges. Moſes prayeth for Pharao. The plage of flyes.*

ſcrale, *crawl, creep, Lev. xi 41, 42.*

V. 22 malefici Ægyptiorum 23 nec appoſuit cor etiam hac vice. 27 or viii, 2 terminos tuos 28 or viii, 3 ebulliet fluuius . .

L. 23 vnd keret ſein hertz noch nit dran 27 or viii, 2 deyne grentzen 28 or viii, 3 wymmeln . .

M M. N. 23 *He ſet not his heart therō* that is, the danger moued him nothinge, as is declared in Eſ. xlvii, b.

where thou ſlepeſt ād vppō thy bedd, and in to the
houſſes of thy ſervauntes, and vppon thy people, and
in to thyne ovens, and vppon thy vitels which thou
4 haſt in ſtore And the frogges ſhall come vpon the
and on thy people and apon all thy ſervauntes.

5 And the Lorde ſpake vnto Moſes, ſaye vnto Aaron:
ſtretche forth thine hande with thy rodd ouer the
ſtremes, riuers, ād pondes. And bringe vp frogges
6 apon the londe of Egipte And Aaron ſtretched his
hande ouer the water of Egipte, and the frogges came
7 vp ād couered the londe of Egipte. And the ſorcerers
dyd likewiſe with theire ſorcery, and the frogges came
vp apon the lande of Egipte.

8 Then Pharao called for Moſes and Aarō and ſayde,
praye ye vnto the Lorde that he may take awaye the
frogges from me and from my people, and I will let
the people goo, that they maye ſacrifice vnto the
9 Lorde. And Moſes ſayde vnto Pharao: Appoynte thou
the tyme [Fo. XIII.] vnto me, when I ſhall praye for
the and thy ſervauntes ād thy people, to dryue awaye
the frogges from the and thy houſſe, ſo that they ſhall
10 remayne but in the riuer only. And he ſayde tomorow.
And he ſayde: euen as thou haſt ſayde, that thou mayſt knowe that there is none like vnto the Lorde oure
11 God. And the frogges ſhall departe from the ād from
thyne houſes, and from thy ſervauntes and from thy
people, and ſhall remayne in the riuer only.

12 And Moſes and Aaron went out frō Pharao, and
Moſes cryed vnto the Lorde apō the apoyntment of
13 frogges which he had made vnto Pharao. And the
Lorde dyd accordinge to the ſaynge of Moſes. And
the frogges dyed out of the houſſes, courtes and feldes.

14 And they gathred them to gether vppon heppes:
ſo that the lande ſtanke of them.

15 But when Pharao ſawe that he had reſt geuen

M. 9 Appoynte thou the tyme

V. 28 or viii, 3 reliquias ciborum tuorum. viii, 9 conſtitue . . . a domo tua, *& a ſeruis tuis, & a populo tuo* 12 pro ſponſione ramarum . . . quam condixerat

L. 28 or viii, 3, in deyne teyg. viii, 9 Hab du die ehr für mir, vnd ſtymme mir 12 vmb das gedinge . . . zugeſagt 15 das er lufft kriegen hatte

him, he hardened his herte and herkened not vnto
16 them, as the Lorde had ſayde. And the Lord ſayde
vnto Moſes: Saye vnto Aarō ſtretch out thy rodd and
ſmyte the duſt of the lande that it may turne to lyſe
17 in all the londe of Egipte. And they dyd ſo. And
Aaron ſtretched out his hande with his rodd and ſmote
the duſt of the erth. ād it turned to lyſe both in man
and beeſt, ſo that all the duſt of the lande .P. turned
to lyſe, thorowe out all the lande of Egipte.
18 And the enchaunters aſſayde lykewyſe with their
enchauntmentes to brynge forth lyſe, but they coude
not. And the lyſe were both apon man and beeſt.
19 Then ſayde the enchaunters vnto Pharao: it is the
fingre of God. Neuerthelater Pharaos herte was hardened and he regarded them not, as the Lorde had ſayde.
20 And the Lorde ſayde vnto Moſes: ryſe vp early in
the mornynge and ſtonde before Pharao, for he will
come vnto the water: and ſaye vnto him, thus ſayth
the Lorde: let my people goo, that they maye ſerue
21 me. Yf thou wilt not let my people goo: beholde, I
will ſende all maner flies both apon the and thy ſervauntes ād thy people and into thy houſſes. And the
houſſes of the Egiptians ſhalbe full of flies, and the
22 grounde where on they are. But I will ſeperate
the ſame daye the londe of Goſan where my people
are, ſo that there ſhall no flyes be there: that thou
mayſt knowe that I am the Lorde vppon the erth.
23 And I will put a deuiſion betwene my people and
thine. And euen tomorow ſhall this myracle be done.
24 And the Lorde dyd euen ſo: and there came noy-
ſom flyes in to the houſſe of Pharao [Fo. XIIII.] and
in to his ſervauntes houſſes and in to all the lōde of
Egipte: ſo that the londe was marred with flyes.

V. 16 et ſint cyniphes 18 vt educerent 21 omne genus muſcarum . . . muſcis diuerſi generis 22 Faciamque mirabilem in die illa terram Geſſen in qua populus meus eſt, vt non ſint ibi muſcæ 23 ſignum iſtud 24 muſca grauiſſima . . corruptaque eſt terra

L. 16 das leuſe werden 18 erauſz brechten 22 vnd wil des tages ein ſonders thun 23 erlöſung ſetzen . . . zeichen 24 böſe würm . . . land ward verderbet

M. M. N. 19 What the fynger of God doth ſignifie is expounded in Luke xi, c.

25 Then Pharao ſent for Moſes and Aaron and ſayde:
26 Goo and do ſacrifice vnto youre God in the land. And
Moſes anſwered: it is not mete ſo to do. for we muſt
offer vnto the Lorde oure God, that whiche is an
abhominatyon vnto the Egiptians: beholde ſhall we
ſacrifice that which is an abhominacion vnto the
Egiptians before their eyes, and ſhall they not ſtone
27 vs? we will therfore goo .iii. dayes yournay in to the
deſerte and ſacrifice vnto the Lorde oure God as he
hath cōmaunded vs.

28 And Pharao ſayde: I will late you goo, that ye
maye ſacrifice vnto the Lorde youre God in the wildernes: only goo not ferre awaye, ād ſe that ye praye
29 for me. And Moſes ſayde: beholde, I will goo out
from the and praye vnto the Lorde, and the flyes
ſhall departe frō Pharao and from his ſervauntes and
from his people tomorow. But let Pharao from hēce
forth deſceaue no moare, that he wolde not lett the
people goo to ſacrifice vnto the Lorde.

30 And Moſes went out from Pharao and prayed vnto
31 the Lorde. And the Lorde dyd as Moſes had ſaide:
ād toke awaye the flies frō Pharao and from his ſervauntes ād from hys .P. people, ſo that there remayned
not one. But for all that, Pharao hardened his herte
euen then alſo and wolde not let the people goo,

¶ The .IX. Chaptre.

1 AND the Lorde ſayde vnto Moſes,
goo vnto Pharao and tell him,
thus ſayeth the Lorde God of
the Ebrues: ſende out my peo-
2 ple that they maye ſerue me. Yf thou
wilt not let them goo but wilt holde them
3 ſtyll: beholde, the hande of the Lorde

M.C.S. *The moren of beſtes. The plage of botches and ſores. The horryble hayle, thonder & lyghtenynge.*

M. 29 that he wille not ix, 1, let my people goo that
V. 25 in terra hac. 28 longius ne abeatis 29 noli vltra fallere
31 non ſuperfuit ne vna quidem
L. 28 nicht ferner zihet 29 alleyne theuſche mich nicht mehr

ſhalbe apō thy catell which thou haſt in the feld apon
horſes aſſes, camels, oxen, and ſhepe, with a mightye
4 great morrayne. But the Lorde ſhall make a deuyſion
betwene the beeſtes of the Iſrahelites, ād the beeſtes of
the Egiptiās: ſo that there ſhal nothing dye of all that
5 perteyneth to the children of Iſrael. And the Lorde
appoynted a tyme ſaynge: tomorow the Lorde ſhall do
this thinge in the londe.

6 And the Lorde dyd the thinge on the morow, and
all the catell of Egipte dyed: but of the catell of the
7 childern of Iſrael dyed not one. And Pharao ſent to
wete: but ther was not one of the catell
of the Iſrahelites dead. Notwithſtondinge the hert of
Pharao hardened, and he wolde not let the people
goo.

wete, *know*

8 And the Lorde ſayde vnto Moſes and Aaron: take
youre handes full of aſſhes out of the [Fo. XV.]
fornace, and let Moſes ſprynkel it vp into the ayre in
9 the ſyghte of Pharao, and it ſhall turne to duſt in all
the londe of Egipte, and ſhal make ſwellynge ſoores
with blaynes both on mā and beeſt in all
10 the londe of Egipte. And they toke
aſſhes out of the fornace, and ſtode before Pharao,
ād Moſes ſprynkeld it vp into the ayre: And there brake
11 out ſoores with blaynes both in mā and beeſt: ſo that
the ſorcerers coude not ſtonde before Moſes, by the
reaſon of botches on the enchaunters and
12 apon all the Egiptians, But the Lorde
hardened the herte of Pharao, that he herkened not
vnto them, as the Lorde had ſayde vnto Moſes.

blaynes, *pimples, or puſtules*

botches, *ſwellings, blotches*

13 And the Lorde ſayde vnto Moſes: ryſe vp early in
the mornynge and ſtonde before Pharao and tell him,

M. 11 before Moſes for there were botches vpon the enchaunters

V. 3 peſtis valde grauis 4 inter poſſeſſiones Iſrael, & poſſeſſiones Ægypt. 7 Miſit Phar. ad vidēdum 8 cineris de camino 9 vlcera, & veſicæ turgētes

L. 3 faſt ſchweren peſtilentz 7 Ph. ſandte darnach, vnd ſihe, 8 ruſz auſz der ſewrmaur 9 ſchweren vnd drüſze

M. M. N. 6 This word *all:* is not taken here for euery one, but for a great nombre, or of all ſortes of catell ſome, as in 1 Tim. ii, a.

thus ſayth the Lorde God of the Ebrues: Let my
14 people goo, that they may ſerue me, or els I will
at this tyme ſende all my plages apon thine herte and
apon thy ſervauntes and on thy people, that thou
mayſt knowe that there is none lyke me in all the erth.
15 For now I will ſtretch out my hande and will ſmyte
the and thy people with peſtilence: ſo that thou ſhalt
16 periſſhe from the erth. Yet in very dede for this cauſe
haue I ſterred the vpp, for to ſhewe my power in the,
and to declare my name thorow out all the worlde.
17 ¶. Yf it be ſo that thou ſtoppeſt my people, that thou
18 wilt not let them goo: beholde, tomorow this tyme I
will ſend doune a mightie great hayle: euē ſoch one as
was not in Egipte ſence it was grounded
19 vnto this tyme. Sende therfore and fet
home thy beeſtes and al that thou haſt in the felde,
For apon all the men and beeſtes which are founde in
the felde ād not broughte home, ſhall the hayle fall,
20 ād they ſhall dye And as many as feared the worde
of the Lorde among the ſervauntes of Pharao made
21 their ſervauntes ād their beeſtes flee to houſe: and they
that regarded not the worde of the Lorde, left their
22 ſervauntes and their beeſtes in the felde.

grounded, *eſtabliſhed, founded.*

And the Lorde ſayde vnto Moſes: ſtretche forth thine
hande vnto heauen, that there may be hayle in all the
lande of Egipte: apō mā ād beeſt, ād apō all the herbes
23 of the felde in the feld of Egipte. And Moſes ſtretched
out his rodd vnto heauen, and the Lorde thondered
and hayled ſo that the fyre ran a longe vppon the
grounde. And the Lorde ſo hayled in the lōde of
24 Egipte, that there was hayle ād fyre mēgled with
the hayle, ſo greuous, that there was none ſoch in all
the londe of Egipte, ſence people inhabited it.
25 And the hayle ſmote in the londe of Egip- [Fo.

V. 14 mittam omnes plagas meas 16 Idcirco autem poſui te 18 pluam . . . grandinem 23 discurrentia fulgura ſuper terram 24 ignis miſta pariter ferebantur . . ex quo gens illa condita eſt.

L. 14 alle meyne plagen . . ſenden 16 Doch darumb hab ich dich erweckt 18 hagel regen laſſen 23 fewr auff die erden ſchoſz. 24 hagel vnd fewr vntereinander furen . . der zeyt leut drynnen geweſen ſind.

XVI.] te all that was in the felde: both man and beeſt
And the hayle ſmote all the herbes of the feld and
26 broke all the trees of the felde: only in the lande of
Goſan where the childern of Iſraell were, was there
27 no hayle. And Pharao ſent ād called for Moſes and
Aaron, and ſayde vnto thē: I haue now ſynned, the
Lorde is rightwes and I and my people are weked.
28 Praye ye vnto the Lorde, that the thonder of God and
hayle maye ceaſe, and I will let you goo, and ye ſhall
tarie no longer.

29 And Moſes ſayde vnto him: aſſoone as I am out of
the citie, I will ſprede abrode my handes vnto the
Lorde, and the thunder ſhall ceaſſe, nether ſhall there
be any moare hayle: that thou mayſt knowe, howe that
30 the erth ys the Lordes, But I knowe that thou and
31 thy ſervauntes yet feare not the Lord God. The flaxe
ād the barly were ſmyttē, for the barly was ſhott vp
32 ād the flaxe was boulled: but the whete boulled, *ſwol-*
and the rye were not ſmeten, for they *len, i.e. grown into buds*
were late ſowne.

33 And Moſes went out of the citie frō Pharao ād
ſprede abrode his handes vnto the Lorde, and the
thunder and hayle ceaſed, nether rayned it any moare
34 vppon the erth. whē Pharao ſawe that the rayne and
the hayle and thunder were ceaſed, he ſynned agayn
ād hardened .P. his herte: both he and his ſervauntes.
35 So was the herte of Pharao hardened, that he wolde
not let the childern of Iſrael goo, as the Lord had
ſayde by Moſes.

V. 25 lignum regionis 28 vt deſinant tonitrua dei 31 hordeum eſſet virens

L. 25 bewm auff dē feld 28 gnug ſey des donnern Gotes 31 gerſten geſchoſſet . . knotten gewunnen

M. M. N. 27 *To be weked,* is: to be without the knowledge & felynge of the goodnes of God and without hope to receaue any goodnes at his hande: ſo that we cannot paciently here any of his truthes nor beleue thē nether ſoffer thē to be taught to other, as it apereth in all the pſalmes & in Eſa. lvii, d.

The .X. Chapter.

1 THE Lorde ſayde vnto Moſes: goo
vnto Pharao, neuertheleſſe I
haue hardened his harte and
the hertes of his ſervauntes,
that I mighte ſhewe theſe my ſygnes among-
2 eſt thē and that thou tell in the audience of
thy ſonne and of thy ſonnes ſonne, the pagiantes which I haue played in Egipte
ād the miracles which I haue done amonge them: that
ye may knowe how that I am the Lorde.

M.C.S. *The heart of Pharao is hardened of God. The greſhoppers. The thicke darcknes.*

pagiantes, *feats,exploits*

3 Than Moſes ād Aaron went in vnto Pharao and
ſayde vnto him: thus ſayth the Lorde God of the
Hebrues: how longe ſhall it be, or thou wilt ſubmyt
thy ſelfe vnto me? Let my people goo that they
4 maye ſerue me. Yf thou wilt not let my people goo:
beholde, tomorow will I brynge greſhoppers in to thy
5 lande, and they ſhall couer the face of the erth that it
can not be ſene, ād they ſhall eate the reſidue which
remayneth vnto you and eſcaped the hayle and they
6 ſhall eate all your grene trees vpon the felde, and
they ſhall fill thy houſſes and all thy ſervauntes houſſes,
and the houſſes of all the Egiptiās after ſoch a maner:
as nether thy [Fo. *omitted.*] fathers nor thy fathers
fathers haue ſene, ſence the tyme they were apon the
erthe vnto thys daye. And he turned him ſilfe aboute,
ād went out from Pharao.

7 And Pharaos ſervauntes ſayde vnto hym: Howe
longe ſhall this felowe thus plage vs? Let the men
goo that they maye ſerue the Lorde their God, or els
8 wilt thou ſee Egipte firſt deſtroyed? And than Moſes and

M. 7 How lōge ſhall we be thus euell intreated? . . . God: wilt thou not yet knowe that Egypt is deſtroyed?

V. 2 in auribus . . quoties contriuerim 5 ne quicquam eius appareat . . reſiduum fuerit . . ligna, quæ germinant 7 patiemur hoc ſcandalum?

L. 2 fur den oren . . getrieben hab 5 land nicht ſehen kunde . . vberig vnd erredtet . . . grūnende bewm 7 das weſen verſtricken?

Aaron were brought agayn vnto Pharao, and he ſayde
vnto them: Goo and ſerue the Lorde youre God but
9 who are they that ſhall goo? And Moſes anſwered:
we muſt goo with yonge and olde: ye and with our sonnes
and with oure doughters, ād with our ſhepe and oxē
muſt we goo For we muſt holde a feaſt vnto the Lorde.
10 And he ſayde vnto them: ſhall it be ſoo? The
Lorde be with you, ſhulde I lett you goo, and youre
childern alſo? Take heede, for ye haue ſome myſchefe
11 in honde. Nay not ſo: but goo ye that are men and
ſerue the Lorde, for that was youre deſyre. And they
thruſt thē out of Pharaos preſence.
12 And the Lorde ſayde vnto Moſes: Stretch out thine
hande ouer the lande of Egipte for greſhoppers, that
they come apon the lande of Egipte and eate all the
herbes of the londe, ād all that the hayle left vn-
13 touched. And Moſes .P. ſtretched forth his rodd ouer
the londe off Egipte, ād the Lorde brought an eaſt
wynde vppō the lande, all that daye and all nyghte.
And in the mornynge the eaſt wynde broughte the
14 greſhoppers, ād the greſhoppers wēt vp ouer all the
lande of Egipte and lighted in all quarters off Egipte
verye greuouſly: ſo that before them were there no ſoch
15 greſhoppers, nether after them ſhal be. And they
couered all the face of the erth, ſo that the londe was
darke therwith. And they ate all the herbes of the lande
and all the frutes of the trees which the hayle had
lefte: ſo that there was no grene thinge lefte in the trees
and herbes of the felde thorow all the lande of Egipte.
16 Then Pharao called for Moſes and Aarō in haſte
and ſayde: I haue ſynned agaynſt the Lorde youre God

M. 9 we wyll go 10 vnto them: let it be ſo?

V. 9 eſt enim ſolennitas domini 10 Sic dominus ſit . . cui dubium eſt quod peſſime cogitetis? 13 induxit ventum vrentem 14 innumerabiles 16 Quam ob rem

L. 9 denn wyr haben eyn feſt des Herrn. 10 Awe ia, der Herr ſey mit euch . . . . Sehet da, ob yr nicht boſes fur habt? 13 treyb eynen Oſtwind 14 ſo ſeer viel 16 Da foddert

L. M. N. 11 Diſe hawſchrecken heyſſen hie nicht *Hagab* auff Ebreiſch, wie an etlichen ortten, ſondern *Arbe*, Es ſind aber vierfuſſige fliegende thier vnd reyn zu eſſen, wie *Hagab* Leuit. xi. aber vnd vnbekand, on dz ſie den hewſchrecken glaych ſind.

17 and agaynſt you. Forgeue me yet my ſynne only this
once, and pray vnto the Lorde youre God that he maye
18 take awaye frō me this deth only. And he wēt out
19 frō Pharao ād prayd vnto the Lorde, ād the Lord
turned the wynde in to a myghtie ſtronge weſt wynde,
and it toke awaye the greſhoppers and caſt thē in to
the reed ſee: ſo that there was not one greſhopper left
20 in all the coſtes of Egipte But the Lorde hardened
Pharaos herte, ſo that he wold not let the childern off
Iſrael goo

21 [Fo. XVII.] And the Lorde ſayde vnto Moſes:
Stretch out thy hond vnto heauē ād let there be
darckneſſe vppon the londe of Egipte: euē that thei
22 maye feale the darckneſſe. And Moſes ſtretched forth
his hande vnto heauē, ād there was a darke myſt vppō
23 all the lande off Egipte .iii. dayes longe ſo that no mā
ſawe another nether roſe vp frō the place where he was
by the ſpace of .iii. dayes, but all the childrē of Iſrael
had lighte where they dwelled.

24 Then Pharao called for Moſes and ſayde: goo and
ſerue the Lorde, only let youre ſhepe. and youre oxen
25 abyde, but let youre childern go with you. And Moſes
anſwered: thou muſt geue vs alſo offringes and burnt-
offringes for to ſacrifice vnto the Lord oure God,
26 Oure catell therfore ſhall goo with vs, and there ſhall
not one hooffe be left behinde, for therof muſt we take
to ſerue the Lorde oure God. Moreouer we cā not
knowe wherwith we ſhall ſerue the Lorde, vntyll we
come thither.

27 But the Lorde hardened Pharaos herte, ſo that he

M. 19 greſhopper in all the coſtes 22 there was a thicke darcknes vpō

V. 19 flare fecit ventum ab occid., 21 vt palpare queant. 26 præſertim cum ignoremus

L. 19 wendet der Herr eyn ſeer ſtarcken Weſtwind 21 das mans greyffen mag 26 Auch wiſſen wyr nicht

M. M. N. 26 This was an outward ſeruyce, but the true and ryght ſeruyce of god, is to feare him as a father, to loue hym, kepe hys cōmaundementes and to commyt a mānes ſelfe holy to him, truſtynge in hys mercy only: ſetting al thought & care vpō him. And when we haue offended, to repēt and to be ſory, & knowledge oure offence & beleue that he will forgeue it vs, for his truthes ſake as 1 Pet. v, b. & Ps. xxxvi, a.

28 wold not let thē goo. And Pharao ſayde vnto him:
get the frō me ād take heade to thy ſelfe that thou ſee
my face no moare, For whē ſoeuer thou comeſt in my
29 ſyghte, thou ſhalt dye. And Moſes ſaide: let it be as
thou haſt ſayde: I will ſee thy face no moare.

.P. ¶ The .XI. Chapter.

M.C.S. The Lorde commaundeth to troble the Egypcyans. The deth of all the fyrſt begotten in Egypt.

1 AND the Lorde ſayde vnto Moſes:
yet wil I brynge one plage
moare vppon Pharao and vppon Egipte, and after that he
wyll lett you goo hence. And when he
letteth you goo, he ſhall vtterly dryue
2 you hence. But byd the people that euery man
borowe of his neghbour and euery woman of hir
neghboureſſe: iewels off ſyluer and iewels of golde.
3 And the Lorde gatt the people fauoure in the ſyghte
of the Egiptians. Moreouer Moſes was very great in
the lande of Egipte: both in the ſyghte of Pharao, and
alſo in the ſyghte of the people.
4 And Moſes ſayde: thus ſayth the Lorde. Aboute myd-
5 nyghte will I goo out amonge the Egiptians, and all the
firſtborne in the lande of Egipte ſhall dye: euen from
the firſtborne off Pharao that ſitteth on his ſeate, vnto the
firſtborne of the maydeſervaunte that is in the mylle,
6 and all the firſtborne of the catell. And there ſhall be
a great crye thorow out all the lande off Egipte: ſo that
7 there was neuer none lyke nor ſhall be. And among

V. 28 caue ne vltra videas faciem meam. xi, 1 dimittet vos, et exire compellet. 2 vt poſtulet 3 vir magnus valde 4 egrediar 5 ancillæ . . ad molam

L. 28 hut dich, das du nicht mehr fur meyn augen komſt. xi, 1 laſſen von hynnen . . nicht alleyn alles laſſen . . von hynnen treyben 2 geſeſs foddere . 3 faſt eyn groſſer man 4 ausgehen ynn 5 magd die hynder der mul iſt

M. M. N. 5 *To ſyt,* is for to beare rule or to mynyſtre any maner of office, as in 1 Reg. ii, b.

all the childern of Iſrael ſhall not a dogg move his
tongue, nor yet man or beeſt: that ye may knowe,
how the Lorde putteth a difference betwene the Egip-
8 tiās and Iſrael. And all theſe thy ſervauntes ſhal
come downe vnto me, and fall before me ād ſaye
[Fo. XVIII.] get the out and all the people that are
vnder the, and than will I departe. And he went out
from Pharao in a great anger.
9 And the Lorde ſayde vnto Moſes: Pharao ſhall not
regarde you, that many wondres maye be wrought in
10 the lande of Egipte, And Moſes ād Arō dyd all
theſe wondres before Pharao. But the Lorde hardened
Pharaos herte, ſo that he wolde not let the childern
of Iſrael goo out of his londe.

The .XII. Chapter.

M.C.S. The paſſeouer is eaten. The ſwete brede. They muſt teache their chyldren what the paſſeouer ſignyfyeth. The deſtrucyō of the fyrſt begottē in Egypt. The robbery of the Egypcians. The goynge oute of the Iſraelytes.

1 AND the Lorde ſpake vnto Moſes
and Aaron in the londe of
2 Egipte ſaynge: This moneth
ſhall be youre chefe moneth:
euē the firſt moneth of the yere ſhal it be
3 vnto you Speake ye vnto all the felow-
ſhipe of Iſrael ſaynge: that they take the
x. daye of this moneth to euery houſ-
4 holde, a ſhepe. Yf the houſholde be to few for a ſhepe,
then lett him and his neghbour that is nexte vnto his
houſe, take acordinge to the

That I here cal a ſhepe is in Ebrue a vvorde indifferent to a ſhepe and a gotte both.

M. 8 And theſe thy ſeruaūtes xii, 2 euen of the fyrſt moneth

V. 7 non mutiet canis ab homine vſque ad pecus; . . quanto miraculo diuidat 10 ſigna et oſtenta quæ ſcripta ſunt. xii, 2 principium menſium . . cœtum 3 agnum 4 animarum quæ ſufficere poſſunt ad eſum agni

L. 7 hund mit ſeyner zungen lippern . . wie . . Æg. vnd Iſrael ſcheyde xii, 3 eyn ſchaff 4 vnd rechnets aus, was eyn iglicher eſſen muge

M. M. N. 8 A ſoudayne chaunge of ſpeakyng to dyuerſe perſonnes, as in the Pſal. xv, a. and thys is referred to the ende of the chapter that goeth before. xii, 3 That is here called a *ſhepe* is in Ebrew a worde indifferent to be takē ether for ſhepe or gote.

nombre of ſoulles, and counte vnto a ſhepe acordinge
5 to euery mans eatinge. A ſhepe with out ſpott and
a male of one yere olde ſhall it be, and from amonge
the lambes ād the gootes ſhall ye take it.
6 And ye ſhall kepe him in warde, vntyll
the .xiiii. daye of the ſame moneth. And
euery mā of the multitude of Iſrael ſhall
7 kyll him abou- .P. te euē. And they ſhall take of the
bloud ād ſtrike on the .ii. ſyde poſtes ād on the vpper
8 dorpoſt of the houſes, wher ī they eate hī. And thei
ſhall eate the fleſh the ſame nyght, roſt with fyre,
ād with vnleuēded bread, ād with ſowre
9 herbes they ſhall eate it. Se that ye eate not therof
ſodē in water, but roſt with fyre: both head fete, ād
10 purtenance together. And ſe that ye let nothinge
of it remayne vnto the mornynge: yf oughte remayne
burne it with fyre.
11 Off this maner ſhall ye eate it: with youre loines
girded, ād ſhoes on youre fete, ād youre ſtaves in
youre handes. And ye ſhall eate it in haſte, for it
12 is the Lordes *paſſeouer, for I will go
aboute ī the lāde of Egipte this ſame
nyghte, ād will ſmyte all the firſtborne
in the lande off Egipte: both of mā
ād beeſt, ād apō al the goddes off
Egipte will I the Lorde do execution.
13 And the bloude ſhall be vnto you a

in ward, *in ſeparate confinement*

ſowre, *bitter*

The lambe vvas called paſſeouer that the very name itſelf ſhuld put thē in remēbraunce vvhat it ſignified. for the ſignes that god ordined

M. 6 ſhall kepe hym in, vntyll 9 therof rawe ner ſoden in water, but roſt with fyre: both the head

V. 5 Iuxta quem ritum tolletis & hœdum 6 vniuerſa multitudo 8 aſſas agni, & azymos panes cum lactucis agreſtibus 9 crudum quid, nec coctum aqua, ſed aſſum tantum igni: caput cum pedibus eius & inteſtinis vorabitis. 11 eſt enim phaſe, id eſt tranſitus domini. 12 faciam iudicia, ego dominus.

L. 5 lemmern vnd zigen 8 mit bitter ſalzen 9 mit ſeynen ſchenckeln vnd eyngeweyde 12 gerichte vben

M. M. N. 12 The *lambe* was called the *paſſeouer:* that the very name it ſelfe ſhulde kepe in memorye what was ſignyfyed therby, which phraſe & maner of ſpeakynge the ſcripture vſeth often, callynge the ſigne by the name of the thynge that it ſygnyfieth, as Gen. xvi, b.

L. M. N. 6 Was das oſterlamb bedeut, leret gnugſam. S. Paulus. 1 Cor. 5. da er ſpricht, vnſer oſterlamb is Chriſtus der geopffert iſt.

tokē vppon the houſes where in ye are, for whē I ſee the bloude, I will paſſe ouer you, ād the plage ſhall not be vppō you to deſtroye you, when I ſmyte the londe off Egipte.

ether ſignified the benefites done, or promyſes to come ād vvere not dōme as are the ſignes of oure domme God the Pope.

14 And this daye ſhall be vnto you a remēbraunce, ād ye ſhall kepe it holie vnto
the Lorde: euen thorow out youre generacions after you
ſhall ye kepe it holie daye, that it be a cuſtome for euer
15 vii. dayes ſhal ye eate vnlevēded bre- [Fo. XIX.] ed, ſo
that euen the firſt daye ye ſhall put awaye leuen out off
youre houſſes. For whoſoeuer eateth leuended bread
from the firſt daye vntyll the .vii. daye, that ſoule ſhall be
16 plucked out frō Iſrael. The firſt daye ſhall be a holie
feaſt vnto you, and the .vii. alſo. There ſhal be no maner
off worke done in thē, ſaue aboute that only which euery
17 man muſt eate that only may ye do. And ſee that ye
kepe you to vnleuēded breed.

For vppō that ſame daye I will brynge youre armyes out off the londe of Egipte, therfore ye ſhall obſerue this daye and all youre childern after you, that yt be a cuſtume for euer.

18 The firſt moneth and the .xiiii. daye off the moneth at euen, ye ſhall eate ſwete brede vnto the .xxi. daye off the moneth at euen agayne.

19 Seuen dayes ſe that there be no leuended bred foūde
in youre houſſes. For whoſoeuer eateth leuended bred,
that ſoule ſhall be roted out frō the multi- roted, *rooted*
tude of Iſrael: whether he be a ſtraunger or borne in
20 the londe. Therfore ſe that ye eate no leuended bred,
but in all youre habitacions eate ſwete bred.

21 And Moſes called for the elders off Iſrael and ſayde vnto them: chouſe out and take to euery houſholde a

V. 14 in monimentum . . cultu ſempiterno. 16 ſancta atque ſolennis . . . . eadem feſtiuitate venerabilis: 17 exercitum veſtrum 19 de cœtu Iſrael 21 tollentes animal

L. 14 zum ewigen brauch 16 on was zur ſpeys gehoret fur allerley ſeelen 17 heer

M. M. N. 14 *Euer* is not here takē for a tyme without ende, but for a longe ceaſon whoſe end is not determyned, as in Gen. xiii, d. and Ex. xxviii, g.

22 shepe, ād kyll passeouer. And take a bunch of ysope,
ād dyppe it in the bloud .P. that is in the basyn, and
stryke it vppon the vpperposte and on the .ii. syde
postes, and se that none of you goo out at the doore
23 of his house vntyll the mornynge. For the Lorde will
goo aboute and smyte Egipte. And when he seyth
the bloude vppon the vpper doorposte ād on the .ii
syde postes, he will passe ouer the doore and will not
suffre the destroyer to come in to youre housse to plage
24 you. Therfore se that thou obserue this thinge, that
it be an ordinaunce to the, and thy sonnes for euer.
25 And when ye be come in to the land which the
Lorde will geue you acordinge as he hath promysed,
26 se that ye kepe this seruice.* And when
youre childern axe you what maner off
27 seruice is this ye doo. Ye shall saye, it is
the sacrifice of the Lordes passeouer which
passed ouer the housses of the childern of
Israel in Egipte, as he smote the Egiptians
and saued oure housses. Than the people
28 bowed them selues and worshipped. And
the childern of Israel went and dyd as
the Lorde had commaūded Moses and
Aaron.
29 And at mydnyghte the Lorde smote
all the firstborne in the lōde of Egipte:
from the first borne of Pharao that satt
on his seat, vnto the firstborne of the
captyue that was in presone, and all first-
30 borne of the catell. Than Pharao [Fo. XX.] arose
the same nyghte and al his servauntes ād all the
Egiptians, and there was a great crieng thorowe out
Egipte, for there was no housse where there was not
one dead.

Oure signes be dōme, vve knovv not the reason of oure baptim: ye and vve must saye oure prayers ād oure beleffe in a tōge vve vnderstonde not. And yet yf vve ansvvere not our prelates vvhen thei be angrie, euen as thei vvolde haue it, vve must to the fyre vvith out redemption, or forsvver god

V. 22 in limine . . . ostium domus 23 percussorem . . . lædere. 25 obseruabitis ceremonias istas 26 ista religio ?

L. 23 verderber . . . zu plagen 25 disen dienst 26 fur eyn dienst?

M. M. N. 23 To passe ouer is a maner of speache of the scrypture, & signyfieth no more, but that as he wolde plage the wycked, as he dyd here the Egypcyās, euē so he wold shew mercye to the faythfull, as he dyd to the Israelytes, as in Ex. xxxiii, d.

31 And he called vnto Moſes and Aaron by nyghte
ſaynge: Ryſe vp and gett you out from amonge my
people: both ye and alſo the children of Iſrael, and goo
32 and ſerue the Lorde as ye haue ſayde. And take
youre ſhepe and your oxen with you as ye haue ſayde,
33 ād departe ād bleſſe me alſo. And the Egiptians were
ferce vppon the people and made haſte to ſend thē out
of the lād: for they ſayde: we be al deed mē
34 And the people toke the dowe before it was ſowered which they had in ſtoare, and bounde it in clothes
35 ād put it vpō their ſhulders And the childern of Iſrael dyd acordinge to the ſaynge of Moſes: ād they
borowed of the Egiptians: iewels of ſyluer, and iewels
36 of gold, and rayment. And the Lorde gat the people
fauoure in the ſyghte of the Egiptians: ād ſo they bor-
37 owed and robbed the Egiptians.
Thus toke the childern of Iſrael their yourney frō Ra-
38 emſes to ſuchoth .vi. hundred thouſand mē of foote, beſyde
childern. And moch comon people went alſo with thē,
39 ād ſhepe ād oxen ād catell exceadinge moch. And they
baked ſwete cakes of the dowe which they brou- .¶.
ghte out of Egipte, for it was not ſowered: becauſe they
were thruſt out of Egipte and coude not tarie, nether
had they prepared them any other prouiſion of meate.
40 And the tyme of the dwellinge of the childern of
Iſrael which they dwelled in Egipte, was .iiii. hundred
41 and .xxx. yere. And whē the .iiii. hundred and .xxx
yeres were expyred, euē the ſelfe ſame daye departed
all the hoſtes of the Lorde out of the lande of Egipte.
42 This is a nyghte to be obſerued to the Lorde, becauſe
he broughte them out of the lande of Egipte. This is
a nyghte of the Lorde, to be kepte of all the childern
of Iſrael and of their generacions after them.
43 And the Lorde ſayde vnto Moſes ād Aaron, this is

M. 37 Suchoth, margin: otherwyſe Socoth

V. 31 immolate domino 32 vt petieratis 35 veſtemque plurimam 36 vt commodarent eis: & ſpoliauerunt 37 ſexcenta fere millia peditum virorum 39 dudum de Æg., conſperſam . . & nullam facere ſinentibus moram

L. 32 wie yhr geſagt habt (*bis*) 33 verſturtzt auff das volck 34 zu yhrer ſpeyſe 36 leyheten, vnd entwandtens 39 ſonſt keyne zehrung zubereyt.

the maner of Paſſeover: there ſhall no ſtraunger eate
44 there of, but all the ſeruauntes that are bought for
money ſhall ye circumciſe, and then let them eat
45 there of. A ſtraũger and a hyerd ſeruaunte ſhall not
46 eate thereof. In one houſſe ſhall it be eatē. Ye ſhall
carie none of the fleſh out at the doores: moreouer, ſe
47 that ye breke not a bone there of. All the multitude
48 of the childern of Iſrael ſhall obſerue it

Yf a ſtraunger dwell amonge you ād wyll holde Paſſeover vnto the Lorde, let him circũciſe all that be males, ād
thē let him come and [Fo. XXI.] obſerue it ād be takē as one
that is borne ĩ the lōde. No vncircũciſed perſone ſhall
49 eate there of. One maner of lawe ſhalbe vnto thē that
are borne in the lōde, ād vnto the ſtraũgers that dwell
50 amōge you. And all the childern of Iſrael dyd as the
51 Lorde cōmaũded Moſes ād Aarō. And euē the ſelfe
ſame daye dyd the Lorde brynge the childern of Iſrael
out of the londe of Egipte with their armies.

The .XIII. Chapter.

1 AND the Lorde ſpake vnto Moſes
2 ſaynge: ſanctifie vnto me all the
firſtborne that opē all maner
matrices amōge the childern
of Iſrael, as well of mē as of beeſtes: for

M.C.S. *The fyrſt begotten muſt be ſanctyfyed vnto the Lorde. The memoryall of their delyuer-*

V. 43 religio phaſe 47 cœtus 48 in veſtram voluerit tranſire coloniam 49 colono 51 per turmas ſuas. xiii, 2 Sanctifica . . . mea ſunt enim omnia

L. 43 die weyſe 45 mietling 48 der beſchneytte 51 mit yhrem heer.

M. M. N. 49 Thoſe that were borne in the lande, are only thoſe that were borne amonge thē: not deſcendynge of the ſtocke or lynage of Iſrael. And the ſtraungers were thoſe that dwelt amōge the Iſraelites, and were not borne among thē, as aboue in this ſame chapter at the letter .d. [i. e. v. 15 ſq.] xiii, 2. Sanctifyĩg loke Gene ii, a.

L. M. N. 43 *Paſſah*, heyſt eyn gang, darumb das der herr ynn Egyptēland des nachts gieng, vnd ſchlug alle erſtegepurt todt, bedeut aber Chriſtus ſterbē vn aufferſtehen, damit er von diſer wellt gangen iſt, vnnd ynn dem ſelben ſund, tod, vnd teuffel geſchlagen vnd vns aus dem rechten Egypten gefurt hat zum vater, das iſt vnſer Paſſah oder oſtern

3 they are myne. And Moſes ſayde vnto
the people: thīke on thys daye ī which ye
came out of Egipte and out of the houſſe
of bondage: for with a myghtie hāde the
Lorde broughte you out frō thēce. Se
therfore that ye eate no leuended bred.
4 This daye come ye out of Egipte in the
moneth of Abib.

aunce. Why they were caryed thorow the wyldernes. The bones of Ioſeph. The pyler of the clowde.

5 whē the Lorde hath broughte the ī to the lōde of
the Canaanites, Hethites, Amorites, Heuites ād Iebuſites, which he ſware vnto thi fathers that he wolde
geue the: a londe where in milke ād honye floweth,
thē ſe that thou kepe this ſervyce in this ſame moneth.
6 Seuē dayes thou ſhalte eate ſwete bred, ād the .vii
7 daye ſhal be feaſtfull vnto the Lorde. Therfore thou
.P. ſhalt eate ſwete bred .vii. dayes, and ſe that there
be no leuended bred ſene nor yet leuē amonge you in
all youre quarters.

8 And thou ſhalt ſhewe thy ſonne at
that tyme ſaynge: this is done, becauſe
of that which the Lorde dyd vnto me
9 when I came out of Egipte. Therfore
it ſhall be a ſigne vnto the vppon thine
hande and a remembraunce betwene thine
eyes, that the Lordes lawe maye be in thy
mouth. For with a ſtronge hāde the Lorde
10 broughte the out of Egipte, ſe thou kepe
therfore this ordinaūce in his ſeaſon from yere to yere.

The fathers novv a dayes maye not be ſofred to knovv ought of God them ſelves, hovv can they then teach their childern vvhat the ceremonie meaneth.

M. 9 hande a remembraūce

V. 4 menſe nouarum ſrugum . 5 hunc morem ſacrorum 7 in cunctis finibus tuis. 9 monimentum ante oculos . . ſemper ſit in ore 10 ſtatuto tempore a diebus in dies.

V. 7 an allen deynen ortten 8 ſon ſagen 9 fur deynen augen.

M. M. N. 4 *Abib:* That is the moneth of Apryll. 9 *With a ſtronge hande:* Looke Pſal. cxxxv, b.

L. M. N. 4 *Abib.* Abib iſt der mond den wyr April heyſſen, denn die Ebreer heben yhr new iar an nach der natur wenn alle ding widder new grunet and wechſet vnd ſich zichtiget, darumb heyſſt er auch Menſis nouorum, das denn alles new wirt. 6 *Ungeſewrt brod.* So hart wyrt der ſawerteyg verpoten, das man ia dz lautter Euangelion vnd Gottis gnade, nicht vnſer werck vnd geſetz ſoll predigen nach der aufferſtehung Chriſti, wie Paulus 1 Cor. v. auch zeygt, vnd iſt ſolch eſſen nichts anders denn glawben ynn Chriſto.

11 Moreouer when the Lorde hath broughte the in to
the londe of the Canaanytes, as he hath ſworne vnto
12 the and to thi fathers, and hath geuen it the, thē thou
ſhalt appoynte vnto the Lorde all that appoynte, *aſ-*
openeth the matrice, and all the firſt- *ſygn, ſeparate*
borne among the beeſtes which thou haſt yf they be
13 males. And all the firſtborne of the aſſes, thou ſhalt
redeme with a ſhepe: yf thou redeme him not, then
breake hys necke. But all the firſtborne amonge thi
childern ſhalt thou bye out.
14 And when thi ſonne axeth the in tyme to come
ſaynge: what is this? thou ſhalt ſaye vnto *Teach youre*
him: with a mightie hande the Lorde *chyldern.*
broughte us out of Egipte, out of the houſſe of bon-
15 [Fo. XXII.] dage. And when Pharao was looth to
lete us goo, the Lorde ſlewe all the firſtborne in the
lande of Egipte: as well the firſtborne of men as of
beaſtes. And therfore I ſacrifice vnto the Lorde all
the males that open the matrice, but all the firſtborne
16 of my childern I muſt redeme. And this ſhall be as a
token in thine hande, and as a thinge hanged vpp betwene thine eyes: becauſe the Lorde broughte vs out
of Egipte with a mightie hande.
17 when Pharao had let the people goo, God caried
them not thorow the londe of the Philiſtines, though
it were a nye waye. For God ſayde: the people
myghte happly repent when they ſe warre, and ſo
18 turne agayne to Egipte: therfore God led thē aboute
thorow the wyldernеſſe that bordreth on the redd ſee.
The childern of Iſrael went harneſſed out harneſſed,
19 of the lāde of Egipte. And Moſes toke *armed*

M. 12 matryce, all

V. 12 ſeparabis . . conſecrabis domino 13 mutabis oue . . . interficies . 14 filius tuus cras 16 appenſum quid, ob recordationem, ante oculos 17 quæ vicina eſt 18 & armati aſcenderunt

L. 13 loſen mit eynem ſchaff . . . brich yhm das genick 16 fur deynen augen 17 die am nehiſten war 18 vmb, auff die ſtraſſe 18 gewapnet

L. M. V. 18 *Schilffmeer.* Die kriechen heyſſen es, dz rote meer vō dem roten ſand vnd boden, aber die Ebreer heyſens ſchilffmeer von dem ſchilff, vnd bedeut die welt mit yhrem pracht, dadurch die heyligen mit viel leyden gehen muſſen.

the bones of Ioſeph with him: for he made the childern
of Iſrael ſwere ſaynge: God will ſurely vyſet you, take
my bones therfore away hence with you,
20 And they toke their iorney from Suchoth: and
pitched their tentes in Etham in the edge of the wyl-
21 derneſſe. And the Lorde went before them by daye
in a piler of a cloude to lede them the waye: and by
nyghte in a piler of fyre to geue thē lighte: that they
22 myghte goo both .N. by day ād nyghte. And the
piler of the cloude neuer departed by daye nor the
piler of fyre by nyghte out of the peoples ſighte.

The .XIIII. Chapter.

1 THAN the Lorde ſpake vnto
2 Moſes ſaynge: byd the childern of Iſrael that they turne
and pytch their tentes before
the entrynge of Hiroth betwene Migdole
and the ſe toward Baal zephon: euen before that ſhall ye pytch apon the ſee.
3 For Pharao will ſaye of the childern of
Iſrael: they are tāgled in the lōd the
4 wilderneſſe hath ſhott thē in. And I
will hardē his harte, that he ſhall folowe after thē,
that I maye gett me honoure vppō Pharao ād vppō all
his hoſte, that the Egiptians maye knowe that I am
the Lorde. And they dyd euen ſo.
5 And whē it was tolde the kynge of Egipte that the
people fled, thā Pharaos harte and all his ſeruaūtes
turned vnto the people ād ſayde why haue we this
done, that we haue let Iſrael go out of oure ſeruyce?

M.C.S. *Pharaos heart is hardened & foloweth the Iſraelites with all his hooſt & capitaynes and is drowned. The Iſraelites grudge. They go thorow the red ſee.*

V. 20 in extremis finibus ſolitudinis. 21 ignis: vt dux eſſet itineris vtroque tempore. xiiii, 2 eregione Phi-hahiroth . . Magdalum . . mare contra Beel-ſephon 3 Coartati 5 immutatumque . . ſuper populum.

L. 20 forn an der wuſten 22 die wolckſeule vnd fewrſ. weych nymer von dem volck. xiiii, 2 gegen dem tall Hiroth 3 wiſſen nicht wo aus 5 verwandelt . . . gegen

6 and he made redie his charettes ād toke his people
7 with hym ād toke .vi. hūdred chosen charettes ād all
the charettes of Egipte ād captaynes vppō all his
8 people. For the Lorde hardened the harte of Pharao
kynge of Egipte, that he folowed after the childern of
Israel which for all that went out thorow an hye hāde,
9 And the Egiptiās folo- [*Fo. XXV.]
wed after thē ād ouertoke thē where they
pitched by the see, with all the horsses ād
charrettes of Pharao ād with his horsse-
mē ād his hoste: euē fast by the entrynge
10 of Hiroth before Baal Zephon. And
Pharao drewe nye, ād whē the childern
of Israel lyft vp their eyes and sawe how the Egiptiās
folowed after thē, they were sore a fraide ād cried out
vnto the Lorde

** Folios XXIII, XXIIII are wanting in the original; a typographical error without a break in the text.*

11 Thā sayde they vnto Moses? were there no graues for
us in Egipte, but thou must bringe us awaye *
for to dye in the wyldernesse? wherfore hast thou serued
12 us thus, for to carie us out of Egipte? Dyd we not tell
the this in Egipte sayinge, let us be in rest and serue
the Egiptians? For it had bene better for us to haue
serued the Egiptians, than for to dye in the wildernesse.
13 And Moses sayde vnto the people: feare ye not but
stonde still and beholde how the Lorde shall saue you
this daye: For as ye se the Egiptians this daye, shall ye
14 see them nomore for euer till the worldes ende. The
Lorde shall fighte for you and ye shall holde youre peace.
15 The Lorde sayde vnto Moses: wherfore criest thou

F. 6 Iunxit ergo currum 7 duces totius exercitus. 9 vestigia præcedentium 13 Nolite timere: state & videte magnalia domini 14 & vos tacebitis. 15 vt proficiscantur.

L. 6 spannet . . . an 8 die doch durch eyn hohe hand 14 yhr werdet styll schweygen.

M. N. 9 *An hye hande:* Loke in Psalme. cxxxv, b. 14 *Ye shall holde youre peace:* that is, ye shall be in rest and quyetnes. 15 *To crye vnto the Lorde,* is to praye vnto him wyth full harte & feruēt desyer, as Moses here dyd, & yet spake neuer a worde. And so doth this word cryenge & makynge of noyes sygnifye thorow oute all the Psalmes, as in Psal. v, a. & ix, b &c.

L. M. N. 15 *Was schreyestu:* merck hie eyn treflich exempel, wie der glawbe, kempst zappelt vnd schreyet ynn notten vnd ferlickeyt, vnd wie er sich an Gottis word blos hellt, vnd von Gott trost empfehet vnd vberwindt.

vnto me ? ſpeake vnto the childern of Iſrael that they
16 goo forwarde. But lifte thou vp thi rodd and ſtretch
out thi hande ouer the ſee and deuyde it a ſondre, that
.P. the childern of Iſrael may goo on drye groũde
17 thorow the myddeſt thereof. And beholde I will
harden the hertes of the Egiptians that they maye
folowe you. And I will gett me honoure vpon Pharao
and vpon all his hoſte, vpon his charettes ād vpon his
18 horſe mē. And the Egiptians ſhall knowe that I am
the Lord whan I haue gotten me honoure vpō Pharao
vpon his charettes and vpon his horſemen.
19 And the angell of God which went before the hoſte
of Iſrael, remoued ād went behinde them. And the
cloudēpiler that was before them remoued ād ſtode
20 behinde them ād wēt betwene the hoſte of the Egiptians ād the hoſte of Iſrael. Yt was a darke clowde,
and gaue lighte by nyghte: ſo that all the nyghte long
the one coude not come at the other.
21 when now Moſes ſtretched forth his honde ouer the
ſee, the Lorde caried awaye the ſee with a ſtronge eaſt
wynde that blewe all nyghte, and made the ſee drie
22 londe ād the water deuyded it ſilfe. And the childern
of Iſrael went in thorow the myddeſt of the ſee vppon
the drie grounde. And the water was a walle vnto
them, both on their right hande ād on their lefte hande.
23 And the Egiptians folowed ād went in after them to
the myddeſt of the ſee, with all Pharaos horſes, and
his charettes and [Fo. XXVI.] his horſſemen.
24 And in the mornynge watch, the Lorde loked vnto
the hoſte of the Egiptiās out of the fyery and clowdie
25 piler, and troubled their hoſte and ſmote of their charett wheles and caſt them doune to the grounde. Than
ſayde the Egiptians: Let vs ſle from Iſrael, for the
26 Lorde fyghteth for them agaynſt vs. Than ſayde the
Lorde vnto Moſes: ſtretch out thine hand ouer the ſee,
that the water maye come agayne vppō the Egiptians

V. 20 ad ſeinuicem . . . accedere non valerent. 21 flante vento vehementi & vrente 24 interfecit exercitum eorum 25 fereban-turque in profundum.

L. 24 ſchuttert jr getzellte 25 ſturtzet ſie mit vngeſtüm

27 vppon their charettes ād horſemen. Than ſtretched
forth Moſes his hande ouer the ſee, and it came agayne
to his courſe erly ī the mornīg, ād the Egiptiās fledd
agaynſt it. Thus the Lorde ouerthrewe the Egiptians
28 in the middeſt of the ſee, ād the water returned and
couered the charettes and the horſemē: ſo that of all
the hoſte of Pharao that came in to the ſee after them,
there remayned not one.

29 But the children of Iſrael went vpon drie lōde in the
myddeſt of the ſee, ād the water was a walle vnto them:
both on the righte hand of them and alſo on the liſte.

30 Thus the Lorde delyuered Iſrael the ſelfe ſame daye
out of the honde of the Egiptians, and Iſraell ſawe the
31 Egiptians deade vpō the ſee ſyde. And when Iſrael
ſawe that myghtye .P. hande which the Lorde had
ſhewed vppō the Egiptians, they feared the Lorde:
and beleued both the Lorde and alſo his ſervaunte
Moſes

❡ The .XV. Chapter.

M.C.S. Moſes and the people wyth the wemen ſynge. At the prayer of Moſes, the bytter waters were ſwete. God muſt be hearCed. They come to Elim.

1 THEN Moſes and the childern off Iſrael ſange this ſonge vnto the Lorde ād ſaide

Let vs ſynge vnto the Lorde, for he is become glorious, the horſe and him that rode vpon him hath he ouerthrowne in the ſee.

2 The Lorde is my ſtrength ād my ſonge,
ād is become my ſaluation.

He is my God and I will glorifie him, he is my fathers God and I will lifte him vp an hie

3 The Lorde is a mā off warre, Iehouah ys his name:
4 Pharaos charettes ād his hoſte hath he caſt in to the ſee.

V. 1 glorioſe enim magnificatus 3 quaſi vir pugnator
L. 30 Egypter hand, vnd ſie ſahen 31 das volck forchtet xv, 3 rechts kriegsman

His iolye captaynes are drowned in the iolye, *ſpir-*
5 red ſee, the depe waters haue couered *ited, brave*
them: thei ſoncke to the botome as a ſtone.
6 Thine hande Lorde is glorious in power, thine hād
Lord hath all to daſhed the enemye. to daſhed,
7 And with thy great glorie thou haſt *thruſt through*
deſtroyed thine aduerſaries, thou ſenteſt forth thy
wrath ād it conſumed them: euē as ſtobell.
8 with the breth off thine anger the water gathered
together and the flodes ſtode ſtyll as a rocke ād the
depe water congeled together in the myddeſt off the
ſee.
9 [Fo. XXVII.] The enymye ſayde, I will folowe and
ouertake thē ād will deuyde the ſpoyle: I will ſatyſfie
my luſt apon thē: I will drawe my ſwerde and myne
hand ſhall deſtroye them.
10 Thou blueſt with thy breth ād the ſee couered thē,
11 and they ſanke as leed in the myghtye waters. ¶ who
is like vnto the o Lord amōge goddes: who is like
the ſo glorious in holynes, feerfull, laudable ād that
ſheweſt wondres?
12 Thou ſtretchedeſt out thy righte hande. ād the erth
ſwalowed them.
13 And thou cariedeſt with thy mercie this people
which thou deliueredeſt, ād broughteſt thē with thy
ſtrength vnto thy holie habitacion.
14 The nations herde ād were afrayde, pāges came
vpon the Philiſtines.
15 Thā the dukes of the Edomites were amaſed,
ād trēblinge came apon the myghtieſt off the Moabites, and all the inhabiters of Canaā waxed faynte
harted.

V. 4 electi principes 6 magnificata eſt in fortitudine: dextera tua . . percuſſit 7 depoſuiſti 8 ſpiritu furoris tui . . ſtetit vnda fluens 9 euaginabo gladium 10 Flauit ſpiritus tuus . . aquis vehementibus. 11 ſimilis tui in fortibus . . terribilis atque laudabilis, faciens mirabilia? 13 Dux fuiſti in miſer. 14 Aſcenderunt populi (Heb. audierunt) 15 conturbati ſunt principes Edom . . obriguerunt

L. 4 auſerwelten hawbtleut 7 deine widderwertigen zuſtoſſen 8 geyſt deyns zorns . . . tieffe plumpten ynn eynander 9 mut an yhn kulen. 11 loblich vnd wunderthettig? 13 geleyttet . . heyligen hauſe. 15 Canaan . . feyg.

16 Let feare and dreade fall apon thē thorow the greatnesse off thyne arme, and let them be as styll as a stone,
while thy people passe thorow o Lorde while the people passe thorowe, which thou hast goten. goten, *ac-*
17 Brynge them in and plante them in *quired*
the mountayns of thine enherytaũce, the place Lorde
whyche thou hast made for the to dweld in .𝔓. the
sanctuarye Lorde which thy handes haue prepared.
18 The Lorde raygne euer and allwaye.
19 For Pharao wēt in an horsebacke wyth his charettes
and horsemen in to the see, and the Lorde broughte
the waters of the see apō thē. And the childern of
Israel went on drie lande thorow the myddest of the see.
20 And mir Iam a prophetisse the sister of Aaron toke
a tymbrell in hir hande, and all the wemen came out
21 after her with tymbrells in a daunse. And mir Iam
sange before them: syng ye vnto the Lorde, for he is
become glorious in deade: the horse and his ryder hath
he ouerthrowne in the see.
22 Moses broughte Israel from the redd see, ād they
went out in to the wildernesse of Sur.
And they went thre dayes longe in the wildernesse
23 ād coude finde no water. At the last they came to Mara:
but they coude not drynke off the waters for bitternesse,
for they were better. therfore the name of the place
24 was called Mara. Then the people mur- ⁂
mured agaynst Moses saynge: what shall we drinke?
25 And Moses cried vnto the Lorde and he shewed him a
tre· and he cast it in to the water, and they waxed swete.

𝔐. 17 made for to dwell in, 25 waters

𝔙. 16 formido et pauor . . donec pertranseat 17 plantabis . . sanctuarium tuum . . firmauerunt 18 in æternum & vltra. 20 Maria prophetissa . . tympanis & choris 23 vnde & congruum loco nomen imposuit, vocans illum Mara, id est amaritudinem.

𝔏. 16 erstarren wie die steyne . . erworben hast. 17 hand bereyt hat. 20 Mir Iam 23 Mararath . . fast bitter

𝔐. 𝔐. 𝔑. 16 *Greatnesse of thyne arme:* Loke in Iob xl, a. 18 *To raygne euer & all waye* is a maner of speaking of the ebrews, which signifieth without ende: because that euer is taken for a lōg tyme whose ende is not apoynted, & not for all waye, as in Exod. xii, c.

𝔏. 𝔐. 𝔑. 23 *Mara* heyst bitter Und bedeut leyden vnd anfechtunge, wilche durch das creutz, Christi, ym glauben auch susse werden. Math. xi. Meyn ioch ist suss.

There he made them an ordinaunce and a [Fo.
XXVIII.] lawe, and there he tempted them and ſaide:
26 Yf ye will herken vnto the voyce of the Lord youre God,
and will do that which is righte in his
ſyght and will geue an eare vnto his
cōmaūdmentes, and kepe all his ordinaunces: thā will I put none of this diſeaſes apon the whiche I brought vpon the
Egiptiās: for I am the Lorde
thy ſurgione.

Vve muſt do that vvhich is right in gods ſight ād as his vvorde teacheth vs and not aftir our avvne imaginacion,

ſurgione, *phyſician, healer*

ℭ The .XVI. Chapter.

27 AND they came to Elim where
were .xii. welles of water
and .Lxx. date trees, and they
pitched there by the water.
XVI,1 And they toke their yourney frō Elim,
and all the hole cōpanye of the childern
of Iſraell came to the wilderneſſe of Sin, which lieth
betwene Elim ād Sinai: the .xv. daye of the ſeconde
moneth after that they were come out of the lande of
2 Egipte. And the hole multitude of the ⁂
childern of Iſrael murmured agaynſt Moſes ād Aarō in
3 the wilderneſſe and ſayde vnto them: wold to God we
had dyed by the hande of the Lorde in the lande of
Egipte, when we ſatt by the fleſſh pottes and ate bred
oure belies full for ye haue broughte vs out in to this
wilderneſſe to kyll this hole multitude for honger.
4 Than ſayde the Lorde vnto Moſes: beholde, I will
rayne bred frō heauē doune to you, ād let the people

M.C.S. *The Iſraelites come into the deſert of Sin. It rayneth quaylles & Manna. They grudge.*

M. 26 of theſe diſeaſes
V. 26 cunctum langorem . . ſanator tuus. xvi, 3 Vtinam mortui eſſemus . . ollas carnium . . panem in ſaturitate . . occider. omnem multitudinem fame?
L. 26 kranckeyt keyne . . artzt. xvi, 3 Wollt Gott . . bey den fleyſch topffen . . die gantze gemeyne
M. M. N. 26 We muſt *do that whych is right* in gods ſyght & as hys worde teacheth vs, & not after our awne ymagynacyon.

goo out ād gather daye by da- .P. ye, that I maye
proue thē whether they wil walke in my lawe or no.
5 The .vi. daye let thē prepare that which they will
brīge in, ād let it be twiſe as moch as they gather in
6 dayly. And Moſes ād Aarō ſayde vnto all the childerē of Iſrael: at euen ye ſhall knowe that it is the
Lorde, which broughte you out of the lāde of Egipte
7 ād in the mornynge ye ſhall ſe the glorie of the Lorde:
becauſe he hath herde youre grudgynges agaynſt the
Lorde: for what are we that ye ſhuld murmure againſt
8 vs. And moreouer ſpake Moſes. At euē the Lorde
will geue you fleſh to eate ād in the mornynge bred
ynough, becauſe the Lord hath herde youre murmur
whiche ye murmur agaynſt hī: for what ar we? youre
murmurynge is not agaynſt vs, but agaynſt the Lorde.
9 And Moſes ſpake vnto Aarō: Say vnto all the cōpanye of the childerē of Iſrael, come forth before the
10 Lorde, for he hath herde youre grudgīges. And as
Aarō ſpake vnto the hole multitude of the childerē
of Iſrael, they loked toward the wilderneſſe: ād beholde, the glorie of the Lord apeared ī a clowde.
11, 12 And the Lorde ſpake vnto Moſes ſayng: I haue
herde the murmurīg of the childrē of Iſrael, tell thē
therfore ād ſaye that at euē they ſhall eate fleſh, ād
ī the morninge they ſhall be filled with bred, ād [Fo.
XXIX.] ye ſhall knowe that I am the Lorde youre
god
13 And at euē the quayles came ād couered the groūde
where they laye. And in the mornynge the dewe laye
14 rounde aboute the hoſte. And whē the dewe was fallē:
behold, it laye apō the grounde in the wilderneſſe,
ſmall ād roūde ād thyn as the hore froſt on the groūde.
15 when the childrē of Iſrael ſawe it, they ſayde one to

M. 6 at euen ye ſhall

T. 5 parent 8 panes in ſaturitate 14 minutum, & quaſi pilo tuſum

L. 5 bereytten 12 zwiſchen dem abent 13 bedeckten die getzellte

M. M. N. 7 *The glory of the Lorde* is here taken for the bryghtnes and lyght that was ſene in the clowde. Of whiche glorye the Apoſtle maketh mencyon 2 Cor. iii, c. d.

another: what is this? for they wist not what it was
And Moses sayde: this is the breed which the Lorde
16 hath geuē you to eate. This is the thinge which the
Lorde hath cōmaūded, that ye gather euery mā ynough
for hī to eate: a gomer full for a mā acordīge to the
nōbre off you, ād gather euery mā for thē which are in
his tente.
17 And the childern of Israel dyd euen so, ād gathered
18 some more some lesse, and dyd mete it with a gomer.
And vnto him that had gathered moch remayned
nothinge ouer, ād vnto hī that had gathered litle was
there no lacke: but euery mā had gathered sufficiēt for
19 his eatinge. And Moses sayde vnto them. Se that
no mā let oughte remayne of it tyll the morninge.
20 Notwithstondinge they harkened not vnto Moses: but
some of thē lefte of it vntyll the mornynge, and it
waxte full of wormes ād stāke and Moses was angrie
wyth them.
21 And they gathered it all mornīges: Euery mā .P.
as moch as suffised for his eatinge, for as sone as the
22 hete of the sonne came it moulte. And moulte, *melted*
the .vi. daye they gathered twise so moch bred: .ii
gomers for one mā, ād the ruelars of the multitude
23 came ād tolde Moses. And he sayde unto thē, this is
that which the Lorde hath sayde tomorow is the Sabbath of the holie rest of the Lord: bake that which ye
will bake ād seth that ye will seth, ād that which
remayneth lay vp for you ād kepe it till the mornynge.
24 And they layde it vp till the mornynge as Moses bad
ād it stāke not nether was there any wormes therī.
25 And Moses sayde: that eate this daye: for todaye it
is the Lordes Sabbath: to daye ye shal finde none in

V. 15 ad inuicem, Man hu? quod significat, Quid est hoc? 18 habuit amplius . . . reperit minus 21 incaluisset sol, liquefiebat. 23 requies sabbathi sanctificata

L. 16 zall der seelen ynn seyner hutten. 18 vbrigs . . feyls 23 der Sabbath der heyligen ruge des Herrn

L. M. N. 15 *Man* heyst auff Ebreisch eyn gabe odder teyl, bedeut das vns das Euangelion on vnser verdienst vnd gedancken, aus lautter gnaden von hymel geben wirt, wie dis Man auch geben wart.

26 the feld, Sixte dayes ye ſhal gather it, for the .vii. is
the ſabbath: there ſhal be none there in.
27 Notwithſtondinge there went out of the people in
the ſeuenth daye for to gather: but they founde none.
28 Thē the Lorde ſeyde vnto Moſes: how longe ſhall it
be, yer ye will kepe my cōmaundmētes ād lawes?
29 Se becauſe the Lorde hath geuē you a Sabbath, therfor he geueth you the .vi. daye bred for .ii. dayes.
Byde therfore euery mā athome, ād let no mā go out
30 of his place the ſeuenth daye. And the people reſted
31 the ſeuenth daye. And the houſſe of Iſrael called it
Man, And it was lyke vnto Coriander [Fo. XXX.] ſeed
and white, and the taſte of it was lyke vnto wafers
made with honye.

32 And Moſes ſayde: this is that which the Lord
commaundeth: fyll a Gomor of it, that it
maye be kepte for youre childern after
you: that they maye ſe the bred wherewith he fedd you in wylderneſſe, when he had
33 broughte you out of the lande of Egipte. And Moſes
ſpake vnto Aaron: take a cruſe and put a Gomer full
of man therin, and laye it vppe before the Lorde to be
34 kepte for youre childern after you as the Lorde commaunded Moſes. And Aaron layed it vppe before the
teſtimonye there to be kepte.

Reliques ought to be but a remembraunce only.

35 And the childern of Iſrael ate man .xl. yere vntill
they came vnto a lande inhabited. And ſo they ate
Man, euen vntill they came vnto the bordres of the
36 lādc of Canaan, And a Gomer is the tenth parte of
an Epha.

M. 26 Sixe dayes
V. 28 Vſquequo non vultis 31 ſimilæ cū melle. 34 in tabern. reſeruandum. 35 in terram habitabilem
L. 31 ſemlen mit honig. 33 kruglin 34 fur dem zeugnis zu behalten.

The .XVII. Chapter.

1 AND all the companye of the children of Iſrael went on their iourneys from the wilderneſſe of Sin at the commaundment of the Lorde, and pitched in Raphidim: where was no water for
2 the people to drynke. And the people * chode with Moſes and ſayde: geue us water to drynke. And Moſes ſayde vnto them: why chyde ye with me, * and wherfore do .P. ye tempte the Lorde?

M.C.S. The Iſraelites come into Raphidim. They grudge. Water is geuē them out of the rocke. Moſes holdeth vp his handes & they ouercome the Amelechytes.

3 There the people thyrſted for water, and murmured
agenſt Moſes ād ſayde: wherfore haſt thou broughte
us out of Egipte, to kyll us and oure childern and
oure catell with thyrſte?
4 And Moſes cried vnto the Lorde ſaynge what ſhal
I do vnto this people? they be al moſt redye to ſtone
5 me. And the Lorde ſayde vnto Moſes: goo before the
people, and take with the of the elders of Iſrael: ād
thi rod wherwith thou ſmoteſt the riuer, take in thine
6 hande and goo. Beholde, I will ſtonde there before
the vppon a rocke in Horeb: and thou ſhalt ſmyte the
rocke, ād there ſhall come water out there of, that
the people maye drynke. And Moſes dyd euen ſo
7 before the elders of Iſrael And he called the name
of the place: Maſſa and Meriba: becauſe of the chid-
ynge of the childern of Iſrael, and becauſe they tempted
the Lorde ſaynge: ys the Lorde amonge us or not?
8 Then came Amalech ād foughte with Iſrael in Ra-

M. 4 all moſt redye

V. 1 per manſiones ſuas 2 iurgatus . . iurgamini 3 præ aquæ penuria: & murmurauit 6 coram te, ibi 7 Tentatio, propter iurgium (Hebr. & iurgium)

L. 1 tage reyſze 2 zanckten 3 murreten 6 daſelbs ſtehen 7 Da hies man den ort, Maſſa Meriba

M. M. N. 2 *To tempte the Lorde:* is to prouoke the Lorde to be angry with them as Sapiē. 1, a.

L. M. N. 7 *Maſſa* heyſt verſuchung. *Meriba* heyſt zanck.

9 phidim. And Moses sayde vnto Iosua: chose out men
and goo fighte with Amelech Tomorow I will stonde
on the toppe of the hyll and the rodd of God in myne
10 hande. And Iosua dyd as Moses bade him, and foughte
with the Amalechites. And Moses, Aa- [Fo. XXXI.]
11 ron and Hur went vp to the toppe of the hyll. And
when Moses helde vp his hande, Israel had the better.
And when he late his hande doune, Amelech had the
better.
12 when Moses handes were weery, they toke a stone
and put it vnder him, and he satt doune there on. And
Aaron and Hur stayed vpp his handes the one on the
one syde and the other on the other syde. And his
13 handes were stedie vntill the sonne was doune. And
Iosua discomfeted Amalech ād his people with the edge
of his swerde.
14 And the Lorde sayde vnto Moses: write this for a remembraunce in a boke and tell it vnto Iosua, for I will
put out the remembraunce of Amalech from vnder hea-
15 uen. And Moses made an alter ād called the name of it
16 *Iehouah Nissi, for he sayde: the hande is
on the seate of the Lorde, that the Lorde
will haue warre with Amalech thorow out
all generations.

Iehouah nissi the Lorde is he that exalteth me.

T. 11 vincebat Israel: sin autem paululum remisisset, superabat Amal. 12 ex vtraque parte . . non lassarentur 13 Fugauitque 14 trade auribus 15 Dominus exaltatio mea 16 manus solii domini & bellum domini erit

L. 11 lag . . oben 12 schweer . . auff iglicher seytten eyner . . hend gewiss 14 ynn die oren 16 durch eyn hand vnter Gottis schutz

M. M. N. 15 *Iehouah Nissi:* that is, the Lord is he that exalteth.

L. M. N. 12 *Gewiss*, das ist trew, das sie nicht feyleten noch abliesen wie eyn trewloser ablessit, bedeut aber, wie die werck des gesetzs vntreglich vnd vntuchtig sind, wo sie nicht durch Christum ym glawben vnterhalten werden. 16 *Nissi*, heyst, mein zeychen, wie eyn panier, wappen odder fenlin ym streyt ist, bedeut das Euangelion das auff geworffen wirt zum streyt zeichen, widder sund, fleysch, tod vnd teuffel.

The .XVIII. Chapter.

M.C.S. Iethros councell is receaued of Moses.

1 IETHRO the preſt of Madian
Moſes father in lawe herde
of all that God had done vn-
to Moſes and to Iſrael his people, how that
2 the Lorde had broughte Iſrael out of Egipte. And he
toke Ziphora Moſes wyfe, P. after ſhe was ſente backe,
3 and hir .ii. ſonnes, of which the one was called Gerſon,
for he ſayde: I haue bene an alient in a ſtraunge lande.
4 And the other was called Elieſar: for the God of my
father was myne helpe ād delyuered me from the ſwerde
of Pharao.
5 And Iethro Moſes father in lawe came wyth his two
ſonnes and his wife vnto Moſes in to the wilderneſſe:
where he had pitched his tente by the mounte of God.
6 And he ſent worde to Moſes: I thi father in law Iethro
am come to the, and thi wyfe alſo, and hir two ſonnes
7 with her. And Moſes went out to mete his father in
lawe and dyd obeyſſaunce and kyſſed him, and they
ſaluted etch other ād came in to the tente.
8 And Moſes tolde his father in lawe all that the
Lorde had done vnto Pharao and to the Egiptians for
Iſraels ſake, and all the trauayle that had happened
them by the waye, and how the Lorde had delyuered
9 them. And Iethro reioeſed ouer all the good which
the Lorde had done to Iſrael, and becauſe he had de-
10 lyuered them out of the hande of the Egiptians. And
Iethro ſayde: bleſſed be the Lorde which hath delyuered you out of the hande of the Egiptians ād out of
the hande of Pharao, which hath delyuered his people
from vnder the power of [Fo. XXXII.] the Egiptians.
11 Now I knowe that the Lorde is greater thē all goddes,
12 for becauſe that they dealte prowdly with them. And

V. 2 quam remiſerat 3 Gerſam, dicente patre 4 Deus enim, ait 7 ſe mutuo verbis pacificis . Cumque intraſſet 8 vniuerſumque laborem 11 eo quod ſuperbe egerint contra illos.
L. 8 Muhe 10 der weys ſeyn volck 11 vermeſſen geweſen ſind an yhn

Iethro Moſes father in lawe offred burntoffrynges and
ſacrifyces vnto God. And Aaron and all the elders of
Iſrael came to eate bred with Moſes father in lawe
before God.
13 And it chaunced on the morow, that Moſes ſatt to
iudge the people, and the people ſtode aboute Moſes
14 from mornynge vnto euen. when his father in lawe
ſawe all that he dyd vnto the people, he ſayde: what
is this that thou doeſt vnto the people? why ſytteſt
thou thi ſelf and letteſt all the people ſtonde aboute
15 the frō mornynge vnto euen? And Moſes ſayde vnto
his father in lawe: becauſe the people came vnto me
16 to ſeke councell of God. For whē they haue a matter,
they come vnto me, and I muſt iudge betwene euery
man and his neyboure, and muſt ſhewe them the or-
dinaūces of God and his lawes.
17 And his father in lawe ſayde vnto him: it is not
18 well that thou doſt. Thou doeſt vnwyſely and alſo
this people that is with the: becauſe the thinge is to
greuous for the, and thou art not able to do it thi ſelfe
19 alone. But heare my voyce, and I will geue the councell, and God ſhalbe with the. Be thou vnto the people to .⁋. Godwarde, and brynge the cauſes vnto God
20 and prouyde them ordinaunces and lawes, ād ſhewe
them the waye wherin they muſt walke and the werkes
that they muſt doo.
21 Moreouer ſeke out amonge all the people, men of
actiuite *which feare God and men that
are true ād hate covetuouſnes: and make
them heedes ouer the people, captaynes
ouer thouſandes, ouer hundredes, ouer fyf-
22 tie, and ouer ten. And let them iudge

Oure prelates nether feare God, for they preach not his vvorde truely: ner are lesse covetouse

V. 13 qui aſſiſtebat 14 cur ſolus ſedes 16 vt iudicem inter eos 18 ſtulto labore cōſumeris . . vltra vires tuas 19 Eſto tu pop. in his quæ ad deum pertinent . 20 oſtendaſque pop. ceremonias & ritum colendi 21 tribunos & centuriones & quinquagenarios & decanos.

L. 13 ſtund vmb 18 du thuſt nerricht . . ſchweer 21 redlichen leuten

M. M. N. 21 The condicions that Iudges ſhuld haue. 22 To Iudge look in Gen. xlix, c.

the people at all feafons: Yf there beany
greate matter, let them brynge that vnto
the, and let them iudge all fmall caufes
them felues, and eafe thi felfe, ād let
23 them bere with the. Yf thou fhalt doo
this thinge, then thou fhalt be able to
endure that which God chargeth the with
all, and all this people fhall goo to their
places quietly.
24 And Mofes herde the voyce of his father in lawe,
25 and dyd all that he had fayde, and chofe actyue men
out of all Ifrael and made them heedes ouer the people, captaynes ouer thoufandes, ouer hundreds, ouer
26 fiftie and ouer ten And they iudged the people at
all feafons, ād broughte the harde caufes vnto Mofes:
27 and iudged all fmall maters them felues. And thā
Mofes let his father in lawe departe, and he went in
to his awne londe.

thē Iudas: for they haue receaued of the devill the kyngdomes of the erth and the glorie thereof vvhich chrift refufedMathe. 4.

The .XIX. Chapter. [Fo. XXXIII.]

1 THE thyrde moneth after the
childern of Ifrael were gone
out of Egipte: the fame daye
they came in to the wilder-
2 neffe of Sinai. For they were departed
from Raphidim, and were come to the
deferte of Sinay and had pitched their
tentes in the wilderneffe. And there If-
3 rael pitched before the mounte. And
Mofes went vpp vnto God.

M.C.S. *The chyldren of Ifrael come to the mounte Sinai. The people of God are holy & a royall prefthode. He that toucheth the hill dyeth. God appereth vnto Mofes vpon the*

V. 22 leuiufque fit tibi, partito in alios onere. 23 implebis imp. dei, & præc. eius poteris fuftentare . . . ad loca fua cum pace. 24 fuggefferat. 27 reuerfus abiit. xix, 2 in eodem loco . . eregione montis.

L. 23 mit friden an feynen ort. xix, 2 gegen dem berg

L. M. N. 24 Naturlich vernunft ift ynn weltlichen fachen zu handeln kluger, denn die heiligen leutte, wie Chriftus auch fagt Luc. 16. das die kinder difer wellt kluger find, denn die kinder des liechts. Darumb was vernunfft meyftern kan, da gibt Gott kein gefetz, fondern left die vernunfft, als feyn Creatur (datzu verordnet Gen. i.) hie handeln.

And the Lorde called to him out of *mounte in thonder & lyghtenyng.*
the mountayne saynge: thus saye vnto
4 the housse of Iacob and tell the childern of Israel, Ye
haue sene what I dyd vnto the Egiptians and how I
toke you vpp apon Egles wynges and haue broughte
5 you vnto my selfe. Now therfore yf ye will heare my
voyce and kepe myne appoyntment: ye shall be myne
6 awne aboue all nations, for all the erth is myne. Ye
shall be vnto me a kyngdome of preastes and an holie
people: these are the wordes which thou shalt saye
vnto the childern of Israel.
7 And Moses came and called for the elders of Israel,
and layde before them all these wordes which the
8 Lorde had commaunded him. And the people answered all together and sayde: All that the Lorde
hath sayde, we will doo. And Moses broughte the
9 wordes of the people vnto the Lorde .P. And the
Lorde sayde vnto Moses: Loo, I will come vnto the in
a thicke clowde, that the people maye heare when I
talke with the and also beleue the for euer. And
Moses shewed the wordes of the people vnto the
Lorde
10 And the Lorde sayde vnto Moses: Go vnto the
people and sanctifie them to daye and tomorow, and
11 let them wash their clothes: that they maye be redie
agaynst the thyrde daye.
For the thyrde daye the Lorde will come doune in
12 the sighte of all the people vpon mounte Sinai. And
sett markes rounde aboute the people and saye: beware that ye go not vp in to the mounte and that ye
twych not the bordres of it, for whoso- twych, twich-
euer twicheth the mounte, shall surely eth, *touch, toucheth*
13 dye There shall not an hande twych it,

V. 4 portauerim vos . . et assumpserim mihi. 5 in peculium
7 natu populi 12 Constituesque terminos populo per circumitum
. . morte morietur

L. 4 getragen . . zu mir bracht. 5 eygentumb 12 stecke zeychen
vmb das volck her . . seyn ende anruret

M. M. V. 10 *To sanctyfye* is here to purge & clense them
from the fylthynes of bothe their body and garmentes, as is in
this same chapter beneth c. d. & xxxi, c.

but that he ſhall ether be ſtoned or els ſhot thorow:
whether it be beeſt or man, it ſhall not lyue. when the
horne bloweth: than let thē come vp in to the mounten
14 And Moſes went doune from the mounte vnto the
people and ſanctifyed them, ād they waſſhed their
15 clothes: And he ſayde vnto the people: be redie
agenſt the thirde daye, and ſe that ye come not at
16 youre wiues. And the thirde daye in the mornynge
there was thunder, and lightenynge and a thicke clowde
apō the mounte, ād the voyce of the horne waxed ex-
[Fo. XXXIII.] ceadynge lowde, and all the people that
17 was in the hoſte was afrayde. And Moſes brought the
people out of the tētes to mete with God. and they
ſtode vnder the hyll.
18 And mounte Sinai was all togither on a ſmoke: becauſe the Lorde deſcended doune vpon it in fyre. And
the ſmoke therof aſcēded vp, as it had bene the ſmoke
of a kylle, and all the mounte was ex-
19 ceadinge fearfull. And the voyce of the
horne blewe and waxed lowder, ād lowder. Moſes
ſpake, ād God anſwered hī ād that with a voyce.
20 And the Lord came doune vppon mounte Sinai: euen
in the toppe of the hyll, ād called Moſes vp in to the
toppe of the hyll. And Moſes went vppe.
21 And the Lorde ſayde vnto Moſes: go doune and
charge the people that they preaſe not vp
vnto the Lorde for to ſe hī, ād ſo many off thē periſſh.
22 And let the preaſtes alſo which come to the Lordes
preſence, ſanctifie them ſelues: leſt the Lorde ſmyte
23 them, Then Moſes ſayde vnto the Lorde: the people
can not come vp in to mounte Sinai, for thou charged-

kylle, *kiln, furnace*

preaſe, *preſſe*

V. 13 conſodietur iaculis . . buccina 16 & mane inclaruerat . . . clangorque buc. vehementius perſtrepebat 17 ad radices montis. 19 creſcebat in maius, & prolixius tendebatur . . deus reſpondebat ei. 20 Deſcenditque 22 ſanctificentur

L. 13 mit geſchoſz erſchoſſen . . . horns dohn dehnet, 16 poſaunen 17 vnden an den berg. 18 ſeer erſchrecklich 19 Gott antwortet yhm laut. 21 nicht erzu brechen 22 nicht zu ſcheyttere

M. M. X. 15 *Come not at youre wyues*, that is, when ye wyll ſerue the Lord ye ſhall put frō you all luſtes and fleſhly concupiſcenſes, geuing your ſelfe holy to prayer & abſtynence, as Paul teacheth 1 Cor. vii, c. that they that haue wyues ſhulde be as though they had none.

eſt vs ſaynge: ſett markes aboute the hyll and ſanctifie it.
24 And the Lorde ſayde vnto him: awaye, and get the
doune: and come vp both thou ād Aaron with the.
But let not the preaſtes and the .P. people preſume for
25 to come vp vnto the Lorde: leſt he ſmyte them. And
Moſes wēt doune vnto the people and tolde them.

ℂ The .XX. Chapter.

1 AND God ſpake all theſe wordes
2 ād ſaide: I am the Lorde thy
God, which haue brought the
out of the londe of Egipte ād
3 out of the houſe of bondage. Thou ſhalt haue none
other goddes in my ſyght.

M.C.S. *The .x commaundements are geuen. The altare of erth.*

4 Thou ſhalt make the no grauen ymage, nether any
ſymilitude that is in heauen aboue, ether in the erth
5 beneth, or in the water that ys beneth the erth. Se
that thou nether bowe thy ſylf vnto them nether ſerue
them: for I the Lorde thy God, am a gelouſe God, and
viſet the ſynne of the fathers vppon the childern vnto
the third and fourth generacion of thē that hate me:
6 and yet ſhewe mercie vnto thouſandes amonge them
that loue me and kepe my commaundmentes.
7 Thou ſhalt not take the name of the Lorde thy
God in vayne, for the Lord wil not holde him giltleſſe
that taketh his name in vayne.
8 Remēbre the Sabbath daye that thou ſanctifie it.
9 Sixe dayes mayſt thou laboure ād do al that thou haſt
10 to doo: but the ſeuenth daye is the Sabbath of the
Lorde thy God, in it thou [Fo. XXXV.] ſhalt do no

V. 24 interficiat illos. xx, 4 eorum quæ ſunt in aquis 5 deus tuus fortis zelotes

L. 4 des das oben . . des das vnden . . oder des das 5 eyn ſtarcker eyfferer 7 vnſchuldig

M. M. N. 5 *I am gelouſe* that is; I am the Lorde that watcheth and looketh narowly vnto your wekednes, & wyll punyſſhe it ſtraytly. And agayne, that feruently loueth youre godlynes & will rewarde it aboundātly.

maner worke: nether thou nor thy ſonne, nor thy
doughter, nether thy manſervaunte nor thy maydeſervaunte, nether thy catell nether yet the ſtraunger
11 that is within thi gates For in ſixe dayes the Lorde
made both heauen and erth and the ſee and all that
in them is and reſted the ſeuenth daye: wherfore the
Lorde bleſſed the Sabbath daye and halowed it.

12 Honoure thy father ād thy mother, that thy dayes
may be lōge in the lōde which the Lorde thy God
geueth the.

13 Thou ſhalt not kyll.

14 Thou ſhalt not breake wedlocke.

15 Thou ſhalt not ſteale.

16 Thou ſhalt bere no falſe witneſſe agēſt thy neghboure

17 Thou ſhalt not couet thy neghbours houſſe: nether
ſhalt couet thy neghbours wife, his māſervaunte, his
mayde, his oxe, his aſſe or aughte that is his.

Thelavvecauſeth vvrath ād maketh a mā fle from God: but the Goſpelldravveth ād maketh a mā bolde to come vnto God.

18 And all the people ſawe the thunder
ād the lyghteninge and the noyſe of the
horne, ād howe the mountayne ſmoked.
And whē the people ſawe it, they re-
19 moued ād ſtode a ferre of ād ſaide vnto
Moſes: talke thou with vs and we wil
heare: but let not god talke with vs, leſt
20 we dye. And Moſes ſayde vnto the people feare not,
for God is come to proue you, and .P. that his feare
may be amonge you that ye ſynne not.

21 And the people ſtode aferre of, ād Moſes went in
22 to the thicke clowde where God was And the Lorde
ſayde vnto Moſes: thus thou ſhalt ſaye vnto the childern of Iſrael: Ye haue ſene how that I haue talked

V. 18 videbat voces et lampades . . . & perterriti ac pauore concuſſi

L. 12 geben wirt. 14 nicht ehebrechen. 17 noch alles das deyn nehiſter 18 ſahe 19 vnd wancketen vnd tratten von ferne 20 euch fur augen

M M. N. 12 *To honor father and mother* is not only to ſhew obedience to them: but alſo to helpe them in their age yf they be poore & nedy, as Ephe. vi, a. Col. iii, d. Marc. vii, b. Matt. ix, c. Rom. xiii, b.

23 with you from out of heauen. Ye ſhal not make therfore with me goddes of ſyluer nor goddes
24 of golde: in no wyſe ſhall ye do it. An alter of erth
thou ſhalt make vnto me ād there on offer thy burntofferinges ād thy peaceoffringes, and thy ſhepe ād thine
oxen. And in all places where I ſhall put the remēbraunce of my name, thither I will come vnto the and
bleſſe the.

with, *beſide*

25 But and yf thou wilt make me an alter off ſtone, ſe
thou make it not of hewed ſtone, for yf thou lyfte vp thy
26 tole vpon it, thou ſhalt polute it. Moreouer
thou ſhalt not goo vp wyth ſteppes vnto
myne alter, that thy nakedneſſe be not ſhewed there on

tole, *tool, chiſel or knife*

The .XXI. Chapter.

1 THESE are the lawes which thou
2 ſhalt ſet before thē. Yf thou
bye a ſervaunte that is an he-
brue, ſixte yeres he ſhall ſerue, and the ſeuenth he ſhall goo out fre paynge noth-
3 inge. Yf he came alone, he ſhall goo out
alone: Yf he came maried, his wife ſhall go out with
4 hī. [Fo. XXXVI.] And yf his maſter haue geuen him
a wife and ſhe haue borne him ſonnes or doughters:
then the wife and hir childern ſhalbe hir maſters ād he
5 ſhall goo out alone. But and yf the ſervaunte ſaye I
loue my maſter and my wife and my children, I will
6 not goo out fre. Then let his maſter bringe him vnto
the Goddes ād ſet him to the doore or the
dorepoſt, ād bore his eare thorow with a
naule, ād let him be his ſervaunte for euer.

M.C.S. *Temporall and cyuile ordinaunces.*

Lawes Bondemen

Goddes are the iudges vvhich are in gods ſtede.

a naule, *an awl*

V. 23 Non facietis mecum deos 24 mei: veniam ad te 25 leuaueris cultrum xxi, 3 Cum quali veſte intrauerit, cum tali exeat. 6 ſubula
L. 23 neben myr machen 25 deym meſſer 26 fur yhm. xxi, 3 alleyne komen 6 pfrymen
M. M. T. 6 Iudges and princes are called in the ſcripture oftentymes *goddes:* becauſe they receaue their office of God, as in Ex. xxii, b. which the apoſtle calleth the myniſters of God. Rom. xiii, a.

7 Yf a man ſell his doughter to be a ſervaunte: ſhe
8 ſhall not goo out as the men ſervauntes doo. Yf ſhe
pleaſe not hir maſter, ſo that he hath geuen her to no
man to wife, then ſhal he let hir goo fre: to ſell her
vnto a ſtraunge nacion ſhal he haue no power, becauſe
9 he deſpiſed her. Yf he haue promyſed her vnto his
ſonne to wife, he ſhal deale with her as men do with
10 their doughters. Yf he take him another wife, yet hir
fode, rayment and dutie off mariage ſhall he not myn-
11 iſſhe. Yf he do not theſe thre vnto her, then ſhall ſhe
goo out fre and paye no money.
12 He that ſmyteth a man that he dye, *Murther*
13 ſhalbe ſlayne for it. Yf a mā laye not awayte but God
delyuer him in to his hande, then I wyll poynte the
14 a place whether he ſhall fle. Yf a man whether, *whither*
come preſumptuouſly vppon his neygh- gile, *guile*
boure ād .P. ſlee him with gile, thou
ſhalt take him fro myne alter that he dye. *But the pope ſaith come to myne altare.*
15 And he that ſmyteth his father or his
mother, ſhall dye for it.
16 He that ſtealeth a mā ād ſelleth him (yf it be
17 proued vppon him) ſhall be ſlayne for it. And he
that curſeth his father or mother, ſhall be put to deth
18 for it. Yf men ſtryue together and one ſmyte another
with a ſtone or with his fyſte, ſo that he dye not, but
19 lyeth in bedd: yf he ryſe agayne and walke without
vpon his ſtaffe then ſhall he that ſmote hī goo quyte:
ſaue only he ſhal bere his charges while he laye in bed
and paye for his healinge.
20 Yf a man ſmite his ſervaunte or his mayde with a
ſtaffe that they dye vnder his hande, it ſhalbe auenged.
21 But ād yf they contynue a daye or two, it ſhall not be
auenged for they are his money.
22 when men ſtryue and ſmyte a woman with childe

V. 7 ſicut ancillæ 8 Si diſplicuerit oc. dom. ſui, cui tradita fuerit, dimittet eam . . . . ſi ſpreuerit eam. 10 prouidebit puellæ nupt., & veſt., & pretium pudicitiæ non negabit. 12 volens occidere, morte moriatur. 20 criminis reus erit. 22 ſed ipſa vixerit

L. 8 verſchmecht 10 futter, decke vnd eheſchuld 12 tods ſterben 15 muter ſchlegt 20 rach drumb leyden

ſo that hir frute departe from her and yet no myſ-
fortune foloweth: then ſhall he be merſed,
acordynge as the womans huſbonde will
laye to his charge, and he ſhall paye as
23 the dayesmen appoynte him. But and yf
any myſſfortune folowe, then ſhall he paye lyfe for lyfe,
24 eye for eye, toth for toth, hande for hande, fote for fote,
25 burnynge for burnynge, wonde for [Fo. XXXVII.]
wonde and ſtrype for ſtrype.

merſed, *amerced;* dayeſmen, *judges;* appoynte, *adjudge*

26 Yf a man ſmyte his ſervaunte or his mayde in the
eye and put it out, he ſhall let thē goo fre for the eyes
27 ſake. Alſo yf he ſmyte out his ſervauntes or his
maydes toth, he ſhall let thē go out fre for the tothes
ſake.

28 Yf an oxe gore a man or a woman that
they dye, then the oxe ſhalbe ſtoned,
and hys fleſh ſhall not be eaten: and his
maſter ſhall go quyte.

God ſo abhorreth murther, that the vnreſonable beſtes muſt dye therfore, and there fleſh caſt avvay.

29 Yf the oxe were wont to runne at men
in tyme paſt and it hath bene tolde his
maſter, and he hath not kepte him, but that he hath
kylled a man or a woman: then the oxe ſhalbe ſtoned
and hys maſter ſhall dye alſo.

30 Yf he be ſette to a ſumme of money,
then he ſhall geue for the delyueraunce
off his lyfe, acordynge to all that is put vnto him.

ſette to, *fined in*

31 And whether he hath gored a ſonne or a doughter,
32 he ſhalbe ſerued after the ſame maner But yf it be a
ſervaunt or a mayde that the oxe hath gored, then
he ſhall geue vnto their maſter the ſumme of .xxx
ſicles, ād the oxe ſhall be ſtoned.

33 Yf a man open a well or dygge a pytt and couer

V. 22 arbitri iudic. 23 Sinautem mors eius fuerit ſubſecuta 26 luſcos eos fecerit 29 bos cornupeta 30 impoſitum . . pro anima ſua . . poſtulatus. 32 inuaſerit 33 ciſternam, & foderit

L. 22 keyn ſchade widerferet . . teydings leut 23 ſeel vmb ſeel 29 vorhyn ſtoſſig geweſen 30 ſeyn ſeel zurloſen 33 gruben . . grube

M. M. N. 28 God ſo abhorreth *murther*, that the vnreaſonable beaſtes muſt dye therfore. and their fleſh caſt awaye. 32 *Sicle*, after the Ebrewes is an ounce: but after the grekes & Latynes it is but the fourth part of an ounce. And it cōteyneth .xx. geras as in Ex. xxx, b. whych is ten pence ſterlyng or thereaboute.

34 it not, but that an oxe or an aſſe fall theryn, the
owner off the pytte ſhall ma- .P. ke it good and geue
money vnto their maſter and the dead beeſt ſhalbe his.
35 Yf one mans oxe hurte anothers that he dye: then
they ſhall ſell the lyue oxe and deuyde the money,
36 and the deed oxe alſo they ſhall deuyde. But and yf
it be knowne that the oxe hath vſed to puſſhe in tymes
paſt, then becauſe his maſter hath not kepte hī, he
ſhall paye oxe for oxe. and the deed ſhalbe his awne.

❡ The .XXII. Chapter

1 YF a man ſteale an oxe or ſhepe
ād kylle it or ſelle it, he ſhall
reſtore .v. oxen for an oxe,
and .iiii. ſhepe for a ſhepe.

M.C.S. *Soche lyke lawes as are in the chapter aboue.*

2 *Thefte* Yf a thefe be founde breakynge vpp ād
be ſmytten that he dye, there ſhall no bloude be ſhed
3 for him: excepte the ſonne be vpp when he is founde,
then there ſhalbe bloude ſhed for him,
A thefe ſhall make reſtitucyon: Yf he haue not
4 wherewith, he ſhalbe ſolde for his thefte. Yf the
thefte be founde in his hande alyue (whether it be oxe,
aſſe or ſhepe) he ſhall reſtore double.
5 Yf a man do hurte felde or vyneyarde, ſo that he
put in his beeſt to fede in another mans felde: off the
beſt off hys owne felde, [Fo. XXXVII.] and of the beſt
of his awne vyneyarde, ſhall he make reſtitucyon.
6 Yf fyre breake out and catch in the thornes, ſo that
the ſtoukes of corne or the ſtōdynge corne ſtoukes, *ſtacks*
or felde be conſumed therwith: he that kynled the fyre
ſhall make reſtitucyon.
7 Yf a man delyuer his neghboure money or ſtuffe to

V. 36 cadauer integrum accipiet. xxii, 2 effringens . . ſiue ſuffodiens 3 homicidium perpetrauit & ipſe morietur. 5 pro damni æſtimatione

L. 36 vnd das aſs haben. xxii, 2 blut gericht (*bis*) 6 die mandel odder getreyde.

kepe, and it be ſtolen out of his houſſe: Yf the theſe
8 be foūde, he ſhal paye double. Yf the theſe be not
founde, then the goodmā of the houſſe
ſhalbe brought vnto the goddes and ſwere,
whether he haue put his hande vnto his neghbours good.

goodman, *maſter*

9 And in all maner of treſpace, whether it be oxe,
aſſe, ſhepe, rayment or ony maner loſt thynge which
another chalēgeth to be his, the cauſe of both parties
ſhall come before the goddes. And whom
the goddes condēne: the ſame ſhall paye
10 double vnto his neghboure. Yf a man delyuer vnto
his neghboure to kepe, aſſe, oxe, ſhepe or what
ſoeuer beeſt it be and it dye or be hurte or dryu-
11 en awaye and no man ſe it: then ſhall an othe of
the Lorde goo betwene them, whether he haue put
his hande vnto his neghbours good, and the owner
of it ſhall take the othe, and the other ſhall not make
it good:

goddes, *judges, as xxi, 6*

12 Yf it be ſtollen from him, then he ſhall make reſti-
13 tucion vnto the owner: Yf .P. it be torne with wylde
beeſtes, thē let him bringe recorde of the teerynge:
and he ſhall not make it good.

14 when a man boroweth oughte of his neghbour yf it
be hurte or els dye, and yf the owner therof be not
15 by, he ſhall make it good: Yf the owner there of
be by, he ſhall not make it good namely yf it be an
hyred thinge ād came for hyre.

16 Yf a man begyle a mayde that is not betrouthed
and lye with her, he ſhall endote her and
17 take her to his wife: Yf hir father refuſe to geue her
vnto him, he ſhall paye money acordynge to the
dowrie of virgens.

endote, *endow*

V. 8 dominus domus applicabitur ad deos 10 vel captum ab hoſtibus 13 deferat ad eum quod occiſum 16 dotabit eam

L. 8 hauſswirt fur die Gotter bringen

M. M. N. 11 An othe is the ende of ſtryfe and deuiſyon, the which is lawfull to be done, when it is ether to the glorie of God or proffyt of our neyboure or for the comen wealth, or elles not, as Math. v, f.

L. M. N. 8 *Gotter* heyſſen die richter, darumb dz ſie an Gottis ſtat, nach Gottis geſetz vnd wort, nicht nach eygen dunckel richten vnd regirn muſten, wie Chriſtus zeugt, Iohan. 10

18 Thou ſhalt not ſuffre a witch to lyue, *vvyches*
19 who ſoeuer lyeth with a beeſt, ſhalbe ſlayne for it.
20 He that offreth vnto ony goddes ſaue vnto the Lorde
21 only, let him dye without redemption vexe not a
ſtraunger nether oppreſſe him for ye were ſtraungers
in the londe of Egipte.

22 Ye ſhall trouble no wedowe nor fa- *Let all op-*
23 therleſſe childe: * Yf ye ſhall trouble thē: *preſſars of the pore take hede*
they ſhall crye vnto me, ād I wyll *to this texte.*
24 ſurely heare their crye and then will my wrath
waxe hoote and I will kyll you with ſwerde, and
youre wyues ſhalbe wedowes and youre childern
fatherleſſe. [Fo. XXXVIII.]

25 Yf thou lende money to ani of my *Lend.*
people that is poore by the, thou ſhalt not be as an
vſurer vnto him, nether ſhalt oppreſſe him with
vſerye.

26 Yf thou take thi neghbours raymēt to *Plegge.*
pledge, ſe that thou delyuer it vnto him agayne by
27 that the ſonne goo doune. For that is his couerlet
only: euē the rayment for his ſkynne wherin he
ſlepeth: or els he will crye vnto me ād I will heare
him, for I am mercyfull.

28 Thou ſhalt not rayle vppon the goddes, *Goddes.*
nether curſe the ruelar of thi people.

29 Thy frutes (whether they be drye or moyſt) ſe thou
kepe not backe. Thi firſtborne ſonne thou ſhalt geue
30 me: likewiſe ſhalt thou doo of thine oxen and of thy

M. 24 yͤ ſwerde

V. 20 diis, occidetur, præter dom. 25 vrgebis eum quaſi exactor, nec vſuris opprimes. 27 indumentum carnis eius nec . . in quo dormiat.

L. 19 der ſey verbannet. 26 ſeyn eynige decke ſeyner haut, darynn er ſchlefft. 29 fulle vnd threnen

M. M. N. 22 Let all oppreſſars of the pore take hede to this texte. 29 By tythes & fyrſt frutes are vnderſtōde geuynge of thākes wher by the heart knowledgeth & confeſſeth to haue receaued it of God, as in 1 Tim. iiii, a.

L. M. N. 29 *Fulle* heyſt er alle hartte fruchte als da ſind, korn, gerſten, epffel, byrn, da man ſpeyſe von macht, *Threnen* heyſt er alle weych fruchte, da man ſäft vnd tranck von macht, Als da ſind weyndrauben ole. Bedeut aber das Euangelion dz da ſpeyſet vnd trenckt geyſtlich.

ſhepe. Seuen dayes it ſhall be with the dame, and
the .viii. daye thou ſhalt geue it me.
31 Ye ſhalbe holye people vnto me, and therfore ſhall
ye eate no fleſh that is torne of beeſtes in the feld.
But ſhall caſt it to dogges.

The .XXIII. Chapter.

1 THOU ſhalt not accept a vayne
tale, nether ſhalt put thine
hande with the wiked to
be an vnrightous witneſſe.
2 *Falſevvitneſſe.* Thou ſhalt not folowe a multitude to do euell: nether anſwere in a
mater of plee that thou woldeſt to folow
3 many turne a ſyde .P. from the trueth,
nether ſhalt thou paynte a porre mans
cauſe.

M.C.S. *Here I ſet no ſome: becauſe I wolde all men ſhuld reade the chapter thorow oute, and the two that are next before alſo.*

paynte, *favor his cauſe, ſee Hebrew.*

4 whē thou meteſt thine enimies oxe or aſſe goynge
a ſtraye, thou ſhalt brynge thē to him agayne.
5 Yf thou ſe thine enimies aſſe ſynke vnder his burthen, thou ſhalt not paſſe by and let him alone: but
ſhalt helpe him to lyfte him vp agayne.
6 Thou ſhalt not hynder the right of the poore that
are amonge you in their ſute.
7 Kepe the ferre from a falſe mater, and the Innocent
and righteous ſe thou ſley not, for I will not iuſtifye
the weked.
8 Thou ſhalt take no giftes, for gyftes *Gyftes.*
blinde the ſeynge and peruerte the wordes of the
righteous.

V. 1 non ſuſcipies vocem mendacii 2 vt a vero deuies. 3 non miſereberis 5 ſed ſubleuabis cum eo. 6 non declinabis in iud. pauperis. 7 quia averſor impium. 8 ſubuertunt verba

L. 1 annehmen vnnutzer teydinge 2 vom rechten weycheſt 6 recht . . beugen 7 rechtfertige keynen gotloſen. 8 rechten ſachen.

M. M. N. 8 By receauyng of gyftes is vnderſtonde all thynge by which one ſeketh hys awne profijt and honoure and not godes, as in Deut. xvi, d. xxvii, d. & Ecclī. xx, d.

9 Thou ſhalt not oppreſſe a ſtraunger, *Straunger.*
for I knowe the herte of ſtraunger, becauſe ye were
ſtraungers in Egipte.
10 Sixe yeres thou ſhalt ſowe thi londe ād gather in the
11 frutes theroff: and the ſeuenth yere thou ſhalt let it
reſt and lye ſtyll, that the poore of thi people maye
eate, and what they leaue, the beeſtes of the felde
ſhall eate: In like maner thou ſhalt do with thi vyneyarde ād thine olyue trees.
12 Sixe dayes thou ſhalt do thi worke ād the [Fo.
XXXIX.] ſeuenth daye thou ſhalt kepe holie daye,
that thyne oxe and thine aſſe maye reſt ād the ſonne
of thi mayde and the ſtraunger maye be refreſſhed.
13 And in all thinges that I haue ſayde vnto you be
circumſpecte.

And make no reherſall of the names of the ſtraunge
goddes, nether let any man heare thē out of youre
mouthes.
14 Thre feaſtes thou ſhalt holde vnto me in a yere.
15 Thou ſhalt kepe the feaſt of ſwete bred that thou eate
vnleuend bred .vii. dayes lōge as I cōmaunded the in
the tyme appoynted of the moneth of Abib, for in that
moneth thou cameſt out of Egipte: ād ſe that noman
16 appeare before me emptie. And the feaſt of Herueſt,
when thou reapeſt the firſtfrutes of thy laboures which
thou haſt ſowne in the felde. And the feaſt of ingaderynge, in the ende of the yere: when thou haſt gathered in thy laboures out of the felde.
17 Thre tymes in a yere ſhall all thy menchildern appere before the Lorde Iehouah.
18 Thou ſhalt not offer the bloude of my ſacrifyce with

V. 9 ſcitis enim ad. animas 12 refrigeretur 13 cuſtodite . . non iurabitis neque audietur 15 menſis nouorum 16 menſis primitiuorum

L. 9 yhr wiſſet vmb der fremdling herz 17 Herrn des hirſchers

L. M. N. 14 Das iſt, das oſterfeſt ym april, Pfingſten ym brachmond vnd das lauberhutten feſt ym weynmond, davon lies am 23. Cap. des dritten buchs. Des iars ausgang heyſt er den weyn mond, das als denn aus iſt mit frucht wachſen vnd ſamlen. 18 Das blut etc. das iſt du ſolt das oſter lamb nicht opffern ehe denn all geſeurt brod aus deynem hauſe kompt, Bedeut das Chriſtus blut nicht neben ſich leydet eygē menſchen leer vnd werck, Matth. 16, hut euch fur dem ſaurteyg der Phariſeer.

leuended bred: nether ſhall the fatt of my feaſt remayne vntill the mornynge.
19 The firſt of the firſtfrutes of thy lōde thou .P. ſhalt
bringe in to the houſſe of the Lorde thy God thou
ſhalt alſo not ſeth a kyde in his mothers mylke.
20 Beholde, I ſende mine angell before the, to kepe
the in the waye, and to brynge the in to the place
21 which I haue prepared Beware of him and heare his
voyce and angre him not: for he wyll not ſpare youre
22 myſdedes, yee and my name is in him. But and yf
thou ſhalt herken vnto his voyce ād kepe all that I
ſhall tell the, thē I wilbe an enimye vnto thyne enimies
and an aduerſarie vnto thine aduerſaries.
23 when myne angell goth before the ād hath broughte
the in vnto the Amorites, Hethites Pherezites, Canaanites, Heuites and Iebuſites and I ſhall haue de-
24 ſtroyed them: ſe thou worſhippe not their goddes nether ſerue them, nether do after the workes of them: but
ouerthrowe them and breake doune the places of them
25 And ſe that ye ſerue the Lorde youre God, ād he
ſhall bleſſe thi bred and thy water, ād I will take all
ſyckneſſes awaye from amonge you.
26 Moreouer there ſhalbe no woman childleſſe or vnfrutefull in thi londe, and the nombre of thi dayes I
27 will fulfyll. I will ſende my feare before the and will
kyll all the people whether thou ſhalt goo. And I
will make all thine enemies turne their backes vnto
28 the, ād I will [Fo. XL.] ſend hornettes before the,
and they ſhall dryue out the Heuites, the Cananites
and the Hethites before the.

V. 18 ſuper fermēto 24 confringes ſtatuas eorum. 25 vt benedicam . . auferam infirm. 26 dier. tuor. implebo. 28 emittēs crabrones prius, qui fug.

L. 18 neben dem ſawrteyg 19 an ſeyner mutt. milch 24 gotzen abthun vnd zubrechen 26 eynſame noch vnfruchtbar . . alter vol machen 28 horniſſen . . ausjagen

M. M. N. 19 That is, thou ſhalt not ſethe it ſo longe as it ſoucketh, or as ſome thynke: they ſhuld not kyll bothe the dāme & the kyd. 28 A hornet is lyke a waſpe—ſhe is of a more venemous nature & ſtyngeth moche ſorer, as in Deut. vii. & Ioſu. xxiiii. c.

L. M. N. 19 Das bocklin etc. das iſt die ſchwachglewbigen vnd iunge Chriſten ſolltu nicht ergern noch mit ſtarcker lere vnd wercken beladen.

29 I will not caſt them out in one yere, leſt the lande
growe to a wylderneſſe: and the beeſtes of the felde
multiplye apon the.
30 But a litle and a litle I will dryue them out before
the, vntill thou be increaſed that thou mayſt enherett
31 the londe. And I will make thi coſtes frō the red ſee
vnto the ſee of the Philiſtenes and from the deſerte
vnto the ryuer. I will delyuer the inhabiters of the londe in to thine hande,
and thou ſhalt dryue them out before the.
32 And thou ſhalt make none appoyntment with them
33 nor wyth their goddes. Nether ſhall they dwell in
thi londe, leſt they make the ſynne agaynſt me: for yf
thou ſerue their goddes, it will ſurely be thy decaye.

By the ryuer vnderſtonde the river Euphrates,

The .XXIIII. Chapter.

1 AND he ſayde vnto Moſes: come
vnto the Lorde: both thou and
Aaron, Nadab and Abihu, and
the .Lxx. elders of Iſrael,
2 and worſhippe a ferre of. And Moſes
went him ſelf alone vnto the Lorde, but
they came not nye, nether came the people vp with him.
3 And Moſes came ād tolde the people
al the .P. wordes of the Lorde and all the lawes. And
all the people anſwered with one voyce and ſayde: all
the wordes which the Lorde hath ſayde, will wee doo.
4 Then Moſes wrote all the wordes of the Lorde and
roſe vp early ād made an alter vnder the hyll, and .xii

M.C.S. *Moſes aſſendeth vp to the mount and wryteth the wordes of the Lorde. The bloude of the couenaunt. The elders of Iſrael iudge the people.*

V. 31 tradam in man. veſtris 32 inibis . . . fœdus 33 quod tibi certe erit in ſcandalum. xxiiii, 1 Aſcēde 3 iudicia 4 ad radices montis

L. 30 meylich 32 bund machen 33 zum ergernis geratten. xxiiii, 1 Steyg erauff 4 vnden am berge

L. M. N. 3 *Eyner ſtym:* Das geſetz zwinget wol euſerlich eynerley zu ſagen oder geloben, aber das hertz iſt nicht da, drumb iſt hie des volcks wol eyne ſtym, aber keyn hertz.

pilers acordynge to the nombre of the .xii. trybes of
5 Israel, ād ſent yonge men of the childern of Israel to
ſacrifyce burntoffrynges ād to offre peaceoffrynges of
oxen vnto the Lorde.
6 And Moſes toke halfe of the bloude and put it in
baſens, and the otherhalfe he ſprenkeld on the alter.
7 And he toke the boke of the appoynt- ment and red it in the audience of the people. And they ſeyde. All that the Lorde hath
8 ſayde, we will do and heare. And Moſes toke the
bloude ād ſprinkeld it on the people ād ſayde: beholde, this is the bloude of the appoyntment which
the Lorde hath made with you apon all theſe wordes.
9 Then went Moſes and Aaron, Nadab ād Abihu and
10 the .Lxx. elders of Iſrael vppe, and ſawe the God of
Iſrael, and vnder his fete as it were a brycke worke
of Saphir and as it were the facyon of
11 heauen when it is cleare, and apō the
nobles of the childern of Iſrael he ſett not his hande.
And when they had ſene God [Fo. XLI.] they ate and
dronke.

appoyntment, *covenant*

facyon, *appearance, v. 17.*

12 And the Lorde ſayde vnto Moſes: come vpp to me
in to the hyll and be there, ād I will geue the tables
of ſtone and a lawe and commaundmentes, which I
13 haue written to teach them. Then Moſes roſe vppe
ād his miniſter Ioſua, and Moſes went vppe in to the
14 hyll of God, ād ſeyde vnto the elders: tarye ye here
vntill we come agayne vnto you: And beholde here is
Aaron and Hur with you. Yf any man haue any
maters to doo, let him come to them

V. 5 victimas pacificas 7 volumen fœderis . . erimus obed. 8 ſuper cunct. ſerm. 10 opus lapidis ſapphirini . . cælum cum ſerenum 11 eos qui procul receſſ. 12 doceas eos. 14 referetis ad eos.

L. 5 fridopffer 7 buch des bunds . . gehorchen 8 vber allen diſ. wortten 10 zigel von Sapphir werck . . geſtalt des hymels, wens klar iſt, 11 furnemiſten 14 an die ſelben gelangen.

M. M. T. 5 *Peace offrynge* is to reconcile God toward mē, to be at peace wyth them & to forgiue thē their treſpace: or as ſome men ſaye for peace obtayned after victorie in batayle, as afore in the .ix. chapter, d and here after xxxii, b. 10 *They ſawe God*, that is: they knewe certenly thatt he was there preſent, and they ſawe him as in a viſyon, not in his godly maieſtie: but as it were by a certen reuelacion.

15 when Moſes was come vpp in to the mounte, a
16 clowde couered the hyll, and the glorye of the Lorde
abode apon mounte Sinai, and the clowde couered it
vi. dayes. And the ſeuenth daye he called vnto Mo-
17 ſes out of the clowde. And the facyon of the glorie
of the Lorde was like conſumynge fyre on the toppe
of the hyll in the ſyghte of the childern of Iſrael.
18 And Moſes went in to the mountayne And Moſes
was in the mounte .xl. dayes and .xl. nyghtes.

The .XXV. Chapter

1 AND the Lorde talked with Moſes
2 ſaynge: ſpeake vnto the childern of Iſrael that they geue
me an heueoffrynge, and of
euerey man that geueth it willingly wyth
3 his herte, ye ſhall take it. And this is
the heue- .P. offrynge which ye ſhall take of them:
4 gold, ſiluer ād braſſe: and Iacyncte coloure, ſcarlet, purpull, byſſe and gootes
5 here: rams ſkynnes that are red, and the ſkynnes of
6 taxus and ſethimwodd, oyle for lightes and ſpices for
7 a noyntynge oyle and for ſwete cenſe: Onix ſtones
and ſett ſtones for the Ephod and for the
breſtlappe.

M.C.S. *The Lord ſheweth Moſes the faſſyon of the holy place and the thynges pertaynynge therto.*

iacyncte, *hyacinth, blue*

Ephod is a garment lyke an amyce.

8 And they ſhall make me a ſanctuarye that I maye
9 dwell amonge them. And as I haue ſhewed the the
facion of the habitaciō and of all the ornamentes therof, euē ſo ſe that ye make it in
all thynges.

facion, *pattern v, 40.*

M. 9 And I ſhall ſhewe the

V. 15 op. nubes mont. 16 medio caliginis. 17 ignis ardens 18 Ingreſſuſque M. medium nebulæ, aſcendit in . . xxv, 2 primitias 4 purpuram, coccumque bis tinctum 5 pelleſque hyac. 7 ephod ac rationale.

L. 17 vertzehrend fewr. . xxv, 1 Hebopffer 4 gelle ſeyden, ſcharlacken, roſynrodt, 5 dachs fell 7 bruſt latzen.

M. M. N. 16 Of this glorie is ſpoken before in the .xvi. Chapter, c. xxv, 7 *Ephod* is a garment lyke an amyce.

10 And they ſhall make an arke of ſethim wodd .ii. cubittes and an halfe longe, a cubite ād an halfe brode
11 and a cubitt and an halfe hye. And thou ſhalt ouerleye it with pure golde: both within and without, and
ſhalt make an hye vppon it a crowne of golde rounde
12 aboute. And thou ſhalt caſt .iiii. rynges of golde for
it and put them in the .iiii. corners there of .ii. rynges
13 on the one ſyde of it and .ii. on the other. And thou
ſhalt make ſtaues of ſethim wodd and couer them with
14 golde, and put the ſtaues in the rynges alonge by the
15 ſydes of the arke, to bere it with all. And the ſtaues
ſhall abyde in the rynges of the arke, and ſhall not be
16 taken awaye. [Fo. XLII.] And thou ſhalt put in the
arke, the wytneſſe which I ſhall geue the.
17 And thou ſhalt make a merciſeate of pure golde .ii
cubytes and an halfe longe and a cubete and an halfe
18 brode. And make .ii. cherubyns off thicke golde on
19 the .ii. endes of the mercyſeate: and ſett the one cherub
on the one ende and the other on the other ende of
the mercyſeate: ſo ſe that thou make them on the .ii
20 endes there of. And the cherubyns ſhall ſtretch theyr
wynges abrode ouer an hye, ād couer the mercy ſeate
with their wynges, and theyr faces ſhall loke one to
another: euē to the mercyſeate warde, ſhall the faces of
21 the cherubyns be. And thou ſhalt put the mercyſeate
aboue apon the arke, ād in the arke thou ſhalt put the
wytneſſe which I will geue the.
22 There I will mete the and will comon comon, *com-*
with the from apon the mercyſeate from *mune*
betwene the two cherubyns which are apon the arke
of witneſſe, of all thynge which I will geue the in
commaundment vnto the childern of Iſrael.
23 Thou ſhalt alſo make a table of ſethim wod of two

V. 11 ſupra coronam 16 teſtificationē 18 productiles facies ex vtraque parte oraculi. 22 Inde præcipiam, & loquar

L. 11 oben vmbher 12 geuſs 13 foern holtz 16 zeugnis 17 Gnaden ſtuel 22 Von dem ort

L. M. N. 22 *Dyr zeugen:* das iſt, dabey als bey eym gewiſſen zeichen vnd zeugnis will ich dich wiſſen laſſen, das ich da bin gegenwertig, das ich daſelbs reden werde etc. Bedeut aber Chriſtum ynn der menſcheyt. Ro. 3.

cubittes longe and one cubett brode ād a cubett ād an
24 halfe hye. And couer it with pure golde and make
25 there to a crowne of golde rounde aboute. And
make vnto that .P. an whope of .iiii. fyngers brode,
rounde aboute, And make a goldē crowne alſo to the
26 whope rounde aboute. And make for it .iiii. rynges
of golde and put them in the corners that are on the
27 iiii. fete therof: euē harde vnder the whope
ſhall the rynges be, to put in ſtaues to
28 bere the table with all. And thou ſhalt make ſtaues
of Sethim wodd and ouerleye thē with golde, that the
29 table maye be borne with them And thou ſhalt make
his diſſhes, ſpones, pottes and flatpeces to poure out
30 withall, of fyne golde. And thou ſhalt ſett apon the
table, ſhewbred before me allwaye.
31 And thou ſhalt make a candelſticke of
pure thicke golde with his ſhaft, braunches,
bolles, knoppes ād floures proceadynge
32 there out Syxe braunches ſhall procede
out of the ſydes of the candelſticke .iii. out of the one
33 ſyde and .iii. out of the other. And there ſhalbe .iii
cuppes like vnto almondes with knoppes
ād floures vppon euery one of the .vi
braunches that procede out of the cādel-
34 ſtycke: and in the candelſticke ſelfe .iiii. cuppes like
35 vnto almondes with their knoppes and floures: that
there be a knope vnder eueri .ii. braūches of the ſyxe
36 that procede out of the cādelſtycke. And the knoppes
and the braunches ſhal be altogether, one pece of pure
thicke golde.

harde vnder, *immediately under*

Shevvbred because it vvas alvvay in the preſence and ſight of the Lorde

knoppes, *buds of a flower, now ſpelled* knob

[Fo. XLIII.] *Woodcut with the inſcription:* ☙ The forme of the arke of witneſſe with his ſtaues and two cherubyns.

.P. *Verſo of* Fo. XLIII. *Woodcut with the inſcrip-*

V. 24 labium aureum 25 coronam interraſilem 29 libamina, ex auro puriſſimo 30 panes propoſitionis 36 vniuerſa ductilia de auro puriſſ.

L. 29 aus lauter golt 30 ſchawbrod 36 alles eyn ticht lautergolt.

M. M. N. 30 *Shewbreed*, becauſe it was alwaye in the preſence and ſyght of the Lorde.

tion: ¶ The table of ſhewbreed with the loves of breed vppon it, and his other veſſels.

[Fo. XLIIII.] *Woodcut with the inſcription*: ¶ The facion of the cādelſticke with his lampes, ſnoffers and other neceſſaryes. F. S. by H. [*in lower right hand corner.*]

37 .P. *Verſo of folio, but marked* [Fo. XLV.] And thou
ſhalt make .vii. lampes and put them an hye there on,
to geue lighte vnto the other ſyde that is ouer agaynſt
38, 39 it: with ſnoffers and fyre pannes of pure golde. And
hundred pounde weyghte of fyne golde ſhall make it
40 with all the apparell. And ſe that thou make them
after the facyon that was ſhewed the in the mounte.

The. .XXVI. Chapter.

1 AND thou ſhalt make an habi-
tatyō with ten curteynes of
twyned byſſe, Iacyncte ſcarlet and purpull, and ſhalt
make them with cherubyns of broderd
2 worke. The lenghte of a curtayne ſhalbe .xxviii. cubyttes, and the bredth .iiii. and they ſhalbe all of one
3 meaſure: fyue curtaynes ſhalbe coupled together one to
a nother: and the other fyue likewiſe ſhalbe coupled
together one to another.

𝔐.𝔆.𝔖. *This chapter alſo deſcrybeth the thynges pertaynynge to the holy place.*

4 Then ſhalt thou make louppes of Iacyncte coloure,
a longe by the edge of the one curtayne even in the
ſelvege of the couplinge courtayne. And likewiſe
ſhalt thou make in the edge of the vtmoſt curtayne

𝔐. 39 And an hundred

𝔙. 37 vt luceant ex aduerſo. xxvi, 1 opere plumario 2 Vnius menſuræ fient vniuerſa tentoria. 4 anſulas hyac.

𝔏. 1 cherubim ſolltu dran machen kunſtlich.

𝔐. 𝔐. 𝔑. 1 *Byſſe* loke in xxxv. of Exo. 4 *Iacynct* is a floure that we call: a vyolet: & it is alſo a precious ſtone or the coloure therof: but here it is taken only for the colore of Iacynct of which colore the curtayns ſhuld be of, as afore in the xxv, a.

𝔏. 𝔐. 𝔑. 4 *Gell ſeyden:* diſe farbe nennen viel, blawbefarb odder hymelfarb. So doch beyde kriechiſch vnd latinſch Bibel Hiacinthen farb ſagt, Nu iſt yhre Hiacinht beyde die blume vnd der ſteyn gell oder goltfarb, darumb zu beſorgen, das hie aber mal die ſprach verfallen vnnd vngewiſz ſey.

5 that is coupled therwith on the other ſyde. Fyſtie
louppes ſhalt thou make in the one curtayne, ād
fiftie in the edge of the other that is couppled therwith on the other ſyde: ſo that the louppes be one
6 ouer agenſte a nother. And thou ſhalt make fyſtie

.P. *Recto of folio, but without a folio numeral. Woodcut with the inſcription:* ¶ The forme of the ten cortaynes of the tabernacle with their cherubins and fiftye loupes. F. S. by H. [*in lower right hand corner.*]

buttons of golde, and couple the curtaynes together
with the buttons: that it maye be an habitacyon.
7 And thou ſhalt make .xi. curtaynes of gotes heere,
8 to be a tente to couer the habitacyō The lenght of
a curtayne ſhalbe .xxx. cubettes, and the bredth .iiii
9 ād they ſhalbe all .xi. of one meaſure. And thou ſhalt
couple .v. by thē ſelues, and the other ſixe by them
ſelues, ād ſhalt double the ſixte in the forefront of the
10 tabernacle, And thou ſhalt make fyſtie loupes in the
edge of the vtmoſt curtayne on the one ſyde: euen in
the couplynge courtayne, and as many in the edge
11 of the couplynge curtayne on the other ſyde. And
thou ſhalt make fyſtie buttones off braſſe and put them
on the louppes, and couple the tente together with
all: that there maye be one tabernacle.
12 And the remnaunt that reſteth in the curtaynes of
the tente: euē the bredeth of halfe a curtayne that
reſteth, ſhalbe lefte on the backe ſydes of the habita-
13 cyon: a cubite on the one ſide and a cubite on the
other ſyde, of that that remayneth in the length of
the curtaynes off the tabernacle, which ſhall remayne
of ether ſyde of the habitacion to couer it with all.
14 And thou ſhalt make another coueringe for the
tente of rams ſkynnes dyed red: ād yet ano- [Fo.
XLVI.] ther aboue all of taxus ſkynnes.
15 And thou ſhalt make bordes for the
16 habitacion of ſethim wod to ſtonde vp righte: ten cubettes long ſhall euery borde be, ād a cubette and an

taxus, *badger, cf. German* Dachs

V. 6 circulos aureos 7 ſaga cilicina 11 vnum ex omnib. operimētum fiat. 14 ſuper hoc . . de hyac. pellibus 15 tabulas ſtantes
L. 7 zigen haar 14 dachs fellen. 15 bretter machen

17 halfe brode. Two fete ſhall one borde haue to couple
them together with all, and ſo thou ſhalt make vnto
18 all the bordes of the habitacion. And thou ſhalt
make .xx. bordes for the habitacion on the ſouth ſyde,
19 and thou ſhalt make, xl. ſokettes of ſyluer ād put them
vnder the .xx. bordes: two ſokettes vnder euery borde,
20 for their two fete. In lyke maner in the northſyde of
21 the habitacyon there ſhalbe .xx. bordes ād .xl. ſokettes
22 off ſyluer: two ſokettes vnder eueryborde. And for
the weſt ende off the habitacyon, ſhalt thou make ſyxe
23 bordes, ād two bordes moo for the two weſt corners of
24 the habitaciō: ſo that these two bordes be coupled to
gether beneth and lykewyſe aboue with clampes. And
25 ſo ſhall it be in both the corners. And ſo there ſhalbe
viii. bordes in all and .xvi. ſokettes of ſyluer: ii. ſokettes
vnder euery borde.

26 And thou ſhalt make barres off ſethimwod fiue for
27 the bordes of the one ſide of the tabernacle, and fyue
for the other ſyde, and fyue for the bordes off the weſt
28 ende. And the mydle barre ſhall goo alonge thorow
the myddes

.P. *Verſo of* Fo. XLVI. *Woodcut with the inſcription*: ¶ The facion of the bordes of the tabernacle, with their fete, ſockettes and barres,

[Fo. XLVII.] *Woodcut with the inſcription*: ¶ The facion of the corner bordes with their fete ſockettes and barres.

29 .P. of the bordes and barre them together frō the
one ende vnto the other. And thou ſhalt couer the
bordes with golde and make golden rynges for them to
30 put the barres thorow, ād ſhalt couer the barres with
golde alſo. And rere vp the habitacion acordinge to
the facion ther of that was ſhewed the in the mount.
31 And thou ſhalt make a vayle off Iacyncte, of ſcarlett,
purpull and twyned byſſe, and ſhalt make it off broderd
32 worke and full of cherubyns. And hange it vppon .iiii

V. 18 latere merid. quod vergit ad auſtrum. 28 per medias tabulas a ſummo vſque ad ſummum 31 & pulchra variet. contextum
L. 24 eynem klammer 26 rigel 31 geller ſeyden, ſcharlacken vnd roſinrodt vnd getzw. weyſſer ſeyde

pilers of ſethim wodd couered with golde ād that their
knoppes be coured with golde alſo, and ſtonde apon
33 iiii. ſokettes of ſyluer. And thou ſhalt hāge vp the
vayle with rynges, and ſhall brynge in within the vayle,
the arke of wittneſſe. And the vayle ſhall deuyde the
holye from the moſt holye.
34 And thou ſhalt put the mercyſeate vppon the arcke
35 of witneſſe in the holyeſt place. And thou ſhalt put
the table without the vayle and candelſticke ouer
agaynſt the table: vppon the ſouth ſyde of the habitacion. And put the table on the north ſyde.
36 And thou ſhalt make an hangynge for the doore of
the tabernacle: of Iacyncte, off ſcarlett, off purpull and
37 off twyned byſſe, wroughte with nedle worke. And thou
ſhalt [Fo. XLVIII.] make for the hangynge, fiue pilers
off ſethim wodd, and couer both them ād their knoppes
with golde, and ſhalt caſt .v. ſokettes off braſſe for them.

¶ The .XXVII. Chapter

M.C.S. *Yet mo thynges pertaynynge to the holye place.*

1 AND thou ſhalt make an altare
of ſethim wodd: fyue cubettes
longe ād .v. cubettes brode,
that it be foureſquare, and .iii
2 cubettes hye. And make it hornes proceding out in
3 the .iiii. corners of it, and couer it with braſſe. And
make his aſſhepannes, ſhovels, baſens, fleſhhokes, fyre-
4 pannes and all the apparell there of, of braſſe after the
faſcyon of a net, ād put apon the nette .iiii. rynges:

M. 33 ſhalt brynge. xxvii, 4 and thou ſhalt make a gredyern alſo lyke a net of braſſe, vpon whoſe .iiii. corners ſhalbe .iiii. braſen rynges: and the gredyern ſhall reache vnto the myddes of the altare. And thou ſhalt make

V. 33 quo et ſanct. & ſanct. ſanctuaria diuidentur. xxvii, 2 ex ipſo erunt 4 in modum retis . . annuli æ nei.

L. 33 dem Heyligen vnd dem Aller heyligſten. 36 tuch machen . . . geſtrickt von geller ſeyden, roſinr., ſcharl., vnd getzwyrnet weiſſ. ſeyden. xxvi, 3 ertz 4 gitter . . ehern netz

M. M. N. 33 *The moſt holy place,* was the ſecrete and inwarde place of the ſanctuary wherī ſtode the arcke & the mercyeſeate, and into which none but the preſtes only might come, and that but once a yere. The figure of which thynge is declared in the Hebrewes ix, a. iii. Reg. vi, c.

5 euen in the .iiii. corners of it, and put it beneth vnder
the compaſſe of the altare, and let the net reache vnto
6 the one half of the altare, And make ſtaues for the
7 altare of ſethim wodd, and couer thē wyth braſſe, and
let them be put in rynges alonge by the ſydes off the
altare, to bere it with all.
8 And make the altare holowe with bordes: euen as
it was ſhewed the in the mount, ſo lett them make it,
9 And thou ſhalt make a courte vnto the habitacion,
which ſhall haue in the ſouth ſyde hāgynges of twyned
10 byſſe, beyng an hundred cubettes longe, and .xx
pilers thereof with there .xx. ſockettes of braſſe: but
the knoppes of the

.P. *Verſo of* Fo. XLVIII. *containing a woodcut with the inſcription:* ☾ The forme of the alter of the burnt-offrynge with his hornes, ringes ſtaues, gredyernes and other ornamētes.

11 [Fo. XLIX.] pilers and their whopes ſhalbe ſyluer.
In like wiſe on the north ſyde there ſhalbe hāgynges
of an hundred cubettes longe and .xx. pilers with their
12 ſokettes of braſſe, and the knoppes and the whopes of
ſyluer. And in the bredth of the courte weſtwarde,
there ſhalbe hangynges of fyftye cubettes longe, and
13 x. pilers with their .x. ſokettes. And in the bredth of
the courte eaſtwarde towarde the ryſynge of the ſonne,
14 ſhalbe hangynges of .L. cubyttes. Hāgynges of .xv
cubittes in the one ſyde of it with .iii. pilers, and .iii
15 ſokettes: and likewiſe on the other ſyde ſhalbe hangynges of .xv. cubettes with .iii. pilers and .iii. ſokettes.
16 And in the gate of the courte ſhalbe a vayle of .xx
cubettes: of Iacyncte, ſcarlet, purpul and twyned byſſe
wroughte with nedle worke, and .iiii. pilers with their
17 iiii. ſokettes. All the pilers rounde aboute the courte
ſhalbe whoped with ſyluer, and their knoppes of ſyluer,
18 and their ſokettes of braſſe. The length of the courte,
ſhall be an hundred cubettes, and the bredth fiftye, and

V. 5 ſubter arulam . . ad alt. medium. 8 Non ſolidū, ſed inane & cauum 10 viginti cum baſibus . . . capita cum caelaturis

L. 5 vnden auff vmb 9 hoff

M. M. N. 9 *The cowrte* is that whych we call a church yarde.

the heygth fyue, and the hangynges ſhalbe of twyned
19 byſſe and the ſokettes of braſſe. And all the veſſels of
the habitacion to all maner ſeruyce ād the pynnes there
of: ye and the pynnes alſo of the courte, ſhalbe braſſe.

.P. *Verſo of* Fo. XLIX. *containing a woodcut with the inſcription*: ℂ The figure of the orderinge of all the ornamētes which muſt ſtande in the tabernacle.

20 [Fo. L.] And commaunde the childern of Iſrael that
they geue the pure oyle olyue beaten for the lyghtes
21 to poure all way in to the lampes. In the tabernacle
of witneſſe without the vayle which is before the wytneſſe, ſhall Aaron ād his ſonnes dreſſe it both even and
mornynge before the Lorde: And it ſhalbe a dewtie
for euer vnto youre generacyons after you: to be geuen
of the childern of Iſrael.

The .XXVIII. Chapter.

1 AND take thou vnto the, Aaron
thi brother and his ſonnes with
him, from amonge the childern
of Iſrael, that he maye minyſtre vnto me: both Aaron, Nadab, Abihu,
2 Eleazar and Ithamar Aarons ſonnes. And
thou ſhalt make holye rayment for Aaron
thy brother, both honorable and glory-
3 ous Moreouer ſpeake vnto all that are
wyſe harted which I haue fylled with
the ſprete of wyſdome: that they make
Aarons rayment to conſecrate him wyth,
that he maye myniſtre vnto me.

M.C.S. *Aarons apparell, & hys ſonnes.*

Frō hēce vnto the bokes ende ād thorovve out all the nexte boke, thou ſhalt ſe vvhat moued the Pope and vvhence he toke the faſcion of the garmētes and ornamētes that are novve vſed in the chyrche

M. 21 and Aaron and hys ſonnes ſhall dreſſe

V. 19 cuncta vaſa 20 vt ardeat lucerna ſemper 21 collocab. eam . . . vt vſque mane luceat . . . cultus per ſucceſſiones eorum. xxviii, 1 vt ſacerdotio fungantur 2 in gloriam et decorem.

L. 19 negel 21 von morgen bis an den abent. xxviii, 1 meyn Prieſter ſey 2 zu ehren vnd ſchmuck 3 weyſen hertzen

M. M. N. 21 It is called the *tabernacle of witneſſe:* becauſe therin was contayned the couenaūt & witneſſe whervnto god wold that the chyldren of Iſrael ſhuld truſt, as Leu. iii. c. *Foreuer:* loke in Geneſis xiii, d.

4 These are the garmentes which they
shall make: a brestlappe, Ephod, a tunycle, a strayte cote, a myter and a
girdell. And they shall make holye
garmentes for Aaron thi brother ād
his sōnes, that he maye mynistre vnto
5 me. And they shal take there to,
golde, Iacincte, scarlet,

and the maner of halovvenge off the church, altare, chalice, fonte, belles, ād so forth, ād is become as it vvere a prest of the olde lavve, ād hath brought vs in to captiuite as it vvere vnder the ceremonies of the old lavve, saue theirs spak and ours be domme.

.P. *Verso of* Fo. L. *containing a wood-cut with the inscription*: ❙ The forme of Aaron with all his apparell.

[Fo. LI.] purpull and bysse.

6 And they shall make the Ephod: of
golde Iacyncte, scarlett, purpull ād white twyned
7 bysse with broderdworke, The two sydes shall come
8 to gether, clossed vppe in the edges thereof And
the girdell of the Ephod shalbe of the same worke-
manshippe ād of the same stuffe: euen of golde, Iacyncte, scarlete, purpull ād twyned bysse,
9 And thou shalt take two onyx stones and graue
10 in them the names of the childern of Israel: sixe in
the one stone, and the other sixe in the other stone:
11 acordinge to the order of their birth. After the
worke of a stonegrauer, euē as sygnettes are grauen,
shalt thou graue the .ii. stones with the names of
the childern of Israel, ād shalt make thē to be set
12 in ouches of golde. And thou shalt put
the two stones apō the two shulders of
the Ephod, ād they shalbe stones off remembraunce vnto the childern off Israel.
And Aaron shall bere their names before the Lorde
vppon hys two shulders for a remembraunce.
13, 14 And thou shalt make hokes off golde and two

ouches, *ornaments fit to display jewels or precious stones.*

V. 4 Rationale & superhumerale, tunicam et lineam strictam 6 bysso retorta, opere polymito. 7 Duas oras iunctas, 10 iuxta ordinem natiuit. eorum. 11 Opere sculptoris & cælatura gemmarii 12 memoriale fil. Israel, . . . ob recordationē. 13 vncinos ex auro

L. 4 weyhe . . brustlatz, leybrock, seyden rock, engen rock 10 orden yhrs alters 12 gedechtnis (*bis*)

M. M. N. 4 *Brestlappe* or brestflappe is soche a flappe as is ī the brest of a cope.

cheynes off fine golde: lynkeworke and wrethed, and
faſten the wrethed cheynes to the hokes.
15 And thou ſhalt make the breſtlappe of en- .P.
ſample with broderd worke: euē after the worke of
the Ephod ſhalt thou make it: of golde, Iacyncte,
ſcarlet, purple ād twyned byſſe ſhalt thou make it.
16 Foureſquare it ſhall be ād double, an hande brede
17 longe and an hande brede brode. And thou ſhalt fyll
it with .iiii. rowes of ſtones. In the firſt rowe ſhalbe
18 a Sardios, a Topas and Smaragdus. The ſeconde rowe:
19 a Rubyn, Saphir and a Diamonde. The thyrd: Lygu-
rios an Acatt and Amatiſt.
20 The fourth: a Turcas, Onix and Iaſpis. And they
ſhalbe ſett in golde in their incloſers.
21 And the ſtones ſhalbe grauen as ſygnettes be grauē:
with the names of the childern of Iſrael euen with
xii. names euery one with his name acordynge to
the .xii. trybes.
22 And thou ſhalt make vppon the breſtlappe .ii
faſteninge cheynes of pure golde ād wrethen worke.
23 And thou ſhalt make likewyſe vppon the breſtlappe
ii. rynges of golde and put them on the edges of the
24 breſtlappe, and put the .ii. wrethen cheynes of golde in
the .ii. rynges which are in the edges of the breſtlappe,
25 And the .ii. endes of the .ii. cheynes thou ſhalt faſten
in the .ii. rynges, and put them vppon the ſhulders
of the Ephod: on the foreſyde of it.
26 And thou ſhalt yet make .ii. rynges of gol- [Fo.
LII.] de ād put them in the .ii. edges of the breſtlappe
euē in the borders there of towarde the inſyde of the

M. 15 breſtlappe of iudgemēt 19 Rubye

V. 15 rationale quoque iudicii 17 Poneſque in eo . . ordines lapidum 17 in primo verſu 20 in quarto chryſolitus, onych., et beryllus 21 cælabuntur 25 quod rationale reſpicit.

L. 15 bruſtlatz des rechts . . nach der kunſt 17 fullen mit vier rigen 25 ecken am leybrock gegen ander vber.

M. M. N. 17 *Smaragdus:* Or an emeraude. 18 *Rubye:* Some rede a carbuncle.

L. M. N. 15 *Des rechts:* Mit dem wort zeygt er an, was der bruſtlatz bedeut, nemlich, das ynn Chriſto dem hohen prieſter die macht ſtehet das geſeze aus zu legen vnnd zu lēncken nach gelegenheyt der ſachen vnnd notturſt der gewiſſen, wie Chriſtus Matth. 12 mit dem Sabbath thut.

27 Ephod that is ouer agaynſt it. And yet .ii. other
rīges of golde thou ſhalt make, ād put thē on the
ii. ſydes of the Ephod, beneth ouer agaynſt the breſtlappe, alowe where the ſydes are ioyned together
28 vppō the brodered girdell of the Ephod. And they
ſhall bynde the breſtlappe by his rynges vnto the
rynges of the Ephod with a lace of Iacyncte, that
it maye lye cloſſe vnto the brodered girdell of the
Ephod, that the breſtlappe be not lowſed from the
Ephod.

29 And Aarō ſhall bere the names of the childern of
Iſrael in the breſtlappe of enſāple vppō his herte, whē
he goth in to the holy place, for a remēbraūce before
30 the Lorde allwaye. And thou ſhalt put ī the breſtlappe of enſāple* lighte and perfectneſſe:
that they be euē vpon Aarōs herte whē
he goeth ī before the Lorde ād Aarō
ſhall bere the enſāple of the childern of
Iſrael vpō his herte before the Lorde
alwaie

31 And thou ſhalt make the tunycle vnto
the Ephod, all to gether of Iacyncte.
32 And ther ſhalbe an hole for the heed in

Light ād perfecteneſſe: *In Hebrue it is lightes and perfectneſſes: ād I thynke that the one vvere ſtones that did gliſter ād had light in them and the other clere ſtones*

M. 27 bordered 29 breſtlappe of iudgement, ſo v. 30. 30 Vrim and Thumin

V. 28 vitta hyacinthina, vt maneat iunctura fabrefacta 29 ſuper pectus 30 doctrinam et veritatem 32 capitium, & ora per gyrum eius textilis

L. 30 Liecht vnd vollickeyt

M. M. X. 30 *Vrym and Thumin*, are Hebrue wordes: Vrim ſignifieth light & Thumin perfectnes: and I thynke that the one were ſtones that dyd glyſter and had light in thē, the other clere ſtones as criſtall. And the lighte betokened the light of Godes worde & the pureneſſe cleane lyuynge acordynge to the ſame, & was therfore called the enſample of the chyldern of Iſrael, becauſe it put them in remembraunce to ſeke Gods worde & to doo therafter.

L. M. X. 30 *Liecht* etc. Ebreiſch heyſſen diſe wort Urim and Thumim, Urim heyſt liechte odder glentze, Thumim heyſt, vollige vnd on wandel, was ſolchs ſey geweſen leyplich, weyſs man itzt nit mehr, Bedeut aber on zweyffel, das Chriſtus lere iſt vnd wirt behalten lauter, hel vnd on wandel ynn des prediger hertzen, wie paulus. Tito gepeut, das er das wort heylſam, redlich vnd vnſtrefflich furen ſol, vnd Timotheo befilt, eyn gutte beylage zu bewarē, das heyſt auch hie, das recht der kinder Iſrael auff Aarons hertzen tragen.

the myddes of it, ād let there be a bonde
of wouen worke rounde aboute the colore
of it: as it were the colore
of a partlet, that it rent not·
33 And beneth .P. vppon the
hem thou ſhalt make pomgranates of Iacyncte, of ſcarlet, and of purpull rounde
aboute the hem, and belles of golde be-
34 twene them rounde aboute: that there be
euer a golden bell and a pomgranate, a
golden bell and a pomgranate rounde
aboute vppon the hem of the tunicle.
35 And Aaron ſhall haue it vppon him
when he minyſtreth, that the ſounde
maye be herde when he goeth in to the holy place
before the Lorde and when he cometh out, that
he dye not.

colore of a partlet, *collar of a ruff, or neckband.*

as criſtall. And the lighte betokened the light of Godes vvorde and the pureneſſe cleane livinge acordynge to the ſame and vvas therefore called the enſample of the childern of Iſrael, becauſe it put thē in remembraunce to ſeke Gods vvorde ād to do there after.

36 And thou ſhalt make a plate of pure golde, and
graue there on (as ſignettes are grauen) the ho-
37 lynes of the Lorde, and put it on a lace
of Iacyncte and tye it vnto the mytre,
38 vppon the forefrunt of it, that it be apon
Aarōs foreheed: that Aaron bere the
ſynne of the holy thynges which the
childern of Iſrael haue halowed in all their holye
giftes. And it ſhalbe alwayes vpon Aarons foreheed,
that they maye be accepted before the Lorde

That he calleth the holyneſſe of the Lorde I ſuppoſe it be this name Iehouah.

39 And thou ſhalt make an albe of byſſe, and thou
ſhalt make a mytre of byſſe ād a girdell of nedle
worke.

40 And thou ſhalt make for Aarons ſonnes alſo cotes,

V. 35 vt audiatur ſonitus 36 Sanctum domino. 38 muneribus et donariis 40 tunicas lineas

L. 35 an haben wenn er dienet 36 die heylickeyt dem Herrn 38 gaben vnd heylthum . . das er ſie verſune

M. M. N. 36 *The holynes of the Lord,* was a name of God made with .iiii. letters, which the Hebrues durſt not name for honoure wyich they had to God, in ſtede wherof they ſayd Adonay. Which we haue interpret in Ex. vi, a. by his name Iehouah. 38 *The ſynne:* for the offryng made for ſynne, as Rom. viii, a.

41 girdels and bonettes honourable and glorious, and
thou ſhalt put them vppon Aaron thy brother ād on
his ſonnes with him [Fo. LIII.] and ſhalt anoynte
them and fyll theyr handes and conſecrate them,
42 that they maye myniſtre vnto me. And thou ſhalt
make them lynen breches to couer their preuyties:
43 from the loynes vnto the thyes ſhall they reach. And
they ſhalbe apon Aaron and his ſonnes, whē they goo
in to the tabernacle of wytneſſe, or when they
goo vnto the altare to myniſtre in holynes, that
they bere no ſynne and ſo dye. And it ſhalbe a
lawe for euer vnto Aaron ād his ſeed after him.

The .XXIX. Chapter.

M.C.S. The conſecracion of Aaron and his ſonnes.

1 THIS is the thinge that thou
ſhalt doo vnto them when
thou haloweſt them to be
my preaſtes. Take one oxe and two
2 rammes that are without blemyſh, ād vnleuēded
bred and cakes of ſwete bred tempered with oyle
and wafers of ſwete bred anoynted with oyle (of
3 wheten floure ſhalt thou make them) and put
them in a maunde and brynge thē in
the maunde with the oyle and the .ii
rammes.

maunde, *a hand baſket.*

M. 3 maunde with the oxe

V. 41 cunct. confec. manus 43 vt min. in ſanctuario, ne iniq. rei moriantur. xxix, 2 cruſtulam abſque fermento . . lagana 3 in caniſtro . . vitulū autem

L. 40 zu ehren vnd ſchmuck. 41 hende fullen 42 nydderkleyd 43 yhr miſſethat tragen.

M. M. X. 43 *Tabernacle of witneſſe:* Loke in Ex. xxvii, d. *Foreuer:* Loke in Gen. xiii, d.

L. M. X. 41 *Fullen:* Dis fullen iſt ein Ebreiſch ſprach, der man mus gewonen, vnd war das, wie ym folgend capitel ſteht, das ynn der weyhe den Prieſtern die hende mit opfer gefullet wurden fur dem herrn, Bedeut, das die prediger ſollen vol gutter werck ſeyn fur allen, wie Chriſtus Math, 5. leret laſt ewr gutte werck fur den menſchen leuchten.

4 And brynge Aaron ād his ſonnes vnto
the doore of the tabernacle of wytneſſe, ād
5 waſſh them with water, and take the garmentes, and put apon Aaron: the ſtrayte
cote, and the tunycle of the Ephod, and
the Ephod ād the breſtlappe: and gerth
thē to him with the brodered girdel of
6 the Ephod. And put the mitre vppō .P. his heed and
7 put the holy crowne vpon the mytre. Then take the
anoyntynge oyle and poure it apon his heed and
8 anoynte him. And brynge his ſonnes and put albes
9 apon them, ād gerth them with girdels: as well Aaron
as his ſonnes, And put the bonettes on them that
the preaſtes office maye be theirs for a perpetuall
lawe.

Of thys they take the conſecratynge of biſſhoppes ād annoyntynge of preaſtes, though they haue altered the maner ſome vvhat.

And fyll the handes of Aaron and of hys ſonnes,
10 and brynge the oxe before the tabernacle of witneſſe.
And let Aaron ād his ſōnes put their hādes apō his
11 heed ād kyll hī before the Lord in the dore of the
12 tabernacle of witneſſe And take of the bloud of the
oxe ād put it apō the hornes of the alter with thi
finger ād poure all the bloude apon the botome of the
13 alter, ād take all the fatt that couereth the inwardes,
ād the kall that is on the lyuer, and the .ii. kydneys
with the fatt that is apō thē: and burne thē apō the
14 alter. But the fleſh of the oxe and his ſkynne and his
donge, ſhalt thou burne with fyre, without the hoſte.
For it is a ſynneofferynge.

15 Then take one of the rammes, ād let Aaron and
his ſonnes put their hondes apon the heade of the ram,
16 and cauſe him to be ſlayne, ād take of his bloude, and
17 ſprenkell it rounde aboute apon the alter, and cutt
the ram in peces and [Fo. LIIII.] wheſh the inwardes
of him and his legges, ād put them vnto the peces

M. 17 waſh

V. 7 atque hoc ritu conſecrabitur. 9 eruntque ſacerd. mihi religione perpetua . 9 initiaueris manus 12 reliquum autem 13 et offeres incenſum

L. 6 heylige kron an den huet 9 hend fullen 10 hutte des zeugnis 12 alles ander blut 14 ſundopffer.

18 ād vnto his heed, ād burne the hole ram apon the
alter. For it is a burntofferyng vnto the Lorde, and a
ſwete ſauoure of the Lordes ſacrifice.
19 And take the other ram and let Aaron and hys
20 ſonnes, put their hondes apon hys heed and let him
than be kylled. And take of his bloude and put it
apon the typpe of the righte eare of Aaron and of
his ſonnes, and apon the thombe of their righte handes,
and apon the great too of their ryghte fete: and
ſprenkell the bloude apon the alter rounde aboute.
21 Than take of the bloude that is apon the alter and
of the anoyntynge oyle, ād ſprēkell it apon Aaron
and his veſtimētes, ād apō his ſonnes ād apō their
garmētes alſo. Thā is he ād his clothes holy ād his
ſonnes ād their clothes holye alſo
22 Than take the fatt of the ram and hys rompe and
the fatt that couereth the inwardes and the kall of
the lyuer and the two kydneys, and the fatt that is
apon them and the righte ſhulder (for that ram is a
23 fulloffrynge) and a ſymnell of bred ād
a cake of oyled bred ād a wafer out of
the baſkett of ſwete bred that is before
24 .P. the Lorde, and put all apon the handes of Aaron
and on the handes of his ſonnes: and waue thē in and
25 out a waueoffrynge vnto the Lorde. Than take it
from of their handes and burne it apon the alter: euen
apon the burntoffringe, to be a ſauoure of ſwetneſſe
before the Lorde. For it is a ſacrifice vnto the Lorde.
26 Then take the breſt of the ram that is Aarons fulloffrynge and waue it a waueoffrynge before the Lorde,
27 ād let that be thy parte. And ſanctifie the breſt of
the waueoffrynge and the ſhulder of the heueoffrynge
whiche is waued and heued vp of the ram whiche is

ſymnell, *a kind of cake, cf. Germ.* Semmel.

V. 18 oblatio eſt domino, odor ſuauiſſimus victimæ domini. 20 ac pedis, dextri 22 aruinā quæ operit vitalia . . aries conſecrationis 24 eleuans coram dom. 25 holocauſtum, odorem ſuauiſſimum 26 in partem tuam.

L. 18 den gantzen wider antzunden . . . brandopffer, eyn ſuſſer geruch des opffers dem HERRN. 22 eyn widder der fulle 24 webe es 25 zunde es an . . des HERRN opffer. 27 gewebet vnd gehebet

M. M. N. 18 What a *ſwete ſauoure* is ye ſhall fynd in Leui. i, c. and Ez. xx, f.

28 the full offrynge of Aaron ād of his ſonnes. And it
ſhal be Aarons ād his ſonnes dutye for euer, of the childrē of Iſrael: for it is an heueoffrynge. And the heueoffrynge ſhalbe the Lordes
dutie of the childern of Iſrael: euen of the ſacrifice
of their peaceoffrynges which they heue vnto the
Lorde.

dutye,' *due, i. e. that which belongs to him.*

29 And the holye garmentes of Aaron ſhalbe his
ſonnes after him, to anoynte them therin, and to fyll
30 their handes therin. And that ſonne that is preaſt
in his ſtede after him, ſhall put them on ſeuen dayes:
that he goo in to the tabernacle of witneſſe, to miniſtre in the holye place.
31 Thā take the ram that is the fullofferyng ād [Fo.
32 LV.] ſeth his fleſh in an holye place. And Aarō and
his ſonnes ſhall eate the fleſh of hī, ād the bred that
is in the baſket: euen in the dore of the tabernacle
33 of witneſſe. And they ſhall eat thē, becauſe the at-
tonmēt was made therewith to fyll their handes and
to ſanctifie thē: but a ſtraunger ſhal not eate therof,
becauſe they are holie
34 Yf oughte of the fleſh of the fulloffrynges, or of the
bred remayne vnto the mornyng, thou ſhalt burne it
with fyre: for it ſhall not be eaten, becauſe it is holye.
35 And ſe thou do vnto Aaron and his ſonnes: euen ſo
in all thynges as I haue commaunded the: that thou
36 fyll their handes ſeuen dayes and offre euery daye an
oxe for a ſynneoffrynge for to recōcyle with all. And
thou ſhalt halowe the alter when thou reconcyleſt it,
37 and ſhalt anoynte it to ſanctifie it. Seuē dayes thou
ſhalt reconcyle the alter and ſanctifie it, that it maye

V. 26 quo initiatus eſt Aaron (and v. 28) 28 quia primitiua ſunt & initia de victimis eorum pacificis 29 conſecrentur manus 33 placabile ſacrificium et ſanct. off. manus. 36 conſecrabis manus 36 Mundabiſque alt . cum immol. exp. hoſtiam

L. 28 todopffern vnd hebungen 36 vmb der willen die verſunet werden

M. M. N. 33 *Sanctifie:* Loke in Geneſis .ii, a.

L. M. N. 36 *Entſundigen:* das iſt abſoluieren vnd los ſprechen wie Ps. 50 *aſperges me yſopo,* das iſt, entſundige vnd abſoluir mich mit Iſopen.

be an alter most holye: so that no mā maye twich it
but thei that be consecrate.
38 This is that which thou shalt offre vpō
the alter: ii. lambes of one yere olde daye
39 by daye for euer, the one thou shalt offre
in the morninge and the other at euen.
40 And vnto the one lābe take a tenth
deale of floure myngled with the fourth parte of an
hin of beaten oyle, and the fourth parte of an hin of
41 wyne, for a drinc- .P. keoffrynge. And the other
lambe thou shalt offer at euen and shalt doo thereto
acordynge to the meateoffrynge and drinkeoffrynge
in the mornynge, to be an odoure of a swete sauoure
42 of the sacrifice of the Lorde. And it shalbe a con-
tinuall burntoffrynge amonge youre children after you,
in the doore of the tabernacle of witnesse before the
Lorde, where I will mete you to spake vnto you there.
43 There I will mete wyth the childern of Israel, and wilbe
44 sanctified in myne honoure. And I will sanctifie the
tabernacle of witnesse and the alter: and I will sanctifie also both Aaron and his sonnes to be my preastes.
45 And moreouer I will dwell amōge the children of
46 Israel and wilbe their God. And they shal knowe
that I am the Lorde their God that broughte them out
of the lond of Egipte for to dwell amonge them: euen
I the Lorde their God,

Toch not the chalyce nor the altare stōne nor holy oyle and holde youre hande out off the fonte.

❡ The .XXX. Chapter.

1 AND thou shalt make an alter to
burne cēse therin, of sethim
2 wod: a cubet longe, and a
cubet brode, euen foursquare
shall it be and two cubettes hye: with hornes proced-

M.C.S. *The altare of incense. The brasen lauer. The anoyntynge oyle.*

V. 38 iugiter 40 & vinum ad libandum eiusdem mensuræ 41 et iuxta ea quæ diximus 42 oblat. perpetua . . . vbi cōstituam 43 Ibique præcipiam filiis Isr., . . altare in gloria mea. xxx, 1 ad adolendum thymiama

L. 37 wer . . anruren wil, der sol geweyhet seyn. 39 zwisschen abents (v. 41) 42 betzeugen vnd mit dyr reden

3 yng out of it, ād thou ſhalt ouerlaye it with fyne golde
both the roffe ād the walles round aboute, ād his
hornes alſo, ād ſhalt make vnto it a crowne of gold
4 roūde aboute, ād .ii. goldē ringes

Fo. LVI. *containing a woodcut with the inſcription*:
¶ The forme of the altare of incenſe with all that belongeth vnto it.

.P. on ether ſyde, euen vnder the croune, to put ſtaues
5 therin for to bere it with all. And thou ſhalt make
the ſtaues of ſethim wodd and couer them with golde.
6 And thou ſhalt put it before the vayle that hangeth
before the arcke of witneſſe, and before the mercyſeate
that is before the witneſſe, where I will mete the.
7 And Aaron ſhall burne thereon ſwete cenſe euery
8 mornynge when he dreſſeth the lampes: and lykewyſe
at euen when he ſetteth vpp the lampes he ſhall burne
cenſe perpetually before the Lorde thorow out youre
9 generacions Ye ſhall put no ſtraunge cenſe thereon,
nether burntſacrifice nor meateoffrynge: nether poure
10 any drynkeoffrynge thereon. And Aaron ſhall reconcyle his hornes once in a yere, wyth the bloude
of the ſynneoffrynge of reconcylīge: euen once in the
yere ſhall he reconcyle it thorow youre generacions.
And ſo is it moſt holye vnto the Lorde.
11,12 And the Lorde ſpake vnto Moſes ſaynge: when
thou takeſt the ſumme of the childern of Iſrael ād
telleſt them, they ſhall geue euery mā a
reconcylinge of his ſoule vnto the Lorde,
that there be no plage amonge them when thou tel-
13 leſt them. And thus moch ſhall euery man geue that
goeth in the nombre: halfe a ſycle, after the holye
ſycle: a ſycle is .xx. geeras: [Fo. LVII.] and an halfe
14 ſycle ſhalbe the heueoffrynge vnto the Lorde. And

telleſt, *numbereſt*.

M. 10 reconcyle vpon the hornes of it 13 after the ſycle of the ſanctuarye

V. 3 coronam aureolam per gyrum 6 propitiatorio . . . vbi loquar tibi. 8 collocat eas ad veſp. 9 compoſitionis alterius 10 deprecabitur . . . ſuper cornua 12 tuleris ſummam . . recenſiti 13 menſuram templi . . obolos

L. 3 ſeyn dach 6 Gnaden ſtuel der auff dem zeugnis . . . zeugen. 9 fremd gereuch 10 auff ſeynen h. verſunen 12 verſunung ſeyner ſeel 13 ſeckel des heyligthums

all that are numbred of thē that are .xx. yere olde
and aboue ſhall geue an heueoffrynge vnto the Lorde.
15 The rych ſhall not paſſe, and the poore ſhall not goo
vnder halfe a ſycle, when they geue an heueoffrynge
16 vnto the Lorde for the attonemēt of their ſoules. And
thou ſhalt take the reconcylinge money of the children
of Iſrael and ſhalt put it vnto the vſe of the tabernacle of witneſſe, and it ſhall be a memoriall of the
childern of Iſrael before the Lorde, to make attonement for their ſoules.
17,18 And the Lorde ſpake vnto Moſes ſaynge: thou
ſhalt make a lauer of braſſe and his fote alſo of braſſe
to waſh with all, and ſhalt put it betwene the tabernacle of witneſſe and the alter and put water there-
19 in: that Aaron and hys ſonnes maye weſh both their
20 handes ād theyr fete thereout, whē they go in to the
tabernacle of witneſſe, or whē they goo vnto the
altare to miniſtre and to burne the Lordes offrynge,
21 leſt they dye. And it ſhalbe an ordinaunce for euer
vnto him and his ſeed amonge youre childern after you.
22,23 And the Lorde ſpake vnto Moſes ſaynge: take
principall ſpices: of pure myrre fiue hundred ſycles, of
ſwete cynamone half ſo moch

.P. *Verſo of* Fo. LVII. *containing a woodcut with the inſcription*: ℂ The figure of the lauer of braſſe with his fote.

[Fo. LVIII.] two hundred and fyftie ſicles: of ſwete
24 calamyte, two hundred and .L. Of caſſia, two hundred
and .L. after the holye ſycle, and of oyle olyue an hin.
25 And make of them holye anoyntynge oyle euen an oyle
26 compounde after the crafte of the apoticarye. And noynt

M. 16 an attonement

V. 14 dabit pretium. 16 monim. eorum 20 offerant . . . thymiama domino 23 aromata primæ myrrhæ & electæ 24 pondere ſanctuarii

L. 18 handfaſs 19 draus waſſchen 23 ſpecerey der beſten myrrhen 25 nach der apotecker kunſt.

M. M. N. 25 *Anoyntynge oyle:* This holy anoynting oyle doth figure the vertue of the holy ghooſt declared or ſhewed by the worde of god: & deſcendynge downe fyrſt on the hed of Aarō which is Chriſt & conſequently vpon the Apoſtles & all the faythfull, as in Ps. cxxxii, a.

the tabernacle off wytneſſe therewyth, and the arcke
27 of witneſſe, and the table with all his apparell, and the
candelſticke with all his ordinaunce, and the alter of
28 incenſe, and the alter of burntſacrifice and all his
29 veſſels, and the lauer and his fote. And ſacrifie them
that they maye be moſt holye: ſo that no man twyche
30 them but they that be halowed. And anoynte Aaron
and his ſonnes and conſecrate thē to miniſtre vnto me.
31 And thou ſhalt ſpeake vnto the childrē of Iſrael
ſaynge: this ſhalbe an holye oyntynge oyle vnto me,
32 thorow out youre generacions. No mans fleſh ſhalbe
anoynted therewith: nether ſhall ye make any other
after the makynge of it for it is holye, ſe therfore that
33 ye take it for holye. whoſoeuer maketh like that, or
whoſoeuer putteth any of it apon a ſtraunger, ſhall
peryſh from amonge his people.
34 And the Lord ſayd vnto Moſes: take vnto the ſwete
ſpices: ſtacte, onycha, ſwete galbanū ād pure frākē-
35 ſens, of etch like moch: ād make .P. cens of them cō-
pounde after the crafte of the apoticarye, myngled
36 together, that it maye be made pure and holye. And
beat it to powder and put it before the witneſſe in the
tabernacle of witneſſe, where I will mete the, but let it
37 be vnto you holye. And ſe that ye make none after
the makinge of that, but let it be vnto you holye for
38 the Lorde. And whoſoeuer ſhall make like vnto that,
to ſmell thereto, ſhall periſh from amonge his people.

¶ The .XXXI. Chapter

1 AND the Lorde ſpake vnto Moſes
2 ſaynge: beholde, I haue called
by name, Bezaleel the ſonne
of Vri ſōne to Hur of the
3 tribe of Iuda. And I haue filled hī with

M.C.S. The callynge of Bezaleel and Ahaliab the woorkmen. The Sabboth is commaunded.

M. 29 ſacrifye
V. 28 vniuerſam ſupellectilem quæ ad cult. eor, pertinet. 34 thus lucid. . 35 & ſanctificatione digniſſimum. 36 pones ex eo . . ſanctum ſanctorum erit vobis thym. 38 vt od. illius perf., peribit
L. 29 das allerheyligſt ſeyen . . . anruren wil der ſol geweyhet ſeyn. 33 ausgerottet

the ſprete of God, with wiſdome, vnderſtondinge ād knowlege: euē in all maner
4 worke, to finde out ſotle faytes, to worke
5 in golde ſyluer ād braſſe and with the
crafte to graue ſtones, to ſet ād to carue in tībre, ād
6 to worke in all maner workmāſhipe. And beholde,
I haue geuē him to be his companion Ahaliab the
ſonne of Ahiſamach of the tribe of Dan, and in the
hertes of all that are wiſe harted I haue put wiſdom
7 to make all that I haue commaunded the: the tabernacle of witneſſe, and the arcke of witneſſe, and the
mercyſeate that is there vppon, all the ornamentes
8 of the tabernacle and [Fo. LIX.] the table with his
ordinaunce, ād the pure cādleſticke with al his appar-
9 ell, ād the alter of incens, ād the alter of burntoff-
10 rynges with al his veſſels, ād the lauer with his fote,
ād the veſtimētes to miniſtre in, ād the holye garmētes
for Aarō the preaſt, ād the garmētes of his ſonnes to
11 miniſtre in, and the anoyntinge oyle and the ſwete
cenſe for the ſanctuarye: acordinge to al as I haue
commaunded the ſhall they doo.
12, 13 And the Lorde ſpake vnto Moſes ſayng: ſpeake
ūto the childern of Iſrael ād ſaye: ī any wyſe ſe that
ye kepe my Sabbath, for it ſhalbe a ſygne
betwene me and you in youre generacions
for to knowe, that I the Lorde doo ſanctifie
14 you. Kepe my Sabbath therfore, that
it be an holye thynge vnto you. He
that defileth it, ſhal be ſlayne therfore.
For whoſoeuer worketh therein, the ſame
ſoule ſhalbe roted out from amonge his
15 people. Sixe dayes ſhall men worke, but

The tables of ſtone are geuen Moſes.

faytes, *ſkilful works.*

The ſabbath beſide that it ſerved to come ād heare the vvorde of god and to ſeke his vvil ād to offer ād reconcile thē ſelues vnto god, it vvas a ſigne vnto them alſo ād

𝔙. 4 ad excogitandum quic. fabrefieri poteſt 10 vt fungantur officio ſuo in ſacris. 14 ſanctum eſt enim

𝔏. 6 allerley weyſen die weysheyt 14 wer yhn entheyliget . . des tods ſterben (v. 15)

𝔐. 𝔐. 𝔑. 13 *Sabboth:* The Sabboth beſyde that it ſerued to come and heare the worde of God and to ſeke hys wil & to offer & recōcyle them ſelues vnto God. It was a ſygne vnto thē alſo & dyd put thē in remembraunce that it was god that ſanctyfied thē with his holye ſprete & not they thē ſelues with their holy workes.

the seuenth daye is the Sabbath of the
holye reste of the Lorde: so that whosoeuer doeth any worke in the Sabbath daye,
16 shal dye for it. wherfore let the childern
of Israel kepe the Sabbath, that they obserue it thorowe out their generacions, that
17 it be an appoyntement for euer. For it
shalbe a sygne betwene me, and the childern of Israel for euer. For in sixe dayes the Lorde
made heauen and erth, and the .P. seuenth daye he
rested and was refresshed.

did put thē in remēbraūce that it vvas god that sanctified thē vvith his holy sprete ād not thei them selues vvith their holy vverkes.

18 And whē he had made an end of comening with
Moses vppon the mounte Sinai, he gaue him two tables
of witnesse: which were of stone and written with the
finger of God.

¶ The .XXXII. Chapter

1 AND when the people sawe that it
was lōge or Moses came doune
out of the mountayne, they
gathered them selues together
ād came vnto Aaron and sayde vnto him:
Vp ād make vs a god to goo before vs:
for of this Moses the felowe that brought
vs out of the londe of Egipte, we wote
not what ys become.
2 And Aaron saidē vnto them: plucke
of the golden earynges which are in the
eares of youre wyues, your sonnes ād of
youre doughters: and brynge them vnto
3 me. And all the people plucked of the
golden earinges that were in their eares,

M.C.S. *The Israelytes worship the golden calffe. Moses prayeth for them puttynge God in remembraunce of his promyse. He breaketh the tables for anger. He chydeth Aaron. The ydolaters are slayne. Moses prayeth God to forgeue them, or to put him oute of the booke of lyfe.*

V. 15 requies sancta domino 16 Pactum est sempiternum . 17 signumque perpetuum. xxxii, 1 congregatus aduersus Aaron . . deos

L. 15 Sabbath, die heylige ruge des HERRN 17 wart erquicket. xxxii, 1 widder Aaron . . Götter

M. M. N. 18 *Wyth the fynger of god,* that is: wyth the spyrite of God, or with the power of god, as Luc. xi, c.

4 and broughte them vnto Aaron And he receaued
them of their handes and facyoned it with a grauer
and made it a calfe of molten metall. And they fayde:
This is thi god, O Ifrael, whiche brought the out of the
londe of Egipte.
5 And when Aaron fawe that, he made an al- [Fo. LX.]
tare before it, and made a proclamacion faing tomor-
6 row fhalbe holy daye vnto the Lorde. And they rofe
vp in the mornynge and offred burntoffrynges, and
brought offrynges of attonement alfo. And than they
fatt them doune to eate and drynke, and rofe vpp
agayne to playe.
7 Than the Lorde fayde vnto Mofes: go get the doune,
for thi people which thou broughteft out of the lāde
8 of Egipte, haue marred all they are turned at once out
of the waye whiche I cōmaunded thē, ād haue made
thē a calfe of molten metall, ād haue worfhipped it and
haue offred therto and haue faide: This is thy God
thou Ifrael, which hath brought the out of the lande
9 of Egipte. And the Lorde fayde vnto Mofes: beholde,
10 I fee this people, that it is a ftife necked people, and
now therfore fuffre me that my wrath maye waxe hote
vppō thē, and that I may confume thē:
and than will I make of the a mightie
people,
11 Than Mofes befoughte the Lorde his
God and fayde: O Lord, why fhuld thy
wrath waxe hote apō thy people which
thou haft brought out of the lande of
Egipte with great power and with a
12 mightie hande? wherfore fhuld the
Egiptians fpeake and faye: For a mifchefe dyd he

The pope vvolde curfe .xx. hundred thoufande as blacke as coles, and fend thē to hell for to haue foche a profre, and vvolde not haue prayed as Mofes did.

V. 4 opere fuforio . . dii tui 5 præconis voce clam. 9 duræ ceruicis

L. 4 entwarffs mit eym griffel . . gotter 9 halfftarrig 10 fie auff freffe

L. M. N. *4 *Entwarffs:* das ift er malet es yhn fur was fie fur eyn bild machen folten. Das bedeut, das menfchen lere, dem volck fur bilden, was fie fur werck thun follen da mit fie Gott dienen, denn hie fiheftu, das die ynn difem kalb vermeynet haben dem rechten Gott zu dienen, weyl Aaron rufen left. Es fey des Herrn feft vnnd bawet ym eyn altar.

brynge them out: euen for to ſlee .P. them in the
mountayns, and to conſume them from the face of
the erth. Turne from thi fearſe wrath, ād haue com-
13 paſſion ouer the wikedneſſe of thi people. Remēbre
Abrahā, Iſaac ād Iſrael thy ſervauntes, to whō thou
ſworeſt by thyne owne ſelfe ād ſaideſt vnto thē: I wil
multiplye youre ſeed as the ſtarres of heauen, ād al
this lande which I haue ſaide, I will geue vnto youre
14 ſeed: ād they ſhall ēheret it for euer. And the Lorde
refrayned him ſelfe from that euell, which he ſayde
he wolde do vnto his people.
15 And Moſes turned his backe and wente doune frō the
hyll, and the .ii. tables of witneſſe in his hande: which
were wryttē on both the leaues and were the worke
16 of God, ād the writīge was the writinge of God grauē
17 apon the tables. And when Ioſua herde the noyſe of
the people as they ſhouted, he ſaide vnto Moſes: there
18 is a noyſe of warre in the hoſte. And he ſayde: it is
not the crye of thē that haue the maſtrye, nor of thē
that haue the worſe: but I doo heare the noyſe of
ſynginge.
19 And as ſoone as he came nye vnto the hoſte and
ſawe the calfe and the daunſynge, his wrath waxed
hote, and he caſt the tables out of his hande, and
20 brake them euen at the hyll fote. And he toke the
calfe which they had made [Fo. LXI.] ād burned it
with fyre, ād ſtampt it vnto powder and ſtrowed it in
the water, and made the childern of Iſrael drynke.
21 And thā Moſes ſayde vnto Aarō: what dyd this people
vnto the that thou haſt brought ſo great a ſynne apon
them.
22 And Aaron ſayde: let not the wrath of my Lorde
waxe fearſe, thou knoweſt the people that they are

V. 12 callide eduxit . . eſto placabilis 13 & poſſidebitis 15 ex vtraque parte 16 ſculpta in tabulis. 17 Vlulatus pugnæ 18 clamor adhort. ad pugnam . . vociferatio compell. ad fugam . . vocem cant. 19 & choros 20 contriuit vſque ad 22 pronus ſit ad malum

L. 13 deyne diener . . . deyner knechte 14 gerewet 17, 18 geſchrey (*thrice*) . . ſingentantzs. 19 den reygen . . malmetz 22 volck boſe iſt

23 euen ſett on myſchefe: they ſayde vnto me: make
vs a god to goo before us, for we wote not what
is become of Moſes the felow that brought us out
24 of the lande of Egipte. And I ſayde vnto them:
let them that haue golde, take and brynge it me:
and I keſt it in to the fyre, and there of came out
this calfe

25 when Moſes ſawe that the people were
naked (for Aaron had made them naked
vnto their ſhame when they made inſur-
26 rection) he went and ſtode in the gate of
the hoſte ād ſayde: Yf any man perteyne
vnto the Lorde, lett him come to me. And all the
ſonnes of Leui gathered them ſelues together and came
27 vnto him. And he ſayde vnto them, thus ſayeth the
Lorde of Iſrael: put euery man his ſwerde by his ſyde,
and goo in and out from gate to gate thorow out the
hoſte: and ſlee euery man his brother, euery man his
28 frende and euery man his neghboure. And the childern of Leui dyd .P. as Moſes had ſayde. And there
were ſlayne of the people the ſame daye,
29 aboute thre thouſande men. Then Moſes
ſayde: fyll your handes vnto the Lorde this
daye, euery man vppō his ſonne and vppon
his brother: to brynge vppō you a bleſſynge
this daye

naked, *bareheaded* (*Luther*), *more probably* unruly (*lxx. Onkel. Syriac*).

The popis bull ſleeth moo thā Aarons calfe, euē an hundred thouſand for one heere of them.

30 And on the morowe, Moſes ſayde vnto the people:
Ye haue ſynned a great ſynne. But now I will goo
vpp vnto the Lorde, to witt whether I can make an
attonement for youre ſynne.
31 And Moſes went agayne vnto the Lorde and ſayde:

V. 24 Quis . . aurum? 25 nudatus . . propter ignom. ſordis & inter hoſtes nudū cōſtituerat 29 Conſecraſtis . . vt detur vobis ben.

L. 25 entbloſſet . . auffrichtet . . entbloſſet zur ſchande 29 fullet heutte . . . das heutte vber euch

L. M. N. 25 *Entbloſſet:* dis bloſſen iſt, des heubts, wenn das heubt on decke vnnd ſchmuck iſt, vnd iſt die meynung, das Aaron hatte das volck Gotte entzogen, das er nicht mehr vber ſie regirt, ſondern giengen barheubt ynn eygen wercken, denn diſe geſchicht iſt eyn exempel, aller die on glauben, ynn eygen wercken wandeln, wilche ſchande zu richten die prieſter mit menſchen lere, vnd meynen doch die leut damit auff zurichten vnd wol zu helfen.

Oh, this people haue ſynned a great ſynne and haue
32 made thē a god of golde: Yet forgeue them their ſynne
I praye the: Yf not wype me out of thy boke which thou
33 haſt written. And the Lorde ſayde vnto
Moſes: I will put him out of my boke that
34 hath ſynned agaynſt me. But goo and
brynge the people vnto the lande which
I ſayde vnto the: beholde, myne angell
ſhall goo before the. Neuerthelater in
the daye when I vyſet, I will vyſett their ſynne vppon
35 them. And the Lorde plaged the people, because
they made the calfe which Aaron made.

O pitiful Moſes, ād likewiſe O mercifull Paul Rom. ix. And o abhominable pope vvith all his mercileſſe Idoles.

The .XXXIII. Chapter

1 AND the Lorde ſayde vnto Moſes:
departe ād goo hence: both
thou ād the [Fo. LXII.] people which thou haſt brought
out of the lād of Egipte, vnto the lande
which I ſwore vnto Abrahā, Iſaac ād Iacob, ſaynge: vnto thi ſeed I will geue it.
2 And I will ſende an angell before the,
and will caſt out the Canaanytes, the
Amorites, the Hethites, the Pherezites,
3 the Heuites and the Iebuſites: that thou
maſt goo in to a lande that floweth with
mylke ād honye. But I will not goo
among you my ſelfe, for ye are a ſtyfnecked people:
leſt I conſume you by the waye.

M.C.S. *The Lord ſendeth an angell before his people. The Lorde denyeth to goo vp with the people. The people lament their ſynne. Moſes talketh wyth the Lorde & deſyreth to ſe his face: and is commaunded to ſtande vpon the rocke.*

V. 31 obſecro, peccauit 32 aut dimitte . . aut 34 iſtum quo locutus . . in die vltionis 35 pro reatu. xxxiii, 3 diſperdam te in via.

L. 31 Ach, das volck 34 dahyn ich dyr . . heymſuchunge . . heymſuchen. 35 plaget . . gemacht, . . machet. xxxiii, 3 vnter wegen auff freſſen

M. M. N. 32 *To wype him oute of the booke*, is to put him oute of the nombre of the choſen and to caſt him cleane oute from god, as Rom. ix, a. 34 *To vyſet their ſynne*, is to haue their ſynne in remēbraunce to ponyſhe it as in Gen. i, d.

4 And when the people heard this euell tydinges,
they ſorowed: ād no mā dyd put on his beſt rayment.
5 And the Lorde ſpake vnto Moſes, ſaye vnto the
childern of Iſrael: ye are a ſtyffnecked people: I muſt
come ons ſodenly apon you, ād make an
ende of you. But now put youre goodly
raymēt from you, that I maye wete what to do vnto
6 you. And the childern of Iſrael layde their goodly
raymēt from them euē vnder the mount Horeb.

ons, *once, cf. Lat.* ſemel, *Germ.* einmal.

7 And Moſes toke the tabernacle ād pitched it without the hoſte a ferre of frō the hoſte, ād called it
the tabernacle of wytneſſe. And al that wold axe
any queſtiō of the Lorde, went out vnto the taber-
8 nacle of wytneſſe which was without the hoſte. And
when Moſes wēt out vnto the tabernacle, all the
people roſe .P. vp and ſtode euery man in his tentdore and loked after Moſes, vntill he was gone in to
9 the tabernacle. And as ſone as Moſes was entred
in to the tabernacle, the clouden piler deſcended and
ſtode in the dore of the tabernacle, ād he talked with
10 Moſes. And when all the people ſawe the clouden
piler ſtonde in the tabernacle dore, they roſe vp and
worſhipped: euery man in his tentdore.

11 And the Lorde ſpake vnto Moſes face to face, as a
man ſpeaketh vnto his frende. And when Moſes
turned agayne in to the hoſte, the ladd Ioſua his
ſeruaunte the ſonne of Nun departed not out of the
12 tabernacle. And Moſes ſayde vnto the Lorde: ſe,
thou ſaydeſt vnto me: lede this people forth, but
thou ſheweſt me not whom thou wilt ſend with me.
And haſt ſayde moreouer: I knowe the by name and
thou haſt alſo founde grace in my ſyghte:

V. 4 indutus eſt cultu ſuo. 7 Tabernaculum fœderis . . aliquam quæſtionem 8 reſpiciebantque tergum Moyſi . . tentorium 11 miniſter eius Ioſue filius Nun, puer

L. 5 alle machen 7 hutte des zeugnis 10 wolcken ſeule 11 ſeyn diener Ioſua der ſon Nun der iungling

M. M. N. 11 *To ſe God or to ſpeake to God face to face,* is: to haue a manyfeſte & a ſure knowledge of him as in Gen. xxxii, g.

L. M. N. 8 **Den rucken Moſe ſehen alle werck heyligen, die das geſetz nicht verſtehen noch vnter augen kennen.**

13 Now therfore, yf I haue founde fauoure in thi ſyghte,
thē ſhewe me thy waye ād let me know the: that I
maye fynde grace in thi ſighte. And loke on this alſo,
how that this nacyon is thi people.
14 And he ſayde: my preſence ſhall goo
15 with the, and I will geue the reſt. And
he ſayde: Yf thi preſence goo not with
16 me, carye us not henſe for how ſhall it
be knowne now that both [Fo. LXIII.]
I and thi people haue founde fauoure in
thi ſighte, but in that thou goeſt with us: that both
I and thi people haue a preemynence before all the
17 people that are vpon the face of the erth. And the
Lorde ſayde vnto Moſes: I will doo this alſo that thou
haſt ſayde, for thou haſt founde grace in my ſighte,
and I knowe the by name.
18 And he ſayde: I beſech the, ſhewe me thi glorye:
19 And he ſayde: I will make all my good goo before
the, and I will be called in this name Iehouah before the, ād wil ſhewe mercy to whom I ſhew mercy,
and will haue compaſſion on whom I haue compaſſion.
20 And he ſayde furthermore: thou mayſt not ſe my face,
for there ſhall no man ſe me and lyue.
21 And the Lorde ſayde: beholde, there is a place by

The popiſh ſaye, my chyrch, mi pareſh my dioceſe, and the monkes and fires ſaye all is oures.

V. 13 vt ſciam te . . reſpice populū tuum gentē hāc. 14 Facies mea præcedet te . . requiē dabo 16 vt glorificemur ab omnib. pop. 19 oſtendam omne bonum tibi . . miſerebor . . clemens ero . . mihi placuerit

L. 13 las mich deynen weg wyſſen, damit ichs erkenne 14 meyn angeſicht wirt gehen 16 etwas beſonders werden 19 alle meyn gut . . . gnedig . . . gnedig . . . erbarme . . . erbarme 20 kanſt . . nicht ſehen

M. M. N. 20 *There ſhal no man ſe my face and lyue.* Not that the face of God which is the face of lyfe, is the cauſe of death to them that ſe it, for the ſayntes that are in heuen do in dede ſe it. But that none that lyueth in the bodye can ſe ner cōprehend the maieſtye of his face: but muſt be fyrſt purifyed by death, as Paule declareth . 1 Cor. xv, g.

L. M. N. 19 Das iſt alles geſagt von Chriſto, wie der ſolt leben, predigen, ſterben, vnd aufferſtehen vnter dem volck Moſis, vnd ſie ſeyn angeſicht nicht ſehen ſondern yhm hynden nach ſehen wurden, das iſt, ſie ſolten Chriſtum ym glawben ſeyner menſcheyt vnd noch nicht ynn der gottheyt ſehen, vnd das iſt der rawm vnnd der fels, darauff alle glewbigen ſtehen ynn diſem leben. Aber dz iſt alles Gottis gabe on vnſer verdienſt, drum ſpricht er, wem ich gnedig byn dem byn ich gnedig etc.

22 me, and thou ſhalt ſtonde apon a rocke, and while
my glorye goeth forth I will put the in a clyſte of
the rocke, and will put myne hande apon the while I
23 paſſe by. And then I will take awaye myne hande,
and thou ſhalt ſe my backe partes: but my face ſhall
not be ſene.

The .XXXIIII. Chapter.

M.C.S. The tables are renued. The mercye of God. To haue felowſhip with the gentyles is forbidden, and their ydolatrie alſo. The feaſt of ſwete breade. The firſt begottē. The Saboth. The feaſt of iii. wekes. The firſt frutes. Moſes faſt, Moſes face glyſtreth.

1 AND the Lorde ſayde vnto Moſes:
hew the .ii. tables of ſtone like
vnto the firſt that I maye write
in thē the wordes which we-
.P. re in the fyrſt .ii. tables which thou
2 brakeſt. And be redye agaynſt the morn-
īge that thou mayſt come vpp early vnto
the mount of Sinai and ſtōde me there apō
3 the toppe of the mount. But let no man
come vp with the, nether let any man be
ſene thorow out all the mount, nether let
ſhepe nor oxen fede before the hyll.
4 And Moſes hewed .ii. tables of ſtone like
vnto the firſt ād roſe vp early in the morninge ād went vp vnto the moūt of Sinai as the Lorde
cōmaunded him: ād toke in his hāde the .ii. tables of
5 ſtone. And the Lorde deſcēded in the cloude, ād ſtode
with him there: ād he called apō the name of the Lorde.
6 And whē the Lorde walked before him, he cryed: Lorde
Lorde God full of compaſſion ād mercy, which art not
7 lightly angrye but abundāt in mercy ād trueth, ād kepeſt
mercy in ſtore for thouſandes, ād forgeueſt wikedneſſe,
treſpace ād ſynne (for there is no man ynnocēt before
the) and viſeteſt the wikydneſſe of the fathers vpō the

V. 22 protegam dextera mea 23 poſteriora mea, faciem . . . non poteris. xxxiiii, 1 Ac deinceps præcide, ait, tibi duas 2 ſtabiſque mecum 4 Excidit ergo 6 Dominator domine deus 7 apud te per ſe innocens

L. 23 ſol nicht geſehen werden. xxxiiii, 2 zu myr trettiſt 6 HERR HERR GOTT

childern ād apon childerns childern, euen vnto the
8 thryd ād fourth generatiō. And Moſes bowed hymſelf
9 to the erth quykly, ād worſhipped ād ſayde: Yf I haue
foūde grace in thi ſighte o Lorde, than let my Lorde
goo with us (for it is a ſtuburne people) and haue
mercy [Fo. LXIIII.] apō oure wikedneſſe ād oure
ſynne, and let us be thyne enheritaunce.
10 And he ſayde: beholde, I make an appoyntment
before all this people, that I will do maruells: ſoch as
haue not bene done ī all the worlde, nether amōge
any nacyon. And all the people amonge which thou
art, ſhall ſe the worke of the Lorde: for it is a terryble
11 thinge that I will doo with the: kepe all that I commaunde the this daye, and beholde: I will caſt out
before the: the Amorites, Canaanites, Hethites, Pher-
12 ezites, Heuites and Iebuſites. Take hede to thi ſelfe,
that thou make no compacte with the inhabiters of the
lōde whether thou goeſt leſt it be cauſe of ruyne
13 amonge you. But ouerthrowe their alters and breke
14 their pilers, and cutt doune their grooues, for thou
ſhalt worſhippe no ſtraunge God For the Lorde is
15 called gelous, becauſe he is a gelous God: leſt yf thou
make any agreament with the inhabiters of the lande,
when they go a whoorynge after their goddes ād do
ſacrifyce vnto their goddes, they call the and thou eate
16 of their ſacrifyce: ād thou take of their doughters vnto
thi ſonnes, and when their doughters goo a whoorynge
after their goddes, they make thi ſonnes goo a whoorynge after their goddes alſo.
17 .P. Thou ſhalt make the no goddes of metall
18 The feſt of ſwete bred ſhalt thou kepe, ād .vii. dayes
thou ſhalt eate vnleuended bred (as I commaunded
the) in the tyme apoynted in the moneth of Abib: for
19 in the moneth of Abib thou cameſt out of Egipte. All

V. 8 curuatus eſt pronus in terrā & adorans 9 & auferas iniq. . . . noſque poſſideas 10 Ego inibo pactum . . opus dom. terribile quod facturus ſum. 12 ne vnquam . . . iungas amicitias, . . in ruinam. 14 Dominus zelotes . . æmulator. 15 ineas pactum . . adorauerint ſimulachra 18 menſis nouorum: menſe enim verni temp.

L. 8 neyget ſich eylend . . bettet yhn an . . deyn erbgut ſeyn. 10 denn ſchrecklich ſols ſeyn 14 eyfferer . . eyfferiger Gott

that breaketh vp the matryce ſhalbe mine, and all
that breaketh the matryce amonge thi catell, yf it be
20 male: whether it be oxe or ſhepe. But the firſt of the
aſſe thou ſhalt by out with a ſhepe, or yf thou redeme
him not: ſe thou breake his necke. All
the firſtborne of thi ſonnes thou muſt nedes
redeme. And ſe that no mā appeare before me emptye.

That is a god texte for the pope.

21 Sixe dayes thou ſhalt worke, and the ſeuēth thou
ſhalt reſt: both from earynge and reap-
22 ynge. Thou ſhalt obſerue the feaſt of
wekes with the fyrſt frutes of wheate
herueſt, ād the feaſt of ingaderynge at the yeres ende.

earynge, *ploughing, or tilling; cf. Latin* aro.

23 Thriſe in a yere ſhall all youre men childern appeare
24 before the Lorde Iehouah God of Iſrael: for I will caſt
out the nacyons before the and will enlarge thi coſtes,
ſo that no man ſhall deſyre thi londe, while thou goeſt
vp to appeare before the face of the Lorde thi God,
thryſe in the yere.
25 Thou ſhalt not offre the bloude of my ſacrifyce with
leuended bred: nether ſhall ought [Fo. LXV.] of the
sacrifyce of the feaſt of Paſſeover, be lefte vnto the
26 morninge. The firſt of the firſtfrutes of thy lōde, thou
ſhalt brynge vnto the houſe of the Lorde thy God.
And ſe, that thou ſeth not a kydd in his mothers mylke.
27 And the Lorde ſayde vnto Moſes: write theſe wordes,
for vppon theſe wordes I haue made a couenaunt with
28 the and with the childern of Iſrael. And he was there
with the Lorde .xl. dayes ād .xl. nyghtes, ād nether
ate bred nor dronke water. And he wrote in the
tables the wordes of the couenaunt: euen ten verſes.
29 And Moſes came doune from mount Sinai and the
ii. tables of witneſſe in his hande, and yet he wyſt not
that the ſkynne of his face ſhone with beames of his

V. 20 dederis, occidetur. 23 omnipotentis domini dei Iſrael. 24 tulero gentes a facie tua 27 quibus . . . pepigi fœdus. 29 cornuta eſſet facies ſua ex conſortio ſermonis domini.

L. 20 brich yhm das genig. 23 dem hirſcher dem Herrn vnd Gott yſrael. 26 noch an ſeyner mutter milch 28 die zehen wort. 29 die haut ſeyns angeſichts glentzet, dauon, das

M. M. N. 19 *All that breaketh vp the matryce*, that is all the fyrſt born, as in Gen. xxxviii.

30 comenynge with him. And when Aaron and all the
childern of Israel loked apon Moses and sawe that the
skynne of his face shone with beames, they were a frayde
31 to come nye him. But he called thē to him, and then
Aaron and all the chefe of the companye came vnto
him, ād Moses talked with them.
32 And at the last all the childern of Israel came vnto
him, and he commaunded them all that the Lorde had
33 sayde vnto him in mount Sinai. And as soone as he
had made an ende of comenynge with them, he put a
34 couerynge .P. apō his face. But whē he went before
the Lorde to speak with him, he toke the couerīge of
vntill he came out. And he came out and spake vnto
the childern of Israel that which he was
35 commaunded. And the childern of Israel
sawe the face of Moses, that the skynne
of his face shone with beames: but Moses
put a couerynge vppon his face, vntill he went in, to
comen with him.

The Pope speaketh that vvhiche he is not commaunded.

The .XXXV. Chapter.

1 AND Moses gathered all the companye of the childern of Israel
together, and sayde vnto them:
these are the thinges which
the Lorde hath commaunded to doo:
2 Sixe dayes ye shall worke, but the seuenth daye shal be vnto you the holy
Sabbath of the Lordes rest: so that who-
3 soeuer doth any worke therein, shall dye. Moreouer
ye shall kyndle no fyre thorow out all youre habita-
cyons apō the Sabbath daye.

M.C.S. *The Saboth. The fyrst frutes are requyred. Theredynes of the people to offer. Bezaleel and Ahaliab are praysed of Moses and sett to worke.*

V. 31 principes synagogæ. 33 velamen. xxxv, 1 Israel, dixit ad eos 2 sanctus, sabbathum & requies domini . . . . occidetur.

L. 31 vbirsten der gemeyne 33 eyn deck. xxxv. 2 eyn Sabbath der ruge des Herrn

M. M.N. 30 The shynynge of Moses face is expounded in 2 Cor. iii, b.

4 And Moſes ſpake vnto all the multitude of the childern of Iſrael ſainge: this is the thinge which the Lorde
5 cōmaūded ſaynge: Geue frō amōge you an heueoffringe,
vnto the Lorde. All thatt are willynge in their hartes,
ſhall brynge heueoffringes vnto the Lorde: golde, ſyl-
6 uer, braſſe: Iacyncte, ſcarlet, purpull, byſſe ād gootes
7 hare: rams ſkynnes red and taxus ſkyn- [Fo. LXVI.]
8 nes and Sethim wodd: and oyle for lightes ād ſpices
9 for the anoyntynge oyle ād for the ſwete cens: And
Onixſtones and ſtones to be ſett for the Ephod and
for the breſtlappe.

10 And let all them that are wyſeharted amōge you,
come and make all that the Lorde hath commaunded:
11 the habitacion and the tent there of with his couerynge ād his rynges, bordes, barres, pilers and ſokettes:
12 the arke and the ſtaues thereof with the mercyſeate
13 ād the vayle that couereth it: the table and his ſtaues
with all that perteyneth thereto ād the ſhewebred:
14 the candelſticke of lighte with his apparell and his
15 lampes ād the oyle for the lyghtes: the censalter and
his ſtaues, the anoyntynge oyle and the ſwete cens ād
16 the hangynge before the tabernacle dore: the alter of
burntſacrifyces ād his braſen gredyren that longeth
there to with his ſtaues ād all his ordynaūce ād the
17 lauer and his fote: the hangynges of the courte with
his pilers and their ſokettes, and the hangynge to the
18 dore of the courte: the pynnes of the habitacion and
19 the pynnes of the courte with their boordes: the myn-
yſtrynge garmentes to mynyſtre with in holyneſſe, and
the holy veſtimentes of Aaron the preaſt and the veſtimentes of his ſonnes to mynyſtre in.

20 .¶. And all the companye of the childern of Iſrael
21 departed from the preſence of Moſes. And they went
(as many as their hartes coraged them and as many

V. 12 velum quod . . . oppanditur 13 menſam cum vectibus & vaſis 16 craticulā eius æneā cum vect. & vaſis 18 paxillos tabernaculi atrii 21 mente promptiſſima atque deuota

L. 5 von freyem hertzen 13 tiſch mit . . alle ſeynem geredt 21 hertzen gabe, vnd . . aus freyem willen

M M. N. 6 *Iacynct* is before in the xxvi, a. *Gotes hearre* is that which we call chāblet.

as their ſpirites made them willynge) and broughte
heueoffrynges vnto the Lord, to the makynge of the
tabernacle of wytneſſe and for all his vſes and for
22 the holy veſtmentes. And the men came with the
wemen (euen as manye as were willynge harted) and
brought bracelettes, earynges, rynges and girdels and
all maner Iewels of golde.
23 And all the men that waued waueoffrynges of golde
vnto the Lorde and euery man with whom was founde
Iacyncte, ſcarlet, purpull, byſſe or gootes hayre or
red ſkynnes of rammes or taxus ſkynnes, brought it.
24 And all that houe vpp golde or braſſe, brought an
heueoffrynge vnto the Lorde. And all men with whom
was founde ſethim wodd mete for any maner worke or
ſeruyce, broughte it.
25 And all the wemen that were wiſe herted to worke
with their handes, ſpanne, and brought the ſponne
worke, both of Iacyncte, ſcarlet, purpull and byſſe.
26 And all the wemen that excelled in wyſdome of herte,
27 ſpãne the gotes hayre. And the lordes brought Onix
ſtones and ſettſtones for the Ephod, and for the breſt
28 lappe, and ſpyce and oyle: both for the lightes [Fo.
LXVII.] and for the anoyntyng oyle and for the ſwete
29 cens. And the childern of Iſrael brought wyllynge
offrynges vnto the Lorde, both men ãd women: as
many as their hartes made thẽ wyllynge to brynge,
for all maner workes which the Lorde had commaunded to make by the hande of Moſes.

V. 22 armillas & inaures, annulos & dextralia . . Omne vas aureũ in donaria dom. ſeparatum eſt. 25 mulieres doctæ . . dederunt 26 ſponte propria cuncta tribuentes. 29 mente deuota obtulerunt donaria

L. 22 armſpangen, ohr rincken, ringe vnd gurttel vnd allerley gulden geredich 25 ſpunnen mit yhren henden . . ſpynwerck 26 ſpunnen zigen har

M. M. N. 23 *Byſſe* is fyne white, whether it be ſylke or lynen.

L. M. N. 22 Diſe zwey wort, *Heben* vnd *Weben*, müſſen wir lernen brauchen vnd verſtehen, denn eyn opffer oder gabe zu Gottis dienſt heyſt darumb eyn Hebe, odder Hebopffer das mans dem herrn ſtracks empor hub. Webe aber heyſt es, das mans hyn vnd her zog ynn vier ortter gegen morgen, abent, mittag vnd mitternacht, Bedeut alles, das Euangeliſch weſen, das ſich zuerſt gegen got hebt mit rechtem glauben, vnd darnach ſich ausbreyt ynn alle welt, durch predigen vnd bekentnis des glaubens zu leren auch den nehiſten.

30 And Moſes ſayde vnto the childern of Iſrael: beholde, the Lorde hath called by name Bezabeel the
31 ſon of Vri the ſon of Hur of the trybe of Iuda, and
hath fylled him with the ſprete of God, with wiſdome,
vnderſtōdinge and knowlege, euen in all maner worke,
32 ād to fynde out curyous workes, to worke in golde,
33 ſyluer and braſſe: and with grauynge of ſtones to ſett,
and with keruynge in wodd, and to worke in all maner
34 of ſotle workes. And he hath put in hys harte the
grace to teach: both him and Ahaliab the ſon of
35 Ahiſamach of the trybe of Dan hath he fylled with
wiſdome of herte, to worke all maner of grauen worke:
they are alſo broderers and workers with nedle, In
Iacyncte, ſcarlet, purple and byſſe, and are weuers
that can make all maner worke, and can deuyſe ſotle
workes.

The .XXXVI. Chapter.

1 AND Bezaleel wrought and Ahaliab ād all wyſe harted mē to
whom the Lorde .P. had geuen
wyſdome and vnderſtondynge,
to knowe how to worke all maner worke

M.C.S. The thynges that Bezaleel and Ahaliab made for the holy place of the Lorde.

for the holye ſervice, in all that the Lorde commaunded.
2 And Moſes called for Bezaleel Ahaliab and all the
wiſe harted men in whoſe hertes the Lorde had put
wyſdome, euē as many as their hartes coraged to
3 come vnto the worke to worke it. And they receaued
of Moſes all the heueoffrynges which the childern of

M. 30 by name Bezaleel

V. 31, 32 & omni doctrina ad excogitandū 33 & opere carpentario quicquid fabre adinueniri poteſt, 34 dedit in corde eius. 35 abietarii, polymitarii, ac plumarii . . & texant omnia, ac noua quæque reperiāt. xxxvi, 1 quæ in vſus ſanct. neceſſaria 2 opus, 3 tradidit eis vniuerſa donaria

L. 33 allerley kunſtlich erbeyt 34 vnd hat yhm vnterweyſung ynn ſeyn hertz geben 35 machen allerley werck, . . . vnd kunſtlich erbeyt erfinden. xxxvi, 1 allerley werck . . . zum dienſt des heyligthums

Iſrael had brought for the worke of the holye ſervice
to make it with all. And they brought beſyde that
wyllyngeoffringes euery mornyng.
4 And all the wyſe men that wrought all the holye
worke, came euery man from his worke which they
5 made, and ſpake vnto Moſes ſaynge: the people brynge
to moch and aboue that is ynough to ſerue for the
werke which the Lorde hath commaunded to make.
6 And then Moſes gaue a commaundment, and they
cauſed it to be proclamed thorow out the hoſte ſaynge:
ſe that nether man nor woman prepare any moare
worke for the holy heueoffrynge, and ſo the people
7 were * forboden to brynge: for the ſtuffe
they had, was ſufficyent for them vnto all
the worke, to make it and to moch.

when wil the Pope ſaye hoo, and forbid to offere for the byldinge of ſaint Peters chyrch: and when will our ſpiritualtie ſaye hoo, and forbid to geue thē more londe ād to make moo fūdacions? neuer verely vntill they haue all.

8 [Fo. LXVIII.] And all the wyſe harted
men amonge them that wroughte in the
worke of the habytacyon made: euen .x.
corteynes of twyned byſſe, Iacyncte, ſcarlet and purple, and made them full of
9 cherubyns with broderd worke. The
length of one curtayne was .xxviii. cubettes and the bredth .iiii. and were all
10 off one ſyſe. And they coupled fyue cur-
teyns by them ſelues, and other fyue by them ſelues.
11 And they made fyſtye louppes of Iacincte alonge by the
edge of the vtmoſt curtayne, euen in the ſilvege of the
couplynge courtayne: And likewiſe they made on the
ſyde of the vtmoſt couplinge curtayne on the other
12 ſyde, fyftye louppes they made in the one curtayne,
and fyftye in the edge of the couplynge curtayne on
the other ſyde: ſo that the loupes were one oueragenſt
13 another. And they made fyftye rynges of golde, and
coupled the curtaynes one to another with the rynges:
and ſo was it made a dwellinge place.

M. 6 forbidden
V. 3 Qui cum inſtarent operi quotidie, mane vota populus offerebat. 6 præconis voce cantari 7 ſufficerent & ſuperabūdarent. 8 opere vario & arte polymita 13 qui morderent cortinarum anſas
L. 3 yhr willige ſteure zu yhm.

14 And they made .xi. curtaynes of gootes heere to be
15 a tent ouer the tabernacle .xxx. cubettes longe a pece
and .iiii. cubettes brode, and they all .xi. of one ſyſe.
16 And they coupled .v. by them ſelues, and .P. vi. by
17 them ſelues, and they made fyſtye louppes alonge by
the border of the vtmoſt couplinge curtayne on the
one ſyde, and fyſtye in the edge of the couplynge cur-
18 tayne on the other ſyde. And they made fyſtye
rynges of braſſe to couple the tent together that it
19 myghte be one. And they made a couerynge vnto
the tent of rammes ſkynnes red, and yet another of
taxus ſkynnes aboue all.
20 And they made bordes for the dwellynge place of
21 ſethim wodd that ſtode vpright euery borde .x. cubetes
22 longe and a cubet ād an halfe brode. And they made
ii. fete to euery boorde of the dwellinge place ioyninge
23 one to another. And they made .xx. boordes for the
24 ſouth ſyde of the habytacyon, and .xl. ſokettes of ſyluer
vnder the .xx. boordes .ii. ſokettes vnder euery boorde,
25 euen for the .ii. fete of thē. And for the other ſyde of
the dwellynge towarde the north, they made other .xx
26 boordes with .xl. ſokettes of syluer .ii. ſokettes vnder
27 euery boorde. And behynde in the ende of the taber-
28 nacle towarde the weſt, they made .vi. boordes and .ii
29 other bordes for the corners of the habitacyon behynde,
and they were ioyned cloſſe both beneth and alſo aboue
with clampes, and thus they dyd to both the corners:
30 ſo they were in all .viii. boordes and .xvi. ſokettes,
vn-[Fo. LXIX.] der euery borde two ſokettes.
31 And they made barres of ſethim wodd .v. for the
32 bordes of the one ſyde of the habitacion and .v. for the
other, ād fiue for the bordes of the weſt ende of the
33 habitacion. And they madė the myddell barre to
ſhote thorowe the bordes: euen from the one ende to
34 the other, and ouerlayde the bordes with golde, and

V. 14 ſaga vndecim 18 quib. necteretur tectū, vt vnum pallium ex omnibus ſagis fieret. 22 Sic fecit in omnibus tabern. tabulis. 27 contra occidentem vero, id eſt, ad eam partē tabernaculi quæ mare reſpicit 29 & in vnam compaginem pariter ferebantur. 32 occidentalem . . . contra mare.

L. 20 fœrn holtz ſtrack

made thē rynges of golde to thruſt the barres thorow,
35 and couered the barres with golde. And they made
an hangynge of Iacincte, of ſcarlett purple ād twyned
36 byſſe with cherubyns of broderd worke. And made
thervnto .iiii. pilers of ſethim wodd and ouerlayde them
with golde. Their knoppes were alſo of gold, ād they
37 caſt for them .iiii. ſokettes of ſyluer. And they made
an hangynge for the tabernacle dore: of Iacincte, ſcar-
38 let, purple and twyned byſſe of nedle worke, and the
pilers of it were fiue with their knoppes, and ouerlayde
the heades of them and the whooppes with golde, with
their fiue ſokettes of braſſe.

The .XXXVII. Chapter

M.C.S. *The arcke of witneſſe. The mercyſeate. The table. The candelſtycke. The lyghtes. The altare and the incenſe.*

1 AND bezaleel made the arcke of
ſethim wodd two cubettes and
an halfe longe and a cubette
and a halfe brode, and a cu-
2 bett and a halfe hye: and ouerlayde it
with fyne gol- .P. de both within and
without, and made a crowne' of golde to
3 it rounde aboute, and caſt for it .iiii. rynges of golde
for the .iiii. corners of it: twoo rynges for the one ſyde
4 and two for the other, and made ſtaues of Sethim wodd,
5 and couered them wyth golde, and put the ſtaues in
the rynges alonge by the ſyde of the arcke to bere it
with all.

6 And he made the mercyſeate of pure golde two
cubettes and a halfe longe and one cubette and a
7 halfe brode, and made two cherubyns of thicke golde

V. 35 varium atque diſtinctum. xxxvii, 2 coronam auream per gyrum 6 propitiatorium, id eſt oraculum 7 Duos et. cher. ex auro ductili

L. 35 Vnd machet Cherubim am furhang kunſtlich. xxxvii, 7 Cher. von tichtem golt

M. M. N. 6 *Mercyſeate* was the place where God ſpake vnto the children of Iſrael, whyche was vpō the arcke of witneſſe fygurynge Chriſt, as it is ſayde Hebr. ix, b.

8 apon the two endes off the mercyſeate: One cherub
on the one ende, and another cherub on the other
9 ende of the mercyſeate. And the cherubyns ſpredde out
their wynges aboue an hye, and couered the mercyſeate therewith, And their faces were one to another:
euen to the mercyſeate warde, were the
faces of the cherubins.

mercyſeate warde, *i. e. toward the mercy ſeat*

10 And he made the table of ſethim wodd
two cubettes longe and a cubette brode, and a cu-
11 bette and an halfe hyghe, and ouerlayde it with fine
golde, and made thereto a crowne of golde rounde
12 aboute, and made thereto an whope
of an hande brede rounde aboute, and
made vnto the whope a crowne of
13 golde rounde aboute, and caſt for it .iiii. rynges of
golde ād put the rynges in the .iiii. corners by the fete:
14 [Fo. LXX.] euen vnder the whope to put ſtaues in to
15 bere the table with all. And he made ſtaues of Sethim
wodd and couered them with golde to bere the table
16 with all, and made the veſſels that were on the table
of pure golde, the dyſſhes, ſpones, flattpeces and pottes
to poure with all,

hande brede. *the breadth of a hand cf. xxxix, 9.*

17 And he made the candelſticke of pure thicke golde:
both the candelſticke and his ſhaft: with braunces,
18 bolles, knoppes ād floures procedynge out of it. Sixe
braunches procedinge out of the ſydes thereof .iii. out
19 of the one ſyde and .iii. out of the other. And on
euery braunche were .iii. cuppes like vnto almondes,
wyth knoppes and floures thorow out the ſixe
20 braunches that proceded out of the candelſticke. And
apon the candelſticke ſelfe, were .iiii. cuppes after the
21 facyon of almondes with knoppes and floures: vnder

F. 8 in ſummitate . . . duos cherub. 9 ſeque mutuo & illud reſpicientes. 12 coronam aur. interraſilem quatuor digit., & ſuper eandem alteram cor. aur. 19 ſphærulæque ſimul & lilia

L. 13 an ſeynen fuſſen 14 hartt an der leyſten 16 aus vnd eyn goſſe. 26 ſeyn dach vnd ſeyne wende rings vmb her vnd ſeyne horner

L. M. N. 19 *Wie mandelnuſſe:* das iſt diſe koppfe oder becher waren auſswendig vmbher bocklicht oder knorricht, als weren gulden nuſs ſchalen vmbher dreyn geſetzt.

22 eueri two braunches a knoppe. And the knoppes and
the braunches proceded out of it, and were all one pece
23 of pure thicke golde. And he made ſeuen lampes
thereto, and the ſnoffers thereof, ād fyrepānes of pure
24 golde. An hundred weyghte of pure golde, made both
it and all that belonged thereto.

25 And he made the cēsalter of ſethī wodd of a cubett
lōge ād a cubett brode: euē .iiii. ſquare .P. and two cu-
26 bettes hye with hornes procedynge out of it. And he
couered it with pure golde both the toppe ād the ſydes
rounde aboute ād the hornes of it, and made vnto it
27 a crowne of golde rounde aboute. And he made two
rynges of golde vnto it, euen vnder the croune apon
ether ſyde of it, to put ſtaues in for to bere it with al:
28 and made ſtaues of ſethim wodd, ād ouerlayde them
29 with golde. And he made the holy anoyntinge oyle
and the ſwete pure incēs after the apothecarys crafte.

The .XXXVIII. Chapter

M.C.S. The altare of burntofferynges. The braſen lauer. The ſomme of that the people offred to the buyldyng of the habytacyon of the Lorde.

1 AND he made the burntoffryngealter of ſethim wodd, fiue cubettes longe ād .v. cubettes
brode: euen .iiii. ſquare, and
2 iii. cubettes hye. And he made hornes
in the .iiii. corners of it procedinge out of
3 it, and ouerlayde it with braſſe. And he
made all the veſſels of the alter: the
cauldrons, ſhovels, baſyns, fleſhokes and
colepannes all of braſſe.

4 And he made a braſen gredyren of networke vnto
the alter rounde aboute alowe beneth vnder the compaſſe of the alter: ſo that it reached vnto half the
5 altare, and caſt .iiii. rynges of braſſe for the .iiii. endes
6 of the gredyren to put ſtaues in. And he made ſtaues
7 of ſethim wodd and couered them with braſſe, and put

V. 26 cum craticula ac parietibus & cornibus.
L. 29 reuchwerck von reyner ſpecerey

the ſtaues in the rynges alonge by the alter ſy-[Fo.
LXXI.] de to bere it with all, and made the alter
holowe with bordes.
8 And he made the lauer of braſſe and the fote of it
alſo of braſſe, in the ſyghte of them that dyd watch*
before the dore of the tabernacle of witneſſe.
9 And he made the courte with hangynges of twyned
byſſe of an hundred cubettes longe vppon the ſouthſyde,
10 ād xx. pilers with .xx. ſokettes of braſſe: but the knoppes
11 of the pilers, ād the whoopes were ſyluer. And on the
north ſyde the hanginges were an hundred cubettes
longe with .xx. pilers and .xx. ſokettes of braſſe, but
the knoppes and the whopes of the pilers were of ſyl-
12 uer. And on the weſt ſyde, were hangynges of .L.
cubettes longe, and .x. pilers with their .x. ſokettes,
and the knoppes ād the whoopes of the pilers were
13 ſyluer. And on the eaſt ſyde towarde the ſonne ryſynge,
14 were hangynges of .L. cubettes: the hangynges of the
one ſyde of the gate were .xv. cubbettes longe, and
15 their pilers .iii. with their .iii. ſokettes. And off the
other ſyde of the court gate, were hanginges alſo of
xv. cubettes longe, and their pilers .iii. with .iii. ſok-
16 ettes. Now all the hanginges of the courte rounde
17 aboute, were of twyned byſſe, ād the ſokettes of the
pilers were braſſe: but the knoppes ād the whoopes of
the pilers we-.P. re ſyluer, and the heedes were ouer-

V 7 Ipſum autem altare non erat ſolidum, ſed cauum 8 de ſpeculis mulierū, quæ excubabant

L. 8 auff dem platz der heere die fur der thur der hutten des zeugnis lagen 9 gezwirnter weyſſer ſeyden (and ſo throughout)

L. M. N. 8 *Der heere:* Diſe heere waren die andechtigen witwynn vnd weyber, die mit faſten vnd beten fur der hutten Gott riterlich dieneten, wie .i. Reg. 2. zeygt, vnd Paulus .i. Tim. 5. beſchreybt, wie auch S. Lucas die heylige prophetyn Hanna rumet Luc. 2. Es reden aber hie die Iuden vnd viel andere, von frawen ſpiegeln, die da ſolten am handfaſs geweſen ſein, die laſſen wyr yhrs ſynnes walden. Es bedeut aber geyſtlich, die hiſtorien des alten teſtamēts die man prediget durchs Euangelion, wilche gar ritterlich ſtreytten den glawben zu beweyſen ynn Chriſto widder die werckheyligen etc.

---

* NOTE.—Tyndale's rendering is suggested by the Latin *excubabant*, while Luther's is an ingenious inferential rendering drawn from the Greek. The Hebrew *mareah* may be rendered *sight*, or *mirror;* the latter is the rendering of the LXX., which, if correct, imports that the laver of brass was made of the brazen mirrors, offered by the women. This meaning is sustained also by the Targums and good critics.

layde wyth ſyluer, ād all the pilers of the courte were
18 whoped aboute with ſyluer. And the hanginge of the
gate of the courte was nedleworke: of Iacincte, ſcarlet, purple, and twyned byſſe .xx. cubettes longe and
fiue in the bredth, acordynge to the hangynges of the
19 courte. And the pilers were .iiii. with .iiii. ſokettes of
braſſe, ād the knoppes of ſyluer, ād the heedes ouer-
20 layde with ſyluer and whoped aboute with ſyluer, ād
all the pynnes of the tabernacle ād of the courte rounde
aboute were braſſe.

21 This is the ſumme of the habitacyō of witneſſe,
whiche was counted at the commaundment of Moſes:
and was the office of the Leuites by the hande
22 of Ithamar ſonne to Aaron the preaſt. And Bezaleel ſonne of Vri ſonne to Hur of the trybe of
Iuda, made all that the Lorde commaunded Moſes,
23 and with hī Ahaliab ſonne of Ahiſamach of the tribe
of Dan, a cōnynge grauer ād a worker of nedle worke
In Iacincte, ſcarlett, purple ād byſſe.

24 All the golde that was occupyde apon occupyde, *uſed*
all the worke of the holy place (whiche was the golde
of the waueofferynge) was, .xxix. hundred weyght and
ſeuen hundred and .xxx. ſycles, acordynge to the holy
25 ſycle. And the ſumme of ſyluer that came of the multitude, was .v. [Fo. LXXII.] ſcore hundred weyght and
a thouſande ſeuen hundred and .Lxxv. ſycles of the
holye ſycle.

26 Euery man offrynge halfe a ſycle after the weyght
of the holye ſycle amonge them that went to be nombred from .xx. yere olde and aboue, amonge .vi. hundred thouſande ād .iii. thouſande ād .v. hundred ād .L. men.

27 And the .v. ſcore hundred weyght of ſyluer went to
the caſtynge of the ſokettes of the sanctuary and the
ſokettes of the vayle: an hundred ſokettes of the fiue
ſcore hundred weigh an hundred weyght to euery
28 ſokette. And the thouſande ſeuen hundred and .Lxxv
ſycles, made knoppes to the pilers ād ouerlayde the
heedes and whoped them.

V. 24 ad menſuram ſanctuarii
L. 24 nach dem ſeckel des heyligthums

29 And the braſſe of the waueofferynge was .Lxx.
hundred weyght and two thouſande, and .iiii. hundred
30 ſycles. And therewith he made the ſokettes to the
doore of the tabernacle of witneſſe, and the braſen
altare, and the braſen gredyren that longeth thereto,
31 and all the veſſels of the alter, and the ſokettes of the
courte rounde aboute, and the ſokettes of the courte
gate, and all the pynnes off the habitacyon, and all
the pynnes of the courte rounde aboute.

.P. ¶ The .XXXIX. Chapter.

M.C.S. The makynge of Aaron and his ſonnes apparell. All that the Lorde commaunded was offred.

1 AND of the Iacyncte, ſcarlet, purple and twyned byſſe, they
made the veſtimẽtes of min-
iſtracion to do ſeruyce in in
that holye place, and made the holye
garmentes that perteyned to Aaron, as
the Lorde commaunded Moſes.
2 And they made the Ephod of golde, Iacinte, ſcar-
3 let, purple, and twyned byſſe. And they dyd beate
the golde in to thynne plates, ãd cutte it in to
wyres: to worke it in the Iacincte, ſcarlet, purple,
4 and the byſſe, with broderd worke. And they made
the ſydes come together, and clooſed them vp by the
5 two edges. And the brodrynge of the girdel that
was vpon it, was of the ſame ſtuffe and after the
ſame worke of golde, Iacincte, ſcarlet, purple and
twyned byſſe, as the Lorde commaunded Moſes.
6 And they wrought onix ſtones clooſed in ouches
of golde and graued as ſygnettes are grauen with the
7 names of the children of Iſrael, and put them on the
ſhulders of the Ephod that they ſhulde be a remembraunce off the childern of Iſrael, as the Lorde commaunded Moſes.
8 And they made the breſtlappe of conning worke,

V. 6 duos lap. onychinos, aſtrictos & incluſos auro

after the worke of the Ephod: euen of golde, Iacincte,
9 ſcarlet, purple ād twyned byſſe [Fo. LXXIII.] And
they made it .iiii. ſquare ād double, an hāde bredth
10 longe and an hande bredth brode. And thei filled it
with .iiii. rowes of ſtones (the firſt rowe: Sardios, a
11 Topas ād ſmaragdus. the ſecōde rowe: a Rubin, a
12 Saphir ād a Diamōde. The .iii. rowe: Ligurios, an
13 Achat ād a Amatiſt. The fourth rowe: a Turcas,
an Onix ād a Iaſpis) cloſed in ouches of gold in their
14 incloſers. And the .xii. ſtones were graue as ſygnettes with the names of the childern of Iſrael: euery ſtone with his name, acordinge to the .xii. trybes.

incloſers, *settings*

15 And they made apon the breſtlappe, twoo faſten-
16 ynge cheynes of wrethen worke ād pure golde. And
they made two hokes of golde and two golde rynges,
and put the two rynges apō the two corners of the
17 breſtlappe. And they put the two chaynes of golde
in the .ii. rynges, in the corners of the breſtlappe.
18 And the .ii. endes of the two cheynes they faſtened
in the .ii. hokes, ād put them on the ſhulders of the
Ephod apon the forefront of it.

19 And they made two other rynges of golde and put
them on the two other corners of the breſtlappe alonge
apon the edge of it, toward the inſyde of the Ephod
20 that is ouer agaynſt it And they made yet two other
golde rynges, ād put them on the .ii. ſydes of the
Ephod, beneth .P. on the fore ſyde of it: euē where
the ſydes goo together, aboue apon the brodrynge
21 of the Ephod, ād they ſtrayned the breſtlappe by his rīges vnto the ringes of the Ephod, with laces of Iacincte, that it mighte lye faſt apon the brodrynge of the Ephod, and ſhulde not be lowſed from of the Ephod: as the Lorde cōmaūded Moſes.

ſtrayned, *tied, bound*

22 And he made the tunycle vnto the Ephod of wo-

V. 10 gemmarum ordines quatuor. in primo verſu 11 ſapphirus & iaſpis 12 amethyſtus 13 chryſolithus

L. 10 die erſte riege 11 Demant

M. M. N. 10 *Smaragdus*, or an Emeraude. 11 *Rubye*, or a carbuncle.

uen worke and all together of Iacincte, heade, *i. e. the opening for the head to pass through, see xxviii, 32.*
23 ād the heade of the tunycle was in the
middeſt of it as the color of a partlet,
with a bonde rounde aboute the color,
24 that it ſhulde not rent, And they made beneth apon
the hem of the tunycle: pomgranates of Iacincte,
25 ſcarlet, purple, and twyned byſſe, And they made
litle belles of pure golde, ād put them amonge the
pomgranates roūde aboute apō the edge of the tuny-
26 cle a bell ād a pomgranate, a bell ād a pomgranate
rounde aboute the hemmes of the tunycle to myniſtre
in, as the Lorde commaunded Moſes.
27 And they made cotes of byſſe of wouē worke for
28 Aaron and his ſonnes, and a mytre off byſſe, and goodly
bonettes of byſſe, and lynen breches off twyned byſſe,
29 and a gyrdell of twyned byſſe, Iacyncte, ſcarlett and purple: euen of nedle worke, as the Lorde cōmaūded Moſes,
30 [Fo. LXXIIII.] And they made the plate of the
holy croune of fine golde, ād wrote apō it with
31 grauē worke: the holynes of the Lorde. ād tyed it
to a lace of Iacincte to faſten yt an hye apon the
mytre, as the Lorde commaunded Moſes.
32 Thus was all the worke of the habitacyon of the
tabernacle of witneſſe, finyſſhed. And the childern of
Iſrael dyd, acordynge to all that the Lorde had com-
33 maunded Moſes. And they brought the habitacyon
vnto Moſes: the tent and all his apparell thereof: the
34 buttones boordes, barres, pilers and ſokettes: and the
couerynge of rams ſkynnes red, and the couerynge of
35 taxus ſkynnes, and the hanginge vayle, and the arcke
of witneſſe with the ſtaues thereof, and the mercyſeate:
36 the table and all the ordinaunce thereof, and the
37 ſhewbred, and the pure candelſticke, and the lampes

V. 23 capitium in ſuperiori parte contra medium 26 quibus ornatus incedebat pontifex. 30 Sanctum domini 32 Perfectum eſt igitur omne opus tabernac. et tecti teſtimonii. [The references are to the Authorized Version; in the Vulgate see instead vv. 21, 24, 29, 31.]

L. 23 ſeyn loch oben mitten ynn 30 Die heylickeyt des HERRN 32 Alſo ward vollendet das gantze werk der wonung der hutten des zeugnis.

prepared therevnto with all the veſſells thereof, and
38 the oyle for lyghtes, and the golden altare and the
anoyntynge oyle and the ſwete cens, and the hang-
39 ynge of the tabernacle doore, ād the braſen alter, and
the gredyern of braſſe longynge therevnto with his
barres and all hys veſſels, and the lauer with his fote,
and the hanginges of the courte with his pilers and
40 ſokettes, and the hangynge to the courte gate, hys
boordes and pynnes, ād all the ordinaunce that .P.
ſerueth to the habitacion of the tabernacle of witneſſe,
41 and the miniſtringe veſtimentes to ſerue in the holy
place, and the holy veſtimentes of Aaron the preaſt
42 and his ſonnes raymētes to miniſtre in: acordyng to
all that the Lorde commaunded Moſes: euen ſo the
43 childern of Iſrael made all the worke. And Moſes
behelde all the worke: and ſe, they had done it
euen as the Lorde commaunded: and thā Moſes
bleſſed them.

The .XL. Chapter

M.C.S. *The tabernacle is reared vp. The glorye of the Lorde appereth in a clowde coueryng the tabernacle.*

1 AND the Lorde ſpake vnto Moſes
2 ſaynge: In the firſt daye of
the firſt moneth ſhalt thou
ſett vp the habitaciō of the
3 tabernacle of witneſſe, ād put therī the
arcke of witneſſe, and couer the arcke
with the vayle, ād brynge in the table and apparell
4 it, and brynge in the candelſticke and put on his
5 lampes, and ſett the cenſalter of golde before the
arcke of witneſſe, and put the hangynge of the dore
6 vnto the habitacion. And ſett the burntoffrynge
alter before the dore of the tabernacle of witneſſe,

V. 43 Quæ poſtq. Moyſes . . benedixit eis. xl, 2 tabernaculum teſtimonii

L. 43 Und Moſes ſahe an . . vnd ſegnet ſie. xl, 2 die wonung der hutten des zeugnis 5 das tuch ynn der thur

7 ād ſett the lauer betwene the tabernacle of witneſſe,
8 ād the alter, ād put water therī, and make the
courte roūde aboute, ād ſet vp the hāgynge of the
courte gate.

9 [Fo. LXXV.] And take the anoyntinge oyle and
anoynt the habitacion and all that is
there in, and halow it and all that be-
longe there to: that it maye be holye.
10 And anoynte the altar of the burntoffringes and all his veſſels, and ſanctifye
the altar that it maye be moſt holye.
11 And anoynte alſo the lauer and his fote,
and ſanctifye it.

12 Than brynge Aaron and his ſonnes
vnto the dore of the tabernacle of wit-
13 neſſe, and waſh them with water. And
put apon Aaron the holye veſtmentes.
and anoynte him and ſanctifye him that
14 he maye miniſtre vnto me, that their *
15 anoyntīge maie be an euerlaſtinge preaſt-
hode vnto thē thorow out their genera-
16 cions. And Moſes dyd acordīge to all
that the Lorde commaunded him.

Of this texte the ſcole men diſpute that the very ſmeringe alone maketh the preſt now alſo with out the breſtlapp of light and perfectneſſe ſo that they haue all power thereby and what thei ſaye is done immediatly whether thei ſend to heven or hell, and that with out preachynge ether of the lawe of God or of his holy Goſpell.

17 Thus was the tabernacle reared vp the first moneth
18 in the ſecōde yere. And Moſes rered vp the tabernacle ād faſtened his ſokettes, ād ſet vp the bordes
19 ād put in their barres, ād rered vp the pillers, ād ſpred
abrode the tēt ouer the habitaciō ād put the coueringe
of the tent an hye aboue it: as the Lorde commaunded
Moſes.

20 And he toke ād put the teſtimonye in the arke ād
ſett the ſtaues to the arcke and put the merciſeate an
21 hye apon the arcke, and brough- .P. te the arcke in to

M. 17 reared vp the fyrſt daye in the fyrſt

V. 7 quod implebis aqua. 19 ſicut dom. imperauerat. 20 Poſuit & teſtimonium . . ſubditis infra vectib. 21 vt expleret dom. iuſſionem.

L. 7 waſſer dreyn thun 13 prieſter ſey, 14 Vnd ſeyne ſone auch ertzu furen vnd yhn die enge rocke antzihen vnd ſie ſalben wie du yhren vater geſalbet haſt 16 wie yhm der Herr gepotten hatte. [and ſo throughout the chapter, viz. vv. 19, 21, 23 etc.] 20 vnd nam das zeugnis

the habitaciō and hanged vp the vayle ād couered
the arcke of witneſſe, as the Lorde commaunded
Moſes.
22 And he put the table in the tabernacle off witneſſe
in the north ſyde of the habitaciō with out the vayle,
23 and ſet the bred in ordre before the Lorde, euē as the
Lorde had commaunded Moſes.
24 And he put the candelſticke in the tabernacle of
witneſſe ouer agaynſt the table in the ſouth ſyde
25 of the habitacion, and ſet vp the lampes before the
26 Lorde: as the Lorde commaunded Moſes. And he
put the golden alter in the tabernacle of witneſſe be-
27 fore the vayle, ād brent ſwete cens there on as the
28 Lorde commaunded Moſes. And ſet vp the hangynge
29 in the dore of the habitacion, and ſet the burntoffringe
alter before the dore of the tabernacle of witneſſe, and
offred burntoffringes and meatofferinges there on as
the Lorde commaunded Moſes.
30 And he ſet the lauer betwene the tabernacle of
witneſſe and the alter, and poured water there in to
31 waſh with all. And both Moſes Aaron and his ſonnes
32 waſhed their hādes and their fete there at: both when
they went in to the tabernacle of witneſſe, or whē they
went to the alter, as the Lorde cōmaunded Moſes.
33 [Fo. LXXVI.] And he rered vp the courte rounde
aboute the habitacion and the alter, and ſet vp the
hanginge of the courte gate: and ſo Moſes fyniſhed the
worke.
34 And the clowde couered the tabernacle of witneſſe,
35 and the glorye of the Lorde fylled the habitacion: ſo
that Moſes coude not entre in to the tabernacle of
witneſſe, becauſe the clowde abode there in, and the
glorye of the Lorde fylled the habitacion.

V. 25 lucernis, iuxta præceptum domini. 27 aromatum. ſicut iuſſerat dominus Moyſi. 29 ſacrificia, vt dom. imperauerat. 30 implens illud aqua 32 ad altare, ſicut præceperat dominus Moyſi. 33 Poſtquam omnia perfecta 35 nube operiēte omnia, & maieſt. dom. coruſcante [The references are to A. V., in the Vulgate, see instead vv. 17, 18, 19, 23, 25, 27, 28, 31, 33, 34, 35, 37.]

L. 24 leuchter auch hyneyn 30 vnd thet waſſer dreyn zu waſſchen 31 draus, 32 denn ſie muſſen ſich wachen 34 Da bedeckt eyn wolcke 35 die wolck drauff bleyb

36 When the clowde was taken vp from of the habitacyō, the childern of Israel toke their iornayes as oft as
37 they iornayed. And yf the clowde departed not, they
38 iornayed nott till it departed: for the clowde of the
Lorde was apon the habitacion by daye, and fyre by
nyghte: in the sighte of all the house of Israel in all
their iornayes.

The ende of the seconde boke of Moses:

M. 36 had iorneyed
V. 36 per turmas suas 37 si pēdebat desuper 38 Nubes . . . incubabat . . cunctas mansiones suas.
L. 38 denn die wolcke des HERRN war des tags auff der wonung, vnd des nachts war fewr drynnen . . . so lang sie reyseten.

A PRO=

LOGE IN TO THE

thirde boke of Moſes

called Leuiticus.

¶ A prologe in to the thirde boke of Moses, called Leuiticus.

THE ceremonies which are deſcribed in the boke folowinge, were cheflye ordined off God (as I ſayde in the ende of the prologe vppon Exodi) to occupye the mindes of that people the Iſraelites, and to kepe them from ſervinge of God after the imaginacyon of their blinde zele and good entent: that their conſciences might be ſtabliſhed and they ſure that they pleaſed God therein, which were impoſſible, yf a man did of his awne heed that which was not commaunded of God nor depēded of any appoyntement made betwene him and God.

Soch ceremonies were vnto them as an A. B. C. to lerne to ſpelle and read, and as a nurce to fede them with milke and pappe, and to ſpeake vnto them after their awne capacyte and to liſpe the wordes vnto them acording as the babes and childern of that age might ſounde them agayne. For all that were before Chriſt were in the infancye and childhod of the worlde and ſawe that ſonne which we ſe openlye, but thorowe a cloude and had but feble and .P. weake imaginacions of Chriſt, as childern haue of mennes deades, a fewe prophetes excepte, whiche yet deſcribed him vnto other in ſacrifices and ceremonies, likeneſſes, rydles, prouerbes, and darke and ſtraunge ſpeakinge vntyll the full age were come that God wold ſhewe him openlye vnto the whole worlde and delyuer them from their ſhadowes and cloudelight and the hethen out of their dead ſlepe of ſtarcke blinde ignorancye. And as the ſhadowe vaniſheth awaye at the comynge of the light, euen ſo doo the ceremonyes and ſacrifices at the comynge of Chriſt, and are henceforth no moare neceſſarye then a token left in remembraunce of a bargayne is neceſſary whē the bargayne is fulfilled. And though they ſeme playne childiſh, yet they be not altogither fruteleſſe: as the popettes and .xx. maner of tryfles which mothers permitte vnto their yonge childern be not all in vayne. For all be it that ſoch phantaſyes be permytted to ſatiſfie the childers luſtes, yet in that they are the mothers giſte and be done in place and tyme at hir cōmaundement, they kepe the childern in awe and make them knowe the mother and alſo make them more apte agenſte a more ſtronger age to obaye in thinges of greater erneſte.

.¶. And moraouer though ſacrifices and ceremonies can be no ground or fundacion to bild apon: that is, though we can proue noughte with them: yet when we haue once found oute Chriſt and his miſteries, then we maye borow figures, that is to ſaye allegoryes, ſimilitudes or examples to open Chriſt and the ſecrettes off God hyd in Chriſt euen vnto the quycke, and to declare them more lyuely and ſenſebly with them than with all the wordes of the worlde. For ſimilitudes haue more vertue and power with them than bare wordes, and lead a mans wittes further in to the pithe and marye and ſpirituall vnderſtondinge of the thinge, than all the wordes that can be imagined. And though alſo that all the ceremonies and ſacrifices haue as it were a ſterrelyght of Chriſt, yet ſome there be that haue as it were the lighte of the brode daye a litle before the ſonne riſinge, and expreſſe him, and the circumſtaunces and vertue of his deth ſo playnly as if we ſhulde playe his paſſyon on a ſcaffold or in a ſtage play opēlye before the eyes of the people. As the ſcape gote, the braſen ſerpent, the oxe burnt without the hoſte, the paſſeouer-lambe &c. In ſo moch that I am fully perſuaded and can not but beleue that God had ſhewed Moſes the ſecrettes of Chriſt and the verey maner of his deth be- .¶. fore hande, and commaunded him to ordene them for the confirmacion of oure faythes whiche are now in the cleare daye lighte. And I beleue alſo that the prophetes whiche folowed Moſes to confirme his propheſyes and to mayntayne his doctrine vnto Chriſtes cominge, were moued by ſoch thinges to ſerche further of Chriſtes ſecrettes. And though God wold not haue the ſecrettes of Chriſt generallye knowne, ſaue vnto a few familier frendes which in that infancye he made of mans witte to helpe the other babes: yet as they had a generall promyſſe that one of the ſeed of Abrahā ſhuld come and bleſſe them, euen ſo they had a generall fayth that God wold by the ſame man ſaue them, though they wiſt not by what meanes as the very apoſtles when it was oft told them yet they coude neuer comprehend it, till it was fulfilled in deade.

And beyonde all this their ſacrifices ād ceremonies as farforth as the promyſes annexed vnto them extende, ſo farforth they ſaued thē and iuſtified them and ſtode them in the ſame ſteade as oure ſacramentes doo vs: not by the power of the ſacrifice or deade it ſelfe, but by the vertue of the faith in the promyſſe whiche the ſacrifice or ceremonye preached and wherof it was a token or ſygne. For the ceremonies .P. and ſacrifices were lefte with them and commaunded them to kepe the promyſſe in remēbraunce and to wake vpp their fayth. As it is not ynough to ſende manye on errandes and to tell them what they ſhall doo: but they muſt haue a remembraunce with them, and it be but a ringe of a ruſh aboute one of their fingers. And as it is not ynough to make a bargayne with wordes onlye, but we muſt put thereto an oth and geue erneſt to confirme the faithe off the perſon with whom it is made. And in like maner yf a man promyſſe, what ſoeuer trifull it be, it is not beleued excepte he hold vppe his finger alſo, ſoch is the wekeneſſe of the world. And therfore chriſt him ſilf vſed oftymes diuerſe ceremonyes in curynge the ſeke, to ſturre vpp their faith with all. As for an enſample it was not the bloud of the lambe that ſaued thē in Egipte, when the angell ſmote the Egiptians: but the mercye of God and his truth wherof that bloude was a token and remembraunce to ſturre vppe their faythes wyth all. For though God make a promyſſe, yet it ſaueth none finallye but them that longe for it and praye God with a ſtronge fayth to fulfill it for his mercye and truthe onlye and knowlege theyr vnworthyneſſe. And euen ſo oure ſacramen- .P. tes (yf they be truelye miniſtred) preach Chriſt vnto vs and leade oure faythes vnto Chriſt, by whiche faithe oure ſynnes are done awaye and not by the deade or worke of the ſacrament. For as it was impoſſible that the bloude off calues ſhuld put awaye ſynne: euen ſo is it impoſſible that the water of the ryuer ſhuld waſh oure hartes. Neuertheleſſe the ſacramentes clēſe vs and abſolue vs of oure ſynnes as the preaſtes doo, in preachinge of repentaunce and faith, for which cauſe ether other of them were ordened, but yf they preach not, whether it be the preaſt or the ſacrament, ſo profitte they not.

And yf a man allege Chriſt Iohan in the .iii. chapter ſayeng: Excepte a man be borne agayne of water and the holye goſte he can not ſe the kingdome of God, and will therfore that the holy goſt is, preſent in the water and therfore the verye deade or worke doth put awaye ſynne: then I will ſend him vnto Paule which axeth his Galathians whether they receaued the holy goſte by the deade of the lawe or by preachinge of faith, and there concludeth that the holy goſt accōpanyeth the preaching of faith, ād with the worde of faith, entreth the harte ād purgeth it, which thou mayſt also vnderſtonde by ſaynt Paule ſayenge: ye are borne .P. a new out of the water thorowe the worde. So now if baptim preach me the waſſhing in chriſtes bloude, ſo doth the holy goſt accompany it and that deade of preachinge thorow fayth doth put awaye my ſynnes. For the holy goſt is no dome god nor no god that goeth a mummīge. Yf a man ſaye of the ſacrament of Chriſtes bodye ād bloude that it is a ſacrifice as well for the dead as for the quycke and therfore the very deed it ſelf iuſtifieth and putteth away ſynne. I anſwere that a ſacrifice is the ſleynge off the body of a beeſt or a man: wherfore yf it be a ſacrifice, then is chriſtes body there ſlayne ād his bloude there ſhed: but that is not ſo. And therfore it is properly no ſacrifice but a ſacrament and a memoriall of that euerlaſtinge ſacrifice once for all which he offered apon the croſſe now apon a .xv. hundred yeres a go and preacheth only vnto them that are alyue. And as for them that be dead, it is as profitable vnto them as is a candell in a lantrene without light vnto them that walke by the waye in a darke night, and as the goſpell ſong in laten is vnto them that vnderſtond none at all, and as a ſermon preached to him that is dead and hereth it not. It preacheth vnto them that are a lyue only, for they that be dead, yf they dyed in the faith which that ſacrament preacheth, they .P. be ſaffe and are paſt all ieopardye. For when they were alyue their hartes loued the lawe off God and therfore ſynned not, and were ſory that their membres ſynned and euer moued to ſynne, and therfore thorow faith it was forgeuen them. And now their ſynnefull membres be dead, ſo that they can now ſynne no more, wherfore it is vnto them that be dead nether ſacrament nor ſacrifice: But vnder the pretence of their ſoule health it is a ſervaunt vnto oure ſpiritualtyes holy couetouſneſſe and an extorcyonar and a bylder of Abayes, Colleges, Chauntryes and cathedrall chirches with falſe gotē good, a pickpurſe, a pollar, ād a bottomleſſe bagge.

Some man wold happely ſaye, that the prayers of the maſſe helpe moch: not the lyuinge only, but alſo the dead. Of the hote fire of their farvent prayer which conſumeth faſter then all the world is able to bringe ſacrifice, I haue ſayde ſufficiently in other places. Howe be it it is not poſſible to bringe me in beleffe that the prayer which helpeth hir awne maſter vnto no vertue, ſhuld purcheſſe me the forgeueneſſe of my ſynnes. If I ſawe that their prayers had obtayned thē grace to lyue ſoch a liffe as goddes worde did not rebuke, then coud I ſone be borne in hande that what ſoeuer they axed off .P. God their prayers ſhuld not be in vayne. But now what good can he wyſh me in his prayers that envieth me Chriſte the fode and the liffe of my ſoule? What good can he wiſh me whoſe herte cleaveth a ſundre for payne when I am taught to repent of my euell?

Forthermore becauſe that fewe knowe the vſe of the olde teſtament, and the moſte parte thinke it nothinge neceſſarye but to make allegoryes, which they ſayne euery mā after hys awne brayne at all wyle advēture without any certayne rule: therfore (though I haue ſpoken off them in another place) yet leſt the boke come not to all mennes handes that ſhall reade this, I will ſpeake off them here alſo a worde or twayne.

We had nede to take hede euery where that we be not begyled with falſe allegories, whether they be drawne out of the new teſtament, or the olde, ether out of any other ſtorye or off the creatures of the worlde, but namely in this boke. Here a man had nede to put on all his ſpectacles and to arme him ſelfe agenſt inviſible ſpretes.

Firſt allegories proue nothinge (and by allegories vnderſtonde examples or ſimilitudes borowed of ſtraunge matters and of another thinge than that thou entreateſt off) As thou- .¶. gh circumcyſyon be a figure of baptim, yet thou canſt not proue baptim by circumcyſion.

For this argumēt were verye feble, the Iſraelites were circūcyſed therfore we muſt be baptiſed. And in like maner though the offering of Iſaac were a figure or enſample off the reſurrection, yet is this argument nought, Abraham wold haue offered Iſaac, but God delyuered him from deth, therfore we ſhall ryſe agayne, and ſo forth in all other.

But the very vſe of allegories is to declare and open a texte that it maye be the better perceaved and vnderſtonde. As when I haue a cleare texte of Chriſt and of the apoſtles, that I muſt be baptyſed, then I maye borowe an enſample of circumcyſion to expreſſe the nature power and frute or effecte of baptim. For as circumcyſion was vnto them a comen bagge ſygnifienge that they were all ſodiars off God to warre his warre and ſeparatinge them from all other nacyons diſobedient vnto God: euen ſo baptim is oure comen bagge and ſure erneſt and perpetuall memoriall that we pertayne vnto Chriſt and are ſeparated from all that are not chriſtes. And as circumciſion was a token certifyenge them that they were receaved vnto the fauoure off God and theyr .¶. ſynnes forgeven them: euen ſo baptim certefyeth vs that we are waſſhed in the bloude of chriſt ād receaued to fauoure for his ſake. and as circumcyſion ſignifyed vnto thē the cuttynge awaye of theyr awne luſtes and ſleynge of their fre will, as they call it, to folowe the will of god even ſo baptim ſignyfyeth vnto vs repentaunce and the mortefyinge of oure vnruly mēbres and body of ſynne, to walke in a newe lyffe and ſo forth.

And likewyſe though that the ſavinge of Noe and of them that were with him in the ſhyppe, thorow water, is a figure, that is to ſaye an enſample and likeneſſe of baptim, as Peter maketh it .1. Petri 3. yet I can not proue baptim therwith, ſaue deſcribe it only. for as the ſheyppe ſaued thē in the water thorow faith, in that they beleved god and as the other that wold not beleve Noe peryſhed: even ſo baptim ſaveth vs thorow the worde of faith which it preacheth when all the world of the vnbelevinge peryſh. And Paule .1. Corin. 10. maketh the ſee ād the cloude a figure of baptim, by which and a thouſand mo I might declare it but not proue it. Paule alſo in the ſayde place maketh the rocke out of which Moſes brought water vnto the childerne of Iſrael a figure or enſample of chriſt not to proue chriſt (for that were impoſſi- .P. ble) but to deſcribe chriſt only: even as chriſt hī ſilf Iohānis .3 boroweth a ſimilitude or figure of the braſen ſerpent to lead Nichodemus frō his erthy imaginacyon in to the ſpirituall vnderſtondinge of chriſt ſayenge: As Moſes lyfted vpp a ſerpent in the wilderneſſe, ſo muſt the ſonne of man be lifted vpp, that none that beleue in him peryſh but haue everlaſtinge liffe. by which ſimilitude the vertue of chriſtes deth is better deſcribed then thou coudeſt declare it with a thouſande wordes. for as thoſe murmurars agenſt god as ſone as they repented were healed of their deadly woundes thorow lokynge on the braſen ſerpent only without medicyne or any other helpe, yee ād without any other reaſon but that god hath ſayed it ſhuld be ſo, and not to murmoure agayne, but to leue their murmuringe: even ſo all that repent ād beleue in chriſt are ſaved from euerlaſtinge deth, of pure grace without and before their good workes, and not to ſynne agayne, but to fight agaynſt ſynne ād henceforth to ſynne no moare.

Even ſo with the ceremonyes of this boke thou canſt

prove nothinge ſaue deſcribe and declare only the puttyng awaye. of oure ſynnes thorow the deth of chriſt. for chriſt is Aaron and Aarons ſonnes and all that offer the ſacrifyce to purge ſynne, And chriſt is all maner .℗. offering that is offered: he is the oxe, the ſhepe, the gote, the kyd and lambe: he is the oxe that is burnt without the hoſt and the ſcapegote that caryed all the ſynne of the people awaye in to the wilderneſſe. for as they purged the people frō their worldly vnclenneſſes thorow bloud of the ſacrifices, even ſo doth chriſt purge vs from the vnclenneſſes of everlaſtinge deth with his awne bloude. and as their worldly ſynnes coude no otherwyſe be purged then by bloude of ſacrifyce, even ſo can oure ſynnes be no otherwyſe forgeven then thorow the bloude of chriſt. All the deades in the world, ſaue the bloude of chriſt, can purchaſe no forgeveneſſe of ſynnes: for oure deades do but helpe oure neyghboure and morteſye the fleſh ād helpe that we ſynne no moare, but and if we haue ſynned, it muſt be frely forgeven thorow the bloude of chriſt or remayne ever.

And in lyke maner of the lepers thou canſt prove nothinge: thou canſt never coniure out confeſſiō thenſe, how be it thou haſt an handſome example there to open the bindinge and lowſinge of oure preaſtes with the kaye of goddes word. for as they made no man a lepre even ſo oures haue no power to commaunde any man to be in ſynne or to go to purgatory or hell. And therefore (in as moch as bindinge .℗. and lowſinge is one power) As thoſe preaſtes healed no man, euen ſo oures can not of their inviſeble and domme power dryve any mannes ſynnes awaye or delyver hym from hell or fayned purgatorye. how be it if they preached gods word purely which is the authorite that chriſt gaue them, then they ſhuld binde ād lowſe, kylle and make alyue agayne, make vncleane and cleane agayne, and ſend to hell ād fett thence agayne, ſo mighty is gods word. for if they preached the lawe of god, they ſhuld bind the conſciences of ſynners with the bondes of the paynes of hell and bringe them vnto repētaunce. And then if they preached them the mercye that is in chriſt, they ſhuld lowſe them and quiet their raginge conſciences and certefie them of the fauoure of god and that their ſynnes be forgeven.

Fynallye beware of allegoryes, for there is not a moare handſome or apte a thinge to be gile withall then an allegorye, nor a more ſotle and peſtilent thinge in the world to perſuade a falſe mater then an allegorye. And contrary wyſe there is not a better, vehementer or myghtyer thinge to make a man vnderſtond with all then an allegory. For allegoryes make a man qwick witted and prynte wyſ- .¶. dome in him and maketh it to abyde, where bare wordes go but in at the one eare and out at the other. As this with ſoch like ſayenges: put ſalt to all youre ſacrifices, in ſteade of this ſentence, do all youre deades with diſcrecion, greteth and biteth (yf it be vnderſtond) moare thē playne wordes. And when I ſaye in ſteade off theſe wordes boſt not youre ſelf of youre good deades, eate not the bloude nor the fatt of youre ſacrifice, there is as great differēce betwene them as there is diſtaunce betwene heauen ād erth. For the liffe and beutye of all good deades is of God and we are but the caren leane, we are onlye the inſtrument wherby god worketh only, but the power is his. As god created Paule a newe, poured hys wiſdome in to him gaue him mighte and promyſed him that his grace ſhulde neuer fayle him &c. and all without deſervinges, excepte that nurteringe* the ſayntes and makinge them curſe and rayle on Chriſt be meritorious. Now as it is death to eate the bloude or fatte of any ſacrifice, is it not (thinke ye) damnable to robbe god of his honoure and to glorifye my ſelf with his honoure?

* Probably a misprint for *murtheringe*, i. e., murdering; *nurtering* is given in Daye's folio of 1573.

¶ The

THYRDE BO=

ke of Moses. Cal=

led Leuiti=

cus.

◖ THE THIRDE BOKE
OF MOSES, CALLED LEUITICUS.

◖ The firſte Chapter.

M.C.S. The order of burnt-offringes, whether it be of ſmal or great catell or foules.

1 AND the Lorde called Moſes,
And ſpake vnto him oute off
the tabernacle of witneſſe ſay-
2 enge, Speake vnto the childern
of Iſrael, and ſaye vnto them. Who ſo-
euer of you ſhall bringe a gifte vnto the Lorde, ſhall
bringe it of the catell: euen of the oxen and of the
ſhepe.
3 Yf he brynge a burntoffrynge of the oxen he ſhall
offre a male without blimeſh, and ſhal brynge him to
the dore of the tabernacle of witneſſe, that he maye be
4 accepted before the Lorde. And let him put his hande
apon the heed of the burntſacrifice, and fauoure ſhalbe
5 geuen him to make an attonemēt for hym, ād let him
kyll the oxe before the Lorde. And let the preaſtes
Aarons ſonnes brynge the bloude and let them ſprinckell
it rounde aboute apon the alter that is before the dore
6 of the tabernacle of witneſſe. And let the burntoff-
7 rynges be ſtrypped and hewed in peces. And thē let
the ſonnes of Aaron the preaſt put fire apō the alter
8 and put wodd apon the fire, and let them laye the
peces with the heed and the fatte, apon the wod that
9 is on the fire in the alter. .P. But the inwardes ād the
legges they ſhall waſh in water, and the preaſt ſhall
burne altogither apon the alter, that it be a burntſac-

V. 2 Homo qui obtulerit 3 ad placādū ſibi dominū 4 caput hoſtiæ & acceptabilis erit, atque in expiationē eius proficiēs. 6 detractaque pelle hoſtiæ 7 ſtrue lignorū ante cōpoſita 8 & cuncta quæ adhærēt iecori

rifice, and an offerynge of a ſwete odoure vnto the
Lorde.
10 Yf he will offer a burntſacrifice of the ſhepe whether
it be of the lambes or of the gootes: he ſhall offer a
11 male without blimeſh. And let him kyll it on the
north ſyde of the alter, before the Lorde. And let the
preaſtes Aarons ſonnes ſprinkle the bloude of it,
12 rounde aboute apon the alter. And let it be cut in
peces: euen with his heed and his fatte, and let the
preaſt putte them apon the wodd that lyeth apon the
13 fire in the alter. But let him waſh the inwardes and
the legges with water, and than bringe altogether and
burne it apon the alter: that is a burntoffrynge and a
ſacrifice of ſwete ſauoure vnto the Lorde.
14 Yf he will offer a burntoffrynge of the foules he
ſhall offer eyther of the turtyll doues or of the ionge
15 pigeons. And the preaſt ſhall brynge it vnto the alter,
and wrynge the necke a ſundre of it, and burne it on
the alter, and let the bloude runne out apon the ſydes
16 of the alter, ād plucke awaye his croppe ād his fethers,
ād caſt thē beſyde the alter on the eaſt parte vppō the
17 hepe of aſſhes, ād breke his winges but [Fo. III.] plucke
thē not a ſundre. And thē let the preaſt burne it vpō
the alter, euē apō the wodd that lyeth apō the fire, a
burntſacrifice ād an offerynge of a ſwete ſauoure vnto
the Lorde.

V. 9 inteſtinis 12 diuidentque membra, caput & omnia quæ adh. iecori 13 Et oblata omnia adol. ſacerdos 15 capite, ac rupto vulneris loco, 17 & nō ſecabit, neque ferro diuidet eā

L. 10 von lemmern odder zygen eyn brando. 13 Vnd der prieſter ſoles alles opffern 15 forn den hals abſtechen 17 ſpalten, aber nicht abbrechen

M. M. N. 9 This *ſwete odoure* is: the ſacryfyce of fayth & of pure affeccyon, in whych God is as delited, as a man is delited in the good ſauoure of meates, as it is ſayd of Noe, Gen. viii, d.

¶ The seconde Chapter.

1 YF any soule will offer a meatoffrynge vnto the Lorde, his offerynge shalbe fine floure, and
he shall poure thereto oyle ād
2 put frankencens theron and shall bringe
it vnto Aarons sonnes the preastes. And
one of them shall take thereout his handfull of the floure, and of the oyle with all
the frankencēs, ād burne it for a memoriall
apō the alter: an offryng of a swete sauoure vnto the
3 Lord. And the rēnaunt of the meatofferynge shalbe
Aarons ād his sonnes, as a thinge most holye of the
sacrifices of the Lorde.

M.C.S. The order of meatoffrynges, of swete cakes, of fyne flower, of franckencens. &ce. with oute leuen, & with oute hony, but not with oute salt.

4 Yf any mā bringe a meatoffrynge that is bakē in the
ouē, let him brynge swete cakes of fine floure mingled
with oyle, ād vnleuended wafers anoynted with oyle.
5 Yf thy meatoffrynge be baken in the fryenge pan, then
6 it shalbe of swete floure mingled with oyle. And thou
shalt mynce it small, ād poure oyle thereon: ād so is it
a meatoffrynge.

7 Yf thy meatofferynge be a thynge broyled vppon
the greadyerne, of floure myngled with oyle it shalbe.
8 And thou shalt brynge the .P. meatoffryng that is
made of these thinges vnto the Lorde, and shalt delyuer it vnto the preast, and he shall brynge it vnto the
9 altare and shall heue vppe parte of the meatoffrynge
for a memoriall, and shall burne it apon the alter: an
10 offerynge of a swete sauoure vnto the Lorde. And
that which is left of the meatofferynge shalbe Aarons
and his sonnes, as a thynge that is most holye of the
offerynges off the Lorde.

11 All the meatoffrynges which ye shall brynge vnto

T. 2 ad filios A. sacerdotis 4 coctum in clibano 6 & fundes super eam oleum. 7 Si autem de craticula 9 tollet memoriale de sacrificio

L. 2 Semel mehl 4 gebacken ym offen 7 so ists eyn speysopffer.

M. M. X. 2 This *swete sauoure* figureth the prayers of the meake & faithfull, as it is interpretate in Apoc. viii, a the which prayers do withstand the furie of the Lorde.

the Lorde, ſhalbe made without leuē. For ye ſhall nether burne leuen nor honye in any offerynge of the
12 Lorde: Notwithſtondinge ye ſhall bryng the firſtlynges
of them vnto the Lorde: But they ſhall not come apon
the alter to make a ſwete ſauoure.
13 All thy meatofferynges thou ſhalt ſalt with ſalt:
nether ſhalt thou ſoffre the ſalt of the couenaunt of thy
God to be lackynge from thy meatofferynge: but apon
all thyne offerynges thou ſhalt brynge ſalt.
14 Yf thou offer a meatofferynge of the firſtripe frutes vnto
the Lorde, then take of that which is yet grene and drye
it by the fire ād beat it ſmall, and ſo offer the meat-
15 offerynge of thy firſtrype frutes. And than poure oyle
there to, and put frankencens thereon: and ſo it is a
16 [Fo. IIII.] meatoffrynge. And the preaſt ſhall burne
parte of the beten corne and parte of that oyle, with
all the frākencens: for a remembraunce. That is an
offerynge vnto the Lorde.

The thyrde Chapter

1 YF any man brynge a peaceofferynge of the oxen: whether it
be male or female, he ſhall
brynge ſuch as is without
2 blemyſh, before the Lorde, and let him

M.C.S. *The order of peace-offringes, whyche were offered for the kepynge of peace, made*

M. 14 then take that

T. 12 Primitias tantum eorum 13 de ſacrificio tuo. 14 munus primitiarū . . . de ſpicis adhuc virentibus . . confringes in morem farris 16 farris fracti [The Latin has nothing to represent Tyndale's: "That is an offerynge vnto the Lorde."]

L. 15 weyr. drauff legen, ſo iſts eyn ſpeyſsopffer. iii, 1 Iſt aber ſeyn opffer ein tödopffer von rindern

M. M. N. 13 All offringes muſt be *ſalted with ſalt,* whiche ſignyfieth that all our good workes muſt be directed after the doctryne of the Apoſtles & prophetes, for then ſhall they be acceptable in the ſyghte of the Lorde, yf they ſauer of the ſalt therof, & elles not.

L. M. N. 1 *Tödopffer* ſoll hie nicht eyn *todtopffer* heyſſen das nicht lebet, ſondern das da todtet vnd wurget vnnd des dings eyn end macht, vollend aus richt, Denn es bedeut das opffer, da S. Paulus Ro. 12. vnd Petrus 1. Pet. 2. von leren, das wir nach dem glauben, ſollen vnſern leyb vnd ſeyne luſte vollend todten vnd aufferbeytten, dz frid werd zwiſchen geyſt vnnd fleyſch, vnd weret, wie die andern die leben lang.

put his hande apon the heed of his offerynge, and kyll it before the dore of the
tabernacle of witneſſe. And Aarons ſonnes the preaſtes,
ſhall ſprinkle the bloude apon the alter rounde aboute.

of oxen, ſhepe, lambes and gootes.

3 And they ſhall offre of the peaceofferynge to be a ſacrifice vnto the Lord: the fatt that couereth the in-
4 wardes and all the fatt that is apon the inwardes: and
the two kydneys with the fatt that lyeth apon the
loynes: and the kall that ys on the lyuer, they ſhall
5 take awaye with the kydneyes. And Aarons ſonnes
ſhall burne them apon the alter with the burntſacrifice
which is apon the wodd on the fire. That is a ſacrifice
of a ſwete ſauoure vnto the Lorde.

6 Yf a man brynge a peaceoffrynge vnto the Lorde
from of the flocke: whether it be male, or female,
7 it ſhalbe without blemyſh. Yf he offre a lambe, he
8 ſhall brynge it before the Lord .P. and put his hande
apon his offrynges heede, and kyll it in the doore off
the tabernacle off wytneſſe, and Aarons ſonnes ſhall
ſprinkle the bloude thereof rounde aboute the alter.

9 And of the peaſeoffringe they ſhall brynge a ſacrifyce vnto the Lorde: the fatt there of ād the rompe
altogether, which they ſhall take off harde by the
backe bone: and the fatt that couereth the inwardes
10 and all the fatt that is apon the inwardes and the .ii
kydneyes with the fatt that lyeth apon them and apon
the loynes, and the kall that is apon the lyuer he
11 ſhall take awaye with the kydneyes. And the preaſt
ſhall burne them apon the alter to fede the Lordes
offrynge withall.

V. 9 offerent de pacificorum hoſtia ſacrificium domino 10 operit ventrem atque vniuerſa vitalia, & vtrumque ren. c. adipe qui eſt iuxta ilia 11 in pabulū ignis et oblationis dom.

L. 6 Iſt aber ſeyn fridopffer (alſo v. 9) 11 zur ſpeyſe des opffers dem HERRN.

M. M. N. 4 By the takyng awaye of the fat, the inwardes, the .ii. kydneys & the kalle is ſignifyed vnto us, that yf we wylbe a ſwete ſacrifice vnto the Lorde we muſt cut of all concupiſcēces & naughty deſyres of the fleſſhe, and the euell vſe of all our mēbres, and muſt ſubdue & mortyfye our affectiōs, & offre thē to God, by the mortificacyon of the croſſe, as ſayth the Prophete Ps. xxv, a.

12 Yf the offrynge be a goote, he ſhall brynge it be-
13 fore the Lorde and put his hande apon the head of it
and kyll it before the tabernacle of witneſſe, and the
ſonnes of Aaron ſhall ſprinkle the bloude thereof apon
14 the alter rounde aboute. And he ſhall brynge thereof
his offrynge vnto the Lordes ſacrifyce: the fatt that
couereth the inwardes and all the fatt that is apō the
15 inwardes and the .ii. kydneyes and the fatt that lyeth
apon them and apon the loynes, and the kall that is
apō the lyuer he ſhall take awaye with the kydneyes.
16 And the preaſt ſhall burne them apō the alter to fede
the Lordes ſacrifyce [Fo. V.] wyth all ād to make a
ſwete ſauoure. And thus ſhal all the fatt be the Lordes,
17 and it ſhalbe a lawe forever amonge youre generacions
after you in youre dwellynge places: that ye eate
nether fatt nor bloude.

ℭ The .IIII. Chapter.

M.C.S. The offryng made for ſynnes done of ignoraunce.

1 AND the Lorde talked with Moſes
2 ſaynge: ſpeake vnto the childern of Iſrael ād ſaye: when a
ſoule ſynneth thorow igno-
raunce and hath done any of thoſe thinges which the
Lorde hath forbydden in his commaundmentes to be
3 done: Yf the preaſt that is anoynted ſynne and make
the people to doo amyſſe, he ſhall brynge for his ſynne
which he hath done: an oxe wythout blemyſh vnto
4 the Lorde for a ſynneoffrynge. And he ſhall brynge
the oxe vn to the dore of the tabernacle of wytneſſe before the Lorde, and ſhall put his hande apon the oxes
heade and kyll him before the Lorde.
5 And the preaſt that is anoynted ſhall take of the

M. 1 Lorde ſpake vnto Moſes 4 vpon the oxe heade

V. 13 altar. circumitū, 14 tollentque ex ea in paſtū ignis dominici ad. qui operit ventrē, & qui tegit vniv. vital., 15 duos ren. cum reticulo quod eſt ſuper eos iuxta ilia 16 in alimoniā ignis & ſuauiſſimi od. iiii, 2 et de vniuerſis mādatis domini . . vt non fierent 3 delinquere faciens

L. 16 zur ſpeyſz des opffers zum ſuſſen geruch.

oxes bloude and brynge it in to the tabernacle of wit-
6 nesse and shall dyppe his fynger in the bloude and
sprinkle thereof .vii. tymes before the Lorde: euen be-
7 fore the hangynge of the holy place. And he shall
put some of the bloude apon the hornes of the alter of
swete cens before the Lorde which is in the .P. tabernacle of witnesse, and shall poure all the bloude of the
oxe apon the botome of the alter of burntofferynges
which is by the dore of the tabernacle of witnesse.
8 And he shall take awaye all the fatt of the oxe that
is the synne-offerynge: the fatt that couereth the in-
9 wardes and all the fatt that is aboute them, and the
ii. kydneyes with the fatt that lyeth apon thē and
apon the loynes, and the kall apon the lyuer let them
10 take awaye also with the kydneyes: as it was taken
from the oxe of the peaceoffrynge and let the preast
11 burne them apon the altare of burntofferynges. But
the skynne of the oxe and all his flesh with his heede,
12 his legges, his inwardes with his donge, shall he carye
altogither out of the hoste vnto a clene place: euen
where the asshes are poured out, and burne hī on wodd
with fyre: euen apon the heape of asshes.

13 Yf the hole comynalte of the childern
of Israel synne thorow ygnoraunce and the
thynge be hyd from their eyes: so that they
haue commytted any of these thinges which the Lorde
hath forbidden to be done in his commaundmentes
14 ād haue offended, ād the synne which they haue synned
be afterwarde knowne, than shal they offre an oxe for
a synneofferynge ād shall brynge him before the taber-
15 nacle of wit- [Fo. VI.] nesse, and the elders of the
multitude shall put their handes apon his heed before
16 the Lorde And the preast that is anoynted shall
brynge of his bloude in to the tabernacle of witnesse,

comynalte, *community, congregation.* *v. 21.*

M. 5 of the oxe bloude

V. 6 cōtra velum sanctuarii 7 thym. gratissimi domino 8 tam eum qui vitalia operit, quam omnia quæ intrinsecus sunt 11 omnes carnes 12 & reliquo corpore . . . cin. effundi solent . . quæ in loco effusorū ciner. cremabuntur. 13 omnis turba Isr. ignorauerit & per imperitiā fecerit 15 seniores populi

L. 9 fett das ynnwendigst ist 13 eyn gantze gemeyne ynn Israel

17 and ſhall dyppe his finger in the bloude, and ſprinkle
it ſeuen tymes before the Lorde: euen before the uayle.
18 And ſhall put of the bloude apon the hornes of the
alter whiche is before the Lorde in the tabernacle of
witneſſe, and ſhall poure all the bloude apon the
botome of the alter of burntoffrynges which is by the
19 dore of the tabernacle of witneſſe, and ſhall take all
20 his fatt from him and burne it apon the altare, and
ſhall do with his oxe as he dyd wyth the ſynneoff-
ryngeoxe. And the preaſt ſhal make an attonement
21 for them, ād ſo it ſhalbe forgeuen them. And he ſhall
brynge the oxe without the hoſte, ād burne him as
he burned the firſt, ſo is this the ſynneofferynge of the
comynalte.

22 When a Lorde ſynneth and committeth thorow
ignoraunce any of theſe thynges whiche the Lorde his
God hath forbydden to be done in his commaund-
23 mentes and hath ſo offended: when his ſynne is ſhewed
vnto him which he hath ſynned, he ſhall brynge for
24 hys offerynge an he goote without blemyſh and laye
his hande apon the heed of it, and kyll it in .P. the
place where the burntofferynges are kylled before the
25 Lorde: this is a ſynneoffrynge. Thā let the preaſt take
of the bloude of the ſynneoffrynge with his finger, and
put it apon the hornes of the burntofferyngalter, and
poure his bloude apon the botome of the burntoffer-
26 yngealter and burne all his fatt apon the alter as he
doth the fatt of the peaceofferynges.

And the preaſt ſhall make an attonement for him as concernynge his ſynne, and so it ſhalbe forgeuen him.

27 Yf one of the comē people of the londe ſynne thorowe
ignoraunce and committe any off the thinges which
the Lorde hath forbidden, in his commaundementes
28 to be done, and ſo hath treſpaſed, when his ſynne

V. 20 ſic faciēs & de hoc vitulo quomodo fecit & prius & rog. pro eis ſac., propitius erit eis dom. 21 quia eſt pro peccato multitud. (v. 24) 22 quod domini lege prohibetur. 25 & reliquum fundēs (v. 30) 26 ſicut in vict. pacific. fieri ſolet (v. 31) 27 de populo terræ
L. 18 alles ander blut 24 Das ſey ſeyn ſundopffer 25 vnd das ander blut

whiche he hath ſynned is come to his knowlege, he
ſhall bringe for his offerynge, a ſhe goote without blem-
29 iſh for his ſynne which he hath ſynned, and laye his
hande apon the heed of the ſynneofferynge ād ſlee it
30 in the place of burntoffrynges. And the preaſt ſhall
take of the bloude with his finger ād put it apō the
hornes of the burntoffryngealter and poure all the
31 bloude apō the botome of the alter, ād ſhall take
awaye all his fatt as the fatt of the peaceoffrynges is
takē awaye. And the preaſt ſhal burne it apō the
alter for a ſwete ſauoure vnto the Lorde, and [Fo. VII.]
the preaſt ſhall make an attonemēt for him ād it ſhalbe
forgeuen him.
32 Yf he bringe a ſhepe ād offer it for a ſynneofferynge, he ſhall bringe a yewe without blemiſh and
33 laye his hande apon the heed of the ſynneofferynge
and ſlee it in the place where the burntoffrynges are
34 ſlayne. And the preaſt ſhal take of the bloude of
the ſynneofferynge with his finger, ād put it apō the
hornes of the burntoffryngealter, ād ſhall poure all
the bloude thereof vnto the botome of the alter.
35 And he ſhall take awaye all the fatt thereof, as the
fatte of the ſhepe of the peaceoffringes was takē a
waye. And the preaſt ſhall burne it apō the alter
for the lordes ſacrifice, and the preaſt ſhal make an
attonemēt for his ſynne, and it ſhalbe forgeuen him.

¶ The ,V. Chapter.

1 WHĒ a ſoule hath ſynned ād herde
the voyce of curſynge ād is a
witneſſe: whether he hath ſene
or knowne of it yf he haue not
2 vttered it, he ſhall bere his ſynne. Ether

M.C.S. Of oothes. The cleanſynge of hym that toucheth vncleane thynges. The pur-

M. 32 a lambe . . . bringe a female

V. 35 adeps arietis, qui immolatur pro pacificis. v, 1 aut ipſe vidit, aut conſcius eſt

L. 35 lam des tödopffers. v, 1 eyn fluch horet

when a mā toucheth any vnclene thinge:
whether it be the caryon of an vnclene
beeſt or of vnclene catell or vnclene
worme and is not warre of
it, he is alſo vnclene and
hath offended.

gacyon of an othe and of ſynne done by ignoraunce. [*vi, 1.*] *The offringes for ſynnes which are done wyllyngly.*

worme, *any creeping thing*

3 Ether when he toucheth any vnclen-
neſſe of mā (whatſoeuer vnclenneſſe it be that a man
is defyled with all) and is not warre of it
and after- .P. warde cometh to the knowledge of it, he
4 is a treſpaſer. Ether when a ſoule ſweareth: ſo that
he pronounceth with his lippes to do euell or to do
good (what ſoeuer it be that a man pronounceth with
an othe) and the thinge be out of his mynde and
afterwarde cometh to the knowledge of it, than he
hath offended in one of theſe.

warre, *aware*

5 Than when he hath ſynned in one of theſe thinges,
6 he ſhall confeſſe that wherein that he hath ſynned, and
ſhall bringe his treſpaceofferynge vnto the Lorde for
his ſynne which he hath ſynned. A female from the
flocke, whether it be an yewe or a ſhe goote, for a ſynneofferynge. And the preaſt ſhall make an attonement
7 for him for his ſynne. But yf he be not able to brynge
a ſhepe, then let him brynge for his treſpace which he
hath ſynned, two turtyll doues or two yonge pygeons
vnto the Lorde one for a ſynneoffrynge and another
8 for a burntofferynge. And he ſhall brynge them vnto
the preaſt, which ſhall offer the ſynneoffrynge firſt and
wringe the necke a ſundre of it, but plucke it not clene
9 of. And let him ſprinkle of the bloude of the ſynneofferynge apon the ſyde of the alter, and let the reſte
of the bloude blede apon the botome of the alter, and
10 than it is a ſynneofferynge. And let him offer the ſe-

M. 5 that wherin he hath 6 whether it be a lambe

V. 2 immundum, ſiue quod occiſū a beſtia eſt, aut per ſe mortuum, aut quodlibet aliud reptile . . . rea eſt & deliquit. 3 poſtea, ſubiacebit delicto. 4 iuramento & ſermone 5 agat pœnitentiam 6 agnam ſiue capram 8 retorq. caput eius ad pennulas, ita vt collo adhæreat, & nō penitus abrumpatur. 9 faciet diſtillare ad fundamentum eius

L. 4 wie denn eym menſchen eyn ſchwur entfaren mag 6 die da tragen haben 8 vnd yhr fornen den hals abſtechen 9 ausblutten

[Fo. VIII.] conde for a burntoffrynge as the maner is:
ād ſo ſhall the preaſt make an atonement for him for
the ſynne which he hath ſynned, and it ſhal be forgeuen
him.
11 And yet yf he be not able to brynge .ii. turtyll doues
or two yonge pigeons, then let hym brynge his offerynge for his ſynne: the tenth parte of an Epha of fine
floure for a ſynneofferynge, but put none oyle thereto
nether put ony frankencens thereon, for it is a ſynne-
12 offeringe. And let him brynge it to the preaſt, and
the preaſt ſhall take his handfull of it and burne it
apon the alter for a remembraunce to be a ſacryfice
13 for the Lorde: that is a ſynneoffrynge. And let the
preaſt make an atonement for him for his ſynne (what
ſoeuer of theſe he hath ſynned) and it ſhalbe forgeuen.
And the remnaūte ſhalbe the preaſtes, as it is in the
meateofferynge.
14 And the Lorde comyned with Moſes
15 ſayenge: when a ſoule treſpaceth ād ſynneth thorow ignoraunce in any of the holy
thinges of the Lorde, he ſhall brynge for his treſpace
vnto the Lord, a ram without blymeſh out of the flocke
valowed at two ſycles after the holy ſycle, for a treſpace-
16 offerynge. And he ſhall make amendes for the harme
that he hath done in the holy thynge, and put the fifte
parte moare .P. there to and geue it vnto the preaſt.
And the preaſt ſhall make an attonemēt for him with
the ram of the treſpaceofferynge, and it ſhalbe forgeuē
hym.
17 When a ſoule ſynneth and committeth any of theſe
thinges which are forbiddē to be done by the cōmaundmentes of the Lorde: though he wiſt it *
18 not, he hath yet offended and is in ſynne, ād ſhall

comyned, *communed*, i. e. *converſed*, *ſpoke*

M. 15 ſycles after the ſycle of the ſanctuary 16 ſyfte parte more to. [The following 7 verses in Tyndale are transferred in Matthew's Bible to ch. vii.]

V. 11 manus eius duos offere turt. 12 in monimentum eius qui obtulit 13 hab. in munere. 17 & peccati rea, intellexerit iniquitatem ſuam

L. 12 zum gedechtnis, vnd antzunden 13 Vnd ſol des prieſters ſeyn 15 ſeckel des heyligthums

brīge a ram without blymesh out of the flocke that
is estemed to be worthe a synneofferynge, vnto the
preast. And the preast shall make an attonement
for him for the ignoraunce whiche he dyd and was
19 not ware, and it shalbe forgeuen him. This is a trespaceofferynge, for he trespaced agaynst the Lorde.
VI, 1, 2 And the Lorde talked with Moses sayenge: when
a soule synneth ād trespaceth agaynst the Lorde and
denyed vnto his neyghboure that which was taken him
to kepe, or that was put vnder his hande, or that which
he hath violently taken awaye, or that whiche he hath
3 deceaued his neyghboure off wyth sotylte, or hath founde
that whiche was loste and denyeth it, and swereth falsely, in what soeuer thinge it be that a man doth and
4 synneth therein, Then when he hath synned or trespaced, he shall restore agayne that he toke violently
awaye, [Fo. IX.] or the wronge whiche he dyd, or that
whiche was delyuered him to kepe, or the lost thinge
5 which he founde, or what soeuer it be aboute which
he hath sworne falsely, * he shall restore it
agayne in the whole sūme and shal adde
the fifte parte moare thereto and geue
it vnto him to whome it pertayneth, the
same daye that he offereth for his tres-
6 pace, and shall brynge for his trespace
offerynge vnto the Lorde, a ram without
blymesh out of the flocke, that is estemed
worth a trespaceofferynge vnto the preast.
7 And the preast shall make an atonemēt for him before
the Lorde, ād it shall be forgeuē hī in what soeuer
thinge it be that a mā doth ād trespaceth therein.

Vnto my neybour pertayneth satiffaciō, but vnto god repētaunce: and thē the sacrifice of christes bloude is a ful satisfaccion, ād attonemēt ād apeasinge of al wrath.

V. 19 quia per errorem deliquit in domino. vi, 2 fidei eius creditum . . aut calumniam fecerit 3 & inficians insuper peierauerit 5 voluit obtinere, integra & quintam 7 pro singulis quæ faciendo peccavit.

L. 18 eyn shuldopffers werd ist (cf. vi. 5) 19 das er dem HERRN verfallen ist. vi, 2 zu trawer hand 3 mit eym falschen eyde

M. M. N. 24 Vnto my neybour pertayneth satiffaccyon, but vnto god repētaunce & then the sacrifice of Christes bloude is a full satiffacciō & attonement & apeasyng of all wrath.

ℭ The .VI. Chapter.

8 AND the Lorde ſpake vnto Moſes
9 ſaynge. Commaunde Aaron
and his ſonnes ſaynge: this is
the lawe of the burntoffrynge.
The burntofferynge ſhalbe apon the herth
of the alter all nyghte vnto the mornynge,
and the fire of the alter ſhall burne there-
10 in. And the preaſt ſhall put on his lynen
albe and his lynen breches apon his fleſh,
and take awaye the aſſhes whiche the fire
of the burntſacrifice in the altare hath
11 made, and put them beſyde the alter, ād thē put off
his raymēt ād put on other .P. and carye the aſſhes
out without the hoſte vnto a clene place.
12 The fire that is apon the alter ſhall burne therein
and not goo out. And the preaſt ſhall put wodd on
the fire euery morninge ād put the burntſacrifice apon
it, and he ſhall burne thereon the fatt of the peace-
13 offerynges. The fire ſhall euer burne apon the alter
and neuer goo out.
14 This is the lawe of the meatoffrynge: Aarons ſonnes
15 ſhall bringe it before the Lorde, vnto the alter: and
one of them ſhall take hys handfull of the floure of the
meatoffrynge ād of the oyle with all the frankencens
whiche ys thereon and ſhall burne it vnto a remēbraunce apon the alter to be a ſwete ſauoure of the
16 memoriall of it vnto the Lorde. And the reſt thereof,
Aaron ād his ſonnes ſhall eate: vnleuended it ſhalbe
eaten in the holy place: euē in the courte of the tab-
17 ernacle of witneſſe they ſhall eate it. Their parte
whiche I haue geuen them of my ſacrifice, ſhall not be

M.C.S. *The offringes for ſynnes which are done wyllyngly. The lawe of the burntoffrynges. The fyre muſt abyde euermore vpon the aulter. The offrynges of Aaron and hys ſonnes.*

V. 9 Cremabitur in altari . . . ignis, ex eodem altari 10 cineres, quos vorās ignis exuſſit 11 mūdiſſimo vſque ad fauillā cōſumi faciet . 12 ignis autem . . ſemper ardebit 13 ignis . . qui nunquam deficiet 14 lex ſacrificii & libamentorum . . coram . . . coram

L. 9 brennen auff dem altar . . alleyn des altars feuer 12, 13 brennen vnd nymmer verleſſchen (*bis*) 15 Es ſol eyner Heben 17 backen yhr teyl, das ich yhn geben hab

baken with leuen, for it is moſt holye, as is the ſynne-
18 offerynge, and treſpaceoffrynge. All the males amonge
the childern of Aaron, ſhall eate of it: and it ſhalbe a
dutye for euer vnto youre generacyons of the ſacrifices
of the Lorde, nether ſhal any man twytche
it, but he that is halowed.

twytche, twych [often], *touch*.

19 [Fo. X.] And the Lorde ſpake vnto Moſes ſayenge:
20 this is the offrynge of Aaron ād of his ſonnes which
he ſhall offer vnto the Lorde in the daye when they are
anoynted: the tenth parte of an Epha of floure, which is
a dayly meatofferinge perpetually: halfe in the morninge
21 and halfe at nighte: ād in the fryenge pan it ſhalbe made
with oyle. And whē it is fryed, thou ſhalt brynge it in as
a baken meatofferynge mynſed ſmall, and ſhalt offer it for
22 a ſwete ſauoure vnto the Lorde. And that preaſt of his
ſonnes that is anoynted in his ſteade, ſhall offer it: ād it
ſhall be the lordes dutye for euer, and it
23 ſhal be burnt altogether. For all the meatoffrynges of
the preaſtes ſhalbe burnt altogether, ād ſhal not be eaten.

dutye, *due*

24, 25 And the Lorde talked with Moſes ſayenge: ſpeake
vnto Aaron and vnto his ſonnes and ſaye. This is the
lawe of the ſynneoffrynge, In the place where the
burntofferynge is kylled, ſhall the ſynneofferynge be
26 kylled alſo before the Lorde, for it is moſt holy. The
preaſt that offereth it ſhall eate it in the holye place:
27 evē in the courte of the tabernacle of witneſſe. No
man ſhall touche the fleſh thereof, ſaue he that is halowed. And yf any rayment be ſprynckled therewyth,
28 it ſhalbe waſſhed in an holy place, and the erthē pott
that it is ſoddē in .P. ſhalbe broken. Yf it be ſodden
in braſſe, then the pott ſhalbe ſcoured and plunged in
29 the water. All the males amonge the childern of
30 Aarō ſhall eate therof, for it is moſt holy. Notwith-

M. 28 ſcoured and ryneſed 29 amonge the Preaſtes ſhall eate

V. 17 ideo autem non fermentabitur, quia pars eius in domini offertur incenſum. 18 Legitimum ac ſempiternum 21 Offeret autem eam calidam in odorem 23 Omne enim ſacrificium ſacerd. 28 defricabitur, & lauabitur aqua. 29 veſcetur de carnibus eius

L. 18 Das ſey ewigs recht 21 gebacken dar bringen vnd geſtuckt 27 eyn kleyd beſprenget, der ſoll ſich waſſchen 28 mit waſſer ſpulen

M. M. N. 27 There ſhall none touche it, but he that is halowed, that is, but he that is dedicated, ordeyned and appoynted to mynyſter before the Lorde, as it is Agge. ii, c.

ſtōdinge no ſynneofferynge that hath his bloude
brought in to the tabernacle of witneſſe to reconcyle with all in the holy place, ſhalbe eaten: but
ſhalbe burnt in the fire.

¶ The .VII. Chapter.

1 THIS is the lawe of the treſpaceofferynge which is moſt holy.
2 In the place where the burntoffrynge is kylled, the treſpaceoffrynge ſhalbe kylled alſo: ād his
bloude ſhalbe ſprīkled rounde aboute apon
3 the alter. And all the fatt thereof ſhalbe offered: the rompe and the fatt that couered the
4 inwardes, and the .ii. kydneyes with the fatt that
lyeth on them and apon the loynes: and the kall on
5 the lyuer ſhalbe taken awaye with the kydneyes, And
the preaſt ſhall burne them apon the altare, to be an
offerynge vnto the Lorde: this is a treſpace offerynge.
6 All the males amonge the preaſtes ſhal eate there-
7 of in the holy place, for it is moſt holy. As the ſynneofferynge is, ſo is the treſpaceofferynge, one lawe
8 ſerueth for both: and it ſhall be the preaſtes that re-
concyleth therwith. [Fo. XI.] And the preaſt that
offered a mans burntofferynge, ſhall haue the ſkyn of
9 the burntofferynge which he hath offered. And all
the meatofferynges that are baken in the ouen, ād all
that is dreſſed apon the gredyerne ād in the fryenge
10 pan, ſhalbe the preaſtes that offereth them. And all
the meatofferynges that are myngled with oyle or drye,
ſhall pertayne vnto all the ſonnes of Aaron, and one
ſhall haue as moche as another.

M.C.S. *Treſpaceoffrynges. Synne offrynges and peaceoffrynges. The fatte and the bloude maye not be eaten.*

V. 2 per gyrum altaris fundetur 5 incēſum eſt domini pro delicto. 7 ad ſacerdotem .. pertinebit 10 mēſura æqua per ſingulos diuidetur.

L. 5 altar antzunden zum opffer 10 mit ole gemenget odder treuge

M'M.N. 1 *Treſpace offringe* that is, an offring for a treſpace. Treſpace after the order of the ſcrypture ſignifyeth ſomtyme all the lyffe paſt which we haue lyued in infidelyte, being ignoraunt of the veritie, not only in doyng opē ſynnes, but alſo when we haue walked in oure awne rightweſnes, as in the Pſalme xviii, d. & .ii. Paral. xxviii, c.

11 This is the lawe of the peaceoffringes whiche ſhalbe
12 offered vnto the Lorde. Yf he offer to geue thanckes,
he ſhall brynge vnto his thanckofferynge: ſwete cakes
myngled with oyle and ſwete wafers anoynted with oyle,
13 and cakes myngled with oyle of fine floure fryed, ād he
ſhall brynge his offerynge apon cakes made of leuended
bred vnto the thanckoffrynge of his peaceofferynges,
14 ād of them all he ſhall offer one to be an heueoffrynge
vnto the Lorde, ād it ſhalbe the preaſtes that ſprynkleth
15 the bloude of the peaceofferynges. And the fleſhe
of the thankofferynge of his peaceofferynges ſhalbe
eaten the ſame daye that it is offred, and there ſhall
none of it be layde vpp vntyll the mornynge.

16 Yf it be a vowe or a fre willofferynge that he bryngeth, the ſame daye that he offereth it, .P. it ſhalbe eaten,
17 and that which remayneth may be eaten on the morowe:
18 but as moche of the offered fleſh as remaneth vnto the
thirde daye ſhalbe burned with fire For yf any of the
fleſh of the peaceoffrynges be eaten the thirde daye then
ſhall he that offered it optayne no fauour, nether ſhall it
be rekened vnto him: but ſhalbe an abhomynacion, and
the ſoule that eateth of it ſhall beare the ſynne thereof.

19 The fleſh that twycheth any vnclene thinge ſhall
not be eaten, but burnt with fire: and all that be clene
in their fleſh, maye eate fleſh.

20 Yf any ſoule eate of the fleſh of the peaceofferynges,
that pertayne vnto the Lorde and hys vnclenneſſe yet
apon him, the ſame ſoule ſhall periſſhe from amonge
21 his people. Moreouer yf a ſoule twych any vnclene
thinge, whether it be the vnclenneſſe of man or of any
vnclene beeſt or any abhominacion that is vnclene: ād
thē eate of the fleſh of the peaceoffrynges whiche per-

F. 14 ex quibus vnus pro primitiis offertur domino 18 irrita fiet eius oblatio, nec proderit offerenti . . anima tali ſe edulio cont., præuaricationis rea erit.

L. 18 Es wirt yhm auch nicht zu gerechnet werden, ſondern es wirt verworffen ſeyn . . iſt eyner miſſethat ſchuldig. 21 was ſonſt greulich iſt

M. M. N. 16 By *vowes* are vnderſtand the gyftes which are acouſtomed to be offred and geuen to God by any outwarde ceremonye, as it was to rounde their heares, or to dryncke no wyne. etc. Num. vi, a.

tayne vnto the Lord, that ſoule ſhall periſſh from his
people.
22, 23 And the Lorde ſpake vnto Moſes ſaynge: ſpeake
vnto the childern of Iſrael ād ſaye. Ye ſhall eate no
24 maner fatt of oxen, ſhepe or gootes: neuerthelater the
fatt of the beeſt that dyeth alone ād the fatt of that
which is torne with wilde beeſtes, maye be occupide,
occupide in all maner [Fo. XII.] vſes: but *employed, uſed*
25 ye ſhal in no wiſe eate of it. For whoſoeuer eateth
the fatt of the beeſt of which mē bring an offring vnto
the Lorde, that ſoule that eateth it ſhall periſſh frō
26 his people. Moreouer ye ſhall eate no maner of bloud,
whereſoeuer ye dwell, whether it be of foule or of
27 beeſt. What ſouer ſoule it be that eateth any maner
of bloude the ſame ſoule ſhal periſſhe frō his people.
28, 29 And the Lorde talked with Moſes ſayenge: ſpeake
vnto the childrē of Iſrael ād ſaye He that offereth his
peaceofferynge vnto the Lord, ſhall bringe his gifte
30 vnto the Lord of his peaceoffrynges: his owne handes
ſhal bringe the offrynge of the Lorde: euē the fatt apō
the breſt he ſhall bringe with the breſt to waue it a
31 waueoffrynge before the Lorde. And the preaſt ſhall
burne the fatt apon the alter, ād the breſt ſhalbe Aarōs
32 ād his ſonnes. And the right ſhulder they ſhall geue
vnto the preaſt, to be an heueoffrynge, of their peace-
33 offringes. And the ſame that offreth the bloud of the
peaceoffringes ād the fatt, amōg the ſōnes of Aarō,
34 ſhall haue the right ſhulder vnto his parte, for the
wauebreſt ād the heueſhulder I haue takē of the childern of Iſrael, euen of their peace offringes, ād haue
geuē it vnto Aarō the preſt and vnto his ſonnes: to be
a dutie for euer of .P. the childern of Iſrael.
35 This is the anoyntinge of Aaron ād of the ſacryfices
of the Lorde, in the daye when they were offered to

V. 21 interibit de populis ſuis,(peribit vv. 25, 27.)25 adipem, qui offeri debet in incenſum domini 30 tenebit manibus adipem . . . cumque ambo oblata domino 32 armus quoque dexter . . cedet in primitias ſacerd. 35 in ceremoniis domini

L. 30 mit ſeyner hand hertzu bringen 32 zur Hebe von yhren tödopffern. 34 zum ewigen recht. 35 vberantwort worden prieſter zu ſeyn

36 be preaſtes vnto the Lorde, whiche the Lorde commaunded to be geuen them in the daye when he
anoynted them, of the childern of Iſrael, and to be a
dutie for euer amonge their generacions.
37 This is the lawe of burntoffrynges, of
meatoffrynges, of ſynneoffrynges, of treſpaceoffrynges,
38 of fulloffrynges, of peaceoffrynges, which the Lorde
commaunded Moſes in the mount of Sinai, in the daye
when he commaunded the childern of Iſrael to offer
their offrynges vnto the Lorde in the wilderneſſe of
Sinai.

dutie, *law, ſtatute.*

The .VIII. Chapter.

1 AND the Lorde ſpake vnto Moſes
2 ſaynge: take Aaron and his
ſonnes with hī, and the veſtures
and the anoyntinge oyle, and
an oxe for a ſynneofferynge and two
3 rammes ād a baſkett of ſwete bred: ād
gather all the comentye together vnto the dore of the
4 tabernacle of witneſſe. And Moſes dyd
as the Lorde commaunded him, and the
people gathered them ſelues togither vnto
the doore of the tabernacle of witneſſe.
5 And Moſes ſayde vnto the people: this is the thinge
which the Lorde commaunded to do.
6 [Fo. XIII.] And Moſes broughte Aaron and his
7 ſonnes, and waſſhed them with water, and put apon
him the albe and gyrde him with a girdel and put
apon him the tunycle and put the Ephod thereon, and
gyrded him with the broderd girdel of the Ephod,

comentye, *community, congregation*

𝔐.𝔆.𝔖. *The anoyntynge and conſecracyon of Aaron and his onnes.*

Hence the pope fett holowenge of chirches, alters, font, belles ād ſo forthe, and the anoyntinge of biſſhopes preaſtes, and ſoch like.

𝔙. 2 caniſtrū cū azymis 6 Cumque lauiſſet eos
𝔏. 36 zum ewigen recht 37 fulleopffer . . tödopffer. viii, 6 wuſch ſie mit waſſer.

8 and bounde it vnto him therewith. And he put the
breſtlappe thereon, ād put in the breſtlappe lighte ād
9 perfectneſſe. And he put the myter apon his heed
ād put apō the myter euē apō the forefrōt of it, the
golden plate of the holy croune, as the Lorde commaunded Moſes.
10 And Moſes toke the anoyntynge oyle and anoynted
the habitacion and all that was therein and ſanctified
11 them, and ſprynkled thereof apon the alter .vii. tymes
and anoynted the alter and all his veſſels, and the lauer
12 with hys fote, to ſanctifie them. And he poured of the
anoyntynge oyle apon Aarons heed and anoynted him
13 to ſanctifie him. And he broughte Aarons ſonnes and
put albes apon them, and gyrde them with gyrdels,
ād put bonettes apō their heedes: as the Lorde cōmaunded Moſes
14 And the ſynneoffrynge was brought. And Aaron
and his ſonnes put their handes apon the heed of the
15 oxe of the ſynneoffryng. And when it was ſlayne,
Moſes toke of the bloude, and put it apon the hornes
of the alter rounde .P. aboute with his finger and puri-
fied it, ād poured the bloud vnto the botome of the
16 alter ād ſanctified it ād reconcyled it. And he toke
all the fatt that was apon the inwardes ād the kal that
was on the lyuer ād the two kydneyes with their fatt
17 ād burned it apō the alter. But the oxe, the hide,
his fleſh ād his donge, he burnt with fire without the
hoſte, as the Lorde commaunded Moſes.
18 And he broughte the ram of the burntofferynge,
and Aaron ād his ſonnes put their handes apon the
19 heed of the ram, and it was kylled. And Moſes ſprink-
20 led the bloud apō the alter roūde aboute, ād cutt the
ram in peces ād burnt the heed, the peces ād the fatte,
21 ād waſſhed the inwardes ād the legges in water, and
burnt the ram euery whitt apō the alter. That was a

M. 8 Vrim and Thumim

V. 8 doctrina & veritas. 9 laminā auream cōſecratam in ſanctificatione 15 quo expiato & ſanctificato

L. 8 Liecht vnd Vollickeyt. 15 entſündiget den altar . . das er yhn verſunet. 20 zehyeb den widder yn ſtuck

M. M. N. 8 Loke in Exo. xxviii, c. & Num. xxvii. d.

burntſacrifice of a ſwete ſauoure ād an offrynge vnto
the Lorde, as the Lorde cōmaunded Moſes.
22 And he broughte the other ram that was the fullofferynge, and Aaron and his ſonnes put their hādes
23 apō the heed of the ram: And when it was ſlayne,
Moſes toke of the bloude of it, and put it apon the
typpe of Aarons ryght eare and apon the thombe of
his right hande, and apon the great too of his right
fote.
24 Then were Aarons ſonnes broughte, ād Mo- [Fō.
XIIII.] ſes put of the bloude on the typpe of the right
eare of them, and apon the thombes of theire righte
handes, and apon the great tooes of their righte fete,
and ſprinkled the bloud apō the alter rounde aboute.
25 And he toke the fatt ād the rompe ād all the fatt
that was apon the inwardes, ād the kall of the lyuer,
ād the .ii. kydneyes with their fatt ād their righte ſhul-
26 der. And out of the baſket of ſwete bred that was
before the Lorde, he toke one ſwete cake of oyled bred
ād one wafer, ād put thē on the fatt ād apon the righte
27 ſhulder, ād put altogether apō Aarons handes ād apō
his ſonnes handes, ād waued it a waueofferynge before
28 the Lorde. And thā Moſes toke thē from of their handes
agayne ād burnt thē apō the alter, euen apon the burntoffrynge: These are the fulloffrynges of a ſwete ſauoure
ād a ſacrifice vnto the Lorde.
29 And Moſes toke the breſte and waued it a waueoffrynge before the Lorde, of the ram of the ful offrynges:
ād it was Moſes parte, as the Lorde commaunded
Moſes.
30 And Moſes toke of the anoynting oyle ād of the
bloude whiche was apon the alter, and ſprinkled it
apō Aarō ād apon his veſtimētes ād apō his ſōnes ād
on their veſtimētes with hī ād ſanctified Aarō ād his
veſturs ād his ſōnes .P. and his ſonnes veſtures alſo.
31 Then Moſes ſayde vnto Aaron and his ſonnes: boyle
the fleſh in the doore of the tabernacle of witneſſe,

V. 24 reliquum fudit ſuper altare 27 qui poſtquam leuauerunt ea 28 eo quod conſecrationis eſſet oblatio
L. 22 widder des fulleopffers 24 gos das blut

and there eate it with the bred that is in the baſket
of fullofferynges, as the Lorde commaunded ſayenge.
32 Aaron and his ſonnes ſhall eate it: ād that which
remayneth of the fleſh and of the brede, burne with
fire.

33 And ſe that ye departe not from the doore of the
tabernacle of witneſſe ſeuen dayes longe: vntill the
dayes of youre fullofferynges be at an ende. For .vii
34 dayes muſt youre hādes be filled, as they were this
daye: euē ſo the Lorde hath commaūded to do, to
35 reconcyle you with all. Se therfore that ye abyde
in the dore of the tabernacle of witneſſe daye and
nyghte ſeuen dayes longe: and kepe the watch of the
Lorde that ye dye not: for ſo I am commaunded.
36 And Aaron and his ſonnes dyd all thynges which the
Lorde commaunded by the hande of Moſes.

ℭ The .IX. Chapter.

1 AND the .viii. daye Moſes called
Aaron and his ſonnes and the
2 elders of Iſrael, and ſayde vnto
Aaron: take a calfe for a ſynne
offrynge, and a ram for a burntoffrynge:
both without blemiſh, and brynge them
3 before the Lorde. And vnto the childern
of Iſrael he ſpa- [Fo. XV.] ke ſayenge:
take ye an he goote for a ſynneofferynge,
and a calfe and a lambe bothe two of a
yere olde, and without blemyſh for a
4 burntſacrifice, and an oxe and a ram for peaceoffrynges,
to offer before the Lorde, and a meateofferyng myngled
with oyle, for to daye the Lorde will appere vnto you.

M.C.S. *The fyrſt offringes of Aaron, for hym ſelfe and for the people. Aaron bleſſeth the people. The glorye of the Lorde is ſhewed. The fyre commynge from aboue conſumeth the ſacrifice.*

V. 31 panes quoque conſecrationis edite 33 complebitur tēpus conſecrationis veſtræ. 34 ſicut impræſentiarum factum eſt, vt ritus ſacrificii compleretur. ix, 4 immolate eos coram domino in ſacrificio ſingulorum

L. 33 bis an den tag, da die tage ewrs fullopffers aus ſind

M. M. N. 36 Loke in the .iiii. of the kinges in the .xix. ch. b.

5 And they brought that which Moſes commaunded
vnto the tabernacle of witneſſe, ād all the people came
6 and ſtode before the Lorde. And Moſes ſayde, this is
the thynge which the Lorde commaunded that ye
ſhulde do: ād then the glorye of the Lorde ſhall appere
7 vnto you. And Moſes ſayde vnto Aaron: go vnto the
alter and offer thy ſynneofferynge, and make an attonement for the and for the people: and then offer the
offerynge of the people and reconcyle them alſo, as
the Lorde cōmaunded Moſes.
8 And Aaron went vnto the alter, and ſlewe the calfe
9 that was his ſynneoffrynge. And the ſonnes of Aaron
broughte the bloude vnto him, and he dypte his finger
in the bloude and put it apon the hornes of the alter,
and poured the bloude vnto the botome of the alter.
10 And the fatt and the two kydneyes with the kall of
the lyuer of the ſynneoffrynge, he burnt vppon the
11 alter, as the Lorde commaunded Moſes: .¶. but the
fleſh and the hyde, he burnt with fyre without the
hoſte.
12 After warde he ſlewe the burntofferynge, ād Aarons
ſonnes brought the bloude vnto him, and he ſprinkled it
13 rounde aboute apon the alter. And they brought the
burntofferynge vnto him in peces and the heed alſo,
14 and he burnt it apon the alter, and dyd waſſhe the
inwardes and the legges, and burnt them alſo apon the
burntofferynge in the alter.
15 And than he broughte the peoples offerynge and toke
the goote that was the peoples ſynneofferynge, and ſlewe
it and offered it for a ſynofferynge: as he dyd the firſt.
16 And then broughte the burntofferynge and offered it
17 as the maner was, and broughte the meatofferynge
and fylled his hande thereof, and burnt it apon the
alter, beſydes the burntſacrifyce in the mornynge.
18 Then he ſlewe the oxe and the ram that were the

V. 7 et deprecare pro te & pro populo. cumque mactaueris hoſtiam populi, ora pro eo, ſicut præcepit dominus. 15 expiatoque altari 17 abſque ceremoniis hol. matutini.

L. 7 deyn ſundopffer vnd deyn brandopffer . . verſüne dich vnd das volck 13 zu yhm zuſtucket vnd den kopff 17 auſſer des morgens brandopffer.

peoples peaſeofferynges, and Aarons ſonnes broughte
the bloude vnto him, and he ſprinkled it apon the alter
19 rounde aboute, and toke the fatt of the oxe and of the
ram: the rōpe and the fatt that couereth the inwardes
20 and the kydneyes and the kall of the lyuer: and put
them apon the breſtes and burnt it apon the alter:
21 but the breſtes and the righte ſhulders Aaron waued
before the Lorde, as the Lorde cō- [Fo. XVI.] maunded
Moſes.

22 And Aaron liſte vpp his hande ouer the people and
bleſſed thē, and came doune from offerynge
of ſynofferynges, burntofferynges and
23 peaſeofferynges. Then Moſes and Aaron
wēt into the tabernacle of witneſſe and
came out agayne and bleſſed the people,
and the glorye of the Lorde apered vnto
24 all the people. And there came a fyre
out from before the Lorde, and conſumed
apon the alter: the burntofferynge and the fatt. And
all the people ſawe it and ſhowted, and fell on their
faces.

Of ſoch places the biſſhopes toke their domme bleſſynge with .ii. fingers: But numery vi. thou maiſt read the goodly prayer of his bleſſynge.

The .X. Chapter

M.C.S. Nadab and Abihu are ſlayne. Iſrael mourneth for them. The Preaſtes are forbydden wyne. The reſydew of the ſacrifice the Preaſtes eate.

1 AND Nadab and Abihu the ſonnes
of Aaron toke ether of them
his cenſor ād put fyre therein and put cens apō, and
broughte ſtraunge fyre before the Lorde: which he
2 cōmaunded thē not and there
went a fyre out frō the Lorde

Hereof ye ſe the frute of a mans good entent with out Gods word. As we maye

V. 24 turbæ, laudauerunt dominū x, 1 ignem alienum
L. 22 ſteyg herab vom werck 24 frolocketen ſie. x, 1 frembd
feur
M. M. N. 1 Herof ye ſe the frute of a mans good entent wythout Goddes word. As we maye do no leſſe, ſo doeth thys enſample teache that we may do no moare then is commaunded.

do noleſſe, ſo doeth this enſample teach that we mayc do no moare than is cōmaunded.

and cōſumed thē, and they dyed before the
3 Lorde. Then Moſes ſayde vnto Aarō this
is it that the Lorde ſpake ſaynge: I will be ſanctifyed in
them that come nye me, ād
before all the people I wilbe glorifyed.
And Aaron helde his peaſe.

God is ſanctified when we obey him ād mortify oure wyll to doo his.

4 And Moſes called Miſael and Eleſaphā the ſonnes
of Vſiel the vncle of Aaron, and ſayde vnto thē: goo
to and carye youre brethrē from the holy place out
5 of the hoſte. And they went to them and caryed
them in their albes out of the hoſte, as Moſes bad.

6 .¶. And Moſes ſayde vnto Aaron and vnto Eleazar
and Ithamar his eldeſt ſonnes: vncouer not youre heed
nether rent youre clothes, leſt ye dye and wrath come
apon all the people lett youre brethren the hole houſe
of Iſrael, bewepe the burnynge which the Lorde hath
7 burnt. But goo ye not out from the dore of the tabernacle of wytneſſe, leſt ye dye: for the anoyntynge oyle of
the Lorde is apon you. And they dyd as Moſes bad.

8 And the Lorde ſpake vnto Aaron ſa-
9 ynge: drynke no wyne nor ſtronge drynke,
nether thou nor thi ſonnes with the: when
ye go in to the tabernacle of witneſſe, leſt
ye dye. And let it be a lawe foreuer vnto
10 youre childern after you: that ye maye
put difference betwene holy and vnholy,
11 and betwene vnclene and clene, and that
ye maye teach the childern of Iſrael:
all the ordynaunces which the Lorde
hath cōmaunded them by the handes of
Moſes.

Oure prelates be dronke wyth deſyre of honoure and haue brought the world oute of their wittes to ſatiſfie their luſtes, and liue not ſobirly to teach vs what chriſt commaunded by the handes of the appoſtels..

12 And Moſes ſayde vnto Aaron and vnto Eleazar ād

V. 3 tacuit Aaron. 5 tulerunt eos ſicut iacebant . . . vt ſibi fuerat imperatum. 6 incendium, quod dominus ſuſcitauit 10 vt habeatis ſcientiam diſcernendi

L. 3 ſchwyg ſtille. 6 brand . . gethan hat 10 das yhr kund vnterſcheyden

M. M. N. 3 God is ſanctified when we obey hym, and mortyſye oure wyll to do his. 4 Loke in Gen. xiii, b. 9 *For euer,* it is here taken for a tyme that hath an ende, and not euer laſting as it is alſo in Gen. xiii, d & Ex. xii, c.

Ithamar his ſonnes that were lefte: take the meatofferynge that remayneth of the ſacrifyces of the Lorde,
and eate it without leuen beſyde the alter, for it is
13 moſt holy: eate it therfore in the holy place, becauſe it
is thy dutye and thi ſonnes dutye of the
ſacrifyce of the Lorde: for ſo I am com-
14 maunded. And the [Fo. XVII.] wauebreſt and heueſhulder eate in a clene place: both thou and thy
ſonnes and thy doughters with the. For it is thy
dutye and thy ſonnes dutye with the, of the peace-
15 offerynges off the childern of Iſrael. For the heueſhulder ād the wauebreſt whiche they brynge with the
ſacrifices of the fatt, to waue it before the Lorde, ſhalbe thyne and thy ſonnes with the, and be a lawe for
euer, as the Lorde hath commaunded.

dutye [often], *due*

16 And Moſes ſoughte for the goote that was the
ſynneofferynge, and ſe, it was burnt. And he was
angrye with Eleazar and Ithamar the ſonnes of Aaron,
17 which were lefte alyue ſayenge: wherefore haue ye not
eaten the ſynneofferynge in the holy place, ſeynge it is
moſt holye: and for as moch as it is geuen you to bere
the ſynne of the people, and make agrement for them
18 before the Lorde? Beholde, the bloude of it was not
brought in within the holy place therfore ſhulde ye
haue eaten it in the holy place as I commaunded.
19 And Aaron ſayde vnto Moſes: behold, this
daye haue they offered their ſynneoffrynge
and their burntoffrynge before the Lorde,
and it is chaunced me after thys maner.
Yf I ſhulde eate of the ſynneofferynge to
20 daye, wolde the Lorde be content with all? And
when Moſes herde that, he was content.

The offeringes muſt haue bene eaten in gladneſſe: but Aaron coude not but morne for his ſonnes.

V. 17 portetis iniquitatem multitudinis & rogetis pro ea 18 ſicut præceptum eſt mihi? 19 mihi autem accidit quod vides . . aut placere domino in cerem. mente lugubri? 20 recepit ſatiſfactionem.

L. 17 miſſethat der gemeyne tragen . . . ſie verſunet 19 es iſt myr gangen, wie es da iſt . . vnd gutter ding ſeyn 20 lies ers yhm gefallen.

M. M. N. 19 The offringes muſt haue bene eatē in gladneſſe, but Aaron coulde not but morne for hys ſonnes.

.¶. The .XI. Chapter.

M.C.S. Of beastes which be cleane & which vncleane.

1 AND the Lorde ſpake vnto Moſes
2 and Aaron ſayenge: ſpeake
vnto the childrẽ of Iſrael and
ſaye, theſe are the beeſtes
whiche ye ſhall eate amonge all the beeſtes that
3 are on the erth: what ſoeuer hath hoffe and dyuydeth it in to two clawes ād cheweth cud among the
4 beeſtes, that ſhall ye eate. Neuertheleſſe, theſe ſhall
ye not eate of them that chewe cud and haue hoffes.
The camel, for he cheweth cud but he deuydeth not
the hoffe in to two clawes therfore he ſhall be vnclene
5 vnto you. And the Conye, for he cheweth the cud
but deuydeth not the hoffe in to two clawes, therfore
6 he is vnclene to you. And the hare, for he likewiſe
cheweth the cud, but deuydeth not the hoffe in to two
7 clawes, he is therfore vnclene to you. And the ſwyne,
for though he deuyde the hoffe in to two clawes,
yet he cheweth not the cud ād therfore is vnclene to
8 you, Of their fleſh ſee that ye eate not ād their carkaſſes ſe that ye twych not for they are vnclene to you.
9 Theſe ſhall ye eate of all that are in the waters:
what ſoeuer hath finnes and ſkales in the waters, ſees
10 and ryuers, that ſhall ye eate And all that haue not
finnes ād ſkales in the ſees ād ryuers of all that moue
and lyue in the waters, [Fo. XVIII.] ſhall ye abhorre.
11 Se that ye eate not of their fleſh, ād alſo that ye ab-
12 horre their carkaſes: for all that haue no finnes nor
ſcales in the waters, ſhalbe abhominacion vnto you.
13 Theſe are the foules which ye ſhall abhorre and
which ſhall not be eaten, for they are an abhomina-
14 cion. The egle, the gooſhauke, the cormoraunte, the
15 kyte, the vultur and all his kynd and all kynde of

V. 5 Chirogryllius 7 Et ſus . . . ruminat. 8 horum carnibus 9 tam in mari quam in fluminibus & ſtagnis 11 morticina vitabitis. 13 Aquilam, & gryphẽ, & haliæetum 14 miluũ . .

L. 5 die Canynchen 7 Vnd eyn ſchweyn 9 ynn waſſern, ym mehr vnd bechen

16 rauens, the eſtrich, the nightcrowe, the cocow, the
17 ſparowhauke, and al the kynde: the litle oule, the
18 ſtorcke, the great oule the backe, the pellicane,
19 the pye, the heron, the Iaye with the kynde, the
20 lappwynge ād the ſwalowe. And all foules that
crepe ād goo apō all .iiii. ſhalbe an abhominacion
vnto you.
21 Yet theſe maye ye eate of all the foules that moue
and goo apon .iiii. fete: euen thoſe that haue no knees
aboue vppon their fete to lepe with all apon the erthe,
22 euen theſe of them ye maye eate: the arbe and all
his kynde: the Soleam with all his kynde: the Hargol and all the kynde, ād the Hagab ād all his kynd.
23 Al other foules that moue ād haue .iiii. fete, ſhalbe
24 abhominacion vnto you. In ſoch ye ſhalbe vnclene
whoſoeuer touch the carkeſſe of thē ſhalbe vnclene
25 vnto the euen, ād whoſoeuer bereth the carkeſſe of thē,
ſhal waſh his clothes ād ſhalbe .P. vnclene vntyll euen.
26 Amonge all maner beeſtes, they that haue hoffes
and deuyde them not in to two clawes or that chewe
not the cud, ſhalbe vnclene vnto you: and all that
27 twicheth them ſhalbe vnclene. And all that goeth
apon his handes amonge all maner beeſtes that goo
on all foure, are vnclene vnto you: and as many as
twych their carkeſſes, ſhalbe vnclene vntyll the euen.
28 And he that beareth the carkeſſe of them, ſhall waſſhe
his clothes ād be vnclene vntyll the euen, for ſoch are
vnclene vnto you.

M. 22 Selaam . . kynde, the Hagab 27 foure fete
V. 16 larum, & accipitrem 17 bubonem et mergulum et ibin 18 cygnum et onocrotalum, et porphyrionem, 19 herodionem, charadrion . . vpupam . . veſpertilionem. 21 longiora retro crura 22 brucus . . attacus . . ophiomachus, ac locuſta 25 & ſi neceſſe fuerit vt portet
L. 21 das keyne knye oben an den beynen hat, da mit es auff erden hupffe 27 auf tappen geht
M. M. N 22 *Arbe, Selaā, Hargol, Hagab* are kyndes of beaſtes that crepe or ſcraul on the grounde which the Hebrues them ſelues do not now a dayes know.
L. M. N. 22 Diſe vier thier ſind ynn vnſern landen nicht, wie wol gemeyniglich *Arbe* vnnd *Hagab*, fur Hewſchrecken gehaltē werden, die auch vierfuſſige vogel ſind, aber es iſt gewiſſer, diſe Ebreiſche namen zu brauchen, wie wyr mit *alleluia* vnd andern frembder ſprach namen thun.

29 And these are also unclene to you amonge the
thinges that crepe apon the erth: the wesell the
30 mouse, the tode and all his kynde, the hedgehogge,
31 stellio, the licerte, the snayle and the moule. These
are vnclene to you amonge all that moue, and all
that twych them when they be dead, shalbe vnclene
32 vntyll the euen. And what soeuer any of the dead
carkesses of them fall apon, shalbe vnclene: what
soeuer vessel of wodd it be, or rayment, or skynne,
or bagge or what soeuer thinge it be that any worke
is wroughte with all. And they shalbe plunged in
the water and be vnclene vntill the euē, and then
they shalbe clene agayne.

33 All maner of erthen vessel where in to any of them
falleth, is vnclene with all that therein [Fo. XIX.] is:
34 and ye shall breake it. All maner meate that is eaten,
yf any soch water come apon it, it shall be vnclene.
And all maner drynke that is drōke in all maner soch
vessels, shalbe vnclene.

35 And whether it be ouen or kettel, it shalbe broken.
For they are vnclene and shalbe vnclene vnto you:
36 Neuerthelater, yet the fountaynes ād welles and
pondes of water, shalbe clene styll. But whosoeuer
twycheth their carkesses, shalbe vnclene.

37 Yf the dead carkesse of any soch fall apō any seed
38 vsed to sowe, yt shall yet be clene styll: but ād yf
any water be poured apō the seed ād afterward the
dead carkesse of them fall thereō, then it shalbe vnclene vnto you.

39 Yf any beest of whiche ye eate dye, he that twitcheth the dead carkesse shalbe vnclene vntyll the euen.
40 And he that eateth of any soche dead carkesse, shall
wasshe his clothes and remayne vnclene vntyll the
euen. And he also that beareth the carkesse of
it, shall wasshe his clothes and be vnclene vntyll
euen.

V. 29 mus & crocodilus 30 migale, & chamæleon, & stellio & lacerta 32 pelles & cilicia 34 fusa fuerit super eum 36 & omnis aquarum congregatio

L. 35 es sey ofen odder kessel

41 All that ſcrauleth vpon the erth, is an
abhominacyon and ſhall not be eaten.
42 And what ſoeuer goeth apon the breſt
ād what ſoeuer goeth apon .iiii. or moo fete amonge
all that ſcrauleth apon the erth, of that ſe ye eate
not: for they are abhomynable. Make not youre ſoules
43 .P. abhominable. Make not youre ſoules abhomynable
with no thinge that crepeth, nether make youre ſoules
vnclene with them: that ye ſhulde be defiled thereby.
44 For I am the Lorde youre God, be ſanctified therfore
that ye maye be holy, for I am holy: and defile not
youre ſoules with any maner thinge that crepeth apon
45 the erth. For I am the Lorde that brought you out
of the londe off Egipte to be youre God: be holy therfore, for I am holy.
46 This is the lawe of beeſt and foule and off all
maner thinge that lyueth ād moueth in the water
47 ād of all thinges that crepe apō the erth, that ye may
put differēce betwene vnclene ād clene, ād betwene
the beeſtes that are eatē and the beeſtes that are
not eaten.

ſcrauleth, *crawleth*, *creepeth* v. 42

The .XII. Chapter.

1 AND the Lorde ſpake vnto Moſes
2 and ſayde: ſpeake vnto the
childern of Iſrael ād ſaye: whē
a womā hath conceaued ād
hath borne a man childe, ſhe ſhalbe vnclene .vii. dayes:
euen in like maner as when ſhe is put aparte in tyme
3 of hir naturall diſeaſe. And in the .viii. daye the fleſh

M.C.S. *A lawe howe wemen ſhulde be purged after their delyuerance.*

M. 42 *omits* Make not youre ſoules abhominable
V. 42 quadrupes graditur, & multos habet pedes 43 Nolite cōtaminare animas 47 differētias noueritis
L. 41 was auff erden ſchleicht (42, 44) 42 auff vier odder mehr fuſſen 43 ſeelen vervnreynigen
M. M. N. 2 Some call it the monethes dyſeaſe, ſome the floures.

4 of the childes foreſkynne ſhalbe cut awaye. And ſhe
ſhall cōtynue in the bloude of hir purifienge .xxxiii
dayes, ſhe ſhal [Fo. XX.] twytch no halowed thinge
nor come in to the ſanctuary, vntyll the tyme of hir
5 purifienge be out. Yf ſhe bere a maydechilde, then ſhe
ſhalbe vnclene two wekes as when ſhe hath hir naturall
diſeaſe. And ſhe ſhall contynue in the bloude of hir
purifienge .Lxvi. dayes.

6 And when the dayes of hir purifienge are out:
whether it be a ſonne or a doughter, ſhe ſhall brynge
a lambe of one yere olde for a burntoffrynge and a
yonge pigeon or a turtill doue for a ſynneoffrynge
vnto the dore of the tabernacle of witneſſe vnto the
7 preaſt: which ſhall offer them before the Lorde and
make an attonement for her, and ſo ſhe ſhalbe
purged of hir yſſue of bloude. This is the lawe of
her that hath borne a childe, whether it be male or
female.

8 But and yf ſhe be not able to bringe a ſhepe, then
let her brynge two turtyls or two yonge pigeons: the
one for the burntofferynge, and the other for the
ſynneofferynge. And the preaſt ſhall make an attonement for her, ād ſhe ſhalbe clene.

The .XIII. Chapter.

1 AND the Lord ſpake vnto Moſes
2 ād ūto Aarō ſaynge: whē
there apeareth a ryſinge in
any mās fleſh ether a ſcabbe
or a gliſtrīge .P. whyte: as though the

M.C.S. The Preaſtes are appoynted to iudge who are the Lepers.

F. 7 mundabitur a profluuio ſanguinis ſui 8 Quod ſi non inuenerit manus eius, nec pot. offerre agnum . . . orabitque pro ea ſacerdos. xiii, 2 diuerſus color ſiue puſtula

L. 4 tage yhrer reynigung aus ſind 5 da heym bleyben ynn dem blut yhrer reynigung. 6 aus ſind 7 reyn von yhrem blutgang 8 Vermag aber yhre hand nicht eyn ſchaff . . verſünen. xiii, 2 eytter weys (4, 19, 23, 39).

plage of leprosye were in the skynne of
his flesh, then let him be brought vnto
Aaron the preast or vnto one of hys sonnes
3 the preastes, and let the preast loke on
the sore that is in the skynne of his fleshe.
Yf the heer in the sore be turned vnto
whyte, and the sore also seme to be lower
than the skynne of his fleshe, then it is
suerly a leprosye, and let the preast loke
on him and make hym vnclene.
4 Yf there be but a white plecke in the
skynne of his fleshe and seme not to be
lower than the other skynne nor the heer
thereof is turned unto white: then let the
5 preast shitt him vpp seuen dayes. And let
the preast loke apon him the .vii. daye: yf
the sore seme to him to abyde styll and to
go no further in the skyne, then let the
preast shutt him vppe yet .vii. dayes moo.
6 And let the preast loke on him agayne
the .vii. daye. Then yf the sore be waxed
blackesh and is not growen abrode in the
skynne, let the preast make him clene, for it is but a
skyrfe. And let him wasshe his clothes, and then he is
7 clene But and yf the scabbe growe in the skynne after
8 that he is sene of the preast agayne. Yf the preast
se that the scabbe be growen abrode in the skynne,
let him make him vnclene: for it is suerly a leprosye.

This chapter maketh not for cōfession in the eare, but is an exāple of excommunicacion off open sinners As these prestes make vncleane ād sende out of company, euen so ours binde ād excommunicat out of the cōgregaciō: and as these make cleane, so doo ours lowsse, and absolue. Now thē that sinne secretly thei binde with preachīge gods word ād yf thei repēt, with preachinge thei lowse thē agayne.

M. 3 iudge hym vnclene.

V. 3 humiliorem cute & carne reliqua . . . et ad arbitrium eius separabitur. 7 & redditus munditiæ . . adducetur ad eum, 8 & immunditiæ condēnabitur.

L. 3 vrteylen 4 verschliessen sieben tage 6 mal geschwungen

M. M. N. 2 The lepre signifyeth properly mannes doctrine, whyche spreadeth abroade lyke a canker: & to be short all infeccyon of vngodlynes, therfore must the Leuytes geue dylygent hede therto: for a lytell leuen soureth the whole loumpe of doughe.

L. M. N. 4 Hie ists offinbar das Moses *aussatz* heyst allerley grind vnd blattern odder mal, da ausfatz aus werden kan oder dem aufzsatz gleych ist. Aussatz aber bedeut eygentlich, menschen lere auffer der lere Gottlichs wort, die selbe bluet vnnd grunet fur den leuten vnd frisset vmb sich, darumb den priestern hie mit fleys auffzusehen gepotten wirt.

9 [Fo. XXI.] Yf the plage of leprosye be in a man, let
10 hī be broughte vnto the preast, and let the preast se
him. Yf the rysinge apeare white in the skynne ād
haue also made the heer white, ād there be rawe flesh
11 in the sore also: then it is an olde leprosye in the
skynne of his flesh. And the preast shall make him
vnclene, ād shall not shutte him vp for he is vnclene.
12 Yf a leprosye breake out in the skynne and couer all
the skynne from the heed to the fote ouer all where-
13 soeuer the preast loketh, then let the preast loke apon
him. Yf the leprosye haue couered all his flesh, let
him make the disease clene: for in as moch as he is
14 altogether white he is therfore cleane. But and yf
there be rawe flesh on him when he is sene, then he
15 shalbe vncleane. Therfore when the preast seeth the
rawe flesh, let him make him vnclene. For in as moch
as his flesh is rawe, he is vnclene and it is suerly a true
16 leprosye. But and yf the rawe flesh departe agayne
and chaunge vnto white, then let him come to the
17 preast and let the preast se him: Yf the sore be
chaunged vnto white, let the preast make the disease
cleane, ād then he is cleane.
18 When there is a byele in the skynne
19 of any mans flesh and is helede and after
in the place of the byele there appeare a whyte rysyng
ether .[illegible]. a shynynge white somwhat redysh, let him
20 be sene of the preast. Yf when the preast seeth hī it
appeare lower than the other skynne and the heer
thereof be chaunged vnto white, let the preast make
hī vncleane: for it is a very leprosye, that is broken
21 out in the place of the byele. But and yf when the

byele [often], *boil*

M. 11 iudge him vnclene 13 iudge the disease 15 iudge 17 iudge 20 iudge

V. 11 inolita cuti. 12 quicquid sub aspectu oculorum cadit 15 sacerd. iudicio polluetur, & inter immundos reputabitur 18 Caro autem et cutis

L. 10 rho fleysch ym geschwyr

M. M. N. 13 *Couered all his flesh*, etc. Here is that called a leper which yet is none in dede, but semyth to be one: whereas the rotnesse of humoures brekyng forth into the vtter partes all the body ouer, is called a leper, and yet must it be iudged to be cleane.

preaſt loketh on it there be no white heeres therein
nether the ſcabbe lower than the other ſkynne and be
ſomewhat blackeſh, then the preaſt ſhall ſhutt him
22 aparte .vii. dayes. Yf it ſprede abrode in the meane
ſeaſon, then let the preaſt make him vnclene: for it is
23 a leproſye. But ād yf the gliſtringe white abyde ſtyll in
one place and go no further, then it is but the prynte
of the byele, and the preaſt ſhal make him cleane.
24 When the ſkynne of any mās fleſh is burnt with fire
that it be rawe and there apere in the burnynge a
gliſtringe white that is ſomwhat redyſh or altogether
25 white, let the preaſt loke apon it. Yf the heer in that
brightneſſe be chaunged to white and it alſo appeare
lower than the other ſkynne, than it is a leproſye that
is broken out in the place of the burnynge. And the
preaſt ſhall make him vncleane, for it is a leproſye. But
26 and yf (when the preaſt loketh on it) he ſe that there
is no white heer in the bryghteneſſe and that it is no
lower than the other [Fo. XXII.] ſkynne and that it
is alſo blackeſh, then let the preaſt ſhutt him upp ſeuen
27 dayes. And yf (when the preaſt loketh on him the
ſeuenth daye) it be growen abrode in the ſkynne, lett
28 him make him vncleane: for it is a leproſye. But and
yf that bryghtneſſe abyde ſtyll in one place and goo
no further in the ſkynne ād be blackeſh, than it is but
a ryſyng in the place of the burnynge, and the preaſt
ſhall make hym cleane: for it is but the prynte of the
burnynge only.
29 Whē ether man or woman hath a breakinge
30 out apon the heed or the beerde, let the preaſt
ſe it. And yf it apeare lower than the other ſkynne
and there be therein golden heeres ād thyn, let the
preaſt make him vncleane, for it is a breaking out
31 of leproſye apō the heed or berde. yf (whē the

M. 22 iudge 23 iudge 25 out of the place . . iudge 27 iudge 30 iudge

V. 23 vlceris eſt cicatrix 28 quia cicatrix eſt combuſturæ. 30 capillus flauus

L. 23 die narbe von der druſs 28 geſchwyr des brandmals 30 har daſſelbs gulden vnd dunne

preaſt loketh on the breakīge out) he ſe that it is no
lower thā the other ſkynne ād that there are blacke
32 heeres therein let hī ſhutt hī vp .vii. dayes. And let
the preaſt loke on the diſeaſe the ſeuenth daye: ād yf
the breakynge oute be gone no forther nether be any
golden heeres therein nether the ſcabbe be lower than
33 the other ſkynne, then lett him be ſhauen, but lett hym
not ſhaue the ſcabbe, and let the preaſt ſhutt him vpp
34 ſeuen .P. dayes moo. And let the preaſt loke on the
breakynge out the .vii. daye agayne: Yf the breakynge
out be gone no further in the ſkynne nor moare lower
thē the other ſkynne, then lett the preaſte make him
cleane, and let him waſſhe his clothes and then he is
35 cleane. Yf the breakynge out growe in the ſkynne
36 after that he is once made cleane, let the preaſt ſee
him. Yf it be growne abrode in dede in the ſkynne,
let the preaſt ſeke no further for ony golden heeres, for
37 he is vncleane. But and yf he ſe that the ſcabbe ſtonde
ſtyll and that there is blacke heer growne vpp there
in, thē the ſcabbe is healed and he is cleane: and the
preaſt ſhall make him cleane.

38 Yf there be founde in the ſkynne of the fleſh of man
39 or woman a gliſterynge white, let the preaſt ſe it. Yf
there appeare in their fleſh a gliſterynge white ſomwhat blackeſh, thē it is but frekels growē vpp in the
ſkynne: ād he is cleane

40 Yf a mans heer fall of his heed, thē he is heedbaulde
41 and cleane. yf his heer fall before in his foreheade,
42 then he is foreheadbalde and cleane. yf there be in
the baulde head or baulde forehead a redyſh white
ſcabbe, then there is leproſye ſpronge vpp in his baulde
43 head or baulde foreheade. And let the preaſt ſe it:
and yf the ryſynge of the ſore be reddyſhwhite in his
baul- [Fo. XXIII.] de heade or foreheade after the
44 maner of a leproſye in the ſkynne of the fleſh, then he
is a leper and vncleane: ād the preaſt ſhall make him
vncleane, for the plage of his heede.

M. 34 iudge 35 iudged 37 iudge 44 iudge
V. 37 hom. ſanatum eſſe, & confid. eum pronuntiet mundum. 43 cōdemnabit eum . . lepræ
L. 31 nicht falb 44 ſolchs mals halben auff ſeym heubt

45 And the leper in whome the plage is, ſhall haue his
clothes rent and his heade bare ād his mouth moffeld,
and ſhalbe called vncleane.
46 And as longe as the dyſeaſe leſteth apon him, he ſhalbe
vncleane: for he is vncleane, and ſhall therfore dwell
alone, ād even without the hoſt ſhall his habitacion be.
47 When the plage of leproſye is in a cloth: whether it be
48 lynen or wollen, yee and whether it be in the warpe or
wolfe of the lynen or of the wollen: ether
in a ſkynne or any thinge made of ſkynne,

wolfe [often], *woof*

49 yf the diſeaſe be pale or ſomwhat redyſh in the cloth or
ſkynne: whether it be in the warpe or the wolfe or any
thinge that is made of ſkynne, thē it is a very leproſye
50 and muſt be ſhewed vnto the preaſt. And whē the
preaſt ſeeth the plage, lett him ſhutt it vpp .vii. dayes,
51 and let him loke on the plage the ſeuenth daye. yf it
be increaſed in the cloth: whether it be in the warpe or
wolfe or in a ſkynne or in anythynge that is made of
ſkynne, then the plage is a fretynge lep-
52 roſye and it is vncleane: And that cloth
ſhalbe burnt, ether warpe or wolfe,
whether it be wollen or lynen or any
thynge that is made of ſkynne where in
the plage is, for it is a fretyn- .P. ge leproſye, and
ſhalbe burnt in the fyre.

fretynge [often], *eaten away;* cf. freten, v. 53, and xiv, 44, and German *freſſen.*

53 Yf the preaſt ſe that the plage hath freten no further
in the cloth: ether in the warpe or wolfe or in what
54 ſoeuer thynge of ſkynne it be, then let the preaſt cōmaunde thē to waſſhe the thynge wherein the plage is,
55 and let him ſhutt it vpp .vii. dayes moo. And let the
preaſt loke on it agayne after that the plage is waſſhed:
Yf the plage haue not chaunged his faſcion though it
be ſpred no further abrode, it is yet vncleane.
And ſe that ye burne it in the fyre, for it is fretē
inwarde: whether in parte or in all together.

M. 55 freat
V. 45 contam. ac ſordidum ſe clamabit.
L. 45 vnreyn genennet werden 51 freſſend mal
M. M. N. 47 Of the leproſye of clothes which was vſed amonge the Iewes, let thē iudge. This is euydēt that we in oure tyme ſoffer ouer many leproſyes in clothes.

56 But and yf the preaſt ſe that it is ſomwhat blackyſh
after that it is waſſhed, let him rent it out of the clothe,
or out of the ſkynne or out of the warpe or wolfe.
57 But and yf it apeare any moare in the cloth ether in
the warpe or in the wolfe or in anythynge made of
ſkynne, than it is a waxynge plage. And ſe that ye
58 burne that with fyre, where in the plage is. Moreouer the cloth ether warpe or wolfe or what ſoeuer
thinge of ſkynne it be which thou haſt waſſhed and
the plage be departed from it, ſhalbe waſſhed once
agayne: and then it is cleane.
59 This is the lawe of the plage of leproſye in a cloth
whether it be wollē or lynen: eyther whether it be in
the warpe or wolfe or in any thynge made of ſkynnes,
to make it cleane or vncleane.

[Fo. XXIIII.] .XIIII. Chapter.

M.C.S. The cleanſynge of the leper, and of the houſe that he is in.

1 AND the Lorde ſpake vnto Moſes
2 ſaynge: this is the lawe of a
leper when he ſhalbe clēſed.
he ſhalbe broughte vnto the
3 preaſt, and the preaſt ſhall goo out without the hoſte
and loke apō him. Yf the plage of leproſye be healed
4 in the leper, thē ſhall the preaſt commaunde that there
be brought for hī that ſhalbe clenſed .ii. lyuynge byrdes
that are cleane, ād cipreſſe wodd, and a pece of purple
5 cloth and yſope. And the preaſt ſhall cōmaunde that
one of the byrdes be kylled ouer an erthē veſſell of
6 runnynge water. And the preaſt ſhall take the lyuynge byrde and the cypreſſe wodd and the purple ād
the yſope, ād ſhall dyppe thē and the lyuynge byrde
in the bloude of the ſlayne byrde and in the rēnynge
7 water and ſprinkle it apon him that muſt be clenſed

M. 59 iudge. xiiii, 4 cedar wodd 5 in an erthen 6 cedar
V. 58 pura ſunt, ſecundo, & munda erunt. xiiii, 4 præcipiet ei qui purificatur . . paſſeres . . lignum cedrinum (vv. 49, 50, 51, 52) 5 in vaſe fictile ſuper aquas viuentes
L. 4 cedern holtz (throughout the chapter) 6 tuncken am lebendigen waſſer

of his leprosye .vii. tymes and clense him, and shall
8 let the lyuynge byrde goo fre in to the feldes.
And he that is clẽsed shall wasshe his clothes and shaue
off all his heer ãd wasshe himselfe in water, and thẽ he
is cleane. And after that he shall come in to the
9 hoste, but shall tarye without his tẽt .vii. dayes. Whẽ
the seuenth daye is come, he shall shaue off al his heer
both apõ his heade ãd his berde ãd on his browes:
ãd euẽ all the heer that is on him, shalbe shauen off.
And he shall wasshe his clothes and his flesh in water,
and then he shalbe cleane.
10 .¶. And when the .viii. daye is come, let him take
ii. lambes without blemysh and a yewelambe of a
yere olde without blemysh, and .iii. tenthdeales of fyne
floure for a meatofferynge myngled with oyle, and a
11 logge of oyle. Than let the preast that maketh him
cleane, brynge the man that is made cleane with those
thynges before the Lorde vnto the dore of the taber-
12 nacle of witnesse. And lett the preast take one of
the lãbes and offer him for a trespaceofferynge, and
the logge of oyle: and waue them before the Lorde.
13 And than let him slee the lambe in the place where
the synofferynge and the burntofferynge are slayne:
euẽ in the holy place. for as the synofferynge is, euẽ
so is the trespace offerynge the preastes: for it is most
holy.
14 Than lett the preast take of the bloude of the trespaceofferynge, and put it apõ the typpe of the right
eare of him that is clensed, and apon the thombe of
his righte hande and apon the greate too of his righte
15 fote. Then let the preast take of the logge of oyle
16 and poure it in to the palme of his lefte hande, ãd
dippe his righte finger in the oyle that is in the
palme of his lefte hand, ãd let him sprinkle it with
17 his fynger .vii. tymes before the Lorde. And of the

V. 7 vt in agrum auolet 10 et seorsum olei sextariũ.
L. 7 frey feld 10 Log oles 15 aus dem Log nemen
M. M. N. 15 *A logge of oyle* is a certayn measure contaynyng .vi. egges, in Grec *Sextarius*.
L. M. N. 10 *Log* ist eyn kleyn maslyn auff Ebreisch also genennet, aber noch vngewis wie gros es sey.

reſt of the oyle that is in his hande, ſhall the preaſt
put apon the typpe of the righte eare of him that [Fo.
XXV.] is clenſed, and apon the thombe of his righte
hande, and apon the great too of his righte fote: euē
18 apon the bloude of the treſpaceofferynge. And the
remnaunte of the oyle that is in the preaſtes hande,
he ſhall poure apon the heede off hym that is clenſed:
and ſo ſhall the preaſte make an attonement for him
before the Lorde,

19 Then let the preaſt offer the ſynneofferynge, ād
make an attonement for him that is clenſed for his
20 venclēneſſe. And thā let the burntoffrynge be ſlayne,
ād let the preaſt put both the burntofferynge and the
meateoffrynge apō the alter; ād make an attonement
for him, ād thā he ſhalbe cleane.

21 Yf he be poore ād can not gett ſo moch, thā let
him bringe one lambe for a treſpaceoffrynge to waue
it and to make an attonement for him, ād a tenth
deale of fine floure myngled with oyle for a meatoff-
22 rynge ād a logge of oyle, ād two turtyll doues or two
yonge pygeons which he is able to gett ād let the one
be a ſynneoffrynge and the other a burntoffryng.
23 And let him brynge them the .viii. daye for his clenſ-
ynge vnto the preaſt to the dore of the tabernacle of
witneſſe before the Lorde.

24 And let the preaſt take the lambe that is the treſ-
25 paceoffrynge and the logge of oyle, ād wa- .P. ue them
before the Lorde. And whē the lambe of the treſpaceoffrynge is kylled, the preaſt ſhall take of the bloude of

V. 19 faciet ſacrificium

L. 21 mit ſeyner hand nicht ſo viel erwirbt 22 mit ſeyner hand erwerben kan

L. M. N. 21 Gleych wie der ausſatz bedeut falſch lere, falſchen glauben, vnnd falſch heyligs leben, ſonderlich das auff eygen werck vnnd nicht auff lauter Gottis gnade Alſo bedeut diſs reynigen wie man ketzerey vnnd ſolch falſch lere vertreyben ſol. Nemlich dz die prediger ſollen dz ole yn der hand haben vnd mit dem finger handeln, dz iſt ſie ſollen das Gottis wort von der gnaden ym leben beweyſen vnd ynn geyſt krafft predigen, damit die leut gehorchen vnd mit der hand faſſen vnd folgen das dis ſprengen fur dem herrn vnnd das ſalben der leut nichts anders iſt, Denn das Euangelion fur Gott predigen vnd die leut alſo vom yrthum furen. Denn fewr vertilget keyn ketzerey ſondern alleyn Gottis wortt ym geyſt gefurt.

the trefpaceoffrynge, and put it apon the typpe of his
righte eare that is clenfed, and apon the thombe of
26 his righte hande, and apon the greate too of hys righte
fote. And the preaft fhall poure of the oyle in to his
27 righte hande, and fhall fprinkle with his finger of the
oyle that is in his lefte hande .vii. tymes before the Lord.
28 And the preaft fhall put of the oyle that is in his
hande (apon the typpe of the righte eare of hĩ that is
clenfed, and apõ the thombe of his righte hande and
apon the great too of his righte fote: euen in the place
where the bloude of the trefpaceofferynge was put,
29 And the refte of the oyle that is in his hande, he fhall
poure apon the heede of him that is clenfed: to make
30 an attonemẽt for him before the Lorde. And he fhall
offer one of the turtyll doues or of the yonge pigeons,
31 foch as he can gett: the one for a fynneofferynge and
the other for a burntoffrynge apõ the alter. And fo
fhall the preaft make an attonemẽt for him that is
32 clenfed before the Lorde. This is the lawe of him
that hath the plage of leprofye, whofe hand is not
able to gett that which pertayneth to hys clenfynge.
33 [Fo. XXVI.] And the Lorde fpake vnto Mofes ãd
34 Aarõ faynge: when ye be come vnto the lond of Canaan which I geue you to poffeffe: yf I put the plage
of leprofye in any houffe of the lande of youre poffef-
35 fion, let him that oweth the houfe go ãd tell the
preaft faynge, me thinke that there is as it were a
36 leprofy in the houffe. And the preaft fhall cõmaunde
them to ryd all thinge out of the houffe, before the
preafte goo in to fe the plage: that he make not all
that is in the houffe vncleane, and then the preaft fhall
goo in and fe the houffe.
37 Yf the preaft fe that the plage is in the walles of
the houffe ãd that there be holowe ftrakes pale or

M. 28put on the oyle

V. 29 vt placet pro eo dominum 35 Quafi plaga lepræ videtur mihi effe in domo mea.

M. M. N. 37 The lepre of the howfes is any thynge ther to pertaynynge, wherby the dweller might take harme in helth of body, in hurtyng of hys goodes or otherwyfe as yf it ftoode in an euel ayre etc.

rede which ſeme to be lower than the other partes of
38 the wall, then let the preaſt go out at the houſſe dores
39 ād ſhett vp the houſſe for .vii. dayes. And let the
preaſt come againe the ſeuenth daye ād ſe it: yf the
40 plage be encreaſed in the walles of the houſſe, let the
preaſt cōmaunde thē to take awaye the ſtones in which
the plage is, ād let thē caſt thē in a foule place with-
41 out the citie, ād ſcrape the houſe within rounde aboute,
ād poure oute the duſt without the citie in a foule
42 place. And let them take other ſtones and put them
in the places of thoſe ſtones, and other morter: ād
playſter the houſſe with all.

43 .P. Yf now the plage come agayne ād breake out
in the houſſe, aſter that they haue taken awaye the
ſtones and ſcraped the houſſe, and after that the
44 houſſe is playſterd anew: let the preaſt come and ſe
it. And yf then he perceaue that the plage hath eatē
further in the houſſe, then it is a fretynge leproſye that
45 is in the houſſe ād it is vncleane. Then they ſhall
breake doune the houſſe: both ſtones, tymbre ād all
the morter of the houſſe, and carye it out of the citye
46 vnto a foule place. Moreouer he that goeth in to the
houſſe all the whyle that it is ſhett vp, ſhalbe vncleane
47 vntyll nighte. And he that ſlepeth in the houſſe ſhall
waſſhe his clothes, and he alſo that eateth in the houſſe
ſhall waſſhe his clothes.

48 But and yf the preaſt come and ſe that the plage
hath ſprede no further in the houſſe after that it is new
playſtered, thē let him make it cleane for the plage is
49 healed. And let hym take to clenſe the houſſe with
all: two birdes, cypreſſe wodd, ād purple clothe ād
50 yſope. And let him kyll one of the birdes ouer an
51 erthen veſſel of runnynge water, ād take the cipreſſe
wodd, the yſope, the purple ād the lyuynge byrde, ād
dyppe them in the bloude of the ſlayne byrde and in
the runninge water, and ſprinkle apon the houſſe ſeuen

M. 49 cedar wodd 50 byrdes in 51 cedar wodd

V. 42 & luto alio liniri domum. 51 in ſanguine paſſ. . . in aquis viuentibus

L. 41 ringſumb ſchaben 42 das haus bewerffen 44 ein freſſender ausſatz 50 ynn eym erden gefeſs an eym lebendigen waſſer.

52 tymes, and clenſe the houſſe with [Fo. XXVII.] the
bloude of the byrde, and with the runninge water, ād
with the lyuyng byrde, ād with the cypreſſe wodd, ād
53 the yſope ād the purple clothe And he ſhall lett
the lyuynge bird flee oute off the towne in to the
wyide feldes, and ſo make an attone-
ment for the houſſe, and it ſhalbe
cleane.

wylde, *open*, cf. wyde xvii, 5

54 This is the lawe of all maner plage of leproſye and
55 breakynge out, and of the leproſye off clothe and
56 houſſe: and of ryſynges, ſcabbes and glyſterynge white,
57 to teache when a thinge is vncleane or cleane. This
is the lawe off leproſye.

ℭ The .XV. Chapter.

M.C.S. *The maner of purging the vnclennes bothe of men and wemen.*

1 AND the Lorde ſpake vnto Moſes
2 and Aaron ſayenge, ſpeake
vnto the children of Iſrael
and ſaye vnto them: euery
mā that hath a runnynge yſſue in his fleſh, is vncleane
3 by the reaſon of his yſſue. And hereby ſhall it be
knowne when he is vncleane. Yf his fleſhe runne, or
yf his fleſh congele by the reaſon off his yſſue, than he
4 is vncleane. Euery couche whereon he lyeth ād euery
thinge whereon he ſytteth ſhalbe vncleane
5 He that twitcheth his couch, ſhall waſſh his clothes
ād bath him ſelfe with water, ād be vncleane vntyll
the euen.
6 He that ſytteth on that whereon he ſatt, ſhall .P.
waſſh his clothes and bathe him ſelfe with water and
7 be vncleane vntill the euenynge And he that twicheth
his fleſh ſhall waſſhe his clothes and bathe him ſelfe in

M. 52 cedar wodd
V. 53 orabit pro domo & iure mūdabitur. 54 lepræ et percuſſuræ, xv, 2 patitur fluxū ſeminis 3 cū per ſingula momenta adhæſerit carni eius, atque cōcreuerit fœdus humor.
L. 56 beulen, gretz vnd eytter weys. xv, 2 ſeym fleyſch eyn flus fleuſſet 3 eyttert odder wund gefreſſen wirt

8 water and be vncleane vnto the euen. Yf any ſoch
ſpytt apon him that is cleane, he muſt waſſhe his
clothes and bathe him ſelfe in water and be vncleane
vntill euen.

9 And what ſoeuer ſadell that he rydeth apō ſhalbe
10 vncleane. And whoſoeuer twicheth any thinge that
was vnder him, ſhalbe vncleane vnto the euē. And
he that beareth any ſoch thinges ſhall waſſh his clothes
and bathe hī ſelf in water ād be vncleane vnto the
11 euē, ād whoſoeuer he twicheth (yf he haue not firſt
waſhed his handes in water) muſt waſſhe his clothes,
ād bathe him ſelfe in water, ād be vncleane vn to the
12 euenynge. And yf he twych a veſſell off erth, it ſhalbe
broken: and all veſſels of wodd ſhalbe renſed in the
water.

13 When he that hath an yſſue is clenſed of his yſſue,
let him numbre .vii. dayes after he is cleane, ād waſſhe
his clothes, and bathe his fleſhe in runnynge water,
14 ād then he is cleane. And the .viii. daye let him take
two turtill doues or two yonge pigeons, and come before the Lorde vnto the dore of the tabernacle of wit-
15 neſſe ād geue them vnto the preaſt. And the preaſt
[Fo. XXVIII.] ſhall offer them: the one for a ſynneofferynge, and the other for a burntofferynge: and
make an attonement for him before the Lord, as cō-
cernynge his yſſue.

16 Yf any mans ſeed departe frō him in his ſlepe, he
ſhall waſh his fleſh in water ād be vncleane vntill euē.
17 And all the clothes or furres whereon furres, *ſkins*
ſoch ſeed chaunceth ſhalbe waſhed with water ād be
18 vncleane vnto the euē. And yf a womā lye with ſoche
a whone, they ſhall waſh thē ſelues with water and be
vncleane vntyll euen.

19 Whē a womās naturall courſe of bloud rūneth, ſhe
ſhalbe put aparte .vii. dayes: ād whoſoeuer twycheth
20 her ſhalbe vncleane vnto the euē. And all that ſhe

M. 12 ryneſed in water.

V. 11 quē tetigerit qui talis eſt 15 rogabitque pro eo . . . vt emūdetur a fluxu ſeminis ſui. 18 Mulier cū qua coierit

L. 18 Eyn weyb, . . . ſollen ſie ſich mit waſſer baden 19 ſieben tage beſeyt gethan

lyeth apō as longe as ſhe is put aparte ſhalbe vnclene.
21 And whoſoeuer twicheth hir couch ſhall waſh his clothes
and bathe hī ſelfe with water ād be vncleane vnto the
22 euē. And whoſoeuer twicheth any thinge that ſhe
ſatt apō, ſhall waſſh his clothes ād waſhe him ſelfe alſo
23 in water, ād be vncleane vnto the euē: ſo that whether
he twich her couche or any thīge whereō ſhe hath ſetē,
24 he ſhalbe vnclene ūto the euē. ād yf a mā lye with
her in the meane tyme, he ſhalbe put aparte as well
as ſhe ād ſhalbe vncleane .vii. dayes, ād all his couch
wherein he ſlepeth ſhalbe vncleane.
25 .P. When a womans bloude runneth longe tyme:
whether out of the tyme of hyr naturall courſe: as
longe as hir vnclenneſſe runneth, ſhe ſhalbe vncleane
26 after the maner as when ſhe is put aparte. All hir
couches whereon ſhe lyeth (as lōge as hir yſſue laſteth)
ſhalbe vnto her as hir couch when ſhe is put a parte.
And what ſoeuer ſhe ſytteth apon, ſhalbe vncleane, as
27 is hir vnclenneſſe whē ſhe is put a parte. And whoſoeuer twicheth them, ſhalbe vncleane, ād ſhall waſſhe
his clothes ād bathe him ſelfe in water ād be vncleane
vnto euen.
28 And when ſhe is clenſed of hyr iſſue, let hyr counte
29 hir ſeuen dayes after that ſhe is cleane. And the .viii
day let her take two turtils or two yonge pigeons and
brynge them vnto the preaſt vnto the dore of the tab-
30 ernacle of witneſſe. And the preaſt ſhall offer the one
for a ſynneoffrynge, and the other for a burntofferynge:
and ſo make an attonement for her before the Lorde.
as concernynge hir vncleane yſſue.
31 Make the childern of Iſrael to kepe them ſelues frō
their venclēneſſe, that they dye not in their vnclēneſſe: whē
they haue defiled my habitacion that is amonge them.

M. 20 And all ẏ ſhe lyeth or ſytteth vpō as longe as ſhe 24 aparte was well 25 longe tyme: out of 28 But yf ſhe be cleane of hir yſſue

V. 25 non in tempore menſtr. vel quæ poſt menſtr. ſanguin. fluere non ceſſat 30 rogabitque pro ea . . & pro fluxu immunditiæ eius.

L. 20 bey ſeyt gethan iſt 25 nicht allein zur gewonlicher zeyt, ſonder auch vber die gew. zeyt. 30 verſunen fur dem HERRN vber dem flus yhrer vnreynickeyt.

32 This is the lawe of him that hath a runninge ſore,
and of him whoſe ſeed runneth from [Fo. XXIX.] him
33 in his ſlepe and is defiled therewith, and of her that
hath an yſſue of bloude as longe as ſhe is put a parte,
and of whoſoeuer hath a runnynge ſore whether it be
man or woman, and of him that ſlepeth with her that
is vncleane.

The .XVI. Chapter.

1 AND the Lorde ſpake vnto Moſes after the deeth of the two
ſonnes of Aaron, when they
had offered before the Lorde
2 and dyed: And he ſayde vnto Moſes:
ſpeake vnto Aaron thy brother that he
go not at all tymes in to the holy
place, that is whithin the vayle that
hangeth before the mercyſeate which is
apon the arcke that he dye not. For
I will appeare in a clowde
vpon the mercyſeate.
3 But of this maner ſhall
Aaron goo in in to the holy place: with a yonge oxe
for a ſynneofferynge, and a ram for a burntoffrynge.
4 And he ſhall put the holy lynen albe apon him, ād
ſhall haue a lynen breche vppon his fleſh, and ſhall
gyrde him wyth a lynen gyrdell, and put the lynen
mytre apon his heede: for they are holy raymentes.
And he ſhall waſſhe his fleſh with water, and put them
5 on. And he ſhall take of the multitude of the childern

M.C.S. What Aarō muſt do or he enter into the holy place. The cleanſyng of the ſanctuary or holy place. Of the feaſte of cleanſyng. Aaron cōfeſſeth the ſynnes of the chyldren of Iſrael ouer the lyue goote & putteth thē vpon hys heed.

By the cloud vnderſtonde the ſmoke off the cence.

M. 3 with a bullock
V. 32 Iſta eſt lex eius qui pat. fluxū ſem., & qui poll. coitu, 33 & quæ men. temp. ſeparatur, vel quæ iugi fluit ſang., & hom. qui dormier. cum ea. xvi, 2 ſuper oraculum 3 niſi hæc ante fecerit 4 cū lotus fuerit
L. 33 vnd wer eyn flus hat, es ſey man odder weyb
M. M. N. 2 By the cloud vnderſtāde the ſmoke of the cenſe.

of Israel two gootes for a synneoffrynge and a ram for
a burntofferynge.
6 .P. And Aaron shall offer the oxe for his synneoffrynge and make an attonement for him ād for his
7 housse. And he shall take the two gootes and present
them before the Lorde in the dore of the tabernacle
8 of witnesse. And Aarō cast lottes ouer the .ii. gootes:
one lotte for the Lorde, ād another for a scapegoote.
9 And Aaron shall bringe the goote apō which the Lordes
10 lotte fell, and offer him for a synneofferynge. But the
goote on which the lotte fell to scape, he shall sett
alyue before the Lorde to recōcyle with ād to let him
11 goo fre in to the wildernesse. And Aaron shall bringe
the oxe of his synoffrynge, ād reconcyle for him selfe
ād for his housholde, and kyll him.

12 And thā he shall take a censer full of burninge coles
out of the alter that is before the Lorde, and his
handfull of swete cens beten small and bringe them
13 within the vayle and put the cens apon the fire before
the Lorde: that the cloude of the cens maye couer the
mercyseate that is apon the witnesse, that he dye not.
14 And he shall take of the bloude of the oxe ād sprinkle
it with his finger before the mercyseate eastwarde: euen
vii. tymes.

15 Then shall he kyll the goote that is the peoples
synneofferynge, and brynge hys bloude within the
vayle, and doo with his bloude as [Fo. XXX.] he
dyd with the bloude of the oxe, and let him sprinkle
it toward the mercyseate and before the mercyseate:
16 ād reconcyle the holy place frō the vnclennesse of the
childern of Israel, and from their trespaces ād all there
synnes. And so let him doo also vnto the tabernacle
of witnesse that dwelleth with them, euē among their
vnclennesses.

M. 6 bullock 11 bullock 14 bullock 15 bullock

V. 8 capro emissario 11 His rite celebratis 12 thuribulo quod de prunis altaris impleuerit 14 contra propitiatorium ad orientem. 15 Cumque mactauerit hircum . . vituli, vt aspergat eregione oraculi 16 quod fixum est inter eos

L. 8 dem freybock 12 eyn pfannen von glut 14 gegen dem Gnadenstuel sprengen fornen an 16 von yhrer vbertrettung, ynn allen yren sunden . . . bey yhn ist, vnter yhrer vnreynickeyt.

17 And there ſhalbe no bodye in the tabernacle of
witneſſe, when he goeth in to make an attonement in
the holy place, vntyl! he come out agayne. And he
ſhall make an attonement for him ſelfe and for his
18 houſholde, ād for all the multitude of Iſrael. Then he
ſhall goo out vnto the alter that ſtondeth before the
Lorde, and reconcyle it, and ſhall take of the bloude
of the oxe and of the bloude of the goote, and put it
19 apon the hornes of the altare rounde aboute, and
ſprynckle of the bloude apon it with his finger ſeuen
tymes, and clenſe it, and halowe it frō the vnclenneſſes
of the childern of Iſrael.

20 And whē he hath made an ende of recōcylinge the
holy place and the tabernacle of witneſſe ād the alter,
21 let him bringe the lyue goote ād let Aarō put both
his handes apon the heede of the lyue goote, and confeſſe ouer him all the myſdeades of the childern of
Iſraell, .P. and all their treſpaces, and all their
ſynnes: and let him put them apō the heed of the
goote ād ſende him awaye by the handes of one that
22 is acoynted in the wyldterneſſe. And the
goote ſhall bere apon him all their myſdeades vnto the wilderneſſe, and he ſhall let the goote
goo fre in the wilderneſſe.

acoynted, *acquainted*

23 And let Aaron goo in to the tabernacle of wytneſſe
and put off the lynē clothes which he put on when he
24 wēt in in to the holy place, ād leaue them there. And
let him waſſhe his fleſh with water in the holy place,
and put on his owne rayment, and then come out and
offer his burntofferynge and the burntofferynge of the
people, and make an atonemēt for him ſelfe ād for the
25 people, and the fatt of the ſynofferynge let him burne
26 apon the alter. And let him that caryed forth the
ſcapegoote, waſſhe his clothes and bathe hys fleſh in
water, and then come in to the hoſte agayne.

M. 18 bullock 21 Iſraell, and their treſpaces
V. 18 domino eſt, oret pro ſe, et ſumptum 21 omnes iniquitates . . . vniuerſa delicta atque peccata . . . per hominem paratum
L. 21 alle yhre vbertretung, ynn yhren ſunden . . eyn man der furhanden iſt

27 And the oxe of the ſynofferynge and the goote of
the ſynofferynge (whoſe bloude was brought in to make
an atonemēt in the holy place) let one carye out without the hoſte and burne with fyre: both their ſkynnes,
28 their fleſh ād their donge. And let him that burneth
them, waſſhe his clothes ād bathe his fleſh in water,
and thē come in to the hoſte agayne.
29 [Fo. XXXI.] And it ſhalbe an ordynaunce for euer
vnto you. And euē in the tenth daye of the ſeuenth
moneth, ye ſhall humble youre ſoules and ſhall doo no
worke at all: whether it be one of youre ſelues or a
30 ſtraunger that ſogeorneth amonge you. for that daye
ſhall an attonemēt be made for you to clenſe you from
all youre ſynnes before the Lorde, and ye ſhalbe cleane.
31 It ſhal be a ſabbath of reſt vnto you, and ye ſhall
humble youre ſoules, and it ſhalbe an ordynaunce for
euer.
32 And the preaſt that is anoynted and whoſe hande
was fylled to myniſtre in his fathers ſteade, ſhall make
the attonemēt and ſhall put on the holy lynē veſti-
33 mētes, and reconcyle the holy ſanctuary and the tabernacle of witneſſe ād the alter, and ſhall make an
attonemēt alſo for the preaſtes and for all the people
34 of the congregacion. And this ſhalbe an euerlaſtynge
ordynaunce vnto you to make an atonement for the
childern of Iſrael for all their ſynnes once a yere: and
it was done euē as the Lorde commaunded Moſes.

M. 27 bullock
V. 30 In hac die expiatio erit veſtri atque mundatio 31 religione perpetua 32 manus initiatæ
L. 31 Ein ewig recht ſey das.
M. M. N. 29 *Humble youre ſoules:* Looke in the .xxiii. chapter, e. 34 *Euerlaſtinge:* Loke in Geneſis .xiii, d.

The .XVII. Chapter.

1 AND the Lorde talked with Mo-
2 ses saynge: speake vnto Aarō
and vnto his sonnes and vnto
all the childern of Israel ād
saye .P. vnto them, this is the thynge
3 which the Lorde charged saynge: whatsoeuer he be of the housse of Israel that
kylleth an oxe, lambe or goote in the hoste or out of
4 the hoste and bryngeth thē not vnto the dore of the
tabernacle of witnesse, to offer an offerynge vnto the
Lorde before the dwellynge place of the Lorde, bloude
shalbe imputed vnto that man, as though he had shed
bloude, and that man shall perysh from amonge his
people.

M.C.S. All sacrifyce must be brought to the dore of the tabernacle. To deuels may they not offer. Bloude and all karen is forbydden them.

5 Wherfore let the childern of Israel brynge their
offerynges they offer in the wyde felde, vnto the
Lorde: euen vnto the dore of the tabernacle of witnesse and vnto the preast, and offer thē for peaseoffer-
6 ynges vnto the Lorde. And the preast shall sprinkle
the bloude apon the alter of the Lorde in the dore
of the tabernacle of wytnesse, and burne the fatt to
7 be a swete sauoure vnto the Lorde. And let them no
moare offer their offerynges vnto deuyls, after whom
they goo a whoorynge. And this shalbe an ordynaūce
for euer vnto you thorow out youre generacyons.

8 And thou shalt saye vnto them: what soeuer man
it be of the housse of Israel or of the straungers that
sogeorne amonge you that offereth a burntofferynge
9 or any other offerynge and bryngeth it not vnto the

M. 5 offerynges ẏ they offer . . the peace offerynges

V. 4 sanguinis reus erit 5 hostias suas quas occidunt in agro 7 dæmonibus, cum quibus fornicati sunt.

L. 4 des bluts schuldig seyn 5 yhre tödopffer dem Herrn opffern 7 vnd mit nichte yhre opffere hyn fort . . . mit den sie huren

M. M. N. 7 He offreth vnto deuelles, that offereth vnto any other thinge thē only to God, or that doth hys offeringes after any other maner then God willeth him to do, & the same goeth a whorehuntynge after the deuell as in Psal. lxxii, d.

dore of the taber- [Fo. XXXII.] nacle of wytneſſe to
offer vnto the Lorde, that felow ſhall peryſh from
amonge his people.
10 And what ſoeuer man it be of the houſſe of Iſrael
or of the ſtraungers that ſoiourne amonge you that
eateth any maner of bloude, I will ſet my face agaynſt
that ſoule that eateth bloude, and will deſtroy him
11 from amonge his people. for the life of the fleſh is in
the bloude, and I haue geuen it vnto you apon the alter, to make an attonement for youre ſoules, for bloude
12 ſhall make an attonemēt for the ſoule. And therfore
I ſayde vnto the childern of Iſrael: ſe that no ſoule of
you eate bloude, nor yet any ſtraunger that ſoiourneth
amonge you.
13 Whatſoeuer man it be of the childern of Iſrael or
of the ſtraungers that ſoiurne amonge you that hont-
eth and catcheth any beeſt or foule that maye be eatē,
he ſhall poure out the bloude ād couer it with erthe.
14 for the life of all fleſh is in the bloude, therefore I ſayde
vnto the childern of Iſrael, ye ſhall eate the bloude of
no maner of fleſh. for the life of all fleſh is in his bloude,
15 and whoſoeuer therfore eateth it ſhall peryſh. And
what ſoeuer ſoule it be that eateth that which dyed
alone or that which was torne with wylde beeſtes:
whether it be one of youre ſelues or a ſtraunger, he
ſhall waſſhe his .P. clothes ād bathe him ſelfe in water,
ād ſhalbe vncleane vnto the euē, ād thā is he cleane.
16 But ād yf he waſſhe them not nor waſſhe his fleſh he
ſhall beare his ſynne.

V. 10 obſirmabo faciem meam contra animam illius 11 dedi illum vobis, vt ſuper altare meum expietis pro animabus veſtris . . pro animæ piaculo 13 ſi venatione atque aucupio 14 anima enim omnis carnis in ſanguine eſt.

L. 10 widder den will ich meyn antlitz ſetzen 11 denn des leybs ſeel iſt ym blut, vnd ich habs euch zum alltar geben 13 ſehet auff der iaget 14 denn alles fleyſch lebt ym blut . . Denn alles fleyſch leben iſt ynn ſeym blut.

The .XVIII. Chapter.

M.C.S. What degrees of kynred may marye to geather & what not.

1 AND the Lorde talked with Mo-
2 ſes ſaynge: ſpeake vnto the
childern of Iſrael, ād ſaye vnto
them, I am the Lorde youre
3 God Wherfore after the doynges of the land of
Egipte wherein ye dwelt, ſe that ye doo not: nether
after the doynges of the lande of Canaan, whether
I will bringe you, nether walke ye in their ordi-
4 naunces, but doo after my iudgemētes, and kepe
myne ordynaunces, to walke therein: for I am the
5 Lorde youre God. Kepe therfore myne ordinaunces,
ād my iudgemētes whiche yf a man doo he ſhall lyue
thereby: for I am the Lorde.

6 Se that ye goo to none of youre nygheſt kynred
for to vncouer their ſecrettes, for I am the Lorde.
7 The ſecrettes of thy father and thy mother, ſe thou
vnheale not: ſhe is thy mother, therfore
8 ſhalt thou not diſcouer hir ſecrettes. The
ſecrettes of thy fathers wife ſhalt thou not
diſcouer, for they are thy fathers ſecrettes.

vnheale, *uncover* [often]
diſcouer, *uncover* [often]

9 Thou ſhalt not diſcouer the preuyte of thy ſyſter,
the doughter of thy father or of thy mother: whe-
[Fo. XXXIII.] ther ſhe be borne at home or without.
10 Thou ſhalt not diſcouer the ſecrettes of thy ſonnes
doughter or thy doughters doughter, for that is
11 thyne awne preuyte: Thou ſhalt not diſcouer the
ſecrettes of thy fathers wyues doughter, which ſhe
bare to thy father, for ſhe is thy ſuſter: thou ſhalt
12 therfore not diſcouer hir ſecrettes. Thou ſhalt not
vncouer the ſecrettes of thy fathers ſyſter, for ſhe
13 is thy fathers nexte kyn. Thou ſhalt not dyſcouer

M. 12 nexte kynſwoman

V. 3 iuxta cōſuetudinem terræ Æg., . . . iuxta morem regionis chan. 6 ad proximam ſanguinis ſui . . . turpitudinem 12 turp. ſororis patris . . quia caro eſt patris tui.

L. 3 nach den wercken [*bis*] 6 nehiſten blutfreundyn thun, yhr ſcham zu bloſſen 12 deyns vaters nehiſte blutfreundyn.

the ſecrettes off thy mothers ſyſter, for ſhe is thy
mothers nexte kyn.
14 Thou ſhalt not open the ſecrettes of thy fathers
brother: that is thou ſhalt not goo in to his wife,
15 for ſhe is thyne awnte. Thou ſhalt not diſcouer the
ſecrettes of thy doughter in lawe ſhe is thy ſonnes
16 wyfe: therfore vncouer not hir ſecrettes. Thou ſhalt
not vnheale the ſecrettes of thy brothers wife, for
17 that is thy brothers preuyte. Thou ſhalt not diſcouer
the preuytes of the wife ād hir doughter alſo, nether
ſhalt thou take hir ſonnes doughter or hir doughters
doughter to vncouer their ſecrettes: they are hir nexte
18 kyn, it were therfore wikydneſſe. Thou ſhalt not take
a wife and hir ſiſter thereto, to vexe hir that thou wold-
19 eſt open hir ſecrettes as longe as ſhe lyueth. Thou
ſhalt not goo vnto a woman to open hir ſecrettes, as
.P. longe as ſhe is put aparte for hir vnclenneſſe.
20 Thou ſhalt not lye with thy neghbours wife, to
21 defyle thi ſelfe with her. Thou ſhalt not geue of thi
ſeed to offer it vnto Moloch, that thou defile not the
name of thi God, for I am the Lorde.
22 Thou ſhalt not lye with mankynde as with wo-
23 mankynde, for that is abominacion. Thou ſhalt
lye with no maner of beeſte to defile thy ſelfe there-

M. 13 nexte kynſwoman 14 Thou ſhalt not vncouer

V. 13 caro ſit matris tuæ. 14 quæ tibi affinitate coniungitur. 15 ignominiā eius. *Et vxorem fratris ſui nullus accipiat.* 17 Turpitud., . . . ignominiam eius . . quia caro illius ſunt, & talis coitus incæſtus eſt. 18 in pellicatum illius . . adhuc illa viuente. 19 reuelabis fœditatem eius. 20 nec ſeminis commiſtione maculaberis. 21 vt conſecretur idolo

L. 13 deyner mutter nehiſte blutfreundyn. 17 vnd iſt eyn laſter. 18 weyb nemen ſampt yhrer ſchweſter . . . weyl ſie noch lebt. 20 ſie zu beſamen 21 dem Molech verbrant werde

M. M. N. 21 *Thy ſeede*, that is thy generacion, thy ſonnes, thy daughters etc.—*Moloch* loke in the .xx. chap. of Leu. 1, a.

L. M. N. 21 *Molech* war eyn abgott, dem ſie yhr eygen kinder zu dienſt verbrantten, wie Manaſſe thet der konig Iuda, vnd meyneten Gott damit zu dienen wie Abraham thet da er Iſaac ſeynen ſon opffert, Aber weyl das Gott nicht befolhen hatte, wie er Abraham thet, war es unrecht, darumb ſpricht hie Gott, das ſeyn name da durch entheyligt werde, Denn es geſchach vnter Gottis namē vnd war doch teuffeliſch, wie auch itzt kloſtergelubd vnd ander menſchen auff ſetze viel leutt verderben, vnter gottlichem namen als ſey es Gottis dienſt.

with, nether ſhall any woman ſtonde before a beeſt
to lye doune thereto, for that is abhominacion.
24 Defile not youre ſelues in any of theſe thinges, for
with all theſe thinges are theſe nacions defiled whiche
25 I caſt out before you: and the lande is defiled, and I
will viſett the wykedneſſe thereof apon it. and the
26 lande ſhal ſpewe out hir inhabiters. Kepe ye therfore myne ordinaunces and iudgementes, and ſe
that ye commytt none of theſe abominacions: nether any of you nor ony ſtraunger that ſoiourneth
27 amonge you (for all theſe abhominacions haue the
men of the lande done whiche were there before
28 you, and the lande is defiled) leſt that the lande
ſpewe you out when ye haue defiled it, as it ſpewed
29 out the nacions that were there before you. For
whoſoeuer ſhall cõmytt any of theſe abhominacions,
the ſame ſoules that [Fo. XXXIIII.] commytt them
30 ſhall periſh from amonge their people. Therfore ſe
that ye kepe myne ordinaunces, that ye commytt
none of theſe abhominable cuſtomes which were commytted before you: that ye defile not youre ſelues
therewith for I am the Lorde youre God.

¶ The .XIX. Chapter.

1 AND the Lorde ſpake vnto Moſes
2 ſayenge: ſpeake vnto all the
multitude of the childern of
Iſrael, and ſaye vnto them.
Be holy for I the Lorde youre God am
3 holye. Se that ye feare: euery man his
father and his mother, ãd that ye kepe
my Sabbathes, for I am the Lorde youre
4 God. Ye ſhall not turne vnto ydolls nor
make you goddes of metall: I am the
Lorde youre God.

M.C.S. A repetycion of certayne lawes pertayning to the .x. commaundemẽtes. A conſyderacion for the poore. How we ought to iudge righteouſly. How we ought not to be auenged. Wytchcraft is forbydden.

V. 23 non ſuccumbet iumento . . . quia ſcelus eſt.
L. 23 thier zu ſchaffen haben

5 When ye offre youre peaceofferynges vnto the
Lorde, ye ſhall offer them that ye maye be accepted.
6 And it ſhalbe eaten the ſame daye ye offer it and
on the morowe, but what ſoeuer is lefte on the
7 thirde daye ſhalbe burnt in the fire. Yf it be eaten
the thirde daye, it ſhalbe vncleane ād not accepted.
8 And he that eateth it ſhall bere his ſynne: becauſe
he hath defiled the halowed thinges of the Lorde,
ād that ſoule ſhall periſh from amonge his people.

9 .¶. When ye repe doune the rype corne of youre
lande, ye ſhal not repe doune the vtmoſt borders of
youre feldes, nether ſhalt thou gather that which is
10 left behynd in thy harueſt. Thou ſhalt not pluck in
all thy vyneyarde clene, nether gather in the grapes
that are ouerſcaped. But thou ſhalt
leaue them for the pore ād ſtraunger.
I am the Lord youre God.

ouerſcaped, *overlooked*

11 Ye ſhall not ſteale nether lye, nether deale falſely
12 one with another. Ye ſhal not ſwere by my name
falſelye: that thou defileſt not the name of thy God,
I am the Lorde.

13 Thou ſhalt not begile thy neyghboure
with cauellaciōs, nether robbe him violently, nether ſhall the workmans laboure abide with
the vntyll the mornynge.

cauellacions, *overreaching, fraud*

14 Thou ſhalt not curſe the deaffe, nether put a ſtom-
blinge blocke before the blynd: but ſhalt feare thy
God. I am the Lorde.

15 Ye ſhall doo no vnrightuouſnes in iudgement. Thou
ſhalt not fauoure the poore nor honoure the mightye,
but ſhalt iudge thy neghboure rightuouſly.

16 Thou ſhalt not go vp ād doune a *
preuy accuſer amōge thy people, nether

Yes for God ād with his awne cōfeſſiō

V. 7 prophanus erit & impietatis reus 9 vſque ad ſolum 13 Non facies calumniam 15 Non facies quod iniquum eſt, nec iniuſte iudicabis. Non conſyderes perſonam pauperis, nec honores vultū potentis. 16 criminator nec ſuſurro in populis.

L. 9 an den enden vmbher abſchneyden 16 keynen verleumbder vnter deynem volck

M. M. N. 10 Here ſhuld we lerne to make a prouiſyon for the poore.

shalt thou helpe to shed the bloude of thy neyghboure: I am the Lorde.

shalt thou accuse him, to stablishe the holye fathers kingdome,

17 Thou shalt not hate thy brother in thyne hart [Fo. XXXV.] but shalt in any wyse rebuke thy neghbour: that thou bere not synne for his sake.

18 Thou shalt not avenge thy selfe nor bere hate in thy mynde against the childern of thi people, but shalt loue thy neghboure euē as thy self I am the Lorde.

19 Kepe myne ordinaunces. Let none of thy catell gendre with a cōtrary kynde, nether sowe thy felde with myngled seed, nether shalt thou put on ony garment of lynen and wollen

20 Yf a man haue to doo with a woman that is bonde and hath bene medled with al of another man which nether is boughte nor fredome geuen her, there shalbe a payne apon it: but they shall not dye,
21 because she was not made fre. And he shall brynge for his trespaceofferynge vnto the Lorde: euen vnto the dore off the tabernacle of witnesse, a ram for a trespaceoffrynge. And the preast shall make an attonement for him with the ram of the trespace-
22 offerynge before the Lord, for his synne which he hath done: and it shalbe forgeuen him, as concerninge the synne which he hath done.

payne, *punishment*

V. 16 . . . stabis contra sanguinem 18 iniuriæ ciuium tuorum 19 ex duobus texta 20 ancilla etiam nobilis . . vapulabunt ambo

L. 19 wolle vnd leyn gemenget 20 vnd von eym andern verrucket

M. M. N. 19 Catell maye not gēdre with a cōtrarykinde agaynst the order of nature: moche lesse reasonable creatures made to the ymage of God as mē & wemē. ¶ The felde maye not be sowen wyth mixt seede, that is, oure dedes & wordes maye not be myngled with ypocresy. Nether maye our garmētes be made of lynē & wollē, that is we maye not myngle false doctrine wyth true, or shew a carnall and worldly lyfe vnder pretence of relygion.

L. M. N. 20 *Verruckt:* dis gesetz redet vō solchē weyb, das zuuor von yemand beschlaffen vnd doch nicht zur ehe genomen ist, wie es seyn solt nach dem gesetz am. 21 capitel ym andern buch, vileicht, das sie yhr herr dem nicht hat wollen geben, vnd als nu gleych eyner witwyn ist vnd zum andern mal beschlaffen wirt, wilchs denn widder ehebruch noch hurerey ist, vnd doch sund, die strefflich ist.

23 And when ye come to the lande ād haue plāted
all maner of trees where of mē eate, ye ſhal holde
them vncircumcifed as concerning their frute: euē
thre yere ſhal they be vncircūcyſed vnto you ād
24 ſhall not be eatē of, ād the fourth .P. yere all the
frute of thē ſhalbe holy ād acceptable to the Lorde.
25 And the fifth yere maye ye eate of the frute of thē,
ād gather in the encreaſe of them: I am the Lorde
youre God.
26 Ye ſhall eate nothinge with the bloude, ye ſhall
vſe no witchcrafte, nor obſerue diſmall diſmall, *evil, unlucky;* xx, 6, 27
27 dayes, ye ſhall not rounde the lockes of
youre heedes, nether ſhalt thou marre the tuftes of
thy beerde.
28 Ye ſhall not rent youre fleſh for any ſoules ſake, nor
printe any markes apon you: I am the Lorde.
29 Thou ſhalt not pollute thi doughter, that thou woldeſt maintene her to be an whoore: leſt the lāde fall to
30 whoredome, ād waxe ful of wekedneſſe. ¶ Se that
ye kepe my Sabbathes and feare my ſanctuary: I am
the Lorde.
31 Turne not to thē that worke with ſprites, nether regarde thē that obſerue diſemall dayes: that ye be not
defiled by thē, for I am the Lorde youre God.
32 Thou ſhalt ryſe vp before the hoorehed, hoorehed, *hoary head*
ād reuerence the face of the old mā ād
33 dread thy god, for I am the Lorde. Yf a ſtraunger
ſoiourne by the in youre lande, ſe that ye vexe him
34 not: But let the ſtraunger that dwelleth with you, be
as one of youre ſelues, and loue him as thi ſelfe, for
ye were ſtraungers in the lande of [Fo. XXXVI.]
Egipte. I am the Lorde youre God.
35 Ye ſhall do no vnrightuouſnes in iudgemēt nether
36 in meteyerde, weyght or meaſure. But ye ſhal haue

V. 23 ligna pomifera, auferetis præputia 26 augurabimini, nec obſ. ſomnia. 29 impl. piaculo. 31 declinetis ad magos, nec ab ariolis aliquid ſciſcitemini 33 Si habitauerit aduena . . & moratus fuerit

L. 23 beuwme pflantzt. . . vorhaut beſchneytten 26 vogel geſchrey achten noch tage welen. 28 buchſtaben . . pfetzen 31 warſagern . . . zeychen deutern

true balāces, true weightes, A true Epha ād a true
hin. I am the Lorde youre god which broughte you
37 out of the land of Egipte, that ye ſhulde obſerue all
myne ordinaunces and iudgementes and that ye ſhulde
kepe them: I am the Lorde.

☙ The .XX, Chapter,

1 AND the Lorde talked with Moſes
2 ſaynge: tell the childern of
Iſrael, whoſoeuer he be of the
childern of Iſrael or of the
ſtraungers that dwel in Iſrael, that geueth
of his ſeed vnto Moloch he ſhall dye for
it: the people off the lande ſhall ſtone hī
3 with ſtones. And I will ſett my face apon that ſelowe,
and will deſtroye him from amonge his people: becauſe he hath geuen of his ſeed vnto Moloch, for to defile
my ſanctuary and to polute myne holy
4 name. And though that the people of
the lande hyde their eyes from that ſelowe,
when he geueth of his ſeed vnto Moloch,
5 ſo that they kyll him not: yet I will put
my face apon that man and apon his houſſ-
holde, and will deſtroy him and all that
goo a whooringe with him and cōmytt
hoordome with Moloch from amonge
their people.

M.C.S. *They that geue of their ſeede to Moloch ſhall dye therfore. Other goodly lawes neceſſarye to be vſed in cōmen wealthes.*

If we tranſgreſſe gods commaundemētes we may happelye eſcape worldlye iudges, but we cā not avoid the firſe wrath of god, but it wil ſurely find vs out.

M. 5 and vpon hys generacion

V. 36 iuſtus modius, æquuſque ſextarius. xx, 4 Quod ſi negligens populus terræ, & quaſi paruipendens imperium meum, dimiſerit hominem 5 et cognationem eius

L. 36 recht Epha, recht Hin. xx, 4 durch die finger ſehen wurd, dem menſchen

M. M. N. 2 *Moloch*, vnder this name moloch is forbidden almaner of ydolatrie, ſpecially the exerciſynge of children therto for that is abhominable before the Lorde. Moloch was an Idolle of the children of Ammon, whoſe Image was holowe hauyng in it ſeuē cloſettes, one was to offer therin fyne floure, another for turtell dowues, the thyrd for a ſhepe, the fourth for a Ram, the fyſth for a calffe, the ſyxt for an oxe, And for hym that wolde offre his ſonne was opened the ſeuēth cloſet. And the face of this Idoll was lyke the face of a calffe, his handes made playne ready to receaue of them that ſtode by.

6 ℙ. Yf any ſoule turne vnto them that worke with
ſpirites or makers of dyſemall dayes and goo a whoorynge after them, I wil put my face apon that ſoule
7 and will deſtroye him from amonge his people. Sanctifie youre ſelues therfore and be holye, for I am the
8 Lorde youre God. And ſe that ye kepe myne ordinaunces and doo them. For I am the Lorde which
ſanctifie you.

9 Whoſoeuer curſeth his father or mother, ſhall dye for it, his bloude on his heed, becauſe he hath curſed his father or mother.

10 He that breaketh wedlocke with another mans wife ſhall dye for it: becauſe he hath broke wedlocke with his neghbours wife, and ſo ſhall ſhe likewiſe.

11 Yf a man lye with his fathers wife ād vncouer his fathers ſecrettes, they ſhall both dye for it, their bloude be apon their heedes.

12 Yf a man lye with his doughter in lawe thei ſhall dye both of them: they haue wrought abhominacion, their bloude vpon their heedes.

13 Yf a man lye with the mankynde after the maner as with womā kynd, they haue both cōmitted an abhominacion and ſhall dye for it. Their bloude be apon their heed.

14 Yf a man take a wife ād hir mother thereto, it is wekedneſſe. Mē ſhall burne with fire both [Fo. XXXVII.] him and them, that there be no wekedneſſe amonge you.

15 Yf a man lye with a beeſt he ſhall dye, and ye ſhall flee the beeſt.

16 Yf a womā go vnto a beeſt ād lye doune thereto: thou ſhalt kyll the womā ād the beeſt alſo they ſhal dye, ād their bloud be apō their hedes

M. 6 him to enchaūters or expounders of tokens 9 his bloud on his head 13 with mankynde . . heades.

V. 6 Anima quæ declin. ad magos & ariolos 9 ſanguis eius ſit ſuper eum. 11 dormierit cum nouerca ſua 15 iumento & pecore 16 Mulier qui ſuccubuerit

L. 6 warſagern vnd zeychen deuttern 11 ſeyns vaters weyb ſchlefft

17 Yf a mā take his ſyſter his fathers doughter or his
mothers doughter, ād ſe hir ſecrettes, and ſhe ſe his
ſecrettes alſo: it is a weked thinge.
Therfore let them periſh in the ſyghte of their people, he hath ſene his ſyſters ſecretneſſe, he ſhall therfore
bere his ſynne.
18 Yf a man lye with a woman in tyme of hyr naturall
diſeaſe and vnheale hir ſecrettes and vncouer hir fountayne, ād ſhe alſo open the fountayne of hir bloude,
they ſhall both periſhe from amonge their people.
19 Thou ſhalt not vncouer the ſecrettes of thy mothers
ſyſter nor of thy fathers ſyſters, for he that doth ſo,
vncouereth his nexte kyn: ād thei ſhall bere their
myſdoynge.
20 Yf a mā lye with his vncles wife, he hath
vncoured his vncles ſecrettes: they ſhall
bere their ſynne, and ſhall dye childleſſe.
21 Yf a mā take his brothers wife, it is an
vnclene thinge, he hath vncouered his
brothers ſecrettes, they ſhalbe childleſſe
therfore.

Thei ſhall dye immediatly ād not tary the byrth, as Iuda wold haue burnt Thamar being great with childe.

22 .¶. Se that ye kepe therfore all myne ordinaunces
and all my iudgementes, and that ye doo them: that
the londe whether I brynge you to dwell therein, ſpewe
23 you not oute. And ſe that ye walke not in the maners
of the nacyons whiche I caſt oute before you: For they
commytted all theſe thinges, and I abhorred them.
24 But I haue ſayde vnto you that ye ſhall enioye their
londe, and that I will geue it vnto you to poſſeſſe it:
euē a londe that floweth with milke and honye. I am
the Lord youre God, whiche haue ſeparated you from
25 other nacions: that ye ſhulde put difference betwene
cleane beeſtes and vncleane, and betwene vncleane
foules and them that are cleane. Make not youre
foules therfore abhominable with beeſtes ād foules,

M. 18 vncouer her ſecrettes and open 19 father ſyſter

V. 17 turpitudinem ſuam mutuo reuelauerint 19 ignom. carnis ſuæ 20 vxore patrui, vel auunculi ſui, & reu. ignom. cognationis ſuæ . . abſque liberis morientur.

M. M. N. 20, 21 They ſhall dye immediatly & not tary the byrth as Iuda wolde haue burnt Thamar being great wyth chylde. Gen. xxviii, f.

and with all maner thinge that crepeth apon the
grounde, which I haue ſeparated vnto you to holde
26 them vncleane. Be holy vnto me, for I the Lorde am
holy and haue ſeuered you from other nacyons: that
ye ſhulde be myne.

27 Yf there be mā or womā that worketh with a ſprite
or a maker of dyſemall dayes, thei ſhall dye for it. Mē
ſhall ſtone them with ſtones, ād their bloude ſhalbe
apon them.

ℂ The .XXI. Chapter.

[Fo. XXXVIII.] XXI. Chapter.

1 AND the Lorde ſayde vnto Moſes: ſpeake vnto the preaſtes
the ſonnes of Aaron and ſaye
vnto them. A preaſt ſhall
defile him ſelfe at the deth of none of
2 his people, but apon his kyn that is nye
vnto him: as his mother, father, ſonne,
3 doughter and brother: and on his ſyſter
as lōge as ſhe is a mayde ād dwelleth
nye him and was neuer geuen to man:
4 on her he maye defile him ſelfe. But
he ſhall not make him ſelfe vncleane
vpon a ruelar of his people to polute
him ſelfe with all.

5 They ſhall make thē no baldneſſe
apon their heedes or ſhaue off the lockes
of their beerdes, nor make any markes
6 in their fleſh. Thei ſhalbe holy vnto
their God, ād not polute the name of

M.C.S. *The preaſt is forbyddē to be at the death of any of his people, a fewe of his kynne except. Preaſtes may not be ſhauē nether on the head nor yet of the bearde. The preaſtes wyfe muſt be a mayde. The preaſtes daughter may not be an harlott.*

Of the hethē preaſtes therfore toke our prelates the enſample off their balde pates.

M. 27 or that expoundeth tokens

V. 27 pythonicus, vel diuinationis fuerit ſpiritus xxi, 2 niſi tantum in conſanguineis, ac propinquis 6 Incenſum enim domini

L. 27 warſager oder zeychen deutter

M. M. N. 1 The preaſtes be warned that they ſhall not come at the cōmē waylynges & lamētacyons of the deed leſt they ſhuld therby be the moare vnapte to do their ſacryſyces wherunto they were properly appoynted, and leſt they ſhulde by theire wepyng geue an occaſion to deſtroye the beleue of the reſurreccion of the dead.

their god, for the ſacrifices of the Lorde ād the bred
of their God thei do offer: therfore they muſt be holy.
7 Thei ſhall take no wife that is an whoore, or poluted, or put frō hir huſbonde: for a preaſt is holy
8 vnto his God. Sanctifie him therfore, for he offereth
vp the bred of God: he ſhal therfore be
holy vnto the, for I the Lorde whiche
ſanctifie you, am holy.
9 Yf a preaſtes doughter fall to playe
the whore, ſhe poluteth hir father: therfore ſhe ſhall be burnt with fire.

By bred vnderſtonde all fode, fleſh, frute, or whatſoeuer it be.

10 He that is the hye preaſt among his brethern .P.
vppon whoſe heed the anoyntynge oyle was poured
and whoſe hande was fylled to put on the veſtimētes, ſhall not vncouer his heed nor rent his clothes,
11 nether ſhall goo to any deed body nor make him
12 ſelfe vncleane: no not on his father or mother, nether ſhall goo out of the ſanctuarye, that he polute
not the holy place of his God. for the croune of the
anoyntynge oyle of God, is apon him.
I am the Lorde.
13 He ſhall take a mayden vnto his wife:
14 but no wedowe nor deuorſed nor poluted
whoore.

The anoyntynge was the coronacion both of kynges ād of preſtes alſo

But he ſhall take a mayden of his awne people to
15 wife, that he defyle not his ſeed apō his people. for
I am the Lorde which ſanctifye him.
16, 17 And the Lorde ſpake vnto Moſes ſaynge, ſpeake
vnto Aaron and ſaye: No man of thi ſeed in their
generacions that hath any deformyte
apon him, ſhall preſe for to
offer the bred of his God.
18 ffor none that hath any blemyſh ſhall come
nere: whether he be blynde, lame, ſnot

preſe, *approach*, v. 21.

Thepope forbideth all ſoch lyke wiſe tyll they haue payd for diſpenſaciōs.

M. 17 preace 18 any myſſhapē mēbre

V. 7 marito: quia conſecratus eſt deo ſuo, 8 & panes propoſ. offert. 10 veſtituſque eſt ſanctis veſtibus 12 oleum ſanctæ vnctionis . . ſuper eum 14 repudiatam, & ſordidam, atque meretricem 15 ſtirpem generis ſui vulgo gentis ſuæ 18 torto naſo

L. 10 vnd ſeyne hand gefullet iſt, das er anzogen wurde mit den kleydern 12 die kron des ſalboles 15 nicht ſeynen ſamen entheylige vnter ſeym volck 18 vngeheurem gelied

19 nosed, or that hath any monstrous mēbre, or broken
20 foted, or broken handed, or croke backed, or perleyed,
or gogeleyed, or maunge or skaulde, or hath his stones
broken.
21 No man that is deformed of the seed of Aaron
the preast, shall come nye to offer the sacrifyces of the
Lorde. Yf he haue a deformyte, he shall not prese
to offer the bred of his God.
22 [Fo. XXXIX.] Notwithstondynge he shall eate of
the bred of his God: euen as well of the most holy,
23 as of the holy: but shall not goo in vnto the vayle
nor come nye the alter, because he is deformed that
he polute not my sanctuary, for I am the Lorde
24 that sanctifye them. And Moses tolde it vnto Aaron
and to his sonnes, and vnto all the childern of Israel.

❡ The .XXII. Chapter.

1 AND the Lorde comened with
2 Moses saynge: byd Aaron and
his sonnes that they absteyne
from the halowed thynges of
the childern of Israel which they haue
halowed vnto me, that they polute not
myne holy name: for I am the Lorde.
3 Saye vnto them: whosoeuer he be of all
youre seed amonge youre generacion after you, that
goeth vnto the halowed thinges which the childern
of Israel shall haue halowed vnto the Lorde, his vnclennes shalbe apon him: and that soule shal perysh
from out of my syghte. I am the Lorde.

M.C.S. *What maner persones ought to abstayne from eatyng the thynges that were offred. How, what, & when they shulde be offerd.*

M. 21 preace
V. 20 si lippus, si albuginem 24 Israel cuncta quæ fuerāt sibi imperata. xxii, 2 & non cōtaminent nomen sanctificatorum mihi, quæ ipsi offerunt. 3 in quo est immunditia
L. 20 fell auffem auge . . schehl 21 nicht erzu thun zu opffern . . . nicht nahen

4 None of the ſeed of Aaron that is a leper or that hath
a runnynge ſore, ſhall eate of the halowed thinges vntill
he be cleane. And whoſoeuer twytcheth any vncleane
ſoule or man whoſe ſeed runneth frō him by nyghte,
5 or whoſoeuer twitcheth any worme that worme, *any*
is vncleane to him, or man that is vn- *creeping thing*
cleane to him, what- .P. ſoeuer vnclenneſſe he hath:
6 the ſame ſoule that hath twyched any ſoch thynge,
ſhalbe vncleane vntill euen, and ſhall not eate of the
halowed thynges vntill he haue waſſhed his fleſh with
7 water. And than when the ſonne is doune he ſhalbe
cleane ād ſhall afterward eate of the halowed thynges:
8 for they are his fode. Off a beeſt that dyeth alone or
is rent with wylde beaſtes, he ſhall not eate, to deſyle
9 him ſelfe therwith: I am the Lorde. But let them
kepe therfore myne ordynaunce, leſt they lade ſynne
apō them and dye therein when they haue deſyled
them ſelues: for I am the Lorde which ſanctiſye them.
10 There ſhall no ſtraunger eate of the halowed
thinges, nether a geſt of the preaſtes, or an hyred
11 ſeruaunte. But yf the preaſt bye any ſoule with
money he maye eate of it, and he alſo that is borne
in his houſſe maye eate of his bred.
12 Yf the preaſtes doughter be maryed vnto a ſtraunger, ſhe maye not eate of the halowed heueoffer-
13 ynges. Notwithſtondynge yf the preaſtes doughter
be a wedowe or deuorſed and haue no childe but is
returned vnto hir fathers houſſe agayne, ſhe ſhall eate
of hir fathers bred as wel as ſhe dyd in hyr youth.
But thereſhall no ſtraunger eate there of.
14 Yf a man eate of the halowed thynges vn- [Fo. XL.]
wyttingly, he ſhall put the fyſte parte there vnto, and
15 make good vnto the preaſt the halowed thynge. And

M. 6 that hath any ſoch thynge

V. 4 patiens fluxum ſeminis 5 & quodlibet immundum 9 non ſubiaceant peccato 12 cuilibet ex populo nupta 13 ſicut puella conſueuerat

L. 5 gewurm . . . das yhm vnreyn . . menſchen der yhm vnreyn iſt, vnd alles was yhn vervnreynigt 7 ſeyn futter. 9 ſund auff ſich laden 12 nicht von der Hebe der heylickeyt 13 wie andere dyrnen.

let the preaſtes ſee, that they defyle not the halowed
thynges of the childern of Iſrael which they haue
16 offered vnto the Lorde, leſt they lade them ſelues with
myſdoynge and treſpace in eatynge their halowed
thinges: for I am the Lorde which halowe them.
17, 18 And the Lorde ſpake vnto Moſes ſaynge: ſpeake
vnto Aaron and his ſonnes and vnto all the childern
of Iſrael and ſaye vnto them, what ſoeuer he be of
the houſſe of Iſrael or ſtraunger in Iſrael that will
offer his offerynge: what ſoeuer vowe or frewillofferynge it be which they will offer vnto the Lorde for a
19 burntofferynge to reconcyle them ſelues, it muſt be
a male without blemyſh of the oxen, ſhepe or gootes.
20 let them offer nothynge that is deformed for they
ſhall gett no fauoure there with.
21 Yf a man will offer a peaſeoffrynge vnto the
Lorde and ſeparate a vowe or a frewill offerynge of
the oxen or the flocke, it muſt be without deformyte,
that it maye be accepted. There maye be no blemyſh
22 therein: whether it be blīde, brokē, wounded or haue
a wen, or be maunge or ſcabbed. ſe that ye offre no
ſoch vnto the Lorde, nor put an offerynge of any ſoch
apon the alter vnto the Lorde.
23 .P. An oxe or a ſhepe that hath any membre out of
proporcion, mayſt thou offer for a frewillofferynge: but
24 in a vowe it ſhal not be accepted. Thou ſhalt not
offer vnto the Lorde that which hath his ſtones brooſed
brokē, plucked out or cutt awaye, nether ſhalt make
25 any ſoch in youre lande, nether of a ſtraungers hande
ſhall ye offer an offerynge to youre God of any ſoch.
For they marre all in that they haue deformytes in
them, and therfore can not be accepted for you.
26, 27 And the Lorde ſpake vnto Moſes ſaynge: when
an oxe, a ſhepe or a goote is brought forth, it ſhalbe
ſeuē dayes vnder the damme. And from the .viii

M. 24 that which is brooſed, broken, plucked

V. 18 domini, 19 vt auferatur per vos 23 Bouem & ouem aure & cauda amputatis 25 non offeretis panes deo . . quia corrupta & maculata ſunt omnia, non ſuſcipietis ea. 27 ſub vbere matris

L. 21 tödopffer 23 vngehewre gelied oder keyn ſchwantz

daye forth, it ſhalbe accepted vnto a gifte in the ſacri-
28 fice of the Lorde. And whether it be oxe or ſhepe, ye
ſhall not kyll it, and hir yonge: both in one daye.
29 When ye will offre a thankofferynge vnto the
Lorde, ye ſhall ſo offre it that ye maye be accepted.
30 And the ſame daye it muſt be eatē vp, ſo that ye
leaue none of it vntill the morowe. For I am the
31 Lorde, kepe now my commaundementes and do them,
for I am the Lorde.
32 And polute not my holy name, that I maye be
halowed amonge the childern of Iſrael. For I am
33 the Lorde which halowe you, and broughte you out
of the londe of Egipte, to be youre [Fo. XLI.] God:
for I am the Lorde.

¶ The .XXIII. Chapter.

M.C.S. Of the holy dayes, as the Saboth, Eſter, whytſontyde, the feaſt of the fyrſt frutes. The feaſt of cleanſyng. The feaſt of trompettes. The feaſt of the tabernacles.

1 AND the Lorde ſpake vnto Moſes
2 ſaynge: ſpeake vnto the childern of Iſrael, and ſaye vnto
them. Theſe are the feaſtes
off the Lorde which ye ſhal call holy
3 feaſtes. Sixe dayes ye ſhall worke, ād
the ſeuenth is the Sabbath of reſt an holy
feaſt: ſo that ye maye do no worke therein, for it is the Sabbath of the Lorde,
whereſoeuer ye dwell.
4 Theſe are the feaſtes of the Lorde whiche ye ſhall
5 proclayme holy in their ceaſons. The .xiiii. daye of
6 the firſt moneth at euē is the Lordes Paſſeouer, And
the .xv. daye of the ſame moneth is the feaſt of ſwete
bred vnto the Lorde: .vii. dayes ye muſt eate vnleuended bred.
7 The firſt daye ſhalbe an holy feaſte vnto you, ſo

V. 3 ſabbathi requies 5 phaſe domini 6 azymorum domini
L. 3 feyr des Sabbaths
M. M. N. 29 *A thankofferynge*, that is, an offeryng of thanckes geuynge. Thankes geuynge is when the benefytes of God are recyted, wherby the fayth to Godward is ſtrēgthened the more faſtly to loke for the thyng that we deſyre of God. Eph. v, a. 1 Tim. iii, a. & b.

8 that ye maye do no laborious worke therein But ye
ſhall offer ſacrifices vnto the Lorde .vii. dayes, and the
ſeuenth daye alſo ſhalbe an holy feaſt, ſo that ye maye
doo no laborious worke therein.
9, 10 And the Lorde ſpake vnto Moſes ſayenge: ſpeake
vnto the childern of Iſraell and ſaye vnto them: when
ye be come in to the lande whiche I geue vnto you
and repe doune youre harueſt, ye ſhall brynge a ſhefe
11 of the firſt frutes of youre harueſt vnto the preaſt, and
he ſhall wa- .P. ue the ſhefe before the Lorde to be
accepted for you: and euen the morow after the Sab-
12 bath the preaſte ſhall waue it. And ye ſhall offer the
daye when he waueth the ſhefe, a lãbe without blemyſh
13 of a yere old for a burntofferynge vnto the Lorde: and
the meatoffrynge thereof, two tenth deales of fine floure
mengled with oyle to be a ſacrifice vnto the Lorde of
a ſwete ſauoure: and the drinkofferinge thereto, the
14 fourth deale of an hin of wyne. And ye ſhall eate
nether bred, nor parched corne, nor furmentye of new
corne: vntyll the ſelfe ſame daye that ye haue broughte
an offrynge vnto youre God. And this ſhalbe a lawe
for euer vnto youre childern after you, where ſoeuer
ye dwell.
15 And ye ſhall counte from the morowe after the
Sabbath: euen from the daye that ye broughte the
16 ſheffe of the waueoffrynge, vii. wekes complete: euen
vnto the morow after the .vii. weke ye ſhall numbre
L. dayes. And thẽ ye ſhal bringe a newe meatoffrynge
17 vnto the Lorde. And ye ſhall brynge out of youre
habitacions two waueloaues made of two tenthdeales
off fine floure leuended and baken, for firſt frutes vnto
18 the Lorde. And ye ſhall bringe with the bred ſeuen
lambes without deformyte of one yere of age, and one
yonge oxe, and .ii. rambes, [Fo. XLII.] which ſhall

V. 8 dies autem ſeptimus erit celebrior & ſanctior 10 manipulos ſpicarum 11 eleuabit faſciculum 14 ex ea deo veſtro. 17 panes primitiarum

L. 10 garben der erſtling ewr erndten

M. M. N. 10 The *fyrſtfrutes* & *tythes* were the ſygnes of the faith knowleagynge to haue receaued their goodes & catell of the Lorde, as it is ſayde Ex. xxii, d. and .xxiii, c.

ſerue for burntoffrynges vnto the Lorde, with meat-
offringes and drinkoffringes longinge to the ſame, to
be a ſacrifice of a ſwete ſauoure vnto the Lorde.
19 And ye ſhall offer an he goote for a ſynneofferinge:
and two lambes of one yere old for peaceoffringes,
20 And the preaſt ſhall waue thē with the bred of the firſt
frutes before the Lorde, and with the two lambes.
And they ſhalbe holy vnto the Lorde, and be the
21 preaſtes. And ye ſhall make a proclamaciō the ſame
daye that it be an holy feaſt vnto you, and ye ſhall do
no laborious worke therein: And it ſhalbe a lawe for
euer thorowe out all youre habitacions vnto youre
childern after you,
22 When ye repe doune youre harueſt, thou ſhalt not
make cleane ryddaunce off thy felde, nether ſhalt thou
make any aftergatheringe of thy harueſt: but ſhalt leue
them vnto the poore and the ſtraunger. I am the
Lorde youre God.
23, 24 And the Lorde ſpake vnto Moſes ſaynge: ſpeake
vnto the childern of Iſrael ād ſaye. The firſt daye of
the ſeuenth moneth ſhalbe a reſt of remembraunce vnto
25 you, to blowe hornes in an holy feaſt it ſhalbe, and ye
ſhall do no laborious worke therein, and ye ſhall offer
ſacrifice vnto the Lorde.
26, 27 ¶. And the Lorde ſpake vnto Moſes ſayenge: alſo
the tenth daye of the ſelfe ſeuēth moneth, is a daye
of an attonement, and ſhalbe an holy feaſt vnto you,
ād ye ſhall humble youre ſoules and offer ſacrifice vnto
28 the Lorde. Moreouer ye ſhall do no worke the ſame
daye, for it is a daye of attonement to make an at-
29 tonemēt for you before the Lord your God. For
what ſoeuer ſoule it be that humbleth not him ſelfe
that daye, he ſhalbe deſtroyde from amonge his peo-
30 ple. And what ſoeuer ſoule do any maner worke that
daye, the ſame I will deſtroye from amonge his peo-

V. 20 cedēt in vſum eius. 22 vſque ad ſolum 27 dies expiat. erit celeberrimus . . . affligetiſque animas

L. 22 nicht gar auff demfeld eynſchneytten 27 ſeelen demutigen [3 times cf. vv. 29, 32.]

M. M. T. 27 *To humble the ſoule* is, to chaſtyce the bodye by abſtynence & affliction, as is ſayde Eſaie, lviii. a.

31 ple. Se that ye do no maner worke therfore. And it
ſhalbe a lawe for euer vnto youre generacions after
32 you in all youre dwellynges. A ſabbath of reſte it
ſhalbe vnto you, and ye ſhall humble youre ſoules.
The .ix. daye of the moneth at euen and ſo forth
from euē to euen agayne, ye ſhall kepe your Sabbath.
33, 34 And the Lorde ſpake vnto Moſes ſayenge: ſpeake
vnto the childern of Iſrael ād ſaye: the .xv. daye of
the ſame ſeuenth moneth ſhalbe the feaſt of tabernacles
35 vii. dayes ūto the Lorde. The firſt daye ſhalbe an
holy feaſt, ſo that ye ſhall do no laborious worke there-
36 in. Seuen dayes ye ſhall offer ſacrifice vnto the Lorde,
and the .viii. daye ſhalbe an holy feaſt vnto you
[Fo. XLIII.] ād ye ſhall offer ſacrifice vnto the Lorde.
It is the ende of the feaſt, and ye ſhall do no laborious
worke therein.

37 Theſe are the feaſtes of the Lorde whiche ye ſhall
proclayme holy feaſtes, for to offer ſacrifice vnto the
Lorde, burntofferynges, meatofferynges, and drink-
38 offrynges euery daye: beſyde the ſabbathes of the
Lorde, ād beſyde youre giftes, and all youre vowes,
and all your frewillofferynges whiche ye ſhall geue
vnto the Lorde.

39 Moreouer in the .xv. daye of the ſeuenth moneth
after that ye haue gathered in the frutes of the lande,
ye ſhall kepe holy daye vnto the Lorde .vii: dayes
longe. The firſt daye ſhall be a daye of reſt, and the
40 viii. daye ſhalbe a daye of reſt. And ye ſhall take you
the firſt daye, the frutes of goodly trees and the
braunches off palme trees and the bowes of thicke

V. 32 & affligetis animas veſtras 35 dies primus vocabitur celeberrimus atque ſanctiſſimus 36 & ſeptem diebus offeretis holocauſta domino. dies quoque octavus erit celeberr. atque ſanct. et offer. holocauſtum . . cœtus atque collectæ 37 libamenta iuxta ritum vniuſcuiuſque diei. 40 fructus arboris pulcherrimæ

L 36 es iſt der ſteur tag

M. M. N. 32 *Sabbothes, feſtes* & *newe mones* ſygnifie the Ioye & gladnes of the conſciēce the renewyng of mā and the reſt wherin we reſt from oure awne woorckes, not doynge oure wylles but godes, which woorcketh in vs thorou hys Goſpell & glad tidynges whyle we erneſtly beleue it. Ezech. xx, b.

L. M. N. 36 *Steuer:* Das iſt die collect odder ſamlung, da man zuſammen trug vnd gab den armen als ynn ein gemeynen beuttel.

trees, ād wylowes of the broke, and ſhall reioyſe be-
41 fore the Lorde .vii. dayes. And ye ſhall kepe it holy
daye vnto the Lorde .vii. dayes in the yere. And it
ſhalbe a lawe for euer vnto youre childern after you,
42 that ye kepe that feaſt in the ſeuenth moneth. And
ye ſhall dwell in bothes ſeuen dayes: euen all that are
43 Iſraelites borne, ſhall dwell in bothes, that youre children after you maye knowe howe that I made .P. the
childern of Iſrael dwell in bothes, when I broughte them
out of the lande of Egipte: for I am the Lorde youre
44 God. And Moſes told all the feaſtes of the Lorde
vnto the childern of Iſrael.

¶ The .XXIIII. Chapter.

1 AND the Lorde ſpake vnto Moſes
2 ſaynge: commaunde the childern of Iſrael that they bringe
vnto the, pure oyle olyue betē
for lightes to poure in to the lampes all-
3 waye, without the vayle of teſtimonye
within the tabernacle of witneſſe. And
Aaron ſhall dreſſe them both euen and
morninge before the Lorde alwayes. And
it ſhalbe a lawe for euer amōge youre childern after
4 you. And he ſhal dreſſe the lampes apon the pure
candelſticke before the Lorde perpetually.

M.C.S. *The oyle for the lampes and lyghtes of the bredde of remembraunce or ſhewbrede. He that curſeth muſt be ſtoned. He that kylleth ſhalbe kylled etc.*

5 And thou ſhalt take fine floure ād bake .xii. waſtels
thereof, two tenthdeales ſhall euery waſtell
6 be. And make two rowes of them, ſixe on
7 a rowe apon the pure table before the Lorde, and put
pure frankencens vppon the rowes. And it ſhalbe bred
8 of remembraunce, ād an offerynge to the Lorde. Euery

waſtell, *fine bread, cake*

M. 3 vayle of wytneſſe
V. 3 velum teſtimonii in tabernaculo fœderis . . cultu rituque perpetuo 7 panis in monimentum oblationis domini.
L. 2 bawm ole 3 furhang des zeugnis ynn der hutten des zeugnis. 7 Denckbrot zum opffer dem HERRN
M. M. N. 5 *Waſtels.* The ſhewe bredes or the halowed loues.

Sabbath he ſhall put them in rowes before the Lorde
euermore, geuen off the childern of Iſrael, that it be
9 an euerlaſtynge couenaunte. And they ſhal- [Fo.
XLIIII.] be Aarons and his ſonnes, and they ſhall
eate them in the holy place. For they are moſt holy
vnto him of the offerynges of the Lorde, dutye, *law,*
and ſhalbe a dutye for euer. *ſtatute*
10 And the ſonne of an Iſraelitiſh wife whoſe father
was an Egiptian, went out amonge the childern of
Iſrael. And this ſonne off the Iſraelitiſh wife and a
11 man of Iſrael, ſtrooue togither in the hoſte. And the
Iſraelitiſh womans ſonne blasphemed the name and
curſed, and they broughte him vnto Moſes.
And his mothers name was Selamyth, the doughter
12 off Dybri off the trybe of Dan: and they putt him in
warde, that Moſes ſhulde declare vnto them what the
Lorde ſayde thereto.
13, 14 And the Lorde ſpake vnto Moſes ſayenge, bringe
him that curſed without the hoſte, and let all that herde
him, put their handes apō his heed, and let all the mul-
15 titude ſtone him. And ſpeake vnto the childern of
Iſrael ſayenge: Whoſoeuer curſeth his God, ſhall bere
16 his ſynne: And he that blaſphemeth the name of the
Lorde, ſhall dye for it: all the multitude ſhall ſtone him
to deeth. And the ſtraunger as well as the Iſraelite
yf he curſe the name, ſhall dye for it.
17, 18 .P. He that kylleth any man, ſhall dye for it: but
he that kylleth a beeſt ſhall paye for it, beeſt for beeſt.
19 Yf a man mayme his neyghboure as he hath done, ſo
20 ſhall it be done to him agayne: broke for broke, *breach,*
broke, eye for eye and toth for toth: euen *fracture*

M. 14 hym that blaſphemed

V. 11 nomen domini 12 donec noſſent quid iuberet dominus. 16 nomen domini 17 percuſſ. & occiderit 18 animam pro anima

L. 11 nennet den namen 12 bis yhn aus gelegt wurd durch den mund des HERRN. 15 ſoll ſeyne ſund tragen 16 den namen nennet 18 Seele vmb Seele.

M. M. N. 11 Hebrue *ſchem* that is, name that is bleſſed aboue all names. 15 *Curſeth:* he curſeth God & blaſphemeth the name of God, that deſpyſeth and deſyeth godes ordynaunces ſtatutes & commaundemētes, or that magnifyeth mennes tradicions and lawes aboue Godes, or ſetteth as moch therby, as by the preceptes of the moſt mercyfle God.

as he hath maymed a man, ſo ſhall he be maymed
21 agayne. So nowe he that kylleth a beeſt, ſhall paye
for it: but he that kylleth a man, ſhall dye for it.
22 Ye ſhall haue one maner of lawe amonge you: euē for
the ſtraunger as wel as for one of youre ſelues, for I
am the Lorde youre God.

23 And Moſes tolde the childern of Iſrael, that they
ſhulde bringe him that had curſed, out of the hoſte,
and ſtone him with ſtones. And the childern of Iſrael
dyd as the Lorde cōmaunded Moſes.

The .XXV. Chapter.

M.C.S. The Saboth of the vii. yeres and of the yere of iubelie, otherwyſe called thefyftyeyere.

1 AND the Lorde ſpake vnto Moſes
in mount Sinai ſayenge, ſpeake
2 vnto the childern of Iſrael and
ſaye vnto thē. When ye be
come in to the lande whiche I geue you,
3 let the londe reſt a Sabbath vnto the Lorde. Sixe
yeres thou ſhalt ſowe thi felde, and sixe yere thou ſhalt
4 cut thi vynes and gather in thy frutes. But the ſeuenth
yere ſhall be a Sabbath of [Fo. XLV.] reſt vnto the
londe. The Lordes Sabbath it ſhalbe, ād thou ſhalt
nether ſowe thi felde, nor cut thy vynes.

5 The corne that groweth by it ſelfe thou ſhalt not
repe, nether gather the grapes that growe without thy
dreſſynge: but it ſhalbe a Sabbath of reſt vnto the
6 londe. Neuertheleſſe the Sabbath of the londe ſhalbe
meate for you: euen for the and thy ſervaunte and for
thy mayde and for thy hyred ſervaunte and for the
7 ſtraunger that dwelleth with the: and for thi catell
and for the beeſtes that are in thy londe, ſhall all the
encreaſe thereof be meate.

V. 21 Qui perc. iumentum, reddet aliud. Qui perc. hominem, punietur. 23 lapidibus oppreſſerunt. xxv, 2 ſabbathizet ſabbathum domino. 4 ſabbathum erit terræ requietionis domini . . vineam non putabis.

L. 3 weynberg beſchneyttiſt 4 weynb. beſchn. ſolt. 7 alles getreyde ſoll ſpeyſe ſeyn.

8 Then numbre ſeuen wekes of yeres, that is, ſeuen
tymes ſeuen yere: and the ſpace of the ſeuen wekes of
9 yeres will be vnto the .xlix. yere. And then thou ſhalt
make an horne blowe: euen in the tenth
daye of the ſeuenth moneth, which is the
daye of attonement. And then ſhall ye
make the horne blowe, euen thorowe out
10 all youre lande. And ye ſhal halowe the
fiftith yere, and proclayme libertie thorowe
out the lande vnto all the inhabiters thereof, It ſhalbe a yere of hornes blowynge
vnto you and ye ſhall returne: euery man
vnto his poſſeſſion and euery man vnto
11 his kynred agayne. A yere of hornes blowynge ſhall
that fiftieth yere be vnto you. Ye ſhall not ſowe
nether re- .P. pe the corne that groweth by it ſelfe, nor
gather the grapes that growe without thi laboure
12 For it is a yere of hornes blowinge and ſhalbe holy vnto
you: how be it, yet ye ſhall eate of the encreaſe of the
13 felde. And in this yere of hornes blowinge ye ſhall
returne, euery man vnto his poſſeſſion agayne.

This horne in ebrue is called iobel, ād of this toke the pope an occaſiō to make eueri .l. yere a iubelye, ſo that he contrafaiteth god in eueri point ād wyl not be one ace behinde him.

14 When thou ſelleſt oughte vnto thy neyghboure or
byeſt off thy neyghboures hande, ye ſhall not oppreſſe
15 one another: but accordynge to the numbre of yeres
after the trompett yere, thou ſhalt bye of thy neyghboure, and accordynge vnto the numbre off frute-

M. 10 a yere of iubilee 11 a yere of iubilee 12 a yere of iubelye 13 a yere of iubelye 15 iubelye yere

V. 9 clanges buccina 10 ipſe eſt enim iubileus. 12 ob ſanctificationem iubilei, ſed ſtatim oblata comedetis .14 cōtriſtes fratrem tuum

L. 8 die zeyt der ſieben iar Sabbath 9 hall der poſaunen 10 denn es iſt das Halliar [and so throughout the chapter] 14 bruder ſchinden

M. M. N. 8 *Wekes of yeres:* A weke is ſometyme taken for the nombre of .vii. dayes as before. xxiii, c. ſometyme for the nombre of ſeuen yeres, as here & in Daniel .ix, f. g. 10 *Iubelye* of this Hebrewe woorde iobell, which in Englyſhe ſygnifieth a trumpet. A yere of ſynguler myrth and ioye and of moche reſt, wher in their corne and all their frutes cam forth wythout ſowynge, tyllynge or any other laboures. 15 By this *iubelye* is ſygnified the reſtorynge of all thinge vnto his perfeccion, which ſhal be after the generall iudgement in that floryſſhynge worlde, when the choſen ſhal be admytted in to lybertye frō all wretchednes, pouertye, anguyſhe & oppreſſion, when all ſhalbe fully reſtored againe in Chriſt, that thorow the ſynne of the fyrſt man was taken awaye.

16 yeres, he ſhall ſell vnto the. Accordinge vnto the
multitude of yeres, thou ſhalt encreaſe the price thereof and accordinge to the fewneſſe of yeres, thou ſhalt
myniſh the price: for the numbre of frute he ſhall ſell
17 vnto the. And ſee that no mā oppreſſe his neyghboure, but feare thi God.

18 For I am the Lorde youre God. Wherfore do after
myne ordinaunces and kepe my lawes ād doo them,
19 that ye maye dwell in the lande in ſaftie. And the
lande ſhall geue her frute, and ye ſhall eate youre fille
and dwell therein in ſaftie.

20 Yf ye ſhall ſaye, what ſhall we eate the ſeue- [Fo.
XLVI.] nth yere in as moche as we ſhall not ſowe nor
21 gether in oure encreaſe. I wyll ſende my bleſſynge
apon you in the ſixte yere, and it ſhall brynge forth
22 frute for thre yeres: and ye ſhall ſowe the eyghte yere
and eate of olde frute vntill the .ix. yere, and euen
vntyll hir frutes come, ye ſhall eate of olde ſtoare.
23 Wherfore the londe ſhall not be ſolde for euer, becauſe
that the lande is myne, and ye but ſtraungers and ſo-
24 iourners with me: and ye ſhall thorowe oute all the
lande of youre poſſeſſion, let the londe go home fre
agayne.

25 When thy brother is waxed poore and hath ſolde
awaye of his poſſeſſion: yf any off his kyn come to
redeme it, he ſhall by out that whiche his brother ſolde.
26 And though he haue no man to redeme it for him, yet
yf hys hande can get ſufficyent to bye it oute agayne,
27 then let him counte how longe it hath bene ſolde, and
delyuer the reſt vnto him to whome he ſolde it, ād ſo
28 he ſhall returne vnto his poſſeſſion agayne. But and
yf his hande cā not get ſufficiēt to reſtore it to him
agayne, then that whiche is ſolde ſhall remayne in the
hande of him that hath boughte it, vntyll the horne-
yere: and in the horne yere it ſhall come out, and he
ſhall .ℙ. returne vnto his poſſeſſion agayne.

M. 28 the yere of iubelye [*bis*], so vv. 30, 31, 33, 40, 50, 52, 54.
V. 16 tempus enim frugum 17 Nolite affligere contribules veſtros 19 nullius impetum formidantes. 23 & vos aduenæ & coloni mei 27 ſicque recipiet poſſeſſionem ſuam. 28 non inuenerit manus eius
L. 18 ym land ſicher wonen mugt

29 Yf a man ſell a dwellynge houſe in a walled cytie,
he maye bye it out agayne any tyme withī a hole yere
after it is ſolde: and that ſhalbe the ſpace in which he
30 maye redeme it agayne. But and yf it be not bought
out agayne within the ſpace of a full yere, then the
houſſe in the walled cytie ſhalbe ſtabliſhed for euer
vnto him that boughte it and to his ſucceſſoures after
31 hī and ſhall not goo out in the trompet yere. But the
houſſes in villagies which haue no walles rounde aboute
them, ſhalbe counted like vnto the feldes of the cuntre,
and maye be boughte out agayne at any ſeaſon, and
ſhall goo out fre in the trompett yere.

32 Notwithſtondynge the cityes of the leuytes and the
houſſes in the cities of their poſſeſſiōs the leuytes maye
33 redeme at all ceaſons. And yf a man purchace ought
of the leuytes: whether it be houſe or citie that they
poſſeſſe, the bargayne ſhall goo out in the trōpet
yere. for the houſſes of the cyties of the leuites, are
34 their poſſeſſions amonge the childern of Iſrael. But
the feldes that lye rounde aboute their cyties, ſhall
not be bought: for they are their poſſeſſions for euer.

35 Yf thi brother be waxed poore ād fallē in decaye
with the, receaue him as a ſtraunger or [Fo. XLVII.]
36 a ſoiourner, and let him lyue by the. And thou ſhalt
take none vſurye of him, nor yet vantage. But ſhalt
feare thi God, that thi brother maye lyue with the.
37 Thou ſhalt not lende him thi money apon vſurye, nor
38 lende him of thy fode to haue avantage by it for I am
the Lorde youre God which broughte you out of the
lande of Egipte, to geue you the lande of Canaan and
to be youre God.

39 Yf thi brother that dwelleth by the waxe poore and
ſell him ſelfe vnto the, thou ſhalt not let him laboure
40 as a bondſeruaunte doeth: but as an hyred ſeruaunte
and as a ſoiourner he ſhalbe with the, and ſhall ſerue
41 the vnto the trompetyere, and then ſhall he departe

V. 29 intra vrbis muros, hab. licentiam redimendi 31 villa . . quæ muros non habet, agrorum iure vendetur. 35 & infirmus manu 37 frugum ſuperabundantiam non exiges. 40 mercennarius & colonus
L. 35 frembdlingen oder hausgnoſs 37 deyn ſpeyſe auff vberſatz austhun.

frō the: both he and his childern with him, and ſhall
returne vnto his awne kynred agayne and vnto the
42 poſſeſſions of his fathers. for they are my ſeruauntes
which I brought out of the lande of Egipte, and ſhall
43 not be ſolde as bondmen. Se therfore that thou reigne
not ouer him cruelly, but feare thi God.

44 Yf thou wilt haue bondſeruauntes and maydens,
thou ſhalt bye them of the heythen that are rounde
45 aboute you, and of the childern of the ſtraungers that
are ſoiorners amonge you, ād of their generaciōs that
46 are with you, which they begate in youre lāde. And
ye ſhall poſſeſſe .P. them and geue them vnto youre
childern after you, to poſſeſſe them for euer: and they
ſhalbe youre bond men: But ouer youre brethern the
childern of Iſrael, ye ſhall not reigne one ouer another
cruelly.

47 When a ſtraunger and a ſoiourner waxeth rych by
the ād thi brother that dwelleth by him waxeth poore
and ſell him ſelfe vnto the ſtraunger that dwelleth by
48 the or to any of the ſtraungers kyn: after that he is
ſolde he maye be redemed agayne. one of his brethren
49 maye bye him out: whether it be his vncle or his
vncles ſonne, or any that is nye of kynne vnto him of
his kynred: ether yf his hande can get ſo moch he
50 maye be looſed. And he ſhall reken with him that
boughte him, from the yere that he was ſolde in vnto
the trompet yere, and the pryce of his byenge ſhalbe
acordynge vnto the numbre of yeres, and he ſhalbe
51 with him as a hyred ſeruaunte. Yf there be yet many
yeres behynde, acordynge vnto them he ſhall geue
agayne for his delyueraunce, of the money that he was
52 ſolde for. Yf there remayne but few yeres vnto the
trompet yere, he ſhall ſo counte with him, and acordynge vnto his yeres geue him agayne for his redemp-
53 cion, and ſhalbe with him yere by yere as an hyred
ſeruaunte, [Fo. XLVIII.] and the other ſhall not reygne

F. 43 affligas eum per potentiā 46 fratres . . ne opprimatis per potentiam 47 inualuerit apud vos manus 53 non affliget eum violēter in cōſpectu tuo

L. 43 mit der ſtrenge vber ſie hirſchen 50 vnd ſol ſeyn tagelon der gantzen zeyt mit eyn rechen [*bis*].

54 cruelly ouer him in thi ſyghte. Yf he be not bought
fre in the meane tyme, then he ſhall goo out in the
55 trompet yere and his childern with him. for the childern of Iſrael are my ſeruauntes which I broughte out
of the lande of Egipte. I am the Lorde youre God.
XXVI, 1 Ye ſhall make you no ydolles, nor grauen
ymage, nether rere you vpp any piler, nether ye ſhall
ſett vp any ymage of ſtone in youre lande to bowe
youre ſelues there to: for I am the Lorde youre God.
2 kepe my ſabbathes and feare my ſanctuary. for I am
the Lorde.

ℭ The .XXVI. Chapter.

3 YF ye ſhall walke in myne ordynaunces and kepe my com-
maundmentes and do them,
4 then I will ſende you rayne
in the ryght ceaſon ād youre londe ſhall
yelde her encreaſe and the trees of the
5 felde ſhall geue their frute. And the
threſhynge ſhall reach vnto wyne harueſt, and the wyneharueſt ſhall reach
vnto ſowyng tyme, and ye ſhall eate
youre bred in plenteouſnes and ſhall
6 dwell in youre lande peaſably. And I
wil ſende peace in youre londe, that
ye ſhall .P. ſlepe, and no man ſhal
make you afrayde. And I will ryd euell

M.C.S.**Images are forbydden. Bleſſed are they that kepe thoſe thynges that God byddeth and moſt curſed are they that kepe them not.* [**In Matthew's Bible this chapter begins with xxvi, 1 as in the Authorized Verſion, while Tyndale connects xxvi, 1, 2 with ch. xxv.*]

V. 2 pauete ad ſanctuarium meum. 4 terra gignet germē ſuum, & pomis arbores replebuntur. 5 abſque pauore

L. 4 bewme auff dem felde 5 ſicher ynn ewrm land

M. M. N. 2 *Feare my ſanctuary:* To feare the ſanctuarie, is dylygently to performe the true worſhyppyng & ſeruyce of God, to leue of nothynge, to obſerue and kepe the purenes both of bodye & mynde, verely & not ypocritelike to beleue that he knoweth, beholdeth, doeth & ruleth all thynges: to bewarre of offendynge hym and with all feare and dylygence to walke in the pathes of his lawes.

beeſtes out of youre londe, and there ſhall no ſwerde
goo thorowe out youre lande.
7 And ye ſhall chace youre enemyes, and they ſhall
8 fall before you vppon the ſwerde. And fiue of you
ſhall chace an hundred, and an hundred of you ſhall
put .x. thouſande to flighte, and youre enemyes
9 ſhall fall before you apon the ſwerde. And I wil
turne vnto you and encreaſe you and multiplye
10 you, and ſett vpp my teſtament with you. And
ye ſhall eate olde ſtore, ād caſt out the olde for
11 plentuouſnes of the newe. I will make my dwellynge
place amonge you, and my ſoule ſhall not loothe
you.
12 And I will walke amonge you and wilbe youre
13 God, and ye ſhalbe my people. For I am the Lorde
youre God whiche broughte you out off the lande of
the Egiptians, that ye ſhulde not be their bondemen,
and I brake the bowes of youre yockes, and made you
go vp righte.
14 But and yf ye will not harken vnto me, nor will
15 do all theſe my commaundementes, or yf *Note well.*
ye ſhall deſpyſe myne ordinaunces ether yf youre ſoules
refuſe my lawes, ſo that ye wil not do all my commaundmentes: but ſhall breake myne appoyntment:
16 then I will do this agayne vn- [Fo. XLIX.] to you:
I will viſet you with vexations, ſwellynge and feuers,
that ſhall make youre eyes daſell and with ſorowes
of herte. And ye ſhall ſowe youre ſeed in vayne, for
17 youre enemyes ſhall eate it. And I will ſet my face
agenſte you and ye ſhal fall before youre enemyes, and
they that hate you ſhal raigne ouer you, ād ye ſhal
flee whē no man foloweth you.
18 And yf ye will not yet for all this herken vnto me,

V. 9 firmabo pactum meum 13 cōfregi catenas ceruicū veſtrarū 14 omnia mandata mea 15 ſed ſpreu. leges meas, & iudicia mea cont. vt non fac. ea quæ a me conſtituta ſunt, & ad irritum perduc. pactum meum 16 velociter in egeſtate & ardore, qui conficiat ocul. veſt. & conſumat animas veſtras.

L. 8 Ewr funffe . . . iagen . . . iagen 9 bund . . . auffrichten 11 ſeele . . nicht verwerffen 15 meynen bund laſſen anſtehen 16 ſchwulſt vnd fiber 17 fliehen . . niemant iaget.

than will I punifh you feuen tymes more
19 for youre fynnes, and will breake the
pride off youre ftrength. For I will make
the heauē ouer you as harde as yerne, and
20 youre londe as hard as braffe. And fo
youre laboure fhalbe fpent in vayne. For
youre londe fhall not geue hir encreafe, nether the
trees of the londe fhall geue their frutes.

God beginneth ād augmenteth his plages moare ād moare as the people hardē their hertes agēfte him.

21 And yf ye walke contrary vnto me and will not
herken vnto me, I will bringe feuen tymes moo plages
22 apon you acordinge to youre fynnes. I will fende in
wylde beeftes apon you, which fhall robbe you of youre
childern and deftroye youre catell, and make you fo
fewe in numbre that youre hye wayes fhall growe
vnto a wilderneffe.

23 And yf ye will not be lerned yet for all this
24 but fhall walke contrarye vnto me, then will I
alfo walke contrarye vnto you and will punifh .P.
25 you yet feuen tymes for youre fynnes. I will fende
a fwerde apon you, that fhall avenge my teftament
with you. And when ye are fled vnto youre cities,
I will fende the peftelence amonge you, ye fhall
be delyuered in to the handes of youre enemyes.
26 And when I haue broken the ftaffe of youre bred:
that .x. wyues fhall bake youre bred in one ouen
and men fhall delyuer you youre bred agayne by
weyghte, thā fhal ye eate and fhall not be fatiffied.

27 And yf ye will not yet for all this harken vnto me,
28 but fhall walke contrarye vnto me, then I will walke
contrary vnto you alfo wrathfully and will alfo chaf-
29 tice you feuen tymes for youre fynnes: fo that ye fhall

V. 18 addam correptiones veftr. 19 fuperbiam duritiæ 23 Quod fi nec fic 25 gladium vltorem fœderis mei. 28 & ego incedam aduerfus vos in furore contrario

L. 19 hoffart ewr ftercke 20 ewr muhe vnd erbeyt 25 ein rachfchwerd

M. M. X. 18 God begineth & augmenteth his plages moare and moare as the people harden their hertes agenfte him. 21 *Seuen tymes:* by that nombre vnderftande all tymes, as in this chapter, c. 26 *To breake the ftaffe of their breade,* is, to breake the ftrēgth therof and to mynifhe hyt fo that they fhuld not haue ynowghe to lyue by.

eate the fleſh of youre ſonnes and the fleſh of youre
30 doughters. And I will deſtroye youre alters bylt
apon hye hylles, and ouerthrowe youre images, and
caſt youre carkaſſes apon the bodies of youre ydolles,
31 and my ſoule ſhall abhorre you. And I will make
youre cities deſolate, and bringe youre ſanctuaries
vnto nought, and will not ſmell the ſauoures of youre
ſwete odoures.

32 And I will bringe the londe vnto a wilderneſſe: ſo
that youre enemyes which dwell there in ſhall wondre
33 at it. And I will ſtrawe you amonge the heethen, and
will drawe out a ſwerde after you, and youre lande
34 ſhalbe waſt, and [Fo. L.] youre cities deſolate. Then
the lande ſhall reioyſe in hir Sabbathes, as longe as
it lyeth voyde and ye in youre enemies londe: euen
then ſhall the londe kepe holye daye and reioyſe in
35 hir Sabbathes. And as longe as it lyeth voyde it
ſhall reſt, for that it coude not reſte in youre Sabbathes,
when ye dwelt therein.

36 And vppon them that are left alyue of you, I
will ſende a feyntneſſe in to their hertes in the londe
of their enemies: ſo that the ſounde of a leef that
falleth, ſhall chace them and they ſhall flee as though
thei fled a ſwerde, and ſhall fall no man folowinge
37 them. And they ſhall fall one uppon another, as it
were before a ſwerde euen no man folowinge them,
and ye ſhall haue no power to ſtonde before youre
38 enemyes: And ye ſhall periſh amonge the hethen, ād
the londe of youre enemyes ſhall eate you vpp.

39 And thei that are left of you, ſhall pyne awaye in
their vnrightuouſnes, euen in their enemies londe, and
alſo in the myſdeades of their fathers ſhall they con-
40 ſume. And they ſhall confeſſe their miſdedes and the
miſdeades of their fathers in their treſpaſes which thei

V. 30 Cadetis inter ruinas idol. veſtrorum, & abhominabitur vos anima mea 35 ſabbathizabit, & req. in ſabbathis . . . ſolitudinis ſuæ 36 terrebit eos ſonitus folii volantis 37 quaſi bella fugiētes 39 tabeſcent in iniquit., . . . affligentur: 40 donec confiteantur

L. 30 ewre hohen altar . . ewre leychnam . . gotzen leychnam 31 ewre kirchen eynreyſſen 36 eyn feyg hertz machen . . . eyn rauſſchend blat iagen 39 verweſen ynn der feynde land

haue trespased againſt me, and for that alſo that they
41 haue walked contrary vnto me. Therfore I alſo will
walke contrary vnto them, and will brynge them in
to the londe of their enemyes.

.P. And then at the leeſt waye their vncircumcyſed
hertes ſhall be tamed, ād then they ſhall make an
attonement for their miſdedes.

42 And I wil remembre my bonde with
Iacob and my teſtamēt with Iſaac, and
my teſtament with Abraham, and will
thinke on the londe.

Mercy is neuer denyed vnto him that repenteth:

43 For the londe ſhall be lefte of them and ſhall haue
pleaſure in hir Sabbathes, while ſhe lyeth waſt without them, and they ſhall make an attonement for
their miſdeades, becauſe they deſpyſed my lawes and
44 their ſoules refuſed myne ordinaunces. And yet for
all that when thei be in the londe of their enemyes,
I will not ſo caſt them awaye nor my ſoule ſhall not
ſo abhorre them, that I will vtterlye deſtroye thē ād
breake myne appoyntment with them: for I am the
45 Lorde their God. I will therfore remēbre vnto thē
the firſt couenaunt made when I broughte them out
of the lond of Egipte in the ſighte of the hethen to
be their God: for I am the Lorde.

46 Theſe are the ordinaunces, iudgemētes, ād lawes
which the Lorde made betwene him ād the childern
of Iſrael in mount Sinai by the hāde of Moſes.

☙ The .XXVII. Chapter.

M. 44 lande of their enemye

V. 41 donec erubeſcat incircūciſa 43 Ipſi vero rogabunt pro peccatis ſuis 44 non penitus abieci eos 45 record. fœd. mei priſt.

L. 41 vnbeſchnyttens hertz 46 ſatzung vnd rechte vnd geſetze

M. M. N. 42 Mercy is never denyed vnto him that repenteth

XXVII. Chapter. [Fo. LI.]

M.C.S Of diuerse vowes and the redemynge of the same. Of tythes &c.

1 AND the Lorde spake vnto Moses
2 sayinge: speake vnto the childern of Israel and saye vnto
them: Yf any man will geue
a' synguler vowe vnto the Lorde acord-
3 ynge to the value of his soule, then shall the male from
xx. yere vnto .Lx. be set at fyftie sycles of syluer, after
4 the sycle of the sanctuary, and the female at .xxx
5 sycles. And from .v. yeres to .xx. the male shalbe set
6 at .xx. sycles, and the female at .x. sycles. And from
a moneth vnto .v. yere, the male shalbe set at .v. sycles
7 of syluer, and the female at thre. And the man that
is .Lx. and aboue, shalbe valowed at .xv. sicles, ād the
8 woman at .x. Yf he be to pore so to be set, thē let him
come before the preast: and let the preast value him,
acordynge as the hande of him that vowed is able
to gete.

9 Yf it be of the beestes of which men bringe an offeringe vnto the Lorde: all that any man geueth of soch
vnto the Lorde, shalbe holy.

10 He maye not alter it nor chaunge it: a good for a
bad or a bad for a goode. Yf he chaunge beest for
beest, then both the same beest and it also where with
11 it was chaunged shall be holy. Yf it be any maner
of vncleane beest of which men maye not offer vnto
the Lorde, let him brynge the beest before the preast
12 and let the preast value it. And whether it be good
or bad .P. as the preast setteth it, so shall it be. And
yf he will bye it agayne, let him geue the fyfte part
moare to that it was set at.

V. 2 & spospōderit deo animam suam, 3 sub æstimatione dabit pretium. 8 & viderit eū posse reddere, tantū dabit. 12 malum sit, statuet pretium.

L. 2 besonder glubde 3 schetzen auff [throughout] 8 priester sol yhn schetzen, Er sol yhn aber schetzen nach dem seyne hand, des der gelobd hat, erwerben kan.

14 Yf any man dedicate his houſſe, it ſhalbe holy vnto
the Lorde. And the preaſt ſhall ſet it. whether it be
good or bad, and as the preaſt hath ſet it, ſo it ſhalbe.
15 Yf he that ſanctifyed it will redeme his houſſe, let him
geue the fyfte parte of the money that it was iudged at
thereto, and it ſhalbe his.
16 Yf a man halowe a pece of his enhereted londe vnto
the Lorde, it ſhalbe ſet acordynge to that it beareth.
Yf it bere an homer of barlye, it ſhall be ſet at fyftie
17 ſicles of ſyluer. yf he halowe his felde immediatly
from the trompet yere, it ſhalbe worth acordynge as it
18 is eſtemed. But and if he halowe his felde after the
trõpetyere, the preaſt ſhall rekẽ the price with him
acordynge to the yeres that remayne vnto the trõpet
yere, ãd there after it ſhalbe lower ſett.
19 Yf he that ſanctifyed the felde will redeme it agayne,
let him put the fyfte parte of the pryce that it was ſet
20 at, there vnto and it ſhalbe his yf he will not it ſhalbe
21 redemed nomoare. But when the felde goeth out in
the trompet yere, it ſhalbe holy vnto the Lorde: euen as
a thinge dedycated, ãd it ſhall be the preaſtes poſſeſſion.
22 Yf a man ſanctifie vnto the Lorde a felde. [Fo. LII.]
which he hath boughte and is not of his enheritaunce,
23 then the preaſt ſhall reken with him what it is worth
vnto the trompet yere, and he ſhall geue the price that
it is ſet at the ſame daye, and it ſhalbe holy vnto the
24 Lorde. But in the trompet yere, the felde ſhall returne vnto him of whome he boughte it, whoſe enheritaunce of londe it was.
25 And all ſettinge ſhalbe acordinge to the holy ſycle.
One ſycle maketh .xx. Geras.

M. 17 yere of iubely 21 yere of iubelye 23 yere of iubelye 24 yere of iubelye

V. 14 conſyderabit eam ſacerdos . . . & iuxta pret. quod ab eo fuerit conſtitutum, venundabitur 18 poſt aliquantulum temporis 21 & poſſeſſio cõſecrata ad ius pertinet ſacerdotum. 24 in ſortem poſſeſſionis ſuæ. 25 viginti obolos

L. 21 wie eyn verbannet acker, vnd ſol des prieſters erbgut ſeyn.

M. M. N. 16 To *halow* & to *ſanctifie* are bothe one, what ſanctyfieng is loke Gen. iii, a. 25 *Holy ſycle* or *ſycle of the ſanctuarye:* they be both one.

26 But the firſtborne of the beeſtes that pertayne vnto
the Lorde, maye no mā ſanctifie: whether it be oxe or
27 ſhepe, for they are the Lordes allredy. Yf it be an
vncleane beeſt, then let him redeme it as it is ſett at,
and geue the fifte parte moare thereto. Yf it be not
redemed, thē let it be ſolde as it is rated.
28 Notwithſtondinge no dedicated thinge that a man
dedicateth vnto the Lorde, of all his goode, whether
it be man or beeſt or lande off his enheritaunce, ſhalbe
ſolde or redemed: for all dedicate thīges are moſt holy
29 vnto the Lorde. No dedicate thinge therfore that is
dedicate of mā, may be redemed, but muſt nedes dye
30 All theſe tithes of the londe, whether it be of the
corne of the felde or frute of the trees, ſhalbe holy vnto
31 the Lorde. Yf any man will redeme oughte of his
tithes, let him adde the fifte .V. parte moare thereto.
32 And the tithes of oxen and ſhepe and of all that
goeth vnder the herdemans kepinge, ſhalbe holye tithes
33 vnto the Lorde. Men ſhal not loke yf it be good or
bad nor ſhall chaunge it. Yf any man chaunge it then
both it and that it was chaunged with all, ſhalbe holy
and maye not be redemed.
34 Theſe are the commaundmentes whiche the Lorde
gaue Moſes in charge to geue vnto the childern of
Iſrael in mount Sinai.

¶ The ende of the thyrde boke
of Moſes.

V. 29 Et omnis conſecratio . . morte morietur. 32 ſub paſtoris virga tranſeunt

L. 28 keyn verbantes verkeuffen . . . verbannet . . . verbante 29 verbanten . . todts ſterben. 32 was vnter der rutten gehet

¶ A prolo
ge in to the fourth boke of
Mofes, called Nu=
meri.

¶ A Prologe in to the fourth boke of Moses, called Numeri.

IN the ſeconde ād thirde boke they receaved yͤ lawe. And in this .iiii. they begynne to worke and to practyſe. Of which practiſynge ye ſe many good enſamples of vnbeleffe & what frewill doth, when ſhe taketh in hand to kepe the lawe of her awne power with out help of fayth in the promyſes of god: how ſhe leueth her maſters carkeſſes by the way in the wilderneſſe and bringeth them not in to the londe of reſt. Why coude they not entre in? Becauſe of their vnbeleffe Hebre. iii. For had they beleved, ſo had they bene vnder grace, and their old ſynnes had bene forgeuen thē, ād power ſhulde haue bene geuē them to haue fulfilled the lawe thenceforth & they ſhuld haue bene kepte from all temptaciōs that had bene to ſtronge for them. For it is wrytten Iohan .i. He gaue them power to be the ſonnes of god, thorow belevynge in his name. Nowe to be the ſonne of god is to loue god and his commaundmentes and to walke in his waye after the enſample of his ſonne Chriſt. But theſe people toke vppon them to worke without faith as thou ſeyſte in the .xiiii. of this boke, where they wold fight and alſo did, without the worde of promyſſe: euē when they were warned that they ſhuld not. And in yͤ .xvi. agayne they wolde pleaſe god .P. with their holye faithleſſe workes (for where gods worde is not there can be no faith) but yͤ fyre of god conſumed their holy workes, as it did Nadab and Abihu Leui. x. And frō theſe vnbeleuers turne thyne eyes vnto the phareſyes which before the comynge of Chriſt in his fleſh, had layde the fundacion of frewill after the ſame enſample. Wher on thei bilt holy workes after their awne imaginacion with out faith of the worde, ſo fervently that for the greate zele of them they ſlew the kinge of all holy workes and the lorde of frewill which only thorow his grace maketh the will fre and lowſeth her from bondage of ſynne, and geueth her loue and luſt vnto the lawes of god, and power to fulfyll them. And ſo thorowe their holye workes done by the power of frewill, they excluded them ſelues out of the holy reſt of forgeueneſſe of ſynnes by faith in the bloude of Chriſt.

And then loke on oure ypocrites which in like maner folowinge the doctryne of Ariſtotle and other hethen paganes, haue agenſte all the ſcripture ſett vpp frewill agayne, vnto whoſe power they aſcribe the kepynge of ỹ cōmaundmētes of god. For they haue ſet vp wilfull povertye of a nother maner then any is cōmaunded of god. And the chaſtite of matrimony vtterlye defyed, they haue ſet vp a nother wilfull chaſtite not required of god, whiche they ſwere, vowe & profeſſe to geue god, .P. whether he will geue it them or no, and compell all their diſciples there vnto, ſayenge that it is in the power of euery mans frewill to obſerue it, contrarye to Christ and his apoſtle Paule.

And the obedience of god and man excluded they haue vowed a nother wilfull obedience condemned of all the ſcripture whiche they will yet geue God whether he will or wyll not.

And what is become of their wilfull pouertye? hath it not robbed the whole worlde & brought all vnder them? Can there be ether kynge or emperoure or of what ſoeuer degre it be, excepte he will hold of them ād be ſworne vnto them to be their ſervaunte, to go and come at their luſte and to defende their quarels be they falſe or true? Their wilfull pouertye hath all readye eaten vpp the whole worlde & is yet ſtill gredyar then euer it was in ſo moche that ten worldes mo were not ynough to ſatiſfye the hongre thereof.

Moreouer beſydes dayly corruptinge of other mens wyues and open whoredome, vnto what abominacions to fylthye to be ſpokē off hath their voluntarye chaſtite broughte them?

And as for their wilfull obediēce what is it but ẏ diſobediēce & the diffiaūce both of all ẏ lawes of god & mā: in ſo moch ẏ yf any prīce begīne to execute any law of mā vppō thē, .P. they curſe him vnto the botom of hell & proclayme him no right kinge & that his lordes ought no lenger to obaye him, and interdite his comen people as they were hethē turkes or ſaracenes. And yf any man preache them gods lawe, him they make an heretike and burne him to aſſhes. And in ſteade of gods lawe and mans, they haue ſette vpp one off their awne imaginacion which they obſerue with diſpenſacions.

And yet in theſe workes they haue ſo greate confidence that they not onlye truſte to be ſaued therby, and to be hyer in heauen then they that be ſaued thorow chriſt: but alſo promeſſe to all other forgeueneſſe of their ſynnes thorow the merites of the ſame. Wherin they reſt and teach other to reſt alſo, excludynge the whole worlde from the reſte of forgeueneſſe of ſynnes thorowe faith in Chriſtes bloude.

And now ſeynge that faith only letteth a mā in ūto reſt & vnbeleffe excludeth hī, what is the cauſe of this vnbeleffe? verely no ſynne ẏ the world ſeyth, but a pope holyneſſe & a rightuouſnes of theire awne imaginacion as Paule ſayeth Roma. x. They be ignoraūte of ẏ rightuouſnes wherwith god iustifieth & haue ſet vp a rightuouſnes of their awne makīge thorow which they be disobediēt vnto ẏ rightuouſnes of god. And Chriſt rebuketh not the phariſeys for groſſe ſynnes whiche .P. the worlde ſawe, but for thoſe holye deades whiche ſo blered the eyes of the worlde that they were takē as goddes: euē for long prayers, for faſtynge, for tythīge ſo diligētly that they lefte not ſo moch as their herbes vntithed, for their clenneſſe in waſſhynge before meate and for waſhynge of cuppes, diſhes, and all maner veſſels, for buyldinge the prophetes ſepulchres, and for kepinge the holy daye, and for turnynge the hethen vnto the fayth, and for gevynge of almes. For vnto ſoch holy deades they aſcribed rightuouſnes and therfore when the rightuouſneſſe of god was preached vnto them they coude not but perſecute it, the devell was ſo ſtronge in thē. Which thinge Chriſt well deſcribeth Luce. xi. ſayenge that after the devell is caſt out he cometh agayne and fyndeth his houſe ſwepte and made gaye and then taketh ſeuen worſe then him ſelfe and dwelleth therein, and ſo is the ende of that man worſe then the beginnynge. That is, when they be a litle clenſed from groſſe ſynnes whiche the worlde ſeyth and then made gaye in their awne ſyght with the rightuouſnes of tradicions, then cometh ſeuen, that is to ſaye the hole power of ẏ devell, for ſeuē with ẏ hebrues ſignifieth a multitude without nūbre & the extremyte of a thinge & is a ſpeach borowed (I ſuppoſe) out of leuiticus where is ſo oft mencion made of ſeuē. Where I wolde ſaye: I will puniſh the .¶. that all the world ſhall take an enſample of the, there the Iewe wold ſaye, I will circumcyſe the or baptiſe the .vii. tymes. And ſo here by ſeuen is ment all the devels of hell & all ẏ might & power of the devell. For vnto what further blindneſſe coude al the deuels in hell bringe thē, then to make them beleue ẏ they were iustified thorow their awne good workes. For whē they once beleued ẏ they were purged frō their ſynnes & made rightuouſſe thorowe their awne holye workes, what rowme was there lefte for ẏ rightuouſnes ẏ is in chriſtes bloudeſhedinge? And therfore whē they be fallen in to this blindneſſe they cā not but hate & perſecute the light. And the more cleare & evidently their deades be rebuked ẏ furiouſſer & maliciouſſer blind are thei vntill they breake out in to opē blaſphemye & ſynnynge agenſt ẏ holy goſt, which is ẏ malicious perſecutīge of the cleare trouth ſo manifeſtly proued that they cā not once hijſh agenſt it. As the pharesyes perſecuted Chriſt becauſe he rebuked their holy deades. And when he proued his doctrine with ẏ ſcripture & miracles, yet though they coude not improue him nor reaſon agenſt him they tought ẏ the ſcripture muſt haue ſome other meaninge becauſe his interpretacion vndermyned their fundacion & plucked vpp by the rootes the ſectes which they had plāted, & they aſcribed alſo his miracles to the deuell. And in like .¶. maner though oure ypocrites can not denye but this is ſcripture, yet becauſe there can be no nother ſens gathered thereof, but that ouerthroweth their byldynges, therfore they euer thinke that it hath ſome other meanynge than as the wordes ſounde and that no man vnderſtondeth it or vnderſtode it ſens the tyme of the Apoſtles. Or yf they thynke that ſome that wrote vppon it ſens the apoſtles vnderſtode it: they yet thynke that we in like maner as we vnderſtonde not the texte it ſelfe, ſo we vnderſtande not the meanynge of the wordes of that doctoure.

For when thou layeſt the iuſtifyinge of holy workes and denyeſt the iuſtifyinge of fayth, howe canſt thou vnderſtond ſaynt Paule, Peter, Iohan and the Actes of the apoſtles or any ſcripture at all, ſeynge the iuſtifyinge of faith is almoſt all that they entende to proue.

Fynally, concernynge vowes whereof thou readeſt chaptre .xxx. there maye be many queſtyons, whereunto I anſwere ſhortly that we ought to put ſalt to all oure offerynges: that is, we ought to miniſtre knowledge in all ovre workes and to do nothinge whereof we coude not geue a reaſon out off gods wordes. We be now in the daye light, and all the ſecretes of God and all his counſell and will is opened vnto vs, and he ỷ was promyſed ſhuld come and bleſſe vs, is .P. come all readye and hath ſhed his bloud for vs and hath bleſſed vs with all maner bleſſynges and hath obtayned all grace for vs, and in him we haue all. Wherfore god henceforth will receaue no moare ſacrifices of beeſtes of vs as thou readeſt Hebre. x. Yf thou burne vnto god the bloud or fatt of beeſtes, to obtayne forgeueneſſe of ſynnes therby or that god ſhuld the better heare thy requeſt, then thou doeſt wronge vnto the bloude of chriſt, and chriſt vnto the is dead in vaine. For in him god hath promyſed not forgeueneſſe of ſynnes only, but alſo what ſoeuer we axe to kepe vs from ſynne and temptacion with all. And what yf thou burne frankencens vnto him, what yf thou burne a cādle, what yf thou burne thi chaſtite or virginite vnto him for the ſame purpoſſe, doeſt thou not like rebuke vnto chriſtes bloude?

Moreouer yf thou offer gold ſyluer or any other good

for the ſame entent, is there any difference? And euen ſo if thou go in pilgrymage or faſtiſt or goeſt wolward or ſprīcleſt thy ſelfe with holy water or els what ſoeuer dead it is, or obſerueſt what ſoeuer ceremonye it be for like meanynge, then it is like abhominacion. We muſt therfore bringe the ſalt of the knowledge of gods worde with all oure ſacrifices, or els we ſhall make no ſwete ſauoure vnto God thereof. Thou wilt axe me, ſhall I vowe nothynge at all? yes, gods .P. commaundement whiche thou haſt vowed in thy baptyme. For what entent? verely for the loue of Chriſt whiche hath bought the with his bloude & made the ſonne &. heyre of god with him, ẏ thou ſhuldeſt wayte on his will & cōmaundmentes and puryfye thy mēbres acordinge to ẏ ſame doctryne that hath puryfyed thyne harte, for if the knowlege of gods worde haue not puryfyed thyne harte, ſo that thou conſenteſt vnto the lawe of god that it is rightuouſſe & good and ſoroweſt, that thy membres moue the vnto the contrarye, ſo haſt thou no parte with Chriſte.

For yf thou repent not of thy ſynne, ſo it is impoſſible that thou ſhuldeſt beleue that Chriſte had delyuered the from the daunger therof. Yf thou beleue not that Chriſte hathe delyuered the, ſo is it impoſſible that thou ſhuldeſt loue goddes commaundementes. Yf thou loue not the commaundementes, ſo is Chriſtes ſprete not in the whiche is the erneſte off forgeueneſſe of ſynne and of ſaluacion.

For ſcripture teacheth, firſt repentaunce then ſayth in Chriſt, that for his ſake ſynne is forgeuen to them that repent: then good workes, whiche are nothynge ſaue the commaundement of god only. And the commaundemētes are nothinge els ſaue the helpinge of oure neyghboures at their neade & the tamyinge of oure mēbres that they myghte .P. be pure alſo as the harte is pure thorow hate of vice and loue of vertue as gods worde teacheth vs which workes muſt procede out of faith: ẏ is, I muſt do them for the loue which I haue to god for that greate mercye which he hath ſhewed me in chriſt, or els I do them not in yͤ ſight of god. And that I faynte not in the payne of the ſleyinge of the ſynne that is in my fleſh, myne helpe is the promeſſe of the aſſiſtence of the power of god and yͤ comforte of the rewarde to come which rewarde I aſcribe vnto the goodneſſe, mercye ād truth of the promiſer that hath choſe me, called me, taught me and geuen me the erneſt therof, ād not vnto the merites of my doenges or ſoferīges. For all that I do & ſoffre is but yͤ waye to the rewarde ād not the deſeruinge thereof. As if the kinges grace ſhuld promeſſe me to defend me at whome in myne awne royalme yet the waye thyther is thorow the ſee wherin I might happlye ſoffre no litle trouble. And yet for all that, yf I might lyue in reſt when I come thither, I wold think & ſo wold other ſaye, that my paynes were well rewarded: which reward & benefyte I wold not proudlye aſcribe vnto the merites of my paynes takynge by the waye: but vnto the goodneſſe, mercyfulneſſe and conſtaunt truth of the kinges grace whoſe gifte it is and to whome yͤ prayſe ād thanke thereof belongeth of duetye and right. So now a rewarde is a gift geuē .ꝑ. frelye of the goodneſſe of the geuer and not of the deſeruinges of the receauer. Thus it appeareth, that if I vowe what ſoeuer it be, for any other purpoſſe then to tame my membres and to be an enſample of vertue ād edefyenge vnto my neyghboure, my ſacrifice is vnſauery and cleane without ſalt and my lāpe without oyle and I one of the folyſh virginis and ſhalbe ſhutt out from the feaſt of the bruydegrome when I thinke my ſelf moſt ſure to entre in.

Yf I vowe voluntary pouerty, this muſt be my purpoſſe, that I will be content with a competent lyuinge which cometh vnto me ether by ſucceſſion of myne elders or which I gette truly with my laboure in miniſtringe and doynge ſeruice vnto the comen welth in one office or in a nother or in one occupatyon or other, becauſe that riches and honoure ſhall not corrupte my mynde and drawe myne harte from god, and to geue an enſample of vertue and edefyinge vnto other and yͤ my neyghboure may haue a lyuinge by me as well as I, if I make a cloke of diſſimulacion of my vowe, laynge a net of fayned beggerye to catch ſuperfluous aboundaunce of ryches and hye degre ād authorite & thorow the eſtimacion of falſe holineſſe to fede and maītayne my ſlowthfull ydleneſſe with ỹ ſweate, laboure, lādes, & rentes of other mē (after ỹ enſample of oure ſpiritualtye) robbinge thē .P. of their faythes and god of his honoure turnynge vnto myne ypocriſye that confidence, which ſhuld be geuē vnto ỹ promyſes of god only, am I not a wilye fox & a raueninge wolfe in a lābes ſkynne & a paynted ſepulchre fayre without ād filthye with in? In like maner though I ſeke no worldlye promocyon therebye, yet if I do it to be iuſtifyed therwith ād to gett an hyer place in heauen, thinkynge that I do it of myne awne naturall ſtrength & of the naturall power of my frewill & ỹ euery man hath might euen ſo to doo and that they do it not is their faute & negligēce and ſo with the proude phareſye in cōparyſon of my ſelf deſpiſe the ſinfull publicanes: what other thinge do I then eate ỹ bloude & fatt of my ſacrifice devowringe ỹ my ſelf which ſhuld be offered vnto god alone and his chriſte. And ſhortly what ſoeuer a man doeth of his naturall giftes, of his naturall witte, wiſdom, vnderſtondinge, reaſon, will, & good entent before he be otherwyſe & cleane cōtrary taught of goddes ſprete & haue receaued other witt and vnderſtondinge, reaſon ād will, is fleſh, worldlye and wrought ī abominable blīdneſſe, with which a man can but ſeke him ſelf, his awne profyte, glory & honoure, euē in very ſpirituall matters. As if I were alone in a wilderneſſe where no man were to ſeke profite or prayſe of yet if I wold ſeke heuē of god there, I coude of myne awne naturall gyftes ſeke it no no- .P. ther wayes then for the merites and deſeruinges of my good workes and to entre therin by a nother waye then by ỹ dore chriſt, which were very theſte, for chriſt is lord ouer all and what ſo euer any man wil haue of god, he muſt haue it geuen him frelye for chriſtes ſake. Now to haue heauen for myne awne deſeruinge, is myne awne prayſe and not chriſtes. For I can not haue it by fauoure & grace in chriſt and by myne awne merites alſo: For fregeuinge and deſeruinge can not ſtōd to gether.

Yf thou wilt vowe of thy goodes vnto god thou muſt put ſalt vnto this ſacrifice: that is thou muſt miniſtre knowlege in this deade as Peter teacheth. 2 pet. i. Thou muſt put oyle of gods worde in thy lāpe & do it accordinge to knowlege, if thou wayte for the comynge of the bridegrome to entre in with him in to his reſt. Thou wilt hāge it aboute the image to moue men to deuocyon. Deuocyon is a feruent loue vnto gods cōmaūdmentes and a deſyre to be with god and with his euerlaſtinge promyſes. Now ſhall the ſight of ſoch riches as are ſhewed at ſaynt thomas ſhryne or at walſingham moue a man to loue the cōmaundmētes of god better and to deſyre to be looſed from his fleſh and to be with god, or ſhall it not rather make his poore herte ſigh because he hath no ſoch at home and to wyſh parte of it in a nother place?

.P. The preaſt ſhall haue it in gods ſtead. Shall the preaſt haue it? Yf the preaſt be bought with chriſtes bloude, thē he is chriſtes ſeruaūte & not his awne & ought therefore to feade chriſtes flocke with chriſtes doctryne & to miniſtre chriſtes ſacramētes vnto thē purely for very loue & not for felthy lucres ſake or to be lord ouer thē as Peter teacheth 1 pet. v. & paule Actes .xx. Beſyde this chriſt is oures ād is a gifte geuen vs, & we be heyres of chriſt & of all that is chriſtes Wherfore the preaſtes doctryne is oures & we heires of it, it is yͤ fode of oure ſoules. Therfore if he miniſtre it not truly ād frely vnto vs with out ſellinge, he is a theſe & a ſoule murtherar: ād euen ſo is he if he take vppon him to fede vs & haue not wherewith. And for a like conclusyon becauſe we alſo with all that we haue be chriſtes, therfore is the preaſt heyre with vs alſo of all that we haue receaued of god, wherfore in as moch as yͤ preaſt wayteth on yͤ worde of god ād is oure ſeruaunte therin, therfore of right we are his dettars & owe him a ſufficyent lyuinge of oure goodes, ād euen therto a wiffe of oure doughters owe we vnto him if he requyre her. And now when we haue appoynted him a ſufficiēt liuinge, whether in tythes rentes or in yerelye wages, he ought to be cōtent & to require no more nor yet to receaue any more, but to be an enſample of ſoberneſſe & of diſpyſinge worldly thinges vnto the en- .¶. ſample of his paryſheonars.

Wilt thou vowe to offre vnto yͤ poore people? that is pleaſaunte in yͤ ſight of god, for they be lefte here to do oure almes apō in chriſtes ſtead & they be yͤ right heyres of all oure abundaūce & ouerplus. Moreouer we muſt haue a ſcole to teach goddes worde ī (though it neded not to be ſo coſtely) & therfore it is lawfull to vowe vnto the buyldynge or mayntenaūce therof & vnto helpinge of all good werkes. And we ought to vowe to paye cuſtome, tolle, rent & all maner dutyes and what ſoeuer we owe: for that is gods commaundmēt.

Yf thou wilt vowe pilgrimage, thou muſt put ſalt therto in like maner if it ſhalbe accepted, if thou vowe to go ād viſet the poore or to here gods worde or what ſoeuer edifieth thy ſoule vnto loue & good worke after knowlege or what ſoeuer god cōmaūdeth, it is well done and a ſacrifyce that ſauoreth well ye will happlye ſaye, that ye will go to this or yͭ place becauſe god hath choſen one place more then a nother and will heare youre peticyon more in one place then a nother. As for youre prayer it muſt be accordīge to goddes worde. Ye may not deſyer god to take vēgeaunce on him whō goddes worde teacheth you to pytye & to praye for. And as for yͤ other gloſe, yͭ god will heare you more ī one place thē in a nother, I ſuppoſe it ſal infatuatum, ſalt vnſauerye, for if it were wiſdome how coude .¶. we excuſe the deeth of ſteuē Acts vii. which dyed for yͤ article that god dwelleth not in tēples made with hādes we that beleue in god are yͤ temple of god ſayth paule, if a man loue god & kepe his worde he is the tēple of god & hath god preſently dwellinge in him, as witneſſeth chriſt Iohan .xiiii. ſayēge: If a mā loue me he will kepe my worde, & thē my father will loue him & we will come vnto him and dwell with him. And in the .xv. he ſayth: if ye abyde in me and my wordes alſo abyde in you, then axe what ye will & ye ſhall haue it. If thou beleue in chriſt & haſt the promyſes which god hath made the in thyne harte, thē go on pilgrymage vnto thyne awne harte ād there praye & god will heare ẏ for his mercy and truthes ſake and for his ſonne chriſtes ſake and not for a few ſtones ſakes. What careth god for the temple? The very beeſtes in that they haue liffe in them be moch better then an hepe of ſtonnes couched to gether.

To ſpeake of chaſtite, it is a gifte not geuen vnto all perſones teſtifyeth both chriſt and alſo his apoſtle Paule, wherfore all perſones maye not vowe it. Moreouer there be cauſes wherfore many perſones maye better lyue chaſt at one tyme then at a nother. Many maye lyue chaſt at twentye and thirtye for certayne colde diſeaſes folowinge them, which at .xl. when their helth is come can not do ſo. Many be occupyed with wylde .¶. phantaſyes in their youth ẏ they care not for mariage which ſame when they be waxē ſad ſhalbe greatly deſyrouſe, yt is a daungerous thynge to make ſynne where none is ād to forſwere ẏ beneſyte of god & to bynde thy ſelf vnder payne of dānacyon of thy ſoule that thou woldeſt not vſe the remeadye that god hath created if nead requyred. ¶ A nother thinge is this, beware that thou gett the not a falſe fayned chaſtite made with ẏ vngodly perſwaſions of ſaynte Hierō or of Ouide in his ſylthye boke of the remedye agenſt loue, leſt when thorow ſoch imaginacyons thou haſt vtterlye deſpyſed, defyed ād abhorred all woman kynde, thou come in to ſoch caſe thorow the ſirce wrath of god, ẏ thou canſt nether lyue chaſt nor fynde in thy harte to marye ād ſo be cōpelled to faule into the abhominacion of the pope agenſt nature and kynde.

Moreouer god is a wyſe father & knoweth all ẏ infirmityes of his children & alſo mercyfull, ād therfore hath created a remedye without ſynne ād geuen therto his fauoure and bleſſinge.

Let vs not be wyſer then god with oure ymaginacyōs nor tēpte him, for as godly chaſtite is not euery mās gyfte: euen ſo he ẏ hath it to daye hath not power to continue it at his awne pleaſure, nether hath god promyſed to geue it him ſtill & to cure his infirmytyes with out his naturall remeadye no more then he hath promyſed to ſlake his hongre .¶. with out meate or thirſt with out drinke.

Wherſore other let all thinges byde fre as wiſe god hath created them & nother vowe that which god requyreth not nor forſwere that which god permitteth the with his fauoure and bleſſinge alſo: or els if thou wilt neades vowe, then vowe godly & vnder a cōdityon, yͭ thou wilt contynue chaſt, ſo longe as god geueth the yͤ gyfte ād as longe as nether thyne awne neceſſyte nether cheryte toward thy neighboure nor yͤ authorite of thē vnder whoſe power thou arte dryue yͭ vnto the contrarye.

The purpoſſe of thy vowe muſt be ſalted alſo with yͤ wiſdom of god. Thou mayeſt not vowe to be iuſtefyed therbye or to make ſatiſſaction for thy ſynnes or to wynne heauē nor an hyer place: for then dideſt thou wrōge vnto the bloude of chriſt & thy vowe were playne Idolatrye & abhominable in yͤ ſight of god. Thy vowe muſt be only vnto yͤ furtheraunce of yͤ commaūdmētes of god, which are as I haue ſayde nothinge but yͤ taminge of thy mēbres & the ſeruice of thy neyghboure: that is if thou thyncke thy backe to weake for the burthen of wedlocke & yͭ thou canſt not rule thy wiff, children ſeruaūtes and make prouiſion for thē godlye & with out ouermoch buſyenge and vnquyetynge thy ſelf ād drounynge thy ſelf in worldly buſyneſſe vnchriſtenlye or that thou canſt ſerue thy neyghboure in ſome office better beynge chaſt then maryed. And then .¶. thy vowe is good & lawfull. And euē ſo muſt thou vowe abſtinēce of meates & drynkes ſo far forth as it is profitable vnto thy neyghbours & vnto yͤ tamīge of thy fleſh: But thou mayſt vowe nether of them vnto yͤ ſleynge of thy bodye. As Paule cōmaūdeth tymothe to drincke wyne & no moare water becauſe of his diſeaſes. Thou wilt ſaye yͭ timothy had not happlye forſworne wyne. I thinke the ſame and that the apoſtles forſware not wedlocke though many of them lyued chaſt nother yet any meate or drincke, though they abſteyned from thē, & that it were good for vs to folow their enſample. How be it though I vowe & ſwere ād thynke on none exceptyon, yet is the breakynge of gods cōmaūdmētes except & all chaunces that hāge of god. As if I ſwere to be in a certayne place at a certayne houre to make a louedaye with out exception, yet if the kinge in the meane tyme commaunde me a nother waye, I muſt goo by gods commaūdment ād yet breake not myne othe. And in like caſe if my father and mother be ſeke and requyre my preſence, or if my wiff, children or houſhold be viſited that my aſſiſtence be requyred, or if my neyghbours houſe be a fyre at the ſame houre and a thouſand ſoch chaunces: in which all I breake myne oth and am not forſworne and ſo forth. Read gods word diligently and with a good herte and it ſhall teach the all thynges.

The four

the boke of Mofes called

Numeri.

☙ THE .IIII. BOKE
OF MOSES, CALLED NUMERI.

𝔐.𝔆.𝔖. All that are apte for batell are nombred. The trybe of Leuy is appoynted to mynistre to the tabernacle.

1 AND the Lorde ſpake vnto Moſes in the wilderneſſe of Sinai,
in the tabernacle of witneſſe,
the fyrſt daye of the ſeconde
moneth, ād in the ſeconde yere after they
were come out of yͤ londe of Egipte ſay-
2 enge: take ye the ſumme of al the multitude of the childern of Iſrael, in their kynredes and
houſholdes of their fathers and numbre thē by name
3 all that are males, pollie by polle, frō .xx. yere &
aboue: euen all yͤ are able to goo forthe in to warre
in Iſraell, thou & Aarō ſhall nūbre thē in their armies,
4 & with you ſhalbe of euery trybe a heed man in the
houſe of his father.
5 And theſe are the names of yͤ mē yͤ ſhall ſtōde with
6 you: in Rubē, Elizur yͤ ſonne of Sedeur: In Simeō,
7 Selumiel yͤ ſonne of Suri Sadai: In yͤ tribe of Iuda,
8 Naheſſon yͤ ſonne of Aminadab: In Iſachar, Nathaneel
9 yͤ ſonne of Zuar: In Sebulō, Eliab yͤ ſonne of Helō.
10 Amōge yͤ childern of Ioſeph: In Ephraī, Eliſama yͤ
ſonne of Amihud: In Manaſſe, Gamaliel yͤ ſōne of Peda
11, 12 zur: In Bē Iamin, Abidan the ſonne of Gedeoni: In
13 Dan, Ahieſer the ſonne of Ammi Sadai: In Aſſer,
14 Pagiel the ſonne of Ochran: In Gad, Eliaſaph the ſōne
15 of Deguel: In Naphtaly, Ahira the ſonne of Enan.

𝔐. 5 ſtande . . . of Ruben 6 of Simeon 7 of . . of Iuda 8 of Iſachar 9 of Zabulon 10 of Ephraim . . of Manaſſe 11 of Ben Iamin 12 of Dan 13 of Aſer 15 of Nephthali

𝔙. 1 tabernaculo fœderis 2 quicquid ſexus eſt maſculini . . . 3 omnium virorum fortium 13 Phegiel filius Ochran.

𝔏. 2 heuſer, bey der zal der namen . . . von heubt zu heubt

𝔐. 𝔐. 𝔑. 13 or Phegiel

16 .P. Thefe were councelers of the congregacion and
lordes in the trybes of their fathers & captaynes ouer
17 thoufandes in Ifrael. And Mofes and Aaron toke
18 thefe men aboue named and gathered all the congregacion together, the fyrft daye of the feconde moneth,
and rekened them after their byrth & kinredes and
houfes of their fathers by name frō .xx. yere & aboue
19 hed by hed: as the Lorde cōmaunded Mofes, euē fo
he numbred them in ẏͤ wilderneffe of Sinai.

20 And the childern of Ruben Ifraels eldeft fonne in
their generacions, kynredes ād houfes of their fathers,
whē they were numbred euery man by name, all
that were males frō .xx. yere and aboue, as many
21 as were able to goo forth in warre: were numbred in
the trybe off Ruben, .xlvi. thoufande and fiue hundred.

22 Among the childern of Simeon: their generacion
in their kynredes and houffes of their fathers (when
euery mans name was tolde) of all the males from .xx
yeres and aboue, whatfoeuer was mete for the warre:
23 were numbred in the trybe of Simeon .Lix. thoufande
and .iii. hundred.

24 Amonge the childern of Gad: their generacion in
their kynredes and houfholdes of their fathers, when
thei were tolde by name, frō .xx. yere and aboue, all
25 that were mete for the warre: were numbred in the tribe
of Gad .xlv. [Fo. III.] thoufande, fixe hundred and fyftie.

26 Amonge the childern of Iuda: their generacion in
their kinredes and houffes of their fathers (by the
numbre of names) from .xx. yere and aboue, all that
27 were able to warre, were tolde in the trybe of Iuda
Lxxiiii. thoufande and fixe hundred.

28 Amonge the childern of Ifachar: their generacion,

T. 18 recēfentes eos 19 Numeratique funt in deferto Sinai. 20 de Ruben . . procedentiū ad bellum 24 omnes qui ad bella procederent 26 poterant ad bella procedere (fo of Iuda, Iffachar, Zabulon, Ephraim, Manaffe, Benjamin, Dan, Afer and Nephtali, and 45.)

L. 16 die namhafftigen der gemeyne . . heubter vnd furften 20 Ruben . . . yns heer zu zihen tuchte 24 Gad . . tuchtig war 26 Iuda . . yns heer zu zihen tuchte (fo vv. 20, 24, 28, 30, 32, 34, 36, 38.)

M. M. X. 20 Of Ruben 22 Of Simeon 24 Of Gad 26 Of Iuda 28 Of Ifachar

in their kinredes and houſes of their fathers (when
their names were counted) from .xx. yere ād aboue,
29 what ſoeuer was apte for warre: were numbred in ỷ
trybe of Iſachar .Liiii. thouſande and .iiii. hundred.
30 Among the childern of Sebulon: their generacion,
in their kynredes and houſes of their fathers (after the
numbre of names) from .xx. yere and aboue, whoſo-
31 euer was mete for the warre: were counted in ỷ trybe
of Sebulō .Lvii. thouſande and .iiii. hundred.
32 Amonge the childern of Ioſeph: fyrſt amōge the
childern of Ephraim: their generacion, in their kynredes and houſſes of theyre fathers (when the names
of all that were apte to the warre were tolde) from .xx
33 yeres and aboue: were in numbre in the trybe off
Ephraim, .xl. thouſande and ſyxe hundred.
34 Amonge the childern of Manaſſe: their generacion,
in their kynredes and houſes of their fathers (when
the names of all ỷ were apte to warre were tolde) from
35 xx. and aboue .P. were numbred in the tribe of Manaſſe .xxxii. thouſand and two hundred.
36 Amonge the childern of Ben Iamin: their generacion, in their kynredes and houſſes of their fathers
(by the tale of names) from twentye yere
and aboue of all that were mete for warre,
37 were numbred in the trybe off Ben Iamin .xxxv. thouſande and .iiii. hundred.

tale, *number*, cf. German *Zahl*

38 Amonge the childern of Dan: their generacion in
theyr kynreddes and houſſes off their fathers (in the
ſumme of names) off all that was apte to warre from
39 twentye yere and aboue, were numbred in the trybe
of Dan .Lxii. thouſande and .vii. hundred.
40 Amonge the childern of Aſer: their generacyon, in
their kynredes & houſes of their fathers (when thei
were ſummed by name) from .xx. yeres & aboue, all
41 that were apte to warre were numbred in the tribe
of Aſer .xli. thouſande and .v. hundred.
42 Amōge the childern of Nepthali: their generacion,

L. 40 Aſſer . . . yns heer zihen mochte (ſo vv. 42, 45.)
M. M. X. 30 Of Zabulon 32 Of Ioſeph 34 Of Manaſſes 36 Cf Bē Iamin. 38 Of Dan 40 Of Aſer 42 Of Nephtali

in their kynredes & houſſes of their fathers (when their
names were tolde) from .xx. yeres ād aboue, what ſo-
43 euer was mete to warre: were numbred in the trybe
of Nephtali .Liii. thouſande and .iiii. hundred.
44 Theſe are the numbres which Moſes ād Aarō numbred with ẏ .xii. princes of Iſrael: of euery houſſe of
45 their fathers a man. And all the numbres of the childern of Iſrael, in [Fo. IIII.] the houſſes of their fathers, from twentye yere and aboue, what ſoeuer was
46 mete for the warre in Iſraell, drewe vnto the ſumme
47 of ſyxe hundred thouſande, ſyue hundred and .L. But
the leuites in the tribe off their fathers were not numbred amonge them.
48, 49 And the Lorde ſpake vnto Moſes ſayenge: only
ſe that thou numbre not the trybe of Leui, nether take
the ſumme of them amonge the childern of Iſrael.
50 But thou ſhalt appoynte the leuites vnto the habitaciō of witneſſe, and to all the apparell thereof and
vnto all that longeth thereto. For they
ſhall bere the tabernacle and all the ordinaunce thereof, and they ſhall miniſtre it and ſhall
51 pitche their tentes rounde aboute it. And when the
tabernacle goeth forth the leuites ſhall take it doune:
and when the tabernacle is pitched, they ſhall ſett it
vpp: for yf any ſtraunger come nere, he ſhall dye.
52 And the childern of Iſrael ſhall pitch their tentes,
euery man in his owne companye and euery mā by
his awne ſtandert thorow out all their hoſtes.
53 But the leuites ſhall pitche rounde aboute the habitacion of witneſſe, that there fall no wrath vpon the
congregacion of the childrē of Iſrael, and the leuites
54 ſhall wayte apon the habitacion of witneſſe. And the
childern of Iſrael dyd acordinge to all that the Lord
commaunded Moſes.

longeth, *belongeth, vi, 15*

M. 43 thrye and fyftye 46 ſyxe hundred and thre thouſande

V. 46 ſexcēta tria millia virorum quingenti quinquaginta. 50 vaſa eius, & quicquid ad ceremonias pertinet. 52 per turmas & cuneos atque exercitū ſuum. 53 ne fiat indignatio . . & excubabunt in cuſtodiis tabern.

L. 50 wonung des zeugnis 53 Leuiten der hutt wartten an der wonung des zeugnis.

.P. ¶ The .II. Chapter.

1 AND the Lorde ſpake vnto Mo-
2 ſes and Aaron ſayenge: The
childern of Iſrael ſhall pitch:
euery man by his owne ſtand-
ert with the armes of their fathers houſes,
a waye, *away* a waye from the preſence of
the tabernacle of witneſſe,
3 On the eaſt ſyde towarde the ryſynge
of ẏ ſonne, ſhall they of the ſtandert of the
hoſte of Iuda pitch with their armes: And
Naheſſon the ſonne of Aminadab ſhalbe captaine ouer the
4 ſonnes of Iuda. And his hoſte and the numbre of them
5 Lxxiiii. thouſande and .vi. hundred. And nexte vnto
him ſhall the trybe of Iſachar pitche and Nathaneel the
6 ſonne of Zuar captayne ouer ẏ childrē of Iſachar: his
hoſte and the numbre of them .Liiii. thouſande and
7 iiii. hundred. And than the trybe of Zabulon: with
Eliab the ſonne of Helon, captayne ouer the childern
8 of Zabulon, and his hoſte in the numbre of them: .Lvii
9 thouſande and .iiii. hundred. So that all they that perteyne vnto the hoſt of Iuda, are an hundred thouſande
Lxxxvi. thouſande ād .iiii. hundred in their companies:
and theſe ſhall goo in the forefront, wen they iurney.
10 And on the ſouthſyde, the ſtandert of the hoſte of
Ruben ſhall lye with their companyes and the captayne
ouer the ſonnes of Ruben, Elizur the ſonne of Sedeur,
11 and his hoſte and the numbre of them .xlvi. thouſande,
12 [Fo. V.] and .v. hundred. And faſt by him ſhall ẏ
trybe of Simeon pitche, and the capteyne ouer ẏ ſonnes

M.C.S. The order of the pytchyng of the tentes rounde aboute the tabernacle of wytneſſe. The heades and chefe Lordes of the kynredes of Iſrael are named.

V. 2 per turmas, ſigna atque vexilla 3 Iudas . . per turmas exercitus ſui 4 ſumma pugnantium 5 Iſſachar 6 numerus pugnatorum 7 Zabulon 8 exercitus pugnatorum 10 Ruben 11 & cūctus exercitus pugnatorum

L. 2 panir vnd zeychen nach yhrer veter haus 9 Iuda . . . heer, (and ſo throughout the chapter)

M. M. N. 3 On the eaſt ſyde the cōpanye of Iuda, Iſachar & Zabulon. 10 On the ſouthſyde the companye of Ruben, Simeō & Gad.

13 of Simeon. Selumiel the ſonne of zuri Sadai, & his hoſte
and the nũbre of them .Lix. thouſande and .iii. hundred
14 And the trybe of Gad alſo: And the captayne ouer the
15 ſonnes of Gad, Eliaſaph the ſonne of Deguel and his
hoſte and the numbre of them .xlv. thouſande .vi. hun-
16 dred and .L. So that all ỷ numbre that pertayne vnto
the hoſte of Ruben, are an hundred thouſande .Li
thouſande .iiii. hundred & fyftie, with their companyes,
and they ſhall be the ſeconde in the iourney

17 And the tabernacle of witneſſe with the hoſte of
the leuites, ſhall goo in the myddes of ỷ hoſtes: as they
lye in their tẽtes, euen ſo ſhall they procede in the
iurney, euery man in his quarter aboute their ſtandertes.

18 On the weſt ſyde, the ſtandarte and the hoſte of
Ephraim ſhall lye with their companies. And the
captayne ouer the ſonnes of Ephraim, Eliſama the
19 ſonne of Amihud: & his hoſte and the numbre of them
20 xl. thouſande & .v. hundred. And faſt faſt by, *cloſe to*
by him, the trybe of Manaſſe, and the captayne ouer
the ſonnes of Manaſſe, Gamaleel ỷ ſonne of Peda zur
21 and his hoſte and the numbre of them .xxxii. thouſande
22 and .ii. hundred. And the trybe of Ben Iamin alſo: and
the captayne ouer the ſonnes of Ben Iamin, Abidan
23 the ſonne of Gedeoni, ãd his hoſte and the numbre of
24 thẽ .P. xxxv. thouſande and .iiii. hundred. All the
nũbre that perteyned vnto the hoſte of Ephraim, were
an hundred thouſand .viii. thouſande and an hundred
in their hoſtes: and they ſhalbe the thryde in the
iurneye

25 And the ſtandert and the hoſte of Dan ſhall lye on
the north ſyde with their companyes: & the captayne
ouer ỷ childrẽ of Dan, Ahiezer the ſonne of Ammi
26 Sadai: and his hoſte and the nũbre of them .Lxii. thou-

V. 12 Simeon 13 & cunctus exercitus pugnat. (so 15, 19, 21, 23, 26, 28, 30) 16 Omnes qui recẽſiti ſunt 17 Leuabitur autẽ tabernac. teſtim. per officia leuitarum & turmas eorum. quomodo erigetur, ita et deponetur. 24 caſtris Ephraim . . . per turmas ſuas

L. 18 Gezelt vnd panier Ephraim

M. M. X. 17 The leuytes with the tabernacle in the myddes. 18 On the weſt ſyde the cõpany of Ephraim Manaſſe and Ben Iamin 25 On the north ſyde the company of Dan, Aſſer and Nephthali.

27 sande & .vii. hundred. And fast by him shall the trybe
of Asser pitche: and the captayne ouer the sõnes of
28 Asser, Pagiel the sonne of Ochran: & his hoste & the
29 nũbre of them .xli. thousande & .v. hundred. And the
trybe of Naphtali also, and the captayne ouer yͤ chil-
30 dern of Naphtali: Ahira the sonne of Enan: & his hoste
and the nũbre of them .Liii. thousande & .iiii. hũdred
31 So yͭ the hole nũbre of all that perteyned vnto yͤ hoste
of Dan, was an hũdred thousande .Lvii. thousande &
vi. hũdred. And they shalbe the last in yͤ iurney with
their stãdertes.
32 These are yͤ sũmes of yͤ childern of Ysrael in the
housses of their fathers: euen all the nũbres of the hostes
with their cõpanies .vi. hũdred thousande .iii. thou-
33 sande .v. hũdred and fyftie. And yet yͤ leuites were
not nũbred amõge the childern of Ysrael, as the Lorde
34 commaunded Moses. And yͤ childern of Ysrael dyd
acordynge to all that the Lorde cõmaũded Moses,
& so they pitched with their stan- [Fo. VI.] dertes,
and so they iurneyd: euery man in his kynred, and in
the housshólde of his father.

❡ The .III. Chapter.

1 THESE are the generacions of
Aaron and Moses, when the
Lorde spake vnto Moses in
2 Mount Sinai, and these are
the names of the sonnes of Aaron: Nadab
the eldest sonne, and Abihu Eleazar and
3 Ithamar. These are the names of the
sonnes of Aaron which were preastes
anoynted and their handes fylled to myn-

M.C.S. *The Leuites are not nombred to go to batell, but to mynistre to the holy place or sanctuary. They must also pitch their tentes next to the habytacyon.*

F. 31 castris Dan, fuerunt 32 per domos cognationum suarum & turmas diuisi exercitus 34 Castrametati sunt per turmas suas, & profecti per familias ac domos patrum suorum. iii, 3 vncti sunt, & quorũ repletæ & consecratæ manus vt sacerdotio fungerentur.

L. 34 lagerten sich vnter yhre panier, vnd zogen aus, eyn iglicher ynn seynem geschlecht nach yhrer veter haus. iii, 3 zu priester gesalbet . . hende gefullet zum priesterthum.

4 iſtre but Nadab and Abihu dyed before the Lorde, as
they broughte ſtraunge fyre before the Lorde in the
wyldernesſe of Sinai, and had no childern. And
Eleazar and Ithamar myniſtred in the ſyght of Aaron
their father.
5, 6 And the Lorde ſpake vnto Moſes ſaynge brynge
the trybe of leui, and ſet them before Aaron the preaſt,
7 and let them ſerue him ād wayte apon him, & apon all
the multitude, before the tabernacle of witneſſe, to doo
8 the ſeruyce of the habitacion. And they ſhall wayte
apō all ẏͤ apparell of ẏͤ tabernacle of witneſſe & apon
ẏͤ childern of Yſrael, to doo ẏͤ ſeruyce of the habitaciō.
9 And thou ſhalt geue the leuites vnto Aaron & his
ſonnes, for they are geuen vnto him of ẏͤ childern of
10 Yſrael. And thou ſhalt appoȳte Aarō & his ſonnes to
wayte on their preaſtes office: & the ſtraūger ẏͭ cometh
nye, ſhall dye for it.
11, 12 And ẏͤ Lorde ſpake vnto Moſes ſaynge: beholde,
I haue takē the leuites frō amonge ẏͤ .𝔓. childern of
Yſrael, for all the firſtborne that openeth the matryce
amonge the childern of Yſrael, ſo that the leuites ſhall
13 be myne: becauſe all the firſt borne are myne: for ẏͤ
ſame daye that I ſmote all the fyrſtborne in the lande
of Egipte, I halowed vnto me all the firſtborne in
Yſrael, both man and beeſt, and myne they ſhall be:
for I am the Lorde.
14 And the Lorde ſpake vnto Moſes in the wilderneſſe
15 of Sinai ſayenge: Numbre the childern of Leui in ẏͤ
houſſes of their fathers and Kynredes, all ẏͭ are males
16 from a moneth olde and aboue. And Moſes numbred
them at the worde of the Lorde, as he was cōmaūded.
17 And theſe are ẏͤ names of ẏͤ childrē of Leui: Gerſon,
18 Cahath, & Merari. And ẏͤ ſe are the ẏͤ ſe, *theſe*
names of the childern of Gerſon in their kynredes:

𝔙 6 vt miniſtrēt ei 7 & excubēt & obſeruēt 10 ſuper cultū ſacerdotii . Externus qui ad miniſtrandum acceſſerit

𝔏. 4 hatten keyne ſone. 7 gemeyne hutt wartten 8 hutt der kinder Iſrael zu dienen am dienſt der wonung.

𝔐. 𝔐. 𝔛. 12 Leuyte ſomtyme ſygnifyeth only a mynyſter or ſeruaunt, as here and Eſa. lxvi, g.

19 Libni and Semei. And the sōnes of Cahath in their
kynredes were Amram. Iezehar. Hebron and Vsiel.
20 And the sonnes of Merari in their kynredes were
Maheli and Musi. These are the kynredes of Leui in
the housses of their fathers.
21 And of Gerson came the kynred of ẏ Libnites and
the Semeites, which are the kynredes of the Gersonites.
22 And ẏ summe of them (when all the males were
tolde) from a moneth olde and aboue, were .vii. thousande and fyue hundred. tolde, *numbered*
23 And the kynredes of the Gersonites pitched behynde
24 the habitacion west warde. And the captayne of the
most awnciēt [Fo. VII.] housse amonge ẏ Gersonites,
25 was Eliasaph the sonne of Lael. And the office of the
childern of Gerson in the tabernacle of witnesse was
the habitacion and the tente with the coueringe theroff and the hangynge of the dore of the tabernacle of
26 witnesse, and the hangynges of the courte, and the
curtayne of the dore of the courte: which courte went
rounde aboute the dwellynge, and the alter, and the
cordes ẏ perteyned vnto all the seruyce therof
27 And of Cahath came the kynred of ẏ Amramites
and the kynred of the Iezeharites & of the Hebronites
and of the Vsielites: And these are the kynredes of ẏ
28 Cahathites. And the numbre of all the males from a
moneth olde and aboue, was .viii. thousande and sixe
29 hundred: which wayted on ẏ holy place. And the
kynred of the childern of Cahath, pitched on ẏ south
30 syde of ẏ dwellynge And ẏ captayne in ẏ most auncyent housse of the kynredes of the Cahathites, was
31 Elizaphan the sonne of Vsiel, and their office was: the
arcke, the table, the candelsticke, and the alter and
the holy vessels to minystre with and the vayle with

M. 25 was to kepe the habitacyon 31 was to kepe the arcke

V. 21 De Gerson fuere familiæ duæ 25 Et habebunt excubias in tab. fœderis 26 quicquid ad ritum altaris pertinet 28 habebunt excubias sanctuarii 30 Oziel 31 & custodient arcam

L. 25 vnd sie sollen warten 31 Heyligthums, daran sie dienen, vnd des tuchs

M. M. N. 21 The Gersonites pitch on the west syde. 27 The Cahathites are assygned to the southsyde.

32 all that ferued there to. And Eleazar ẏ fonne of Aaron
the preaft, was captayne ouer all the captaynes of the
Leuites, and had the ouer fyghte of them that wayted
vppon the holythynges.

33 And of Merari came the kynredes of the Mahelites
and of the Mufites: and thefe .II. are the kynredes
34 of the Merarites. And the nūbre of them (when all
the males frō a moneth olde ād aboue was tolde)
drewe vnto .vi. thoufande & .ii. hundred. drewe vnto,
35 And ẏ captayne of the moft auncient *amounted to*
houffe amonge the kynredes of the Merarites, was
Zuriel the fonne of Abihail which pitched on the north
36 fyde of the dwellynge. And the office of the fonnes
of Merari was: the bordes of ẏ dwellynge & the barres,
pilers with the fokettes thereof, and all the inftrumētes
37 there of & all that ferued thereto: & the pilers of the
courte rounde aboute and their fokettes, with their
38 pynnes & cordes. But on ẏ fore front of ẏ habitaciō
ād before the tabernacle of witneffe eaft warde, fhall
Mofes and Aaron & his fonnes pytch and wayte on the
fanctuary in the fteade of ẏ childern of Yfrael. And the
39 ftraunger ẏ cometh nye, fhall dye for it. And the hole
fumme of the leuites which Mofes & Aaron nūbred, at
ẏ cōmaūdmēt of ẏ Lorde thorow out their kynredes
euen, of all ẏ males of a moneth olde & aboue, was
xxii. thoufande.

40 And the Lorde fayde vnto Mofes: Numbre all ẏ
firft borne that are males amōge the childern of Yfrael,
frō a moneth olde & aboue and take ẏ numbre of their
41 names. And thou fhalt appoynte ẏ leuites to me the
Lorde, for all the firftborne amōge ẏ childern of Yfrael
and the catell of ẏ leuites for the firftborne of the
42 childern of Yfrael. And Mofes nūbred [Fo. VIII.] as
ẏ Lorde cōmaūded him, all the firftborne of ẏ chil-

M. 36 was to kepe ẏ bordes

V. 32 erit fuper excubitores cuftodiæ fanctuarii. 36 Erunt fub cuftodia eorum tabulæ 38 habentes cuftod. fanctuarii in medio filiorum Ifrael. 42 Recenfuit Moyfes

L. 32 Eleafar . . . vber die verordnet find zu wartten

M. M. N. 33 The Merarites affygned on the north fyde. 38 Mofes & Aaron & their fonnes on the eaft fide. 39 kynredes, euen

43 dern of Yſrael. And all the firſtborne males, in ẏ
ſumme of names, from a moneth olde and aboue, were
numbred .xxii. thouſande .ii. hundred and .Lxxiii.
44, 45 And the Lorde ſpake vnto Moſes ſayenge: take
the leuites for all the fyrſtborne of the childern of Iſrael,
ād the catell of the leuites for their catell: & the
46 leuites ſhalbe myne whiche am the Lorde. And for
the redemynge of the two hundred and .Lxxiii. whiche
are moo than the leuites in the firſtborne of the chil-
47 dren of Iſrael, take .v. ſycles of euery pece, after the
48 ſycle of ẏ holy place .xx. geras the ſycle. And geue
ẏ money wherewith the odde numbre of them is re-
49 demed, vnto Aaron ād his ſonnes. And Moſes toke
the redempciō money of the ouerplus that were moo
50 then the leuites, amonge the firſtborne of the childern
of Iſrael: & it came to a thouſande .iii. hundred &
51 Lxv. ſycles, of the holye ſycle. And he gaue that re-
dempcionmoney vnto Aaron & his ſonnes at the worde
of the Lorde, euen as the Lorde commaunded Moſes.

¶ The .IIII. Chapter.

1 AND ẏ Lord ſpake vnto Moſes &
2 Aarō & bade thē take ẏ ſumme
of ẏ childern of Cahath frō
amonge ẏ ſonnes of leui, in
their kynredes and houſſes of their fathers,
3 from .xxx. yere and aboue vntill fyftie, all that were
able to warre, for to doo the worke in .P. the tabernacle
4, 5 of witneſſe: euen in the moſt holy place. And when

M.C.S. *The offyces of the Leuytes, euery one after the flocke that he came of.*

M. iiii, 4 witneſſe. [Tyndale omits the following clause] This ſhalbe the office of the chyldrē of Kahath in the tabernacle of witneſſe which is mooſt holy.

V. 47 viginti obolos. iiii, 3 qui ingrediūtur vt ſtent & miniſtrēt 4 Hic eſt cultus filiorū Caath

L. 46 vberlengen erſten gepurten . . . vber der Leuiten zal 48 daſſelb gelt, das vberleng iſt vber yhre zal 49 Loſegelt das vberlenge war. iiii, 3 alle die yns heer tugen, das ſie thun die werck ynn der hutten des zeugnis

ŷ hoſte remoueth, Aaron ād his ſonnes ſhall come and
take doune the vayle and couer the arcke of witneſſe
6 there with, and ſhall put there on a couerynge of
taxus ſkynnes, and ſhall ſprede a cloth ŷ is altogether
of Iacyncte aboue all, and put the ſtaues thereof in.
7 And apon the ſhewe table, they ſhall ſprede a cloth
of Iacyncte, and put thereō, the diſhes, ſpones, flat
peces and pottes to poure with, and the dayly bred
8 ſhal be thereon: and they ſhall ſpred apon them a
couerynge of purple, and couer the ſame with a couerynge of taxus ſkynnes, and put the ſtaues thereof in.
9 And they ſhall take a cloth of Iacyncte & couer
the candelſticke of light and hir lāpes and hir ſnoffers
and fyre pannes and all hir oyle veſſels which they
10 occupye aboute it, & ſhall put apon her and on all hir
inſtrumentes, a couerynge of taxus ſkynnes, and put
11 it apon ſtaues. And apon the golden alter they ſhall
ſprede a cloth of Iacyncte, and put on hir ſtaues.
12 And they ſhall take all the thīges which they occupye to minyſtre with in ŷ holy place, & put a
cloth of Iacyncte apon them and couer them with a
couerynge of taxus ſkynnes and put them on ſtaues.
13 And they ſhall take a waye the aſſhes out of the alter,
14 and ſprede a ſcarlet cloth thereon: & put aboute it,
the fyre pannes, the fleſh hokes, the ſho- [Fo. IX.]
uels, the baſens, and all that belongeth vnto the alter,
and they ſhall ſprede apon it a coueryng of taxus
ſkynnes and put on the ſtaues of it
15 And when Aaron and his ſonnes haue made an
ende of couerynge the ſanctuary ād all the thinges
of the ſanctuarye, agenſt that the hoſte remoue, then
the ſonnes of Cahath ſhall come in for to bere,

V. 6 velamine hyacinthinarum pellium . . . pallium totum hyacinthinum 7 hyac. pallio. . . panes ſemper in ea erunt 8 pallium coccineum . . velamento hyac. pellium 10 operimentum hyac. pellium, & inducent 11 inuoluent hyac. veſtimento & ext. deſuper oper. hyac. pellium 12 ſanctuario inuoluent hyac. pallio . . oper. hyac. pellium 13 altare . . . purpureo veſtimento 14 ſimul vel. hyac. pellium

L. 6 dachs fellen [ſo throughout the chapter where Tyndale renders *taxus ſkynnes*] 7 ſchawtiſch auch eyn gel kleyd [ſo throughout the chapter where Tyndale renders *Iacyncte*]

and so let them not twich the sanctuary lest they
dye. And this ys the charge of the sonnes of Ca-
16 hath in the tabernacle of witnesse. And Eleazar
the sonne of Aaron the preast, shall haue the charge
to prepare oyle for the lightes and swete cens, & the
dayly meatofferynge and the anoyntinge oyle, and
the ouersyghte of all the dwellynge and of all that
therein is: both ouer the sanctuary & ouer all that pertayneth thereto.
17 And the Lorde spake vnto Moses & Aaron sayenge:
18 destroye not the trybe of the kynredes of the Cahathites,
19 from amonge the leuites. But thus doo vnto them that
they maye lyve and not dye, whē they goo vnto ỹ
most holy place. Aaron and his sonnes shall goo in
and put them, euery man vnto his seruyce and vnto
20 his burthen. But let them not goo in to se when they
couer the sanctuarye, lest they dye.
21, 22 And the Lorde spake vnto Moses sayenge Take
the summe of the childern of Gerson, in the houses of
23 their fathers ād in their kyn- .P. redes: from .xxx. yere
and aboue, vntyll .L. all that are able to goo forth in
warre, for to doo seruyce in the tabernacle of witnesse.
24 And this is the seruyce of the kynred of the Gersonites,
25 to serue and to beare. They shall bere the curtaynes
of the dwellynge and the roffe of ỹ tabernacle of witnesse and his couerynge ād the coueryng of taxus
skynnes that is an hye aboue apon it, and
the hangynge of the dore of the tabernacle of witnesse:
26 and the henginge of the courte and the hangynge of
the gate of the courte that is rounde aboute the dwellynge and the altare, and the cordes of them, and all
the instrumentes that serue vnto them and all that is

an hye, *on high*

V. 15 filii Caath vt portent inuoluta . . onera filior. Caa. in tabernaculo fœderis, 16 super quos erit Eleazar . . sacrificium quod semper offertur 18 Nolite perdere 20 Alii nulla curiositate videāt quæ sunt in sanctuario priusquam inuoluantur 22 Tolle summam etiam fil. Gerson. 23 Numera omnes qui ingred. et ministr. in tab. fœderis. 25 & tectum fœd. operimentum aliud . . . velamen hyac.

L. 16 das tegliche speysopffer 18 nicht verderben vnter den Leuiten 20 zu schawen vnbedacht das Heyligthum 22 Gerson 23 zum heer tuchtig

27 made for them. And at the mouth of Aaron and his
ſonnes, ſhall all the ſeruyce of the childern of the Gerſonites be done, in all their charges and in all their ſeruyce, and ye ſhall appoynte them vnto al their charges
28 that they ſhall wayte apō. And this is the
ſeruyce of the kynred of the children of
the Gerſonites in ẏ tabernacle of witneſſe,
and their wayte ſhalbe in the honde of Ithamar the
ſonne of Aaron the preaſt.

wayte, *watch, ſervice, charge* cf. Germ. *Hut*

29 And thou ſhalt numbre the ſonnes of Merari in their
30 kynredes and in the houſes of their fathers, from .xxx
yeres and aboue vnto .L. All that is able to goo
forth in warre, to doo the ſeruyce of the tabernacle
of witneſſe.

31 And this is the charge that they muſt way- [Fo. X.]
te vppon in all that they muſt ſerue in the tabernacle
of witneſſe: The bordes of the dwellynge, and the
32 barres, pylers, and ſokettes thereof, and the pylers of
the courte rounde aboute, and their ſokettes, pynnes
and cordes with all that pertayneth and ſerueth vnto
them. And by name ye ſhall reken the thynges that
33 they muſt wayte apon to bere. Thys is the ſeruyce
of the kynreddes of the ſonnes of Merari in all theyr
ſeruyce in the tabernacle of witneſſe by the hande of
Ithamar the ſonne of Aaron the preaſt.

34 And Moſes and Aaron and the princes of the multitude numbred the ſonnes of the Cahathites in their
35 kynredes and houſſes of theire fathers, from .xxx. yere
and aboue vnto fyftie, all that were able to goo forth in
the hoſte and to do ſeruyce in the tabernacle of witneſſe.
36 And the numbre of them in their kynredes were two
37 thouſande, ſeuen hundred and .L. Theſe are the numbres of the kynredes of the Cahathites, of all that dyd
ſeruyce in the tabernacle of witneſſe, whyche Moſes and

V. 27 et ſcient ſinguli cui debeant oneri mancipari. 28 eruntque ſub manu Ithamar 29 Merari . . . recenſebis 30 omnes qui ingred. ad officium miniſterii ſui & cultū fœd. teſtimonii. 31 Hæc ſunt onera eorū 31 Portabunt 32 ad numerum accipient 35 omnes qui ingred. ad min. tab. fœd.

L. 29 Merari 30 alle die yns heer tugen 32 ſeyn teyl der laſt am gered zu warten 34 Kahathither 35 alle die yns heer tuchten

Aaron dyd numbre at the commaundment of the
Lorde of by the hāde of Moſes.
38 And the ſonnes of Gerſon were numbred in their
39 kynredes and in the houſſes of their fathers, from .xxx
yere vp vnto fyftye, .P. all that were able to goo forth
in the hoſte for to doo ſeruyce in the tabernacle of wit-
40 neſſe. And the numbre of them in their kynredes, and
in the houſſes of their fathers, was two thouſande, ſixe
41 hundred and .xxx. This is the numbre of the kynredes of the ſonnes of Gerſon, of all that dyd ſeruyce
in the tabernacle of witneſſe, which Moſes and Aaron
dyd numbre at the commaundement of the Lorde.
42 And the kynredes of the ſonnes of Merari were
numbred in their kynredes and in the houſes of their
43 fathers, from .xxx. yere vp vnto fyftie. all that were
able to goo forth with the hoſte, to doo ſeruice in ỷ
44 tabernacle of witneſſe. And the numbre of them was
in theyr kynredes, thre thouſande and two hundred.
45 This is the numbre of the kynredes of ỷ ſonnes of
Merari, whiche Moſes and Aaron numbred at the byd-
dynge of the Lorde, by ỷ hande of Moſes.
46 The whole ſumme which Moſes, Aaron and the
lordes of Iſraell numbred amonge the leuites in their
47 kynredes and houſholdes of their fathers, from .xxx
yere vpp vnto .L. euery man to doo his office and ſeruyce and to bere his burthen in the tabernacle of wit-
48 neſſe: was .viii. thouſande, fyue hundred ād .Lxxx
49 which they numbred at the commaundement of the
Lorde by the honde of Moſes euery man vnto his ſeruyce
and burthen: as [Fo. XI.] the Lorde commaunded
Moſes.

V. 38 Gerſon 39 omnes qui ingred. vt min. in tab. fœd. 41 populus Gerſonitarum 42 Merari 43 omnes qui ingred. ad explēdos ritus tab. fœd. 47 ingredientes ad miniſterium tabernaculi & onera portanda

L. 38 Gerſon 39 alle die yns heer tuchten 42 Merari 43 alle die yns heer tuchten 49 zu ſeynem ampt vnd laſt

The . fyſte Chapter.

1 AND the Lorde ſpake vnto Moſes
2 ſayenge: commaunde the childern of Iſrael that they put
out of the hoſte, all the lepers
and all that haue yſſues and all that are
3 defyled apon the deed, whether they be
males or females ye ſhall put them out
of the hoſte, that they defyle not the tentes
4 amōge which I dwell. And the childern
of Iſrael dyd ſo, and put them out of the hoſte: euen as the
Lorde cōmaunded Moſes, ſo dyd the childern of Iſrael.
5, 6 And the Lorde ſpake vnto Moſes ſayenge: ſpeake
vnto the childern of Iſrael: whether it be man or
woman, whē they haue ſynned any maner of ſynne
which a man doeth wherewith a man treſpaſeth agenſt
the Lorde, ſo that the ſoule hath done amyſſe:
7 then they ſhall knowlege their ſynnes
which they haue done, and reſtore a gayne
the hurte that they haue done in the hole,
and put the fyſte parte of it moare there-
8 to, and geue it vnto him whom he hath
treſpaſed agenſte. But and yf he that
maketh the amendes have no man to
doo it to, then the amendes that is
made ſhalbe the Lordes and the preaſtes,
beſyde the ram of the attonementoffer-
ynge where with he maketh an attonemēt
9 for hymſelfe .P. And all heueofferynges
of all the halowed thinges which the childern of

M. C. S. *Who they be that ought to be caſt out of the hoſte. The knowlegynge of ſynne. The cleanſyng of ſynne done of ignoraunce. The lawe of the fyrſt frutes & of gelouſye.*

knowlege, *acknowledge, confeſs*

in the hole, *in the whole,* i. e. *the principal*

Yf ye haue false gotten goodes & no mā to reſtore it vnto, then bringe it vnto ỹ pope ād he will diſpēce with it.

M. 3 amōge which ye dwell.

V. 2 leproſum, & qui ſemine fluit 3 cum habitauerint vobiſcum. 8 excepto ariete 9 Omnes quoque primitiæ

L. 2 alle die eytter fluſſe haben 3 darynnen ich vnter yhnen wone 6 hat die ſeel eyn ſchuld auff yhr 7 verſunen mit der ſumma 8 prieſter, ausgenomen den widder

M. M. N. 6 This text is to be vnderſtāded of ſoche treſpaces, wherwith we hurt oure neybours in worldly goodes (as they cal thē) & therfore muſt the hurt be reſtored and the fyſth parte moare therto: If the partye remayned not to whom the reſtitucyon was due, ner any of his leafull heares, then muſt it be the preaſtes wages, whiche at that tyme had no nother lyuehode.

Iſrael brynge vnto the preaſte, ſhalbe the preaſtes, and
10 euery mans halowed thinges ſhalbe his awne, but what
ſoeuer any man geueth the preaſt, it ſhalbe the preaſtes.
11, 12 And the Lorde ſpake vnto Moſes ſayenge: ſpeake
vnto the childern of Iſraell and ſaye vnto them.
Yf any mans wyfe goo a ſyde and treſpaſe agaynſt
13 hym, ſo that another man lye with her fleſhely and
the thynge be hydd from the eyes of hir huſbonde and
is not come to lighte that ſhe is defyled (for there is
no witneſſe agenſt her) in as moche as ſhe was not taken
14 with the maner, and the ſprete of gelouſye
cometh apon him and he is gelouſe ouer
his wife and ſhe defyled, Or happely the ſprete of
gelouſye cometh apon him, and he is gelouſe ouer hys
15 wyfe ād ſhe yet vndefyled. Thē let hyr huſbonde
bringe her vnto the preaſte and brynge an offerynge
for her: the tenthe parte of an Epha of barlye meele,
but ſhall poure none oyle there vnto, nor put frankencens thereon: for it is an offerynge of gelouſye, and an
offerynge that maketh remembraunce of ſynne.

with the maner, *in the act*

16 And let the preaſt brynge her and ſett her before the
17 Lorde, and let him take holy water in an erthen veſſell
& of the duſt that is in ẏ flore of the habytacyon, and
18 put it in to the [Fo. XII.] water. And the preaſt ſhall
ſet the wyfe before the Lorde and vncouer
hir heed, and put the memoryall of the
offerynge in hyr handes whiche is the
gelouſye offerynge, and ẏ preaſt ſhall haue bytter and
19 curſynge water in his hande, and he ſhall
coniure her and ſhall ſaye vnto her. Yf

wyfe, *woman* vv. 22, 25, 31 & xxv, 6

coniure, *adjure*

V. 13 hoc maritus deprehendere nō quiuerit, ſed latet adulterium . . . inuenta in ſtupro 14 polluta eſt, vel falſa ſuſpicione appetitur 15 ſacrificium zelotypiæ eſt, & oblatio inueſtigans adulterium. 18 ſacrif. recordationis, & oblationem zelotypiæ . . . aquas amariſſimas, in quibus cum execratione maledicta congeſſit.

L. 14 eyffergeyſt entzundet yhn 15 eyn eyffer opffer vnd eyn rüge opffer, das miſſethat rüget. 18 bitter verflucht waſſer

M. M. N. 14 The hole lawe of gelouſie ſemeth to be a feare & a certen nourtour of wyues that they ſhulde be obediēt to their huſbādes, chaſte, manerly & faythfull, and ſoche as geue no occaſiō to be ſuſpect: & therto ſerued thys lawe whyle it kept thē vnder & gaue thē no licēs to rēne at large wherby they might haue come in ſome ſuſpect & ſo haue come to thys greate ſhame before the congregacyon.

no man haue lyen wyth the nether haſte gone aſyde,
and defyled thy ſelfe behynde thy huſbonde, then haue
thou no harme of this bytter curſynge water.
20 But and yf thou haſt gone aſyde behynde thyne
huſbonde and art defyled and ſome other man hath
21 lyen with the beſyde thyne huſbonde (and let the
preaſte coniure her with the coniuracyon of the curſe
and ſaye vnto her.) the Lorde make the a curſe and a
coniuracyon amonge thy people: ſo that the Lorde
22 make thy thye rotte, and thy bely ſwell and thys
bytter curſynge water goo in to the bowels of the, that
thy bely ſwell and thy thye rotte, and the wyfe ſhall
ſaye Amen Amen.
23 And the preaſt ſhall wrytte this curſe in a byll and
24 waſſhe it out in the bytter water. And when the curſ-
25 ynge water ys yn her that it is bytter, then let the
preaſt take the parentſyofferynge out of the wyfes hande,
and waue it before the Lorde, and brynge it vnto the
26 altare: and he ſhall take an hande- .P. full off the
memoryall offerynge and burne it apon the alter, and
27 then make her dryncke the water and when he hath
made her dryncke the water. Yf ſhe be defyled and
haue treſpaſed agenſt her huſbond, then ſhall the curſynge water goo in to her and be ſo bitter, ẏ hir bely
ſhall ſwell and hir thye ſhall rotte, & ſhe ſhalbe a curſe
28 amonge hir people. And yf ſhe be not defyled but is
cleane, then ſhe ſhall haue no harme, but that ſhe
maye conceaue.
29 This is the lawe of gelouſye, when a wyfe goeth a
30 ſyde behynde hyr huſbonde ād is defyled, or when the

V. 19 ſi nō polluta es deſerto mariti thoro . . amariſſimæ, in quas maledicta congeſſi 20 altero viro, 21 his maledictionibus ſubiacebis . . tumens vterus tuus diſrumpatur. 23 congeſſit 24 & dabit ei bibere. Quas cum exhauſerit, 25 tollet ſacerdos 26 & ſic potū det mulieri 27 mulier in maledictionem & in exemplū omni populo.

L. 21 ſetze dich zum fluch vnd zum ſchwur . . bauch berſten laſſe 22 deyn bauch berſte 24 das yhr bitter wirt 27 ynn ſie gehen vnd ſie verbittern . . berſten 31 weyb ſoll ſeyn miſſethat tragen.

M. M. N. 22 Amen is an Hebrew word & ſygnifyeth euen ſo be it, or be it faſt and ſewer, approuynge & alowing the ſentēce going before: and when it is doubled it augmenteth the confyrmacyon, as in many pſalms & Iohn .v. & .vi.

ſpirite of gelouſye cometh apon a man, ſo that he is
gelouſe ouer his wife: then he ſhall bringe her before
the Lorde, and the preaſt ſhall miniſtre all this lawe
31 vnto her, & the man ſhalbe giltleſſe, & the wyfe ſhall
bere hir ſynne.

ℂ The .VI. Chapter.

M.C.S. The lawe of them that toke vpon them abſtynence. The maner of bleſſyng the people.

1 AND the Lorde ſpake vnto Mo-
2 ſes ſaynge: ſpeake vnto ẏ
childrē of Iſrael & ſaye vnto
them: when ether man or
woman appoynteth to vowe
a vowe of abſtinence for to abſtene vnto
3 the Lorde, he ſhall abſtene from wyne and ſtronge
drynke, and ſhall drycke no vynegre of wyne or of
ſtronge drynke, nor ſhal drynke what ſoeuer is preſſed
out of grapes: & ſhal eate no freſh grapes nether yet
4 dry- [Fo. XIII.] ed, as lōge as his abſtinēce ēdureth.
Moreouer he ſhall eate nothyng ẏ is made of the vyne
tre, no not ſo moch as ẏ cornels or the
huſke of the grape.

appoynteth, *reſolveth*

cornels, *kernels*

5 And as longe as the vowe of his abſtinēce endureth,
there ſhall no raſure nor ſheres come apon his heed,
vntill his dayes be out which he faſteth vnto the Lorde,
and he ſhalbe holy and ſhall let the lockes of his heer
6 growe. As longe as he abſteneth vnto the Lorde he

V. 2 vt ſanctificentur, & ſe voluerint domino conſecrare 3 a vino, & omni quod inebriare poteſt

L. 2 eyn zucht gelubd, das er dem herrn zuchtet 3 weyns vnd ſtarcks getrencks

M. M. N. 2 Here it appereth what a *vowe* is after the olde teſtament, whyche was a fygure of the vowe that a Chriſtē man ought to do, geuyng & dedicatinge hymſelfe to God: as it is ſpoken Roma. xii. a.

L. M. N. 2 Auff Ebreiſch heyſt diſe zucht *Neſer* vnd der ſie helt heyſt *Naſir*, wilchem nach auch vnſer herr Iheſus Chriſtus *Naſarenus* heyſt, vnd er der rechte Naſir iſt, weyl wir aber keyn deutſch wort drauff haben muſſen wyrs die weyl zucht vnd Naſir nennen. Denn auff deutſch ſagen wyr von ſolchen leuiten. Er zuchtet alſo theur etc.

7 ſhall come at no deed bodye: he ſhall not make him
ſelfe vncleane at the deeth of his father, mother,
brother or ſyſter. for the abſtinēce of his God is
8 apon his heed. And therfore as longe as his abſtynence laſteth, he ſhalbe holy vnto the Lorde.

9 And yf it fortune that any man by chaunce dye
ſodenly before him, and defyle the heed of his abſtinēce, then muſt he ſhaue his heed the daye of his
clēſynge: euen the ſeuenth daye he ſhall ſhaue it.
10 And the eyght daye he ſhall brynge .ii. turtels or .ii
yonge pigeons to the preaſt, vnto ẏ dore of ẏ taber-
11 nacle of witneſſe And ẏ preaſt ſhall offer the one for
a ſynofferynge and the other for a burntofferynge &
make an atonement for him, as concernynge that
he ſynned apon the deed, and ſhall alſo halowe his
12 heed the ſame daye and he ſhall abſtene vnto the
Lorde the tyme of his abſtinencye, and ſhall brynge
a lambe of an yere olde for a treſpace offerynge: but
the dayes ẏ .P. were before are loſt, becauſe his abſti-
13 nence was defyled. ¶ This is the lawe of the ab-
ſteyner, when the tyme of his abſtinēce is out. he ſhalbe broughte vnto ẏ dore of
14 ẏ tabernacle of witneſſe & he ſhall brynge his offerynge
vnto ẏ Lord: an he lābe of a yere olde with out blemyſh for a burntofferynge & a ſhe lambe of a yere olde
without blemyſh for a ſynofferynge, a ram without
15 blemyſh alſo for a peaſeofferynge, & a baſket of ſwete
breed of fyne floure myngled with oyle & wafers of
ſwete bred anoyntyd with oyle with meatofferynges
ād drynkofferynges that longe thereto.

is out, *completed*

16 And the preaſt ſhall brynge him before ẏ Lorde &
17 offer his ſynofferynge & his burntofferynge, & ſhall
offer ẏ ram for a peaſeofferynge vnto ẏ Lorde with

V. 7 cōſecratio dei ſui 9 in eadem die . . & rurſum ſeptima. 11 ſuper mortuo

L. 7 Denn die zucht ſeyns Gottis 9 das iſt am ſiebenden tage 11 an eym todten 14 tödopffer (17, 18.)

M. M. N. 7 To haue *the abſtynence of God* vpon his heed is, to ſhew a token of refuſing the care of bodely thynges by that he ſetteth not by the hayre of hys heed, or by the trymmynge of hys buſſhe or bearde, which thīg the world ſo greatly eſteameth.

the baſket of ſwete brede, ãd the preaſt ſhall offer alſo
18 his meat offerynge & his drynckofferynge. And ẏ
abſteyner ſhall ſhaue his heed in ẏ dore of ẏ tabernacle
of witneſſe ãd ſhall take the heer of his ſober heed &
put it in ẏ fyre which is vnder the peaſeofferynge.
19 Then the preaſt ſhall take the ſodden ſhulder of ẏ
ram ãd one ſwete cake out of ẏ baſket & one ſwete
wafer alſo ãd put them in the hãde of the abſteyner
20 after he hath ſhauē his abſtinēce of, & the preaſt ſhall
waue them vnto the Lorde, which offerynge ſhalbe
holy vnto the preaſt with ẏ wauebreſt and heue
ſhulder: & then the abſteyner maye drynke wyne.
21 This is the lawe of the abſtey- [Fo. XIIII.] ner which
hath vowed his offerynge vnto ẏ Lorde for his abſtynence, beſydes that his hãde can gete And acordyng
to the vowe which he vowed, euen ſo he muſt doo in
the lawe of his abſtinence.

22, 23 And the Lorde talked with Moſes ſayenge: ſpeake
vnto Aaron and his ſonnes ſayẽge: of this wiſe ye ſhall
bleſſe the childern of Yſrael ſaynge vnto them.

24 The lorde bleſſe the and kepe the.
25 The lorde make his face ſhyne apon
the & be mercyfull vnto the.
26 The lorde lifte vpp his countenaunce
27 apō the, and geue the peace For ye
ſhall put my name apon the childern of
Yſrael, that I maye bleſſe them.

Here of ye ſe that Aarō, when he lift vpp his hande and bleſſed the people, was not dumme as oure biſſhopes be.

V. 18 radetur Nazaræus 20 Suſceptaque rurſum ab eo. . . ſacerdotis erunt, ſicut pectuſculum quod ſeparari iuſſum eſt, & femur. 21 exceptis his quæ inuenerit manus eius 25 Oſtendat dom. faciem, 26 Conuertat dom. vultū ſuum ad te

L. 18 Vnd ſoll dem zuchter . . . beſcheren 19 nach dem er ſeyn zucht beſchoren hat 20 zu der Webebruſt vnd der Hebeſchuldern 21 auſſer dem das ſeyne hand erwerben kan 25 erleuchte ſeyn angeſicht 26 hebe ſeyne angeſicht auff dich

M. M. N. 25 *To make his face to ſhijne* is to geue a token of his louyng kyndenes.

The .VII. Chapter.

1 AND when Moſes had full ſett vp
the habitacion and anoynted
it ād ſanctifyed it and all
the apparell thereof, and had
anoynted & ſanctifyed yͤ alter alſo and all

M.C.S. The offryng of the Lordes and heades of Iſraell when the tabernacle was ſett vp.

2 the veſſels there of: then the prynces of Yſrael heedes
ouer the houſſes of their fathers which were the lordes
3 of the trybes that ſtode ād numbred, offered ād broughte
their giftes before the Lorde ſixe couered charettes
and .xii. oxen: two and two a charet and an oxe euery
man, and they broughte them before the habitacion.
4, 5 .¶. And the Lorde ſpake vnto Moſes ſaynge take
it of them and let them be to do the ſeruyce of yͤ tabernacle of witneſſe, and geue them vnto the leuites,
6 euery man acordynge vnto his office And Moſes toke
the charettes ād the oxen, & gaue them vnto the leu-
7 ites: .ii. charettes and .iiii. oxen he gaue vnto the ſonnes
8 of Gerſon acordynge vnto their office. And .iiii. charettes and eyght oxen he gaue vnto yͤ ſonnes of Merari
acordynge vnto their offices, vnder the handes of
9 Ithamar the ſonne of Aaron the preaſt. But vnto the
ſonnes of Cahath he gaue none, for the office that
perteyned to them was holy, & therfore they muſt
bere vppon ſhulders.
10 And the princes offered vnto the dedycatynge of
the alter in the daye yͤ it was anoynted, and brought
11 their giftes before the alter And the Lorde ſayde vnto
Moſes: let the prīces brynge their offerynges, euery
daye one prynce, vnto the dedicatynge of the alter.

V. 2 principes Iſrael & capita familiarum, quæ erant per ſingulas tribus præfecti eorum qui numerati fuerant 3 duo duces 7 iuxta id quod habebant neceſſarium. 8 Merari ſecundum officia & cultum ſuum, 9 Caath non dedit plauſtra & boues: quia in ſanctuario ſeruiunt 10 obtulerunt duces

L. 2 die heubtleut Iſrael, die die vbirſten waren ynn yhrer veter hauſe. Denn ſie waren die heubtleut vnter den geſchlechten vnd ſtunden vber den getzeleten. 3 zween heubtleut 7 nach yhrem ampt 8 nach yhrem ampt 9 gab er nicht, darumb das ſie eyn heylig ampt auff yhn hatten 10 Vnd die heubtleut

12 He that offered his offerynge ẏͤ firſt daye, was Naheſſon the ſonne of Aminadab of the trybe of Iuda.
13 And his offerynge was: a ſyluer charger, of an hundred
and .xxx. ſicles weight: and a ſyluer boule of .Lxx
ſicles of the holy ſicle, both of them full of fyne whetē
14 floure myngled with oyle for a meat offerynge: & a
15 ſpone of .x. ſicles of golde full of cens: & an oxe, a ram
16 ād a lambe of a yere olde for burnt offerynges, and an
17 he goote for a ſynnofferyn- [Fo. XV.] ge: and for peaſe
offerynges .ii. oxen .v. rammes .v. he gootes and .v
lambes of a yere olde. and this was the gifte of
Naheſſon the ſonne of Aminadab.
18 The ſeconde daye, dyd Nathaneel offer, ẏͤ ſonne of
19 Zuar, captayne ouer Yſachar. And his offerynge
which he broughte was: a ſyluer charger of an hundred
& .xxx. ſicles weyght, and a ſyluern boule of .Lxx
ſicles, of ẏͤ holy ſicle: [* and both full of fyne floure
20 myngled with oyle for a meatofferynge:] and a golden
21 ſpone of .x. ſicles full of cens: and an oxe, a ram and
a lambe of a yere olde for burntofferynges: [22 see foot
23 note**] ād for peaſeofferynges .ii. oxen .v. rammes
v. he gootes and .v. lambes of one yere olde. And
this was ẏͤ offerynge of Nathaneel the ſonne of
Zuar.
24 The thyrde daye, Eliab the ſonne of Helon the
cheſeſt amonge the childern of Zabulon, brought his
25 offerynge. And his offerynge was, a ſyluer charger
of an hundred and .xxx. ſicles weyghte, and a ſyluern
boule of .Lxx. ſicles of the holy ſicle, & both full of
fyne floure myngled with oyle for a meat offerynge:
26, 27 and a golden ſpone of .x. ſicles full of cēs: and an
oxe and a ram and a lambe of a yere olde for burntof-
28, 29 ferynges, and an he goote for a ſynofferynge: and
for peaſeofferynges .ii. oxen .v. rammes .v. he gootes

M. 15 & an bullock 19 and both full of fyne floure myngled with oyle for a meatofferynge: 21 a bullock

M. M. N. 12 The offerynge of Naheſſon. 18 The offrynge of Nathanael. 24 The offrynge of Eliab.

---

* The passage in brackets, omitted by Tyndale, has been supplied from *Matthew's Bible*.

** Tyndale and Matthew omit v. 22, which by analogy of v. 16 may be supplied thus: and an he goote for a synofferynge.

and .v. lambes of one yere olde. And this was the
offerynge of Eliab the ſonne of Helon.
30 The fourt daye, Elizur the ſonne of Sedeur, chefe
lorde amonge the childern of Ru- .P. ben, broughte his
31 offerynge. And his gifte was: a ſyluer charger of an
hundred and .xxx. ſicles weyghte, and a ſyluern boule
of .Lxx. ſicles of the holy ſicle, & both full of fyne
32 floure myngled with oyle for a meatofferynge: and a
33 golden ſpone of .x. ſicles full of cens: and an oxe, a
34 ram & a lambe of a yere olde for burntofferynges, and
35 an he goote for a ſynofferynge: and for peaſeofferynges
ii. oxen .v. rammes .v. he gootes and .v. lambes of one
yere olde. And this was the offerynge of Elizur the
ſonne of Sedeur.
36 The fyfth daye, Selumiel yͤ ſonne of Zuri Sadai,
chefe lorde amonge the childern of Simeon, offered.
37 whoſe gifte was: a ſyluer charger of an hundred & .xxx
ſicles weyghte: and a ſyluer boule of .Lxx. ſicles of the
holy ſicle: ād both full of fyne floure myngled with oyle
38 for a meatofferynge: & a golden ſpone of .x. ſicles full
39 of cens. And an oxe, a ram ād a lābe of a yere olde
40 for burntofferynges, ād an he goote for a ſynofferynge:
41 & for peaſeofferīges .ii. oxen .v. rāmes .v. he gootes
ād .v. lābes of a yere olde. And this was the offerynge
of Selumiel the ſonne of Zuri Sadai.
42 The ſixte daye, Eliaſaph yͤ ſonne of Deguel the
chefe lorde amonge the childern of Gad, offered.
43 whoſe gifte was: a ſyluer charger of an hundred and
xxx. ſicles weyghte: and a ſyluern boule of .Lxx. ſicles
of the holy [Fo. XVI.] ſicle: & both full of fyne floure
44 myngled with oyle for a meatofferynge: and a golden
45 ſpone of .x. ſicles full of cens. And an oxe, a ram ād a
46 lambe of a yere olde for burntofferynges, & an he goote
47 for a ſynofferynge: And for peaſeofferynges .ii. oxen .v
rammes .v. he gootes and .v. lābes of one yere olde.
And this was the offerynge of Eliaſaph the ſonne of
Deguel.

M. 33 a bullock 39 a bullock
M. M. N. 30 The offrynge of Elizur. 36 The offrynge of Selumiel. 42 The offrynge of Eliaſaph.

48 The ſeuenth daye, Eliſama the ſonne of Amiud, ỹ
49 chefe lorde of ỹ childern of Ephraim, offered. And his
gifte was a ſyluern charger of an hundred and .xxx. ſicles
weyght: ād a ſyluern boule of .Lxx. ſicles of the holy
ſicle: ād both full of fyne floure myngled with oyle for
50 a meatofferynge: and a golden ſpone of .x. ſicles, full of
51 cens. And an oxe, a ram and a lambe of a yere olde
52 for burntofferynges, ād an he goote for a ſynofferynge:
53 and for peaſeofferynges .ii. oxen .v. rammes .v. he
gootes & .v. lambes of a yere olde. And this was ỹ
offerynge of Eliſama the ſonne of Amiud.
54 The .viii. daye, offered Gamaliel the ſonne of Peda-
55 zur, the chefe lorde of the childern of Manaſſe. And
his gifte was: a ſylueren charger of an hundred and
xxx. ſicles weyght: and a ſyluern boule of .Lxx. ſicles
of the holy ſicle: ād both full of fyne floure myngled
56 with oyle for a meatofferynge: & a golden ſpone of .x
57 ſycles, full of cēs. And an oxe, a ram .P. and a lambe
58 of a yere olde for burntofferynges, and an he goote for
59 a ſynofferynge: and for peaſeofferynges .ii. oxen .v
rammes, fyue he gootes and fyue lābes of a yere olde.
And this was the offerynge of Gamaliel the ſonne of
Peda zur.
60 The .ix. daye, Abidan ỹ ſonne of Gedeoni ỹ chefe
61 lord amōge ỹ childern of Ben Iamin offered. And his
gifte was: a ſyluern charger of an hundred and .xxx
ſicles weyght: & a ſyluern boule of .Lxx. ſicles of the
holy ſicle, and both full of fyne floure myngled with
62 oyle for a meatofferynge: and a golden ſpone of .x. ſicles,
63 full of cens. and an oxe, a ram and a lambe of one
64 yere olde for burntofferynges: & an he goote for a
65 ſynofferynge: and for peaſeofferynges .ii. oxen .v. rammes
v. he gootes & .v. lambes of one yere olde. And this
was the offerynge of Abidan the ſonne of Gedeoni.
66 The .x. daye, Ahieſer the ſonne of Ammi Sadai,
67 chefe lorde amōge ỹ childern of Dan offered. And his

M. 51 a bullock 57 a bullock 63 a bullock
M. M. N. 48 The offerynge of Eliſama. 54 The offerynge of Gamaliel. 60 The offryng of Abidan. 66 The offryng of Ahiezer.

gifte was: a ſyluern charger of an hundred and .xxx
ſycles weyght: a ſyluern boule of ſeuentye ſicles of
the holy ſycle: and both full of fyne floure myngled
68 with oyle for a meatofferynge: and a golden ſpone of .x
69 ſicles full of cens: and an oxe, a rā and a lambe of a
70 yere olde for burntofferynges, and an he goote for
71 a ſynofferynge: and for peaſeofferynges .ii. oxen .v
rammes, fyue he gootes and fyue lābes of a yere olde.
And [Fo. XVII.] this was the offrynge of Ahieſer the
ſonne of Ammi Sadai.

72 The .xi. daye, Pagiel the ſonne of Ochran the chefe
73 Lorde amonge the childern of Aſſer offered: And his
gifte was: a ſyluerē charger of an hundred and .xxx
ſycles weyghte: a ſylueren boule of .Lxx. ſycles of the
holye ſycle and both full of fyne floure myngled with
74 oyle for a meateoffrynge: and a golden ſpone of .x. ſycles,
75 full of cens. And an oxe, a ram and a lambe of one
76 yere olde for burntofferinges: and an he goote for a
77 ſynneofferynge: ād for peaceofferynges: two oxen,
fyue rammes .v. he gootes and .v. lambes of one yere
olde. And this was the offerynge of Pagiel ỹ ſonne
of Ochran.

78 The .xii. daye, Ahira the ſonne of Enan, chefe lorde
79 amonge the childern of Nephtali offered. And his
gifte was: a ſylueren charger of an hundred and .xxx
ſycles weyghte: a ſylueren boule of .Lxx. ſycles of the
holye ſycle, both full of fyne floure myngled with oyle
80 for a meatofferynge: and a golden ſpone of twentye
81 ſycles, full of cens. And an oxe, a ram and a lambe
82 of one yere olde for burntofferynges: and an he goote
83 for a ſynneofferinge: and for peaceofferynges, two oxen
v. rāmes .v. he gootes and .v. lambes of one yere olde.
And this was the offerynge of Ahira, the ſonne of
Enan.

84 Of this maner was the dedicacyon of the .P. alter,
when it was anoynted: vnto the whiche was broughte of

M. 69 a bullock 75 a bullock 81 a bullock
T. 72 Phegiel
M. M. T. 72 The offryng of Pagiell, or Phegiell. 78 The offryng of Ahira.

the prynces of Iſrael .xii. chargers of ſyluer .xii. ſyluern
85 boules and .xii. ſpones of golde: euery charger con-
taynynge an hundred and .xxx. ſycles of ſyluer, and
euery boule .Lxx. ſo that all the ſyluer of all the veſſels, was two thouſande and .iiii. hundred ſycles of the
86 holy ſycle. And the .xii. golden ſpones which were
full of cens, contayned ten ſycles a pece of the holy
ſycle: ſo that all the golde of the ſpones, was an hundred and .xx. ſycles.
87 All the oxen that were broughte for the burntoffrynges were .xii. and the rāmes .xii. & the lābes .xii
of a yere olde a pece, with the meateofferynges: with
88 he gootes for ſynne offrynges. And all the oxē of the
peaceofferynges were .xxiiii. the rammes .Lx. the gootes
Lx. and lambes of a yere olde a pece .Lx. & this was
the dedicacion of the alter, after ỷ it was anoynted.
89 And when Moſes was gone in to the tabernacle of
witneſſe to ſpeke with hī, he harde the voyce of one
ſpeakinge vnto him from of the mercyſeate that was
apon the arcke of witneſſe: euen from betwene the two
cherubyns he ſpake vnto him.

¶ The .VIII. Chapter.

[Fo. XVIII.] VIII. Chapter.

1 AND the Lorde ſpake vnto Mo-
2 ſes ſaynge: ſpeake vnto Aaron
and ſaye vnto hym: when thou
putteſt on the lampes ſe that
they lighte all ſeuen apon the forefront
3 of the candelſticke. And Aaron dyd euen

M.C.S. The diſpoſicion and order of the lampes. The forme of the candelſtyck. The cleanſyng and

V. 84 principibus 88 altaris quando vnctum 89 vt conſuleret oraculum . . vnde & loquebatur ei. viii, 2 lucernas, — candelabrum in auſtrali parte erigatur. Hoc igitur præcipe vt lucernæ contra boream eregione reſpiciant ad menſam panum propoſitionis: . . contra eam partem quam candelabrum reſpicit, lucere debebunt.

L. 84 heubtleut 88 nachdem er geſalbet wart. 89 von dannen wart mit yhm geredt.

ſo, and put the lampes apon the forefrõt
of the candelſticke, as the Lorde com-
4 maunded Moſes, and the worke of the candelſticke was of ſtiffe golde: both the ſhaft
and the floures thereof. And accordinge vnto the viſyon whiche the Lorde had ſhewed
Moſes, euen ſo he made the candelſticke.

offryng of the Leuytes. The age of the ſame.

ſtiffe, *solid, beaten*

5, 6 And the Lorde ſpake vnto Moſes ſayenge: take
the leuites from amonge the childern of Iſrael, and
7 clenſe them. And this doo vnto them when thou
clenſeſt them, ſprinckle water of puriſyenge apon them
and make a raſure to runne alonge apon all the fleſhe
of them, and let them waſhe their clothes, and then
8 they ſhall be cleane. And let them take a bollocke
and his meatofferynge, ſyne floure myngled with
oyle: & another bollocke ſhalt thou take to be a
ſynneofferynge.

9 Than brynge the leuites before the tabernacle of
witneſſe and gather the hole multitude of the chyldern
10 of Iſrael together. And bringe the leuites before the
Lorde, and let the childern of Iſrael put their handes
11 apon the leuites. And let Aaron heue the leuites
before the LORDE, for an heueoffe- .P. rynge geuen
of the childern of Iſrael, ãd thẽ let them be appoynted
to wayte apon the ſeruyce of the Lorde.

12 And let the leuites put their handes vpõ the heedes
of the bollockes, and then offer them: the one for a
ſynneofferynge and the other for a burntofferynge vnto
the Lorde, to make an attonement for the leuites.
13 And make the leuites ſtonde before Aaron & hys
ſonnes, and heue them to be a heueofferynge vnto the
14 Lorde. And thou ſhalt ſeparate the leuites, from
amonge the childern of Iſrael, that they be myne:
15 and after that let them goo and do the ſeruice of the

V. 4 iuxta exemplum 7 iuxta hunc ritum . . aqua luſtrationis, et radant omnes pilos carnis 9 omni multitudine 11 vt ſeruiant in miniſterio eius

L. 4 nach dem geſicht 9 gantze gemeyne 11 auf das ſie dienen mugen an dem ampt des Herrn.

L. M. N. 7 *Entſund Waſſer:* Entſunden iſt ſo viel als abſoluiren oder los ſprechen, daher das waſſer damit ſie abſoluirt wurden von ſunden heyſt entſund waſſer.

tabernacle of witnesse. Clense them and waue them,
16 for they are geuen vnto me from amonge the childrē of
Israel: for I haue taken them vnto me for all ẏ firstborne
that opē any matrice amōge the childern of Israel.
17 For all the fyrstborne among the childern of Israel are
myne both man and beest: because the same tyme that I
smote the fyrstborne in the lande of Egipte, I sanctyfyde
18 them for my selfe: and I haue taken the Leuites for all
the fyrstborne amonge the childern of Israel, and haue
19 geuen them vnto Aaron and his sonnes from amonge
the childern of Israel, to doo the seruyce of the childern of Israel in the tabernacle of witnesse and to
make an attonement for the chyldern of Israell, that
there be no plage amonge the childern [Fo. XIX.] of
Ysraell, yf they come nye vnto the sanctuarye
20 And Moses and Aaron and all the congregacion
of the childern of Israel dyd vnto the leuites acordynge
21 vnto all that ẏ Lorde commaunded Moses. And the
leuites purifyed them selues, and wasshed their clothes.
And Aaron waued them before ẏ Lorde, and made
22 an attonement for them to clense them. And after
that they went in to doo their seruyce in the tabernacle
of wytnesse, before Aaron and his sonnes. And acordinge as the Lorde had commaunded Moses as concernynge the leuites, euen so they dyd vnto them.
23, 24 And the Lorde spake vnto Moses sayenge: this
shalbe the maner of the leuites: from .xxv. yere vpp-
warde they shall goo in to wayte vppon the seruyce in
25 the tabernacle of witnesse, and at fyftye they shall ceasse
waytynge apon the seruyce thereof, and shall laboure
26 no moare: but shall ministre vnto their bretheren in
the tabernacle of witnesse, and there wayte, but shall
doo no moare seruyce.

And se that thou doo after this maner vnto the
leuites in their waytynge tymes.

¶ The .IX. Chapter.

V. 15 ingrediantur 16 accepi eos. 17 Ex die quo 19 dono Aaron 22 vt purificati ingrederentur 25 annum ætatis impleuerint

L. 15 hyneyn gehen 16 vnd hab sie myr genomen 19 zum geschencke Aaron 22 Darnach giengen sie hyneyn

.¶. .IX. Chapter.

M.C.S. The eſter or paſſe-ouer offringe of the cleane and vncleane. A cloude couerynge the tabernacle leadeth the hoſte.

1 AND the Lorde ſpake vnto Moſes in the wilderneſſe of Sinai,
in the fyrſte moneth of the
ſeconde yere, after they were
come out of the londe of Egipte ſayeng:
2 let ẏ childern of Iſrael offer Paſſeouer in
3 his ſeaſon: euen the .xiiii. daye of this
moneth at euen they ſhall kepe it in his ſeaſon, accordynge to all the ordinaunces & maners thereof.
4 And Moſes bade the childern of Yſrael that they
5 ſhulde offer Paſſeouer, & they offered Paſſeouer the
xiiii. daye of the firſt moneth at euen in the wilderneſſe of Sinai: and dyd acordinge to all that the Lorde
commaunded Moſes.

6 And it chaunced that certayne men whyche were
defyled with a deed corſe that they myghte not offer
Paſſeouer the ſame daye, came before Moſes and Aaron
7 the ſame daye, and ſayde: we are defyled apon a deed
corſe, wherfore are we kepte backe that we maye not
offer an offerynge vnto the Lorde in the due ſeaſon,
8 amonge the childern of Iſraell? And Moſes ſayde vnto
them: tary, that I maye heare what the Lorde wille
9 commaunde you. And the Lord ſpake vnto Moſes
10 ſayengė: ſpeake vnto the childern of Iſraell and ſaye.
Yf any man amonge you or youre childern after you
be vncleane by the reaſon of a corſe or is in the waye
ferre of, then lett hym offer Paſſeouer vnto ẏ Lorde:
11 the .xiiii. [Fo. XX.] daye of the ſeconde moneth at
euen, and eate it with ſwete bred and ſoure herbes,
12 ād let them leaue none of it vnto the mornynge nor
breake any boone of it. And acordynge to all the
ordinaunce of the Paſſeouer let them offer it.

13 But yf a man be cleane and not let in a iurney, and

V. 5 Qui fecerunt tempore ſuo 7 quare fraudamur vt non vale-amus 11 lactucis agreſtibus

yet was negligent to offer Paſſeouer, the ſame ſoule
ſhall periſh from his people, becauſe he brought not
an offerynge vnto the Lorde in his due ſeaſon: and
14 he ſhall bere his ſynne. And when a ſtraunger dwelleth amonge you and will offer Paſſeouer vnto the
Lorde, accordynge to the ordinaunce of Paſſeouer
and maner thereof ſhall he offre it. And ye ſhall
haue one lawe both for the ſtraunger and for him
that was borne at home in the lande.
15 And the ſame daye that the habitaciō was reered
vpp, a cloude couered it an hye apon the tabernacle
of witneſſe: and at euen there was apon the habitacyon, as it were the ſymilitude of fyre vntyll the
16 mornynge. And ſo it was allwaye, that the cloude
couered it by daye, and the ſymylitude of fyre by
17 nyghte. And when the cloude was taken vpp from
of the tabernacle, then the childern of Iſrael iurneyed:
and where the cloude abode there the childern of
18 Iſrael pitched their tentes. At the mouthe of the
Lorde the childern of Iſraell iurneyed, and at the
mouthe of .P. the Lorde they pitched. And as longe
as the cloude abode apon the habitacion, they laye
19 ſtyll, and when the cloude taryed ſtill apon the habitacion longe tyme, the childern of Iſraell wayted
apon the Lorde and iurneyed not.
20 Yf it chaunced that the cloude abode any ſpace
of tyme apon the habitacion, then they kepte their
tentes at the mouth of the Lorde: and they iurneyed
21 alſo at the commaundement of the Lorde. And yf
it happened that the cloude was apon the habitacion
from euen vnto mornynge and was taken vpp in ẏ

V. 15 quaſi ſpecies ignis 19 in excubiis domini v. 23.

L. 15 ein geſtalt des fewrs v. 16. 19 wartten . . . auff die hutt des Herrn v. 23.

M. M. N. 13 In lyke mān̄er is it with vs in oure *ſpirituall eſter* or *paſſeouer*, who ſoeuer doth not reuerently beleue the redēpcyon of mankynde whyche was thoroulye fyniſhed in offrynge the true lābe chriſt and amendeth not his life, nor turneth frō vyce to vertue in the tyme of this mortal life ſhall not belōge vnto the glory of the reſurreccion, which ſhall be geuen vnto the true worſhippers of chriſt: but ſhall be roted oute frō the companye of the ſaynctes.

mornynge, then they iurneyed. Whether it was by
daye or by nyghte that ẏ cloude was taken vpp, they
22 iurneyed. But when ẏ cloude taryed two dayes or a
moneth or a longe ſeaſon apon the habitacion, as
longe as it taried thereon, the childern of Iſrael
kepte their tentes and iurneyed not. And as ſoone
as the cloude was taken vpp, they iurneyed.
23 At the mouth of the Lorde they reſted, and at the
commaundment of the Lorde they iurneyed. And
thus they kepte the wayte of the Lorde, at the commaundement of the Lorde by the hande of Moſes.

ℭ The .X. Chapter.

M.C.S. The trompettes of ſyluer and the vſe therof. The Iſraelites depart from Sinai. The captaynes of the hoſte are nombred. Hobab refuſeth to go with Moſes.

1 AND the Lorde ſpake vnto Moſes
2 ſayenge: Make the two trompettes of harde ſyluer, that thou
mayſt vſe thē to call the congregacion together, and when [Fo. XXI.]
3 the hoſte ſhall iurney. when they blowe
with them, all the multitude ſhall reſorte
to the, vnto the dore of the tabernacle of
4 witneſſe. Yf but one trumpet blowe only,
then the princes which are heedes ouer the thouſandes of
5 Yſrael ſhall come vnto the. And when ye
trompe the firſt tyme, the hoſtes that lye
6 on the eaſt partes ſhall goo forwarde. And when ye
trōpe the ſeconde tyme, then the hoſtes that lye on ẏ
ſouth ſyde ſhall take their iurney: for they ſhall trompe
7 when they take their iurneyes. And in gatherynge

trompe, *to sound a trumpet*

M. 2 beaten ſyluer

V. 4 principes, & capita multitudinis 6 & iuxta hunc modum reliqui facient vlulantibus tubis in profectionem.

L. 4 vbirſten vber die tauſent ynn Iſrael.

M. M. N. 22 *Two dayes etc.*, after the grekes certayne dayes, a fewe or ſome dayes. x, 4 *To blowe with one trumpet* is, to ſhew the worde of helth ſynglye after the vnytye of the faith.

the congregacion together, ye ſhall blowe and not
8 trompe. And the ſonnes of Aaron the preaſtes ſhall
blowe the trompettes and ſhall haue them and it ſhalbe a lawe vnto you for euer & amonge youre childern
after you.
9 And when ye ſhall goo to warre in youre londe
agenſt youre enymies that vexe you, ye ſhall trompe
with the trompettes and ye ſhalbe remēbred before the
10 Lorde youre God and ſaued from youre enymies. Alſo
when ye be mery in youre feſt dayes and *Hēce oure*
in the firſtdayes of youre monethes, ye *belles were ſett.*
ſhall blowe the trompettes ouer youre burnt ſacrifices
and peaſeofferynges, that it maye be a remēbraūce of
you before youre God. I am the lorde youre God.
11 And it came to paſſe the .xx. daye of the ſeconde
moneth in ẏ ſeconde yere, that the cloude was take
12 vpp from of the habitacion of .P. witneſſe. And the
childern of Iſrael toke their iurney out of the deſerte
of Sinai, and the cloude reſted in ẏ wilderneſſe of Parā.
13 And ẏ firſt toke their iurney at the mouth of the Lorde,
14 by the honde of Moſes: euen the ſtanderte of ẏ hoſte
of Iuda remoued firſt with their armies, whoſe captayne
15 was Naheſſon ẏ ſonne of Aminadab. And ouer the hoſte
of ẏ trybe of the childern of Iſachar, was Nathaneel
16 the ſonne of zuar. And ouer the hoſte of ẏ trybe of
the childern of Zabulon, was Eliab the ſonne of Helon.
17 And the habitacion was taken doune: and the ſonnes
of Gerſon and Merari went forth bearynge the
habitacion
18 Then the ſtandert of the hoſte of Ruben went forth
with their armies, whoſe captayne was Elizur the
19 ſonne of Sedeur. And ouer the hoſte of the trybe of

M. 13 they firſt

V. 7 ſimplex tubarum clangor erit, & non conciſe vlulabunt. 10 canetis tubis 13 Moueruntque caſtra primi

L. 7 blaſen vnd nicht drometen.

M. M. N. 7 *Blowe and not trompe:* The cōmen people muſt they teache playnely, and with oute curioſitye. 9 *Trompe with the trompettes:* In tyme of warre muſt they trumpe with trumpetes: which ſygnifyeth when moſte neade is at hande then muſt faithe prayer and lyftyng vp of the mynde to God be cheſely exercyſed.

ẏ childern of Simeon, was Selumiel the ſonne [of
20 Suri ſaddai. And ouer the hoſte of the tribe of the
chyldren of Gad was Eliaſaph the ſonne]* of Deguel.
21 Then the Cahathites went forwarde and bare the
holy thinges, and the other dyd ſet vp the habitacion
agenſt they came.

22 Then the ſtandert of the hoſte of the childern of
Ephraim went forth with their armies, whoſe captayne
23 was Eliſama the ſonne of Amiud. And ouer the hoſte
of the trybe of the ſonnes of Manaſſe, was Samaleel the
24 ſonne of Peda zur. And ouer the hoſte of the trybe of
the ſonnes of Ben Iamin, was Abi- [Fo. XXII.] dan the
ſonne of Gedeoni.

25 And hynmoſt of all the hoſte came the ſtandert of
the hoſte of the childern of Dan with their armies:
whoſe captayne was, Ahiezar the ſonne of Ammi Sadai.
26 And ouer the hoſte of the trybe of the childern of
27 Aſſer, was Pagiel the ſonne of Ochran. And ouer the
hoſte of the trybe of the childern of Naphtali, was
28 Ahira the ſonne of Enan, of this maner were the
iurneyes of the childern of Iſrael, with their armies
when they remoued.

29 And Moſes ſayde vnto Hobab the ſonne of Raguel
the Madianyte, Moſes father lawe: we goo vnto the
place of which the Lorde ſayde I will geue it you.
Goo with us ād we will doo the good, for the Lorde
30 hath promyſed goode vnto Iſrael. And he ſayde vnto

M. 19 Salamiel ẏ ſonne of Suri ſaddai. And ouer the hoſte of the tribe of the chyldren of Gad was Eliaſaph the ſonne of 23 Gamaliel 29 father in lawe

V. 21 Tamdiu tabernaculum portabatur, donec venirent ad erectionis locum.

L. 21 vnd richteten auff die wonung bis ſie hyneyn kamen. 29 das beſte bey dyr thun

M. M. N. 26 *Pagiel:* or phegiell. 29 *Hobab* is the ſame which before is called Iethro euē as Salamō is called ī ſome places Idida, & as Oſias is alſo called Azarias. He was the ſonne of Raguell & father to zephora Moſes wyfe: all be it that in the ſecond of exod. Raguell be called her father, not becauſe he was ſo in deade but becauſe he was her fathers father: which maner of ſpeakyng is not a fewe tymes vſed in the ſcrypture.

---

* The passage in brackets omitted by Tyndale, has been supplied from ***Matthew's Bible.***

him: I will not: but will goo to myne awne londe and
31 to my kynred. And Moses sayde oh nay, leaue us not,
for thou knowest where is best for us to pitche in the
32 wildernesse: and thou shalt be oure eyes And yf thou
goo with us, loke what goodnesse the Lorde sheweth
apon us, the same we will shewe apon the
33 And they departed from the mount of the Lorde
iii. dayes iurney, and the arcke of the testament of the
Lorde went before .P. them in the .iii. dayes iurney
34 to serche out a restynge place for them. And the
cloude of the Lorde was ouer them by daye, when they
went out of the tentes.
35 And when the arcke went forth, Moses sayde Ryse
vp Lorde and lat thine enemies be scatered, and let
36 them that hate the flee before the. And when the
arcke rested, he sayde returne Lorde, vnto the many
thousandes of Ysrael.

The .XI. Chapter.

1 AND the people waxed vnpacient,
and it displeased the eares of
the Lorde. And when the
Lorde herde it he was wroth,
and the fyre of the Lorde burnt amonge
them and consumed the vttermost of
2 the hoste. And the people cried vnto
Moses, & he made intercession vnto the
3 Lorde and the fyre qwenched. And they
called ẏ name of the place Tabera be-

M.C.S. *The people murmureth & is punyshedwith fyre. They loothe māna. The murmuryng and waueryng fayth of Moses. The Lorde dyuydeth the burden of Moses to seuentye*

M. 1 complayned

V. 32 quicquid optimum fuerit 36 ad multitudinem exercitus Israel. xi, 2 absorptus est ignis.

L. 30 meyn land zu meyner freuntschafft 36 zu der menge der tausent Israel. xi, 2 verschwand das feur

M. M. N. 31 *Eyes:* or gyde. xi, 1 *Complained:* Or waxed discontent, some tyme dyd wekedly. 3 *Thaberah* signyfyeth, kyndlyng inflamyng or fyryng.

cause the fyre of the Lorde burnt amonge
them.
4 And the rascall people
that was amonge them fell
a lustynge, And the chil-
dern of Ysrael also went to
and wepte and sayde: who
5 shall geue us flesh to eate? we remembre
the fysh which we shulde eate in Egipte for noughte,
and of the Cucumbers and melouns, lekes, onyouns
6 and garleke. But now oure soules ar dryed a waye,
for oure eyes loke on nothynge els, saue apon Manna.
7 The Manna was as it had bene corian- [Fo. XXIII.]
8 der seed, and to see to lyke Bedellion. And ỷ people
went aboute and gathered it, & groũde it in milles, or
bett it in morters and boke it in pannes
and made cakes of it. And the tast of it was like vnto
9 the tast of an oylecake And when the dewe fell aboute
ỷ hoste in the nyghte, the Manna fell therewithe.
10 And when Moses herde the people wepe in their
housholdes euery man in the dore of his tent, then the
wrath of the Lorde waxed whote exced-
11 yngly: and it greued Moses also. And
Moses sayde vnto the Lorde: wherfore dealest thou so
cruelly with thi seruaunte? wherfore doo I not fynde
fauoure in thi syghte, seynge that thou puttest the
12 weyght of this people apon me? haue I conceyued
all this people, or haue I begote them, that thou shuld-
est saye vnto me, carye them in thi bosome (as a nurse
beareth the suckynge childe) vnto the londe which
13 thou swarest vnto their fathers? where shulde I haue
flesh to geue vnto all this people? For they wepe
vnto me sayenge: geue us flesh that we maye eate.
14 I am not able to bere all this people alone, for it is
15 to heuy for me. Wherfore yf thou deale thus with

of the auncyentes, and they prophesye. Eldad and Medad do also prophesye in the hoste. It rayneth quayles. The flesh raueners are punnyshed.

rascall people, *rabble*, cf. French, *racaille* and *racler*, to scrape together

boke, *baked*

whote, *hot*

v. 33

M. 8 baked . . . kakes

V. 6 Anima n. arida 10 Moysi intoleranda res visa est 12 nutrix infantulum 14 grauis est mihi.

L. 6 vnser seele verdorret 10 verdros Mosen auch 14 es ist myr zu schweer

me, kyll me, I praye the, yf I haue founde ſauoure in
thi ſyght and let me not ſe my wrechidneſſe.
16 And the Lorde ſayde vnto Moſes: gather vnto me
Lxx. of the elders of Yſrael, which thou knoweſt that
they are the elders of ẏ pe- .P. ple and officers ouer
them, and brynge them vnto the tabernacle of witneſſe,
17 and let them ſtonde there with the. And I wyll come
doune and talke with the there, and take of ẏ ſpirite
which is apon the and put apon them, ād they ſhall
bere with the in the burthen of the people, and ſo
ſhalt thou not beare alone.
18 And ſaye vnto ẏ people: halowe youre ſelues agenſt
to morow, that ye maye eate fleſh for ye
haue whyned in the eares of the Lorde
whyned, *wept* cf. German *weinen*
ſaynge: who ſhall geue vs fleſh to eate, for we were
happie when we were in Egipte? therefore the Lorde
19 will geue you fleſh, and ye ſhall eate: Ye ſhall not eate
one daye only ether .ii. or .v. dayes, ether .x. or .xx
20 dayes: but euen a moneth longe, ād vntill it come out
at the noſtrels of you, that ye be ready to perbrake:
becauſe that ye haue caſt ẏ Lorde a ſyde which is amonge
you, and haue wepte before him ſaynge: why came we
out of Egipte.
21 And Moſes ſayde: ſixe hundred thouſande fotemen
are there of the people, amonge which I am. And
thou haſt ſayde: I will geue them fleſh and they ſhall
22 eate a moneth lōge. Shall the ſhepe ād the oxen
be ſlayne for them to fynde them ether ſhall all
the fyſh of the ſee be gathered together to ſerue
23 them? And the Lorde ſayde vnto Moſes: is the
lordes hande waxed ſhorte? Thou ſhalt ſe whe-

M. 17 put apon the and apon them

V. 15 ne tantis afficiar malis. 18 Sanctificamini: cras comedetis 20 exeat per nares veſtras, & vertatur in nauſeam 22 boum multitudo 23 manus dom. inualida eſt?

L. 15 das ich nicht meynen iamer ſehen muſſe. 18 heyliget euch auff morgen 20 euch zur naſen ausgehe, vnd auch eyn ekel ſey 23 hand . . verkürtzt?

M. M. N. 17 I wyll come doune: loke Gene. ix, a. *Take of ẏ ſpirite:* That is I wyll enſpyre them with the ſame ſpryte. 20 *Noſtrels:* Or mouthes.

[Fo. XXIIII.] ther my worde ſhall come to paſſe
vnto the or not.
24 And moſes went out and tolde the people the ſayenge of the Lorde, and gathered the .Lxx. elders of
the people, and ſett them rounde aboute the taber-
25 nacle. And the Lorde came doune in a cloude and
ſpake vnto him, ād toke of the ſprete that was apon
him, ād put it apon the .Lxx. elders. And as the
ſpirite reſted apon them, they prophecied and did
26 nought els. But there remayned .ii. of ẏ mē in the
hoſte: the one called Eldad, ād the other Medad.
And the ſpirite reſted apon them for they were of
them that were written, but they wēt not out
vnto the tabernacle: and they prophecied in the
hoſte.
27 And there ran a younge man & tolde Moſes and
ſayed: Eldad ād Medad do prophecye in the hoſte.
28 And Ioſua the ſonne of Nū the ſeruaunte of Moſes
which he had choſen out, anſwered and ſayed: maſter
29 Moſes, forbyd them. And Moſes ſayed vnto him:
enuyeſt thou for my ſake? wolde God that all the
Lordes people coude prophecye, and that
the Lorde wolde put his ſpirite apon them.
30 And then both Moſes and the elders of
Iſrael, gat them in to the hoſte.
31 And there went forth a wynde frō ẏ

The pope wold that none of the lordes people coud prophecie & that none had his ſpirite.

lorde and brought quayles from the ſee and let .P.
them fall aboute the hoſte, euen a dayes iurney rounde
aboute on euery ſyde of the hoſte, and .ii. cubetes hye
32 apon the erth. And the people ſtode vpp all that
nyghte and on the morowe, ād gathered quayles. And

M. 32 ſtode vp all that daye & all that nyghte

V. 31 volabantque in aere duobus cubitis altitudine ſuper terram 32 & ſiccauerunt eas

L. 29 wolt Gott

M. M. N. 23 *ſhall come to paſſe* etc: After the greke & the chalde: Some, of what value it ſhalbe. 25 *Did nought els:* To prophecye is other to preache the worde to the people, as it is i. corin. xiiii, a. or to ſhewe the wōderful workes of God, or to ſhewe thinges to come: but to prophecye & do nought elles is here to rule the people of God accordyng to the ſpyryte & to gouerne theyr ſubiectes with iudgement, Iuſtyce and truthe.

he that gathered the left, gathered .x. homers full.
And they kylled them rounde aboute the hoste
33 And whyle the flesh was yet betwene their teeth,
yer it was chewed vpp, the wrath of the
Lorde waxed whote apon the people, and the Lorde
slewe of the people an exceadynge myghtie slaughter.
34 And they called the name of the place, the graues of
lust: because they buried the people that lusted there.
35 And the people toke their iurney from the graues
of lust vnto hazeroth, and bode at hazeroth.

yer, *ere, before*

¶ The .XII. Chapter.

1 AND Mir Iam and Aaron spake
agēst Moses, because of his
wife of inde which he had
taken: for he had taken to
2 wyfe one of India. And they sayed: doth
ỷ Lorde speake ōly thorow Moses? doth
he not speake also by us? And the Lorde
3 herde it. But Moses was a very meke man aboue all
4 the men of the erthe. And ỷ Lorde spake attonce
vnto Moses vnto Aaron & Mir Iam: come out ye .iii
vnto the tabernacle of witnesse: and they came out all
thre.
5 And the Lorde came doune in the piler of the cloude
and stode in the dore of the taber- [Fo. XXV.] nacle
and called Aaron ād Mir Iam. And they went out
6 both of them. And he sayed: heare my wordes. Yf
there be a prophet of the Lordes amonge you, I will
shewe my selfe vnto him in a vision and will speake

M.C.S. *Aaron and Mir Iam grudge agaynst Moses. Miriam was strycken with the leper and healed at the prayer of Moses.*

M. 34 place kibrath hathauah 35 kibrash hathauah

V. 33 nec defecerat huiuscemodi cibus. xii, 1 vxorem eius Æthiopissam 2 nonne & nobis similiter est loquutus? 6 in visione apparebo

L. 33 ehe es auff war. xii, 1 der morynnen . . . darumb das er eyne morynne zum weybe 6 ynn eym gesicht

M. M. N. 35 *Kibrath hathauah:* That is the graues of lust. xii, 5 *came doune:* Loke Gene. xii, a.

7 vnto him in a dreame: But my ſervaunte Moſes is not
8 ſo, which is faythfull in all myne houſſe. Vnto him I
ſpeake mouth to mouth and he ſeeth the ſyght and
the facyon of the Lorde, ād not thorow rydels. Wherfore thē were ye not afrayed to ſpeake agenſt my ſervaunte Moſes?

9 And the Lorde was angrye with them and went his
10 waye, and the cloude departed from the tabernacle.
And beholde, Myr-Iam was become leprous, as it were
ſnowe And when Aaron looked apon Mir Iam and
11 ſawe that ſhe was leprous, he ſayed vnto Moſes: Oh
I beſeche the my lorde, put not the ſynne apon vs
12 which we haue foliſhly commytted and ſynned. Oh,
let her not be as one that came deed oute of his mothers
wombe: for halfe hyr fleſhe is eaten awaye.

13 And Moſes cryed vnto the Lorde ſayenge: Oh god,
14 heale her. And the Lorde ſayed vnto Moſes: Yf hir
father had ſpitte in hyr face, ſholde ſhe not be aſhamed
15 vii. dayes? let her be ſhut out of the hoſte .vii. dayes,
& after that let her be receyued in agayne. And Mir
Iam was ſhett out of the hoſte .vii. dayes: ād the people remoued not, till ſhe was .P. broughte in agayne.
16 And afterwarde they remoued from Hazeroth, and
pitched in ẏ wilderneſſe of Pharan.

V. 8 ore enim ad os loquor 9 abiit 10 apparuit candens lepra quaſi nix. 12 quaſi mortua, & vt abortiuū . . . medium carnis eius devoratum eſt a lepra. 14 reuocabitur. 15 reuocata eſt Maria.

L. 8 Mundlich rede ich mit yhm 9 wand ſich weg 10 war . . ausſetzig 12 wie eyn todes, das von ſeyner mutter leybe kompt 14 widder auff nemen 15 auffgenomen wart.

M. M. N. 8 *Mouth to mouth*, that is I ſpeake not to hym ī dreames but by manifeſt tokens and vyſyble ſygnes & vndoutefully geue I hym knowledge of my mynde: here is no bodely mouth meant. 14 *To ſpytte in her face* is, to punnyſhe her & cauſe her to ſe her offēce. The Lorde is a father & punnyſſheth his choſē not to dāme thē but to correct & feare thē, & to dryue thē to erneſt repētaunce. After .viii. dayes was ſhe receaued agayne into the hoſte, ſo after repentaunce had muſt we be receaued in to the congregacion.

❡ The .XIII. Chapter.

M.C.S. Certen are ſend to ſearche the land of Canaan: which bryng with thē a clouſter of grapes for a ſigne of fertylytye and frutefulnes.

1 AND the Lorde ſpake vnto Moſes
2 ſayenge: Sende men out to
ſerche the londe of Canaan,
which I geue vnto the childern
of Iſrael: of euery trybe of their fathers a
man and let them all be ſoche as are rue-
3 lars amonge them. And Moſes at the commaundement of the Lorde ſent forth out of
the wilderneſſe of Pharan: ſoche men as were all heedes
4 amonge the childern of Iſrael, whoſe names are theſe.
5 In the trybe of Ruben, Sammua ẏ ſonne of Zacur: In
6 the trybe of Symeon, Saphat the ſonne of Hori. In the
7 trybe of Iuda Caleph the ſonne of Iephune. In the trybe
8 of Iſachar, Igeal the ſonne of Ioſeph. In the trybe of
9 Ephraim, Hoſea the ſonne of Nun. In the trybe of
10 Ben Iamin, Palti the ſonne of Raphu. In the trybe
11 of Zabulon, Gadiel the ſonne of Sodi. In the trybe of
Ioſeph: In the trybe of Manaſſe, Gaddi the ſonne of
12 Suſi. In the trybe of Dan, Amiel the ſonne of Gemali.
13 In the trybe of Aſſer, Sethur the ſonne of Micheel.
14 In the trybe of Nephtali, Nahebi the ſonne of Vaphſi.
15, 16 In the trybe of Gad, Guel the ſonne of Machi. Theſe
are the names of the men whiche Moſes ſent to [Fo.
XXVI.] ſpie out the londe. And Moſes called the
name of Hoſea the ſonne of Nun, Ioſua.
17 And Moſes ſent them forth to ſpie out the lande of
Canaan, and ſayed vnto them: get you ſouthwarde and
18 goo vpp in to the hye contre, and ſe the londe what
maner thynge it is ād the people that dwelleth therein:
whether they be ſtronge or weke, ether fewe or many,
19 and what the londe is that they dwell in whether it

M. 11 Ioſeph: that was of Manaſſe, Gaddi

V. 2 conſyderent terram 4 principes 18 cumque veneritis ad montes 19 conſiderate

L. 2 Canaan erkunden 18 auff das gepirge 19 beſehet

M. M. N. 16 *Hoſea:* Hoſea or oſee ſygnifieth ſauyng or ſaiour. Ioſua or Iehoſua ſignifyeth the ſaluaciō of the Lorde.

be good or bad, and what maner of cities they dwell
20 in: whether they dwell in tentes or walled townes, ād
what maner of londe it is: whether it be fatt or leane,
& whether there be trees therein or not. And be of
a good corage, and brynge of the frutes of the londe.
And it was aboute the tyme that grapes are firſt rype.
21 And they went vp and ſerched out the lande from
the wilderneſſe of Zin vnto Rehob as men goo to He-
22 math, and they aſcended vnto the ſouth and came vnto
Hebron, where Ahiman was and Seſai and Thalmani
the ſonnes of Enacke. Hebron was bylt .vii. yere be-
23 fore Zoan in Egipte. And they came vnto the ryuer of
Eſcol and they cutte doune there a braunch with one
clouſter of grapes & bare it apō a ſtaffe betwene twayne,
& alſo of the pomgranates & of the fygges of the place.
24 The ryuer was called Eſcol, becauſe of the clouſter of
grapes whiche the childern of Iſrael cutt doune there.
25 .P. And they turned backe agayne from ſerchinge the
26 londe, at .xl. dayes ende. And thei went and came to
Moſes and Aaron & vnto all the multitude of the childern of Iſrael, vnto the wilderneſſe of Pharan: euen vnto
Cades, and broughte them worde and alſo vnto all the
congregacion, and ſhewed them the frute of the lande.
27 And they tolde him ſayenge: we came vnto the londe
wether thou ſendedſt vs, & ſurely it is a lōde that floweth
28 with milke & honye & here is of the frute of it Neuertheleſſe the people be ſtronge ŷ dwell in the londe, and
the cities are walled and exceadinge greate, and more-

M. 24 Nehel Eſcol

V. 20 vrbes quales, muratæ, an abſque muris 22 explorauerunt terram 24 ad torrentem botri 25 qui appellatus eſt Nehel eſchol, id eſt Torrens botri, eo quod botrum portaſſent 27 Pharan quod eſt in Cades. 28 vt ex his fructibus cognoſci poteſt

L. 20 mit mauren verwaret ſind odder nicht 22 erkundeten 24 bach Eſcol 25 der ort heyſt bach Eſcol . . daſelbs abſchnytten. 27 Paran gen Kades 28 vnd dis iſt yhre frucht

M. M. N. 22 *Enacke:* Loke Iudi. i, d. *Zoan:* Otherwyſe Tanis, after the Chalde. 24 *Nehel Eſcol* ſygnifyeth by interpretacion the ryuer of the grape or as ſome wyll the valeye of the clouſter. 27 *Floweth with mylcke & honye* that is, full of good paſtures, herbes, bees, catell, vynes, trees, pleaſaunt woodes ſo that vnder heuē ther was not a moare choſen peace of grounde for aboundance and plenteouſnes.

L. M. N. 24 *Eſcol* heyſt eyn drauben, daraus wirt der name draubenbach.

29 ouer we ſawe the childrē of Enack there. The amaleckes
dwel in the ſouth cuntre, and the Hethites, Iebuſites and
the Amorites dwell in the moūtaynes, and the Cananites
dwell by the ſee ād alonge by the coſte of Iordayne.
30 And Caleb ſtylled the murmure of the people agenſt
Moſes ſayenge: let vs goo vp and conquere it, for we
31 be able to ouercome it. But the men that went vpp
with him, ſayde: We be not able to goo vpp agenſt
32 the people, for they are ſtronger than we: And they
broughte vpp an euell reporte of the londe which they
had ſerched, vnto the childern of Iſrael ſayenge. The
londe which we haue gone thorowe to ſerche it out, is a
londe that eateth vpp the inhabiters thereof, and the people that we ſawe in it are men of ſtature. [Fo. XXVII.]
33 And there we ſawe alſo geantes, the childrē of Enack
which are of the geaūtes. And we ſemed in oure ſyght
as it were greſhoppers and ſo we dyd in their ſighte.

The .XIIII. Chapter.

1 AND the multitude cryed out, &
the people wepte thorow out
2 that nyght, & all the childern
of Yſrael murmured agenſt
Moſes & Aaron. And the hole congregacion ſayed vnto them: wolde god that
we had dyed in the lond of Egipte, ether
we wolde that we had dyed in thys
3 wilderneſſe. Wherfore hath the Lorde
broughte vs vnto this londe to fall apon
the ſwerde, that both oure wyues, & alſo
oure childrē ſhulde be a praye? is it not

M.C.S. *The people diſpearyng of cōmyng to the land promyſed, do murmur agaynſt God, and woold haue ſtoned Caleb and Iosue. The ſearchers of the land dye. Amalech kylleth the Iſraelites.*

V. 31 Caleb compeſcens murmur populi 33 terra quam luſtrauimus, deuorat 34 quibus comparati . . . videbamur. xiiii, 3 ducantur captiui.

L. 31 Caleb aber ſtillet das volck 32 land da durch wyr gangen ſind zu erkunden 34 fur vnſern augen . . . auch ynn yhren augen. xiiii, 3 vnſer kinder eyn raub werden

M. M. X. 32 *Eateth up etc.* that is, ſuffereth them not to lyue, but with battell & vyolēce of geauntes conſumeth them.

4 better that we returne vnto Egipte agayne? And
they ſayde one to another: let vs make a captayne and
returne vnto Egipte agayne.
5 And Moſes & Aaron fell on their faces before all the
congregacion of the multitude of the childern of Yſrael.
6 And Ioſua the ſonne of Nun, and Caleb the ſonne of
Iephune which were of them that ſerched the londe
7 rent their clothes and ſpake vnto all the companye of
the childern of Yſrael ſaynge: The londe which we
8 walked thorowe to ſerche it, is a very good lande. Yf
the Lorde haue luſt to vs, he will bring vs
in to this londe & geue it vs, which is a
9 lond ẏ floweth with mylke & hony. But in any wiſe
rebell not agenſt .𝔓. the Lorde, Moreouer feare ye not
the people of the londe, for they are but bred for vs.
Their ſhylde is departed from them, & the Lorde is
with vs: feare them not therfore.
10 And all the whole multitude bade ſtone them with
ſtones. But the glorie of the Lorde appered in the
tabernacle of witneſſe, vnto all the childern of Iſrael.
11 And the Lorde ſayed vnto Moſes: Howe longe ſhall
thys people rayle apon me, and how longe will it be,
yer they beleue me, for all my ſignes whiche I haue
12 ſhewed amonge them? I will ſmyte them with the
peſtilence & deſtroy thē, and will make of the a greatter
nacion and a mightier then they.
13 And Moſes ſayed vnto the Lorde: then
the Egiptians ſhall heare it, for thou
broughteſt this people with thy mighte
14 from amonge them. And it wilbe tolde
to the inhabiters of this lande alſo, for they haue herde
likewiſe, that thou the Lorde art amōge this people,

luſt to, *delight in*

The Pope wolde not ſo haue prayed if thei had been aboute to ſtone him.

𝔙. 4 Conſtituamus nobis ducem 6 qui et ipſi luſtrauerunt 12 gentem magnam et fortiorem

𝔏. 4 heuptman auffwerfen 6 die auch das land erkundet hatten 12 groſſern vnd mechtigern volck

𝔐. 𝔐. 𝔑. 6 *Rent their clothes*, loke Gene. xxxvii, f. 11 *To rayle apon the Lorde*, to prouoke him, to refyſt withſtand or ſtryue agaynſt hym: all ſoche maners of ſpeache where ſoeuer ye fynde them, do ſygnifye no thyng elles: but not to beleue his wordes, as in the Pſal. v, c. & .ix, f.

ād ỷ thou art ſene face to face, & ỷ thy cloude ſtondeth
ouer them & that thou goeſt before them by daye tyme
15 in a piler of cloude, & in a piler of fyre by nyght. Yf
thou ſhalt kill all this people as thei were but one mā
then the nacions which haue herde the fame of the,
16 will ſpeake ſayenge: becauſe ỷ Lorde was not able to
bringe in this people in to ỷ londe which he ſwore vnto
them, therfore he ſlewe them in the wilderneſſe.
17 [Fo. XXVIII.] So now lat the power of my Lord
18 be greate, acordynge as thou haſt ſpoken ſayenge: the
Lorde is longe yer he be angrye, ād full of mercy, and
ſuffereth ſynne and treſpace, and leaueth no man innocent,
and viſiteth the vnryghtuouſneſſe of the fathers vppon
19 ỷ childern, euē vpō ỷ thirde & fourth generacion. be
mercyfull I beſeche ỷ therfore, vnto ỷ ſynne of this
people acordinge vnto thi greate mercy, & acordinge
as thou haſt forgeuē this people from Egipte euen vnto
this place.
20 And the Lorde ſayed: I haue forgeuē it, acordynge
21 to thy requeſt. But as trulye as I lyue, all the erth
22 ſhalbe fylled with my glorye. For of all thoſe mē
whiche haue ſene my glorye & my miracles which I dyd
in Egipte & in ỷ wilderneſſe, & yet haue tempted me
now this .x. tymes & haue not herkened vnto my voyce,
23 there ſhall not one ſe the lond whiche I ſware vnto
their fathers, nether ſhall any of thē that rayled apō
24 me, ſe it. But my ſervaūte Caleb. becauſe there is another maner ſprite with hī, & becauſe he hath folowed
me vnto the vttmoſt: him I will bringe in to the lond
which he hath walked in, & his ſeed ſhall conquere it,
25 & alſo the Amalechites ād Cananites which dwell in
the lowe contrees Tomorowe turne you and gete you in
to the wilderneſſe: euen the waye towarde the red ſee.
26 .¶. And the Lorde ſpake vnto Moſes ād Aaron ſayenge:

V. 24 terram hanc quam circumiuit
L. 24 dareyn er kommen iſt
M. M. N. 21 *The erth ſhalbe fylled with my glory:* That he wyl haue the erth fylled with his glorye is, that he wyll be magnyfyed, preached ſpoken of honoured and prayſed thorou oute the erth. Ps. xvii, d.

27 how longe ſhall this euell multitude murmure agenſt
me? I haue herde ỳ murmurynges of ỳ childern of
28 Yſrael whyche they murmure agenſte me. Tell them,
ỳ the Lorde ſayeth. As truely as I lyue, I wil do vnto
29 you euen as ye haue ſpoken in myne eares. Youre
carkaſſes ſhall lye in this wilderneſſe, nether ſhall any
of theſe numbres which were numbred from .xx. yere
& aboue of you which haue murmured agenſt me
30 come in to the londe ouer which I liſted myne hande
to make you dwell therein, ſaue Caleb the ſonne of
Iephune, and Ioſua the ſonne of Nun.
31 And youre childern whiche ye ſayed ſhuld be a
praye, thē I will bringe in, & they ſhall knowe the
32 londe which ye haue refuſed, and youre carkeſſes ſhall
33 lye in this wilderneſſe And youre childern ſhall wādre
in this wilderneſſe .xl. yeres & ſuffre for youre whoredome vntill your carkaſſes be waſted in the wilderneſſe,
34 after the numbre of the dayes in which ye ſerched out
ỳ londe .xl. dayes, & euery daye a yere: ſo that they
ſhall bere your vnrightuouſnes .xl. yere, & ye ſhall fele
35 my vengeaunce I the Lorde haue ſayed ỳ I will do it
vnto all this euell congregacion ỳ are gathered together
agenſt me: euen in thys wilderneſſe ye ſhalbe conſumed,
and here ye ſhall dye.
36 [Fo. XXIX.] And the men which Moſes ſent to
ſerche the londe, and which (when they came agayne)
made all the people to murmure agenſt it in that they
37 broughte vpp a ſlaunder apon ỳ londe: dyed for their
bryngenge vp that euell ſlaunder apon it, and were
38 plaged before the Lorde. But Ioſua the ſonne of Nun
and Caleb the ſonne of Iephune which were of ỳ mē
39 that went to ſerche the londe, lyued ſtill. And Moſes

V. 29 iacebunt cadauera veſtra. 33 Filii . . vagi . . . conſumantur cadauera patrum 34 et ſcietis vltionem meam 35 deficiet & morietur. 37 mortui ſunt et percuſſi

L. 29 Ewre leiber . . verfallen 32 yhr ſampt ewern leiben . . verfallen 33 kinder ſollen hirten ſeyn 35 ſollen ſie alle werden . . ſterben. 36 alſo ſtorben vnd worden geplagt

M. M. N. 30 *I lyfted etc.* Loke Exod. vi, b. 33 *Whoredome* for infydelytye or Idolatrye as in .iiii. Regū. ix, c. & Sapien. xiiii, b.

tolde these sayenges vnto all the childern of Ysrael,
and the people toke great sorowe.
40 And they rose vp yerlee in the mornynge & gatt them vpp in to the toppe
of the mountayne sayenge: lo we be here,
ād will goo vpp vnto the place of which
the Lorde sayed, for we haue synned.
41 And Moses sayed: wherfore will ye goo
on this maner beyonde the worde of the
42 Lorde? it will not come well to passe goo not vpp for
the Lorde is not amonge you that ye be not slayne be-
43 fore youre enemyes. For the Amalechytes and the
Cananites are there before you, & ye will fall apon the
swerde: because ye are turned a waye from ȳ Lorde,
and therfore the Lorde wyll not be with you.
44 But they were blynded to goo vpp in
to ȳ hylltoppe: Neuer the lather, the arke
of the testament of the Lorde and Moses
45 departed not out of the hoste. Then the Amalekytes
ād the Cananites which dwelt in that hill, came .P.
doune and smote them and hewed thē: euen vnto
Horma.

Blinde reasō which yerwhile wolde not let them beleue in Gods worde, teacheth them now to trust in their awne workes.

blynded, *darkened as to the mind*, cf. Latin *contenebratus*

The .XV. Chapter.

1 AND the Lorde spake vnto Mo-
2 ses sayēge: speake vnto the
childern of Israel & saye vnto
them: when ye be come in to
ȳ londe of youre habitacion which I geue
3 vnto you, and will offre an offerynge apon

M.C.S. *The drynckofferinges of thē that enter ī to the lāde. The punyshment of hym that synneth*

V. 42 ne corruatis 44 contenebrati 45 percutiens eos atque concidens, persecutus xv, 2 terram habitationis

L. 42 geschlahen werdet 44 verblendet 45 schlugen vnd zuschmissen xv, 2 land ewr wonung

M. M. N. 40 sq. Blinde reason which yer while wolde not let them beleue in Gods worde, teacheth them now to trust in their awne workes.

the fyre vnto the Lorde, whether it be
a burntofferynge or a speciall vowe or
frewill offerynge or yf it be in youre
principall festes to make a swete sauoure vnto the Lorde, of the oxen or
of the flocke.
4 Then, let him that offereth his offerynge vnto the Lorde, brynge also a meatofferynge of a tenth deale of floure myn-
5 gled with the fourth parte of an hin of
oyle, and the fourth parte of an hin of wine for a drynkofferynge and offer with ẏ burntofferynge or any other
6 offerynge when it is a lambe. And vnto a rā thou
shalt offer a meatofferynge of .ii. tenth deales of floure,
7 myngled with ẏ thyrde parte of an hin of oyle, and
to a drynkofferynge thou shalt offer the thyrde parte
of an hin of wyne, to be a swete sauoure vnto the
Lorde.
8 When thou offerist an oxe to a burntofferynge or
in any speciall vowe or peaseofferinge vnto the Lorde,
9 then thou shalt brynge vnto an oxe, a meatofferynge
of .iii. tenth deales [Fo. XXX.] of floure myngled with
10 half an hin of oyle. And thou shalt brynge for a
drynkofferynge halfe an hin of wyne, that is an offer-
11 ynge of a swete sauoure vnto the Lorde. This is the
maner that shalbe done vnto one oxe, one ram a
12 lambe or a kyd. And acordynge to the numbre of
soche offerynges, thou shalt encrease ẏ meatofferynges
and the drynkofferynges
13 All that are of youre selues shall do these thinges
after this maner, when he offereth an offerynge of swete
14 sauoure vnto the Lorde And yf there be a straunger
with you or be amonge you in youre generacions, and
will offer an offerynge of a swete sauoure vnto ẏ Lorde:
15 euen as ye do, so he shall doo. One ordynaunce shall

of arrogāce or pryde. The man is stooned that gethered styckes on the Saboth. Gardes must be made vpō the quarters of theyr garmentes.

deale, *part, portion,* cf. German *Theil*

V. 4 quartam partem hin: 5 & vinum . . . eiusdem mensuræ [cf. the Hebrew and Latin vv. 10–24] . . Per agnos singulos 6 & arietes 8 pacificas victimas

L. 4 vierden teyls (cf. *deale*) 8 zum besonderen gelübdopffer . . tödtopffer 14 der sol thun, wie sie thun

ſerue both for you of the congregacion, and alſo for
the ſtraunger. And it ſhalbe an ordynaunce for euer
amonge youre childern after you, that the ſtraunger
16 and ye ſhalbe lyke before the Lorde. One lawe and
one maner ſhall ſerue, both for you and for ẏ ſtraunger
that dwelleth with you.

17, 18 And the Lorde ſpake vnto Moſes ſayenge: ſpeake
vnto the childern of Iſrael ād ſaye vnto them: when
ye be come in to the londe whether I will brynge you,
19 then whē ye will eate of the bred of the londe, ye
20 ſhall geue an heue offerynge vnto the Lorde. Ye ſhall
geue a cake of the firſt of youre dowe vnto an heue
offerynge: as ye do the heue offerynge of the barne,
21 euen ſo ye ſhall heue it .¶. Of the firſt of youre dowe
ye muſt geue vnto the Lorde an heue offerynge, thorow
out youre generacions.

22 Yf ye ouerſe youre ſelues and obſerue
not all theſe commaundmētes which the
23 Lorde hath ſpoken vnto Moſes, & all that
the Lorde hath commaunded you by ẏ
hāde of Moſes, from the firſt daye forwarde that the Lorde commaunded amonge youre
24 generacion: when oughte is commytted ignorantly
before the eyes of the congregacion, then all the
multitude ſhall offer a calfe for a burntofferynge to
be a ſwete ſauoure vnto the Lorde, & the meatofferynge and the drynkofferynge there to, acordynge to
the maner: and an he goote for a ſynof-
25 ferynge. And the preaſt ſhall make an
atonement for all the multitude of ẏ chil-

ouerſe youre ſelues, *err through ignoraunce or inadvertence*, cf. Germ. *überſehen, verſehen*

maner, *cuſtom, uſage as preſcribed by law*

V. 23 a die qua cœpit iubere & vltra 24 oblitaque fuerit facere multitudo . . vt ceremoniæ poſtulant

L. 15 Der gantzen gemeyn ſey eyn ſatzung . . . eyne ewige ſatzung ſoll das ſeyn ewrn nachkomen das fur dem Herrn der frembling ſey, wie yhr 23 von dem tage an da er anfieng zu gepieten 24 die gemeyne etwas vnwiſſent thet . . . wie es recht iſt 25 Vnd der prieſter

M. M. N. 15 This cōmaundement was a fore token of gethering the gentyles & the hebrues in to one church of Chriſte, Iohan. x, c. wherin there is no dyfference betwene the Hebrue or Iewe and the grecyan, ryche and poore, cytezen and ſtraunger or forener.

dern of Israel, ād it shalbe forgeuen thē for it was ignoraunce. And they shall brynge their giftes vnto
the offerynge of the Lorde, and their synofferynge
26 before the Lorde for their ignoraunce. And it shalbe
forgeuen vnto all the multitude of the childern of
Israel, & vnto the straunger that dwelleth amōge
you: for the ignorauncye perteyneth vnto all the people.
27 Yf any one soule synne thorow ignoraunce he shall
brynge a she goote of a yere olde for a synneofferynge.
28 And the preast shall make an atonement for the soule
that synned ignorauntly with the synofferynge before
the [Fo. XXXI.] Lorde and reconsyle him, and it
29 shalbe forgeuen him. And both thou that art borne
one of the childern of Israel and the straunger that
dwelleth amonge you shall haue both one lawe, yf ye
synne thorow ignorauncye.
30 And the soule that doth ought presumptuously,
whether he be an Israelite or a straūger, the same
hath despysed the Lorde. And that soule shalbe de-
31 stroyed from amonge his people, because he hath
despised the worde of the Lorde & hath brokē his
cōmaūdmentes, ẏ soule therfore shall perysh ād his
synne shalbe apon him.
32 And whyle the childern of Ysrael were in the wildernesse, they founde a man gatherynge stickes vppon
33 the Sabath daye. And they ẏ founde him gatherynge
stickes, brought him vnto Moses and Aaron and vnto
34 all ẏ congregacion: ād they put him in warde, for it
was not declared what shulde be done vnto him.
35 And the Lorde sayed vnto Moses: ẏ mā shall dye.
let all the multitude stone him with stones without

V. 25 nihilominus 26 quoniam culpa est omnis populi per ignorantiam. 29 Tam indigenis quam aduenis vna lex erit omnium qui peccauerint ignorantes. 30 Anima vero quæ per superbiam . . quon. aduersus dominum rebellis fuit 34 nescientes quid super eo facere deberent. 35 Morte moriatur

L. 26 das gantze volck ist ynn solcher vnwissenheyt. 29 Vnd es soll eyn gesetz seyn 30 eyn seele aus hoffart . . . der hat den Herrn geschmecht 34 Denn es war nicht ausgedruckt, was man mit yhm thun solte 35 des todts sterben

M. M. N. 32 Necessytye droue him not to gether styckes & therfore was he woorthye this cruell death, for as moche as he dispysed to heare the woorde of the Lorde wher vnto he was so straytlye cōmaunded to geue eare on the saboth daye.

36 the hoſte. And all ẏ multitude broughte him with
out the hoſte ād ſtoned him with ſtones, and he dyed
as the Lorde commaunded Moſes.
37, 38 And the Lorde ſpake vnto Moſes ſayenge: ſpeake
vnto the childern of Yſrael and byd them, that they
make them gardes apon the quarters of
their garmētes thorow out their gener-
acions, ād let them make the gardes .P. of ribandes of
39 Iacyncte And the garde ſhall be vnto
you to loke apon it, that ye remembre all
the commaundmentes of the Lorde and
doo them: that ye ſeke not a waye after
youre awne hertes and after youre awne
eyes, for to goo a whooringe after them:
40 but that ye remembre and doo all my
commaundmentes and be holy vnto youre
41 God, for I am ẏ Lorde youre God, which
broughte you out of ẏ londe of Egipte, to be youre
God. I am the Lorde God.

gardes, *fringes*
quarters, *corners*
Iacyncte, *blue*
Gods ſignes were to put men in remēbraunce of his worde, that they ſhuld not ſeke a waye to pleaſe God after their awne imaginacion.

ℭ The .XVI. Chapter.

1 AND Corah the ſonne of Iezehar
the ſonne of Cahath the ſonne
of Leui: & Dathan & Abiram
the ſonne of Eliab, and On
the ſonne of Peleth, the ſonne of Ruben:
2 ſtode vpp before Moſes, with other of the
childern of Iſrael .ii. hundred and fyftie,
heedes of the congregacion, and councelers, and men

M.C.S. *The rebelliō & reſyſtaunce of Corah, Dathan & Abiram. The erth opened and ſwalowed them vp.*

M. 41 Egipte, for to be youre God
V. 38 fimbrias per angulos . . . vittas hyacinthinas 40 ſintque ſancti deo ſuo. xvi, 2 contra Moyſen . . . viri proceres ſynagogæ, & qui tempore concilii per nomina vocabantur.
L. 38 lepplin machen an den fittichen . . . gelle ſchnurlin 40 heylig ſeyn ewrem Gott. xvi, 2 fur Moſe . . heubtleut der gemeyne, radtsherrn vnd berumpt leut
M. M. N. 38 Soche *gardes* ſhulde the chriſten haue depely fixed in their hertes, conſydering what they are bounde to the Lorde, of what god what a ſeruyce they haue takē vpō thē: that they myght with al dyligēce & cyrcumſpectiō fullfyl that, which they haue promiſed etc. xvi, 1 Some wryte Koreh the ſonne of Izachar. Some wryte Abirom.

3 of ſame, and they gathered thē ſelues together agenſt
Moſes and Aaron & ſayed vnto them: ye haue done
ynough. For all the multitude are holy euery one of
them, and the Lorde is amonge them. Why therfore
heue ye youre ſelues vpp aboue the con- heue, *lift*
gregacion of the Lorde.

4, 5 When Moſes herde it, he fell apon his face and
ſpake vnto Corah and vnto all his companye ſayenge:
tomorow the Lorde will ſhewe who is his and who is
holy, and will take them vnto him, and whom ſo euer
he [Fo. XXXII.] hath choſen, he will cauſe to come
6 to him. This doo: take fyrepannes, thou Corah and
7 all thi companye, and do fyre therein ād put cēs thereto before the Lorde tomorowe: And then whom ſoeuer
the Lorde doeth choſe, the ſame is holy. Ye make
ynough to doo ye childern of Leui.

8 And Moſes ſayed vnto Corah: heare ye childern of
9 leui, Semeth it but a ſmall thynge vnto you, that ẏ
God of Iſrael hath ſeparated you frō the multitude of
Iſrael to brynge you to him, to doo the ſeruyce of the
dwellynge place of the Lorde, and to ſtonde before the
10 people to minyſtre vnto them? he hath taken the to
him and all thi brethern the ſonnes of leui with the,
11 and ye ſeke the office of ẏ preaſt alſo. For which cauſe
both thou and all thi companye are gathered together
agenſt the Lorde: for what is Aaron, that ye ſhulde
murmure agenſt him.

12 And Moſes ſent to call Dathan ād Abiram the
ſonnes of Eliab, and they anſwered: we will not come.
13 Semeth it a ſmall thynge vnto the that thou haſt
broughte us out of a londe that floweth with mylke
and honye, to kyll us in ẏ wilderneſſe. But that thou
14 ſhuldeſt reygne ouer us alſo? More ouer thou haſt
broughte us vnto no londe that floweth with mylke
and honye, nether haſt geuen us poſſeſſions of feldes or

V. 5 quos elegerit appropinquabūt ei. 10 vt vobis etiam ſacerdotium vendicetis 14 Reuera induxiſti nos in terram . .

L. 5 Wilchen er erwelet der ſol ſich zu yhm nahen 10 vnd yhr ſucht nu auch das prieſterthum 14 wie feyn haſtu vns bracht ynn eyn land

of vynes. Ether wilt thou pull out the eyes of theſe
men? we wyll .P. not come.
15 And Moſes waxed very angrye and ſayed vnto the
Lorde: Turne not vnto their offerynges. I haue not
taken ſo moch as an aſſe from them, ne- *Can oure prelates ſo ſaye?*
16 ther haue vexed any of them. Then
Moſes ſayed vnto Corah: Be thou ād all thy companye
before the Lorde: both thou, they and Aaron to
17 morowe. And take euery man his cenſer and put cens
in them, & come before the Lorde euery man with hys
cenſer: two hundred and fyſtie cenſers, and Aaron with
18 his cenſer. And they toke euery man his cenſer and
put fyre in them & layed cens thereon, and ſtode in
the dore of the tabernacle of witneſſe, and Moſes &
19 Aaron alſo. And Corah gathered all the congregacyon agenſt them vnto the dore of the tabernacle of
witneſſe.
And the glorye of the Lorde appered vnto all the
20 congregacion. And the Lorde ſpake vnto Moſes and
21 Aaron ſayenge: ſeparate youre ſelues from this con-
22 gregacion, that I maye conſume them atonce. And
they fell apon their faces and ſayed: O moſt myghtie
God of the ſpirites of all fleſhe, one mā hath ſynned,
23 and wylt thou be wroth with all the multitude? And
24 the Lorde ſpake vnto Moſes ſayenge: ſpeake vnto the
congregacion and ſaye: Gett you awaye from aboute the
dwellynge of Corah, Dathan & Abiram.
25 And Moſes roſe vpp and went vnto Da- [Fo.
XXXIII.] than & Abirā, & the elders of Iſrael folowed
26 him. And he ſpake vnto the congregacyon ſayenge:
departe from the tentes of theſe weked men and twyche
nothinge of theres: leſt ye peryſhe in all there ſynnes.
27 And they gate them from the dwellynge of Corah,

V. 14 an & oculos noſtros vis eruere? 15 Ne reſpicias 16 & Aaron die craſtino ſeparatim. 22 Fortiſſime deus ſpirituum vniverſæ carnis . . . ira tua deſæuiet? 26 ne inuoluamini in peccatis eorum.

L. 14 Wiltu den leutten auch die augen aus brechen? 15 wende dich nicht 16 morgen . . . du, ſie auch vnd Aaron 22 Gott Gott der geyſter alles fleyſchs . . vber die gantze gemeyne wueten? 26 das yhr nicht villeicht vmbkompt ynn yrgent yhrer ſunden eyne.

Dathan and Abiram, on euery ſide. And Dathan and
Abiram came out & ſtode in ẏ dore of there tētes with
their wyues, their ſonnes and their childern.
28 And Moſes ſayed: Hereby ye ſhall knowe that the
Lorde hath ſent me to doo all theſe workes, and that
29 I haue not done them of myne awne mynde: Yf theſe
men dye the comon deth of all men or yf they be
viſyted after the viſitacion of all men, then the Lorde
30 hath not ſent me. But and yf the Lorde make a new
thinge, and the erth open hir mouthe and ſwalowe
them and all that pertayne vnto them, ſo that they
goo doune quycke in to hell: then ye ſhall vnderſtōd,
that theſe mē haue rayled apon the Lorde.
31 And as ſoone as he had made an ende of ſpeakynge
all theſe wordes, the grounde cloue aſunder that was
32 vnder them, and ẏ erth opened hir mouthe and
ſwalowed them and their houſſes and all the mē that
33 were with Corah and all their goodes. And they
and all that pertayned vnto them, went doune alyue
vnto hell, and the erthe cloſed apon them, and they
34 peryſhed from amonge the .P. congregacyon. And all
Iſrael that were aboute them, fledde at the crye of them.
For they ſayed: The erthe myghte happelye ſwalowe
35 vs alſo. And there came oute a fyre from the Lorde and
conſumed the two hundred and fyftye men that offred cens.
36, 37 And the Lorde ſpake vnto Moſes ſayenge: Speake
vnto Eleazer the ſonne of Aaron the preaſte and
let him take vppe the cenſers oute of the burnynge
38 and ſcater the fyre here and there, for the cenſers
of theſe ſynners are halowed in theyr deethes: and

V. 27 a tentoriis eorū per circumitum . . . & liberis, omnique frequentia. 28 & non ex proprio ea corde protulerim. 30 ſcietis quod blaſphemauerint dominum. 33 deſcenderuntque viui in infernum operti humo 34 fugit a clamore pereuntium 37 quoniam ſanctificata ſunt 38 in mortibus peccatorum

L. 27 traten an die thur yhrer hutten mit yhren weyben vnd ſonen vnd kindern 28 vnd nicht von meynem hertzen 30 erkennen, das diſe leut den Herrn geleſtert haben 33 vnd furen hyn vntern lebendig ynn die helle 34 floh fur yhrem geſchrey

M. M. N. 29 *Viſited:* That is pūnyſhed with the punnyſhement. 30 *To go doune quycke or a lyue into hell* is, to peryſh by ſoudayne deeth and to be ouerwhelmed with the erth.

let them be beten in to thyne plates thyne, *thin*
and faftened apon the altare. For they offred thē before the Lorde, and therfore they are holye and they
fhalbe a fygne vnto the childern of Ifrael.
39 And Eleazar the preaft toke the brafen cenfers
which they that were burnt had offered, and bet them
40 and faftened them vppon the altare, to be a remembraunce vnto the childern of Ifrael, that no ftraunger
whiche is not of the feed of Aaron, come nere to offer
cens before the Lorde, that he be not made like vnto
Corah and his companye: as the Lorde fayed vnto him
by the hande of Mofes.
41 And on the morowe all the multitude of the childern of Ifraell murmured agenfte Mofes and Aaron fayenge: ye haue kylled [Fo. XXXIIII.] the people of
42 the Lorde. And when the multitude was gathered
agenfte Mofes and Aaron, they loked towarde the tabernacle of witneffe. And beholde, the cloude had
couered it and the glorye of the Lorde appeared.
43 And Mofes and Aaron went before the tabernacle of
44 witneffe. And the Lorde fpake vnto Mofes fayenge:
45 Gett you from this congregacyon, that I maye confume
them quyckelye. And they fell apon theyr faces.
46 And Mofes fayde vnto Aaron: take a cenfer and put
fyre therein out of the alter, and poure on cens, and goo
quyckly vnto the cōgregacion and make an attonement for thē. For there is wrath gone oute from the
47 Lorde, and there is a plage begone. And Aaron toke

V. 38 eo quod oblatum fit . . . et fanctificata fint . . pro figno & monimēto 42 Cumque oriretur feditio & tumultus increfceret 43 Moyfes & Aaron fugerūt . . Quod poftquam ingreffi funt, operuit nubes, & apparuit gloria domini. 44 Dixitque dominus 45 etiam nunc delebo eos. 46 et plaga defæuit. 47 Quod cum feciffet Aaron

L. 38 denn folche pfannen der funder find geheyligt, durch yhre feele . . . denn fie find geopffert fur dem Herrn vnd geheyliget, vnd follen den kindern Ifrael zum zeychen feyn. 42 gemeyne verfamlet widder Mofe vnd Aaron, wandten fie fich zu der hutten des zeugnis. Vnd fihe, da bedecket es die wolcken, vnd die herlickeyt des Herrn erfcheyn 45 ich will fie bald freffen 47 Vnd Aaron nam. . .

M. M. N. 38 The cenfers were *halowed in theyr deathes* becaufe that by them was geuen an enfample vnto other to feare.

as Moſes commaunded him, and ran vnto the congregacion: and beholde, the plage was begone amonge
the people, and he put on cens, and made an attone-
48 ment for the people. And he ſtode betwene the deed,
49 and them that were alyue, and the plage ceaſed. And
the numbre of them that dyed in the plage, were
xiiii. thouſande and ſeuen hundred: beſyde them that
50 dyed aboute the buſynes of Corah. And Aaron went
agayne vnto Moſes vnto the dore off the tabernacle of
witneſſe, and the plage ceaſed.

ℂ The .XVII. Chapter.

.V. XVII. Chapter.

M.C.S. Aarons rodde buddeth and beareth bloſſomes.

1 AND the Lorde ſpake vnto Mo-
2 ſes ſayenge: ſpeake vnto the
childern of Iſrael and take
of them, for euery pryncypall
houſſe a rod, of their princes ouer the houſſes of their
fathers: euen .xii. roddes, and wryte euery mans name
3 apon his rod. And wryte Aarons name apon the ſtaffe
of Leui: for euery heedman ouer the houſſes of their
4 fathers ſhall haue a rod. And put thē in the taber-
5 nacle of witneſſe where I wyll mete you. And his
rod whom I choſe, ſhall bloſſome: So I wyll make ceaſe
from me the grudgynges of the childern of Iſrael which
they grudge agenſt you.
6 And Moſes ſpake vnto the childern off Iſrael, and

V. 48 & ſtans inter mortuos ac viuentes 50 poſtquam quieuit interitus. xvii, 4 coram teſtimonio vbi loquar ad te. 5 et cohibebo a me querimonias filiorum Iſrael, quibus contra vos murmurant.

L. 47 vnd die plage iſt angangen vnter 48 vnd ſtund zwiſchen den todten vnd lebendigen 50 vnd der plage wart geweret. xvii, 4 fur dem zeugnis da ich euch zeuge 5 das ich das murren der kinder Iſrael, das ſie widder euch murren, ſtille.

M. M. N. 48 Aaron is heare a fygure of Chriſt which is the medyatoure betwene God and the churche which reſtraineth the iuſt vengeaunce of God for the ſynnes of the worlde, which helpeth the choſen whē they be in ieopardye.

all the prynces gaue him for euery prynce ouer their
fathers houſſes, a rod: euen .xii. roddes, and the rod
7 of Aaron was amonge the rodes. And Moſes put ȳ
roddes before the Lorde in the tabernacle of witneſſe.
8 And on the morowe, Moſes went in to the tabernacle:
and beholde, the rod of Aaron of the houſſe of Leui
9 was budded & bare bloſomes and almondes. And
Moſes broughte out all the ſtaues from before the
Lorde, vnto all the childern of Iſrael, & thei loked
apon them, and toke euery man his ſtaffe.
10 And the Lorde ſayed vnto Moſes: brynge Aarons
rod agayne before the witneſſe to be kepte for a token
vnto the childern of re- [Fo. XXXV.] bellyon, that
their murmurynges maye ceaſſe fro me, that they
11 dye not. And Moſes dyd as the Lorde commaunded
12 him. And the childern of Iſrael ſpake vnto Moſes
ſayenge: beholde, we are deſtroyed and all come to
13 nought: for whoſoeuer cometh nye the dwellynge of
the Lord, dyeth. Shall we vtterly conſume awaye?

❡ The .XVIII. Chapter.

1 AND the Lorde ſayed vnto Aaron: Thou and thy ſonnes and thy fathers houſſe with the, ſhall bere the faute of that whiche is done amyſſe in the holy place.

faute, *fault, iniquity.*

M.C.S. *The offyce of the Leuites. The tythes and fyrſt frutes muſt be geuen them. Aarons herytage.*

And thou and thy ſonnes with the, ſhall beare the

V. 6 et dederunt ei omnes principes virgas per ſingulas tribus fueruntque virgæ duodecim abſque virga Aaron. 10 in ſignum re bellium filiorum 12 Ecce cōſumpti ſumus, omnes periimus 13 num vſque ad internecionem cuncti delendi ſumus?

L. 6 gaben yhm zwelff ſtecken, eyn iglicher heubtman eynen ſtecken nach dem haus yhrer veter, Vnd der ſtecke Aaron war auch vnter yhren ſtecken. 10 zum zeichen den widderſpenſtigen kindern 12 Sihe, wyr nemen ab vnd komen vmb, werden all vnd komen vmb 13 Sollen wyr denn allerding abnemen?

M. M. N. 1 *Holy place:* Vnderſtāde yf ye take not heade that it be not touched.

faute of that whiche is done amyſſe in youre preaſt-
2 hode. And thy brethern alſo ẏ tribe of leui, ẏ trybe
of thy father take with the, and let them be yoyned
vnto the and miniſtre vnto the.

And thou and thy ſonnes with the ſhall miniſtre
3 before the tabernacle of witneſſe. And let them wayte
apon the and apon all the tabernacle: only let them
not come nye the holy veſſels & the alter, that both
4 they ād ye alſo dye not. And let them be by the and
wayte on the tabernacle of witneſſe, and on all the
ſeruyce of the tabernacle, and let no ſtraunger come
nye vnto you.

5 Wayte therfore apon the holye place and .P. apon
the alter, ẏ there fall no moare wrath apon the childern
6 of Iſrael: beholde, I haue taken youre brethern the
leuites from amonge [the] childern of Iſrael, to be
youres, as giftes geuen vnto the Lorde to doo the
7 ſeruyce of the tabernacle of witneſſe. And ſe that
both thou and thy ſonnes with the take hede vnto
youre preaſtes office, in all thinges that pertayne
vnto the alter and within the vayle. And ſe that
ye ſerue, for I haue geuē youre preaſtes office vnto
you for a gifte to do ſeruyce: & the ſtraunger that
cometh nye, ſhall dye.

8 And the Lorde ſpake vnto Aaron: beholde, I haue
geuen the the kepynge of myne heueofferynges in all
the halowed thynges of the childern of Iſrael. And
vnto the I haue geuen them vnto anoyntynge ād to
9 thy ſonnes: to be a dutye for euer. This
ſhall be thyne of moſt holy ſacrifyces: All
their giftes, thorow out all their meatofferynges ſynne-

dutye, *due*, noun

M. 6 from amonge the chyldren

V. 1 peccata ſacerd. 2 fratres tuos de tribu Leui, ſceptro patris tui ſume tecum . . in tabernaculo teſtimonii. 3 Excubabuntque Leuitæ ad præcepta tua . . . ne & illi moriantur, vt vos pereatis ſimul. 4 Alienigena non miſcebitur vobis. 5 ne oriatur indignatio 7 per ſacerdotes adminiſtrabuntur. 8 dedi tibi cuſtodiam primitiarum mearum. 9 & cedit in ſancta ſanctorum

L. 1 miſſethat ewrs prieſterthums 2 deyne bruder des ſtams Leui deyns vatters . . . fur der hutten des zeugnis 4 Vnd keyn frembder ſol ſich zu euch nahen 5 das furt nicht mehr eyn wueten kome 7 denn ewr prieſterthum gebe ich euch eyn zum ampt fur eyn gabe 8 meyne Hebeopffer 9 das aller heyligſt ſeyn,

offrynges and trespaceoffrynges whiche they bringe
vnto me: They shalbe most holy vnto the ād vnto
10 thy sonnes. And ye shall eate it in the most holye
place: all that are males shall eate of it: for it shalbe
holye vnto the.
11 And this shalbe thyne: the heueofferynge of their
giftes, thorow out all the waueofferynges of the childern of Israel, for I haue geuen them vnto the and thy
sonnes, [Fo. XXXVI.] and thy doughters with the,
to be a dutye for euer: and all that are cleane in thy
12 house, shall eate of it, all the fatt of the oyle, of the
wyne and of the corne: their firstfrutes which they geue
13 vnto the Lorde that haue I geuen vnto the. The first
frutes of all that is in their londes whiche they brynge
vnto the Lorde, shalbe thyne: and all that are cleane
in thyne housse, shall eate off it.
14, 15 All dedicate thinges in Israel, shalbe thine. All
that breaketh the matrice of all flesh that men bringe
vnto the Lorde, bothe of man and beest, shalbe thyne.
Neuerthelater the firstborne of man shalbe redemed,
and the firstborne of vncleane beestes shalbe redemed.
16 And their redemptions shalbe at a moneth olde, valowed at .v. sycles of syluer, of the holy sycle. A sycle
17 maketh twentye Geras. But the firstborne of oxen,
shepe & gootes shall not be redemed. For they are
holy, and thou shalt sprinkle their bloud apon the
alter, and shalt burne their fatt to be a sacrifyce of a
swete sauoure vnto the Lorde.
18 And the flesh of them shalbe thyne, as the waue
19 brest and all the right shulder is thyne. All the holy
heueofferynges whiche the childern of Israel heue vnto
ẏ Lorde, I geue the & thy sonnes & thi doughters
with the to be a dutye for euer. And it shalbe a

V 10 mares tantum edent ex eo, quia consecratum est tibi 13 Vniuersa frugum initia, quæ gignit humus 14 Omne quod ex voto 15 ita duntaxat 16 obolos 17 quia sanctificata sunt domino 19 Omnes primitias sanctuarii . . .

L. 10 Am allerheyligsten ort soltu es essen . . . Was menlich ist . . . denn es sol dyr heylig seyn. 13 Die erste frucht, alles das ynn yhrem land 14 Alles verbannete ynn Israel 15 doch das du die erste menschen frucht 16 Gera. 17 denn sie sind heylig 19 Alle Hebopffer die die kinder Israel heyligen . . .

ſalted couenaunte for euer, before the Lorde: vnto
the and to thy ſeed with the.
20 .P. And the Lorde ſpake vnto Aaron: thou ſhalt haue
none enheritaunce in their lande, nor parte amonge
them. For I am thy parte and thy enheritaunce
21 among the childern of Iſrael. And beholde I haue
geuen the childern of Leui, the tenth in Iſrael to en-
herite, for the ſeruyce whiche they ſerue in the taber-
22 nacle of witneſſe, that the childrē of Iſrael henceforth
come not nye the tabernacle of witneſſe, and beare
23 ſynne and dye. And the leuites ſhall do the ſeruyce
in the tabernacle of witneſſe and beare their ſynne,
and it ſhalbe a lawe for euer vnto youre childern after
you: But amonge the childern of Iſrael they ſhall en-
24 heret none enheritaunce. For the tithes
of the childern of Iſrael whiche they heve
vnto the Lorde, I haue geuen the Leuites
to enherett. Wherfore I haue ſayed vnto
them: Amonge the chyldern off Iſraell ye
ſhall enherett none enheritaunce.

Oures, will haue tithes & landes & rētes & kingdomes & emperies and all.

25, 26 And the Lorde ſpake vnto Moſes ſayenge: ſpeake
vnto the leuites and ſaye vnto thē: when ye take of
the childern of Iſrael the tithes whiche I haue geuen
you of them to youre enheritaunce, ye ſhall take an
heueoffrynge of that ſame for the Lorde: euen the
27 tenth of that tythe. And it ſhalbe rekened vnto you
for youre heueofferynge, euen as though ye gaue corne
out of the barne or a fullofferynge from the wynepreſſe.
28 [Fo. XXXVII.] And of this maner ye ſhall heue an
heueofferynge vnto ẏ Lorde, of all youre tithes which
ye receaue of the childern of Iſrael, & ye ſhall geue

V. 19 Pactum ſalis eſt 21 in poſſeſſionem pro miniſterio 22 nec cōmittant peccatū mortiferū 24 decimarum oblatione contenti, quas in vſus eorum & neceſſaria ſeparaui.

L. 19 eyn vnuerweſenlich bund 21 alle zehenden geben ynn Iſrael zum erbgut 22 das hynfurt . . nicht nahen . . ſund auff ſich zu laden vnd ſterben.

M. M. N. 19 *Salted couenaūt* for a fyrm ſuer and ſtable couenaunt.

L. M. N. 19 Im Ebreiſchen heyſſt es eyn ſaltzbund, das wie das ſaltz erhelt das fleyſch vnuerweſlich, alſo ſoll auch diſer bund vnuerrucklich ſeyn. So redet die ſchrifft auch .2. Paralip. 13. Gott hatt das reych Dauid geben vnd ſeynen mit eym ſaltzbund.

there of the Lordes heueofferinge vnto Aaron the
29 preaſt Of all youre giftes, ye ſhall take out the Lordes
heueofferynge: euen the fatt of all their halowed
thynges.
30 And thou ſhalt ſaye vnto them: when ye haue take
a waye the fatt of it from it, it ſhalbe counted vnto
31 the leuites, as yͤ encreaſe of corne and wyne And ye
ſhall eate it in all places both ye and youre houſholdes,
for it is youre rewarde for youre ſeruyce in the taber-
32 nacle of witneſſe. And ye ſhall beare no ſynne by yͤ
reaſon of it, when ye haue taken from it the fatt of it:
nether ſhall ye vnhalowe yͤ halowed thynges of the
childern of Iſrael, and ſo ſhall ye not dye.

¶ The .XIX. Chapter.

M.C.S. Of the redde cowe. The lawe of him that dyeth in the tabernacle: and of hym alſo that toucheth any vncleane thyng.

1 AND the Lorde ſpake vnto Moſes
2 and Aaron ſayenge: this is the
ordynaunce of the lawe which
yͤ Lorde cōmaūdeth ſayenge:
ſpeake vnto yͤ childern of Iſrael and let
them take the a redd cowe with out ſpot
wherein is no blemyſh,& which neuer bare
3 yocke apō her. And ye ſhall geue her
vnto Eleazer the preaſt, and he ſhall brynge her with
out the hoſte and cauſe her to be ſlayne before him.
4 And Eleazar yͤ preaſt ſhall take of hir bloude vppon
his fynger, and ſprynkle it ſtreght .P. towarde the tab-
5 ernacle of witneſſe .vii. tymes And he ſhall cauſe the

F. 29 Omnia quæ offeretis ex decimis, & in donaria domini ſeparabitis 30 reputabitur vobis 32 ne polluatis oblationes filiorum Iſrael, & moriamini. xix, 2 religio victimæ . . . vaccam rufam ætatis integræ 3 in conſpectu omnium

L. 30 ſo ſols den leuiten gerechnet werden 32 vnd nicht entweyhen das geheyligete der kinder Iſrael, vnd nicht ſterben. xix, 2 Diſe weyſe ſol eyn geſetz ſeyn . . . eyn rodlichte kue . . . auff die noch nie keyn ioch komen iſt 3 daſelbs fur yhm 4 ſtracks gegen die hutten

cowe to be burnt in his ſyghte: both ſkyn, fleſh and
6 bloude, with the doũge alſo. And let the preaſt take
cipreſſe wodd, and Iſope and purple cloth, and caſt
7 it apon the cowe as ſhe burneth. And let the preaſt
waſh his clothes and bathe his fleſh in water, and then
come in to the hoſte, and ẏ preaſt ſhalbe vncleane
vnto the euen.

8 And he that burneth her, ſhall waſh his clothes in
water & bathe his fleſh alſo in water, ād be vncleane
9 vntill euen. And one that is cleane, ſhall goo and
take vpp the aſſhes of the cowe, and put them without
the hoſte in a cleane place, where they ſhall be kepte to
make ſprynklynge water for the multitude *Hēce came*
of the childern of Iſrael: for it is a ſynoffer- *holy water*
10 ynge And let him that gathereth the aſſhes of the
cowe, waſh his clothes, and remayne vncleane vntill
euen. And this ſhalbe vnto the childern of Iſrael ād
vnto the ſtraunger ẏ dwelleth amonge them, a maner
for euer.

11 He that twycheth any deed perſone, ſhalbe vn-
12 cleane .vii. dayes. And he ſhall purifye him ſelfe with
the aſſhes the thyrde daye ād then he ſhalbe cleane
the ſeuenth daye. And yf he purifye not himſelfe the
thyrde daye, thē the ſeuenth daye, he ſhall not be
13 cleane. Whoſoeuer twicheth any perſone ẏ dyeth &
ſprynkleth not him ſelfe, defyleth the dwellynge of
[Fo. XXXVIII.] the Lorde: ād therfore that ſoule
ſhalbe roted out of Iſrael, becauſe he hath not ſpryn-

M. 6 Cedar wood 13 whoſoeuer toucheth

V. 5 comburetque eam cunctis videntibus 6 in flammam, quæ . . . vorat 7 corpore ſuo 9 in loco puriſſimo . . . quia pro peccato vacca combuſta eſt. 10 ſanctum iure perpetuo. 13 Omnis qui . . . et peribit ex Iſrael . . . et manebit ſpurcitia eius ſuper eum.

L. 5 kue fur yhm verbrennen 6 auff die brennende kue 7 ſeyn leyb (v. 8) 9 an eyne reyne ſtette . . . denn es iſt eyn ſundopfer. 10 eyn ewigs recht 13 ſolche ſeele ſol ausgerotet werden

M. M. N. 10 *For euer* loke gene. xiii, d. 13 As they were defyled with the touchyng of the deed, ſo are the ſoules of the chriſten defyled when they commyt deedly ſynne: which is cleanſed with chriſtes ſacryfyce and merytes onely: and that cleāſyng obtayned by the paſſyon and deth of Chriſt oure Lorde who ſoeuer contēneth his ſoule ſhall be rooted oute frō among the choſen.

kled the ſprynklynge water vppon him. he ſhalbe vncleane, and his vnclenneſſe ſhall remayne vppon him.
14 This is the lawe of the man that dyeth in a tent: all
that come in to the tent and all ẙ is in the tent, ſhalbe
15 vncleane .vii. dayes. And all the veſſels that be opē
which haue no lyd nor couerynge apon them, are vn-
16 cleane. And who ſoeuer twicheth one that is ſlayne
with a ſwerde in the feldes, or a deed perſone, or a
bone of a deed man, or a graue: ſhall be vncleane .vii
dayes.
17 And they ſhall take for an vncleane perſone, of the
burnt aſſhes of the ſynofferynge, & put runnynge water
18 thereto in to a veſſell. And a cleane perſone ſhall take
Iſope and dyppe it in the water, and ſprynkle it apon
ẙ tent and apon all the veſſells and on the ſoules that
were there, and apon him that twyched a bone or a
19 ſlayne perſone or a deed body or a graue. And the
cleane perſone ſhall ſprynkle apon the vncleane the
thyrde daye and the ſeuenth daye. And the ſeuenth
daye he ſhall purifie him ſelfe and waſſhe his clothes
and bathe him ſelfe in water, and ſhalbe cleane at euen.
20 Yf any be vncleane and ſprynkle not himſelfe, the
ſame ſoule ſhalbe deſtroyed frō amōge the congregacion: for he hath defyled .P. the holy place of the
Lorde. And he that ſprynkleth ẙ ſprynklynge water,
ſhall waſſh his clothes.
21 And he that twicheth the ſprynklynge water, ſhal-
22 be vncleane vntill euē. And whatſoeuer ẙ vncleane
perſone twicheth, ſhalbe vncleane. And the ſoule that
twicheth it, ſhalbe uncleane vntill the euen.

M. 20 holy place of ẙ Lorde, & is not ſprynkled with ſprinklyng water therfore is he vncleane. And this ſhalbe a perpetual lawe vnto thē.

V. 16 aut per ſe mortui 17 cineribus combuſtionis atque peccati 18 & homines huiuſcemodi contagione pollutos 20 Si quis hoc ritu non fuerit expiatus . . . de medio eccleſiæ 22 et anima quæ horum quippiam tetigerit

L. 16 oder eyn todten 17 nemen der aſſchen diſes verbranten ſundopffers 18 vnd alle ſeelen die drynnen ſind. Alſo auch denen der eyns todten beyn, odder erſchlagenen, odder todten, odder grab angeruret hat 20 Wilcher aber vnreyn ſeyn wirt vnd ſich nicht entſundigen wil 22 Vnd wilche ſeel er anruren wirt

¶ The .XX. Chapter.

M.C.S. Mir Iam dyeth. The people murmur. They haue water euen oute of the rocke. Edom denyeth the Israelites passage thorow his reaulme. The death of Aaron in whose roume Eleazar succedeth.

1 AND the whole multitude of ẏ
childern of Israel, came in to
the deserte of Sin in the first
moneth, & the people dwelt
at cades. And there dyed Mir Iam, &
2 was buried there. More ouer there was
no water for the multitude, wherfore they
gathered thē selues together agēst Moses
3 and agēst Aaron. And the people chode
with Moses and spake sayenge: wold God
that we had peryshed when oure brethern
4 peryshed before ẏ Lorde. Why haue ye brought the
congregacion of the Lorde vnto this wildernesse, that
5 both we & oure catell shulde dye here? Wherfore
brought ye us out of Egipte, to brynge us in to this vn-
gracious place, which is no place of seed nor of fygges
nor vynes nor of pomgranates, nether is there any
water to drynke?

6 And Moses and Aaron went from the congregacion
vnto the dore of the tabernacle of witnesse, and fell
apon their faces. And ẏ glorye of the Lorde appered
7 vnto them. And [Fo. XXXIX.] the Lorde spake vnto
8 Moses sayenge: take ẏ staffe, and gather thou and thi
brother Aarō the congregacion together, and saye vnto
the rocke before their eyes, that he geue forth his
water. And thou shalt brynge thē water out of the
rocke and shalt geue the company drynke, and their
beesse also.

V. 3 & versi in seditionem . . . Vtinam periissemus inter fratres nostros 4 ecclesiam domini 6 Ingressusque Moyses & Aaron dimissa multitudine in tabernaculum fœderis . . . — *clamaueruntque ad dominum, atque dixerunt, Domine deus audi clamorem huius populi, & aperi eis thesaurū tuum fontē aquæ viuæ, vt satiati cesset murmuratio eorum* . . 8 loquimini ad petram

L. 2 haddert mit Mose . . Ach das wyr vmbkomen weren da vnser bruder vmbkamen 4 gemeyne des Herrn 6 von der gemeyne zur thur der hutten des zeugnis 8 redet mit dem fels

9 And Moſes toke the ſtaffe from before ẏ Lorde, as
10 he commaunded him. And Moſes and Aaron gathered
the congregacion together before the rocke, ād he
ſayed vnto thē heare ye rebellyons, muſt we ſett you
11 water out of this rocke? And Moſes liſte vp his hāde
with his ſtaffe and ſmote the rocke .ii. tymes, and the
water came out abundantly, & the multitude dranke
and their beeſſe alſo.
12 And the Lorde ſpake vnto Moſes & Aaron: Becauſe
ye beleued me not, to ſanctifye me in the eyes of the
childern of Iſrael, therfore ye ſhall not brynge this congregacion in to the londe which I haue geuen them.
13 This is the water of ſtryffe, becauſe the childern of
Iſrael ſtroue with the Lorde, & he was ſanctifyed
apon them.
14 And Moſes ſent meſſengers from cades vnto the
kynge of Edome. Thus ſayeth thi brother Iſrael:
Thou knoweſt all the trauell ẏ hath happened us,
15 how oure fathers wēt doune in to Egipte, and how we
haue dwelt in Egipte a longe tyme, and how the
16 Egiptians vexed both us and oure fathers. Then .P.
we cryed vnto the Lorde and he herde oure voyces,
and ſent an angell and hath fett us out of Egipte.
And beholde, we are in Cades a citie harde by the
17 borders of thi contre let us goo a good
felowſhipe thorow thi contre we wyll not
goo thorow the feldes nor thorow the
vyneyardes, nether will we drynke of the water of the
fountaynes: but we will goo by the hye waye and nether turne vnto ẏ ryghte hande nor to ẏ lefte, vntill
we be paſt thi contre.
18 And Edom anſwered him: Se thou come not by me,
19 leſt I come out agēſt the with the ſwerde And the

a good felow-ſhipe, *peace-ably* cf. xxii, 6

V. 10 Audite rebelles et increduli 13 aqua cōtradictionis 14 omnem laborem 16 Cades, quæ eſt in extremis finibus tuis 17 via publica 18 alioquin armatus occurram tibi.

L. 10 Horet yhr widderſpenſtigen 13 das hadder waſſer 14 alle die muhe 16 Kades ynn der ſtadt an deynen grentzen 17 die land ſtraſſe 18 dyr mit dem ſchwerdt entgegen zihen

M. M. N. 12 *To ſanctifye* here is, to ſhewe and declare to be holy as in Math. vi, b.

childern of Iſrael ſayed vnto him: we will goo by the
beeten waye: & yf ether we or oure catell drynke of thi
water, we will paye for it, we wyll doo nomoare but
20 paſſe thorow by fote only. And he ſayed: ye ſhall not
goo thorow. And Edom came out agenſt him with
21 moch people and with a mightie power. And thus
Edom denyed to geue Iſrael paſſage thorow his contre.
And Iſrael turned a waye from him.
22 And the childern of Iſrael remoued frō Cades and
went vnto mount Hor with all the congregacion.
23 And the Lorde ſpake vnto Moſes and Aaron in mount
Hor, harde vppon the coſtes of the londe harde vppon,
24 of Edom ſayenge: let Aaron be put vnto *near to*
his people, for he ſhall not come in to the londe which
I haue [Fo. XL.] geuen vnto the childern of Iſrael: becauſe ye diſhobeyed my mouth at the water of ſtryffe
25 Take Aaron and Eleazer his ſonne, & brynge them
26 vpp in to mount Hor, and ſtryppe Aaron out of his
veſtimentes and put them apon Eleazer his ſonne, ād
let Aaron be put vnto his people and dye there.
27 And Moſes dyd as the Lorde commaunded: and
they went vpp in to mount Hor in the ſyghte of all the
28 multitude. And Moſes toke off Aarons clothes and
put them apon Eleazer his ſonne, and Aaron dyed
there in the toppe of the mount. And Moſes &
29 Eleazer came doune out of the mount. And all ẏͤ
houſſe of Iſrael morned for Aarō .xxx. dayes

V. 19 Per tritam gradiemur viam . . . dabimus quod iuſtum eſt 20 cum infinita multitudine, & manu forti 22 Hor, qui eſt in finibus terræ Edom 23 vbi 24 eo quod incredulus fuerit ori meo 25 Tolle Aaron & filium eius cum eo 26 nudaueris patrem veſte ſua . . Aaron colligetur, & morietur ibi. 28 deſcendit cum Eleazaro. 30 per cunctas familias ſuas.

L. 19 auff der gebeenten ſtraſs . . ſo wollen wyrs betzalen 20 mit mechtigem volck vnd ſtarcker hand. 22 Hor am gepirge 23 Hor am gepirge an den grentzen des lands der Edomiter 24 darumb das yhr meynem mund widderſpenſtig geweſt ſeyd 25 Nym Aar. vnd ſeynen ſon Eleaſar 26 Aaron ſol ſich daſelbs ſamlen vnd ſterben. 28 Moſe aber vnd El. ſtygen erab vom berge 29 Aaron dahyn war . . . das gantze haus Iſrael.

The .XXI. Chapter.

1 AND when kynge Arad the ca-
nanite which dwelt in the
ſouth parties, harde tell that
Iſrael came by the waye that
the ſpies had founde out: he
came and foughte with Iſrael
and toke ſome of them preſ-
2 oners. Then Iſrael vowed a
vowe vnto the Lorde and
ſayed: Yf thou wilt geue this
people in to oure hādes, we
will deſtroye their cities.
3 And the Lorde herde ẏ
voyce of Iſrael, ād dely-
uered them the Cananites And they
deſtroyed both them and their cities,
and called the place Horma.

Hence couetouſnes fett monethes myndes and hath encreaſed thē with yeres myndes ād ſeuen yeres mīdes ye as longe as the wife liveth ſhe muſt once in the yere offer ſomewhat for her olde huſbond.

M.C.S. *Iſrael vanqueſſheth kyng Arad. The fyerye ſerpentes ſtynge them: but when they loke at the braſen ſerpent which the Lord commaunded Moſes to lyft vp, they are healed. The kynges, Sehon and Og are ouercome in batell.*

4 .P. Then they departed from mount hor towarde
the redd ſe: to compaſſe the londe of Edō. And the
5 ſoules of the people faynted by the waye. And
the people ſpake agenſt God and agenſt Moſes:
wherfore haſt thou brought us out of Egipte, for
to dye in the wilderneſſe for here is nether bred nor
water, and oure ſoules lotheth this lyghte bred.
6 Then the Lorde ſent fyrie ſerpentes amōge the
people, which ſtonge them: ſo that moch people dyed
7 in Iſrael. And the people came to Moſes and ſayed:
we haue ſynned, for we haue ſpoken agenſt the Lorde

V. 1 et victor exiſtens, duxit ex eo prædam. 3 quem ille interfecit ſubuerſis vrbibus eius: & vocauit nomen loci illius, Horma, id eſt anathema. 4 Et tædere cœpit populum itineris ac laboris 5 anima noſtra iam nauſeat ſuper cibo iſto leuiſſimo 6 ad quorum plagas & mortes

L. 1 vnd furet etlich gefangen 3 Vnd hies die ſtett Harma. 4 dem volck wart die ſeele vnluſtig auff dem wege 5 vnſer ſeele ekelt vber diſer loſen ſpeyſe. 6 die biſſen das volck

M. M. N. 5 *Lyghte bread:* Or that is ſo lytell woorth. 6 The plage of ſerpentes

L. M. N. 3 *Harma* heyſt eyn bann

and agenſt the make interceſſion to the Lorde, that
he take awaye the ſerpentes from us And Moſes
8 made interceſſion for the people. And the Lorde
ſayed vnto Moſes: make the a ſerpent ād hāge it vpp
for a ſygne, and lett as many as are bytten loke apon
9 it and they ſhall lyue. And Moſes made a ſerpent of
braſſe ād ſett it vpp for a ſygne And when the ſerpentes had bytten any man, he went and behelde the
ſerpent of braſſe and recouered.

10 And the childern of Iſrael remoued and pitched in
11 Oboth. And they departed from Oboth and laye at
Egebarim in the wilderneſſe which is before Moab on
12 the eaſt ſyde. And they remoued thence, and pitched
13 apon the ryuer of zarad. And they departed thence
and pitched on the other ſyde of Arnō, which ryuer
is in the wilderneſſe, and cometh out of [Fo. XLI.]
the coſtes of the Amorites: for Arnon is the border of Moab, betwene Moab and the Amorites.
14 Wherfore it is ſpoken in the boke of the warre
of the Lorde: goo with a violence, both on the
15 ryuer of Arnon and on the ryuers heed, whiche
ſhoteth doune to dwell at Ar, and leneth vppon the
coſtes of Moab.

16 And from thence they came to Bear, whiche is the
well whereof the Lorde ſpake vnto Moſes: gather the
17 people together, that I maye geue them water. Then
Iſrael ſange this ſonge: Aryſe vpp well, ſynge thereto:
18 The well whiche the rulers dygged and the captaynes
of the people with the helpe of the lawegeuer and with
their ſtaues.

V. 9 quem cum percuſſi aſpicerent, ſanabantur. 13 & prominet in finibus Amorrhæi . . . diuidēs Moabitas & Amorrhæos. 14 Sicut fecit in mari rubro, ſic faciet in torrētibus Arnon. 15 Scopuli torrentium inclinati ſunt, vt requieſcerent in Ar, & recumberent in finibus Moabitarum. 16 Ex eo loco apparuit puteus 17 Aſcendat puteus. Concinebant 18 in datore legis, & in baculis ſuis.

L. 9 vnd bleyb leben 13 vnd eraus fleuſſt an der grentze der Amoriter . . zwidſſchen Moab vnd den Amoritern 14 Vnd far mit vngeſtum beyde an den bechen Arnon 15 vnd der beche quellen, wilcher neygt ſich hyn, das er wone zu Ar, vnd lehnet ſich an, das er der Moabiter grentze wirt. 16 Vnd von dannen zogen ſie zum brunnen. 17 ſungen eyns vmbs ander vber dem brun. 18 durch den lerer vnd yhre ſtebe.

M. M. N. 14 Some thinck it to be the boke of iudges.

19 And from this wildernesse they went to Matana, and
from Matana to Nahaliel, and from Nahaliel to Bamoth,
20 and from Bamoth to the valay that is in the felde of
Moab in the toppe of Pisga which boweth towarde the
wildernesse.

21 And Israel sent messengers vnto Sihō, kynge of the
22 Amorites sayenge: let vs goo thorow thy londe. we
will not turne in to thy feldes nor in to thy vyneyardes,
nether drynke of the water of the welles: but we will
goo alonge by the comon waye, vntill we be past thy
23 contre. And Sihō wolde geue Israel no licence to
passe thorow his contre, but gathered all his people
together & went out agēst .P. Israel in to the wildernesse. And he came to Iaheza and foughte with Israel.

24 And Israel smote him with the edge of the swerde
and conquered his londe, from Arnon vnto Iabock:
euen vnto the childern of Ammon. For the borders
25 of the childern of Ammon, are stronge. And Israel
toke all these cities & dwelt in all ẏ cities of ẏ Amorites: in Esbon and in all the townes that longe there
26 to. For Esbon was the citie of Sihon the kinge of the
Amorites which Sihon had fought before with the kinge
of the Moabites, ād had taken all his londe out of his
hande, euen vnto Arnon.

27 Wherfore it is a prouerbe: goo to Hesbō and let the
28 citie of Sihon be bylt ād made redye for there is a
fyre gone out of Hesbon & a flame frō the citie of Sihō
ād hath cōsumed Ar of the Moabites and the men of
29 the hylles of Arnon. Wo be to the Moab: o people
of Chemos ye are forloren. His sonnes
are put to flighte & his doughters brought
captyue vnto Sihon kinge of the Amorites.

forloren, *lost*, cf. German *verloren*

M. 20 Phasgah which boweth toward Iesimon. 29 Chamos ẏ are vndone

V. 22 via regia 24 A quo percussus est in ore gladii 25 in Hesebon scilicet, & viculis eius. 28 & habitatores excelsorum Arnon.

L. 22 die landstrasse 24 Israel aber schlug yhn mit der scherff des schwerds 25 Hesbon mit allen yhren tochtern 28 vnd die burger der höhe Arnon

M. M. N. 20 *Phasgah:* After the commen translacyon. Chald. a hylle. *Iesimon:* Grec. wyldernesse. 29 *Chamos* is the name of a certen image.

30 There lighte is out from Heſbon vnto Dibon and
we made a wilderneſſe euen vnto Nopha whiche reach-
eth vnto Mediba.
31 And thus Iſraell dwelt in the londe of the Amorites.
32 And Moſes ſent to ſerche oute Iaezer, & they toke
the townes belongynge thereto ād conquered the Amorites that were there.
33 [Fo. XLII.] And then they turned and went vppe
to warde Baſon. And Og the kynge of Baſon came out
agenſt them, both he and all his people, to warre at
34 Edrei. And the Lorde ſayed vnto Moſes: feare him
not, for I haue delyuered him in to thy handes with
all his people and his lande. And thou ſhalt do with
him as thou dydeſt with Sihon the kynge of the
35 Amorites which dwelt at Heſbon. And they ſmote
him and his ſonnes and all hys people, vntyll there
was nothinge left him. And they conquered his lande.
xxii, 1 And ỹ children of Iſrael remoued and pitched
in the feldes of Moab, on the other ſyde of Iordane, by
Iericho.

☙ The .XXII. Chapter.

2 AND Balac the ſonne of Ziphor
ſawe all that Iſrael had done
3 to the Amorites, and the Moabites were ſore afrayed of the
people, becauſe they were many, and ab-
4 horred the childern of Iſrael: And Moab

M.C.S. Kyng Balac ſendeth for Balam to thyntent that he ſhulde curſe Iſrael: but Balam can do nothynge

V. 30 Iugum ipſorum diſperiit ab Heſebon vſque Dibon 32 cuius ceperunt viculos,& poſſederunt habitatores. 35 vſque ad internecionem xxii, 1 vbi trans Iordanem Iericho ſita eſt. 2 Iſrael Amorrhæo 3 & impetum eius ferre non poſſent

L. 30 yhr herlickeyt iſt zu nicht worden von Hesbon bis gen Dibon 32 vnd gewonnen yhre töchter, vnd namen die Amoriter eyn die drynnen waren. 35 bis das keyner vberblieb. xxii, 1 ienſid dem Iordan bey Ieriho. 2 den Amoritern 3 grawet fur

L. M. N. 32 *Tochter:* das iſt die dorffer vnd flecken vmb die ſtad her ligend.

ſayed vnto the elders of Madian, now this
companye hath lickte vpp all that are
rounde aboute vs, as an oxe lycketh vp
the graſſe of the felde. And Balac the
ſonne of Ziphor was kinge of the Moabites at that tyme.

agaynſt the wyll of the Lorde. Balams aſſe ſpeaketh to him in the waye.

5 And he ſent meſſangers vnto Balam the ſonne of
Beor, the interpreter whiche dwelt vppon the ryuer
of the lande of the childern .P. of his folke, to call him
ſayenge: beholde, there is a people come out of Egipte
which couereth the face of the erthe and lye euen harde
6 by me. Come nowe a felaſhippe and curſe me this people. For they are to myghtie for me, ſo perauenture
I myghte be able to ſmyte them and to dryue them
oute of the londe. For I wote that whome thou bleſſeſt ſhalbe bleſſed, and whome thou curſeſt ſhalbe curſed.
7 And the elders of Moab went with the elders of
Madian, and the rewarde of the ſothe ſayenge in their
handes. And they came vnto Balam and tolde him
8 the wordes of Balac. And he ſayed vnto them: tary
here all nyghte and I will bringe you worde, euen as
the Lorde ſhall ſaye vnto me. And the lordes of Moab
abode with Balam.
9 And god came vnto Balam and ſayed: what men
10 are theſe which are with the? And Balam ſayed vnto
god: Balac the ſonne of Ziphor kynge of Moab hath
11 ſent vnto me ſayenge: beholde, there is a people come
out of Egipte and couereth the face of the erthe: come
now therfore and curſe me them, that ſo peraduenture
I maye be able to ouercome them in batell, and to
12 dryue thē out. And god ſayed vnto Balam: thou ſhalt
not goo with them, nether curſe the people, for they
are bleſſed.

M. 5 lyeth euen harde
V. 4 delebit hic populus 5 Balaam filium Beor ariolum . . . terræ filiorum Ammon . . . ſedens contra me 6 de terra mea. 7 omnia verba Balac 9 Quid ſibi volunt 10 Reſpondit, Balac
L. 4 Nu wirt diſer hauffe auff nagen 5 Bileam dem ſon Beor, der eyn ausleger war 6 vnd ligt gegen myr . . denn es iſt myr zu mechtig 8 ſo wil ich euch widder ſagen 9 Wer ſind die leut? 10 Bileam ſprach zu Gott

13 [Fo. XLIII.] And Balam rose vp in the mornynge &
sayed vnto the lordes of Balac: gett you vnto youre
lande, for the Lorde will not suffre me to goo with you.
14 And the lordes of Moab rose vpp and went vnto Balac
15 and sayed Balam wolde not come with vs. And Balac
sent agayne a greatter companye of lordes ād more
16 honorable than they. And they came to Balam and
tolde him: Thus sayeth Balac the sonne of Ziphor:
17 oh, let nothynge lett the to come vnto me, for I will
greatly promote the vnto great honoure, ād will doo
whatsoeuer thou sayest vnto me, come therfore I praye
the, curse me this people.

18 And Balam answered and sayed vnto the servauntes
of Balac: Yf Balac wolde geue me his houssull of syluer
and golde, I can goo no further than the worde of the
19 Lorde my god, to do lesse or moare. Neuerthelesse
tarye ye here all nyghte: that I maye wete, what
20 the Lorde will saye vnto me once moare. And God
came to Balam by nyghte and sayed vnto him: Yf
the men come to fett the, ryse vppe and goo with
them: but what I saye vnto the, that onlye thou
shalt doo.

21 And Balam rose vppe early and sadelde his asse and
22 went with the lordes of Moab, But God was angrye because he went.

And the angell of the Lorde stode in the waye
agenste hym. And he ryd vppon hys .P. asse and two
23 seruauntes with him. And when the asse sawe the
angell of the Lorde stonde in the waye and his swerde
drawen in his hande, she turned a syde oute of the waye
and went out in to the felde. And Balam smote the
asse, to turne her in to the waye.

24 And the angell of the Lorde went and stode in a

M. 20 God came vnto Balam by nyghte

V. 13 quia prohibuit me dominus 15 Rursum ille 16 Ne cuncteris venire ad me 17 et quicquid volueris dabo 18 non potero immutare 21 asina . . . cum eis. 22 contra Balaam

L. 13 denn der Herr wils nicht gestatten das ich mit euch zihe 15 Da sandte Balak 17 Lieber were dich nicht zu myr zu zihen 18 doch nicht vbergehen das wort des Herrn 21 eselyn . . mit den fursten der Moabiter. 22 das er hinzoch . . . das er yhm widder stunde

path betwene the vyneyardes, where was a wall on the
25 one ſyde and another on the other. When the aſſe ſawe
the angell of the Lorde, ſhe wrenſhed vnto the walle and thruſt Balams fote vnto
wrenſhed, *puſhed, thruſt*
26 the wall, and he ſmote her agayne. And the angell
of ẏ Lorde went forder and ſtode in a narowe place,
where was no waye to turne, ether to the right hande
27 or to the lyſte. And when the aſſe ſawe the angell of
the Lorde, ſhe fell downe vnder Balam: & Balam was
wroth & ſmote the aſſe with a ſtaffe.
28 And the Lorde opened the mouthe of the aſſe, and
ſhe ſayed vnto Balam: what haue I done vnto the,
29 that thou ſmyteſt me this .iii. tymes? And Balam
ſayde vnto the Aſſe: becauſe thou haſt mocked me?
I wolde that I had a ſwerde in myne hande, that I
30 myghte now kyll the. And the aſſe ſayed vnto Balam: am not I thyne aſſe whiche thou haſt rydden vppon ſence thou waſt borne vnto this daye? Was I
euer wont to do ſo vnto [Fo.XLIIII.] the? And he
ſayed, nay.
31 And the lorde opened the eyes of Balam that he
ſawe the angell of the Lorde ſtondinge in the waye,
with his ſwerde drawen in his honde. And he bowed
32 him ſelfe and fell flatt on his face. And ẏ angell of ẏ
Lord ſayed vnto him: Wherfore ſmyteſt thou thyne
aſſe this .iii. tymes? beholde, I came oute to reſyſt the,
33 for the waye is contrarye vnto me: and the aſſe ſawe
me and avoyded me thre tymes: or elſe (had ſhe not
turned fro me) I had ſuerly ſlayne the and ſaued her
alyue.
34 And Balam ſayed vnto the angell of ẏ Lorde: I
haue ſynned: for I wiſt not that thou ſtodeſt in the
waye agenſt me. Now therfore yf it diſpleaſe thyne
35 eyes, I will turne agayne. And the angell ſayde vnto

M. 28 ſmyteſt me thus .iii. tymes 33 thus .iii. tymes?

V. 27 concidit ſub pedibus ſedentis . . . fuſte latera eius. 29 Quia commeruiſti & illuſiſti mihi 30 cui ſemper 31 pronus in terram. 32 quia peruerſa eſt via tua, mihique contraria.

L. 27 auff yhre knie vnter dem Bileam 29 Das du meyn geſpottet haſt 30 zu deyner zeyt 32 denn der weg iſt myr entgegen 33 auch itzt erwurget . . . haben.

Balam, goo with the men: but in any wiſe, what I ſaye
vnto the, that ſaye. And Balam went with the lordes
of Balac.
36 And when Balac herde that Balā was come he went
out agenſt him vnto a cytie off Moab that ſtode in the
border of Arnō, whiche was the vttmoſt parte of his
37 contre. And Balac ſayed vnto Balam: dyd I not ſende
for the, to call the? wherfore cameſt thou not vnto me?
thinkeſt thou that I am not able to promote the vnto
38 honoure? And Balam ſayed vnto Balac: Loo I am
come vnto the. But I can ſaye nothynge at all .P.
ſaue what God putteth in my mouthe that muſt I ſpeake.
39 And Balam went with Balac, and they came vnto the
40 cytie of Huzoth. And Balac offered oxen and ſhepe,
& ſent for Balam and for the lordes that were with
hym.

¶ The .XXIII. Chapter.

M.C.S. Balam bleſſeth the people, where he was required to curſe thē and propheſyeth that they ſhalbe a greate people.

41 AND on the mornynge Balac toke
Balam and brought him vpp
in to the hye place of Baall,
ād thēce he ſawe vnto the vtt-
XXIII, 1 moſt parte of the people. And Balam ſayed vnto Balac: bylde me here
ſeven alters and prouyde here ſeuē oxen
2 and ſeuen rammes. And Balac dyd as Balam ſayed.
And Balac and Balam offered on euery alter an oxe
and a ram.

M. 39 came vnto the large cytie. xxiii, 1 ſeuen bullockes 2 alter a bullock

V. 35 caue ne aliud quam 36 Quod cum audiſſet Balac, egreſſus eſt in occurſum eius in oppido Moabitarum, quod ſitum eſt in extremis finibus Arnon. 37 cur non ſtatim . . . an quia mercedem aduētui tuo reddere nequeo? 39 vrbem quæ in extremis regni eius finibus erat. 40 miſit ad Balaam . . . munera.

L. 35 aber nichts anders denn was ich 36 die da ligt an der grentze 39 vnd kamen in die gaſſenſtadt 40 ſandte nach Bileam

M. M. N. 39 The large cytie: Ebre. of places or of ſtreates. Some full of people in the ſtreates.

3 And Balam ſayed vnto Balac: ſtonde by the ſacrifyce, whyle I goo to wete whether the Lorde will come
ād mete me: & what ſoeuer he ſheweth me, I will tell
the, and he went forthwith.
4 And god came vnto Balam, and Balam ſayed vnto
him: I haue prepared .vii. alters, and haue offered apō
5 euery alter, an oxe & a ram. And ỷ Lorde put a
ſayenge in Balās mouth & ſayed: goo agayne to Balac
6 & ſaye on this wyſe. And he went agayne vnto him
and loo, he ſtode by his ſacrifice, both he ād all the
7 lordes of Moab. And he began hys parable and ſayed:
Balac the kinge of [Fo. XLV.] Moab hath fett me fro
Meſopotamia out of the mountaynes of the eaſte ſayenge: come & curſe me Iacob, come and deſye me
8 Iſrael. How ſhall I curſe whom God curſeth not and how ſhall I deſye whom
The pope cā tell howe.
9 the Lorde deſyeth not? from the toppe of ỷ rockes I
ſe him and from the hylles I beholde him: loo, ỷ people ſhall dwell by him ſelfe and ſhall not be rekened
10 amōge other nacions. Who can tell the duſt of Iacob
& the numbre of the fourth parte of Iſrael. I praye
God that my ſoule, maye dye the deeth of the righteous, ād that my laſt ende maye be like his.
11 And Balac ſayed vnto Balam, what haſt thou done
vnto me? I fett ỷ to curſe myne enemyes: and be-
12 holde, thou bleſſeſt them. And he anſwered and ſayed:
muſt I not kepe that and ſpeake it, which the Lorde
13 hath put in my mouthe? And Balac ſayed vnto him:
Come I praye the with me vnto another place, whence
thou ſhalt ſe them, and ſhalt ſe but ỷ vtmoſte parte of
them ād ſhalt not ſe them all and curſe me them there.

M. 4 alter, a bullock

V. 3 Sta paulifper . . . donec 7 propera et deteſtare Iſrael. 10 & noſſe numerum ſtirpis Iſrael? 12 Num aliud poſſum loqui niſi quod iuſſerit dominus? 13 vnde partem Iſrael videas, & totum videre non poſſis

L. 7 kom ſchilt Iſrael 10 die zahl des vierden teyls Iſrael? 12 Mus ich nicht das halten vnd reden, das myr der Herr ynn den mund gibt?

M. M. N. 9 *To dwell by him ſelfe* is, to lyue in lybertye with oute trouble and oute of the ſubieccion of other people as in Deutero. xxxiii, d. *Rekened:* After the chald. deſtroyed.

14 And he brought him in to a playne felde where
men myght ſe farre, euen to the toppe of Piſga, and
bylt .vii. alters and offered an oxe and a rā on euery
15 alter. And he ſayed vnto Balac: ſtonde here by thi
16 sacrifyce whyle I goo yonder. And the Lorde mett
Balam and put wordes in his mouth and ſayed: goo
17 agayne vnto Balac ād thus ſaye. And when .P. he
came to him: beholde, he ſtode by his ſacrifyce and
the lordes of Moab with him And Balac ſayed vnto
him: what ſayeth ẏͤ Lorde?

18 And he toke vp his parable and ſayed: ryſe vpp
Balac and heare, and herken vnto me thou ſonne of
19 Ziphor The Lorde is not a mā, that he can lye, nether the ſonne of a mā that he can repent: ſhulde he
ſaye and not doo, or ſhulde he ſpeake and not make it
20 good? beholde, I haue begon to bleſſe and haue bleſſed,
21 and can not goo backe there fro. He beheld no wikedneſſe in Iacob nor ſawe Idolatrye in Iſrael: The Lorde
his God is with him, and the trompe of a kynge amonge
22 thē. God that broughte them out of Egipte, is as the
23 ſtrength of an vnycorne vnto them, for there is no
ſorcerer, in Iacob, nor ſothſayer in Iſrael. When the
tyme cometh, it wylbe ſayed of Iacob & of Iſrael, what
24 God hath wrought Beholde, ẏͤ people ſhall ryſe vp as

F. 14 locum ſublimem ſuper verticem montis Phaſga 19 vt mutetur 21 Non eſt idolum in Iacob, nec videtur ſimulachrum in Iſrael. Dominus deus eius cum eo eſt, & clangor victoriæ regis in illo. 23 Non eſt augurium in Iacob, nec diuinatio in Iſrael.

L. 14 eyn freyen platz auff der hohe Piſga 19 das yhn etwas gerewe 21 keyn muhe in Iacob noch keyn erbeyt ynn Iſrael, der Herr ſeyn Gott iſt bey yhm vnd das drometen des konigs vnter yhm 23 keyn zeuberey ynn Iacob vnd keyn warſager ynn Iſrael . . . was Gott thut

M. M. N. 21 *He behelde no wikedneſſe:* Ther is no people wythoute ſynne nether yet Iſrael, but God loketh not on hit, he waxeth not angrye in the ende, he auengeth it not accordynge as it deſerueth, but amendeth it by his grace. *Triumphe of a kynge:* Chal. habitacion dwellyng place or courte.

L. M. N. 21 *Muhe vnd erbeyt* heyſt die ſchrifft die groſſen gutten werck on glawben gethan Pſal. 10. Vnter ſeyner zungē iſt muhe vnd erbeyt, Denn ſolch lere vnd werck macht boſe ſchwere gewiſſen die der glaube leicht vnd frolich macht.—*Drometen des konigs*, das iſt, die leyplichen drometen gottis yhres konigs, der ſie zu machen befolen hatt, darumb, ſie vnvber windlich waren ym ſtreyt. Bedeut aber das Euangelion in der Chriſtenheyt.

a lyoneſſe and heue vpp hym ſelfe as a lion, & ſhall not
lye downe agayne, vntill he haue eaten of the praye
and dronke of the bloude of them that are ſlayne.
25 And Balac ſayed vnto Balam: nether curſe them
26 nor bleſſe thē. And Balam anſwered ād ſayed vnto
Balac: tolde not I the ſayēge, all that the Lorde
27 byddeth me, yͤ I muſt doo? And Balac ſayed vnto
Balam: come I praye the, I will brynge the yet vnto
another place: ſo perauenture it ſhall pleaſe God, that
28 [Fo. XLVI.] thou mayſt curſe thē there. And Balac
broughte Balam vnto the toppe of Peor, that boweth
29 towarde the wilderneſſe. And Balam ſayed vnto Balac: make me here .vii. alters, & prepare me here .vii. bol-
30 lockes and .vii. rāmes And Balac dyd as Balam had
ſayed, and offered a bollocke and a ram on euery alter.

¶ The .XXIIII. Chapter.

M.C.S. Balam prophesieth of the kyngdome of Israel and of the comyng of Christ. Balac is angrie with Balam. The destruccion of the Amelickites and of the Kenytes.

1 WHEN Balam ſawe that it pleaſed
yͤ Lorde that he ſhulde bleſſe
Iſrael, he went not as he dyd
twyſe before to ſett ſothſay-
enge, but ſett his face towarde yͤ wilder-
2 neſſe, and lyfte vpp his eyes and loked
apon Iſrael as he laye with his trybes, and
3 the ſpirite of God came apon him. And
he toke vp his parable and ſayed: Balā
the ſonne of Beor hath ſayed, and the
4 man whoſe eye is open hath ſayed: he hath ſayed which
heareth the wordes of God and ſeeth the viſions of the
allmightie, which falleth downe & his eyes are opened.

V. 4 qui viſionem omnipotentis intuitus eſt, qui cadit & ſic aperiuntur oculi eius

L. 24 eyn iunger lewe. xxiiii, 4 der des almechtigen geſicht ſahe, der da nydder fiel

L. M. N. 1 Hyraus merckt man, das Bileam droben altzeyt ſey zu zeuberey gangen vnter Gottis namen. Aber der Herr iſt yhm ymer begegenet vnd hat die zeuberey gehyndert, das er hat muſſen das recht gottis wort ſaſſen an ſtatt der zeuberey.

5 How goodly are the tentes of Iacob and thine ha-
6 bitacions Iſrael, euen as the brode valeyes and as
gardens by the ryuers ſyde, as the tentes which the
Lorde hath pitched & as ciperstrees apon the water.
7 The water ſhall flowe out of his boket and his ſeed
ſhall be many waters, and his kynge ſhalbe hyer then
8 Agag, And his kyngdome .P. ſhalbe exalted. God
that broughte him out of Egipte is as the ſtrenght of
an vnycorne vnto him, and he ſhall eate the nacions
that are his enemies and breake their bones and perſe
9 them thorow with his arowes. He couched him ſelfe
and laye doune as a lion and as a lyoneſſe, who ſhall
ſtere him vp? bleſſed is he that bleſſeth the, ād curſed
is he that curſeth the.
10 And Balac was wroth with balam and ſmote his
handes together, and ſayed vnto him: I ſent for the
to curſe myne enemyes: & beholde, thou haſt bleſſed
11 them this thre tymes, and now gett the quyckly vnto
thi place. I thoughte that I wolde promote the vnto
honoure, but the Lorde hath kepte the backe from
12 worſhepe. And Balam ſayed vnto Balac: tolde I not
13 thi meſſēgers which thou ſenteſt vnto me ſayenge: Yf
balac wolde geue me his houſe ful of ſyluer ād golde, I
can not paſſe the mouth of the Lorde, to doo ether
good or bad of myne awne mynde. What the Lorde
14 ſayeth, that muſt I ſpeake. And now beholde, I goo
vnto my people: come let me ſhewe the, what this
people ſhall doo to thi folke in the later dayes.
15 And he began his parable ād ſayed: Balam the
ſonne of Beor hath ſayed, and ẏ man that hath his eye

M. 5 thyne habitacion. 8 Egypt his ſtrenght is as the ſtrenght

V. 6 cedri 7 in aquas multas. 8 Deuorabunt gentes hoſtes illius . . . et perforabunt ſagittis. 13 non potero præterire 14 quid populus tuus populo huic faciat extremo tempore

L. 6 cedern 7 eyn groſs waſſer 8 Seyne freydigkeyt iſt wie eyns Eynhorns . . . pfeylen zu ſchmettern 9 wie eyn iunger lewe 13 ſo kund ich doch fur des Herrn wort nicht vber 14 was dis volck mit deynem volck thun ſolle

M. M. N. 5 By all theſe ſimilitudes wolde Balam declare the felycitye of the people of Iſrael which came of God. as ye haue in the Pſal. cxi, & Iere. xvii, b.

16 open hath ſayed, & he hath ſayed that heareth the
wordes of God & hath the knowlege of the moſt hye
and beholdeth ẏ [Fo. XLVII.] viſion of the allmightie,
17 and when he falleth downe hath his eyes opened. I
ſe him but not now, I beholde him but not nye. There
ſhall come a ſtarre of Iacob and ryſe a cepter of Iſrael,
which ſhall ſmyte ẏ cooſtes of Moab and vndermyne
18 all the childern of Seth. And Edom ſhalbe his poſſeſſion, and ẏ poſſeſſion of Seir ſhalbe their enimyes, and
19 Iſrael ſhall doo manfully. And out of Iacob ſhall
come he that ſhall deſtroye the remnaũt of the cities.
20 And he loked on Amaleck and began his parable
and ſayed: Amaleck is the firſt of the nacions, but his
21 latter ende ſhall peryſh utterly. And he loked on the
Kenites, and toke his parable and ſayed: ſtronge is thi
22 dwellynge place and put thi neſt apon a rocke, Neuer
thelater thou ſhalt be a burnynge to Kain, vntill Aſſur
23 take ẏ priſoner. And he toke his parable & ſayed:
24 Alas, who ſhall lyue when God doeth this? The
ſhippes ſhall come out of the coſte of Cittim and ſubdue Aſſur and ſubdue Eber, and he him ſelfe ſhall
25 peryſh at the laſt. And Balam roſe vp and went and
dwelt in his place: and Balac alſo went his waye.

M. 24 Chittim

V. 17 conſurget virga de Iſrael . . . duces Moab, vaſtabitque omnes filios Seth. 18 Iſrael vero fortiter aget. 19 qui dominetur, et perdat 22 & fueris electus de ſtirpe Cin 24 Venient in trieribus de Italia . . . vaſtabuntque Hebræos & ad extremum etiam ipſi peribunt. 25 Balac quoque via qua venerat, rediit.

L. 17 eyn ſcepter aus Iſrael auff komen, vnd wirt zu ſchmettern die vberſten der Moabiter vnd vberweldigen alle kinder Seth. 18 Iſrael aber wirt redlich thatten thun. 19 der hirſcher komen, vnd vmb bringen 22 aber du wirſt eyn antzundung werden Kain 24 Er aber wirt auch gar vmbkomen 25 vnd Balak zoch ſeynen weg.

M. M. N. 24 *Chittim:* Chalde & the cõmen tranſl. Italy.—*Eber:* That is the Hebrues or thoſe that are be yonde the floude of Euphrates.

L. M. N. 17 Diſer ſtern is Dauid, wilcher ſolche leut vnd lender vnter ſich bracht hat, Denn Bileam redet nichts võ Chriſto, ſondern nur vom leybliche͞ reych des volcks Iſrael, wie wol da durch Chriſtus allenthalben bedeut iſt. 20 Amalek war der erſte vnter den heyden den die kinder Iſrael anfochten Exod. 17. aber durch Saul vertilget. 1. Re. 15.—23, 24 Diſer ſpruch iſt auff die Romer biſher gedeutte, Aber der text laut, als ſey der gros Alexander damit bedeut.

The XXV. Chapter.

1 AND Iſrael dwelt in Sittim, and
2 the people began to commytt
whoredome with the dough-
ters of Moab, which called the
people vnto ẏ ſacrifyce of their god- .¶.
des. And the people ate and worſhipped
3 their goddes, and Iſrael coupled him ſelfe
vnto Baal Peor. Then ẏ Lorde was angrie
with Iſrael, and ſayed vnto Moſes: take
all ẏ heedes of the people, and hange them vp vnto
ẏ Lorde agenſt the ſonne, that the wrath of the Lorde
5 maye turne awaye from Iſrael. And Moſes ſayed vnto
the iudges of Iſrael: goo and ſlee thoſe men that ioyned
thē ſelues vnto Baal Peor.

6 And beholde, one of the childern of Iſrael came and
broughte vnto his brethern, a Madianitiſh wife euen in
the ſighte of Moſes & in the ſighte of all the multitude
of ẏ childern of Iſrael, as they were wepynge in the
7 dore of the tabernacle of witneſſe. And when Phineas
the ſonne of Eleazer the ſonne of Aarō the preaſt ſawe
it, he roſe vp out of the companye and toke a wepon
8 in his hande, and wēt after the man of Iſrael in to the
horehouſſe, & thruſt them thorow: both the man of
Iſrael and alſo the woman euen thorow the belye of
hir. And the plage ceaſed from the childern of Iſrael.
9 And there dyed in the plage .xxiiii. thouſande.

M.C.S. *The people cōmitteth fornication with the daughters of Moab. Phinehes kylleth Zamri and Cozbi. God commaundeth to kyll the Madianites.*

V. 2 At illi comederunt & adorauerunt deos earum. 3 Initiatuſque eſt Iſrael Beelphegor 4 et ſuſpende eos contra ſolem in patibulis: vt auertatur furor meus ab Iſrael. 6 intrauit coram fratribus ſuis ad ſcortum Mad. 7 et arrepto pugione 8 in lupanar . . . in locis genitalibus.

L. 2 zu huren mit der Moab. töchter . . . aſs vnd bettet yhr gotter an . . . vnterwarff ſich dem Baal Peor. 4 henge ſie dem Herrn an die ſonne, auff das der grymmige zorn . . . gewand werde. 6 lies Moſe zu ſehen 7 eyn meſſer yn ſeyne hand 8 ynn das hurhaus . . . durch yhren bauch

M. M. N. 4 *To hang agaynſt the ſonne* is, to be put to execucion openly before all people. 8 *Thorow* etc. After the chald. The Grec & the cōmen tranſl. throwe the ſhamelie or fyltye membres. Some reade, euen in the ſtewes.

10, 11 And the Lorde ſpake vnto Moſes ſayenge: Phineas the ſonne of Eleazer the ſonne of Aaron the preaſt,
hath turned myne anger awaye from the childern of
Iſrael, becauſe he was gelous for my ſake amonge them,
that I had not cōſumed the childern of Iſrael in my
12 [Fo. XLVIII.] gelouſye. Wherfore ſaye: beholde, I
13 geue vnto him my couenaunte of peaſe, and he ſhall
haue it and his ſeed after him, euen the couenaunte of
the preaſtis office for euer, becauſe he was gelous for
his Gods ſake and made an atonement for the childern
of Iſrael.

14 The name of the Iſraelite which was ſmytten with
the Madianitiſh wife, was Simri the ſonne of Salu, a
lorde of an auncīet houſſe amonge the Simeonites.
15 And the name of the Madianitiſh wife, was Coſbi the
doughter of Zur and heed ouer the people of an auncient
houſſe in Madian.

16, 17 And the Lorde ſpake vnto Moſes ſayenge: vexe
18 the Madianites and ſmyte them, for they haue troubled
you with their wiles with the which they haue begyled
you, thorow Peor and thorow their ſyſter Cosby ẏ
doughter of a lorde in Madian, which was ſlayne in ẏ
daye of the plage for Peors ſake.

❡ The .XXVI. Chapter.

1 AND after the plage, ẏ Lorde
ſpake vnto Moſes and vnto
2 Eleazer ſayenge: take the number of all the multitude of the
childern of Iſrael from .xx. yere ād aboue
thorow out their fathers houſſes, all that

M.C.S. The chyldrē of Iſraell are nombred a gayne when they ſhulde entre in to the lande of Canaan.

M. 15 Zur a heed

V. 11 quia zelo meo . . . in zelo meo. 12 pacem fœderis mei 13 zelatus eſt 14 dux de cognatione, & tribu Simeonis. 15 principis nobiliſſimi 17 Hoſtes vos ſentiant Madianitæ 18 per idolum Phogor . . . pro ſacrilegio Phogor.

L. 11 ſeynen eyffer . . . in meynem eyffer 12 meynen bund des frydes 14 eyn heubtman des haus des vatters der Simeon. 15 eyn vberſter der leut war eyns geſchlechts 17 thut den Midianitern leyd

3 are able to goo to warre in Israel. And Moses &
Eleazer the preast tolde them in the feldes .P. of Moab,
by Iordane fast by Iericho, from .xx. yere and aboue,
as the Lorde commaunded Moses. And the childern
of Israel that came out of Egipte were.
5 Ruben the eldest sonne of Israel. The childern of
Ruben were, Hanoch, of whome cometh the kynred
of the Hanochites: & of Palu, cometh the kynred of
6 the Paluites: And of Hesron, cometh the kynred of the
Hesronites: and of Carmi, cometh the kynred of the
7 Carmites. These are the kynredes of the Rubenites,
which were in numbre .xliii. thousande .vii. hūdred
8, 9 and .xxx. And the sonnes of Palu were Eliab. And
the sonnes of Eliab were: Nemuel, Dathan and Abiram.
This is that Dathan and Abiram councelers in the
cōgregacion, which stroue agēst Moses and Aaron in
the companye of Corah, when they stroue agenst the
10 Lorde. And the erth opened hir mouth ād swalowed
thē and Corah also, when the multitude dyed, what
tyme the fyre consumed .ii. hundred and fiftie men, and
11 they became a signe: Notwithstondynge, the childern
of Corah dyed not.
12 And the childern of Simeon in their kynredes were: Nemuel, of whom cometh ẏ kynred of the Nemuelites: Iamin, of whom cometh the kynred of the Iaminytes: Iachin,
13 of whom cometh the kynred of the Iachinites: Serah, of
whom cometh the kynred of the Serahites: Saul, of
whom cometh the kyn- [Fo. XLIX.] red of the Saulites.
14 These are the kynredes of the Simeonites: in numbre
xxii. thousande and .ii. hundred.
15 And the childern of Gad in their kynredes were:
Zephon, of whom cometh the kynred of the Zephonites:
and of Haggi, cometh the kynred of the Haggites: and

V. 3 Locuti sunt itaque Moyses, & Eleazar 4 sicut dominus imperauerat, quorum iste est numerus 9 in seditione Core 10 morientibus plurimis . . . et factum est grande miraculum

L. 3 Vnd Mose redet mit yhn 4 wie der Herr Mose gepotten hatte vnd den kindern Israel, die aus Egypten zogen waren. 9 in der rotten Korah 10 da die rotte starb 12 vnd waren zum zeychen

M. M. N. 5 The kynred of Ruben. 12 The kynred of Simeon. 15 The kynred of Gad.

16 of Suni, cometh the kynred of the Sunites: and of
17 Aſeni, cometh the kynred of the Aſenites: and of Eri
cometh the kynred of the Erites: and of Arod cometh
the kynred of the Arodites: and of Ariel cometh the
18 kynred of the Arielites. Theſe are the kynredes of the
children of Gad, in numbre .xl. thouſande and .v
hundred.
19 The childern of Iuda: Er and Onā, whiche dyed in
20 the londe of Canaan. But the childern of Iuda in
their kynred were: Sela of whom cometh the kynred
of the Selamites: and of Phares cometh the kynred of ẏ
Phareſites: and of Serah cometh the kynred of the
21 Serahites. And the childern of Phares were Heſron,
of whom cometh the kynred of the Heſronites: and of
22 Hamul cometh ẏ kynred of the Hamulites. Theſe are
the kynredes of Iuda, in numbre .Lxxvi. thouſande
and .v. hundred.
23 And the childern of Iſachar in their kynredes were:
Tola, of whō cometh ẏ kynred of the Tolaites : & Phuva,
24 of whō cometh ẏ kinred of the Phuuaites: and of Iaſub
cometh .P. the kynred of the Iaſubites: and of Symron
25 cometh the kynred of the Simronites. Theſe are ẏ
kynredes of Iſachar in numbre .Lxiiii. thouſande and
iii. hundred.
26 The childern of Zabulon in their kynredes were:
Sered, of whom cometh the kynred of the Seredites:
and Elon, of whom cometh the kynred of the Elonites:
and of Iaheliel, cometh the kynred of the Iehalelites.
27 Theſe are the kynredes of Zabulon: in numbre .Lx
thouſand & .v. hundred.
28 The childern of Ioſeph in their kinredes were:
29 Manaſſe ād Ephraim. The childern of Manaſſe: Machir, of whom cometh the kynred of the Machirites.
And Machir begat Gilead, of whom cometh the kinred
30 off the Gileadites. And theſe are the childern of Gilead: Hieſer, of whom cometh the kynred of the Hieſerites:
and of Helech cometh the kynred of the Helechites:

M. 23 Thola . . . Tholaites
M. M. N. 19 The kynred of Iuda. 23 The kynred of Iſachar. 26 The kynred of Zabulon. 28 The kynred of Ioſeph.

31 and of Asriel ẏ kinred of the Asrielites: and of Sichem
32 cometh the kinred of the Sichimites: & of Simida
cometh the kinred of the Simidites: & of Hepher
33 cometh the kinred of the Hepherites. And Zelaphead
the sonne of Hepher had no sonnes but doughters And
ẏ names of ẏ doughters of Zelaphead were: Mahela,
34 Noa, Hagla, Milcha ād Thirza. These are the kinredes of Manasse, in numbre .Lii. thousande and seuen
hundred.

35 These are the childern of Ephraim in the- [Fo. L.]
ir kinredes: Suthelah, of whom cometh the kinred of
the Suthelahites: and Becher, of whom cometh the kinred of the Becherites: & of Thaha cometh the kynred
36 of the Thahanites. And these are the childern of
Suthelah: Eran, of whom cometh the kynred of the
37 Eranites. These are the kynredes of the childern of
Ephraim in numbre .xxxii. thousande & .v. hundred.
And these are the childern of Ioseph in their kinredes.

38 These are the childern of Ben Iamin in their kinredes: Bela, of whom cometh the kinred of the Belaites:
and of Asbel cometh the kinred of the Asbelites: and
39 of Ahiram, the kinred of the Ahiramites: and of Suphā
the kinred of the Suphamites: and of Hupham the kin-
40 red of the Huphamites. And the childern of Bela were
Ard and Naamā fro whence come the kinredes of the
41 Ardites and of the Naamites. These are the childern
of Ben Iamin in their kinreddes, and in numbre .xlv
thousande and syxe hundred.

42 These are the childern of Dan in their kynreddes:
Suham, of whom cometh the kynred of the Suhamites.
These are the kynreddes of Dan in their generacyons.
43 And all the kynreddes of the Suhamites were in numbre .Lxiiii. thousande ād .iiii. hundred.

44 The childern of Asser in their kynredes .P. were:
Iemna, of whom cometh the kynred of the Iemnites:
ād Isui, of whom cometh the kinred of the Isuites: & of
45 Bria cometh the kinred of Briites. And the childern

M. M. N. 35 The kynred of Ephraim. 38 The kynred of Ben Iamin. 42 The kynred of Dan. 44 The kynred of Aser.

of bria were Heber, of whom cometh ẏ kynred of the
Heberites: and of Malchiel came the kynred of the Mal-
46 chielites. And ẏ doughter of Aſſer was called Sarah.
47 Theſe are the kinredes of Aſſer in numbre .Liii. thou·
ſande and .iiii. hundred.
48 The childern of Nephtali in their kynreddes were:
Iaheziel, of whom came the kynred of the Iahezielites:
and Guni, of whom came the kynred of the Gunites:
49 & of Iezer, came the kynred of the Iezerites: and of
50 Silem the kynred of Silemites. Theſe are the kinredes
of Naphtali in their generaciōs in numbre .xlv. thou-
51 ſande and .iiii. hundred. Theſe are the numbres of the
childern of Iſrael: ſixe hundred thouſande, & a thouſande .vii. hundred and .xxx.
52, 53 And the Lorde ſpake vnto Moſes ſayenge: vnto
theſe the londe ſhalbe deuyded to enherett, acordinge
54 to the numbre of names: to many thou ſhalt geue ẏ
moare enheritaunce & to fewe ẏ leſſe: to euery tribe
ſhall ẏ enheritaūce be geuē acordinge to ẏ numbre
55 therof. Notwithſtondinge, ẏ londe ſhalbe deuyded by
56 lott, & acordinge to ẏ names of ẏ tribes of their fathers,
thei ſhall enherett: & acordinge to their lott thou
ſhalt deuyde their lond, both [Fo. LI.] to the many
and to the fewe.
57 Theſe are the ſummes of ẏ leuites in their kinredes:
of Gerſon, came the kynred of ẏ Gerſonites: and of
Cahath came the kinred of the Cahathites: and of
58 Merari came the kinred of the Merarites. Theſe are
the kynredes of Leui: the kinred of the Libnites, the
kynred of the Hebronites, the kynred of the Mahelites,
the kynred of the Muſites, the kynred of the Karahites.
59 Kahath begate Amram, and Amrams wife was
called Iochebed a doughter of leui, which was borne
him in Egipte. And ſhe bare vnto Amram, Aaron,

V. 54 ſingulis ſicut nunc recenſiti ſunt tradetur poſſeſſio: 55 ita duntaxat vt ſors terram tribubus diuidat & familiis.

L. 54 iglichen ſol man geben nach yhrer zal, 55 Doch man ſol das land durchs los teylen, nach den namen der ſtemme yhrer veter ſollen ſie erb nemen

M. M. N. 48 The kynred of Nephthali. 57 The nombre of the Leuites.

60 Moſes and Mir Iam their ſyſter. And vnto Aaron were
61 borne, Nadab, Abihu, Eleazer and Ithamar. But Nadab and Abihu dyed, as they offered ſtraunge fyre
62 before the Lorde. And the numbre of them was
xxiii. thouſande, of all the males from a moneth olde
and aboue For they were not numbred amonge ẏͤ
children of Iſrael, becauſe there was no enheritaunce
geuen them amonge the childern off Iſrael.
63 Theſe are the numbres of the childern of Iſrael
which Moſes and Eleazer the preaſt numbred in the
64 feldes of Moab, faſt by Iordane nye to Iericho. And
amonge theſe there was not a man of the numbre of
the children of Iſrael which Moſes and Aaron tolde in
65 the wilderneſſe of Sinai. For the Lor- .¶. de ſayed
vnto them, that they ſhulde dye in ẏͤ wilderneſſe &
that there ſhulde not be lefte a man of them: ſaue
Caleb the ſonne of Iephune & Ioſua the ſonne of Nun.

❡ The .XXVII. Chaptre

M.C.S. The lawe of the herytage of the daughters of Zelaphead. The land of promeſſe is ſhewed vnto Moſes: in whoſe ſteade is appoynted Ioſue.

1 AND the doughters of Zelaphead
the ſonne of Heber the ſonne
of Gilead, the ſonne of Machir
the ſonne of Manaſſe, of the
kinredes of Manaſſe the ſonne of Ioſeph
(whoſe names were Mahela, Noa, Hagla,
2 Melcha and Thirza) came & ſtode before
Moſes and Eleazer the preaſt ād before
the lordes & all the multitude in the
3 dore of the tabernacle of witneſſe ſayenge: oure father
dyed in the wilderneſſe, & was not amonge the companye of them that gathered them ſelues together
agenſt the Lorde in the congregation of Corah: But

V. 62 nec eis cum cæteris data poſſeſſio eſt. 65 Prædixerat enim dominus. xxvii, 3 nec fuit in ſeditione quæ concitata eſt contra dominum ſub Core . . . hic nō habuit mares filios . . . inter cognatos patris noſtri.

L. 62 denn man gab yhn keyn erbe vnter den K. Iſrael. xxvii, 3 vnd war nicht mit vnter der gemeyne die ſich widder den Herrn auflehnten ynn der rotten K.

4 dyed in his awne ſynne, and had no ſonnes. Wherfore
ſhulde the name of oure fathers be taken awaye from
amonge hys kynred, becauſe he had no ſonne? Geue
vnto vs a poſſeſſyon amonge the brethern of oure
father.

5 And Moſes broughte their cauſe before the Lorde.
6, 7 And ỹ Lorde ſpake vnto Moſes ſayenge: The doughters of Zelaphead ſpeke righte: thou ſhalt geue them a
poſſeſſion to en- [Fo. LII.] herett amonge their fathers
brethern, & ſhalt turne the enheritaunce of their fa-
8 ther vnto them. And ſpeake vnto the childern of
Iſrael ſayenge: Yf a man dye and haue no ſonne ye
9 ſhall turne his enheritaunce vnto his doughter. Yf he
haue no doughter, ye ſhall geue his enheritaunce vnto
10 his brethern. Yf he haue no brethern, ye ſhall geue
11 his enheritaunce vnto his fathers brethern. Yf he haue
no fathers brethern, ye ſhall geue his enheritaunce vnto
him that is nexte to him of his kinred, & let him poſſeſſe it. And this ſhalbe vnto the childern of Iſrael an
ordynaunce, and a lawe, as the Lorde hath commaũded
Moſes.

12 And the Lorde ſayed vnto Moſes: get ỹ vpp in to
this mount Aabrim, and beholde, the londe which
13 I haue geuen vnto the children of Iſrael. And whẽ
thou haſt ſene it, thou ſhalt be gathered vnto thy
people alſo, as Aaron thy brother was gathered vnto
14 his people. For ye were diſobedient vnto my mouthe
in the deſerte of Zin in ỹ ſtryfe of the congregacion,
that ye ſanctified me not in the water before their eyes.
That is the water of ſtryfe in cades in the wilderneſſe

M. 12 Abarim

V. 4 Retulitque Moyſes cauſam earum ad iudicium domini. 6 Iuſtam rem poſtulant filiæ Salphaad . . . & ei in hæreditate ſuccedant. 8 ad filiam eius tranſibit hæreditas. 10 dabitis hæred. fratribus patris eius. 11 dabitur hær. his qui ei proximi ſunt. 12 daturus ſum 14 quia offendiſtis me . . . ſuper aquas.

L. 5 Moſe bracht yhr recht fur den Herrn 7 die t. Zel. haben recht geredt . . . vnd ſolt yhrs vaters erbe yhn zu wenden. 8 ſo ſolt yhr ſeyn erbe ſeyner tochter zu wenden 10 ſeynen vettern geben 11 ſeynen nehiſten freunden die yn anhören ynn ſeynem geſchlecht 12 geben werde 14 wie yhr meynem wort vngehorſam geweſen ſeit . . . durch das waſſer

15 of Zin. And Moses spake vnto the Lorde
16 sayenge: let the Lorde God of the spirites
of all flesh, sett a man ouer the congrega-
17 cion, which maye goo in & out before them,
and to lede them in and oute that the congregacion
of the Lorde be not as a flocke of shepe without a
sheparde.

O faithfull & mercifull Moses ful onlike oure Balams.

18 And ẏ Lorde sayed vnto Moses: take Iosua the
sonne of Nun in whom there is spirite, and put thyne
19 handes apon him, and set him before Eleazer the preast
and before all the congregacion and geue him a charge
20 in their syghte. And put of thi prayse apon him that
all the companye of ẏ childern of Israel maye heare.
21 And he shall stonde before Eleazar ẏ preast which shall
axe councell for him after ẏ maner of the
* lighte before ẏ Lorde: And at the mouth
of Eleazer shall both he and all the childern of Israel with him and all the congregacion, goo in and out.
22 And Moses dyd as the Lorde com-
23 maũded him, and he toke Iosua and sette
him before Eleazer the preast and be-

There was of likelyhod a bryght stonne in the ephod, whereĩ the hie preast loked & sawe the will of God in tymes of neade, as thou mayst se in the story of Dauid:

M. 21 After the iudgemẽt of Vrim

V. 16 dominus deus spirituum omnis carnis 17 sicut oues absque pastore. 18 in quo est spiritus 20 & partem gloriæ tuæ, vt audiat eum 21 Eleazar sacerdos consulet dominum.

L. 16 der Herr der Gott vber die geyster alles fleyschs 17 wie die schaff on hirten. 18 ynn dem der geyst ist 19 vnd gepeut yhm fur yhren augen 20 vnd lobe yhn mit deynem lobe, das yhm gehorche 21 der sol fur yhn radt fragẽ, durch die weyse des Liechts fur dem Herrn

M. M. N. 17 *To go in and oute before them* is to gouerne, teache, counfort, leade, & defende them etc. 21 *After the Iudgement of Vrim*, that is, after the iudgemẽt of the light, loke Exodi. xxviii, e. It is very lyke that in the Ephod was some bryght stone, wherin the hye preste loked & sawe the wyll of God, as it appereth in the storye of Dauid

L. M. N. 20 *Vnd lobe yhn:* das ist, lobe du yhn vnd sage viel guttis von yhm, damit du yhn ehrlich vnd angenehm machist fur dem volck, das leget St Pau. aus Rom. 3 da er spricht Gottis gerechtickeyt die Christus ist sind bezeuget, von dem gesetz vnd propheten. 21 *Des liechts:* das ist das liecht auff der brust des hohen priesters. Exo. 28. daher sagen etlich, wenn Gott habe auffs priesters frage geantwortet dz hat sollen, ia, seyn, so habe das liecht glentz von sich geben.

fore all the congregacion, & * put his
handes apon him & geue him a charge,
as the Lorde commaunded thorow the
hande of Moſes.

This was the maner of the Ebrues to make their offícers & of this maner did the apoſtle make deakons, preaſtes & biſhopes, with oute any other ceremony as thou ſeiſt ĩ thactes, ãd mayſt gather of paul to Tìmothe:

❡ The .XXVIII. Chaptre

M.C.S. What muſt be offered on euery feaſt daye.

1 AND the Lorde ſpake vnto Mo-
2 ſes ſayenge: geue ẏ childern
of Iſrael a charge and ſaye
vnto them, that they take hede to offer
vnto me ẏ offryng of my * bred in the
ſacrifyce of ſwete ſauoure, in his due ſea-
3 ſon. And ſaye vnto thẽ. This is ẏ offerynge which ye ſhall offer vnto ẏ Lorde
ii. lãbes [Fo. LIII.] of a yeare olde with out ſpot daye
4 by daye to be a burntofferynge perpetually. One
lambe thou ſhalt offer in the mornynge, and ẏ other
5 at euen, And thereto ẏ tẽth parte of an Epha of floure
for a meatofferynge myngled with beten oyle, the
6 fourth parte of an hin: which is a dayly offerynge ordened in the mount Sinai vnto a ſwete ſauoure in the
7 ſacrifyce of ẏ Lorde. And the drynkofferynge of the
ſame: the fourth parte of an hin vnto one lambe, &
poure the drynkofferynge in the holy place, to be good
8 drynke vnto the Lorde. And ẏ other lambe thou ſhalt
offer at euen, with the meatofferynge and the drynkofferynge after ẏ maner of the mornynge: a ſacrifyce of
a ſwete ſauoure vnto the Lorde.

Bred is here borowed & takẽ for all maner of fode generally:

M. 2 offer vnto the offeryng.

V. 23 replicauit quæ mandauerat dominus. xxviii, 3 quotidie in holocauſtum ſempiternum (v. 10, 15) 4 ad veſperum 6 holocauſtum iuge eſt 8 ad veſperam

L. 23 vnd gepot yhm wie der Herr mit Moſe geredt hatte. xxviii, 3 zum teglichen brandopffer 4 zwiſſchen abents (v. 8) 6 das iſt eyn teglich brandopffer (v. 10) 7 yns Heyligtum goſſen werden zur gabe dem Herrn.

9 And on the Sabbath daye .ii. lambes of a yere olde
a pece and with out ſpot, and two tēthdeales of floure
for a meatofferynge myngled with oyle, and the drynk-
10 offerynge thereto. This is the burntofferynge of euery
Sabbath, beſydes the dayly burntofferynge and his
drynkofferynge.
11 And in the firſt daye of youre monethes, ye ſhall
offer a burntofferynge vnto the Lorde: two yonge
bollockes, and a ram, and .vii. lambes of a yere olde
12 without ſpott, and .iii. tēthdeales of floure for a meatofferynge mingled with oyle vnto one bollocke, and
ii. tēth deales of floure for a meatofferynge myngled
13 with oyle vnto one rā. And euer moare, .P. a tēth
deale of floure myngled with oyle, for a meatofferinge
vnto one lābe. That is a burntofferynge of a ſwete
14 ſauoure in the ſacrifyce of the Lorde. And their
drynkofferynges ſhalbe halfe an hin of wyne vnto
one bollocke, ād the thyrde parte of an hin of wyne
vnto a ram and the fourth parte of an hin vnto a
lambe. This is the burntofferynge of euery moneth
15 thorow out all the monethes of the yere: & one he
goote for a ſynofferynge vnto the Lorde, which ſhalbe
offered with the dayly burntofferynge and his drynkofferynge.
16 And the .xiiii. daye of the firſt moneth ſhalbe Paſſe-
17 ouer vnto the Lorde. And ẏ .xv. daye of the ſame
moneth ſhalbe a feaſt, in which .vii. dayes men muſt
18 eate vnleuēded bred The firſt daye ſhalbe an holy
feaſt, ſo that ye ſhall do no maner of laboryous worke
19 therein. And ye ſhall offer a burntofferynge vnto the
Lorde .ii. bollockes, one ram, and .vii. lambes of a yere
20 olde without ſpott, and their meatofferynge of floure
myngled with oyle .iii. tenthdeales vnto a bollocke,
21 and .ii. tenthdeales vnto a ram, and euermoare one

M. 19 two younge bullockes

V. 13 holocauſtum ſuauiſſimi odoris atque incenſi eſt domino. 14 per omnes menſes, qui ſibi anno vertente ſuccedunt. 16 phaſe domini erit 18 dies prima venerabilis & ſancta erit

L. 13 Das iſt das brandopffer des ſuſſen geruchs eyn opffer dem Herrn. 14 eyns iglichen monden ym iar. 16 Oſtern dem Herrn 18 Der erſte tag heyſt heylig

tenthdeale vnto a lambe, thorow out the .vii. lambes:
22 & an hegoote for a ſynofferynge to make an atone-
23 ment for you. And ye ſhall offer theſe, beſyde the
burntofferynge in ẏͤ mornynge that is allway offered.
24 And after this maner ye ſhall offer thorow out the .vii
dayes, the fode of the ſacrifice of ſwete ſauoure vnto
the Lor- [Fo. LIIII.] de. And it ſhalbe done beſyde
25 the dayly burntofferynge and his drynkofferynge. And
the ſeuenth daye ſhalbe an holy feaſt vnto you, ſo that
ye ſhall doo no laboryous worke therein.
26 And the daye of youre firſt frutes when ye brynge
a new meatofferynge vnto the Lorde in youre wekes,
ſhalbe an holy feaſt vnto you: ſo that ye ſhall doo no
27 laboryous worke therein. And ye ſhall offer a burntofferynge of a ſwete ſauoure vnto the Lorde .ii. younge
bollockes, and a ram, and .vii. lambes of a yere olde
28 a pece, with their meatofferynges of floure myngled
with oyle .iii. tenthdeales vnto a bollocke .ii. tenthdeales
29 to a ram, ād euermoare one tenthdeale vnto a lambe
30 thorow out the .vii. lambes, ād an he goote to make an
31 atonement for you. And this ye ſhall doo beſydes the
dayly burntofferynge, and his meatofferynge: & they
ſhalbe without ſpot, with their drynkofferynges.

¶ The .XXIX. Chapter.

1 AND ẏͤ firſt daye of ẏͤ .vii. moneth
ſhalbe an holy feaſt vnto you,
ād ye ſhall doo no laboryous
worke therein. It ſhalbe a
2 daye of trompetblowynge vnto you. And ye ſhall

M.C.S. *What muſt be offred the .viii. firſt dayes of the ſeuenth mone.*

F. 22 & hircum pro peccato vnum, vt expietur pro vobis 23 matutinum quod ſemper 24 Ita facietis per ſingulos dies ſeptem dierum in ſomitem ignis 25 Dies quoque ſeptimus celeberrimus & ſanctus erit vobis 26 quando offeretis nouas fruges 29 hircum quoque vnum 30 qui mactatur pro expiatione 31 cum libationibus ſuis. xxix, 1 quia dies clangoris eſt & tubarum.

L. 22 das man euch verſune 23 wilchs eyn teglich brandopffer iſt 24 Nach diſer weyſe 27 heylig heyſſen. xxix, 1 Es iſt ewr drometen tag

offer a burntofferynge of a ſwete ſauoure vnto ẏ Lorde:
one younge bollocke & one rā & .vii. lābes of a yere
3 olde a pece that are pure. And their meatofferinges
of floure .P. myngled with oyle: .iii. tenthdeales vnto
4 the bollocke, and .ii. vnto the ram, and one tenthdeale
5 vnto one lambe thorow the .vii. lambes And an he
goote for a ſynofferynge to make an atonement for
6 you, beſyde the burntofferynge of the moneth and his
meatofferynge and beſyde the dayly burntofferynge
and his meatofferynge, and the drynkofferynges of the
ſame: acordynge vnto the maner of them for a ſauoure
of ſwetneſſe in the ſacrifice of ẏ Lorde.
7 And the tenth daye of that ſame ſeuenth moneth
ſhalbe an holy feaſt vnto you, and ye ſhall humble
youre ſoules and ſhall doo no maner worke therein.
8 And ye ſhall offer a burntofferynge vnto the Lorde
of a ſwete ſauoure: one bollocke, and a ram, and .vii
9 lambes of a yere olde a pece, without faute & their
meatofferynges of floure myngled with oyle: iii. tenth-
10 deales to a bollocke, ād .ii. to a rā and all waye a
tenthdeale vnto a lambe, thorow out the .vii. lambes
11 And one he goote for a ſynofferynge, beſyde ẏ ſynofferynge of atonement and the dayly burntofferynge, and
ẏ meate and drynkofferynges that longe to the ſame.
12 And the .xv. daye of the ſeuenth moneth ſhalbe
holy daye & ye ſhall doo no laboryous worke therein,
and ye ſhall kepe a feaſt vnto ẏ Lorde of .vii. dayes
13 longe. And ye ſhall offer a burntofferynge of a ſwete
ſauoure vnto the [Fo. LV.] Lorde: .xiii. bollockes .ii
rammes and .xiiii. lābes which are yerelynges and pure,
14 with oyle .iii. tenthdeales vnto euery one of the .xiii
15 bollockes .ii. tēthdeales to ether of the rammes, and
16 one tenthdeale vnto eche of the .xiiii. lambes. And
one he goote vnto a ſynofferynge, beſyde ẏ dayly burntofferynge with his meate and drynkofferynges.

V. 6 præter holocauſtum calendarum . . . holocauſtum ſempiternum (vv. 11, 16, 19, 22, 25, 28, 31, 34, 38) cum libationibus ſolitis. 7 ſancta atque venerabilis (v. 12), et affligetis animas veſtras
L. 6 on das brandopffer des monden . . . nach yhrem rechten 7 ſoll . . heylig heyſſen, vnd ſolt ewre ſeelen demutigen 11 tegliche brandopffer (vv. 16, 19, 22, 25, 28, 31, 34, 38) 12 heylig heyſſen

17 And the ſeconde daye .xii. younge bollockes .ii
18 rammes & .xiiii. yerlynge lambes without ſpot: & their
meatofferynges and drynkofferynges vnto the bollockes,
rammes and lambes, acordynge to the numbre of them
19 & after the maner And an he goote for a ſynofferynge, beſyde the dayly burntofferynge ād his meate
and drynkofferynges.

20 And the thyrde daye .xi. bollockes .ii. rammes &
21 xiiii. yerelynge lambes without ſpot: & their meate and
drynkofferynges vnto the bollockes, rammes & lambes,
after the numbre of thē & acordynge to the maner.
22 And an he goote for a ſynofferynge, beſyde the dayly
burntofferynge & his meate and drynkofferynges.

23 And the fourth daye .x. bollockes .ii. rammes & .xiiii
24 lābes, yerelynges & pure: ād their meate & drynkofferynges vnto the bollockes rāmes & lābes, acordynge
25 to their nūbre and after the maner. And an hegoote
for a ſynofferynge, beſyde the dayly burntofferynge
ād his meate and drynkofferynges.

26 .P. And the fyfte daye .ix. bollockes .ii. rāmes and
xiiii. lambes of one yere olde a pece without ſpott.
27 And their meat and drynkofferynges vnto the bollockes, rāmes and lambes, acordynge to the numbre
28 of them and after the maner. And an hegoote for a
ſynofferynge, beſyde the dayly burntofferynge and his
meate and drynkofferynges.

29 And the ſyxte daye .viii. bollockes .ii. rammes ād
30 xiiii. yerelynge lambes without ſpot And their meate
and drynkofferynges vnto the bollockes, rammes and
31 lambes, acordynge to the maner. And an hegoote
for a ſynofferynge, beſyde the dayly burntofferynge
and his meate and drynkofferynges.

32 And the ſeuenth daye .vii. bollockes .ii. rāmes and
33 xiiii. lambes that are yerelynges & pure. And their
meate and drynkofferynges vnto the bollockes, rammes
and lābes, acordynge to their numbre & to the maner.

M. 23 yerelynges pure 24 accordyng to the nombre of them 32 .xiii. lambes
V. 18 rite celebrabitis (vv. 21, 24, 27, 30, 33, 37)
L. 18 nach dem recht (vv. 21, 24, 27, 30, 33, 37)

34 And an hegoote for a ſynofferynge, beſyde ẏ dayly
burntofferynge and his meate and drynkofferynges.
35 And the eyght daye ſhalbe the con-
cluſion of ẏ feaſte vnto you, & ye ſhall doo
36 no maner laboryous worke therein. And
ye ſhall offer a burntofferynge of a ſwete
ſauoure vnto the Lorde: one bollocke, one rā & .vii
37 yerelynge lābes without ſpott. And the meate &
drynkofferynges vnto the bollocke, rā and lābes, acordynge to their nūbres & acordynge to ẏ ma- [Fo. LVI.]
38 ner. And an he goote for a ſynofferynge beſyde the
dayly burntofferynge and his meate & drynkofferynges.
39 Theſe thinges ye ſhall doo vnto the Lorde in youre
feaſtes: beſyde youre vowes and frewyll offerynges, in
youre burntofferinges meatofferynges, drynkofferynges
40 and peaſe offerynges. And Moſes tolde the childern
of Iſrael, acordynge to all that the Lorde commaunded
him.

Out of ſoch come oure octaues ād feaſtes of eight dayes longe.

ℭ The .XXX. Chapter.

1 AND Moſes ſpake vnto the heedes
of the trybes of ẏ childern
of Iſrael ſayēge: this is the
thynge which the Lorde com-
2 maundeth. Yf a man vowe a vowe vnto
the Lorde or ſwere an othe ād bynde his
ſoule, he ſhall not goo backe with his
worde: but ſhal fulfyll all ẏ proceadeth
out of his mouth
3 Yf a damſell vowe a vowe vnto ẏ

M.C.S. *Of vowes when they ſhalbe kept and when not.*

Hēce was ſett the exāple of oure vowes of chaſtite, obediens and willfull pouertie: oure offerynges ād oure pilgremage.

F. 39 præter vota & oblationes ſpontaneas xxx, 2 ad principes tribuum . . . Iſte eſt ſermo

L. 39 ausgenomen was yhr gelobd vnd freywillig gebt xxx, 2 vbirſten der ſtemme . . Das iſts . .

M. M. N. 2 *If a man vowe etc.* This vowe here is that which a man voweth for a certayne ſpace, whether it be to faſt or to chaſtyce the bodye, or any other thyng, as it is ſayd Leui. vii, d.

L. M. N. 35 *Am achten tage, ſolt yhr ſteur thun:* Diſe ſteuer war das man fur die armen zu hauff trug eyn gemeyn gutt von allerley was Gott geben hatte.

Lorde & binde herſelfe beynge in hir fathers houſſe
4 and vnmaried: Yf hir father heare hir vowe & bonde
which ſhe hath made vppon hir ſoule, & holde his
peaſe thereto: then all hir vowes & bōdes which ſhe
5 hath made vppō hir ſoule ſhall ſtonde in effecte. But
& yf hir father forbyd her the ſame daye that he heareth it, none of hir vowes nor bondes which ſhe hath
made vppon hir ſoule ſhalbe of value, ād the Lorde
ſhall forgeue her, becauſe hir father forbade her.
6 Yf ſhe had an huſbonde when ſhe vowed .P. or pronounſed oughte out of hir lippes wherewith ſhe bonde
7 hir ſoule, and hir huſbonde herde it and helde his peace
thereat the ſame daye he herde it: Then hir vowes and
hir bondes wherewith ſhe bounde hir ſoule, ſhal ſtonde
8 in effecte. But ād yf hir huſbonde forbade her the
ſame daye that he herde it, than hath he made hir
vowe which ſhe had vppō her of none effecte, and
that alſo whiche ſhe pronounſed with hir lippes wherewith ſhe bounde hir ſoule, and the Lorde ſhall forgeue
her.
9 The vowe of a wedowe and of her that is deuorſed,
& all that they haue bound their ſoules with all, ſhall
ſtonde in effecte with them.
10 Yf ſhe vowed in her huſbandes houſſe or bounde her
11 ſoule with an oth, and her huſbande herde it and helde
his peace and forbade her not: then all her vowes and
bondes wherewith ſhe bound her ſoule, ſhall ſtōde.
12 But yf her huſbande diſanulled them ẏ ſame daye that
he herde them, then nothing that proceded out of her
lippes in vowes ād boundes wherewith ſhe bounde her

V. 3 non faciet irritum verbum ſuum 4 voti rea erit 6 ſtatim vt audierit . . . irrita erunt, nec obnoxia tenebitur ſponſioni 9 propitius erit ei dominus. 10 Vidua & repudiata quicquid vouerint, reddent. 11 Vxor in domo 12 ſi audierit vir

L. 3 ſoll ſeyn wort nicht ſchwechen 5 ſo gilt alle yhr gelubd vnd alle yhr verbundnis, des ſie ſich vber yhr ſeele verbunden hat. 6 des Tags wenn ers horet . . . Vnd der Herr wirt yhr gnedig ſeyn (v. 13) 10 verſtoſſene 11 geſinde 12 hausherr . . . ſo gilt all daſſelb gelubd vnd alles wes es ſich verbunden hat vber ſeyn ſeele

L. M. N. 3 *Seyn ſeele:* das iſt, wenn ſie ſich verbunden zu faſten odder ſonſt wz zu thun mit yhrem leybe Got zu dienſt das ſeele hie heyſſe, ſo viel, als der lebendige leyb wie die ſchrifft allenthalben braucht.

ſoule ſhall ſtonde in effecte: for her huſbande hath
lowſed them, and the Lorde ſhall forgeue her.
13 All vowes and othes that binde to humble the ſoule,
14 maye her huſbande ſtabliſh or breake. But yf her huſbande hold his peace from one daye vnto another, then
he ſtabliſheth [Fo. LVII.] all her vowes and boundes
whiche ſhe had vppon her, becauſe he helde his peace
15 the ſame daye that he herde them. And yf he afterwarde breake them, he ſhall beare her ſynne him ſelf.
16 Theſe are the ordinaunces which ÿ Lorde commaunded
Moſes, betwene a man and his wife, and betwene the
father and his doughter, beyenge a damſell in hir
fathers houſſe.

ℭ The .XXXI. Chapter.

1 AND the Lorde ſpake vnto Moſes
2 ſayenge: auenge the childern
of Iſrael of the Madianites,
and afterwarde be gathered
3 vnto thy people. And Moſes ſpake vnto
the folke ſayenge: Harneſſe
ſome of you vnto warre, and
let them goo apon the Madianites and auenge the Lorde of the Madi-
anitis. Ye ſhall ſende vnto the warre
4 a thouſande of euery trybe thorow out all the trybes
5 of Iſrael. And there were taken oute of the thouſandes
of Iſrael .xii. thouſande prepared vnto warre, of euery

harneſſe, *arm*, vv. 20, 21, cf. vv. 17,26,30,32

M.C.S. The Madianytes & Balā are ſlayne. The praye was brought to Moſes & equallye deuyded. A preſent geuē of Iſrael becauſe none of their men were ſlayne.

V. 13 ſinautem extemplo contradixerit . . . quia maritus contradixit, & dominus ei propitius erit. 14 affligat animam ſuam: in arbitrio viri erit ſiue faciat, ſiue non faciat. 15 quod ſi audiens vir tacuerit 16 ſin autem contrad. . . . portabit ipſe iniquitatem eius. xxxi, 2 Vlciſcere prius . . . & ſic colligeris 3 Statimque Moyſes, Armate, inquit . . . qui poſſint vltionem domini expetere 5 Dederuntque

L. 13 Machts aber der hausherr des tags los . . . denn der hausherr hats los gemacht 14 hausherr krefftigen odder ſchwechen 15 Wenn er dazu ſchweygt . . . ſo bekrefftiget er 16 Wirt ers aber ſchwechen . . . ſo ſol er die miſſetat tragen. xxxi, 2 darnach dich ſamleſt 3 mit dem volck . . . Ruſtet 5 Vnd ſie namen an

6 trybe a thousande. And Moses sent them a thousande
of euery trybe, with Phineas the sonne of Eleazer the
preaste to warre, and the holye vessels & the trompettes
to blowewith in his honde.
7 And they warred agenst the Madianites, as the
Lorde commaunded Moses, ād .P. slewe all the males.
8 And they slewe the kynges of Madian among other
that were slayne: Eui, Rekem, Zur, Hur and Reba:
fyue kynges of Madian. And they slewe Balā the
9 sonne of Beor with the swerde. And the childern of
Israel toke all the wemen of Madian presoners and
their childern, and spoyled all their catell, their sub-
10 stance and their goodes. And they burnt all their
cities wherein they dwelt, and all their castels with
11 fyre. And they toke all the spoyle and all they coude
12 catche, both of men and beestes. And they broughte
the captyues and that which they had taken and all
the spoyle vnto Moses and Eleazer the preast ād vnto
the companye of the childern of Israel: euen vnto the
hoste, in ỹ feldes of Moab by Iordane nye to Iericho.
13 And Moses and Eleazer the preast and all the lordes
of the congregacion went out of the hoste agenst them.
14 And Moses was angrie with the officers of the hoste,
with ỹ captaynes ouer thousandes and ouer hundredes,
15 which came from warre and batayle, and sayde vnto
16 them: Haue ye saued the wemen alyue? beholde, these
caused the childern of Israel thorow Balam, to commytt
trespace agēst ỹ Lorde, by ỹ reason of Peor, & their
folowed a plage amōge ỹ congregacion of the Lorde.
17 Nowe therfore slee all the men childern and the wemen
18 that haue lyen [Fo. LVIII.] with men fleshlye: But all
the wemen children that haue not lyen with men, kepe

V. 6 vasaque sancta, & tubas ad clangendum 9 & cunctam supellectilem. quicquid habere potuerant depopulati sunt. 12 ad omnem multitudinem 14 principibus, exercitus 15 Cur fœminas reseruastis? 16 super peccato Phogor 17 quæ nouerunt viros in coitu, iugulate 18 reseruate vobis

L. 6 den heyligen gezeug vnd die Hall drometen 9 namen gefangen . . . all yhr habe, vnd alle yhre gutter 14 heubtleut . . . die aus dem heer vnd streyt kamen 15 habt yhr allerley weyber leben lassen? 16 vber dem Peor 17 So erwurget . . . die man erkand vnd bey gelegen haben 18 last fur euch leben

19 alyue for youre ſelues. And lodge without the hoſte
vii. dayes all that haue killed any perſone & all that
haue twiched any dead body, & purifye both youre
20 ſelues & youre preſoners the .iii. daye & the .vii. And
ſprinkle all youre raymentes & all that is made of
ſkynnes, & all worke of gootes heer, ād all thynges
made of wodd.
21 And Eleazer the preaſt ſayed vnto all ỹ mē of warre
which went out to batayle: this is the ordinaunce of
22 the lawe which the Lorde commaunded Moſes: Gold,
23 ſyluer, braſſe, yeron, tyn & leed, & all that maye abyde
ỹ fyre, ye ſhall make it goo thorow the fyre, ād then
it is cleane. Neuerthelater, it ſhalbe ſprinkled with
ſprinklinge water. And all ỹ ſoffereth not the fyre,
24 ye ſhall make goo thorow the water. And waſh youre
clothes the ſeuenth daye, & then ye are cleane. And
after warde come in to the hoſte.
25, 26 And the Lorde ſpake vnto Moſes ſayenge: take
the ſumme of the praye that was taken, both of the
wemē & of catell, thou & Eleazer the preaſt and the
27 auncient heedes of ỹ congregacion. And deuyde it in
to two parties, betwene them that toke the warre vppō
thē and went out to batayle and all the congregacion.
28 And take a porcion vnto the Lorde of the men of warre
whiche went oute to .P. batayle one of fyue hundred,
of the wemen and of the oxen and of the aſſes and of the
29 ſhepe: and ye ſhall take it of their halfe and geue it
vnto Eleazer the preaſt, an heueofferynge vnto the
30 Lorde. And of the halfe of ỹ childern of Iſrael, take
one of fyftye, of ỹ wemen, of the oxen, of the aſſes and
of the ſhepe, and of all maner of beeſtes, & geue them
vnto the leuites which wayte apon ỹ habitacion of the
Lorde.
31 And Moſes and Eleazer the preaſt did as the Lorde

V. 19 luſtrabitur 20 expiabitur. 23 igne purgabitur . . . aqua expiationis ſanctificabitur 26 principes vulgi 27 omnem reliquam multitudinem 28 vnam animam 29 quia primitiæ domini ſunt. 30 qui excubant in cuſtodiis (v. 47)

L. 19 entſundiget (v. 20) 23 mit dem Sprenge waſſer entſundiget 26 die vbirſten veter der gemeyne 27 der gemeyne 28 eyn ſeele 29 zur Hebe dem Herrn. 30 die der hut warten (v. 47)

32 commaunded Moses. And ẏ botye and the praye
which the men of warre had caught, was .vi. hundred
33 thousande & .Lxxv. thousande shepe: ād .Lxxii. thou-
34, 35 sande oxen: & .Lxi. thousande asses: & .xxxii. thousande wemen that had lyen by no man.

36 And the halfe which was the parte of thē that wēt
out to warre, was .iii. hundred thousande and .xxxvii
37 thousande and fyue hundred shepe: And the Lordes
38 parte of the shepe was .vi. hundred and .Lxxv. And
the oxen were .xxxvi. thousande, of which the Lordes
39 parte was .Lxxii. And the asses were .xxx. thousande
and fyue hundred, of whiche the Lordes parte was
40 Lxi. And the wemen were .xvi. thousande, of which
41 the Lordes parte was .xxxii. soules. And Moses gaue
that summe which was the Lordes heueofferynge vnto
Eleazer the preast: as the Lorde cōmaunded Moses.

42 [Fo. LIX.] And the other halfe of the childern of
Israel whiche Moses seperated from the men of warre
43 (that is to wete, the halfe that pertayned vnto the
congregacion) was .iii. hundred thousande and .xxxvii
44 thousande and fyue hundred shepe: and .xxxvi. thou-
45 sande oxen: and .xxx. thousande asses and fyue hūdred:
46, 47 and .xvi. thousande wemen. And Moses toke of this
halfe that pertayned vnto the childern of Israel: one
of euery fyftie, both of the wemen & of the catell, and
gaue them vnto the leuites which wayted vppon the
habitacion of the Lorde, as the Lorde commaunded
Moses.

48 And the officers of thousandes of the hoste, the
captaynes ouer the thousandes and the captaynes ouer
49 the hundreds came forth & sayed vnto Moses: Thy
servauntes haue taken the summe of the men of warre,
which were vnder oure hande, & there lacked not one
50 man of them. We haue therfore broughte a present
vnto the Lorde what euery man founde of Iewels of

V. 37 in partem domini supputatæ sunt 40 cesserunt in partem domini 41 numerum primitiarum domini 43 reliquæ multitudini
L. 32 der vbrigen ausbeutte 41 solch Hebe 43 der gemeyne zustendig
M. M. N. 43 *vnto the congregacion:* which was not at the warre.

golde, cheyns, bracelettes, ringes, earynges & ſpangels,
to make an attonement for oure ſoules before the
Lorde.
51 And Moſes & Eleazer toke the golde off them:
52 Iewels of all maner facions. And all the golde of the
heueoffrynge of the Lord, of the captaynes ouer thouſandes & hundreds was .xvi. thouſand .vii. hundred &
53 L. ſycles, .P. which ẏ mē of warre had ſpoyled, euery
54 man for him ſelfe. And Moſes & Eleazer ẏ preaſt toke
the golde of the captaynes ouer the thouſandes & ouer
the hundreds, & brought it in to the tabernacle of witneſſe: to be a memoriall vnto ẏ childern of Iſrael, before ẏ Lorde.

The .XXXII. Chapter.

1 THE childern of Rubē & the
childern of Gad, had an exceadinge greate multitude of
catell. And whē they ſawe
the lōde of Iaeſer & the lōde of Gilead ẏ
2 it was an apte place for catell, they came
& ſpake vnto Moſes & Eleazer ẏ preaſt &
vnto ẏ lordes of ẏ cōgregaciō ſayenge.
3 The lōde of Ataroth Dibo & Beon,
4 whiche contre ẏ Lorde ſmote before the
congregacion of Iſrael: is a londe for catell and we

M.C.S. *To Ruben and Gad and to halfe the trybe of Manaſſes, is promeſed the poſſeſſion beyounde Iordan eaſtward: yf they bryng their brethren into the lande of promeſſe.*

M. 3 Ataroth & Dibō & Iazer, and Nemrah & Heſbon & Elealeh & Sabam & Nebo & Beon

V. 50 vt depreceris pro nobis dominum. 53 Vnuſquiſque enim quod in præda rapuerat, ſuum erat. xxxii, 1 pecora multa, & erat illis in iumentis infinita ſubſtantia . . . aptas animalibus alendis terras 3 Ataroth, & Dibon, & Iazer, & Nemra, & Heſebon, & Eleale, & Sabam, & Nebo, & Beon 4 regionis vberrimæ . . . iumenta plurima

L. 50 vnſer ſeelen verſunet werden fur dem Herrn 53 denn die kriegs leutt hatten geraubt eyn iglicher fur ſich xxxii, 1 hatten viel vnd ſeer eyn gros viech . . bequeme ſtet 3 Atroth, Dibon, Iaeſer, Nimra, Hesbon, Eleale, Sebam, Nebo vnd Beon 4 iſt bequeme . . . haben viech.

5 thy ſervauntes haue catell wherfore (ſayed they) yf
we haue founde grace in thy ſyghte, let this londe be
geuen vnto thy ſervauntes to poſſeſſe, and bringe vs
not ouer Iordane.
6 And Moſes ſayed vnto the childrē of Gad and of
Ruben: ſhall youre brethern goo to warre and ye
7 tarye here? Wherfore diſcorage ye the hertes of the
children of Iſrael for to goo ouer in to the londe which
8 the Lorde hath geuē them? This dyd youre fathers,
whē I ſent them from Cades bernea to ſe the londe.
9 And they went vp euen vnto the ryuer of Eſcol & ſawe
the londe, & diſcoraged the hertes of the childern of
Iſrael, that they ſhulde [Fo. LX.] not goo in to the
londe whiche the Lorde had geuen them.
10 And the Lorde was wroth the ſame tyme and ſware
11 ſayenge: None of the men that came out of Egipte frō
twentye yere olde and aboue, ſhall ſe the londe whiche
I ſwore vnto Abraham, Iſaac and Iacob, becauſe they
12 haue not continually folowed me: ſaue Caleb the ſonne
of Iephune the Keneſite, & Ioſua the ſonne of Nun, for
13 they haue folowed me continually. And the Lorde
was angrie with Iſrael, and made them wandre in
the wilderneſſe .xl. yere, vntill all the generacion
that had done euell in the ſyghte of the Lorde were
conſumed.
14 And beholde, ye are ryſen vp in youre fathers ſtede,
the encreaſe of ſynfull men, to augmente the ferſe
15 wrath of the Lorde to Iſrael warde. For yf ye turne
awaye from after him, he wyll yet agayne leue the
people in the wilderneſſe, ſo ſhall ye deſtroy all this
folke. folke, *people*
16 And they went nere him ād ſayed: we will bylde
ſhepefoldes here for oure ſhepe and for oure catell, and

M. 14 ſteade, to ẏ encreaſe . . . & to augmēte
V. 5 in poſſeſſionem, nec facias 7 Cur ſubuertitis mentes (v. 9) 9 vallem Botri 12 iſti impleuerunt voluntatem meam. 14 incrementa, & alumni hominum peccatorum 15 et vos cauſa eritis necis omnium. 16 vrbes munitas
L. 5 ſo wollen wyr nicht vber den Iordan zihen. 7 macht . . . hertz wendig (v. 9) 11 ſollen ia . . . nicht ſehen . . . das ſie myr nicht gentzlich nach gefolgt haben (cf. v. 12).

17 cities for oure childern: But we oure ſelues will go
ready armed before ŷ childern of Iſrael, vntill we haue
broughte them vnto their place. And oure childrē
ſhall dwell in the ſtronge cities, becauſe of the inhabi-
18 ters of the londe. And we will not returne vnto oure
houſſes, vntill the childern off .P. Iſrael haue enhereted:
19 euery man his enheritaunce. For we will not enheret
with them on yonder ſyde Iordane forwarde, becauſe
oure enheritaunce is fallen to vs on this ſyde Iordane
eaſtwarde.

20 And Moſes ſayed vnto them: Yf ye will do this
thinge, that ye will go all harneſſed before the Lorde
21 to warre, and will go all of you in harneſſe ouer Iordane before ŷ Lorde, vntill he haue caſt out his ene-
22 myes before him, & vntill the londe be ſubdued before
ŷ Lorde: then ye ſhall returne & be without ſinne
agenſt the Lorde & agenſt Iſrael, & this lōde ſhalbe
23 youre poſſeſſion before the Lorde. But & yf ye will
not do ſo, beholde, ye ſynne agenſt the Lorde: ād be
24 ſure youre ſynne will fynde you out. Bilde youre
cities for youre childern & foldes for youre ſhepe, &
ſe ye do ŷ ye haue ſpoken.

25 And the childern of Gad & of Ruben ſpake vnto
Moſes ſayenge: thy ſervauntes will do as my lorde
26 commaundeth. Oure childrē oure wiues ſubſtāce &
all oure catell ſhall remayne here in the cities of Gilead.
27 But we thi ſervauntes will goo all harneſſed for the
warre vnto batayle before the Lorde, as my lorde hath
ſayed.

28 And Moſes cōmaūded Eleazer ŷ preaſt & Ioſua ŷ
ſonne of Nun & the aunciēt hedes of the tribes of the
29 childern of Iſrael, & ſayed vnto them: Yf the childern
of Gad and Ru- [Fo. LXI.] ben will goo with you ouer

M. 17 fenced cyties

V. 17 nos autem ipſi armati & accincti . . . ad loca ſua . . . propter habitatorum inſidias. 18 in domos noſtras 20 expediti . . . ad pugnam 21 et omnis vir bellator armatus 22 inculpabiles 23 nulli dubium eſt quin peccetis 27 omnes expediti

L. 17 an yhren ort 21 ruſtet zum ſtreyt . . . wer vnter euch gerüſt iſt (cf. vv. 27, 29, 30, 32) 22 vnſchuldig 23 vnd werdet ewr ſunden ynnen werden, wenn ſie euch finden wirt.

Iordane, all prepared to fyghte before the Lorde: then
when the lande is ſubdued vnto you, geue them the
30 londe of Gilead to poſſeſſe, but & yf they will not
goo ouer with you in harneſſe, then they ſhall haue
their poſſeſſions amonge you in ỹ londe of Canaan.
31 And the childern of Gad & Ruben anſwered ſayenge:
that which ỹ Lorde hath ſayed vnto thi ſeruaũtes
32 we will doo We wil goo harneſſed before the Lorde
in to the londe of Canaan, & the poſſeſſion of oure
enheritaunce ſhalbe on this ſyde the Iordane.
33 And Moſes gaue vnto ỹ childern of Gad and of
Ruben & vnto halfe the trybe of Manaſſe the ſonne
of Ioſeph, the kyngdome of Sihon kynge of the Amorites, and the kyngdome of Og kynge of Baſan, the
lande that longed vnto the cities thereof in the coſtes
34 of the contre rounde aboute. And the childern of Gad
35 bylt Dibō, ataroth, Aroer, Atroth, Sophan, Iaeſer,
36 Iegabeha, Bethnimra & Betharan ſtronge cities, and
37 they bylt foldes for their ſhepe. And the childern of
38 Ruben bylt Heſebon, Elalea, Kiriathaim, Nebo, Baal
Meon and turned their names, and Sibama alſo: &
gaue names vnto the cities which they bylt.
39 And the childern of Machir the ſonne of Manaſſe
went to Gilead and toke it, and put out the Amorites
40 ỹ were therein. And Mo- .P. ſes gaue Gilead vnto
41 Machir the ſonne of Manaſſe & he dwelt therein. And
Iair the ſonne of Manaſſe wēt & toke ỹ ſmall townes
42 thereof, & called thē the townes of Iair. And Nobah
went & toke kenath with the townes longinge thereto,
& called it Nobah after his awne name.

M. 36 Betharan fencend cyties [fenced]
V. 29 omnes armati 30 armati (v. 32) 32 trans Iordanem. 36 vrbes munitas 41 Auoth iair, id eſt villas Iair.
L. 32 diſſeyt des Iordans 36 verſchloſſen ſtedte 41 Hauoth 42 mit yhren tochtern

The .XXXIII. Chapter

1 THESE are the iurneyes of the
children of Iſrael which went
out of the lande of Egipte
with their armies vnder Mo-
2 ſes ād Aaron. And Moſes wrote their
goenge out by their iurneyes at yͤ cō-
maundment of the Lorde: euen theſe
3 are yͤ iurneyes of their goenge out. The childern of
Iſrael departed from Rahēſes the .xv. daye of the firſt
moneth, on yͤ morowe after Paſſeouer & went out with
4 an hye hande in the ſyghte of all Egipte, while the
Egiptians buried all their firſtborne which the Lorde
had ſmoten amonge thē. And vppō their goddes alſo
5 the Lorde dyd execucion. And yͤ childern of Iſrael
remoued from Rahemſes and pitched in Sucoth.
6 And they departed frō Sucoth & pitched their tentes
7 in Ethā, which is in the edge of yͤ wylderneſſe. And
they remoued frō Ethā ād turned vnto the entrynge
of Hiroth which is before baall Zephon, & pitched be-
8 fore Migdol. And they departed frō before Hiroth &
went thorow the myddes of the ſee in to the wilderneſſe, & wēt .iii. dayes iurney in yͤ wil- [Fo. LXII.]
9 derneſſe of Ethā, & pitched in Marah. And they
remoued frō Marah & wēt vnto Elim where were .xii
fountaynes ād .Lxx. datetrees and they pitched there.
10 And they remoued from Elim & laye faſt by the
11 red ſee. And they remoued frō the red ſee & laye in
12 yͤ wilderneſſe of Sin. And they toke their iurney out
of yͤ wilderneſſe of Sin, & ſett vpp their tentes in Daphka.
13 And they departed from Daphka, and laye in Alus.
14 And they remoued from Alus, & laye at Raphedim,

M.C.S. *The iourneys and departynges frō place to place of Iſrael are nombred. They are cōmaunded to kyll the Canaanites.*

M. 4 ſmyttē 9 .Lxx. paulmetrees

V. 3 altera die phaſe . . . in manu excelſa 4 nam & in diis eorum exercuerat vltionem 9 & palmæ ſeptuaginta

L. 2 beſchreyb yhren auszug 3 des andern tags der oſtern, durch eyn hohe hand

15 where was no water for the people to drynke. And
they departed from Raphedim, and pitched in the
wildernesse of Sinai

16 And they remoued from the deserte of Sinai, &
17 lodged at the graues of lust. And they departed from
18 the sepulchres of lust, ād laye at Haseroth. And they
19 departed from Hazeroth, & pitched in Rithma. And
departed frō Rithma and pitched at Rimon Parez.
20 And they departed from Rimon Parez, & pitched in
21 Libna. And they remoued from Libna, & pitched at
22 Rissa And they iurneyed frō Rissa ād pitched at Ke-
23 helatha. And they went frō Kehelatha, & pitched in
24 moūt Sapher And they remoued from mount Sapher,
25 and laye in Harada. And they remoued from Harada,
and pitched in Makeheloth.

26 And they remoued from Makeheloth, & laye at
27 Tahath, ād they departed frō Tahath & pitched at
28 Tharath And they remoued frō .P. Tharath, and
29 pitched in Mithca. And they went from Mithca, and
30 lodged in Hasmona. And they departed frō Has-
31 mona, and laye at Moseroth. And they departed
from Moseroth, and pitched amonge the childern of
32 Iaecon. And they remoued from the childern of Iae-
33 con, ād laye at Hor gidgad. And they went from Hor
34 gidgad, and pitched in Iathbatha. And they remoued
35 from Iathbatha, and laye at Abrona. And they departed
36 from Abrona, and laye at Ezeon gaber. And they remoued from Ezeon gaber, and pitched in the wildernesse
of Zin, which is Cades.

37 And they remoued from Cades, & pitched in mount
38 Hor, in ẏ edge of the londe of Moab. And Aaron the
preast went vpp in to mount Hor at the commaūdment
of ẏ Lorde & dyed there, euen in the fortieth yere after
the childern of Israel were come out of ẏ londe of

M. 31 pytched in Bane Iakan. 32 And they remoued from Bane Iakan, and laye at Hor gadgad. Hor gadgad 37 land of Edom

V. 16 ad Sepulchra concupiscentiæ. 17 Sep. concup. 31 castrametati sunt in Bene-iaacan. 32 Profectique de Bene-iaacan venerunt in montem Gadgad.

L. 16 lustgreber (v. 17) 31 lagerten sich ynn Bne Iaekon, Von Bne Iaekon zogen sie aus vnd lagerten sich in Hor gidgad

39 Egipte, & in the firſt daye of the fyfte moneth. And
Aaron was an hundred ād .xxxiii. yere olde when he
dyed in mount Hor
40 And kinge Erad the canaanite which dwelt in ỹ
ſouth of ỹ lond of canaā, herd ỹ the childern of Iſrael
were come.
41 And they departed frō mount Hor, & pitched in
42 Zalmona. And they departed from Zalmona, & pitched
43 in Phimon, & they departed from Phimon, & pitched in
44 Oboth. And they departed frō Oboth, & pitched in Igim
45 [Fo. LXIII.] Abarim in the borders of Moab. And they
46 departed from Igim, and pitched in Dibon Gad. And
they remoued from Dibon Gad, and laye in Almon Dibla-
47 thama. And they remoued from Almon Diblathama, ād
48 pitched in ỹ mountaynes of Abarim before Nibo. And
they departed from the mountaynes of Abarim, &
pitched in the feldes of Moab faſt by Iordane nye to
49 Iericho. And they pitched apon Iordayne, from Beth
Haieſmoth vnto ỹ playne of Sitim in ỹ feldes of Moab
50 And the Lorde ſpake vnto Moſes in the feldes of Moab
51 by Iordayne nye vnto Iericho, ſayēge: ſpeake vnto the
childern of Iſrael and ſaye vnto them: when ye are
52 come ouer Iordane in to the londe of Canaan, ſe that
ye dryue out all the inhabiters of the londe before you,
& deſtroy their Ymaginacions & all their Ymages of
Metall, ād plucke downe all their alters bylt on hilles:
53 And poſſeſſe ỹ londe & dwell therein, for I haue geuen you
54 the londe to enioye it. And ye ſhall deuyde the enheritaunce of the londe by lott amonge youre kynreddes,
ād geue to the moo the moare enheritaunce, & to the
fewer the leſſe enheritaunce. And youre enheritaunce
ſhalbe in ỹ trybes of youre fathers, in ỹ place where
euery mans lott falleth.

M. 44 Iehabarim 46 Iehabarim 49 Abelſatim 52 deſtroye their chappelles

V. 52 confringite titulos, & ſtatuas comminuete, atque omnia excelſa vaſtate

L. 52 vertreyben fur ewrem angeſicht, vnd alle yhre ſeulen vnd alle yhre gegoſſene bilder vmbringen vnd alle yhre höhe vertilgen

M. M. N. 52 *Chapelles:* After the Chald. Ra. Salo. and Ra. Abr. graued pauing ſtones.

55 But and yf ye will not dryue out the inhabiters of
ŷ londe before you, then these which ye let remayne
of thē, shalbe thornes in youre .P. eyes and dartes in
youre sydes, & shall vexe you in the lōde wherein ye
56 dwell. More ouer it will come to passe, ŷ I shall doo
vnto you as I thought to doo vnto them.

¶ The .XXXIIII. Chapter.

1 AND the Lorde spake vnto Moses
2 sayenge: cōmaūde the childern
of Israel and saye vnto them:
when ye come in to the londe
of Canaan, this is the londe that shall fall
vnto youre enheritaunce, the londe of
3 Canaan with all hir costes. And youre south quarter
shalbe from the wildernesse of Zin alonge by the coste
of Edom, so that youre south quarter shalbe from the
4 syde of the salte see eastwarde, & shall set a compasse
frō the south vpp to Acrabim, & reach to Zinna. And
it shall goo out on ŷ south side of Cades Bernea, & goo
out also at Hazar Adar, and goo alōge to Azmon.
5 And shall set a cōpasse from Azmon vnto the ryuer of
Egipte, and shall goo out at the see.

6 And youre west quarter shall be the greate see,
which coste shalbe youre west coste.

7 And this shalbe youre north quarter: ye shall com-
8 passe from the great see vnto moūt Hor. And from

M.C.S. *The Coostes and borders of the land of promesse. Certen are assygned to deuyde the lande.*

M. 55 those which

V. 55 claui in oculis, & lanceæ in lateribus, et aduersabuntur vobis xxxiiii, 2 sorte ceciderit 3 mare salsissimum 4 per ascensum scorpionis . . . ad villam nomine Adar 5 ad torrentem Ægypti, & magni maris litore finietur. 6 a mari magno incipiet, & ipso fine claudetur. 7 montem altissimum

L. 55 zu dornen werden in ewern augen vnd zu stachel ynn ewern seytten, vnd werden euch drengen 56 So wirts denn gehen, das ich euch gleich thun werde xxxiiii, 2 euch zum erbteyl fellet 3 ecke . . saltz meers 4 Hazor Adar 5 den bach Egypti

M. M. N. 55 *Thornes in youre eyes* that is, they shall be youre rodde scourge and vndoars.

mount Hor, ye ſhall compaſſe & goo vnto Hemath,
9 and the ende of ẏ coſte ſhalbe at Zedada, & the coſte
ſhall reach out to Ziphron and goo out at Hazor Enan.
And this ſhalbe youre north quarter.
10 [Fo. LXIIII.] And ye ſhall compaſſe youre eaſt
11 quarter frō Hazar Enan to Sepham And the coſte
ſhall goo downe from Sepham to Ribla on the eaſt ſyde
of Ain. And then deſcende and goo out at the ſyde
12 of the ſee of Chinereth eaſtwarde. And then goo
downe alonge by Iordayne, and leue at the ſalte ſee.
And this ſhall be youre lōde with all the coſtes thereof rounde aboute.
13 And Moſes commaunded the childern of Iſrael,
ſayēge: this is the lōde which ye ſhall enherett by
lotte, and which the Lorde cōmaūded to geue vnto
14 ix. trybes and an halfe: for the trybe of the childern
of Ruben haue receaued, in the houſſholdes of their
fathers, and the trybe of the childern of Gad in their
fathers houſſholdes, & halfe the trybe of Manaſſe, haue
15 receaued their enheritaunce, that is to wete .ii. trybes
and an halfe haue receaued their enheritaunce on ẏ
other ſyde of Iordayne by Iericho eaſtwarde, towarde
the ſonne ryſynge.
16, 17 And the Lorde ſpake to Moſes ſayenge: Theſe
are the names of ẏ men, which ſhall deuyde you the
londe to enherett. Eleazer ẏ preaſt, ād Ioſua the
18 ſonne of Nun. And ye ſhall take alſo a lorde of euery
19 trybe to deuyde the londe, whoſe names are theſe: In
20 the trybe of Iuda, Caleb ẏ ſonne of Iephune. And in
ẏ trybe of ẏ childern of Simeon, Demuel ẏ ſōne of
21 Amiud, ād in ẏ tribe of Bē Iamin, Eli- .P. dad the
22 ſonne of Ciſlon. And in the trybe of ẏ childern of
23 Dan, the lorde Bucki the ſonne of Iagli. And amonge
the childern of Ioſeph: in the trybe of the childern of
24 Manaſſe, the lorde Haniel the ſonne of Ephod. And

M. 20 Semuel the ſonne of Amiud.
V. 9 villam Enan (v. 10). 11 Reblatha contra fontem Daphnim 15 trans Iordanem contra Iericho ad orientalem plagam.
L. 9 Hazor Enan (v. 10) 15 diſſeyt des Iordans gegen Iericho gegen dem morgen.

in the trybe of the childern of Ephraim, yͤ lorde Cemuel
25 the ſonne of Siphtan. And in the trybe of the ſonnes
of Zabulon, yͤ lorde Elizaphan the ſonne of Parnac.
26 And in the trybe of the childern of Iſachar, the lorde
27 Palthiel yͤ ſonne of Aſan. And in the trybe of the
ſonnes of Aſſer, the lorde Ahihud yͤ ſonne of Selomi.
28 And in the trybe of the childern of Naphtali, the lorde
29 Peda El the ſonne of Ammihud. Theſe are they which
the Lorde commaũded to deuyde the enheritaũce vnto
the childern of Iſrael, in the londe of Canaan.

¶ The .XXXV. Chapter.

1 AND the Lorde ſpake vnto Moſes
in yͤ feldes of Moab by Ior-
2 dayne Iericho ſayenge: commaunde the childern of Iſrael,
that they geue vnto the leuites of the enheritaũce of their poſſeſſion: cities to dwell
in. And ye ſhall geue alſo vnto the cities
of yͤ leuites, ſuburbes rounde aboute them.
3 The cities ſhalbe for them to dwell in, and
yͤ ſuburbes for their catell, poſſeſſion and
all maner beſtes of theirs.

M.C.S. *Vnto the Leuites muſt be geuen Cytyes and ſuburbes. The Cyties of refuge or ſanctuaryes. The lawe of manquellyng. For one mannes wytneſſe ſhall no man be condempned.*

4 And the ſuburbes of the cities which ye ſhall geue
vnto the leuites, ſhall reach from the wall of yͤ citie
outwarde, a thouſande cu- [Fo. LXV.] bites rounde
5 aboute. And ye ſhall meaſure without the citie, and
make the vtmoſt border of the eaſtſyde: two thouſande
cubites, And the vtmoſt border of the ſouth ſyde: two
thouſande cubetes, And the vtmoſt border of the weſt
ſyde: two thouſande cubetes: and the vtmoſt border
of the north ſyde: two thouſande cubetes alſo: and the

M. 1 Iordan ouer againſt Ericho

V. 3 et ſuburbana earum per circũitum . . . ſint pecoribus ac iumentis, 4 quæ a muris ciuitatum forinſecus per circumitum . . . tendentur. 5 æquali termino finietur. eruntque vrbes in medio, & foris ſuburbana

L. 3 allerley thier haben 5 an der ecken (3 times)

citie ſhalbe in the myddes. And theſe ſhall be the
ſuburbes of their cities.
6 And amonge the cities which ye ſhall geue vnto
the leuites, there ſhall be ſixe cities of
fraunches which ye ſhall geue to that
intent that he which killeth, maye flye
7 thyder. And to them ye ſhall adde .xlii
cities mo: ſo that all the cities which ye
ſhall geue the leuites ſhalbe .xlviii. with
their ſuburbes.

fraunches, *franchiſe,* i.e. *a ſanctuary ſecuring to the criminal freedom from arreſt,* cf. vv. 27, 32

8 And of the cities which ye ſhall geue oute of the
poſſeſſyons of the childern of Iſrael, ye ſhall geue many
out of their poſſeſſions that haue moche and fewe out
of their poſſeſſiōs that haue litle: ſo that euery tribe
ſhall geue of his cities vnto the leuites, acordinge to
the enheritaunce which he enhereteth.
9, 10 And the Lorde ſpake vnto Moſes ſayenge: ſpeake
vnto the childern of Iſrael and ſaye vnto them: when
ye be come ouer Iordayne in to the londe of Canaan,
11 ye ſhall bylde cities whiche ſhalbe preuyleged townes for
you: that he whiche fleeth a man vnwares, maye flye thi-
12 ther. And the cities ſhalbe to .¶. flee from the executer
of bloude, that he whyche kylled dye not, vntill he
13 ſtonde before the congregacion in iudgement. And
of theſe .vi. fre cities which ye ſhall geue
14 .iii. ye ſhall geue on this ſyde Iordayne
15 and .iii. in ỹ londe of Canaan. And theſe
ſixe fre cities ſhalbe for the childern of Iſrael & for
the ſtraunger & for him that dwelleth amonge you, ỹ
all thei which kill any perſone vnwares, maye flee
thither.

The righte vſe of ſenctuaryes.

16 Yf any man ſmyte another with a wepō of yerne
that he dye, than he is a murtherer, & ſhall dye for it.

V. 6 ſex erunt in fugitiuorum auxilia ſeparata 11 decernite quæ vrbes eſſe debeant in præſidia fugit. qui nolentes, ſanguinem fuderint 12 cognatus occiſi . . . & cauſa illius iudicetur. 14 trans Iordanem 16 reus erit homicidii, & ipſe morietur.

L. 6 ſechs frey ſtedte geben 12 blut recher, das der nicht ſterben muſſe, der eyn todſchlag than hat, bis das er fur der gemeyne zu gericht geſtanden ſey.

M. M. N. 11 The ryght vſe of ſanctuaries.

17 Yf he ſmyte him with a throwinge ſtone that he
dye therwith, then he ſhall dye: For he is a murtherer
and ſhalbe ſlayne therfore.
18 Yf he ſmyte him with a handwepon of wodd that
he dye therwith, then he ſhall dye: for he is a murtherer and ſhalbe ſlayne therfore.
19 The iudge of bloude ſhall ſlee the murtherer, as
20 ſone as he fyndeth him: Yf he thruſt him of hate or
21 hourle at him with layenge of wayte that he dye or
ſmyte him with his hande of enuye that he dye, he that
ſmote him ſhall dye, for he is a murtherer. The iuſtice
of bloude ſhall ſlee him as ſoone as he fyndeth him.
22 But and yf he puſſhed him by chaunce & not of
hate or caſt at him with any maner of [Fo. LXVI.]
23 thynge and not of layenge of wayte: or caſt any maner
of ſtone at him that he dye therewith, and ſawe him
not: And he caſt it apon him and he dyed, but was
24 not his enemye, nether ſoughte him ony harme: Then
the cōgregacion ſhall iudge betwene the ſleer ād the
25 executer of bloude in ſoche caſes. And the congregacion ſhall delyuer the ſleer out of the hande of the
iudge of bloude, and ſhall reſtore him agayne vnto
the frauncheſed cytye, whother he was ſleed. And he
ſhall byde there vnto the dethe off the hye preaſte
whiche was anoynted with holy oyle.
26 But and yf he came without the borders of his
27 preuyleged citie whether he was fled, yf the bloudvenger
fynde him without the borders of his fre towne, he
28 ſhall ſlee the murtherer and be giltleſſe, becauſe he
ſhulde haue bidden in his fre towne vntyll the deth of
the hye preaſte, and after the deth of the hye preaſte,
he ſhall returne agayne vnto the londe of his poſſeſſyon.

M. 19 the iuſtice of bloude 26 yf the aūeger of bloud

V. 17 Si lapidem iecerit, & ictus occubuerit: ſimiliter punietur. 18 percuſſoris ſanguine vindicabitur. 19 Propinquus occiſi, homic. interficiet: ſtatim vt apprehenderit eum, interficiet. 21 inimicus . . . cognatus occiſi ſtatim vt inuenerit eū, iugulabit. 23 & inimicitiis quicquam horum fecerit 24 inter percuſſorem & propinquum ſanguinis quæſtio ventilata 25 liberabitur innocens de vltoris manu 26 quæ exulibus deputatæ ſunt

L. 25 frey ſtad (cf. vv. 26, 27, 28) 28 widder zum land ſeynes erbguts komen

29 And this ſhalbe an ordinaunce and a lawe vnto you,
amonge youre childern after you in all youre habitacions.
30 Whoſoeuer ſleeth, ſhalbe ſlaine at ŷ mouthe of witneſſes. For one witneſſe ſhall not anſwere agenſte one
31 perſone to put him to deeth. Moreouer ye ſhall take
none amendes for the lyfe of the murtherer whiche is
32 .P. worthy to dye: But he ſhall be put to deeth. Alſo
ye ſhall take none atonement for him ŷ is fled to a fre
citie, that he ſhulde come agayne and dwell in the
londe before the deeth of the hye preaſt.
33 And ſe that ye polute not the londe which ye are
in, for bloude defyleth the londe. And the londe can
none other wyſe be clenſed of ŷ bloude that is ſhed
34 therein, but by the bloude of it that ſhed it. Defyle
not therfore the londe which ye inhabitt, & in the
myddes of which I alſo dwell, for I am ŷ Lorde which
dwell amonge the childern of Iſrael.

¶ The .XXXVI. Chapter.

M.C.S. An order for the maryage of the daughters of Zelaphead. One of the trybes may not marye wyth a nother: but euery one muſt take hym a wyfe of hys awne trybe.

1 AND the auncyēt heedes of the
childern of Gilead the ſonne
of Machir ŷ ſonne of Manaſſe
of the kynred of ŷ childern of
Ioſeph, came forth and ſpake before Moſes
and the prynces which were auncyēt heedes
2 amōge the childern of Iſrael & ſayed: The
Lorde commaunded my lorde to geue ŷ
lande to enherette by lotte to the childern of Iſrael. And then my lord commaunded in ŷ

M. 33 bloude of hym 34 I alſo dwell amonge the chyldren of Iſrael.

V. 30 Homicida ſub teſtibus punietur 34 Atque ita emūdabitur veſtra poſſeſſio xxxvi, 2 Tibi domino noſtro præcepit dominus, vt terram ſorte diuideres filiis Iſrael & vt filiabus

L. 32 Vnd yhr ſolt keyne verſunung nehmen 33 wenn wer blut ſchuldig iſt, der ſchendet das land. xxxvi, 2 Lieber herr

M. M. N. 30 For one mannes wytneſſe ought no man to be condemned.

name of the Lorde to geue the enheritaunce of Zela-
3 phead oure brother vnto his doughters. Now when
any of the ſonnes of the trybes of Iſrael take them to
wyues, then ſhall their enheritaunce be taken from
the enheritaunce of oure fathers, and ſhall be put vnto
the enheritaunce of the trybe in which they [Fo.
LXVII.] are and ſhalbe taken from the lott of oure
4 enheritaunce. And when the fre yere cometh vnto
the childern of Iſrael, then ſhall their enheritaunce be
put vnto the enheritaunce of the trybe where they are
in, and ſo ſhall their enheritaunce be taken awaye
from the enheritaunce of the trybe of oure fathers.

5 And Moſes commaunded the childern of Iſrael at
the mouth of the Lorde ſayenge: the trybe of ỹ chil-
6 dern of Ioſeph haue ſayed well. This therefore doeth
the Lorde commaũde the doughters of Zelaphead ſayenge: let them be wyues to whom they thẽ ſilfe thynke
beſt, but in the kynred of the trybe of their fathers
7 ſhall they marye, that the enheritaunce of the children
of Iſrael roole not from trybe to trybe. But that the
childern of Iſrael maye abyde, euery man in the enherit-
8 aunce of the trybe of his fathers And euery doughter
that poſſeſſeth any enheritaunce amonge the trybes of the
childern of Iſrael, ſhalbe wife vnto one of the kynred of
the trybe of hir father, that the childern of Iſrael maye
enioy euery man the enheritaunce of his father, &
9 that the enheritaunce goo not from one trybe to
another: but that the trybes of the childern of Iſrael,
maye abyde euery man in his awne enheritaunce.

10 And as the Lorde commaunded Moſes euen ſo dyd
11 the doughters of Zelaphead: Mahela, Thirza, Hagla,

M. 4 And when the yere of iubelye . . wherin they are

V. 3 quas ſi alterius tribus homines vxores acceperint . . . de noſtra hæreditate minuetur 4 iubileus, id eſt quinquageſimus annus remiſſionis aduenerit, confundatur ſortium diſtributio, & aliorum poſſeſſio ad alios tranſeat. 5 Reſpondit Moyſes filiis Iſrael, & domino præcipiente ait, Recte . . . locuta eſt 7 ne commiſceatur poſſeſſio filiorum Iſrael de tribu in tribum. Omnes enim 9 nec ſibi miſceantur tribus, ſed ita maneant 10 vt a domino ſeparatæ ſunt.

L. 5 hat recht geredt. 7 vnd nicht eyn erbteyl von eym ſtam falle auff den andern 9 ſondern eyn iglicher hange an ſeynem erbe

Milca and Noa, .P. ād were maried vnto their fathers
12 brothers ſonnes, of the kynred of the childern of Manaſſe the ſonne of Ioſeph: ād ſo they had their enheritaunce in the trybe of the kynred of their father.
13 Theſe are the commaundmentes & lawes which the
Lorde commaunded thorow Moſes, vnto the childern
of Iſrael in the feldes of Moab apon Iordayne nye vnto
Iericho.

¶ The ende of the .iiii. boke of Moſes.

V. 11 filiis patrui ſui 12 et poſſeſſio quæ illis fuerat attributa, manſit 13 per manum Moyſi
L. 11 den kindern yhrer vettern 12 Alſo bleyb yhr erbteyl.

A PRO

LOGE IN TO THE

fyfte boke of Moſes, cal=

led Deuteronomye.

W T

THIS is a boke worthye to be rede in daye and nyghte and neuer to be oute of handes. For it is the moſt excellent of all the bokes of Moſes It is eaſye alſo and light and a very pure goſpell that is to wete, a preachinge of fayth and loue: deducinge the loue to God oute of faith, and the loue of a mans neyghboure oute of the loue of God. Herin alſo thou mayſt lerne right meditacion or contemplacyon, which is nothing els ſaue the callynge to mynde and a repeatyng in the hert of the gloriouſe ād wonderfull deades of God, and of his terreble handelinge off his enemyes and mercyfull entreating of them that come when he calleth them which thinge this boke doth and almoſt nothinge els.

In the .iiii. firſt chaptres he reherſeth the benefites of God done vnto thē, to prouoke thē to loue, ād his mightie deades done aboue all naturall power ād beyonde all naturall capacite of faith, that they might beleue God ād truſt in him and in his ſtrength. And thyrdlye he reherſeth the firce plages of God vppon hys enemyes and on them which thorowe impacientie and vnbeleffe fell from him: partelye to tame .¶. and abate the appetites of the fleſhe whiche alwaye fyght agenſt the ſpirite, and partely to bridle the wilde raginge luſtes of thē in whom was no ſpirite: that though they had no power to do good of loue, yet at the leſt waye they ſhulde abſteyne from outwarde euell for feare of wrath and cruell vengeaunce whiche ſhuld fall vppon them and ſhortly finde them oute, yf they caſt vpp goddes nurter and runne at ryotte beyonde his lawes and ordinaunces. Moreouer he chargeth them to put nought to nor take oughte awaye from goddes wordes, but to be diligent onlye to kepe them in remēbraunce and in the harte and to teache theire childern, for feare of forgettinge. And to beware ether of makynge imagerye or of bowinge them ſelues vnto images ſayenge: Ye ſawe no image when God ſpake vnto you, but herde avoyce onlye and that voyce kepe and therunto cleaue, for it is youre liffe and it ſhall ſaue you. And finally yf (as the frayltie of al fleſh is) they ſhall haue fallen from God and he haue brought them in to troble, aduerſyte, ād cōbraunce ād all neceſſite: yet yf they repent and turne, he promyſeth them that God ſhall remēbre his mercie ād receave thē to grace agayne

In the fifte he repeteth the .x. commaūdmētes and that they myght ſe a cauſe to do them .ꝑ. of loue, he biddeth them remembre that they were bounde in Egipte and how God delyuered them with a mightie hande and a ſtretchedout arme, to ſerue him and to kepe his commaundmentes: as Paule ſayeth that we are bought with Chriſtes bloude ād therfore are his ſervauntes ād not oure awne, ād ought to ſeke his will and honoure onlye ād to loue ād ſerue one another for his ſake.

In the ſixte he ſetteth out the fountayne off all commaundmentes: that is, that they beleue how that there is but one God that doeth all, and therfore ought onlye to be loued with all the herte, all the ſoule and all the myghte. For loue only is the fulfillinge of the commaundementes, as Paule alſo ſayeth vnto, the Romaynes and Galathians likewiſe. He warneth thē alſo that they forgett not the commaundmentes, but teach thē their childern ād to ſhew their childern alſo how God delyuered thē out of the bondage of the Egiptiās to ſerue him and his commaundmētes, that the childern myght ſe a cauſe to worke of loue, likewiſe.

The ſeuēth is all together of faith: he remoueth all occaſiōs that might withdrawe them from the fayth, and pulleth them alſo from all confidence in them ſelues, and ſturreth thē vp to truſt in god boldlye and onlye.

.¶. Of the eyght chaptre thou ſeyſt how that the cauſe of all temptation is, that a mā might ſe his awne herte. For whē I am brought in to that extremite that I muſt ether ſuffre or forſake god, then I ſhall feale how moch I beleue and truſt in him, and how moch I loue him. In like maner, yf my brother do me euel for my good, then yf I loue him when there is no cauſe in him, I ſe that my loue was of god, ād euē ſo yf I then hate him, I feale and perceave that my loue was but wordly, And finallye he ſturreth thē to the fayth ād loue of god, ād dryveth them frō all confidence of theire awne ſelves.

In the nynth alſo he moueth thē vnto faith and to put their truſt in god, and draweth thē from confidence of them ſelues by rehearſinge all the wekedneſſe which they had wrought from the firſt daye he knew them vnto that ſame daye. And in the end he repeteth how he coniured god in horeb ād ouercame him with prayer, where thou mayeſt lerne the right maner to praye.

In the tenth he rekeneth vpp the pith of all lawes and the kepinge of the lawe in the harte: which is to feare god loue him ād ſerue him with all their harte ſoule and mighte ād kepe his commaundmentes of loue. And he ſheweth a reaſon why they ſhuld that doo: euen .¶. becauſe god is lord of heuen and erth ād hath alſo done all for them of his awne goodneſſe without their deſervinge. And then out of the loue vnto god he bringeth the love vnto a mans neyghboure ſayenge: god is lorde aboue all lordes and loveth all his ſeruauntes indifferently, as well the poore and feble and the ſtraunger, as the rich and mightye, ād therfore wil that we loue the poore and the ſtraunger. And he addeth a cauſe, for ye were ſtraungers and god deliuered you and hath brought you vnto a londe where ye be at home. Loue the ſtraunger therfore for his ſake.

In the .xi. he exhorteth them to loue and feare god, and reherſeth the terrible dedes off god vppon his enemies, and on them that rebelled agenſt him. And he teſtifyeth vnto thē both what will folow yf they loue and feare god, and whate alſo yf they deſpiſe him ād breake his commaundment.

In the .xii. he cōmaundeth to put out of the waye all that might be an occaſion to hurte the fayth and forbiddeth to do ought after their awne mindes, or to altre the worde of god.

In the .xiii. he forbiddeth to herken vnto ought ſaue vnto gods worde: no though he which coūſeleth cōtrarye ſhuld come with miracles, as Paule doth vnto the Galathians.

.¶. In the .xiiii. the beeſtes are forbiddē, partely for the vnclenneſſe of thē, ād partely to cauſe hate betwene the hethē ād thē, that they haue no cōuerſatiō to gether, in that one abhorreth whatt the other eateth. Vnto this xv. chaptre all pertayne vnto faith and loue cheflye. And in this .xv. he beginneth to entreate moare ſpeciallye of thinges pertayninge vnto the comen welth ād equite ād exhorteth vnto the loue of a mans neyghboure. And in the .xvi. amonge other he forgetteth not the ſame. And in the .xvii. he entreateth of right and equite chefly, in ſo moche that when he loketh vnto faithe and vnto the, punyſhment of ydolatres, he yet endeth in a lawe of loue and equite: forbiddinge to condemne any man vnder leſſe *then twoo witneſſes at the leſt and commaundeth to bringe the treſpacers vnto the open gate of the citye where all men goo in and out, that all men might heare the cauſe and ſe that he had but right. But the pope hath founde a better waye, even to appoſſe him with out any accuſare ād that ſecretlye, that no man knowe whether he haue right or no, ether hare his articles or anſwere: for feare leſt the people ſhuld ſerch whether it were ſo or no.

In the .xviii. he forbiddeth all falſe and develiſh craftes that hurte true fayth. Moreouer .¶. becauſe the people coude not heare the voyce of the lawe ſpokē to thē in fire, he promiſeth thē a nother prophete to brīge thē better tydinges which was ſpokē of chriſt oure ſauiour.

The .xix. ād ſo forth vnto the ende of the .xxvii. is almoſt al to gether of love vnto oure neyboures ād of lawes of equite ād honeſtye with now ād then a reſpecte vnto fayth.

* The original has: them.

The .xxviii. is a terreble chaptre ād to be trēbled at: A chriſtē mans harte might wel bleed for ſorow at the readinge of it, for feare of the wrath that is like to come vpō us accordinge vnto all the curſes which thou there readeſt.

For acordinge vnto theſe curſes hath god delt with all nacions, after they were fallē in to the abhominacions of blindneſſe.

The .xxix. is like terreble with a godly leſſō in the ende that we ſhuld leue ſerchīge of goddes ſecrettes ād geue diligēce to walke accordinge to that he hath opened vnto us. For the kepīge of the cōmaūdmētes of god teacheth wiſdome as thou mayeſte ſe in the ſame chapter, where Moſes ſayeth, kepe the cōmaūdmētes, that ye maye vnderſtōd whate ye ought to do. But to ſerch goddes ſecretes blīdeth a mā as it is wel proved by the ſwarmes of oure ſophiſters, whoſe wiſe bokes are now whē we loke ī the ſcripture, foūde but ful of foliſhneſſe.

THE FYFTE

BOKE OF MOSES. CAL=

led Deuteronomye.*

** This title page does not form part of the Lenox copy of the Pentateuch of 1530; the copy recently added to the Astor Library is also without it. The subjoined entries, in the latter, made by an English hand, and signed D., are given as curiosa.*

On the Fly Leaf: "According to the various readings of Bp. Wilson's Bible by his Editor, these four last books of Moses are translated by Matthews. D."

"A. D. 1433 seems to be on a piece of parchment bound in with them. Is this the year of binding and Translin? D."

In the margin of Fo. I. Deuteronomye: "This, accordg. to Bp. Wilson's Editor, is Matthews, Transln. D."

M.C.S. *A briefe rehersall of thynges done before, from the pytchynge at mounte Horeb vntyll they came to Cades barne.*

1 THESE be the wordes which
Moses spake vnto all Israel, on
the other syde Iordayne in the
wildernesse and in the feldes
by the red see, betwene Pharã ãd Tophel,
2 Laban, Hazeroth and Disahab .xii. dayes
iurney from Horeb vnto Cades bernea, by
3 the waye that leadeth vnto mount Seir. And it fortuned the first daye of the .xi. moneth in the fortieth
yere, that Moses spake vnto the childern of Israel
acordinge vnto all that the Lorde had geuen him in
4 commaundment vnto them, after that he had smote
Sihon the kynge of the Amorites which dwelt in Hesbon, and Og kinge of Basan which dwelt at Astaroth
in Edrei.

5 On the other syde Iordayne in the londe of Moab,
6 Moses begane to declare this lawe sayinge: the Lorde
oure God spake vnto vs in Horeb sayenge: Ye haue
7 dwelt longe ynough in this mount: departe therfore
and take youre iurney and goo vnto the hilles of the
Amorites and vnto all places nye there vnto: both
feldes, hilles and dales: and vnto the south and vnto
the sees syde in the londe of Canaan, and vnto libanon:
8 euen vnto the greate ryuer Eu- .P. phrates. Beholde,
I haue set the londe before you: goo in therfore and

M. 2 .xi. dayes . . barne 4 Sehon . . Edrai.

V. 1 trans Iordanem (v. 5.) . . Aseroth vbi auri est plurimum. 4 habitauit . . mansit 5 explanare legem 6 in hoc monte 7 & iuxta litus maris . . vque ad flumen magnum Euphraten. 8 En, inquit tradidi vobis

L. 1 iensyd (v. 5) 5 aus zulegen dis gesetz 6 an disem berge 7 gegen den anfurt des meeris . . bis an das grosse wasser Phrath, 8 Sihe da ich hab das land fur euch geben (v. 21)

M. M. N. 6 Horeb and Sinai are both one.

possesse the londe which the Lord sware vnto youre
fathers Abraham, Isaac and Iacob, to geue vnto them
and their seed after them.
9 And I sayde vnto yov the same season: I am not
10 able to bere you myselfe alone. For the Lorde youre
God hath multiplyed you: so that ye are this daye
11 as the starres of heauen in numbre (the Lorde god of
youre fathers make you a thousande tymes so many
moo as ye are, and blesse you as he hath — moo, *more*
12 promysed you) how (sayde I) can I myselfe alone, beare
the combraunce, charge and stryffe that is amonge you:
13 brynge therfore men of wisdome and of vnderstondinge
and expert knowne amonge youre trybes, that I maye
make them ruelars ouer you.
14 And ye answered me and sayed: that which thou
15 hast spoken is good to be done. And then I toke the
heedes of youre trybes, men of wysdome and that were
expert, and made them ruelers ouer you: captaynes
ouer thousandes and ouer hundredes ouer fyftye and
ouer ten, and officers amonge youre trybes.
16 And I charged youre Iudges the same — *Iudges.*
tyme sayenge: heare youre brethern and iudge [Fo.
II.] righteously betwene euery man and his brother
17 and the straunger that is with him. Se that ye knowe
no man in Iudgement: but heare the small as well as
the greate and be afrayed of no man, for the lawe is
Gods. And the cause that is to harde for you, brynge
18 vnto me and I will heare it. And I commaunded you
the same season, all the thinges which ye shulde doo.
19 And then we departed from Horeb and walked
thorow all that greate and terreble wildernesse as ye

M. 17 for the iudgement is Gods

V. 10 solus sustinere vos . . . sicut stellæ cæli, plurimi. 12 negotia vestra . . . & pondus ac iurgia. 13 & quorum conuersatio sit probata 14 quam vis facere. 15 ac decanos, qui docerent vos singula 16 Præcepique eis, dicens, Audite illos, & quod iustum est iudicate: siue ciuis sit ille, siue peregrinus. 17 Nulla erit distantia personarum

L. 9 nicht alleyn ertragen 10 wie die menge der stern am hymel 12 muhe. last. hadder 14 das du es thun wilt. 16 richtet recht zwisschen yderman vnd seynem bruder vnd dem frembdlingen 17 niemants person euch schewen

M. M. N. 16 Iudges.

haue ſene alonge by the waye that ledeth vnto the
hilles of the Amorites, as the Lorde oure God com-
20 maunded us, and came to Cades bernea. And there
I ſayed vnto you: Ye are come vnto the hilles of the
Amorites, which the Lorde oure God doth geue vnto
21 us. Beholde the Lorde thi God hath ſett the londe
before the, goo vpp and conquere it, as the Lorde God
of thy fathers ſayeth vnto the: feare not, nether be
diſcoraged.

22 And then ye came vnto me euery one and ſayed:
Let us ſende men before us, to ſerche us out the londe
and to brynge us worde agayne, both what waye we
ſhall goo vpp by, and vnto what cities we ſhall come.
23 And the ſayenge pleaſſed me well .P. and I toke .xii
24 men of you, of euery trybe one. And they departed
and went vp in to the hye contre and came vnto the
25 ryuer Eſcoll, and ſerched it out, and toke of the frute
of the londe in their hondes and brought it doune vnto
us and brought us worde agayne and ſayde: it is a
good lande which the Lorde oure God doeth geue us.

26 Notwithſtondinge ye wolde not conſente to goo
vpp, but were diſhobedient vnto the mouth of the
27 Lorde youre God, ād murmured in youre tentes and
ſayde: becauſe the Lorde hateth us, therfore he hath
brought us out of the londe of Egipte, to delyuer us in
to the handes of the Amorites and to deſtroye us.

28 How ſhall we goo vpp? Oure brethern haue diſcoraged oure hartes ſayenge: the people is greater and
taller than we, ād the cities are greatte and walled
euen vpp to heauen, and moreouer we haue ſene the
ſonnes of the Enakimes there.

M. 20 barne

V. 20 daturus eſt vobis. 21 dabit . . nec quicquam paueas. 24 Vallem botri 25 attulerunt ad nos, atque dixerunt 28 Quo aſcendemus? nuntii terruerunt

L. 20 geben wirt 22 furcht dich nicht vnd ſchew 23 Das gefiel myr wol 25 ſagten vns widder 28 Wo ſollen wyr hynauff?

M. M. N. 21 *Before the:* That is, at thy commaundement. 26 *But were dyſobedyent:* The people beyng vnfaithfull wolde not go vnto the land promeſed. 27 *Hateth vs:* God is ſayd to hate a man whē he putteth him forth of hys hert, & geueth him not of his grace. Pſal. v, b and .xxx, b.

29 And I ſayed vnto you: dreade not nor be afrayed
30 of thē: The Lorde youre God which goeth before you,
he ſhall fyghte for you, acordynge to all that he dyd
31 vnto you in Egipte before youre eies ād in the wilderneſſe: as thou haſt ſene how that the Lorde thy God
bare the as a man ſhulde beare his ſonne, thorow [Fo.
III.] out all the waye which ye haue gone, vntill ye
32 came vnto this place. And yet for all this ſayenge ye
dyd not beleue the Lorde youre God which goeth the
33 waye before you, to ſerche you out a place to pitche
youre tentes in, in fyre by nyght, that ye myghte ſe
what waye to go and in a cloude by daye.

34 And the Lorde herde the voyce of youre wordes
35 and was wroth and ſwore ſayenge, there ſhall not one
of theſe men of this frowarde generacion ſe that good
36 londe which I ſware to geue vnto youre fathers, ſaue
Caleb the ſonne of Iephune, he ſhall ſe it, and to him
I will geue the londe which he hath walked in ād to
his childern, becauſe he hath contynually folowed the
37 Lorde. Likewiſe the Lorde was angrye with me for
youre ſakes ſayenge: thou alſo ſhalt not go in thither.
38 But Ioſua the ſōne of Nun which ſtondeth before the,
he ſhall go in thither. Bolde him therfore
39 for he ſhall deuyde it vnto Iſrael. Moreouer youre childern which ye ſayed ſhulde be a praye,
and youre ſonnes which knowe nether good nor bad
this daye, they ſhall goo in thither ād vnto them I will
40 geue it, ād they ſhall enioye it. But as for you, turne
backe and take youre iurneye in to the wilderneſſe:
euen the waye to the reed ſee.

bolde, *verb, to encourage*

41 Than ye anſwered and ſayed vnto me: We .P. haue
ſynned agenſt the Lorde: we will goo vp and fyghte,
acordinge to all that the Lorde oure God cōmaunded

M. 38 Boldē

V. 30 qui ductor eſt veſter 32 Et nec ſic quidem credidiſtis 33 metatus eſt locum 35 ſub iuramento pollicitus ſum 36 quia ſecutus eſt dominum. 37 Nec miranda indignatio in populum 38 ſorte terram diuidet 39 qui hodie

L. 30 zeucht fur euch hyn 32 Aber das gallt nichts bey euch . . . hettet gegleubt 33 euch die ſtette zu weyſen 36 volliglich . . . gefolget hat 39 die heuts tags

us. And whē ye had gyrde on euery man his wepons
42 of warre and were ready to goo vp in to the hilles, the
Lorde ſayed vnto me: ſaye vnto thē, ſe that ye go not
vp and that ye fighte not, for I am not amōge you:
leſt ye be plaged before youre enemies.
43 * And whē I told you ye wold not
heare: but diſobeyed the mouth of the
Lorde, and went preſumptouſly vp in to
the hilles.
44 Thē the Amorites which dwelt in thoſe
hilles, came out agenſt you and chaſed you
as bees doo, and hewed you in Seir, euē
45 vnto Horma. And ye came agayne and
wepte before the Lorde: but the Lorde wolde not
46 heare youre voyce nor geue you audience. And ſo ye
abode in Cades alōge ſeaſon, acordinge vnto the tyme
that ye there dwelt.

Here thou ſeiſt the verey image of the papiſtes. For thei like wiſe where Gods wordeis, there they beleue not ād where it is not there they be bold.

The .II. Chapter.

1 THEN we turned and toke oure
iurney in to the wilderneſſe,
euen the waye to the red ſee
as the Lord cōmaunded me.
And we compaſſed the mountayns of Seir
2 a lōge tyme Thē the Lorde ſpake vnto
3 me ſaienge: Ye haue cōpaſſed this mountayns lōge ynough, turne you northwarde.
4 And warne the people ſay- [Fo. IIII.]
enge: Ye ſhall goo thorow the coſtes of youre brethern

M.C.S. *A reherſall of that which was done from the tyme that they departed from Cades barne, vnto the battell agaynſt the kynges Sehon & Og.*

M. 46 *omits:* acordinge vnto the tyme that ye there dwelt.

V. 41 inſtructi armis 42 ne cadatis 43 tumentes ſuperbia 44 ſicut ſolent apes perſequi: & cecidit de Seir vſque Horma. ii, 1 circumiuimus

L. 41 Da yhr euch nu ruſtet eyn iglicher mit ſeynem harnſch 42 geſchlagen werdet 43 wart vermeſſen 44 wie die byenen thun, vnd ſchlugen euch zu Seir bis gen Harma, ii, 1 vmbzogen

M. M. T. 43 *Ye wold not heare:* Here thou ſeyſt the verye Image of vs that lyue ī this moſt perlouſe tyme, for euen we lyke-wyſe, where goddes worde is, here beleue we not: and where it is not, there be we bolde.

the childern of Eſau which dwell in Seir, and they
ſhalbe afrayed of you: But take good hede vnto youre
5 ſelues that ye prouoke thē not, for I wil not geue you
of their lōde, no not ſo moch as a fote breadeth: becauſe I haue geuē mount Seir vnto Eſau to poſſeſſe.
6 Ye ſhall bye meate of thē for money to eate, and ye
7 ſhall bye water of thē for money to drīke. For the
Lorde thy God hath bleſſed the in all the workes of
thine hāde, ād knew the as thou wēteſt thorow this
greate wilderneſſe. Moreouer the Lorde thi God hath
bene with the this .xl. yeres, ſo that thou haſt lacked
nothinge.

8 And whē we were departed from oure brethern the
childern of Eſau which dwelt in Seir by the felde waye
from Elath ād Ezion Gaber, we turned ād went the
9 waye to the wilderneſſe of Moab. Thē the Lorde ſayed
vnto me ſe that thou vexe not the Moabites, nether
prouoke thē to batayle for I will not geue the of their
lōde to poſſeſſe: becauſe I haue geuē Ar vnto the chil-
10 dern of loth to poſſeſſe. The Emimes dwelt there in in
tymes paſt, a people greate, many ād tal, as the Ena-
11 kimes: which alſo were takē for geantes as the
Enakimes: And the Moabites called thē Emymes.
12 In like maner the Horimes dwelt in Seir before time
which .☛. the childern of Eſau caſt out, ād deſtroyed
thē before them and dwelt there in their ſtede: as
Iſrael dyd in the londe of his poſſeſſiō which the Lorde
gaue them

13 Now ryſe vpp (ſayed I) ād get you ouer the ryuer
14 Zared: ād we went ouer the ryuer Zared. The ſpace

M. 11 Emims. 12 Horims

V. 5 ne moueamini contra eos 8 de Aſion-gaber, venimus ad iter 9 Non pugnes . . . nec ineas aduerſus eos prælium . . . filiis Lot 13 venimus ad eum.

L. 5 nicht reytzet, denn ich werd euch yhres lands nicht eynen ſuſs breyt geben 6 das yhr eſſet . . . trincket 8 Ezeongaber, wandten wyr vns vnd giengen 9 nicht beleydigen noch ſie reytzen zum ſtreyt

M. M. N. 10 *Emims:* Emym a kynd of Geauntes ſo called becauſe they were terrible & cruell for Emym ſygnifyeth terryble-neſſe. *Enakyms* loke Iudic. i, d. 12 *Horims* a kynde of Ge-auntes and ſygnifyeth noble, becauſe that of pryde they called thē ſelues nobles or gentels.

in which we came from Cades bernea vntill we were
come ouer the ryuer Zared was .xxxviii. yeres: vntill
all the generacion of the men of warre were wafted
15 out of the hoft as the Lorde fware vnto thē. For in
dede the hande of the Lorde was agēft thē, to deftroye
them out of the hoft, till they were confumed.
16 And as foone as all the men of warre were confumed
17 and deed from amonge the people, then the Lorde
18 fpake vnto me fayenge. Thou fhalt goo thorow Ar
19 the cofte of Moab this daye, and fhalt come nye vnto
the childern of Ammon: fe that thou vexe them not,
nor yet prouoke them. For I will not geue the of the
londe of the childern of Ammon to poffeffe, becaufe I
haue geuen it vnto the childern of loth to poffeffe.
20 That alfo was taken for a londe of geauntes and geauntes
dwelt therin in olde tyme, and the Ammonites called
21 them Zamzumyms. A people that was great, many
and taule, as the Enakyms. But the [Fo. V.] Lorde
deftroyed them before the Ammonites, and they caft
22 them out and they dwelt there ī their fteade: as he
dyd for the childern of Efau which dwell in Seir: euē
as he deftroyed the horyms before them, ād they caft
them out and dwell in their fteade vnto this daye.
23 And the Avims which dwelt in Hazarim euē vnto
Aza, the Caphthoryms which came out of Caphthor
deftroyed them and dwelt in their rowmes.
24 Ryfe vp, take youre yourney and goo ouer the ryuer
Arnon. Beholde, I haue geuen in to thy hād Sihō the
Amorite kynge of Hefbō, ād his londe. Goo to and
25 conquere and prouoke hī to batayle. This daye I will
begynne to fend the feare and dreade of the vppon all

M. 14 barne 20 Zamzumims 21 Enakims 24 Sehon

V. 14 donec confumeretur 15 vt interirent de caftrorum medio. 18 vrbem nomine Ar 20 reputata eft 22 quam poffident vfque in præfens. 24 incipe poffidere

L. 14 eyn ende nemen 15 vmbkemen . . . bis das yhr eyn ende wurde. 20 gefchetzt 22 befitzen, das fie da an yhrer ftat woneten, bis auff difen tag. 24 heb an zu eintzunem

M. M. N. 20 *Zāzumims:* Zamzumim a kynde of geauntes and fygnyfyeth myfcheuoufe. They were tyrauntes, cruell theues & pollars. 24 *Sehon & his lande before the:* Or at thy cōmaundement

nacions that are vnder al portes of heauen: ſo that whē
they heare ſpeake of the, they ſhall tremble and quake
for feare of the.
26 Then I ſent meſſengers out of the wilderneſſe of
kedemoth vnto Syhon kynge of Heſbon, with wordes
27 of peace ſaynge: Let me goo thorow thy londe. I
will goo allweyes alonge by the hye waye and will
nether turne vnto the righte hande nor to the left.
28 Sell me meate for money for to eate, and geue me
drinke for money for to drynke: I will goo thorowe
29 by fote only (as the childern of Eſau dyd vnto me
whi- .P. che dwell in Seir and the Moabites whiche
dwell in Ar) vntyll I be come ouer Iordayne, in to
the londe which the Lorde oure God geueth vs.
30 But Sihon the kinge of Heſbon wolde not let vs
paſſe by him, for the Lord thy God had hardened his
ſprite and made his herte tough becauſe he wold delyuer him into thy hondes as it is come to paſſe this
daye.
31 And the Lorde ſayed vnto me: beholde, I haue begonne to ſet Sihon and his londe before the: goo to
32 and conquere, that thou mayſt poſſeſſe his londe. Then
both Sihon and all his people came out agenſt vs
33 vnto batayle at Iahab. And the Lorde ſet him before
vs, and we ſmote hym and his ſonnes and all hys
people.
34 And we toke all his cities the ſame ſeaſon, and
deſtroyed all the cities with men, wemen, and childern
35 ād let nothinge remayne, ſaue the catell only we

M. 26 wilderneſſe of the eaſte . . Sehon 29 Iordan 30 Sehon 32 Sehon . . . Iahaza

V. 25 ſub omni cælo: vt . . . paueāt, & in morem parturentium contremiſcant, & dolore teneantur. 27 publica grad. via 28 Tantum eſt vt nobis concedas tranſitum 29 ad Iordanem 30 indurauerat dominus deus tuus ſpiritum eius, & obfirmauerat cor illius . . . ſicut nunc vides. 32 incipe poſſidere eam.

L. 25 vnter allen hymeln, das wenn ſie von dyr horen, toben vnd ſich engſten fur deyner zukunfft. 28 Ich wil nur zu fuſs durch hyn gehen 29 vber den Iordan 30 verhertet ſeynen mut vnd verſtockt yhm ſeyn hertz . . . wie es iſt itzt am tage. 31 eyn zu nemen zu beſitzen ſeyn land 34 alle ſeyne ſtedte vnd verbanten alle ſtedte

M. M. N. 32 *Iahaza:* Otherwyſe Iaſa.

caught vnto oure ſelues and the ſpoyle of the cities
36 which we toke, from Aroer vppon the brynke off the
riuer off Arnon, and the citie in the ryuer, vnto Gilead:
there was not one citye to ſtronge for vs. The Lorde
37 oure God delyuered all vnto vs: only vnto the londe
of the childern of Ammon ye came not, nor vnto all
the coſte of the riuer Iabock [Fo. VI.] ner vnto the
cities in the mountaynes, nor vnto what ſoeuer the
Lorde oure God forbade vs.

¶ The .III. Chapter.

M.C.S. A reherſall of thynges that chaunſed from the vyctorye of the .ii. kynges Sehon & Og, vnto the Inſtitucion of Ioſue in Moſes ſteade.

1 THEN we turned and went vpp
the waye to Baſan. And Og
the kinge of Baſan came out
agenſt vs: both he and all his
2 people to batayle at Edrey. And the
Lorde ſayed vnto me: feare him not, for
I haue delyuered him and all his people
ād his lande in to thy hande ād thou ſhalt
deale with hī as thou dealeſt with Sihon kynge of the
3 Amorites which dwelt at Heſbon. And ſo the Lorde
oure God delyuered in to oure handes, Og alſo the
kynge off Baſan and al his folke, And we ſmote him
vntyll noughte was left him.
4 And we toke all his cities the ſame ceaſon (for there
was not a citie whiche we toke not from them) euen
iii. ſcore cities, all the region of Argob, the kyngdome
of Og in Baſan.
5 All theſe cities were made ſtronge with hye walles,
gates and barres, beſyde vnwalled townes a greate

M. 36 Galaad. iii, 1 Edrai 2 Sehon

V. 35 Abſque iumentis 36 torrentis Arnon, & oppido, quod in valle . . Non fuit vicus & ciuitas 37 Abſque terra . . . torrenti Ieboc iii, 2 traditus eſt 3 percuſſimuſque eos vſque ad internecionem 4 vno tempore. 5 abſque oppidis innumeris

L. 36 des bachs Arnon 37 on zu dem land . . . bach Iabok iii, 2 ich hab . . . geben 3 ſchlugen bis das yhm nichts vberbleyb.

M. M. N. 5 *Vnwalled townes:* As thorouſares and vyllages.

6 maynye. And we vtterly deſtroyed them, as we
played with Sihon kynge off Heſbon: bringing to
nought al the cities with men, wemen and childern.
7 But all the catell and the ſpoyle of the cities, we
caughte for .P. oure ſelues.

8 And thus we toke the ſame ceaſon, the lōde out of
the hande of two kynges of the Amorites on the other
ſyde Iordayne, from the ryuer of Arnon vnto mount
9 Hermon (which Hermon the Sidons call Sirion, but
10 the Amorites call it Senyr) all the cities in the playne
ād all Gilead and all Baſan vnto Salcha and Edrei,
11 cities of the kingdome of Og in Baſan. For only
Og kynge of Baſan remayned of the remnaūt of
the geauntes: beholde, his yernen bed is yet at
Rabath amonge the childern off Ammō .ix. cubettes longe ād, .iiii. cubetes brode, of the cubettes
of a man.

12 And when we had conquered this londe the ſame
tyme, I gaue from Aroer which is apon the riuer of
Arnon, and halfe mount Gilead and the cities thereof
13 vnto the Rubenites, and Gadites. And the reſt of Gilead and all Baſan the kingdome of Og, I gaue vnto the
halfe trybe of Manaſſe: all the regiō of Argob with all
14 Baſan was called the londe of geauntes. Iair the ſonne
of Manaſſe toke all the region of Argob vnto the coſtes
of Geſuri ād Maachati, and called the townes of Baſan
after his owne name: the townes of Iair vnto thys daye.
15,16 And I gaue half Gilead vnto Machir. And vnto
Ruben ād Gad, I gaue from Gile- [Fo. VII.] ad vnto
the ryuer of Arnon ād half the valey ād the coſte, euē
vnto the ryuer Iabock which is the border of the chil-
17 dern of Ammon, and the feldes ād Iordayne with the

M. 6 Sehon 10 Galaad . . Salecha . Edrai 12 Galad 13 Galaad 14 & called them after his owne name: Baſan Hauoth Iair vnto this daye. 15 Galaad 16 Galaad

V. 8 trans Iordanem 11 Et monſtratur lectus 14 Baſan, Auoth-Iair, id eſt Villas Iair

L. 6 vnd verbanneten (*bis*) 8 ienſyd dem Iordan 11 alhie zu Rabath

M. M. N. 14 *Hauoth Iair:* That is ſuburbes or vyllages belongyng to Iair.

coste, from Cenereth even vnto the see in the felde
which is the salt see vnder the sprynges off Pisga
eastwarde.
18 And I commaunded you the same tyme (ye Ruben
ād Gad) sayeng: the Lorde your God hath geuen you
this londe to enioye it: se that ye go harnessed before
youre brethern the childern of Israel, all that are mē
19 of warre amonge you. Youre wyues only youre childern ād youre catell (for I wote that ye haue moch
catell) shall abyde in youre cities which I haue geuen
20 you, vntyll the Lorde haue geuē rest vnto your brethern as well as vnto you, and vntyll they also haue
conquered the londe which the Lorde youre God
hath geuen them beyond Iordayne: and then returne agayne euery mā vnto his possession which I
haue geuē you.
21 And I warned Iosua the same tyme sayeng thyne
eyes haue sene all that the Lorde youre God hath
done vnto these two kynges, euē so the Lorde will doo
22 vnto all kyngdomes whither thou goest. Feare them
not, for the Lorde youre God he it is that fighteth for
you.
23 And I besoughte the Lorde the same tyme .P. say-
24 enge: O lorde Iehoua, thou hast begonne to shewe
thy servaunte thy greatnesse and thy mightie hande
for there is no God in heauen nor in erth that can do
25 after thy workes and after thy power: let me goo ouer ād
se the good londe that is beyonde Iordayne, that goodly
26 hye contre and Libanon. But the Lorde was angrie with
me for youre sakes and wolde not heare me, but sayed

M. 17 Ceneroth . . Phasgah 24 O lorde God

V. 17 & planitiem solitudinis . . . ad mare deserti, quod est salsissimum ad radices montis Phasga 20 trans Iordanem 21 quæ fecit dominus deus vester duobus his regibus: sic faciet omnibus regnis ad quæ transiturus es. 24 comparari fortitudini tuæ. 25 montem istum egregium

L. 17 vnden am berge Pisga 20 iensyd dem Iordan 24 der es deynen wercken vnd deyner macht kunde nach thun? 25 dis gutte gepirge . . .

M. M. N. 17 *Vnder ẏ springes of Phasgah:* Some the hyll fote. Heb. Esdoth which signifyeth sprīges, although some wyll that it be the name of a towne.

vnto me, be content, and ſpeake henceforth no moare
27 vnto me of this matter, Get the vp in to the toppe
of Piſga ād liſte vpp thine eyes weſt, north, ſouth ād
eaſte, ād beholde it with thyne eyes for thou ſhalt not
28 goo ouer this Iordayne. Moreouer, charge Ioſua and
corage him and bolde him.
For he ſhall go ouer before
his people, and he ſhall deuyde the londe which thou
29 ſhalt ſe vnto them. And ſo we abode in the valaye
beſyde Beth Peor.

corage, *verb, to encourage,*

bolde, *verb, to encourage*

The .IIII. Chapter.

1 AND now herken Iſrael vnto the
ordinaunces ād lawes which
I teache you, for to doo them,
that ye maye lyue ād goo ād
conquere the londe which
the Lorde God of youre
2 fathers geueth you. Ye
ſhall put nothinge vnto the
worde which I commaunde
you nether doo ought there
from, that ye maye kepe
[Fo. VIII.] the commaundmentes off the Lorde youre
3 God which I commaunde you. Youre eyes haue ſene
what the Lorde dyd vnto Baal Peor: for al the men
that folowed Baal Peor, the Lorde youre God hath

No: ner yet corrupt it with falſe gloſes to cō-firme Ariſtotle: but rebuke Ariſtotles falſe lerninge therewith.

M.C.S. *An exhortacyon to geue dylygent heede vnto the lawe, & that they ſhulde not take awaye or adde any thyng therto. Images may not be worſhypped nor yet made. The .iii. Cytyes of refuge.*

M. 27 Phaſgah

V. 26 Sufficit tibi, nequaquam vltra loquaris de hac re ad me. 27 et oculos tuos circunfer . . . & aſpice. 28 corrobora . . . conforta 29 contra phanum Phogor. iiii, 1 doceo te . . . daturus eſt 2 verbum quod vobis loquor . . cuſtodite 3 contra Beel-phegor, quomodo contriuerit

L. 26 Las gnug ſeyn, ſage myr dauon nicht mehr 29 Alſo blieben wyr ym tal gegen dem haus Peor. iiii, 1 euch lere . . gibt 2 nichts dazu thun, das ich euch gepiete . . . auff das yhr behaltet 3 vber dem Baal Peor

M. M. N. 2 *To put to the woord and to take awaye therfro* is, to Iudge & thynck otherwyſe of the wyll of god then is ſhewed vs in the ſcrypture, as in Deut. xii, d. Prouer. xxx, a.

4 deſtroyed from amōge you: But ye that claue vnto
the Lorde youre God, are alyue euery one of you this
5 daye. Beholde, I haue taught you ordinaunces and
lawes, ſoche as the Lorde my God commaūded me,
that ye ſhulde do euē ſo in the londe whether ye goo
to poſſeſſe it

6 Kepe them therfore and doo them, for that is youre
wiſdome and vnderſtandynge in the ſyghte of the nacyons: whiche when they haue herde all theſe ordinaunces, ſhall ſaye:

O what a wyſe and vnderſtondynge people is this
7 greate nacion. For what nacyon is ſo greate that hath
Goddes ſo nye vnto hym: as the Lorde oure God is
nye vnto vs, in all thinges, when we call vnto hym?
8 Yee, and what nacyon is ſo greate that hath ordinaunces
and lawes ſo ryghtuouſſe, as all thys lawe which I ſett
before you this daye.

9 Take hede to thy ſelfe therfore only ād kepe thy
ſoule diligently, that thou forgett not the thinges which
thyne eyes haue ſene and that they departe not out of
thyne harte, all the dayes of thine life: but *Teach youre*
teach them thy ſon- .P. nes, ād thy ſonnes *childern.*
10 ſonnes. The daye that I ſtode before the Lorde youre
god in Horeb, whē he ſayed vnto me, gather me the
people together, that I maye make them heare my
wordes that they maye lerne to fere me as longe as
thei lyue vppon the erth and that they maye teache
11 their childern: ye came ād ſtode alſo vnder the hyll
ād the hyll burnt with fire: euen vnto the myddes
of heauē, ād there was darckneſſe, clowdes ād myſt.

M. 9 thy lyfe

V. 4 adhæretis 5 Scitis . . . ſic facietis ea in terra quā poſſeſſuri eſtis 6 ſapientia, & intellectus coram populis . . . gens magna. 7 natio tam grandis . . . deos appropinquantes ſibi 8 alia gens ſic inclyta . . . ceremonias, iuſtaque iudicia, & vniuerſam legem . . . proponam hodie ante oculos veſtros? 9 cunctis diebus vitæ tuæ. 11 ad radices montis . . . tenebræ, et nubes, & caligo.

L. 4 anhienget 5 Sihe . . das yhr alſo 6 weyſzheyt vnd verſtand fur allen volckern . . . vnd eyn trefflich volck 7 Gotter alſo nahe ſich thun . . ſo offt wir yhn an ruffen? 8 furlege? 9 alle deyn leben lang 11 vnden an dem berge . . . finſternis, wolcken vnd tunckel.

M. M. N. 9 Teache your chyldrē.

12 And the Lorde ſpake vnto you out of the fire ād ye
herde the voyce of the wordes: But ſawe
no ymage, ſaue herde a voyce only,
13 And he declared vnto you his couenaunt, which he commaunded you to doo,
euen .x. verſes and wrote them in two
14 tables of ſtone. And the Lorde commaunded me the
ſame ſeaſon to teache you ordynaunces and lawes, for
to doo them in the londe whether ye goo to poſſeſſe it
15 Take hede vnto youre ſelues diligently as pertayninge vnto youre ſoules, for ye ſawe no maner of ymage
the daye when the Lorde ſpake vnto you in Horeb out
16 of the fire: leſt ye marre youre ſelues and make you
grauen ymages after what ſoeuer likeneſſe it be: whe-
17 ther after the likeneſſe of mā or womā or any maner
beeſt that is on the erth or of any maner fether- [Fo.
18 IX.] red foule that fleth in the ayre, or of any maner
worme that crepeth on the erth or of any maner fyſh
19 that is in the water beneth the erth: Ye and leſte thou
lyſte vpp thyne eyes vnto heuen, and when thou ſeyſt
the ſonne and the mone and the ſtarres and what ſoeuer is
contayned in heauen, ſhuldeſt be diſceaued and ſhuldeſt bow thi ſelfe vnto them ād ſerue the thinges which
the Lorde thy God hath diſtributed vnto all nacions
that are vnder al quarters of heauen.
20 For the Lorde toke you and broughte you out of
the yernen fornace of Egipte, to be vnto him a people
21 of enheritaunce, as it is come to paſſe this daye. For-
thermoare, the Lorde was angrye with me for youre
ſakes and ſware, that I ſhulde not goo ouer Iordane
and that I ſhulde not goo vnto that good londe, which

The voice is all to gether: vnto that image ought men to bowe there hertes.

V. 12 formam penitus non vidiſtis. 16 ſculptam ſimilitudinem, aut imaginem 19 omnia aſtra cæli, & errore deceptus . . quæ creauit . . in miniſterium cunctis gentibus 21 propter ſermones veſtros . . . terram optimam quam daturus eſt vobis.

L. 13 nemlich die zehen wort 19 das gantze heer des hymels (corrected into: yrgent eyn heer des hymels) 21 vmb ewres thuns willen

M. M. N. 12 *The voyce of the wordes:* The voyce is al to gether: vnto that ymage ought men to bowe there hertes. 20 *Yron fornace:* By the yron fornace is vnderſtande anguyſh & greate ſorowe & carefulnes of hert .iii. Reg. viii, f. & Ierem. xi, a.

22 the Lorde thy God geueth te to enherytaunce. For I
muſt dye in this londe, and ſhall not goo ouer Iordane:
But ye ſhall goo ouer and conquere that good londe
23 Take hede vnto youre ſelues therfore, that ye forgett
not the appoyntment of the Lorde youre appoyntment,
God which he made with you, and that *covenant*
ye make you no grauen ymage of whatſoeuer it be that
24 the Lorde thi God hath for- .P. bidden the. For the
Lorde thi God is a cōſuminge fyre, and a gelouſe
God.
25 Yf after thou haſt gotten childern and childerns
childern and haſt dwelt longe in the londe, ye ſhall
marre youre ſelues and make grauen ymages after the
likneſſe of what ſo euer it be, and ſhall worke wekedneſſe in the ſyghte of the Lorde thy God, to prouoke
him.
26 I call heauen and erth to recorde vnto you this daye,
that ye ſhall ſhortely pereſſh from of the londe whether
ye goo ouer Iordayne to poſſeſſe it: Ye ſhall not prolonge
27 youre dayes therin, but ſhall ſhortly be deſtroyed. And
the Lorde ſhall ſcater you amonge nacions, and ye ſhalbe
lefte few in numbre amonge the people whother the
28 Lorde ſhall brynge you: and there ye ſhall ſerue goddes
which are the workes of mans hande, wod and ſtone
which nether ſe nor heare not eate nor ſmell.
29 Neuer the later ye ſhall ſeke the Lorde youre God
euen there, and ſhalt fynde him yf thou ſeke him with
30 all thine herte and with all thy ſoule. In thi tribulacion and when all theſe thinges are come apon the,
euen in the later dayes, thou ſhalt turne vnto the Lorde

V. 22 Ecce morior . . . terram egregiam. 23 quæ fieri dominus prohibuit. 24 deus æmulator. 25 patrantes malum . . . ad iracundiam prouocetis 27 et remanebitis pauci 29 & tota tribulatione animæ tuæ. 30 Poſtquam te inuenerint omnia quæ prædicta ſunt, nouiſſimo autem tempore reuerteris

L. 22 ſondern . . . gutt land 23 wie der Herr deyn Got gepotten hat 27 eyn geringe pobel vberig ſeyn

M. M. X. 24 *Conſuminge fyre:* Becauſe God proueth his by afflyccion, therfore is he called a conſumyng fyre. Hebr. xii, g. & becauſe he conſumeth the vnfaithfull remedyleſſe, for ther is nothing that can reſyſt his anger toward thē. And he is called gelouſe becauſe he can not ſuffer that any ſhuld fall from hym.

thy God, and ſhalt herken vn- [Fo. X.] to his voyce.
31 For the Lorde thy God is a pitiefull God: he will not
forſake the nether deſtroye the, nor forgett the ap-
poyntmēt made with thy fathers which he ſware vnto
them.
32 For axe I praye the of the dayes that are paſt which
were before the, ſence the daye that God created man
vppon the erth and from the one ſyde of heauen vnto
the other whether any thinge hath bene lyke vnto this
greate thinge or whether any ſoche thinge hath bene
33 herde as it is, that a nacion hath herde the voyce of
God ſpeakinge out of fyre as thou haſt herde, and yet
34 lyued? ether whether God aſſayed to goo and take him
a people from amonge nacions, thorow temptacions and
ſygnes and wonders and thorow warre and with a
mightie hande and a ſtretched out arme and wyth
myghtye terreble ſightes, acordynge vnto all that
the Lorde youre God dyd vnto you in Egipte before
youre eyes.
35 Vnto the it was ſhewed, that thou myghteſt knowe,
how that the Lorde he is God and that there is none
but he.
36 Out of heauen he made the heare his voyce to
nurter the, and vppon erth he ſhewed
.P. the his greate fyre, and thou hardeſt
37 his wordes out of the fyre. And becauſe he loued thy
fathers, therfore he choſe their ſeed after them and
broughte the out with his preſence and with his
38 myghtye power of Egipte: to thruſt out nations
greater ād myghtyer then thou before the, to bringe
the in and to geue the their londe to enheritaunce:
as it is come to paſſe this daye.
39 Vnderſtonde therfore this daye and turne it to
thine herte, that the Lorde he is God in heauen aboue

nurter, *verb, to bring up, educate*

V. 31 nec omnino delebit 34 ſi fecit deus . . . de medio nationum . . . & horribiles viſiones . . . oculis tuis: 35 vt ſcires 36 vt doceret te 37 Eduxitque te præcedens in virtute ſua magna ex Ægypto 38. in introitu tuo: & introduceret te

L. 34 Oder ob Got verſucht habe . . . durch groſſe geſichte 36 dz er dich zuchtiget 37 ausgefurt mit ſeym angeſicht durch groſſe krafft aus Egypten

and vppon the erth beneth there is no moo: moo, *besides, else*
40 kepe therfore his ordynaunces, and his
commaundmentes which I commaunde the this daye,
that it maye goo well with the and with thi childern
after the and that thou mayst prolonge thy dayes vppon
the erth which the Lorde thi God geueth the for euer.
41 Then Moses seuered .iii. cities on the other syde
42 Iordane towarde the sonne rysynge, that he shulde fle
thiter which had kylled his neyghboure vnwares and
hated him not in tyme past and therfore shulde fle vnto
43 one of the same cities and lyue: Bezer in the wildernesse euen in the playne contre amonge the Rubenites:
and Ramoth in Gilead amonge the Gaddites and Solan
in Basan amonge the Manassites.
44 [Fo. XI.] This is the lawe which Moses set before
45 the childern of Israel, and these are the witnesse, ordinaunces and statutes which Moses tolde the childern
46 of Israel after they came out of Egipte, on the other
syde Iordayne in the valey besyde Beth Peor in the
londe of Sihō kinge of the Amorites which dwelt at
Hesbon, whom Moses and the childern of Israel smote
47 after they were come out of Egipte, ād conquered his
lande and the lande of Og kinge of Basan .ii. kynges
of the Amorites on the other syde Iordayne towarde
48 the sonne rysynge: from Aroar vppon the bancke of
the ryuer Arnon, vnto mount Sion which is called
49 Hermon ād all the feldes on the other syde Iordayne
eastwarde: euen vnto the see in the felde vnder the
springes of Pisga.

M. 40 geueth the thy lyfe longe 43 Galaad 45 witnesses 46 Sehon 49 Phasgah

V. 40 Custodi . . : vt bene sit tibi . . quam dom. deus tuus daturus est tibi. 42 nec sibi fuerit inimicus ante vnum & alterum diem, & ad harum aliq. vrbium possit euadere 44 proposuit 46 trans (vv. 47, 49) Iordanem in valle contra phanum Phogor . . . quem percussit Moyses. Filii quoque Israel egressi ex Ægypto 48 qui est & Hermon 49 & vsque ad radices montis Phasga.

L. 40 das du haltest . . . so wirt dyrs . . . wolgehn . . . gibt deyn leben lang. 42 nicht feynd gewesen ist, der sol ynn der stedte eyne fliehen 45 fur legt 46 iensid (vv. 47, 49) dem Iordan ym tal gegen dem haus Peor . . den Mose vnd die kinder Israel schlugen, da sie aus Egypten zogen waren 49 vnden am berge Pisga.

The .V. Chapter.

1, AND Moſes called vnto all Iſraell
and ſayed vnto them: Heare
Iſrael the ordynaunces and
lawes which I ſpeke in thyne
eares this daye, and lerne them and take
2 hede that ye doo them. The Lorde oure God made
an appoyntment with us in Horeb.
3 The Lorde made not this bonde with oure fathers,
but with us: we are they, which are .P. al heare a lyue
4 this daye. The Lord talked with you face to face in
5 the moūt out of the fyre. And I ſtode betwene the
Lorde and you the ſame tyme, to ſhewe you the
ſayenge of the Lorde. For ye were afrayed of
the fyre and therfore went not vpp in to the mount
and he ſayed.
6 I am the Lorde thy God which brought the out of
7 the lōde of Egipte the houſſe of bōdage. Thou ſhalt
haue therefore none other goddes in my preſence.
8 Thou ſhalt make the no grauen Image
off any maner lykeneſſe that is in heauen aboue, or
in the erth beneth, or in the water beneth the erth.
9 Thou ſhalt nether bowe thy ſelf vnto them nor ſerue
them, for I the Lorde thy God, am a gelouſe God,
viſettinge the wikedneſſe of the fathers vppon the childern, euen in the thyrde and the fourth generacion,
10 amonge them that hate me: and ſhew mercye apon
thouſandes amonge them that loue me and kepe my
commaundmentes.

M.C.S. *The .x commaundementes of the lawe. No Image maye be made.*

Image

M. 8 in erth benethe
V. 1 Vocauitque . . . diſcite ea, & opere complete. 4 locutus eſt nobis 5 Ego ſequeſter & medius fui . . . vt annuntiarem 7 in conſpectu meo. 8 in aquis 9 deus æmulator . . generationem
L. 1 rieff 4 mit vns 5 anſagete 7 fur myr 8 keyn bildnis . . . ym waſſer 9 eyn eyfferiger Gott . . . gelied
M. M. N. 4 *Face to face* the Chaldees woorde to worde, that is to ſaye, with ſo manyfeſt woordes and ſygnes that it cannot be denyed but that it was god. 8 *Images.*

11 Thou ſhalt not take the name of the Lorde thy God
in vayne: for the Lorde will not holde him giltleſſe,
that taketh his name in vayne.
12 Kepe the Sabbath daye that thou ſancti- [Fo. XII.]
fie it, as the Lorde thy God hath commaunded the.
13 Syxe dayes thou ſhalt laboure and doo all that thou
14 haſt to doo, but the ſeuenth daye is the Sabbath of the
Lorde thy God: thou ſhalt doo no maner worke, nether
thou nor thy ſonne nor thy doughter nor thy ſeruaunte
nor thy mayde nor thine oxe nor thyne aſſe nor any
of thi catell nor the ſtraunger that is within thy cytye,
that thy ſeruaunte and thy mayde maye reſt as well
15 as thou. * And remembre that thou waſt
a ſeruaunte in the londe of Egypte and
how that the Lorde God, brought the
out thence with a myghtye hande and a
ſtretched out arme. For which cauſe the
Lorde thy God commaundeth the to kepe the Sabbath
daye.

God ſheweth a cauſe why we oughte to kepe his commaundmentes the pope doth not.

16 Honoure thi father and thi mother, as the Lord
thi God hath cōmaūded the: that thou mayſt prolonge
thi dayes, and that it maye go well with the on the
londe, which the Lorde thi God geueth the.
17 Thou ſhalt not ſlee.
18 Thou ſhalt not breake wedlocke.
19 Thou ſhalt not ſteale.
20 Thou ſhalt not beare falſe witneſſe agenſt thy
neghboure,
21 Thou ſhalt not luſte after thi neghbours .P. wife:
thou ſhalt not couet thi neyghbours houſſe, felde, ſeruaunte, mayde, oxe, aſſe nor ought that is thi neghbours.
22 Theſe wordes the Lorde ſpake vnto al youre multitude in the mount out of the fyre, cloude and darckneſſe, with a loude voyce and added nomoare there

V. 11 Non vſurpabis nomen . . . fruſtra . . qui ſuper re vana nomen eius aſſumpſerit. 14 Septimus dies ſabbathi eſt, id eſt requies 18 mœchaberis. 22 multitudinem veſtrā in monte de medio ignis

L. 11 Du ſolt den namen . . . nicht vergeblich furen, denn der HERR wirt den nicht vnſchuldig halten, der ſeynen namen vergeblich furet. 18 ehebrechen. 22 gemeyne auff dem berge . . .

to, and wrote them in .ii. tables of ſtone and delyuered
them vnto me.
23 But as ſoone as ye herde the voyce out off the
darckneſſe and ſawe the hill burne with fyre, ye came
vnto me all the heedes of youre tribes and youre
24 elders: and ye ſayed: beholde, the Lorde oure God
hath ſhewed us his glorye and his greatneſſe, and we
haue herde his voyce out of the fyre, and we haue ſene
this daye that God maye talke with a man and he
25 yet lyue. And now wherfore ſhulde we dye that this
greate fyre ſhulde conſume us: Yf we ſhulde heare the
voyce of the Lorde oure God any moare, we ſhulde
26 dye. For what is any fleſh that he ſhulde heare the
voyce of the lyuynge God ſpeakynge out of the fyre as
27 we haue done and ſhulde yet lyue: Goo thou ād heare
all that the Lorde oure God ſayeth, and tell thou vnto
us all that the Lorde oure God ſayeth vnto the, and
we will heare it and doo it.
28 [Fo. XIII.] And the Lorde herde the voyce of
youre wordes when ye ſpake vnto me, and he ſayed
vnto me: I haue herde the voyce of the wordes of this
people which they haue ſpokē vnto the they haue well
ſayed all that they haue ſayed.
29 Oh that they had ſoche an herte with them to feare
me ād kepe all my commaundmentes alwaye, that it
myghte goo well with them and with their childern
30 for euer. Goo ād ſaye vnto them: gett you in to
31 youre tentes agayne, but ſtonde thou here before
me and I will tell the all the commaundmentes, ordinaunces ād lawes which thou ſhalt teache thē, that
they may doo them in the londe whiche I geue them
to poſſeſſe.
32 Take hede therfore that ye do as the
Lorde youre God hath commaunded you,

walke ſtrayght

V. 22 in duabus tabulis 23 de medio 24 maieſtatem & magnitudinem ſuam . . . , & probauimus hodie 26 Quid eſt omnis caro 27 Tu magis accede 29 Quis det talem eos habere mentem 30 Reuertimini 31 hic ſta mecum . . in poſſeſſionem.

L. 22 auff zwo ſteynern taffeln 24 herlickeyt vnd ſeyne groſſe 26 Denn was iſt alles fleyſch 30 Gehet heym 31 hie fur myr

M. M. N. 32 Walke ſtraight.

and turne not asyde: ether to the righte hande or to
33 the lefte: but walke in all the wayes which the Lorde
youre God hath cōmaunded you, that ye maye lyve
and that it maye goo well with you ād that ye maye
prolonge youre dayes in the lond which ye shall possesse.

☙ The .VI. Chapter

1 THESE are the commaundmentes,
ordinaunces and lawes which the
Lorde youre God commaund-
ed to teach you, that ye might
doo them in the londe whother ye goo to
2 pos- .P. sesse it: that thou mightest feare
the Lorde thy God, to kepe all his ordinaunces and his commaundmentes which
I commaunde the, both thou and thy
sonne and thy sonnes sonne all dayes off
3 thy lyfe, that thy dayes maye be prolonged. Heare
therfore Israel and take hede that thou doo thereafter,
that it maye goo well with the and that ye maye encrease myghtely: euē as the Lord God of thy fathers hath
promysed the, a lōde that floweth with mylk ād hony
4, 5 Heare Israel, the Lorde thy God is Lorde only and
thou shalt loue the Lorde thy God with all thyne harte,
with all thy soule and with all thy myght.
6 And these wordes which I commaunde
7 the this daye, shalbe in thine herte ād
thou shalt whett them on
thy childern, and shalt talke of them when
thou art at home in thyne housse and as

M.C.S. The lawe must be ernestly prynted in their hartes and to kepe it in memorye they must wryte it on the dores and poostes of their houses, And teache it vnto their chylderne.

It is heresy with vs for a laye mā to loke of gods worde or to reade it.

whett on, *to sharpen, discipline, stimulate*

V. 33 sed per viam quam . . . ambulabitis . . . & protelentur dies vestri in terra possessionis vestræ. vi, 1 vt docerem vos 2 tibi & filiis ac nepotibus tuis . . . vt prolongentur dies tui. 3 sicut pollicitus est . . . terram lacte & melle manantem. 5 fortitudine tua. 7 & narrabis ea . . & meditaberis sedens . . .

L. 33 sondern wandelt ynn allen wegen. vi, 2 du vnd deyne kinder vnd deyns kinds kinder 3 dyr geredt hat 7 scherffen

M. M. N. 2 To feare God is to honoure him in putting thy confydence in him, and in hauyng a good and rightwes conuersacion in hys syght. 7 *Whett them on thy children* that is, exercyse thy chyldren in them & put thē in vre with them.

thou walkeſt by the waye, and when thou lyeſt doune and
8 when thou ryſeſt vpp: and thou ſhalt bynde them ſor a
ſygne vppon thyne hande. And they ſhalbe papers
9 off remembraunce betwene thyne eyes, and ſhalt write
them vppon the poſtes of thy houſſe ād vppon thy
gates.

10 And when the Lorde thy God hath brought the in
to the lond which he ſware vnto thy fathers Abraham,
Iſaac and Iacob, to geue the with greate and goodly
11 cities which thou byl- [Fo. XIIII.] deſt not, and houſſes
full of all maner goodes which thou filledeſt not, and
welles dygged which thou dyggedeſt not, ād vynes
and olyue trees which thou plantedeſt not, ād whē
12 thou haſt eaten, and art full: Then beware leſt thou
forget the Lorde which broughte the out off the lande
of Egipte the houſſe of bondage.

13 But feare the Lorde thy God and ſerue hym, and
14 ſwere by his name, and ſe that ye walke not after
ſtraunge goddes of the Goddes off the nacyons whiche
15 are aboute you. For the Lorde thy God is a gelouſe
God among you leſt the wrath of the Lorde thy God
waxe hotte vppon the and deſtroye the from the erth.

16 Ye ſhall not tempte the Lorde youre God as ye
17 dyd at Maſa. But ſe that ye kepe the commaundmentes of the Lorde youre God, his witneſſes and his
18 ordinaunces which he hath commaunded the, and ſe
thou doo that which is right and good in
the ſyghte of the Lorde: that thou mayſt
proſpere and that thou mayſt goo ād cōquere that good lāde which the Lorde ſware vnto thy
19 fathers, and that the Lorde maye caſt out all thine
enemies before the as he hath ſayed.

Right in goddes ſight is that he commaundeth

V. 8 & mouebuntur inter oculos tuos 11 quas non extruxiſti 13 & illi ſoli 15 de ſuperficie terræ. 16 Non tentabis . . in loco tentationis. 18 in conſpectu domini

L. 8 eyn denckmal fur deynen augen 11 ausgehawen brunne 15 von der erden 17 ſondern 18 fur den augen des HERRN

M. M. N. 13 *Swere by his name:* Loke beneth in the .x. chapter d. 15 *Gelouſe* loke Exod. xx, a and the chapter next afore this. 16 *Maſa:* or Maſah. 18 Right ī goddes ſyght is that which he commaundeth.

20 When thy ſonne axeth the in tyme to
come ſayenge: What meaneth the witneſſ-
es, ordina-.P. unces and lawes which the Lorde oure God
21 hath commaunded you? Then thou ſhalt ſaye vnto thy
ſonne: We were bondmen vnto Pharao in Egipte, but
the Lorde brought vs out of Egipte with a mightie hande.
22 And the Lorde ſhewed ſignes and won-
dres both greate ād evell vppon Egipte,
Pharao and vppon all his houſholde, before
23 oure eyes and broughte vs from thence: to
brynge vs in ād to geue vs the londe
24 which he ſware vnto oure fathers. And
therfore cōmaunded vs to do all theſe
ordinaunces ād for to feare the Lord
oure God, for oure welth
alwayes and that he might
ſaue vs, as it is come to paſſe
25 this daye. Moreouer it ſhalbe rightuouſnes vnto vs before the Lorde oure God,
yf we take hede to kepe all theſe cōmaundmētes as he hath commaunded vs,

Teach youre childern.

The outwarde deade is rightuouſneſſe vnto the avoidinge of puniſhmēt, threteninges ād curſes ād to opteine temporall bleſſīges: but vnto the life to come thou muſt haue the rightuouſneſſe of faith ād there by receaue forgeueneſſe of ſinnes ād promiſe of enheritaunce ād power to worke of loue.

welth, *proſperity, happineſs*

V. 20 cras 22 fecitque ſigna . . . contra Pharaonem . . in conſpectu noſtro 24 omnia legitima hæc . . vt bene ſit nobis cunctis diebus vitæ noſtræ 25 Eritque noſtri miſericors

L. 20 heut odder morgen 22 Vnd der HERR thet groſſe vnd boſe zeychen vnd wunder . . . fur vnſern augen 24 allen diſen ſitten . . . auff das vns wol gehe all vnſer lebtage 25 vnd es wirt vns zur gerechtickeyt gedeyen fur dem HERRN

M. M. N. 20 Teach youre chyldren. 25 *Righteouſnes vnto vs*, etc: The outwarde deade is righteouſneſſe vnto the auoydinge of punniſhemēt, threteninges & curſes & to optayne tēporall bleſſynges: but vnto the life to come thou muſt haue the ryghteouſneſſe of faith & thereby receaue forgeueneſſe of ſinnes & promiſe of enheritaunce & power to worke of loue.

ℭ The .VII. Chapter.

1 WHĒ the Lorde thy God hath
brought the in to the lond whither thou goeſt to poſſeſſe it, and
hath caſt out manye nacions
before the: the Hethites, the Girgoſites,
the Amorites, the Cananites, the Phere-
ſites, the Heuites and the Iebuſites: vii
nacions moo in numbre ād mightier than
2 thou: ād whē the Lorde thy God hath ſett
them before the that thou ſhuldeſt ſmyte
them ſe that thou vtterly deſtroye them
and make no couenaunt [Fo. XV.] with
3 them nor haue compaſſion on them. Alſo
thou ſhalt make no mariages with them,
nether geue thy doughter vnto his ſonne nor take his
4 doughter vnto thy ſonne. For they will make youre
ſonnes departe fro me and ſerue ſtraunge Goddes, and
then will the wrath off the Lorde waxe whote vppon
you ād deſtroye you ſhortely.
5 But thus ye ſhall deale with them: ouerthrowe their
alters, breake doune their pilers, cut doune their groves
6 ād burne their ymages with fyre. For thou art an holy
nacion vnto the Lorde thy God the Lorde thy God
hath choſen the to be a ſeuerall people vnto
him ſilf of all nacions that are vppon the erth.
7 It was not becauſe of the multitude of
you aboue all nacions, that the Lorde
had luſt vnto you and choſe you. For ye

𝔐.𝔆.𝔖. *The Iſraelites may make no couenaūt or appoyntment with the Gentyles. They muſt deſtroye their Idolles. Them that keape the cōmaundementes doth God loue and bleſſe, and the contrary hateth & puneſheth. Idolaters muſt be ſlayne.*

ſeuerall, *ſeparate*

Gods awne goodneſſe ād his awne trueth cauſeth hī to worke.

𝔐. 1 Gergeſites 2 not haue compaſſyon
𝔙. 1 et deleuerit 2 tradideritque eas 4 quia ſeducet filium tuum 5 ſubuertite, & confringite ſtatuas 6 populus peculiaris 7 vobis iunctus eſt dominus
𝔏. 1 vnd aus wortzelt 2 Vnd wenn ſie . . . fur dyr gibt . . . noch yhn gonſt erzeygeſt 5 yhr ſeulen zu brechen 7 Nicht hat euch der HERR vmbfangen vnd euch erwelet [*corrected* into: nicht hat der HERR luſt zu euch gehabt]
𝔐. 𝔐. 𝔑. 7 Gods awne goodneſſe & his awne trueth cauſeth him to worke.

8 were fewest of all nacions: But because the Lorde loued
you and because he wolde kepe the othe which he had
sworne vnto youre fathers, therfore he brought you out
of Egipte with a mightie hande ād delyuered you out of
the housse of bondage: euē frō the hande of Pharao kinge
of Egipte.
9 Vnderstonde therfore, that the Lorde thy God he
is God and that a true God, which kepeth poyntment
and mercy vnto them that loue him and kepe his commaundmentes, euen .P. thorowe out a thousande gen-
10 eracions and rewardeth them that hate him before his face so that he bringeth them to
noughte, and wil not defferre the tyme
vnto him that hateth hī but will rewarde
11 him before his face. Kepe therfore the commaundmentes, ordinaunces and lawes which I commaunde
you this daye, that ye doo them.

Before his face in his presēce, while he loketh on.

12 Yf ye shall herken vnto these lawes ād shall obserue
and do them, then shall the Lorde thy God kepe
poyntment with the and the mercy which he swore
13 vnto thy fathers and will loue the, blesse the and multiplye the: he will blesse the frute of thy wombe and
the frute of thi felde, thy corne, thy wyne and thy
oyle, the frute of thyne oxen and the flockes of thy
shepe in the londe which he swore vnto thy fathers to
14 geue the. Thou shalt be blessed aboue all nacions,
there shalbe nether man nor woman vnfrutefull amonge
you, nor any thinge vnfrutefull amonge youre catell.
15 Moreouer the Lorde will turne from the all maner
infirmityes, and will put none off the euell dyseases off
Egipte (whiche thou knowest) apon the, but wyll sende
them vppon them that hate the.

M. 13 thyne oyle

V. 8 Eduxitque vos in manu forti 9 quia dominus deus tuus, ipse est deus fortis & fidelis 10 statim . . . & vltra non differat, protinus eis restituens quod merentur. 12 Si postquam audieris 13 oleo, & armentis, gregibus ouium 14 inter omnes populos . . . vtriusque sexus, tam in hominibus quam in gregibus tuis. 15 sed cunctis hostibus tuis.

L. 8 hat er euch ausgefuret mit mechtiger hand 10 fur seynem angesicht 14 vber allen volckern 15 allen deynen hessern

M. M. N. 10 *Before his face:* Before his face in his presence, whyle he loketh on.

16 Thou ſhalt bringe to nought all nacions which the
Lorde thy God delyuereth the, thy- [Fo. XVI.] ne
eye ſhall haue no pitie vppon them nether ſhalt thou
17 ſerue their goddes, for that ſhalbe thy decaye. Yf thou
ſhalt ſaye in thine hert theſe nacions are moo than I,
18 how cā I caſt them out? Feare thē not,
but remēbre what the Lorde thy god dyd
19 vnto Pharao ād vnto all Egipte, ād the
greate temptacions which thine eyes ſawe,
ād the ſignes ād wonders ād mightie hāde ād ſtretched
out arme wherewith the Lord thy god broughte the
out: euē ſo ſhall the Lorde thy God doo vnto all
the nacions of which thou art afrayed.

God is as able now alſo to deliuer vs out of the captiuite of the pope

20 Thereto, the Lorde thy God will ſend hornettes
amonge them vntyll they that are lefte, and hyde them
21 ſelues frō the, be deſtroyed. Se thou feare thē not
for the lord thi god is amōg you a mightie god ād a
22 terrible. The Lord thy god will put out theſe naciōs
before the a litle ād a litle: thou maiſt not cōſume thē
at ōce leſt the beeſtes of the felde encreaſe vpō the.
23 And the lorde thy god ſhall delyuer thē vnto the ād
ſterre vp a mightie tēpeſt amōge thē, vntil thei be
24 brought to nought. And he ſhal deliuer their kinges
in to thine hāde, ād thou ſhalt deſtroye their names
frō vnder heauē. There ſhal no mā ſtonde before the,
25 vntill thou haue deſtroyed them. The images of their
goddes thou ſhalt burne with fire, ād ſe that thou couet
not .P. the ſyluer or golde that is on them nor take it

V. 16 Deuorabis omnes populos 17 delere eas ? 18 noli metuere ſed 19 plagas maximas . . . ſic faciet cunctis 20 qui te fugerint, & latere non potuerint. 22 ipſe conſumet . . . paulatim atque per partes . . . pariter 23 et interficiet illos 25 Sculptilia eorum . . . de quibus facta ſunt

L. 16 Du wirſt alle volcker freſſen . . . denn das wurde dyr eyn ſtrick ſeyn. 19 durch groſſe verſuchung 20 vnd ſich verbirget fur dyr 22 Er der Herr deyn Gott wirt diſe leut aus wurtzelen fur dyr, eyns nach dem andern . . . nicht eylend alle machen 23 wirt ſie mit groſſer ſchlacht erſchlahen 25 Die bild yhrer Gotter . . . das dran iſt

M. M. N. 20 What hornettes are loke Exod. xxiii, d. 25 *Syluer or golde:* Whatſoeuer golde or ſyluer honoure or profet, calleth frō the woorde of God, belōgeth to the Images of their goddes & muſt be therfore abhorred: yee yf they be good worckes whē thou thynkeſt that thou doeſt thē of thyne awne ſtrenght & not helped of God.

vnto the, left thou be ſnared therewith. For it is an
26 abhominacyon vnto the Lorde thy God. Brynge not
therfore the abhominacyon to thyne houſſe, leſt thou
be a damned thynge as it is: but vtterlye defye it and
abhorre it, for it is a thinge that muſt be deſtroyed.

The .VIII. Chaptre.

1 ALL the commaundmentes which
I commaunde the this daye ye
ſhal kepe for to do them, that
ye maye lyue and multiplye
and goo and poſſeſſe the londe whiche the
2 Lorde ſware vnto youre fathers. And
thinke on all the waye which the Lorde
thy God led the this .xl. yere in the wilderneſſe, for to humble the ād to proue

M.C.S. *Moſes putteth the Iſraelites in remembraunce of the afflicyons and benifytes that they hadde the xl. yere which they were in the wilderneſſe.*

the, to wete what was in thine herte, whether thou
3 woldeſt kepe his commaundmentes or no, He humbled the and made the hongre and fed the with
man which nether thou nor thy father knewe of. to
make the know that a man muſt not lyue by bred
only: but by al that procedeth out of
the mouth of the Lorde muſt a man lyue.

The word is life

4 Thy rayment waxed not olde vppon the, nether dyd
thy fete ſwell thys .xl. yere.

V. 26 quippiam ex idolo . . . ne fias anathema . . . Quaſi ſpurcitiam deteſtaberis, & velut inquinamentum ac ſordes abominationi habebis viii, 2 Et recordaberis . . vt affligeret te atque tentaret 3 Afflixit te penuria . . vt oſtenderet tibi . . . in ſolo pane . . . in omni verbo 4 Veſtimentum tuum quo operiebaris, nequaquam vetuſtate defecit

L. 25 nicht drynnen verſehiſt 26 ſondern du ſolt eyn ekel vnd grewel daran haben. viii, 2 vnd gedenckſt . . demutiget vnd verſucht 3 am brot alleyn, ſondern an allem 4 veraltet an dyr . . geſchwollen

M. M. N. 26 *Damned*, Or curſed. viii, 3 *Humbled the:* Humbled loke after .xxi, c.—The word is lyfe. 4 *Thy rayment*, etc.: Here mayſt thou ſe that they ſhall want nothyng that beleue the woorde & lyue after it, but that God careth for them in all thynges yf they cōmytt them ſelues wholy to his prouiſyon. i. Pet. v, d.

5 Vnderſtonde therfore in thine herte, that as a man
nurtereth his ſonne, euen ſo the Lorde thy God nurter-
6 eth the. Kepe therfore the com- [Fo. XVII.] maundmentes of the Lorde thy God that thou walke in
7 his wayes and that thou feare him For the Lorde
thy God bringeth the in to a good lande, a
londe of riuers of water, of foūtens and of ſpringes
8 that ſpringe out both in valayes and hylles: a
londe of whete and of barly, of vynes, figtrees and
pomgranates, a lond of olyuetrees with oyle and of
9 honye: a lande wherin thou ſhalt not eate bred in
ſcarceneſſe, and where thou ſhalt lacke nothinge, a
londe whoſe ſtones are yerne, and out of whoſe hylles
10 thou ſhalt dygge braſſe. When thou haſt eaten therfore and filled thy ſelfe, then bleſſe the Lord for the
good lond which he hath geuen the.
11 But bewarre that thou forgett not the Lorde thy
God, that thou woldeſt not kepe his cōmaundmentes,
lawes and ordinaunces which I commaunde the this
12 daye: yee and when thou haſt eatē ād filled thy ſelfe
13 ād haſt bylt goodly houſſes ād dwelt therin, ād when
thy beeſſe ād thy ſhepe are waxed manye ād thy ſyluer
ād thy golde is multiplied ād all that thou haſt en-
14 creaſed, then bewarre leſt thine herte ryſe ād thou forgett the Lorde thy God which brought the out of the
15 londe of Egipte the houſſe of bondage, ād which led
the in the wilderneſſe both greate ād terreble with firye
ſerpentes ād ſcor- .P. piōs ād thurſte where was no
water which brought the water out of the rocke of
16 flynt: whiche fed the in the wilderneſſe with Man where
of thy fathers knewe not, for to humble the and to

M. 15 and drouth

V. 5 Vt recogites 6 vt cuſtodias 7 terram riuorum, aquarumque, & fontium: in cuius campis & montibus erumpunt fluuiorum abyſſi 9 abſque vlla penuria . . . & rerum omnium abundantia perfrueris . . . æris metalla 10 vt cū comederis 13 armenta boum, & ouium greges 14 eleuetur cor tuū 15 ſerpens flatu adurens 16 Et poſtquam . . .

L. 7 beche. brunnen. tieffen . . . die an den bergen vnd ynn den awen flieſſen 8 ölebewm vnd honnig ynnen wechſt. 9 ertz aus den bergen 11 So hütt dich nu 14 deyn hertz ſich nicht erhebe 15 feuer ſpeyeten

proue the, that he might doo the good at thy later
ende.
17 And beware that thou ſaye not in thine herte, my
power and the might of myne awne hãde hath done
18 me all theſe actes: But remembre the Lorde thy God,
how that it is he which gaue the power
to do mãfully, for to make good the promeſſe which he ſware vnto thy fathers, as it is come to
paſſe this daye,

Gods power worketh and not we

19 For yf thou ſhalt forget the Lorde thy god and ſhalt
walke after ſtraunge goddes and ſerue them and wor-
ſheppe them, I teſtyfye vnto you this daye, that ye
20 ſhall ſurely peryſh. As the nacyons whiche the Lorde
deſtroyeth before the, euen ſo ye ſhall peryſhe, becauſe
ye wolde not herken vnto the voyce of the Lord youre
God.

¶ The .IX. Chapter.

1 HEARE Iſrael, thou goeſt ouer
Iordayne this daye, to goo
and conquere nacions greater
and mightier than thy ſelfe:
and cities greate ãd walled vp to heauen,
2 ãd people greate and tall, euen the childern of the Enakims, which thou knoweſt
and of whom thou haſt [Fo. XVIII.] herde
ſaye who is able to ſtond before the chil-
3 dern of Enack? But vnderſtonde this

M.C.S. *They are forbiddẽ to truſt in their awne ſtreãgth. A reherſall of certen thynges that were done after the lawe was geuen, vnto the murmuring at the Graues of Luſt.*

V. 16 ad extremũ miſertus eſt tui 18 vt impleret pactum ſuum . . . ſicut præſens indicat dies. 19 omnino diſpereas. 20 quas deleuit dominus in introitu tuo ix, 1 & ad cælũ vſque muratas 2 quibus nullus poteſt ex aduerſo reſiſtere.

L. 16 das er dyr hernach wol thett 7 diſs vermugen 18 auffricht ſeynen bund . . . wie es gehet heuts tags. ix, 1 vermauret bis yn den hymel 2 Wer kan widder die kinder Enak beſtehen?

M. M. N. 17 *And beware*, etc.: By the helpe of God onely doeſt thou what ſoeuer good is, & not by thyne awne helpe, no not by the helpe of any of the ſaynctes were he neuer ſo holy. ix, 1 *Walled vp to heauẽ* is a fyguratyue ſpeache, ſygnyfyẽg that the walles were hye and not eaſye to be wõne.

daye that the Lorde thy God which goeth ouer before
the a conſumyng fire, he ſhall deſtroye them and he
ſhall ſubdue them before the. And thou ſhalt caſt
them out, and brynge them to noughte quyckely as
the Lorde hath ſayed vnto the.
4 Speake not in thyne hert, after that the Lorde thy
God hath caſt them out before the ſayenge: for my
rightuouſnes the Lorde hath brought me *where is mās*
in to poſſeſſe this lōde. Nay, but for *rightewesneſſe.*
the wekedneſſe of theſe nacions the Lord doth caſt
5 thē out before the. It is not for thi rightuouſnes ſake
ād right hert that thou goeſt to poſſeſſe their lōd: But
partely for the wekedneſſe of theſe naciōs, the Lord
thy god doth caſt thē out before the, and partly to
performe that which the Lorde thy God ſware vnto
thi fathers, Abraham, Iſaac and Iacob.
6 Vnderſtond therſore that it is not for thy rightuouſnes ſake, that the Lorde thy God doth geue the this
good lond to poſſeſſe it, for thou art a ſtiffenecked
7 people. Remēbre ād forget not how thou prouokedeſt
the Lorde thi god in the wilderneſſe: for ſens the daye
that thou cameſt out of the lond of Egipte vntyll ye
came vnto this place, ye haue rebelled agenſt the
8 .P. Lorde. Alſo in Horeb ye angred the Lorde ſo
that the Lorde was wroth with you, euē to haue de-
9 ſtroyed you, after that I was gone vpp in to the mount,
to fett the tables of ſtone, the tables of appoyntment
which the Lorde made with you. And I abode in the
hyll .xl. dayes ād .xl. nightes and nether ate bred nor
10 dranke water. And the Lorde delyuered me two tables
of ſtone writen with the finger of God, and in them
was acordynge to all the wordes which the Lorde

M. 3 caſt thē out, and brynge them out, and brynge them to noughte 4 in to poſſeſſe.

V. 3 ignis deuorans atque cōſumens, qui conterat eos & deleat atque diſperdat ante faciē tuā velociter 6 cum duriſſimæ ceruicis ſis populus. 7 ad iracundiam prouocaueris . . . ſemper aduerſum dominum contendiſti. 8 prouocaſti eum

L. 3 er wirt ſie vertilgen . . . vnd vmbringen bald 6 ſyntemal du ein halſtarrig volck biſt 7 erzorntiſt ynn der wuſten 8 ynn Horeb ertzurntet

M. M. N. 4 Where is mans rightweſnes?

ſayed vnto you in the mount out of the fire in the daye
whē the people were gathered together.
11 And whē the .xl. dayes and .xl. nyghtes were ended,
the Lorde gaue me: the two tables off ſtone, the tables
12 of the teſtament, and ſayed vnto me: Vpp, and get the
doune quyckely from hence, for thy people which thou
haſt broughte out of Egipte, haue marred
them ſelues.

marred, *hurt, injured, damaged*

They are turned attonce out of the waye, whiche I
commaunded them, and haue made thē a god of metall.
13 Furthermore the Lorde ſpake vnto me ſayenge: I ſe
14 this people how that it is a ſtiffenecked people, let me
alone that I maye deſtroye them and put out the name
off them from vnder heauen, and I will make off the a
nacion both greater ād moo than they.
15 [Fo. XIX.] And I turned awaye and came doune
from the hyll (and the hyll burnt with fire) and had
16 the two tables of the appoyntment in my handes. And
when I loked and ſawe that ye had ſynned agenſt the
Lorde youre God and had made you a calfe of metall
and had turned attonce out of the waye whiche the
17 Lorde had commaunded you. Thē I toke the two
tables and caſt them out of my two handes, and brake
18 thē before youre eyes. And I fell before the Lorde:
euen as at the firſt tyme .xl. dayes ād .xl. nightes and
nether ate bred nor dranke water ouer all youre ſynnes
whiche ye had ſynned in doynge wekedly in the ſyght
19 of the Lorde ād in prouokinge him. For I was afrayed
of the wrath and fearſneſſe wherwith the Lord was
angrie with you, euē for to haue deſtroyed you But
the Lorde herde my peticion at that tyme alſo.
20 The Lorde was very angrie with Aaron alſo, euē
for to haue deſtroyed him: But I made interceſſion
21 for Aarō alſo the ſame tyme. And I toke youre
ſynne, the calfe which ye had made ād burnt him

V. 10 quando concio populi congregata eſt. 12 Ægypto, deſeruerunt velociter viam, quam demonſtraſti eis, feceruntque ſibi conflatile. 14 dimitte me 16 vitulum conflatilem 18 procidi . . . & eum ad iracundiam prouocaſtis. 20 ſimiliter

L. 12 eyn gegoſſens bild 14 las ab von myr 16 eyn gegoſſen kalb 18 fiel fur . . . yhn zu erzurnen 20 zur ſelben zeyt

with fire ād ſtampe him and grounde him a good, euē vnto ſmal duſt. And I caſt the duſt thereof in to the broke that deſcended out of the mount.

ſtampe, *verb, paſt tenſe*
a good, *thoroughly*

22 Alſo at Thabeera and at Maſa and at the .P. ſepul-
23 chres of luſt ye angred the Lorde, yee ād when the
Lorde ſent you from Cades Bernea ſayenge: goo vpp
and conquere the lond whiche I haue geuen you, ye
diſobeyed the mouth of the Lorde youre God, and
24 nether beleued hī nor herkened vnto his voyce. Thus
ye haue bene diſobediēt vnto the Lord, ſence the daye
that I knew you.

25 And I fell before the Lorde .xl. dayes
and .xl. nightes whiche I laye there, for
26 the Lorde was minded to haue deſtroyed you. But I
made interceſſion vnto the Lorde and ſayed: O Lorde
Iehoua, deſtroye not thy people and thyne enheritaūce which thou haſt delyuered thorow thi greatneſſe
and which thou haſt brought out of Egipte with a
27 mightie hand. Remēbre thy ſervauntes Abraham,
Iſaac and Iacob and loke not vnto the ſtoburneſſe
28 of this people nor vnto their wekedneſſe and ſynne: leſt
the londe whence thou broughteſt them ſaye: Becauſe
the Lorde was not able to brynge them in to the londe
which he promyſed them and becauſe he hated them,
therfore he caried them out to deſtroye them in the
29 wilderneſſe. Moreouer they are thy people and thine
enheritaunce, whiche thou broughteſt out with thy
myghtye power and wyth thy ſtretched out arme.

Lerne to praye.

M. 22 Thaberah 23 Barne

V. 22 In incendio quoque, & in tentatione, & in Sepulchris cōcupiſcentiæ 23 & contempſiſtis imperium domini 24 ſed ſemper fuiſtis rebelles a die qua noſſe vos cœpi. 25 quibus eum ſuppliciter deprecabar . . . vt fuerat comminatus 26 in magnitudine tua 28 dicāt habitatores terræ . . . quam pollicitus eſt eis

L. 22 zu Thabeera vnd zu Maſſa vnd bey den Luſtgrebern 24 denn yhr ſeyt vngehorſam dem Herrn geweſt, ſo lang ich euch kand habe. 25 die ich da lag, Denn der Herr ſprach 28 das land ſage . . . das er yhnen geredet hatte

M. M. N. 25 Lerne to praye.

[Fo. XX.] ℭ The .X. Chapte .

M.C.S. A repeticyon of ſome of the Iourneys of the Iſraelites. The renuyng of the tables. An exhortacyon to geue heede to the Lawe.

1 IN the ſame ceaſon the Lord ſayed
vnto me hewe the two tables
of ſtone like vnto the firſt and
come vp vnto me in to the
2 mount ād make the an Arke of wod, and
I will wryte in the table, the wordes that
were in the firſt tables which thou brakeſt,
3 ād thou ſhalt put thē in the arcke. And I made an
arke of ſethī wod ād hewed two tables of ſtone like
vnto the firſt, ād went vp in to the mountayne and the
ii. tables in myne hande.
4 And he wrote in the tables, acording to the firſt
writinge (the .x. verſes whiche the Lorde ſpake vnto
you in the mount out of the fire in the daye when the
5 people were gathered) ād gaue thē vnto me. And I
departed ād came doune frō the hyll and put the tables
in the arcke which I had made: ād there they remayned, as the Lorde commaunded me
6 And the childern of Iſrael toke their iurney from
Beroth Bē Iakē to Moſera, where Aarō dyed ād where
he was buried, ād Eleazer his ſonne became preaſt ī
7 his ſteade. And frō thēce they departed vnto Gudgod:
ād frō Gudgod to Iathbath, a lōd of riuers of water.
8 And the ſame ceaſon the Lorde ſeparated the trybe
of Leui to beare the arcke of the appoyntment .P. of
the Lorde and to ſtonde before the Lorde, ād to min-

M. 2 in the tables 4 mount of the fire . . . people gethered together 6 Beroth of the childrē of Iakan 7 Gadgad (*bis*)

V. 2 in his quas ante cōfregiſti 3 habens eas in manibus. 4 quādo populus cōgregatus eſt 5 quæ hucuſque ibi ſunt 6 Beroth filiorū Iacan 7 in terra aquarū atque torrentiū. 8 arcam fœderis domini . . . ac benediceret in nomine illius

L. 2 die auff den erſten waren, die du zu brochen haſt 4 zur zeyt der verſamlung 5 das die daſelbs weren 7 eyn land da beche ſind. 8 die lade des bunds des Herrn . . . vnd ſeynen namen zu loben

M. M. N. 7 *Gadgad:* Or Gadgadah: Iathbath: or Iatebath.

iſtre vnto him and to bleſſe in his name vnto this
9 daye. Wherſore the Leuites haue no parte nor enheritaunce with their brethern. The Lorde he is their
enheritaunce, as the Lorde thy God hath promyſed
them.
10 And I taried in the mount, euē as at the firſt tyme
xl. dayes and .xl. nyghtes and the Lorde herkened
vnto me at that tyme alſo, ſo that the Lorde wolde
11 not deſtroye the. And the Lorde ſayed vnto me: vpp
ād goo forth in the iurney before the people and let
them goo in ād conquere the lond which I ſware vnto
their fathers to geue vnto them.
12 And now Iſrael what is it that the Lord thi God
requyreth of the, but to feare the Lord thi God and to
walke in all his wayes and to loue him and to ſerue the
Lorde thy God with all thyne herte and with all thy
13 ſoule, that thou kepe the commaundmentes of the
Lorde ād his ordinaunces which I commaunde the this
14 daye, for thy welth. Beholde, heauen
and the heauen of heauens is the Lordes
thy god, and the erth with all that there-
15 in is: only the Lorde had a luſt vnto thy fathers to
loue them, and therfore choſe you theire ſeed after
them off all nacyons, as it is come to paſſe this
daye.

welth, *happineſs, welfare*, cf. *weal*

16 [Fo. XXI.] Circumcyſe therfore the foreſkynne of
17 youre hartes, and be no longer ſtiffnecked. For the
Lorde youre God, he is God of goddes and lorde of
lordes, a greate God, a myghtye and a terreble which
18 regardeth no mans perſon nor taketh giftes: but doeth
right vnto the fatherleſſe and wedowe and loueth the
19 ſtraunger, to geue him fode and rayment. Loue therefore the ſtraunger, for ye were ſtraungers youre ſelues
in the londe of Egipte.

V. 9 non habuit Leui . . . ſicut promiſit ei 11 poſſideat terram 15 & tamen patribus tuis cōglutinatus eſt dominus, . . . id eſt vos 17 dominus dominantium

L. 9 die Leuiten . . . yhnen geredt hat. 11 das land eynnemen 15 Noch hat er alleyn zu deynen vetern luſt gehabt 17 keyn perſon achtet

20 Thou ſhalt feare the Lorde thi God and ſerue him
21 and cleaue vnto him ād ſwere by his name, for he is
thi prayſe ād he is thi God that hath done theſe greate
and terreble thinges for the, which thine eyes haue
22 ſene. Thi fathers went doune in to Egipte with .Lxx
ſoules, ād now the Lorde thi God hath made the as
the ſtarres of heauen in multitude.

☙ The .XI. Chapter.

1 LOUE the Lorde thi God and
kepe his obſeruaunces, his
ordinaunces, his lawes and
his commaundmentes alwaye.
2 And call to mynde this daye that which
youre childern haue nether knowen nor
ſene: euen the nurture of the Lorde youre
God, his greatneſſe, his myghtye hande
3 and his ſtretched out arme: his miracles
and his actes which he dyd amonge .P.
the Egiptiās, euen vnto Pharao the kinge
4 off Egipte and vnto all his lōde: ād what
he dyd vnto the hoſt of the Egiptiās, vnto
their horſes ād charettes, how he brought
the water of the red ſee vppon thē as they chaſed you,
and how the Lorde hath brought them to nought vnto

M.C.S. *An exhortacion to regarde the Lawe, and how they ought to haue it in their hertes alwayes and before theire eyes, and to talck of hit when they ryſe, when they ſytt doune and when they walke by the waye &c.*

V. 20 & ei ſoli ſeruies: ipſi adhærebis, iurabiſque in nomine illius. xi, 1 obſerua præcepta eius 2 Cognoſcite hodie . . . diſciplinam domini 4 omnique exercitui . . et deleuerit

L. 20 yhm ſoltu dienen, yhm ſoltu anhangen, vnd bey ſeynem namen ſchweren 21 bey dyr. xi, 1 vnd ſeyne hut 2 erkennet . . . nemlich die zuchtigung 4 an der macht der Egypter . . . da ſie euch nach iagten . . vmbracht

M. M. N. 20 *Swere by his name:* To ſweare that which is true in a cauſe of fayth ether to the honoure of God or profet of thy neyghboure is leafull. And then wyll Moſes that the othe be made by the name of God: by which he meaneth, that yf we muſt neades ſweare, we refer the othe to God onely although thou ſweare by a boke or other thyng: as paull dyd by his conſcience. Roma. ix. a.

5 this daye: ād what he dyd vnto you in the wildernesse,
6 vntill ye came vnto this place: ād what he dyd vnto
Dathan and Abiram the sonnes of Eliab the sonne of
Ruben, how the erth opened hir mouth ād swalowed
thē with their housholdes and their tentes, ād all their
substāce that was in their possessiō, in the myddes of
Israel.

7 For youre eyes haue sene all the greate deades of
8 the Lorde which he dyd. Kepe therfore al the cōmaundmentes which I cōmaunde the this daye that
ye maye be stronge ād goo and conquere the londe
9 whother ye go to possesse it, ād that ye maye prolonge
youre dayes in the londe which the Lorde sware vnto
youre fathers to geue vnto them ād to their seed, a
londe that floweth with mylke and honye.

10 For the londe whother thou goest to possesse it, is
not as the londe of Egipte whence thou camest out,
where thou sowedest thi seed and wateredest it with
11 thi laboure as a garden of herbes: but the londe whither
ye goo ouer [Fo. XXII.] to possesse it, is a londe of
hilles and valeyes and drynketh water of the rayne of
12 heauē, and a londe which the Lorde thi God careth
for. The eyes of the Lord thi God are always apō it,
from the begynnynge of the yere vnto the later ende
of the yere.

13 Yf thou shalt herken therfore vnto my commaundementes which I commaunde you this daye, that ye loue
the Lorde youre God and serue him with all youre
14 hertes and with all youre soules: then he will geue
rayne vnto youre londe in due season, both the fyrst
rayne and the later, and thou shalt gather in thy corne,

V. 6 in medio Israelis. 10 vbi iacto semine in hortorum morem aquæ ducuntur irriguæ 12 semper inuisit

L. 6 yhrem gesind . . mitten vnter dem gantzen Israel. 8 gesterckt werdet 10 da du deynen samen sehist vnd trenckest es zu fussen, wie eyn kol garten, 12 nach wilchem land der Herr . . . fraget . . . ymer dar drynen 14 so wil ich . . . regen geben

M. M. N. 6 *Abiram:* Or Abirom. 10 *Waterdest,* etc: By this is meant that water was wonte to be brought ouer all Egypt oute of the ryuer Nilus by laboure because they wanted rayne. 14 *Rayne & the later:* That is after the Hebre. the rayne in october which is after heruest, & in spring tyme.

15 thy wyne and thyne oyle. And he will ſende graſſe
in thy feldes for thy catell: and thou ſhalt eate and
fyll thy ſelfe.

16 But bewarre that youre hertes diſceaue you not that
ye turne aſyde and ſerue ſtraunge goddes and worſhepe
17 them, and thē the wrath of the Lorde waxe hote vpon
you ād ſhott vp the heauen that there be no rayne and
that youre londe yeld not hir frute, and that ye pereſh
quickly from of the good lōde which the Lorde geueth
you.

18 Putt vp therfore theſe my wordes in youre hertes
and in youre ſoules, and bynde them for a ſygne vnto
youre handes, and lett .P. them be as papers of re-
19 membraunce betwene youre eyes, and teach them
youre childern: ſo that thou * talke of them
when thou ſytteſt in thyne houſſe, and
when thou walkeſt by the waye, and when
20 thou lyeſt doune and when thou ryſeſt vpp: yee and
write them vppon the dorepoſtes of thine houſſe and
21 vppon thi gates, that youre dayes may be multiplyed ād the dayes of youre childern apon the erth
which the Lorde ſware vnto youre fathers to geue
them, as longe as the dayes of heauē laſt vpon
the erth.

Talke of robynhod ſaye oure prelates

22 For yf ye ſhall kepe all theſe cōmaundmentes which
I cōmaunde you, ſo that ye doo thē and loue the Lorde
youre God and walke in all his wayes and cleaue vnto
23 him. Then will the Lorde caſt out all theſe nacions
24 both greatter and myghtyer then youre ſelues. All
the places where on the ſoles of youre fete ſhall treade,
ſhalbe youres: euen from the wilderneſſe and from

M. 23 all theſe nacions & ye ſhall conquere thē which are both greatter

V. 17 iratuſque dominus claudat cælum . . de terrā optima . . . daturus eſt 18 & ſuſpendite ea pro ſigna in manibus, & . . . collocate. 19 vt illa meditētur 21 quamdiu cælum immineret terræ. 23 poſſidebitis 24 Omnis locus quem calcauerit

L. 15 vnd wil . . . gras geben 16 das ſich ewr hertz nicht vberreden laſſe 18 bindet ſie zum zeichen auff ewre hand, das ſie eyn denckmal fur ewren augen ſeyen. 19 leret ſie . . . das du dauon rediſt 21 ſo lange die tage von hymel auff erden weren. 24 Alle ortter darauff ewr fuſs ſolen trit

Libanon and from the ryuer Euphrates, euen vnto the
25 vttemoſt ſee ſhall youre coſtes be. There ſhall no man
be able to ſtonde before you: the Lorde youre God ſhal
caſt the feare and dreade of you vppō all londes whether ye ſhall come, as he hath ſayed vnto you.
26 Beholde, I ſett before you this daye a ble- [Fo.
27 XXIII.] ſſynge and a curſe: a bleſſynge: yf ye herkē
vnto the commaundmentes of the Lorde youre God
28 which I cōmaūde you this daye: And a curſe: yf ye will
not herkē vnto the cōmaundmentes of the Lord youre
God: but turne out of the waye which I commaūde
you this daye to goo after ſtraunge goddes which ye
haue not knowen.
29 When the Lorde thi God hath brought the in to
the londe whother thou goeſt to poſſeſſe it, then put
the bleſſinge vppon mount Griſim and the curſe vppon
30 mount Ebal, which are on the other ſyde Iordane on
the backe ſide of the waye towarde the goynge doune
of the ſonne in the lōde of the Cananites which dwell
in the feldes ouer agenſt Gilgal beſyde moregroue.
31 Fo ye ſhall goo ouer to goo and poſſeſſe the londe
which the Lorde youre God geueth you, and ſhall con-
32 quere it ād dwell there in. Take hede therfore that
ye doo al the cōmaundmentes and lawes, which I ſett
before you this daye.

M. 29 Garizim 30 agenſt Galgal beſyde the groue of Moreh.
V. 24 a flumine magno Euphrate vſque ad mare occidentale 25 ſuper omnem terram quā calcaturi eſtis 28 quam ego nunc oſtendo vobis 30 poſt viam quæ vergit ad ſolis occubitum . . . Galgalam, quæ eſt iuxta vallem tendentem & intrantem procul. 32 Videte ergo
L. 24 bis ans letzte meer 25 darynnen yhr reyſet 29 den ſegen geben 30 der ſtraſſen nach von der ſonnen nyddergang . . . blachen felt wonen gegen Gilgal vber, bey dem hayn More 32 So behaltet nu

The .XII. Chapter.

1 THESE are the ordinaunces and
lawes which ye ſhall obſerue
to doo in the londe which the
Lorde God of thy fathers geueth
the to poſſeſſe it, as longe as ye lyue vppon
2 the .P. erth. Se that ye deſtroye all places
where the nacyons which ye conquere
ſerue their goddes, vppon hye mountaynes
3 and on hye hilles and vnder euery grene tree. Ouerthrowe their alters and breake their pylers and burne
their groues with fyre and hewdowne the ymages off
theyr goddes, and brynge the names of them to noughte
out of that place.

M.C.S. Idolatrye muſt the Iſraelytes deſtroye and flee fro. They muſt eate no bloude. They muſt onely do that thyng whych God commaundeth.

4, 5 Se ye doo not ſo vnto the Lorde youre God but
ye ſhall enquere the place which the Lorde youre God
ſhall haue choſen out of all youre trybes to put his
name there and there to dwell. And thyther thou
6 ſhalt come, and thyther ye ſhall brynge youre burnt-
ſacryfices and youre offerynges, youre tithes and heueofferynges off youre handes, youre vowes and frewillofferynges and thy fyrſt borne off youre oxen and off
7 youre ſhepe. And there ye ſhall eate before the
Lorde youre God, and ye ſhall reioyſe in all that ye
laye youre handes on: both ye and youre houſholdes,
becauſe the Lord thy God hath bleſſed the.

8 Ye ſhall doo after nothinge that we doo *
here this daye, euery man what ſemeth hī good in his
9 awne eyes. For ye are not yet come to reſt nor vnto the

M. 6 and the fyrſt borne

V. 1 daturus eſt 2 omnia loca . . mōtes excelſos, & colles . . . . lignum frondoſum. 3 Diſſipate aras . . & idola comminuite: diſperdite nomina eorum de locis illis. 5 ad locum . . . venietis 6 et offeretis in loco illo 7 miſeritis manum vos & domus 8 Non facietis ibi quæ nos hic facimus hodie

L. 1 geben hat 2 auff hohen bergen, auff hugelln odder vnter grünen b. 3 brecht ab . . die gotzen yhrer Gotter . . aus dem ſelben ort. 5 ſolt yhr forſchen vnd dahyn komen 7 eſſen vnd frolich ſeyn 8 der keyns thun

enheritaunce which the Lorde [Fo. XXIIII.] youre God
10 geueth you. But ye ſhal goo ouer Iordayne ād dwell
in the lōde which the Lorde youre God geueth you to
enheret, ād he ſhal geue you reſt frō al youre enemies
rounde aboute: and ye ſhall dwell in ſafetie.
11 Therfore when the Lorde youre God hath choſen a
place to make his name dwell there, thither ye ſhall
brynge all that I commaunde you, youre burntſacry-
fices and youre offerynges, youre tithes and the heueofferynges of youre handes and all youre godly vowes
which ye vowe vnto the Lorde.
12 And ye ſhall reioyſe before the Lorde youre God,
both ye, youre ſonnes and youre doughters, youre ſeruauntes and youre maydes and the leuite that is within
youre gates for he hath nether parte nor enheritaunce
with you.
13 Take hede that thou offer not thi burntofferynges
14 in what ſoeuer place thou ſeyſt: but in the place which
the Lorde ſhall haue choſen amonge one of thy trybes,
there thou ſhalt offer thi burntofferynges and there
15 thou ſhalt doo all that I commaunde the. Not withſtondynge thou mayſt kyll ād eate fleſh in al thi cities,
what ſoeuer thi ſoule luſteth after acordinge to the
bleſſinge of the Lorde thi God which he hath geuen
the both the .P. * vncleane and the cleane
mayſt thou eate, euen as the roo and the
16 hert: only eate not the bloude, but poure
it apon the erth as water.
17 Thou mayſt not eate within thi gates
the tythe of thi corne, of thy wyne and
of thi oyle, ether the firſtborne of thine

Vncleane as pertayninge vn to ſacrifice as beeſtes that had deformities: but not of the vncleane that was forbiddē

V. 9 daturus eſt (v. 10) 10 et abſque vllo timore habitetis 11 & quicquid præcipuū eſt in muneribus quæ vouiſtis 12 Ibi epulabimini 13 holocauſta 14 offeres hoſtias 15 Si autem comedere volueris, . . . dedit tibi in vrbibus tuis: ſiue immundū fuerit, hoc eſt maculatū, & debile: ſiue mūdum, hoc eſt integrū & ſine macula, quod offerri licet

L. 10 vnd werdet ſicher wonen. 11 brandopffer, ewr ander opffer 15 beyde reyn vnd vnreyn mugens eſſen

M. M. N. 15 *Vncleane:* Vncleane as pertayninge vnto ſacrifyce, as beaſtes that had deformyties: but not of the vncleane that was forbidden.

oxen or of thy ſhepe, nether any of thi vowes which
thou voweſt, nor thi frewilofferinges or heueofferynges
18 of thyne handes: but thou muſt eate them before the
Lorde thi God, in the place which the Lorde thi God
hath choſen: both thou thi ſonne and thi doughter, thi
ſeruaunte and thy mayde ād the leuite that is within
thi gates: ād thou ſhalt reioyſe before the Lorde thi
19 God, in al that thou putteſt thine hande to. And be
warre that thou forſake not the leuite as lōge as thou
lyueſt vppon the erth.
20 Yf (when the Lorde thi God hath enlarged thi coſtes
as he hath promyſed the) thou ſaye: I will eate fleſh,
becauſe thi ſoule longeth to eate fleſh: then thou ſhalt
21 eate fleſh, whatſoeuer thi ſoule luſteth. Yf the place
which the Lorde thi God hath choſen to put his name
there be to ferre from the, then thou mayſt kylle of thi
oxen and of thi ſhepe which the Lorde hath geuen the
as I haue commaunded the and thou mayſt eate in thine
awne citie what [Fo. XXV.] ſoeuer thi ſoule luſteth.
22 Neuer the later, as the roo and the herte is eaten, euen
ſo thou ſhalt eate it: the vncleane and the cleane in-
23 differently thou ſhalt eate. But be ſtrong that thou
eate not the bloude. For the bloude, that is the lyfe:

V. 18 Leuites, qui manent (manet, *Complut.*) 20 ſicut locutus eſt tibi, et volueris veſci carnibus . . . 21 locus autem

L. 18 ſoltu ſolchs eſſen laſſen 20 weyl deyne ſeele fleyſch zu eſſen geluſtet, ſo iſs fleyſch nach aller luſt deyner ſeele 22 wie man eyn rehe odder hirs iſſet, . . . beyde reyn odder vnreyn mugens zu gleych eſſen

M. M. N. 22 *Eate not the bloude:* By that they ſhulde eate no bloude is ſygniſyed that they ſhulde abhorre from bloude ſhedyng, & mãquellyng.

L. M. N. 21 *So opffere:* Wie ſollen ſie opffern vnd doch nicht opffern, an iglichem ort? Item, wie ſollen ſie von den zehenden eſſen &c. ſo ſie doch ſolchs den leuiten vnd prieſtern geben muſten? Antwort, am 14. ca. hernach legt er das aus nemlich alſo, wenn die ſtett zu fern war, ſo ſolten ſie die zehendē, vnd alles was, zu opffern war frey eſſen odder verkeuffen vnd zu gelde machen, vnd dasſelb an den ort bringen, vnd anders ſo viel keuffen vnd opffern, vnd den prieſtern geben. Drumb mus hie das wortlin opffern heyſſen, ſo viel als das opffer eſſen, oder mit gelde gedencken zu uergleychen. Vnd eſſen von den zehenden odder gelubden ſo viel, als eſſen laſſen, nemlich die prieſter. Doch iſt mit ſolchen wortten daneben angezeigt, das alles volck fur Got prieſter ſeyen, wie er ſagt Exo. 19.

24 and thou mayſt not eate the life with the fleſh: thou
maiſt not eate it: but muſt power it vppō the erth as
25 water. Se thou eate it not therfore that it maye goo
well with the and with thy childern after the, when
thou ſhalt haue done that whyche is ryghte in the
ſyghte off the Lorde.
26 But thy holye thinges which thou haſt and thy
vowes, thou ſhalt take and go vnto the place which
27 the Lorde hath choſen, and thou ſhalt offer thy burntoffrynges, both fleſh ād bloude apon the alter of the
Lorde thy God, and the bloude of thine offrynges thou
ſhalt poure out vppon the alter of the Lorde thy God,
28 and ſhalt eate the fleſh. Take hede and heare all theſe
wordes which I commaunde the that it maye goo well
with the and with thy children after the for euer, whē
thou doeſt that whiche is good and right in the ſighte
of the Lorde thy God.
29 When the Lorde thy God hath deſtroyed the nacions before the, whother thou goeſt to conquere them,
and when thou haſt conque- .P. red them, and dwelt
30 in their landes: Bewarre that thou be not taken in a
ſnare after thē, after that they be deſtroyed before the,
and that thou axenot after their goddes ſaynge: how
dyd theſe nacyons ſerue their goddes, that I maye doo
31 ſo likewyſe? Nay, thou ſhalt not doo ſo vnto the
Lorde thy God: for all abhominacyons which the Lorde
hated dyd they vnto their goddes. For they burnt
both their ſonnes ād their doughters with fire vnto their
32 goddes. But what ſoeuer I commaunde
you that take hede ye do: ād put nought
thereto, nor take ought there from.

Put noughte to ner take ought awaye.

V. 23 ſanguis enim eorum pro anima eſt, & idcirco non debes 27 offeres oblationes tuas 28 bonum eſt & placitum 29 diſperdiderit . . poſſidendas, & poſſederis 30 caue ne imiteris eas . . Sicut coluerunt . . ita & ego colam. 32 hoc tātum facito domino.

L. 23 alleyn faſſe . . . denn das blut iſt der ſeelen, Darumb ſoltu die ſeele nicht mit dem fleyſch eſſen 26 heyligſt etwas das deyn iſt 28 recht vnd gefellig 30 das du nicht ynn den ſtrick felleſt yhnen nach . . nicht frageſt noch . . Wi diſe volcker haben . . gedienet, alſo wil ich auch thun

M. M. N. 32 Put noughte to nor take ought awaye.

❡ The .XIII. Chapter.

1 YF there aryse amonge you a prophett or a dreamer of dreames and
geue the a sygne or a wondre,
2 and that sygne or wonder which
he hath sayed come to passe, and then saye:
lat vs goo after straunge Goddes which thou
3 hast not knowen, and let vs serue them: herken not vnto
the wordes of that prophete or dreamer of dreames.
For the Lorde thy God tēpteth you, to
wete whether ye loue the Lord youre God
with all youre hertes ād with al youre soules.
4 For ye must walke after the Lorde youre
God ād feare him and kepe his cōmaū-
[Fo. XXVI.] dmentes and herken vnto
his voyce and serue him and cleaue vnto
5 him. And that prophete or dreamer of
dreames shall dye for it, because he hath
spokē to turne you awaye frō the Lorde youre God
which broughte you out of the londe of Egipte ād
delyuered you out of the housse of bondage, to thrust
the out of the waye whiche the Lorde thy God commaunded the to walke in: and so thou shalt put euell
awaye from the.
6 Yf thy brother the sonne of thy mother or thyne
awne sonne or thy doughter or the wife that lieth in
thy bosome or thy frende which is as thyne awne soule
vnto the, entyce the secretly sayenge: let vs goo and
serue straunge goddes which thou hast not knowē nor

M.C.S. The falsse prophete must be put to death. God proueth oure fayth by falsse myracles.

God geueth vs his worde ād cōfirmeth it with miracles to proue who hath a true herte. we must take hede to the scripture, lest false prophetes or false miracles deceave vs.

F. 2 & euenerit quod locutus est 3 tentat 4 adhærebitis. 5 fictor somniorum . . . quia locutus est vt vos auerteret . . . vt errare te faceret de via . . . & auferes malum 6 vxor quæ est in sinu tuo, aut amicus quē diligis vt animam tuam

L. 3 versucht euch 4 Denn . . anhangen. 5 den bosen 6 weyb ynn deynen armen

M. M. N. 3 *For the Lorde thy God tēpteth you, etc:* God geueth vs his worde & confirmeth it with myracles to proue who hath a true herte. We must take hede to the scripture, lest falsse prophetes or falsse myracles deceaue vs

7 yet thy fathers, of the goddes of the people whiche
are roūde aboute the, whether thei be nye vnto the or
farre of from the, from the one ende of the lande vnto
8 the other: Se thou consente not vnto him nor herken
vnto him: no let not thyne eye pitye him nor haue
9 compassyon on hym, nor kepe him secrett, but cause
him to be slayne: Thine hande shalbe first apon hym to
10 kyll him: and then the handes off all the people. And
thou shalt stone hym with stones that he dye, because
he hath gone .P. aboute to thrust the awaye from the
Lord thy God which brought the out of Egipte the
11 housse of bondage. And all Israel shall heare and feare
ād shall doo no moare any soche wekednesse as this is,
amonge them.
12 Yf thou shalt heare saye of one of thy cities which
13 the Lorde thy God hath geuen the to dwell in, that
certen beyng the childern of Beliall are gone out from
amonge you and haue moued the enhabiters of their
citie sayeng: lat vs goo and serue straunge Goddes
14 whiche ye haue not knowen. Then seke and make
serche and enquere diligently. Yf it be true and the
thinge of a suertie that soch abhominacion is wrought
15 among you: then thou shalt smyte the dwellers of
that citie with the edge of the swerde, and destroye it
mercylesse and all that is therin, and euen the very
16 catell thereof with the edge of the swerde. And gather
all the spoyle of it in to the myddes of the streates there·

M. 15 destroye hit 16 spoyle of hit

V. 7 ab initio vsque ad finem terræ 9 sed statim interficies. sit primum manus tua super eum, & post te omnis populus mittat manum. 10 quia voluit te abstrahere 11 & nequaquam vltra faciat quippiam huius rei simile. 13 et auerterunt habitatores 14 quære solicite, & diligenter . . . certum esse quod dicitur 15 ore gladii, & delebis eam, omniaque quæ in illa sunt vsque ad pecora 16 quicquid etiam supellectilis

L. 7 von eym end der erden bis an das ander 10 Denn er suchte dich auszustossen 11 nicht mehr solchs vbel furneme 14 so soltu wol suchen, forschen vnd fragen . . . die warheyt das gewis also ist 16 raub

M. M. T. 13 *Belial:* Belial by interpretacion sygnifieth malyce, or as some wyll wyckednesse, wherfore all myscheuouse, wycked and cursed mē that cast the youcke of God of their neckes & wil not obeye God, are called the chyldren of Belial or men of Belial. Iudicū. xix, f. and Regum. i, c.

of, and burne with fire: both the citie and all the ſpoyle
thereof euery whitte vnto the Lord thy God. And it
ſhalbe an hepe for euer and ſhall not be bylt agayne.
17 And ſe that their cleaue nought of the damned thinge
in thine hande, that the Lorde maye turne frō his fearſe
wrath and ſhewe the mercye ād haue compaſſion on the
and multiplye the, as he hath ſworne vnto [Fo. XXVII.]
18 thy fathers: when thou haſt herkened vnto the voyce
of the Lorde thy God, to kepe all his cōmaundmentes
which I cōmaunde the thys daye ſo that thou doo
that which is right in the eyes of the Lorde thy God.

¶ The .XIIII. Chapter.

M.C.S. The maners of the gentyles may not befolowed. What beaſtes are cleane to be eaten & what not.

1 YE are the childern of the Lorde
youre God, cut not youre ſelues
nor make you any baldnes betwene the eyes for any mās
2 deeth. For thou art an holy people vnto
the Lord thy God, ād the Lorde hath
choſen the to be a ſeuerall people vnto him ſelfe, of
all the nacyons that are vppon the erth.
3, 4 Ye ſhall eate no maner of abhominacyon. Theſe
are the beeſtes which ye ſhall eate of: oxen, ſhepe and
5 gootes, hert, roo and bugle, hertgoote, vnicorne, origen
6 and Camelion. And all beeſtes that cleaue the hoffe
and ſlytte it in to two clawes and chewe the cud, them
7 ye ſhal eate. Neuertheleſſe, theſe ye ſhall not eate of

M. 5 bugle wyldegoote, vnicorne

V. 17 de illo anathemate . . . & miſereatur tui, multiplicetque te xiiii, 1 nec facietis caluitiū 2 populum peculiarem 3 immunda 4 Hoc eſt animal 5 bubalum, tragelaphum, pygargum, orygem, camelopardalum.

L. 17 von dem grym ſeyns zorns . . . vnd gebe dyr barmhertzickeyt vnd erbarme ſich deyner. xiiii, 1 kalh zwiſſchen ewren augen 3 grewel 4 Dis iſt aber das viech 5 Hirs, Rehe, Hemps, Steynbock, Eynhorn, Vrochs, vnd Elend

M. M. N. 1 *Chyldren of the Lorde:* They are here called the chyldren of the Lorde, becauſe a boue al other people of the worlde they were Indued with the gyftes and benifites of the Lorde Pſal. xxviii, a.

them that chew cud ād of thē that deuyde and
cleaue the hoffe: the camell, the hare ād the conye.
For they chew cud, but deuyde not the hoffe: ād ther-
8 fore are vncleane vnto you: ād alſo the ſwyne, for
though he deuyde the hoffe, yet he cheweth not cud,
ād therfor is vncleane vn- .P. to you: Ye ſhall not
eate of the fleſh of thē nor twich the deed carkaſſes
of them.

9 Theſe ye ſhall eate off all that are in the waters: All
that haue fynnes and ſcales.

10 And what ſoeuer hath not finnes and ſcales, of that
ye may not eate, for that is vncleane vnto you.

11, 12 Of all cleane byrdes ye ſhall eate, but theſe are
they of which ye maye not eate: the egle, the goſhauke,
13 the cormerant, the ixion, the vultur, the kyte and hyr
14, 15 kynde, and all kynde off rauens, the Eſtrich, the
nyghtcrowe, the kuckoo, the ſparowhauke and all hir
16, 17 kynde, the litle oule, the greate oule, the backe, the
18 bytture, the pye the ſtorke, the heron, the Iaye in his
19 kynde, the lapwynge, the ſwalowe: And all crepynge
foules are vncleane vnto you and maye not be eaten
20 of: but of all cleane foules ye maye well eate.

21 Ye ſhall eate of nothinge that dyeth alone: But
thou mayeſt geue it vnto the ſtraunger that is in thy
citie that he eate it, or mayſt ſell it vnto an Aliēt.
For thou art an holy people vnto the Lorde thy God.
Thou ſhalt not ſeth a kyd in his mothers mylke.

22 Thou ſhalt tyeth all the encreaſe of thy ſeed that
cometh out of the felde yere by yere.

23 And thou ſhalt eate before the Lorde thy [Fo.
XXVIII.] God in the place whiche he hath choſen to
make his name dwell there the tyth off thy corne, of
thy wyne and of thyne oyle, and the firſtborne of thine

V. 7 chirogryllium 10 quia immunda ſunt. 12 Immundas ne comedatis 21 Peregrino . . . da . . aut vende ei . . . Non coques hœdum in lacte matris ſuæ. 22 ſeparabis 23 & comedes

L. 10 denn es iſt euch vnreyn. 11 Alle reyne vogel eſſet 21 dem frembdlingen ynn deynem thor magſtus geben . . eym frembden Du ſolt das bocklin nicht kochen, weyl es noch ſeyn mutter ſeuget 22 abſondern 23 vnd ſolts eſſen

M. M. T. 21 Sethe a kyd: Loke exod. xxiii, c.

oxen and of thy flocke that thou mayst lerne to feare
the Lorde thy God allwaye.
24 Yf the waye be to longe for the, so that thou art
not able to carie it, because the place is to farre from
the whiche the Lorde thy God hath chosen to set his
name there (for the Lorde thy God hath blessed the)
25 then make it in money and take the money in thyne
hande, and goo vnto the place which the Lorde thy
26 God hath chosen, and bestowe that moneye on what soeuer thy soule lusteth after: on oxen shepe, wyne and
good drynke, and on what soeuer thy soule desyreth,
and eate there before the Lorde thy God and be mery:
27 both thou and thyne housholde and the Leuite that is
in thy cytye. Se thou forsake not the Leuite, for he
hath nether parte nor enheritaunce with the.
28 At the ende of thre yere, thou shalt brynge forth
all the tithes of thine encrease the same yere and laye
29 it vpp within thyne awne cytye, and the Leuite shall
come because he hath nether parte nor enheritaunce
with the, and the straunger and the fatherlesse and the
wedo- .P. we which are whithin thy citie and shall
eate and fyll them selues: that the Lorde thy God
maye blesse the in all the workes of thine hond which
thou doest.

M. 26 lusteth after: of oxen
V. 23 omni tempore. 24 elegerit . . . tibique benedixerit 25 vendes omnia, & in pretium rediges 26 & emes ex eadem pecunia quicquid tibi placuerit . . . & epulaberis 27 intra portas tuas (v. 29.) 28 separabis . . . & repones intra ianuas tuas.
L. 23 deyn leben lang. 25 so gibs vmb gelt 26 vnd sey frolich 27 ynn deynem thor (vv. 28, 29) 28 auszihen . . . vnd solts lassen

The .XV. Chapter.

1 AT the ende of ſeuen yere thou
2 ſhalt make a fre yere. And
this is the maner off the fre
yere, whoſoever lendeth ought
with his hande vnto his neyghboure, maye
not axe agayne that which he hath lent,
of his neyghboure or of his brother: be-
3 cauſe it is called the lordes fre yere, yet
of a ſtraunger thou maiſt call it home
agayne. But that which thou haſt with
4 thy brother thyne hande ſhall remytt, and that in any
wyſe, that there be no begger amonge you. For the
Lorde ſhall bleſſe the lande whiche the Lorde thy God
5 geueth the, an heritaunce to poſſeſſe it: ſo that thou
herken vnto the voyce of the Lorde thy God, to obſerue
ād doo all theſe commaundmentes which I commaunde
6 you this daye: ye and then the Lorde thy God ſhall
bleſſe the as he hath promyſed the, and thou ſhalt
lende vnto many nacyons, and ſhalt borowe of no
man, and ſhalt raygne ouer many nacyons, but none
ſhal reygne ouer the.
7 [Fo. XXIX.] When one of thi brethern amonge you
is waxed poore in any of thi cities within thi lōde which
the Lorde thi God geueth the, ſe that thou harden not
thine hert nor ſhetto thyne hande from thi poore bro-
8 ther: But open thyne hand vnto him and lende him
9 ſufficient for his nede which he hath. And beware that

M.C.S. The forgeuencs of dettes in the ſeuenth yere. If the Iſraelites obey God they are promeſed that they ſhall not ſuffre pouertye. How and after what maner we ought to lende.

M. 2 aſke agayne 4 enheritaũce

V. 1 remiſſionem 2 quæ hoc ordine celebrabitur. Cui debetur aliquid ab amico vel proximo ac fratre ſuo, repetere non poterit 3 exiges: ciuem & propinquum repetendi non habebis poteſtatem. 4 omnino indigens, & mendicus . . . vt 5 Si tamen . . . quæ iuſſit, & quæ . . . præcipio 5 vt pollicitus eſt. 7 Si vnus . . . ad paupertatem deuenerit 8 quo eum indigere perſpexeris.

L. 1 Freyiar 2 Alſo ſols aber zugehen . . eynmanen (v. 3) . . . denn es heyſt 4 Es ſol aller dinge keyn . . . denn 5 alleyn

there be not a poynte of Belial in thine hert, that thou
woldeſt ſaye. The ſeuenth yere, the yere of fredome is
at honde, and therfore it greue the to loke on thy poore
brother and geueſt him nought and he then crye vnto
10 the Lorde agenſt the and it be ſynne vnto the: But
geue him, and let it not greue thine hert to geue. Becauſe that for that thinge, the Lorde thy God ſhall
bleſſe the in all thi workes and in all that thou putteſt
11 thine hande to. For the londe ſhall neuer be without
poore. Wherfore I cōmaunde the ſayenge: open thine
hande vnto thi brother that is neady ād poore in thy
lande.

12 Yf thi brother an Hebrue ſell him ſelf to the or an
Hebruas, he ſhall ſerue the ſyxe yere and the ſeuenth
13 yere thou ſhalt lett him go fre from the. And when
thou ſendeſt hym out fre from the, thou ſhalt not let
14 him goo awaye emptye: but ſhalt geue him of thy ſhepe
and of thi corne and of thy wyne, and geue him off .
that where with the Lorde thi God hath bleſſed the.
15 And remembre that thou waſt a ſeruaunte in the londe
of Egipte, and the Lorde thi God delyuered the thence:
wherſore I commaunde the this thinge to daye.

16 But and yf he ſaye vnto the, I will not goo awaye
from the, becauſe he loueth the and thine houſſe and
17 is well at eaſe with the. Then take a naule a naule, *an awl*
and nayle his eare too the doore there with ād let him
be thi ſeruaunte foreuer and vnto thi mayde ſeruaunte
18 thou ſhalt doo likewiſe. And let it not greue thine

V. 9 ſubrepat tibi impia cogitatio, & dicas in corde tuo . . . & auertas oculos tuos (18) . . clamet contra te 10 nec ages quippiam callide in eius neceſſitatibus ſubleuandis . . . ad quæ manum miſeris. 12 Hebræus aut Hebræa 14 ſed dabis viaticum 15 & liberauerit te 17 & perforabis aurem eius

L. 9 eyn Belial tuck ſey, das da ſprech . . . vnd ſiheſt deynen . . . vnfreuntlich an 10 ſondern du ſolt yhm geben vnd deyn hertz nicht verdriſſen laſſen, das du yhm gibſt 12 Ebreer odder Ebreeryn 17 bore yhm durch ſeyn ohr an der thur 18 Vnd las dichs nicht ſchwer duncken

M. M. N. 9 *A poynte of Belial in thine herte:* A poynt of Belial here for the wycked and frowarde councell of Belial. 17 *Then take a naule and nayle, etc:* The entent of this lawe is to cauſe thē to abhorre bōdage wherunto this open ſhame ſhulde dryue them for God wyll not that the loue of any man ſhulde be dearer vnto hym then lybertye.

eyes to lett him goo out from the, for he hath bene
worthe a double hired seruaunte to the in his seruyce
vi. yeres. And the Lorde thi God shall blesse the in
all that thou doest.
19 All the firstborne that come of thine oxen and of thi
shepe that are males, thou shalt halowe vnto the Lorde
thi God. Thou shalt do no seruyce with the firstborne
20 of thi shepe: but shalt eate thē before the Lorde thi
God yere by yere in the place which the Lorde hath
chosen both thou and thine houssholde.
21 Yf there be any deformyte there in, whether it be
lame or blinde or what soeuer euell faueredneffe it hath,
22 thou shalt not offer it vnto the Lorde thi God: But
shalt eate it in thine awne citie, the vncleane and the
cleane in- [Fo. XXX.] differently, as the roo and the
23 hert. Only eate not the bloude there of, but poure
it vppon the grounde as water.

V. 18 quoniam iuxta mercedem mercennarii 19 deo tuo. Non operaberis in primogenito bouis, & non tondebis primogenita ouium. 21 aut in aliqua parte deforme vel debile 22 tam mundus quam immundus similiter vescentur eis

L. 18 denn er hat dyr als eyn zwiffeltig tagloner 19 heyligen. Du solt nicht ackern mit dem erstling deyner ochsen, vnd nicht bescheren die ersthling deyner schaff 21 odder sonst yrgen eyn bosen feyl 22 sondern ynn deynem thor soltu es essen (du seyst vnreyn oder reyn)

M. M. T. 22 *The vncleane and the cleane indifferētly*, etc.: Or whether thou be cleane or vncleane, & lyke wyse in the .xii chapter b, and c. In the Hebrue it is indifferēt in al these places, to aplye the cleanes or vncleanes to the person that eateth it, or to the beast that is eaten.

¶ The .XVI. Chapter.

1 OBSERUE the moneth of Abyb, and offer passeover vnto the Lorde thi God. For in the moneth of Abib, the Lorde thy God brought the out of Egipte by nyght.

M.C.S. *Of Easter, whytsontyde, & the feast of tabernacles. what offycers ought to be ordeyned.*

2 Thou shalt therfore offer passeover vnto the Lorde
thi God, and shepe and oxen in the place which the
3 Lorde shall chose to make his name dwell there. Thou
shalt eate no leuēded bred there with: but shalt eate
there with the bred of tribulaciō .vii. dayes lōge. For
thou camest out of the lōde of Egipte in hast, that thou
mayst remembre the daye when thou camest out of
4 the londe of Egipte, all dayes of thi life. And se that
there be no leuended bred sene in all thi costes .vii
dayes longe, and that there remayne nothinge of the
flesh which thou hast offered the fyrst daye at euen,
vntil the mornynge.
5 Thou mayst not offer passeover in any of thi cities
6 which the Lord thi god geueth the: But in the place
which the Lorde thi God shall chose to make his name
dwell in, there thou .P. shalt offer Passeouer at euen
aboute the goyngdoune of the sonne, euen in the
7 season that thou camest out of Egipte. And thou
shalt seth and eate in the place which the Lorde thi
God hath chosen, and departe on the morowe and
8 gette the vnto thi tente. Sixe dayes thou shalt eate

V. 1 mensem nouarum frugum, & verni primū temporis . . . in isto mense 2 de ouibus 3 Non comedes in eo . . absque fermento, afflictionis panem . . in pauore egressus 4 immolatum 5 immolare . . phase . . daturus est 7 maneque consurgens vades

L. 1 bey der nacht 2 Vnd solt . . . zu Ostern opffern 3 vngeseuerts brod deyns elends 5 Ostern opffern (v. 6) 7 vnd darnach dich wenden des morgens vnd heym gehen

M. M. N. 1 *Abib:* Abib, that is of apryll, when all thynges do sprynge of freasshe Exod. xxiii, b.

ſwete bred, and the ſeuenth daye is for the people to
come together to the Lorde thi God, that thou mayſt
do no worke.

9 Then reken the .vii. wekes, and begynne to rekē
the .vii. wekes when the ſyccle begynneth in the corne,
10 and kepe the feaſt of wekes vnto the Lorde thi God,
that thou geue a frewilofferinge of thine hāde vnto the
Lord thi God acordinge as the Lorde thi God hath
11 bleſſed the. And reioyſe before the Lorde thi God
both thou, thi ſonne, thi doughter, thi ſeruaunte and
thi mayde, and the leuite that is within thi gates, and
the ſtraunger, the fatherleſſe ād the wedowe that are
amonge you, in the place which the Lorde thi God
12 hath choſen to make his name dwel there. And
remēbre that thou waſt a ſeruaūte in *why.*
Egipte, that thou obſerue and doo theſe ordinaunces.
13 Thou ſhalt obſerue the feaſt of tabernacles .vii. dayes
longe, after that thou haſt gathered in thi corne and
14 thi wyne. And thou ſhalt reioyſe in that thi feaſt,
both thou and thi ſonne, [Fo. XXXI.] thi doughter,
thi ſeruaunte, thi mayde, the leuite, the ſtraunger, the
fatherleſſe and the wedowe that are in thi cities.
15 Seuen dayes thou ſhalt kepe holy daye vnto the
Lorde thi God, in the place which the Lorde ſhal
choſe: for the Lorde thi God ſhall bleſſe the in all thi
frutes and in all the workes of thine handes, and thou
16 ſhalt be all together gladneſſe. Thre tymes in the
yere ſhall al youre males appere before the Lorde thi
God in the place which he ſhal choſe: In the feaſt of

M. 15 handes, & therfore ſhalt thou be glad.

V. 8 collecta eſt domini 9 Sept. hebd. numerabis tibi ab ea die qua falcem in ſegetem miſeris 10 diem feſtum hebdomadarum 11 & epulaberis (v. 14) 12 cuſtodieſque ac facies quæ præcepta ſunt. 14 feſtiuitate tua 15 eriſque in lætitia.

L. 8 die ſteur 9 zelen, vnd an heben zu zehlen 11 frölich ſeyn (v. 14) 12 haltiſt vnd thuſt nach diſen ſitten. 15 das feſt halten 16 erwelet hat

M. M. N. 11 *Gates:* By gates is oft tymes vnderſtande cytyes Iuriſdycyon rule and gouernaunce as in this ſame chapter beneth in d. (v. 18).

ſwete bred, in the feaſt of wekes and in the booth feaſt.
And they ſhal not appere before the Lorde emptie:
17 but euery mā with the gifte of his honde, acordynge
to the bleſſinge of the Lorde thi God, which he hath
geuen the.

The .XVII. Chapter.

18 IVDGES and officers thou ſhalt
make the in all thi cities which
the Lorde thi God geueth the
thorow out thi trybes. and lett
Iudges. thē iudge the people right-
19 eouſly. Wreſt not the lawe nor knowe
any perſone nether take any rewarde: for
giftes blynde the wiſe and peruerte the
20 wordes of the righteous. But in all thinge
folowe righteouſneſſe, that thou mayſt lyue
and enioye the londe which the Lord thi
God geueth the.

M.C.S. *The payne and punyſhement for Idolatrie. The doutefull ſentence muſt be referred vnto the greate Iudges. The punyſhement of a rebeller or preſumptuouſe withſtander of the lawe. The Inſtitucyon of a Kynge.*

21 .¶. Thou ſhalt plante no groue of what ſoeuer trees
it be, nye vnto the altare of the Lorde thi God which
22 thou ſhalt make the. Thou ſhalt ſett the vpp no piler,
XVII, 1 which the Lorde thy God hateth. Thou ſhalt
offer vnto the Lorde thy God no oxe or ſhepe where
in is any deformyte, what ſoeuer euell faueredneſſe it
be: for that is an abhominacion vnto the Lorde thi
God.

2 Yf there be founde amonge you in any of thi cities

M. 16 feaſt *of tabernacles (* Margin, see below. This chapter ends in Matthew's Bible as in the Authorized Version; v. 17 of the latter is the last verse of Ch. xvi. in Tyndale). xvii, 2 the cytyes

V. 18 Iudices & magiſtros 19 nec in alteram partem declinent. . . . excæcant oculos . . . mutant verba 20 Iuſte quod iuſtum eſt, perſequeris. xvii, 1 macula aut quippiā vitii

L. 18 richten mit rechtem gericht 19 Du ſolt das recht nicht beugen . . . verleytten die rechten ſachen 20 Was recht iſt dem ſoltu nach iagen. xvii, 1 etwas boſes

M. M. N. 16 *Of tabernacles:* Or bothes. 18 Iudges.

which the Lord thi God geueth the man or woman
that hath wrought wekedneſſe in the ſighte of the Lord
thi God, that they haue gone beyonde his appoynt-
3 ment, ſo that they haue gone and ſerued ſtraūge goddes
ād worſhipped thē, whether it be the ſonne or mone or
4 any thinge contayned in heauē which I forbade, and
it was tolde the ād thou haſt herde of it: Then thou
ſhalt enquere diligently.

And yf it be true and the thinge of a ſuertye that
5 ſoch abhomynacion is wrought in Iſrael, thē thou ſhalt
bringe forth that mā or that woman whiche haue cō-
mytted that weked thinge, * vnto thi gates
ād ſhalt ſtone thē with ſtones ād they ſhall
6 dye. At the mouth of .ii. or .iii. witneſſes
ſhal he that is worthy of deeth, dye: but
at the mouth of one witneſſe he ſhall not
7 dye. And the handes of the witneſſes
ſhalbe fi- [Fo. XXXII.] rſt vppon hym
to kyll him, ād afterwarde the handes of
all the people: ſo ſhalt thou put wekedneſſe awaye from the.

Opinly in the gates and not ſecretlye in preſon: with lawfull witneſſe and not tormentynge them or makēge them ſwer agenſt thē ſelves or forſwere thē ſelves.

8 Yf a matter be to harde for the in iudgemēt betwene bloud and bloude, plee and plee, plage and
plage in maters of ſtriſe within thi cities: Then Ariſe
and gett the vpp vnto the place which the Lorde thi
9 God hath choſen, and goo vnto the preaſtes the leuites
and vnto the iudge that ſhalbe in thoſe dayes, and axe,
10 and they ſhall ſhewe the how to iudge. And ſe that

𝔐. 5 vnto the gates 9 dayes, and aſke

V. 2 malum 3 omnem militiam cæli, quæ non præcepi 4 inquiſieris diligenter 5 et lapidibus obruentur. 6 peribit qui interficietur 7 vt auferas malum de medio tui (v. 12). 8 Si difficile & ambiguū . . . lepram & non lepram, & iudicum intra portas tuas videris verba variari 9 qui indicabunt tibi iudicii veritatem.

𝔏. 2 vbels thut 3 yrgent eyn heer des hymels, das ich nicht gepotten habe 5 vnd ſolt ſie zu todt ſteynigen 7 das du den boſen von dyr thueſt (v. 12). 8 zwiſſchen plage vnd plage, vnd was zenkiſche ſachen ſind ynn deynen thoren 9 die ſollen dyr das vrteyl ſprechen

𝔐. 𝔐. 𝔑. 5 *Vnto the gates:* Opēly in the gates & not ſecretly in preſon With lawful witneſſe and not tormentinge them or makynge thē ſwere agaynſt them ſelues or forſwere them ſelues.

thou doo acordinge to that which they of that place
which the Lorde hath chosen shew the and se that thou
obserue to doo acordinge to all that they enforme the.
11 Acordinge to the lawe which they teach the and maner
of iudgement which they tell the, se that thou doo and
that thou bowe not from that which they shewe the,
nether to the right hande nor to the lyste.
12 And that man that will doo presumptuously, so that
he will not herken vnto the preast that stondeth there
to mynistre vnto the Lorde thi God or vnto the iudge,
shall dye: and so thou shalt put awaye euell from Israel.
13 And all the people shall heare and shall feare, and
shall doo nomare presumptuosly,
14 ¶. When thou art come vnto the lõde which the Lorde
thi God geueth the and enioyest it and dwellest therin:
Yf thou shalt saye, I will sett a kinge ouer *kynges.*
me, like vnto all the nacions that are aboute me:
15 Then thou shalt make him kinge ouer the, whom the
Lorde thi God shal chose. One of thi brethern must
thou make kinge ouer the, and mayst not sett a straunger
16 ouer the which is not of thi brethern. But in ani wyse
let hĩ not holde to many horsses, that he bringe not the
people agayne to Egipte thorow the multitude of horsses,
for as moch as the Lorde hath sayed vnto you: ye shall
17 hence forth goo no moare agayne that waye. Also
he shall not haue to many wyues, lest his hert turne
awaye, nether shall he gather him syluer and golde to
moch.
18 And when he is seten vppon the seate off his

M. 18 And when he is sett

V. 11 iuxta legem eius, sequerisque sententiam eorum, nec declinabis 12 Qui autem superbierit . . . ex decreto iudicis 13 vt nullus deinceps intumescat superbia. 14 possederis eam, habitauerisque in illa 15 Non poteris alterius gentis hominem regem facere, qui non sit frater tuus. 16 Cumque fuerit constitutus . . . equitatus numero subleuatus . . . vt nequaquam amplius per eandem viam reuertamini. 17 quæ alliciant animum eius

L. 10 nach allem das sie dich leren werden 11 soltu dich halten . . . nicht abweychest 12 vermessen handeln . . . ampt stehet 14 nymest es eyn vnd wonest drynnen 16 nicht viel rosser halte . . . vmb der rosse menge willen . . . fort nicht widder durch disen weg komen solt 17 das seyn hertze nicht abgewand werde

M. M. X. 14 Kynges.

kingdome, he ſhall write him out this ſeconde lawe in
a boke takynge a copye of the preaſtes the leuites.
19 And it ſhalbe with him and he ſhall reade there in
all dayes of his lyfe that he maye lerne to feare the
Lorde his God for to kepe all the wordes *
20 of this lawe ād theſe ordinaunces for to doo them: that
his hert aryſe not aboue his brethern and that he turne
not from the commaundment: ether to the righte hande
or to the lifte: that both he ād his [Fo. XXXIII.]
childern maye prolonge their dayes in his kingdome in
Iſrael.

The .XVIII. Chapter.

1 THE preaſtes the Leuites all the
trybe off Leui ſhall haue no
parte nor enheritaunce with
Iſrael. The offrynges of the
Lorde ād his enheritaunce
2 they ſhall eate, but ſhall
haue no enheritaunce amonge
their brethern: the Lorde he
is their enheritaunce, as he
3 hath ſayed vnto them. And this is the
dutie of the preaſtes, of the people and of them that
offer, whether it be oxe or ſhepe: They muſt geue vnto
the preaſt, the ſhulder and the two chekes and the
4 maw, the firſtfrutes of thy corne, wyne and oyle,
and the firſt of thy ſhepeſheryng muſt thou geue
5 him. For the Lorde thy God hath choſen him out

I meruel that oure diſſigured coude make no figure of this all this while.

M.C.S. *The Leuytes myght haue no poſſeſſyons. Idolatrye muſt be fledde. The prophet Chryſt is promyſed. The falſe prophet muſt be ſlayne, & how he may be knowē.*

F. 18 deſcribet ſibi Deuteronomium legis huius in volumine, accipiens exemplar a ſacerdotibus Leuiticæ tribus 19 & ceremonias eius quæ in lege præcepta ſunt. 20 in ſuperbiam ſuper fratres ſuos . . . vt . . regnet ipſe & filii eius ſuper Iſrael. xviii, 1 quia 3 Hoc erit iudicium ſacerdotum

L. 18 alle wort diſes geſetzs vnd diſe ſitten 20 auff ſeynem konigreych. xviii, 3 das recht der prieſter

of all thy trybes to ſtonde and to miniſtre in the
name of the Lorde: both hĩ and his ſonnes for euer.
6 Yf a Leuite come out of any of thy cities or any
place of Iſrael, where he is a ſegeorner, ād come with
all the luſt of his herte vnto the place which the Lorde
7 hath choſen: he ſhall there miniſtre in the name of
the Lorde his god as all his brethern the Leuites doo
8 whiche ſtonde there before the Lord. And they ſhall
haue lyke porcyons to eate, beſyde that whiche cometh
to hym of the patrimonye of hys .P. elders.
9 When thou art come in to the londe which the
Lorde thy God geueth the, ſe that thou lerne not to
10 doo after the abhominacyōs of theſe nacyons. Let
there not be founde amonge you that maketh his
ſonne or his doughter go thorow fyre, ether
a bruterar or a maker of diſmale dayes or
11 that vſeth witchcraft or a ſorcerar or a
charmar or that ſpeaketh with a ſpirite or a ſothſayer
12 or that talketh with them that are deed. For all that
doo ſoch thinges are abhominacion vnto the Lorde:
and becauſe of theſe abhominacyons the Lorde thy
13 God doeth caſt them out before the, be pure therfore
14 with the Lorde thy God. For theſe nacyons whiche
thou ſhalt conquere, herken vnto makers off dyſemall
dayes and bruterars.

bruterar, *murmurer*
diſmale dayes, *unlucky days*

M. 5 all the trybes 10 ſonne or daughter to go thorow the fyre, or that vſeth withcraſt, or a choſer oute of dayes or that regardeth the flyēg of ſoules, or a ſorcerar 11 or a charmar, or that counceleth with ſpretes, or a propheciar or that aſketh the aduyſe of the deed. 14 herken vnto choſers oute of dayes and prophecyars.

V. 6 deſyderans locum 8 ex paterna ei ſucceſſione debetur. 9 dabit . . . ne imitari velis 10 qui luſtret . . . ducens per ignem: aut qui ariolos ſciſcitetur, & obſeruet ſomnia atque auguria. nec ſit maleficus, 11 nec incātator, neque qui pythones conſulat, nec diuinos, & quærat a mortuis veritatē. 12 delebit eos in introitu tuo. 13 perfectus eris & abſque macula 14 tu autem . . aliter inſtitutus es.

L. 6 vnd kompt nach aller luſt ſeyner ſeele 8 on was er hat von dem verkaufften gutt ſeyner veter. 9 geben wirt 10 odder eyn weyſſager, odder eyn tage weler, odder der auff vogel geſchrey achte, odder zeuberer, 11 odder beſchwerer, odder warſager, odder eyn zeychen deutter, odder der die todten frage. 13 on wandel

M. M. N. 10 *Withcrafte:* Or arte magyke. *Choſer oute of dayes:* Some that haue regarde to tymes. 11 *Aſketh the aduyſe of the deed:* They aſke ye aduyſe of ye deed that cōiure ſprytes in the nyght thinckyng that they are ſoules departed

But the Lorde thy God permytteth not that to the.
15 The Lorde thy God will ſterre vpp a prophete
amonge you: euē of thy brethern like vnto me: and
16 vnto him ye ſhall herken acording to all
that thou deſyredeſt of the Lorde thy god
in Horeb in the daye when the people
were gathered ſayenge: Let me heare the
voyce of my Lorde God nomoare nor ſe
17 this greate fire any moare, that I dye not. And the
18 Lorde ſayed vnto me: they haue well ſpoken, I will
[Fo. XXXIIII.] rayſe them vpp a prophett from amonge
their brethern like vnto the ād will put my wordes in
to his mouth and he ſhall ſpeake vnto thē al that I
19 ſhall commaunde him. And whoſoeuer will not herken
vnto the wordes which he ſhall ſpeake in my name, I
will requyre it off him.
20 But the prophete which ſhall preſume to ſpeake
ought in my name which I commaunded him not to
ſpeake, and he that ſpeaketh in the name of ſtraunge
21 Goddes, the ſame prophete ſhall dye. And yf thou
ſaye in thine hert, howe ſhall I knowe that whiche
22 the Lorde hath not ſpoken? When a prophete
ſpeaketh in the name of the Lorde, yf the thynge
folow not nor come to paſſe, that is the thinge
which the Lorde hath not ſpoken. But the prophete
hath ſpoken it preſumptuouſly: be not aferde therfore
of him.

Chriſt is here promyſed a preacher off better tydinges then Moſes.

M. 20 commaunded not to ſpeake

V. 15 de gente tua & de fratribus tuis 16 quando contio congregata eſt 17 Bene omnia ſunt locuti 19 ego vltor exiſtam. 21 ſi tacita cogitatione 22 hoc habebis ſignum: . . . ſed per tumorem animi ſui propheta confinxit, & idcirco

L. 14 nicht alſo ſtellen dem Herrn 16 am tage der verſamlung 19 von dem wil ichs ſuchen. 20 vermeſſen 22 mit vermeſſenheyt geredt, darumb

M. M. X. 15 Chriſt is here promyſed a preacher of better tydynges then Moſes.

L. M. X. 15 Hie wirt klerlich eyn ander predigt verheyſſen denn Moſes predigt, wilche kan nicht das geſetze ſeyn, das gnugſam durch Moſe geben, drum mus es das Euangelion ſeyn, Vnd diſer prophet niemant denn Iheſus Chriſtus ſelbs der ſolch newe predigt auff erden hat bracht.

The .XIX. Chapter.

1 WHEN the Lorde thy God hath
destroyed the nacyons whose
londe the Lorde thy God geueth
the, and thou hast conquered
thē and dwellest in their cities and in their
2 housses: thou shalt appoynte .iii. cities in the lande
whiche the Lorde thy God geueth the to .P. possesse
3 it: thou shalt prepare the waye and deuyde the costes
of thy lande whiche the Lorde thy God geueth the to
enheret, in to .iii. partes that whosoeuer committeth
murthur may flee thither.

M.C.S. *The fraunchesed townes. The punyshement of hym that beareth false wytnesse.*

4 And this is the cause of the sleyer that
shal flee thither and be saued: Yf he smyte
his neghboure ignorantly and hated him
5 not in tyme passed: As when a man goeth
vnto the wodd with his neghboure to hew
wod, and as his hāde fetcheth a stroke
with the axe, the head slippeth from the
helue and smyteth his neghboure that he dye: the
same shall flee vnto one off the same cities ād be saued.
6 Lest the executer of bloude folowe after the sleyer
while his hert is whote and ouertake him, because

The popis setuaries are of an other purpose. For he had leuer haue the frenshep of the euel, thē to saue them that are Good.

V. 2 separabis tibi 3 sternens diligenter viam 4 Hæc erit lex homicidæ fugientis . . . nesciens, & qui heri & nudiustertius nullum contra eum odium habuisse comprobatur 5 ferrumque lapsum de manubrio . . ad vnam supradictarum vrbium 6 dolore stimulatus

L. 2 ausfondern 4 Vnd das sol die sach seyn . . . vnwissend, vnd hat vorhyn keyn hass auff yhn gehabt 5 das eysen fure vom stiel 6 der blut recher dem todschleger nach iage, weyl seyn hertz erhitzt ist

M. M. N. 4 *If he smyte, etc.:* Here are shewed .ii. maner of māquellyng one done wyllyngly & of set purpose, the other vnwyllinglye: for euē he that kylleth with the hande maye before God be no māquellare: and agayne he that is angrye and enuyeth althoughe he kyll not wyth the hāde, cānot but be a manslear before God: because he wylleth hys neyghboure euyll. As it is sayde .i. Iohan .iii, c.

the waye is longe, and ſlee him, and yet there is
no cauſe worthy of deeth in him, in as moch as he
hated not his neghbour in tyme paſſed. *As hate maketh the dead*
7 Wherfore I commaunde the ſayeng: ſe *euell: ſo love*
that thou appoynte out .iii. cities *maketh it*
8 And yf the Lorde thy God enlarge *good.*
thy coſtes as he hath ſworne vnto thy fathers and geue
the all the londe which he ſayed he wold geue vnto
9 thy fathers (ſo that thou kepe all theſe commaundmentes to doo them, which I commaunde the this
daye, that thou loue the Lord thy god ād walke in his
wayes euer) then thou [Fo. XXXV.] ſhalt adde .iii
10 cities moo vnto thoſe .iii. that innocent bloude be not
ſhed in thi lande which the Lorde thy God geueth the
to enheret, and ſo bloude come vppon the,
11 But and yf there be any man that hateth his neyghboure and layeth awayte for him and ryſeth agenſt
him and ſmyteth him that he dye, and fleeth vnto any of
12 theſe cities. Then let the elders of his citie ſende and
fetche him thence and delyuer him in to the hondes
13 of the iuſtice of bloude, and he ſhall dye, Let thyne
eye haue no pitie on him, and ſo thou ſhalt put awaye
innocent bloude from Iſrael, and happie arte thou.
14 Thou ſhalt not remoue thy neghbours marke which
they of olde tyme haue ſett in thyne enheritaunce that
thou enheretteſt in the londe which the Lorde thy God
geueth the to enioye it.
15 One witneſſe ſhall not ryſe agenſt a man *Yee in all*
in any maner treſpace or ſynne, what ſo- *mater of hereſie agenſt*
euer ſynne a man ſynneth: But at the *holye churche:*
mouthe of two witneſſes or of .iii. witneſſes ſhall all
maters be tryed.
16 Yf an vnrighteous witneſſe ryſe vp agenſt a man to

V. 6 qui non eſt reus mortis: . . contra eum qui occiſus eſt, odium . . . monſtratur. 8 quam eis pollicitus eſt 9 omni tempore . . . et ſupradict. trium vrbium numerum duplicabis 10 ne ſis ſanguinis reus. 12 de loco effugii . . proximi, cuius ſanguis effuſus eſt 13 Non miſereberis eius . . vt bene ſit tibi. 15 ſtabit omne verbum.

L. 6 ſo doch keyn vrteyl des todts an yhm iſt 7 ausſonderſt. 8 geredt hat 9 deyn leben lang 10 vnd kome blut auff dich. 12 des blut rechers 13 deyn augen ſollen ſeyn nicht verſchonen (v. 21) . . das dyrs wol gehe. 15 ſol alle ſache beſtehen. 16 eyn freueler zeuge

17 accuſe him of treſpace: then let both the men which
ſtryue together ſtonde before the Lorde, before the
preaſtes and the iudges .P. which ſhalbe in thoſe dayes,
18 and let the iudges enquyre a good. And
yf the witneſſe be founde falſe and that
he hath geuen falſe witneſſe agenſt his
19 brother thē ſhall ye do vnto hī as he had thought to
do vnto his brother, and ſo thou ſhalt put euel away
20 frō the. And other ſhal heare ād feare ād ſhal hēceforth comytt no more any ſoch wekedneſſe amōg you.
21 And let thyne eye haue no compaſſiō, but life for life,
eye for eye, toth for toth, hande for hand, and fote
for fote.

a good, *in good earnest, thoroughly*

❡ The .XX. Chapter

1 WHEN thou goeſt out to batayle
agenſt thine enemyes, and
ſeeſt horſes and charettes and
people moo then thou, be not
aferde of them, for the Lorde thy God is
with the whiche broughte the out of the
2 londe off Egipte. And when ye are come
nye vnto batayle, let the preaſt come forth and ſpeake
3 vnto the people and ſaye vnto them: Heare Iſrael, ye
are come vnto batayle agenſte youre enemyes, let not
youre hartes faynte, nether feare nor be amaſed nor a
dreade of them.

4 For the Lorde thy God goeth with you to fyghte
for you agenſte youre enemyes and to ſaue you.

M.C.S. *Who ought to go to battel. The Lawe of Armes amonge the Iſraelites. The Canaanytes muſt they kyll.*

F. 18 Cumque diligentiſſime perſcrutantes 19 & auferes malum de medio tui 20 talia audeant facere. 21 Non miſereberis eius, ſed . . . exiges. xx, 1 ad bellum . . . equitatus & currus, & maiorem quam tu habeas, aduerſarii exercitus multitudinem 2 prælio, ſtabit ſac. ante aciem 4 contra aduerſarios dimicabit, vt eruat vos de periculo.

L. 18 wol forſchen 19 das boſe von dyr weg thuſt 20 ſolche boſe ſtuck furnemen zu thun. xx, 1 ynn eyn krieg . . . roſs vnd wagen des volcks das groſſer ſey, denn du 2 zum ſtreyt 3 furcht euch nicht, vnd zappelt nicht

5 And let the officers ſpeake vnto the peo- [Fo.
XXXVI.] ple ſayenge: Yf any man haue bylt a new
houſſe and haue not * dedicate it, let him
6 goo and returne to his houſſe leſt he dye
in the batayle, and another dedicate it.
And yf any man haue planted a vyneyarde and haue not made it comen *, let
him goo and returne agayne vnto his
houſe, leſt he dye in the batayle
and another make it comen. And
7 yf any man be betrothed vnto a wyfe
and haue not taken hyr, let hym goo
and returne agayne vnto his houſſe, leſt
he dye in the batayle and another take
her.

Dedicat: the leuites I ſuppoſe, halowed thē as we doo oure ſhippes.

Comē: the iii. firſt yeres the frute myghte not be eatē the fou.'h it might be offred ād the fifte eaten ād that ys to make it comē to bringe it to the vſſe of the laye people.

8 And let the officers ſpeake further vnto the people
and ſaye. Yf any man feare and be faynte herted, let
him goo and returne vnto his houſſe, leſt his brothers
9 hert be made faynte as well as his. And when the
officers haue made an ende off ſpeakynge vnto the
people, let thē make captaynes of warre ouer them.
10 When thou comeſt nye vnto a citie to fight agenſt
11 it, offre them peace. And yf they anſwere the agayne
peaſably, and open vnto the, then let all the people
that is founde therein be tributaries vnto the and ſerue
12 the. But and yf they will make no peace with the,
then make warre agenſte the citie and beſege it.
13 .¶. And when the Lord thy God hath delyuered it
in to thine handes, ſmyte all the males thereof with

V. 6 fecit eam eſſe communem, & de qua veſci omnibus liceat? . . . & alius homo eius fungatur officio. 8 ſicut ipſe timore perterritus eſt. 9 ſiluerint duces exercitus . . .vnuſquiſque ſuos ad bellandum cuneos præparabit. 10 offeres ei primum pacem. 11 Si receperit . . . ſaluabitur, & ſeruiet tibi ſub tributo. 12 ſinautem fœdus inire noluerit, & cœperit contra te bellum

L. 5 die heubtleut ſollen mit dem volck reden 6 noch nicht gemeyn gemacht 8 ſeyner brüder hertz feyg mache wie ſein hertz iſt. 9 die heubtleut . . . ſollen ſie die vbirſten des heers fur das volck an die ſpitzen ſtellen. 11 Antworttet ſie dyr fridelich . . . dyr zinsbar vnd vnterthan ſeyn. 12 Wil ſie aber nicht fridelich mit dyr handeln, vnd wil mit dyr kriegen

M. M. N. 5 *Dedicat:* Same note as in Tyndale. 6 *Comē.* Same note as in Tyndale.

14 the edge of the ſwerde, ſaue the wemē and the childern
and the catell and all that is in the citie and all the
ſpoyle thereof take vnto thy ſelfe and eate the ſpoyle
of thyne enemies which the Lord thy God geueth the.
15 Thus thou ſhalt doo vnto all the cities whiche are a
greate waye of from the ād not of the cities of theſe
nacions.

16 But in the cities of theſe nacions which the Lorde
thy God geueth the to enheret, thou ſhalt ſaue alyue
17 nothinge that bretheth. But ſhalt deſtroye them with
out redempcion, both the Hethites, the Amorites, the
Cananites, the Pherezites, the Heuites and the Iebuſites, as the Lorde thy God hath commaunded the,
18 that they teach you not to doo after all their abhominacyons whiche they doo vnto theire goddes, and ſo
ſhulde ſynne agenſt the Lorde youre God

19 When thou haſt beſeged a citie longe tyme in makinge warre agenſt it to take it. deſtroye not the trees
thereof, that thou woldeſt thruſt an axe vnto them.
For thou mayſt eate of thē, and therſore deſtroye them
not. For the trees of the feldes are no men, that they
20 myght come agenſt the to beſege the. Neuerthelater
thoſe [Fo. XXXVII.] trees which thou knoweſt that
mē eate not of them, thou maiſt deſtroye and cutte
them doune and make bolwerkes agenſt the citie that
maketh warre with the, vntyll it be ouerthrowne.

V. 14 Omnem prædam exercitui diuides .. de ſpoliis 15 & non ſunt de his vrbibus quas in poſſeſſionem accepturus es. 17 ſed interficies in ore gladii 19 nec ſecuribus per circūitum debes vaſtare regionem . . . nec poteſt bellantium contra te augere numerum. 20 non ſunt pomifera, ſed agreſtia & in cæteros apta vſus, ſuccide & inſtrue machinas

L. 14 allen raub ſoltu vnter dich austeylen . . . von der ausbeut 15 vnd nicht hie von den ſtedten ſind diſer völcker. 17 ſondern ſolt ſie verbannen 19 das du mit exten dran fariſt . . . Iſts doch holtz auff dem feld . . . vnd kan nicht zum bolwerg komen widder dich. 20 bolwerg draus bawen.

¶ The .XXI. Chapter.

1 YF one be founde ſlayne in the
land whiche the Lorde thy
God geueth the to poſſeſſe it,
and lieth in the feldes, and
2 not knowne who hath ſlayne him: Then
let thine elders and thy iudges come forth
ād meet vnto the cities that are rounde
3 aboute the ſlayne. And let the elders of
that citie which is nexte vnto the ſlayne
mā, take an heyffer that is not laboured
4 with nor hath drawen in the iocke, and
let them bringe her vnto a valeye where
is nether earinge nor ſowenge, ād ſtrike
of hir heed there in the valey.

M.C.S. *The purgacion of hym that is founde deed & is not knowen how he was ſlayne. How we ought to take to wyfe her that is takē in warre. The ryght of thefyrſt begotten. The punnyſhment of the ſonne that is dyſobedyent to hys father and mother.*

5 Then let the preaſtes the ſonnes of Leui come forth
(for the Lorde thy God hath choſen them to miniſtre
and to bleſſe in the name off the Lorde and therfore at
6 their mouthe ſhall all ſtrife and plage be tryed). And
all the elders of the citie that is nexte to the ſlayne
man ſhall waſſhe their handes ouer the heyffer that is
7 beheded in the playne, and ſhall anſwere ād ſaye: oure
handes haue not ſhed this bloude ne- .P. ther haue oure
8 eyes ſene it. Be mercifull Lord vnto thy people Iſrael
which thou haſt delyuered and put not innocent bloude
vnto thy people Iſrael: and the bloude ſhalbe forgeuen

V. 2 & metientur a loco cadaueris ſingularum per circumitum ſpatia ciuitatum 3 quæ non traxit iugum, nec terram ſcidit vomere 4 vallem aſperam et ſaxoſam, quæ nunquam arata eſt, nec ſementem recepit 5 & ad verbum eorum omne negotium pendet: & quicquid mundum vel immundum eſt, iudicetur. 7 & dicent 8 Et auferetur ab eis reatus ſanguinis

L. 2 vnd von dem erſchlagenen meſſen an die ſtedte die vmbherliegen 3 da mit man nicht geerbeyttet hat, noch am ioch gezogen hat 4 ynn eynen kieſichten grund, der widder geerbeytet noch beſeet iſt 5 nach yhrem mund ſollen alle ſach vnd alle plage gehandelt werden 7 vnd ſollen antwortten vnd ſagen 8 So werden ſie vber dem blut verſunet ſeyn

9 thē And ſo ſhalt thou put innocent bloud frō the,
when thou ſhalt haue done that which is
right in the ſyght of the Lorde.
10 When thou goeſt to warre agenſt thyne
enemies and the Lorde thy God hath delyuered them
in to thine handes and thou haſt take them captyue,
11 and ſeiſt amonge the captyues a bewtifull woman and
haſt a fantaſye vnto her that thou woldeſt
12 haue her to thy wyfe. Then bringe her
home to thine houſſe and let her ſhaue hir heed and
13 pare hir nayles ād put hir rayment that ſhe was taken
in from hir, and let hir remayne in thine houſſe and be
wepe hir father and hir mother a moneth long and
after that goo in vnto her ād marie her ād let her be
14 thi wife. And yf thou haue no fauoure vnto her, then
let her go whother ſhe luſteth: for thou mayſt not ſell
her for monye nor make cheueſaūce of her,
becauſe thou haſt hūbled her.
15 Yf a man haue two wyues, one loued and a nother
hated, and they haue borne him children, both the loued
and alſo the hated. Yf the firſtborne be the ſonne of the
16 hated: then whē [Fo. XXXVIII.] he deal-
eth his goodes amonge his childern, he
maye not make the ſonne of the beloued firſtborne before the ſonne of the hated whiche is in deade the firſt-
17 borne: But he ſhall knowe the ſonne off the hated for

Right in the lordes ſighte, ād not in thyne imaginacion.

fantaſye, *liking, fondneſs*

cheueſaunce, *bargain*

dealeth, *divideth*

V. 9 tu autem alienus eris ab innocentis cruore qui fuſus eſt, cum feceris quod præcepit dominus. 11 adamaueris eam 13 & poſtea intrabis ad eam, dormieſque cum illa 14 non ſederit animo tuo . . . nec opprimere per potentiam 17 ſed filium odioſæ agnoſcet

L. 9 Alſo ſoltu das vnſchuldige blut von dyr thun, das du thueſt was recht iſt fur den augen d. H. 11 haſt luſt zu yhr . . . 12 beſcheren 14 wenn du aber nicht luſt zu yhr haſt 14 verkeuffen noch verſetzen 17 ſondern . . . erkennen

M. M. N. 9 *Innocēt bloud:* The Chald. interpre. him that ſhedeth innocēt bloude. 11 *Haue her to thy wyfe:* Here were they permytted to take a wife of the gentyles but fyrſt to ſhaue her head & cut her nayles &c. which ceremony ſygnifyed that ſhe ſhuld be inſtruct to cutt a waye the wantoneſſe, & ſuperfluouſe deckyng with the delycate condycions of the gentyles, leſt the cleane people of the Iewes ſhulde in ſhort ſpace abhorre her, yf ſhe contynued in her olde maners. 14 *Haſt humbled her,* that is, afflyct vexed & greued her by takīg awaye her father contrey & goodes &c. as in the Pſal. xxxvii, b.

his firſtborne, that he geue him dowble off all that he
hath. For he is the firſt off his ſtrength, and to him
belongeth the right of the firſtborneſhippe.
18 Yf any man haue a ſonne that is ſtuburne, and diſobedient, that he will not herken vnto the voyce of
his father and voyce of his mother, and they haue
taught him nurture, but he wolde not herken vnto
19 them: Then let his father and his mother take him
and brynge hym out vnto the elders of that citie and
20 vnto the gate of that ſame place, ād ſaye vnto the
elders of the citie. This oure ſonne is ſtoburne and
diſobedient and will not herken vnto oure voyce, he
21 is a ryoter and a dronkarde. Then let all the men of
that citie ſtone him with ſtones vnto deeth. And ſo
thou ſhalt put euell awaye from the, and all Iſrael ſhall
heare and feare.
22 Yf a man haue commytted a treſpace worthy of
deeth and is put to deeth for it and hanged on tree:
23 let not his body remayne all nyghte vppon the tree,
but burye hym .P. the ſame daye. For the curſe off
God is on him that is hanged. Defile not thy londe
therfore, whiche the Lorde thy God geueth the to
enherett.

The .XXII. Chapter.

1 YF thou ſe thy brothers oxe or
ſhepe goo aſtraye, thou ſhalt
not with drawe thy ſelfe from
them: But ſhalt brynge them
2 home agayne vnto thy brother. Yf thy

M.C.S. *What thou oughteſt to do when thou fyndeſt thy neyghboures beaſt goyngaſtraye.*

M. 21 And t .u ſhalt put

V. 17 iſte eſt enim principium liberorum eius 19 ad portam iudicii 20 contemnit, comeſſationibus vacat, & luxuriæ atque conuiuiis 21 vt auferatis malum 22 morte plectendum eſt, & adiudicatus morti appenſus fuerit in patibulo. xxii, 1 Non videbis . . . & præteribis: ſed reduces

L. 17 Denn der ſelb iſt der anfang ſeynes vermugens 20 vnd iſt eyn ſchwelger vnd truncken bolt 21 das boſe 22 des todes wirdig iſt, vnd wirt alſo getodt das man yhn auff eyn holtz henget. xx, 1 Wenn du . . . ſiheſt . . . ſo ſoltu dich nicht entzihen

brother be not nye vnto the or yf thou
knowe him not, then bringe them vnto
thine awne houſſe and lett them be with
the, vntyll thy brother axe after them, and
3 then delyuer him them agayne. In like
maner ſhalt thou doo with his aſſe, with
his rayment and with all loſt thinges of
thy brother which he hath loſt and thou
haſt founde, and thou maiſt not withdrawe thy ſelfe.
4 Yf thou ſe that thy brothers aſſe or oxe
is fallen doune by the waye, thou ſhalt
not withdrawe thy ſelfe from them: but
ſhalt helpe him to heue them vp agayne.
5 The woman ſhall not weere that whiche pertayneth
vnto the man, nether ſhall a man put on womans rayment. For all that doo ſo, are abhomynacyon vnto
the Lorde thi God.
6 Yf thou chaunce vppon a byrds neſt by the [Fo.
XXXIX.] waye, in what ſoeuer tree it be or on the
groũde, whether they be younge or egges, ãd the
dame ſittenge vppon the younge or vppõ the egges:
7 Thou ſhalt not take the mother with the younge.
But ſhalt in any wyſe let the dame go and take the
younge, that thou mayſt proſpere and prolonge thy
dayes.
8 When thou byldeſt a new houſſe, thou ſhalt make

A man ſhall not were wemens clothyng or a womã manes clothyng. To weare a cote of woolle & of flaxe is also forbiddẽ. The punnyſhement of hym that accuſeth a man vnrighteouſly: of an aduowtrer also & of hym that rauyſheth a mayde.

M. 2 aſke

V. 2 quærat . . . & recipiat. 3 ne negligas quaſi alienam. 4 non deſpicies, ſed ſubleuabis cum eo. 5 apud deum 7 abire patieris

L. 2 ſuche, vnd denn yhm widder gebiſt 3 du kanſt dich nicht entzihen. 4 ſondern ſolt yhm auff helffen. 7 ſolt die mutter fliegen laſſen

M. M. X. 5 It is not here forbyddẽ but that to cxtue (*sic*) or auoyde Ieopardye, or to paſſe the tyme merely or to begile oure enemyes a womã may were a mans harneſſe or veſtimentes & contrarywyſe a man womãs clothes: but that they be not erneſtly & cuſtomablye vſed, that due honeſty & dignitye may be obſerued of bothe kyndes: ſeyng to do other wyſe is vncomely. 6 *The mother with the younge:* Thou ſhalt not kil the mother, etc. This lawe will no moare but that in dealinge mercifully with beaſtes we ſhulde lerne mercyfulneſſe vnto oure neyghboures. 8 *A new houſe:* The houſes be flat in thoſe contreys.

a batelmēt vnto the roffe, that thou lade not bloude vppon thine houſſe, yf any mā fall there of.

The houſſes be flattin thoſe cōtres.

9 Thou ſhalt not ſowe thy vyneyarde with dyuerſe ſede: leſt thou halowe the ſede whiche thou haſt ſowen with the frute off thy vyneyarde.

10 Thou ſhalt not plowe with an oxe ād an aſſe togetherr

11 Thou ſhalt not weere a garment made of woll and flax together.

12 Thou ſhalt put rybandes vpō the .iiii. quarters of thy veſture wherewith thou coulereſt thy ſelfe.

13 Yf a man take a wyfe and when he hath lyen with
14 her hate her ād leye ſhamefull thinges vnto hyr charge
and brynge vp an euell name vppon her and ſaye: I
toke this wyfe, and whē I came to her, I founde her
15 not a mayde: Thē let the father of the damſell and the
mother .P. brynge forth the tokens of the damſels virginite, vnto the elders of the citie, euen vnto the gate.
16 And let the damſels father ſaye vnto the elders, I gaue
my doughter vnto this man to wife and he hateth her:
17 and loo, he layeth ſhamefull thinges vnto hir charge
ſaynge, I founde not thy doughter a mayde. And yet
theſe ar the tokens of my doughters virginite. And
let them ſprede the veſture before the elders off the citie.

V. 8 murum tecti per circūitum: ne effundatur ſanguis in domo tua, & ſis reus labente alio, & in præceps ruente. 9 ne & ſementis quam ſeuiſti, & quæ naſcuntur ex vinea, pariter ſanctificētur. 11 contextum 12 quatuor angulos pallii tui 13 & poſtea odio habuerit eam, 14 quæſieritque occaſiones . . . obiiciens ei nomen peſſimum 15 tollent eam . . . & ferent 17 imponit ei nomen peſſimum . . . hæc ſunt ſigna

L. 8 eyn lehnen drumb auff d. dache, auff das du nicht blut auff deyn haus ladiſt 9 das du nicht zur fulle heyligeſt . . . ſampt dem eynkomen des weynbergis. 11 zu gleych gemenget. 12 an den vier ſittigen deynes mantels 13 vnd wirt yhr gram, wenn er ſie beſchlaffen hat, 14 vnd legt yhr was ſchendlichs auff 15 ſie nemen, vnd fur die Eltiſten der ſtad yn dem thor eraus bringen 17 vnd legt eyn ſchendlich ding auff ſie

M. M. N. 9 *With diuerſe ſeede* for then the one ſhulde hurte the other: ſo the maners & dealig of men may not be double but ſingle ſymple agreable in opinions & not of contrary ſectes & dyuerſe doctrynes. 10 To not plowe with an oxe and an aſſe and not to were a garmēt of wollen & lynē do meane both one thyng, and are expounded in Leuiti. xix, d.

18 Then let the elders of that citie take that man and
19 chaſtyce him and merce him in an hundred ſycles of
ſyluer and geue them vnto the father of the damſell,
becauſe he hath brought vpp an euell name vppon a
mayde in Iſrael. And ſhe ſhalbe his wife, and he maye
20 not put her awaye all his dayes. But and yf the thinge
be of a ſuertie that the damſell be not founde a virgen,
21 let them brynge her vnto the dore of hir fathers houſſe,
and let the men of that citie ſtone her with ſtones to
deeth, becauſe ſhe hath wrought folye in Iſrael, to
playe the whore in hir fathers houſſe. And ſo thou
ſhalt put euell awaye from the.

22 Yf a man be founde lyenge with a woman, that
hath a wedded huſbonde, then let thē
dye etherother of thē: both the man that
laye with the wife and alſo the wife: ſo
ſhalt thou put awaye euell from Iſrael.

etherother, *both the one and the other*

23 Yf a mayde be hanſaſted vnto an huſbonde, and then a man finde her in the
24 towne and leye with her, then ye ſhall
brynge them both out vnto the gates of that ſame citie
and ſhall ſtone them with ſtones to deeth: The damſell
becauſe ſhe cried not beynge in the citie: And the man,
becauſe he hath humbled his neyghbours wife, and thou
ſhalt put awaye evell from the.

hanfaſted, i. e. *handfaſted, betrothed*

25 But yf a man finde a betrothed damſell in the felde
and force her and leye with her: Thē the man that
26 laye with her ſhall dye alone, and vnto the damſell
thou ſhalt doo no harme: becauſe there is in the damſell no cauſe of deeth. For as when a man ryſeth

V. 19 quos dabit . . diffamauit nomen peſſimum . . . non poterit dimittere eam 20 non eſt in puella inuenta virginitas: 21 eiicient eam . . . quoniam fecit nefas in Iſrael . . . & auferes malum (vv. 22, 24) 22 morietur, id eſt, adulter & adultera 23 Si puellam. deſponderit vir . . . 24 quia humiliauit vxorem proximi ſui. 25 & apprehendens concubuerit cum ea, ipſe morietur ſolus 26 quoniam ſicut latro

L. 19 ſeyn leben lang nicht laſſen muge. 20 Iſts aber die warheyt, das . . . nicht iſt iungfraw funden 21 torheyt in Iſr. begangen hat . . das boſe (vv. 22, 24) 22 der man vnd das weyb, bey dem er geſchlaffen hat 23 yemand vertrawet iſt 24 geſchrien hat 25 auff dem felde krieget, vnd ergreyfft ſie vnd ſchlefft bey yhr . . . der man alleyne ſterben 26 Sondern gleych wie yemand

agenſte his neyghboure and ſleyeth him, euē ſo is this
27 matter. For he founde her in the feldes and the betrothed damſell cried: but there was no mā to ſuccoure
her.

28 Yf a man finde a mayde that is not betrothed ād
29 take her ād lye with her ād be founde: Then the man
that laye with her ſhall geue vnto the damſells father
L. ſycles of ſyluer. And ſhe ſhall be his wife, becauſe
he hath humbled her, and he maye not put her awaye
all hys dayes.

30 No man ſhall take his fathers wife, nor vnheale his
fathers couerynge.

ℭ The .XXIII. Chapter

M.C.S. What maner of men may not be admyt in to the churche. Pollucios that happe in the night. Vſurie.

1 NONE that is gelded or hath his
preuey membres cutt of, ſhall
come in to the congregacion
2 of the Lorde. And he that is
borne of a comen woman ſhall not come
in- the congregacion of the Lorde, no in
the tenth generacyon he ſhall not entre in to the con-
3 gregacyon of the Lorde. The Ammonites and the
Moabites ſhall not come in to the cōgregacyon of the
Lorde, no not in the tenth generacion, no they ſhall

M. 2 in to the congregacyō

T. 26 animam eius: ita et puella perpeſſa eſt. 27 liberaret eam. 28 & res ad iudicium venerit 29 cunctis diebus vitæ ſuæ. 30 nec reuelabit operimentum eius. xxiii, 1 eunuchus attritis vel amputatis teſticulis, & abſciſo veretro 2 mamzer, hoc eſt de ſcorto natus . . . vſque

L. 26 ſchluge ſeyne ſeele todt, ſo iſt dis auch 27 ſchrey, vnd war niemant der yhr halff. 28 vnd werden gefunden 29 nicht laſſen ſeyn leben lang. 30 nicht auff decken ſeyns vaters decke. xxiii, 1 gebrochener noch verſchnyttener 2 hurkind . . . auch nach dem zehenden gelid, ſondern ſol ſchlecht nicht

M. M. N. 29 What humble ſignifieth here loke Thren. v. b. xxiii, 1 *To come into the cōgregacyon* is to haue office or myniſtracion, amōg the congregacion: which no deformed perſon myght haue: leſt his deformytye ſhuld be an occaſyon to deſpyſe the offyce or admynyſtracion wherin he was ordeyned.

4 neuer come in to the cōgregacion of the Lorde, because they met you not with bred and water in the
waye when ye came out of Egipte, and because they
hyred agenst the Balaam the sonne of Beor the inter-
5 preter of Mesopotamia, to curse the. Neuerthelesse
the Lorde thy God wolde not herken vnto Balaam, but
turned the curse to a blessinge vnto the, because the
6 Lorde thy God loued the. Thou shalt neuer therfore
seke that which is prosperouse or good for them all
thy dayes for euer.

7 Thou shalt not abhorre an Edomite, for he is thy
brother: nether shalt thou abhorre an Egiptian, because
8 thou wast a straunger in hys londe. The childern that
are begotten of them shall come in to the congregacyon of the Lorde in the .iii. generacion.

9 [Fo. XLI.] When thou goest out with the host
agenst thine enemies, kepe the frō all wekednesse for
the Lorde is amonge you.

10 Yf there be any man that is vncleane by the reason
of vnclennesse that chaunceth hym by nyght, let him
11 goo out of the host and not come in agayne vntyll he
haue washed him selfe with water before the euen: ād
then whē the sonne is doune, let him come in to the
host agayne.

12 Thou shalt haue a place without the host whother
13 thou shalt resorte to and thou shalt haue a sharpe poynte
at the ende of thy wepon: and when thou wilt ease thy
selfe, digge therewith and turne and couer that which

V. 4 quia conduxerunt contra 6 Non facies cum eis pacem, nec quæris eis bona 7 nec Ægyptium 9 re mala. 10 Si fuerit inter vos . . . nocturno pollutus sit somnio 12 ad requisita naturæ 13 gerens paxillum in balteo

L. 4 widder euch dingeten 6 Du solt yhn widder glück noch heyl wundschen deyn leben lang ewiglich. 7 nicht fur grewel halten 9 fur allem bosen. 10 Wenn yemand vnter dyr ist, der nicht reyn ist, das yhm des nachts was widder faren ist 12 zur nott hynaus

M. M. N. 13 *Wepon:* If soche polycies must be hadde in sowdyars tentes to kepe thē cleane, moch moare in cyties and townes. If soche a thyng, which of it selfe is not euell, must be so ernestly seene to: what syngular prouysyō ought ther to be hadde that no opē whoredom̄e, aduowtrye, theft, pollyng, exaccion etc. were vsed.

14 is departed from the. For the Lorde thy God walk-
eth in thyne hoſt, to rydd the and to ſett thine enemyes before the. Let thine hoſt be pure that he ſe no vncleane thinge amonge you and turne from you.
15 Thou ſhalt not delyuer vnto his maſter the ſeruaunt
16 which is eſcaped from his maſter vnto the. Let him dwel with the, euẽ amonge you in what place he him ſelſe liketh beſt, in one of thi cities where it is good for him, and vexe him not.
17 There ſhalbe no whore of the doughters of Iſrael,
18 nor whorekeper of the ſonnes of Iſrael .¶. Thou ſhalt nether brynge the hyre of an whore nor the pryce of a dogge in to the houſſe of the Lorde thy God, in no maner of vowe: for euẽ both of them are abhominacion vnto the Lorde thy God.

The pope wil take tribute of them yet ād biſſhopes, ād abottes deſire no better tenauntes.

19 Thou ſhalt be no vſurer vnto thy brother, nether in mony nor in fode, nor in any maner thinge that is lent
20 vppon vſerye. Vnto a ſtraũger thou maiſt lende vppon vſerye, but not vnto thy brother, that the Lorde thy God maye bleſſe the in all that thou ſetteſt thyne hande to in the londe whother thou goeſt to conquere it.
21 When thou haſt vowed a vowe vnto the Lorde thy God, ſe thou be not ſlacke to paye it. For he will ſurely requyre it of the, and it ſhalbe ſynne vnto the.
22 Yf thou ſhalt leue vowinge, it ſhalbe no ſynne vnto
23 the: but that which is once gone out off thy lippes, thou muſt kepe and doo, accordynge as thou haſt vowed vnto the Lorde thy god a frewiloffrynge whiche thou haſt ſpoken with thy mouth.
24 When thou comeſt in to thy neghboures vyneyarde,

V. 14 vt eruat te 16 in loco qui ei placuerit . . . ne contriſtes eum. 17 ſcortator 20 ſed alieno. Fratri autem tuo abſque vſura id quod indiget, cõmodabis 23 ſicut promiſiſti domino deo tuo, & propria voluntate & ore tuo locutus es.

L. 14 das er dich erredte 16 ſolt yhn nicht ſchinden. 17 hurer 20 An dem frembden magſtu wuchern

M. M. N. 18 *The hyre,* etc. There be now many that deſyre no beter rentes.

thou mayſt eate grapes thy belyfull at thine awne pleaſure: but thou ſhalt put none in thy bagge.
25 When thou goeſt in to thy neyghbours corne,
thou mayſt plucke the eares with thine hād [Fo. XLII.] but thou mayſt not moue a ſycle vnto thy neghbours corne.

ℂ The .XXIIII. Chapter.

1 WHEN a man hath taken a wyfe
and maried her, yf ſhe finde
no fauoure in his eyes, becauſe
he hath ſpied ſome vnclenneſſe
in her. Then let him write her a bylle
of devorcement and put it in hir hande
2 and ſende her out of his houſſe. Yf when
ſhe is departed out of his houſſe, ſhe goo
3 and be another mans wife and the ſeconde
huſbonde hate her and write her a letter of deuorcement and put it in hir hande and ſende her out of his houſſe, or yf the ſeconde man dye whiche toke her to
4 wyfe. Hir firſt man whiche ſent hir awaye maye not
take her agayne to be his wyfe, in as moche as ſhe is defiled. For that is abhominacyon in the ſyght of the Lorde: that thou defile not the lōde with ſynne, which the Lorde thy God geueth the to enherett.
5 When a man taketh a newe wyfe, he ſhall not goo
a warrefare nether ſhalbe charged wyth any buſyneſſe: but ſhalbe fre at home one yere and reioyſe with his wife whiche he hath taken.

M.C.S. Deuorcement is permytted. He that is newly maryed ſhall not be compelled to go to warre. The remnaunte of corne muſt be left in herueſt for the poore.

F. 24 quantum tibi placuerit: foras autem ne efferas tecum. 25 falce autem non metes. xxiiii, 1 propter aliquam fœdidatem 2 Cumque egreſſa alterum maritum duxerit 3 oderit eam, . . domo ſua, . . fuerit 4 polluta eſt, & abominabilis facta . . ne peccare facias terram tuam 5 non procedet ad bellum, nec ei quippiam neceſſitatis iniungetur publice

L. 24 bis du ſatt habiſt, aber du ſolt nichts ynn deyn geſeſs thun. 25 nicht drynnen hyn vnd her faren. xxiiii, 1 vmb etwa eyner vnluſt willen 4 nach dem ſie iſt vnreyn vnd eyn grewel fur dem HERRN, Auff das du das land nicht zu ſunden machiſt 5 yhm nichts aufflegen.

6 .P. No mā ſhall take the nether or the vpper milſtone to pledge, for then he taketh a mans lyfe to pledge.
7 Yf any man be founde ſtealynge any of his brethern
the childern of Iſrael, ād maketh cheueſaunce of him
or ſelleth him, the thefe ſhall dye. And thou ſhalt
put euell awaye from the.
8 Take hede to thy ſelfe as concernynge the plage of
leproſye, that thou obſerue diligently to doo acordinge
to all that the preaſtes the leuites ſhall
teach the, as I commaunded them ſo ye
9 ſhall obſerue to doo. Remembre what
the Lorde thy God dyd vnto Mir Iam
by the waye, after that ye were come out
off Egipte.

Do as the preaſtes teache you: but as I haue taughte thē and not as they fayne.

10 Yf thou lende thy brother any maner ſoker, thou
11 ſhalt not goo in to his houſſe to fetche a pledge: but
ſhalt ſtonde without and the man to whom thou lend-
12 eſt, ſhall brynge the the pledge out at the dore. Forthermore yf it be a pore body, goo not to ſlepe with
his pledge: but delyuer hym the pledge agayne by that
13 the ſonne goo doune, and let him ſlepe in his owne
rayment and bleſſe the. And it ſhalbe rightuouſnes
vnto the, before the Lorde thy God.
14 Thou ſhalt not defraude an hyred ſervaunte that is
nedye and poore, whether he be off thy [Fo. XLIII.]
brethern or a ſtraunger that is in thy lond with in thy
15 cities. Geue him his hyre the ſame daye, and let not the

V. 6 quia animam ſuam appoſuit tibi. 7 Iſrael, & vendito eo acceperit pretium 8 ſacerdotes Leuitici generis . . . & imple ſolicite. 10 Cum repetes 11 proferet quod habuerit. 14 indigentis, & pauperis fratris tui

L. 6 denn er hat dyr die ſeel zu pfand geſetzt. 7 eyn ſeele ſtilet . . . verſetzt odder verkeufft ſie 10 yrgent eyne ſchuld borgeſt 14 nicht vervorteylen das lohn des bnöttigeten vnd armen

M. M. X. 6 By the nether or vpper mylſtone is ſignyfyed any thinge which is neceſſarily requyred to a borower or debtour, wherof he nouryſſheth & ſuſtayneth hym ſelfe, that may no creditoure take frō him, in eſpeciall his crafte & occupacyō wherō he chefely liueth may he not, by enpreſonnement (which ſome moſt cruelly do) kepe hym from: Leſt he be compelled to paye his dett with double diſprofet. One, that his milſtone is idell in the meane tyme. Another, that he is conſtrayned to come further in dett otherwayſe: or to ſell his neceſſary goodes with out which he cannot lyue, to makepayment.

ſonne goo doune thereon. For he is nedye ād therewith ſuſteyneth his life, leſt he crye agenſt the vnto
the Lorde ād it be ſynne vnto the.
16 The fathers ſhal not dye for the childern nor the
childern for the fathers: but euery mā ſhall dye for
his awne ſynne.
17 Hynder not the right of the ſtraunger nor of the
18 fatherleſſe, nor take wedowes rayment to pledge. But
remembre that thou waſt a ſervaunte in Egipte, ād how
the Lord thy God delyuered the thēce. Wherfore I
cōmaūde the to doo this thinge.
19 When thou cutteſt doune thyne herueſte in the felde
and haſt forgotte a ſhefe in the felde thou ſhalt not
goo agayne and fett it: But it ſhalbe for the ſtraunger, the fatherleſſe and the wedowe, that the Lorde
thy God maye bleſſe the in all the workes of thyne
20 hande. When thou beateſt doune thyne oylue, trees thou
ſhalt not make cleane riddaunce after the: but it ſhalbe
21 for the ſtraunger, the fatherleſſe and the wedowe. And
when thou gathereſt thy vyneyarde, thou ſhalt not
gather cleane after the: but it ſhalbe for the ſtraunger,
22 the fatherleſſe and the wedowe. And remembre that
thou waſt a .P. ſeruaunte in the lond of Egipte: wherfore I cōmaunde the to doo this thinge.

¶ The .XXV. Chapter.

1 WHEN there is ſtrife betwene men,
let thē come vnto the lawe,
and let the iudges iuſtifie the
rightuous and condemne the
2 treſpeaſer. And yf the treſpeaſer be wor-

M.C.S. The punnyſhment of offendars. The lawe of reaſyng ſeed to the brother that is deed.

M. 1 If there be

V. 15 ſuſtentat animam ſuam 17 Non peruertes 20 collegeris . . non reuerteris vt colligas 21 non colliges remanentes racemos xxv. 1 & interpellauerint iudices, . . . iuſtitiæ palmam dabunt: . . . condemnabunt impietatis.

L. 15 erhelt ſeyne ſeele darauff 17 nicht beugen 20 abgeleſen . . . genaw ableſen . . . 21 weinberg geleſen . . genaw auffleſen. xxv, 1 fur gericht bringen . . . den gerechten rechtfertigen vnd den gotloſen verdamnen.

thy of ſtrypes, then let the iudge cauſe to take him doune and to bete him before *Meaſures and weyghtes.*
his face accordynge to his treſpace, vnto a certayne
3 numbre. XL. ſtripes he ſhall geue him and not paſſe:
leſt yf he ſhulde exceade and beate him aboue that with
many ſtripes, thi brother ſhuld appere vngodly before
thyne eyes.

4 Thou ſhalt not moſell the oxe that treadeth out
the corne.

5 When brethren dwell together and *It were hard to proue this a ceremonye*
one of them dye ād haue no childe, the
wyfe of the deed ſhall not be geuen out vnto a ſtraunger: but hir brotherlawe ſhall goo in vnto her and take
6 her to wife and marie her. And the eldeſt ſonne which
ſhe beareth, ſhall ſtonde vp in the name of his brother
which is deed, that his name be not put out in
Iſrael.

7 But and yf the man will not take his ſyſterlawe,
then let her goo to the gate vnto the el- [Fo. XLIIII.]
ders and ſaye: My brotherlawe refuſeth to ſterre vpp
vnto his brother a name in Iſrael, he will not marie
8 me. Then let the elders of his citie call vnto him and
comen with him. Yf he ſtonde and ſaye: I will not
take her, then let his ſyſterlawe goo vnto him in the
preſence of the elders and looſe his ſhowe of his fote
and ſpytt in his face and anſwere and ſaye.

9 So ſhall it be done vnto that man that will not
10 bylde his brothers houſſe. And his name ſhalbe called
in Iſrael, the vnſhoed houſſe.

M. 3 vngoodly 7 ſyſter in lawe (v. 8)

V. 2 Pro menſura peccati, erit & plagarum modus 3 non exedant: ne fœde laceratus 6 & primogenitum ex ea filium nomine illius appellabit 7 accipere vxorem frat. ſui quæ ei lege debetur . . . ad portam ciuitatis, & interpellabit . . dicetque 10 Domus diſcalceati.

L. 2 nach der mas vnd zal ſeyner miſſethat 3 ſo man mehr ſchlege gibt, er zu viel geſchlagen werd, vnd deyn bruder ſcheuſlich fur deynen augen ſey. 7 ſchwegeryn neme, ſo ſol ſie, ſeyne ſchwegeryn hinauff gehen vnter das thor . . . eyn namen zu erwecken 8 Wenn er denn ſteht 10 des Barfuſſers haus.

M. M. N. 3 *XL. ſtrypes:* Therfore had S. Paul no mo at any tyme. 2 Cor. xi, f. 6 *Which is deed:* So that he ſhulde be the chylde of the brother that deed was, & not his that gatt him

11 Yf when men ſtryue together, one with another, the
wife of the one rūne to, for to ryd hyr huſbonde out
of the handes of him that ſmyteth him and put forth
12 hir hande and take him by the ſecrettes: cutt of hir
hande, and let not thine eye pitie her.
13 Thou ſhalt not haue in thy bagge two maner
14 weyghtes, a greate and a ſmall: nether ſhalt thou haue
in thine houſe dyuerſe meaſures, a great ād a ſmall.
15 But thou ſhalt haue a perfect ād a iuſt meaſure: that
thy dayes maye be lengthed in the londe whiche the
16 Lorde thy God geueth the, For all that do ſoche thinges
ād all that doo vnright, are abhominacion vnright, *wrong*
vnto the Lorde thy God.
17 .P. Remembre what Amalech dyd vnto the by the
18 waye after thou cameſt out of Egipte, he mett the by
the waye and ſmote the hynmoſt of you, all that were
ouer laboured and dragged by hynde, when thou waſt
19 faynted and werye, and he feared not God. Therfore
when the Lorde thy God hath geuen the reſt from all
thyne enemyes rounde aboute, in the londe whiche
the Lorde thy God geueth the to enheret and poſſeſſe:
ſe that thou put out the name of Amalech from vnder
heauen, ād forget not.

M. 13 two maner of weyghtes

V. 11 iurgium viri duo, & vnus contra alterum rixari cœperit 12 nec flecteris ſuper eam vlla miſericordia. 15 pondus habebis iuſtum & verum, & modius æqualis & verus 16 abominatur . . . & auerſatur omnem iniuſtitiam. 19 requiem, & ſubiecerit . . . delebis

L. 11 leufft zu 12 auge ſol yhr nicht verſchonen. 15 vollig vnd recht gewicht . . . Epha 19 austilgen.

M. M. N. 11 *Put forth her hande* etc.: God wyll that a woman be moare ſhame faſt then ether to exercyſe the feate of a mā in feyghtynge or to touche that mēbre.

The .XXVI. Chapter.

1 WHEN thou art come in to the
londe whiche the Lorde thy
God geueth the to enherett
and haſt enioyed it and dwell-
2 eſt there in: take of the firſt of all the
frute of the erthe, which thou haſt brought in out of
the lande that the Lorde thy God geueth the and put
it in a maunde and goo vnto the place
which the Lorde thy God ſhall choſe to
3 make his name dwell there. And thou ſhalt come
vnto the preaſt that ſhalbe in thoſe dayes ād ſaye
vnto him I knowledge this daye vnto the Lorde thy
God, that I am come vnto the contre whiche the
Lorde ſware vnto oure fathers for to geue vs.
4 [Fo. XLV.] And the preaſt ſhall take the maunde out
of thine hande, and ſet it doune before the alter of the
5 Lorde thy God. And thou ſhalt anſwere ād ſaye before
the Lorde thy God: The Sirians wolde haue deſtroyed
my father, and he went doune in to Egipte ād ſogeorned
there with a few folke and grewe there vnto a nacyon
6 greate, myghtie and full of people. And the Egiptians
vexed vs ād troubled vs, and laded vs with cruell bond-
7 age. And we cried vnto the Lorde God of oure fathers,

M.C.S. *The fyrſt frutes and tythes to the Leuites, fatherleſſe, wedowes, and ſtraungers.*

maunde, *baſket*

V. 1 daturus eſt poſſidendam, & obtinueris eam 2 de cunctis frugibus tuis primitias, & pones . . vt ibi inuocetur nomen 3 Profiteor hodie coram domino 5 loqueris . . Syrus perſequebatur . . . in pauciſſimo numero . . . & infinitæ multitudinis.

L. 1 zum erbe geben wirt, vnd nympſt es eyn 2 die aus der erden komen 3 Ich verkundige heutt dem Herrn deynem Gott 5 antworten . . . Die Syrer wolten meynen vater vmb bringen

M. M. N. 5 *The Siriās would haue deſtroyed etc.:* The Chaldee interpret. readeth, The Sirian went aboute to deſtroye my father meanyng (as ſome ſuppoſe) laban, of whom Gene. xxxi. The .Lxx. my father left or forſoke Siria. The comē tranſlacyon readeth, the Sirian did perſequute my father: ſignifying, as ſome interpretate, that Siria the contrey of their fathers had expelled thē and thruſt them out.

and the Lorde herde oure voyce and loked on oure
8 aduersyte, laboure and oppressyon. And the Lorde
brought vs out of Egipte with a mightye hande and a
stretched out arme and with greate tereblenesse and
9 with sygnes and wonders. And he hath brought vs
in to this place and hath geuē vs this londe that floweth
10 with mylke and honye. And nowe loo, I haue brought
the first frutes off the londe whiche the Lorde hath
geuen me. And set it before the Lorde thy God and
11 worshepe before the Lorde thy God and reioyse ouer
all the good thinges whiche the Lorde thy God
hath geuē vnto the and vnto thyne housse, both
thou the Leuite and the straunger that is amonge
you.
12 When thou hast made an ende of tithynge .P. all
the tithes of thine encrease the thyrde yere, the yere
of tythynge: and hast geuen it vnto the Leuite, the
straunger, the fatherlesse ād the wedowe, and they
13 haue eaten in thy gates ād fylled them selues. Then
saye before the Lorde thy God: I haue brought the
halowed thinges out of myne housse: and haue geuen
them vnto the Leuite, the straunger, the fatherlesse and
the wedowe acordynge to all the commaundmentes
which thou commaundest me: I haue not ouerskypped
14 thy commaundmentes, nor forgetten them. I haue
not eaten thereof in my moornynge nor taken awaye
thereof vnto any vnclennesse, nor spente thereof aboute
any deed corse: but haue herkened vnto the uoyce of the
Lorde my God, and haue done after all that he com-
15 maūded me, loke doune from thy holy habitacyon
heauen and blesse thy people Israel and the lande which

V. 7 humilitatem nostram, & laborem atque angustias 8 et eduxit nos 9 introduxit 10 Et idcirco nunc offero . . . dominus dedit mihi. 12 Quando compleueris . . . vt comedant intra portas tuas, & saturentur 13 non præteriui mandata tua, nec sum oblitus imperii tui. 14 in re funebri . . . sicut præcepisti mihi. 15 sanctuario tuo, & de excelso cælorum habitaculo

L. 7 zwang, erbeyt and leyd 8 vnd furet vns aus 9 vnd bracht vns 10 Nu bringe ich . . . das der Herr vns geben hat. 12 zusammen bracht hast . . . das sie essen ynn deynem thor vnd satt werden. 14 nicht zu den todten dauon gegeben . . . wie du myr gepotten hast. 15 heyligen wonung vom hymel

thou haſt geuen vs (as thou ſwareſt vnto oure fathers)
a lond that floweth with mylke and honye.
16 This daye the Lorde thy God hath commaunded
the to doo theſe ordinaunces and lawes. Kepe them
therfore and doo them with all thyne hert and all thy
17 ſoule. Thou haſt ſett vpp the Lorde this daye to be
thy God and to walke in hys wayes and to kepe his
ordinaunces, his commaundmentes and his lawes, and
18 [Fo. XLVI.] to herken vnto his voyce. And the Lord
hath ſett the vp this daye, to be a ſeuerall
people vnto him (as he hath promyſed
19 the) and that thou kepe his commaundmentes, and to
make the hye aboue all nacyons which he hath made,
in prayſe, in name and honoure: that thou mayſt be an
holy people vnto the Lord thy God, as he hath ſayed.

ſeuerall, *ſeparate*

☙ The .XXVII. Chapter.

1 AND Moſes with the elders of
Iſrael cōmaunded the people
ſayenge: kepe all the commaundmentes which I com-
2 maunde you this daye. And when ye
be come ouer Iordayne vnto the londe
which the Lorde thy God geueth the,
ſett vpp greate ſtones and playſter them with playſ-
3 ter, and write vpō thē all the wordes of this lawe,

M.C.S. *An aultare muſt be bylded before they go ouer Iordan. The bleſſynges in the hyll Garizim. The Curſes in the hyll Eball.*

V. 17 Dominum elegiſti hodie . . 18 populus peculiaris, ſicut locutus eſt tibi 19 & faciat te excelſiorem cunctis gentibus quas creauit in laudem, & nomen, & gloriam ſuam xxvii, 2 dabit tibi (v. 3) . . calce leuigabis (v. 4)

L. 17 Dem Herrn haſtu heutte geredt 18 Vnd der Herr hatt dyr heut geredt . . . ſeym volck des eygenthums ſeyn ſolt wie er dyr geredt hat . . . vnd er dich das hohiſte mache zu lob, namen, vnd preyſs vber alle völcker. xxvii, 1 ſampt den Eltiſten 2 geben wirt (v. 3) . . kalck tunchen (v. 4)

M. M. N. 17 *Thou haſt ſett vp the Lorde etc.:* Or thou haſte cauſed to be ſayde that ẏ Lorde ſhulde be vnto the for thy God: or, as many will, he made the to ſaye, that is, he was the cauſe that thou ſhuldeſt ſaye, that the Lorde ſhulde be vnto ẏ for thy God.

when thou arte come ouer: that thou mayſt come
in to the londe whiche the Lorde thy God geueth the:
a londe that floweth with mylke and honye, as the
Lorde God off thy fathers hath promyſed the.
4 When ye be come ouer Iordayne, ſe that ye ſet vpp
theſe ſtones which I commaunde you this daye in
5 mount Eball, and playſter them with playſter. And
there bylde vnto the Lord thy God, an altare of
ſtones and ſe thou lifte .P. vpp no yerne uppon them:
6 But thou ſhalt make the altare of the Lorde thy God
of rughſtones and offer burntoffrynges thereon vnto
7 the Lorde thy God. And thou ſhalt offer peaceoffrynges and ſhalt eate there and reioyſe before the Lorde
8 thy God. And thou ſhalt write vppon the ſtones all
the wordes of this lawe, manyfeſtly and well
9 And Moſes with the preaſtes the Leuites ſpake vnto
all Iſrael ſayenge: take hede ād heare Iſrael, this daye
thou art become the people of the Lorde thy God.
10 Herken therfore vnto the voyce of the Lorde thi God
ād do his cōmaundmētes ād his ordinaunces which I
commaunde you this daye.
11 And Moſes charged the people the ſame daye ſay-
12 enge: theſe ſhall ſtonde vppon mount Griſim to bleſſe
the people, when ye are come ouer Iordayne: Symeon,
13 Leui, Iuda, Iſachar, Ioſeph and Ben Iamin. And theſe
ſhall ſtonde apon mount Eball to curſe: Ruben, Gad
14 Aſſer, Zabulon, Dan and Neptaly. And the Leuites
ſhall beginne ād ſay vnto all the men of Iſrael with a
loude voyce.
15 Curſed be he that maketh any carued
image or image of metall (an abhominacion vnto the Lorde, the worke of the
handes of the crafteſman) and putteth it
in a ſecrett place: [Fo. XLVII.] And all
the people ſhall anſwere and ſaye Amen.

Here of take the popes an occaſiō to curſe .iiii tymes in the yere

M. 12 Garizim

V. 5 quos ferrum non tetigit 6 ſaxis informibus & impolitis 8 plane et lucide. 10 audies vocem eius 15 ponetque illud in abſcondito.

L. 5 dar vber keyn eyſen feret 6 gantzen ſteynen 7 todopffer 8 klar vnd wol. 10 das du der ſtym des Herrn deyns Gottis gehorſam ſeyſt 15 vnd ſetzt es verporgen

16 Curſed be he that curſeth his father or hys mother,
and all the people ſhall ſaye Amen.
17 Curſed be he that remoueth his neghbours marke
and all the people ſhall ſaye Amen.
18 Curſed be he that maketh the blynde goo out off
his waye, and all the people ſhall ſaye Amen,
19 Curſed be he that hyndreth the right of the ſtraunger, fatherleſſe and wedowe, and all the people ſhall
ſaye Amen.
20 Curſed be he that lieth with his fathers wife becauſe
he hath opened his fathers coueringe, ād all the people
ſhall ſaye Amen.
21 Curſed be he that lieth with any maner beeſt, and
all the people ſhall ſaye Amen.
22 Curſed be he that lieth with his ſyſter whether ſhe
be the doughter of his father or off his mother, and all
the people ſhall ſaye Amen
23 Curſed be he that lieth with his mother in lawe, and
all the people ſhall ſaye Amen.
24 Curſed be he that ſmyteth his neghboure ſecretly,
and all the people ſhall ſaye Amē.
25 Curſed be he that taketh a rewarde to ſlee innocent
bloude, and all the people ſhall ſaye Amen.
26 Curſed be he that mātayneth not all the wor- .P. des
of this lawe to doo them, ād all the people ſhall ſaye
Amen.

V. 16 non honorat patrem 17 tranſfert 18 errare facit 19 peruertit iudicium 20 dormit cum vxore . . reuelat operimentum lectuli eius. 24 clam percuſſerit —*Maledictus qui dormit cum vxore proximi ſui. & dicet omnis populus, Amen* . . 25 animam ſanguinis innocentis. 26 permanet in ſermonibus legis huius, nec eos opere perficit.

L. 16 ſeym vater . . . flucht 17 grentze engert 18 yrren macht 19 das recht . . . beuget 20 bey ſeynes vaters weyb ligt . . . den flugel 24 heymlich ſchlecht 25 die ſeele des vnſchuldigen bluts 26 alle wort diſes geſetzs auffrichtet das er darnach thue

❡ The .XXVIII. Chapter

1 YF thou ſhalt herken diligently
vnto the voyce of the Lorde
thy God, to obſerue and to
do all his commaundmentes
whiche I commaunde the this daye. The
Lorde wil ſet the an hye aboue all nacions
2 of the erth. And all theſe bleſſynges ſhall
come on the and ouer take the, yf thou ſhalt herken
3 vnto the voyce of the Lorde thy God. Bleſſed ſhalt
4 thou be in the towne and bleſſed in the feldes, bleſſed
ſhalbe the frute of thy body, the frute of thy grounde
and the frute of thy catell, the frute of thine oxen, and
5 thy flockes of ſhepe, bleſſed ſhall thine
6 almery be ād thy ſtore. Bleſſed ſhalt
thou be, both when thou goeſt out, ād bleſſed whē
thou comeſt in.

M.C.S. *The promyſes of the bleſſynges vnto them that regarde the commaundementes: and the curſes to the contrarye.*

almery, *a cupboard*

7 The Lorde ſhall ſmyte thyne enemyes that ryſe
agenſt the before thy face. They ſhall come out agenſt
8 the one waye, and flee before the ſeuen wayes. The
Lorde ſhal commaunde the bleſſynge to be with the in
thy ſtore houſſes ād in all that thou ſetteſt thine hande
to, and will bleſſe the in the lande which the Lord thi
god geueth the.
9 The Lorde ſhall make the an holye people [Fo.
XLVIII.] vnto himſelfe, as he hath ſworen vnto the:

V. 1 Si autem audieris 2 & apprehendent te: ſi tamen . . audieris. 4 ventris . . . greges armentorum . . caulæ ouium 5 reliquiæ tuæ (v. 17). 6 Benedictus eris ingrediens & egrediens. 7 in conſpectu tuo. 8 Emittet dom. benedictionem ſuper cellaria . . opera manuum tuarum . . in terra quam acceperis.

L. 1 Vnd wenn . . . gehorchen wirſt 2 werden vber dich komen . . dich treffen (v. 15) darumb das du . . . biſt gehorſam geweſt. 4 fruchte deyner ochſen . . . fruchte deyner ſchaff 5 deyn vbrigs 6 Geſegnet . . . Geſegenet 8 gepieten dem ſegen . . . keller . . . fur handen nimpſt

L. M. N. 5 *Deyn korb:* das iſt alles was du beſeyt legeſt zu behalten vnd alles was du braucheſt.

yf thou ſhalt kepe the commaundmentes of the Lorde
thy God and walke in hys wayes.
10 And all nacyons of the erthe ſhall ſe that thou arte
called after the name of the Lorde, and they ſhalbe
11 aferde off the. And the Lorde ſhall make the plenteous in goodes, in the frute of thy body, in the frute
off thy catell and in the frute of thy grounde, in the
londe whiche the Lorde ſware vnto thy fathers to
geue the.
12 The Lorde ſhall open vnto the his good treaſure, euen the heauen, to geue rayne vnto thy
londe in due ceaſon and to bleſſe all the laboures
of thine hande. And thou ſhalt lende vnto many
nacyōs, but ſhalt not nede to borowe thy ſelfe.
13 And the Lorde ſhall ſett the before and not behinde,
and thou ſhalt be aboue only and not beneth: yf that
thou herken vnto the commaundmentes of the
Lorde thy God which I commaunde the this daye to
14 kepe and to doo them. And ſe that thou bowe not
from any of theſe wordes which I commaunde the this
daye ether to the right hande or to the lefte, that thou
woldeſt goo after ſtraung goddes to ſerue them.
15 But and yf thou wilt not herken vnto the voyce of
the Lorde thy God to kepe and to .P. doo all his commaundmentes and ordinaunces which I commaunde
the this daye: then all theſe curſes ſhall come vppon
16 the and ouertake the: Curſed ſhalt thou be in the
17 towne, and cursed in the felde, curſed ſhall thyne almery
18 be and thi ſtore. Curſed ſhall be the frute of thy body
ād the frute of thy lond be ād the frute of thine oxen
19 ād the flockes of thy ſhepe. And curſed ſhalt thou be
when thou goeſt in, ād whē thou goeſt out.
20 And the Lorde ſhall ſende vppon the curſynge,

V. 9 ſi cuſtodieris 11 fructu terræ tuæ quam iurauit 13 in caput, et non in caudam (v. 44): & eris ſemper ſupra, & non ſubter 14 non declinaueris 15 & apprehendent te.

L. 9 darumb das du . . . heltiſt 10 nach dem namen 13 zum heubt . . nicht zum ſchwantz (v. 44) vnd . . . oben ſchweben vnd nicht vnten liegen 14 nicht gewichen biſt

M. M. N. 14 *Bowe not from any* etc.: To bowe vnto the ryght hāde is to adde to the woorde of God, And to bowe vnto the lefte is to take awaye, as in the prouer .iiii, d.

goynge to nought and complaynyng in all that thou
ſetteſt thine hande to what ſoeuer thou doeſt: vntyll
thou be deſtroyed ād brought to nought quyckely, becauſe of the wekedneſſe of thyne invencyons in that
21 thou haſt forſaken the Lorde. And the Lorde ſhall
make the peſtilence cleaue vnto the, vntyll he haue
conſumed the from the londe whether thou goeſt to
22 enioye it. And the Lorde ſhall ſmyte the with ſwellynge, with feuers, heet, burnynge, wetherynge, with
ſmytynge and blaſtinge. And they ſhall folowe the,
vntyll thou periſhe.
23 And the heauen that is ouer thy heed ſhalbe braſſe,
and the erth that is vnder the, yerne.
24 And the Lorde ſhall turne the rayne of the lāde
vnto powder ād duſt: euen frō heauen they [Fo. XLIX.]
ſhal come doune vpō the, vntyll thou be brought to
25 nought. And the Lorde ſhall plage the before thine
enemyes: Thou ſhalt come out one waye agenſt them,
and flee ſeuen wayes before them, ād ſhalt be ſcatered
26 amonge all the kingdomes of the erth. And thy car-
caſſe ſhalbe meate vnto all maner foules of the ayre ād
vnto the beeſtes of the erth, and no man ſhall fraye
them awaye.
27 And the Lorde will ſmyte the with the botches of
Egipte and the emorodes, ſcalle and maungyneſſe,
28 that thou ſhalt not be healed thereof. And the Lorde
ſhall ſmyte the with madneſſe, blyndneſſe and daſynge

V. 20 famem & eſuriem, & increpationem . . . velociter, propter adinuentiones tuas peſſimas 21 Adiungat . . . peſtilentiam 22 egeſtate, ſebri & frigore, ardore & æſtu, et aere corrupto ac rubigine, & perſequatur 23 terra quam calcas 24 puluerem, & de cælo . . cinis 25 Tradat te dom. corruentem 26 abigat. 27 vlcere Ægypti, & partem corporis per quam ſtercora digeruntur, ſcabie quoque & prurigine 28 furore mentis

L. 20 bald vmbringe, vmb deynes boſen thuns willen 22 ſchwulſt, fiber, hitze, brand, brunſt, durre vnd bleyche, vnd wirt dich verfolgen 24 ſtaub, vnd aſſchen fur regen . . aſſchen vom hymel 26 ſcheucht. 27 druſen Egypti, mit feygwartzen, mit grind vnd kretz 28 raſen des hertzen . . .

L. M. N. 20 *Klagen:* das iſt wenn das volck klagt, heulet vnd ſchreyet vber die theurung vnd iamer ym land da alles ſich weg friſſet vnd vnterhenden verſchwindet, wilches geſchicht, das Gott dem land nicht ſegenet, ſondern flucht vnd ſchilt.

29 of herte. And thou ſhalt grope at none daye as the
blynde gropeth in darkeneſſe, and ſhalt not come to
the right waye.
And thou ſhalt ſuffre wronge only and
be polled euermore, and no man ſhall
30 ſoker the, thou ſhalt be betrothed vnto a
wiſe, and another ſhall lye with her. Thou ſhalt bylde
an houſſe and another ſhall dwell therein. Thou ſhalt
plante a vyneyarde, and ſhalt not make it comen.
31 Thine oxe ſhalbe ſlayne before thyne eyes, ād thou
ſhalt not eate thereof. Thine aſſe ſhalbe violently
taken awaye euen before thi face, and ſhall not be
reſtored the agayne. Thy ſhepe ſhalbe geuen vnto
thine enemyes, ād no .P. man ſhall helpe the.
32 Thy ſonnes ād thy doughters ſhall be geuē vnto
another nacion, and thyne eyes ſhall ſe and daſe vppon
them all daye longe, but ſhalt haue no myghte in thyne
33 hande. The frute of thy londe and all thy laboures
ſhall a nacyon which thou knoweſt not, eate, ād thou
ſhalt but ſoffre violence only and be oppreſſed alwaye:
34 that thou ſhalt be cleane beſyde thy ſelfe for the ſyghte
of thyne eyes whiche thou ſhalt ſe.
35 The Lord ſhall ſmyte the with a myſcheuous botche
in the knees ād legges, ſo that thou cāſt not be healed:
euē from the ſole of the fote vnto the toppe of the heed.
36 The Lorde ſhall brynge both the and thy kynge
which thou haſt ſett ouer the, vnto a nacyon whiche
nether thou nor thy fathers haue knowne, and there
thou ſhalt ſerue ſtraunge goddes: euen wodd ād ſtone.
37 And thou ſhalt goo to waſt ād be made an enſample
ād a geſtyngeſtocke vnto al naciōs whether the Lord ſhall carye the.
38 Thou ſhalt carie moch ſeed out in to

polled, *plundered, robbed*

ſoker, *ſuccor*

geſtyngeſtocke *a laughing-ſtock*

M. 29 at none dayes . . . ẏ ryght awaye 30 betrawthed

V. 29 non dirigas vias tuas . . . calumniam ſuſtineas, & opprimaris violentia 30 non habites in ea . . . non vindemies eam. 32 deficientibus ad conſpectum eorum 33 ſemper calumniam ſuſtinens, & oppreſſus 34 ſtupens ad terrorem eorum 37 eris perditus, in prouerbium ac fabulam

L. 30 nicht drynnen wonen 31 nicht gemeyn machen. 32 alle werden vber yhnen 34 wanſynnig 37 vnd wirſt verwuſtet, vnd eyn ſprich wort vnd fabel

the felde, and ſhalt gather but litle in: for the locuſtes
39 ſhall deſtroye it, Thou ſhalt plante a vyneyarde and
dreſſe it, but ſhalt nether drynke off the wyne nether
gather of the grapes,[Fo. L.] for the wormes ſhall eate
40 it. Thou ſhalt haue olyue trees in all thy coſtes, but
ſhalt not be anoynted with the oyle, for thyne olyue
41 trees ſhalbe rooted out. Thou ſhalt get ſonnes ād
doughters, but ſhalt not haue them: for they ſhalbe
42 caried awaye captyue. All thy trees and frute of thy
londe ſhalbe marred with blaſtynge.

43 The ſtraungers that are amonge you ſhall clyme
aboue the vpp an hye, ād thou ſhalt come doune be-
44 neth alowe. He ſhall lende the ād thou ſhalt not lende
him, he ſhalbe before ād thou behynde.

45 Moreouer all theſe curſes ſhall come vppō the and
ſhall folowe the and ouertake the, tyll thou be deſtroyed: becauſe thou herkenedeſt not vnto the voyce
of the Lorde thy God, to kepe his cōmaundmētes ād
46 ordinaunces whiche he cōmaūded the, ād they ſhalbe
vppō the as miracles ād wonders ād vppon thy ſeed
47 for euer. And becauſe thou ſeruedeſt not the Lorde
thy God with ioyfulneſſe and with a good herte for the
48 abundaunce of all thinges, therfore thou ſhalt ſerue
thyne enemye whiche the Lorde ſhall ſende vppon the:
in hunger and thruſt, in nakedneſſe and in nede off all
thynge: and he ſhall put a yocke off yerne vppon thyne
necke, vntyll he haue broughte .P. the to noughte.

49 And the Lorde ſhall brynge a nacion vppon the
from a farre, euen from the ende off the worlde, as
50 ſwyfte as an egle fleeth: a nacion whoſe tonge thou

M. 38 for the greſhoppers 49 flyeth

V. 40 quia defluent, & deperibunt 41 et non frueris eis 42 rubigo 43 deſcendes, & eris inferior. 46 Et erunt in te ſigna atque prodigia 47 in gaudio, cordiſque lætitia 49 in ſimilitudinem aquilæ volantis cum impetu

L. 40 ausgeriſſen 43 erunder ſteygen vnd ymer vnterligen 46 darumb werden zeychen vnd wunder an dyr ſeyn 47 mit frolichem vnd gutem hertzen 49 wie eyn Adeler fleuget

M. M. N. 42 *blaſtynge:* Or greſhoppers, ſome reade vermyn. 46 *as miracles and wonders:* Myracles do ſometyme ſtreangthen the weakneſſe of the faithfull and blynde the vnfaythfull, and be vnto them a wytneſſe of dānacyon.

ſhalt not vnderſtonde: a herde fauoured nacion whiche
ſhall not regarde the perſon of the olde nor haue com-
51 paſſiō on the younge. And he ſhall eate the frute of
thy londe and the frute of thy catell vntyll he haue
deſtroyed the: ſo that he ſhall leaue the nether corne,
wyne, nor oyle, nether the ēcreaſe of thyne oxen nor
the flockes of thy ſhepe: vntyll he haue brought the
52 to nought. And he ſhall kepe the in all thy cities,
vntyll thy hye ād ſtronge walles be come doune whereī
thou truſtedeſt, thorow all thy londe. And he ſhall
beſege the in all thy cities thorow out all thy land
whiche the Lorde thy God hath geuen the.
53 And thou ſhalt eate the frute of thyne awne bodye:
the fleſſh of thy ſonnes and off thy doughters which the
Lorde thy God hath geuen the, in that ſtrayteneſſe and
54 ſege wherewith thyne enemye ſhall beſege the: ſo that
it ſhall greue the man that is tender and exceadynge
delycate amonge you, to loke on his brother and vppon
his wife that lyeth in hys boſome ād on the remnaunte
55 of his childern, whiche he hath yet lefte, for feare of
geuynge [Fo. LI.] vnto any of them of the fleſh of hys
childern, whiche he eateth, becauſe he hath noughte
lefte him in that ſtrayteneſſe and ſege wherewith thyne
enemye ſhall beſege the in all thy cytyes.
56 Yee and the woman that is ſo tender and delycate
amonge you that ſhe dare not auenture to ſett the ſole
of hyr foote vppon the grounde for ſoftneſſe and ten-
derneſſe, ſhalbe greued to loke on the huſbonde that
leyeth in hir boſome and on hyr ſonne and on hyr
57 doughter: euen becauſe of the afterbyrthe that ys
come out from betwene hyr legges, and becauſe of hyr
childern whiche ſhe hath borne, becauſe ſhe wolde eate

M. 52 kepe the in, in all thy cities . . . thorow all the lande 56 aduēture

V. 50 gentem procaciſſimam, quæ non deferat 52 conterat . . . Obſideberis 53 in anguſtia & vaſtitate qua opprimet 55 in obſidione & penuria qua vaſtauerint 56 Tenera mulier & delicata (v. 54) . . . propter mollitiem & teneritudinem nimiam, inuidebit

L. 52 engſten . . . geengſtet werden 53 angſt vnd not (vv. 55, 57) 54 ein man der zuuor zertlich vnd ynn luſten . . vergonnen (cf. v. 56 Eyn weyb, etc.) 55 engſten 57 die affterburd die zwiſſchen yhr eygen beynen ſind ausgangen

them for nede off all thynges secretly, in the ſtrayteneſſe
and ſege wherewith thine enemye ſhall beſege the in
thy cities.
58 Yf thou wilt not be diligent to doo all the wordes
of this lawe that are wrytten in thys boke, for to feare
this glorious and fearfull name of the Lorde thy God:
59 the Lorde will ſmyte both the and thy ſeed with wonderfull plages and with greate plages and of longe contin-
uaunce, and with euell ſekeneſſes and of longe duraunce.
60 Moreouer he wyll brynge vppon the all the diſeaſes
off Egipte whiche thou waſt afrayed off, and they ſhall
61 clea- .P. ue vnto the. Thereto all maner ſekeneſſes
and all maner plages whiche are not wrytten in the
boke of this lawe, wyll the Lorde brynge vppon the
62 vntyll thou be come to noughte. And ye ſhalbe lefte
fewe in numbre, where to fore ye were as the ſtarres
off heauen in multitude: becauſe thou woldeſt not herkē
vnto the voyce of the Lorde thy God.
63 And as the Lorde reioyſed ouer you to do you good
and to multiplye you: euen ſo he will reioyſe ouer you,
to deſtroye you and to brynge you to nought. And
ye ſhalbe waſted from of the lande whother thou goeſt
64 to enioye it, And the Lorde ſhall ſcater the amonge
all nacyons from the one ende of the worlde vnto the
other, and there thou ſhalt ſerue ſtraunge goddes, which
nether thou nor thy fathers haue knowne: euen wod
and ſtone.
65 And amonge theſe nacyons thou ſhalt be no ſmall
ſeaſon, and yet ſhalt haue no reſte for the ſole of thy
foote. For the Lorde ſhall geue the there a trēblynge
66 herte ād daſynge eyes and ſorowe of mynde. And thy
lyfe ſhall hange before the, and thou ſhalt feare both daye

V. 58 nomen . . . hoc eſt dominum deum tuum 59 plagas magnas & perſeuerantes, infirmitates peſſimas & perpetuas 60 omnes afflictiones Ægypti 64 a ſummitate terræ vſque ad terminos eius 65 non quieſces . . . cor pauidum, & defic. oculos, & animam conſumptam mœrore 66 vita tua quaſi pendens ante te.

L. 58 namen den Herrn deynen Gott 59 wunderlich mit dyr vmbgehen 60 alle ſeuge Egypti 62 ewer wenig pubels vberbleyben 64 von eym end der welt bis ans ander 65 keyn wehre haben . . . bebendes hertz . . ammacht der augen . . verſchmachte ſeele, 66 das deyn leben wirt fur dyr hangen

67 and nyghte ād ſhalt haue no truſt in thy lyfe. In the
mornynge thou ſhalt ſaye, wolde God it were nyghte.
And at nyghte thou ſhalt ſaye, [Fo. LII.] wolde God
it were mornynge. For feare off thyne herte whiche
thou ſhalt feare, and for the ſyghte of thyne eyes whiche
thou ſhalt ſe.

68 And the Lorde ſhall brynge the in to Egipte agayne
with ſhippes, by the waye which I bade the that thou
ſhuldeſt ſe it nomoare. And there ye ſhalbe ſolde vnto
youre enemyes, for bondmen and bondwemen: and yet
no man ſhall bye you.

¶ The .XXIX. Chapter.

M.C.S. The people are exhorted to obſerue the cōmaundementes, for the conſyderacion of benefytes receaued: which yf they breake they are threatned to be plaged.

1 THESE are the wordes of the ap-
poyntmēt which the Lorde
commaunded Moſes to make
with the childern of Iſrael in
the londe of Moab, beſyde the appoyntment whiche he made with them in Horeb.
2 And Moſes called vnto all Iſrael and
ſayed vnto them: Ye haue ſene all that
the Lorde dyd before youre eyes in the
lande of Egipte, vnto Pharao and vnto all his
3 ſeruauntes, and vnto all his londe, and the greate
temptacyons whiche thyne eyes haue ſene and thoſe
4 greate myracles and wonders: and yet the Lorde
hath not geuen you an herte to perceaue, nor eyes
to ſe, nor eares to heare vnto this daye.
5 .P. And I haue led you .xl. yere in the wilderneſſe: and
youre clothes are not waxed olde vppon you, nor are
6 thy ſhowes waxed olde vppon thy fete. Ye haue eaten

V. 67 propter cordis tui formidinem, qua terreberis 68 per viam de qua dixit tibi xxix, 2 in terra Ægypti 3 ſigna illa portentaque ingentia 4 cor intelligens 5 Adduxit vos . . . attrita veſtimenta . . . calceamenta . . . vetuſtate conſumpta ſunt

L. 67 Wer gibt . . . Wer gibt . . . fur groſſer furcht . . die dich ſchrecken 68 durch den weg, dauon ich geſagt hab. xxix, 2 ynn Egypten . . 3 groſſe zeychen vnd wunder 4 eyn hertz, das verſtendig were 5 Er hat euch . . . laſſen wandeln . . veraltet . . veraltet

no bred nor droncke wyne or ſtrounge drryncke: that
ye myghte knowe, howe that he is the Lorde youre
God.
7 And at the laſt ye came vnto this place, ād Sihon the
kynge of Heſbon and Og kynge of Baſan came out agenst
8 you vnto batayle, and we ſmote them and toke their
londe and gaue it an heritaunce vnto the Rubenites
9 and Gadites and to the halfe tribe of Manaſſe. Kepe
therfore the worde of this appoyntment and doo them,
that ye maye vnderſtonde all that ye ought to doo.
10 Ye ſtonde here this daye euery one of you before
the Lorde youre God: both the heedes of youre trybes,
youre elders, youre officers ād all the mē of Iſrael:
11 youre childern, youre wyues and the ſtraungere that
are in thyne hoſt, from the hewer of thy wod vnto the
12 drawer of thy water: that thou ſhuldeſt come vnder the
appoyntment of the Lorde thy God, and vnder his othe
which the Lorde thy God maketh with the this daye.
13 For to make the a people vnto him ſelfe, and that he
maye be vnto the a God, as he hath ſayed vnto the and
[Fo. LIII.] as he hath ſworne vnto thi fathers Abraham, Iſaac and Iacob.
14 Alſo I make not this bonde and this othe with you
15 only: but both with him that ſtōdeth here with us
this daye before the Lorde oure God, and alſo with
16 him that is not here with us this daye. For ye knowe
how we haue dwelt in the londe of Egipte, and how
we came thorow the myddes of the nacions which we
17 paſſed by. And ye haue ſene their abhominaciōs and
their ydolles: wod, ſtone, ſiluer and golde which they
had.

M. 9 wordes
V. 6 vt ſciretis 7 et veniſtis . . . occurrentes nobis ad pugnam. 9 verba . . . vt intelligatis vniuerſa quæ facitis. 10 atque doctores, omnis populus Iſrael 11 exceptis lignorum cæſor. 12 vt tranſeas in fœdere 15 ſed cunctis præſentibus & abſentibus. 17 abominationes & ſordes, id eſt idola eorum . . . quæ colebant.

L. 6 auff das du wiſſeſt 7 Vnd da yhr kamet . . . mit vns zu ſtreytten 9 die wort . . . auff das yhr klug ſeyt ynn allem das yhr thut. 10 die vberſten ewr ſtemmen, ewr Eltiſten, ewr amptleut, eyn yderman 12 eynhergehen 15 mit denen, die heutte nicht mit vns ſind, 17 yhr grewel vnd yhre gotzen . . . die bey yhn waren.

18 Leſt there be amonge you man or woman kynred or
trybe that turneth awaye in his hert this daye from
the Lord oure God, to goo ād ſerue the goddes of theſe
nacions: and leſt there be amonge you ſome roote that
19 bereth gall and wormwod, ſo that when he heareth the
wordes of this curſe, he bleſſe him ſelfe in his hert ſayenge: I feare it not, I will ther fore walke after the luſt
of myne awne hert, that the drounken deſtroye the
thurſtie.

20 And ſo the Lorde will not be mercyfull vnto him,
but then the wrath of the Lorde ād his gelouſye,
ſmoke agenſt that man, ād al the curſes that are written in this boke light vppō him, and the Lorde doo out
21 his name frō vnder heauen, and ſeparate him vnto euell
out of .P. all the trybes of Iſrael acordynge vnto all
the curſes of the appoyntement that is written in the
boke of this lawe.

22 So that the generacion to come of youre childern
that ſhal ryſe vpp after you ād the ſtraunger that ſhall
come from a ferre londe, ſaye when they ſe the plages

M. 19 ſayinge. I ſhall haue peace. I will therfore worcke . . . that the dronckē may peryſh with the thryſtye.

V. 18 mulier, familia . . . radix germinans fel & amaritudinem. 19 iuramenti huius . . . Pax erit mihi, & ambul. in prauitate cordis mei: & aſſumat ebria ſitientem 20 quammaxime furor eius fumet . . . & deleat 21 & conſumat eum in perditionem . . in libro legis huius ac fœderis

L. 18 eyn weyb, odder eyn geſind . . . galle vnd wermut trage 19 diſes fluchs dennoch ſich ſegene . . . ſpreche, Es wirt ſo boſe nicht, Ich . . . wie es meyn hertz dunckt, das die trunckne mit der durſtigen verloren werde. 20 austilgen 21 abſondern zum vbel . . . lautts aller fluche des bunds

M. M. N. 19 *The dronckē man etc.:* By this is ſygnyfyed, that bothe the wycked teacher & the dyſcyple which receaueth euell doctryne ſhall peryſh together. Some reade that the droncken maye be put to the thriſye (*ſic*). Some, that dronckneiſe maye be put to thriſt.

L. M. N. 19 *Es wirt ſo boſe nicht:* Das iſt der rauchloſen leut wort vnd gedancken, Ey die helle iſt nicht ſo heyſs, Es hat nicht nott, der teuffel iſt nicht ſo grewlich als man yhn malet, wilchs alle werckheyligen frech vnd turſtiglich thun, ia noch lohn ym hymel gewarten. *das die trunckene:* Das iſt, das lerer vnd iunger miteynander verloren werden, Der lerer iſt der truncken von ſeynem tollen weyn, da Eſaias von ſagt, der gehet vber vnd verfuret mit ſich die durſtigen vnd ledigen ſeelen, die da ymer lernen, vnd nymer zur warheit komen, wie Sanct Paulus ſagt.

of that londe, and the diseases where with the Lorde
23 hath smytten it how all the londe is burnt vpp with
bremstone and salt, that it is nether sowne nor beareth
nor any grasse groweth therein, after the ouerthrowenge
of Sodome, Gomor, Adama ād Zeboim: which the
Lorde ouerthrewe in his wrath and angre.

24 And than all nacions also saye: wherfore hath the
Lorde done of this facion vnto this londe? O how
25 fearse is this greatt wrath? And men shall saye: because they lefte the testamēt of the Lorde God of their
fathers which he made with them, whē he brought
26 them out of the lande of Egipte. And they went ād
serued straunge goddes and worshipped them: goddes
which they knewe not and which had geuen them
27 nought. And therfore the wrath off the Lorde waxed
whote vppon that londe to brynge vppon it all the
28 curses that are written in this boke. And the Lorde
cast them out of their londe in angre, wrath and greate
furyou- [Fo. LIIII.] snesse, and cast thē in to a straunge
londe, as it is come to passe this daye.

29 The secrettes perteyne vnto the Lorde oure God
and the thinges that are opened perteyne vnto us and
oure childern for euer, that we doo all the wordes of
this lawe.

M. 23 salt, & ẏ it is 24 And then shall 29 The secrettes of the Lorde oure God are opened vnto us

V. 23 ita vt vltra non feratur . . in exemplum subuersionis Sod. . . . quas subuertit 24 quæ est hæc ira furoris eius immensa? 25 Ægypti: 26 & seruierunt . . . & quibus non fuerant attributi 28 in indignatione maxima . . . sicut hodie comprobatur. 29 Abscondita, domino . . . : quæ manifesta sunt, nobis

L. 23 gleych wie Sodom . . . vmbkeret sind 24 Was ist das fur so grosser grymmiger zorn? 26 vnd sind hyngangen . . . vnd den nichts zu geteylet ist. 28 mit grossem zorn, grym vnd vngnaden . . . wie es stehet heuttigs tages. 29 Das geheymnis des Herrn vnsers Gottis ist vns vnd vnsern kindern eroffnet ewiglich

M. M. N. 29 *are opened:* That is, the Lord hath opened vnto vs his wyll before all other people.

L. M. N. 29 *Das geheymnis:* wil so sagen, Vns Iuden hat Got fur allen volckern auff erden, seynen willen offenbart, vnd was er ym synn hatt, drumb sollen wir auch deste vleissiger seyn.

The .XXX. Chapter.

1 WHEN all theſe wordes are come
vpō the whether it be the
bleſſinge or the curſſe which I
haue ſet before the: yet yf thou
turne vnto thyne hert amonge all the nacions whother the Lorde thi God hath
2 thruſte the, and come agayne vnto the Lorde thi God
ād herken vnto his voyce acordinge to all that I cōmaunde the this daye: both thou and thi childern with
3 all thine hert and all thi ſoule: Then the Lorde thi
God wil turne thi captiuite ād haue cōppaſſion vpō the
ād goo ād fett the agayne from all the nacions, amōge
which the Lorde thi God ſhall haue ſcatered the.

M.C.S. The worde of God is not farre from thē that ſeke for it, but in their mouthes and hertes.

4 Though thou waſt caſt vnto the extreme partes of
heauen: euen from thence will the Lorde thi God gather
5 the and from thence ſett the and brynge the in to the
lande which thi fathers poſſeſſed,and thou ſhalt enioye
it. And he will ſhewe the kyndneſſe and .P. multiplye
6 the aboue thi fathers. And the Lorde thi God will
circumcyſe thine hert and the hert of thi ſeed for to
loue the Lorde thi God with all thine hert and all thi
7 ſoule, that thou mayſt lyue. And the Lorde thi
God will put al theſe curſes vpō thine enemyes and on
thē that hate the and perſecute the.

8 But thou ſhalt turne and herken vnto the voyce of
the Lorde and doo all his commaundmentes which I
9 commaunde the this daye And the Lorde thi God
will make the plenteous in all the workes of thine
hande and in the frute of thi bodye, in the frute of thi

V. 1 & ductus pœnitudine cordis tui in vniuerſis gentibus 2 & reuerſus (vv. 8, 9, 10) fueris ad eum 3 reducet . . . te ante diſperſit. 4 inde te retrahet 7 conuertet ſuper inimicos tuos 9 & abundare . . . in ſobole vteri tui

L. 2 vnd bekeriſt (vv. 8, 9, 10) dich zu dem Herrn deynem Got 3 deyn gefengnis wenden 7 auff deyne feynde legen 9 dich laſſen vberfluſſig ſeyn

catell and frute of thi lande and in riches. For the
Lórde will turne agayne and reioyſe ouer the to doo the
10 good, as he reioyſed ouer thi fathers: Yf thou herken
vnto the voyce of the Lorde thy God, to kepe his commaundmentes and ordynaunces which are written in
the boke of this lawe, yf thou turne vnto the Lord thi
God with all thine hert and all thi ſoule.
11 For the commaundment which I commaunde the
this daye, is not ſeparated from the nether ferre of.
12 It is not in heauen, that thou neadeſt to ſaye: who
ſhall goo vpp for us in to heauen, and fett it us, that
13 we maye heare it ād doo it: Nether is it beyonde the
ſee, that thou ſhuldeſt ſaye: who ſhall goo ouer ſee for us
and fett [Fo. LV.] it us that we maye heare it and doo
14 it: But the worde is very nye vnto the: euen in thi
mouth and in thine hert, that thou doo it.
15 Beholde I haue ſett before you this daye lyfe and
16 good, deeth and euell: in that I commaunde the this
daye to loue the Lorde thi God and to walke in his
wayes and to kepe his commaundementes, his ordynaunces and his lawes: that thou mayſt lyue and multiplye, and that the Lorde thy God maye bleſſe the in
the londe whother thou goeſt to poſſeſſe it.
17 But and yf thyne hert turne awaye, ſo that thou
wilt not heare: but ſhalt goo aſtraye and worſhepe
18 ſtraunge goddes and ſerue them, I pronounce vnto you
this daye, that ye ſhal ſurely pereſh and that ye ſhall
not prolonge youre dayes vppon the londe whother
thou paſſeſt ouer Iordayne to goo and poſſeſſe it.
19 I call to recorde this daye vnto you, heauen and
erth, that I haue ſett before you lyfe and deeth, bleſſynge and curſynge: but choſe lyfe, that thou and thi

M. 12 for vs to heauen

V. 9 in vbertate terræ tuæ, & in rerum omnium largitate. 11 non ſupra te 13 vt cauſeris, & dicas . . . poterit transfretare mare . . audire & facere quod præceptum eſt ? 15 bonum, & econtrario mortem & malum: 16 vt diligas . . . atque multiplicet 17 atque errore deceptus 18 prædico tibi 19 Elige ergo vitam

L. 9 an der frucht deyns lands, zum gutten. 11 nicht zu wunderlich, noch zu ferne 14 faſt nah 15 das boſe, 16 der ich dyr heute gepiete 17 ſondern felleſt aus 19 das du das leben erweleſt

20 ſeed maye lyue, in that thou loueſt the Lorde thi God
herkeneſt vnto his voyce and cleaueſt vnto him. For
he is thi life and the lengthe of thi dayes, that thou
mayſt dwell vppon the erth which the Lorde ſware
vnto thi fathers: Abraham, Iſaac and Iacob to .P. geue
them.

ℂ The .XXXI. Chapter.

1 AND Moſes went and ſpake theſe
2 wordes vnto all Iſrael and ſayed
vnto them I am an hundred
ād .xx. yere olde this daye,
ād can nomoare goo out and in. Alſo
the Lorde hath ſayed vnto me, thou ſhalt
3 not go ouer this Iordayne. The Lord
youre God he will go ouer before the ād
he will deſtroye theſe nacions before the,
ād thou ſhalt cōquere thē. And Ioſua he
ſhall goo ouer before the, as the Lorde
4 hath ſayed. And the Lorde ſhall doo
vnto them, as he dyd to Sihon ād Og kynges of the
Amorites ād vnto their landes which kinges he deſtroyed.
5 And when the Lorde hath delyuered them to the,
ſe that ye doo vnto them acordynge vnto all the cō-
6 maundmentes which I haue cōmaunded you. Plucke
vpp youre hartes and be ſtronge, dreade not nor be
aferde of them: for the Lorde thi God him ſelfe will
goo with the, and wil nether let the goo nor forſake
the:

M.C.S. *Moſes beyng readye to dye ordereth Ioſue to rule the people in his ſteade, This boke Deuteronomye is wrytten and layde in the tabernacle beſyde the arcke The Leuites are charged to reade hit to the people.*

M. 2 an hūdred & .xx. yere this daye 4 Sehon
V. 20 et illi adhæreas (ipſe eſt enim vita . . .) xxxi, 2 præſertim cum 3 deus tuus . . omnes gentes has 4 delebitque eos. 5 ſimiliter facietis 6 Viriliter agite, & confortamini . . . nec paueatis ad conſpectum eorum
L. 20 vnd yhm anhanget, Denn das iſt deyn leben. xxxi, 3 Der Herr deyn Gott . . das du ſie eynnemeſt 6 Seyt getroſt vnd freydig
M. M. N. 2 *Go out and in:* To go in and oute is to exercyſe the offyce of a myniſtre & leader of thē: as chriſt ſayth of the miniſters aud paſtoures. Iohan. x, a.

7 And Mofes called vnto Iofua and fayed vnto him in
the fighte of all Ifrael: Be ftrōge and bolde, for thou
muft goo with this people vnto the londe which the
Lorde [Fo. LVI.] hath fworne vnto their fathers to
geue them, and thou fhalt geue it them to enheret.
8 And the Lorde he fhall goo before the ād he fhall be
with the, and wil not let the goo nor forfake the, feare
not therfore nor be difcomforted.
9 And Mofes wrote this lawe and delyuered it vnto the
preaftes the fonnes of Leui which bare the arke of the
teftament of the Lorde, and vnto all the elders of Ifrael,
10 and commaunded them fayenge: At the ende of .vii
yere, in the tyme of the fre yere, in the feft of the tab-
11 ernacles, when all Ifrael is come to appere before the
Lorde thi God, in the place which he hath chofen: fe
that thou reade this lawe before all Ifrael in their eares
12 Gather the people together: both men, wemen and
childern and the ftraungers that are in thi cities, that
they maye heare, lerne and feare the Lorde youre God,
and be diligent to kepe all the wordes of this lawe,
13 and that theyr childern which knowe nothinge maye
heare and lerne to feare the Lorde youre God, as longe
as ye lyue in the londe whother ye goo ouer Iordayne
to poffeffe it.
14 And the Lorde fayed vnto Mofes:
Beholde thy dayes are come, that thou .P. muft dye.
Call Iofua and come and ftonde in the tabernacle
of witneffe, that I maye geue him a charge. And
Mofes and Iofua went and ftode in the tabernacle
off witneffe.
15 And the Lorde apeared in the tabernacle: euen in
the pyler off the cloude. And the piler of the cloude
ftode ouer the dore of the tabernacle.

V. 7 Confortare . . . eam forte diuides. 8 nec paueas. 13 filii . . . qui nunc ignorant: vt audire poffint, & timeant . . verfantur 14 prope funt dies mortis 15 dominus ibi in columna nubis quæ ftetit

L. 7 vnter fie austeylen 8 mit dyr feyn . . . erchrick nicht. 11 ort, den er erwelen wirt 12 fur der verfamlung des volcks . . . ynn deynem thor 13 kinder die nichts wiffen 14 deyne zeyt . . das du fterbift . . yhm befelh thue 15 ynn der hutten

16 And the Lorde ſayed vnto Moſes: beholde, thou
muſt ſlepe with thi fathers, and this people will
goo a whorynge after ſtraunge goddes off the londe
whother they goo and will forſake me and breake
the appoyntement which I haue made with them.
17 And then my wrath will waxe whote agenſt them,
and I will forſake them and will hyde my face from
them, and they ſhalbe conſumed. And when moch
aduerſyte and tribulacion is come vppon them, then
they will ſaye: becauſe oure God is not amonge us,
18 theſe tribulacions are come vppon us. But I wil hyde
my face that ſame tyme for all the euels ſake which
they ſhall haue wrought, in that they are turned vnto
ſtraunge goddes.

19 Now therfore write ye this ſonge, and teach it the
childern of Iſrael and put it in their mouthes that
this ſonge maye be my witneſſe [Fo. LVII.] vnto
20 the childern of Iſrael. For when I haue brought
them in to the londe whiche I ſware vnto their fathers that runneth with mylke ād honye, then they
will eate and fyll them ſelues and waxe fatt and
turne vnto ſtraunge goddes and ſerue them and
21 rayle on me and breake my teſtament. And then
when moch myſchefe and tribulacion is come vppon them, this ſonge ſhall anſwere before them, and
be a witneſſe. It ſhall not be forgetten out of the
mouthes of their ſeed: for I knowe their imaginacyon whiche they goo aboute euen now before I haue
22 broughte them in to the londe which I ſware. And

V. 16 irritum faciet fœdus 17 & erit in deuorationem . . . omnia mala . . . non eſt deus mecum, inuenerunt me 18 abſcondam, & celabo faciem 19 vt memoriter teneant & ore decantent 20 Introducam . . Cumque comederint 21 reſpondebit ei canticum . . terram quam ei pollicitus ſum.

L. 16 den bund faren laſſen (v. 20) 17 viel vngluck vnd angſt . . mich . . myr 19 legts ynn yhren mund 20 ich wil ſie . . bringen . . . mich leſtern 21 fur yhn antwortten 22 Alſo ſchreyb Moſe

M. M. X. 17 *hyde my face:* To hyde hys face is as moch as not to heare & to take a waye the tokens of hys kyndneſſe, as whē he geueth no eare to vs or oure prayers nor ſheweth vs any tokē of loue but ſetteth before oure eyes greuouſe afflyccions and euen verye death. As in Iob .xiii, d & Miche. iii, b.

Moses wrote this songe the same season, and taught it
the childern of Israel.
23 And the Lorde gaue Iosua the sonne off Nun a
charge and sayed: be bolde and stronge for thou shalt
brynge the childern of Israel in to the lond which I
sware vnto them, ād I will be with the.
24 When Moses had made an ende of wrytynge out the
wordes of this lawe in a boke vnto the ende of them
25 he commaunded the Leuites which bare the arcke of
26 the testamēt of the Lorde sayenge: take the boke off
thys lawe and put it by the syde of the arcke of the
testament of the Lorde youre God, and let it .P. be there
27 for a witnesse vnto the. For I knowe thi stubernesse and
thi stiffe necke: beholde, while I am yet a lyue with you
this daye, ye haue bene dishobedient vnto the Lorde:
ād how moch moare after my deeth.
28 Gather vnto me al the elders of youre trybes and
youre officers, that I maye speake these wordes in their
eares and call heauē ād erth to recorde agenst them.
29 For I am sure that after my deeth, they will vtterly
marre them selues and turne from the waye which I
commaunded you, and tribulacion will come vppon you
in the later dayes, when ye haue wrought wekednesse
in the sight of the Lorde to prouoke him with the
30 workes of youre handes. And Moses spake in the eares
of all the congregacion of Israel the wordes of this
songe, vnto the ende of them.

M. 29 wickednesse.
V. 26 Tollite librum istum . . contra te 27 semper cont. egistis
28 atque doctores 29 inique agetis . . mala in extremo tempore
L. 23 Vnd befalh Iosua . . getrost vnd frisch 24 gantz ausgeschrieben 25 laden des zeugnis 26 zeuge sey widder dich 29 das
yhrs . . . verderben werdet . . vngluck begegen hernach

The .XXXII. Chapter.

1 HEARE o heauen, what I ſhall ſpeake and heare o erth the wordes of my mouth.
2 My doctrine droppe as doeth the rayne, ād my ſpeach flowe as doeth the dewe, as the meſellynge vpō the herbes,
3 ād as the droppes vppō the graſſe. For I wil call on the name of the Lorde: Magnifie the might of oure God.

M.C.S. *The ſong of Moſes. He gothe vp vnto the toppe of Abarim to ſee the lande of promeſſe.*

meſellynge, *ſmall rain, drizzle*

4 [Fo. LVIII.] He is a rocke and perfecte are his deades, for all his wayes are with diſcrecion. God is faithfull and without wekedneſſe, both rightuous and iuſte is he.

5 The frowarde and ouerthwarte generacion hath marred them ſelues to himward, ād are not his ſonnes for their deformities ſake,

ouerthwarte, *adj. oppoſite, perverſe*

6 Doeſt thou ſo rewarde the Lorde? O fooliſh nacyon ād vnwyſe. Is not he thy father ād thyne owner? hath he not made the and ordeyned the?

7 Remembre the dayes that are paſt: conſydre the

V. 1 cæli . . . Concreſcat in pluuiam doctrina . . imber . . . ſtillæ 3 date magnificentiam 4 Dei perfecta ſunt opera, & omnes viæ eius iudicia. 5 Peccauerunt ei, & non filii eius: in ſordibus, gen. praua atque peruerſa. 6 pater tuus, qui poſſedit 7 cogita generationes ſingulas

L. 4 On wandel ſind die werck des Felſen 5 verkerete vnd verruckte art . . verterbet . . vmb yhrs taddels willen. 6 nerricht vnd vnweyſes volck? . . bereyttet? 7 iar der vorigen geſchlechten.

M. M. N. 1 *Heare O heauē:* The Prophetes couſtomably, when they ſpeake with a feruent affeccion, do ſpeake vnto thynges that haue no lyſe, as thoughe they ſpake to men, as in Eſai. the fyrſt a. And here Moſes thynkyng that the chyldren of Iſrael wold not erneſtly heare hym, and that he ſhulde loſe hys laboure willeth yet heuen and erth to heare him & to be his wytneſſes that he recyted this ſong vnto them. 4 *Rock.* God is called a Rock, becauſe he & hys worde laſteth for euer, he is ſuer to truſt to, & a perfect confort to beleuers, and their ſinguler defence at all times 2 Reg. xxii, a.

L. M. N. 4 *Felſen:* die Ebreiſch ſprach heyſt Got eynen Fels, das iſt, eyn trotz, troſt, hord, vnd ſicherung, allen die ſich auff yhn verlaſſen vnd yhm trawen. *Gerichte:* das iſt das ſie yderman recht verſchaffen vnd niemant vnrecht thun.

yeres from tyme to tyme. Axe thy father ād he will
ſhewe the, thyne elders and they wyll tell the.
8 Whē the moſt hygheſt gaue the nacyons an enheritaunce, ād diuided the ſonnes of Adam he put the borders of the nacions, faſt by the multitude of the childern
of Iſrael.
9 For the Lordes parte is his folke, ād Iſrael is the
porcion of his enheritaunce.
10 He founde him in a deſerte londe, in a voyde ground
ād a rorynge wilderneſſe. he led hī aboute and gaue
him vnderſtondynge, ād kepte him as the aple of his eye.
11 As an egle that ſtereth vpp hyr neſt and flotereth
ouer hyr younge, he ſtretched oute his wynges and
toke hym vpp and bare hym .P. on his ſhulders.
12 The Lorde alone was his guyde, and there was no
ſtraunge God with him.
13 He ſett him vpp apon an hye londe, and he ate the
encreaſe of the feldes. And he gaue hī honye to ſucke
out of the rocke, ād oyle out of the harde ſtone.
14 With butter of the kyne and mylke of the ſhepe,
with fatt of the lambes ād fatt rammes and he gootes
with fatt kydneyes and with whete. And of the
bloude of grapes thou drōkeſt wyne.
15 And Iſrael waxed fatt and kyked. Thou waſt fatt,
thicke and ſmothe, And he let God goo that made hī
and deſpyſed the rocke that ſaued him.

M. 9 and Iacob is the porcion 14 of kyne

V. 8 diuidebat . . conſtit. term. pop. iuxta numerum filiorum Iſr. 9 funiculus hæred. 10 loco horroris, & vaſtæ ſolitudinis. 11 prouocans ad volandum . . volitans . . . in humeris ſuis. 14 & hircos cum medulla tritici 15 Incraſſatus eſt dilectus, & recalcitrauit, incraſſatus, impinguatus, dilatatus . . 15 a deo ſalutari ſuo.

L. 8 austeylet . . der menſchen kinder . . nach der zal der kinder Iſrael. 9 ſchnur ſeyns erbs. 10 eynode da es heulet. 11 auffweckt ſeyn neſt . . ſchwebt . . trug yhn auff ſeynen flugeln. 13 vnd etzet yhn 14 vnd böcke mit fetten nieren, vnd weytzen. 15 wart er geyl. Du biſt fett vnd dick vnd glat worden . . Gott faren laſſen

M. M. N. 9 *Iacob:* Onely the faythfull, which are ſygniſyed by Iacob, are Goddes porcion: the vnbeleuers be longe not to him. 11 *Bare hym on his ſhoulders:* To beare thē on his ſhoulders is to ſaue & kepe thē from euell, & let thē haue the fruicyon of hys goodnes, as in Nume. xi, c. 14 *butter of kyne etc.:* By theſe thynges named, are ſygniſyed aboundaūce of all good thynges as it is ſayd in Pſal. Lxii, b.

16 They angred him with ſtraūge goddes ād with
abhominacions prouoked him.
17 They offered vnto feldedeuels and not feldedeuels, *ſatyrs*
to God, ād to goddes which they knewe
not ād to newe goddes that came newly vpp whiche
their fathers feared not.
18 Of the rocke that begat the thou arte vnmyndefull
and haſt forgott God that made the.
19 And when the Lorde ſawe it, he was angre becauſe
of the prouokynge of his ſonnes and doughters.
20 [Fo. LIX.] And he ſayed: I will hyde my face
from thē and will ſe what their ende ſhall be. For
they are a froward generacion ād childern in whō is
no fayth.
21 They haue angred me with that whiche is no god,
and prouoked me with their vanities And I agayne
will angre them with thē whiche are no people, and
will prouoke thē with a foeliſh nacion.
22 For fire is kyndled in my wrath, ād ſhal burne
vnto the botome of heell. And ſhall conſume the
erth with her encreaſe, and ſet a fire the botoms of the
mountaynes.
23 I will hepe myſcheues vpon the ād will ſpēde all
myne arowes at them.
24 Burnt with hungre ād conſumed with heet and with
bitter peſtilence. I will alſo ſende the tethe of beeſtes
vppon them and poyſon ſerpentes.
25 Without forth, the ſwerde ſhall robbe thē off theire
childern: and wythin in the chamber, feare: both younge
men and younge wemen and the ſuckelynges with the
mē of gray heedes.

V. 20 generatio enim peruerſa eſt, & infideles filii. 22 vſque ad inferni nouiſſima . . . germine 24 Conſumentur fame, & deuorabunt eos aues morſu amariſſimo . . cum furore trahentium

L. 16 zu eyffer gereytzet durch frembde. 17 felt teuffeln geopffert . . . den newen die newlich komen ſind . . ewr veter 18 fels der dich geporn hat (cf. v. 16) 20 kinder da keyn glawb ynnen iſt. 22 bis ynn die vnterſten hell . . . gewechs 23 vngluck . . heuffen 24 verzehret werden vom fiber, vnd von bittern ſeuchen 25 berauben, vnd ynn den kamern

M. M. N. 20 *I wyll hyde etc.:* Loke afore in the .xxxi, d.

26 I haue determened to ſcater thē therowout the
worlde, ād to make awaye the remēbraunce of them
from amonge men.
27 Were it not that I feared the raylynge off .P. theyr
enemyes, leſt theire aduerſaries wolde be prowde and
ſaye: oure hye hande hath done al theſe workes and
not the Lorde.
28 For it is a nacion that hath an vnhappye forcaſt,
29 and hath no vnderſtonge in them. I wolde
they ware wyſe and vnderſtode this ād
wolde conſider their later ende.

vnderſtonge, *underſtanding*

30 Howe it cometh that one ſhall chace a thouſande,
and two putt ten thouſande off them to flyghte? except
theire rocke had ſolde them, and becauſe the
Lorde had delyuered them.
31 For oure rocke is not as their rocke, no though
oure enemyes be iudge.
32 But their vynes are of the vynes of Sodom, and of the
feldes of Gomorra. Their grapes are grapes of gall,
and theire cluſters be bytter.
33 Their wyne is the poyſon of dragons, ād the cruell
gall of aſpes.
34 Are not ſoch thinges layed in ſtore with me, ād
ſeeled vpp amonge my treaſures?
35 Vengeaunce is myne and I will rewarde: their fete
ſhall ſlyde, when the tyme cometh. For the tyme
of their deſtruction is at honde, and the tyme that ſhall
come vppon them maketh haſt.
36 For the Lorde will doo iuſtice vnto hys [Fo. LX.]
people, and haue compaſſion on his ſervauntes. For it

V. 26 dixi, Vbi nam ſunt? ceſſare faciam ex hominibus memoriam eorum. 28 Gens abſque conſilio 29 ac nouiſſima prouiderent. 30 Quomodo . . . deus ſuus . . . dominus concluſit illos? 31 Non enim eſt deus noſter, vt dii eorum, & inimici 32 de ſuburbanis Gom. 33 Fel drachonum . . . & venenum aſpidum inſanabile. 34 condita . . . ſignata 35 retribuam eis in tempore

L. 26 Ich wil ſagen, wo ſind ſie? 28 keyn radt yn iſt 30 Wie gehets zu . . yhr fels verkaufft 31 fels . . . fels 32 acker Gomora . . trachen grym, Vnd wutiger ottern gall. 34 verſigelt 35 zu ſeyner zeyt ſol yhr ſuſs gleytten

ſhalbe ſene that theire power ſhall fayle, and at the
laſt they ſhalbe preſoned and forſaken.
37 And it ſhalbe ſayed: where are their goddes ād their
rocke wherein they truſted?
38 The fatt of whoſe ſacrifices they ate and drancke
the wyne of their dryncköfferynges, let them ryſe vpp
and helpe you and be youre protection.
39 Se now howe that I, I am he, and that there is no
God but I. I can kyll and make alyue, ād what I haue
ſmyten that I can heale: nether ys there that can delyuer any man oute off my honde.
40 For I will lifte vp my hande to heauē, ād will ſaye:
I lyue euer.
41 Yf I whett the lyghtenynge of my ſwerde, and myne
hande take in hande to doo iuſtyce, I will ſhewe vengeaunce on myne enemyes and will rewarde them that
hate me.
42 I will make myne arowes dronkē with bloude, and
my ſwerde ſhall eate fleſh of the bloud of the ſlayne
and of the captyue and of the bare heed of the enemye.
43 Reioyſe hethen wyth hys people, for he will auenge
the bloude off his ſervauntes, and wyll auenge hym off
hys aduerſaryes, .P. and wilbe mercyfull vnto the londe
off hys people.

M. 41 whett the edge of my ſwerde 43 Prayſe ye hethen his people

V. 36 Videbit quod infirmata ſit manus, & clauſi quoque defecerunt, reſiduique conſumpti ſunt. 37 dii eorum, in quibus 38 & in neceſſitate vos protegant. 39 percutiam & ego ſanabo 41 Si acuero vt fulgur gladium 42 Inebriabo . . . & de captiuitate nudati inimicorum capitis. 43 Laudate gentes populum eius

L. 36 Vnd aus iſt auch mit dem der verſchloſſen vnd vbrig war. 37 fels 39 was ich zu ſchlagen hab das kan ich heylen 41 Wenn ich den blitz meyns ſchwerds wetzen werde 42 ſol fleyſch freſſen, vber dem blutt . . . vnd das des feynds heubt entbloſſet ſeyn wirt. 43 mit ſeym volck

M. M. N. 42 *Of the ſlayne:* Here recyteth he .iii. plages of the ſwerde, that many ſhalbe ſlayne, that they ſhall be leade captyue and brought in to bondage, & that their head ſhuld become bare, that is, their kyngdom and preſthode ſhulde be taken awaye frō thē.

L. M. N. 42 *Vber dem blut:* das ſind drey ſtraffen des ſchwerds, die erſt, das yhr vil erſchagen wirt, die ander das ſie gefangen gefurt werden, die drit, das yhr heubt blos ſolt werden, das iſt konigreich vnd prieſterthum ſolt von yhn genomen werden, wilche durchs har auff dem heubt bedeut wart.

44 And Mofes went ād fpake all the wordes of this
fonge in the eares of the people, both he and Iofua
45 the fonne of Nun. And when Mofes had fpoken all
46 thefe wordes vnto the ende to all Ifrael, then he
fayed vnto them.
Sett youre hertes vnto all the wordes whiche I teftifye vnto you this daye: that ye commaunde them
vnto youre childern, to obferue and doo all the wordes
47 off thys lawe. For it is not a vayne worde vnto you:
but it is youre lyfe, and thorow thys worde ye fhall
prolonge youre dayes in the lond whother ye goo ouer
Iordayne to conquere it.
48 And the Lorde fpake vnto Mofes the felfe fame daye
49 fayenge: get the vpp in to this mountayne Abarim
vnto mount Nebo, which is in the londe of Moab ouer
agenft Ierícho.
And beholde the londe of Canaan whiche I geue
vnto the childern of Ifrael to poffeffe.
50 And dye in the mount whiche thou goeft vppon,
and be gathered vnto thy people: As Aaron thy brother dyed in mounte Hor ād was gathered vnto his
51 people. For ye trefpafed agenft me amonge the childern of Ifrael at the waters off ftriffe, at Cades in the
wylderneffe of Zin: becaufe ye fanctified me not a- [Fo.
52 LXI.] monge the childern of Ifrael. Thou fhalt fe the
londe before the, but fhall not goo thither vnto the
londe which I geue the childern off Ifrael.

V. 46 Ponite corda . . . teftificor vobis . . . vniuerfa quæ fcripta funt in volumine legis huius 49 Abarim, id eft, tranfitum, in montem Nebo 50 iungeris populis tuis . . appofitus

L. 46 Nempt zu hertzen 50 wenn du hynauff komen bift . . . verfamle . . . verfamlet 51 an myr vergriffen 52 das land gegen dyr . . . nicht hyneyn komen.

M. M. N. 46 *the wordes which I teftifye:* To teftifye the worde is to preache the worde & therfore is the worde called a teftymonye or witneffe. Pfal. cxviii, b.

The .XXXIII. Chapter.

1 THIS is the blessinge where with Moses gods man blessed the childern of Israel before his
2 deeth sayenge: The Lord
came frō Sinai and shewed his beames from Seir vnto them, and appered gloriously from mount Paran, and he came with thousandes of sayntes, and in his right
3 hande a lawe of fyre for them How loued he the people? All his sayntes are in his honde. They yoyned thē selues vnto thy fote and receaued thi wordes.
4 Moses gaue us a lawe which is the enheritaunce of
5 the cōgregacion of Iacob. And he was in Israel kinge when he gathered the heedes of the people and the tribes of Israel to gether.

M.C.S. *Moses dying blesseth all the trybes of Israel.*

6 Ruben shall lyue and shall not dye: but his people shalbe few in numbre.

7 This is the blessynge of Iuda. And he sayed: heare Lorde the voyce of Iuda and bringe him vnto his people: let his handes fyght for him: but be thou his helpe agenst his enemies.

8 And vnto Leui he sayed: thy perfectnesse .P. ād thi light be after thy mercifull mā whō thou temptest at

M. 2 Pharan 8 tēptedest at Masah

V. 2 ortus est nobis 3 sancti . . . & qui appropinquant pedibus eius, accipient de doctrina illius. 5 Erit apud rectissimum rex 7 adiutor illius . . . erit. 8 & doctrina tua a viro sancto tuo

L. 2 vnd ist yhnen auffgangen . . feurigs gesetz an sie 3 heyligen sind ynn deyner hand 5 Vnd er war in der fulle des konigs 7 seyne hende lasse sich mehren 8 Deyn Vollickeyt vnd deyn Liecht sey nach dem man deyner barmhertzickeyt

M. M. N. 3 *All his sayntes:* That is, let thy preastes offyce be happye and fortunate before God & men; by prayer, teachynge and good ensample geuynge, as it was in Moses. 8 *Thy perfectnesse and thy light:* This is the light & perfectnesse, which Moses put ī the breast lappe of iudgemēt Exo. xxviii, c & Num. xxvii, d. The Chald. interpr. readeth with perfectnesse & light induedst thou the man that was founde holye.

L. M. N. 5 *Fulle des konigs:* die fulle ist das volck Israel, das Christi seyns konigs fulle ist, wie Paulus die Christenheyt nennet die fulle Christi Ephe. i. 8 *Vollickeyt:* Das ist, wie Exo. 28 stehet das Heyligthum auff dem brustlatzen, wil also sagen, Dein priesterlich ampt sey gluckselig fur Gott vnd den menschen, mit beten vnd leren wie es war an Mose, der yhn von gottis gnaden geben war.

Masa ād with whom thou ſtriuedſt at the waters of ſtrife.
9 He that ſaieth vnto his father ād mother. I ſawe him not
ād vnto his brethern I knewe not, and to his ſonne I wote
not: for they haue obſerued thi wordes and kepte thi teſ-
10 tament. They ſhall teach Iacob thi iudgementes ād Iſrael thi lawes. They ſhall put cens before thi noſe and
11 whole ſacrifices apon thine altare. Bleſſe Lorde their
power and accepte the workes of their hondes: ſmyte
the backes of them that ryſe agēſt them and of them
that hate them: that they ryſe not agayne.

12 Vnto Ben Iamin he ſayed: The Lordes derlynge
ſhall dwell in ſaffetye by him and kepe him ſelfe in
the hauen by hym contynually, and ſhall dwell betwene his ſhulders.

13 And vnto Ioſeph he ſayed: bleſſed of the Lorde is
his londe with the goodly frutes off heauen, with dewe
14 and with ſprynges that lye beneth: and with frutes of
the encreaſe of the ſonne and wyth rype frute off the
15 monethes, and with the toppes of mountaynes that
were from the begynnynge and with the dayntes of
16 hilles that laſt euer and with goodly frute of the erth
and off [Fo. LXII.] the fulneſſe there of. And the
good will of him that dwelleth in the buſh ſhall
come vppon the heed of Ioſeph and vppon the
toppe of the heed of him that was ſeparated frō
17 amonge his brethern his bewtye is as a firſtborne
oxe and his hornes as the hornes of an vnycorne.
And with them he ſhall puſh the nacions to gether,
euen vnto the endes of the worlde. Theſe are the

M. 9 wyth whom thou ſtryuedeſt 11 hate them: they ryſe

V. 9 Neſcio vos . . . & neſcierunt filios ſuos . . . ſeruauerunt, 10 iudicia tua o Iacob & legem (Heb. docebunt Iacob iudicia tua, & Iſrael legem tuam) . . . thymiama in furore tuo 12 quaſi in thalamo tota die 13 rore, atque abyſſo ſubiacente. 15 de pomis collium 16 nazaræi 17 in ipſis ventilabit

L. 10 reuchwerg fur deyne naſe legen 12 Den gantzen tag wirt er vber yhn halten 13 vom taw, vnd von der tieffen die hunden ligt 16 Der gutte wille des der ynn dem puſch wonet . . des Naſir 17 wie eynhorners horner . . . ſtoſſen zu hauff

L. M. N. 13 *Edle fruchte:* Das iſt vom konigreich Iſrael geſagt wilchs hoch geſegenet wart mit allem dz hymel, ſonn, mond, erden, berg, tal, waſſer vnd alles zeytlich gutt, trug vnd gab, dazu auch Propheten vnd heilig regentē hatte.

many thouſandes of Ephraim and the thouſandes off
Manaſſe.
18 And vnto Zabulon he ſayed: Reioyſe Zabulon in thi
19 goenge out, and thou Iſachar in thi tentes. They ſhall
call the people vnto the hill, and there they ſhall offer
offerynges of righteouſnes. For they ſhall ſucke of the
abundaunce of the ſee and of treaſure hyd in the ſonde.
20 And vnto Gad he ſayed: bleſſed is the rowmmaker
Gad. He dwelleth as a lion and caught the arme ād
21 alſo the toppe of the heed He ſawe his begynnynge,
that a parte of the teachers were hyd there ād come
with the heedes of the people, and executed the righteouſnes of the Lorde and his iudgementes with Iſrael.
22 And vnto Dan he ſayed: Dan is a lions whelpe, he
ſhall flowe from Baſan.
23 .P. And vnto Nepthali he ſayed: Nepthali he ſhall
haue abundance of pleaſure and ſhalbe fylled with the
bleſſinge of the Lorde ād ſhall haue his poſſeſſions in
the ſouthweſt.
24 And of Aſſer he ſayed: Aſſar ſhalbe bleſſed with
childern: he ſhalbe acceptable vnto his brethern and
25 ſhall dyppe his fote in oyle: Yern and braſſe ſhall hange
on thi ſhowes and thine age ſhalbe as thi youth.
26 There is none like vnto the God of the off Iſrael: he
that ſitteth vppon heauen ſhalbe thine helpe, whoſe

M. 17 Manaſſes. 21 a parte of the teacher was . . . and came 26 vnto the God of Iſrael

V. 17 multitudines Ephraim, . . . millia Manaſſe. 19 quaſi lac ſugent 20 in latitudine Gad 21 principatum ſuum, quod in parte ſua doctor eſſet repoſitus 22 fluet largiter 23 abundantia perfruetur . . . mare & meridiem 26 vt deus rectiſſimi . . Magnificentia eius diſcurrunt nubes

L. 20 der raum macher . . . der lerer hauffe verborgen lagen 23 gegen abend vnd mittag 26 Got des richtigen.

M. M. N. 19 *Sucke of the abundance etc.:* That is, they ſhall haue aboundaunce of rycheſſe, what of marchaundyſe cōmyng by ſee, and of metalles of the erthe. 20 *Roumemaker*, becauſe with warre he made roume: for he was a valyaunt warryer. 21 *Teacher:* Or (as ſome will) lawgeuer. *Was hyd there:* The Chald. interpre. was buryed there. 26 *There is none lyke etc.*; Why Simeō is left oute there appeareth no cauſe, that is euydēt and worthye to be beleued.

L. M. N. 20 Den ſegen Gad, hat der konig Iehu aufgericht 4 reg. x. da er Baal vertilget vnd das volck wider zu recht bracht vnd ſchlug zween konige todt dazu auch Iſabel.

27 glorie is in the cloudes, that is the dwellinge place of
God from the begynnynge and from vnder the armes
of the worlde: he hath cast out thine enemies before
28 the and sayed: destroye. And Israel shall dwell in
saffetye alone. And the eyes of Iacob shall loke appon
a londe of corne and wyne, moreouer his heauen shall
29 droppe with dewe. Happye art thou Israel, who is
like vnto the? A people that art saued by the Lorde
thy shilde and helper and swerde of thi glorye. And
thyne enemyes shall hyde them selues from the, and
thou shalt walke vppon their hye hilles.

The .XXXIIII. Chapter

1 AND Moses went frō the feldes of
Moab vpp in to mount Nebo
which is the [Fo. LXIII.] toppe
of Pisga, that is ouer agenst
Iericho.

M. C. S. *Moses dyeth. Israell wepeth. Iosua succedeth in Moses roume.*

And the Lorde shewed him all the londe off Gilead
2 euen vnto Dan, and all nephtali and the londe of Ephraim and Manasse, ād all the londe of Iuda: euen vnto
3 the vtmost see, ād the south and the region of the playne
4 of Iericho the citye of datetrees euen vnto Zoar. And
the Lorde sayed vnto him. This is the londe which I
sware vnto Abraham, Isaac and Iacob sayenge: I will
geue it vnto thy seed. I haue shewed it the before thyne
eyes: but thou shalt not goo ouer thither.

5 So Moses the seruaunte of the Lorde dyed there in
the londe of Moab at the commaundment of the Lorde.
6 And he buryed him in a valey in the londe of Moab

M. 1 Galaad 3 paulmetrees

V. 27 habitaculum eius sursum, & subter brachia sempiterna 29 negabunt te. xxxiiii, 3 Segor. 4 Vidisti eam oculis tuis

L. 27 wonung Gottis von anfang 29 Deyne feynde werden verschmachten. xxxiiii, 3 Zoar 4 Du hast es mit deynen augen gesehen

M. M. N. 28 *In safety alone:* loke Numeri. xxiii, b. vpō this worde to dwell by him selfe.

besyde Beeth Peor: but no man wyst of his sepulchre
7 vnto this daye. And Moses was an hundred an
xx. yere olde when he dyed, ād yet his eyes were
8 not dym nor his chekes abated. And the childern
of Israel wepte for Moses in the feldes off Moab .xxx.
dayes. And the dayes off wepynge and mornynge for
Moses were ended.
9 And Iosua the sonne of Nun was full of the spirite of
wisdome: for Moses had put his hande vppon him. And
all the childern of Israel herkened vnto him and dyd
10 as the Lorde .P. cōmaunded Moses. But there arose
not a prophett sense in Israel lyke vnto Moses, whom
11 the Lorde knewe face to face, in all the miracles and
wonders which the Lorde sent him
to doo in the londe of Egipte vnto Pharao
and all his seruauntes and vnto all his
12 londe: and in all the myghtye deades and greate tereble thinges which Moses dyd
in the sight of
all Isra-
el

¶ The ende of the fifth boke of Moses.

Avims, A kinde of geauntes, and the worde signifieth crooked vnright or weked.

Belial weked or wekednesse, he that hath cast the yoke of God of his necke ād will not obeye god.

Bruterar, prophesiers or sothsayers.

Emims, a kinde of geaūtes so called be cause they were terreble and cruell for emin signifieth terreblenesse.

Enack, a kinde of geauntes, so called happlye be-

V. 6 Moab contra Phogor 7 non caligauit oculus eus, nec dentes illius moti sunt. 8 dies planctus lugentium 11 quæ misit per eum . . . terræ illius, 12 & cunctam manum robustam

L. 6 gegen dem hause Peor 7 seyne augen waren nicht tunckel worden vnd seyne wangen waren nicht verfallen 8 die tag des weynens vnd klagens 12 zu aller diser mechtiger hand vnd grossen gesichten

caufe they ware cheynes aboute their neckes, for enack fignifieth foch a cheyne as men weer aboute their neckes.

.P. [*Recto.* No numeral]. Horims, A kinde of geauntes, ād fignifieth noble, becaufe that of pride they called thē felues nobles or gentles.

Rocke, God is called a rocke, becaufe both he ād his worde lafteth euer.

Whett thē on thy childern, that is exercyfe thy childern in thē ād put them in vre.

Zamzumims, a kinde of geaūtes, ād fignifieth myf-cheuous or that be all waye imaginīge.